THE CAMBRIDGE HISTORY OF JAPAN

General editors

JOHN WHITNEY HALL, MARIUS B. JANSEN, MADOKA KANAI,
AND DENIS TWITCHETT

Volume 4
Early Modern Japan

THE CAMBRIDGE HISTORY OF JAPAN

Volume 4
Early Modern Japan

Edited by
JOHN WHITNEY HALL
James L. McClain, *assistant editor*

The right of the
University of Cambridge
to print and sell
all manner of books
was granted by
Henry VIII in 1534.
The University has printed
and published continuously
since 1584.

CAMBRIDGE UNIVERSITY PRESS
CAMBRIDGE
NEW YORK PORT CHESTER MELBOURNE SYDNEY

Published by the Press Syndicate of the University of Cambridge
The Pitt Building, Trumpington Street, Cambridge CB2 1RP
40 West 20th Street, New York, NY 10011, USA
10 Stamford Road, Oakleigh, Melbourne 3166, Australia

© Cambridge University Press 1991

First published 1991

Printed in the United States of America

Library of Congress Cataloging-in-Publication Data
(Revised for volume 4)
The Cambridge history of Japan.
Includes bibliographical references.
Contents: v. 4. Early modern Japan /
edited by John W. Hall   – v. 5. The nineteenth century /
edited by Marius B. Jansen   – v. 6. The twentieth
century / edited by Peter Duus.
1. Japan – History.   I. Hall, John Whitney, 1916–
DS835.C36   1990   952   88-2877

British Library Cataloguing in Publication Data
Hall, John Whitney 1916–
The Cambridge history of Japan.
Vol. 4, Early modern Japan
1. Japan, history
I. Title
952

ISBN 0-521-22354-7 (v. 3) hardback
0-521-22355-5 (v. 4) hardback
0-521-22356-3 (v. 5) hardback
0-521-22357-1 (v. 6) hardback

GENERAL EDITORS' PREFACE

Since the beginning of this century the Cambridge histories have set a
pattern in the English-reading world for multivolume series containing chapters written by specialists under the guidance of volume editors. Plans for a Cambridge history of Japan were begun in the 1970s
and completed in 1978. The task was not to be easy. The details of
Japanese history are not matters of common knowledge among Western historians. The cultural mode of Japan differs greatly from that of
the West, and above all there are the daunting problems of terminology and language. In compensation, however, foreign scholars have
been assisted by the remarkable achievements of the Japanese scholars
during the last century in recasting their history in modern conceptual
and methodological terms.

History has played a major role in Japanese culture and thought,
and the Japanese record is long and full. Japan's rulers from ancient
times have found legitimacy in tradition, both mythic and historic,
and Japan's thinkers have probed for a national morality and system of
values in their country's past. The importance of history was also
emphasized in the continental cultural influences that entered Japan
from early times. Its expression changed as the Japanese consciousnes
turned to questions of dynastic origin, as it came to reflect Buddhist
views of time and reality, and as it sought justification for rule by the
samurai estate. By the eighteenth century the successive need to explain the divinity of the government, justify the ruler's place through
his virtue and compassion, and interpret the flux of political change
had resulted in the fashioning of a highly subjective fusion of Shinto,
Buddhist, and Confucian norms.

In the nineteenth century the Japanese became familiar with Western forms of historical expression and felt the need to fit their national
history into patterns of a larger world history. As the modern Japanese
state took its place among other nations, Japanese history faced the
task of reconciling a parochial past with a more catholic present. Historians familiarized themselves with European accounts of the course of

civilization and described Japan's nineteenth-century turn from mili-tary to civilian bureaucratic rule under monarchical guidance as part of a larger, worldwide pattern. Buckle, Guizot, Spencer, and then Marx successively provided interpretative schema.

The twentieth-century ideology of the imperial nation state, how-ever, operated to inhibit full play of universalism in historical interpre-tation. The growth and ideology of the imperial realm required cau-tion on the part of historians, particularly with reference to Japanese origins.

Japan's defeat in World War II brought release from these inhibi-tions and for a time replaced them with compulsive denunciation of the pretensions of the imperial state. Soon the expansion of higher education brought changes in the size and variety of the Japanese scholarly world. Historical inquiry was now free to range widely. A new opening to the West brought lively interest in historical expres-sions in the West, and a historical profession that had become cau-tiously and expertly positivist began to rethink its material in terms of larger patterns.

At just this juncture the serious study of Japanese history began in the West. Before World War II the only distinguished general survey of Japanese history in English was G. B. Sansom's *Japan: A Short Cultural History*, first published in 1931 and still in print. English and American students of Japan, many trained in wartime language pro-grams, were soon able to travel to Japan for study and participation with Japanese scholars in cooperative projects. International confer-ences and symposia produced volumes of essays that served as bench-marks of intellectual focus and technical advance. Within Japan itself an outpouring of historical scholarship, popular publishing, and his-torical romance heightened the historical consciousness of a nation aware of the dramatic changes to which it was witness.

In 1978 plans were adopted to produce this series on Japanese his-tory as a way of taking stock of what has been learned. The present generation of Western historians can draw upon the solid foundations of the modern Japanese historical profession. The decision to limit the enterprise to six volumes meant that topics such as the history of art and literature, aspects of economics and technology and science, and the riches of local history would have to be left out. They too have been the beneficiaries of vigorous study and publication in Japan and in the Western world.

Multivolume series have appeared many times in Japanese since the beginning of the century, but until the 1960s the number of professionally trained historians of Japan in the Western world was too small to sustain such an enterprise. Although that number has grown, the general editors have thought it best to draw on Japanese specialists for contributions in areas where they retain a clear authority. In such cases the act of translation itself involves a form of editorial cooperation that requires the skills of a trained historian whose name deserves acknowledgment.

The primary objective of the present series is to put before the English-reading audience as complete a record of Japanese history as possible. But the Japanese case attracts our attention for other reasons as well. To some it has seemed that the more we have come to know about Japan the more we are drawn to the apparent similarities with Western history. The long continuous course of Japan's historical record has tempted historians to look for resemblances between its patterns of political and social organization and those of the West. The rapid emergence of Japan's modern nation state has occupied the attention of comparative historians, both Japanese and Western. On the other hand, specialists are inclined to point out the dangers of being misled by seeming parallels.

The striking advances in our knowledge of Japan's past will continue and accelerate. Western historians of this great and complex subject will continue to grapple with it, and they must as Japan's world role becomes more prominent. The need for greater and deeper understanding of Japan will continue to be evident. Japanese history belongs to the world, not only as a right and necessity but also as a subject of compelling interest.

JOHN WHITNEY HALL
MARIUS B. JANSEN
MADOKA KANAI
DENIS TWITCHETT

CONTENTS

MAPS, FIGURES, AND TABLES

PREFACE TO VOLUME 4

Each volume in this series has its own identity and editorial history. Volume 4 derives its special tone from the fact that it relies more heavily on contributions prepared by Japanese scholars than do most of the other books in the series. In order to handle the problem of accurate translation for this multicultural study, an effort has been made to select translators from among established American scholars who have a sensitivity toward the interests and intent of the Japanese author whose essay they were assigned to translate. This method has been tested previously in a number of bilingual seminars held on the Muromachi, Sengoku, and early Edo periods. The Introduction to this volume acknowledges the contributions made by the authors, but little is said about the translators. We have been fortunate in attracting a number of talented scholars as translators, and I feel the results have proven the soundness of our policy.

One who deserves special mention is James L. McClain who has served as assistant editor. Aside from his work as author and translator he has prepared the historical chronology and has been invaluable in facilitating the production process throughout the entire procedure. I am especially grateful to him for negotiating several complicated editorial issues and in serving as a link with authors on his visits to Japan.

My retirement in 1983 meant the transfer of editorial work from Yale and the setting up of a home office and computer center. Michael Cutler, whose natural ability to make the computer friendly was crucial at this time, compiled the chart of the Tokugawa genealogy; and, armed with his own bilingual word processor, he also prepared the list of Works Cited. The meticulous care shown by Luke S. Roberts in preparing the Glossary-Index proved invaluable.

Two of the general editors of the *Cambridge History of Japan* series were most generous with their time and editorial help: Kanai Madoka whose encyclopedic knowledge of Japanese history was called upon to read portions of the manuscript and later the proofs, and Marius

Jansen whose vision stirred this project from its beginnings and whose good natured companionship has made it all worthwhile.

In this volume Japanese is romanized according to the Hepburn system, and Chinese according to the Wade–Giles system. Japanese and Chinese personal names follow their native form, with surname preceding given name, except in citations of Japanese authors writing in English. We wish to thank the Japan Foundation for grants that facilitated the production of this series.

Throughout the unexpectedly long time it has taken to bring this volume into being there has been one invaluable assistant who deserves special recognition. My wife Robin has worked closely with me as general facilitator and encourager. At a time when she was anticipating the leisure of retirement from her own professional duties she has patiently endured the invasion of her home by computer equipment and the indignity of having to learn to master it for this project.

JOHN WHITNEY HALL

CHRONOLOGY

Era names (*nengō*) are indicated in bold type; months and days correspond to the Japanese lunar calander.

1532   **Tenbun** era begins on 7/29.

1534   Oda Nobunaga is born; the process of national unification begins.

1536   Toyotomi Hideyoshi is born, perhaps on Tenbun 6/2/6.

1542   Tokugawa Ieyasu is born; Portuguese traders arrive in Japan and introduce Western muskets and cannon.

1549   Francis Xavier (1506–52) lands at Kagoshima and initiates the Christian mission.

1555   **Kōji** era begins 10/23.

1558   **Eiroku** era begins 2/28; Hideyoshi (Kinoshita Tōkichirō) enters the service of Nobunaga.

1560   Nobunaga gains national prominence by defeating Imagawa Yoshimoto, the foremost power in the Kantō region, in the battle of Okehazama.

1562   Nobunaga concludes alliance with Ieyasu.

1568   Nobunaga marches into Kyoto and installs Ashikaga Yoshiaki as shogun; Nobunaga issues the *rakuichi–rakuza* decrees in Kanō and abolishes toll gates in all provinces.

1569   Nobunaga issues *erizeni* decrees (Eiroku 12/3); the city of Sakai submits to Nobunaga.

1570   **Genki** era begins 4/23; Nobunaga launches campaign against the True Pure Land sect, with warfare to continue for nearly ten years.

1571   Nobunaga destroys Enryakuji, headquarters of the Tendai sect on Mt. Hiei.

1572   Nobunaga confines the shogun Ashikaga Yoshiaki to Nijō Castle, burns much of the inner city of Kyoto, and then drives Yoshiaki from Kyoto, in effect putting an end to the Ashikaga shogunate.

1573   **Tenshō** era begins 7/28.

1576   Nobunaga moves to Azuchi and begins to construct a new castle.

1580   English trading vessels visit Hirado; Nobunaga orders a cadastral survey for Yamato and Harima provinces.

1582   Akechi Mitsuhide betrays Nobunaga; Hideyoshi avenges Nobunaga's death
        by slaying Mitsuhide in the battle of Yamazaki and torches Azuchi Castle;
        Hideyoshi orders a cadastral survey for Yamashiro Province, initiating what
        ultimately will become a nationwide land survey (*kenchi*).

1583   Hideyoshi enters Osaka Castle.

1585   Hideyoshi is appointed *kampaku* (imperial regent).

1587   Hideyoshi conquers Kyushu and issues an edict restricting the practice of
        Christianity.

1588   The exiled Ashikaga Yoshiaki resigns the office of shogun, bringing a legal
        end to the Ashikaga shogunate; Hideyoshi initiates a sword hunt in many
        provinces.

1589   Hideyoshi orders the brothels of Kyoto to be brought together in one li-
        censed quarter known as Nijō Yanagimachi.

1590   Hideyoshi completes his military hegemony by defeating the Go-Hōjō at
        Odawara; the final resistance in northern Japan ceases by the following year;
        Ieyasu resettles in the Kantō and builds a castle at Edo.

1591   Hideyoshi issues a three-clause order prohibiting changes of status from
        samurai to merchant or from farmer to merchant.

1592   Hideyoshi's armies invade Korea; **Bunroku** era begins 12/8.

1594   Hideyoshi constructs a grand palace at Momoyama and a castle at Fushimi.

1596   **Keichō** era begins 10/27; Hideyoshi's field generals arrange a truce with the
        Chinese that fails to meet Hideyoshi's military objectives.

1597   Hideyoshi orders the death of twenty-six Christians in Nagasaki (Keichō 1/
        11); Hideyoshi moves to Osaka Castle (Keichō 1/11); Hideyoshi orders the
        second invasion of Korea (Keichō 2/1); Ashikaga Yoshiaki dies.

1598   Hideyoshi dies, and the Japanese invasion armies are recalled from Korea.

1600   The first Dutch ship arrives in Japan; Ieyasu grants an audience to Will
        Adams at Osaka; Ieyasu asserts military hegemony with a victory in the
        battle of Sekigahara.

1603   Ieyasu is appointed shogun; Okuni, a priestess of Izumo Shrine, performs
        kabuki dances in Kyoto; the bridge at Nihonbashi is constructed in Edo.

1604   The Confucian scholar Hayashi Razan is employed by Ieyasu; he later
        founds a private school in Edo.

1605   Ieyasu retires as shogun and the post passes to his son Hidetada; Ieyasu takes
        the title of retired shogun (*ogosho*) and names the family castle at Sumpu as
        his official residence; Hayashi Razan has his first audience with Ieyasu.

1607   Envoys from Korea arrive in Edo, their first visit to Japan since Hideyoshi's
        invasions.

1609   The Dutch East India Company receives permission from the shogunate to
        trade at Nagasaki.

1612   The shogunate issues prohibitions against Christianity.

1614   The shogunate expels 148 Christians from Japan; Ieyasu launches his winter campaign against Hideyori at Osaka Castle.

1615   The summer campaign culminates with the fall of Osaka Castle and the death of Hideyori; the shogunate issues its "one province, one castle" edict and the Buke shohatto (ordinances pertaining to warrior houses); **Genna** era begins 7/13.

1616   Ieyasu dies and his remains are interred first at Mt. Kunō in Shizuoka and later at Nikkō; all foreign ships, except Chinese, are restricted to Nagasaki and Hirado.

1617   The shogunate authorizes the establishment of a licensed quarter at Yoshiwara; the first kabuki theaters are licensed in Kyoto.

1618   The shogunate issues injunctions against those who disguise themselves as mountain ascetics (*yamabushi*).

1619   Fujiwara Seika, regarded as the founder of early modern Japanese Neo-Confucianism, dies; Christians in Kyoto are executed.

1621   The shogunate issues edicts against overseas travel, the construction of ships capable of sailing to foreign countries, and the exportation of weapons.

1622   Fifty-five Christians are executed at Nagasaki; a period of intense persecution begins.

1623   Hidetada retires as shogun and is succeeded by Iemitsu; the English close their shops at Hirado and leave Japan.

1624   **Kan'ei** era begins 2/30; Saruwaka (Nakamura) Kanzaburō forms a kabuki troupe in Edo.

1628   "Women's kabuki" (*onna kabuki*) becomes popular in Edo.

1629   The Buke shohatto is amended and reissued; the shogunate bans women from the kabuki stage; Hayashi Razan publishes his *Shunkanshō*, an exposition of the tenets of Neo-Confucianism.

1630   Ieyasu's great-granddaughter is enthroned as the empress Meishō.

1631   The Shimmachi licensed quarter opens in Osaka.

1633   Shamisen are first used in kabuki performances.

1635   The shogunate restricts foreign ships and foreign trade to Nagasaki and prohibits overseas Japanese from returning home (commonly referred to as the *sakoku* laws); the *sankin kōtai* system of alternate residence is institutionalized as *tozama* daimyo are ordered to participate in the system.

1636   A barrier guard post (*sekisho*) is established at Hakone to protect Edo from the West.

1637   The Shimabara Rebellion begins, continuing into the next year. Ieyasu's spirit is deified as Tōshō-dai-gongen at Nikkō.

1638   The shogunate issues its most severe edicts against Christianity; the phenomenon of Ise pilgrimages sweeps the nation during the summer.

1639   The shogunate prohibits Portuguese ships from calling at Japanese ports.

1640   The shogunate establishes an anti-Christian inquisition (*shūmon aratame yaku*); brothels in Kyoto are transferred to a new location, Shimabara.

1641   The Dutch trading posts are transferred from Hirado to Deshima at Nagasaki.

1642   The *fudai* daimyo are instructed to participate in the alternate residence system.

1644   **Shōhō** era begins 12/16.

1645   Takuan Sōhō, a leading figure in the Zen reform movement, dies.

1648   The shogunate issues a legal code regulating the lives of commoners in Edo; **Keian** era begins on 2/15; two months later codes concerning urban life and commerce are issued in Osaka.

1649   The shogunate issues the Keian furegaki, impressing on the peasants the necessity of diligence and frugality.

1651   Ietsuna succeeds Iemitsu; the shogunate uncovers a plot by Yui Shōsetsu.

1652   "Young men's kabuki" (*wakashū*) is banned in Edo; **Jōō** era begins 9/18.

1655   **Meireki** era begins 4/13; the Confucian scholar Yamazaki Ansai opens a private school in Kyoto.

1656   Illicit bath houses become popular in Edo.

1657   A great fire destroys large portions of Edo; a new licensed quarter, the Shin Yoshiwara, is established near Asakusa; the daimyo of Mito, Tokugawa Mitsukuni, begins compilation of the *Dai Nihonshi* (The history of great Japan).

1658   **Manji** era beings 7/23.

1661   **Kambun** era begins 4/25; Kimpira *jōruri* enters period of great popularity in Edo.

1662   The Takeda theater is established in Osaka.

1663   The Buke shohatto is revised to prohibit warriors from committing suicide upon the death of their lord; fireworks are banned in Edo.

1665   Asai Ryōi publishes his *Ukiyo monogatari* (A tale of the floating world); the shogunate issues regulations governing temples and priests (*shoshūjiin hatto*).

1666   The twenty-volume illustrated lexicon *Kimmō zui* (Illustrations and definitions to train the untutored) appears.

1672   Under the direction of Kawamura Zuiken, preparations are completed for the western and eastern coastal shipping circuits.

1673   **Empō** era begins 9/21; the Mitsui family opens its textile store, the Echigoya, in Edo.

1679   The shogunate executes the masterless samurai Hirai Gompachi, who had taken refuge in the Yoshiwara licensed quarter and robbed townspeople.

1680   Tsunayoshi is appointed shogun; he asserts his authority by dismissing Grand Councilor Sakai Tadakiyo and confiscating part or all of the domains of forty-six daimyo, beginning with Matsudaira Mitsunaga of Takada in 1681; a revised and expanded edition, containing more than thirty thousand entries, of the fifteenth-century dictionary *Setsuyō shū* is published in Edo.

1681   **Tenna** era begins on 9/29.

1682   Kinoshita Jun'an becomes Confucian adviser to the shogunate; Yamazaki
        Ansai, prominent Neo-Confucian scholar and founder of the Suiga school of
        Shinto, dies; Ihara Saikaku publishes his first book, *Kōshoku ichidai otoko*
        (The life of an amorous man).

1684   **Jôkyô** era begins 2/21; codes regulating the publishing business are promul-
        gated in Edo.

1685   A guide to Kyoto, *Kyō habutae*, appears, listing 241 master teachers offering
        private instruction in forty-seven specialties.

1686   A protective association (*kabunakama*) is formed by cotton cloth wholesalers
        in Edo; regulations concerning trade with Korea are issued; Saikaku pub-
        lishes *Kōshoku ichidai onna* (The life of an amorous woman) and *Kōshoku
        gonin onna* (Five women who loved love); Chikamatsu Monzaemon writes
        Kagekiyo (Victorious).

1688   Saikaku publishes *Nihon eitaigura* (The eternal storehouse of Japan);
        Genroku era begins on 9/30; Yanagisawa Yoshiyasu becomes grand chamber-
        lain for the shogun Tsunayoshi; the shogunate limits to seventy the number
        of Chinese ships visiting Nagasaki each year.

1689   Bashō departs on his journey along "Narrow Roads to Distant Places."

1690   *Ukiyo-zōshi* literature reaches new hights of popularity; the wood-block
        print artist Torii Kiyomori begins to draw actors, producing his first poster
        for the Ichimura-za; the school founded by Hayashi Razan is named as the
        shogunate's official school.

1693   The shogunate completes a census of Edo, recording a *chōnin* population of
        more than 353,000.

1694   The Group of Ten Wholesale Associations is formed in Edo; Bashō dies.

1696   Miyazaki Antei writes *Nōgyō zensho* (The complete agriculturalist) barely
        one year before his death.

1698   Tsunayoshi orders his first debasement of currency.

1702   The forty-seven *rōnin* carry out their celebrated vendetta.

1703   Chikamatsu's *Sonezaki shinjū* (The love suicides of Sonezaki) is first per-
        formed; more than twenty domains have by now established schools for
        educating samurai.

1704   Ichikawa Danjūrō, first head of the Ichikawa kabuki troupe, dies; **Hōei** era
        begins 3/13.

1705   Thousands across Japan join in *okagemairi* pilgrimages to Ise; the shogunate
        confiscates the wealth of Yodoya Saburōemon.

1711   **Shōtoku** era begins 4/25.

1712   Arai Hakuseki completes his influential history, the *Tokushi yoron*.

1714   Kaibara Ekken dies, a prolific writer on such topics as ethics for common-
        ers, education for women, natural history, and Neo-Confucian metaphysics
        and cosmology.

1715   Nagasaki trade limited to thirty ships annually for the Chinese, two for the
        Dutch; Arai Hakuseki writes his *Seiyō kibun* (A report on the Occident).

1716   Yoshimune becomes shogun and launches the first major reform of the
        shogunate; **Kyōhō** era begins 6/22.

1719   Nishikawa Joken completes his *Chōnin bukuro* (A bagful of advice for
        merchants).

1720   Yoshimune allows Chinese translations of Western books into Japan.

1721   Nishikawa Joken writes his *Hyakushō bukuro* (A bagful of advice for farm-
        ers), encouraging literacy among farmers.

1723   The shogunate prohibits depictions of double love suicides in publications or
        on stage in Osaka; the shogunate introduces the *tashidaka* system of augment-
        ing stipends in order to facilitate the promotion of capable officials; a protec-
        tive association of book dealers is formed in Osaka; censorship of new publi-
        cations is carried out.

1724   Oil, rice, and other commodity dealers are instructed to form closed associa-
        tions in Edo; the shogunate issues the Kyōhō-do hōritsurui, a collection of
        legal precedents and instructions.

1726   Edo wholesalers dealing in fifteen different products, including rice and cook-
        ing oils, are required to submit account books and price lists to the shogunate.

1727   Nakagawa Seizaburō and other Osaka merchants join to open the Dōjima
        rice market; Ogyū Sorai publishes *Seidan* (Political essays).

1728   Trade in rice futures is permitted in Osaka; Kada Azumamaro petitions the
        shogunate to establish a "school of national learning."

1729   Dazai Shundai completes his *Keizairoku,* a widely read work on political
        economy.

1730   The City Office in Edo issues regulations concerning the establishment of
        fire-fighting services.

1732   Famine conditions prevail in Kinki and portions of southern and western
        Japan.

1733   *Chōnin* residents in Edo and other major cities attack the shops of rice
        merchants to protest high rice and commodity prices, the first instance of
        violent demonstrations by commoners in Edo.

1735   Several daimyo abolish licensed quarters in their castle towns.

1736   **Gembun** era begins 4/28.

1737   Kamo Mabuchi arrives in Edo to promote the study of ancient Japanese texts
        such as the *Man'yōshū.*

1738   The evolution of popular protest into a major factor in domestic politics is
        exemplified by the rioting of 84,000 farmers in Iwakitaira and the interven-
        tion of troops from thirteen daimyo domains to crush a protest near the
        Ikuno silver mines.

1741   **Kampō** era begins 2/27.

1742   The shogunate compiles the Kujikata osadamegaki, a codification of its legal
        codes and procedures.

1744	**Enkyō** era begins 2/21; the Kyoto merchant Ishida Baigan, who founded the commoner teaching known as *Shingaku*, dies.
1745	Aoki Konyō issues a Dutch–Japanese dictionary.
1748	**Kan'en** era begins 7/12; the first performance of the eleven-act puppet play *Kanadehon chūshingura* (A copybook of the treasury of loyal retainers) depicts the classic act of samurai revenge, the 1702 vendetta of the forty-seven *rōnin*.
1751	**Hōreki** era begins 10/27.
1760	Ieshige resigns and his son Ieharu becomes the tenth Tokugawa shogun.
1763	A merchant association handling Korean ginseng is founded in the Kanda district of Edo.
1764	**Meiwa** era begins 6/2.
1769	Tanuma Okitsugu begins his rise to prominence under the patronage of Ieharu.
1770	Licensing procedures are put into place for oil producers in Osaka and surrounding areas.
1772	**An'ei** era begins 11/16; the shogunate issues the *nanryō nishugin* coin in an effort to increase the amount of currency in circulation.
1777	Russian authorities approach the authorities of Matsumae domain in Hokkaido with a request for trade.
1781	**Temmei** era begins 4/2.
1783	Mt. Asama erupts, and much of the agricultural land in the Kantō is severely damaged.
1786	The shogun Ieharu dies; Tanuma and several of his assistants are dismissed from office.
1788	Matsudaira Sadanobu is appointed as chief senior councilor for the shogun Ienari and initiates the Kansei Reforms; Ōtsuki Gentaku publishes his *Rangaku kaitei* (Explanation of Dutch studies).
1789	**Kansei** era begins 1/25.
1790	Sadanobu initiates the so-called prohibitions against unorthodox teachings.
1791	The Sumitomo family opens the Besshi copper mines.
1792	Adam Laksman, a lieutenant in the Russian navy, arrives in Nemuro with instructions from Catherine the Great to seek the repatriation of Russian castaways and the opening of diplomatic and commercial relations; the shogunate orders coastal defenses improved.
1793	Matsudaira Sadanobu is stripped of his position as senior councilor.
1794	The shogunate's bibliographer Hanawa Hokiichi completes the *Gunsho ruijū* (Classified documents).
1798	The scholar Honda Toshiaki publishes his *Keisei hisaku* (Secret proposals on political economy), calling for the creation of a national merchant marine.
1801	**Kyōwa** era begins 2/5.
1804	**Bunka** era begins 2/11.

1809   Compilation of the *Tokugawa jikki* (Veritable records of the Tokugawa house) begins.

1811   The shogunate establishes an office to translate works from the West.

1818   **Bunsei** era begins 4/22.

1830   **Tempō** era begins 12/10.

1837   Ōshio Heihachirō leads riots in Osaka; several domains launch reform programs.

1841   Mizuno Tadakuni abolishes protective associations, begins the shogunate's Tempō Reforms.

MAPS

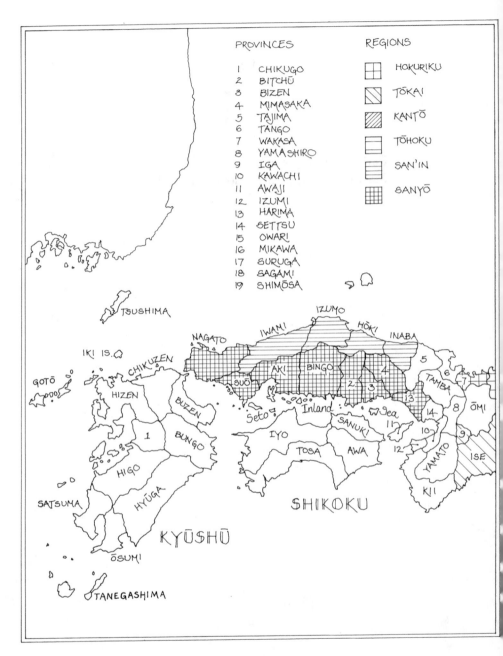

Provinces and regions of early modern Japan.

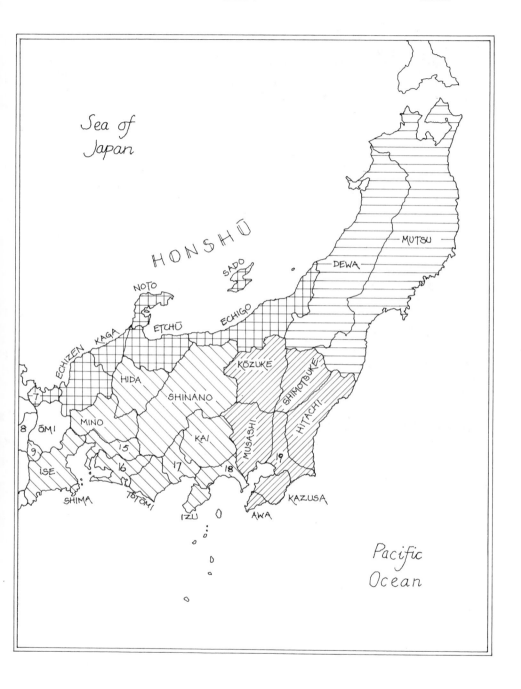

Sea of Japan

HONSHŪ

NOTO

SADO

MUTSU

DEWA

ECHIGO

ECHIZEN KAGA ETCHŪ

KŌZUKE

SHIMOTSUKE

HIDA

SHINANO

HITACHI

7

ŌMI MINO

MUSASHI

8

KAI

9

15

19

ISE

16

17

18

SHIMA

TŌTŌMI

KAZUSA

IZU

AWA

Pacific Ocean

Maritime routes, early modern East Asia.

CHAPTER 1

INTRODUCTION

JAPAN'S EARLY MODERN TRANSFORMATION

In 1543 some Portuguese traders in a Chinese junk came ashore on the island of Tanegashima south of Kagoshima, the headquarters city of the Satsuma domain of southernmost Kyushu. This first, and presumably accidental, encounter between Europeans and Japanese proved to be an epochal event, for from the Portuguese the Japanese learned about Western firearms. Within three decades the Japanese civil war that had been growing in intensity among the regional military lords, or *daimyō*, was being fought with the new technology. In 1549 another Chinese vessel, this time purposefully, set on Japanese soil at Kagoshima the Jesuit priest Francis Xavier, one of the founders of the Society of Jesus. This marked the start of a vigorous effort by Jesuit missionaries to bring Christianity to Japan. For another hundred years Japan lay open to both traders and missionaries from the West. And conversely Japan became known to the world beyond its doors.[1]

From a strictly Japanese perspective, the century or so from the middle of the sixteenth century is distinguished by what can be called the "daimyo phenomenon," that is, the rise of local military lords who first carved out their own domains and then began to war among themselves for national hegemony. Between 1568 and 1590 two powerful lords, Oda Nobunaga (1534–82) and Toyotomi Hideyoshi (1536–98), managed to unite all daimyo under a single military command, binding them together into a national confederation. The most important political development of these years was without question the achievement of military consolidation that led in 1603 to the establishment of a new shogunate, based in Edo. The shogunate itself, the government of the Tokugawa hegemony, gave form to the "Great Peace" that was to last until well into the nineteenth century.

---

1 The use of the term "Christian century" has been applied to this era by Western scholars, but I have avoided using it in this introduction because of its possible overemphasis on the foreign factor. The best-known general work on this subject in English is C. H. Boxer's *The Christian Century in Japan, 1549–1650* (Berkeley and Los Angeles: University of California Press, 1951).

Japan's sixteenth-century unification, as it was both observed by Europeans and influenced by the introduction of Western arms, has naturally suggested to historians various points of comparison between European and Japanese historical institutions. In fact, European visitors of the time found many similarities between the Europe they knew and the Japan they visited.[2] Will Adams (1564–1620), for one, who landed in Japan in 1600, found life there quite amenable. Japan to him was a country of law and order governed as well or better than any he had seen in his travels. Since his time, historians, both Western and Japanese, have given thought to whether Japan and Western Europe were basically comparable in the mid-sixteenth century. Was there in fact a universal process of historical development in which two societies, though on the opposite sides of the globe, could be seen to react to similar stimuli in comparable ways? The first generation of modern Japanese and Western historians to confront this question readily made the intellectual jump and put Japan on the same line of historical evolution as parts of Europe. The pioneer historian of medieval Japanese history, Asakawa Kan'ichi, typified this positivistic approach. As a member of the Yale University faculty from 1905 to 1946, he spent much of his scholarly life in search of a definition of feudalism that could be applied to both Europe and Japan.[3]

Historians today are more cautious about suggesting that a tangible continuum might underlie two such distant but seemingly similar societies. Yet they continue to be intrigued by questions of possible comparability in the Japanese case.[4] We think of early modern Western Europe in political terms as an age of the "absolute monarchs," starting with the heads of the Italian city-states, the monarchies of Spain and Portugal, and finally England under the Tudors and France under the Bourbons. Underlying these state organizations were certain common features of government and social structure. First there was a notable centralization and expansion of power in the hands of the monarchy, and this tended to be gained at the expense of the landed aristocracy and the church. Characteristic of these states was the

2 A conveniently arranged anthology of excerpts from the writings of European visitors to Japan is available in Michael Cooper, comp. and ed., *They Came to Japan: An Anthology of European Reports on Japan, 1543–1640* (Berkeley and Los Angeles: University of California Press, 1965).
3 Kan'ichi Asakawa's most pertinent articles on the subject of feudaliam in Japan have been gathered in *Land and Society in Medieval Japan* (Tokyo: Japan Society for the Promotion of Science, 1965).
4 See the discussion of feudalism in Japan in Joseph R. Strayer, "The Tokugawa Period and Japanese Feudalism," and John W. Hall, "Feudalism in Japan – A Reassessment," in John W. Hall and Marius B. Jansen, eds., *Studies in the Institutional History of Early Modern Japan* (Princeton, N.J.: Princeton University Press, 1968).

growth of centralized fiscal, police, and military organizations and the increasing bureaucratization of administration. There were certain attendant social changes, particularly what is commonly described as the "breakdown" of feudal social class divisions, and the "rise" of the commercial and service classes. Often this process was furthered by an alliance between the monarchy and commercial wealth against the landed aristocracy and the clergy. And finally, common to all, was the growing acceptance of the practice of representation in government. The establishment of diets or parliaments was the truest test of postfeudal society.

Japan during the sixteenth and seventeenth centuries underwent several similar political and social changes. The country achieved a new degree of political unity. The Tokugawa hegemony gave rise to a highly centralized power structure, capable of exerting nationwide enforcement over military and fiscal institutions. Yet centralization did not go as far as it had in Europe. Daimyo were permitted to retain their own armies and also a considerable amount of administrative autonomy.

However, in contrast with Europe, Edo military government did not nurture an independent and politically powerful commercial class. There was no parliamentary representation of the "Third Estate." Rather, the samurai were frozen in place as the "ruling class" and reinforced at the expense of the merchant class. Although internal events in Japan showed certain patterns that invited comparison with Western Europe, the methodology for making such comparisons has not been convincingly developed. To be sure, there have been numerous attempts at one-on-one comparison based on the premise that the unification of Japan under the Tokugawa hegemony was comparable to the appearance of the monarchal states of Europe. Specifically, Marxist theory has been used to equate changes in sixteenth-century Japan with the presumed universal passage of society from feudalism to the absolute state.[5]

The effort to explain Japanese history using concepts of change derived from a reading of European history has its advocates as well as its critics. This point is touched on in several chapters in this volume, especially that by Wakita Osamu. As more is discovered about the political and social institutions of the late sixteenth century in Japan,

5 For a discussion of the controversy over concepts of periodization, see John Whitney Hall, Keiji Nagahara, and Kozo Yamamura, eds., *Japan Before Tokugawa: Political Consolidation and Economic Growth, 1500–1650* (Princeton, N.J.: Princeton University Press, 1981), pp. 11–14.

the more complex the problem of comparison across cultural boundaries appears to be. It is important to note that the vocabulary of
historical explanation that has evolved among historians working
strictly in documents primary to Japan is perfectly capable of identifying and analyzing the Japanese case on its own terms.

The traditional landmarks of Japanese historical periodization help
identify the primary boundary-setting events of the period. We start
with the Ōnin–Bummei War of 1467 to 1477 that marked the beginning of the final downward slide of the Muromachi shogunate. According to traditional historiography, the period from the Ōnin War to
1568 – the year in which Oda Nobunaga occupied Kyoto and thereby
initiated the period of military consolidation – is referred to as the
Sengoku period, the Age of the Country at War. Between this date and
1582, when Nobunaga was killed by one of his own generals, traditional historiography has applied the label *Azuchi*, the name of
Nobunaga's imposing castle on Lake Biwa. The period from Nobunaga's death to 1598, during which Hideyoshi completed the unification of the daimyo, is given the name *Momoyama*, from the location of
Hideyoshi's castle built between Osaka and Kyoto. The victory of
Tokugawa Ieyasu's forces against the Toyotomi faction at the battle of
Sekigahara in 1600 marked the beginning of the Tokugawa hegemony.
Tokugawa Ieyasu (1542–1616) received appointment as shogun in
1603, but his status was not fully consummated until 1615, when he
occupied Osaka Castle and destroyed the remnants of the Toyotomi
house and its supporters. The Tokugawa, or Edo, period was to last
until 1868.

We have already noted that for purposes of distribution and coverage of subject matter, the temporal scope of this the fourth volume of
our series is roughly from 1550 to 1800. The years covered do not
conform to any single traditional historical era but, rather, include
both the Azuchi and Momoyama periods and the first two centuries of
the Edo, or Tokugawa, period. This time span is justified on the
grounds that it covers the birth and the ultimate maturation of the
form of political organization referred to by modern Japanese historians as *bakuhan*, namely, the structure of government in which the
shogunate (*bakufu*) ruled the country through a subordinate coalition
of daimyo, whose domains were referred to as *han*. Although historians have commonly treated the Azuchi–Momoyama and the Edo periods as distinct entities, more recently they have come to recognize that
the origin of the Tokugawa hegemony and the formation of Edo polity
cannot be explained without reference to the fundamental institutional

changes that occurred under Oda Nobunaga and Toyotomi Hideyoshi. Hence, we now commonly link the earlier age as a preamble to the longer Edo period.[6]

There is, of course, no intent to deny the separate identities of the Azuchi–Momoyama and Edo periods as meaningful units of historical periodization, especially from the point of view of the cultural historian. Similarly, Azuchi–Momoyama still stands for half a century of massive military consolidation and political and social transformation, as the leading regional warlords created the compact domains that were eventually hammered together into a national coalition in 1590 by Toyotomi Hideyoshi.

Most of the events of this era have been described with superlatives and absolutes. Unification was not simply a matter of conquest by one all-powerful daimyo. Rather, unification was companion to a more universal development, namely, the establishment of the warrior estate (the *bushi* or samurai) as the primary ruling authority in the country. Gathered into the castle towns that served as headquarters for the more than two hundred daimyo, the samurai enforced a rigorous administration over disarmed peasant and merchant classes. Despite the weight of military rule, the general national mood was one of openness to social change and to the outside world. Japanese adventurers engaged in commerce and piracy along the China mainland and into the waters of Indochina and the Philippines. Conversely, when Japan's shores were first visited by European traders and missionaries, they were warmly welcomed. We have noted already that Japan learned of firearms and Christianity from the West. The first had an immediate bearing on the nature of domestic warfare, hastening appreciably the process of military consolidation. The spread of Christianity was basically divisive in its impact, giving rise to deep suspicions and tensions among Japanese of all classes. This ultimately became a contributory factor that led the authorities to close Japan's doors to all Europeans except the Dutch, adopting the so-called *sakoku*, or seclusion, policy. But that was not until 1639 and was the work of the more conservative Tokugawa shogunate.

More characteristic of the ages of Nobunaga and Hideyoshi were the private figures of the first two unifiers themselves. Nobunaga appears as the ruthless destroyer, wholly determined to eliminate all obstacles

---

6 For recent studies of this transition era, see George Elison and Bardwell L. Smith, eds., *Warlords, Artists, & Commoners: Japan in the Sixteenth Century* (Honolulu: University of Hawaii Press, 1981). Pages 245 to 279 of this volume comprise an extensive bibliography of works in Western languages.

to his national unification. On the other hand, Hideyoshi is remembered as the creator of institutions that became the building blocks for the subsequent Tokugawa hegemony. Yet for all of this, he remains the colorful military upstart, indulging in flamboyant social displays, erecting gilded monuments to the emperor (*tennō*) or to himself. His most grandiose exploit was the controversial invasion of Korea in 1592–8.

The Edo period that followed also projected its own historical image exemplified in the figure of Ieyasu, the only one of the unifiers who succeeded in establishing a hegemony that survived his own death. National unity was institutionalized to safeguard a lasting peace. The major decisions made by Ieyasu and his first two successors as shogun were taken in the name of consolidation and stability. This was evident in the efforts to shape the bakufu as a national instrument of political control. Christianity was interdicted, and foreign contacts were brought under strict regulation. The stamp of *sakoku* that colored the Edo bakufu's relations with the outside world was a reversal of the previous mood of openness. But it should not be thought that all the policies of the Edo shogunate were negative in their intent. Indeed, it was under the Tokugawa that Japan successfully made the transition from military to civil government, something that Hideyoshi had had little time to consider. Moreover, it was Tokugawa policy that permitted or even encouraged the growth of a new urban class, the *chōnin*, and the urban cultural environment that it nurtured. In the area of foreign affairs, the Tokugawa shogunate was to continue to keep its eyes on the outside world indirectly through the Chinese, the Koreans, and the Dutch, who were given restricted access to Japan.

THE ODA–TOYOTOMI INSTITUTIONS OF UNIFICATION

The reason that historians today place such emphasis on the factors of continuity between the Oda–Toyotomi age and the succeeding Edo period comes from a new appreciation of the institutional changes that took place between the last half of the sixteenth century and the first half of the seventeenth. Earlier writers were not oblivious to this point, but as more has been discovered about the domestic changes of the last half of the sixteenth century, it has become clear that Japan experienced in those years a major transformation in social and political organization, military and economic capacity, and cultural style. Moreover, this transformation was more than a by-product of the unification movement or a reflection of the personal leadership of the three unifiers. Of late, historians have looked for explanations of the forces of change in two broad areas: the evolving relationships between the peasantry and the land, and between the samurai and the sources of their political power. Both approaches are concerned at bottom with the phenomenon of *hei-nō-bunri*, the process whereby the samurai class was moved into the daimyo's newly formed headquarter towns, leaving a disarmed peasantry confined to the villages in the countryside.

A new look at the agrarian foundations of sixteenth-century Japan was initiated in the 1950s by Araki Moriaki in his study of the massive cadastral survey (the so-called Taikō *kenchi*) conducted by Hideyoshi.[7] It was Araki's claim that the survey marked a major watershed in national organization. By giving rise to a farming class of small independent farm families under the direct control of regional military lords, it gave shape for the first time in Japan to what Araki claims to be a true serf class. As a consequence, Japan entered a state of feudalism, in Araki's terms.

Araki's work created a stir in Japanese historical circles that has not yet subsided. But whether or not one agrees with his conceptual premises, historians in general have acknowledged that what happened to Japan in the wake of the sixteenth-century cadastral surveys was of fundamental historical importance. The *kenchi* was instrumental in drawing a clear line between the samurai and the *hyakushō* (peasantry). Moreover, it gave rise to the *kokudaka* system of land management and taxation. This remarkable practice converted large numbers of samurai into absentee fief holders possessing proprietary rights of taxation, but not of free disposal, on their lands held in fief. It affirmed the existence of the self-regulated village unit (*mura*) and the cultivators' rights of occupancy.

At the other end of the political spectrum, formation of the Tokugawa hegemony has been studied in terms of the relationship between the bakufu as the central government and the *han* as units of local rule. Before our own time, historians had placed their attention chiefly on the bakufu as the central government – a regime they saw as the willful creation of the Tokugawa house. The growing interest in the study of daimyo domains that began in the late 1930s, however, led to the practice of referring to the government structure of the Tokugawa

---

7 This spectacular accomplishment by the military aristocracy of the sixteenth century was not fully appreciated until the 1950s. With the appearance of Araki Moriaki's *Bakuhan taisei shakai no seiritsu to kōzō* (Tokyo: Ochanomizu shobō, 1959), the nationwide land survey became a major focus of attention for Japanese historians.

period as a combined *bakuhan* system.[8] Thus they gave the *han* a position of equal standing with the bakufu.

The present consensus among historians is that government organization during the Edo period was the consequence of the evolution of two political systems: the shogunal system of national control and the daimyo system of local control. Both of these aspects of government were necessary and mutually dependent. In other words, the hegemonic power ultimately acquired by the shogun rested significantly on the ability of the daimyo who made up the shogun's vassal band to assert effective command over their provincial domains. These in fact accounted for no less than three-quarters of the national land base. The shogun, although in possession of the remaining one-quarter, was not prepared to abolish the daimyo and take on the administration of the entire country through a private officer corps. The shogun's government was essentially an expanded version of *han* government. Many features of Tokugawa administration, including its policy of proprietary authority, derived from precedents established when Ieyasu himself was still a daimyo in the province of Mikawa.

The current emphasis on the *bakuhan* and *kokudaka* systems as explanatory concepts for the Edo period has eased the controversy over interpretation in the Marxist sense of whether Edo Japan should be considered a feudal society. As shown in the chapter by Wakita Osamu, so distinctive are the *bakuhan* and *kokudaka* systems, so difficult to compare with other historical models, particularly European, that the use of feudalism as an explanatory device has become less attractive.

Having made this point, however, it must be admitted that scholars are still divided over matters of periodization. A persistent issue is how to interpret the term *kinsei*. Japanese historians customarily apply this term to the Edo period as a whole, now generally adding to it the last three decades of the sixteenth century. Having done this, they assume that in terms of social organization, the Edo period was still essentially feudal. This approach is reflected in the work of Western scholars who have used such phrases as "late feudalism" or "centralized feudalism" as labels to translate *kinsei*. But since the 1960s, Western historians have used the term "early modern" as the preferred translation. What this reveals, as Wakita Osamu notes in his chapter in this volume, is that between the two bodies of scholars, the Japanese tend to think of

8 Two pioneer historians who opened up the study of the *han* in the *bakuhan* context, and their primary works, are Itō Tasaburō, "Bakuhan taisei ron," in *Shin Nihonshi kōza* (Tokyo: Chūō kōronsha, 1947); and Nakamura Kichiji, *Bakuhan taisei ron* (Tokyo: Yamakawa shuppansha, 1972).

the Edo period as being more feudal than modern, whereas the Western historians think of the same era as more modern than feudal.[9]

THE ROLE OF LOCAL STUDIES

Today's interpretations of the Edo period have changed not simply as a result of shifts in theoretical approach but also as a result of new research methods and interests. Since the 1940s there has been a vast change in the kinds of documents being worked on by Japanese historians, part of an ever-deepening probe into the basic raw materials of the past. The boom in *han* studies came as a result of, and a stimulus to, the gathering and sorting of large quantities of *han* archival materials, much of it still kept in old domain capitals.[10] Local history and village studies were strengthened through the use of documents, such as cadastral registers, tax records, legal briefs on water and land ownership disputes, village headmen's diaries, and the remarkable religious affiliation registers preserved at the village level. Materials of this type contrast with those used by scholars in the 1930s. The latter, as exemplified in the great printed collections produced by economic historians like Honjō Eijirō and Takimoto Seiichi, were in many cases one level removed from what we would call primary, being mainly contemporary historical accounts, scholarly memoranda, laws, and injunctions. Inevitably such materials carried either a conservative establishment-oriented bias or the reverse, an antiestablishment, polemical bias.[11]

The explosive growth of primary materials now available from the Edo period has given today's historians the means of posing and answering an increasing number of fundamental questions, especially in the field of institutional history. Moreover, the historian finds in such materials an abundant vocabulary with which to explain these data. At the base of the marching and countermarching of vast armies and the violent competition for land and status that the Japanese have called Sengoku was the drive toward hegemony, unification, and the achievement of political stability. The sixteenth-century buildup of effective daimyo power fed the aspiration of provincial lords to reach beyond regional control toward national supremacy. Real power of command gave substance to dreams of national conquest, and these in turn

9 See Chapter 3 in this volume.
10 For an example of the materials contained in the archives of one daimyo house, see my "Materials for the Study of Local History in Japan: Pre-Meiji Daimyo Records," reprinted in Hall and Jansen, eds., *Studies*, pp. 143–68.
11 See Ono Takeo, comp., *Kinsei jikata keizai shiryō*, 10 vols. (Tokyo: 1931); and Takimoto Seiichi, ed., *Nihon keizai taiten*, 54 vols. (Tokyo: Keimei shuppansha, 1928–30).

evoked new expressions of legitimacy. Hideyoshi, the first to bring all daimyo under single command, became in his own words "first within the realm," *tenka-bito*. The Ashikaga shoguns of the medieval period, for all the noble status they had acquired, were obliged to share political power with other court families, other members of the military aristocracy, and the religious orders. Theirs was a national command limited by the fragmentation of sovereignty and by the precedents and structures of the court-centered institutions of governance.

The creation of a unified national organization based on the exercise of hegemonic military power was not brought about by the assertion of new monarchal powers by forces at the center of the political arena. No member of the Ashikaga house, for instance, fought his way to become "king." Rather, unification resulted from the emergence of increasingly stronger and larger units of local military lordships, beginning with the small-scale village-level proprietors called variously *kunishū* or *kokujin* (men of the provinces) and then step by step to the formation of the regional lordships of daimyo size. These in turn became the building blocks of a national unity. At the heart of the local military power structure was the lord–vassal relationship among members of the samurai class. Although the shape of shogunal authority changed relatively little during the Muromachi period, the emerging daimyo domains underwent fundamental changes, especially in the strength and spread of the lord–vassal relationship that lay at the center of military house organization. From their early appearance as small military lordships in the Muromachi age, the incipient daimyo domains underwent a long process of evolution, changing shape in response to the different political environments that enveloped them. Modern historians have claimed to be able to identify four different types, or stages, of daimyo development, to which they have assigned the names *shugo*, *sengoku*, *shokuhō*, and *kinsei*, each exhibiting progressively greater strength of control from the center.[12]

Daimyo rule exhibited many regional differences at the start. Hayami Akira makes a case for the existence of three regional zones of economic development: (1) the developed central Kinai region surrounding the capital city; (2) the middle fringe area surrounding Kinai, particularly the provinces of Ōmi and Mikawa; and (3) the Kantō, or eastern provinces.[13] It was the middle fringe area that, being able to profit from

12 See my "Foundations of the Modern Japanese Daimyo," republished in Hall and Jansen, eds., *Studies*, pp. 65–77.

13 Shōda Ken'ichirō and Hayami Akira, *Nihon keizaishi*, vol. 4 of *Keizaigakkō zenshū* (Tokyo: Sekai shoin, 1965), pp. 57–58.

innovations developed in the two other zones, was the launching ground for each of the unifiers. Within their own domains, daimyo worked to extend central control over their vassals. By the middle of the seventeenth century most daimyo had reduced their retainers from independent fief holders to highly dependent stipendiaries. The ability to exert this degree of command was facilitated by the new nationwide land survey that provided the daimyo with the means to make an informed calculation of the land and manpower resources of the domain. By the same token, this gave to the national hegemon reasonably trustworthy evidence on the size and resources of the domains of the daimyo under his command. In particular it provided the groundwork for the assignment of military services (*gun'yaku*).[14]

One of the most pervasive features that identified Edo period government was the domain's tremendous increase in size and effectiveness as a power-holding structure. This fact is so obvious that it is easy to overlook. During the Sengoku period there was a dramatic increase in both the size of the units of local control and the density and effectiveness of the means of exercising that control. These two factors were, of course, interrelated. Under the Muromachi bakufu, authority over the land and its cultivators had been fragmented into scattered proprietorships held at various levels of completeness. *Shugo* appointed by the Ashikaga shoguns over provincewide jurisdictions did not govern anything like unified domains. During the fifteenth and sixteenth centuries, proprietary rights (*ryōshuken*) were acquired in increasing amounts by members of the provincial military aristocracy. The concentration of proprietary tenures in the hands of the provincial military lords became widespread during the first half of the sixteenth century. But it did not become universal until Hideyoshi's unification of the daimyo and his acquisition of all superior proprietary rights to registered land as national military overlord. It was not until Hideyoshi's military conquest was completed in 1591 that the military hegemon became the supreme proprietor as well. This meant that all daimyo, at some time in the past, had surrendered their lands to Hideyoshi and subsequently had received them back as fiefs (*ryōchi* or *chigyō-chi*) after swearing allegiance to him.

What was the nature of the land rights defined by these terms? The era of civil wars had been a struggle for proprietory control of land by

---

14 A leader in the recent interest that Japanese historians have directed toward the practice of assigning military duty (*gun'yaku*) is Sasaki Junnosuke. See his "Gun'yaku ron no mondaiten," pt. 1, in Toyoda Takeshi et al., eds., *Bakuhan taisei*, vol. 7 of *Ronshū Nihon rekishi* (Tokyo: Yūseidō shuppan, 1973), pp. 62–79.

the samurai class, and an effort to protect rights of cultivation by the farming class. The bushi, who until this point had been widely dispersed as land managers in estates whose superior proprietory authority was held by court nobles, religious institutions, and other military houses, were now differentiated by decree as a class given a monopoly over the exercise of higher civil and military administration. It was this condition, in which government above the level of agricultural village and urban ward self-administration had become the sole prerogative of the military aristocracy, that distinguished Japanese society of the Edo period. And because the size of the warrior class remained roughly the same as it had been at the end of the era of military consolidation, Japan was burdened with a heavy load of hereditary fighters and administrators during the centuries of peace that followed.

Shogun and daimyo, leaders of the bushi assemblage, were not unmindful of the burden created by the size of the bushi estate. The three unifiers vigorously cultivated new forms of justification and legitimation for themselves and for the samurai as a body. During the years of active fighting, the aspiring unifiers matched their military exploits with the acquisition of lands and official titles that served to justify their acts of military aggression. Hideyoshi, as national hegemon, came to rely heavily on the symbolic support of the Kyoto court. Referring to their status as *kōgi*, the unifiers took the high moral stand that acknowledged the responsibility of superior government to serve the needs of the common people. Ikeda Mitsumasa, daimyo of Bizen, could write in 1652 that the common people were placed under the care of the samurai officialdom. "The shogun receives authority over the people of Japan as a trust from heaven. The daimyo receives authority over the people of the province as a trust from the shogun. The daimyo's councilors and retainers should aid the daimyo in bringing peace and harmony to the people."[15]

Asao Naohiro, in his contribution to this volume, explains how concepts like *tenka* and *kōgi*, or the evocation of Confucian precepts of benevolent rule, set the contours of the larger polity within which shogun and daimyo claimed rightful places. Not since the eighth-century adoption of the Chinese institutions of imperial government had Japan been ruled under as comprehensive a system of laws and administrative procedures, and historians have been quick to expand

---

15 Ikeda Mitsumasa, in Ishii Ryōsuke, ed., *Hampōshū* vol. 1, doc. 335 (Hōreishū, sec. 36). An English translation may be found in John Whitney Hall, *Government and Local Power 500 to 1700: A Study Based on Bizen Province* (Princeton, N.J.: Princeton University Press, 1966), p. 403.

on its significance. When Hideyoshi spoke of himself as *tenka*, he was laying claim to a position of absolute authority over the land. Should later historians call his regime a "monarchy," a "despotism," or an "absolutism"?

Recent attempts to answer such questions and to comprehend the larger structure within which the *bakuhan* system took its place has led to the use of the concept of *kokka*, or state. Wakita Osamu is one of the few Japanese historians to expand on this theme in English. As he put it, "The central question now asked is not how the creation of central power evolved from a medieval base but how the central powers that emerged came to possess what we can regard as the powers of state."[16] Historians have been inclined to take the easy route in answer: that is, to credit the great regional lords with the motivation and the drive to establish a central power by personal ability alone. But the drive toward military hegemony was due as much to the existence of preconditions that led in that direction as it was to the personal charisma of the individual unifiers.

The course by which the daimyo were brought under unified command, though basically a struggle for power among members of the warrior aristocracy, involved other contestants as well. Most of these other groups were at cross purposes to the interests of the military aristocracy. Such were the various types of *ikki* – local uprisings or compacts organized for collective action.[17] *Ikki* were organized by groups of peasants or by communities of adherents to religious sects in protest against the harsh rule exerted by military proprietors in the provinces. *Ikki* could be formed among village samurai who banded together to resist territorial encroachments from larger neighboring daiymo. Among these groups, the militant communities of Ikkō and Nichiren sect adherents gave the most trouble to the daimyo. In fact, each of the unifiers at the start of his rise to power had to combat militant religious communities that had put down roots in the villages and newly emerging urban societies within their domains. There they offered powerful resistance to the expanding daimyo authority. But the *ikki* were best organized for purposes of defense and resistance. They had little staying power. In the long run, therefore, they gave way to the daimyo, who were better able to organize local administra-

---

16 Osamu Wakita, "The Emergence of the State in Sixteenth Century Japan," *Journal of Japanese Studies* 8 (Summer 1982): 343–67.
17 For an overview of the various types of *ikki* that took place during the fifteenth and sixteenth centuries, see David L. Davis, "Ikki in Late Medieval Japan," in John W. Hall and Jeffrey P. Mass, eds., *Medieval Japan: Essays in Institutional History* (New Haven, Conn.: Yale University Press, 1974), pp. 226–47.

tion and to set up the mechanisms for the management of land and local communities and for the exploitation of the wealth and military resources of a given area.

THE EMERGENCE OF THE SAMURAI CLASS

Ultimately the daimyo system won out over its competitors in the countryside, but not without certain conspicuous consequences. The movement of nearly the entire body of rural samurai into castle towns that served as daimyo headquarters was occasioned in part by the attraction that service under the daimyo could offer to the samurai class. But it is equally true that withdrawal of the samurai from the countryside was motivated by defensive considerations as well. In the provinces, small-sized military proprietors found that submission to the armies of larger regional hegemons could be the lesser of evils. They preferred to accept the command of a rising military lord rather than face possible destruction at the hands of a militant popular religious uprising. The so-called sword hunts, *katanagari*, that were carried out at various times – first by individual daimyo and later under the command of Hideyoshi – was evidence of the fear that members of the samurai class who still lived in the village environment had of the possibility of losing out to militant mass attacks.

Fear of resistance from below helps explain why neither Nobunaga nor Hideyoshi, in the course of his national conquest, did not simply abolish all daimyo as they were defeated, and add their vacated territories to his own granary lands. The answer is evident in the nature of the warfare in which the unifiers were engaged. The victories won over their rivals were achieved not by a single all-powerful army but by mixed forces drawn from the unifier's daimyo followers, many of them only recently acquired. As a general practice, contingents from the most recently defeated daimyo were placed in the vanguard in the next battle, thus obliging them to prove their loyalty. The armed forces that won the hegemony for the unifiers, from first to last, consisted of contingents drawn from a coalition of daimyo. Rather than destroy the daimyo, the unifiers found themselves heavily reliant on them, for both military support and field administration. Hideyoshi, in particular, made every effort to win over opposing daimyo by compromise rather than a fight to the finish. This mutual dependence was to remain an integral part of the *bakuhan* system throughout the Edo period.

The *bakuhan* system was the result of processes that had been under way well before the appearance of the Tokugawa shogunate. Further-more, the processes continued to undergo change well beyond the first shogun's lifetime. But how far beyond? On what basis are we to judge when a given institution has reached its stable form? Itō Tasaburō and Nakamura Kichiji, historians who first developed the concept of the *bakuhan* system, early on directed special attention to a common prac-tice that they believed served as an indicator of just such an institu-tional change.[18] This is the method by which samurai retainers of daimyo received their financial support.

Typical of daimyo domains of the early sixteenth century was the large percentage of enfeoffed vassals (*chigyō-tori*) among the daimyo's vassal band, and the relatively small amount of the daimyo's private holdings (less than 25 percent in some cases). This condition reflected the fact that the daimyo had won control over the lesser lordships only recently. In fact, during the Sengoku period the typical domain was literally a coalition of individual fief holders over whom the daimyo had only an uncertain hold.[19] But the daimyo's central authority in-creased steadily. The form this ultimately took was one in which all retainers had been deprived of their proprietory rights and were paid out of the daimyo's granary. Whereas in earlier times the daimyo's men exercised direct proprietary authority over the inhabitants of their fief lands, by the end of the seventeenth century most of the retainers of the shogun and daimyo had become officers possessing only those powers delegated by the daimyo's superior authority. The evolution from fief to stipend and from personal to bureaucratic au-thority was one of the crucial subcurrents that marked the passage of Japanese society into the Edo age. But this did not happen automati-cally or uniformly. At no time was the transformation from fief to stipend complete in all respects and in all parts of Japan. In fact, there were certain areas in which the Edo ideal was never fulfilled.

Enfeoffed samurai remained on the land in a number of areas, mostly in the long-established domains like Satsuma, Aizu, and Sendai that were located in the frontier regions of the Japanese islands farthest from the traditional centers of military and political power. But on closer examination, even in these cases a good measure of the rural samurai's rights over land and its cultivators had been absorbed

18 An early statement by Itō Tasaburō on the *bakuhan* system is found in his "Bakuhan taisei ron." The same series contains Nakamura Kichiji's "Hōken jidai kōki sōsetsu." Both articles reflect the changes in historical interpretation that appeared in Japan following the end of World War II.

19 This is seen clearly in the map showing the distribution of fiefs in Bizen province under the command of the Ukita house. See Hall, *Government and Local Power*, p. 314.

into the daimyo's superior authority. In many parts of the country, what appeared to be a retention of functional fiefs was actually a fiction. Because possession of fief land was considered more prestigious than the receipt of granary rights, retainers were often given certificates of enfeoffment but in actual practice were treated like stipendiaries. Centralization of the *han* around the daimyo's granaries had become the normal expectation by the beginning of the Edo period, and the adoption of the rice stipend could be considered a mark of institutional maturity.[20]

FORMATION OF THE EARLY MODERN VILLAGE

Much of the same pattern of development was evident in the case of the village, or *mura*. Here the specific changes that marked the conversion of the medieval agricultural community into the mature administrative mura must be defined in terms of specific land rights held by the cultivator class and the manner in which samurai government interacted with village administration. The land survey became the foundation on which rested both the mura and the legal structure by which the samurai class related to the peasantry and the peasantry related to the land. The key elements in this connection were the formation of a legally defined farming class (the *hyakushō*), the designation of village officials such as the headmen (*nanushi*, *shōya*), and the placement of the daimyo's regional field administrators (*daikan* or *kōribugyō*). The status of *hyakushō*, who in simplest terms can be thought of as taxpaying villagers, was very much the product of the land survey. Up to the middle of the sixteenth century the line between the village head and the estate land-steward was not clearly drawn. Village samurai were able to participate in both worlds. The eventual form of this relationship was one in which both the village internal administration and the control mechanism descending from the daimyo had been effectively bureaucratized.

Before that could happen, however, two practices held over from the Oda–Toyotomi years had to be eradicated. On the one hand, a number of legal rights over land and its workers, including setting the annual tax rate, continued to be held by the former village samurai, even though they had taken up residence in the daimyo's castle town.

---

20 For a recent analysis of the formation of what he has called the "mature daimyo domain," see Junnosuke Sasaki, with Ronald P. Toby, "The Changing Rationale of Daimyo Control in the Emergence of the Bakuhan State," in Hall, Nagahara, and Yamamura, eds., *Japan Before Tokugawa*, pp. 286–91.

On the other hand, various economic and social privileges that the village samurai held during periods of widespread warfare remained in the hands of former village samurai, even though they had reduced their political and legal status to that of *hyakushō*. It was common practice that village landholders of this type would be able to monopolize village offices like that of headman, especially in the early years of Tokugawa rule. But it was to the interest of both the military hegemon and the daimyo that private powers exercised arbitrarily on a hereditary basis should be discontinued in favor of administrative authority based on legal precedent. The battle between impersonal bureaucratic government and rule by private influence was fought at all levels of government. Under the Tokugawa bakufu, the principle of administration according to precept and precedent was never enforced absolutely: hereditary privilege and status inevitably remained a part of the political process. But it was not considered a desirable condition, especially at the lower levels.

Studies of the two fundamental institutions – *bakuhan* government and *kokudaka* land management – have opened important new vistas into the nature of the structural legacies of the Oda–Toyotomi years. One of the most significant consequences of the reforms adopted by the unifiers was the manner in which society became divided into the separate classes of samurai, *hyakushō*, *chōnin*, and a number of subclasses. From the early years of the sixteenth century, a growing volume of legislation, especially from the large regional daimyo, began to reflect a conscious effort to define and separate the several classes or estates. The enforcement of the Taikō land survey, the sword hunts, and the census surveys, though motivated primarily by political and economic objectives, had a fundamental impact on social organization and behavior. Today we debate whether the elaborate system of class separation reflected the actual dynamics of the time or whether they were imposed arbitrarily from above. Were they in fact basically repressive, serving primarily the interests of the military aristocracy? Indeed, scholars who view the Hideyoshi settlement as imposing on Japan a revitalized feudal despotism are of such an opinion.[21]

But the social legislation of the time can be viewed in another light. As Asao Naohiro points out in this volume, in the course of the drive toward unification, Nobunaga "promoted policies that released society from the restrictions that had fettered the daily lives of the medieval

---

21 The prime advocate of this thesis in English is E. H. Norman. See his "Late Feudal Society," in John W. Dower, ed., *Origins of the Modern Japanese State: Selected Writings of E. H. Norman* (New York: Random House, 1975), pp. 321–51.

populace."[22] Bitō Masahide directs his attention to the concept of *yaku*, or function, that applies to the entire society, defining the expectations that society had for each class, subclass, and group.[23] By Tokugawa times this had led to what can be called "rule by status," a condition in which individuals, as long as they remained in their proper place and performed their given roles, were treated impartially under the law and according to precedent.[24] Granted, seventeenth-century social theory did not subscribe to concepts of individual rights or political representation; yet the bakufu, *han*, and mura governments did provide for dispute resolution and arbitration. Bitō Masahide points out that the *ie* system of family organization offered a mechanism that protected the individual from arbitrary demands from outside the system.

THE EDO BAKUFU IN THE EIGHTEENTH CENTURY

Our analysis so far has explored the institutional legacies of the Oda–Toyotomi era to the Edo period. As we pursue this inquiry farther into the Edo period, we encounter conditions of a different sort. Eighteenth-century Japan confronted problems that were the consequences of the decisions made during the latter half of the sixteenth century, such as the necessary adjustments to civil rule, the side effects of political centralization, the separation of classes, urbanization, economic growth, and technological change – all problems that put new pressure on the *bakuhan* system as a whole.

When in the late 1940s Western historians directed their attention to the evolution of political life under the *bakuhan* system, the most common explanation of why the Edo bakufu took the shape it did was that it reflected the power of the military aristocracy. George B. Sansom's often-quoted characterization of Tokugawa government as an "extension into times of peace of the supreme command in times of war. It was not based upon any theory of the state" expresses neatly the popular conception of the Edo government as a military absolutism that sought to survive through the exercise of autocratic power.[25]

Postwar literature on the Tokugawa government's exercise of power

---

22 See Chapter 2.
23 This is discussed in English in Masahide Bitō, "Society and Social Thought in the Tokugawa Period," in *Japan Foundation Newsletter* 9 (June–September 1981): 4–6.
24 Quite similar to Bitō's *yaku* thesis is the concept of status, or *mibun*. See my "Rule by Status in Tokugawa Japan," *Journal of Japanese Studies* 1 (Autumn 1974): 38–49.
25 G. B. Sansom, *Japan, a Short Cultural History* (New York: Appleton Century, 1943), p. 455.

has, to varying degrees, borrowed from Marxist and Weberian theories of types of authority. Western writers, among them Edwin O. Reischauer and E. H. Norman, identified the cohesive ingredient in Edo period political organization as the bond between lord and vassal. The image of "centralized feudalism" is used to account for the effectiveness of Tokugawa rule. Absolute and arbitrary power, they believe, became their own justification.[26]

But it was obvious that reliance on military power alone had its limitations. Shogun and daimyo were engaged in a nationwide effort to routinize administrative procedures and to codify basic legal precepts. The first task at hand was the necessary conversion from military to civil government. During the 1930s, Kurita Mototsugu developed the classic explanation of how this process benefited from the spread of Confucian philosophy.[27] The concept of "benevolent rule" (bunji-seiji), according to Kurita, had helped humanize military government. The conversion of the samurai class into urban-based administrators, as promoted in the first clause of the "Buke shohatto" (ordinances pertaining to the warrior class), was matched by a strenuous enforcement of laws against possession of arms by others than the samurai. And once peace was attained, the bakufu took elaborate means to curtail and regulate the size and armament of the standing forces permitted to the daimyo. Improvements in military technology were largely discontinued under a conscious policy that played down the use of firearms.[28]

From the 1940s, and culminating in Kitajima Masamoto's analysis of the Edo power structure, the most vigorous school of interpretation concentrated on the study of the administrative devices by which shogun and daimyo exercised their rule.[29] The key ingredients in such a polity were, of course, the possession of hegemonic military power and the acquisition of legitimacy as a public authority. As Asao Naohiro explains in his chapter, the sources of legitimacy other than military strength were the symbolism of proximity to the tennō (emperor) and the actual creation of a political and social order that could claim to be dedicated to the good of the people, in other words, the acquisition of the status of kōgi.

26 Edwin O. Reischauer, Japan. The Story of a Nation (New York: Knopf, 1970).
27 Kurita Mototsugu, Edo jidai shi (Tokyo: Kokushi kōza kankōkai, 1934), pp. 85–108, contains a summary of his treatment of the subject.
28 For descriptions of bakufu and daimyo military organizations, see Conrad Totman, Politics in the Tokugawa Bakufu, 1600–1843 (Cambridge, Mass.: Harvard University Press, 1967), pp. 43–63.
29 Kitajima Masamoto, Edo bakufu no kenryoku kōzō (Tokyo: Iwanami shoten, 1964).

THE POLITICAL PROCESS

One characteristic of the Edo age is that the long stretch of domestic peace and the structural continuities within the bakufu and *han* enforcement agencies meant that there were few easily identifiable period-defining events. The Edo period, therefore, has left to the viewer much of the task of giving it meaningful shape. And because historians differ widely in their sense of the relative importance of events, the periodization of the Edo era remains a matter of controversy.

But implicit in much of the work on the Edo period by specialists in the field is the reliance on what is essentially a dynastic approach to periodization. Although careful to avoid the appearance of reliance on the great-man approach to causation, they have found useful the traditional chronology based on the sequence of individual shoguns, if only as a convention. For this reason it seems desirable for this general introduction to the political history of the Edo period to set down an outline of the Tokugawa "dynasty." (In what follows, the years in office of the successive shoguns are shown in parentheses.)

1. Ieyasu (1603–5), Hidetada (1605–23), Iemitsu (1623–51). The first three shoguns are generally linked together as the founders of the bakufu and the framers of basic political institutions and policies.
2. Ietsuna (1651–80). The fourth shogun, being a minor when he was named shogun, was obliged to rely on advisers assigned from among the high-ranking members of the Tokugawa vassal band. This was the first appearance of a pattern of bakufu politics in which members of the *fudai* daimyo, that is, the hereditary house daimyo, exerted superior influence on bakufu policy through the Senior Council.
3. Tsunayoshi (1680–1709). The fifth shogun was the first to be selected from among several possible candidates. Iemitsu's fourth son, Tsunayoshi had served as a daimyo as the adopted head of the Tatebayashi house and thus had developed his own ideas regarding shogunal policy before assuming that office. Although a patron of Confucian political philosophy, his reputation was tarnished by some of his extreme policies, exemplified by his ordinances protecting animals, notably dogs. He was the first shogun to use the office of grand chamberlain (*sobayōnin*) as a means of bypassing the Senior Council, thus earning the resentment of many entrenched *fudai* daimyo.
4. Ienobu (1709–12) and Ietsugu (1713–16). The sixth and seventh

shoguns were not in good health, and both died after only a few years in office. Bakufu policy depended on shogunal advisers, and, again, they were drawn from the "inner" staff close to the individual shoguns rather than from the Senior Council. Ienobu's adviser was the remarkable Confucian scholar Arai Hakuseki (1657–1725), who was instrumental in rationalizing several aspects of bakufu policy, including finance and trade.

5. Yoshimune (1716–45). The eighth shogun was selected from the Kii branch of the Tokugawa house. Having served as a daimyo for some ten years, he came to the office of the shogunate with a reputation as a strong administrator. Upon his transfer to Edo Castle he undertook the first major "revision" of the bakufu system: the so-called Kyōhō Reforms. Proclaimed as a "return to Ieyasu's legacy," it sought to expand the bakufu's finances, clean up corruption in the land-tax system, and improve morale among lesser vassals of the shogun by bettering their financial status.

6. Ieshige (1745–60) and Ieharu (1760–86). Both the ninth and tenth shoguns had physical problems and were less than vigorous administrators. The combination of weak shoguns and advisers who were personal favorites created conditions that contemporaries criticized as leading to corruption in government. Ieharu's favorite, Tanuma Okitsugu (1719–88), was to go down in history as the archetypical corrupt influence in shogunal government. Although modern historians are less critical of Tanuma, his contemporaries attacked him for his policies that benefited the shogunate at the expense of the daimyo's interests.

7. Ienari (1787–1837). The eleventh shogun's rule was divided into two parts. It began when the shogun was still a minor. During his early years he served as legitimizer for the reform-minded Matsudaira Sadanobu (1758–1829) who mounted what has been called the "Kansei Reforms" dedicated to cleaning up what he believed to be the evil influences of Tanuma. In 1817, however, Ienari found himself free of influence from conservative members of the bakufu senior officialdom. There followed a period of conspicuous spending under Grand Chamberlain Mizuno Tadaakira.

8. Ieyoshi (1837–53). As an individual the twelfth shogun seemed an ordinary person without strong expectations for bakufu policy. He nonetheless gave his support to Senior Councilor Mizuno Tadakuni's (1794–1851) extreme program of bakufu reform – the so-called Tempō Reform. The results were disastrous and led to further weakening of the Tokugawa hegemony.

9. Iesada (1853–8), Iemochi (1858–66), and Keiki (Yoshinobu, 1866–7). The last three shoguns were largely overwhelmed by events following the arrival of the Perry expedition and the demands by the Western powers that Japan open its ports to foreign trade. The story of how the *bakuhan* system performed in the face of this foreign crisis is discussed in the fifth volume of the *Cambridge History of Japan*.

PATTERNS OF POLITICAL DEVELOPMENT

The preceding outline of Tokugawa dynastic succession provides a backdrop on which historians have plotted the events that they have found most significant. This in turn has depended on the questions that individual scholars have asked. Historians, both premodern and modern, have been concerned with issues that relate to the success or failure of the *bakuhan* system. Traditional interpretations, reflecting the opinions of Confucian-trained scholars, long put their emphasis on the character of individual shoguns and their advisers. Conditions of crisis presumably were brought on by the failure of those in high places to maintain discipline, to guard against the progressive deterioration of the capacity to command. What were the signs that presumably brought on times of crisis? These, as understood by the Japanese of that time, can best be discovered by analyzing the reform movements that periodically broke through the surface of the Tokugawa political calm.

As we noted, the Edo bakufu experienced three major attempts at reform. These were Shogun Yoshimune's reform of the Kyōhō era (1716–35), the reform pushed by Matsudaira Sadanobu in the Kansei era (1789–99), and that of Mizuno Tadakuni during the Tempō era (1830–44).[30] Each of these reforms aimed at specific targets: the extravagance of shoguns like Tsunayoshi and Ienari, the corruption of advisers like Tanuma Okitsugu, or the failure to control the commercial sector and maintain an acceptable level in the price of rice. In other words, the problems were mainly economic and social, but they were seen as failures of political leadership.

The practice of attaching primary significance to the individual actors on the bakufu stage has not been abandoned, but scholars today have taken care to base their explanations of political events on general concepts of political authority combined with a thorough familiarity

---

30 Honjō Eijirō, ed., *Kinsei Nihon no san dai kaikaku*, vol. 4 of *Keizai shiwa sōsho* (Tokyo: Ryūginsha, 1949).

with documents that deal directly with the events under study. This has led to a number of new types of historical inquiry, among them the careful study of the motivations of the central actors through the use of new levels of documentation, and the application of social scientific hypotheses in the fields of economic, social, and demographic analysis.

An outstanding example of this approach is found in the work of Tsuji Tatsuya.[31] We owe to him the opening up of the middle years of Edo bakufu political history. This has touched importantly on our assessment of the politics of the shogunates of Tsunayoshi and Yoshimune and the advisory roles of Arai Hakusaki, Tanuma Okitsugu, and Matsudaira Sadanobu. Tsuji concludes that when all of the expressions of Confucian moral judgment are stripped away, the policy objectives of Tsunayoshi and Yoshimune were not so different from each other. Nor does there seem to be so great a difference among the basic economic policies of the various leaders. Obviously the tensions and disputes that built up between the holders of power – that is, the bakufu, shogun, daimyo, as against the commoner merchants and farmers – had political origins. More significant has been the discovery of the gradual professionalization of offices in the bakufu bureaucracy, particularly in the Finance Office. Rather than seeing high-level bakufu policy as the work of ideologues striking out blindly, it appears that there was increasing input from experienced administrators at the level just below that of the Senior Council. The same pattern was duplicated in many of the daimyo domains; in fact, many daimyo were far in advance of the shogunate in their use of mercantilist fiscal policy.

GROWTH AND CONFLICT

The simple fact that the Tokugawa hegemony lasted for over two and a half centuries evokes our admiration. What was the secret of bakufu success as peacekeeper of the nation? We think immediately of the balance of power within the political structure – the remarkable network of checks and balances at almost every level. From the start of the Tokugawa regime, there had been a competition for power between the central interests of the bakufu, as these were being defined by the shogun, and those of the daimyo. These were not by any means identical. Much of the animosity that the upper level of the shogun's house daimyo directed at the influence of shogunal favorites was motivated by the realization that a Tanuma represented the interests of the

31 Tsuji Tatsuya, *Kyōhō kaikaku no kenkyū* (Tokyo: Sobunsha, 1963).

bakufu against those of the house daimyo. Harold Bolitho analyzed the policy controversies within the bakufu and concluded that men like Tokugawa Tsunayoshi, Arai Hakuseki, and Tanuma Okitsugu projected negative images because they were advocating policies that appeared to be to the disadvantage of the house daimyo.[32] Why these tensions did not break into the open is a reflection of the comparatively crisis-free condition of the great Tokugawa peace. It reveals as well the high degree of accommodation – the capacity to satisfy basic needs – that resulted from the relatively low intensity of domestic tension and the strong pressures applied to avoid open confrontation.

From the 1920s, Marxist theory had had a strong influence on Japanese interpretations of Edo history. Up to the 1950s, in fact, the dominant view of the state of the peasantry under the *bakuhan* system was fundamentally Marxist and hence class oriented. According to this view, the daimyo, conceived of as "feudal lords," enforced a harsh exploitive policy from above, whereas at the village level, "parasitic" landlords joined with samurai administrators to squeeze out whatever surplus might remain after payment of annual land dues. Thus, it was explained, conditions inevitably worsened as time passed, forcing the peasantry to use protest and mass demonstration to express their grievances.[33]

The phenomenon of rural and urban popular protest has occupied an important place in the effort of modern historians to understand Edo society. As already noted, the story of the enforcement of samurai rule over the agrarian populace told of many types of popular resistance to higher authority in the name of local self-interest. A common practice was the organization of autonomous groups, or *ikki*, and we have seen that the movement toward consolidation of local power under the daimyo required the forcible elimination of *ikki* communities that sought to retain their independence. The consolidation of rule by the bushi estate under the Tokugawa shogunate resulted in a general quieting of the rural population under the mura system. But the causes of rural unrest were not fully eliminated. Moreover, because the system of rural administration incorporated few opportunities for the legal presentation of grievances, the practice of mass protest was often the only method of self-expression available.

---

32 Harold Bolitho, *Treasures Among Men: The Fudai Daimyo in Tokugawa Japan* (New Haven, Conn.: Yale University Press, 1974), pp. 169–85, 190–205.

33 Traditional historiography backed by Marxist theory has painted a harsh image of the peasant under the *bakuhan* system. For a description of the controversy over the condition of the Edo period peasantry, see my "E. H. Norman on Tokugawa Japan," in *Journal of Japanese Studies* 3 (Summer 1977): 365–74.

Studies of Edo society since the introduction of Marxist historiography have adopted the evidence of popular protest as an index to the intensity of class struggle. Among the early Japanese scholars in this field were Ono Takeo and Kokushō Iwao, who began gathering first-hand accounts of peasant disturbances and took the first steps in analyzing and classifying the many types of such occurrences.[34] Hugh Borton's pioneering study of Edo peasant uprisings reflects this approach. The most recent effort to record an inventory of rural protest is the work of Aoki Kōji, who identified over 6,889 occurrences.[35]

What was the significance of these occurrences? The major issues that attract the attention of historians of the Edo period concern the manner in which the uprisings exposed the nature of the social problems of that time. Among these incidents were large-scale peasant uprisings and mass demonstrations that required the use of government troops to control. But many, in the opinion of some observers, were hardly more than the equivalent of "union collective bargaining."[36] Clearly, Japan did not experience unrest so severe as to bring about the overthrow of either rural administration or the central government. Thus the Japanese narrative is concerned with the formation of class identity within an acknowledged national historical frame.

Contradictory views of Edo society still divide the scholarly world, both in Japan and the West. But the early simplistic assumptions that the inhabitants of Edo rural society were from beginning to end motivated by fear and hatred have given way to a more realistic analysis in the works of scholars like Sasaki Junnosuke, who place their main emphasis on the spiritual foundations of village solidarity.[37]

Equally positive in their interpretation of the economic foundations of Edo society are modern economic historians. This group bases its argument on evidence of an agricultural and commercial revolution encouraged by what to them appears to be a remarkable surge of economic growth.[38] The effort to quantify this eighteenth-century economic growth has focused on the pattern of population growth. Na-

34 Kokushō Iwao, *Hyakushō ikki no kenkyū* (Tokyo: Iwanami shoten, 1928).
35 Hugh Borton, "Peasant Uprisings in Japan of the Tokugawa Period," *Transactions of the Asiatic Society of Japan*, 2nd series, vol. 16 (1938), pp. 1–219; Aoki Kōji, *Hyakushō ikki sōgō nempyō* (Tokyo: Sanichi shobō, 1971).
36 Irwin Scheiner, "Benevolent Lords and Honorable Peasants: Rebellion and Peasant Consciousness in Tokugawa Japan," in Tetsuo Najita and Irwin Scheiner, eds., *Japanese Thought in the Tokugawa Period – Methods and Metaphors* (Chicago: University of Chicago Press, 1978), p. 60.
37 Sasaki, "The Changing Rationale."
38 The thesis that Japan underwent an agricultural revolution under the Edo bakufu rule is vigorously stated in Kozo Yamamura, "Returns on Unification: Economic Growth in Japan, 1550–1650," in Hall, Nagahara, and Yamamura, eds., *Japan Before Tokugawa*, p. 329 or 7–372.

tional demographic figures are sketchy for the early years of the period. But it is thought that both population and the size of the land base probably doubled within the first century of Tokugawa rule. The remarkable fact is that the overall population appears to have remained at roughly the same man–land ratio throughout the Edo period. Bear in mind that this was the very time when China was experiencing a fantastic explosion of its own population. How were the Japanese able to keep their population growth under control? Was there a conscious effort to do so? Village family records exist in abundance, in the form of annual temple registers whose main purpose was to screen out Christian believers. These documents have provided demographic historians with the documentary base from which they can demonstrate that population growth was consciously curtailed using a wide variety of methods: late marriages, restrictions on length of childbearing for women, abortion, infanticide, and the like.[39] But there are also those who believe that the failure of the population to grow was due primarily to the ill effects of the feudal system.[40]

Not yet fully factored into our analysis is the effect of the city on the process of economic growth. Urban growth was spectacular. The city headquarters of bakufu and daimyo establishments were witness to the almost total urbanization of the samurai class and to the creation of a new class, the urban service class, or chōnin. Other than the studies of the great cities of Kyoto, Osaka, and Edo, the analysis of urbanization as a general theme began with the castle town phenomenon. One of the most revealing insights into Edo life has come from recent studies of han structure and the accompanying development of the han castle town.[41]

A further question that still has not been answered satisfactorily is whether the Tokugawa "Great Peace" resulted in a general improvement in the quality of life for all classes. That it indeed did so for the upper levels of the three primary classes is irrefutable. But what of the less fortunate? Certainly, as Furushima Toshio makes clear, the Japanese of the seventeenth century made great advances in agricul-

---

39 For an assessment of the living standard in the most economically advanced area of Japan, see Susan B. Hanley and Kozo Yamamura, *Economic and Demographic Change in Preindustrial Japan, 1600–1868* (Princeton, N.J.: Princeton University Press, 1977), pp. 17–25.
40 See Norman, "Late Feudal Society," p. 324.
41 Among the growing number of studies of the Edo period *han* in English, see James L. McClain, *Kanazawa, a Seventeenth Century Castle Town* (New Haven, Conn.: Yale University Press, 1982). Also Madoka Kanai, "Fukui, Domain of a Tokugawa Collateral Daimyo: Its Tradition and Transition," in Ardath Burks, ed., *The Modernizers, Overseas Students, Foreign Employees and Meiji Japan*, (Boulder, Colo.: Westview Press, 1985), pp. 33–65. An early synthetic study of the castle town can be found in John Whitney Hall, "The Castle Town and Japan's Modern Urbanization," in Hall and Jansen, eds., *Studies*.

tural technology, manufacturing, civil engineering, and transportation. These achievements invite comparison with contemporary developments in China and Europe. And although it may not be demonstrated that the Japanese led the way in the invention of new technologies, they were clearly far advanced in the adaptation of known technologies and especially the social systems that ensured their most effective application. Hideyoshi's invasion of Korea, though politically misguided, exemplifies both of these factors. His mobilization of two invasion armadas of over 140,000 men each is a truly remarkable achievement. Recent studies of Japan's involvement in foreign trade revealed the surprising fact that Japan led the world in the export of silver during the seventeenth century.[42] In the following pages, Professors Nakai, McClain, Furushima, and Hanley write cautiously about a possible general improvement. They cite at the same time evidence of extreme conditions of hardship that affected certain regions and certain levels of society that remained troublesome throughout the Edo period.

THOUGHT AND RELIGION

The cultural implications of the separation of classes, the cessation of active warfare, and the reasonable distribution of economic means were made evident in many ways. Class separation made for the parallel but separate growth of arts and letters and patterns of patronage according to social class capability or preference. The new cities became not only points of economic concentration but also environments in which all levels and classes of society could maintain their separate identities. Samurai participated in higher learning and patronized the "genteel" arts, building lavishly decorated residences and mausoleums. Despite the scattering of daimyo headquarters over the entire extent of the Japanese islands, the alternate attendance (*sankin-kōtai*) system that required daimyo to reside in Edo in alternate years became a powerful force drawing the upper samurai class together culturally. The system required daimyo to spend enormous sums to maintain their establishment in Edo. Meanwhile the urban-based *chōnin* were spreading out across the land. The creative centers of urban culture began in Kyoto and Osaka but soon moved to Edo as well. It was especially in these large urban environments that samurai and *chōnin*

---

42 Hayami Akira, "Tokugawa Nihon seiritsu no sekaishi – Philip II to Toyotomi Hideyoshi," *Mitagakkai zasshi* 77 (February 1985): 50–61.

intermingled to create the new urban style of life, as Donald Shively demonstrates in his chapter.

During the battles for unification, one of the most troublesome problems faced by the three unifiers was the control of religious bodies. Daimyo who sought to participate in the unification movement first had to eliminate the armed Buddhist communities in their home territories before they were free to mobilize their military resources to meet challenges from outside their boundaries. By the time of the establishment of the Edo shogunate, the great monastic fortresses and the armed Ikkō and Nichiren communities had been brought under control.[43] Christianity had also gone through a cycle of toleration that later turned to persecution. Government control of religion was symbolized by the requirement that all Japanese adopt a temple of registry (dannadera) and submit to the enforcement of the annual religious scrutiny conducted at the temple.[44]

It is generally assumed that this double policy of the elimination of militant religious groups and the enforcement of temple registry literally swept away the religious content of life for the Japanese people. To the contrary, Bitō Masahide suggests that various combinations of Buddhism, fused with Shinto, spread widely among the common people, giving rise to what he calls a "national" or "people's" religion. Medieval religion had offered the prospect of individual salvation. The new religious practices spoke directly to the living, "offering the means of sustaining life in the real world." The result was, according to Bitō, an "affirmation of reality."[45]

The addition of Confucian and native historical studies to the repertory of the samurai led to the most active outpouring of Japanese scholarship before modern times. By the Edo period Japanese society had clearly reached a new level of cultural sophistication. Prewar studies of this aspect of Edo life had gone a long way to identify the primary thinkers and writers of the day. But their works were not appreciated fully by students outside Japan. Since World War II Western scholars have acquired the necessary tools with which to make their own inquiries into the thought world of Tokugawa Japan. Much of this recent scholarship has sought to play down the importance of

43 For the story of Nobunaga's suppression of the military powers of the Buddhist monasteries, see Neil McMullin, *Buddhism and the State in Sixteenth Century Japan* (Princeton, N.J.: Princeton University Press, 1984), pp. 100–61.
44 The office of religious scrutiny was established by the bakufu in 1640. See McMullin, *Buddhism and the State*, pp. 245ff. Also see George Elison, *Deus Destroyed: The Image of Christianity in Early Modern Japan* (Cambridge, Mass.: Harvard University Press, 1973).
45 See Chapter 8.

Confucianism as the official ideology of the Edo samurai establishment. A concrete measure of the influence of the Confucian scholar on the Japanese thought world can be found in the status of the Confucian adviser in samurai government. Although shoguns and daimyo patronized Confucianists in their governments, such advisers, known as *jusha*, were clearly subordinate to the primary interests of samurai government.[46]

Although much of the work of Western historians of Edo Japan has been devoted to the study of political and social institutions, there has been of late a remarkable upsurge of interest in the intellectual foundations of Edo society and culture. It began with the work of Robert N. Bellah, who in his *Tokugawa Religion* sought to apply the concepts of Max Weber to Edo society.[47] More recently this interest has been reflected in the work of the continuing seminar on Tokugawa intellectual history. The purpose of the first conference volume, edited by Tetsuo Najita and Irwin Scheiner, was to demonstrate that the Tokugawa era should be regarded as one of Japan's great creative ages. They also observed that Japan's eighteenth-century value system was as relevant a legacy for modern Japan as were the principles adopted from the West.[48] Symbolic of the new look of the Edo era was the magnificent museum display, *The Great Japan Exhibition: Art of the Edo Period 1600–1868*, held in London in 1981.[49] Once the shadows of feudalism and militarism are withdrawn, we have on view a cultural display of magnificent proportions and vigor. We are only now realizing how much post–Edo Japan depended on the cultural norms of the Edo period.

What of the role of Christianity in the century from 1530 to 1630? By the 1620s the foreign religion had become a thorn in the side of unification politics. The cycle from acceptance to prohibition was played out in the atmosphere of diminishing trade relations in the East Asian area. Adoption of the seclusion policy, though it restrained the natural urge of the Japanese to take to the sea for trade, did not turn off all foreign contact. Most recently, scholars have looked upon the

---

46 John Whitney Hall, "The Confucian Teacher in Tokugawa Japan," in David S. Nivison and Arthur F. Wright, eds., *Confucianism in Action* (Stanford, Calif.: Stanford University Press, 1959). This is the main theme of the volume of essays entitled *Confucianism and Tokugawa Culture*, ed. Peter Nosco (Princeton, N.J.: Princeton University Press, 1984).
47 Robert N. Bellah, *Tokugawa Religion: The Values of Pre-Industrial Japan* (Glencoe, Ill.: Free Press, 1957).
48 Najita and Scheiner, eds., *Japanese Thought in the Tokugawa Period*.
49 For the catalog of this exhibition, see William Watson, ed., *The Great Japan Exhibition: Art of the Edo Period 1600–1868* (New York: Alpine Fine Arts Collection, 1981).

"Christian century" less simplistically and negatively. In fact, Japan did maintain a highly regulated contact with the outside world through Korea, the Ryūkyū Islands, and, of course, Nagasaki. The factor of isolation (*sakoku*) in Tokugawa history has been subjected to rethinking by scholars in the 1970s, but considerable controversy still surrounds the question of how closed Japan really was, the motives that led the Tokugawa government to reduce the scope of Japan's relations with the outside world, and the consequences of closure on Japan's long-term development.[50]

On reflection, it is possible to turn the concept of *sakoku* around and come to different conclusions. Relative isolation from foreign contacts, particularly Western, for some two centuries did indeed force the Japanese back on their own resources. But this was not a prelude to general stagnation. The Japanese homeland was of a sufficient size and diversity and its inhabitants sufficiently vigorous that they were able to pursue an energetic development without having to depend on outside stimulus.

By comparison with European societies under similar circumstances, one is struck by the lack of effort on the part of central authority, the bakufu, to increase its powers after the mid-seventeenth century. The balance between daimyo landholdings and those of the shogun remained little changed. And no other general effort to create a monarchic sovereignty was attempted. On the other hand, under the influence of the alternate attendance regulations, the samurai as a class was fused into a single cultural homogeneity. The cultural styles of the great urban centers became standard for the other major cities of the entire country. By 1800, then, we can see that the many special features of the Azuchi–Momoyama legacy had been fulfilled and Japan was beginning to encounter new conditions that were to lead the country into its modern revolution.

THE EDO PERIOD: A NEW FIELD OF STUDY

The preceding pages have argued that the field defined for this volume has emerged as a combination of the research and writing of scholars both Japanese and Western. Although the greater volume of scholar-

50 A more skeptical approach to *sakoku* has acquired a number of supporters, beginning with Asao Naohiro's *Sakoku* (Tokyo: Shogakkan, 1975). He emphasizes its use by the Tokugawa shogun, whose claims of political legitimacy were enhanced by their control of foreign relations. These conditions have been explained in detail by Ronald P. Toby in his *State and Diplomacy in Early Modern Japan: Asia in the Development of the Tokugawa Bakufu* (Princeton, N.J.: Princeton University Press, 1984).

ship has come from the work of Japanese historians, the contributions of Western writers is noticeable in several subfields, especially in matters of methodology and interpretation. Of special concern for non-Japanese scholars is the problem of transforming Japanese historical reality in a manner that is easily and accurately understandable to the English-reading audience.

Since the 1940s, studies of the Edo age have generated several cycles of interpretation and emphasis, both inside and outside Japan. The fact that these cycles have not been identical shows that scholarship on each side of the Pacific has responded to different influences and situations. The reader has already been introduced to the major cyclical phases that have distinguished the postwar evolution of Edo historiography. We now must look more closely at the development of the Edo period as a field of study.

In taking up the evolution of the field of Edo history from the Japanese side, we need to go back at least to the 1920s, to a time when the first generation of works that still remain useful to us today made their appearance. It was during the 1920s that Japanese historians followed a number of historical approaches, giving rise to several distinct interpretative schools. Such were the political historians like Kuroita Katsumi, the cultural historians like Nishida Naojirō, the early economic historians like Honjō Eijirō, and the legal and social historians like Takigawa Masajirō.[51]

The beginning of Marxist historical interpretation is identified with Hani Gorō and Hattori Shisō, whose major concerns were the Meiji Restoration and the spread of capitalism in Japan; for them the Edo period served as preparation for Japan's rapid modernization. During the war years all historical writing that did not carry the nationalist spirit was pushed underground. But following Japan's defeat in 1945, with the withdrawal of restrictions on freedom of expression, Marxist historiography quickly became the dominant conceptual methodology. The work most commonly cited as having led the way in the application of Marxist methodology to the analysis of medieval history was Ishimoda Shō's *Chūseiteki sekai no keisei* (The structure of medieval society) (1946). Interpretations of Japanese history based on theories of class identity and interaction spread quickly to affect all aspects of historical analysis. These branches of Japanese scholarship were well represented in new journals that first made their appearance in the

51 A bibliographical analysis of the work of these and other prewar Japanese historians can be found in John W. Hall, *Japanese History: A Guide to Japanese Reference and Research Materials* (Ann Arbor: University of Michigan Press, 1954), esp. pp. 75–85.

1930s. These were *Shakai keizai shigaku* (Journal of the social and economic history society), and *Rekishigaku kenkyū* (Journal of historical studies), which began publishing in 1932. The latter journal was obliged to take a low profile during the war-gripped 1940s, but it rapidly came into its own following the war's end. The most comprehensive view of postwar historical scholarship in Japan can be found in the Iwanami series on Japanese history (*Iwanami kōza Nihon rekishi*). These collections of scholarly articles by the leading Japanese specialists appeared in two series following the war.[52]

From the Iwanami series one gains a clear understanding that the main theme that has dominated the efforts of Japanese historians has been the solution to the question of how political power was achieved and conserved. Their primary concern has been to explain the "power structure" at particular moments in Japanese history, to comprehend the exercise of power, its legitimation, and its passage from one group to another.

Another major thrust of Japanese scholarship has dealt with the structure of society, that is, the composition of classes and the relationship of social groups to government and to the levers of power. The common approach of these scholars can best be described as institutional history, namely, the study of structure. And it is here that Western historians find themselves most closely in communication with their Japanese counterparts.

Turning to the development of the field on the Western side, the obvious point to make at the outset is the surprising newness of the field. At the conclusion of the war there were scarcely a handful of historians who could claim professional training in Edo period history. Before 1945 the field could be defined in terms of G. B. Sansom's *Japan, a Short Cultural History*, E. H. Norman's *Japan's Emergence As a Modern State*, Hugh Borton's "Peasant Uprisings in Japan of the Tokugawa Period," and Kan'ichi Asakawa's work on Japanese feudalism.[53] This was hardly a substantial legacy, even if we add to this list a few of the well-produced English-language translations of the works of some of the outstanding Japanese historians, such as Honjō Eijirō's *The Social and Economic History of Japan* and Tsuchiya Takao's *Economic History of Japan*.[54]

---

52 A prewar series appeared in eighteen cases between 1933 and 1935. The first postwar series was published in twenty-three volumes between 1962 and 1964. Series 3 came out in twenty-six volumes between 1975 and 1977.

53 Kan'ichi Asakawa, trans. and ed., *The Documents of Iriki* (Tokyo: Japan Society for the Promotion of Science, 1955).

54 Published by the Asiatic Society of Japan in 1937 and 1943.

World War II had a profound effect on the development of the field of premodern Japanese history in the West. The war with Japan called for the training of military personnel in the United States and Great Britain to use the Japanese language. It also aroused in Western minds a profound realization of the lack of general knowledge that the world outside Japan had of Japan. The result in the United States was the "area studies" movement that affected all fields of international studies. This movement was to have a major influence through the stimulus it gave to private foundations and government agencies to come to the support of the academic study of foreign areas and peoples. The field of Japanese studies in general reacted rapidly to this stimulus. Facilities for the academic study of Japanese language improved dramatically, as did the numbers of programs of specialized training in the field. It was at this point that the first generation of scholarly research monographs, most of them the edited versions of doctoral dissertations, came onto the scene. Overnight the field became a self-generating phenomenon.

The major contributions to Edo historiography have been, and continue to be, the work of individual scholars. But it is easiest to obtain a general overview of the state of the field by referring to several anthologies and conference symposia that have marked the publication record of the field. The first and the most elaborate of these research projects was the Conference on Modern Japan, a project organized under the Association for Asian Studies, which, beginning in the late 1950s, published a total of six volumes. Although the major theme of these conferences dealt with modernization, several contributions touched on aspects of the Edo period and the way in which premodern institutions laid the groundwork for modern change.[55]

It was characteristic of this approach to Japanese history, however, that it subordinated the Edo period to the modernization process. This is apparent in an anthology of articles under the title *Studies in the Institutional History of Early Modern Japan*, edited by John W. Hall and Marius B. Jansen.[56] By declaring that the Tokugawa period should be called Japan's "early modern" age, this volume challenged the common practice of assuming that Japan during the Edo period was still fundamentally feudal. During the 1960s and 1970s the main concern of Western scholars of the Edo period was directed toward explaining Japan's rapid modernization. Outstanding examples are R. P. Dore's

55 Most useful in this respect is the first volume, Marius B. Jansen, ed., *Changing Japanese Attitudes Toward Modernization* (Princeton, N.J.: Princeton University Press, 1965).
56 Hall and Jansen, eds., *Studies*.

Education in Tokugawa Japan (1965), T. C. Smith's *The Agrarian Origins of Modern Japan* (1959), and S. B. Hanley's and Kozo Yamamura's *Economic and Demographic Changes in Preindustrial Japan* (1977). It would appear that Western scholars were more inclined to look forward rather than backward in their explanations of social change.

The time was approaching, however, when the Edo period would be looked at from the other end of the evolutionary process, namely, from the sixteenth century. Heretofore the sixteenth century had been one of the least understood chapters in Japanese history. Recognizing this as a time of fundamental political and social change, historians nevertheless had difficulty in assigning meaning to these changes or to their results. The personal qualities of the great unifiers were obviously not sufficient to serve as sole causes. Despite their leadership, and that of many powerful daimyo, the momentum of class behavior patterns provided the structure within which these changes were made. But from where did the primary motive power come? An interpretative breakthrough came in the 1950s, as a result of the work of Japanese historians on fundamental questions of land control, political authority, and social organization. This, as already noted, was the work of such scholars as Itō Tasaburō, Nakamura Kichiji, and Toyoda Takeshi, who with others identified the importance of such phenomena as the nationwide cadastral survey, the *kokudaka* system, the process of class separation, and the *han* and mura and other such entities. These elements of Japanese rural life of the sixteenth and seventeenth centuries were not yet permanent features of Western historical writing, although the contents of the anthology compiled by Hall and Jansen show the beginnings of an adoption of these institutions as explanatory devices. The recognition that more attention needed to be placed on medieval Japanese institutions stimulated the organization of two multinational conferences. These were the Conference on Muromachi Japan and the Conference on Sengoku Japan. These gatherings were significant because they brought together the leading specialists in Japan and the West to bring up-to-date the knowledge about two relatively neglected periods of Japanese history. Because the conference procedures were conducted in Japanese and the resulting symposium volumes appeared in Japanese and English, they did a great deal to increase the volume of what was known about the Muromachi and Sengoku periods by historians outside Japan.

The approach to Edo history taken in these symposia was largely what we would term institutional. There were other conferences that dealt with aspects of Tokugawa history from different points of analysis. Among these, the ones on intellectual history were especially significant. Especially influential has been the continuing seminar on Tokugawa intellectual history, out of which have emerged volumes such as *Japanese Thought in the Tokugawa Period: Methods and Metaphors* (1968).[57]

Yet another development that has brought the historical world of Japan and the West closer together resulted from the founding of the *Journal of Japanese Studies* in 1970. A feature of this journal has been the effort to publish the work of leading Japanese historians in English translation, or to publish the results of collaborative enterprises. A noteworthy example of this objective was the conference that produced the article "Terms and Concepts in Japanese Medieval History: An Inquiry into the Problems of Translation."[58]

In the final analysis, of course, it is the work of individual scholars that make up any field of historical concentration. This is especially true for a field that has been in existence for so short a time. At the outset of the postwar era of scholarship, it would have been difficult to identify the existence of a field in which works in English by non-Japanese specialists were in sufficient supply and quality to constitute a legitimate field. But by the 1960s this condition began to change, as a large number of works by Western scholars trained to use Japanese primary materials began to make their presence felt.

A NOTE ON THE ORGANIZATION OF THIS VOLUME

The primary objectives of this the fourth volume of our history of Japan is to lay out, as concisely and professionally as possible, the history of Japan from roughly 1550 to 1800. Naturally the presentation has been selective, depending as it must on the availability of contributors and the existence of prior stocks of scholarship on essential subjects. The division of the time span into "chapters" that could be assigned to specialists was the work of the senior editors. Probably the most delicate problem the editors confronted was to strike a balance in the distribution of assignments between Japanese and non-Japanese writers. Because most of the readers of this collection will not have prior knowledge about the authors, it has seemed appropriate to add a brief note about them and their major contributions to the overall

---

57 Edited by Tetsuo Majita and Irwin Scheiner (Chicago: Chicago University Press, 1978).
58 John W. Hall, *Journal of Japanese Studies* 9 (Winter 1983): 1–32.

content of the volume. These will be taken up in the order in which they appear in the volume.

Chapter 2: Asao Naohiro is a leading specialist on medieval Japanese history, known especially for his contributions to the Iwanami Historical Series. Recently he has been studying the nature of the political legitimacy acquired by Nobunaga and Hideyoshi. In his chapter for this volume, Asao has made the important observation that political authority could not have stood on military might alone but must have rested as well on the projection of an image of the ruler's concern for the general welfare.

Chapter 3: Wakita Osamu made his scholarly reputation through his studies of the social and economic history of the Oda–Toyotomi era. One of his most noteworthy achievements was the several articles published in English translation, in the *Journal of Japanese Studies*. Of special importance is his "The Emergence of the State in Sixteenth Century Japan" (1982). Wakita has been one of the few Japanese historians to discuss directly the difference between Japanese and Western scholarly concepts of feudalism and modernization.

Chapter 4: John Whitney Hall has written on the Muromachi and Edo periods in a number of contexts, although his main interest has been the establishment of the daimyo domain, using the materials of the Ikeda house, the daimyo of Okayama (Bizen), as a case study. He has sought to analyze the evolution of military rule as it moved increasingly from military hegemony to the rule of principle (*kōgi*).

Chapter 5: Harold Bolitho has written extensively on the inner politics of the Edo bakufu, particularly the relationship between the daimyo and the shogun. He was one of the first to point out the potential conflicts of interest between shogun and daimyo over bakufu policy. He also raised the highly pertinent question of why the shogun added so little to his powers of rulership following the consolidation of bakufu power in the latter half of the seventeenth century.

Chapters 6 and 7: Jurgis Elisonas, who has hitherto published as George Elison, is best known for his study of the Christian missionary effort of the seventeenth century. His telling of the Christian episode is a skillful presentation of the story from the Japanese side. His description of the establishment of the "Church domain" of Nagasaki breaks new ground. Particularly noteworthy is his handling of Hideyoshi's Korean invasion in Chapter 6.

Chapter 8: Bitō Masahide is an extremely versatile specialist in Edo period thought and religion. His special talent, well illustrated in his contribution to this volume, is his ability to link social organizations with religious and ideological beliefs. Most recently he has pursued the concept of *yaku,* or function, as a controlling principle for individual performance. The concept of *ie,* with which he begins his chapter, goes to the heart of the question of individual rights in a Confucian context. Bitō also offers new ideas about a theory of religiosity in the seventeenth century. His use of the concept of "national" or "popular" religion is an important addition to our current image of the religious life of the common people of the Edo era.

Chapter 9: Tsuji Tatsuya is a foremost political historian of eighteenth-century Japan. His major contributions to our understanding of bakufu policy issues are his interpretations of the shogun Tsunayoshi, the Confucian adviser Arai Hakuseki, the shogun Yoshimune, and the shogunal favorite Tanuma Okitsugu. In the main he has sought to redress the more spectacular positive hyperboles as they affected someone like Yoshimune, or the biased criticisms of men like Tanuma. What emerges from his approach to the inner workings of the bakufu is a greater sense of professionalism among the bakufu and daimyo officials and the growth of realism in the policy-setting organs of the bakufu.

Chapter 10: Furushima Toshio was one of the first of the great social historians to emerge after World War II. His studies deal with the field of agricultural development, technological change, and village organization and politics. The piece he was asked to write for this volume sums up much of his lengthy career in scholarship. It is interesting to reflect on this essay and to observe how his views have changed in the course of some four decades. Most notable has been a more positive approach to rural society based on new studies by him and his colleagues of Edo period agricultural technology. Though not neglecting to show the evidence of social and economic hardship, Furushima is more positive in his descriptions of improvements in agricultural tools and various other devices that helped increase the efficiency of overall production.

Chapter 11: Nakai Nobuhiko is an important social historian of urbanization during the sixteenth and seventeenth centuries. In designing this chapter it became apparent that the subject of the castle towns deserved expanded coverage. James McClain, his translator, had just published his study of Kanazawa, the castle town of the Maeda domain. Thus it seemed logical to invite McClain to share the authorship of this chapter and to add a significant amount of new material on the castle town.

James McClain has written on Japanese local government, in addition to the study of Kanazawa. The main thrust of his work is to demonstrate the amount of merchant initiative that contributed to the establishment of the castle town.

Chapter 12: Tetsuo Najita, although specializing in the political history of modern Japan, has been turning increasingly to the study of Tokugawa intellectual history. His primary objective is to explain the relevance of Confucian social and political thought to the life experience of the Edo period Japanese. His most significant work in this vein is his study of the Kaitokudo Merchant Academy of Osaka. For the volume at hand he has written an analysis of certain aspects of Confucian thought that served the Edo samurai society in the eighteenth century.

Chapter 13: Susan B. Hanley is a demographer who has specialized in Edo period population trends. As a further dimension of her work she has taken up the study of the quality of life in Edo period Japan. In her chapter for this volume she offers a meticulous analysis of premodern Japanese culture as it contributes to our assessment of Edo period livelihood. One of Hanley's objectives was to devise an anthropological system that permits comparative judgments across cultural boundaries.

Chapter 14: Donald H. Shively, one of the early postwar scholars specializing in Edo period popular culture, is best known for his study of the kabuki play *The Love Suicide at Amijima.* Shively's chapter describes the popular culture of the Edo period as concentrated in the merchant class. Especially noteworthy is the evidence he cites on the remarkable spread of literacy among the urban commoner families and, later, the upper levels of the rural villagers.

A FINAL WORD

The image of the Sengoku–Edo era that emerges from the essays in this volume is quite different from that most commonly held by the writers active before World War II. That image was predominantly negative, depicting Japanese of the Edo period as suffering under a rigid and harshly enforced social class system, a policy of national isolation, and a ruthlessly enforced suppression of Christianity. Government was described as an oppressive military autocracy. The standard indictment of the Edo government was that it was not only feudal, but what could be described as a "centralized feudalism," oppressive in the extreme, especially in its treatment of the nonprivileged populace.

This standard, and basically negative view, came into question following the war, largely in the writings of historians, some of whom appear as contributors to this volume. This new look – if indeed we can give it such a distinction – rested on two important revisionist lines of inquiry. One was the insight it gave into the institutional structure of the country and of the inner balances between the authority system and the needs of the people as a whole. The other came out of new studies of the thought world of the Edo period. The revelations that Japan was not just living out an unchanging destiny under inflexible social and economic restraints, but that in fact basic and creative changes were taking place throughout the Tokugawa shogunate, were of critical importance. Especially significant have been the studies demonstrating that Edo period thinkers were able to discover fundamental values and patterns of behavior that anticipated the demands Japan would face in the mid-nineteenth century. The telling of that story belongs to the volume that follows.

CHAPTER 2

THE SIXTEENTH-CENTURY UNIFICATION

POLITICAL UNIFICATION

The rise of Oda Nobunaga

The prominent details of Oda Nobunaga's rise to power have been well established by historians.[1] We know him as the son of a samurai from Owari and as a man who possessed enough unbridled ambition to slay several of his own kin in a struggle for control of the Oda family holdings. The same raw nerve – and military tactical genius – was equally evident in 1560 when his small band of followers defeated the considerably larger forces of Imagawa Yoshimoto, the military governor of Suruga who was crossing Nobunaga's land in what became a vain attempt to reach Kyoto and seize the symbols of national authority.

This victory at Okehazama in 1560 established Nobunaga as the foremost daimyo within Owari, and he soon moved beyond these narrow boundaries. First, he concluded an alliance with Matsudaira Motoyasu (the future Tokugawa Ieyasu) of Mikawa Province, who had been released as an Imagawa hostage after the defeat at Nobunaga's hands. Then Nobunaga attacked the Saitō of Mino; with their eventual defeat in 1567 he took control of Mino and the balance of Owari and moved his headquarters to Gifu Castle. From this time he began to use the seal inscribed with the slogan "the realm subjected to military

---

1 There are several standard studies in Japanese that discuss the political history of the early modern period. Asao Naohiro, "Shōgun kenryoku no sōshutsu," pts. 1–3, *Rekishi hyōron* 241 (August 1970): 70–8; 266 (August 1972): 46–59; and 293 (September 1974): 20–36; Wakita Osamu, *Oda seiken no kiso kōzō* (Tokyo: Tōkyō daigaku shuppankai, 1975); Okuno Takahiro, "Oda seiken no kihon rosen," *Kokushigaku* 100 (November 1976): 29–58; Katsumata Shizuo, "Rakuichiba to rakuichi-rei," in "Chūsei no mado" dōjin, ed., *Ronshū chūsei no mado* (Tokyo: Yoshikawa kōbunkan, 1977), pp. 87–110, reprinted in Katsumata Shizuo, *Sengokuhō seiritsu shiron* (Tokyo: Yoshikawa kōbunkan, 1979), pp. 61–85. Since the 1960s a number of excellent studies in English have appeared. Access to these is facilitated by Bardwell L. Smith's "Japanese Society and Culture in the Momoyama Era: A Bibliographic Essay," in George Elison and Bardwell L. Smith, eds., *Warlords, Artists, & Commoners: Japan in the Sixteenth Century* (Honolulu: University of Hawaii Press, 1981).

power" (*tenka fubu*), showing his intention to unite all of Japan by military power.

Nobunaga was fortunate to have been born in Owari, for the acquisition of hegemony in this key area rewarded him with several advantages in his quest for national power. First, Owari was near the Kinai region, which at that time was not only the political heartland of Japan but was also blessed with the highest level of agricultural productivity and was closely linked to the Kinai through the constantly expanding commerce and manufacture of the time. Further, although the traditional authorities such as the Muromachi bakufu, as well as the court and the great shrines and temples, were deeply rooted in the Kinai, their influence in Owari was comparatively weak. Consequently, conditions were favorable for newly emergent daimyo, merchants, and others to expand their spheres of influence. In addition, Owari was favored with the fertile fields of great river basins such as the Kiso River delta. Historically advanced features of this region include the early development of flood prevention technology and the spread of communal organizations for constructing riparian works. The most advanced self-governing farming villages of the time had been formed in the province of Ōmi, located between the Kinai and the Owari–Mino region, which was also the home of highly skilled craftsmen, as well as the freight carriers and merchants who dominated the transportation routes feeding into the three highways (Tōkaidō, Tōsandō, and Hokurikudō) and who carried on an active trade on both land and sea. Under these conditions the political situation in Kyoto was rapidly conveyed to the Mino–Owari region.

The end of the Muromachi bakufu

In the ninth month of 1568 Nobunaga entered Kyoto at the head of some fifty thousand troops drawn from Mino, Owari, and neighboring provinces, thus raising the curtain on a new scene in Japan's history. Nobunaga had two causes to justify his entry into Kyoto, even though he was only one of many daimyo who could advance the same claims. The first was a plea for assistance from Ashikaga Yoshiaki, claimant to the post of shogun then held by the puppet Yoshihide. The second was a three-article request from Emperor Ōgimachi asking, among other things, that Nobunaga repair the imperial palace.

Yoshiaki made several requests to Nobunaga from the time of the transfer of the Oda family headquarters to Gifu in 1567. These included a contribution for Crown Prince Kotohito's coming-of-age ceremony, the return of imperial estates located in Owari and Mino, and repairs to the imperial palace. The third item could not be carried out unless Nobunaga were to come to Kyoto, and thus Nobunaga and Yoshiaki, both aiming at Kyoto, joined hands. Yoshiaki was invited to Gifu and obtained the military force that he required. Nobunaga, on the other hand, installed Yoshiaki as shogun and consequently was able to assume the mantle of one who had conquered rebel enemies of the state and could enter Kyoto under the pretext of fulfilling the emperor's requests.

Once in Kyoto, Nobunaga swiftly asserted military control over the Kinai area and then advanced into the neighboring provinces of Tamba, Tajima, and Ise. The puppet shogun Yoshihide had fled, and so Nobunaga was able to install Yoshiaki as the fifteenth Ashikaga shogun and build for him a fortified residence in Kyoto. Nobunaga then took over the civil administration of Kyoto, and he dispatched administrators (*daikan*) to Sakai, Otsu, Kusatsu, and other cities, thereby bringing them under his direct control. For the imperial court, Nobunaga carried out the emperor's three requests, including the repair and restoration of the Naishidokoro, Shishinden, Seiryo-den, and other palace buildings in which governmental affairs had been carried out in classical times. To the citizens of Kyoto he advanced rice loans and designated the interest as income for the imperial family. He also adopted a policy of guaranteeing the current landholdings (*tōchigyō*) of the court nobility (*kuge*) and the shrines and temples located in the capital area. Nobunaga's troops, being orderly at first, received a warm welcome from all, high and low, who were weary of the long years of strife and the dissolution of social order.

Was Nobunaga then the restorer of the medieval order? Did he appear to his contemporaries as the savior of the Muromachi political system? Not at all, as Yoshiaki was soon to discover. When he was appointed shogun, Yoshiaki suggested that Nobunaga become deputy shogun (*kanrei*), but Nobunaga refused. He would not become Yoshiaki's vassal. In 1569 Nobunaga went so far as to issue regulations concerning those who served the shogun and the judicial proceedings that were conducted in the residence that he had constructed for Yoshiaki. This was the first time that a mere warrior had issued regulations to govern the actions of the shogunal house and had then forced the shogun to accede to them. By the end of this year Nobunaga and Yoshiaki had come into open conflict. The court, much concerned about this development, used its good offices to effect a reconciliation.

But a memorandum written at that time makes clear that Nobunaga had seized the real political and military power of the realm (*tenka*) and that he wished to limit the shogun's authority to little more than that of an attendant at court rituals.[2]

Yoshiaki could not accept such treatment and, trusting to the authority vested in the shogun, called on all daimyo in the country to form an anti-Nobunaga league. Takeda Shingen of Kai, Asakura Yoshikage of Echizen, Asai Nagamasa of Ōmi, and also the Honganji, the headquarters of the Ikkō sect located in Ishiyama (Osaka), responded to his call. Between 1570 and 1573 Nobunaga continued the struggle against these enemies in neighboring provinces while being menaced at his base in the Kinai by the militants of the Ikkō confederation. By virtue of his tactical genius and good luck, he was able to subjugate these enemies one after the other; the Asakura and Asai were destroyed militarily, and Takeda Shingen died from natural causes in the midst of the campaign.

After establishing Yoshiaki in Kyoto, Nobunaga had given him the formal trappings of respect, despite his machinations. Yoshiaki naturally had no military power of his own and so posed no direct military threat. But the shogun could stimulate and organize opposition that came from others. In 1573, therefore, Nobunaga finally drove the shogun out of Kyoto. He now obtained his desire to have the court issue a new era name, Tenshō, the era of Heavenly Righteousness. The Muromachi bakufu, which had lasted for more than 230 years since the time of Ashikaga Takauji, thus came to an end, and this meant in turn the destruction of the Muromachi political system that had been structured with the bakufu at its center.

Ascendancy over the religious powers

The kind of institutional structure that Nobunaga envisaged as a replacement for the old Muromachi bakufu is lost to historians, as Nobunaga was killed before he could achieve a national military hegemony, a precondition to more sweeping and permanent institutional change. Surely Nobunaga was determined to achieve such a hegemony, for he threw his full force first at the monks at Enryakuji and then at the Ikkō sect's adherents in Echizen and at Ishiyama Honganji. He was bold in his purpose, ruthless in his execution: "There are so

---

2 The struggle between Nobunaga and Yoshiaki is treated in detail in George Elison, "The Cross and the Sword: Patterns of Momoyama History," in Elison and Smith, eds., *Warlords, Artists, & Commoners*, pp. 245–79.

many corpses in Fuchu that there is no room for more," he claimed after leading more than thirty thousand troops into Echizen.[3]

Yet in the destruction of the past, one can glimpse something of the new future that Nobunaga hoped to construct. His new castle at Azuchi, for instance, symbolized his conception of a new national (*tenka*) unity. This became his center of government, and it was from this base that Nobunaga ordered the preparation of a cadastral survey in the form of land and tax statements (*sashidashi*) from Yamato and Izumi provinces. It was also from Azuchi that he arbitrated the famous dispute between the monks of the Pure Land and the Lotus (Nichiren) sects, reducing by his decision the sect to an existence "graciously permitted" by his own magnanimity as the secular leader of the lay world. Nobunaga drew another public picture of his superiority over religious sects when he compelled various Buddhist temples to move their headquarters to the foot of Azuchi Castle. Just as graphic was the art that decorated the seven floors of the castle: paintings of T'ang Confucians, wizards, wise men, the Buddha's Ten Great Disciples, dragons, phoenixes, demons, and rulers and great men of East Asia such as the Three Emperors, the Five Sovereigns, and the Ten Accomplished Disciples of Confucius. Nobunaga, the master of this keep, presented himself as the greatest of the great, standing above all the leading figures of the physical and spiritual world.[4]

Nobunaga preached to the people that he, as the most powerful figure of authority in Japan, would guarantee them peaceful lives, and he sought to drag the medieval peasantry, who out of the poverty and insecurity of their daily lives had had to count on salvation in a future existence, into a new society that offered a stable secular life full of promise. To accomplish this he promoted policies that released society from the restrictions that had long fettered the daily lives of the medieval populace. These policies included the introduction of Western medicine, the construction of castle towns filled with a new entrepreneurial spirit, the establishment of free markets (*rakuichi, rakuza*), and the destruction of toll barriers (*sekisho*).

But the rapidity of these changes gave rise to disharmony within his own ranks, and this became his undoing. His confrontation with the

3 Okuno Takahiro, ed., *Oda Nobunaga monjo no kenkyū* (Tokyo: Yoshikawa kōbunkan, 1970), vol. 2, p. 62 (doc. 533).
4 Asao Naohiro, "Shōgun kenryoku no sōshutsu," pt. 2, and Tsuji Zennosuke, ed., *Nihon bukkyōshi*, vol. 7 (Tokyo: Iwanami shoten, 1953, reprinted 1970), pp. 47–9. A careful study in English of the meaning of the paintings at Azuchi can be found in Carolyn Wheelwright, "A Visualization of Eitoku's Lost Paintings at Azuchi Castle," in Elison and Smith, eds., *Warlords, Artisits, & Commoners*, pp. 87–111.

Ikkō sect taught him that the continued existence of the warrior class was imperiled unless he could transform the relatively autonomous groups of warriors, whose means of survival were derived from their own private domains (*shiryō*), into bands of retainers whose members were cut off from their fiefs and could be moved at their lord's will. Nobunaga commenced this transformation of his followers from fief holders to stipendiary retainers, but his actions must have seemed to be nothing more than the cruel and merciless deeds of a despot.

After subduing the temples and shrines that had held much actual power in the Kinai, and the peasant federations (*ikki*) allied with those institutions, Nobunaga then for the first time turned to the pacification of the east; in 1581 he entered Shinano and Kai provinces. Having destroyed the Takeda, he advanced into a portion of the Kantō. In 1582 he turned to the west and was on the verge of a decisive battle with the Mōri, the leaders of the provinces at the western end of Japan's main island. On his way to join in the attack on the Mōri, he stopped off at the Honnōji in Kyoto. There he was attacked and murdered by his vassal Akechi Mitsuhide. Nobunaga's life thus ended when he was only forty-nine, with the unification of Japan only half accomplished.

The unification of Japan by Toyotomi Hideyoshi

At the time of Nobunaga's death, Hideyoshi, the general who was to succeed Nobunaga, was engaged at the front in Bitchū Province. Hideyoshi was from a farming family in the Aichi district of Owari.[5] His father had served Oda Nobuhide as a foot soldier but is said to have returned to his fields after having been wounded in battle. Hideyoshi himself left home when he was sixteen and traveled through Owari, Mikawa, and Totomi provinces looking for a master to serve. A number of episodes from this period have been handed down, relating how Hideyoshi supported himself on his travels by buying needles to sew cotton thread with the cash given to him by his stepfather and then exchanging the needles for food and straw sandals, or how he at one time joined a band of peasant warriors (*nobushi*) – episodes that are meant to suggest that Hideyoshi came from the low social station of bound servants (*nuhi*) and that he was open to new trends in commerce and manufacturing.

---

5 The first full biography of Toyotomi Hideyoshi in English is Mary Elizabeth Berry's *Hideyoshi* (Cambridge, Mass.: Harvard University Press, 1982).

Whatever his exact origins, Hideyoshi entered the service of a rural samurai of Tōtōmi but before long deserted him for Nobunaga. The tale of how he began as Nobunaga's sandal bearer, gradually rising in the ranks as his intelligence and abilities were recognized and finally emerging as one of Nobunaga's influential generals, is a success story well known to almost every Japanese. When Nobunaga built his castle at Gifu, Hideyoshi had adopted the name Kinoshita Tōkichirō and had attained sufficient rank to be given a small but strategically important castle.

Talent on the battlefield earned Hideyoshi additional promotions, and by the early 1580s, he had become one of Nobunaga's leading generals. Thus, when news of Nobunaga's death reached him, Hideyoshi moved quickly to grasp Nobunaga's legacy. Returning rapidly to the Kinai, he avenged Nobunaga's murder by destroying Akechi Mitsuhide, whose preparations for defense were not yet complete. The critical battle took place at Yamazaki in Settsu Province. In the following year (1583), Hideyoshi defeated Shibata Katsuie, a leading contender for Nobunaga's mantle, at the battle of Shizugatake in Ōmi. With his position as Nobunaga's successor now established, he built a castle in Osaka to serve as his headquarters. But there were still competitors for national leadership among the great daimyo.

Nobunaga's ally Tokugawa Ieyasu had joined Nobunaga's second son Nobuo (Nobukatsu) and checked Hideyoshi's advance to the east at the battles of Komaki and Nagakute in Owari, but in military terms the results were indecisive. Consequently, Hideyoshi sought to gain ascendance over Ieyasu by political means. He continued the task, which Nobunaga had left unfinished, of mopping up the *ikki* in the Kinai and neighboring provinces. He also gave permission for the Enryakuji and the Honganji (temples), which had been destroyed by Nobunaga, to rebuild as religious institutions divorced from political power.

As one means of acquiring legitimacy, Hideyoshi approached the court on his own initiative and received promotions in court rank. In 1585 he had himself adopted by Konoe Sakihisa, who could boast of the most exalted lineage within the Fujiwara line, the family that had monopolized the position of imperial regent (*kampaku*), the highest post in the imperial court system save that of the emperor. No previous example exists of a person other than a Fujiwara being appointed to this post. Endowed now with the Fujiwara surname, Hideyoshi had himself so appointed. Further, in 1586, he married his sister to Tokugawa Ieyasu, sent his mother to him as a hostage, and summoned Ieyasu to Osaka Castle to offer to Hideyoshi a pledge of allegiance. At the same time Emperor Ōgimachi abdicated, and Hideyoshi had the sixteen-year-old Go-Yōzei installed as his successor. It was as though Go-Yōzei were "Hideyoshi's emperor." Hideyoshi now dominated the imperial authority and, as grand minister of state (daijōdaijin) at the junior first court rank, was clearly superior in terms of the imperial court system to Ieyasu, who had achieved only junior third court rank.

Hideyoshi took this opportunity to change his name yet again: He petitioned the court and established the surname Toyotomi. His reasoning was that just as each existing name had its respective progenitor, it was only proper that he, who had risen so high from so low a starting point, should be permitted to found a new family name. Finally Hideyoshi built the Jurakutei Palace in Kyoto as his administrative headquarters. There in 1588 he invited Go-Yōzei for a grand reception. By this act he displayed his status in accordance with precedents set by Ashikaga Yoshimitsu and Yoshimasa. But Hideyoshi added a new element to the interplay between the military and court aristocracies. On this occasion twenty-nine daimyo, including Ieyasu, attended and gave thanks to Hideyoshi for giving them the privilege of attending court as high court nobles (kugyō). They swore to protect the holdings of the emperor and the nobility, and they pledged absolute obedience to the imperial regent, Hideyoshi.[6]

Even Ashikaga Yoshiaki, the shogun in name only who had fled to Bingo-no-tomo after his expulsion by Nobunaga, was pardoned at this time. He returned to Kyoto, entered holy orders with the name Shōzan, and was granted ten thousand koku. Because there was no longer any shogun, Hideyoshi was the leader of the warrior bands in name as well as in fact. The Toyotomi regime took its final shape with the imperial progress to the Jurakutei. This act symbolized the fact that under Hideyoshi the daimyo class had taken control of the country from the imperial court. That Hideyoshi, a former farmer, should have brought this about was an epochal event in Japanese history.

"Peace" was the slogan that Hideyoshi carried with him as he unified the country. He followed Nobunaga in destroying the fortresses in the areas that he conquered, but he explained that such a policy was

6 Asao Naoshiro, "Toyotomi seiken ron," Iwanami kōza Nihon rekishi, 2nd (kinsei 1) (Tokyo: Iwanami shoten, 1963), pp. 159–210; Niki Seiichirō, "Taikō kenchi to Chōsen shuppei," Iwanami kōza Nihon rekishi, 3rd series (kinsei 1) (Tokyo: Iwanami shoten, 1975), pp. 81–116; and Fujiki Hisashi, Toyotomi heiwa rei to sengoku shakai (Tokyo: Tōkyō daigaku shuppankai, 1985). This event is well covered in English in George Elison, "Hideyoshi, the Bountiful Minister," in Elison and Smith, eds., Warlords, Artists, & Commoners, pp. 236–44.

for the purpose of "bringing peace to the provinces for fifty years."[7] When this slogan was applied to the daimyo in areas that had not yet come under Hideyoshi's control, it served to inhibit them from die-hard resistance. In other words, the projection of a national order in which individual daimyo could be given secure positions served to weaken the determination of daimyo to resist Hideyoshi. From an early stage Hideyoshi had declared that his main political concern was in "redistributing holdings" (*kuniwake, chigyōwake*). This meant putting a stop to the struggles of the daimyo and warrior bands throughout the country, who were trying to secure or expand their territories by military means, and instead doing so "peacefully" under Hideyoshi's control. Now imperial regent and grand minister of state, Hideyoshi dictated this to all the daimyo in Japan fom his position as the leader of the military estate.

At the time when Hideyoshi succeeded to Nobunaga's still-incomplete hegemony, various bands of warriors, large and small, were competing with one another in many parts of Japan to establish control over their territories, but gradually there began to appear in each region a powerful daimyo who united that area under his own military power. Chief among these were Date Masamune of Mutsu Province, Hōjō Ujimasa in the Kantō, Uesugi Kagekatsu in Hokuriku, Tokugawa Ieyasu in Tōkai, Mōri Terumoto in Chūgoku, Chōsokabe Motochika in Shikoku, and Shimazu Yoshihisa in Kyushu. Among them the Tokugawa and the Uesugi had had the opportunity to learn firsthand the control and centralizing policies employed by Nobunaga and Hideyoshi. The Mōri and the Chōsokabe had been engaged in hostilities with Hideyoshi's forces and had come to respect their power; they submitted to Hideyoshi early in his regime. However, those daimyo who lived far from the scene of Hideyoshi's activities and whose attention was taken up by the unification of their own regions had not yet felt the full strength of Hideyoshi's power. They refused to take seriously orders from a man who, though bearing the title of imperial regent, had risen from low birth and about whom many unfavorable rumors circulated.

First among such daimyo were the Shimazu, a military family with a proud tradition extending back to the Kamakura period, who were seeking to unify Kyushu. When in 1587 Shimazu ignored Hideyoshi's order to submit peacefully, Hideyoshi displayed the imperial mandate to maintain peace and labeled the Shimazu as enemy of the imperial

7 Tōkyō daigaku shiryō hensanjo, ed., *Dai Nihon shiryō*, series 11, vol. 4 (Tokyo, 1902–), p. 817.

realm. He then sent an order to thirty-two provinces to raise troops by provincial units. He set out for Kyushu, defeated the Shimazu in battle, and made them submit to him. But the Shimazu were not totally destroyed; rather, they were reduced in territory but were still recognized as the daimyo of the two provinces of Satsuma and Ōsumi.

The Hōjō family of the Kantō stood out as another major power who refused to accept Hideyoshi's overlordship. At first it seemed as if they would submit to Hideyoshi through the mediation of Tokugawa Ieyasu, but then they violated the regulations regarding the distribution of holdings made by the Toyotomi regime and encroached on other domains. Hideyoshi announced their transgressions to the nation and gathered a huge army of 150,000 troops with which he advanced to the Kantō, laid siege to the Hōjō headquarters at Odawara Castle in Sagami, and destroyed it. During this campaign Date Masamune came to Hideyoshi's camp and swore allegiance to him. Hideyoshi then led his army as far as Aizu in Mutsu, placing daimyo and distributing territories not only in the Kantō but also in the northern provinces of Mutsu and Dewa, the last area of Japan to be conquered. With this, the pacification of the entire country was complete.

Hideyoshi ordered that the wives and children of the daimyo who submitted to him must live in Kyoto as hostages, while the daimyo themselves were made to serve him in Kyoto with a fixed number of their troops. This method of ensuring the loyalty of vassals to their lord was commonly practiced within daimyo domains as well. Daimyo, in other words, frequently required the wives and children of their chief retainers to take up residence in the daimyo's castle, and the retainers themselves also had to serve there in turn. The practice of taking hostages and requiring attendance spread over the now-united country. Military service in the form of attendance (*sankin gun'yaku*) was required of the daimyo, and powerful daimyo such as the Tokugawa and Shimazu were granted holdings to maintain a residence in Kyoto (*zai-Kyō makanai ryō*) in or near the Kinai to offset living expenses.

Hideyoshi's "peace" extended not only to the daimyo but also to every social class, including farmers and fishermen. It was implemented by his sword hunt edict and his ban on piracy, both issued and carried out in 1588.[8] The sword hunt edict ordered the confiscation of all weapons held by farmers, including long swords, short swords, bows, spears, and firearms. The ordinance stipulated that the confiscated weapons would be used to make the nails and clamps for the

8 Berry, *Hideyoshi*, pp. 102–3, 133–4.

Hall of the Great Buddha at the Hōkōji, which Hideyoshi was then building in Kyoto. It was explained that this meant that the farmers would be saved not only in this life but in the hereafter as well: If the farmers would take up their farming implements and devote themselves to cultivating the fields, the prosperity of their children and grandchildren for generations would be assured. The second edict strictly forbade piracy and directed the domain holders to make a survey of shipmasters, fishermen, and others in each province who made their living from the sea and to put them under their control.

These two edicts put an end to activities by confederations of farmers and fishermen against the domain proprietors. Their significance in this respect was well understood at the time. One step beyond Nobunaga's suppression of the *ikki*, their aim was to institutionalize the results of this suppression into a social system. Seen in the light of subsequent history, they served as a final contribution to the tendency of society in the sixteenth and seventeenth centuries to abandon the practice of solving disputes among the various groups by recourse to arms.

The social system of heinō bunri

Hideyoshi's cadastral surveys followed his conquests. These surveys were much more thorough than those conducted by either Nobunaga or any of the daimyo up to that time, and we know them as "Taikō's cadastral surveys" (Taikō *kenchi*) from the title Taikō that Hideyoshi took when he retired from the post of imperial regent. Until Hideyoshi's surveys began in 1584, the medieval standard of land measurement, in which one *tan* equaled 360 *bu*, was employed, and land area was expressed in units labeled as "large" (240 *bu*), "middle" (180 *bu*), and "small" (120 *bu*). Hideyoshi then introduced the *tan–se–bu* system, with one *tan* equal to 300 *bu*, one *se* equal to 30 *bu*, and one *bu* being one square *ken* in area. This method of land measurement has lasted to modern times, although in the Edo period the length of the *ken* was shortened slightly. The Taikō *kenchi*, as will be revealed in several subsequent chapters in this volume, aside from introducing a more effective method of land measurement and taxation, became the foundation for one of the greatest transformations of the land system in Japanese history.

Hideyoshi also adopted throughout his domain the *kokudaka* system, a method of assessing the yield (*taka*) of each parcel of land in terms of a quantity of rice (expressed in *koku* units). The land so measured included not only paddy and dry fields but also residential land and sometimes even undeveloped fields, mountains, forests, and marshland. In the process, the various volume measures (*masu*) that until that time had varied according to region, proprietary lord, or purpose (receiving versus paying out) also were unified, and the "Kyoto measure" (*Kyō-masu*) was adopted as the national standard.

Of course, some regional differences were visible in the survey procedures and results. In the Kinai and neighboring provinces, which had come under Hideyoshi's control from an early date, the land surveys were conducted repeatedly. In contrast, in backward regions of low productivity such as Kyushu or the northern provinces, it was impossible to take measurements according to the established standards. There were cases, therefore, in which the former tenurial records were merely recalculated and converted to fit the new cadastral registers. Despite various discrepancies, the survey made it possible to know the "proprietary amount" (*ryōchidaka*) of the entire country. In fact a unified cadastral survey on a national scale was carried out in 1591, just one year after unification, and there is evidence that this was updated in 1593–4. From these measures it appeared that the total *kokudaka* of the entire country amounted to approximately 18 million *koku*.

The cadastral survey recorded various kinds of information for each parcel of land: the name of the person who held the rights of cultivation to that land, the area, assessed productive capacity (*kokudaka*), and quality, ranked as superior, medium, or inferior paddy or dry field. This information was compiled in a cadastral register for each village. In medieval times it was common for several persons to hold overlapping rights to a given parcel of arable land, but Hideyoshi's cadastral surveys established the principle of "one cultivator per parcel of land." The Toyotomi regime refused to acknowledge the existence of a landlord–tenant relationship *within* the peasant class and did not recognize the existence of any intermediate level of exploitation between the domain lords and the actual cultivators of the soil.

Consequently, the farmers registered in the cadastral surveys as the direct cultivators would logically have been the ones obliged to pay taxes, but the realities of the system made the village the unit of taxation and the agency responsible for submitting the payment of taxes. The annual grain tax (*nengu*) was levied as a percentage of the assessed productive capacity. The Toyotomi regime determined the standard rate as "two to the lord, one to the farmer," and indeed, tax documents show that taxes were in fact collected in approximately this ratio. The amount of tax that each villager had to pay was determined within the village in proportion to the amount of *kokudaka* he held. If a farmer could not pay the amount of taxes he owed, the village paid for him, according to the principle of collective responsibility.

Farmers were liable for corvée duty (*yaku*) in addition to land taxes. The term *yaku* originally referred to the use of a person's labor, and it took many forms, extending back to ancient times. By the sixteenth century, the word was used to mean not only military service (*gun'yaku*) and the usual corvée but also service to a domain lord offered in exchange for specific rights. Labor services were levied by the court or shogunate, by the daimyo, or by individual fief holders. The labor requirement was frequently commuted to a payment in cash or in kind, such as rice or other products.

It is thought that in large Sengoku domains each daimyo made the province (the *kuni*) the unit of his rule and had the right in time of war to require military service from the farmers in his domain. But the lord's authority did not extend to the labor services that each of his vassals levied on the farmers who lived on the vassals' fiefs (*chigyōchi*). Thus the interests of the daimyo and his vassals were frequently in conflict. The Toyotomi regime's policy was to take the right to extract labor services away from the vassals and to reserve for the national military hegemon and the daimyo the right to levy all labor services.

Hideyoshi's cadastral surveys also brought about a major change in the form of fiefs assigned to samurai retainers. The survey imposed the requirement that there could be only one proprietor entitled to collect the taxes from a given parcel of land. That proprietor, however, was not a law unto himself. As a member of a daimyo's band of retainers, he had been granted a fief. But his proprietory authority was based on the laws of his superior. In other words, the entire warrior class had by now been organized into daimyo units, and although fief holders could collect taxes by virtue of their warrior status, this status could now be obtained only by subordinating themselves to a daimyo's superior authority. For example, during the cadastral survey in the Shimazu domain, Hideyoshi ordered that the indigenous military proprietors be cut off from their holdings and moved elsewhere. This transfer of vassals within a daimyo's domain was conducted in the name of "fairness" in the distribution of fiefs; there even were cases in which daimyo assigned fiefs by lot.

Further, during the course of national unification Hideyoshi began to transfer daimyo, together with their bands of retainers, to new domains, and in this process the vassals were often deprived of several of their former rights to hold fiefs. There were many such cases in which daimyo from provinces such as Mino, Owari, and Ōmi were relocated to the northern provinces, the Kantō, or Kyushu. This broad principle of withdrawal of proprietary rights over fief land held by the members of the warrior class below the rank of daimyo constituted one of the chief objectives of the cadastral surveys as well. Until this time the vassals had been the holders (*shoyūsha*) of proprietary rights over their own fiefs. However, farmers became the registered holders (*hoyūsha*) of the land as a result of the cadastral surveys, and in this way private ownership of land was forbidden to members of the warrior class. Although vassals were in fact granted fiefs whose geographic contours contained specifically designated villages, they were enjoined from cultivating the land in those villages themselves or making any other use of it, even land that for one reason or another had no designated productivity or that was not being lived on or cultivated by any farmer. Their proprietory rights were thus reduced to the authority to collect as a form of taxes (*nengu*) a portion of the wealth produced on the land.

In sum, Hideyoshi's cadastral surveys had a profound influence on Japanese society. The warriors were deprived of fiefs but won the right to collect taxes. The farmers, on the other hand, were bound to the land and were obliged to pay those taxes in return for a guarantee of their right to cultivate the soil. The warriors, in another contrast, carried swords as members of the lord's standing army, and they were stationed in the castle towns where they became bureaucrat-warriors and a major consuming class. The farmers, meanwhile, lived in the villages where they had to devote themselves strictly to farming. As the ruled, the farmers were stripped of weapons, and they became the producers of the food and many other items consumed by samurai. As this engineered situation congealed into a social system, the overthrow of superior by inferior, which characterized the previous age, was systematically brought to a halt, and a new society was formed, identified by the strict definition and separation of the warrior and peasant classes.

THE MILITARY AND ECONOMIC BASE

Military strength and organization

The strength of Nobunaga's armies is usually attributed to his companies of musketeers (*teppōtai*), composed chiefly of foot soldiers (*ashi-*

garu). The term *ashigaru* means literally "a person who advances on foot." Its currency testified to the tendency from the fourteenth century for battles between masses of foot soldiers gradually to assume more importance than did individual combat between mounted samurai. By the sixteenth century, *ashigaru* had become trained infantrymen organized into spear, bow, and musket corps. Nobunaga placed particular importance on the musket corps and used them effectively. For instance, at the critical battle of Nagashino in Mikawa (1575), Nobunaga's musketeers, separated into three ranks firing in rotation, defeated, indeed slaughtered, Takeda's mounted warriors. This defeat of the warrior elite by the lowest stratum of that professional class signaled a revolution in the accepted style of combat.

Another outstanding feature of Nobunaga's army was its mobility. He showed at the battle of Okehazama that he could assemble an effective military force at the necessary time and place with a speed that his opponents could not even imagine. Nobunaga's superior military capacity was not a matter of accident or luck; it was well planned. To facilitate the rapid movement of large forces, he widened and repaired the main strategic roads, such as those between Gifu and Kyoto, and Kyoto and Azuchi; built pontoon bridges across rivers; and constructed large hundred-oar galleys to transport troops and military gear across Lake Biwa. This made possible the employment of a union of *ashigaru* infantry battalions with the corps of mounted samurai of higher status. And usually Nobunaga was in the lead, whether at the front in a battle or, having decided that the odds were against him, in a swift retreat.

Nobunaga's military genius was also apparent in his ability to come up with new strategies that defied tradition. During his siege of the Honganji fortress of Osaka, Nobunaga suffered casualties inflicted by the naval forces of the Mōri, who were aiding the Honganji. To counter this, Nobunaga ordered the Kuki family (daimyo of Shima Province) to construct seven vessels armored with large iron plates, the first armored ships built in Japan. Armed with cannon and muskets, these ships annihilated the Mōri fleet, which was composed of conventional small-scale wooden ships.

Mass troop movements required a variety of ancillary units, such as transport and engineering corps, to support soldiers engaged in actual combat. As a result, warfare increasingly demanded the mobilization of a domain's total resources. Unlike Nobunaga, Hideyoshi hardly ever took the lead in battle, but he inherited Nobunaga's legacy with regard to the conduct of warfare and greatly expanded it. The unique features of warfare as waged by Hideyoshi could already be seen when he served as Nobunaga's general in the struggle against the Mōri at the sieges of Tottori Castle in Inaba Province in 1581 and of Takamatsu Castle in 1582. At Tottori he dug moats around the castle, ringed it with watchtowers, and brought the defenders to the verge of starvation. At Takamatsu, Hideyoshi took advantage of rivers swollen by the heavy rains of the rainy season. He constructed earthen dikes seven meters high, twenty meters wide at the base, ten meters wide at the top, and three kilometers in length and diverted the rivers to flood the castle. Cut off from supplies and aid, the defenders were forced to surrender. Hideyoshi ordered the defeated castellans to commit ritual suicide but spared their retainers. On other occasions, he mobilized miners to dig tunnels to undermine castles. In all such projects Hideyoshi employed superior methods of manpower mobilization, dividing up the work into sections or stages and allotting them to the generals and daimyo under his command, with labor supplied by impressed bands of retainers and the peasantry.

Hideyoshi ordered such massive mobilizations everywhere as he unified the country. During the siege of the Hōjō's Odawara Castle, for instance, he not only built fortifications but also constructed shops for entertainers and merchants so as to help the besieging troops pass the hours while they waited for battle. The preparations for the invasions of Korea were awesome in their dimensions. Hideyoshi established his headquarters at Nagoya Castle and soon gathered a huge army of 200,000 troops at what had been an impoverished fishing village, transforming it into a large castle city. The labor was mobilized on a similarly large scale to construct Osaka Castle, Jurakutei Palace, and other projects. Similar mobilizations were used after unification to construct dikes and riparian works as the daimyo settled down to improving living conditions for the populace.

For the campaign against the Hōjō, Hideyoshi appointed Natsuka Masaie as his magistrate in charge of procurement. The previous practice in time of war had been for each band of warriors to come to camp carting its own provisions from the home domain. But Natsuka commissioned a fleet of ships to transport 200,000 *koku* of rice and fodder for twenty thousand horses to supply the entire invading army, and he spent ten thousand pieces of gold to buy supplies. Thus Hideyoshi made his armies dependent on his own officers for most of their supplies of food and ammunition, and this assured him the ability to assemble promptly in one place large-scale military forces. For this reason alone the Toyotomi regime came to rely to an unprecedented degree on the merchants and shipping agents who contracted to under-take these tasks.

Army organization in Nobunaga's time adhered to patterns em-ployed throughout the Sengoku period. At the nucleus of an army was a band of direct retainers, in this instance, called "horse guards" (umamawari). Nobunaga's army also consisted of smaller armies led by generals with a strong sense of independence. By Hideyoshi's time, control of territory by the daimyo had progressed to the extent that the main unit of military service assessment was the province or domain that the daimyo ruled. Then, as Hideyoshi's cadastral surveys were carried out more thoroughly, assessment of military service came to be based more and more on assessed yields of fief land, with an obligation of so many men per one hundred koku.

The first nationwide military service plan based on the kokudaka system was implemented in 1592 in preparation for the invasion of the continent. It was done in a systematic manner: For every one hundred koku the Kyushu daimyo were obliged to provide five men; the daimyo of Shikoku and Chūgoku, four. Daimyo of provinces in the Kinki region and to the east were assessed a lighter levy, in part because their provinces were farther from the Nagoya headquarters and in part to compensate for the fact that two years before, they had shouldered a heavy burden during the campaign against the Hōjō.

The Toyotomi regime's practice of linking military service to fief output as determined by the cadastral surveys was still beset by several internal problems. It was not a permanent system but had been set up to meet certain immediate contingencies – the unification campaigns and the invasion of the continent. Because accommodations were made for previous military service and physical distance from the scene of battle, it fell short of being the completely standardized sys-tem of military service later instituted by the Tokugawa shogunate, in which levies were precisely determined by a domain's total kokudaka rating. Moreover, domains granted by Hideyoshi to many daimyo often contained holdings that were exempt from military services (muyakubun). For example, the domain grant to Miyabe Keijun in 1589, awarded in anticipation of the campaign against the Hōjō, desig-nated ten thousand koku from his domain of more than fifty thousand koku as exempt from the military service levy. Miyake was expected to supply two thousand men as part of the military levy against the remaining forty thousand koku. The exempt portion was directly de-scended from what had been the daimyo's "original domain" (honryō), which was "confirmed as an [original] fief" (ando chigyō). The portion on which military service was assessed was gift land awarded by the lord and was thus treated as a "boon fief" (*kyūon chigyō*).[9]

The Toyotomi regime instituted several measures that touched off an evolution of lord–general relations. After national unification had been completed, for instance, Hideyoshi began to require military service in the form of attendance even on what previously had been "exempt lands." Almost all of the fiefs of daimyo established by Hideyoshi were subsumed into the military service system in this way, and the same formula was applied in settlement with powerful daimyo such as the Mōri, Shimazu, Kobayakawa, and Tokugawa. Still, the total disappearance of fief grants with a portion exempt from military service had to await the establishment of the Tokugawa regime.

Commerce, manufacturing, and the growth of cities

Nobunaga's abolition of toll barriers (*sekisho*) and his expansion of the road system aided both the military and the merchant class that was taking shape in major cities. The merchants also benefited because the region that first came under Nobunaga's control, with the provinces of Mino, Ise, and Ōmi at the center, formed a ring of vital nodes in what was emerging as a national distribution network that linked the outlying provinces with the Kinai. Nobunaga also abolished the special privileges of the markets (*ichi*) and guilds (*za*) in the main cities in some areas, permitting what were called "free markets" (*rakuichi*) and "free guilds" (*rakuza*). He guaranteed the merchants' freedom to travel and to conduct business without interference. When the merchants came under his direct control, Nobunaga exempted them from the various imposts that had been exacted from them by different types of proprietary authorities such as court nobles, temples, shrines, and other warriors. These imposts included market taxes, business taxes, urban residential taxes, property taxes, and a variety of assessments that had to be given as "offerings of appreciation" in return for permission to conduct business.

While Nobunaga sought to free merchants from such burdensome exactions, he also tried to concentrate commercial activity in the newly emerging castle towns. His ordinance for the governance of the castle town of Azuchi reflected these urban policies.[10] Illustrative of the

9 Cited in Asao, "Toyotomi seiken ron," p. 183. English translations of these documents can be found in David John Lu, comp., *Sources of Japanese History* (New York: McGraw-Hill, 1974), vol. 1, pp. 186–90.
10 Okuno, ed., *Oda Nobunga monjo no kenkyū*, vol. 2, pp. 300–4 (doc. 722). For a translation in English see Lu, *Sources*, pp. 184–5.

effort to draw commercial activity into Azuchi was Nobunaga's order to redirect the Nakasendō highway, a main trunk route, so that it ran through the city. At the same time he stipulated that merchants had to pass through Azuchi and also to stay overnight. New regulations governing the punishment of criminals and the collection of debts provided a better environment for the growth of commerce. On the other hand, Nobunaga guaranteed and confirmed the privileges of the guilds composed of merchants and artisans who lived in Kyoto, Sakai, and the other cities and towns in the Kinai region, the center of traditional commerce and craft manufacture. His intention was to use these guilds to gain control of commerce and craft manufacture, which had been dominated by their organizations.

Nobunaga's policies toward the guilds might seem inconsistent, as he abolished some and confirmed the rights of others. But this was done with a purpose. Rather than maintaining a system that relied on the extraction of small-scale cash income from individual merchants in the form of dues, and realizing that the territorial expansion of his authority required that the cities as a whole function as mechanisms for the conversion into cash of vast quantities of taxes collected in kind, he sought to make the cities the supply nodes for military equipment, firearms, ammunition, and the consumer goods needed for the daily lives of his retainers.

Accordingly, market and guild privileges that might have hindered these objectives were abolished, whereas guilds, such as those for imported items and the handicraft products of the economically advanced regions and those that handled rice and oil – products vital to the stability of daily life within the domains – were protected and their rights confirmed. This trend toward economic expansion necessarily gave rise to the construction and enlargement of cities and towns. The building of the castle town at Azuchi is a dramatic example of this. There Nobunaga built houses for his retainers and made them live in the castle town. He even went so far, on occasion, as to enforce this policy by burning to the ground the rural dwellings of those retainers who did not obey his orders to move to Azuchi.

The policies adopted by Nobunaga to utilize commerce and craft manufacture and to build towns and cities were promoted on an even larger scale by Hideyoshi. It is well known that Nobunaga depended on Imai Sōkyū of Sakai to manufacture firearms and provide gunpowder. Under the Toyotomi regime, Sen-no-Rikyū, Konishi Ryūsa, Kamiya Sōtan, Shimai Sōshitsu, and other leading merchants from Sakai, Kyoto, Hakata, and elsewhere were linked to the regime in a variety of ways. Sen-no-Rikyū, for example, served as a financial adviser to the Toyotomi family from an early stage, and Konishi Ryūsa and others became fiscal administrators. Merchants participated actively in distributing the produce of the granary lands under Hideyoshi's direct control throughout the country, in developing and managing mines, in transporting troops, and in constructing castles and castle towns. The shipping route on the Yodo River between Kyoto and Osaka, the land freight route between Kyoto and Ōtsu, and its extension east across Lake Biwa formed the economic arteries that fed supplies to the Toyotomi regime. Consequently, the regime put these under its direct control and levied transport taxes on their use.

Policies affecting the guilds also became more fully defined under Hideyoshi. From about 1584 the guilds patronized by court nobles, temples, and shrines were abolished, and the right to collect guild fees was denied. Craft guilds affiliated with temples and shrines, such as those for carpenters, smiths, tatami makers, and roof tile makers, were abolished in rapid succession. These prohibitions severed guild ties with the court nobles and the temples and shrines. This practice was carried out in the daimyo domains as well, but it should not be supposed that the guilds themselves were abolished completely. Instead, the antiguild policy was directed mainly against those organizations that were dominated by the medieval proprietory class. This strengthened control of commerce and craft manufacture by the daimyo (and, by extension, by the Toyotomi regime that stood above them) and facilitated their direct control over their domain economies.

Commerce and craft manufacture now came to be concentrated in the more open environment of the castle towns. There it could be mobilized for town construction projects or to supply goods to the bands of retainers. The Toyotomi regime itself was constantly engaged in urban construction: the castle and city of Osaka, the Jurakutei Palace and the reconstruction of Kyoto, the castle and castle town at Nagoya in Kyushu, and the castle and surrounding town at Fushimi are prominent examples. All these were carefully planned projects with several common characteristics. The typical castle town included an administrative headquarters surrounded by the residences of the daimyo and his attendant retainers, a sector for the townspeople, and frequently a zone where temples and shrines could be concentrated. Labor and construction materials such as stone and lumber were requisitioned from daimyo throughout Japan, and merchants were required to contribute capital. Daimyo retainer bands participated in the construction work alongside farmers.[11]

This construction took place not only in central Japan but also in the provinces – Hideyoshi's stepbrother Hidenaga built Kōriyama; his nephew Hidetsugu constructed Ōmi Hachiman; and Hideyoshi himself rebuilt Hakata in Chikuzen after he subjugated Kyushu. Daimyo could boast of equally proud achievements, as when – to cite but a few examples – the Mōri oversaw the construction and growth of Hiroshima, and the Maeda and Date lords did likewise at Kanazawa and Sendai. The Gamō family built a new castle town each time it was transferred: at Hino in Ōmi, Matsuzaka in Ise, and Wakamatsu (Aizu) in Mutsu. The Japanese archipelago was caught up in an unprecedented urban construction boom that lasted into the middle of the seventeenth century. In keeping with the evolution in the function of cities, there was also a marked change in the conditions for the location of daimyo castles. Previously, castles had been located on hilltops for strategic reasons, but they were now being built at key transportation nodes on plains or near harbors, the main concerns being the political and economic dimensions of territorial rule. As a result, castles and cities tended to coalesce spatially.[12]

Once the city was founded, the daimyo and his band of retainers, as well as merchants and artisans, congregated from the towns, markets, and villages throughout the domain. Commerce and handicraft industry were removed from the farming villages and relocated in the new cities, systematically creating a separation in status between the townspeople and the farmers. In conjunction with the separation of the warriors and peasants (heinō bunri), the formation of such cities gave shape to the warrior–farmer–artisan–merchant (shi-nō-kō-shō) status system that prevailed throughout the Tokugawa period.

The minting of coins and the monopoly of international trade

In sixteenth-century Japan, the production of gold and particularly silver grew so significantly that it left a mark on world economic

---

11 A case study of the construction of Osaka Castle under the Tokugawa regime appears in William E. Hauser, "Osaka Castle and Tokugawa Authority in Western Japan," in Jeffrey P. Mass and William B. Hauser, eds., The Bakufu in Japanese History (Stanford, Calif.: Stanford University Press, 1985), pp. 153–72.

12 For an early study in English of the sixteenth-century castle town in Japan, see John Whitney Hall, "The Castle Town and Japan's Modern Urbanization," in John W. Hall and Marius B. Jansen, eds., Studies in the Institutional History of Early Modern Japan (Princeton, N.J.: Princeton University Press, 1968), pp. 169–88.

history. Indeed, Japan may have accounted for as much as one-third of the world's silver output at the end of the sixteenth and the beginning of the seventeenth century. This expanded production began in the 1530s and had an important impact on the form and content of trade in East Asia. The Oda and Toyotomi regimes were quick to respond to this situation.

In the third month of 1569, only a year after he had entered Kyoto, Nobunaga established official exchange rates for gold, silver, and copper coins (ten *ryō* of gold were to equal fifteen copper *kammon*, and ten *ryō* of silver were to equal two *kammon*) and laid down rules for trading in gold and silver; for example, imported items such as raw silk, medicines, damask, and tea bowls had to be traded in gold and silver. This establishment of official exchange rates was a completely new policy; nothing similar had been attempted by the Muromachi shogunate.[13] It was also the predecessor of the triple coinage system that would prevail through the Tokugawa period to the 1870s. Nobunaga placed Imai Sokyū in charge of operating the Ikuno silver mine (in Tajima), which was under Nobunaga's direct control, and it is recorded that he had Gotō Tokujō strike gold coins, although none of these coins has survived.

In 1588, Hideyoshi commissioned the Gotō family to mint *ōban* gold coins, which were followed by the *koban* and *ichibuban*. Further, he assigned twenty silver refiners to Daikoku (Yuasa) Jōze of Sakai to mint silver coins. In return for these privileges, the Gotō's gold guild paid fees to the regime of 1,000 pieces of gold per year, and the silver guild (*jōzeza* or *ginza*) paid 10,000 pieces of silver. All the gold and silver mines in the nation, including the Sado gold mine and the Iwami silver mine, were placed under Hideyoshi's direct control; the amount of fees he received from these in 1598 came to more than 3,397 pieces of gold and 79,415 pieces of silver.[14]

This striking and issuance of gold and silver coins was an epochmaking event in Japan's monetary history. It is well known that the ancient Japanese imperial state was modeled on the Chinese system as exemplified by the T'ang dynasty. In the eighth century, twelve types of copper coins and one variety of silver coin were minted in Japan.

13 See Asao Naohiro, " 'Kinsei' no hajimari – Higashi Ajiya no keizai hendō to sankasei," *Geppō* 8; Kodama Kōta, ed., *Azuchi Momoyama jidai*, vol. 8 of *Zusetsu Nihon bunkashi taikei* (Tokyo: Shōgakkan, 1966), pp. 1–3.
14 The sources are "Nihon fuzei" (Naikaku Bunko) and the "Keichō sannen zōnō mokuroku," in Nonaka Jun, comp., *Dai Nihon sozeishi* (Tokyo: Chōyōkai, 1926–27), vol. 2, pp. 585–91). One detailed analysis of these documents is contained in Yamaguchi Keiji, *Bakuhansei seiritsushi no kenkyū* (Tokyo: Azekura shobō, 1974), pp. 47–116.

After that time, no coins were issued, and in medieval times, Japan relied entirely on imported Sung, Yuan, and Ming coins. Later, with the growth of trade in the late medieval period, the striking and circulation of private coins of inferior quality, both domestic and foreign, became a problem, which the shogunate and individual daimyo attempted to resolve through the frequent issue of "coinage selection regulations" (erizeni rei), edicts designed to regulate the kinds of coins in circulation and the exchange rates among them. Although these were not very effective, they can be seen as serving to accelerate the process by which Japan's coinage became independent of the Chinese economic sphere. The completion of this process came under the Tokugawa shogunate in the first half of the seventeenth century, when not only many varieties of gold and silver coins but also vast quantities of copper and brass coins were minted and issued.

The rapid increase in the production of gold and particularly silver involved Japan perforce in world commerce and transformed the structure of trade in East Asia. The Muromachi shogunate's trade with China had taken the standard form of sending tribute to the Ming emperor. But this ended in the 1540s, and with the decline of the Ming empire and its antimaritime policies, the East Asian seas witnessed the expansion of private trade. The Portuguese, the first Europeans to appear on the scene, served as intermediaries in a triangular trade among Japan, China, and other Asian countries. They established their base at Macao, which had been ceded to them by the Ming as a reward for suppressing piracy, and carried on trade between Japan and China by exchanging Japanese silver for Chinese raw silk, which was in great demand in Japan, where it was processed into textiles of extraordinary quality.

This official trade was conducted via the "Great Ship" commanded by a Portuguese captain-major who wielded military, administrative, and economic powers in the name of the king of Portugal. The Macao–Nagasaki route became from 1570 an indispensable part of the long sea journey from Goa. A portion of the profits of this trade was allotted to the Society of Jesus as funds for proselytizing. Nagasaki, the headquarters for this trade in Japan, together with the neighboring area of Mogi, was ceded in 1580 to the Jesuits by the lord of the region, Ōmura Sumitada, and his son Yoshisaki. The Society of Jesus then held all rights pertaining to possession of land, administration, and judicial matters there and also received the anchorage fees levied on Portuguese ships.

Hideyoshi learned of this when he went to Kyushu in 1587 and immediately issued an edict expelling the missionaries. In the following year he revealed his intention to take control of all trade by confiscating Nagasaki and by appointing Nabeshima Naoshige, daimyo of Hizen, as his administrative representative. To exert his control over trade there, Hideyoshi in 1588 sent Konishi Ryūsa to Nagasaki with a large quantity of silver and instructions to buy up all of the raw silk brought by the Portuguese vessel, and the next year he sent Ishida Mitsunari, magistrate of Sakai, to purchase the entire stock of raw silk carried by a Portuguese ship that had landed in the Shimazu domain. In 1594 Toyotomi Hidetsugu was ordered to send thirteen thousand *koku* of rice from lands under Hideyoshi's direct control to the Iwami silver mine, there to have it exchanged for silver to be forwarded to Nagasaki to buy up the lead carried by a Portuguese ship. It is also clear that Hideyoshi planned to monopolize the purchase of the gold, mercury, and Luzon jars that came by ship from Manila. The raw silk and other goods were resold to domestic merchants, with the price difference remaining as profit in the coffers of the Toyotomi house. The details of this trade are not entirely known, but it has been established that Hideyoshi's wife Kita-no-mandokoro (Nei) held the right to sell raw silk to the citizens of Kyoto.[15]

Hideyoshi issued an edict forbidding piracy in 1588, making an effort to seize and control all seafarers in Japan. Concurrently the daimyo, particularly those in Kyushu, were ordered to suppress piracy and private trade, an initiative that complemented the regime's policy of monopolizing foreign trade. As a result, the Toyotomi regime established in principle a system of official trade managed by the state and seized both economic profits and military goods, a high proportion of which (particularly lead and gunpowder) at that time had to be imported.

Expansion of landholdings under direct control

The source of the economic power that sustained the Toyotomi regime's rule over the entire nation was the huge amount of land under its direct control (*chokkatsu-ryō* or *kurairi-chi*, literally "granary lands"). Oda Nobunaga's domain was limited to the Kinai and neighboring provinces, and almost all of the land under his direct control consisted of territory formerly administered by the Muromachi shogunate. It must

---

15 "Kinoshita monjo," in Sanyō shimbunsha, ed., *Nene to Kinoshita-ke monjo* (Okayama: Sanyō shimbunsha, 1982), pp. 126–7.

be noted that he endeavored to seize cities such as Sakai, Kyoto, and Ōtsu and that he was greatly concerned about securing mines such as the Ikuno silver mine. But Nobunaga was not able to achieve stable territorial control. The Toyotomi regime, however, succeeded in expanding the holdings under its direct control while confiscating and redistributing fiefs in the course of national unification. Near the end of the Toyotomi regime (in 1598), it had direct holdings valued at 2,223,641 *koku,* or about 12.2 percent of the total national land base of 18,509,143 *koku.*[16] Although this figure does not match the 4,120,000 *koku* (16.5 percent of the nation's total) held by the Tokugawa shogunate at its peak in the first half of the eighteenth century, it does represent a concentration of holdings whose size had no precedent in Japanese history up to that time.

The geographic distribution of land under Hideyoshi's direct control had two centers: The first was made up of the three provinces of Settsu, Kawachi, and Izumi, where he held approximately 60 percent of the total *kokudaka,* as well as the two remaining provinces of the Kinai region, Yamashiro and Yamato, and the five provinces of Ōmi, Echizen, Tamba, Harima, and Awaji, where he directly controlled lands whose output came to 20 to 40 percent of the total productivity.[17] In all, more than half of all the land held by Hideyoshi was located in these provinces. The other core area under his control was in northern Kyushu and centered on Chikuzen and Bungo provinces. He brought under his direct control more than 55 percent of Chikuzen's *kokudaka* and more than 40 percent of Bungo's. The first center, needless to say, was the Toyotomi regime's home territory and base; the second served as the mustering point for the invasions of the continent and as a source of military stores. The remaining lands under direct control were located mainly in the Chūbu region, the Toyotomi family's original home province of Owari, and along the shores of the Inland Sea between Osaka and Kyushu. In addition, also placed under direct control were the mines and major cities throughout Japan.

Originally, the chief purpose of placing land under direct proprietary control was to ensure a supply of commissariat rice (*hyōrōmai*) for the standing army, in order to maintain the bands of retainers who had been cut away from their holdings. By obliging the rural samurai to

---

16 See Asao, "Toyotomi seiken ron," pp. 185ff; and Yamaguchi, *Bakuhansei seiritsu shi,* pp. 47–116.

17 These provinces formed a link connecting transportation to the east, using the Tōkaidō and Tōsandō and the Sea of Japan shipping routes, with transportation to the west via the San'indō and Sanyōdō and Inland Sea shipping routes.

give up their village residences and to move into the lord's castle headquarters, the daimyo had placed his samurai retainers in a position in which they could be called to arms at any moment. Hideyoshi entrusted strategically important castles to generals who had been in his service since their youth, and he established his granary lands in the areas immediately around these castles. During the wars of unification, castles frequently served as granaries. Land under direct control was located so as to protect the castles, which in turn served to guard that land.

In areas that were pacified and came under stable control as national unification drew closer to realization, Buddhist priests, merchants, and others were appointed as administrators to make use of their financial skills and local influence. A form of control over broad areas of lands under direct daimyo influence that required almost no military force was ultimately established. According to a 1591 administrator's account book kept by the Shomyōji (temple) in Ōmi Province, the temple showed an annual outlay of 9,860 *koku* from its granary land. Of this, most was used for new grants or fief increments from the Toyotomi regime to daimyo, vassals, temples, Buddhist monks, and so forth. The lands under direct control came in this way to function less as a source of commissariat rice and more as a temporary reserve of land for the reallocation of fiefs during the course of unification. Then, toward the end of the regime, two other functions gradually assumed more importance. First, land held under direct control served as a source of stipendiary rice (*fuchimai*) for low-ranking vassals who had no landed fiefs. Second, it was used to meet the expenses of castle construction and public works undertaken by the Toyotomi regime.

Hideyoshi also managed to make his continuing presence felt in even the peripheral areas of Japan, by requiring daimyo to set aside within their domain a portion of land that would technically be under Hideyoshi's direct proprietary control but that would be administered on his behalf by the daimyo. For example, in 1595 Satake Yoshinobu of Hitachi was granted a domain of 545,800 *koku*, of which 10,000 *koku* was designated as land remaining under Hideyoshi's direct control. This land corresponded to an area of paddy that comprised Satake's original fief (*honryō*) and functioned as a commissariat rice granary for the eastern provinces. It presumably fed a fund that the Toyotomi regime could draw on to accumulate special products of the domains (in this case, gold).[18]

18 See Yamaguchi, *Bakuhansei seiritsushi*, pp. 71ff.

To take another example, land under Hideyoshi's direct control was established in the domain of the Akita family of Dewa that amounted to one-third of the domain territory. According to the account books submitted every three years by the daimyo, this land was used to supply the central government with lumber for use in building ships and castles. Granary lands placed in distant daimyo domains had yet a third function. Subject to periodic inspection by officials sent out from the central government, they provided the excuse for administrative oversight and also the opportunity to convey to daimyo in distant regions, whose fiscal policies were comparatively backward, the more advanced techniques of the capital.

CHANGES IN INTERNATIONAL RELATIONS

Seizure of the right to conduct diplomacy

The unification of Japan by Nobunaga and Hideyoshi required the binding together of the many separate political entities that constituted Japan's domestic body politic. It also drew the two unifiers into involvement in the affairs of the world outside Japan. Foreign relations was an integral part of the domestic order. As of 1530, international relations in East Asia took place within a structure dominated by Ming China, and Japan was considered a part of this order. The shogun Ashikaga Yoshimitsu had been invested as "king of Japan" by the second Ming emperor Chu Yün-wen (r. 1398–1402). Yoshimitsu, employing this title, sent ambassadors to China and Korea. Formal diplomatic relations were opened from this time in which the Korean kings, who had also been invested by the Chinese, treated the Ashikaga shoguns as the "kings of Japan" on a level equal to themselves. The Ming emperor was at the apex of this structure, and only those who had been recognized by him as "king" had the right to conduct foreign relations and to engage in trade. The Ashikaga shoguns who followed after Yoshimitsu did not obtain this investiture and even avoided using the title "king of Japan" in their correspondence, because there had been in Japan since ancient times a strong feeling of superiority to Korea. But the basis of foreign relations remained unchanged in the eyes of the Ming government; relations between Japan and China continued mainly as trade in the form of tribute until the end of the Muromachi shogunate; and in addition, Japan and Korea exchanged more than sixty official diplomatic missions.

The system by which the Muromachi shogunate ruled Japan was

not suited to the unitary diplomatic relations of the kind conceived by the Ming emperors. Instead, diplomacy took a pluralistic form in which daimyo such as the Hosokawa and Ōuchi came to share in the China trade with the shogun, and the actual enterprise of sending the tribute ships was entrusted to merchants of Sakai and other cities. These conditions did not conform to Ming requirements. But the Korean government accommodated these realities by granting the special status of ruler or chieftain (kyoshū) to daimyo or other participants in this trade, according them treatment second only to that given to a "king."[19] Although the Koreans eagerly sought trade with Japan, they were even more interested in obtaining Japanese cooperation in suppressing the so-called Japanese pirates.

The decline of the Ming empire accelerated the trend toward pluralistic relations and brought about a transformation in the pattern of relations among the medium-sized and small states and peoples on the Chinese periphery. The formal relationships among the kings and the system of official diplomatic relations authorized by the state began to crumble, and illicit trade and private diplomacy made their appearance. The suspension of the Japan–China tally trade after the final voyage in 1547 marked the end of the old system. Overseas, the emergence of the Ryūkyūs as a trading country from the fifteenth to the sixteenth centuries, and its multifaceted activities in the East China Sea, represented the transition from the old system to the new.

The Oda and Toyotomi regimes appeared in the midst of these developments. The changes that were taking place in Japan were one aspect of the decline of the world order centered on the Ming empire. The Muromachi shogunate, which was linked to that order, collapsed and was replaced by the new political order founded by Nobunaga and Hideyoshi. Given these circumstances, the task of pacifying the nation and uniting the daimyo and merchants made it inevitable that Japan's new national leadership would intervene in, and eventually reorganize, the pluralisitic international relations and private trade established by the daimyo and the merchants. Further, the decline of Ming power encouraged the new Japanese rulers to form a new international order more suitable to their specific needs.

In addition, a new element appeared in East Asia at this time, first, the Portuguese and then the other European powers. Establishing a new state in place of the Muromachi shogunate burdened Hideyoshi

19 Tanaka Takeo, Chūsei taigai kankei shi (Tokyo: Tōkyō daigaku shuppankai, 1975); Arano Yasunori, "Taikun gaikō taisei no kakuritsu," in Katō Eiichi and Yamada Tadao, eds., Sakoku, vol. 2 of Kōza Nihon kinsei shi (Tokyo: Yūhikaku, 1981), pp. 117–221.

with two problems simultaneously: What role should this state assume in the changing East Asian world? What conception of authority and the international order should inform its diplomatic relations with other countries?

At each stage of national unification, Hideyoshi seized and redefined the rights to conduct diplomacy that had been fragmented under the old system. In 1587, after the pacification of Kyushu, for instance, Hideyoshi confirmed the lord of Tsushima, Sō Yoshishige, in his proprietorship of that island and made him solely responsible for relations with Korea. The Sō had established their authority in a unique form, using Tsushima's geographic and political situation to assume what amounted to a monopoly on relations with Korea, and they retained specialists who had acquired the techniques and knowledge required to exercise diplomacy. Hideyoshi brought under his own control diplomatic relations with Korea, by forming a lord–vassal relationship with Sō Yoshishige. Then Hideyoshi decided to attack Korea because the Korean king had not sent tribute to him, the unifier of Japan. But Yoshishige persuaded Hideyoshi to postpone the attack, by promising to persuade the Korean king to send tribute. What Yoshishige did in fact was to invite the Koreans to send an envoy. When the Korean ambassadors came to Japan in 1590, Hideyoshi granted them an audience at Jurakutei. As a reward for his success in bringing this about, Yoshishige was promoted to chamberlain (jijū) at the junior fourth rank lower grade and was granted the Hashiba name, a surname that Hideyoshi had once used.

The Shimazu of Satsuma attained a similar position with respect to the Ryūkyūs. The kingdom of the Ryūkyūs had once held an independent status in East Asian diplomatic relations and trade. But this was now being eroded by Japanese, Chinese, and Portuguese traders, and the Ryūkyūs were eventually reduced to conducting intermediary trade between China and Japan. This took the form of tribute trade with China to obtain goods that were then sold to Japan. Hideyoshi attempted to regulate this trade by using the Shimazu as intermediaries to negotiate with the king of the Ryūkyūs. He was particularly anxious to have an envoy sent to congratulate him on his unification of the country, an act that would acknowledge the Ryūkyūs' recognition of Japanese sovereignty. Before this objective was fully realized, however, the Japanese invasions of Korea began. Hideyoshi assigned the Ryūkyūs to the Shimazu and ordered them as his rear vassals to cooperate with the Korean invasion. Although this order was not carried out, Hideyoshi gained control of Japan's relations with the Ryūkyūs by confirming the exclusive position of the Shimazu family over diplomatic relations with the Ryūkyūs and by placing the Shimazu under his own control.

Hideyoshi's diplomatic concerns moved in still other directions. In 1590, Kakizaki Yoshihiro, lord of Matsumae in Hokkaido, came to Kyoto and submitted to Hideyoshi, who brought him under his overlordship by acknowledging Yoshihiro's right to rule his territory as daimyo and by having him appointed to a court post and the rank of junior fifth rank lower grade. Most of Hokkaido in this period was under the control of two Ainu communities, and the Kakizaki domain constituted only a small area in the southern part of the island. Yoshihiro had established his authority by unifying the small commercial towns that had grown up to trade with the Ainu. When in 1592 Yoshihiro joined the forces assembled in northern Kyushu for the attack on Korea, Hideyoshi recognized Yoshihiro's right to oversee the seamen, merchants, and others on Japanese commercial ships that sought trade with the Ainu and to prohibit them from treating the Ainu unfairly. Yoshihiro's right to collect a customs tax from these ships was also acknowledged. This meant not only that Yoshihiro's previously acquired interests were confirmed but also that his right to supervise and control the commercial dealings between the Ainu and the Japanese was recognized. In this way Hideyoshi gained control over the diplomatic channels to the Ainu.

When in 1587 Hideyoshi traveled to Kyushu in his campaign against the Shimazu, he was surprised to find Nagasaki and Mogi in the possession of the Society of Jesus. He therefore confiscated the church's domain the following year and put Nagasaki under his own control, appointing the nearby daimyo Nabeshima Naoshige as his local representative. But this was merely for administrative purposes; Hideyoshi himself took direct charge of diplomatic relations with the countries of Europe.

In his diplomatic initiatives, Hideyoshi appointed as his assistants Buddhist monks from the Kyoto Gozan (the leading Rinzai Zen temples in the capital), who had previously conducted the diplomatic correspondence for the Muromachi shogunate. Monks such as Seishō Jōtai and Gempo Reisan conducted diplomatic negotiations with China and Korea from about 1591, and they drafted Hideyoshi's letters to the viceroy of the Indies (Portuguese Goa), to the governor general of the Philippines (Spain), and to Takasagun (Taiwan). In this way Hideyoshi brought the right to handle Japan's foreign relations into his own hands at the same time that he was completing domestic unification. This involvement in fashioning a new international as well as domestic order ultimately pushed Hideyoshi into yet another massive use of military power.

The invasions of Korea

In the ninth month of 1591 Hideyoshi issued orders to all the daimyo of Japan to muster troops for the invasion of Korea.[20] The Korean ambassadors who had come to Jurakutei the previous year had brought their king's message offering congratulations on Hideyoshi's unification of Japan and seeking to cultivate good neighborly relations. That was completely different from what Hideyoshi had desired, namely, the payment of tribute so as to suggest Korea's subordination to Japan. Nonetheless, Hideyoshi expressed admiration for the "tribute" presented by the Koreans and ordered them to grant passage to the army he planned to send against China. The Korean envoys protested, but to no avail. The Sō family, afraid of losing their special status in Japanese–Korean relations, made great efforts to persuade the Koreans to provide passage for Hideyoshi's army, but their arguments were not successful either. Misunderstandings and discrepancies on both sides remained unresolved, and so the two sides moved toward catastrophe.

Hideyoshi's plan to invade the continent was linked with the task of completing his unification. An incident that took place in 1585 helps explain Hideyoshi's conception of the unified state that he hoped to create. In that year Hideyoshi delivered a reprimand to Katō Mitsuyasu, a retainer who had been in Hideyoshi's service since his youth. Katō had claimed that he found it impossible to support his own vassals on the income drawn just from the relatively small domain that Hideyoshi had granted to him. Consequently Katō requested that he be allowed to assign fiefs to these vassals from that portion of his domain that had been reserved for Hideyoshi's direct control. Greatly

---

20 The mainstream of postwar research on the invasion of Korea sees the cause of the invasion in the Toyotomi regime's internal contradictions; that is, Hideyoshi launched the invasions to complete domestic unification, suppressing the daimyo's desire to increase the size of their domains. The source for this view is the "Iyo Komatsu Hitotsuyanagi monjo" (copy in Tōkyō daigaku shiryō hensanjo). Some research on the activities of the Japanese army in Korea has appeared recently, but the full story has not yet been told. Further, Fujiki Hisashi, in his *Toyotomi heiwa-rei*, revived the interpretation that the purpose of the invasion was the renewal of licensed trade with the Ming. See also the treatment of the invasion of Korea in Chapter 6 of this volume.

angered, Hideyoshi repeated what he thought was obvious to all: that such lands were intended to provide commissariat rice and other supplies for the wars of unification, and he labeled Katō's request as outrageous, claiming that Katō's proposal was akin to invading the domains held by neighboring daimyo. Hideyoshi even went so far as to accuse Katō of harboring a desire for national upheaval and left unsaid the implication that Katō dreamed of replacing Hideyoshi as national hegemon. "Peace" was Hideyoshi's slogan for unification, and he would stop the daimyo from fighting among themselves and have them establish their territories through peaceful procedures under the auspices of his regime. Hideyoshi realized only too well that Katō's request might lead to the dissolution of his own base. Hideyoshi then went on to recount how he had promoted Katō from a lowly thirty-*koku* status to a daimyo holding of more than twenty thousand *koku*, saying, "for his [Katō's] sake, Hideyoshi would go so far as to subjugate not only Japan but also China."[21]

Independent military initiatives by the daimyo to expand their domains at one another's expense would collide directly with Hideyoshi's aim of unification. Hideyoshi felt that he could achieve domestic peace and unity and bring to an end the daimyo's struggles among themselves, by redirecting their tremendous energy for independent action toward the conquest of the continent. He referred to this plan at each successive stage of the unification process: He emphasized it strongly in the 1586 mobilization order for the Kyushu campaign and mentioned it in the 1588 orders for cessation of hostilities sent to daimyo in the Kantō and northern Japan. It was finally realized in the mobilization order of 1591. The fact that this mobilization took place after national unification had been achieved indicates that the contradictions submerged in the peaceful unity made an invasion of the continent a necessity and strongly suggests a close linkage between the two events.

In 1592 a great army of more than 158,000 troops assembled at a base established at Nagoya in Kyushu and crossed to Korea. Their destination was China. The Japanese forces landed at Pusan in the fourth month, took the fortresses at Pusan and Donglae, and occupied Seoul by the second day of the fifth month. After regrouping there they moved north: Konishi Yukinaga occupied P'yŏngyang; Katō Kiyomasa moved toward the east coast and captured Hamhung, then

21 "Iyo Komatsu Hitotsuyanagi monjo"; Iwasawa Yoshihiko, "Hideyoshi no Kara-iri ni kansuru monjo," *Nihon rekishi* 163 (January 1962): 73–5, was the first to introduce this source.

continued north to Hoeryong, seized two Korean princes, and advanced as far as the Tumen River basin. Meanwhile, the other generals moved into the areas to which they had been assigned, so that the Japanese armies completed their invasion of the entire Korean peninsula. They surrounded the main cities in Korea's eight provinces and issued decrees to the populace: Those who obeyed were spared, but those who resisted were annihilated. This was like the process of pacification that had taken place in Japan. Then each army prepared for the invasion of China by collecting taxes and amassing military stores. Two reasons for Japan's victories at the beginning of hostilities were that the Japanese troops were seasoned by domestic warfare and they were organized around powerful companies of musketeers.

In the seventh month, a Ming army crossed the Yalu River at the request of the Koreans and engaged Japanese troops twice in P'yŏng-yang Province; in the second battle the Japanese were defeated and withdrew to Seoul. The Korean army took heart at the withdrawal of the Japanese armies, and local "righteous armies" (guerrilla bands known as uigun) harassed the Japanese everywhere. The Chinese troops under Li Ju-sung attacked Seoul but were defeated in the battle of Pyokchegwan and fled to P'yŏngyang. A truce was then declared between the Japanese and Chinese forces, and a long period of peace negotiations, lasting four years, began in 1592.

Hideyoshi presented seven conditions for peace, including the following: A daughter of the Ming emperor was to become a consort of the Japanese emperor; official licensed trade with China was to be resumed; ministers of China and Japan were to exchange oaths; four provinces of Korea were to be ceded to Japan; and a Korean prince and ministers were to be sent to Japan as hostages. On the other hand, the Chinese saw trade to be the main problem complicating the negotiations, because for the Chinese to recognize trade, an investiture from the emperor was required; this in turn hinged on the Japanese submission to China of a petition to surrender and seek friendship. Hence, the Chinese continued to view the world in terms of a civilized China surrounded by barbarian states. Once again, the persons responsible for carrying out the negotiations for each country, Konishi Yukinaga and Shen Wei-ching, deceived Hideyoshi in order to achieve a peace settlement. The result was a promise for the withdrawal of Japanese forces, approval of Hideyoshi's investiture as "king" of Japan, and friendship with Korea. The Korean royal family, which had fled north as the Japanese armies advanced, also agreed to send envoys when the Ming ambassadors brought the investiture to Japan.

The Chinese and Korean embassies arrived in Japan in 1596 and were given an audience by Hideyoshi at Osaka Castle. Hideyoshi was then presented with the instructions and patents from the Ming emperor, investing him as the king of Japan, and he also received a golden seal and official garb. He was greatly pleased, and he entertained the envoys at a banquet and reception. Hideyoshi, however, was under the mistaken impression that the Chinese had yielded to his demands. The truth soon came out, however, exposed by Katō Kiyomasa and others who were at odds with Konishi Yukinaga over the manner in which the war in Korea was being conducted. Hideyoshi realized that his demands had been deliberately twisted and manipulated in order to provide for a Chinese diplomatic victory, and he thereby became enraged and ordered a second invasion. The Chinese and Korean delegations were expelled, and peace negotiations were summarily broken off.

The second invasion began early in 1597 when more than 140,000 troops sailed to Korea. This time the objective was to win acceptance of the conditions for peace that Hideyoshi had laid down during the peace negotiations, and so emphasis was placed on obtaining the cession of Korea's three southern provinces and gathering as many hostages as possible. The Koreans again sought help from China, and a joint army of Chinese and Korean troops fought the Japanese along with the local guerrillas. The Japanese forces were thus unable to commandeer as many supplies as they had intended from the Korean farming villages, which had been devastated by successive years of warfare.

Faced with fierce resistance by the civilian population and the menace to their supply routes by the Korean navy under Yi Sun-sin, the Japanese were gradually pushed back to the Pusan coastal area. No longer able to maneuver freely, the leaders of the Japanese army became intensely weary of the war and proposed reopening peace talks with the Chinese. But in the eighth month of 1598, Hideyoshi died suddenly, at the age of sixty-three. Tokugawa Ieyasu and others among the Five Elders kept Hideyoshi's death secret while they arranged for the withdrawal of the entire Japanese army. The Japanese forces returned home in rapid succession, and with this the invasions of Korea, which had lasted for over seven years, came to an end without the Toyotomi regime itself or any of the daimyo or their vassals gaining any rewards or a single inch of territory.

Hideyoshi's invasions of Korea had a number of results. The mobilization of a huge army by the Ming dynasty exacerbated already-existing financial difficulties and hastened its collapse. Korea was devastated, especially the southern provinces, which were the country's agricultural heartland, and the country would not recover for several generations. In Japan, the impetus for outward expansion that sustained the domestic unification drive ended in failure. The decline of the Toyotomi regime that was already in evidence was surely hastened.

New conceptions of the state and the world

Hideyoshi sent troops to Korea just as if he were extending to the field of conquest the domestic warfare by which he unified Japan. But he failed. Did Hideyoshi grasp any distinction between "domestic" and "foreign"? I would argue that he did and that by establishing a unified Japanese state, he created a new way for the Japanese to perceive of foreign countries and the world.

In the course of his tumultuous political career, the first time that Hideyoshi was made conscious of an actual, as opposed to an abstract, foreign presence in Japan came in 1587 during the Kyushu campaign. On that occasion he issued an edict expelling the Christian missionaries, the first article of which stated: "Although Japan is the land of the gods (*shinkoku*), there are persons who come here from a Christian country to expound wicked teachings. This is a very evil thing and must not be allowed."[22]

Here Hideyoshi conceived of Japan as the "land of the gods," in contrast with a "Christian country." In the 1540s a few Portuguese became the first Europeans to arrive in Japan when they drifted ashore at Tanegashima aboard a Chinese pirate ship, and in 1549 Francis Xavier of the Society of Jesus landed in Kagoshima to bring Christianity to Japan. At this time the worldview of the medieval Japanese was largely a Buddhist one that perceived of the world as composed of three entities: Japan (Honchō), China (Shintan), and India (Tenjiku). Japan, as "a small country on the periphery of the Buddhist world," asserted its political and cultural identity by advancing the claim of being the land of the gods. Europeans came from an outside world completely beyond what could be imagined by the medieval Japanese.

---

22 This is my own interpretation. On the medieval philosophy of *shinkoku*, see Kuroda Toshio, "Chūsei kokka to shinkoku shisō," in his *Nihon chūsei no kokka to shūkyō* (Tokyo: Iwanami shoten, 1975), pp. 253–330; and Murai Shōsuke, "Chūsei Nihon no kokusai ishiki ni tsuite," in *Minshū no seikatsu, bunka to henkaku shutai (Rekishigaku kenkyūkai 1982 nendo taikai hōkoku)* (Tokyo: Aoki shoten, 1982), pp. 57–67. The source has been published in Kyōto daigaku bungakubu kokushi kenkyūshitsu, ed. *Hirado Matsuura-ke shiryō* (Kyoto, 1951), pp. 115–16.

Thus Christianity was thought at first to be a sect of Buddhism. And because these Europeans had brought with them a powerful new weapon, namely, firearms, they instantly transformed the worldview of Japan's rulers. Hideyoshi's use of the expression "Christian country" for Europe demonstrated that he did recognize the existence of an area in the world that had its own characteristic culture different from that of either Tenjiku or Shintan. He responded to this culture by placing it in an intellectual category that contrasted it with the concept of the land of the gods.

Hideyoshi felt that the activities of the Christian country that he witnessed in Kyushu were potentially dangerous to Japan. The missionaries did not merely convert the populace but ruthlessly destroyed Shinto shrines and Buddhist temples, claiming they were institutions of idol worship. The Christian daimyo Ōmura Sumitada and his son Yoshisaki had even ceded Nagasaki, an excellent natural harbor in their domain, to the Society of Jesus. The Jesuits were given practically a free rein: They administered the town, dispensed justice, owned land, and collected anchorage fees from Portuguese ships. However, they were not granted the right to collect a tax on trade from ships entering the harbor.

Hideyoshi surely was aware of the parallels with an earlier example of ecclesiastical challenge to secular authority: the Ikkō *ikki* that Nobunaga had had such great difficulty in suppressing. The Ikkō believers, too, had destroyed Shinto shrines and Buddhist temples in an attempt to promote a "single-minded, exclusive practice" (*ikkō senju*), built towns within temple compounds that were relatively independent of secular authority, and pitted themselves militarily against daimyo authority.

Hideyoshi was convinced, on the basis of his experience, that such "heresies" would present obstacles to national unification. The Society of Jesus, moreover, was identified as being a foreign lord. Because Hideyoshi was attempting to unite the lords of Japan under his own authority, he could not tolerate the existence of a separate authority that was not integrated into that system of unity. On 1587/6/19 he ordered that trade and foreign travel be permitted only so long as they did not disturb the practices of Buddhism, but he instructed the missionaries to leave Japan within twenty days.

The identity of the new state that Hideyoshi built was based on the land of the gods concept and was enhanced by an additional element, the notion of an inherent conflict between a strong Japan and China dominated by effete aristocrats and Buddhist clergy. This was illustrated by Hideyoshi's instructions for the invasion of the continent in 1592: "With only five hundred or a thousand men I succeeded in uniting Japan, a country of warriors and furious internecine struggles. Since so many of you are in the vanguard against 'the long-sleeved country of the Great Ming,' I am confident of the outcome. Subjugate it speedily."[23]

Two concepts, "Japan, a country of warriors and furious internecine struggles," and "the long-sleeved country of the Great Ming," were used in opposition to each other. The term "long-sleeved" referred to aristocrats and Buddhist clergy; when used by warriors, it expressed contempt. Hideyoshi, who had united the Japan's warrior bands and built a state composed of a national coalition of daimyo, was keenly aware of that state as a nation of warriors. His disdain for the "long sleeves" was particularly strong, perhaps because his regime itself had had to derive its legitimacy from his adopting the title of imperial regent. Although the leaders of the Kamakura and the Muromachi shogunates had been drawn from warrior bands, they were unable ultimately to free themselves from the organizational principles advocated by the "long sleeves." Hideyoshi ruled Japan through the military power that had unified the daimyo. This military power then became the basis of a new state structure that put an end to the nobles' control of the state. In his terms, both the Ming empire and the Muromachi shogunate were "long-sleeved" administrations.

Under the sixteenth-century unifiers, the land of the gods had become a state organized around the daimyo. Opposition to this new state was seen to come from the "long sleeves" of both Japan and China. Moreover, with the Ming empire in a state of collapse and Europeans arriving in Japan in ever-increasing numbers, the new center of authority for a secure international order was not to be "long-sleeved" China but, rather, the militarily powerful "country of warriors and furious internecine struggles": Japan. Hideyoshi thought that because he had pacified both the land and sea and had made travel safe at home and abroad, the Chinese should dispatch a mission to thank him. Obviously, he was applying knowledge gained from his narrow domestic experience in a simpleminded fashion to complex international problems. He had, as well, a haughty, insular view of the outside world. On the other hand, it cannot be denied that he made an

---

23 Tōkyō daigaku shiryō hensanjo, ed., *Dai Nihon komonjo, Iewake 8, Mōri-ke monjo*, vol. 3, pp. 164–8 (doc. 904). Asao Nashiro, "Sakokusei no seiritsu," in Rekishigaku kenkyūkai and Nihonshi kenkyūkai, eds., *Bakuhansei shakai*, vol. 4 of *Kōza Nihonshi* (Tokyo: Tōkyō diagaku shuppankai, 1970), pp. 59–74.

effort to develop a new conception of state that would displace the international order based on China, then in a state of decline.

In 1591 the Jesuit *visitator* Alexandro Valignano, returning to Japan from a trip in which he had taken four young Japanese samurai from Kyushu to Europe, brought to Hideyoshi a letter from the Portuguese viceroy of the Indies (Goa). In his reply to the viceroy, Hideyoshi revealed still more of his idea of Japan's world status. He himself, he wrote, had united by force of arms the more than sixty provinces of Japan that had suffered years of disorder. He had stabilized public affairs so that even foreign nations sent tribute to him. Moreover, he suggested that he was planning to conquer the great Ming empire in an effort to wield his authority beyond Japan's borders. He continued by saying that Japan was the land of the gods (*kami*) and that the gods of Japan were the origin of all things. Worship of the *kami* was equivalent in Japan to Buddhism in India and Confucianism in China. Finally, he had forbidden the Christian missionaries, who remained unaware of these teachings, from coming to Japan, although he promised to guarantee the safety on land and sea of those who would come seeking friendship and trade.[24]

In a letter to the governor general of the Philippines sent in that same year, Hideyoshi omitted the passage about the land of the gods but emphasized the mysterious quality of his authority, by describing the omens that appeared at his birth. He mentioned Korea and the Ryūkyūs as countries that rendered tribute, and he threatened to attack the Philippines immediately if tribute were not forthcoming. He sent a letter of the same import to Taiwan (Takasagun) in 1593, revealing more details of his miraculous birth, such as how the rays of the sun filled the room when his mother and father conceived him. He likened himself to a child of the sun: The sun causes everything to grow, he said, adding that it also had the power to wither everything. The letter went on to say that he had already launched an attack on Korea, that the Chinese ambassador had come to surrender, and that the Europeans (*namban*) and the Ryūkyūs were sending tribute. This claim about tribute was not true in either case; in essence, Hideyoshi was trying to extend the military power by which he had united Japan to be the central principle of a new regional order.

The former international order from the Chinese viewpoint was based on a dichotomy between China and the barbarians. In this sys-

24 Hideyoshi's letter to the viceroy of the Indies (Goa) in English translation appears in Ryusaku Tsunoda, W. Theodore de Bary, and Donald Keene, eds., *Sources of Japanese Tradition* (New York: Columbia University Press, 1958), pp. 316–18.

tem China was the land of culture, rites, and etiquette, and the barbarians were the foreign countries beyond this realm. Hideyoshi put forward a Japanese version of the Chinese–barbarian concept, placing the militarily powerful "country of warriors and furious internecine struggles" at the center and then arranging the neighboring countries around it. It is simple to point out how devoid this concept was of substance, as seen from outside Japan. But to the unifier of the Japanese state, the claim of international hegemony was not farfetched.

Indeed, one can even find some basis for Hideyoshi's claim. From his time Korea and the Ryūkyūs were consistently ranked as tribute-bearing countries. This pattern was continued in the Edo period, when both countries were defined as "emissarial countries" (*tsūshin-koku*) that sent envoys to the shogun, with the Sō and Shimazu daimyo serving as the respective intermediaries. The Ainu suffered military suppression at the hand of the Matsumae and were set on a course of assimilation with Japan in the Edo period. Despite the fall of the Ming dynasty, China continued to hold its place as an entity with a unique culture. India (Tenjiku) disappeared from the three-realm Buddhist worldview formerly held by the Japanese. Europe, as the Christian country with a culture different from either China's or Japan's, came to occupy a prominent place in the Japanese worldview, evidence of which can be seen in Hideyoshi's direct seizure of diplomatic relations with Portugal and Spain, and the relationship between the Tokugawa shogunate and the Netherlands, which later monopolized Europe's diplomatic relations with Japan. In the Edo period the Netherlands and China were given roughly equal status as "trading countries."

THE POWER STRUCTURE OF THE UNIFIED STATE

The transcendental authority of the "men of the realm"

The state created by Oda Nobunaga and Toyotomi Hideyoshi was basically a military hegemony imposed on the heads of all warrior bands of daimyo who had staked out their own local territorial claims. One important feature of the history of this state structure is that it was imposed *from above* by Nobunaga and Hideyoshi, instead of being formed through a process in which the daimyo, as a result of protracted warfare, would have accepted mutually *from below* the rule of a superior authority *after* having attained control over their own territories. Why was the state not formed by the mutual consent of a coalition of independent daimyo?

With the policy of strict separation of the samurai and peasant classes, the daimyo cut off their bands of retainers from private fiefs in the countryside and reconstituted them as a well-defined warrior class that administered the various landholdings that made up the domain and that carried out legislative, judicial, fiscal, and other functions under the lord's direction. This policy was implemented from above by Hideyoshi, to whom the daimyo had sworn allegience. By accepting this scheme, the daimyo were able to safeguard their own positions and achieve greater control over their own domains. Only by entering into lord–vassal relationships with Nobunaga and Hideyoshi could the daimyo ensure their own positions as proprietary lords. The social and economic functions necessary for everyday existence, including agriculture, handicraft production, and commerce and distribution, were left entirely to farmers, merchants, artisans, and others of the ruled populations and were not open to warrior participation. In institutional terms, the rights of rule and administration were lodged in the hands of the legally defined warrior status, but the day-to-day administration in each town or village was for the most part entrusted to functionaries within the ruled statuses of farmers, artisans, and merchants.

The ruled classes of late medieval Japan were clustered in villages (mura) and town wards (*machi*). Customarily, villages would combine to form autonomous groups, that is, self-governing village associations (*sōson*). These self-governing village associations were particularly prominent in the economically advanced regions, such as the Kinai and surrounding provinces, and especially within the domains of the religious proprietary lordships, including the Ikkō *ikki* and also temples such as Kōfukuji, Negoroji, and Enryakuji.

The self-governing village associations sometimes formed district-wide alliances (*gunchūsō*) or even provincewide associations (*sōgoku ikki*). The province and the district (*kōri*) were local administrative units of the ancient state, but their boundaries no longer conformed to the contours of sixteenth-century political realities. Rather, the ancient units served as a basis for the formation of autonomous groups. As a monk of the Ikkō sect of Ōmi Province aptly recorded, these alliances geographically symbolized their abhorrence of ties to the private lord–vassal system maintained by individual warrior lords and, at the same time, demonstrated their preference for the jurisdiction of the court, aristocracy, and religious institutions of Kyoto.[25]

25 *Hompukuji atogaki*, in Kawahara Kasuo and Inoue Toshio, eds., *Rennyo, Ikkō ikki*, vol. 17 of *Nihon shisō taikei* (Tokyo: Iwanami shoten, 1972), pp. 185–236; citation from p. 230.

The farmers, artisans, and merchants insisted that they were not a part of any warrior's band of private followers but, rather, "people" (i.e., citizens) of the provinces and districts. They saw that compared with the rule of military proprietors, the rule of the nobility was more lenient and would intrude less on their autonomy. The slogan of one peasant alliance (*tsuchi ikki*) in Harima Province, "There shall be no samurai in the province," shows this clearly.[26] Moreover, religious *ikki* crossed district or provincial borders to spread insurrection over wide areas, threatening the daimyo's control over their territories. For example, the Ikkō *ikki* under the leadership of the Honganji (temple) waged warfare as a union of believers drawn from more than a dozen provinces. Nobunaga felt keenly the threat posed by this Ikkō *ikki*, and for that reason he resorted to a strategy of total annihilation. But Nobunaga also realized that a government could not continue to exist through such a destructive policy alone. The alternative that he and his successors chose was to become "men of the realm" (*tenka bito*) and as such to establish their own authority and legitimacy in terms more acceptable to the people of Japan.

The term "men of the realm" was a sobriquet used by contemporaries to refer to Hideyoshi and Tokugawa Ieyasu; it meant "the de facto ruler of the realm." The concept of realm (*tenka*) came from China. In ancient Japan, the portion of the Japanese archipelago ruled by the emperor was regarded as the entire world, and so the term *tenka* was frequently used in a political sense to designate the universality of the authority ruling that area. With the advent of the military regimes in the Kamakura period, Minamoto no Yoritomo, the Hōjō regents, and the subsequent Ashikaga shoguns were often called "masters of the realm" (*tenka no shujin*), meaning that they held the right to rule universally.

But it was Oda Nobunaga who used the term "realm" (*tenka*) most effectively. By his time it had acquired four concentric layers of meaning: (1) Japan and the people who lived there; (2) Kyoto and its environs, the locus of the regime that ruled the nation; (3) the regime itself; and (4) the individual rulers of the regime. Nobunaga used the term in the first sense to criticize the shogun: "The realm," he stated, "is reprimanding Ashikaga Yoshiaki." He then overthrew him. In this instance Nobunaga claimed to represent public opinion. But at the same time he continued to maintain that he had been entrusted with

---

26 "Sakkaiki," the diary of Nakayama Sadachika, entry for 1429/1/29 (unpublished; manuscript copies in Tōkyō daigaku shiryō hensanjo and Kyōto daigaku).

the government of the realm and ascribed the third and fourth meanings to himself. Nobunaga was at once the representative of the realm (a ruled object) and the realm itself (the principal of the realm). As the personification of the realm, he felt called upon to replace the old social order. Because Nobunaga was killed halfway on his path to unification, he could not be called a "man of the realm," but he was nonetheless the first to develop and apply the mode of action associated with a man of the realm in actual politics.

Beyond using the notion of *tenka* as justification to dispatch the Ashikaga shogun, Nobunaga's method of dealing with the religious powers, his conception of Azuchi Castle, and his interventions in the retainer bands of his subordinate daimyo all are clearly permeated with the mode of action of the men of the realm, who rose above the various autonomous groups and brought them under their control. Of particular importance was Nobunaga's attitude toward the emperor and the court. When he entered Kyoto in 1568, he fulfilled the emperor's three requests and, in one sense, restored the emperor and court nobility, who were on the verge of being deprived of their income, to their rightful positions in the ancient, Kyoto-based hierarchy. But Nobunaga did not have in mind a resurrection of the ancient court system. Rather, he aimed at creating a state structure based on the hegemonial power of a man of the realm.

After driving out Ashikaga Yoshiaki, the court bestowed high noble rank on Nobunaga, and he advanced rapidly in rank and office until 1578, when he was named to the senior second court rank and was appointed minister of the right (*udaijin*) and great commander of the imperial bodyguards of the right (*udaishō*). But in the same year he resigned his posts and held none thereafter for the rest of his life, remaining at the senior second rank with the honorary title of former minister of the right. Nobunaga refused to be bound by the traditions and restrictions of the court system, which he would have had to accept if he had taken office; instead, he sought to put himself into a position that permitted more freedom. But he did have his eldest son, Nobutada, serve in court ranks and offices. This pattern was repeated by Nobunaga's successors: Hideyoshi became Taikō (retired imperial regent), and Ieyasu became Ōgosho (retired shogun or shogun's father). Bearing these honorary titles, they conducted themselves as the ones with the greatest actual power, setting themselves the task of forming a unified state.

In 1581 a court messenger came to Nobunaga to request that he accept appointment as minister of the left (a more prestigious post than minister of the right). Nobunaga replied that he wished the emperor Ōgimachi to abdicate and that he would in time provide the funds for an accession ceremony for Imperial Prince Kotohito, whose coming of age ceremony Nobunaga had also underwritten. Only then would Nobunaga accept the post. While the construction of Azuchi Castle was under way, Nobunaga also built a residence for himself in Kyoto that served as his point of contact with the ceremonies of the imperial court system that were useful in supporting his claims to legitimacy. But in 1579 he gave this residence, called the Nijō *gosho*, to Prince Kotohito. Here a group of nobles surrounding the twenty-seven-year-old prince worked full time, and a great deal of court business was conducted here rather than at the court of Emperor Ōgimachi, who was then in his late sixties. People called Ōgimachi's residence "the upper palace" from its location north of Prince Kotohito's Nijō *gosho*, which was then termed "the lower palace," thereby recognizing the functional division of court government. There is little doubt that Nobunaga planned sooner or later to install Prince Kotohito as "Nobunaga's emperor."

In 1582, upon Nobunaga's triumphal return from pacifying the eastern provinces, the court sent another messenger with the offer to appoint Nobunaga to the post of shogun, linked traditionally to the conquest of the Kantō. An imperial council at that time even discussed appointing him grand minister of state or imperial regent, the highest offices among the nobility's official posts, an indication that the court was thinking seriously of treating Nobunaga as the highest-ranking person in the imperial court system, save only the emperor himself.

But on this occasion, too, Nobunaga declined the offer. One month later Nobunaga died in Akechi Mitsuhide's rebellion, without revealing his motives for refusing the appointment. But it can be assumed that the complexity of asserting claims to political hegemony by working through the old imperial court system was distasteful to him. First, he would have had to tie his political future to the will of the emperor, whose subject and subordinate he would always remain. Second, he would have had to convince the general populace that he did in fact dominate the emperor and court nobility, despite his outward dependence on the emperor. And in turn, this might mean that Nobunaga would have had to conspire to install a new emperor and high nobility who would be receptive to maintaining the fictive aspects of the dependency–dominance relationship. In the end, this was not a road to power that Nobunaga chose to tread, and so it fell to Hideyoshi to put this plan into practice, with the enthronement of Emperor Go-Yōzei and Hideyoshi's own appointment as grand minister of state.

By establishing their authority as men of the realm, Nobunaga and Hideyoshi also opened up the possibility for the daimyo lords under them to fashion a concept of public authority that they could employ to govern the people below them. Within their domains the daimyo ruled with the legitimacy of state authority and not simply as private entities that used force to compel obedience. Through Hideyoshi, the daimyo were even given rank in the court system. As a result, their jurisdiction over their own territories was recognized as official, their position as public lords confirmed. Now, for the first time the daimyo could use concepts of state and public authority to maintain their claims to hold proprietary lordships, and with time they were able to confront the general populace of the provinces and districts as autonomous public persons.

There was no single means for a daimyo to obtain court rank: Petitions to the emperor could be made through members of the imperial family, the nobility, or a prominent military family. Hideyoshi set out to control the warriors' access to court rank, and he succeeded in building an ingenious structure that would induce the emperor and court to work his will while still preserving the respect due them. The most effective answer to Hideyoshi's need was to claim the authority of the men of the realm to establish "one's own emperor" from whom to receive court rank and high office. Once this public gesture was made, the final step was to return his posts and honors to the emperor and adopt the guise of "the master of the nation," free from the shackles of historical precedent. Thus the emperor was made the basis of a new state structure. He, of course, held the highest authority within it but possessed little actual power. This allowed Hideyoshi to show that the authority of the men of the realm and the daimyo was the legitimate public authority of the imperial court system.

In comparing the concept of the land of the gods with notions of legitimacy in China, an important historical fact becomes apparent. In China the dynasties frequently changed, whereas in Japan the imperial house reigned in an unbroken line. But now in the crucible of change that was late-sixteenth-century Japan, the actual guardian deities of the land of the gods were no longer the spiritual *kami* but, rather, the men of the realm who had assumed that responsibility. Then, to complete the historical circle, these men were themselves deified. After his death Hideyoshi was given the divine name of Toyokuni daimyōjin by the court, just as Ieyasu was to be given the name Tōshō daigongen after his death. Both were thus worshiped as deities. According to the missionary Luís Fróis, Nobunaga even had himself worshiped as a deity at Azuchi a few weeks before his death. In premodern Japan those who had died with hatred in their hearts were worshiped as deities to pacify their spirits, but the men of the realm were the only commoner statesmen to be recognized as Shinto deities.

From shogun and imperial regent to the authority of the retired imperial regent

The men of the realm, whose lives spanned the creation of the new state, faced numerous obstacles and difficulties in legitimizing their authority. Hideyoshi, born into a farming family, underwent particularly great hardships, but it appears that early in his life he dreamed of becoming shogun some day. His lord, Nobunaga, had been asked to accept appointment as shogun by an exceptional decision of the imperial court; consequently, it was only natural that Hideyoshi, who self-consciously played the part of Nobunaga's successor, would choose that course.[27] Indeed, there are indications that soon after Hideyoshi had consolidated his hold over central Japan in the mid-1580s, he began negotiations with Ashikaga Yoshiaki, the nominal shogun who had fled from Nobunaga. Hideyoshi purportedly offered to let Yoshiaki return to Kyoto, in return for which Hideyoshi would become Yoshiaki's adopted heir and future shogun. Had this plan succeeded, Hideyoshi would have obtained painlessly the title of unifier of the daimyo. But it is widely believed that this proposal was rejected by the proud Yoshiaki. Hideyoshi then made plans to "conquer the east," that is, the eight Kantō provinces. Doubtless he had recalled the traditional connection between the subjugation of the eastern provinces and appointment to the post of *sei-i tai-shōgun*. But Ieyasu stood in his way, and in the end Hideyoshi chose the path that led to his becoming imperial regent.

But here too, Hideyoshi encountered strong resistance because of his lowly birth. The Shimazu, daimyo of Satsuma, even went so far as to ignore Imperial Regent Hideyoshi's orders for a cessation of hostilities in 1586, after Ōtomo Sōrin, another Kyushu daimyo, had requested Hideyoshi's help in his long struggle against the Shimazu.

27 It had been thought that only members of the Minamoto lineage could become *sei-i tai-shōgun*. Nobunaga's family had no relationship to either the Minamoto or the Taira, but he claimed to be a Taira in that he had overthrown the Ashikaga house that claimed descent from the Minamoto.

The Shimazu defied both "the low fellow with no antecedents" and the court, which had appointed such a person to the post of imperial regent. Hideyoshi consequently had to confront such resistance with military force. He needed to show those around him that even though he was serving as imperial regent, he still held military power befitting the leader of the great warrior alliance. For this reason, he continued to lead armed forces during the course of national unification. Even in times of peace he made military "progresses" (godōza) to each region of the country, behaving in a way completely different from the style expected of the imperial regent and grand minister of state.[28] Interestingly, Hideyoshi offered a new interpretation of the post of imperial regent: In his view it was an office "that must conquer the realm."[29] For Hideyoshi the invasions of the continent, too, were compelled in part by his need to assert authority.

Although Hideyoshi's difficulties in gaining legitimacy were multiplied by the lowness of his birth, his life followed a path that those who would be men of the realm had to tread. Men of the realm could not stop with just the unification of the daimyo but had to use their authority to unite and rule all of Japan's land and people. The chief difficulty confronting them was to find a way to accomplish both of these tasks at one stroke. Throughout medieval times the feudal fief system had developed chiefly under the shogunate, which was an office in the imperial court system. On the other hand, not only the shogun but also the emperor, nobles, and other court families formed relationships with warriors by appointing them to court rank and office. These two circumstances merged to form Japan's unique feudal fief system: Fiefs were based on the kokudaka system enforced by the military elite, and court rank played a role in the legitimization of the warrior status.

No contradictions between the imperial and military-based system of authority appeared on the surface as long as Hideyoshi held the posts of imperial regent and grand minister of state and at the same time stood at the apex of the hierarchy of military proprietary lords. But in 1591 when he handed over the office of imperial regent to his nephew and adopted son Hidetsugu and began to rule as the retired imperial regent, the structural fault lines inherent in this arrangement

28 The term godōza was used to mean an aristocrat's removal of his residential base to another place, or a general's taking the field.
29 See "Komai nikki," the diary of Hidetsugu's vassal Komai Shigekatsu, entry for 1594/4/13, in Kondō Keizo, ed., Kaitei shiseki shūran, vol. 25 (Kyoto: Rinsen shoten, reprint, 1967–9), p. 560. See also Asao, "Toyotomi seiken ron," p. 208.

gradually broke through to the surface. There was tension between the powers of the court system, of which Hidetsugu was the center, and the powers held and symbolized by Hideyoshi as the man of the realm, the true holder of actual military power. To cite one example, the edict ordering a census issued in Hidetsugu's name in 1592 was a call for a national count of households and individuals to provide a statistical base for requisitioning military laborers for the Korean campaigns.[30] But at that time, camp laborers (*jimpu*) and sailors (*kako*) already were being mobilized in each daimyo domain under orders from Hideyoshi.

In general, Hideyoshi's orders to the daimyo drew their legitimacy from Hideyoshi's private authority, his position as head of the warrior estate. But edicts such as the national census order were different from this – they applied to the nation as a whole and thus had to be grounded in Hidetsugu's public authority as derived from his position as imperial regent. Similarly, decrees that were national in scope, such as regulations on post horses (*temma*), and official documents granting the bearer permission to pass through toll barriers (*kasho*) exceeded the authority of individual lords and consequently were issued in Hidetsugu's name. Moreover, in matters relating to the court system, such as the ceremony for appointing daimyo to court rank or the punishment of nobles, the required procedure was that Hideyoshi's wishes be communicated to Hidetsugu, who would carry them out in his capacity as imperial regent.

It is true that Hideyoshi was the one who had arranged for Hidetsugu to become imperial regent, but once the appointment was made, Hidetsugu stood at the apex of the court system and was subject to the strong influence of the automatic laws of motion that governed the operation of the court institutions based on that framework. Hideyoshi did not have the capability to bypass these precedents and rule on the basis of his own prestige. The resulting situation gave rise to the formation within the regime of two groups, the "*taikō* (Hideyoshi's) group" and the "*kampaku* (Hidetsugu's) group," whose policies might be in opposition.

The friction between these two factions intensified from 1594, the immediate cause probably being the birth of Hideyoshi's natural son Hideyori. Hideyoshi had had no children by his wife, Kita-no-

30 Tōkyō daigaku shiryō hensanjo, ed., *Dai Nihon komonjo, Iewaki* 9, *Kikkawa ke monjo*, vol. 2, pp. 137–9 (doc. 975). Miki Seiichirō has shown that 1591, the date usually given for the census order, is incorrect. "Hitobarai-rei to megutte," in Nagoya daigaku bungakubu kokushi kenkyūshitsu, ed., *Nagoya daigaku Nihonshi ronshū* (Tokyo: Yoshikawa kōbunkan, 1975), vol. 2, pp. 97–136.

mandokoro (Nei), and his beloved son Tsurumatsu, born to his concubine Yodo-dono (Chacha), died in 1591 at the age of two. Thus he chose Hidetsugu, his nephew, as his successor. But when Yodo-dono gave birth to their second child, there then were two persons qualified to succeed Hideyoshi to the headship of the Toyotomi house. This second child created another nucleus around which those who differed over any of a variety of political and military problems might rally.

In 1594 Hideyoshi's magistrates conducted a new cadastral survey in Owari Province, Hidetsugu's domain, and carried out an on-the-spot inspection of his civil government, fiscal affairs, and procedures for collecting taxes from the lands under his direct administrative control. This type of inspection was also conducted on the lands held directly by Toyotomi Hideyasu, Hidetsugu's younger brother and lord of Kōriyama Castle in Yamato Province, as well as on the estate of the recently deceased Gamō Ujisato, a longtime associate of Hideyoshi who had been placed in the critical location of Aizu in northern Japan. In each case this constituted interference with the rights of individual daimyo, prompted by the presumed incompleteness of the cadastral surveys that had been submitted previously. That such an intervention could be directed against the imperial regent, Hidetsugu, demonstrated to all that two reins of authority existed and that Hideyoshi believed his to be of higher purity.

In the seventh month of 1595, when the first invasion of Korea had reached an impasse and peace negotiations were under way, Hidetsugu was interrogated by Hideyoshi's magistrates on suspicion of treason. Ultimately, he was divested of his offices of imperial regent and minister of the left, and banished to Mt. Kōya where he was ordered to take his own life. The leading retainers of his *kampaku* group were later arrested: Some were sentenced to death, and others were banished. Hidetsugu's wife, concubines, and children, numbering more than thirty persons, all were beheaded. Several great daimyo were also implicated, some of whom were ordered into domiciliary confinement for a time. All the magistrates and daimyo submitted one after another oaths of loyalty to Hideyoshi, signed in blood. The first to present theirs were Hideyoshi's magistrates Ishida Mitsunari and Mashita Nagamori, who had carried out Hidetsugu's punishment. Other influential daimyo who submitted oaths included Tokugawa Ieyasu, Maeda Toshiie, Ukita Hideie, Mōri Terumoto, and Kobayakawa Takakage.

It was after this incident that a set of regulations and an accompanying supplement were issued on 1595/8/3 over the signatures of Tokugawa Ieyasu, Ukita Hideie, Uesugi Kagekatsu, Maeda Toshiie, Mōri

Terumoto, and Kobayakawa Takakage.[31] The regulations sought chiefly to control the warrior lords by requiring permission for the daimyo's marriages, urging peaceful solutions to disputes, requiring investigations of falsehoods and accusations, and establishing rules to designate those permitted to use palanquins. The purpose of these regulations was to bring the warrior lords under the aegis of the Toyotomi regime and to make the daimyo themselves conscious of their public role.

Supplementary regulations defined the regime's relationships with the nobility, temples, and shrines, by ordering that nobles and *monzeki* (temples whose abbots were taken from the imperial family or high nobility) remain faithful to the traditions of their own houses and serve the public interest (*kōgi*). Moreover, the monks and priests of temples and shrines were required to obey the laws governing them, to repair and rebuild their religious establishments, and to be diligent in their studies and the conduct of religious services. With respect to land-tax procedures, it was decreed that the "produce of the entire realm" was to be taxed on the basis of formal "inspections" (*kemi*). Military lords were instructed to take two-thirds of the harvest and leave the farmers one-third. The Toyotomi regime had established this two-to-one ratio as the official tax rate in 1586, but this official recognition that one-third was to be allotted to the farmers as "a right to hold the realm" is an extremely important fact when considering the character of the Toyotomi state. The regulations also limited the number of concubines that warriors could keep and, in general, established fief size as the standard for governing warrior behavior. There were new regulations on clothing and family crests, and of special importance were the regulations concerning judicial proceedings. A group of ten persons was established to deal with litigation. Tokugawa Ieyasu and the other "elders" would deal with direct appeals to the retired imperial regent; depending on the circumstances, they could bring the matter to his attention. In this way the regime set up its own internal machinery for processing litigation, however inadequate it may have been.

Thus Hideyoshi's regime was more successful in asserting its control over other power contenders, especially on the local level, than any previous regime in Japan's history. He created fixed rules for the unique organs of authority and internal organization that carried out

31 On the texts of these regulations, see Miki Seiichirō, "On'okite, on'okite tsuika o megutte," in Bitō Masahide, sensei kanreki kinenkai, ed., *Nihon kinsei shi ronsō* (Tokyo: Yoshikawa kōbunkan, 1984), pp. 81–111. English translations can be found in Berry, *Hideyoshi*, pp. 144–5.

his wishes. These in turn were based on obedience to the *"taikō's* laws and edicts," which he deemed superior to those of the imperial court. Hideyoshi's system also had its own weaknesses. The relationship between the two administrative organs, the Five Elders and the Five Magistrates, had not been defined with respect to the formation and execution of the intentions of the retired imperial regent's authority. Among the Five Elders were formidable daimyo such as Ieyasu, Hideyoshi's leading rival, but they also included Ukita Hideie, who would not have been able to maintain such a large domain had he not had Hideyoshi's support. Maeda Toshiie, a former peer of Hideyoshi's, was a member, as were Mōri Terumoto, Kobayakawa Takakage, and Uesugi Kagekatsu, who had joined Hideyoshi's alliance at an early stage in the unification enterprise. All the elders had received their court ranks and offices by virtue of Hideyoshi's political power. In other words, the imperial court institution was influencing the very selection and appointment of the Five Elders. On the other hand, all the Five Magistrates, with the exception of Maeda Gen'i, who was responsible for the administration of Kyoto, were daimyo of middling size who had been in Hideyoshi's service since their youth and were his direct retainers.

There thus were two routes linking Hideyoshi with the daimyo, through the Five Elders and through the Five Magistrates, and not unexpectedly this was a frequent source of conflict. When Hideyoshi died in 1598, his testament was sent to both groups, entrusting them with Hideyori's future. It is telling that the one addressed to the elders used the polite address "Group of Five" but that the one to the magistrates used the more familiar "five persons," suitable for retainers. Thus it was no accident that two years later, at the battle of Sekigahara, the actual leaders of the two opposing sides were the strongest of the Five Elders, Tokugawa Ieyasu, and the most prominent of the Five Magistrates, Ishida Mitsunari.

The structure of kōgi *authority*

The authority of the newly established unified state referred to itself as the *kōgi*, to show that it was a public authority that was subordinate to neither the imperial court system nor the will of the daimyo. *Kōgi* was a comparatively new term that had gradually gained currency in Japan from the middle of the medieval period. The origins of the word are uncertain, but it seems to have two lines of descent. First, it referred to the rites and ceremonies of the court, and second, it referred to the consensus of a meeting of representatives of all the subordinate temples and monks in a headquarters Buddhist temple or monastery. The former gradually came to indicate the constitutional order of the imperial court system, and its relationship to the system of titles and ranks. The latter was used to express the issues common to diverse autonomous groups such as villages, towns, and individual proprietary lords. These two meanings coalesced in the late Muromachi period. In the capital and its environs, the term was used to signify "the shogun" or "the shogun's authority"; in the provinces, Sengoku daimyo such as the Mōri or the Hōjō frequently used the title in reference to themselves and also called others by this term. In any case, it was used to refer to warrior authority because that authority had gradually united the various politically autonomous groups. The use of this term in reference to ruling authorities implied that they expected the lords to perform the public function of maintaining the general security of daily life.

Underlying this, as the "Seikyōsho" explains, was the widespread conception that the "samurai's great law (daihō) and kōgi" consisted of the formalities and etiquette observed whenever a regional warrior band received an emperor's personal edict (rinji), a retired emperor's directive (inzen), a letter of instruction (from a high-ranking noble) (mikyōjo), or a transmittal of an order (hōsho).[32] That is, a document from the emperor or shogun approving an appointment to office or a promotion was received from the messenger in a clean, decorated hall by the entire household in full formal dress. Those attending the ceremony were seated in order of rank: lineages and houses, parents and children, direct and branch lines, clergy and laity, and so on. Attendance by members of warrior bands when their leader (tōryo) was the recipient of an official document meant that their position and standing as warriors in their particular areas had been recognized officially. Their union was based on their common interests as the warrior class that lived in a given region. The main element of their common interest was control of the people in their domains. By nature this military proprietary class was highly exclusive because its cohesion was based on a system of individual relationships between lord and vassal. For them, this was the sole public order through which their position and standing could be recognized. By attending this ceremony and taking part in this group activity, they became members of an official ruling group. In this way, warrior lords were able for the first time to confront as rulers the people (farmers) on their lands.

---

32 "Sekyosho," in Zoku gunsho ruijū, rev. 3rd ed. (Tokyo: Zoku gunsho ruijō kanseikai, 1984), 32 jo (zatsubu), pp. 249–92.

Sengoku daimyo such as the Mōri and the Hōjō established their own regional authority as the *kōgi* of the "provinces" that they ruled, and they consolidated the warrior bands of those areas as members of their own "houses" as "housemen" (*kachū*). In other words, an enfeoffed warrior who enrolled in the houseband of the most prominent local daimyo became a member of the "*kōgi* family," and he thereby was recognized as the proprietor of his fief. On the other hand, a warrior who was expelled from a Sengoku daimyo's "houseband" lost his status as both proprietor and warrior.

Let us now apply the concept of *kōgi* to the unification process. Oda Nobunaga could be called the *kōgi* only from 1579, fully six years after he had driven out Ashikaga Yoshiaki. In that year he set out to unite the realm as the master of the completed Azuchi Castle, placing Prince Kotohito in the Nijō Palace in Kyoto. In this way he united the two senses of *kōgi* and established a sense of authority endowed with both the name and the reality of *kōgi*. Until then, the shogun Yoshiaki, although in exile and shogun in name only, was called the *kōgi* by himself and others. At the same time Nobunaga, although he did not become shogun, was called the *kōgi* as well. Just how did this happen?

Clearly there had been a change in the substance of *kōgi*. The new conception of *kōgi* was formed by preserving the form of the first of its original two meanings while emphasizing the second as its actual substance. When Nobunaga established his own authority, he based it on the claim that he acted on the basis of a public consensus of the realm. He consistently asserted that he overthrew the old authority and established a new one not for his own benefit but for the common good. The destruction of the Ikkō *ikki*, he claimed, was for the sake of the nation, as were his rebukes of daimyo who were concerned only with what would benefit their own domains and who did not cooperate in the unification enterprise. In his own view, Nobunaga's expulsion of the shogun from Kyoto was also done for the sake of the nation. These claims did not end merely with pious platitudes. The desires of the autonomous popular groups in the countryside could not be ignored; people were weary of the long years of warfare and were demanding a tranquil and orderly daily life. Nobunaga used the power of official recognition and direct intervention against his daimyo vassals, in the disposition of lands within their domains, in their methods of granting fiefs, and in the way they engaged their vassals to maintain a policy that favored the common good.

Historically, superior warrior authorities, beginning with the Kamakura and the Muromachi shogunates, had been able to intervene in the problems (suits, disputes) that arose among the military lords under their command, but they had been unable to intervene in the internal problems of a vassal lord's domain. This was true also of the relationship between the *shugo* and the local warriors (*kokujin*) in the Muromachi period, a weakness that even the Sengoku daimyo were unable to overcome. For this reason, Nobunaga's intervention may be considered revolutionary, as it came at a time when the daimyo, by privatizing their holdings and making them the objects of their personal rule, had lost all claim to be acting for the sake of the nation. Here lies the logic behind not placing the daimyo under the authority of the Kyoto court system but creating a new public authority. Nobunaga exemplified the way that military lords should behave under the principles of *Bushidō* (the normative code of behavior for warriors).

Nobunaga exempted the peasants from the corvée labor that they had been obliged to perform for their proprietary lords and drew them under his aegis as the one who wielded *kōgi* authority. Instead, the corvée was levied in "provincial" or domain units. The notion that a fief holder's use of the workers on his land for his own purposes was "a private [antisocial] matter," and that coveting people's labor, which properly belonged to the *kōgi*, was evil, gradually gained currency.

Toyotomi Hideyoshi took up where Nobunaga had left off, carrying out his cadastral survey, severing the bonds that linked the individual vassals to the land and its workers, and institutionalizing a strict separation of the warrior and peasant classes. Within the new legal order, the daimyo became the unit of warrior rule, and the farming village became the unit of peasant control. Hideyoshi denied private possession (*shoyū*) of land by individual vassals and rejected their private control over the peasantry. The principle was established that only he who exercised *kōgi*, and thereby took into account the interests of all the people of a region, could rule legitimately.

This concept of "public" or "official" proprietorship was established in several propositions in 1587 and 1588. The 1587 edict on Christianity asserts that "grants in fief of provinces or districts to vassals are temporary." That is, the fief was viewed not as a permanent private tenure (*shiryō*) but rather as something that had been merely entrusted to the vassal.[33] It further states: "Vassals may be moved

---

33 On the texts of this edict, see Anno Masayuki, " 'Kirishitan kinrei' no kenkyū," in Bitō, ed., *Nihon kinseishi ronsō*, vol. 1, pp. 39–79. An English translation can be found in George Elison, *Deus Destroyed: The Image of Christianity in Early Modern Japan* (Cambridge, Mass.: Harvard University Press, 1973), pp. 117–18.

from one place to another, but farmers may not be moved." In other words, although fiefs could be transferred by reassignment to a different samurai holder, the people were bound to the land and could not be moved. These represented the tenurial principles of the early modern period. It was also stipulated that warriors could not become Christians without permission of the one who exercised *kōgi*.

This body of regulations later gradually broadened in scope and reached its final form in the Tokugawa shogunate's Buke shohatto (Laws for military households) of the 1620s and 1630s.[34] By this time the daimyo had lost many freedoms: They could not marry freely, rebuild their castles as they liked, or enter into alliances with one another. As members of a nationally constructed *kōgi* order, they had to bear the responsibility for maintaining public peace and order in the realm.

In the late 1580s Hideyoshi ordered the daimyo of the nation to cease fighting and to come to Kyoto and formally submit to him. From his position as the realm's hegemonic authority he sought to unite and organize the daimyo of all provinces. The imperial visit to the Jurakutei in 1588 was the finishing touch to unification. He invited Emperor Go-Yōzei to his residence, and under the emperor's aegis Hideyoshi as imperial regent seized at one stroke the right to petition for imperial approval of official ranks for the assembled daimyo. He made the daimyo pledge their gratitude for their promotions in rank and swear absolute obedience to the imperial regent. It was in actuality an investiture ceremony on a national scale, establishing the public authority (*kōgi*) of the realm.

After the hegemonic authority of the realm had been established, the next step was to use this power to promote the acceptance of the daimyo's territorial authority. The case of Shimazu Yoshihisa, daimyo of Satsuma, is illustrative. Yoshihisa was having trouble maintaining control of his family and vassals, and so in 1592 Hideyoshi set about reviving Yoshihisa's authority, using his status of *kōgi* of the realm. He seized the fiefs of rebellious retainers and added them to Yoshihisa's granary lands. He also reclaimed the holdings that Yoshihisa and his family had sold, and he conducted land surveys on the holdings of temples and shrines in Satsuma, confiscating undocumented holdings and placing them under Yoshihisa's direct control. These measures were designed to strengthen Shimazu Yoshihisa's authority within his

---

34 English translation is in Tsunoda, de Bary, and Keene, eds., *Sources of Japanese Tradition*, pp. 335–8.

domain, but they also changed the nature of Yoshihisa's proprietary authority. Whereas previously, the lands were his to sell in times of financial distress, now the entire territory had become the *kōgi*'s holding and no longer could be disposed of at the whim of a daimyo.

The unification of the daimyo and the establishment of the warriors' proprietary authority in the early modern period shows that the daimyo had also come to share public authority, performing a number of recognized public functions. However, just as the meanings contained in the term *kōgi* are neither simple nor clear, the terms "public authority" and "public functions" as used here possess meanings and contents determined historically, which are different from their modern meanings. I conclude this chapter by enumerating the unique characteristics of *kōgi* authority.

First, *kōgi* authority was absolute. Formed as the authority of the men of the realm, it extended gradually from the individual men of the realm to mean authority as a whole; *kōgi* may at times be characterized as transcendent. Thus when Tokugawa Ieyasu set about establishing his own authority after Hideyoshi's death, he had difficulty in freeing himself and the other daimyo from the framework of the *taikō*'s laws and edicts. In the end, he was obliged to destroy the framework itself by defeating the Toyotomi family by force of arms and then establishing the authority of the Tokugawa shogunate.

Second, *kōgi* was a legal norm. The law by which the shogun controlled the daimyo and the daimyo their retainers had already appeared in Hideyoshi's regulations and supplement (of 1595–8), but the first article of the Buke shohatto, which states, "The study of literary texts and the practices of the military arts must be cultivated diligently," is memorable. It enumerated the qualifications by which the daimyo could take possession of the state and act as its public authority. The moral and normative character of Tokugawa law has been pointed out frequently, but until now it has been explained as resulting from the influence of Confucian thought. There is some truth in this, but it is not the full explanation. Emphasis on literary and military training came from the belief that to be accepted as the legitimate ruling authority, the warrior bands must control their selfishness and employ their capacities for the good of the realm.

This sentiment in turn gave rise to the third characteristic. That is, *kōgi* was a mechanism applicable to authority in the context of the lord–vassal relationship, specifically to the relationship between shogun and daimyo and that between the daimyo and their retainers. But *kōgi* did not recognize the existence of lord–vassal relationships between daimyo or between retainers. There were differences in family status and *kokudaka* size among daimyo and among retainers, but before their respective lords, whether the shogun or the daimyo, they were equal, and the free development of superior–inferior relationships among them was suppressed. The lord–vassal relationships between the shogun and the daimyo and between the daimyo and the retainers were public, and any other conditions of subordination were deemed private and were forbidden.

Finally, *kōgi* authority had a group character: The warrior of early modern times was recognized as being of the warrior class only when he was a member of the *kōgi* group. Individual warriors did not possess their own land and live on it independently; their income from a fief or stipend, under conditions created by Hideyoshi and continued by the Tokugawa, was guaranteed by their belonging to the *kōgi* group. The strict separation of the warrior and peasant estate was a precondition for this. Conversely, a warrior was a warrior by virtue of his conducting public service as a member of the *kōgi*; this was also the source of the logic by which the warriors were able to collect taxes (*nengu*) and monopolize government. If a warrior were given to willfulness, he would be punished as one who had departed from the group's rationale. The unification of Japan in the sixteenth century had given risen to such a public authority.

CHAPTER 3

THE SOCIAL AND ECONOMIC
CONSEQUENCES OF UNIFICATION

INTRODUCTION

Japan underwent a major transformation in its social organization and economic capacity during the latter half of the sixteenth century. These changes were of such enormous historical significance that historians see them as marking Japan's transition from its medieval (*chūsei*) to its early modern (*kinsei*) age. The first currents of this transmutation radiated throughout Japan during the late fifteenth and early sixteenth centuries, and the impulses manifested themselves in the appearance of self-administering towns such as Sakai and relatively autonomous, self-governing rural communities, commonly referred to as *sōson*. These communities were the ultimate products of social movements that earlier had begun to shake the foundations of the medieval, *shōen*-based political and economic order. Central to this process was the appearance of organized peasant protest, increasingly common in the Kinai region and its environs in the late medieval period, and the emergence throughout large portions of Japan of local associations, or *ikki*, that were formed for military purposes and reasons of self-defense. Examples of such leagues include the so-called *tsuchi ikki*, peasant organizations formed to resist economic demands made by proprietory lords, a phenomenon especially common in the Kyoto area from the fifteenth through the sixteenth centuries; the *kuni ikki*, larger federations composed chiefly of warriors who hoped to carve out spheres of autonomous control; and the Ikkō *ikki*, confederations associated with the Honganji branch of the True Pure Land sect (Jōdo Shinshū).

Under these unsettled conditions, the aristocratic houses and temple headquarters that had held the highest level of proprietary rights over private estates (*shōen*) were displaced by local bushi proprietors who had fought their way to power during the Sengoku period. These warriors eventually pushed aside the Muromachi shogunate, opening the way for the appearance of the three hegemonic leaders, Oda Nobunaga (1539–82), Toyotomi Hideyoshi (1537–98), and Tokugawa

96

Ieyasu (1542–1616), who forged the military unification of Japan during the latter half of the sixteenth century. The elaboration during the seventeenth century of a strong, unified political structure based on an unchallengable military hegemony also unleashed new forces that generated their own enormous consequences, ushering in what Japanese historians commonly call the *kinsei* period, or what Western historians refer to more often as the early modern age.

Historians have expounded a number of interpretations to account conceptually for how the two processes, the one social and economic and the other military and political, worked together to produce the *kinsei* society. Among the most influential of these interpretations has been Nakamura Kichiji's refeudalization thesis, presented in the 1930s.[1] Nakamura focused on the relationships between warrior lords and their retainers, both in the medieval and Tokugawa periods, and he concluded that the *kinsei* age witnessed the reformulation under the Tokugawa shogunate of the essential components of medieval feudalism in a more politically stable and highly organized form.

In the decades following World War II, Araki Moriaki challenged this idea with his theory of a "revolution into feudalism."[2] Working with documents that presented an opportunity to analyze the structure of familial-based agricultural household units, Araki argued that the medieval *shōen* system owed its existence to what he termed the "patriarchal slave system" (*kafuchōteki doreisei*). But, he claimed, Tokugawa society was organized differently and was characterized by the appearance during the seventeenth century of an agricultural system dependent on labor supplied by the Japanese equivalent of serfs (*nōdo*). This shift from a slave to a serf system, Araki contended, meant that true feudalism first appeared in Japan only during the age of the Tokugawa shogunate.

More recently a third interpretation that has shaped the contours of scholarly debate has been offered by Miyagawa Mitsuru.[3] Like Araki, Miyagawa found his scholarly inspiration in village sources, and he agreed that medieval society was characterized by a serf system and that feudalism prevailed in Japan during the Tokugawa period. But Tokugawa society, he believed, relied not on true serfs but, rather, on what he called *reinō*, a class of partially dependent, partially independent, small-scale serflike families. Consequently, to distinguish Miya-

---

1 Nakamura Kichiji, *Bakuhan taisei ron* (Tokyo: Yamakawa shuppansha, 1972).
2 Araki Moriaki, *Bakuhan taisei shakai no seiritsu to kōzō* (Tokyo: Ochanomizu shobō, 1959).
3 Miyagawa Mitsuru, *Taikō kenchi ron*, 3 vols. (Tokyo: Ochanomizu shobō, 1957–63).

gawa's concept of historical change from that of Araki, we may refer to
his ideas as a theory of "evolutionary feudalism."

American scholarship, of course, has been influenced by the theories developed by Japanese researchers.[4] Yet it is important to note also
that Western historians who work on Japan have independently constructed their own frameworks of analysis and that these in turn have
had their own impact on Japanese scholarship. One particularly prominent and powerful idea has been to use the term "early modern" to
refer to the *kinsei* period, thus avoiding the Marxist categories of
analysis favored by many Japanese and, at the same time, drawing
attention away from the period's feudal aspects and toward those long-
term trends related to the emergence of the modern Japanese state and
economy after 1868.[5]

This chapter will look closely at the events of the late sixteenth
century, the pivotal transitional years that separated the *chūsei* from
the *kinsei* epoch. From the evidence that will be presented, it should
become obvious that many continuities linked the two ages. But it
should be equally evident that enormous changes surged through the
transition years and that the evidentiary scales tilt more to the side of
dissimilarity than similarity. The social and economic trends observed
in the late medieval period did not extend, undisturbed, into the *kinsei*
period, nor did Tokugawa society merely represent a reconstruction of
medieval conditions. Indeed, the medieval and the Tokugawa systems
are so dissimilar that they should be conceived of as entirely different
societal types, and emphasis should be placed on the distinct characteristics of each epoch. Such an understanding requires a clear evaluation
of how the early modern society was molded in the cauldron of change
during the late sixteenth century.[6]

4 See, for instance, Edwin O. Reischauer's reliance on the concept of refeudalization in his
Japan: The Story of a Nation, 3rd ed. (New York: Knopf, 1981), pp. 78–86.
5 See, for instance, John Whitney Hall, "Feudalism in Japan – A Reassessment," in John W.
Hall and Marius B. Jansen, eds., *Studies in the Institutional History of Early Modern Japan*
(Princeton, N.J.: Princeton University Press, 1968). Some of the most promising research on
the major questions concerning the transition from the medieval to the Tokugawa period is
contained in John W. Hall, Keiji Nagahara, and Kozo Yamamura, eds., *Japan Before Tokugawa: Political Consolidation and Economic Growth, 1500–1650* (Princeton, N.J.: Princeton
University Press, 1981); and George Elison and Bardwell L. Smith, eds., *Warlords, Artists, &
Commoners: Japan in the Sixteenth Century* (Honolulu: University of Hawaii Press, 1981).
6 For an introduction to the institutional changes of the late sixteenth century, see the following
by Wakita Osamu, *Kinsei hōkensei seiritsu shiron* (Tokyo: Tōkyō daigaku shuppankai, 1977);
"The Kokudaka System: A Device for Reunification," *Journal of Japanese Studies* 1 (Spring
1975); "The Emergence of the State in Sixteenth Century Japan: From Oda to Tokugawa,"
Journal of Japanese Studies 8 (Summer 1982): 343–67; and (with James L. McClain), "The
Commercial and Urban Policies of Oda Nobunaga and Toyotomi Hideyoshi" in Hall et al.,
eds., *Japan Before Tokugawa*, pp. 224–47.

THE TAIKŌ LAND SURVEYS AND THE EARLY MODERN PEASANTRY

The expansion of the productive capacity of agriculture was the keystone supporting the economic foundations of Japan's early modern society. Agricultural productivity had been increasing even during the fourteenth century, especially in the Kinai region around the ancient imperial capital of Kyoto. Initially, the prime movers behind this expansion were the major proprietors, who financed large-scale land development projects, and influential peasants, who were active on a smaller, more local scale. In the capital area the redevelopment of fields devastated by warfare and neglected during the fifteenth century boosted overall yields. The opening up of entirely new fields also was common in the Kinai environs. On this expanding land base, technological advances increased productivity, as did the spread of certain agricultural innovations such as double cropping. A commercial economy also began to develop, as evident in the growth of towns and periodic local markets. Elements of this commercial economy soon began to penetrate the rural villages. Documents from Tara *shōen* in Wakasa, for instance, reveal how farmers commuted almost daily to the nearby port town of Obama to sell their produce. Another index of commercial growth was the increased payment of the annual land tax in cash rather than produce. Although this sort of economic development was at first the work of rural entrepreneurs, eventually the proprietary lords also attempted to promote commerce in their country estates.[7]

The spread of the commercial economy into agricultural villages had various consequences. Some village landlords (*kajishi jinushi*) withdrew from the active management of fields and lived on the land rents that they collected from the peasants, and other landlords kept a labor force of subordinate personnel in a serflike condition. The more commercialized economy benefited some cultivators, but it caused others to fall into economic ruin, and many fled to nearby cities and port towns, where they became day laborers, menials, or beggars.[8] But on the whole, the trend was toward greater security for

---

7 For additional details concerning economic developments, see Kozo Yamamura, "Returns on Reunification: Economic Growth in Japan 1550–1650," in Hall et al., eds., *Japan Before Tokugawa*, pp. 327–72.
8 For further details, see Wakita Haruko, "Muromachi-ki no keizai hatten" in *Kōza Nihon rekishi*, vol. 7 (Tokyo: Iwanami shoten, 1976), as well as the article by Keiji Nagahara (with Kozo Yamamura), "The Sengoku Daimyo and the Kandaka System"; and Gin'ya Sasaki (with William B. Hauser), "Sengoku Daimyo Rule and Commerce," in Hall et al., eds., *Japan Before Tokugawa*, pp. 27–63 and 125–48, respectively.

the peasant landholder. For instance, the designated portions to income (*shiki*) that were based on one's function within the *shōen* system, such as the landholder, peasant, and cultivator portions, became legally defined entitlements. The peasants' rights to possess land also were strengthened. The end result of these developments was that ordinary farmers gained a great deal of influence within their village communities and then went on to form confederations in order to secure a greater degree of control over the political and economic spheres of local life.

During the sixteenth century, two forces appeared to be in competition: the expanding autonomy of village communities, allied in *ikki* organizations, and the opposing desire of military lords to establish secure domains. These conflicting goals were resolved under the early modern political order by adopting certain fundamental institutions such as the nationwide cadastral survey, the separation of the warrior and farming classes, and the *kokudaka* system of land-tax management. The land policies begun by the Sengoku daimyo were co-opted and carried out on a broader, more national scale by Oda Nobunaga. But the perfection of early modern rural administration was not achieved in his lifetime, and the institutional structure of rural administration took final shape only under the Hideyoshi and Tokugawa regimes.

The main objective of both the Sengoku diamyo as regional overlords and Oda Nobunaga as the emerging national hegemon was to gain systematic control over the productive capacities of the countryside. In the middle of the sixteenth century, landholding, tax collecting, and military service recruitment systems varied greatly from location to location. What the lords most required was information on land area, productive capacities, and the distribution of manpower. Such information could be had in one of two ways, by either direct or indirect measurement.[9]

The complete details of Oda Nobunaga's land policies in his home provinces of Owari and Mino have never been fully revealed, but in those regions that he occupied later, Nobunaga ordered new cadastral surveys. Usually he tried to appoint his own representatives to con-

9 In Japan, one line of interpretation sees Oda Nobunaga's administration as representing the more completely unified authority characteristic of the early modern period and views the Sengoku daimyo as similar to early modern daimyo. The argument presented here identifies Nobunaga as more of a transitional figure with greater access to the elements of centralized political authority than the Muromachi shogunate had, but still weaker than the Tokugawa shoguns. For more details on current research, see Nagahara Keiji, ed., *Sengoku-ki no kenryoku to shakai* (Tokyo: Tōkyō daigaku shuppankai, 1976).

duct them, but where that was not feasible, he required local lords to submit their own land and tax reports, called *sashidashi*. However compiled, the registers listed landholdings and the amounts of annual tax customarily collected.[10] Under Nobunaga, direct land surveys were conducted in Ise, Echizen, Harima, Settsu, and Tango provinces, and the land-tax submission reports were collected in Ōmi, Yamashiro, Yamato, and Izumi. Because the cadastral surveys were direct on-site investigations, they included as much detail as the overlord deemed necessary. Although the land-tax reports were submitted by individual proprietors, who in turn relied on records supplied by village communities, they too contained a considerable amount of detail. Some extant *sashidashi* from the Yamato region in the 1580s, as well as one from Kōfukuji, show that the surveys were based on actual plot-by-plot field inspections by the proprietor and listed precisely the area of the fields, the tax imports, and the cultivators' names.[11]

The cadastral registers and land-tax submissions became the documentary foundations on which Oda Nobunaga based his claim to superior powers of control over provincewide units. The nature of his authority was basically identical to the administrative and proprietary powers that the Sengoku daimyo exercised within their holdings. In other words, they had fashioned what were legally called "complete proprietorships" (*ichien chigyō* or *isshiki shihai*). This meant that within their domains, the daimyo, as proprietary lords, held the right to assign fiefs, command military forces, and exercise police and judicial authority. Of course, Nobunaga's political administration pursued a more complete expression of these powers, in time asserting a rudimentary central authority over the individual Sengoku daimyo that was much stronger than that of the preceding Muromachi shogunate.

Oda Nobunaga was able to impose his claims to this superior authority while at the same time assigning provincial lands as fiefs to the more important members of his houseband, such as Shibata Katsuie

---

10 Those persons who discovered unregistered fields or who developed new paddy had to conduct a survey or submit a *sashidashi* report. Because Owari and Mino constituted the central core of Nogunaga's holdings, he was particularly anxious to impose his authority over outlying areas within those provinces, but even at present, we have discovered no complete set of land survey records for this region.

11 The cadastral surveys were carried out on a province-by-province basis, and the surveyed land was granted to proprietors (*ryōshu*) as fiefs (*chigyō*). In other words, the Oda administration could lay claim to the rights to control land, possess land, and distribute it as fiefs. The *sashidashi* were reports submitted by individual proprietors and, consequently, served as confirmations of fief grants. In these cases, too, the Oda administration claimed superior rights, but the *sashidashi* were different from the cadastral surveys in terms of thoroughness. This was probably because the *sashidashi* reports came from areas where the proprietary rights were claimed by temples and aristocrats.

and Hashiba (Toyotomi) Hideyoshi. Nobunaga authorized these retainers to exercise proprietary rights, especially the collection of dues
and labor services. But there still were regional procedural differences.
Within any one unit of control, the means of measuring productive
capacity (*taka*) had been standardized, but as yet no one method was
applied uniformly across all of Japan. For instance, in the five provinces around Kyoto – Yamashiro, Yamato, Settsu, Kawachi, and
Izumi – as well as in Ōmi, Echizen, Harima, and Tamba, grain was
measured in terms of *koku*. However the *kandaka* system, in which
dues and imposts were expressed in units of cash, was used in Owari,
Mino, and Ise. Both systems indicated the actual amount of tax due in
goods and services from the land. In practice, the annual rents collected under the *kandaka* system included some payments in grain,
and portions of the so-called *kokudaka* imposts could also be paid in
cash.

Despite Nobunaga's effort to exercise total control over the land
base, the fact that he was obliged to accept *sashidashi* submissions
showed that he was still far from achieving this goal. Moreover, the
grant of a fief to a retainer (*kashin*) often merely reconfirmed existing
rights that the retainer already claimed over those units of land. Fiefs
were also granted in which temples and Kyoto-based proprietors continued to exercise their old *shōen*-derived prerogatives. Consequently,
despite surface changes, the old patterns of land possession often continued to prevail. In the same way, although Nobunaga imposed the
burdens of the tax and corvée levies on the peasants, he also recognized the landlord–tenant relationships that already existed in peasant
society. Thus in several documented cases he affirmed that the *myōshu*,
the man who held the plot of land and was responsible for paying the
dues levied against it to the overlord, could continue to receive his
customary profits and the traditional set of miscellaneous dues (*komononari*) imposed on the families living on his holdings.

Following the death of Nobunaga in 1582, Toyotomi Hideyoshi
imposed his own hegemony over the country. At the outset of his
takeover, the pattern of land rights remained as they had been under
Nobunaga, a complicated mix of claims by local military proprietors.
The *kokudaka* system, a product of the cadastral survey ordered by
Toyotomi Hideyoshi and known as the Taikō *kenchi*, cut across this
welter of competing claims and both simplified and clarified rights of
land possession. Hideyoshi was able to carry out a nationwide survey
because he had assembled more military power than Oda Nobunaga
had and thus could extend stronger claims of national legitimacy. In

particular, Hideyoshi was able to justify his action on the basis of having received from the emperor the famous injunction: "You shall exercise administrative functions over the more than sixty provinces of Japan in accordance with what is best for the land and the people."[12] Thus, Hideyoshi's survey might appropriately be called a "public survey over the entire realm" (*tenka no kenchi*). As such, it literally remade the land relationships that had existed up to that time.

The early modern form of landed enfeoffment rested on new principles of land possession as defined by this Taikō cadastral survey. At the highest level, all proprietary rights became securely lodged in the hands of the national hegemon. Now all bushi, and even temples and Kyoto-based aristocrats, could hold territory only as grants-held-in-trust (*azukarimono*) confirmed by the vermilion seal of Hideyoshi. Moreover, certain rights and responsibilities concerning these holdings could be reassigned to lower elements in the power structure. A clause in the famous "Bateren expulsion decree" that Hideyoshi issued in 1587 banning Christianity and ordering the Jesuits to leave Japan within twenty days inadvertently confirmed this practice by stating: "Fiefs granted to vassals belong ultimately to the state, that is, to the provinces and districts, and each vassal holds the land in trust for the present only. Each vassal must obey the laws of the realm (*tenka*)."[13] This use of the concept of land held in trust for the overlord became the basis for the new centralization of power. The rights to collect the grain tax and corvée levies and to exercise judicial judgment, which had been divided under the *shōen* system, were now pulled together and held by a single authority.

To conduct the Taikō survey, inspectors (*bugyō*) were dispatched to the provinces where they were ordered to investigate each parcel of land in each village. This practice of relying solely on officials dispatched by the governing authority was a fuller declaration of the powers of overlordship than Nobunaga had been able to develop. Hideyoshi's intentions in this regard were revealed initially in 1582, when he carried out surveys in Yamashiro without first receiving *sashidashi* reports. This new trend became more evident in the 1584 cadastral survey documents for some portions of Ōmi and then became the normal method of conducting cadastral surveys from the end of the decade of the 1580s.

---

12 "Shimazu-ke monjo," no. 345 in *Dai Nihon komonjo: Shimazu ke monjo*, vol. 1 (Tokyo: Tōkyō daigaku shuppankai, 1942), p. 342.
13 See the "Matsuura-ke monjo." A reproduction of the document is contained in the *Iezusukai Nihon nempyō*, vol. 2 (Tokyo: Yūshōdō shoten, 1969), located in the Matsuura Museum.

Data compiled in the cadasters reveal a wealth of information about land rights at the local level. The following is an entry from the survey register for Fukita village in Ota district (*gun*) of Settsu Province. As other documents of this type, it lists the location (or name) of the field, an assessment of its overall quality, use, area, and expected yield (*kokumori*), as well as the person in whose name the field is registered:

Field name/location:	Kaito
Quality (superior, average, poor):	Superior
Use (paddy, dryfields, house lot):	Paddy
Area:	1 *tan* (993 sq. m)
Yield:	1 *koku* 5 *to* (approx. 7.5 bushels)
Registered to:	Yohei

As this document shows, the Taikō survey relied on the *kokudaka* system, which in turn rested on a new concept of *taka* as being equivalent to yield (*kokumori*). Each plot recorded in the register was assigned a figure that represented an assessment of the field's potential yield. The total yield for all fields within a village was known as the village's *kokudaka*, and this, expressed in units of rice, served as the base on which the taxes and dues were computed. Even land that was not given over to rice production, such as dry fields and house plots, was assigned a computed, theoretical yield expressed in measures of rice. Under the *shōen* system, several different kinds of crops other than rice were grown, and these were delivered separately as taxes. The *kokudaka* system was designed to simplify this procedure by reducing tax collection to a single calculation.

Why did Hideyoshi and the daimyo decide to collect taxes in an agricultural commodity such as rice? The answer lies in the effort of Hideyoshi and his vassal daimyo to gain firmer control over their domains' resources and productive output. Because these domains were composed of many different kinds of land whose productive capacities varied enormously, the overlords needed some universal standard that would allow them to impose uniform tax rates. For some Sengoku daimyo, the *kandaka* system, which required that taxes be paid in cash, served this purpose. But in reality the *kandaka* system was difficult to manage because it was feasible only for those daimyo who were able to regulate the minting and circulation of coins and thereby to exercise some control over the marketplace and the conversion into cash of rice and other products.

The Toyotomi regime, however, was attempting to extend its jurisdiction over the entire country and, in this process, found it impossible to maintain sufficient control over coinage nationwide. The

Toyotomi administration did issue in 1588 the gold coins known as *tenshō ōban*, as well as some silver coins, but these were not intended for practical, everyday use on a mass scale. Nor did the Muromachi shogunate or the Sengoku daimyo enjoy any success with the ordinances known as *erizeni-rei*, which were issued during the sixteenth century in an effort to cope with the problems caused by the circulation of coins of differing purities. It was impossible to use the *kandaka* system on a countrywide scale as long as these kinds of difficulties with coinage continued to exist. On the other hand, rice was a staple of the Japanese people and was grown nearly everywhere. Rice had other advantages as well: It was a commercial product that could be readily converted into cash, and it could easily be stored. Consequently, the Toyotomi administration adopted the *kokudaka* system, with dues calculated and paid in rice.

In one sense, the rice collected under the *kokudaka* system was essentially a land rent paid in produce. The daimyo proprietary lords could use this rice both for their own consumption needs and as military provisions. Rice was also a major commercial product, and the daimyo could expect to sell a certain portion of their tax receipts on the open market. The fact that Hideyoshi kept records on the market value – expressed in denominations of gold and silver coins – of the rice he collected from his own direct holdings shows that he clearly recognized the commercial value of this crop.[14] By collecting the land tax in rice, the daimyo were able to control a very important commercial product and thereby dominate the markets through its sale. On the other hand, the peasants were now being systematically cut off from the most easily marketed product that they themselves grew, and thus they could not improve their living standards by selling their own surpluses commercially.

The *taka*, or assessment figure in the registration documents, expressed the normative production of rice on a plot of land, a theoretical figure based on the area, type, and quality of the plot.[15] Some historians believe that this figure reflected fairly accurately the actual yield, but, in fact, the two were often very different. Whereas the *taka* was

---

14 The market price for a *koku* of rice in both gold and silver is recorded in the "Toyotomi-ke kuramai san'yōjō." From this we know that the price of rice in Tsuruga and Akita was ten *ryō* of gold for 240 *koku* of rice, whereas in Kyoto just 30 *koku* of rice cost that much. This price differential was due to political intervention. Several copies of this document exist. See my *Kinsei hōken shakai no keizai kōzō* (Tokyo: Ochanomizu shobō, 1963), pp. 23–36.

15 Having classified the land as paddy, dry field, and house lot, it was customary, if a "superior"-grade paddy had a theoretical yield of 1.5 *koku* (per *tan*), to assign a computed yield of 1.2 *koku* (per *tan*) to the dry fields and house lots.

calculated with reference to the productive capacity and yield, it was also set in accordance with the historical background of each region and with the character of the proprietor and his fiscal requirements.[16] To arrive at an assessment figure, survey teams inspected fields and assigned a grade of superior, average, or poor to each plot according to the overall conditions within the village, the type of grain (rice or some specialty crop) that was being grown, and the location of the field and village in respect to transportation routes. Finally, the entire range of cultivated lands within a village was assigned a quality rating of superior, average, or poor, and this too played a part in calculating the computed yield of each individual plot.

The annual tax demand on a village was calculated as a percentage of the total assessments for all land within that village. As a general rule, when setting the tax rate, the Toyotomi administration would select a sample set of villages, inspect the actual productive output of the fields in those villages, and then declare a local tax that would amount to approximately two-thirds of the anticipated yield. Of course, the actual harvest in any given year might vary considerably from the assessment figure listed in the cadastral record. But inspection teams could not possibly visit each village every year to ascertain any discrepancy. Thus adjustments could be made by referring to the annual inspection of the sample set of villages.[17]

This method of tax assessment differed significantly from the practices of the medieval period. Most importantly, it permitted the proprietary lords to set the rate each year after taking into account the actual harvest conditions. This could work to the advantage of either the cultivator or the proprietor. The Toyotomi administration generally set the land tax at two-thirds of the actual yield, which left only one-third in the hands of the peasants. This was a much larger proportion of the farmer's income than generally had been collected during the medieval period. Within a *shōen*, tax rates had tended to be permanently fixed, and thus the surpluses resulting from any increases in productivity stayed in the countryside. The new system imposed by the Toyotomi regime ended this and permitted the overlords to lay claim to any surplus production. By Hideyoshi's time, the samurai

16 Nakamura, *Bakuhan taisei ron;* Matsushita Shirō, *Bakuhansei shakai to kokudakasei* (Tokyo: Hanawa shobō, 1984); and Ōmori Eiko, "Daimyō kaieki to bakuhan kankei," in the 1978 special edition of *Rekishigaku kenkyū* entitled *Sekaishi ninshiki ni okeru minzoku to kokka.* (Tokyo: Aoki shoten, November 1978).

17 Previously, historians believed that the *takamori* was the yield of all village fields, that the *nengu* rate was calculated after a land survey, and that this rate was applied to the *takamori* recorded on the survey register.

government apparently felt that farmers could survive on this lesser amount, and several notorious sayings became current, such as "farmers should be taxed at a rate that keeps them suspended between life and death," an apt expression of the essential character of daimyo rule during the early modern period.

But certain other conditions, it must be noted, acted to reduce the actual amount of taxes extracted from the villages. The *kokudaka* system made levies in terms of rice, which meant that when commercial crops such as cotton started to be cultivated on a wide scale from the middle of the seventeenth century, it was difficult to incorporate this activity into the *kokudaka* system. During the Tokugawa period, peasant protests and a variety of other factors also prompted many daimyo to reduce the imposts on their holdings. For example, the actual rate paid by households that grew cotton in the economically advanced area around Osaka in the middle of the seventeenth century had fallen to about 10 percent of the average household's total income. Historians now believe that, on the average, daimyo collected only about 30 percent of the crop in most areas, although, occasionally a tax rate as high as 80 percent of the base assessment was demanded in some domains. In other words, over the course of the early modern period the assessment figure became increasingly arbitrary, serving only as a base figure on which the actual tax demand would be negotiated.

The Taikō survey defined not only the proprietor's claims to the produce of the land but also strengthened the farmer's rights to more secure possession of the land. As Hideyoshi's magistrate Ishida Mitsunari (1560–1600) noted, those peasants whose names were recorded next to plots on the survey register were recognized as having claims of possession to those parcels. These procedures have given rise to problems of historical interpretation. One important question is how to understand the fact that only one name appears on the survey documents for each plot of land. In the medieval period several different persons – the landlord, or the man in whose name the field was registered (*myōshyu*), the peasant (*hyakushō*), and the cultivator (*sakunin*) – each claimed certain specified rights over a given parcel of land. It is not clear which of these various levels of possession was recognized in the Taikō survey. Nonetheless, it is certain that the person recorded on the Taikō survey register was legally assumed to be of peasant status (*hyakushō mibun*). In other words, even if that person had once claimed the prerogatives of a local proprietor and had been a member of the bushi class, he now was assumed to be the cultivator and so was held responsible for the dues assessed on his holdings.

There still exist uncertainties regarding the social composition of the village community that resulted from the enforcement of the Taikō survey. It is doubtful that Hideyoshi and the daimyo were attempting to create a single, undifferentiated society of peasants, for even after the survey, there obviously remained a stratum of wealthy and influential farmers, just as there were landless peasants and other villagers who were heavily dependent on the registered cultivators. In fact, two types of dependent persons resided in the villages. One category lived as slavelike members of large patriarchal families, and in a legal sense, these persons remained unfree even after the cadastral survey was enforced. The other group, however, bore names and were recorded on survey documents as peasants, although they were still considered to be dependent on landowning patrons (*oyakata*) in the village. Dependent cultivators of this type, generally referred to as *hikan* when listed on the cadastral register, possessed formally recognized rights as peasants while still being classified as dependents of a patron to whom they owed service. Their inclusion in survey documents meant only that they had become "taxable registrants," (*naukebyakushō*), but not full-fledged landholding farmers. In this sense, the cadastral surveys did not constitute a systematic attempt to fashion a coherent policy that would create a single class of small, independent cultivators.[18] Viewed in this light, the purpose of Toyotomi policy concerning land relationships in local areas was to respect superior proprietary rights to the land while at the same time assigning more secure rights of possession to the peasantry.

Because the cadastral survey called into question all land claims and even jeopardized the rights of some persons, resistance to the survey could be strong. In Ōmi and Yamashiro provinces, it is recorded that "more than half the peasants fled."[19] Villagers erupted in violence in a famous incident in Higo, and in 1590 in Dewa, in the north of Japan, whole villages rose up in widespread revolt and killed the survey officials. Not unexpectedly, the survey teams often negotiated a compromise with local leaders. In some instances, officials exempted certain paddies from the survey and declared that such parcels would not be subject to the annual levy. In some other places, house plots were

18 One contradictory example comes from documents concerning the survey on Ōmi Province in 1590, which appears to have recognized the land possession rights of this kind of dependent personnel. Miyakawa Mitsuru also claimed that the lower peasants were made independent by the Taikō land survey, but he was generalizing from only a few, isolated examples. Miyakawa, *Taikō kenchi ron*, vol. 2.
19 From a document in the "Katagiri monjo," as cited in Miyakawa, *Taikō kenchi ron*, vol. 3, p. 388.

not included in the land-tax base, and the peasants were also granted exemptions from corvée levies. Yet Hideyoshi could also be ruthless. He wanted to send the survey teams everywhere, even to "the deepest recesses of the mountains and as far to the sea as men might row" (*yama wa oku, umi wa rōkai no tsuzuki sōrō made*). In 1584 Hideyoshi threatened to crucify peasants who hid fields, and in 1590 he angrily instructed Asano Nagamasa (1547–1611) – the person responsible for conducting the survey in Dewa – to put entire villages to the sword if they joined the revolt in that region, a threat made partially good by the forces of Uesugi Kagekatsu (1555–1623), who moved in troops to support Asano.

Because of the difficulty of making informed judgments concerning land rights in the confusion of almost constant warfare, survey inspectors commonly awarded the rights of possession to those peasants who had paid the land tax in previous years and to those who were actually tilling the fields at the time of the survey. These rights of possession became increasingly strong and secure under the Edo shogunate. Both shogun and daimyo added regulations governing the division and sale of land, the best known being the shogunate's "prohibition against the permanent alienation of land" in 1643 and the decree limiting the division of land in 1673. The first of these was nearly unenforceable from the start, however, and was relaxed in 1695 before being totally abandoned in 1723. The same problems with enforcement occurred when governments placed restrictions on the cultivation of certain kinds of commercial crops, and the restraints against growing tobacco that were issued at the end of the seventeenth century were the last major limitations of this sort. Similarly, although formal restrictions were placed on the use and conveyance of land, in fact as long as a farmer continued to pay the annual imposts and did not commit any crimes, his rights of possession were secure, and he could generally buy, sell, and will land.

The requirements of the *kokudaka* system greatly influenced the economic development of the village community in the years after the Taikō survey. Because of the greater importance assigned to rice, its cultivation spread even into the most remote reaches of the northern Tōhoku region. Moreover, because even dry fields and house plots were assigned a theoretical output expressed in units of rice when computing the tax base, the actual percentage of the rice crop collected was greater than the simple tax rate would indicate. Consequently, peasants were obliged to cultivate rice more intensively than they might otherwise have chosen. As mentioned, the collection of the annual tax in rice acted to limit the peasants' participation in the commercial economy. But this limitation was not absolute. As Nakai and McClain point out in Chapter 11 in this volume, the daimyo often vigorously promoted a commercialized economy within their domains. Thus the development of commercial products was to some extent inevitable, and in the latter half of the seventeenth century, peasants around the Osaka area began to grow cotton on their fields and actually had to buy rice on the open market in order to pay their land-tax obligations.

In turn, the spread of the commercial economy influenced the way in which farm families organized their labor. The most common type of farm household contained members of the direct family line, and these families typically owned about two and a half acres of land (one *chō*), an amount that they could farm with family labor. The second major type of farm unit was managed by wealthier farmers who used bound servants and other dependent personnel as tenants (*kosaku*), in order to cultivate some of the land. During the latter half of the seventeenth century, these bound personnel disappeared, to be replaced as the chief form of farm labor by contract servants (*nenki-hōkōnin*) and day laborers (*hiyatoi*). The dependent tenants (*hikan*) also gradually acquired independence, and many of them migrated to urban centers. Ultimately, the style of small-scale management that relied on family labor became the principal mode of production. This made for a labor-intensive style of agricultural management, one that also led to the increased cultivation of crops for sale to urban markets.

COMMERCE AND THE EARLY MODERN CITIES

Commerce and urban centers grew together during the sixteenth century. At this time Kyoto was still Japan's most important political city, as well as a center of a superlative tradition of craft and artisan production. Strung out like satellites around Kyoto were smaller commercial towns such as Sakai, Ōyamazaki, Tennōji, and Hiranogō. Taken together these cities constituted what might be termed a capital marketing area. Here could be found the commerce and craft production that formed the heart of the national economy. Merchants in these cities also engaged in foreign trade with China and Korea. Such activities made Kyoto into Japan's most important node of trade and commerce in the Sengoku period.

Outside this central area, the countryside was dotted with communities that hosted periodic markets (*rokusai-ichi*). These markets were most often found in embryonic castle towns or commercial areas around branch castles such as Yamaguchi, Odawara, and Sumpū (Shizuoka), but even settlements such as Hakata and Nagasaki became sites for periodic markets. Wherever located, the markets stimulated the development of a commodity trade that then began to penetrate the peasant village economy. The periodic markets were also connected with the central markets around Kyoto. The outlying communities sent their specialty products to the capital marketing area and, in turn, bought up manufactured products such as armor and textiles.

One consequence of this development was the emergence of what many historians refer to as urban self-government in such commercially based towns as Sakai and Ōyamazaki. Many of these towns owned their economic existence to their place in the Kyoto-centered marketing structure. Ōyamazaki, for instance, was located on the border between Yamashiro and Settsu provinces, a strategically important point, and from the tenth century many different powers contested for control over this area so that they could construct warehouses and other commercial facilities there. Because there were so many contenders for proprietary control and because proprietary rights in the area were so confused, no single outside lord or institution could achieve undisputed control of Ōyamazaki. Consequently, several local, influential persons – who also nominally served as priests of Iwashimizu Hachiman Shrine – carried out their administrative functions on a self-governing basis. Their economic base was the processing and sale of lamp and cooking oil, and they had the right to buy raw materials and to sell the refined oil in Kyoto.

Many *jinaimachi*, or temple towns, also enjoyed the prerogatives of self-government. In communities that were considered to lie within the precincts of temples associated with the True Pure Land and Nichiren sects, the ultimate political authority remained with the temple administrators, as was the case with Ishiyama Honganji and Imai in Yamato. This contrasts with the patterns in other temple towns, such as Tondabayashi, Daigazuka, and Kaizuka, where the residents themselves exercised political authority. In the last case, temples of the True Pure Land sect were the proprietors of record, but in reality local men of influence, usually referred to as elders (*toshiyori*) carried out all administrative functions. The sphere of self-administration included the rights to arrest criminals and adjudicate crimes, to verify the coverage of debt cancellation edicts, and to negotiate contracts for rents and taxes levied on the town as a whole. Private possession of land was also recognized, and the towns maintained their own defenses. Of special interest are the records showing that towns like Sakai, Amagasaki, and Tsukaguchi were given guarantees of neutrality by military commanders, even in times of warfare. Despite its overwhelming importance as a commercial and shipping center, for instance, Sakai was not attacked by opposing forces, and peace was guaranteed by all sides.

This medieval proprietary order underwent a basic transformation at the start of the early modern period. But the changes came slowly. The Oda regime sponsored many policies that were essentially similar to those of the Sengoku daimyo, assuming a cautious, prudent attitude toward the religious and aristocratic establishment in Kyoto. However, in his home territories of Owari and Mino, Nobunaga adopted more innovative policies, one designed to enhance his domination of cities. For example, as part of an attempt to assert greater control over trade and commerce within his holdings in the provinces of Owari and Mino, Nobunaga appointed Itō Sōjūrō to the post of *shōnin tsukasa*, a position entrusted with the responsibility of overseeing commercial activity,. In the castle towns of Kanō (present-day Gifu) and Azuchi, Nobunaga pursued a similar goal of encouraging economic activity and concentrating it in the urban centers by granting special privileges to castle town merchants and by requiring merchants and artisans to live together in specified areas according to occupation. Furthermore, Nobunaga ordered the abolition of toll barriers (*sekisho*) in order to promote commerce. His "free market" declaration (*rakuichi-rei*) issued for Kanō, together with limited exemptions from land taxes and corvée levies, provided incentives for merchants and artisans to move there and set up business establishments. In order to build up his new headquarters at Azuchi, Nobunaga announced many special policies: The town was declared an open, free market, and existing monopolistic guilds were prohibited; merchants in the castle town were declared exempt from debt moratorium edicts, house taxes, and corvée levies; outside merchants traveling along the Nakasendō highway were required to stop in Azuchi and conduct some business; and merchants in the castle town were granted exclusive monopolies on buying and selling horses within the Oda domain. Nobunaga granted these special privileges to the merchants in his castle towns because, as their overlord, he expected to receive a percentage of the proceeds generated by their commercial activities. Moreover, Nobunaga was particularly interested in attracting to Ōmi those merchants and artisans who were involved in the construction trades or who were otherwise important from a military point of view, such as swordsmiths, tatami makers, sawyers, stonecutters, and carpenters. Nobunaga tapped their talents by imposing on them a *kuniyaku*, a corvée levied for domain-related construction projects, while exempting them from other kinds of corvée imposts.

In Kinai and the capital environs, however, Nobunaga was unable to implement to the same degree the policies he had adopted in his home provinces. The chief obstacle was his inability to do away with the special rights and interests of the aristocrats and historically power-ful religious institutions. For instance, in Kyoto these groups were continuing to assert their proprietary claims to land and to exercise local policing and judicial rights. Thus Nobunaga was obliged to recog-nize the special status of the merchants in self-administered cities like Sakai and Hiranogō, which had come under the patronage of privi-leged nobles and temples in Kyoto. During attacks on the Ishiyama Honganji, Nobunaga received aid from the Nichiren sect, a return on his promise to approve construction of a new temple town at Chōenji in Amagasaki. He even went so far as to guarantee the town's immu-nity from military attack. Later, Araki Murashige, military governor of Settsu Province and a direct retainer of Oda Nobunaga, conferred on the new town the right to investigate and prosecute criminals, a significant grant of self-governing powers.

The same kind of limitations on Nobunaga's powers can be seen in his dealings with the rights and interests of medieval merchant organi-zations. Even after Nobunaga entered Kyoto and gained military con-trol of the Kinai region, the activities of the guild (*za*) organizations remained undiminished. These organizations were accustomed to pay-ing a kind of licensing fee to aristocratic establishments and religious organizations in exchange for patronage and protection. Nobunaga did not touch these. Rather, he reconfirmed the status quo arrangements, as is evident in his actions toward the Tatebe oil guild. Interestingly enough, no documents yield conclusive evidence to show that Nobu-naga destroyed the rights of that guild, although there are several extant documents in which he affirmed the rights of closed merchant associations.[20] These include the acknowledgment to a group at Katata port in Ōmi of its right to oversee shipping on Lake Biwa and to assess port taxes, as well as the confirmation of the rights of an organization in Echizen that specialized in textiles and another in Sakai that traded

20 The only document stating that Nobunaga abolished the oil guild is the "Rikyū Hachimangū monjo" of Ōyamazaki. And although we know of a decree from the shogun Ashikaga Yoshiaki that granted rights to the oil guild, there is no document that abolished those privileges. "Rikyū Hachimangū monjo," no. 313 in Ōyamazaki-machi chōshi hensan iinkai, ed., *Ōyamazaki chōshi, shiryōhen* (Kyoto: Ōyamazaki-machi, 1981), p. 723.

in horses. Nobunaga recognized and guaranteed the historic rights of these closed associations and, except for castle towns, did not attempt to impose a "free markets, free guilds" policy.

Nobunaga's recognition of the ancient rights of these guilds was a compromise. Although some historians have argued that his policies masked a deeper intent to eventually abolish the guilds, it is more plausible that he permitted guilds to continue to function because he could meet his own supply and trade requirements by relying on these existing merchant organizations. Because the guilds were able to ship goods long distances, even through areas controlled by his enemies, it made sense for Nobunaga to co-opt for his official needs those guilds and transportation associations (*nakama*) that specialized in the long-distance transportation of goods such as the Katata group, the Kashosen group on the Yodo River, and the Shashaku group in Toba.

Controversy surrounds Nobunaga's policies toward transport barriers. In medieval Japan, proprietors in most regions established toll barriers, or checkpoints, called *sekisho*, where they collected fees on goods transported through those areas. In the tenth month of 1568, Oda Nobunaga, claiming that he represented public authority (*tenka*) and that he was acting in the best interests of all the people, abolished the toll barriers within his holdings, which at that time officially included just the two provinces of Owari and Mino, although information contained in documents in the "Shinchō kōki" show his intention to extend the measure into the southeastern portions of Ōmi and the Kinai as well.[21] Moreover, he also abolished toll barriers in territories that he occupied later, such as Ise and Echizen, thus advancing a policy of encouraging unrestricted trade.

However, Nobunaga's toll barrier policy did not proceed beyond certain self-imposed limitations. He did not, for example, abolish the imperial checkpoints at the seven entrances to Kyoto. Rather, he reconfirmed them after his grand entrance into the city. He also confirmed similar rights on behalf of the Muromachi shogun. Even as late as 1582, the year of Nobunaga's death, tolls were still being collected on the shogunate's behalf under the direction of the Yamashina family, the officials in charge. The transitional and somewhat ambivalent nature of Nobunaga's policy is further reflected in his handling of merchant transport associations. The four famous merchant houses of Ōmi, under his patronage, retained the exclusive right to ship goods along the two routes that lead from Ōmi through Happū and Chigusa

21 See the "Nobunaga kōki," ms copy, Ōyamazaki Toshokan.

to Ise, whereas other, ordinary merchants had to pay tolls collected along the way, a clear restraint on the free conduct of trade. Clearly, though Nobunaga adopted new commercial and urban policies that reflected the desires of the warrior class, he did not aim to promote conditions of general free trade throughout all of Japan.

Oda Nobunaga also had a mixed record in dealing with the independence of temple towns. Immediately after his arrival in Kyoto, he began to challenge militarily the towns of Sakai and Hiranogō. In time, these communities submitted to him and lost their rights to autonomous self-governance. Yet Nobunaga was never able to impose his will completely over Kyoto and most of the temple towns in the capital region. In Kyoto, for instance, Nobunaga achieved some administrative powers by asserting the right to appoint representatives (*shoshidai*), but at the same time, he still had to acknowledge the landownership rights of the vested order and their partial powers to investigate and prosecute criminals. Beyond this, Nobunaga also reconfirmed the vested interests of the proprietary classes in those temple towns that were not antagonistic toward him, as in the examples of Tondabayashi and Tonda.[22]

Toyotomi Hideyoshi continued these policies concerning guilds for one or two years. In the ninth month of 1585, for example, Hashiba Hidekatsu (1568–85), who was holding down the Settsu region on behalf of Hideyoshi, issued the following seven-article agreement that reconfirmed the existing special rights of the area's self-governing towns:

1. No guilds and no corvée levies.
2. No forcible property seizure or attachment for debt restitution.
3. Administration by city elders.
4. Exemption from military service levies.
5. Cessation of unreasonable demands.
6. Exemption from debt moratorium decrees.
7. No samurai residences in the city.[23]

However, from the mid-1580s Hideyoshi began to enforce ordinances against guilds and self-governing urban communities, and he also initiated his nationwide cadastral survey. Ultimately these measures would bring Japan's cities more fully under the influence of the military lords and also would promote the formation of new types of

22 "Shimizu-ke monjo," in Takatsuki shishi hensan iinkai, ed., *Takatsuki shishi* (Takatsuki: Takatsuki-shi, 1973), vol. 4, pp. 548, 584.
23 "Shimizu-ke monjo." Hashiba (Toyotomi) Hidekatsu was the fourth son of Nobunaga and the adopted son of Hideyoshi.

economic and protective organizations among merchants and artisans. Clearly, Hideyoshi was more successful than Nobunaga had been in asserting his authority over urban areas. One reason for this success was that Hideyoshi articulated his urban policy with other policy initiatives. Important in this context was his cadastral survey, which had an adverse impact on self-governing towns, as the survey recognized all land as coming under the administrative authority of the national overlord. Land survey documents remain for the area incorporated as the modern-day Osaka metropolitan prefecture, except for the old city areas of Osaka and Sakai. These records reveal that temple towns like Tondabayashi and Tonda were legally redefined as villages, which meant that they lost their old special urban privileges. Consequently, all governing rights, including the power to apprehend and punish criminals, were assigned to the military lords who received these areas as parts of their fiefs.

Hideyoshi had a particularly difficult time coping with Kyoto, where the authority of court nobles and religious institutions was so firmly rooted in history. Hideyoshi carried out a cadastral survey in Kyoto but confronted serious political problems when he tried to curtail the rights and interests of these noble and religious proprietors. Finally, following a land survey in 1591, Hideyoshi was able to persuade some noble families and religious institutions in central Kyoto to give up their holdings and accept substitute land in villages surrounding the city of Kyoto.[24] Hideyoshi then went on to rearrange the layout of the city's residential wards, construct an earthen wall around the city, create a special ward for temples, and grant exemptions from corvée and property taxes – all measures of his newly acquired powers.

Hideyoshi also imposed his control over commercial institutions and marketing structures. One major policy initiative came in the ninth month of 1585, when Hideyoshi issued his famous injunction that "the various fees levied by noble families, warriors, and common merchants are to cease, and guilds are to be abolished," a measure that effectively erased from existence the business taxes, tolls, and other miscellaneous imposts that the Kyoto nobility, warriors, and powerful merchants had traditionally collected from merchants and artisans.[25] Hideyoshi also put his seal on a letter severely criticizing the Suzuki family, a member of the court nobility, for levying imposts on the

---

24 Ono Kōji, "Kyōto no kinsei toshika," *Shakai keizai shigaku* 10 (October 1940): 1–32.
25 The quotation is from the "Hideyoshi jiki." Additional details can be found in the "Kanemi kyōki" and "Kobayakawa-ke monjo" in Shiryō hensanjo, ed., *Dai Nihon komojo iewake* (Tokyo: Tōkyō teikoku daigaku, 1929), vol. 11, p. 2 and pp. 401–3.

trading of cattle, and his agent Asano Nagayoshi reprimanded merchant leaders in the town of Imazu in Ōmi for collecting a fee for each traveler and piece of baggage that passed through that post town.[26]

The decree to abolish guilds, however, did not bring in its wake complete freedom of commerce. Hideyoshi's intentions were much more complex, for tied into his promotion of commerce was the desire to terminate the domination of trade by court nobles and religious institutions and to assert his own direct lines of authority over merchants. Thus Hideyoshi could tolerate, and even encourage, certain closed business associations if this were in his own immediate interest. Hideyoshi also permitted a few merchants to dominate the rice market in Kyoto. Warehousing documents of the Toyotomi family dated 1598, for example, record that imposts were still being levied against guilds in Sakai, an indication that the Toyotomi regime allowed some guilds to continue to exist so as to tap them for business taxes.[27] Then, from 1594, Hideyoshi had his nephew and adopted son Hidetsugu (1568–95), who had succeeded him as regent (*kampaku*), require these men to submit monthly reports concerning the prices and the marketing of rice.[28]

Particularly revealing was Hideyoshi's policy toward certain transportation guilds. He abolished the rights of the merchant association that controlled shipping on Lake Biwa, only to turn around and authorize the establishment of the "One Hundred Ship Association" at Ōtsu, as well as another shipping association on the Yodo River. Hideyoshi guaranteed exclusive monopolies to these groups, but in exchange, he issued codes of operating procedures, dictated official prices, levied business fees, and reserved the right to commandeer the ships for official business. Allied daimyo engaged in the same expediences. For example, Hashiba Hidenaga (1541–91), Hideyoshi's stepbrother, abolished all guilds and corvée levies in the towns of Nara and Kōriyama in his home domain of Yamato. But just three months later, he exempted the iron, fish, and salt guilds from that order.[29]

The historical significance of the 1585 decree abolishing guilds had many ramifications. First, it deprived the Kyoto-based court families

26 For the Suzuki case, see doc. 463 in "Kobayakawa-ke monjo," in *Dai Nihon komonjo iewake*, vol. 11, p. 2, pp. 401–3. The Asano document is contained in "Kawarabayashi monjo" in Shiga-ken, ed., *Shiga kenshi* (Tokyo: Sanshūsha, 1928), vol. 5, p. 376.

27 "Keichō sannen Toyotomi-ke zōno mokuroku," in *Dai Nihon sozeishi*, vol. 2 (Tokyo: Choyokai, 1927), pp. 585–91.

28 See the entry for Bunroku 3/3/21 in the "Komai nikki," in *Kaitei shiseki shūran*, vol. 25 (Tokyo: Kondō shuppanbu, 1902), pp. 549–50.

29 See the entry for Tenshō 15/1/16 in the "Taken'in nikki," in *Taken'in nikki*, vol. 4 (Tokyo: Kadokawa shoten, 1967), p. 61.

and central religious institutions of their supervisory powers over the activities of merchant and artisans, and it transferred that control to the hands of the warrior class. Merchants and artisans thus were freed from the domination of medieval guild organizations, but they were made more subject to the emerging forms of daimyo authority. Consequently, the decree did not literally free trade and commerce from all restrictions. Although Hideyoshi eliminated many of the monopolistic privileges of the medieval guild associations, the artisans and merchants themselves came under new restraints devised by the rising military aristocracy, who ultimately proved hostile to the development of the independent, self-governing aspects of cities and of merchant and artisan activities.

The coalescence of political control over cities and commerce was clearly revealed in the castle towns that appeared during the late sixteenth and early seventeenth centuries. Above all, these castle towns became residential centers for the military class of proprietors, the daimyo and their retainers, and the merchant and artisan classes that supported economic development. Because the castle towns served as domain military headquarters, the daimyo lords were concerned about their ability to regulate affairs in these urban centers. One measure of this is the care that daimyo took to plan the layout of these new cities. The central focus for most castle towns was a keep that itself was encircled with moats and canals that protected the daimyo, his chief administrative officers, and the residences of his top military and administrative personnel. Next came a belt of merchant residences, and finally temples and the residences of low-ranking warriors were situated on the outskirts of the cities near natural barriers like rivers or foothills, forming outer defense perimeters.

This type of urban plan showed a sensitivity to the dictates of the emerging status system. The daimyo lived at the center of his domain world, as befitted his status. Living within the safety of the moats were his chief lieutenants, protected by his lordship both symbolically and physically. The merchants resided in undefended parts of the city, and the outcast (*semmin*) subcommunities were located on the outer fringes of the cities, typically near rivers that often flooded. Merchants and artisans did not "own" the land in the modern, legal sense of that term but, rather, merely had the right of usufruct over their plots. Clearly this type of urban layout reflected the needs of Japan's new rulers. When compared with the earlier temple towns, it shows how daimyo had strengthened their claims to political control over the land and the activities of the merchants and artisans.

It is also useful to observe how urban administrative structures were changed to accommodate the ascension of daimyo power. The corporate organizations (*kyōdōtai*) of the old temple towns, which had been formed by merchants to protect their own interests, were now placed at the very bottom of the administrative structure. Daimyo assumed legislative, judicial, and military prerogatives, and the merchant residents who had previously served as community leaders were converted into functionaries in the daimyo's administration, executing decisions made by the daimyo and inner samurai elite. The most important merchant offices were now those of the city elders and ward representatives, who carried out such administrative duties as conducting census reports, investigating crimes, collecting taxes, and transmitting the lord's laws to the urban residents.[30]

The daimyo also entrusted to the merchants and artisans responsibility for constructing and maintaining streets, bridges, and sewage canals in their sections of the city. For instance, of the more than one hundred bridges in Osaka that were called "public bridges," the shogunate actually built and maintained only twelve. In addition, as a general principle, merchants and artisans had to resolve commercial and debt disputes among themselves, with the city elders and ward representatives attempting to negotiate settlements based on techniques of reconciliation.

The early modern marketing structure took shape around this kind of urban nucleus. There was both a central marketing structure and a set of domain markets. Within each domain market, the daimyo manipulated the tax system in order to lay claim to rice and other local products. He then sold these to merchants in the domain, particularly in the castle town, and used the proceeds to buy military equipment and everyday necessities. Moreover, peasants also purchased in the local urban centers items that they could not produce themselves, such as salt and certain farm implements. Consequently the castle town became home to a variety of merchants and artisans who had previously resided in villages and country towns: swordsmiths, armorers, carpenters, plasterers, dyers, weavers, transportation agents, and merchants who dealt in perishables and textiles. This indicated a growing functional separation of village and city, and despite the continuing trade between the two in those goods that were part of the lord's tax system, there were strong restraints on the peasants' participation in the commercial economy.

---

30 Wakita Osamu, "Kinsei toshi no kensetsu to gōshō," in *Nihon rekishi*, vol. 9 (1975).

The internal economies of most domains were not self-sufficient. Moreover, not all rice and specialty products were consumed within the domain, thus leaving a surplus that could be shipped to markets outside the domain. The apex of the central marketing area included the cities of Kyoto, Osaka, Sakai, and Nara in the Kinai region. In 1634, Kyoto probably still had a population of more than 410,000, and Osaka was home to perhaps nearly the same number of people.[31] Edo quickly became a major consumption center as well, and it too eventually became an integral part of the central marketing area.

This national marketing structure was supported by the growth of local, domain economies, and these in turn could not have come into existence without the adoption of the *kokudaka* system and the practice of collecting local specialty products. For fiscal reasons, the daimyo had to develop the capability to market certain goods in the central markets, while at the same time maintaining control over their own domain marketing structures. Thus, they kept themselves informed about rice prices in the central markets and then maintained rice prices within their domains at a higher level. They also created their own independent currency systems, as well as uniform standards of weights and measures.

This domestic marketing system underwent important modifications during the latter half of the seventeenth century. Much of this was a consequence of shogunal policy initiatives, particularly the implementation of measures that led to an extraordinary degree of national seclusion (*sakoku*). During the 1640s the Edo shogunate issued a series of ordinances that prohibited the possession of oceangoing ships, thus throwing the country into relative trade isolation. Indeed, scholars are still troubled by the question of how a policy of national closure could be adopted without disastrous results to the national economy. But the measures did not lead to a complete cessation of trade itself, nor were they so intended. The ongoing growth of domain market economies certainly stimulated commercial expansion, and the lower demand for imports of critical military supplies such as lead and leather brought on by the onset of the "Great Tokugawa Peace" meant, in any case, that Japan was becoming less dependent on foreign trade. Japan also gained increasing self-sufficiency in the production of raw silk thread, which for many years had been the main import item from China. Finally, there was a decline in the output of gold, silver, and copper, Japan's chief items of export. Viewed from the standpoint of

31 Wakita Osamu, "Kinsei shoki no toshi keizai," *Nihonshi kenkyū* 200 (April 11, 1979): 52–75.

market relations, Japan had never been deeply involved in foreign trade, and the closure policy was adopted largely for political reasons, chiefly as an anti-Christian measure.[32]

THE EARLY MODERN SOCIAL SYSTEM

All of the issues we have discussed – the Taikō cadastral survey, the decision to encourage migration to the castle towns, and the separation of warrior and peasant – combined to produce a new social order at the beginning of the early modern period. At the apex of this new structure was the bushi class, secure in its position of military and political dominance and concentrated in the castle towns. The relocation of the bushi from the countryside into urban centers took many decades to complete. In the medieval period, the warriors possessed personal fiefs (*honryō*), and they tended to stay in these home areas, where they put down strong roots, living with their families and their own bands of retainers. As part of his effort to consolidate military control over the country, Toyotomi Hideyoshi adopted policies that severed, or at least weakened, this bond between the warrior and his fief. The key move here was Hideyoshi's efforts to compel increasing numbers of warriors to take up residence in the newly emerging castle towns. He also used rather frequently the practice of transferring daimyo from one domain to another, and this required the daimyo and the entire vassal band of fief holders to relocate.

Such pressures to break the personal tie to specific holdings were applied at different levels, even into the early decades of the Edo period. The Shimazu family of Satsuma, for instance, had been historically prominent from the Kamakura period and was never transferred to a new domain, even by the Tokugawa shoguns. Consequently, the so-called rural samurai, or *gōshi*, system, remained intact in that area of southern Japan. Yet, even though these local samurai continued to hold fiefs after the Taikō cadastral survey, they were instructed to "order [their] affairs and be prepared to transfer to new fiefs."[33] The Tokugawa shogunate continued the policy of transferring daimyo, so much so that the philosopher Ogyū Sorai (1666–1728) compared the life of the samurai with that of travelers, "always living in inns."[34]

The policy of separating the warriors from the peasantry also had a

---

32 Wakita, "Kinsei toshi no kensetsu to gōshō."
33 "Haseba-ke monjo" in Miyagawa, *Taikō kenchi ron*, vol. 3, p. 326.
34 See Ogyū Sorai's "Seidan," in Yoshikawa Kōjirō and Maruyama Masao, eds., *Ogyū Sorai*, vol. 36 of *Nihon shisō taikei* (Tokyo: Iwanami shoten, 1973), p. 295.

significant impact on the shape of early modern society. Although many bushi continued to be granted a fief of record even after an extensive round of cadastral surveys in the early seventeenth century, they now had no permanent home village, no ancestral base to which they could return if they became "masterless samurai" (rōnin). Moreover, the samurai now had no claims to landed property, a condition that transformed the lord–retainer relationship. In the medieval period, the bushi lived in the villages as proprietors, and the warriors and peasants lived together communally, cooperating in the cultivation of fields, the construction of irrigation facilities, and the celebration of festivals. Of course, status differences intruded between the peasants and warriors, but these had been overshadowed by the deep, personal relationships that bound them together. However, in the early modern period, only the peasants lived in the villages. The village had become the peasant's possession, and proprietary landholding was no longer vested in individual samurai.

The policy of separating warriors and peasants was designed to ensure better control over the bushi while still providing a means of governing the peasantry. When the daimyo's vassal retainers lived in villages as minor proprietors, they were self-reliant and often disregarded the higher authority of their daimyo masters, who feared acts of betrayal and perfidy. These rural bushi were also sensitive to the pressures from the peasantry, and, although most bushi had relatives and tenants in the villages, they were clearly in the rural minority. Consequently, in kuni ikki and Ikkō ikki, village-based retainers frequently allied with the peasants. The Honganji sect often served as the nucleus for this kind of confederation. To cite a concrete example, when a large-scale tsuchi ikki occurred in 1465, the shogunate, fearing that its own direct retainers might go over to the side of the farmers, compelled the protesters to assemble in the capital.[35] By doing this, the shogunate strengthened its own position and prevented the rural federation of its rivals. Confronted with these circumstances, the policy of separating peasant from warrior took on a special meaning and can be seen as one step toward severing the connection between bushi and peasant power.

Toyotomi Hideyoshi and his successors also implemented measures to entice merchants and artisans to live in their cities. Especially important was the granting of tax exemptions to those who moved into the

---

35 See "Tōji monjo," in Dai Nihon komonjo, Tōji monjo, vol. 6 (Tokyo: Tōkyō daigaku shuppankai, 1959), pp. 363–71.

castle towns. One goal of the daimyo was to build up their own economic base, but they also used this policy as a political tool for maintaining the economic distinctions between city and peasant village.
The early modern daimyo continued to place heavy tax obligations on
the peasantry, while granting special privileges to the cities. This practice apparently did induce large numbers to migrate to the cities.[36]

Another special characteristic of the early modern social order was
the forced imposition of the status system (*mibun-sei*) on the population. Of course, status distinctions had existed in the medieval period,
but during the sixteenth and early seventeenth centuries the shogun
and daimyo sought new ways to bring about a more complete separation of peasant from warrior and peasant from merchant. Usually the
early modern status system is seen as being fourfold, consisting of
warrior, peasant, merchant, and artisan statuses. Conceptually, however, divisions can also be drawn between warrior-proprietor, peasant,
and townsperson, with various outcast categories such as *eta* and *hinin*
existing outside the specified status groups.

The daimyo enforced these distinctions in several ways. For example, the legal system was based on status considerations, and separate
legal codes were issued for each status group. Bushi carried two
swords and used surnames, but peasants, townspeople, and outcasts
had neither. Marriage between members of different status groups,
particularly between warriors and the ruled status groups, or with
outcasts, was strictly prohibited.[37]

Status groups were also separated spatially according to occupation:
The bushi, merchants, and artisans lived in cities, and the peasants
lived in villages. Some outcast subcommunities were also located in
peasant villages, but administratively they were treated as separate,
detached "branch villages" and could not participate in the selection of
village officials such as the headmen or elders. Within most castle
towns, separately defined areas were created for warriors, townspeople, temples, and outcasts, as well as for "pleasure quarters" of
theaters and houses of prostitution (*yūkaku*). Urban outcast communities were subordinate to urban administrative associations, but they
were typically located on the outskirts of the city, on land of very poor
quality.[38] Furthermore, pleasure quarters, such as the Yoshiwara in

36 See Wakita, *Kinsei hōkensei seiritsu shiron*, chap. 3.
37 There were ways of bypassing this, such as the so-called practice of adopting daughters. But
    if the woman was of *eta* status, and this was later discovered, she would be divorced and
    punished.
38 For more details of outcast subcommunities, see Buraku mondai kenkyūjo, ed., *Burakushi no
    kenkyū: zenkindai-hen* (Kyoto: Buraku mondai kenkyūjo shuppanbu, 1978).

Edo, Shimabara in Kyoto, and Shinmachi in Osaka, were confined to certain geographically defined areas. Status distinctions tended to become blurred in these areas – customers were not usually queried at the entry gates – and if there were fights or disputes, the government did not usually intervene but, rather, let the people settle the issues themselves.

The social distinctions and class separation also became the basis for determining the distribution and use of residential land. The bushi, peasants, and townspeople each had different claims to land. The enfeoffed members of the bushi class held plots of land bestowed by the overlord, and consequently, they could not sell or otherwise convey their holdings. Of course, the majority of the bushi received stipends and hence had no claims to the land at all. In contrast with this, peasants in the early modern period were given certain rights to the use of land. In a technical sense, these might be called "tillage rights" or "user rights," although in actual practice they amounted to a close equivalent to what we would style ownership rights. As we noted, townspeople could own houses and use land.

Fiscal obligations also varied according to status. Peasants were assessed the *nengu*, the annual land tax, as well as corvée. Most daimyo extracted various services from merchants and artisans. Chartered merchants and artisans usually had to pay a service tax in goods of their own specialty, and ordinary townspeople were assessed a tax in cash to pay for the construction and maintenace of the castle. Outcasts, on the other hand, were charged with such duties as keeping up the castle grounds, tanning hides, cleaning prisons, and carrying out the punishment of criminals.

The changing social conditions also had an impact on the lord–retainer relationship. Within the bushi class as a whole, the delegation of powers of governance from the shogun to the various daimyo then down through the lower elements of the bushi class was based on feudalistic practices. The basic principles of this relationship between lord and vassal – ideals of loyalty, service, and obligation – had penetrated the consciousness of the bushi during the medieval period. In the early modern period, these older practices became intertwined with more abstract notions of centralized state authority, as expressed in concepts such as *kōgi*, or a public authority, a term that daimyo began to use from the late sixteenth century. The shift toward the more abstract conceptualization of power tended to put more authority into the hands of the daimyo. This contrasted with relationships between lord and master that had existed during Nobunaga's regime, which, despite Nobunaga's own despotic character, were based on mutual consent and agreement. The customary practice at that time was to decide such matters as military service requirements through joint discussions, without contracting a written agreement. By the early modern period, on the other hand, military service requirements were generally related to fief size, indicating that the master enjoyed more authority over his followers and that his authority was defined in more abstract and universal terms.

The specific characteristics of the early modern social system were also closely associated with the requirements of the commercial economy. It is well known that after the social structure assumed final form, the bushi scorned commerce and left the management of the economy to those who were skilled at it. However, while the system was taking shape, the bushi proved to be financial experts. Indeed, Nobunaga used the symbol of the *eiraku* coin in his flag design. Toyotomi Hideyoshi devised brilliant fiscal policies, and he was known "to be parsimonious with his calculations on the abacus." This concern with precision in fiscal matters was not prompted by greed but reflected Hideyoshi's great need for revenues for warfare and construction projects. Hideyoshi further showed his fiscal acumen when he specified on the fief inventories sent to the Satake and Shimazu daimyo the portion of the holdings that should be administered directly by the daimyo and the portion that should be assigned as retainers' fiefs. Concerning the peasantry, his decision to collect as land tax two-thirds of what they grew was deliberately calculated to keep them at the far edge of existence. Another example of Hideyoshi's fiscal skill is seen in his manipulation of rice prices in order to acquire that grain for consumption in his home base in Kinai and for use in the Korean invasion attempts.

CONCLUSIONS

Japan's early modern society had a clear influence on its modern development. To discuss these in detail would be beyond the scope of this essay, but we can make several general observations. First, although the early modern sociopolitical structure can be considered feudal, it was different from that of the medieval period. For this reason, the transition to a modern state was not a gradual process that took place in installments but, rather, became possible only with the revolutionary upheaval of the Meiji Restoration. One important reason for this was the nature of the governing powers held by the shogun and daimyo, of which the military, despotic authority of the bushi was an essential component. But more than anything else, it was the *bakuhan* system supported by the *kokudaka* fief system that characterized bushi rule under the Edo shogunate. The system's decentralized feudalistic nature is seen in the way the country was governed. The basic right to possess proprietary holdings (*ryōyūken*) did not change, nor did it move into the hands of merchants and artisans. Thus it required a sudden, abrupt upheaval for such power to be transferred from shogun to emperor and for the domains to be abolished and replaced by prefectures.

Having said this, however, we also should observe that the Meiji Restoration and the subsequent elimination of the feudal proprietors grew out of certain developments in the early modern period, such as the emergence of the fief system and the formulation of abstract concepts of state authority. Clearly, during the Edo period, individual independence was weakened because of the continuing feudalistic master–subject relationships and the spread of Bushido, with its emphasis on selfless devotion. The self-governing powers of cities and villages, along with the commercial guilds, were suppressed by the daimyo, and the early modern family system, which also permitted few individual freedoms, was incorporated into the Meiji civil code, both events having a pervasive influence on modern Japan. The early modern status system was inflexible and was not changed until the equality of classes was decreed following the Meiji Restoration. Even after that, the emperor system (*tennō-sei*) and the peerage system were established, and despite the so-called abolition of classes, the outcasts have continued to the present day to be subject to cruel forms of discrimination. Nonetheless, despite the suffering of so many under the status system, the Meiji period laws calling for class equality had some success. In particular they served to stimulate and concentrate the energies of the new nation's citizenry. The absorption of these energies, especially into the bureaucracy and the military, was one reason for Japan's "successful" modernization.

The *kokudaka* system guaranteed that the economic policies of shogun and daimyo would maintain their vitality. The primary problem confronting the system was the need to cope with the growth of a commercial economy. Although most of the daimyo's economic policies were poorly designed, several large domains managed successful economies during the late Tokugawa period. Within the shogunate and many individual domains, there also emerged skillful economic managers. On the other hand, a high level of cultural development, including education, was necessary for the accomplishments of the modern period. In this sense, the standards of sixteenth-century Japan had been very high, and the early modern social order only hindered development.

As is well known, the Edo period peasantry suffered from extreme poverty. Although they had secure rights of possession that were later converted into a modern form of ownership rights, the land reform of the early modern period also meant that the peasantry continued to be saddled with major burdens, and as capitalism developed, so too did landlordism. The *chōnin* (townsmen) participated in the economy and, to some extent, were able to accumulate commercial capital. However, entrepreneurship and the spirit of enterprise were weak, and the direction of commercial development was easily molded by the state and the bureaucracy. This was the system's major defect. These are some of the points that emerge from looking at modernization from the standpoint of early modern society. At the very least, the Edo period had a distinctive character that clearly influenced modern Japan.

CHAPTER 4

THE *BAKUHAN* SYSTEM

The political structure established by the Tokugawa house in the early years of the seventeenth century is now commonly referred to as the *bakuhan* system (*bakuhan taisei*). This term, coined by modern Japanese historians, recognizes the fact that under the Edo bakufu, or shogunate, government organization was the result of the final maturation of the institutions of shogunal rule at the national level and of daimyo rule at the local level.[1] Although Tokugawa Ieyasu became shogun in 1603, it was not until the years of the dynasty's third shogun, Iemitsu, that the Edo bakufu reached its stable form, that is, not until the 1630 and 1640s. And it took another several decades before the *han*, or daimyo domains, completed their evolution as units of local governance.[2] Scholars now agree, however, that most of the institutional components of the *bakuhan* system had made their initial appearance under the first two of the "three great unifiers," Oda Nobunaga and Toyotomi Hideyoshi.

This chapter will trace the formation and the evolution of the *bakuhan* structure of government from the middle of the sixteenth century to the end of the eighteenth century. Because the following chapters will treat separately the daimyo domains as units of local administration, the primary emphasis of this chapter will be the Edo shogunate and the nationwide aspects of the *bakuhan* system. As noted in the introduction to this volume, historians increasingly identify the broader dimensions of shogunal rule by using the concept of *kokka* (nation or state) to replace *taisei* (system), thus coining the expression

1 The use of the term *bakuhan* is essentially a post–World War II phenomenon, although the pioneers in this field had begun to conceive of Edo government as a dyarchy by the late 1930s. See Itō Tasaburō, "Bakuhan taisei ron," in *Shin Nihonshi kōza* (Tokyo: Chūō kōronsha, 1947); and Nakamura Kichiji, *Nihon hōkensei saihenseishi* (Tokyo: Mikasa shobō, 1940).

2 The new interest in the daimyo domain was also led by the two scholars cited in footnote 1. After the war the field was introduced by Fujino Tamotsu, in his *Bakuhan taiseishi no kenkyū* (Tokyo: Yoshikawa kōbunkan, 1961); and by Kanai Madoka, *Hansei* (Tokyo: Shinbundō, 1962). Harold Bolitho describes in greater detail the emergence of the *han* studies field in Chapter 5 in this volume.

bakuhansei-kokka (the *bakuhan* state).[3] Though not explicitly adopting this usage, this chapter will treat the Edo shogunate as a total national polity, not simply as a narrowly defined political system.

The political and social institutions that underlay the *bakuhan* polity had their origins in the "unification movement" of the last half of the sixteenth century, especially in the great feats of military consolidation and social engineering achieved by Toyotomi Hideyoshi during the last two decades of the century.[4] Although neither Nobunaga nor Hideyoshi became shogun, they succeeded in advancing to absolute proportions the capacity to rule over the daimyo and other political bodies that comprised the Japanese nation. In the parlance of the day they succeeded in winning the *tenka* (the realm) and serving as its *kōgi* (its ruling authority).[5] At the same time however, the daimyo enhanced their own powers of private control over their local domains (their *kokka* in a limited local sense), borrowing support from the very central authority that sought to constrain them. The most significant feature of the resulting national polity was that unification was carried only so far. The daimyo domains, though giving up a portion of their hard-won autonomy, managed to survive as part of the system.[6]

Tokugawa Ieyasu and his immediate successors brought to its fullest development the bakufu system of rule under a military hegemon. But despite the preponderance of military power that the Tokugawa shoguns held, their legal status was not qualitatively different from that of the fifteenth-century Muromachi shoguns. On the other hand, the powers exercised by the daimyo within their domains had expanded tremendously since the time of the Muromachi military governors, the *shugo* daimyo. In fact it was probably in the *han* that the machinery of centralized bureaucratic administration proceeded the farthest. In many instances the Edo shogunate based its governing practices on

3 See the treatment of this approach to Japanese political history by Sasaki Junnosuke in "Bakuhansei kokka ron," in Araki Moriaki et al., comps., *Taikei Nihon kokka shi (kinsei 3)* (Tokyo: Tōkyō daigaku shuppankai, 1975).
4 For a recent overview in English of Hideyoshi's social policies, see Bernard Susser, "The Toyotomi Regime and the Daimyo," in Jeffrey P. Mass and William B. Hauser, eds., *The Bakufu in Japanese History* (Stanford, Calif.: Stanford University Press, 1985), pp. 128–52. For greater detail, see Mary Elizabeth Berry, *Hideyoshi* (Cambridge, Mass.: Harvard University Press, 1982).
5 A penetrating treatment of these terms appears in Chapter 2 in this volume. For the early use of these terms by the large regional daimyo of the sixteenth century, see Shizuo Katsumata, with Martin Collcutt, "The Development of Sengoku Law," in John Whitney Hall, Keiji Nagahara and Kozo Yamamura, eds., *Japan Before Tokugawa: Political Consolidation and Economic Growth, 1500–1650* (Princeton, N.J.: Princeton University Press, 1981), pp. 119–24.
6 The previously cited symposium by Mass and Hauser on bakufu rule is a pioneer effort to analyze the evolution of military government in historical–structural terms.

techniques adopted from times when the head of the Tokugawa line was simply one of many daimyo competing for local supremacy in central Japan. In analyzing the creation of the Edo bakufu, then, we must deal with two separate but interrelated strands of institutional development. And it is this that is suggested by the term *bakuhan*.

THE TOKUGAWA HOUSE AND ITS RISE TO POWER

The story of the rise of the Tokugawa family to become the foremost military house of Japan follows a pattern common among a whole class of active regional military families who competed for local dominion during the fifteenth and sixteenth centuries.[7] The stages of growth, from local estate manager (*jitō*) to small independent military lord (*kunishū*), to minor regional overlord (daimyo), and then to the status of major regional hegemon were typical of the day. As of the 1550s, there were daimyo leaders in almost every region of Japan poised to contest the national *tenka*. Why Ieyasu rather than another of his peers managed to gain the prize, rested, no doubt, on his native ability and on such unpredictable factors as the length of his life (he lived to be seventy-three), his ability to father capable sons (he had eleven), and the location of his original power base. The Mikawa–Owari region was clearly one of the more favorable locations from which to take and hold the imperial capital. It was the starting point for all three of the unifiers.

The Tokugawa house genealogy as officially adopted by Ieyasu in 1600 claimed descent from the most prestigious of military lineages, the Seiwa Genji, through the branch line begun by Nitta Yoshishige (1135–1202). The originator of the Nitta line took his name from the locality in the province of Kōzuke to which he was first assigned as estate manager. In the generations that followed, the Nitta line branched, giving rise to numerous sublines, each of which followed the custom of adopting the name of its residential base as its identifying surname. One such branch took the name Tokugawa from the village of that name in the Nitta district of Kōzuke. Eight generations later the head of this Tokugawa family is presumed to have left Kōzuke and established himself as the adoptive head of the Matsu-

7 Among the large number of narrative histories on the rise of the Tokugawa house, I have relied on Tsuji Tatsuya's *Edo kaifu*, vol. 4 of *Nihon no rekishi* (Tokyo: Chūō kōronsha, 1966); and Kitajima Masamoto, *Edo bakufu*, vol. 16 of *Nihon no rekishi* (Tokyo: Shōgakkan, 1975). An outstanding scholarly analysis of the establishment of the Tokugawa hegemony can be found in the work of Kitajima Masamoto, notably his *Edo bakufu no kenryoku kōzō* (Tokyo: Iwanami shoten, 1964).

daira family, chiefs of a village bearing the same name in neighboring Mikawa Province. According to the official genealogy, Ieyasu was the ninth head of this Matsudaira line, and it was he who in 1566 petitioned the Kyoto court to recognize a change of surname to Tokugawa. See Figure 4.1.

There are numerous questions about the authenticity of the official Tokugawa family descent chart, particularly in the Kōzuke years. In premodern society, pedigree played an essential role in the establishment of a family's political status. Descent from noble lineage, whether or not supported by authentic documentation, was commonly claimed by local members of the provincial warrior aristocracy. When such families reached national importance, the need to prove genealogical correctness became critical. In Ieyasu's own case, not only did he change his surname, he also for a time kept two descent charts, thus keeping open a choice of two pedigrees, one tied to the Fujiwara (the foremost court family) and the other to the Minamoto (one of the primary military lineages). His decision to settle for the Minamoto was taken in the wake of his victory at Sekigahara in 1600, when the possibility of becoming shogun seemed within his grasp.

Whether the Kōzuke years recorded in the official genealogy are to be taken seriously is not of great consequence. In fact, most recent studies of the Tokugawa house begin with the Mikawa years, starting roughly from the middle of the fifteenth century. Only then do the sources permit a reasonably reliable account. We begin, then, at a time in Japanese history when the old order that had been maintained by the Muromachi shoguns and their provincial agents, the *shugo* daimyo, was being challenged. A new generation of provincial military lords was on the rise. These Sengoku daimyo, as they have been called, built up tightly knit housebands of increasing size and military effectiveness. The strength of these organizations lay in the closeness of the lord–vassal relationships that held the housebands together. Other than the steady increase in the size of these organizations, the most visible index of the growth of these new organizations could be seen in the nature of their military establishments.

Village samurai were distinguished from common cultivators by their possession of proprietary lordships and residences protected by rudimentary moats and earthen embankments. As fighting became more technologically advanced, these local warrior families took to building small fortifications, usually on the ridges of nearby hills, in which the local chief and his band of followers could take shelter and hold off predators. During the sixteenth century these little "hill cas-

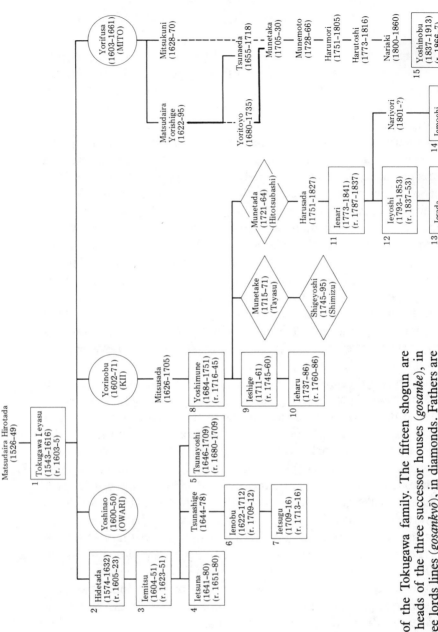

Figure 4.1 Genealogy of the Tokugawa family. The fifteen shogun are enclosed in rectangles; heads of the three successor houses (*gosanke*), in circles; heads of the three lords lines (*gosankyō*), in diamonds. Fathers are connected to actual sons by solid lines, to adopted sons by dashed lines. (Based on *Tokushi sōran*, *Nihonshi sōran*, and *Encyclopedia of Japan*.)

tles" proliferated throughout the country. In Mikawa we can trace the establishment of the Matsudaira branch families by noting the appearance of numerous hilltop forts above the valleys of the Yahagi River and its upper tributaries. The village of Matsudaira was itself on the Asuke River some distance above its confluence with the Yahagi. The first two Matsudaira generations were confined to this mountainous environment, but the third chief, Nobumitsu (?–1488) greatly expanded the family's reach, pushing into the middle plain of Mikawa and occupying the castle of Anjo in 1471.

For roughly fifty years the Matsudaira based themselves at Anjo. But its location to the west and south of Matsudaira village made it hard to hold, particularly in the face of the growing power of the Oda establishment to the west in Owari Province. In 1524 the family chief Kiyoyasu (1511–35) consolidated his position by pulling back to the east of the Yahagi river, adopting the castle of Okazaki as his headquarters. This castle was to serve the Matsudaira on and off until Ieyasu's time. Okazaki was well placed for purposes of military defense and economic growth, and by the 1550s the family had asserted itself over several districts covering roughly the interior one-third of Mikawa Province.[8]

The Matsudaira were not yet in a position to stand on their own. Historically they existed, as did others in this area, within a regional power structure built around the Imagawa house, whose heads were military governors (*shugo*) of Suruga, and at times of Mikawa and Tōtōmi as well. As a vassal of the Imagawa, the Matsudaira aspired to the vice-governorship of Mikawa. But they were hard pressed by the head of the Oda house who, as vice-governor of Owari, was actively pushing beyond its provincial borders. During the 1550s the Matsudaira household split over whether to realign themselves toward the Oda. The move to Okazaki Castle was an implicit decision to continue to look toward the east and the Imagawa. But Kiyoyasu was killed in 1535 by one of his own men over this issue, and when his successor Hirotada (1526–49) (Ieyasu's father) acknowledged the Imagawa overlordship, a faction of the Matsudaira leadership broke off and joined the Oda. As a child Ieyasu was a victim of these unsettled circumstances. From age six to fourteen he was kept as a hostage first by the Oda and then by the Imagawa. Technically he had inherited the family headship following Hirotada's death in 1549. But Okazaki was occu-

8 The Okazaki years are thoroughly covered in the documentary history published by Okazaki City: Shibata Akimasa, ed., *Tokugawa Ieyasu to sono shui*, 3 vols. (Okazaki shi: Okazaki shiyakusho, 1926).

pied by Imagawa officers. It was only in 1556 that Ieyasu was able to return to Okazaki as head of the Matsudaira main line.

Ieyasu found the Matsudaira houseband in disarray. On top of this, between 1556 and 1559 he was constantly in the field fighting at the behest of his overlord, Imagawa Yoshimoto (1519–60). Nevertheless, he did what he could to repair the damage done to the houseband during the years of internal dissension, thereby strengthening the bonds between himself and the numerous cadet houses and several classes of house vassals.

The Tōkai years

By the middle of the sixteenth century, the temptation to contest for national overlordship was becoming increasingly seductive to some of the more powerful daimyo. Imagawa Yoshimoto was one of the first to make the attempt. But when in 1560 he led an army of some 25,000 men across Mikawa on his way to the capital to gain legitimacy from the emperor, his army was decisively defeated, and he himself was killed by a greatly inferior force under the command of Oda Nobunaga. Yoshimoto's death released Ieyasu from his bond to the Imagawa house. As a sign, he adopted the given name Ieyasu at this time. (It had been Motoyasu, the "Moto," of couse, having come from Imagawa Yoshimoto.) Nobunaga was now clearly the coming power in the area, and Ieyasu lost little time in entering into a formal alliance with him.

Thus began a new chapter in the evolution of the Matsudaira house.[9] Using Okazaki as his central castle and protected on his western flank by Nobunaga, Ieyasu began to press eastward at the expense of the now-weakened Imagawa of Tōtōmi and the still-powerful Takeda in Suruga. By 1565 he had succeeded in placing his men in the key castles of Mikawa. In other words, Mikawa was safely his. Symbolic of his new sense of confidence, in 1566 he petitioned the court to have his surname changed to Tokugawa, leaving the name Matsudaira attached to the principal cadet families and also available for use as an honorary "gift name" with which Ieyasu could reward daimyo who became his allies. Along with official recognition of his change of surname, Ieyasu received appointment to the now largely honorary title of governor of Mikawa and to the fourth court rank junior grade.

9 The map of the Matsudaira house's castle holdings in Mikawa Province printed in Kitajima, *Kenryoku kōzō*, p. 7, reveals the close relationship of the Matsudaira house to the province's physical configuration – hills and rivers.

By such means Ieyasu began to acquire recognition as a member of the military aristocracy.

During the next few years Ieyasu beat into shape the kind of houseband and enfeoffment pattern required of a successful daimyo. Whereas the Matsudaira chieftains up to this point had relied heavily on kinsmen as their main supports in battle and administration, Ieyasu adopted the practice of converting even heads of collateral houses into dependent hereditary vassals (*fudai*), thus gaining a firmer grip over his senior military commanders. At the same time he enlarged his vassal band, particularly at the lower levels, by incorporating into his fighting forces large numbers of rural samurai. These he assigned to the command of his enfeoffed vassals to form new and expanded military units. At yet another level he worked to stabilize the relationship between his samurai retainers and the land-cultivating peasantry. As other daimyo were doing at this time, Ieyasu began a systematic survey of the land of his domain. He also confronted the troublesome issue posed in Mikawa by the militant and politically independent Ikkō religious communities, eventually bringing them around to his support.

Nobunaga and Ieyasu worked closely together during the next few years. Ieyasu's hold on Mikawa protected Nobunaga's advance on Kyoto in 1568, whereas the Oda presence in Owari gave Ieyasu the freedom to concentrate on his eastern front. By 1570 the Tokugawa chief had taken all of Tōtōmi from the Imagawa and had moved his castle headquarters to Hamamatsu, a port town in Tōtōmi. Ieyasu now began with Nobunaga's help an all-out effort to destroy the Takeda of Suruga and Kai. It turned out to be a lengthy operation. Not until 1582 were the Takeda finally defeated and Ieyasu could receive investiture of Suruga from Nobunaga.

By this time Ieyasu had acquired control over all or parts of the five provinces of Mikawa, Suruga, Tōtōmi, Kai, and Shinano. These all being in the Tōkaidō circuit, Ieyasu was commonly referred to as "lord of five Tōkai provinces." He stood among the dozen or so largest daimyo of the land, and he was already gaining a reputation for having one of the most effective administrative and military organizations in the country.

Nobunaga's assassination in 1582 by Akechi Mitsuhide threw the existing power structure into momentary confusion. Ieyasu himself, a likely figure to come to the defense of the Nobunaga legacy, was caught without his following in the port city of Sakai. He thus was forced to make his way to Okazaki in secret. Before he could gain full command of his forces for a possible military move, Hideyoshi had already killed Akechi and was in the process of winning over the Oda coalition. Ieyasu had been outmaneuvered, and he realized it. But he also knew that it was not politically wise to give in too precipitously to Hideyoshi's takeover.

Over the next several years Ieyasu worked off the formal obligations of his oath of allegiance to Nobunaga by taking up the cause of Nobunaga's second son Nobukatsu (1558–1630) against Hideyoshi. This involved him in some actual tests of strength with Hideyoshi. In 1589, Ieyasu invaded Toyotomi territory in Owari, winning a limited engagement at Nagakute. But his forces fought to a stalemate at Komaki. Although these at the time seemed to be minor engagements, in retrospect it is clear that they constituted something of a turning point. Militarily they instilled in each man a respect for the other. Modern historians have suggested that this was Ieyasu's first "political war," one that he shrewdly ended by agreeing, for political effect, to a formal compact of submission with Hideyoshi. Obviously Hideyoshi also found it expedient not to push to the limit. The agreement was consummated in 1586 by Ieyasu's formal visit of submission to Hideyoshi at Osaka Castle.[10] Ieyasu's second son was given to Hideyoshi for adoption; one of Hideyoshi's sisters was given in marriage to Ieyasu; and for a period Hideyoshi's mother was kept as a hostage in Ieyasu's household. At the time these exchanges were being negotiated, Ieyasu moved his castle headquarters farther to the east at Sumpu.

From 1586 to Hideyoshi's death in 1598, Ieyasu served as a willing ally. Having stood his own in battle against Hideyoshi, he was treated with respect and caution by the latter. As a consequence he was able to avoid depleting his own military resources by fighting Hideyoshi's battles. While Hideyoshi was sending gigantic armies into Shikoku and Kyushu to carry his conquest into western and southern Japan, Ieyasu managed to stay in the east expanding his holdings, improving his military capacity, and perfecting his administrative machinery. He also greatly enlarged his castle at Sumpu, to which he gathered large bodies of retainers and merchant and service personnel. It was during these same years that he carried forward the systematic survey of cultivated land, now definitely adopting the method preferred by Hideyoshi that stressed payment of the annual land tax in rice. The survey became the base on which an effective system of material extraction was built and the recruitment of military manpower from both samurai and peasants was standardized.

10 Tsuji, *Edo kaifu*, pp. 43–50.

By 1589, after the subjugation of Kyushu, the only major daimyo holdouts requiring Hideyoshi's attention were the Hōjō of the Kantō and the Date, Gamō, Tsugaru, and others in the far north. Hideyoshi attempted to win over the Hōjō by using Ieyasu as a go-between. Ieyasu had previously given his daughter in marriage to Hōjō Ujinao (1562–92). But unlike the daimyo of Shikoku and Kyushu, Ujinao refused to capitulate. Hideyoshi prepared for battle. This time Ieyasu was obliged to assist Hideyoshi in the attack on Odawara Castle, the headquarters of the great Hōjō domain that included the six Kantō provinces of Izu, Sagami, Musashi, Shimōsa, Kazusa, and Awa. In the investment, Ieyasu took the initiative, leading an army of some thirty thousand men in six divisions. The Hōjō held out for some three months, but the end was inevitable. Odawara Castle surrendered in the summer of 1590. Before this the Date and other daimyo to the north sought out Hideyoshi's camp and quickly pledged their allegiance. Hideyoshi had pacified the realm. All daimyo were now his vassals, and he could claim to be the chief of the military estate (*buke no tōryō*).

The early Kantō years

Following the Hōjō surrender, Hideyoshi ordered Ieyasu to move out of his home Tōkai provinces and to occupy the domain vacated by the Hōjō.[11] The assignment was on the surface an advancement. Possession of six of eight Kantō provinces made Ieyasu's holdings the largest in the land, larger in fact than Hideyoshi's. But the transfer moved Ieyasu farther from the center of political affairs, and it uprooted him and his followers from the areas where their historic roots were deepest and most secure. The move thus came as a shock to Ieyasu's senior vassals, who saw it as tantamount to exile.

The rapidity with which Ieyasu accomplished the Kantō transfer is amazing. Literally thousands of families had to pick up their entire households and equipment and find new houses in unfamiliar territory. And this had to be done with great expedition. Ieyasu received Hideyoshi's formal command on the thirteenth day of the seventh month. He had had some prior warning dating back to the fourth month and hence had been able to make some advance plans.[12] He entered the small castle of Edo, his new headquarters, by the first of

11 Kitajima, *Kenryoku kōzō*, pp. 189ff.
12 Kitajima, *Kenryoku kōzō*, p. 190; and Kitajima, *Edo bakufu*, pp. 132ff.

the eighth month. This was the official completion of his move, although it took nearly a year longer to settle in. Just as rapidly, Hideyoshi filled the castles given up by Ieyasu in the Tōkai provinces with his own trusted vassals.

The transfer into the Kantō was a major turning point in the Tokugawa fortunes, with results that were in many ways unanticipated, at least by Hideyoshi. The move out of the ancestral Mikawa homeland was bound to break the long-established ties of command among Ieyasu's vassal band, the lower village samurai, and the peasantry, thereby forcing Ieyasu to establish a network of command over an unfamiliar base.

There is some evidence that Hideyoshi expected the village samurai of the Kantō to give Ieyasu a difficult time. But Ieyasu's earlier experience in handling territories obtained by conquest – Kai Province won from Takeda was a good example – proved critical in the Kantō. Rather than displace the rural samurai and even some enfeoffed vassals left behind by the Hōjō, Ieyasu used them as best he could, recognizing the status they had held under the Hōjō and using them as rural intendants or recruiting them into his and his retainers' vassal bonds.

For all the difficulties that attended the transfer, possession of the Kantō – the historic homeland of the bushi class – provided Ieyasu with what was to prove the ideal base from which to win the national hegemony. Moreover, from the point of view of institutional development, the major difference between the domain structure of the daimyo of the Sengoku era and those of the Edo era was visible in the greater degree to which the latter had reduced the independence of their vassals. During the Sengoku era most bushi remained in the countryside living off their hereditary landholdings. This was true even for the high-ranking military officers with personal fiefs and even castles. Although independent enfeoffment meant that the daimyo overlord was less burdened by the need to provide shelter and maintenance for these members of his vassal band, he was at a disadvantage when it came to asserting his authority over them. The so-called Sengoku daimyo was lord of a decentralized domain made up of a patchwork of daimyo demesne and vassal fiefs. The daimyo of the seventeenth century had drawn their housemen, down to a fairly low level, away from their fiefs, thereby making them dependent on stipends paid out of the daimyo's granaries.[13] This condition is seen by

13 This practice distinguishes the possession of a land fief (*chigyō-chi*) from the rice stipend (*hōroku*). See Kanai, *Hansei*, pp. 38–43.

some scholars as indicative of the degree to which daimyo achieved the ultimate Edo period norm in sociopolitical evolution. Moreover it is apparent that in those parts of Japan where either the daimyo or the rural samurai, or both, had remained in place for several generations, daimyo authority over houseband vassals was harder to achieve. "Daimyo absolutism," as the capacity to exact domainwide compliance with directives from the castle headquarters has been called, flourished best where the private tie between the daimyo's houseband and the peasantry – in other words, the *jizamurai* system – had been completely destroyed.[14] The resulting structure was one in which the samurai had been drawn into the daimyo's castle headquarters and the peasantry had been placed under an impersonal field administration controlled from the central castle. There was thus a hidden advantage for Ieyasu in the forced transfer to the Kantō, for it obliged him to reorganize from scratch the relationship of his vassal band to the peasantry. The domain transfer was an experience that nearly all the daimyo who made the transition into the Edo period were to encounter at least once. One could say that it was almost a precondition for a successful transition into the *bakuhan* era.

Possession of the Kantō made Ieyasu lord of the largest domain in the country, well over twice the size of his Tōkai holdings. There is no accurate record of the total productive base of Ieyasu's Tōkai domain, but it is possible to get a general idea by extrapolation from the holdings of the daimyo who were placed in the territory vacated by Ieyasu in 1590. These add up to just over 1 million *koku*.[15] The extent of the Kantō domain taken over from the Hōjō is also not precisely known because of the complexity of the transfer and the fact that different methods of calculation were used at the time. In gross terms, however, the total was in the neighborhood of 2.5 million to 3.0 million *koku*. The task of administering and defending this greatly expanded territory meant that Ieyasu had either to delegate more authority to officers of his field administration or to expand his military and administrative personnel. He chose the latter method, relying on the services of both old and newly enrolled vassals. He, of course, took with him as many as possible of his own housemen. But he was still shorthanded and had to adopt into his service numerous samurai who had been left behind

---

14 For an analysis of the evolution of the "mature" *han* in terms of the progressive withdrawal of the samurai from their land fiefs, see Junnosuke Sasaki, with Ronald P. Toby, "The Changing Rationale of Daimyo Control in the Emergence of the Bakuhan State," in Hall, Nagahara, and Yamamura, eds., *Japan Before Tokugawa*, pp. 271–94.
15 Nakamura Kichiji, *Tokugawa*, p. 111.

by the Hōjō or who had been cast adrift in other provinces by the fortunes of war.[16]

As a master plan for his new domain, Ieyasu adopted Edo as his capital and distributed his retainers around Edo according to certain guidelines. Lands directly held by the head of the Tokugawa house as granary lands (*kurairi-chi* or *goryō*, later *tenryō*) were located close to Edo; small fief holders were placed not more than a single night's stopover away from Edo; and holders of large domains were placed at a greater distance from the center. These last were, for the most part, set out as castle holders and were situated with an eye to strategic location.

Ieyasu put the actual task of fief assignment into the hands of a team of officers with experience in land-tax administration. The team was under the supervision of Sakakibara Yasumasa (1548–1606), the first among his daimyo-class retainers and shortly to occupy the castle of Tatebayashi. The transition team worked quickly and effectively. It set aside lands with a total assessed value of roughly one million *koku* (the new standard unit of land assessment based on assessed rice production) for Ieyasu's private granary land. This, being about 39 percent of the total, was considerably more than the Hōjō chief had held. Granary land was placed under the administration of Ina Tadatsugu (1550–1610) and a group of subordinate land stewards. The latter were drawn in large part from personnel who remained in their ancestral villages and who had previously served the Takeda, Imagawa, or Hōjō. They were selected for their familiarity with the area.

The remaining territory was divided among Ieyasu's enfeoffed vassals. Of these, thirty-eight were assigned holdings of from 10,000 to 120,000 *koku*. This meant that they were of daimyo size and function, but they were not considered daimyo because they were rear vassals in the eyes of the national overlord. All together, this group held about 1 million *koku*. Thirty-two retainers holding from 2,000 to 5,000 *koku* accounted for another 142,000 *koku*, and several hundred lesser housemen each enfeoffed at less than 2,000 *koku* took up the remaining 426,000 *koku*. The initial fief distribution was carried out on the basis of the cadastral records obtained from the Hōjō. Because the Hōjō had retained the old monetary payment system of calculation (*kandaka*), the Tokugawa soon initiated a round of new surveys using

16 For a more limited example of vassal band organization by accretion, see my "The Ikeda House and Its Retainers in Bizen," in John W. Hall and Marius B. Jansen, eds., *Studies in the Institutional History of Early Modern Japan* (Princeton, N.J.: Princeton University Press, 1968) pp. 79–88. Also see Tsuji, *Edo kaifu*, pp. 54–6.

the rice-tax system.[17] It would take the next several decades for the Tokugawa to convert their Kantō holdings to the specifications of Hideyoshi's survey system (Taikō *kenchi*). Aside from the assignment of his military followers, Ieyasu was occupied with a mass of logistical problems. He faced the construction of a suitable castle, the draining of swampy land for urban construction, the drawing of fresh water into the city, and the improvement of port facilities.

Hideyoshi's last years

In the eight years from the fall of Odawara to the time of his death in 1598, Hideyoshi worked energetically, though rather erratically, to institutionalize his military power into a national government. Despite his domestic military successes, Hideyoshi still felt the need to demonstrate his powers of command over his vassal daimyo, even by compelling them to engage in foreign invasions. This would appear to be his main reason for the conquest of China that he attempted in 1590.[18] When the invasion ended in failure, many of the participating daimyo had been measurably weakened. And because the invasion was still in progress when Hideyoshi died, the fact that several important daimyo were out of the country at the time contributed to the political confusion that followed the hegemon's death.

Meanwhile Ieyasu, and a number of daimyo whose domains were located at great distances from the takeoff point for the invasion of Korea, had been spared a debilitating involvement in the venture. Ieyasu sent only a token backup force to northern Kyushu in 1592, and this did not see action. Ieyasu cleverly took the opportunity to expand and strengthen his Edo Castle and carry out military and civil administrative programs. Thus at the time of Hideyoshi's death in 1598, Ieyasu enjoyed a much more secure and powerful position than he had when he first acquired the Kantō provinces.

Although remarkably successful as a military leader, Hideyoshi proved less capable as a political organizer. Having beaten the daimyo into submission, he had difficulty in devising a governmental framework that would institutionalize his charismatic overlordship. What he eventually did was to graft his military power onto the social pres-

---

17 The earlier *kandaka* system of tax management, calculated in terms of monetary currency, is explained in Keiji Nagahara, with Kozo Yamamura, "The Sengoku Daimyo and the Kandaka System," in Hall, Nagahara, and Yamamura, eds., *Japan Before Tokugawa*, pp. 27–63.
18 The thesis that Hideyoshi used the invasion of Korea to safeguard his legitimacy is developed in Chapter 2 in this volume.

tige of the high nobility, legitimizing himself through the title of *kampaku* and by his close proximity to the throne.[19]

It was not until Hideyoshi realized that he was near the end of his life and that he was putting the fate of his succession on Hideyori (1593–1615), a child of five, that he tried to devise a formal system for delegating political authority. The task of safeguarding Toyotomi rule, he placed in the hands of a board of five regents (*go-tairō*). They were selected from among the most powerful of Hideyoshi's allies: namely, Tokugawa Ieyasu, who was to remain in Fushimi Castle as chief policymaker and head of the board; Maeda Toshiie (1538–99), who was assigned to Osaka Castle as guardian to Hideyori; Mōri Terumoto (1553–1625); Kobayakawa Takakage (1533–97) (later succeeded by Uesegi Kagekatsu); and Ukita Hideie (1573–1655). The more administrative aspects of government became the responsibility of a board of five commissioners (*go-bugyō*): Asano Nagamasa (1544–1611), Maeda Gen'i (1539–1602), Ishida Mitsunari (1560–1600), Mashita Nagamori (1545–1615), and Natsuka Masaie (?–1600). All five had served for many years as members of Hideyoshi's house administration.

This arrangement did create a central authority of sorts, able to make and carry out national policy in the immediate aftermath of Hideyoshi's death, as it did in calling off the Korean campaign. But the structure was inherently unstable, and once Hideyoshi passed from the scene it began to fall apart. The members of the two boards were too involved in their own domestic problems, so that one by one they abandoned the capital area on grounds of urgent business. The death of Maeda Toshiie in 1599 made Ieyasu by far the most experienced and powerful among the regents, and when on his own initiative he moved into the position in Osaka Castle vacated by Maeda Toshiie, he was recognized as the obvious *tenka-dono* (lord of the realm).

Winning the tenka

Ieyasu's path from here to the acquisition of recognized national leadership was not easily traversed. There were a number of powerful daimyo heads of large daimyo leagues, located mainly in western Japan, who were not ready to accept a takeover by Ieyasu without a struggle. There were also a number of lesser daimyo whose entire careers had been spent in the service of Hideyoshi and whose fortunes were thereby tied to a continuation of the Toyotomi polity.

19 See footnote 4.

This group consisted of house daimyo, like the five magistrates, and Hideyoshi's close field generals like Katō Kiyōmasa, Kuroda Naga-masa, and Fukushima Masanori. Their center of activity was Osaka Castle. But their cause lacked a single charismatic leader who could keep them united, and it soon became apparent that major differ-ences of opinion divided the so-called administrative (bugyō) group from the generals.

Ieyasu did not openly declare his ambition to succeed Hideyoshi to national hegemony, but increasingly he began to act the part. For instance, he entered into marriage alliances with other daimyo on his own authority. In early 1600, after Maeda Toshiie's death, he moved from Fushimi into the western enclosure of Osaka Castle. The numer-ous letters he directed to his fellow daimyo at this time were couched in statesmanlike terms of concern for the maintenance of peace.[20] When Uesugi Kagekatsu (1555–1623), who had joined the ranks of the regents after Maeda Toshiie's death, was reported to be mobilizing troops in his domain centered on Aizu, a location that threatened the Tokugawa rear, Ieyasu expressed alarm and called for a counter-mobilization, ordering nearby daimyo to prepare a move again Aizu.

By now Ieyasu was issuing orders as though he had full national authority, and he was being courted by daimyo members of the Toyotomi coalition who began to offer him pledges of support, even sending hostages as a safeguard for the future. Among these were members of the Toyotomi "generals" group and others like the Ikeda (of Bizen) and the Yamanouchi (of Tōtōmi). By the summer of 1600, the country divided increasingly between those who saw an advantage to supporting the Osaka group based on Hideyori's potential as a symbol of national unity and those who saw Ieyasu as the inevitable hegemon of the future. The Osaka faction had among its most power-ful supporters the Ukita, Chōsokabe, Mōri, Konishi, Nabeshima, and Shimazu, daimyo whose lands were mainly in provinces west of Osaka and out of Ieyasu's immediate reach. The supporters who clustered around Ieyasu were mainly based in the east.

Ishida Mitsunari, the prime mover of the western faction, de-nounced Ieyasu's move against Aizu as a usurpation of national author-ity and called for punitive action. He assembled a large military force and began to march toward the Kantō. Ieyasu, having anticipated this move, left the Aizu operation to others, notably Date Masamune and

---

20 Ieyasu's correspondence is conveniently arranged by Kuwata Tadachika in *Tokugawa Ieyasu, sono tegami to ningen* (Tokyo: Shin jimbutsu ōraisha, 1971).

Yūki Hideyasu, and quickly prepared to meet the threat from Osaka. As he led his army out of the Kantō, all the daimyo along the way opened their castles to him, detaching forces to join the mobilization. On the fifteenth day of the ninth month (October 21, 1600), the combined armies of the two factions met in battle at Sekigahara. It is estimated that the eastern league committed some seventy thousand men to the engagement. The western league fielded some eighty thousand men, but they were poorly positioned and of uncertain reliability. Only about half of them went into action. The battle was in doubt throughout the morning, but the defection of Kobayakawa turned the tide. Victory went to the eastern coalition.

Ieyasu used the victory at Sekigahara to assert his national authority over the military estate and to make drastic changes in the composition and placement of the daimyo and their holdings throughout Japan.[21] In the immediate aftermath of the battle, eighty-seven daimyo who had opposed Ieyasu were defeated and their lands confiscated. The lands of three others were drastically reduced in size. All together, a total of 6,221,690 *koku* were taken from Ieyasu's daimyo opponents. Another 1.35 million *koku* were taken from the Toyotomi house and made available for reallocation to other daimyo or for inclusion in Ieyasu's personal holdings. Even greater changes were brought about by the transfer of forty-three daimyo from one location to another and the creation of new daimyo. The authority to invest new daimyo rested on Ieyasu's claim to hegemony over the warrior estate. Prior to the battle Ieyasu counted among his cadet branch heads and hereditary housemen forty whose holdings were of 10,000 *koku* or more. He was now able to set these men out as full-fledged daimyo under his own patent. All were given domain increases. Another twenty members of his houseband who, as of 1600, held fiefs of less than 10,000 *koku* were raised to daimyo status. Finally, he granted daimyo status to eight rear vassals who had distinguished themselves in Ieyasu's eyes.

All these confiscations, reassignments, and new creations added up to the greatest transfer of landholding in Japanese history. As a result, the balance of power was heavily tilted in Ieyasu's favor. But it was not by any means secure or properly legitimized. In the immediate aftermath of Sekigahara, as the troops of the eastern coalition poured into Osaka, Ieyasu undoubtedly had the military capacity to take over Osaka Castle, at the time defended by Mōri Terumoto on behalf of

21 The most recent and detailed treatment of the Sekigahara settlement is found in the work of Fujino Tamotsu, especially *Bakuhan taisei shi no kenkyū*, p. 150.

Toyotomi Hideyori and his mother Lady Yodo. But Ieyasu was a sworn trustee of the Toyotomi polity, and many of his most powerful supporters in the recent confrontation still had strong emotional ties to Hideyoshi. Ieyasu was also sobered by the fact that he had few trustworthy allies in the western provinces. Hideyori, though suffering a loss of nearly two-thirds of the domain left by his father, was therefore allowed to retain Osaka Castle and a 650,000-*koku* domain in the surrounding provinces of Settsu, Kawachi, and Izumi. Although reduced to the status of daimyo in the world of the military hegemon, in the eyes of the court, Hideyori merited high rank as heir to Hideyoshi, who had retired with the high rank of Taikō. It was clear to all that the Tokugawa reality and the Toyotomi memory could not coexist for long, but Ieyasu, hoping to avoid a war that would reopen the question of the ultimate loyalty of the military houses, felt constrained to put off the final confrontation until 1614–15.

FORMATION OF THE EDO BAKUFU

In 1602, the Shimazu house of southern Kyushu acknowledged Ieyasu's overlordship, thus completing the Sekigahara settlement. A year later Ieyasu was installed as *sei-i tai-shōgun* by Emperor Go-Yōzei. In anticipation of this appointment that would legitimize him as chief of the warrior estate (*buke no tōryō*), Ieyasu had put together a genealogy that showed his descent from the Minamoto line. Concurrently with his new appointment he received the traditional designations *Genji no chōja* (chief of the Minamoto lineage), *Junna, Shōgaku ryōin bettō* (rector of the Junna and Shōgaku colleges), second court rank, and *udaijin* (minister of the right). These grandiloquent titles did not in themselves add new political or military weight to Ieyasu, but as tokens of legitimacy, they all were important. And their importance was underlined by the fact that Hideyori, although only ten years of age, received the title of inner minister (*naidaijin*) at the same time. Osaka Castle, because of Hideyori's high court rank, held certain powers of appointment and recommendation to the court that paralleled those of Ieyasu. Obviously Hideyori was the darling of the court and was being used as a means of court involvement in warrior political affairs. The closer the center of warrior officers came to Kyoto, the deeper this involvement became.

In 1605, Ieyasu turned over the office of shogun to his son Hidetada. Adopting the style of *ōgosho* (retired shogun), he established himself in the subsidiary castle of Sumpu where he surrounded himself with advisers of his own selection.[22] Hidetada was inducted as shogun at the Tokugawa residence in Kyoto. Entering Kyoto at the head of more than 100,000 men he used the occasion to impress on the country the power of his house. The great bulk of these troops were provided by the daimyo of eastern Japan who thereby reiterated their loyalty to the shogun.

Ieyasu's move was no retirement, no effort to ease the pressures of official life. Rather, it was a way of making the Tokugawa succession more secure, both by setting a precedent of direct succession and by making sure that the next shogun was safely in place before Ieyasu's death, thus frustrating any effort to promote Hideyori as an alternative head of state. Most important to the future of the bakufu, it gave Ieyasu a free hand to develop basic strategy and policy. At Sumpu, Ieyasu assembled what has been called a private "brain trust" to assist him in devising policy. Among these were the Tendai priest Tenkai (1536–1643), who served as Ieyasu's spiritual adviser and was instrumental in having the first shogun's grave established at Nikkō; Hayashi Razan, the Confucian scholar who assisted Ieyasu in drafting the legal codes; Ina Tadatsugu, a specialist on local administration; Gotō Mitsutsugu, founder of the Silver Mint (Ginza) and adviser on currency policy; and even the English navigator, William Adams.

There was much to be done. The administrative organs of shogunal government were yet to be adequately designed. The organization and assignment of the bakufu officials were not complete. The relocation of daimyo for political and strategic purposes would require many more years and many more moves and confiscations before the Tokugawa house could feel secure. There were numerous problems of overall political control of such groups as the emperor and his court, the temples and shrines, the peasants and merchants, and the foreign intruders from Europe and China.

But what most pressed on Ieyasu's mind was the threat of Toyotomi Hideyori and Osaka Castle. The problem became more acute each year as Hideyori came ever closer to maturity. There was already talk in the court circles of his being ready for appointment as *kampaku*.[23] And there were those in Kyoto who saw no harm in creating a dual head of state, one military and the other civil. In 1611 Ieyasu's greatest fears were confirmed when he arranged to meet Hideyori at Nijō

---

22 Naohiro Asao, with Marius B. Jansen, "Shogun and Tenno," in Hall, Nagahara, and Yamamura, eds., *Japan Before Tokugawa*, pp. 259–60.
23 The Hideyori threat to Ieyasu is analyzed in Harold Bolitho, *Treasures Among Men: The Fudai Daimyo in Tokugawa Japan* (New Haven, Conn.: Yale University Press, 1974), pp. 3–6.

Castle in Kyoto. Ieyasu's nervousness was reflected in his demand shortly thereafter, on the occasion of celebrations in honor of Emperor Go-Mizuno-ō's accession, that all daimyo swear a special oath of allegiance to him as the head of the military estate.

But Ieyasu knew full well that such an oath was not a solution. And so he resorted to a number of strategems to weaken the Osaka faction. One was to encourage them to exhaust the huge bullion supply stored in Osaka Castle to build temple monuments in Hideyoshi's memory. But in the end it took military action. Over a contrived issue in the winter of 1614, Ieyasu launched an attack on Osaka Castle. Although Hideyori failed to recruit a single active daimyo to his cause, Osaka Castle filled with ex-daimyo defeated at Sekigahara and masterless warriors set adrift by the destruction of so many daimyo housebands. An estimated ninety thousand defenders, many of them Christian, managed to hold off a force estimated at twice that number under Tokugawa command. Despite the use of newly acquired firearms by the attacking force, Osaka Castle proved impregnable. The first siege failed at a heavy cost in lives, and Ieyasu realized that a continuation of the assault using the same strategy could lead to humiliating defeat. Clearly, he had come to the most critical juncture of his career: An obvious victory by the Osaka faction would likely turn against him a large number of daimyo who had once been pledged to Hideyoshi but who joined the Tokugawa between 1598 and 1600. In this extremity Ieyasu called for a political compromise and a military truce, one provision of which called for the elimination of parts of the moats and defenses surrounding the castle. Hideyori, or rather his mother Lady Yodo, agreed to the truce only to realize too late that the Tokugawa work gangs brought in to fill in moats had gone too far. Once the castle's defenses had been seriously weakened, Ieyasu renewed his attack in May of 1615. In this so-called summer campaign, he was successful. Osaka Castle was entered and burned. Hideyori and his mother committed suicide. At long last the Toyotomi memory had been destroyed.

Hidetada and Iemitsu

Barely a year after the destruction of the Osaka faction, Ieyasu died. But he left for his successors a firm foundation on which to base an enduring political order. He had achieved what neither Nobunaga nor Hideyoshi had been able to do, the creation of a structure of political allegiances that could transcend the person of the hegemon, making the office of shogun the permanent object of national loyalty and obedience. This obviously was Ieyasu's main intent when he resigned the office of shogun. During the "Ōgosho era" he was able to take a number of important steps toward the institutionalization of the post of shogun. Toward the Kyoto court he exploited every occasion to impose his authority. A particularly sensitive issue was control over the award of court titles to members of the bushi class. In 1613, on the occasion of a court intrigue involving Hideyori, Ieyasu had promulgated a code of regulations, the Kuge shohatto, directed toward the nobility and restricting their involvement in political affairs. Documents of this sort were reworked and resubmitted after the victory at Osaka. The result was the Kinchū narabini kuge shohatto, a set of regulations that applied to the emperor and the Kyoto nobles, restricting them to the traditional arts and ceremonials and limiting their appointment authority. It effectively screened the civil nobility from the military aristocracy and their government.

Toward the daimyo Ieyasu had directed numerous regulations and demands for pledges of loyalty. The first such command following the victory at Osaka was the order limiting each daimyo to a single castle (*ikkoku ichijō rei*), an action that signaled the start of a new order of peace in which warfare among the daimyo was not to be countenanced. A few months later, the Buke shohatto (Laws for military households) was issued in a new and extended form.

Despite all that Ieyasu had achieved, the two shoguns who followed him did not have an easy time, for it was they who were given the task of consolidating the relations among shogun, emperor, and daimyo. As Asao Naohiro has pointed out, neither Hidetada nor Iemitsu received automatic recognition as national hegemon.[24] Whereas Ieyasu was accepted as chief of the military estate on the basis of his military successes, his successors did not have the opportunities to enhance their charisma through military exploits. Hidetada did see action in the Osaka investments, but under his father's command. Following Ieyasu's death he thus felt the need to pursue several lines to back up his claim to leadership of the bushi class. First, he made conspicuous display of the shogun's authority to act in matters of high national policy. His strict enforcement of prohibitions against Christianity and his early steps toward the regulation of foreign trade were calculated to gain general recognition for the shogun as the political head of state. In

24 The problem of legitimation faced by Ieyasu's successors as shogun is discussed by Asao, "Shogun and Tenno," pp. 265–90.

both instances Hidetada could claim to be the "protector" of the Japanese homeland against foreign enemies.

Second, the Tokugawa shoguns, as had Nobunaga and Hideyoshi, used the emperor for political effect. On the one hand, posing as patrons of the emperor, the shogun expended or requisitioned conspicuous financial resources to build palaces and residences for members of the court. On the other hand, he did everything to make the emperor the shogun's private legitimizer. This was accomplished in part by the enforcement of regulations limiting the court's contact with members of the warrior elite and by deepening relations between the Tokugawa house and the court, ultimately through intermarriage. In 1620 Hidetada's daughter was married to Emperor Go-Mizuno-ō. A daughter of this union born in 1623 took the throne as Meishō in 1629. This was the first time since the eighth century that a woman had been named empress, a clear demonstration that the Tokugawa house had succeeded in acquiring supreme status in both the military and noble hierarchies.

We are reminded of the close relationship that existed between the shogun and the imperial institution under the Ashikaga house. But the location of the Edo bakufu in the Kantō, some three hundred miles to the east, meant that the Tokugawa relationship was more institutional than personal. Much greater emphasis was placed on control. The Edo bakufu's presence in Kyoto was exhibited in the massive Nijō Castle, home of the shogun's deputy, the Kyoto *shoshidai*. Furthermore, the provisions that squeezed the more than three hundred aristocratic families into the palace enclosure (*gyoen*) in Kyoto exemplified the restraints that the shogun was capable of imposing.[25]

The crowning touch to the effort to legitimize the Tokugawa house was the successful deification of Ieyasu as Tōshō daigongen (Great shining deity of the east). Under the third shogun, Iemitsu, a shrine to Ieyasu was established at Nikkō. In time, daimyo, presumably on their own initiative, set up in their home territories scaled-down versions of the Nikkō shrine where they could hold services in memory of Ieyasu. The Nikkō Tōshōgu received from the emperor the same rank as the imperial shrine at Ise. The periodic grand progresses to Nikkō called by later shoguns served to direct national attention to Ieyasu's special place in history.[26]

25 For a map of the *kuge* quarters in Kyoto, see my "Kyoto As Historical Background," in John W. Hall and Jeffrey P. Mass, eds., *Medieval Japan, Essays in Institutional History* (New Haven, Conn.: Yale University Press, 1974), pp. 33–8.
26 Willem Jan Boot, "The Deification of Tokugawa Ieyasu," a research report in *Japan Foundation Newsletter* 14, no. 5 (1987): 10–13.

THE *BAKUHAN* POWER STRUCTURE

In the final analysis it was the shogunate's capacity to govern the daimyo that gave stability to the *bakuhan* state. In turn, this capacity rested on the maintenance of a favorable balance of power. The concept of balance implies differences in degree of attachment or of reliability under shogunal command among several categories of daimyo, particularly between the "house" daimyo (*fudai*) and the "outside" daimyo (*tozama*). At the time of Ieyasu's death, the balance could not yet be considered secure from the Tokugawa point of view, and the process of rearrangement continued for the rest of the seventeenth century. (See Map 4.1.) Whereas changes in the composition and location of daimyo were a natural outcome of victory or defeat in battle, in times of peace other justifications had to be given for making such changes. By keeping the relationship between daimyo and shogun a precarious one and by making the daimyo accountable to bakufu regulations and codes of conduct, the shogun was given numerous opportunities to transfer, reduce in size, or disinherit any daimyo. Transfers, of course, were not necessarily ordered for punitive reasons; they most often were ordered as a sign of favor from the shogun, usually involving assignment to a larger domain in a strategically more important location. Reductions and seizures were the result of disciplinary action by the shogun. Using the provisions of the Buke shohatto, the shogun could penalize a daimyo for failing to produce a natural heir, for making repairs on his castle without obtaining permission, for making unauthorized marriage alliances, and many other seemingly minor acts that violated the code.

Fujino Tamotsu calculated the total figures for confiscations of daimyo holdings for each shogun of the Edo regime.[27] The figures for the first five shoguns are shown in Table 4.1. Not counting the Sekigahara settlement, a total of some 13.2 million *koku* (equivalent to one-half of the country's total taxable land base) changed hands under the first five Tokugawa shoguns. These lands were reassigned to other daimyo or added to the shogun's demesne. In the process, a large number of outside daimyo were eliminated, among them such notable participants in the Tokugawa rise to power as Katō Kiyomasa (1562–1611) and Fukushima Masanori (1561–1624), while the number of house daimyo increased in numbers. All told, under these shoguns some 200 daimyo had been destroyed; 172 had been newly created; 200 had received increases in holdings; and 280 had their domains

27 Fujino Tamotsu, "On'ei roku – haizetsu roku," in his *Bakusei to hansei* (Tokyo: Yoshikawa kōbunkan, 79), pp. 42–3.

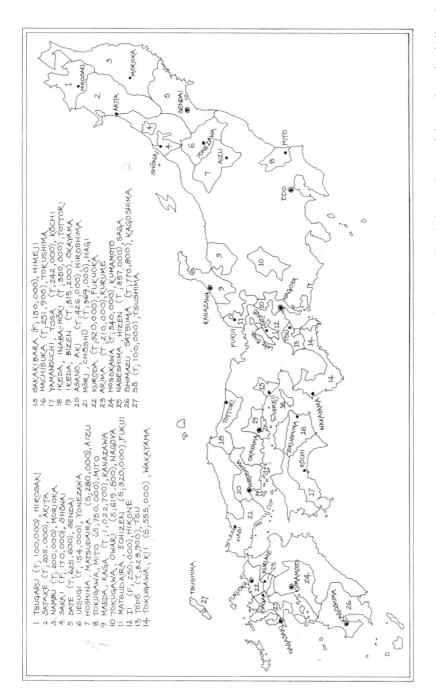

1 TSUGARU (T; 100,000), HIROSAKI
2 SATAKE (T; 205,000), AKITA
3 NAMBU (T; 200,000), MORIOKA
4 SAKAI (F; 170,000), SHŌNAI
5 DATE (T; 625,600), SENDAI
6 UESUGI (T; 154,000), YONEZAWA
7 HOSHINA, MATSUDAIRA (S; 280,000), AIZU
8 TOKUGAWA, MITO (S; 750,000), MITO
9 MAEDA, KAGA (T; 1,022,700), KANAZAWA
10 TOKUGAWA, OWARI (S; 619,500), NAGOYA
11 MATSUDAIRA, ECHIZEN (S; 320,000), FUKUI
12 II (F; 250,000), HIKONE
13 TŌDŌ (T; 323,900), TSU
14 TOKUGAWA, KII (S; 555,000), WAKAYAMA
15 SAKAKIBARA (F; 150,000), HIMEJI
16 HACHISUKA (T; 251,900), TOKUSHIMA
17 YAMANOUCHI, TOSA (T; 242,000), KŌCHI
18 IKEDA, INABA-HŌKI (T; 350,000), TOTTORI
19 IKEDA, BIZEN (T; 315,200), OKAYAMA
20 ASANO, AKI (T; 426,000), HIROSHIMA
21 MŌRI, CHŌSHŪ (T; 369,000), HAGI
22 KURODA (T; 520,000), FUKUOKA
23 ARIMA (T; 210,000), KURUME
24 HOSOKAWA (T; 540,000), KUMAMOTO
25 NABESHIMA, HIZEN (T; 357,000), SAGA
26 SHIMAZU, SATSUMA (T; 770,800), KAGOSHIMA
27 SŌ (T; 100,000), TSUSHIMA

Map 4.1 Major daimyo domains and capital cities, mid-seventeenth century. The information on daimyo domains is listed in the following order: daimyo house name, province, status (T *tozama*, F *fudai*, S *shimpan*), domain size in *koku*, and capital city.

TABLE 4.1
Confiscations of daimyo holdings, 1601–1705

Shogun	Daimyo (No.) (*tozama/fudai*)	Amounts confiscated (*koku*)
Ieyasu (1601–16)	41 (28/13)	3,594,640
Hidetaka (1616–31)	38 (23/15)	3,605,420
Iemitsu (1632–50)	46 (28/18)	3,580,100
Ietsuna (1651–79)	28 (16/12)	728,000
Tsunayoshi (1680–1705)	45 (17/28)	1,702,982
Total	198 (112/86)	(13,211,142)

transferred. By the time of Tsunayoshi's death in 1709 the purposeful reassignment of daimyo had been carried out in sufficient favor of the shogunate that the rate of attainder fell off dramatically.

The structure of power over which the Tokugawa shogun ultimately presided was conceived as a balance among several classes of daimyo and the interests of the shogun. The elements of this balance need further clarification. To begin, at the top of the hierarchy were the collateral houses, the so-called *shimpan* (or *ichimon* or *kamon*). These eventually numbered 23. The house or hereditary daimyo, or *fudai*, by the end of the eighteenth century numbered 145. The remnants of the daimyo who had been brought into being by either Nobunaga or Hideyoshi, the so-called outside lords (*tozama*), numbered 98. The Tokugawa house itself constituted the single largest power bloc. In 1722 the shogun's enfeoffed bannermen (*hatamoto*) numbered as many as 5,200 individuals, while his stipended housemen (*gokenin*) numbered an estimated 17,399. The latter were sustained on stipends derived from the shogun's granary lands. In addition there were nonofficer-grade foot soldiers (*ashigaru*) and clerks (*dōshin*) in the uncounted thousands. At the end of the first century after the founding of the Edo shogunate, the division of taxable landholdings among these several groups was calculated as follows:[28]

Imperial house land	141,151 *koku*
Shogun's granary land (*tenryō*)	4,213,171 *koku*
Shogun's bannermen (*hatamoto*)	2,606,545 *koku*
Shogun's house daimyo (*fudai*) and collateral daimyo (*shimpan*)	9,325,300 *koku*
Outside lords (*tozama*)	9,834,700 *koku*

28 A convenient listing of the 243 daimyo existing in 1698 is reproduced in Kanai, *Hansei*, pp. 60–73. In English, see a similar list in Conrad Totman, *Politics in the Tokugawa Bakufu 1600–1843* (Cambridge, Mass.: Harvard University Press, 1967), pp. 264–8.

Domainal productive capacity, as expressed in *koku*, was the first and most easily demonstrated measure of the relative strength of the several classes of daimyo.[29] Other factors such as geographical distribution and control of strategic and economically valuable locations were taken into account as well. The shogun's granary lands were located in forty-seven of the sixty-eight provinces, accounting for roughly a sixth of the country's productive base. If we add to this the bannermen's holdings, the percentage rises to close to a quarter. These holdings were heavily concentrated in the Kantō and the Tōkai provinces, but they also extended into central and western Japan. The actual distribution of *tenryō* by region shows 1.026 million *koku* in the Kantō, 687,000 in the capital area, 688,000 in the Tōkai provinces, 1.353 million in the region north of the Kantō, 412,000 in western Honshu and Shikoku, and 176,000 in Kyushu.[30] As European visitors to Japan in the seventeenth century commented, it was possible to travel from Osaka to Edo without having to leave bakufu territory. Not only was the *tenryō* well located to serve the tax need of the bakufu, it also contained most of the important urban centers, such as Edo, Osaka, Sakai, Kyoto, Fushimi, Nara, and Nagasaki. The shogun had also gained possession of the country's active silver and copper mines. The bakufu, through its authority over the *tenryō* and the fief lands of the bannermen, was directly in control of a commanding section of the country, whether measured in terms of land, manpower, commercial capacity, or institutional importance. But however large the shogun's direct holdings, government under the Tokugawa house remained a coalition between shogun and daimyo, as the term *bakuhan* reminds us.

To understand the several types of daimyo, their relationship to the shogun, and the significance of their geographic distribution, we need first to look back to origins.[31] There were, first, the self-made daimyo, those who had come into existence before the appearance of Oda Nobunaga. Among these were the Shimazu of southern Kyushu and the Nabeshima of northern Kyushu, the Mōri of western Honshu, and the Satake, Date, Nambu, Mogami, and Uesegi in the provinces north of Edo. These long-established houses had managed to survive the wars of consolidation, in many cases holding on to their original do-

29 Harold Bolitho has cautioned that *kokudaka* figures were not a sure sign of daimyo power, nor should one expect that these figures would hold constant throughout the era. See Chapter 5 in this volume.
30 Kitajima, *Kenryoku kōzō*, p. 332.
31 The difficulty that scholars have in classifying daimyo types is well explained in Chapter 5 in this volume.

mains and gaining acceptance as *tozama* from each of the unifiers, including the Tokugawa shogun. For the most part, their domains were of considerable size but were located on the fringes of the Japanese islands. Next were the daimyo who owed their existence to Oda Nobunaga. Only a few of these survived, among them the Maeda of Kaga, the Ikeda of Bizen, the Yamanouchi of Tosa, and the Kuroda of Buzen. Next came the daimyo created by Hideyoshi. Again, precious few of these survived Sekigahara. Among them were some of the "generals" groups such as Kato Kiyōmasa of Higo, who had managed to cast his lot with Ieyasu before Sekigahara.

In the middle of the seventeenth century, the vast majority of daimyo lines had been created by the heads of the Tokugawa house. The Tokugawa daimyo, as noted earlier, were divided first into the collaterals (*ichimon*) and the house or hereditary daimyo (*fudai*). Ieyasu, in contrast with Nobunaga and Hideyoshi, fathered a large number of capable offspring; moreover, he lived long enough to see to the survival of more than enough cadet branches to safeguard the Tokugawa line. The collaterals were used in two particular ways: first, to protect the Tokugawa family from failure to provide an heir and, second, to hold strategically important locations. Among the collaterals, three lines established by direct descent from Ieyasu were given the privilege of bearing the Tokugawa surname. Ieyasu's ninth son was assigned the Owari domain (619,500 *koku*) centering on Nagoya. His tenth son was given the Kii domain (555,000 *koku*) in Wakayama, and his eleventh son was placed in the province of Hitachi (250,000 *koku*). These three Tokugawa branches, collectively known as the three houses (*sanke*), were available for shogunal succession should the main line started by Hidetada fail to produce an heir. In fact, this did happen following the death of Ietsugu, the seventh shogun, and Yoshimune was brought in from the Kii branch of the house to serve as the eighth shogun.

Strictly for the purpose of safeguarding the succession, three additional collateral lines were established in the mid-eighteenth century, two by Yoshimune and one by his son Ieshige. These were the Hitotsubashi, Tayasu, and Shimizu families, collectively called the three lords (*san kyō*). Not strictly daimyo, they had no domains but were assigned residential quarters in Edo Castle and received stipends of 100,000 *koku* each from the shogun's treasury. These three houses in time played important roles in shogunal politics, as is shown by the fact that both the eleventh and fifteenth shoguns came from the Hitotsubashi line.

There were other collaterals and simulated cadet houses. Under the first three shoguns, various favored sons were given the Matsudaira surname and provided with suitable domains. Such were the Matsudaira houses of Aizu and Echizen. All in all, the Tokugawa house was remarkably successful in safeguarding its succession, thereby avoiding debilitating succession quarrels or the possibility of takeover by a subordinate house exercising power through a puppet shogun.

Fudai daimyo held status within the shogun's houseband in early protocol according to the time and place of the first enrollment in the houseband. The oldest of these lines can be traced back to the Okazaki Castle or the Sumpu Castle years, although the majority were products of later stages in the rise of the Tokugawa house. From the standpoint of power politics, of course, size and location were more significant. At the end of the Edo era, of the 145 house daimyo, 14 held domains of 100,000 *koku* or more; 36 had domains assessed between 50,000 and 99,000 *koku;* 64 between 11,000 and 49,000 *koku;* and 31 held the minimum of 10,000 *koku.*

The majority of the *fudai* were placed in the Kantō close to Edo. This was true particularly for those at the lower levels of the *koku* scale. The larger among the *fudai*, however, were placed at strategically important spots across the country. The Okudaira of Utsunomiya (77,000 *koku*) for instance, were located to provide additional protection to Edo from one of the city's northern approaches. The Ii were given the critically important domain of Hikone (350,000 *koku*) that stood guard at the approach to Kyoto from the east. On the other side of the capital, the domain of Himeji (150,000 *koku*) was considered guardian of the western approach. First held by the Ikeda house (*tozama*), it was eventually placed in the hands of the Sakai house (*fudai*).

Farther to the west, house daimyo were placed at Matsue, Tsuyama, and Fukuyama. On Shikoku, daimyo bearing the Matsudaira surname held Takamatsu and Matsuyama on the island's two northern corners. On Kyushu, however, the Tokugawa were not well represented. The Ogasawara at Kokura (150,000 *koku*) and the Ōkubo of Karatsu (60,000 *koku*) were the prime daimyo representatives of the shogun, and the port of Nagasaki, held in rotation by bakufu-appointed governors, served as the shogunate's main bureaucratic center for the control of foreign trade.

Why, given the number of daimyo destroyed by the shogun in the years after Sekigahara, did not Ieyasu and his successors simply preempt domains at will and assign their own men to them at their own

discretion? To some extent, this is what was done on a small scale by
the expansion of the shogun's granary lands. But the scale was modest.
The fact is that the Tokugawa shoguns, from the first to the last,
considered the daimyo a necessary element of national administration.
That is, the daimyo were not thought of as enemies of effective government but, rather, as necessities. Throughout the formative period of
the Edo shogunate, the effort was to find capable and reliable daimyo,
not to destroy them. Clearly, daimyo could not be artificially fabricated. Experience in the handling of men and lands at one level was a
prerequisite for advancement to a higher level. For example, a small
fief holder, say a bannerman of 1,000 *koku,* could not be raised to
daimyo status in a single move. Among the house daimyo, those who
after the move into the Kantō had received domains of 100,000 *koku*
were later advanced into the 150,000-*koku* range but no higher, and
those in the 30,000 range were held below the 100,000 range. A sense
of proportion was clearly involved.

THE EDO SHOGUNATE: THE AUTHORITY STRUCTURE

By taking the office of shogun as his prime means of legitimation
Tokugawa Ieyasu followed the precedent established by the two previous shogunates. As shogun, he claimed recognition as chief of the
bushi estate and, as the emperor's delegate, the rights and responsibilities of national governance. In describing the Edo regime in its early
phases, historians until recently have dwelt on the factor of rights and
perquisites, almost to the exclusion of responsibilities. But the existence of an implicit compact on the part of the shogun to serve as
guardian of the state (the *tenka*) and protector of its people was acknowledged by the shoguns themselves, particularly with regard to
matters involving foreign relations, as in the cases of the spread of
Christianity in the mid-seventeenth century and of foreign intrusion in
the mid-nineteenth century. It was this publicly acknowledged responsibility, and right, to conduct foreign relations that most clearly distinguished the Edo bakufu's status in the hierarchy of national affairs.
    In domestic affairs the most important of the shogun's rights and
responsibilities derived from his position as the ultimate proprietor of
the country's taxable land. This right was comprehensive and applied
to all proprietary holding of land, whether by members of the court
nobility or of the religious orders. The corresponding responsibility
was the shogun's duty to provide good government, a task that he
shared with the daimyo. Under the Edo polity, the proprietary posses-

sion of land was legally possible only when certified by the shogun's seal. This was particularly significant in the case of the daimyo, all of whom were the shogun's sworn vassals who held their domains as personal grants from him.

As supreme proprietary overlord, the shogun assumed the right to regulate all lesser proprietors, be they courtier, priest, or warrior aristocrat. This regulatory authority was spelled out in a series of codes (*hatto*) directed toward each of these groups. Note has already been taken of the orders covering the court and the daimyo; a closer look needs to be taken of the latter.[32] Ieyasu had anticipated this document in the three-clause oath of allegiance he had demanded of all daimyo in 1611 and 1612. Its provisions called for obedience to bakufu laws and agreement not to harbor disloyal or criminal samurai. The Buke shohatto in its first extended form of thirteen clauses was issued in 1615 following the Tokugawa victory at Osaka. It began with what was to become a trademark of the Edo shogunate's political philosophy for a military government functioning in an era of peace: "The study of letters and the practice of military arts, including archery and horsemanship, must be cultivated diligently." There followed admonitions against unruly conduct, luxurious living, and failure to abide by dress regulations. But the heart of the code was concerned with matters of control. Daimyo must not harbor antibakufu criminals in their domains. They must not repair or enlarge their castles without permission from the bakufu. They must gain shogunal approval before contracting a marriage. And they must report suspicious activities in neighboring domains.

From the time of Ieyasu the Buke shohatto was read before the assembled daimyo at the inauguration of each new shogun. Iemitsu, the third shogun, made the most changes in its content, increasing the provisions to twenty-one with the addition of prohibitions against private trade barriers, against ships of more than a five hundred-*koku* burden, and against the propagation of Christianity. This version clarified as well the provisions of alternate attendance (*sankin-kōtai*) and reiterated the decree that all laws emanating from Edo be obeyed as the law of the land.[33]

Unquestionably the most effective mechanism developed by the

---

32 Translation of this and other Tokugawa bakufu laws can be found in Ryusaku Tsunoda, William Theodore de Bary, and Donald Keene, eds., *Sources of Japanese Tradition* (New York: Columbia University Press, 1958).
33 Toshio G. Tsukahira, *Feudal Control in Tokugawa Japan: The Sankin Kotai System* (Cambridge, Mass.: Harvard East Asia Research Center, 1966).

Tokugawa shoguns was the alternative attendance requirement. At first applied selectively to *tozama* daimyo, it was made mandatory for all daimyo, including *fudai*, by Iemitsu in 1642. This extension of the common practice among the bushi commanders of taking hostages to ensure the loyalty of vassals and military allies obliged all daimyo to establish residences in the environs of Edo Castle so as to be available to pay regular attendance on the shogun. In their Edo residences, daimyo were required to domicile their wives, children, and a certain number of chief retainers, together with the necessary staff to maintain the official residences. Daimyo were permitted to return to their home domains in alternate years (in some instances, in alternate half-years) but were required to leave their wives and children and ranking retainers in Edo as hostages.

As a method of assisting shogunal authority, this practice continually affirmed Edo's political centrality. By means of alternate attendance, the shogun was able continuously to assemble the daimyo in Edo Castle for rituals and other gatherings. Communication between the bakufu and the daimyo was thereby made immediate and personal. Aside from these considerable advantages to the bakufu, there were other, perhaps unintended, side effects of alternate attendance. The maintenance of dual residences, at home and in Edo, and the expenses of frequent travel between them imposed a massive drain on the daimyo's treasury, especially for the lords in western Japan. By the end of the eighteenth century for many daimyo, alternate attendance was costing a third or more of their annual income, and as a result many were in serious debt to merchant financiers.

It should be recognized that the provisions of the Buke shohatto and other similar codes were couched in generalities so that enforcement could be at the whim of the enforcer. The first three shoguns, as we have seen, frequently used presumed violations of the code to justify their numerous attainders. In the early years, the bakufu kept the daimyo under constant scrutiny through such agents as the itinerant inspectors (*junkenshi*), created in 1633 to conduct periodic inquiries into daimyo domains. Their eyes were focused particularly on political conditions, the enforcement of anti-Christian edicts, and the state of daimyo military forces. Another type of bakufu official, the provincial inspectors (*kuni metsuke*) were used to watch over critical periods in a domain's existence, such as when succession passed into the hands of a minor. The bakufu also required the daimyo to submit a great variety of reports. Maps of the domain (*kuni ezu*) gave visual evidence of the location and *kokudaka* figures of the taxpaying villages. Population registers compiled as a by-product of the annual religious inquiry (*shūmon aratame*) were made available to the bakufu's inspector general (*ōmetsuke*). And periodic reports on judicial actions taken by daimyo had to be submitted to bakufu scrutiny.[34]

Although the daimyo gave up critical portions of their political autonomy to the bakufu, in actual practice they were left with considerable freedom in the administration of their domains. The bakufu did not tax them directly, on the principle that the daimyo's responsibilities to maintain order in their domains and to share in the regime's military defense constituted a sufficient contribution to the common good. The maintenance of a domain military force was, for a daimyo, both a right and a responsibility. The rules governing the performance of military service (*gun'yaku*) had both positive and negative implications.[35] The bakufu found itself caught between the desire to reduce daimyo military capacity so as to lessen the likelihood of rebellion, and the necessity, for purposes of defense and the maintenance of domestic peace, to keep a certain level of military force in readiness. The 1615 order restricting "one castle to a province" denied the daimyo the maintenance of more than one military establishment. The 1649 regulation on military service (Gun'yaku ninzuwari) set standard figures on the size of armed forces permitted to, or required of, daimyo according to their domain size. A 100,000-*koku* domain, for instance, was made accountable for 2,155 men, of which 170 were mounted, 350 carried firearms, 30 carried bows, 150 were spearmen, and 20 were trained in signal flags. A samurai with an enfeoffment of 200 *koku* was accountable for 5 men: himself with a horse, a horse leader, a spear bearer, an armor bearer, and a porter.

Although the bakufu tended to discourage the expansion of daimyo military establishments, daimyo were obliged to contribute heavily to the bakufu program of castle building. On the theory that construction for the bakufu was a public service, daimyo were obliged to contribute manpower, material, and funds for the construction and rebuilding of a series of shogunal castle and residences, palaces for the court nobility, and various public works projects. Daimyo were required to build or expand castles at Edo, Nijō (Kyoto), Hikone, Sumpu, Nagoya, and Osaka. Work on Edo Castle continued into the

---

34 The annual religious investigation registers required of all Japanese beginning in the 1630s, as a means of stamping out Christianity, have been used by modern demographers to reconstruct Edo population history. See Susan B. Hanley and Kozo Yamamura, *Economic and Demographic Change in Japan 1600–1868* (Princeton, N.J.: Princeton University Press, 1977).

35 The 1649 regulations for military service are published in Shihōshō, *Tokugawa kinrei kō*, 6 vols. (Tokyo: Yoshikawa kōbunkan, 1931–2), vol. 1, p. 129.

1630s and required the efforts of daimyo from all parts of the country, as far distant as the Mōri of Choshu and the Date of Sendai.[36] Like every centralizing government, the Edo shogunate pursued the objective of standardizing weights and measurements and unifying the currency. The latter goal was facilitated by the shogun's acquisition of the country's major gold, silver, and copper mines. As one after another major city fell within its area of authority, the bakufu was able to exercise a powerful influence on the country's commercial life. The bakufu also succeeded in regulating foreign trade by channeling it through chosen instruments at Nagasaki, Tsushima, and Kagoshima. Thus step by step in the course of its efforts to govern the cities and villages under its direct administration, the bakufu established policies that set the national norm. The so-called Regulations of Keian (Keian ofuregaki) issued to the agricultural population of the shogunal demesne in 1646 and the 1655 Regulations for Edo (Edo machijū sadame) took their place among the principal legal documents of the age.

The dominance of military authority over the great monastic orders had been largely achieved by Oda Nobunaga and Toyotomi Hideyoshi. Until that time, monasteries held independent proprietary rights to extensive territories, and religious communities had built castles and recruited large bodies of armed men for their defense. Under the Edo bakufu, the religious bodies were further reduced in their landholdings, and the priesthood was regulated under the provisions of the 1655 Shoshū jiin hatto. The popular Honganji sect was divided into two branches, east and west, to reduce the sect's influence. But although the Buddhist orders were denied political influence and were greatly reduced in income, they were given a new and secure place in the Tokugawa order as the agents of anti-Christian policy. Under the tera-uke, or temple register, system, all Japanese were obliged to adopt a family temple of registry (dannadera). These temples in turn were given the task of making annual inquiries into the religious belief of their parishioners. The practice of religious inspection (shūmon aratame) was then institutionalized by the creation in 1640 of a bakufu office for that purpose.[37]

Finally, the shogun as national overlord exercised the right and responsibility to settle disputes and hear cases involving daimyo and other elements of the Tokugawa order. Whereas previously such dis-

36 See the example of Osaka Castle in William B. Hauser, "Osaka Castle and Tokugawa Authority in Western Japan," in Mass and Hauser, eds., *The Bakufu*, pp. 153–88.
37 George Elison, *Deus Destroyed: The Image of Christianity in Early Modern Japan* (Cambridge, Mass.: Harvard University Press, 1973), p. 195.

putes had been settled by direct military action, under the Edo bakufu, as spelled out in the Buke shohatto, the bakufu was to provide the mechanisms for settlement. A supreme court (*hyōjōsho*) staffed by daimyo and bannermen members of the shogun's upper administration was established in Edo Castle in 1722.

The commonly given description of the power structure that supported the Edo bakufu inevitably leaves the impression that the Tokugawa shogunate was all-powerful. If this indeed had been true, it would raise the question of how such a structure could have collapsed so suddenly after 1853. The truth is that many of the elements of power in the seventeenth century failed to retain their meaning in the nineteenth. Why did the Tokugawa house not follow the pattern, for instance, of the nearly contemporaneous Tudor monarchy in England and work toward a greater centralization of power?[38] There were, of course, some uncontrollable factors of decline. Mines of precious metals were unexpectedly exhausted. Epidemics, droughts, and famines debilitated whole regions and required the bakufu's material assistance. Economic conditions worsened for the entire samurai class.

Unlike the European monarchs, however, the shogunate, once a stable power structure had been achieved, did little to extend the powers of the central government and instead allowed many of these powers to decay. Not only was there no effort made to do away with the daimyo, but the many restrictions that proved so essential in the early years were softened or even abandoned. The 1651 decision to allow "deathbed adoptions" eliminated one of the most effective weapons the shogun had in finding reasons to dispossess daimyo.

By virtue of its dependence on a balance of power between shogun and daimyo, the *bakuhan* system was particularly vulnerable to the effect of time once the central authority abandoned its aggressive effort to build up its strength at the expense of the daimyo. When control regulations became routine, when the surveillance of the daimyo by bakufu inspectors was carried out halfheartedly, as economic problems affected the samurai class, and as the bakufu's finances deteriorated, the central authority was weakened disproportionately.

BAKUFU ORGANIZATION

The organs of shogunal administration evolved from the Tokugawa house organization as the Tokugawa family worked its way from the

38 Bolitho, *Treasures*, p. 18.

status of village samurai to head of a major regional daimyo coalition and finally to national hegemon. Early patterns of military and civil organization were carried over into the institutions of national governance, expanded, refined, or modified to handle changing requirements. Military and administrative service remained the expected "return" for the "favor" granted by the shogun as overlord. The consequences of this evolutionary process are most clearly seen in the manner in which the shogun staffed his military forces and administrative offices. For although Tokugawa authority extended over the entire country, the bakufu itself was manned only by the houseband, that is, the house daimyo, the bannermen, and the direct retainers or housemen. This was the inner group of dependent personnel under the shogun's direct command. The outside lords and even the cadet and collateral daimyo were treated as allies existing outside this circle.

An early view of the Matsudaira (Tokugawa) house organization comes into focus during the latter years of its Okazaki phase. By this time, the Matsudaira chief had pulled together a houseband consisting of related families (most of them bearing the Matsudaira surname), local gentry (*kunishū*) who had been reduced to vassalage, and stipended housemen (*kenin*). Already the practice was developing whereby the chief, as daimyo, was relying increasingly on direct military subordinates, *fudai* and *kenin*, rather than members of his kinship group, to carry the burden of enforcement and defense. Whereas many daimyo continued to rely heavily on senior collaterals and hereditary vassals with a long history of association with the daimyo's house, the Matsudaira policy, at least under Ieyasu, was more flexible and responsive to the needs of the chief. As head of the Matsudaira (Tokugawa) main line, Ieyasu had persistently kept his options open and relied when possible on nonkin vassals and on direct retainers of the *hatamoto* and *gokenin* variety, on the assumption that they would be more responsive to his command. The problem with kinsmen was that because they were eligible for family succession, they were potential rivals to the existing family head. Thus, when possible, kin branch heads were reduced to military vassalage. This practice was facilitated by the constant move and expansion of the locus of the Tokugawa domain. For example, the Tokugawa houseband that started with a preponderance of members from Mikawa Province was enlarged by recruits from Suruga, Tōtōmi, Kai, and Shinano, as Ieyasu added these provinces to his control.

A document of 1567 is useful for its insight into the military and civil organization of the Tokugawa domain.[39] For command purposes the Tokugawa houseband was organized on two separate levels: at the top between the daimyo and his direct vassal commanders, and below that between the commanders and their own military bands or units (*kumi*). For military purposes the majority of the daimyo's vassals were assigned to two divisions under separate leaders. In one, Sakai Tadatsugu was placed over eighteen vassal commanders (seven bearing the Matsudaira surname). In the other Ishikawa Kazumasa took the lead of thirteen vassal commanders (three of them Matsudaira). In addition there were five commanders of bannermen companies and two commanders of rearguard companies. Units under ten vassal commanders were designated keepers of the castle (*gorusui shū*), and fifteen headed units of foot soldiers (*ashigaru*). Other officers were placed in charge of flags and communications, ships, packhorses, and supplies. The civil affairs of the domain were assigned to the so-called three magistrates (san bugyō), to which Ieyasu appointed his trusted retainers, Ōsuga Yasutaka, Uemura Masakatsu, and Kōriki Kiyoyasa. Under them were three chief intendants (*daikan gashira*) charged with collecting land taxes, and a variety of officers responsible for currencies, weights and measures, the kitchen, the secretariat, documents, and the like. Among special service personnel there were attendant priests and physicians. The establishment of a bureaucracy with numerous functionally specific offices had already begun to take shape. And supporting this were personnel organized into three categories of *karō* (elders), *bugyō* (functional unit heads), and *daikan* (intendants).

As this houseband organization expanded into the Kantō in 1590 and then across the entire nation after 1600, the basic composition of the inner command structure did not change. The Tokugawa bakufu remained essentially an expanded houseband in which the chieftain (now the shogun) governed through his hereditary vassals and other types of direct retainers. But in addition there were now two new groups of daimyo located outside the houseband that had to be accommodated. These were the cadet or collateral houses and the *tozama* allies. Neither of these groups of daimyo routinely held office in the bakufu.

The central bureaucracy

The massive bureaucracy that eventually took shape under the Tokugawa shoguns was not yet fully organized at the time Ieyasu became

---

39 Fujino, *Bakuhan taisei*, p. 29.

shogun.[40] Many offices and administrative procedures we think of as having been part of the bakufu practice from the start actually were not adopted until well into the second half of the century. At the time of Ieyasu's death, a number of basic problems in the transition of governance from charismatic leadership to bureaucratic routine had yet to be solved. Most critical was the continuing disagreement over the locus of policymaking authority, whether it should reside with the shogun alone or in council with the chief advisory positions in the bakufu.[41]

Tokugawa Ieyasu had been fairly successful in defending himself and his immediate successors against interference from the collaterals. As it turned out, it was the leading members of the house daimyo who gave the shoguns the most trouble. The neat table of organization charts of the Edo bakufu, which list upwards of four hundred posts in chain-of-command order, mask the problems of competition for control of policy and enforcement authority that plagued Edo bakufu politics. While Ieyasu was still alive, it would have been hard to imagine that differences of policy would develop between the shogun and the house daimyo, whose interests as a whole were represented by the *rōjū* (senior councilors). Historically, shogun and *fudai* had worked together to win the *tenka*, with the bakufu being simply the mechanism through which the shogun activated the daimyo and governed the country. But as time passed, the *fudai* found their private interests as daimyo diverging from those of the Tokugawa house. As a result, control over bakufu policy became a prize sought by a number of special interests, including the shogun, the collateral daimyo, and the house daimyo.

The first three shoguns managed to assert their political leadership by controlling a circle of personal favorites whom they placed in high advisory posts such as the Senior Council. Ieyasu's use of his own "brain trust" is well documented. Hidetada's reliance on Doi Toshikatsu (1573–1644), his youthful companion, and Iemitsu's reliance on Hotta Masamori (1608–51) exemplify the ability of strong shoguns to govern through chosen instruments. But later shoguns found it increasingly difficult to have their own way in making appointments to high office. Each shogun thereafter was obliged to fight for his own identity, in a number of different ways with varying degrees of success.

40 There are numerous versions of the Edo bakufu's table of organization. A complete and informative one is "Edo bakufu," in Kokushi daijiten henshū iinkai, comp., *Kokushi daijiten* (Tokyo: Yoshikawa kōbunkan, 1980), vol. 2, pp. 331–6.
41 Harold Bolitho has clarified the nature of the tensions between the wishes of the *fudai* daimyo and the interests of the shogun. See his chapter "Fudai Daimyo and Bakufu Policy: 1600–1857," in his *Treasures*, pp. 154ff.

Iemitsu's successor as shogun, Ietsuna, being but ten years old and physically weak, was quickly captured by the senior *fudai* houses. Later shoguns found it expedient to rely on more easily controlled "inner officers" such as the chamberlains. Tsunayoshi, the fifth shogun, who came to the office as a mature man, began his tenure by dismissing the distinguished Tairō Sakai Tadakiyo. It was rumored that Sakai had plotted to install a courtier as a figurehead shogun, in order to gain control of bakufu policy. Tsunayoshi was thus the first to use successfully the inner office route to bypass the senior *fudai*.

The shogun in theory was a despot, accountable to none but the emperor. (See Figure 4.2.) The emperor in turn represented the "will of Heaven" that placed on the shogun the responsibility to ensure the well-being of the people. A child or an incapacitated shogun could be guided by a regent, and on occasion collateral members of the Tokugawa house could intervene in situations affecting the well-being of the extended Tokugawa lineage. A case in point would be the choice of an heir to the shogun. Informal or irregular involvement by members of the three houses and other Tokugawa collaterals was made possible by the fact that the daimyo of this category sat together in the shogun's palace on ceremonial occasions. But in legal terms there was no higher authority between the shogun and "shogunal policy."

In making policy, the head of the Tokugawa house followed the common daimyo practice of recognizing certain senior vassals as "elders." Ieyasu and Hidetada used such terms as *toshiyori* and *shukurō* to designate members of a senior advisory council. Under Iemitsu the term *kahan no retsu* (seal bearer) was applied to senior daimyo with powers to represent the shogun's authority. This practice was eventually formalized by the creation of two advisory boards of retainers. A group of four to six senior councilors (*rōjū*) constituting a high administrative council was brought into place in stages beginning in 1623. Staffed by high-level *fudai* daimyo, the Senior Council was given authority over matters of national scope, including supervision of the Kyoto court, the daimyo of all classes, religious bodies, foreign affairs, defense, taxation, currency, and other matters of major importance. A second board or council of three to five junior councilors (*wakadoshiyori*) was formalized in 1633 to handle the more domestic aspects of shogunal rule. Composed of *fudai* daimyo of lesser rank, it had jurisdiction over the bannermen and housemen, their assignment to office and promotion in rank. The Junior Council also was charged with the peacetime training and assignment of guard units, the procurement of military supplies, and other such military matters.

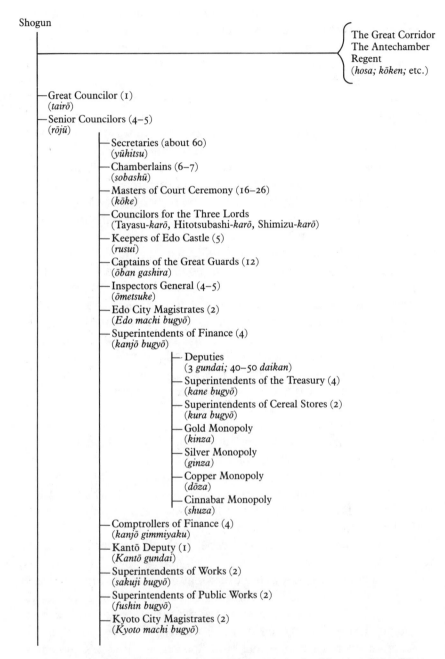

Shogun
> The Great Corridor
> The Antechamber
> Regent
> (*hosa; kōken;* etc.)

—Great Councilor (1)
　(*tairō*)
—Senior Councilors (4–5)
　(*rōjū*)

　　—Secretaries (about 60)
　　　(*yūhitsu*)
　　—Chamberlains (6–7)
　　　(*sobashū*)
　　—Masters of Court Ceremony (16–26)
　　　(*kōke*)
　　—Councilors for the Three Lords
　　　(Tayasu-*karō*, Hitotsubashi-*karō*, Shimizu-*karō*)
　　—Keepers of Edo Castle (5)
　　　(*rusui*)
　　—Captains of the Great Guards (12)
　　　(*ōban gashira*)
　　—Inspectors General (4–5)
　　　(*ōmetsuke*)
　　—Edo City Magistrates (2)
　　　(*Edo machi bugyō*)
　　—Superintendents of Finance (4)
　　　(*kanjō bugyō*)

　　　　— Deputies
　　　　　(3 *gundai;* 40–50 *daikan*)
　　　　— Superintendents of the Treasury (4)
　　　　　(*kane bugyō*)
　　　　— Superintendents of Cereal Stores (2)
　　　　　(*kura bugyō*)
　　　　— Gold Monopoly
　　　　　(*kinza*)
　　　　— Silver Monopoly
　　　　　(*ginza*)
　　　　— Copper Monopoly
　　　　　(*dōza*)
　　　　— Cinnabar Monopoly
　　　　　(*shuza*)
　　—Comptrollers of Finance (4)
　　　(*kanjō gimmiyaku*)
　　—Kantō Deputy (1)
　　　(*Kantō gundai*)
　　—Superintendents of Works (2)
　　　(*sakuji bugyō*)
　　—Superintendents of Public Works (2)
　　　(*fushin bugyō*)
　　—Kyoto City Magistrates (2)
　　　(*Kyoto machi bugyō*)

Figure 4.2 Main offices of the Tokugawa bakufu. [Source: John W. Hall, *Tanuma Okitsugu: Forerunner of Modern Japan* (Cambridge, Mass.: Harvard University Press, 1955), pp. 28–9.]

```
        ├─Osaka City Magistrates (2)
        │ (Ōsaka machi bugyō)
        ├─Magistrates of Nagasaki (2–4), Uraga (1–2), etc.
        │ (Nagasaki bugyō, Uraga bugyō)
─Grand Chamberlain (1)
 (sobayōnin)
─Junior Councilors (4–5)
 (wakadoshiyori)
              ├─Captains of the Body Guard (6)
              │ (shoimban gashira)
              ├─Captains of the Inner Guards (6)
              │ (koshōgumiban gashira)
              ├─Captains of the New Guards (6)
              │ (shimban gashira)
              ├─Superintendents of Construction and Repair
              │ (kobushin bugyō)
              ├─Chiefs of the Pages (6)
              │ (koshō-tōdori)
              ├─Chiefs of the Attendants (3)
              │ (konando-tōdori)
              ├─Inspectors
              │ (metsuke)
              ├─Chiefs of the Castle Accountants (2)
              │ (nando gashira)
              │ Attendant Physicans
              │ (ishi)
              ├─Attendant Confucianists
              │ (jusha)
              └─Superintendents of the Kitchen (3–5)
                (zen bugyō)
─Masters of Shogunal Ceremony (20 or more)
 (sōjaban)
─Superintendents of Temples and Shrines (4)
 (jisha bugyō)
─Kyoto Deputy (1)
 (Kyōto-shoshidai)
─Keeper of Osaka Castle (1)
 (Ōsaka-jōdai)
```

```
├─Supreme Court of Justice
 (hyōjōsho)
     Regular duty:
          Superintendents of Temples and Shrines
          Edo City Magistrates
          Superintendents of Finance
     Irregular duty:
          A Senior Councilor
          The Grand Chamberlain
          Other Magistrates and Superintendents when residing in Edo
     Assisted by:
          Comptrollers of Finance
          Inspectors General and others
```

The composition of the two councils, particularly the Senior Council, reflected at any given time the existing balance of influence within the bakufu, between the shogun and his primary vassals, and among the house daimyo. The position of great councilor (*tairō*) was less clearly defined. Presumably the name implied an advisory role over the senior councilors. But the post was not routinely filled, and its political significance is not at all clear. In the long Tokugawa history, only Ii Naosuke, who in 1858 was the last to be appointed grand councilor, used his position to affect bakufu policy. And for this he was promptly assassinated.

Aside from the councilors, several other offices reported directly to the shogun. The post of grand chamberlain, established in 1681, was an outgrowth of the office of *sobashū*, or chamberlain. The chamberlains waited on the shogun under the direction of the *rōjū*. By placing the grand chamberlain directly under the shogun, the post acquired great potential influence. When occupied by a shogun's favorite, it could be used as a means of circumventing the Senior Council. The most flagrant example of this was the case of Tanuma Okitsugu, who served under Ieharu as both senior councilor and grand chamberlain.

Also reporting to the shogun were the twenty or more masters of shogunal ceremony (*sōjaban*), who functioned as protocol officers, establishing the shogun's schedule, mediating between shogun and daimyo, and organizing the pageantry that attended the shogun's ceremonial routine. Another position concerned with shogunal ritual was that of *kōke* (master of court ceremony). This post was held in hereditary succession by the heads of certain families who had monopolized the technical details of dealing with the Kyoto court since the time of the Muromachi shogunate. They were of low rank but commanded high prestige because of their historical association with the court. They reported to the Senior Council.

Of the offices under direct shogunal command, the position of superintendent of temples and shrines (*jisha bugyō*), customarily assigned to four individuals, had as their main duties the regulation of religious orders and their landholdings. They also were responsible for maintaining law and order in the shogun's lands lying outside the Kantō. The office was frequently held jointly with that of the *sōjaban*. Two positions of particular significance outside Edo were the Kyoto deputy (Kyoto *shoshidai*) and the keeper of Osaka Castle (Osaka *jōdai*). The former was charged with overseeing the affairs of the Kyoto court and the court nobility. The latter was the senior military officer in central Japan, with special responsibility to maintain the military strength of

Osaka Castle as the primary bakufu military presence west of the Kantō. Edo Castle served as headquarters for the bakufu administration. Here was located the business office (*yōbeya*) close by the shogun's daytime apartments. And it was here that the two bodies of councilors attended to the business of government. Under the Senior Council some officials, such as the secretaries (*yūhitsu*), the chamberlains (*sōbashū*), and the superintendents of works (*sakuji bugyō*), saw to the maintenance of the shogun's public posture as head of state. Others, like the keepers of Edo Castle (*rusui*), the captains of the great guards (*ōban gashira*), and the inspectors general (*ōmetsuke*), were chiefly supervisory and defensive in nature. A group of officials who have not been well understood were the *metsuke* (inspectors). Described as "spies" by the early Western observers of Japan in the nineteenth century, and also as "censors" by China hands, they performed police and enforcement duties at numerous levels. Most *metsuke* served under the Junior Council and hence did not form a hierarchy of political control in concert with the inspector general.

The land base and its management

In real terms, once the necessities of military readiness had been taken care of, the most important administrative offices under the Senior Council were the superintendents of finance (*kanjō bugyō*) and the magistrates of major cities (*machi bugyō*). The former were doubly important because their authority covered both the collection of bakufu taxes and the civil administration of the villages that comprised the shogun's direct landholdings. The shogunal lands were administered much as they had been when Ieyasu was still a daimyo in the Tōkai region, that is, by a network of rural intendants (called *gundai* or *daikan*).[42] When Ieyasu moved into the Kantō, he established the office of the superintendent of the Kantō (Kantō *sōbugyō*) to oversee a number of chief intendants (*daikan gashira*). After the battle of Sekigahara, as the Tokugawa acquired more and more houseland in all parts of Japan, the intendant system was expanded, along with various makeshift arrangements for administering distant holdings. For instance, the Kyoto deputy, the keeper of Osaka Castle, and the keeper of Sumpu Castle administered the shogunal land in their vicinities. But the most commonly used expedient was to assign distant lands to

---

42 Kitajima, *Kenryoku kōzō*, pp. 214ff.

nearby daimyo as trust lands (*azukari dokoro*). The daimyo so designated were responsible for administering and collecting taxes on behalf of the bakufu. In the middle of the eighteenth century, between 13 and 18 percent of the *tenryō* was administered in this way. Trust arrangements were not assigned in the Kantō, but in the northern provinces they amounted to more than 387,000 *koku*.

The various temporary arrangements by which the first two shoguns managed their fiscal affairs were finally consolidated in 1642 by the creation of the office of the superintendent of finance (*kanjō gashira*).[43] The office was placed under the Senior Council to coordinate bakufu fiscal administration. At the same time, changes were made both in the type of official named to the intendancies and in their life-style. As he moved into unfamiliar Kantō territory, Ieyasu had found it expedient to appoint village samurai who had experience in village administation under the Hōjō and other eastern daimyo. Many of these officials had been able to aggrandize themselves after the Tokugawa takeover. Some had built fortified residences (*jinya*) and exercised personal, hence undesirable, command over the villages in their territories. The early practice of permitting intendants to deduct their office stipends from the annual tax payment to the bakufu was particularly open to abuse.

Corruption in rural tax collection and the lack of uniformity in the handling of rural administration prompted the bakufu to carry out reforms in this area. Gradually, administrative procedures were systematized under the Finance Office. At the same time the great rural families, like the Ina who had monopolized the posts of chief intendant, were replaced by low-ranking bannermen with stipends that averaged only 100 to 150 *koku*. Whereas in 1681 there had been as many as ninety-nine intendants, by 1734 the number had fallen to about forty-six. Thereafter, throughout the Edo era the number seldom rose above fifty. In the course of their duties *daikan* personally moved between Edo and official residences or headquarters (*daikansho*) located in the territory they administered. These headquarters were supplied with offices, prisons, and modest defenses and, of course, granaries.

Surely the most remarkable feature of the bakufu intendancy system was that so much territory could be administered by such a small number of officials. In essence some fifty low-level bannermen were assigned to administer land rated – if we subtract the trust lands from

43 Ibid., p. 347.

the overall total – at over 3.4 million *koku*. This made for an average of 70,000 *koku* per intendant, the same as a fair-sized daimyo domain. *Daikan* were given an extremely limited staff and no armed forces to speak of. Bakufu regulations carefully prescribed the authorized staff of clerks, guards, and porters at around thirty individuals for each *daikansho*. The intendant, in addition to his regular stipend, received an allowance in cash as well as maintenance allowances of bales of rice (*fuchi mai*) for the staff. But these were also too limited to serve the purpose adequately.

That so small a staff could administer so large a domain can be explained in terms of what can be called the "power content" of the *bakuhan* system. Villages in the *tenryō* were never out of range of well-armed daimyo castle headquarters, and in emergencies, intendants could call for assistance from neighboring daimyo. The relative quiescence of the rural population reflects as well the effectiveness of the mura system in which each village was taxed as a unit and in which the village headman was used as a bridge between samurai authority and farmer self-administration.

There is considerable debate over whether rural communities under the *bakuhan* system were kept as relatively tranquil as it appears they were, by the coercive power of samurai government or by the relatively benign nature of the mura system of rural administration.[44] The remarkable fact remains that in gross terms the income from the bakufu granary lands, although showing minor ups and downs, remained roughly the same throughout the last hundred years of the bakufu's existence. This can be interpreted in contradictory ways: for instance as a sign of weakness or lethargy on the part of the bakufu tax collectors, who failed to exact more taxes, or in the reverse as a sign of the debilitating oppression of samurai rule. But the mura system must surely be given credit for creating a rural environment that was not totally coercive and extractive. With the removal of the samurai class from the countryside, the mura, or village, as the basic unit of rural society and administration, defined a world that was essentially of the peasant's own making. Shogunal and daimyo authority touched this world through the village headman who no longer retained samurai status or authority.

The village as a unit of rural administration was the result of a lengthy evolution of agrarian society to free itself from the direct

44 In Western scholarship the classic controversy is between the Marxist approach, represented by E. H. Norman in his *Japan's Emergence As a Modern State*, and the more recent work of neoclassicist economic historians such as Kozo Yamamura.

control of the rural samurai.[45] Thus as the daimyo of the Sengoku era carried out their new land surveys and drew the samurai away from their fiefs, they brought into being village communities that had bargained with the daimyo to provide an agreed-upon annual tax payment in exchange for varying degrees of village self-management. Mura were composed of registered taxpaying farmers (*hyakushō*), their tenants, and dependent workers. Self-management was provided by an administrative staff composed of villagers and subject to a certain amount of village selection. Each mura had its headman (*nanushi* or *shōya*), and a villagers' representative (*hyakushō dai*). Village families had to form neighborhood groups (*goningumi*) for purposes of mutual assistance but also to serve as units of mutual responsibility and vicarious enforcement of regulations.

To say that this arrangement amounted to village self-administration and that this favored the villagers as a whole may seem too easy a judgment. Throughout the Edo era the village community remained divided between families of wealth and those of economic dependence.[46] At the start of the seventeenth century many of the villagers designated as *hyakushō* in the Taikō land surveys had been rustic samurai (*jizamurai*) before they had faced the option of joining as samurai the local daimyo in his castle town or remaining in the village and losing their samurai status. Within the village, moreover, ex-samurai were able to retain a degree of special influence, owing to the dominant role their families had once played. Such families tended to monopolize the office of headman, and most often had extensive landholdings. The kind of "extralegal" influence exerted by such wealthy villagers, however, was considered undesirable by both shogun and daimyo, so that samurai government sought to convert village headmen as much as possible into simple officeholders performing administrative functions for higher authority. It worked also to regularize rural administration.

As will be described in a later chapter, the bakufu's first noteworthy effort to reform local administration occurred after 1680 when the shogun Tsunayoshi instructed Hotta Masatoshi, at the time a member of the Senior Council, to look into the problem of *tenryō* administration. The result was the discovery of wide areas of mismanagement,

45 This subject is well covered in Chapter 10 in this volume. On the course of village evolution as a political entity, see Keiji Nagahara, with Kozo Yamamura, "Village Communities and Daimyo Power," in John Whitney Hall and Takeshi Toyoda, eds. *Japan in the Muromachi Age* (Princeton, N.J.: Princeton University Press, 1977), pp. 107–23.
46 Thomas C. Smith, "The Japanese Village in the Seventeenth Century," in Hall and Jansen, eds., *Studies*, pp. 263–82.

which led to the dismissal of some thirty-five intendants over the course of several years. Within their domains, daimyo found similar problems. There were two potential trouble spots. The first was the tendency of the enfeoffed vassals to press villagers arbitrarily, particularly over matters of taxation and labor service. The second was the possible high-handed treatment of village members by headmen and senior headmen. Both shogun and daimyo sought to convert the remnants of the local *jizamurai* system into the more prevalent stipendiary system and to bring the village headmen into strict fiscal accountability. The abolition by the bakufu of the post of *ōjoya*, or village group headmen, in 1712 is an example of this effort.

Although the intendancy system, by which the inhabitants of the shogun's granary lands were administered, appeared to be seriously understaffed, it cannot be said that there was any lack of regulatory effort. And because bakufu policies were expected to set the national standard, bakufu regulations took on special importance. Out of the flood of bakufu pronouncements, the 1643 (Kan'ei) edict carried the often-repeated prohibition against the "permanent sale of cultivated land" (*dembata eitai baibai no kinshi*). The one dating from 1649 (Keian *ofuregaki*) is of particular interest for its moralistic and condescending tone. It begins with an exhortation to rise early and work industriously. It then advises against luxurious living and prohibits the drinking of saké and tea and the smoking of tobacco. But military government was not totally restrictive. The 1649 edict contained the remarkable provision that if a farmer found the local intendant's administration unbearable, so long as his taxes were paid up, he could move to another district.[47]

Bakufu finances

The bakufu's Finance Office did more than regulate granary lands; it was charged with collecting revenue from all sources, rural as well as commercial, and with outlay. Under its authority were the central and regional granaries and treasuries. Its personnel handled the payment of stipends to housemen and some of the bannermen, the issuing of currency, and, increasingly, the setting of fiscal policy. Finance Office personnel underwent several dramatic changes during the first century of bakufu history. This was evident in its size, which went from a

47 This document can be found in English translation in David John Lu, comp., *Sources of Japanese History*, 2 vols. (New York: McGraw-Hill, 1974, vol. 1, pp. 209–10.

handful of nonspecialist bannermen to well over a hundred officials, among whom many were highly experienced in financial affairs. Specialization also was evident in the separation of the superintendants themselves into those having either financial (*katte*) or judicial (*kuji*) duties. As part of Tsunayoshi's cleanup of the bakufu finances, a separate office of financial comptrollers (*kanjō gimmiyaku*) was created in 1682 to serve as a check on the activities of the Finance Office. The comptrollers were of relatively low rank; the office was classed at five hundred *koku* and carried an office stipend of three hundred *hyō*. But because they were placed directly under the Senior Council, the comptrollers could report any negative findings directly to a higher authority. By the time of Yoshimune, the practice had come into use of giving one of the senior councilors the duty of financial oversight.[48]

An overall accounting for the finances of the Edo bakufu is not easily made. Not only were the sources of income hard to identify fully, but the items of expenditure also were not systematically recorded. For over a hundred years, it would seem, no nationwide record of income and expenditures was kept. Nor was there a clear difference between the private finances of the Tokugawa house and the bakufu's public fiscal affairs. In practice, regional separation between the Kantō and the Kansai remained strong. This situation improved somewhat after 1716 when, under the influence of the shogunal adviser Arai Hakuseki, uniform financial accounting mechanisms were adopted and eventually an annual budget was drawn up.[49]

From the start the Tokugawa bakufu suffered from certain obvious systemic problems. First, even though the shogunate assumed nationwide political and military obligations, it restricted its base of fiscal and personnel operations to the shogun's personal houseband. Second, in its basic policy, it held to the general principle that the affairs of government were properly handled as a normal function of the members of the samurai class, whose lands and stipends presumably provided them with sufficient income to perform the tasks to which they were assigned. In theory, therefore, all the bakufu had to do was to deliver to the bannermen and housemen the stipends due their rank. But it became evident that the hereditary stipends received by bannermen and housemen were not sufficient to sustain them when

48 The history of the establishment of the Finance Office in the bakufu is analyzed by Ono Mizuo in Kitajima Masamoto, ed., *Bakuhansei kokka seiritsu katei no kenkyū* (Tokyo: Yoshikawa kōbunkan, 1978), pp. 126–57.
49 Arai Hakuseki's autobiographical diary, *Oritaku shiba no ki*, was translated by Joyce Ackroyd as *Told Round a Brushwood Fire: The Autobiography of Arai Hakuseki* (Princeton, N.J.: Princeton University Press, 1979).

they were assigned to bureaucratically demanding jobs. And so a compromise was made.[50] For certain offices, special "office funds" (*yakuryō*) were added, beginning in 1655. Later, the practice of temporarily enhancing the officeholder's base stipend during his tenure, a practice known as *tashidaka*, was adopted, thereby making it possible to assign to an office an individual whose base salary was below that of the office to which he was named. These added expenditures for office and salary support were just one of many categories that required funding beyond normal expectations.

The most important source of bakufu income was, of course, granary land. This had swelled to over 4 million *koku* by the end of the seventeenth century and occasionally rose to over 4.5 million in the ensuing years. From these holdings the bakufu received between 1.4 million and 1.6 million *koku* in taxes annually. There were other sources of income, however, such as the numerous miscellaneous revenues from commercial business, export and import dues, transport taxes, and frontage taxes collected in the major cities. The bakufu also received income from the monopoly of certain commodities such as silk thread imported from China at Nagasaki. The shogun's control of the currency also yielded important revenues, first, as new coins were minted from ore produced from the shogun's mines and, after 1698, when the bakufu resorted to debasing the circulating coins. Because of the lack of documentation, it is difficult to get an overall picture of bakufu finances, but some sense of the complexity of the conditions faced by the bakufu can be gained from Furushima Toshio's Chapter 10 in this volume.[51]

The overall financial and economic health of the Edo bakufu within the *bakuhan* system should be viewed in evolutionary terms.[52] Under the early shoguns, finances were not a problem: The numerous daimyo attainders allowed the confiscation of land and goods. The high productivity of the bakufu mines fed the large stores of bullion that accumulated in Osaka, Edo, and Sumpu storehouses. At his death Ieyasu left some 1.9 million *ryō* of gold, well over the entire annual budget by 1840. This permitted a distribution of inheritance to the Owari and Kii collaterals of 30,000 *ryō* each and 15,000 *ryō* to Mito. Hidetada left to Iemitsu a 3.2 million-*ryō* reserve, permitting a distribu-

50 Kitajima, *Kenryoku kōzō*, pp. 474–9.
51 Furushima Toshio is one of the primary scholars working in this field; see his *Kinsei keizaishi no kiso katei – nengu shūdatsu to kyōdōtai* (Tokyo: Iwanami shoten, 1978). Chapter 10 in this volume reflects his findings in the larger work.
52 See the tightly reasoned survey of bakufu finances in Ono Mizuo, "Kanjōsho," in *Kokushi daijiten*, vol. 3, pp. 834–6.

tion of 32,000 *ryō* in gifts to daimyo. Under Iemitsu the bakufu confronted numerous special expenses such as the building of the Nikkō mausoleum, the giving of largess to the merchants of Edo and Kyoto when the shogun made his progress to Kyoto, and the suppression of the Shimabara Rebellion. Moreover, these were years when the bakufu could still call on the daimyo to pick up the expense of castle construction, the building of residences in Edo and Kyoto, and many other symbols of conspicuous display.

But after the third shogun died, the flow of special financial support began to move in other directions. Beginning with the great Edo fire of 1657, we find the bakufu providing loans and gifts of money to help the rebuilding of daimyo and samurai residences. Fires and periodic natural calamities, such as earthquakes and volcanic eruptions of Mt. Fuji and Mt. Asama, required costly rehabilitation. Fiscal deficits began to appear in 1678. And from this time on, maintaining solvency was a running battle. The discovery of the expedient of currency debasement was the single most useful device for balancing the bakufu budget, and it was used frequently.

Recognition of fiscal realities grew in three stages in the bakufu leadership. First came the realization that corruption was a problem and required immediate and drastic action. Second came the effort to identify special problems for specific remedial action, illustrated by Arai Hakuseki's efforts to reform bakufu policy toward foreign trade. Third, we come to the time of shogun Yoshimune, who attempted to work out an overall, comprehensive fiscal, or economic, policy for the country. He recognized that such a policy would have to include within its purview the country's growing commercial dimension.

Urban administration

From the middle of the eighteenth century a significant portion of bakufu income was derived from taxes on urban property, fees on commercial and transport activities, and other nonagricultural sources. To understand this development we must turn to the urban sector of the Edo government. The standard pattern of city administration was through the bakufu-appointed city magistrate (*machi bugyō*), who for large cities like Edo, Osaka, and Kyoto would be daimyo or bannermen of some size and importance.

The typical city under the *bakuhan* system was the castle town, like Edo, which had grown up in response to the needs of a daimyo as he organized his domains during the warfare of the sixteenth century. As the regional hegemons built fortresses of great size and drew garrison troops around them, new cities developed that became the domiciles for nearly the entire samurai class. These in turn drew large numbers of service personnel: merchants, artisans, and professional groups of all types.[53]

The bakufu set the model for urban administration, as most of the largest cities were held under its direct control. Edo, Osaka, Kyoto, Sumpu, Nagasaki, and Ōtsu, the most important of the tenryō cities, were each quite different in history and function, but the general pattern of administration was similiar. Bakufu administration over the nonsamurai residents was vested in the city magistrate, who maintained an office (bugyōsho) to which were attached a staff of clerks and enforcement officers (yoriki, dōshin). In both Edo and Osaka it became necessary to divide the office into two, on opposite sides of the city. And it was always customary to name two magistrates who rotated on duty on alternate months. Below the magistrates the urban population, referred to as chōnin, was organized much as the rural populace was, under a system of local management. The basic unit was the ward (machi or chō) headed by ward heads (machidoshiyori). Urban householders were required to form mutual responsibility groups (gonin-gumi), as did villagers. Osaka was further divided into districts composed of several wards, and these were headed by elders (sōdoshiyori). Thus there were several layers of chōnin administrators between samurai officialdom and the city dwellers themselves.

In the formative years of the bakuhan system, daimyo and shogun adopted a positive attitude toward the mercantile community, offering merchants and other service groups attractive conditions in order to lure them to their castle headquarters. Although later the chōnin became subject to a variety of excise taxes, license fees, and compulsory loans (both forced and secured), they were never as systematically and heavily taxed as were the agriculturalists. Samurai government placed merchants under various restraints, but it also relied on the mercantile community to bridge the gap between the urban-based samurai and the rural commoners who produced food and other goods. Urbanization and the spread of money economy created conditions that enabled merchants and manufacturers to become essential to the well-being of the warrior class. But the Edo period samurai government had diffi-

53 The study of castle towns has grown in proportion to the study of daimyo domains. Chapter 11, by Nakai Nobuhiko and James L. McClain, in this volume provides a good overview of Edo period urbanization. McClain also has written a thorough survey of Kanazawa as a castle town.

culty working out institutionally a satisfactory relationship between the two segments of the society.

The first three Tokugawa shoguns articulated the shogunate's basic policies toward the commercial sector. Special service, or contract, merchants (*goyō shōnin*) – among them the houses charged with procuring precious metals and minting them into currency – were given new charters. Restrictions were placed on foreign trade to the advantage of chartered merchants who monopolized foreign imports of silk on behalf of the bakufu. The bakufu also issued generic laws and regulations (*furegaki*) that established the national structure within which the commercial economy could operate. The regulations of 1615 that dealt with such matters as the disputes between commercial litigants or problems of family inheritance were typical of the effort of the samurai government to pass on to each class the management of its own internal affairs. But the destinies of the samurai and the *chōnin* were closely linked, and when the bakufu finally woke up to the deterioration of its fiscal condition, the problems it faced were deeply embedded in the underlying economy. The financial expedients undertaken by the fifth shogun, Tsunayoshi, the shogunal adviser Arai Hakuseki, and the eighth shogun, Yoshimune, such as price fixing, currency debasement, and restraints on exports of precious metals, all reflect the effort to deal with ill-understood economic problems that were truly national in scale. Whereas military and political issues had been the primary concerns that had dictated policy choices until now, the bakufu by the time of Tsunayoshi was faced with real fiscal problems that required economically informed solutions. The debate over whether or not to carry out currency debasement discussed in Chapter 9 of this volume is an obvious case in point.

The junior councilors and military organization

The point is often made that *bakuhan* civil government was nothing more than the application to peacetime conditions of an administrative system developed by the daimyo during years of constant warfare. This should not be construed to mean that civil administration from top to bottom was handled as a sideline by officials whose normal functions were military service. During the Sengoku wars, the daimyo had obviously accentuated the military side of their houseband buildup. But the civil administration of the towns and villages within their domains was given due attention. Ieyasu's appointment, during his Okazaki years, of commissioners for civil administration is illustrative. During the years of heavy warfare, members of a daimyo's vassal band were obliged to function in both military and civil positions. When peaceful conditions were assured, these two types of service tended to become separate in practice as the qualification for office became more specialized.

As we noted, the Tokugawa houseband consisted of three major segments: the house daimyo, the bannermen, and the housemen. Whereas the senior councilors handled the affairs of the shogun's daimyo-rank vassals, the junior councilors were made responsible for carrying out functions appropriate to the other two classes of shogunal officials. These were military guard duty and service to the person of the shogun and his household. The office was occupied by four to five daimyo of minor rank.

On paper, a wartime muster of the shogun's armed forces would draw on all levels of support. Army units would be led by the senior councilors, the junior councilors, and the several daimyo. Under the command of the senior councilors were the keepers of Edo Castle, the members of the twelve great guards (ōban), the inspector general, and the necessary signal officers and civil engineers. Under the command of the junior councilors were ten body guard (shoimban) units, ten inner guard (koshōgumiban) groups, eight units of the new guard (shimban), as well as numerous specialized units trained for communication, firearms, naval warfare, and the like.

In peacetime these specialized units were expected to hold themselves in functioning order. The guard groups remained as castle guards, shogunal body guards, and military attendants when the shogun traveled outside Edo Castle. Despite the tedium of guard duty, membership in them was considered more desirable than were civil administrative positions. The more domestic of the positions under the purview of the junior council were in such services as construction and repair (kobushin), shogunal pages (koshō), shogunal attendants (konando), inspectors (metsuke), physicians (ishi), Confucian scholars (jusha), the kitchen (zen bugyō), women's apartments (ōoku), and the like. It should be kept in mind that this list of functions applied to more than just the Edo headquarters; that is, the bakufu establishment was grounded in numerous subsidiary castles, like Sumpu, Osaka, and Kyoto, and administrative positions, like the Kyoto deputy (Kyoto shoshidai), and each of these commands had detachments of military guards and service units assigned by Edo.

Selection for office and administrative procedures

It was frequently observed by foreign visitors to Japan in the mid-nineteenth century that the samurai government was greatly over-staffed. This was the result of carrying over into peacetime the undiminished rosters of shogun and daimyo vassal bands and attached service personnel that had grown to inflated proportions during the warfare of the last half of the sixteenth century. But the financial burden that this decision placed on the samurai government in the nineteenth century was not understood at the time. Nor should we imagine that the bureaucratic system was totally defenseless against the pressures created by the hereditary retention of stipends by so many members of an underused aristocracy.[54]

The samurai's practice of enrolling in the service rosters of the daimyo and shogun was relatively open and fluid when war was being waged. Assignment to office or to military service unit most frequently was tied to battlefield performance, and rewards for courage or loyal service were easily paid in the currency of captured fief land. But once military action had ended, the basis of assignment and promotion in rank or office had to be systematized and ultimately institutionalized. Criticism has been directed toward the hereditary nature of samurai officeholding, especially that toward the end of the Tokugawa regime. It is true that the samurai families appeared to remain, by hereditary right, on the bakufu and daimyo rolls. But what about the holding of office? Appointment to office throughout the *bakuhan* society rested on the concept of family status (*mibun* or *kakaku*). The status of a given house could be expressed in terms of military or bureaucratic rank and in size of income measured in *koku* of rice. Thus what any house inherited was rank and not office.[55]

Positions within the bureaucracy were graded according to the occupant's rank and salary. For any given office, there were obviously many qualified individuals. And for each samurai of a given status there were numerous positions for which he was qualified. Accordingly, the matching of status to office rested on the basic philosophy behind the assignment to office and the requirements of the office.

54 The application of these principles of status inheritance is clearly brought out in the case of a daimyo domain such as the Bizen *han*. See Hall, "The Ikeda House and Its Retainers in Bizen," pp. 87–8.

55 Recruitment procedures were well developed in both the bakufu and the *han*. For an example of the latter, see John Whitney Hall, "The Nature of Traditional Society: Japan," in Robert E. Ward and Dankwart A. Rustow, eds., *Political Modernization in Japan and Turkey* (Princeton, N.J.: Princeton University Press, 1964), pp. 14–41.

Because it was assumed that size of income reflected the individual's stature and administrative experience, it required a person of an appropriate income to fulfill the requirements of a given position. This minimum income requirement for office was termed *yakudaka*, and for a few, such requirements were as follows: senior councilor (25,000 *koku*), chamberlain (5,000 *koku*), inspector general or Edo city magistrate (5,000 *koku*), and page (500 *koku*).

But before long, as bannermen and housemen incurred their own financial problems, the minimum income requirement became increasingly meaningless. Thus beginning in 1665, captains of the great guard were given an office expense allowance (*yakuryō*) of two thousand *hyō* (bales of rice) to take care of office costs. Eventually this practice was applied to nearly all bakufu offices. A few examples: inspector general (one thousand *ryō*), head of the Finance Office (seven hundred *ryō*), and inspector (five hundred *ryō*). A further innovation in office compensation was the practice begun by Yoshimune of offering compensatory salary increases to individuals whose basic house income was below the minimum income requirement for a given post. Called *tashidaka*, a bannerman with a two thousand-*koku* stipend, for example, could receive a temporary salary enhancement of one thousand *koku* so as to qualify for appointment to a post listed at three thousand *koku*. Although these measures were cumbersome in practice, they helped, to some degree, open up the bakufu bureaucracy to talent from below.

Within a system so strongly colored by hereditary constraints, how were the talents of potential officeholders recognized, and how were appointments made from the pool of eligibles? Here another common bureaucratic technique was relied on, namely, the use of the personnel group, or *kumi*. Samurai were enrolled in the service registers of shogun or daimyo at a given rank and assigned to a given personnel group, before being assigned to a post. As a member of a *kumi* he came under the supervision of the *kumi* head (*kumigashira*), who served as personnel officer for the group, assisted in advancing the careers of men under his supervision, and preparing and presenting to a higher authority the petitions for promotion or transfer. The personnel group head was different from the administrative or military command superior, and this separation of the command and status systems made for a more impartial handling of bureaucratic personnel matters.

Finally, we should note that many of the positions in the bakufu bureaucracy were filled by more than one person, which reflects the common practice of multiple authority, or responsibility, and alternation of duty. In the service of both the shogun and the daimyo, especially in sensitive assignments, two or more individuals alternated in office, usually on a monthly rotation basis. This practice served to protect the political process from being dominated by any single individual, for multiple appointment meant that important policy decisions would have to be made collectively by all officials, whether or not on duty. On the other hand, duty rotation meant that minor issues were often allowed to remain undecided, in the hope that they would be handled by the next duty officer. These practices worked against rapid and decisive bureaucratic action. Just as in the practice of retaining the daimyo in a centralizable political organization, the retention of these conservative administrative practices militated against a number of "modern" tendencies in samurai government during the Edo period.

CHAPTER 5

THE *HAN*

The *han,* or daimyo domains, covered some three-quarters of the total area of the Japanese islands. They presided over most of Japan's wealth and garnered most of its taxes. Under their control came the greater part of Japan's military forces, as at least three-quarters of the samurai class were in their service. For the majority of the common people, the only form of government they knew was provided by their *han.* Its borders, seldom if ever passed, formed the edge of their known world, and its officials were the only ones they could ever expect to see. The *han* gave the majority of Japanese their roads, their bridges, their laws, and their order. When villages quarreled over water supply or rights to forage in the mountains, it was the *han* that stepped in to separate them. When crops failed, the *han* doled out rations. Should a river burst its banks, then the responsibility for relief and restoration fell to the *han.*[1]

This is not to say that those who lived in the *han* were not conscious of higher forms of authority. Above the *han* was the Tokugawa bakufu, presided over by a shogun from whom every daimyo, or *han* chief, derived his legitimacy. One step beyond that again stood the emperor and his court, powerless in fact but nevertheless the symbolic fount of all authority, even that of the bakufu itself. Yet to most people living in the *han* – the farmers, craftsmen, shopkeepers, servants, day laborers, and fishermen – shogun and emperor would have been little more than abstractions, dimly perceived and of no immediate relevance. The samurai class, being both educated and traveled to an extent denied other sections of society, would have known of these more exalted bodies – would perhaps have had some degree of personal contact with one or other of them at some time – but for most of them, too, their *han* was paramount. It was the *han* that met their needs, both material and ideological, satisfying the one with stipends and the

---

1 Throughout this chapter the term *han* will denote not only an area of land but also its military, administrative, and fiscal superstructure. This is in accordance with Japanese usage.

other with an opportunity to serve. The stipends may have been far from large, and the service often as much a socially acceptable counterfeit as anything of real substance, but nontheless it defined, as nothing else could, the place of this privileged and shamefully underemployed class within the community. By whatever yardstick, therefore, the *han* formed an integral part of Japanese life.

Nobody in Tokugawa Japan could have doubted the importance of the *han*, just as nobody would seriously contest it now. But such was not always the case. For more than seventy years after the *han* were abolished in 1871, they and their function in Tokugawa society were substantially ignored. During the late nineteenth and early twentieth centuries, Japanese scholars – servants themselves of strong central government – took their own preoccupations with state power and imperial loyalty with them when they studied the Edo period, only rarely looking beyond the bakufu, its individual leaders, and what their attitude toward the imperial court in Kyoto might have been. Insofar as the *han* were considered at all, it was through their association with individual daimyo – Tokugawa Mitsukuni of Mito, for example, or Hoshina Masayuki of Aizu – statesmen whose devotion to the imperial house or to Confucian morality seemed exemplary enough to warrant attention. Of the considerable role played by the *han* themselves in the social, economic, cultural, and institutional life of their time, little notice was taken.[2]

Only after World War II did attention shift significantly in the direction of *han* studies, largely through the leadership of Itō Tasaburō, a historian at the University of Tokyo. Even before the war Itō's research on a number of individual *han* – Mito, Kii, Nakamura, and Tsushima among them – had delineated a whole new field for historical research. Then, in 1956, with the publication of his *Bakuhan taisei* (The bakuhan system), he brought *han* studies to academic prominence. As the title of his book suggests, the *han* were now to be recognized as entities distinct from, and in a sense comparable to, the Tokugawa bakufu with which they shared responsibility for governing Japan. At the same time Itō Tasaburō, and the group of like-minded scholars he gathered around him – Taniguchi Sumio, Kobayashi Seiji, Kanai Madoka, and Fujino Tamotsu, among others – have between them, individually and as members of the Hanseishi kenkyūkai (Soci-

---

2 See, for example, the old standard works on Tokugawa history: Yoshida Tōgo, *Tokugawa seikyō kō*, 2 vols. (Tokyo: Fuzambō, 1894); Ikeda Kōen, *Tokugawa jidai shi* (Tokyo: Waseda daigaku shuppanbu, 1909); and Kurita Mototsugu, *Sōgō Nihonshi gaisetsu ge* (Tokyo: Chūbunkan, 1943).

ety for the study of *han* administrative history), managed to keep *han* studies at the forefront of Japanese historical research ever since. To some extent, the readiness with which academic attention had moved away from the Tokugawa bakufu, the central government, and toward the *han*, which together constituted so much of Tokugawa Japan's local government, may well have reflected a postwar aversion to the old themes of prewar Japan: central power and loyalty to the emperor. To this extent it perhaps also reflected a new freedom of choice in the Japanese academic world. But it is also certain that other factors played a part – the realization, for example, of the existence in former castle towns of an immense volume of untouched documentary material, such as ledgers, diaries, memoranda, and tax records. For scholars, the temptation of these dormant riches was irresistible, particularly once the overall theoretical framework for *han* studies had been hammered out at historical conferences, notably at the 1957 meeting of the Shakai keizaishi gakkai (Society for the study of social and economic history). Also, in a variety of ways, Japanese historians were growing familiar with Western scholarship, itself becoming attuned to local history. One of the most seminal encounters took place in Okayama early in the 1950s, through the cooperative efforts of John Whitney Hall, then at the University of Michigan, and the Okayama historian Taniguchi Sumio.[3]

Over the past twenty-five years there has been little short of a *han* studies explosion, reflected in the volume of publications devoted to the subject.[4] The *han* have been restored to their rightful place in the history of the Tokugawa period. Paradoxically, however, this does not make them any easier to write about, for the overwhelming trend has been toward the dissection of individual *han*, rather than toward synthesis, and because no two *han* were precisely the same, the more minute and penetrating the dissection, the more remote the likelihood of convincing synthesis.[5] At almost any given time during the Tokugawa period there would have been as many as 260 *han* coexisting;

---

3 Part of the results of this collaboration are to be found in John Whitney Hall, *Government and Local Power in Japan, 500 to 1700: A Study Based on Bizen Province* (Princeton, N.J.: Princeton University Press, 1966); and Taniguchi Sumio, *Okayama hansei shi no kenkyu* (Tokyo: Hanawa shobō, 1964).
4 It would be tedious to list the major works in each genre and absolutely impossible to list them all. The eight-volume *Monogatari han shi*, and its seven-volume successor, *Dai ni ki monogatari han shi*, both edited by Kodama Kōta and Kitajima Masamoto and published by Jimbutsu ōraisha, Tokyo, in 1964–5 and 1966, respectively, contain some of the best work intended for the general reader.
5 How does one begin to encompass the experience of *han* so different in size as Sendai, which covered 1,018 villages, and Tannan, which covered a mere 23?

further, some 540 are known to have existed, however briefly.[6] It is therefore difficult to find generalizations capable of embracing the entire *han* experience. To do so would require a retreat to the barest essentials: that a *han* was a fief with a minimum productivity of ten thousand *koku* of rice per year and that it was consigned by the shogun into the custody of a vassal, who thereby merited the title of daimyo. This much can safely be said (although not without some qualification, as not every fief over ten thousand *koku* was a *han*), but not much else, and even that tells us remarkably little. Once past this basic definition, historians have usually found it necessary to divide the *han* into different groups, using for the purpose any one of a number of yardsticks.

One of these, which concentrated on the figure of the daimyo rather than on the domain itself, divided the *han* into three categories on the basis of the daimyo's political relationship to the shogun, namely, *tozama* daimyo, *fudai* daimyo, and *kamon* daimyo. The *tozama*, whose families had been substantial local magnates before the political ascendancy of Tokugawa Ieyasu in 1600, were automatically assumed to be at best neutral, and at worst hostile, to Tokugawa leadership. The *fudai*, the second category, were men who, having been Tokugawa vassals, were rewarded for their service by promotion to the status of daimyo. As the *tozama* were assumed to be either neutral or hostile, so the *fudai* were assumed automatically to be loyal and supportive. The third group, the *kamon* daimyo, sometimes linked with the *fudai*, were members of the manifold branches of the Tokugawa family, whether they bore the Tokugawa surname (as with the daimyo of Owari, Kii, and Mito) or the earlier Matsudaira surname (as with the daimyo of Takamatsu and Kuwana). Such a categorization had one clear advantage, as there was for the most part a general agreement on which daimyo fell into which category, despite a few cases of uncertainty.[7] There was also an apparent thread of logic to it, given that senior positions in the central bakufu bureaucracy were allocated to *fudai* daimyo, but never (or hardly ever) to *tozama*.

In practice, however, this classification, plausible enough in the abstract, was not necessarily a reliable determinant of enduring political complexion. The differences of 1600 do not seem to have persisted into the Tokugawa period for very long. By the early eighteenth century, as Ogyū Sorai noted in his *Seidan*, "the distinction between the

6 Fujii Sadafumi and Hayashi Rikurō, eds., *Han shi jiten* (Tokyo: Akita shoten, 1976).
7 Harold Bolitho, *Treasures Among Men: The Fudai Daimyo in Tokugawa Japan* (New Haven, Conn.: Yale University Press, 1974), p. 47, n. 7.

fudai and tozama daimyō is now merely a matter of name . . . both fudai and tozama are closely related, and, having been reared in Edo, both regard the city as their home."[8] The bakufu, for its part too, did not appear to have discriminated among *han* because of the ancestry of their respective daimyo. This was certainly the case when it offered help to daimyo in difficulties or demanded some measure of assistance from them in its turn, but even on purely formal occasions, when one might have expected due attention to be given to old comrades or their descendants, the bakufu was scrupulously impartial. Precedence at such times was invariably given to the daimyo with the largest *han*, or in the case of daimyo of equal standing, to whoever had succeeded first to his title.[9]

The *fudai–tozama* distinction, though still occasionally used, has largely been discarded as a working concept by modern historians, who have discovered that it is no longer possible to assume that the attitude of any daimyo toward national political issues owed anything to the allegiance of his ancestors; indeed, more significantly, it is no longer possible to assume that any given group of vassals would necessarily be influenced by what their daimyo thought.[10] Like any organization of human beings, the *han* were full of conflicting interests and opinions, and among them the daimyo's voice was not always decisive.

The postwar growth of *han* studies, together with the interest in social and economic history that, if it did not precipitate, then certainly accompanied it, has produced new insight into the origin and development of the *han*. Recent studies concentrate on the *han* itself, rather than the individual daimyo or his ancestry, and they take into account a whole range of phenomena that earlier approaches conspired to ignore, such as the internal social and political structure of the *han* or its size and location. Looked at historically or developmentally, the *han* can be divided into two groups: those tracing their foundation back to 1580 and earlier and those established thereafter.

Typically, in *han* formed before 1580 – that is, at a time when civil war was still very much a fact of life – few daimyo could exert more than a conditional control over their vassals. The sixteenth century was the golden age of the old-style samurai, the *jizamurai*, as they are often called: men who lived out in the countryside, on fiefs with which

8 Quoted in J. R. McEwan, *The Political Writings of Ogyū Sorai* (Cambridge, England: Cambridge University Press, 1962), pp. 75–76.
9 Bolitho, *Treasures*, chap. 3; for precedence, Hōseishi gakkai, ed., *Tokugawa kinreikō* (hereafter cited as TKRK), 11 vols. (Tokyo: Sōbunsha, 1958–61), vol. 4, p. 315.
10 For a differing view, see Conrad Totman, *Politics in the Tokugawa Bakufu, 1600–1843* (Cambridge, Mass.: Harvard University Press, 1967), chap. 8.

they had long associations and over which they exercised a substantial degree of independent control, dispensing rough and ready justice, gathering taxes, and mobilizing the inhabitants for the tasks of both war and peace. Such men presented their daimyo with a constant dilemma. He needed their support, for they and those over whom they presided accounted for a major part of his military strength, but he could seldom command it absolutely. Instead, he usually had to bargain for it, offering guarantees of one sort or another designed to strengthen the samurai's independence at the cost of his own central power. Certainly he could not afford to give offense, for once displeased the *jizamurai* were always free, in an age of civil war, to take their allegiance elsewhere. They could in fact do rather more than that, that is, gather support of their own to overthrow the daimyo, installing themselves in his stead. Some of medieval Japan's most noted families – among them the Akamatsu, once lords of three provinces, and the Ōuchi, who at their height commanded seven – were destroyed in precisely this way. It was, after all, the age of *gekokujō*, when the lesser had often been known to vanquish the greater.

Any daimyo house, to navigate these shoals into the safety of the Tokugawa period, had therefore almost inevitably been obliged to jettison many claims to authority on the way. Quite often, in such *han*, the *jizamurai* were to survive – their existence confirmed in some forty *han* as late as 1690[11] – residing in their own fiefs, taxing them, and governing them just as their ancestors had done. As a formal token of submission they might pay occasional visits to their daimyo's castle town, as the daimyo in his turn visited Edo, but their main concern was with the villages from which they derived their income.

Later daimyo, those created by the great generals of the late sixteenth century – Oda Nobunaga, Toyotomi Hideyoshi, or Tokugawa Ieyasu – or by later Tokugawa shoguns, tended to be spared these problems. For one thing, they and their men were accustomed to being moved about the country in obedience to the strategic interests of their overlord, so they had long since shrugged off much of the invisible luggage – loyalties, affections, expectations – of the past. Further, the age of *gekokujō* was over. Not only were alternative employers diminishing, but also few samurai would take up arms against a daimyo if that also meant pitting oneself against a Nobunaga, a

---

11 Hidemura Senzō, Kuwabata Kō, and Fujii Jōji, "Hansei no seiritsu," in vol. 10 of *Iwanami kōza Nihon rekishi* (Tokyo: Iwanami shoten, 1975), p. 66, claim thirty-eight such *han*; Fujino Tamotsu, *Daimyō: sono ryōgoku keiei* (Tokyo: Jimbutsu ōraisha, 1964), p. 61, claims forty-two.

Hideyoshi, or an Ieyasu. By the circumstances of their creation, therefore, the later daimyo were able to command bands of vassals that
were much more streamlined and much more amenable to central
direction, in fact – to use the terminology of most postwar scholars,
for whom such things signify a shift away from feudalism – more
"modern."

In contrast with their longer-established brothers, these daimyo
were able to build up their *han* along completely new lines, bringing
their vassals into permanent residence in the samurai quarters of the
castle towns, paying them stipends, and integrating them into the
political, economic, administrative, and cultural life of the *han*. For
the most part, in the newer *han*, this transformation was accomplished
with remarkably little ill feeling. The samurai themselves, having long
since left their native villages, no longer had any traditional local
authority to lose, and they were therefore often surprisingly amenable
to such a move, sometimes to the point of initiating it themselves.

In 1625, after only seven years in their new *han* at Nagaoka, senior
vassals of the Makino family had begun to petition for permission to
surrender their fiefs (from which, as they noted, "the income can be
small in some years, because parts of the domain are subject to frequent droughts or floods") and to be given stipends instead. They
knew precisely what terms they wanted: "48 percent of our enfeoffment in rice, fodder for our horses, straw, and money to pay our
servants."[12] This request for stipends rather than fiefs underlines another extension of the problem created by the changing relationship of
the samurai to the workers of their village fiefs. Former *jizamurai*,
when moved into the daimyo's castle headquarters, at first were permitted to retain certain portions of their customary powers over the
workers on these lands. But increasingly, after the middle of the
seventeenth century, the *han* chief absorbed the right to govern the
peasantry.

At first glance, this might seem no more than a classification of *han*
along purely administrative lines, with the newer *han* distinguished by
their centralized and bureaucratic nature and the older ones by the
lack of it. In fact, however, it correlates with a number of other
important phenomena. As long as the samurai continued to reside in
the villages, as they did in Tosa, Satsuma, and Echizen, then anything
other than subsistence farming was discouraged. Once the samurai

12 Imaizumi Shōzō, *Nagaoka no rekishi*, 6 vols. (Sanjō: Yashima Shuppan, 1968–9), vol. 1, pp. 220–1.

were safely out of the way, however, the villagers were free to explore a
range of attractive commercial activities: cash cropping, certainly, but
also tax evasion, unreported land reclamation, small-scale processing,
usury, and land purchases. The small minority of *han* retaining the
jizamurai system (roughly 17 percent of all *han* at the end of the
seventeeth century),[13] therefore, were on the whole among the most
commercially backward parts of Tokugawa Japan. Their farmers were,
at the same time, the most biddable, displaying far less overt evidence
of discontent than those in other, more commercially advanced areas.
On the whole they were spared the strains that all too often accompanied commercial agriculture, such as the polarization between rich and
poor and between landlords and agricultural laborers, which became
so much part of the late Tokugawa countryside.[14]

Another useful categorization of the *han* of the Tokugawa period is
that put forward by Itō Tasaburō, who suggested that they be divided
into three types, large, middling, and small.[15] As Itō saw it, large *han*
were those believed capable of producing upwards of 200,000 *koku* of
rice annually, that is, a matter of 26 *han* in 1614 and 20 in 1732, some
120 years later. Middling domains were those assessed at an annual
productivity of from 50,000 to 200,000 *koku*, or 48 han at the beginning of the seventeenth century, and 78 in the early eighteenth. Anything else, from 50,000 *koku* down to the exiguous 10,000 *koku*, could
be considered small, leaving us with 117 such *han* in 1614 and 161 in
1732.[16]

This particular taxonomy, already familiar to many through the work
of Charles Perrault, is especially convincing, as it was its size, more than
anything else, that determined the range of possibilities and responsibilities of any given *han*. Large *han*, wherever situated, whenever established, and whatever the original political affiliation of their daimyo,
were likely to have greater military authority, more regional influence,
and greater economic diversity than small ones. Their responsibilities,
too, whether to larger numbers of samurai or peasants, were correspond-
ingly more onerous. This in turn predisposed them to a rather higher
degree of assertiveness than would have been the case with smaller *han*,
just as it gave them a greater propensity for faction squabbles, for the
stakes were so much higher. Small *han*, by contrast, had little control

13 Kanai Madoka, *Hansei* (Tokyo: Shibundō, 1962), p. 42.
14 Thomas C. Smith, *The Agrarian Origins of Modern Japan* (Stanford, Calif.: Stanford Univer-
    sity Press, 1959), chaps. 11, 12.
15 Kanai, *Hansei*, p. 33.
16 Daimyo numbers have been calculated from Tōkyō daigaku shiryō hensanjo, ed., *Tokushi
    biyō* (Tokyo: Kōdansha, 1966), pp. 475–94.

over their destiny. Lacking economic flexibility, they had none of the recuperative powers of their larger neighbors and were far more at the mercy of events; without a significant force of samurai, too, there were obvious limits to their political independence or effectiveness.

In the following examination of the *han*, although I have kept such classifications in mind, I have elected to follow none of them. Instead, despite the acknowledged difficulty of producing persuasive generalizations, I have tried to do just that. In the attempt I have been forced to pass over many of the elements that made one *han* different from another, and I can therefore legitimately be accused of leaching out much of the colorful variety from a subject that is nothing if not varied. What I have tried to do, however, has been to focus on those issues with which all *han* were concerned to a greater or lesser degree – their relationship with the central government, their internal economic and political health – in the hope that the picture I present, if not exhaustive, will at least have the virtue of relative clarity.

THE *HAN* AND CENTRAL CONTROL, 1600-1651

No consideration of the *han* can hope to avoid the issue of their relations with the Edo bakufu. True, many *han* were already in existence well before the bakufu was established in 1603; for that matter, almost all of them, in one form or another, were to survive its fall, lingering on uneasily into the Meiji world. Yet ultimately the role of the *han* was defined by the bakufu, for it was the Tokugawa government that confirmed their existence and prescribed the extent of their responsibilities and the limits of their jurisdiction. Certainly they could not have existed in the form they did without the framework that the bakufu provided. Once that was taken away, they did not linger very long.

This interdependence was recognized right from the beginning of the Tokugawa period, for there is every indication that Tokugawa Ieyasu, the founder of the dynasty, was committed to the *han* as an institution. Of course, this did not prevent him from dealing severely with individual daimyo. Accordingly, immediately after his victory at Sekigahara in 1600, he set out to make sure that those who had fought against him were given cause to regret their poor judgment. Eighty-eight daimyo – among them some of Japan's more powerful provincial families, like the Ukita of Bizen, the Chōsogabe of Tosa, the Konishi, and the Masuda – were destroyed. Others lost large tracts of land, the Mōri of Hiroshima being reduced to two of the eight provinces they had once held and the Uesugi of Aizu losing three-quarters of their vast northeastern holdings. The Satake, too, were reduced from over half a million *koku* to a domain at Akita half that size.[17] But none of this could have been considered unusually severe. It was standard treatment for vanquished opponents, and nobody going into battle at Sekigahara in 1600 would have done so in ignorance of the likely consequences of defeat.

Certainly there was no reason to believe that these summary punishments threatened the institution of the *han* itself, whether in principle or practice. Without daimyo cooperation and the resources of their *han*, there would have been no Tokugawa victory at Sekigahara, so all who had assisted the victor could look forward with confidence to a reward. This, too, was part of Sengoku convention. Nor were they disappointed. Yamanouchi Kazutoyo, for example, who had declared for the Tokugawa side on the eve of Sekigahara, was given the old Chōsogabe domain on the Pacific coast of Shikoku, an area three times the size of his former holdings. Kuroda Nagamasa, too, was given a *han* at Fukuoka more than double the size of the one he left. More than that, however, a whole host of new *han* were created and placed in the care of Tokugawa vassals, sixty-eight of whom became daimyo in the two years immediately after Sekigahara, bringing with them into the Japanese political arena a whole new set of names: the Ii, the Sakai, the Mizuno, and the multitudinous branches of the Matsudaira family.[18] Without exception, the *han* of these new daimyo were considerably smaller than those they replaced, and they were, moreover, so distributed as to make it plain that they had a watching brief over less obviously dependable neighbors. But they were *han*, for all that, and as the deliberate creations of the country's single most important political figure, it would have been safe to conclude that the *han* institution itself had a secure future in the government of Japan.

What needed to be defined was the terms on which they would participate, and there could be no doubt of the Tokugawa intention on the score. It was intended that the bakufu would be paramount, and its first move in this campaign was to demand tokens of submission. Some of these were purely practical: to fund a spate of castle building by obliging the *han* to provide men, money, and materials toward the construction of a series of fortifications, among them the Nijō Castle in Kyoto, the bakufu's own fortress in Edo, and provincial castles in

17 Fujino Tamotsu, (*Shintei*) *Bakuhan taisei shi no kenkyū* (Tokyo: Yoshikawa kōbunkan, 1975), app., pp. 36–8.
18 Ibid., app. pp. 46–4.

places like Hikone, Sumpu, Nagoya, Kameyama, and Takada. Other tokens of submission were more symbolic but nonetheless impressive for that, like the obligation imposed on *han* leaders to surrender their own names and acquire new ones – the Matsudaira surname, for example, originally the name of the Tokugawa house, or, in the case of given names, a character from the name of the shogun himself.

As time went on, particularly after the Tokugawa victory in the Osaka campaigns of 1614 and 1615, the bakufu grew increasingly assertive in its relations with the *han*. In 1617, for the first time, the principle was established that all *han* would be distributed by the shogun, as head of the bakufu. In that year every daimyo received a document signed by the shogun, or bearing his vermilion seal, in which the extent of his *han* – the number and location of the villages of which it was composed, together with an estimate of their productive capacity – was formally defined. In some cases this was no more than reasonable, as many of these *han* had been conferred on their daimyo by the Tokugawa in the first place. Others, however, like the pre-1580 *han,* had evolved independently and owed nothing to Tokugawa favor. The daimyo of these domains, therefore, as they received their certificates must have done so with mixed feelings – mixed because, although the bakufu was offering them a formal guarantee of support, it was also, obliquely, suggesting an alarming possibility, namely, that at some future date the guarantee might be withdrawn, and their *han* with it. The importance of this development is obvious. It effectively altered the entire basis on which many Japanese daimyo had until now kept their domains, substituting for right by prior possession and inheritance something much more conditional, namely, right by bakufu recognition.

Two years earlier, in 1615, the daimyo had already been given warning of a new attitude. In the summer of that year, Konchiin Suden, the Zen priest who customarily assisted Tokugawa Ieyasu in religious and foreign policy matters, had read to the assembled daimyo, gathered together for the purpose in Fushimi Castle, a document designed to set the tone for all future relations between their *han* and the Edo government. This was the Buke shohatto, the Laws governing military houses. In its way it was an ostentatiously traditional document, larded with quotations from the Confucian classics, from the *Shoku Nihongi,* and from earlier Japanese legal codes like the Kemmu shikimoku, and it was certainly far more modest in tone than were later versions, which proved both lengthier and far more explicitly ambitious. Nevertheless, this first set of instructions served notice to all *han* that they were to surrender their independence in certain vital areas. That is, they were expressly forbidden to admit within their borders any criminals or traitors – fugitives, in other words, from the bakufu, as both crime and treason would be defined in Edo. It also prohibited new fortifications, or surreptitious repairs to old ones, and demanded that daimyo receive official permission before arranging marriages for members of their families.[19]

To some extent, of course, these instructions would have come as no surprise. Indeed, just a month earlier the Ikkoku ichijō-rei had restricted the *han* to no more than one fortification. Further, the daimyo of Uwajima, Nobeoka, Ushiku, and Odawara had already lost their *han*, the first two for harboring criminals and the others for having contracted unauthorized marriages.[20] Such concerns, being purely negative and defensive, were well within the Sengoku tradition. Yet the Buke shohatto also seemed to foreshadow something new. Its thirteenth and final clause urged the daimyo to appoint none but capable men as *han* administrators, thereby sounding a note to which the granting of formal certificates of enfeoffment two years later was to add resonance. The Tokugawa bakufu was claiming for itself ultimate responsibility in *han* internal affairs. If the *han* were not well governed, was the warning, then they could be forfeited.

The second version of the Buke shohatto, which appeared under the aegis of Tokugawa Iemitsu, the third shogun, in 1635, was to define beyond all ambiguity the new relationship between the *han* and the central government. The thirteen clauses of the original were now expanded to twenty-one.[21] Not all were immediately relevant to the distribution of power and authority between the *han* and the bakufu. Some indeed touched on matters of rather tangential concern (as had the 1615 version), expressing as they did support for filial piety, hostility to Christianity, or eagerness to define just who may or may not wear certain sorts of clothes or ride in palanquins. The kernel of the 1635 version, however, made quite explicit the basis on which the Tokugawa bakufu expected its relationships with the *han* to proceed. Henceforth, in addition to the previous prohibitions, daimyo were to be forbidden a variety of activities once theirs by right. They could not interfere with highways traversing their domains, nor could they install barriers or create new embargoes. Officially designated post towns, together with lands belonging to religious insti-

19 TKRK, vol. I, pp. 61–2.   20 Fujino, *Bakuhan*, pp. 39, 42.
21 TKRK, vol. I, pp. 63–5.

tutions, were also removed from their immediate control. The legal
authority of the *han*, too, was inhibited as never before, as they were
now enjoined to "follow the laws of Edo in all things" and were ordered to leave criminal matters to the adjudication of bakufu officials
and were forbidden to settle disputes among themselves. This latter
prohibition was reinforced later that same year by the creation of a
tribunal, the *hyōjōshō*, in which these and other matters could be
settled. In two other areas, too, the bakufu was now prepared to
extend its authority. An instruction issued to the southwestern *han* in
1609, to the effect that they were not to build large ships, was now
made universal, with a blanket prohibition on the construction of any
vessel with a capacity of more than five hundred *koku*. Similarly, the
informal visits of several daimyo to Edo on a regular basis since 1600
was now – according to the text of the 1635 Buke shohatto – to be
applied to all, with instructions that they were to alternate their visits,
changing guard, as it were, in the fourth month of each year. Although
the text did not make it clear, this applied initially only to *tozama*
daimyo,[22] but by 1642 all apparently came to be included in what is
now known as the *sankin kōtai* system, under which they were obliged
to alternate a year of residence in their *han* with a similar period in
attendance on the shogun in Edo. There were a few exceptions – the
daimyo of Tsushima, whose domain was the most distant from Edo,
was required to come only at three-year intervals, whereas those with
domains in the Kantō – and therefore closest to Edo – worked on a
six-month schedule. The daimyo of Mito, too, and any daimyo holding bakufu office, was expected to spend all his time in Edo.[23]

Quite clearly this was an ambitious program of central control, but
it should be emphasized that like any other laws, the Buke shohatto,
no matter what its aspirations, needed enforcement to be effective,
and it was precisely on this point that the Tokugawa bakufu seemed to
mean what it said. Administrative practice in the first half of the
seventeenth century was to serve warning to the *han*, beyond all possibility of doubt, that the Tokugawa bakufu meant to control them.
Obviously an efficient inspection system was needed, so in 1633 the
bakufu, although already in receipt of confidential reports, created a
group of more than thirty inspectors and charged them with monitor-
ing those developments in the *han* most likely to be of interest to the

22 Asao Naohiro, "Shogun seiji no kenryoku kōzō," in *Iwanami kōza Nihon rekishi*, vol. 10
   (Tokyo: Iwanami shoten, 1975), p. 20.
23 Fujino, *Daimyō*, pp. 93–4.

government in Edo.[24] To supplement the inspectors' activities, the
daimyo were required, in 1644[25] to submit detailed maps – *kuniezu* –
of their *han* to the bakufu; they were of more symbolic than practical
value, perhaps, but important nonetheless.

On the basis of its intelligence, whether from formal or informal
sources, the bakufu was in a position to enforce its will over the *han*,
and daimyo soon came to learn that if they ignored it, they did so at
their peril. After 1615, in fact, their tenure of their *han* suddenly
became insecure, conditional on good behavior or, more significantly,
bakufu pleasure. Over the next thirty-five years, a total of ninety-five
daimyo lost their *han* or substantial parts of them. Some of them,
moreover, had been Tokugawa allies in the past. Fukushima Masanori, having assisted in the victory at Sekigahara, was deprived of his
vast holdings at Hiroshima nineteen years later and was packed off to
retirement in the Shinano mountains, with a modest competence of
45,000 *koku*, all his power and prestige gone. Three years later, the
young Mogami Yoshitoshi, whose *han* in the northeast was one of the
six largest and whose father, Iechika, had been one of Tokugawa
Ieyasu's closest confidants, suffered the same fate. He was given a
pittance of 10,000 *koku* (itself reduced by half ten years later) at Ōmi,
some three hundred miles away from his old domain. Others, equally
important, were to disappear in their turn – the Katō of Kumamoto in
1632, the Horio in 1633, the Gamō finally in 1634, the Kyōgoku in
1637, the Terazawa in 1638, and the Ikoma two years later.

Outright confiscation was not the only way in which the bakufu was
to assert its ultimate authority over the *han*. Over the same thirty-five-
year period in which 95 *han* were confiscated, there would be a total of
250 *han* transfers, in which daimyo, their families, and their vassals
(not to mention their vassals' families) were shifted from one part of
the country to another in obedience to the bakufu's perceived needs. It
was now apparent that if this continued, no *han* could ever be regarded
as being in the permanent possession of any specific daimyo family.
Never in the history of Japan had so much violence been done to local
autonomy.

This was not all, for the years after the fall of Osaka in 1615 were to
produce fresh demands on the *han*, demands on such a scale and so
elaborately conceived as to be literally beyond the experience of any of
those called upon to shoulder them. One of these was the introduction

24 For an outline of the duties of this inspectorate, see TKRK, pp. 326–7.
25 Kitajima Masamoto, *Edo bakufu no kenryoku kōzō* (Tokyo: Iwanami shoten, 1964), p. 326.

of a formal military levy, the *gun'yaku* system, which prescribed just what degree of military support each domain was expected to provide to the central government. There had been earlier intimations, in 1605 and again in 1615, but in 1633 the levy was extended to all *han* with 100,000 or fewer *koku* and – by unspoken implication – to all larger domains as well.[26] Under these scales, the daimyo of, say, a 200,000-*koku han* had to be prepared to contribute 349 horsemen, 700 musketeers, 150 bowmen, 300 pikemen, and 60 standard bearers.[27]

In a sense, impositions of this sort, even if not on this scale, were only to be expected. The daimyo were, after all, military leaders and might have been assumed to wish to maintain as many combat-ready troops as possible. They would not, however, have found other impositions quite so palatable. As we have already noted, they were obliged to contribute to the building or repair of castles, some in domains other than their own, and two in particular – Edo and Osaka – that belonged to no *han* but to the bakufu itself. Edo Castle, the residence of the Tokugawa shogun and the seat of their government, was built entirely from the resources of the Japanese daimyo, almost all of whom contributed to the project at one time or another, sixty-eight of them in one single year, 1629.[28] The same applied to the fortress at Osaka which, having been destroyed by Tokugawa forces in 1615, was thereafter rebuilt between 1620 and 1630 on a far greater scale than before, at the expense of sixty-four daimyo.[29] Thereafter it served as the focal point of bakufu power in western Japan.

The construction of such magnificent edifices passed far beyond the strategic needs of either the nation or the Tokugawa house. So lavishly were they built, and so imposing the final result, that they might more properly be regarded as statements of symbolic authority by which the leaders of each *han* government had been forced to recognize the supremacy of Edo. Certainly such was the intention of other forms of *han* tribute. The elaborate mausoleum erected at Nikkō to house part of the remains of Tokugawa Ieyasu and to enshrine his memory was built at *han* expense, and it was expected that the daimyo themselves would pay homage there from time to time. They did so first in 1617, joining a variety of notables – two lion dancers, a man wearing a

26 TKRK, vol. 1, pp. 89–90; Fujino, *Daimyō*, p. 111; Asao, "Shōgun seiji," p. 13; Takagi Shōsaku, "Edo bakufu no seiritsu," in *Iwanami kōza Nihon rekishi*, vol. 9 (Tokyo: Iwanami shoten, 1975), p. 144.
27 Yamagata-ken, ed., *Yamagata-ken shi* (*Shiryō-hen*), (Yamagata: Gannandō, 1961), pp. 375–8.
28 Murai Masuo, *Edo-jō* (Tokyo: Chūō kōronsha, 1964), pp. 58–59.
29 Kodama Kōta, *Genroku jidai*, vol. 16 of *Nihon no rekishi* (Tokyo: Chūō kōronsha, 1967), p. 249.

goblin mask, thirty-eight children dressed as monkeys – in a procession that, paying tribute to Tokugawa rule, can have done little for their self-esteem.[30] Naturally, too, it was expected that *han* forces would accompany, at their own expense, the shogun on such state occasions as formal visits to the ancestral tombs, whether at Nikkō or closer to hand at the Tōeizan in Ueno or, later, the Zōjōji at Mita. When Tokugawa Hidetada, the second shogun, went down to Kyoto in 1617, he did so in the company of "innumerable daimyo."[31] So too did Iemitsu, the third shogun, seventeen years later, escorted by 307,000 men (the largest force ever assembled in Japan to that date, according to one authority),[32] most of whom were provided by the *han*.

There were other important areas, too, in which well-established regional prerogatives were to be eroded during this period, none more striking than in the matter of foreign contact. Spiritual contact, in the form of Christianity which had gained a substantial foothold in southwestern Japan, was prohibited "in all provinces and places" with great finality, by the 1635 Buke shohatto. More tangible contacts also virtually disappeared. Foreign trade, once enjoyed by many southwestern *han* and eyed enviously by others less advantageously sited (Sendai, for instance), was closed down in several stages. By 1641 most of it had gone, and what remained was either restricted to Nagasaki, under tight bakufu supervision or, in the case of the Korean trade, conducted through Tsushima with official permission.[33]

In all of this the motive was to restrict *han* independence, to intimidate them by constant threats to their tenure, to sap their financial vigor through repeated impositions, to keep them dancing abject attendance on Tokugawa shogun both living and dead, and to curtail their intellectual, commercial, and diplomatic freedom. But that was not all. *Han* autonomy was further compromised by the hostage system, introduced in 1622.[34] Under this system the daimyo and their chief retainers all were obliged to send close relatives – wives, children, and even mothers on occasion – into permanent residence in Edo, where they could serve as surety for continued good behavior. By 1647 two

---

30 *Tokugawa jikki*, vols. 38–47 of Kuroita Katsumi, ed., *Shintei zōho kokushi taikei*, 2nd ed. (Tokyo: Yoshikawa kōbunkan, 1964–6), vol. 39, pp. 124–5.
31 Ibid., vol. 39, p. 132. 32 Asao, "Shogun seiji," p. 13.
33 Hidemura et al., "Hansei no seiritsu," p. 74.
34 Opinions seem to vary on the date. Takagi, "Edo bakufu," p. 151, sets it at 1622; Kanai, *Hansei*, p. 28, mentions 1634 in this context; Fujino, *Daimyō*, p. 93, also refers to 1634, but only in relation to *fudai* daimyo.

senior councilors of one large *han* were between them maintaining eight children as hostages in Edo for precisely this purpose.[35] Of course, much of this was not new; the principles underlying many Tokugawa control mechanisms were already in common use well before 1600. The hostage system, for example, was a familiar phenomenon during the Sengoku era: Much of Tokugawa Ieyasu's own childhood and adolescence had been spent as a hostage, and he had later delivered his wife and firstborn son to Oda Nobunaga in the same capacity. Others, in their turn, had begun to send hostages to Edo long before it was compulsory: Tōdō Takatora as early as 1596, even before Hideyoshi was dead; Maeda Toshinaga and Hori Hideharu before the battle of Sekigahara; and a whole host of people afterwards, including the most powerful daimyo – Date, Nabeshima, Hosokawa, Mōri, and Shimazu.[36] Nor had the Tokugawa invented the twin control devices of fief confiscation and transfer; both Nobunaga and Hideyoshi had employed these on occasion, just as they had called upon daimyo for assistance with their own castles at Azuchi and Fushimi.[37]

Equally, Nobunaga and Hideyoshi had led the way in interfering in the internal workings of the daimyo domains, compelling the destruction of superfluous military fortifications, prohibiting private marriage alliances, and, in Hideyoshi's case, establishing a *gun'yaku* scale of sorts. Hideyoshi had also moved to control *han* external relations, ordering the expulsion of Christian priests in 1587 (although he relaxed this from time to time) and, nine years later, the crucifixion of twenty-six missionaries and converts. The elements of symbolic subjugation – oaths of allegiance, daimyo attendance at state occasions, grants of names, and so on – were also in common use before 1600.[38]

Yet, if the outlines of Tokugawa policy bore the impress of many Sengoku hands (and not just those of its two greatest generals), it must also be recognized that the Tokugawa employed that policy on a totally unprecedented scale. They controlled far more of the country than had either Nobunaga or Hideyoshi; they controlled it for an infinitely longer period; and they enforced that control far more rigorously and consistently. Effectively they had been given an opportunity to develop all of these well-known devices into a coherent system of daimyo control. Through the combined efforts of the first three shoguns in

35 TKRK, vol. 4, p. 393.   36 Kanai, *Hansei*, p. 28; Fujino, *Daimyō*, p. 92.
37 Fujino, *Daimyō*, p. 101; Mary Elizabeth Berry, *Hideyoshi* (Cambridge, Mass.: Harvard University Press, 1982), p. 131.
38 For a full account of Hideyoshi's policies, see Berry, *Hideyoshi, passim.*

particular – Ieyasu, Hidetada, and Iemitsu – the first half-century of Tokugawa rule created a Japan of a very new kind. It is quite clear that in the years between the victory at Sekigahara in 1600 and 1651, the year in which the third shogun died, the traditional independence of the daimyo and their *han* had been severely compromised. This is not to say that it had disappeared entirely. Domain governments were free at any time to interfere in the personal lives of the inhabitants of their *han*, certainly to whatever extent was necessary to preserve the peace, and even beyond that. They could prevent people of all classes from marrying whomever they wished, leaving their villages, traveling outside the domain, eating certain kinds of food, wearing certain kinds of clothes, and holding certain sorts of entertainment at weddings, funerals, and New Year. They could also determine whether or not their people should be free to watch performances by traveling players. But such discretionary power was discretionary only up to a point. It was now circumscribed as never before, for the daimyo and his government were no longer absolute masters of their own house. The events of the first fifty years of Tokugawa rule had made this plain, first by defining the limits of daimyo authority and then by making examples of anyone unwise enough to exceed those limits.

Equally important, it had also been made clear to the daimyo that in some areas they were to have no discretionary powers at all. Their governments could no longer use domain income exclusively for their own needs, could no longer determine their own military requirements, could no longer conduct independent relations with neighbors or the world outside, and – given the exigencies of the *sankin kōtai* system – could no longer be masters of their own movements. There had been, in this first half-century of Tokugawa rule, a complete shift in the basis on which daimyo held their domains. They could be disenfeoffed or moved at the discretion of the bakufu, for a variety of reasons – some valid, others not – but all of them beyond recourse or argument. There was no court of appeal against bakufu decisions, save the emperor, access to whom had already been blocked. So they were now dependent on the bakufu's approval, and many would have come to see themselves simply as custodians of their domains, as civil servants liable to be promoted, demoted, transferred, or dismissed according to the requirements of the government in Edo. Certainly this would have been reinforced to a certain extent by habits engendered by both the *sankin kōtai* and hostage systems, which had radically changed the orientation of samurai leaders.

Edo had become the center of the nation. Five out of every six incumbent daimyo in 1690 had been born there,[39] and all of them could look forward to spending at least half of their working lives there. Edo, where their families lived, was now their home, as Ogyū Sorai was to observe, not the *han* of which they were titular leaders.[40] Within a matter of two generations, therefore, an entire provincial aristocracy had been uprooted. A period of residence in Edo might have represented exile to the first generation of seventeenth-century daimyo, but to their grandsons it was a return home, a feeling no doubt encouraged by Edo's rapid growth as a cultural, commercial, and entertainment center. To many eighteenth-century daimyo, indeed, there seemed little reason to leave it. Sakai Tadazane, daimyo of Shōnai *han*, was so little enamored of his remote domain on the Japan Sea coast that in 1707 his senior vassals had to beg him to come home. Sakai Tadayori, his immediate successor, was apparently no better. He provided his Edo residence with a noh stage, after which, as his family chronicles note rather forlornly, "he did not visit his domain for a long time."[41]

THE *HAN* AND CENTRAL CONTROL AFTER 1651

At the death of Tokugawa Iemitsu in 1651, anybody involved in *han* government, looking back over the developments of the past fifty years, might have been excused a certain pessimism. They had surrendered during that time a great many powers to Edo and seemed likely to be called upon to surrender many more. Regional autonomy, one of the most abiding features of Japanese history, appeared to be all but at an end. Yet, among all the pessimism and despite all the inroads into local prerogatives, there were grounds for optimism, for not all of the developments of the first fifty years of Tokugawa rule had been negative. In many respects, indeed, the *han* had gained from the Tokugawa peace. True, their average size was to fall, from 93,000 *koku* early in the seventeenth century to slightly more than 65,000 *koku* in the eighteenth,[42] but overall their numbers increased. In 1614 there had been only 192 *han*, but there were 229 fifty years later, 241 in 1688 and, by 1720, 262, a number that thereafter remained largely unaltered.[43] Obviously the bakufu entertained no implacable malice toward the *han*,

39 Calculated from information contained in Kanai Madoka, ed., *Dokai kōshūki* (Tokyo: Jimbutsu ōraisha, 1967).
40 See McEwan, *The Political Writings of Ogyū Sorai*.
41 Tsuruoka shiyakusho, ed., *Tsuruoka-shi shi* (Tsuruoka: Tsuruoka-shi, 1962), pp. 323–42.
42 Calculated from Tōkyō daigaku, ed., *Tokushi biyō*, pp. 475–94.
43 Kanai, ed., *Dokai kōshūki*, pp. 46–47.

nor did it wish to increase its own holdings at their expense. Had it done so, it would have confiscated more and distributed less. Certainly it would not have been at such pains to create new *han*.

In many important respects, indeed, the centuries of Tokugawa rule provided the *han* with far more security than they had ever known. To begin with, the Tokugawa peace had freed them from their major Sengoku fear: each other. Alessandro Valignano, who had had occasion to observe Sengoku politics closely during no fewer than three visits to Japan in the late sixteenth century, noted that "none of the lords (or very few of them) are secure in their domains."[44] Now, under the Tokugawa bakufu, if the *han* were restrained as never before, they were also protected. For more than 250 years no *han* took up arms against another. There were disputes among them, of course, but these went to the bakufu for arbitration, and even the smallest *han* could expect protection. Obi *han*, locked in a border dispute with its giant neighbor Satsuma early in the seventeenth century, was able to take its case to the bakufu and win. A scant forty years earlier no *han* of 57,000 *koku* would ever have dared contest anything, let alone so vital a subject as boundaries, with an opponent more than ten times its size.[45]

Tokugawa rule had effectively released all *han* from the need for constant vigilance against each other. Equally, it had done much to enhance their internal stability by making it clear that it would countenance no usurpers from among the *han* vassals. The right to govern each *han* was entrusted to a particular individual as daimyo, and to nobody else, and this right was determined almost entirely by hereditary succession.

This new security enabled the emergence of a new kind of *han*. Sengoku strategy had dictated that they be compact geographical units, to minimize the dangers attending scattered frontiers, extended supply lines, and stretched communications. In the Tokugawa period, however, such considerations no longer applied, and certain *han* were therefore able to take advantage of the positive aspects of fragmentation and diversification. This did not have much significance for *han* like Sendai, of which only 20,000 out of its total of 612,000 *koku* were held elsewhere.[46] For smaller *han*, however, it was often of great significance: In the early eighteenth century, some 20 percent of the Nakatsu domain, in north Kyushu, was held in Hiroshima, a hundred miles

44 Michael Cooper, *They Came to Japan: An Anthology of European Reports on Japan, 1543–1640* (London: Thames and Hudson, 1965), p. 46.
45 Fujii and Hayashi, eds., *Han shi jiten*, p. 521.
46 Takahashi Tomio, *Miyagi-ken no rekishi* (Tokyo: Yamakawa shuppansha, 1969), pp. 124–5.

away. Later in the same century, Sakura *han*, northeast of Edo, held 40 percent of its fief in Dewa, on the other side of Honshu. At one time, too, only 50 percent of Odawara *han* was in the area of the castle town. The remainder was distributed over eleven different counties in six different provinces.[47] Not one of these *tobichi*, as such fragments were called, could have been defended in a civil war, but that – thanks to the Tokugawa bakufu – was no longer an important consideration. What was more significant was that *han* were able to diversify their economic bases in this way, winning access to new kinds of agricultural products or to areas of higher productivity, and insuring themselves to some extent against local crop failure and famine.

Under the Tokugawa, then, the *han* were protected to a degree unimaginable to their Sengoku predecessors. They were also given considerable assistance, for the relationship between the *han* and the bakufu was by no means completely one-sided, with the former giving while the latter took. Justifiably or not, the bakufu believed itself to carry ultimate responsibility for the well-being of the realm, and if from time to time this necessitated making demands of the *han*, it also obliged the bakufu in its turn to respond to their appeals. In such cases, bakufu assistance could take the form of gifts, like the distribution of rice during a famine in the Echigo area in 1676 or subsidies like that announced in 1720, when *han* under 200,000 *koku* (and there would have been some 180 of these) were invited to apply for help with flood control projects.[48]

By far the most common type of assistance, however, took the form of loans, usually repayable over a fixed period of time. Unavailable under normal circumstances, when *han* customarily made use of the great business houses in Kyoto, Edo, and Osaka, these loans were reserved for the emergencies of which Tokugawa Japan seemed able to produce an inordinate number. Fires, floods, typhoons, earthquakes, and volcanic eruptions all were frequent visitors to the *han* of Tokugawa Japan, but whenever a crop was ruined, a castle damaged, or an Edo mansion destroyed, the bakufu could be relied on for aid. In the overwhelming calamities, too, there was no doubt that help would be given. When a plague of grasshoppers devastated crops in western Japan in 1732, loans were immediately made available to the afflicted *han* on a fixed scale – from twenty thousand gold pieces to *han* with

47 Kodama and Kitajima, eds., *Monogatari han shi*, vol. 2, p. 390; *Dai ni ki monogatari han shi*, vol. 7, p. 415; Kimura Motoi and Sugimoto Toshio, eds., *Fudai hansei no tenkai to Meiji ishin* (Tokyo: Bungadō ginkō kenkyūsha, 1963), pp. 29–32.
48 *Yamagata-ken shi (Shiryō-hen)*, vol. 6, pp. 267–8.

300,000 *koku* and over, down to a basic two thousand gold pieces for the smallest *han*.[49] Similar loans were made available in 1784 and the 1830s, during the other great famines of the Tokugawa period.[50] Being loans, such sums were of course repayable – over a ten-year period in the case of those in 1732 – but there are examples of far more indulgent terms: Kokura *han* did not get around to discharging a debt contracted in 1635 until sixty-five years later.[51]

None of this consideration would have been possible had the Tokugawa bakufu been determined to augment its own powers at *han* expense. Had this been the case, one might have anticipated that one of the three great famines would provide the bakufu with the necessary pretext to step in and assume emergency powers that it could thereafter forget to relinquish. That it showed no sign of doing so, at least not until faced with the crisis of the mid-nineteenth century, seems to argue that – as far as the bakufu was concerned – the *han* were there to stay.

Indeed, the bakufu could not have governed without them. Their cooperation was essential, for example, to national defense. The port of Nagasaki, where almost all of Tokugawa Japan's defense and diplomacy was concentrated, depended for its protection not on Tokugawa resources but on those of neighboring *han*, several of which were charged with permanent responsibility for its safety. Hokkaido, too, was an area where the bakufu could not have functioned without the cooperation of *han* like Tsugaru, just across the straits, which was ordered to dispatch three thousand men there during the Russian scare of 1789, or Shōnai, which sent three hundred men to patrol the area during another scare twenty years later.[52] It was also expected that every coastal *han* would take charge of local coast-guard duties, an obligation that gave Nagaoka, for example, a watching brief over nearby Sado Island.[53]

That these responsibilities were observed is indicated by an incident in 1644, when a foreign vessel, presumably Chinese, blundered into Karatsu bay and was sunk by a combined fleet provided by five adjacent *han*.[54] The *han* were also needed to keep the peace, for the bakufu itself had neither the men nor the mobility to deal with any serious insurrection. Certainly the Shimabara Rebellion of 1637–8,

49 *Tokugawa jikki*, vol. 45, p. 611.   50 Ibid., vol. 47, pp. 745–63; vol. 49, p. 282.
51 Kita-Kyūshū, ed., *Buzen sōsho*, 22 vols. (Kita- Kyūshū, 1962–7), vol. 12, p. 51.
52 Furuta Ryōichi hakase kanreki kinen-kai, ed., *Tōhoku shi no shin kenkyū* (Sendai, 1963), p. 288; *Tsuruoka-shi shi*, p. 371.
53 Imaizumi, *Nagaoka no rekishi*, vol. 2, pp. 238–40.
54 Karatsu-shi shi hensan iinkai, ed., *Karatsu-shi shi* (Karatsu, Fukuoka, 1962), p. 570.

which was by far the most serious incident to confront the bakufu before the mid-nineteenth century, could not have been suppressed by Tokugawa forces alone. At the time these numbered no more than 20,000, and it took a force of 125,000 men, provided in the main by the *han* of western Japan, to settle the matter.[55] Similarly, on those occasions when the bakufu ordered the confiscation of a *han*, it relied on the forces of those adjacent to make sure that there was no likelihood of resistance, no matter on how small a scale. Peasant uprisings, too, usually needed *han* cooperation before they could be put down.

In addition to these military obligations, every *han* had an important administrative function. In fact, the *bakuhan* system was firmly based on the full cooperation of these two levels of government. Indeed, it would have been impossible for the bakufu, with its machinery concentrated in Edo, to have governed a country with such a formidable topography as Japan. It was the *han* that provided the tax collectors, magistrates, policemen, and clerks needed for government within their own borders. Further, the bakufu's own landholdings, amounting to 4 million *koku* and scattered over forty-seven provinces, would have been totally ungovernable without regular assistance from nearby *han*. This was obviously the case whenever peasant rebellions broke out.

The bakufu simply did not have – and never seemed anxious to acquire – the number of administrators necessary to govern its own domain. There were of course several coherent and well-defined areas[56] where the bakufu kept its own administrators – Nagasaki, Sado, Kōfu, and Hita among them – but so much bakufu land was strewn around the country in smaller pockets that it was often easier to rely on local *han* administrators, assigning bakufu land to their charge as trust lands (*azukarichi*). A total of twenty-six *han* were to help the bakufu in this capacity, providing caretaker services for what were, in some cases, quite large tracts of land. Aizu bore the heaviest burden, for in addition to its own domain of 230,000 *koku* it also presided over a further 880,000 *koku* of bakufu territory in adjacent parts of Mutsu, Echigo, and Shimotsuke provinces. Others, too, were obliged to carry fairly heavy loads – Nakatsu *han* in north Kyushu, for example, with a domain of 80,000 *koku*, administered almost twice as much bakufu

---

55 Asao, "Shōgun seiji," pp. 21, 31.
56 In fact, as many as forty-two of them; see Chihōshi kenkyū kyōgikai, ed., *Chihōshi kenkyū hikkei* (Tokyo: Iwanami shoten, 1961), pp. 144–5.

land in the same province, gathering its taxes, settling its disputes, and dealing with its criminals.[57]

Clearly, it would have required an immense upheaval to replace the *han* with a totally centralized form of government directed from Edo. Equally clearly, at least after a certain time, the Tokugawa bakufu, though standing to gain most from such a development, appeared to lose interest in the prospect. The death of Tokugawa Iemitsu, the third shogun, in 1651, virtually marked the end of any consistent assault on *han* prerogatives and responsibilities. Thereafter, Tokugawa authority began to deteriorate and, despite sporadic attempts to revive it, never regained its original impetus.

One by one, the original control mechanisms were allowed to run down. The *sankin kōtai* system continued, certainly, but without the underpinning of the hostage system, which was abandoned in 1665 in ostensible commemoration of the fiftieth anniversary of Tokugawa Ieyasu's death.[58] Impositions, too, slackened. Demands for assistance with castle building slowed to a halt by the mid-seventeenth century, to be replaced by much more modest calls for help with river work, canal construction, guard duty, and repairs to the Imperial Palace in Kyoto. True, such demands could occasionally be crippling: Sendai being pressed into providing 6,200 laborers for work on the Koishi-kawa canal in Edo in 1660, for example, and Satsuma laying out more than 300,000 gold pieces in flood control work in Ise, Mino, and Owari, more than four hundred miles to the east, in 1754–5. But overall, the period after 1651 showed nothing as constant or as debilitating as the preceding fifty years.[59] Rather, the bakufu itself came increasingly to shoulder the burden it had once imposed on the *han*, paying, for example, for work on the Ōi River in 1722,[60] a project from which it would never derive any benefit.

The Tokugawa bakufu's inspection scheme, too, lost its early vigor, with surprise visits from parties of *junkenshi*, charged with ferreting out any misgovernment, giving way to formal and perfunctory tours, all announced well ahead of time (even down to the details of their itinerary), all asking predictable questions, and all – inspectors and

---

57 For general information on *azukarichi*, see ibid., p. 146; Shindō Mitsuyuki, "Hansei kaikaku no kenkyū; – jōkamachi shōgyō no kiki o tsūjite mita Nakatsu han hōken kōzō no hōkai katei," *Keizai-gaku kenkyū* 21 (1955): 94–5.
58 Kanai, *Hansei*, p. 29; TKRK, vol. 4, p. 302, states that it was discontinued in 1670.
59 Kitajima Masamoto, ed., *Oie sōdō* (Tokyo: Jimbutsu ōraisha, 1965), p. 149; Fujino, *Daimyō*, pp. 107ff; Yoshizumi Mieko, "Tetsudai bushin ichiran-hyō" *Gakushūin daigaku bungaku-bu kenkyū nempō* 15 (1968): *passim*.
60 Tsuji Tatsuya, *Tokugawa Yoshimune* (Tokyo: Yoshikawa kōbunkan, 1958), p. 69.

inspected alike – hoping earnestly that they might be spared the necessity of presenting a critical report.[61] The *kuniezu*, detailed domain maps demanded of the daimyo in 1644, were required only once more, in 1697.[62]

As a result of this neglect, *han* were able to develop in ways of which the bakufu was to remain ignorant. Land reclamation, which doubled the area of cultivated land in Japan during the Tokugawa period, gave almost every *han* an income considerably in excess of its formal enfeoffment, but this was allowed to escape official notice. Had the bakufu been so inclined, this vast increase could have served as a pretext for a number of legitimate initiatives: It could have increased its own domain by confiscating reclaimed land, for example, or created new *han*, or at the very least it could have incorporated these new areas into the formal enfeoffment of each particular *han* and so provided a more realistic basis for future impositions and military levies. But land reclamation received little formal recognition. Only once, when the Mizuno were transferred from Fukuyama, did the bakufu initiate a new survey and bring hidden productivity out into the open. This done, the bakufu claimed the newly developed land for itself and left what remained to the Mizuno's successors.[63]

There is no doubt that as the flow of information to the bakufu dried up, so did daimyo become much more secure in the possession of their *han*. Bakufu displeasure, formerly enough to shake the largest *han*, was no longer quite such a problem, simply because Edo officialdom no longer knew what it ought to be displeased about. Further, such displeasure as it may have felt came to be expressed with far more diffidence than had once been the case. After 1651 daimyo came to be treated with notable forbearance, receiving, in the main, the lightest of reproofs for offenses that would have cost their fathers and grandfathers dearly. Open dissension among one's vassals, a misdemeanor that had cost at least seven daimyo their fiefs in the first fifty years of the Tokugawa period, was now usually punished with a reprimand, or at most a brief period of house arrest; only the really spectacular cases attracted anything more.

Signs of mental instability, or gross misgovernment, which had once invited bakufu displeasure, continued to do so to some extent, but clearly the definition had changed. The astonishing affair of Matsudaira Sadashige, daimyo of Kuwana, is a case in point. Discovering in 1710

61 Bolitho, *Treasures*, pp. 31–3.   62 Kitajima, *Edo bakufu*, p. 326.
63 Fukuyama-shi shi hensankai, ed., *Fukuyama-shi shi*, 3 vols. (Fukuyama-shi, 1963–7), vol. 2, p. 394.

that one of his officials had been cheating him, the daimyo proceeded to carry out a stupefying number of executions – the guilty man, of course, but also eight of his sons (the youngest only two years old), his grandson (also two years old), his two brothers, ten of his nephews, his octogenarian mother, and several officials. A large number of other officials were also banished or dismissed from their posts. So sensational a loss of control – foreshadowed twenty years earlier by the perceptive compilers of the *Dokai kōshūki*, who had warned of his "quick temper and hotheadedness" and his "severity with his vassals" – would never have been tolerated by the earlier Tokugawa shogun, but by 1710 it was considered to warrant no more than a transfer from one *han* to another.[64]

In 1651, the bakufu offered more evidence of its newfound solicitude for the daimyo, by permitting them the privilege of deathbed adoption. Over the preceding fifty years, forty-one daimyo families had forfeited both *han* and status for failing to produce a convincing heir, an omission that proved them incapable of providing the military and administrative continuity expected of them. Now, after 1651, moribund – or even dead – daimyo, after having had their seals affixed to a petition, could obtain the bakufu's consent to the speedy adoption of a successor and so assure a measure of stability. As a result, the next two centuries of Tokugawa rule could produce only twenty-five attainders under this heading; the bakufu had abandoned its main pretext for confiscation.[65]

It is not surprising, therefore, that with deathbed adoptions, maladministration, and misbehavior freely countenanced after 1651, disenfeoffments should have tailed away so dramatically. Between 1616 and 1651, there had been a total of 95 attainders, an average of just under 3 cases per year. The remainder of the Tokugawa period, from 1652 to 1867, presents a marked contrast, only 118 instances over more than two hundred years, or fewer than 1 a year. Indeed, if one were to exclude the rule of Tokugawa Tsunayoshi, whose incumbency as shogun from 1680 to 1709 produced an extraordinarily large number of disenfeoffments,[66] the total for the remainder of the Tokugawa period would fall to 74, or around 1 every three years.

This new tolerance also lowered the rate of fief transfers, which had been such a feature of the first half-century of Tokugawa rule. Such movements came virtually to an end after 1651, and only a tiny minor-

---

64 Kondō Moku and Hiraoka Jun, eds., *Kuwana-shi shi*, 2 vols. (Kuwana: Kuwana-shi kyōiku iinkai, 1959), vol. 1, pp. 183ff; Kanai, ed., *Dokai kōshūki, p. 258*.
65 Fujino, *Bakuhan*, app. pp. 41–5.   66 Forty-four, to be precise. Ibid.

ity of daimyo were ever moved thereafter. There were some exceptions: The Shirakawa domain changed hands eight times during the
Tokugawa period, and the Yamagata domain twelve, and the Ogyū
branch of the Matsudaira family were relocated no fewer than eleven
times between 1638 and 1764. But the overall statistics leave no room
for doubt that here, too, daimyo had much less to fear after 1651 than
they had earlier. Between 1616 and 1651 there were 205 fief transfers,
at an average rate of something close to 6 per year. The succeeding 215
years could produce only 306, an average of 1.4 per year, a decline of
around 80 percent.[67]

This development, although one that might have been anticipated
of a government now well established after an initial period of uncertainty, did not win total approval. Ogyū Sorai, writing in his *Seidan*
early in the eighteenth century, thought it patently obvious that
"daimyō should be deprived of all their lands when the administration
of their households is bad, or if there are disturbances in their fiefs,"[68]
while several bakufu leaders – Tokugawa Tsunayoshi, Tanuma Okitsugu, and Mizuno Tadakuni among them – seemed willing to revive
some of the old severity.[69] Yet it is possible to see why the bakufu,
seemingly on the very threshold of creating a new and far stronger
kind of central government for Japan, should have called a halt. It
owed its foundation to *han* cooperation. Further, it owed its continued
existence to shogunal forbearance; certainly, with its own domain of
four million *koku* (over six million including *hatamoto* fiefs), it was far
more powerful than even the strongest *han*, but it did not have absolute predominance. Any combination of *han* – as the nineteenth century was to reveal – could muster the resources to topple it, so the
bakufu was forced, even from the beginning, to placate and cosset
them wherever possible.

The apparent ease with which the first three shoguns could dictate
disenfeoffments and fief transfers was deceptive in this respect, for
whenever they invoked their power, as they well knew, they risked
offending all daimyo, who saw, behind the threat to others, a threat to
themselves also. No attainder was ever carried out without some possibility of rebellion – vassals threatening to defy the order, to barricade
themselves inside their castles, and the like – which was why nearby

---

67 Ibid.   68 McEwan, *The Political Writings of Ogyū Sorai*, pp. 76–77.
69 Harold Bolitho, "The Dog Shogun," in Wang Gungwu, ed., *Self and Biography* (Sydney:
    Sydney University Press, 1975); Harold Bolitho, "The Tempō Crisis" in Marius B. Jansen,
    ed., *The Nineteenth Century*, vol. 5 of *The Cambridge History of Japan* (Cambridge, England:
    Cambridge University Press, 1989); see also Bolitho, *Treasures*, pp. 169–79, 190–8; 209–22.

han were always asked to help enforce such decrees. But even more serious was the danger – muted, but there nevertheless – of resistance on a wider scale, in which several *han* might conceivably join forces and come to the aid of one of their number. This fear was clearly uppermost in Iemitsu's mind when, in 1632, having ordered the attainder of Katō Tadahiro (an event that left Tadahiro's neighbor, Hosokawa Tadaoki, "dumbfounded"), the shogun felt constrained to offer a personal explanation to five of Japan's most powerful daimyo – Date Masamune, Maeda Toshitsune, Shimazu Iehisa, Satake Yoshinobu, and Uesugi Sadakatsu.[70]

Other factors also worked to guarantee the *han* a large measure of security against bakufu encroachment. The hereditary principle, for example – important enough at any time in Japanese history – was particularly respected in the Tokugawa period, when it provided the underpinning for the entire social and political fabric. From the emperor down to the humblest farmer, all Japanese were held to have inherited a particular function in society, one that Nature – having allocated their positions – had decreed. The will of Heaven was therefore not to be tampered with unless absolutely necessary, especially not by shoguns who were themselves beneficiaries of the same process. Another explanation may be found in the composition of the bakufu, for its chief administrative and decision-making functions were in the hands of officials who, daimyo themselves, were already convinced both of the desirability of hereditary succession and of the need for *han* to be administered in an atmosphere of stability and security, free from outside interference. Only an extraordinary political figure, a shogun like Hidetada, Iemitsu, or Tsunayoshi or a senior councillor of the caliber of Tanuma Okitsugu or Mizuno Tadakuni, could overrule these men in the interests of the central government.[71]

This is not to say that after 1651 the *han* were entirely free from bakufu intrusion. Disputes among *han* continued to be settled by the bakufu in Edo, for its position as the nation's legal arbiter never changed; their laws, too, in conformity with the 1635 Buke shohatto, were in the main modeled on those of the bakufu. Most *han*, even oldestablished ones, simply found it more convenient to copy Edo laws than to formulate their own, and as society – and the legislation needed to control it – grew more complex, so this tendency increased.[72] This was no more than reasonable, for bakufu laws, for the

70 Asao, "Shōgun seiji," p. 9.   71 Bolitho, *Treasures*, chap. 5.
72 Harafuji Hiroshi, "Kaga han kahō no seikaku," *Kanazawa daigaku hō-bungaku-bu ronshū* (Hōkei hen, 5), 1958. Reprinted in Harafuji Hiroshi, *Bakufu to hampō* (Tokyo: Sōbunsha, 1980).

most part, did no more than reflect the common concerns of the ruling class: concern about Christianity, about fires, about the insubordination of the lower orders, about declining samurai morale, and the lamentable habit common to all classes of eating, drinking, and dressing above their station. Such laws could therefore be adopted by any *han* and displayed on its signboards without doing any violence to existing attitudes. Equally, the bakufu provided services recognizably essential to the nation's commercial health: keeping the major highways in order, standardizing the distance between their milestones, and providing a series of uniform weights and measures. Further, its residual powers, even if seldom used, were available on occasion, and any *han* flouting them ran a risk. It was always open to the bakufu to intervene in domain affairs, here cautioning a daimyo about his behavior, there suggesting a possible candidate for adoption or a consort for his daughter or, as happened in Shōnai in 1811, forcing the retirement of several senior vassals.[73]

Nevertheless, *han* were known to ignore bakufu instructions if they believed their interests required them to do so. Thanks to the decline in disenfeoffments and fief transfers, those interests had been allowed to become concentrated on specific fiefs, and daimyo and vassals alike, anticipating perpetual tenure, accordingly identified their own interests with those of the area assigned to them. Understandably, therefore, they could not be expected to welcome instructions from outside, especially if those instructions seemed to run counter to local interests.

Even in the best of times there was a latent conflict between the *han* and the bakufu, with each able to claim a mandate of a kind – the bakufu on the one hand pledged to govern Japan in the general interest, and the *han* on the other committed primarily to their own prosperity. Usually this conflict stayed hidden well below the surface of Tokugawa life, but on occasion an emergency could thrust the two competing mandates into sharp relief. When this happened, the *han* usually had the upper hand, simply because the bakufu had neither the strength nor the will to compel total obedience.

Most commonly, these clashes took place during famines, or indeed shortages of any kind, when the bakufu, in the interest of Japan as a whole, was obliged to order that supplies be sent where they were most needed. Yet obviously, in an atmosphere of shortage, few *han* had the confidence to part with anything they might subsequently need. Reports of poor harvests in 1660 in Mikawa, Tōtōmi, and Ise prompted a

73 *Tsuruoka-shi shi*, pp. 355; 371–4.

fairly typical reaction elsewhere, with both Aizu and Fukuyama immediately forbidding the export of any cereals, the former noting that
although "it does not seem as though our farmers will starve, it is quite
likely that next year will be very difficult."[74] Reports of drought in the
Kantō and elsewhere eight years later were enough to spur the Aizu
authorities into another embargo of foodstuffs, this time a comprehensive one – not merely rice, wheat, and barley but also soy beans, red
beans, millet, buckwheat, cowpeas, sesame seed oil, and even radishes.[75] Every subsequent famine produced comparable reactions from
those domains fortunate enough to have been spared: Obama banning
the export of cereals and pulse in the mid-eighteenth century, and
Shōnai during the great Tempō famine of the 1830s.[76] In such circumstances, every *han* was really obliged to give priority to its own needs, no
matter how great the crisis elsewhere, and nothing the bakufu could do
was likely to change that.

If the *han* could put their own interests first in even the severest of
national emergencies, as they did all too readily, then there was little to
inhibit a similar approach to lesser issues. The bakufu's attempts to
control the nation's commercial life, successful to some extent in the
seventeenth century, were to evoke little sympathy from the *han* as the
Tokugawa period moved on and as they too had come to depend on
commerce to meet mounting expenses. Economic development had
compelled them all to make the most of such resources as they had or
else fall behind, so they were hardly likely to obey bakufu directives
that, no matter how honestly inspired, were likely to work to their
disadvantage.

A 1730 order to the *han* to stop selling their rice in Osaka until
further notice, for example, was issued with the best possible motives:
There was a glut there, which was making the price artificially low,
and so damaging both the morale and the living standards of the entire
samurai class, almost all of whom had to sell their rice stipends to live.
Effectively, however, the *han*, having priorities of their own, ignored
the command, sending their rice to Osaka as they had always done.
Circumstances hardly permitted them to do anything else. Such
clashes persisted throughout the eighteenth century, with the bakufu's
orders being greeted by *han* noncooperation, and by the nineteenth

74 *Fukuyama-shi shi*, vol. 2, p. 690; Aizu–Wakamatsu-shi shuppan iinkai, ed., *Aizu–
   Wakamatsu-shi* (Aizu–Wakamatsu: Aizu–Wakamatsu-shi, 1967), vo. 9, p. 41.
75 *Aizu Wakamatsu-shi*, pp. 74–75.
76 Fukui-ken, ed., *Fukui-ken shi*, 5 vols. (Tokyo: Sanshūsha, 1921), vol. 2, pt. 2, p. 92;
   Tsuruoka-shi shi, p. 389.

century, as the economic crisis of Tokugawa Japan sharpened, this blossomed into open defiance and competition.[77] Given the chronic financial difficulties that were to overwhelm *han* and bakufu alike, one could hardly have expected anything else.

HAN FINANCES

Traditionally, the *han* derived the bulk of their income – in many cases up to 80 percent and more[78] – from their land tax, calculated as a certain proportion (usually 40 to 50 percent, but sometimes as much as 70 percent)[79] of the estimated annual production of any given piece of land. It applied to rice paddies, of course, but also to the dry fields used to produce almost everything else, from the "miscellaneous cereals" like wheat, barley, and buckwheat, to more overtly commercial crops, like cotton, which was replacing hemp as the popular clothing material, or tobacco, whose production, initially prohibited, was legalized after 1667. Housing sites were also usually subject to land tax, except in newly created castle towns where the authorities had offered tax exemptions in an effort to attract population.[80] There was naturally a great deal of regional variation in methods of tax collection, but on the whole much of the tax on paddy fields was collected in kind, whereas that on dry fields was often, and on housing sites presumably invariably, collected in cash.[81]

There were other, lesser, taxes, known collectively as *komononari*. These had nothing to do with cultivated land but encompassed almost every other kind of economic activity – fishing, seaweed gathering, mining, timber cutting, charcoal burning, bamboo cutting, rush gathering, exploiting hot springs, and whatever other opportunities were offered by *han* natural resources. Nor did those engaged in the manufacturing and service industries escape. The net was cast wide, to include not only the more prosperous members of the community – the local associations of wholesalers, the saké brewers and the pawnbrokers, and others of the kind – but also those involved in more modest activities, like the makers of bean curd, the hairdressers, the thatchers, and the laundrymen, all of whom were obliged to pay a registration fee (*myōgakin*) or a percentage of their turnover (*unjōkin*)

---

77 Tsuda Hideo, "Kansei kaikaku," in *Iwanami kōza Nihon rekishi*, vol. 12 (Tokyo: Iwanami shoten, 1963), p. 257; see also Chapter 9 in this volume, and Bolitho, "The Tempō Crisis."
78 Hiroshima *han* is a case in point. See Aono Shunsui, *Daimyō to ryōmin* (Tokyo: Kyōikusha, 1983), p. 72.
79 See Suwa *han*, for example, in Fujii and Hayashi, eds. *Han shi jiten*, p. 246.
80 Aono, *Daimyō*, p. 182.   81 Fujino, *Daimyō*, pp. 32–3.

or, not uncommonly, both.[82] Such a daunting list, however, suggests a
far greater importance for these miscellaneous taxes than they actually
warranted. True, they tended to increase as economic activity grew
more diverse, but they were never a significant element in *han* finances. In Hiroshima *han* in 1719, as against a land-tax revenue
amounting to almost 80 percent of the total income, these miscellaneous taxes produced only a meager 1.5 percent.[83] The same might be
said of the corvée, from which *han* originally mobilized men for service as porters, carters, messengers, and palanquin bearers in the post
towns, or as laborers for road building, land reclamation, flood control, and repairs to and maintenance of the daimyo's castle. Such
demands, even when commuted into payment in cash or kind, had no
more than a marginal impact on *han* income.[84]

These all were traditional forms of revenue. Local rulers had been
levying land taxes, miscellaneous taxes, and corvée ever since the
beginning of Japanese history and continued to do so free from any
interference by the central government. The trouble was that as traditional taxes, they failed to keep abreast of changing circumstances,
and the *han* were to pay dearly for it. The formal distinction between
wet and dry field agriculture is a case in point. The latter had never
been as highly regarded as the former, for rice was the prestige cereal,
credited with all sorts of benign properties, mystical, as when offered
to the gods (for no other grain would do), and tonic, as when pressed
on the sick as a restorative. Land capable of growing this wondrous
crop, therefore, was far more highly regarded than was any dry field
and so carried a substantially heavier tax burden. Its taxes, too, as we
have seen, were largely collected in kind – that is, as bales of rice –
unlike that on dry fields, for which a vulgar cash settlement was
considered appropriate. Because the precise sum levied on dry fields
was based on a notional estimate, rather than on any realistic calculation involving crop types and market prices, the taxes they paid were
not always related to the returns they brought their cultivators.

Administrators, at least initially, did not readily grasp the fact that a
light sandy soil, totally unsuited to wet-rice production, might nevertheless produce a crop of tobacco, for example, capable of fetching a
high price at Osaka or Edo. Yet, increasingly, such was the case. The
rapid growth and diversification of the economy saw more and more
people moving away from subsistence farming and producing crops

---

82 For Kaga, see ibid., pp. 3–5; for Hikone, see Nakamura Naokatsu, ed., *Hikone-shi shi*, 3
  vols. (Hikone-shi: Hikone shiyakusho, 1960), vol. 1, pp. 607–9.
83 Aono, *Daimyō*, p. 72.   84 Fujino, *Daimyō*, pp. 115–17.

for sale – tobacco and cotton, of course, but also indigo, madder,
rapeseed, and vegetables. In some areas, particularly in central Japan,
commercial agriculture had become the predominant mode by the
eighteenth century: Over 60 percent of the arable land of the provinces
of Settsu and Kawachi was given over to cotton production, which had
proved so lucrative that farmers were even planting it in their paddies.[85] Agriculture, by becoming more varied, had also grown more
profitable, but the *han* (and the bakufu too, for that matter) seemed
unable to take advantage of it.

It is tempting to ascribe such administrative lacunae to ignorance,
inertia, or even to some impermeable precommercial innocence, and
indeed all of these elements may have played a part in the initial failure
of the *han* to react constructively to changes in economic life. But
there was another important element involved as well. For all their
authority over the common people – who were, after all, dragooned
into *goningumi*, or joint responsibility groups, in which all were held
hostage for the good behavior of their fellows, and therefore theoretically totally responsive to direction – very few *han* administrations
were strong enough to do as they pleased. This was particularly so in
matters of taxation. Any intensification of taxes, whether in their rate,
their incidence, or even their administration, was likely to be opposed.
The first stage of such opposition took the form of argument, in which
one of two lines might be pressed. One approach was to label any
variation from former practice a departure from precedent and therefore, by definition, a breach of faith. The other was to draw attention
to nearby *han* where things were done differently, and rather better.
Given the complicated map of Tokugawa Japan, where *han*, portions
of *han*, and fragments of bakufu land lay cheek by jowl, it was never
difficult to point to some neighbor who, under a different administration, was receiving more favorable treatment. Because precedent was
so valued and because there was so much local variation, either of
these gambits could be effective.[86]

If they should fail, then farmers could turn to more emphatic measures. They could, for example, desert their farms en masse, as they did
in Shōnai in 1632, when large numbers trooped across the *han* border
into Akita rather than submit to a new (and presumably more accurate)
land survey, or as 3,000 farmers from Takatō *han* did in 1654 in protest
against administrative "tyranny."[87] The next, and graver, step was an

85 Ōtsuka shigakkai, ed., (*Shimpan*) *Kyōdo shi jiten* (Tokyo: Asakura shoten, 1969), p. 611.
86 Aono, *Daimyō*, p. 219, cites some examples from the Hiroshima area.
87 *Tsuruoka-shi shi*, p. 265; Fujii and Hayashi, eds., *Han shi jiten*, p. 247.

intimidatory show of solidarity, like that displayed by the 300,000 peasants who jammed into Hiroshima in 1718 to protest against a new (and
once again presumably more accurate) survey of their lands, or the
20,000 farmers in Karatsu who joined together to protest the imposition
of a new tax on low-lying land, as well as the fact that their normal taxes
were now being measured out with a far larger measure than usual, and
a heaped one, at that.[88] Such incidents, increasingly spilling over into
violence, were frequent enough in the seventeenth century, but their
rate more than doubled in the eighteenth – upwards of a thousand cases
between 1715 and 1815, as against fewer than five hundred over the
period 1615 to 1715.[89] In almost every case, new taxation initiatives on
the part of the authorities, *han* or bakufu, according to location, was at
the root of the trouble. The more efficiently these governments tried to
tap the traditional sources of income, the more resistance they encountered, and the more effective that resistance was.

Of course, in all but the very largest demonstrations, the *han* had
the military force needed to restore order. They often did so and
frequently none too gently; it was not unknown for protest leaders to
be beheaded for their pains, as a warning to future malcontents.[90] But
nevertheless, the relationship between *han* officals and peasants was a
particularly delicate one. Any dispute, if mishandled, could well bring
about such turmoil that the bakufu would be compelled to intervene,
in which case the daimyo and his officials might not go unscathed.
Kōriki Takanaga lost his domain at Shimabara and Yashiro Tadataka
his at Hōjō in precisely such circumstances.[91]

Peasant protest was possible because the bakufu had recognized as
early as 1603 that peasants, no matter where they lived, had certain
rights, among them the right to formal complaint and the right to
desert their fields and move elsewhere, if necessary.[92] Subsequently,
after experiencing difficulties of its own in this regard, the bakufu was
to regret its magnanimity, but the principle still remained. Once confronted by a determined peasant opposition, *han* often found it politic
to compromise, even to back down, rather than risk a prolonged,
costly, embarrassing, and potentially damaging dispute. The fact was
that *han* needed their peasants and needed them, moreover, to be
reasonably healthy and moderately content. Few daimyo would have

---

88 Aono, *Daimyō*, p. 220; *Karatsu-shi shi*, pp. 592–3.
89 Aoki Kōji, *Hyakushō ikki no nenji-teki kenkyū* (Tokyo: Shinseisha, 1966), p. 17.
90 One of the earliest examples from the Tokugawa period is the beheading in 1608 of twelve
    Chōshū peasant leaders. Minegishi Kentarō, "Seiritsu-ki han keizai no kōzō," in Furushima
    Toshio, ed., *Nihon keizai shi taikei* (Tokyo: Tōkyō daigaku shuppan-kai, 1965), vol. 3, p. 222.
91 Fujii and Hayashi, eds., *Han shi jiten*, pp. 489, 158.   92 TKRK, vol. 5, p. 150.

disagreed with Ikeda Mitsumasa of Okayama *han*, who in 1655 spoke of his concern that "the peasants should be robust and devote themselves to their agriculture."[93] Twenty-odd years later, officials in Fukuyama *han* were warning of exhaustion among the peasantry and urging that they be allowed adequate opportunity for relaxation.[94]

The traditional framework really offered the *han* only one way of augmenting their income without unduly provoking their peasants, and this was land reclamation. If they could increase the area under cultivation and make sure that it all paid taxes at the appropriate rate, then to that extent *han* revenues would rise. The prospect was undeniably attractive, whether achieved by the *han* itself – perhaps using corvée labor – or else by local entrepreneurs working with official knowledge and permission. Many *han*, availing themselves of the opportunity, were able to expand their productive capacity by 30 percent and more: The area of cultivated land in Tsugaru *han* doubled during the seventeenth century, and in both Shōnai, farther down the Japan Sea coast, and Fukuyama, over on the Inland Sea, it increased by at least a third.[95] Between 1600 and 1720, in fact, the area of cultivated land in Japan grew by a colossal 82 percent.[96] But reclamation could not be extended indefinitely, particularly not within the limits of contemporary technology, and by the early eighteenth century those limits appeared to have been reached. The next 150 years could produce an increase of no more than 3 percent.[97] In any case, few *han* would have had a completely free hand with their reclamation; undoubtedly much of it was carried on surreptitiously by peasants who, having cleared or drained small plots for themselves, strenuously resisted the visits of any inspectors who might have discovered them.[98]

It was in the eighteenth century, when reclamation was almost at an end, that many *han* administrators became aware of a new problem. Not only was it now virtually impossible for them to increase returns from traditional sources, but more disturbing still, their revenues were actually shrinking.[99] There were several reasons for this. In part it came about through the concentration of samurai in castle towns, a phenomenon observable in much of Japan by the late seventeenth

93 Quoted in Aono *Daimyō* p. 17.   94 Ibid., p. 99.
95 Miyazaki Michio, *Aomori-ken no rekishi* (Tokyo: Yamakawa shuppansha, 1970), pp. 149–50; *Tsuruoka-shi shi*, p. 296; Aono, *Daimyō*, p. 80.
96 Aono, *Daimyō*, p. 79.   97 Ibid.
98 Miura Toshiaki, "Hamamatsu-han ryōiki no keisei to shukueki joseikin," *Chihō-shi kenkyū* 79 (1966): 85.
99 For some examples, see *Fukuyama-shi shi*, p. 496; Nagaoka shiyakusho, ed., *Nagaoka-shi shi* (Nagaoka: Nagaoka shiyakusho, 1931), p. 109; Taniguchi Sumio, *Okayama han* (Tokyo: Yoshikawa kōbunkan, 1964), pp. 145–6.

century. No matter how greatly this had contributed to the stability and coherence of *han* governments, it had robbed them of their commanding position in the countryside. Village affairs were now left almost completely in the care of the headmen, themselves farmers and therefore subject to precisely the same pressures as their fellows were. Consequently they reacted to their freedom by underreporting yields, by neglecting to register freshly cultivated land, and by concealing the extent of rural commerce.

There were other contributing factors as well. In provinces like Settsu and Kawachi, the transformation of highly taxed rice paddies into more modestly taxed cotton fields inevitably led to reduced revenues. So too did a steady drift of farming population away from the villages and into country towns, castle towns, and the great urban centers of Edo and Osaka.[100] For that matter, agriculture was notoriously unpredictable during the Tokugawa period, and most *han* found themselves compelled to reduce or suspend normal taxation from time to time to help their farmers cope with disasters of one sort or another. In the northeast, where crop failures were common, unseasonable cold was usually the problem; elsewhere the agricultural cycle could be shattered by anything from floods, typhoons, and mud slides to earthquakes and volcanic eruptions. Whatever the cause, every *han* sooner or later had to recognize genuine hardship and make some sort of allowance for it. Even Nagaoka, after three successive years of flooding in the 1680s, was forced to acknowledge the gravity of the situation to the extent of subsidizing rice sales, providing shelter for the homeless, and suspending, albeit temporarily, the torture of those who had defaulted on their taxes.[101]

Naturally, declining incomes made the *han* far more sensitive to their expenses, and these were substantial. Despite the Tokugawa peace, in which no armies took the field between 1638 and 1864, every *han* was compelled to maintain a standing army. The bakufu's *gun'yaku* requirements would admit of nothing else. Paradoxically, it had been far less costly for daimyo to maintain armies in the Sengoku period, when fighting was more or less constant, than it proved to be in the tranquillity of the Tokugawa period.

In the sixteenth century, samurai had been mobilized only when necessary and supported themselves by farming the rest of the time. Whenever they did fight, they were subject to the full rigors of mili-

100 Susan B. Hanley and Kozo Yamamura, *Economic and Demographic Change in Preindustrial Japan, 1600–1868* (Princeton, N.J.: Princeton University Press, 1977), pp. 103–14.
101 Imaizumi, *Nagaoka no rekishi*, vol. 2, pp. 122–3.

tary Darwinism: Only the fittest survived. Under the Tokugawa, however, the situation was totally different; the majority of samurai no longer farmed but lived permanently on the payroll, whether in castle towns or in Edo (where some *han* were known to keep as many as 30 to 40 percent of their samurai stationed permanently).[102] Further, because none of them ever fought, old samurai tended to fade away rather than die, never so enfeebled as to be unable to draw their stipends at twice-yearly intervals. Yet, no matter how crushing the samurai incubus, no *han* could do much about it. Ōgaki actually succeeded in ridding itself of 150 samurai in 1680, after having received special permission from the bakufu, and in the late eighteenth century, Yonezawa, attempting a gentler approach, suggested hopefully that the second and third sons of its samurai families might like to find alternate employment as farmers,[103] but these were the exceptions rather than the rule.

Even by the bakufu's 1649 standardization of *gun'yaku* obligations,[104] which called upon even the smallest *han* to maintain a force of 235 men, Tokugawa Japan would have been spectacularly well endowed with samurai. But the fact was that although the bakufu had established a minimum figure for each *han*, it had deliberately refrained from setting a maximum. In the coda to its 1649 instructions, it had effectively left open the way for *han* to employ as many samurai as they wished, so long as they all were "loyal." It was not uncommon, therefore, for *han* of comparable endowment to differ wildly from one another in samurai numbers. Yonezawa, Takada, and Kōriyama all had much the same assessed productivity – roughly 150,000 *koku* – but although the last two had no more than two thousand samurai each, Yonezawa maintained four times that number.[105] More than anything else, such discrepancies were due to differing histories. Both Takada and Kōriyama owed their creation to Tokugawa patronage in the seventeenth century, and they were therefore able to employ just as many men as required, and no more. Yonezawa, by contrast, had come into being by a different route. It was in the hands of the Uesugi, a family prominent in eastern Japan since the fourteenth century. They had survived to enter the seventeenth century with both lands and military machine largely intact but, on being deprived of half of the

102 *Fukuyama-shi shi*, pp. 469–70; Kimura and Sugimoto, eds., *Fudai hansei*, pp. 26–7.
103 Ōgaki shiyakusho, ed., *Ōgaki-shi shi*, 3 vols. (Ōgaki, 1930), vol. 1, pp. 415–17; Tsuda, "Kansei kaikaku," p. 278.
104 TKRK, vol. 1, pp. 90–2.
105 Hanseishi kenkyūkai, ed., *Hansei seiritsushi no sōgō kenkyū – Yonezawa han* (Tokyo: Yoshikawa kōbunkan, 1963), p. 369.

former in 1664, still found themselves prevented by old ties of loyalty and obligation (and perhaps by fear of repercussions) from shedding anything like half their vassals. Many other *han* – Chōshū among them – were similarly placed.

It was all an immense burden. *Han* did what they could with their samurai, training and educating many of them for useful employment as civil servants of one sort of another – magistrates, censors, schoolmasters, secretaries, gamekeepers, policemen, foresters, bailiffs – and appointing those left over to sonorous and virtually meaningless military positions – guards, lancers, captains of the colors, and buglers (or at least blowers of conch shells).

A glance at the administrative structure of any *han* shows a bewildering range of posts: about 150 of them in Sakura *han* and almost as many in Owari.[106] Yet it was all so much window dressing. There was simply not enough business to engage the services of such a vast number of samurai – probably as many as 350,000 in the service of the various *han* – all of the time. Even with rotation and rostering there was not enough useful work to go around, so few could ever hope for more than temporary employment. Their status, nevertheless, remained constant, and so did their right to a basic salary. They served merely as a standing army (perhaps lounging army would be more apt a description), kept waiting for whatever emergency should arise. Ironically, that emergency did not eventuate for over two hundred years, and when it did, it found them lamentably unprepared.

The other major drain on *han* finances was a by-product of the *sankin kōtai* system, under which daimyo were required to take up residence in Edo every alternate year. No part of this ritual was ever done cheaply. It was unthinkable, for example, that a daimyo should sidle unobtrusively into Edo. Instead, he made it his business to set out on his journey with as splendid an escort as possible. The daimyo *gyōretsu*, or procession, numbering as many as a thousand men with spears and pennants, was one of the most splendid sights Tokugawa Japan had to offer. It was also one of the most costly, for it was no easy matter to move large numbers of men across Japan. In the case of the more distant *han*, like Karatsu in north Kyushu, for example, when the journey needed more than thirty overnight stops, the outlay for food and shelter en route was enormous. Every other year Saga *han*,

---

106 Kimura and Sugimoto, *Fudai hansei*, p. 21; Hayashi Tōichi, *Owari han no kōhōshi no kenkyū* (Tokyo: Nippon gakujutsu shinkōkai, 1962), pp. 153–6.

FINANCES   221

Karatsu's near neighbor, customarily spent 20 percent of that year's
income on the journey alone.[107]
   Nor did the cost diminish once the daimyo and his retinue had
reached Edo. "Above all, we must economize when we are in Edo,"
warned the senior vassals of the daimyo of Karatsu in 1782, and not
without reason.[108] Virtually everything the daimyo and his vassals
needed for their stay in Edo, from food and fuel to paper and ink,
had to be bought there at Edo prices, almost always higher than
those current at home. There were, too, unremitting temptations to
spend – familiar enough to any urban society, but particularly intense in a city where samurai from all over Japan competed with one
another in keeping up appearances. Each daimyo, too, no matter
how frugal by personal inclination, was caught up in the same contest and was obliged to live in a manner befitting his eminence, real
or pretended.
   All of them therefore maintained mansions of some elegance, often
set in notable gardens, traces of which are still to be seen in Tokyo: the
Kōrakuen for example, once the property of Mito *han*, or the
Rikugien, which belonged to the Yanagisawa of Kōriyama. It was
customary for *han* to have more than one such residence. The chief
one, known as the *kami-yashiki*, functioned as a permanent legation,
where a staff of officials attended to the *han*'s Edo business and where
the daimyo was housed during his *sankin kōtai* stays. A secondary
residence, or *naka-yashiki*, accommodated the daimyo's heir apparent
but also provided shelter for the daimyo whenever necessary, as, for
example, on the many occasions when the official residence had been
either destroyed by fire or was being rebuilt in readiness for the next.
It was common, too, for *han* to have yet another residence, this time a
shimo-yashiki, or holiday house, in some distant quarter of the city, to
which the daimyo and his family could repair during the worst of the
summer heat. As reported in the *Edo zusetsu* of 1799, there were 265
official residences and another 734 secondary residences and holiday
houses scattered around the city.[109]
   Compared with such massive outlays, the normal run of expenses
back in the *han* seems rather meager. It was expected, and indeed
often explicitly stated, that the *han* themselves were to be administered

107 *Karatsu-shi shi*, p. 617; Sasaki Junnosuke, *Daimyō to hyakushō*, vol. 15 of *Chūō kōron Nihon no rekishi* (Tokyo: Chūō kōronsha, 1966), p. 156.
108 Matsuyoshi Sadao, *Kanemochi daimyō bimbō daimyō* (Tokyo: Jimbutsu ōraisha, 1964), p. 69.
109 Cited in Fujino, *Daimyō*, p. 95.

as conservatively as possible, eschewing all expenses not absolutely necessary to their primary function of feeding the samurai and maintaining the system. Typically, budgets began and ended with the needs of the samurai class (stipends and education) and their obligations (*han* defense and alternate attendance). The needs of the remaining 90 percent of *han* population figure only occasionally and grudgingly in *han* ledgers, and then only in times of crisis. Under normal circumstances they were left to fend for themselves, their lives, customs, and amusements frequently the subject of *han* regulation, but never its object. All they gained in return for their taxes was the attempted perpetuation of conditions under which their future contributions to *han* finances might be maximized.

In any case, no *han* could really have afforded to do anything more for its common people. As it was, with revenues stagnant or declining and enormous commitments in Edo and to their samurai, it was more and more difficult for the *han* to balance their budgets. It is hardly necessary to go through the dispiriting roll call of those *han* that tottered through the eighteenth and early nineteenth centuries (and even part of the seventeenth century) poised precariously on the knife-edge between indigence and bankruptcy. It was a state common to them all, to a greater or lesser degree, and their responses to it were broadly similar. The instinctive reaction to the crisis, when it first appeared, was for *han* governments to accuse the common people of living above their station and to call upon them to spend less and surrender more. Next came internal economy drives, initially for fixed periods (five years being the favored figure), but sooner or later these periods became consecutive; one such initiative launched by Kanazawa *han* in 1779 was still in force twenty years later.[110] At such times not even the daimyo's own household expenses escaped scrutiny, a fact that was sometimes known to drive needy daimyo into the welcoming arms of the pawnbrokers. It was in precisely such circumstances that Sakai Tadazane of Shōnai came to pledge two family heirlooms – a noted tea bowl and a painting – for a thousand gold pieces. His successor, Tadayori, beset by similar difficulties, did the same with his wife's hair ornaments, originally part of her dowry.[111]

Overwhelmingly, however, *han* governments confronted the financial crisis with the help of moneylenders, usually the great merchant houses of Osaka and Kyoto – the Kōnoike (who had thirty-one indebted *han* on their books by the end of the seventeenth century),[112]

---

110 Ibid., p. 207.   111 *Tsuruoka-shi shi*, pp. 326, 336.   112 Fujino, *Daimyō*, p. 163.

the Sumitomo, the Masuya, and others – but gradually coming to rely on local merchants as well.

The borrowing had in fact begun very early, particularly in the case of *han* like Sendai, Chōshū, Satsuma, Saga, and Tosa, all of which were compelled to contribute heavily to the bakufu's castle-building projects at the beginning of the seventeenth century.[113] By the end of that century, however, and long after the heaviest of bakufu impositions had been met, every *han* had gone into debt. Few of them ever emerged, for the interest on those debts (usually from 5 to 7 percent per annum)[114] was to prove beyond the resources of all but the very richest of *han*. Tosa, by 1688, was spending 34 percent of its budget repaying loans; Hiroshima, across the Inland Sea, unable to meet even the interest on its debt, owed the Kōnoike house a sum that in 1745 had grown precisely ten-fold since 1719; for Okayama, by 1829, payments to moneylenders had come to represent the largest single item in its annual budget.[115] The *han* had thus built such a superstructure of debt for themselves that only the most draconian measures – the unilateral repudiation of all debts, for example[116] – could set them free. Budget deficits and chronic debts were as much a part of *han* life as they are of our own, and no matter how much contemporaries deplored them, it is certain that they, like ourselves, also learned to live with them, at least until the cataclysmic events of the mid-nineteenth century.

There were just two other avenues open to *han* wishing to enhance their finances. In most cases, neither of them proved to be anything more than a mild palliative, leaving the superstructure of *han* debts largely untouched. Both of them, however, were of some political significance. In following one of them, *han* governments found themselves at odds with local residents; in following the other, they were to erode their relations with their own samurai. Nevertheless, given the circumstances in which they found themselves, the *han* had little alternative but to pursue them both.

The first was essentially a reaction to the commercial development of the Tokugawa period, in which the medieval ideal of individual self-sufficiency crumbled under the pressures of commercial farming and specialized manufacture. It was not long before the *han* governments responded to the change, with mercantilist policies that encouraged local products with protection inside the domain (to stop money from

113 Ibid., p. 200; Sasaki, *Daimyō*, pp. 132–3. 114 Fujino, *Daimyō*, p. 164.
115 Hirao Michio, *Tosa han* (Tokyo: Yoshikawa kōbunkan, 1965), pp. 33–34; Aono, *Daimyō*, p. 73; Taniguchi, *Okayama hansei*, p. 160.
116 Bolitho, "The Tempō Crisis," pp. 32–3.

leaving the *han*) and outside with purposeful marketing (to bring money into the *han*). This attention proved a mixed blessing to local producers, however.

Those who benefited by protection – the ink makers of Aizu, for example, freed from competition by a ban on imported ink in 1791 – could not have been more pleased.[117] Such was not the case, though, with producers of more highly prized commodities. As the indigo growers of Tokushima, the madder growers of Yonezawa, the lacquer makers of Aizu, the potters of Saga, and countless other farmers and craftsmen were to discover, few *han* could resist trying to siphon away the profits. The experience of the Karatsu paper-mulberry growers in this regard is fairly typical. With their crop subject to compulsory acquisition orders by the *han* and with severe punishment threatened for anyone attempting to evade such orders, they were obliged to sell what they grew to none but authorized buyers, and at a third of the price obtainable outside the domain.[118] The *han*, having bought cheaply, intended to sell dear elsewhere and to pocket the proceeds. Indeed, quite often in such cases, local producers were to be paid in *hansatsu*, *han* paper currency, worth virtually nothing outside the *han* borders and little more inside. It was a tidy scheme, but it did not often work. Inevitably there was resistance. The Karatsu case is no less typical in this respect, for its paper-mulberry farmers rioted in 1771, as did cotton farmers in Fukuyama in 1752, Matsuyama tea growers in 1741, Oka tobacco growers in 1811, and innumerable other farmers and craftsmen and manufacturers at various times during the Tokugawa period.[119] So fierce were these protests, and so determined and inventive local producers in evading official directives, that few *han* managed to recoup their finances as easily as they had originally hoped. Nevertheless, illusion though it may have been, it was virtually the last one that most *han* had, and they therefore clung to it all the more tenaciously.

The remaining possibility for *han* intent on relieving financial pressures was yet another form of borrowing. This time, however, rather than from the great merchant houses, which always had to be appeased in some way, loans were levied from a captive source – the samurai themselves. Such inroads into samurai salaries began quite early in the Tokugawa period: as early as 1623 in Chōshū, 1639 in Hiroshima, the 1650s in Fukuyama, and the 1670s in

117 *Aizu–Wakamatsu-shi*, vol. 9, p. 238.   118 *Karatsu-shi shi*, p. 621.

119 Ibid., p. 593; *Fukuyama-shi shi*, p. 537; Aono, *Daimyō*, p. 187; Kishida Tsutomu, "Kyūshū no bunjinga," in Mikami Tsugio, ed., *Kyūshū no ega to tōgei* (Tokyo: Heibonsha, 1975), p. 246.

Nagaoka.[120] Initially samurai were called upon only intermittently to give back part of their salaries, usually in reponse to some immediate need, as in the case of Nagaoka, where a special levy was made to pay for a wedding in the daimyo's family.[121] But once the first step had been taken and the principle established that samurai could be expected to surrender part of their stipends in the general interest, then it was much easier the next time there was an emergency.

Ultimately, forced loans from samurai became a constant feature of *han* life. In Shōnai *han* between 1690 and 1797 there were just nine years in which all samurai received their full stipends; the rest of the time anybody with more than two hundred *koku* was obliged to part with a percentage of it (usually 7 percent). In 1741, nobody received any salary at all; instead they were given a daily ration of rice and a small amount of copper cash, just enough to see them through the immediate crisis and no more. Nor was their experience unusual; at Hikone, reduced stipends were so much a matter of course that samurai had to be notified when they were to be paid in full. In Matsushiro *han*, full stipends were granted only once in 138 years.[122]

In all of this the samurai were to prove themselves far more tractable than the peasants were. Such security as they had depended entirely on their *han*, so they could be relied on to make whatever sacrifices were necessary, even if it meant "temporary" salary reductions that were never made good or "loans" that were never repaid. For all of them, the alternative – dismissal and the total loss of salary and status – was generally far less attractive than genteel poverty. Nevertheless, their cooperation was far from enthusiastic, and all *han* were to pay for these exactions in two ways. First, poverty produced a samurai class far too poorly equipped and demoralized to meet even the smallest emergency. Second, in the context of *han* political life, hardship forced samurai of all ranks to take a far keener interest in *han* affairs than they might otherwise have done and so ultimately helped bring about a revolution in government.

HAN POLITICS

It is not to be thought that the samurai had been totally tamed by the conditions of life in Tokugawa Japan. True, many of them had been

120 Fujino, *Daimyō*, p. 210; Aono, *Daimyō*, p. 74; *Fukuyama-shi shi*, p. 5, Imaizumi, *Nagaoka no rekishi*, vol. 1, p. 118.
121 *Nagaoka-shi shi*, p. 114.
122 *Tsuruoka-shi shi*, pp. 322, 339; *Hikone-shi shi*, vol. 1, pp. 624–5; Fujino, *Daimyō*, p. 214.

removed from their old country estates and brought into residence in the new castle towns, but this in itself did not necessarily mean subjection. Certainly they were now under constant scrutiny, utterly reliant on their salaries, and virtually denied alternative employment. They were infinitely more dependent than they had ever been; yet they were far from quiescent. Paradoxically, the establishment of the Tokugawa peace had created circumstances that not only enabled samurai to question their daimyo's prerogative but, on occasion, compelled them to do so and so made inevitable a degree of political ferment.

In theory, of course, no challenge to daimyo authority should have been possible. In accepting each daimyo's submission, the Tokugawa government guaranteed its support to every one of them in turn. Their legal right to govern their *han* was therefore unassailable. So, too, was a certain moral obligation, for Heaven had selected each one of them for precisely that position. As Uesugi Harunori, daimyo of Yonezawa, expressed it in a piece of calligraphy written on his accession in 1767, this obligation was clear: "Father and Mother of the People," the inscription read, followed by a poem, "Inheriting the command of this domain, I must never forget that I am father and mother to my people."[123] There were also practical considerations, as the daimyo, it was thought, were the custodians of secret traditions enabling them to rule far more effectively than ordinary men could. Such, at least, was believed of the daimyo of Saga, alleged in *Hagakure* to have had a number of secret books entrusted to him on his accession.[124] For all of these reasons, it was the clear duty of the samurai to obey their daimyo, even, for some favored samurai in the early seventeenth century, to follow him to the grave in token of their loyalty, devotion, and obedience.

Yet in practice there were difficulties. The daimyo of Tokugawa Japan, no less than their Sengoku predecessors, walked a tightrope – nearer to the ground, perhaps, and slightly slacker, but still needing to be traversed with the utmost care. Many realized how volatile their vassals could be, sometimes feeling impelled to warn them, as did the daimyo of Shōnai in 1648, against "factious, conspiratorial, or obstructive behavior" or, as did the young daimyo of Aizu forty years later, demanding of his senior vassals a special oath of loyalty, signed in

123 Naramoto Tatsuya, Hosokawa Morisada, and Murakami Genzō, eds., *Edo daimyō hyakke*, vol. 22 of *Taiyō bekkan* (Tokyo: Heibonsha, 1978), p. 162.
124 Naramoto Tatsuya, ed., *Hagakure*, vol. 17 of *Nihon no meicho* (Tokyo: Chūō kōronsha, 1969), pp. 54–5.

blood.[125] Paradoxically, these difficulties were directly traceable to bakufu policies. By compelling daimyo to spend at least half of their working lives in Edo under the *sankin kōtai* system, for example, the bakufu had effectively obliged them to leave the larger part of normal decision making in the hands of those senior vassals permanently resident in the *han*. Daimyo therefore were only intermittently in contact with *han* affairs and even when in residence were inevitably tempted to leave decisions to those who were better informed.

Still more serious was the Tokugawa government's commitment to the principle of hereditary succession. This virtually guaranteed the appointment of the fit and unfit alike. Not even the demonstrably infirm, the palpably dull-witted or the openly uninterested were disqualified. A confidential appraisal of daimyo in the late seventeenth century was able to call attention to those who could never have survived in an earlier period: Matsuura Masashi, "who has made friends of every merchant and priest in Edo with a liking for *kemari*";[126] Itami Katsumasa, "devoted to beautiful women and boys"; Date Munezumi, "totally obsessed with sex, spending all day in his bedchamber while feigning indisposition"; and Hoshina Masayoshi, "ignorant and totally lacking in ability."[127] By the eighteenth century, Arai Hakuseki was able to use the term "daimyo's sons" as a derisive epithet, a judgment confirmed 150 years later by Ernest Satow, who met too many daimyo to have any great opinion of them.[128] Not uncommonly, too, the bakufu was prepared to confirm any legitimate heir as daimyo, no matter how young he might be – even indeed before he could walk. Of the 163 daimyo in 1691 for whom such information is available, a total of 85, or more than half, appear to have become daimyo before reaching the age of twenty.[129]

The regular absence of all daimyo from their *han*, combined with the Tokugawa government's almost total support for hereditary succession, was enough to create a power vacuum in many *han*, but not for long. Inevitably it was filled, sometimes by relatives or, increasingly, by senior vassals. By 1691 it was obviously accepted that this was likely; the same confidential report that spoke so freely of daimyo

125 *Yamagata-ken shi (shiryō-hen)*, vol. 5, p. 352; *Aizu Wakamatsu-shi shi*, vol. 9, pp. 106–7.
126 *Kemari*, one of Japan's traditional sports was a football game in which a number of players cooperated in keeping a deerskin ball in the air for as long as possible.
127 Kanai, ed., *Dokai kōshūki*, pp. 701, 616, 478, 578.
128 Miyazaki Michio, ed., *Teihon "Oritaku shiba no ki" shakugi* (Tokyo: Shibundō, 1964), p. 575; Sir Ernest Satow, *A Diplomat in Japan* (Oxford, England: Oxford University Press, 1968), p. 37.
129 Calculated from Kanai, ed., *Dokai kōshūki*.

shortcomings made this clear: "Leaving the government of one's people to senior vassals has both good and bad features," it warned. "It is good when the vassal puts loyalty first and follows the right path selflessly and unswervingly. But if the vassal is deceitful and harbors mischievous designs while counterfeiting loyalty . . . and uses his authority selfishly and unjustly, then that house will surely fall."[130]

Equally, other pressures made sure that vassals were not merely able to supplant their daimyo in all but name but indeed were obliged to. Political power by itself was perhaps not such a prize, offering at the most a massage for the ego, marginally better living conditions, and agreeable opportunities for the exercise of patronage. But the alternative, as far as samurai were concerned, could be disastrous. If a daimyo, selected by no process more discriminating than the accident of birth, were to attempt to rule his *han* personally, then who could say what havoc he might let loose? He might be led by flatterers to overturn the traditional samurai hierarchy; he might prove spendthrift; or he might bankrupt the *han* or even, by attracting Tokugawa displeasure, put his own tenure at risk, and with it that of all his samurai as well.

The dangers inherent in daimyo autocracy were just too great to allow samurai, dependent as they were on their *han* and its well-being, the luxury of meek obedience. Naturally, they preferred their daimyo to be ciphers, like the well-loved Makino Tadataka, who became daimyo of Nagaoka at the age of seventeen. Although he died the following year and would therefore have had neither the years nor the time to do very much, his reputation is nevertheless that of a model ruler: "He was careful not to neglect military matters," the chronicles say, "and was concerned always for the common people. He instructed his government that old ways should be reformed and abuses corrected, that honest men should be promoted and corrupt officials dismissed. . . . He knew how to teach his people through the impartial use of severity and mercy. Conditions improved immediately, and hardships were thankfully forgotten."[131] Such a daimyo was no trouble to anyone and therefore was always appreciated. Even those marginally more active could be controlled with a minimum of effort and within the political conventions; the only evidence of struggle would then be confined to ripples on the surface – resignations, dismissals, appointments, and muted complaints – the last sometimes embodied in appeals to the

130 Ibid., pp. 587–8.   131 Imaizumi, *Nagaoka no rekishi*, vol. I, pp. 82–3.

daimyo's good sense and better nature or, should these prove unsuccessful, in an occasional case of remonstratory suicide.[132] The encomium for the young Makino Tadataka, dead in his nineteenth year, contrasts vividly with the reputations of determined reformers like Mizuno Tadatoki, whose policies in Okazaki *han* so outraged his senior vassals that they placed him under house arrest and forced him to retire.[133] This was playing the game hard, but given what was at stake, it could scarcely have been otherwise. Throughout the Tokugawa period, indeed, a constant succession of *oiesōdō*, spectacular public disputes, was to mark those occasions when daimyo and samurai came into conflict over policy issues or, alternatively, when samurai and samurai came into conflict over the daimyo. Some of the more celebrated of these disputes offer enough drama – father against son (Miyazu *han*), brother against brother (Tokuno *han*), uncle against nephew (Sendai *han*), daimyo against vassals (Yonezawa *han*), vassals against daimyo (Kokura *han*), and vassal against vassal (Suwa *han*), all punctuated with arrests, suicides, executions, assassinations, poison plots, and mass walkouts – to satisfy the most jaded kabuki audience.

Some, indeed, did just that. The famous Sendai incident, heavily fictionalized, first appeared on the stage forty years after it erupted and thereafter provided the framework for some thirty different plays.[134] It is not too difficult to see why. The situation – a power vacuum in the *han* brought on by the enforced retirement of the daimyo, and his replacement by his two-year-old son – was pure kabuki. So were the leading characters in the struggle that soon exploded, a wicked uncle, an even more wicked greatuncle, and a number of unscrupulous vassals, all of them whipping up conspiracies, murder plots, and formal letters of complaint to the government in Edo. The denouement, a meeting of opponents at an inquiry held in the residence of a senior bakufu politician, added a touch of Grand Guignol, as swords were drawn and four men were cut down, two dying instantly and the others receiving mortal wounds.[135]

Such disputes were not without their risks. With tempers running high, violence was not uncommon. But there were more serious hazards still. Once one of these incidents became public, it then invited bakufu intervention, and this could sometimes take an unpalatable

---

132 For an example of a complaint, see *Tsuruoka-shi shi*, pp. 323–4; for a remonstratory suicide, see *Karatsu-shi shi*, p. 607.
133 Kitajima Masamoto, "Meikun no higeki," in Itō Tasaburō, ed., *Kokumin seikatsu shi kenkyū*, vol. 1 of *Seikatsu to seiji* (Tokyo: Yoshikawa Kōbunkan, 1957).
134 Kitajima, ed., *Oiesōdō*, pp. 173–4.   135 Ibid., p. 168.

form, as Edo did not usually approve of troublemakers, and execution or exile was not uncommon. Still more serious, the bakufu could interpret such events as proof of a *han*'s inability to govern itself and issue a confiscation order. This was precisely the way in which the Mogami of Yamagata, the Hiraoka of Tokuno, the Matsudaira of Echigo, and the Kyōgoku of Miyazu came to lose their domains, and how Morioka and Kōriyama *han* both came to be split in two. That samurai were prepared to take such risks indicates just how seriously they viewed their political role. No matter how great the possible perils of action, the probable penalties of inaction were often greater still.

Some degree of conflict is inevitable in politics. Without it, indeed, what we know as politics would cease to exist. But it must be acknowledged that certain aspects of *han* government, by their very secrecy and inefficiency, tended to invite disagreement among the overwhelming majority of samurai, who being ineligible for high office, were not privy to the reasoning of those who were. No *han* could prevent its vassals questioning its policies, although many felt obliged to try from time to time, as did Nakatsu, which in 1738 forbade its samurai even to discuss any of the new domain laws.[136] Nearly a hundred years earlier Ikeda Mitsumasa of Okayama had put the position still more bluntly, warning that "anyone who interferes in any government business whatsoever is not a samurai; he is a malefactor, even if he is our vassal."[137] Given the rules governing selection for *han* office throughout most of the Tokugawa period, a certain measure of discontent was unavoidable, for as with the positions of emperor, shogun, and daimyo, those of senior officials in the *han* had also largely come to be filled by reason of birth. In the wars of the Sengoku period it was usually the case that no man could hold for very long an office he was incapable of filling successfully, but here too, the Tokugawa peace had intervened.

By the middle of the seventeenth century, or even earlier, the samurai hierarchy in most *han* had been stabilized. The head of each samurai family had been allotted a stipend (whether or not he always received it all) that served as an index of his status in the *han*, and this in turn determined his eligibility for positions in the *han* military and administrative hierarchy. The fine calibration to be seen among the samurai of Sakura *han* can serve as a fairly typical example of the

---

136 Kuroya Naofusa, *Nakatsu-han shi* (Tokyo: Hekiun-so, 1940), p. 322.
137 Taniguchi, *Okayama han*, p. 55.

system here: Of the 152 different kinds of official position, the most important advisory posts were limited to the heads of seven families, none of which had a stipend of less than 250 *koku*. To be eligible for the office of censor, a stipend of between 70 and 120 *koku* was needed; to be a secretary, it took an income of between thirty and fifty bales of rice per year; and to work as an assistant accountant, fourteen to sixteen bales.[138]

Of course, many of these 152 positions were of little consequence, demanding neither particular skill nor particular energy for their performance. In an age of peace it mattered as little who was captain of the colors (anyone with from 150 to 500 *koku*) as it did who was chosen to beat drums and gongs (anyone with 3 *koku* and ten bales). Neither was likely to be called upon for anything other than ceremonial duties. But it mattered very much who filled the key advisory and administrative posts, for here was where the important decisions had to be made. Sakura *han*, by allowing seven men to monopolize these positions, was effectively turning its back on the talents and energies of the other two thousand-odd members of its vassal band. It was hardly alone, however. All *han* did so, even the larger ones. Saga drew on the heads of eighteen samurai families when filling its most important positions, and Owari fifty. The largest *han* found their top advisers and administrators from among as many as eighty families, but given the total pool of samurai (roughly thirty thousand in the case of Sendai), we may doubt that even they had so much as begun to exploit the reservoir of samurai talent.[139]

There is no doubt that in the long run the *han* suffered by filling demanding positions with those who were eligible rather than suitable, for senior vassal families were subject to precisely the same genetic limitations as were their daimyo. There was just no guarantee that any group of seven men (or even seventy) could produce enough inspired (or even competent) officials to oversee the increasingly complex business of *han* government. Indeed, the members of such families were prepared to admit as much, preferring to base their authority on grounds other than mere talent: "Although it is desirable that senior councilors be capable and mature," one of them was to observe, "nevertheless men like ourselves, who come from lines of hereditary senior councilors, must themselves become senior council-

138 Kimura and Sugimoto, *Fudai hansei*, pp. 21–3.
139 Fujino Tamotsu, "Hansei kakuritsu-ki no shomondai – seihoku Kyūshū sho han (Hirado, Ōmura, Saga kaku han o chūshin to shite)," in *Shakai keizai shigaku* 24 (1958): 259; Kodama and Kitajima, eds., *Monogatari han shi*, vol. 4, p. 132, vol. 2, pp. 68–69.

ors, even should they be young and untalented. . . . Those families that have traditionally held the office of senior councilor are familiar with the domain laws and so pass on their knowledge to their children and grandchildren. They can also note down memoranda and bequeath them to their children, so that no matter how many generations pass, our ancient laws will be maintained."[140] This was a recipe for conservatism, and on the whole the record of *han* governments during the Tokugawa period does no more than confirm a general impression of stagnation.

It was not impossible for daimyo to interfere with this charmed circle of hereditary advisors, and many did so, sometimes by introducing a system of temporary salaries, or *tashidaka*, by which men might be promoted to positions for which they were otherwise ineligible, or sometimes by showering rewards on favorites. Mizuno Katsusada of Fukuyama did this in the mid-seventeenth century, raising Inekuma Saemon from a stipend of one hundred *koku* to something fifteen times that amount, thereby giving him a status equivalent to that of senior councilor. Such favorites always encountered the implacable hostility of the hereditary councilor class, and their appearance was usually the signal for an outbreak of tension within the domain. The very least such men could expect would be charges of corruption (for how could an outsider be promoted if not dishonestly?) or selfishness (for why would he wish to be if not for his own benefit?) Occasionally, as in the case of Inekuma Saemon, it ended in suicide on the death of the daimyo protector.[141]

In the last resort, the grip of hereditary senior councilors could be loosened only by a crisis grave enough to warrant extraordinary measures. Even then it was not easy. An immediate emergency, like a flood or famine or a particularly severe financial crisis, might confer temporary authority on an outsider with special skills, who would set about rebuilding the dikes, or take charge of famine relief, or slash expenditures, but once the crisis itself had dissipated, then so too would the hierarchical hiccup it had occasioned. Such at least was the case through the seventeenth and much of the eighteenth centuries.

When the chronic financial problems of *han* governments began to bite, however, this situation changed, for reduced salaries, though they affected all samurai, particularly hurt the poorest among them. Not unnaturally, they began to lash out. In some cases, like the mass desertion of samurai from Kokura in 1814 after yet another salary

---

140 Imaizumi, *Nagaoka no rekishi*, vol. 1, p. 172.   141 *Fukuyama-shi shi*, p. 53.

reduction, their target was the *han* itself. In others it was the daimyo, one of whom, the daimyo of Oka *han*, was taken publicly to task for his personal extravagance in 1812, by one of his lower samurai, a poet and painter called Tanomura Chikuden. More generally, however, the discontent of the poorer samurai found its target among their richer and more prominent fellows, the members of the traditional councilor class. Increasingly it was seen as inequitable that there should be so great a discrepancy between the salaries of these *baka karō*, or "idiot councilors," as they came to be called, and their lesser brethren.[142] That discrepancy was certainly glaring enough. In Nakatsu, 78.2 percent of all expenditure on salaries went to a mere 15.5 percent of samurai.[143] More important, in the context of *han* government, it seemed increasingly unwise to leave policy in the hands of men who in the course of two hundred years had shown themselves incapable of adapting to changing circumstances.

The nineteenth century, therefore, ushered in a revolution – sometimes only half-formed and imperfectly articulated, but a revolution nevertheless – in the governments of many *han*. The situation was too grave to be ignored, for to the standard economic worries was added a frightening confluence of new concerns: concern with mounting unrest in the countryside, where the peasantry was rioting on an unprecedented scale; concern with a growing alien interest in Japan's corner of the Pacific; concern therefore that *han* and bakufu alike would need to spend far more in their defense than ever before – money, moreover, that none of them had; concern that with a flagging government in Edo the nation might once more be plunged into turmoil; and concern too, paradoxically, that if the Tokugawa bakufu were to restore its authority it would be at *han* expense.[144] A crisis of such magnitude could not be solved by half-measures. When it was finally confronted, in the last three decades of Tokugawa rule, it was by a new kind of samurai administrator, one caring little for hereditary privilege, as he had climbed from the lower rungs of the samurai ladder, and caring still less for the conventions of *han* government, of which (as neither his father nor grandfather was capable of instructing him) he was mercifully ignorant. The revolution in government such men brought to their *han* in the nineteenth century – characterized by new commercial initiatives, by the creation of peasant militia, by the rationalization of samurai stipends, by independent diplomatic activ-

142 Kishida, "Kyūshū no bunjinga," p. 246; Andō Hideo, ed., *Chiritsubo–Kawai Tsugunosuke nikki*, vol. 257 of *Tōyō Bunko* (Tokyo: Heibonsha, 1974), p. 304.
143 Shindō, "Hansei kaikaku," pp. 117–19.   144 Bolitho, "The Tempō Crisis."

ity, by participation in an internecine race for arms – was perhaps a natural reaction to Japan's problems. Natural or not, however, it ultimately destroyed the bakufu and with it, after three short years, the *han* themselves.

CHAPTER 6

THE INSEPARABLE TRINITY: JAPAN'S RELATIONS WITH CHINA AND KOREA

Krieg, Handel und Piraterie,
Dreieinig sind sie, nicht zu trennen
War, trade, and piracy
Are an inseparable trinity
(Goethe, *Faust*, II, 5:3)

TRADE AND PIRACY

The Sinocentric tributary system

The international order that ideally spanned East Asia when Japan was in the later Middle Ages of its history (1392–1573) may be described as a tributary system, one in which outlying states were bound with real or fictional ties of allegiance to the "Central Country," China. Underlying that system was a culturalist theory, developed by Chinese Confucians, which held that China was a universal empire whose sovereignty had to be acknowledged by the "barbarian" rulers on its periphery if they wanted the benefits of commerce with it. In return for their homage, the Chinese emperor granted them the status of his royal vassals, the privilege of diplomatic relations, and the boon of access to Chinese civilization. They sent him tribute. He, in turn, bestowed gifts upon them out of his bounty.

As far as the Chinese of the Ming period (1368–1644) were concerned, Japan had entered such a tributary relationship with China long ago, during the time of the Han dynasty (202 B.C.–A.D. 220). Their scholars could catalog a long list of Japanese "tribute-bearing missions" stretching back at least to A.D. 57. To be sure, in more recent times that relationship had been disturbed by war and piracy, but it was confirmed and regulated once again at the beginning of the fifteenth century, on the initiative of the Japanese ruler Ashikaga Yoshimitsu (1358–1408), the third shogun of the Muromachi bakufu, who retained his control over Japan's foreign affairs even after formally retiring from the shogunate in 1395.

Yoshimitsu was an ardent seeker of monarchal distinction and just as avid an amateur of Chinese luxury goods. Between 1401 and 1405, he sponsored four embassies to China in pursuit of both those objectives. As a result, he was invested with the title "King of Japan" by the Ming emperors Chien-wen (r. 1398–1402) and Yung-lo (r. 1402–24), acknowledged his status as their subject, and entered an agreement that permitted the Japanese to send periodic missions with tribute to China. These missions were legitimated with visas issued in the form of tallies (Chinese: *k'an-ho;* Japanese: *kangō*) by the Chinese court, and the trade that was part and parcel of such embassies is therefore called the "tally trade." Yoshimitsu's eager acceptance of the Chinese norms of international relations opened the door to commerce, which the Japanese pursued under cover of obeisance.

The Japanese were assigned Ningpo in Chekiang Province as their port of entry into China. From there, a substantial part of their embassy – sometimes more than three hundred persons – would proceed to the Ming capital, which from 1421 was Peking. There they presented their tribute, according to a prescribed list of goods, which included sulfur and such products of Japanese artisanship as swords, suits of armor, gilt fans, and painted screens; the chief envoy was received in audience by the Ming emperor; and the embassy was then dismissed with gifts for the "King of Japan" (i.e., the shogun), including sumptuous silken fabrics, porcelain and other precious objets d'art, as well as large sums of copper cash.

The Ming government made official purchases from the cargoes of the Japanese ships and also allowed the Japanese envoys and their accompaniment of merchants to carry on private trade with licensed Chinese brokers. Ships were sent not only by the shogunate itself but also by religious institutions and regional notables. In the fleet of nine sail that reached China in 1453, for instance, there were vessels chartered by the powerful Ōuchi family of Yamaguchi in western Honshu, the equally prominent Ōtomo family of Bungo in northern Kyushu, the great Zen monastery Tenryūji of Kyoto, as well as the Shinto and Buddhist temple complex of Tōnomine in Yamato Province. The growing volume of imports from Japan, as demonstrated by this large fleet, evidently alarmed the Chinese authorities, for they limited the size of subsequent missions to three ships. Having transacted its business, such a "tribute-bearing mission" sailed back to Japan richly laden with Chinese merchandise. For almost a century and a half – from 1404, when the first official tally mission departed for China, to 1549, when the seventeenth and last returned to Japan – this arrangement provided the framework for largely peaceful (if not entirely incident-free) relations between the two countries.

It must be emphasized that the tally trade was the only form of commerce permitted the Japanese by the Chinese authorities. Indeed, it was the sole legal channel for the direct exchange of commodities between Japan and China. The Ming empire from 1371 repeatedly issued decrees that prohibited Chinese from voyaging overseas for private purposes and thereby rigidly circumscribed the opportunities for foreign trade. The denial of free access to the sea was originally intended to protect the newly founded empire's security against yet-unpacified rebels who had their bases on the littoral of China. In time, however, it became the shibboleth of a state whose governmental institutions were designed to foster and exploit agriculture, not commerce, and whose public ideology, Confucianism, distrusted and even condemned the profit motive behind trade. The Ming regime sought to keep its people from venturing abroad; it restricted and regulated foreigners' entry into China; and it undertook these measures in the name of security, ideological purity, and the control of trade. It thereby constructed the model of an isolationist policy for East Asia. In its own way, Japan was destined to follow that model: The means and motives of what the Chinese of the Ming period called *hai-chin* (J: *kaikin*), or maritime prohibitions, were analogous to those of the Tokugawa period's *sakoku* directives.

The isolationism to which the Ming regime became habituated is a genuine paradox, because that same regime between 1405 and 1433 conducted maritime exploration on a scale unprecedented in the world's history, sending seven fleets with scores of naval vessels and tens of thousands of men to Southeast Asia, the Indian Ocean, and as far away as the east coast of Africa. Once having shown the flag in faraway lands, tied more "barbarian" rulers (if only loosely and temporarily) to the Chinese tributary system, and brought back shiploads of exotica for the court's self-gratulation, the fleets were adjudged superfluous and were disbanded. Exploration was not followed by colonization; trade did not follow the flag. Instead, the regime's attention was redirected inward. Abandoning the quest for distant oceans, the Ming empire did not rule the waves even of the China Sea.

Its maritime prohibitions were, moreover, ineffective. In its anticommercial bias, the regime failed to react positively to the fact that the growth of handicraft and processing industries in places on or near the seacoast of South China – from the silk and cotton manufactures of Soochow and the Yangtze Delta to the iron-utensil production of

Canton – had stimulated mercantile activities that spilled over into large-scale maritime trade. That trade remained illegal. The merchants, however, ignored the government's ban. The gentry of the littoral invested in the trade. The very officials charged with enforcing the maritime prohibitions as often as not connived at the traffic. As a result, by the end of the fifteenth century the trade directed overseas by Chinese merchants exceeded by far the volume of goods carried to and from China in the bottoms of the various official "tribute-bearing missions." The government's efforts to enforce its laws merely encouraged the contrabandists to arm themselves, thus turning merchants into outlaws.

On the Japanese side, too, efforts to regulate commerce with China were doomed by a breakdown of authority. Here the smooth functioning of the tally trade postulated an order kept, if not by the "King of Japan" directly, then by his deputies and provincial constables. By the beginning of the sixteenth century, however, the Ashikaga shoguns had been reduced to utter powerlessness by the internal strife that had swept Japan ever since the Ōnin War of 1467–77. Control over the official trade with China had long since slipped out of their hands and become a bone of contention between two of their principal vassals, the Hosokawa and Ōuchi families.

These two parties exported their quarrel to China itself in 1523, when they sent rival embassies to Ningpo. There Hosokawa agents bribed the superintendent of merchant shipping and obtained precedence for their mission, thereby infuriating the delegation of the Ōuchi. The Ōuchi men vented their rage by killing the Hosokawa side's chief envoy, the priest Rankō Zuisa, and rampaging through the streets of Ningpo. Having burned and looted their way to the harbor, the Ōuchi delegation sailed away in commandeered vessels, carrying with them a kidnapped garrison officer, and fought off a Chinese pursuit squadron, killing its commander.[1]

In the aftermath of this riot, which exposed the Chinese officials' corruption no less than the Japanese voyagers' penchant for violence, the Ming authorities further tightened the procedures governing the tally trade. In the event, only two more missions, those dispatched by the Ōuchi in 1540 and 1549, were to be accepted by the Chinese, although the Japanese sent several others. By the middle of the sixteenth century, political conditions in Japan had become so chaotic

1 *Ming shih, chüan* 322: "Lieh-chuan 210, wai-kuo 3, Jih-pen," vol. 27 (Peking: Chung-hua shu-chü, 1974), pp. 8348–9. Nihon shiryō shūsei hensankai, ed., *Chūgoku, Chōsen no shiseki ni okeru Nihon shiryō shūsei: Seishi no bu* (Tokyo: Kokusho kankōkai, 1975), pp. 290–1.

that there was indeed good reason to question the legitimacy of embassies arriving from that country. Moreover, the entire setting of trade and diplomatic relations between Japan and China was being transformed dramatically with the appearance of the Portuguese and the resurgence of the pirates known as *wakō* (Ch: *wo-k'ou,* Korean: *waegu*), or "Japanese brigands," in East Asian waters. The *wakō* were anything but a new phenomenon. Rather, they were a scourge that had afflicted Korea intermittently for centuries.

The early tide of the wakō

The Chinese-character compound *wakō,* referring to invaders from Japan, first occurs on a Korean stele erected in A.D. 414. By the sixteenth century, seafaring as defined by Goethe's Mephistopheles – "War, trade, and piracy / Are an inseparable trinity" – was a time-honored tradition in the Japanese archipelago. This is not the place to trace the origins of that tradition or to explore all of the regions where it developed. Two benchmarks, however, should be recorded. The first is the rebellion of Fujiwara no Sumitomo in the 930s. Sumitomo, an official ordered to suppress the pirates of Iyo Province in Shikoku, instead joined them, fomenting a disturbance that swept across the Bungo Strait and the Inland Sea to keep much of western Japan in a state of turmoil until he was tracked down and killed in 941. The other benchmark is in the 1220s, when the Matsuura-tō first became notorious as a "band of villains"who sailed abroad to "destroy people's dwellings and plunder their property."[2] The Matsuura-tō was a group of petty military families with eleventh-century roots in the Matsuura region of northern Hizen Province in Kyushu, and the object of their piratical raids was Korea. The myriad coves and islands of the Inland Sea would remain important bases of piracy – or, as the case may be, of maritime enterprise and naval endeavor – into the sixteenth century and beyond. So would the lairs of the Matsuura-tō from Sasebo, Hirado, and the Gotō Islands to Yobuko, Iki, and Tsushima.

The flurry of piratical activity directed against Korea in the 1220s died down abruptly after the Kamakura shogunate's commissioner in Kyushu (*Chinzei bugyō*), Mutō Sukeyori, had ninety suspected brigands decapitated before the eyes of a Korean envoy in 1227. For more than a century thereafter, *wakō* raids to Korea were few and far be-

---

2 Fujiwara Teika, *Meigetsuki,* vol. 2 (Tokyo: Kokusho kankōkai, 1911), pp. 544–5; entries for Karoku 2 (1226).10.16–17.

tween. To start with, the Koreans had been forced into a high state of vigilance and military preparedness by the aggressive designs of an emergent imperial power, the Mongols, who invaded Korea in force six times between 1231 and 1258 before they finally managed to subdue the country and put it under their complete domination. On the Japanese side, the shogunate evidently was able to keep seafaring military groups under control throughout the rest of the Kamakura period (1185–1333). They were mobilized against the threat of a Mongol invasion of Japan, which had to be reckoned with even after the Mongols had been repelled twice, in 1274 and 1281.

By the middle of the fourteenth century, however, the Kamakura shogunate had fallen; the Mongol empire was disintegrating; and its client, the Koryŏ dynasty (918–1392) of Korea, was likewise on the edge of a crisis. Japan was in the throes of a widespread conflict engendered by a dynastic schism in its imperial house. In Kyushu as elsewhere, supporters of the so-called Southern Court contended with adherents of the Northern Court and its principal backer, the Muromachi bakufu. There was, in short, no authority strong enough to keep down the predatory hunger of the sea wolves.

The *wakō* resumed their activities in earnest in 1350, and for the next half-century engulfed Korea with a veritable tide of spoliation.[3] Worst was the decade between 1376 and 1385, when the wave crested with no fewer than 174 recorded instances of pirate raids. Some of these raids amounted to miniature Japanese invasions of Korea. Bands of as many as three thousand intruders, far from being satisfied with ravaging the coasts, penetrated deep into the country's interior before withdrawing again to their ships. The entire southern half of the Korean peninsula was subjected to this rapine: The raiders repeatedly despoiled the environs of Kaesŏng, the Koryŏ dynasty's capital city, and on occasion reached as far north as the mouth of the Taedong River and the general area of P'yŏngyang. These Japanese marauders, who pillaged granaries and waylaid revenue shipments of grain, were at the same time slavers, who carried people away with them into servitude and held them to ransom. Their depredations seriously hurt Korea's society and economy, put a severe strain on the resources of the Koryŏ dynasty, and greatly contributed to its downfall. The pirati-

---

3 See the chronological table prepared by Tanaka Takeo in *Wakō: umi no rekishi*, vol. 66 of Kyōikusha rekishi shinsho "Nihonshi" (Tokyo: Kyōikusha, 1982), pp. 200–1. The estimate of 174 *wakō* raids on Korea between 1376 and 1385 is a conservative figure. The count of 228 (or even 346) incidents can be found in a similar chart set out by Tamura Hiroyuki in *Chūsei Nitchō bōeki no kenkyū* (Kyoto: Sanwa shobō, 1967), pp. 36–7. The number 346 is given in the chart presented by Yi Hyŏng-sŏk, *Imjin Chŏllan sa*, vol. 1 (Seoul: Ch'ungmuhoe, 1975), p. 49.

cal tide of the *wakō* overflowed into China. Some of their bands roved across the Yellow Sea from Korea to the Shantung peninsula. Others struck farther south, at Kiangsu and the coastal provinces south of the Yangtze Delta: Chekiang, Fukien, and Kwangtung. Both China and Korea demanded that Japanese authorities put an end to the piracy. No sooner had the Hung-wu emperor (r. 1368–98) conquered the Yüan dynasty of the Mongols and established the Ming empire in China – in 1369 and 1370, the second and the third years of his reign – than he sent envoys to Prince Kanenaga (1329–83), the Southern Court's "generalissimo for the subjugation of the west" (*seisei daishōgun*) in Kyushu; he warned the Japanese that he would send forces to "capture and exterminate your bandits, head straight for your country, and put your king in bonds" unless the *wakō* raids were stopped, and urged Japan to submit to the suzerainty of Ming.[4] Kanenaga treated the first of these embassies rudely, killing five of its members, but responded deferentially to the second: In 1371, he sent his own envoys to China, where (according to Chinese records) they rendered obeisance in the expected manner and took receipt of the symbols of vassalage for their master. Actually, there is some doubt that Kanenaga would have assumed such a grave diplomatic responsibility. But it is clear that, his grand title notwithstanding, he was by that time hard put to it just to maintain himself in Kyushu and quite unable to deliver on any promises to stamp out the pirates.

In contrast with the Chinese, the Koreans sought redress not from the Southern Court and its agents but from the Muromachi bakufu, its opponent. A Koryŏ embassy was received in 1367 by Shogun Ashikaga Yoshiakira (1330–67) (r. 1359–67) in Kyoto but was told, ingenuously enough, that Kyoto could do nothing abut the lawless actions of the inhabitants of Shikoku and Kyushu, areas over which the bakufu as yet had no control.[5] The Koreans next sought the cooperation of the shogunal deputy (*tandai*) in Kyushu, Imagawa Ryōshun, to whom they sent the first of repeated embassies in 1377. Ryōshun had been successful in the contest against Prince Kanenaga and the Southern Court's other champions in Kyushu, but he had not managed to gain

4 *Ming T'ai-tsu shih-lu*, pt. 39, f. 3, entry for Hung-wu 2 (1369).2.[6]: *Ming shih-lu*, vol. 2 (Taipei: Chung-yang yen-chiu-yüan li-shih yü-yen yen-chiu-so, 1962), p. 787; Nihon shiryō shūsei hensankai, ed., *Chūgoku, Chōsen no shiseki ni okeru Nihon shiryō shūsei: Min jitsuroku no bu*, vol. 1 (Tokyo: Kokusho kankōkai, 1975), pp. 1–2.
5 Gotō Tanji and Okami Masao, eds., *Taiheiki*, vol. 3, in vol. 36 of *Nihon koten bungaku taikei* (Tokyo: Iwanami shoten, 1962), p. 451. The historicity of this account is examined in detail by Nakamura Hidetaka, *Nissen kankeishi no kenkyū*, vol. 1 (Tokyo: Yoshikawa kōbunkan, 1965), pp. 203–6.

the ascendancy over the maritime area of Matsuura and the island provinces of Iki and Tsushima, the principal nests of the pirates who plagued Korea. Hence the *wakō* stayed out of control. The Chinese fortified their seacoasts. The Koreans in 1389 and again in 1419 attacked the pirate bases on Tsushima but were forced to withdraw without inflicting much damage. A major precondition for solving the *wakō* problem was, however, met in 1392, when the conflict between the Southern and Northern courts was finally resolved under the auspices of Shogun Ashikaga Yoshimitsu, who thereby brought the Muromachi bakufu to the height of its authority. Coincidentally, 1392 was also the year when the new Yi dynasty displaced Koryŏ in Korea. Under the new political circumstances, diplomacy had a better chance of prevailing. The results of Yoshimitsu's diplomatic initiative toward the Ming empire – his investiture as "King of Japan" and the inception of a regulated trade with China – have already been noted. In 1404, Yoshimitsu sent an embassy to Korea under that new title, "King of Japan," that is, as one vassal of the Ming to another, his coequal. In sum, through Yoshimitsu's management of foreign affairs, Japan was integrated into the East Asian international order.

To be sure, that by itself did not put down the *wakō*. They went on raiding China in force at least until 1419. In that year, a large pirate fleet of more than thirty sail assembled in Tsushima and headed north along Korea's Yellow Sea coast. Kept under constant observation, it was finally ambushed and smashed off Wang-hai-kuo in Liaotung by the provincial military commander, Liu Jung, who is said to have taken anywhere between seven hundred and fifteen hundred heads.[6] After that, the *wakō* steered clear of Liaotung, although they hit other areas of China sporadically. They had become more of a nuisance than a threat and would remain so until their massive new surge of the 1550s. In the case of Korea, too, it was not simply high-level diplomacy and the radiance of the bakufu's institutional or Ashikaga Yoshimitsu's personal prestige that stopped the *wakō*. Rather, it was action by regional notables of western Japan, whom the Koreans lured with appeals to their self-interest and conciliated by making concessions.

Korean efforts to deal with the wakō

The gist of the Koreans' plan was to try transforming the robber barons of western Japan into instruments for controlling the *wakō*. As

---

6 *Ming shih*, vol. 27, p. 8346; *Seishi no bu*, vol. 1, p. 288. Cf. Nakamura, *Nissen kankeishi*, vol. 1, pp. 309–10.

King Sejong (r. 1418–50) of Korea concluded after hearing the report of Pak Sŏ-saeng, his ambassador to the court of Ashikaga Yoshinori (1394–1441) (r. 1429–41) in 1429, dealing with the Japanese shogun was necessary for ceremonial reasons but apt to prove ineffective if the purpose was the suppression of piracy.[7] Much more, Pak reported, could be expected from a direct approach to the real masters of the shores and islands that harbored the *wakō*.

Among the most important of these were the great *shugo* daimyo family of the Ōuchi, lords over seafaring groups based both in the Inland Sea (e.g., at Kamado and Yashirojima; now Kaminoseki and Ōshima, Yamaguchi Prefecture) and in Kyushu (at Shikanoshima; now part of the city of Fukuoka); the Ōtomo family, who held the military governorship (*shugoshiki*) of Bungo Province and were powerful rivals of the Ōuchi for the control of northern Kyushu; the Munakata, barons of Chikuzen Province and patrons of the seafarers of Ōshima (now an offshore part of Fukuoka Prefecture); and the petty barons who constituted the membership of the Matsuura-tō. Winning the favor of this last group would be tantamount to pacifying the most active pirate bands, those from the in- and offshore region between the Gotō Islands and Iki that had its geographical center at Hirado. Courting the Ōuchi was politic, not least because they could seal off the narrow straits at Akamagaseki (now Shimonoseki) and thereby bottle up the rovers of the Inland Sea. Above all, it was necessary to cultivate the goodwill of the Sō family, the preeminent power on Tsushima, for it was Tsushima, as Pak Sŏ-saeng observed correctly, where all Japanese pirates mustered before attacking Korea, at its closest point less than thirty nautical miles away.

As regards Tsushima, Iki, and Matsuura, Kang Kwŏn-sŏn (another Korean envoy, who visited Iki in 1444) capped Pak's appraisal with the following pithy analysis:[8]

In these regions, the people's dwellings are miserable; land is tight and, moreover, utterly barren, so that they do not pursue agriculture and can scarcely escape starvation; thus they engage in banditry, being of a wicked and violent cast. . . . But if we attend on them with courtesy and nourish

---

7 *Sejong Changhŏn Taewang sillok*, pt. 46, ff. 13v–16 and 16v–17v, entries for Sejong 11.12.[3] and [9] (December 28, 1429 and January 3, 1430): *Chosŏn wangjo sillok*, vol. 3 (Seoul: Kuksa p'yŏnch'an wiwŏnhoe, 1955), pp. 207–9; Nihon shiryō shūsei hensankai, ed., *Chūgoku, Chōsen no shiseki ni okeru Nihon shiryō shūsei: Richō jitsuroku no bu*, vol. 1 (Tokyo: Kokusho kankōkai, 1976), pp. 259–63. Hereafter brackets indicate that the date has been converted from its original citation in the sexagesimal citation; parentheses indicate conversion to Western calendar.

8 *Sejong Changhŏn Taewang sillok*, pt. 104, f. 8, entry for Sejong 26 (1444).4.[30]: *Chosŏn wangjo sillok*, vol. 4, p. 552; *Richō jitsuroku no bu*, vol. 2, (1977), p. 459.

them with generosity, even more so than in previous days, then the pirates will all submit.

The Koreans went to great lengths to appease those who held the pirates in leash. From around 1396, only a few years after coming to power, the Yi dynasty adopted the policy of granting official Korean titles, with appropriate stipends, to *wakō* chiefs who were willing to surrender.[9] Such appointments to titular office were used not only to buy off actual aggressors but also to reward residents of Japan who assisted in repatriating Korean captives of the *wakō*, furnished information on the pirates' plans, or were helpful in other ways. Another device used by the Korean court to coax the picaroons into peaceful partnership was the issuance of copper seals (K: *tosŏ*, J: *tosho*) as a sign of most favored status to Japanese perceived as being influential in maritime affairs. This practice dates back at least to 1418, but many of the recipients of the seals were members of the Matsuura-tō who were granted this distinction in the 1440s and 1450s, perhaps as a result of Kang Kwŏn-sŏn's recommendations. Japanese holders of Korean titles and the bearers of *tosŏ* had legal access to Korea, which they could use for the purpose of trade.

From the 1420s, the Koreans began to develop an elaborate system of allotting the number of ships that could be licensed each year for trade by individual Japanese. The most advantaged in that regard, as in others, was the Koreans' nearest and most strategically placed neighbor, Sō, the overlord of Tsushima. According to an agreement concluded in 1443 (sometimes called the Kakitsu treaty, after the Japanese era name for the years 1441 to 1444), the head of the Sō family was permitted to sponsor fifty regular vessels a year, with the proviso of sending other ships on special missions, and was granted the sizable yearly stipend of two hundred *koku* (about 361 hectoliters) of rice and legumes from the Korean fisc; other members of the Sō family also received various privileges. The Sō were also delegated the task of verifying the bona fides of all Korea-bound Japanese vessels, which were required to stop at a checkpoint in Tsushima and obtain a permit (K: *munin*, J: *bun'in*) before proceeding to their destinations. This was a highly remunerative arrangement for the Sō, who not only levied transit duties on the cargoes but also charged each ship's master a fee for the indispensable *munin*. Few captains could have willfully bypassed the Tsushima checkpoint; for regardless of who sponsored the

---

9 A chronology of the successive steps in the development of Japanese–Korean relations from 1392 to 1868 is found in Nakamura, *Nissen kankeishi*, vol. 3 (1969), pp. 241–4.

voyage, any Japanese ship found in Korean waters without a permit from the Sō was automatically suspect.

In short, the Koreans paid with privileges and direct emoluments for the services of the Sō in policing the Japanese traffic. Logically enough, in view of this inspector's role, Sō Shigemoto (1419–67) was in 1461 at his own request appointed governor of Tsushima by the Korean court. Not surprisingly, this appointment *in partibus* later fed the Korean misconception that the island was a dependency of their country. In actuality, the head of the Sō family used the political and economic advantages he derived from his special relationship with Korea to consolidate his authority over Tsushima. To be sure, there were benefits for the Koreans, too, not just for the Sō: As the fifteenth century wore on, piracy did fade away, even if it did not totally disappear.

Japanese–Korean relations under the Kakitsu treaty

The framework of Japanese–Korean relations that was erected by the Kakitsu treaty of 1443 and stood for a century and a half until destroyed by Toyotomi Hideyoshi's aggression was on the whole an orderly structure. That structure was based on formal agreements between the Korean court and the Sō family of Tsushima. The Sō fell out of grace with the Koreans once or twice but were readmitted to favor and privilege because it was recognized that they were invaluable mediators. Moreover, their self-interest dictated cooperation with the Koreans. Hence, by applying levers on the Sō, the Koreans could hope to moderate, if not perfectly regulate, the level of the Japanese commercial influx into their country. And that, indeed, was a vital consideration for the Yi dynasty. At first, the new and still-insecure dynasty had been eager to appease the Japanese in its anxiety to see piracy replaced by peaceful commerce, but its initial permissive attitude toward the Japanese traders in Korea and fishermen off its shores was not meant to last and was replaced by the desire to constrict their activities. Overall, the Yi dynasty's policy toward Japan in the fifteenth and sixteenth centuries was marked by efforts to limit the traffic from Japan in order to reduce the expense of diplomatic intercourse, diminish the drain of resources caused by the Japanese trade, and keep under control the sometimes-unruly Japanese community in Korea. For all that, the policy was not rigid but retained the capacity for compromise and the accommodation of Japanese interests.

In the course of the fifteenth century, the Koreans restricted the number of Japanese envoys permitted to come as far as their capital city, Seoul, the number of Japanese ships allowed each year to carry on trade, and the number of places where those ships could call. For all these limitations, however, at the century's end, some two hundred sail a year – ships sponsored by the Ashikaga shogun, by daimyo such as the Ōuchi and a whole list of other grandees, by holders of *tosŏ*, and by bearers of Korean titles – continued to have access to Korea. That access was restricted to the "Three Ports" (K: *samp'o*, J: *sampo*) of Pusan, Naeip'o (now part of the city of Chinhae), and Yomp'o (now part of the city of Ulsan) in the southeastern corner of the peninsula, and the Japanese were officially permitted to maintain no more than sixty residential households in these three trading stations.

A census conducted in 1494 revealed, however, that the trading factories had developed into fairly substantial Japanese enclaves within Korea: There were 525 households (almost nine times the permitted total) and 3,205 permanent foreign residents, who maintained fourteen Buddhist temples on Korean soil, farmed rice fields in the vicinity of the harbors, and exploited the nearby fisheries.[10] The inevitable conflicts with the natives over fishing rights occasionally led to Japanese attacks on Korean officials. Moreover, Japanese fishermen, whether from the Three Ports or from Tsushima and beyond, were not unknown to metamorphose into pirates, depending on the catch to be had. It was also clear that the Three Ports were bases for smuggling. The resident Japanese escaped Korean taxation, but the Sō family collected taxes from their settlements through its own delegates (*daikan*).

This type of Japanese presence in the country surely raised questions of the erosion of Korean sovereignty. But the major problem was economic. Along with dyestuffs, spices, and pharmaceuticals from Southeast Asia, which were transshipped through the island kingdom of Ryūkyū and the flourishing entrepôt of Hakata (now Fukuoka) in Kyushu, the Japanese brought to Korea large amounts of copper, lead, and sulfur, products of their own country. They took back from Korea various luxury items, artistic objects, and Buddhist scriptures. Above all, however, they wanted Korean textile goods. In the fifteenth century's last decades, it appeared more and more that an insatiable Japanese demand for Korean cotton cloth was depleting the country's supply of a precious manufactured product, which was also used as a medium of exchange. (The cultivation of cotton in Japan itself was

10 A chart showing the numbers of Japanese residents in the "Three Ports" from 1436 to 1494 can be found in Nakamura, vol. 1, p. 643.

barely beginning as the century turned.) The Korean government did not consider this a favorable balance of trade.

Each year, great sums were drained off from Korea through the entertainment of the numerous Japanese merchants who were in the country theoretically on official missions. Because trade was carried on under the label of diplomatic relations, the hosts were responsible for covering their visitors' living expenses during their stay and for providing supplies for the voyage home.[11] In 1485, the Korean court tried to solve this problem by permitting the bypass of official channels for the disposal of goods and sanctioning private trade between Korean and Japanese merchants in the Three Ports. In 1495, this measure was rescinded, the cure having been found worse than the ailment. But the network of the direct contacts between merchants, once established, could not so easily be unraveled. The prohibition of private trade and the reinstitution of a government monopoly merely amplified the pressures for an increase in the volume of commerce.

That this state of affairs could not be permitted to continue was the conclusion reached in the councils of King Chungjong (r. 1506–44) of Korea early in his reign. By way of remedy, it was decided to start applying strictly the rules that had been set down in the past to govern the relationship between Korea and Japan. The Korean court's resolve stiffened in the face of several provocative incidents that occurred between 1506 and 1509: at least three major cases of piracy, including an armed assault carried out by Korean-speaking Japanese on Kadŏk Island, halfway between Naeip'o and Pusan; arson by Japanese residents of Naeip'o; and demonstratively arrogant if not violent behavior by members of a Japanese embassy in Seoul itself.

Early in 1510, the Korean court therefore sent the lord of Tsushima, Sō Morinobu (later known as Sō Yoshimori, 1476–1521), a message demanding the suppression of piracy and the determined pursuit of the perpetrators of all those illegal activities that poisoned relations between the two countries.[12] Unless the Koreans obtained satisfaction, the message warned, all Japanese residents of the Three Ports, except for the officially permitted sixty households, would be expelled. The

---

11 A good idea of the expenses incurred by the Koreans in official entertainments may be obtained from the rules governing the treatment of Japanese guests that are recorded in the geographic work *Haedong chegukki* (Account of the countries east of the sea) compiled in 1472 by the noted statesman Sin Suk-ju (1417–75); see the facsimile edition, Chōsenshi henshūkai, ed., *Kaitō shokokuki*, vol. 2 of *Chōsen shiryō sōkan* (Keijō: Chōsen sōtokufu, 1933), ff. 111–26v.

12 *Chungjong Taewang sillok*, 10:43v–44, entry for Chungjong 5 (1510).2.[13]: *Chosŏn wangjo sillok*, vol. 14 (1956), pp. 409–10; *Richō jitsuroku no bu*, vol. 5 (1981), pp. 1449–50.

Sō were furthermore cautioned to check carefully before issuing permits to Japanese traders bound for Korea and to make sure that the *tosŏ* they presented as credentials were still valid and did not, in fact, belong to dead souls. In the meantime, Korean officials charged with supervising the Three Ports had begun to enforce rigidly the regulations meant to govern life there. Some of the measures they undertook departed from precedent. In response to these new and unaccustomed rigors, the Japanese rioted.

The rioters could claim that they had been provoked by an overly zealous Korean officer, who had caused the deaths of four Japanese in a squabble over fishing rights. Their actions, however, were not spontaneous but planned with the connivance of the Sō of Tsushima, who agreed to come to their assistance. The incident began on May 11, 1510 (Chungjong 5 - Eishō 7.4.4), when the Japanese residents of Naeip'o and Pusan assaulted and captured their Korean magistrates' offices. On the same day, a fleet sent by the Sō attacked Kŏje Island off Pusan. After having ransacked the environs of the Three Ports and pillaged various localities on Kŏje, the Japanese gathered their forces at Naeip'o with the apparent intention of keeping the place occupied until they had intimidated the Korean government into backing down, abandoning its rigorism, and letting them have their own way in Korea. But they were mistaken if they thought they could bring the Koreans to terms. Although the news of this insurrection by foreigners backed from abroad terrified some Seoul officials, the government's armed forces reacted effectively to the Japanese threat. Thus the "disturbance of the Three Ports" was brought to a speedy conclusion fifteen days after its outbreak, when the Koreans attacked and recaptured Naeip'o, taking 295 heads. The remaining Japanese fled in their ships for Tsushima. Needless to say, in the wake of this incident the Korean government severed its relations with the Sō.

That those relations should have been resumed as soon as they were – in 1512, after Tsushima had asked the shogun and the Ōuchi to intercede – testifies to the accommodative nature of Korean policy and to the perceived indispensability of the Sō. To be sure, under the new agreement the privileges of the Sō were trimmed, the three ports of entry reduced to one (Naeip'o), and the rights of permanent residence and the exploitation of fisheries by Japanese eliminated, but the basic framework of Japanese–Korean relations stayed intact. For all the new restrictions, more than sixty Japanese ships a year were still permitted access to Korea. Moreover, the Japanese for a time succeeded in expanding that access: For example, in 1521 Pusan was reinstated as a port of call, and in 1523 the head of the Sō family was granted the right to add five annual trading vessels to the twenty-five permitted by the agreement of 1512.

Their proclivities toward piracy, however, set the Japanese back again. A raid carried out by twenty or more *wakō* ships on Saryang Island off the southern coast of Kyŏngsang Province in 1544 caused relations between the two countries to be severely curtailed for three years. The so-called Tenbun treaty of 1547 restored an ordered commerce but again restricted Japanese access to one port (this time Pusan) and reduced the Sō to twenty-five vessels each year. Until the last decade of the sixteenth century, when Toyotomi Hideyoshi's invasion of Korea destroyed their prospects, the Sō of Tsushima did not abandon hope of remedying the conditions that governed Japanese commerce with Korea, retrieving their lost privileges, and regaining the status they held before 1510. Paradoxically, their hopes were raised as a result of yet another pirate incident, the 1555 *wakō* raid on Tallyang and other areas of the South Chŏlla coast, Korea's southwestern corner. This raid by more than seventy pirate ships from the Gotō Islands and the rest of the Matsuura region apparently reminded the Koreans of the usefulness of the Sō. In any event, by 1557 the Sō were back up to thirty annual vessels, and by 1567 the Koreans had agreed to restore some of the privileges that had been withdrawn from the holders of *tosŏ*. The *wakō* no longer bothered Korea. And there matters rested until Korea came within the compass of Hideyoshi's aggressive designs.

The second tide of brigandage

To be sure, it was not so much action by the Sō that kept the pirates from bothering Korea after 1555. As it happens, the marauders' attention had already been diverted elsewhere, toward more profitable targets. Even the Tallyang raid, for all its large scale, was actually no more than an aberrant eddy within the great tide of brigandage that swept East Asian waters in the 1550s and 1560s. This resurgent tide did not, however, flow toward Korea but swirled about the coasts of China. It threatened at first to submerge Kiangsu and Chekiang and then shifted to beat on the shores of Fukien. The intensity of this new wave of pillage may be gauged from a telling set of figures: In more than a century, from 1440 to 1550, Chinese sources recorded only 25 *wakō* raids, but they mentioned no fewer than 467 separate incidents in the single decade between 1551 and 1560 and added another 75 for the ten years from 1561 to 1570, when the tide began to ebb.[13]

In contrast with the previous type of *wakō*, however, the pirate bands of the middle sixteenth century no longer consisted preponderantly of Japanese. Although *wakō*, or "Japanese brigands," remained the common label by which they were identified, most of these bandits were in fact, if not in name, Chinese. Moreover, although Japanese are listed among the leadership of some of their groups, the masterminds of the far-flung activities of this new type of *wakō* were unscrupulous Chinese adventurers. The Tallyang raid, for instance, was just one of the notorious exploits of the Chinese buccaneer Wang Chih, who at the time had his headquarters in Japan, in that old *wakō* lair, Hirado, and availed himself of a comfortable base of operations in the Gotō Islands. Wang Chih and his congeners – such as Teng Wen-chün, whose base was Yobuko in that same Matsuura region, and Ch'en Tung, who had close connections with the prominent daimyo family of southern Kyushu, the Shimazu – were part of a syndrome that was more complex than the *wakō* plague that had afflicted Korea and threatened China in previous times.

What were the causes of this new wave of piracy? Contemporary Chinese sources put the onus for the resurgence of the *wakō* on Chinese merchant adventurers, their greed, and their perverse incitation of the Japanese to plunder China. That celebrated "bible of *wakō* studies," *Ch'ou-hai t'u-pien* (A maritime survey: collected plans, 1562), asserts, for instance: "Maritime brigandage originated when rogues from the seacoast of China, seeking profits, broke the prohibitions [of overseas trade]. First they took up with the Western Barbarians and then extended their activities to Japan, which they made the very base and heartland of their banditry."[14] In other words, the appearance of the Portuguese (who are meant here by "Western Barbarians") gave a great boost to the officially proscribed but actually uncontrollable private overseas trade of China. The private commercial networks spread to include Japan just at the time when the official tally trade, inadequate to start with, was petering out. At first, the

---

13 See the chronological chart set out by Tanaka in *Wakō: umi no rekishi*, pp. 203–7. For a detailed descriptive chronology, see Ch'en Mou-heng, *Ming-tai wo-k'ou k'ao-lüeh* (Peking: Jen-min ch'u-pan-she, 1957), chap. 3, pp. 47–128.

14 *Ch'ou-hai t'u-pien*, comp. Cheng Jo-tseng, ed. Shao Fang, under the auspices of Hu Tsung-hsien, governor of Chekiang (revised by Hu Tsung-hsien's descendants Hu Wei-chi, Hu Teng, Hu Ming-kang, and Hu Chieh-ch'ing; prefaces by Mao K'un, 1562, and Hu Ssu-shen, 1624; copy in the Tōyōshi Collection, Library of the Faculty of Letters, Kyoto University), pt. 11, f. 6.

entrepôts of the illicit trade were on or just off the coast of China, but the Ming government's countermeasures eventually forced the traders to seek safer bases as far away as Japan and to enlist the aid or at least the acquiescence of Japanese regional rulers and maritime barons in their schemes.

The Portuguese first intruded into China's commercial sphere in the second decade of the sixteenth century. In 1511, they conquered the Malayan sultanate of Malacca, a place much frequented by Chinese overseas merchants, and by 1513 their own merchants were visiting the China coast. They sought official relations with China through Canton from 1517, but five years later they were forcibly driven away from that area as a result of the piratical behavior of the captain of their 1519 embassy, Simão de Andrade. Thereupon (until in 1554 they finally gained official toleration of their trade in Canton), they engaged in a thoroughly illicit but highly lucrative trade, not at major ports but at island anchorages on the coast of South China. There they exchanged spices, ivory, aromatic woods, and other products of their South and Southeast Asian trading colonies, for Chinese silks and porcelains. Needless to say, these anchorages were not haphazardly chosen. Rather, they were the strategically located offshore bases of the Chinese smuggling bosses, who often operated with the collusion of the coastal officialdom.

The most notorious of these contrabandists' nests, called Liampoo by the Portuguese, was Shuang-hsü-kang in the Chusan Islands off Ningpo, which became important from 1526 onward. In its heyday, the middle 1540s, Shuang-hsü-kang was run by the Hsü brothers, whose theater of operations extended from Malacca to Kyō-domari (now part of the city of Sendai, Kagoshima Prefecture) in Japan. Their chief lieutenant, Wang Chih, traveled to Japan to bring back with him more recruits for the illicit trade. The Portuguese, according to the *Tractado* (1569–70) of the well-informed Dominican friar Gaspar da Cruz, "were so firmly settled" in Liampoo "and with such freedom, that nothing was lacking them save having a gallows and [municipal whipping post]." One would scarcely expect this place, populated by Portuguese freebooters and their Lascar crews, Chinese smugglers and their Japanese partners, to have been a well-ordered, peaceful municipality. Indeed, we are told by da Cruz that "the Chinas who accompanied the Portugals, and some Portugals with them, came to disorder themselves in such a manner that they began to make great thefts and robberies, and killed some of the people." At length, the flagrancy with which its laws were being flouted moved the Ming government to appoint the hardheaded Chu Wan as governor of Chekiang Province, with the clear mandate to eliminate Shuang-hsü and other coastal sore spots in his own province as well as in Fukien and northern Kwantung. From the official Ming standpoint, the traders who gathered at such anchorages were either outlaws guilty of high treason or barbarian brigands. When Chu Wan was ordered "to drive the pirates from all the coast," da Cruz notes, "all the merchants . . . were included in this number of pirates."[15]

Chu Wan did his job energetically. In 1548 he destroyed Shuang-hsü (where his troops captured at least two Japanese alive) and scattered its denizens to the four winds. The next year, he successfully blockaded the coast of Fukien, where his catch included two junks carrying some thirty Portuguese; some of these captives he summarily executed. Because some of the most influential members of the Fukien gentry were among the heaviest investors in the illicit overseas trade, it is not surprising that after this thorough sweep, Chu Wan should have been traduced, disgraced, and driven to suicide. Perhaps more surprisingly, his successes against the contrabandists are often cited as the proximate cause of the regeneration of the *wakō*. Indeed, it is held that deprived of their accustomed bases, the overseas traders had little choice but to transform themselves into bands of armed rovers.

According to this school of thought, when the Ming government cracked down on their illegal activities, the Chinese entrepreneurs enlisted Japanese swashbucklers, known far and wide to be "tough and ferocious" types, into "safeguarding and abetting" their schemes, by force of arms if need be.[16] The armed clashes that resulted between the smugglers assisted by their Japanese strong-arm men and the troops mobilized by the Chinese authorities generated widespread disturbances along the littoral of the South China Sea. Some of the Chinese coastal populace turned to banditry, making common cause with the intruders in preference to being raped and looted by troops who had been quartered on them ostensibly to guard them against the *wakō*.[17] Bands of Chinese robbers with no connection with the sea

15 Padre Frey Gaspar da Cruz OP, *Tractado em que se côtam muito por estëso as cousas da China* (title page: 1569; colophon: Euora em casa de Andre de Burgos impressor (1570); copy in the Lilly Library, Indiana University), chap. 23, unfoliated; C. R. Boxer, trans. and ed., "Treatise in which the things of China are related at great length," in *South China in the Sixteenth Century*, Hakluyt Society, 2nd series, vol. 106 (London: Hakluyt Society, 1953), pp. 192–3.
16 *Ch'ou-hai t'u-pien*, pt. 11, f. 5v.
17 Chang Shih-ch'e, the president of the Board of War, used strong terms in arguing against the practice of saddling the population with levies from distant provinces: "This is their nature – swinish greed and wolflike brutality. They practice extortion and robbery by broad daylight; by night they pollute the women. Should anyone resist, then out comes the sword and that

went about in the guise of Japanese in order to capitalize on the terror universally inspired by the name of *wakō*. And local officials, intent on minimizing the extent of popular discontent in their jurisdictions, labeled all armed disorders, regardless of their cause, as outrages perpetrated by the *wakō*, thereby cravenly libeling the Japanese in order to mask their own malfeasance. Thus the reality was camouflaged at the time, and the false image has persisted in history. That much would appear to be the consensus at least of the Japanese historians who have recently written on this subject.

By and large, Japanese scholars do their best to minimize the number of Japanese participants in *wakō* bands. Moreover, insofar as they do admit the involvement of their sixteenth-century countrymen in these Chinese adventures, they tend to be charitable toward the seafarers, whose motivation (they claim) has been misunderstood and true nature misrepresented. One widely sold text suggests, for instance, that the *wakō* phenomenon was, in effect, a plea for free trade against protectionism and that the Japanese who ventured to China in armed groups were forced to go under arms as a measure of self-defense in the insecure conditions under which they conducted commerce.[18] Another author, who clearly admires the pugnacity of the *wakō*, in apparent seriousness puts them in the "forefront of the people's liberation war" in China.[19] Yet another has meticulously combed Chinese sources to show that in them, terms such as *chen-wo* (J: *shinwa*, "real Japanese") and *ts'ung-wo* (J: *jūwa*, "follower of Japanese"), which imply that Japanese had the chief part in the *wakō* raids, are outweighed by *kou-wo* (J: *kōwa*, "inciters" or "seducers of Japanese") and similar terms, which show that the initiative was Chinese.[20]

Such scholars frequently quote the passage from the official history *Ming shih*, which in referring to the brigands in the great raid of 1555 states that "about three of ten were real Japanese, and seven of ten

person's dead; they don't give murder another thought! Hence the proverb says, 'Cross, if you must, a Japanese bandit's path, but never a garrison soldier's.' Run into a Japanese, and there's still a chance you'll get away. But meet a soldier, and you're done for." *Ch'ou-hai t'u-pien*, pt. 11, f. 66v.

18 Iwami Hiroshi and Taniguchi Kikuo, *Dentō Chūgoku no kansei*, vol. 4 of *Chūgoku no rekishi*, vol. 4 of *Shinsho Tōyōshi*, Kōdansha gendai shinsho, no. 454 (Tokyo: Kōdansha, 1982, 4th printing), p. 91.

19 Yobuko Jōtarō, *Wakō shikō* (Tokyo: Shin jimbutsu ōrai-sha, 1971), p. 272. Alternatively Yobuko speaks of the *wakō* as a "Japanese–Ming allied army [*Nichimin rengōgun*]"; see p. 280.

20 Ishihara Michihiro, *Wakō*, vol. 7 of *Nihon rekishi sōsho* (Tokyo: Yoshikawa kōbunkan, 1964), pp. 71–5, 233–4. Ishihara has also strained all possible references to the quality of mercy among the *wakō* out of the sources; see his "Wakō no onjō ni tsuite," *Nihon rekishi* 166 (April 1962): 38–45.

were persons who subordinated themselves to the Japanese."[21] Or they seek support from other Chinese sources, such as the passage in *Ch'ou-hai t'u-pien* that maintains, "If today's pirates mobilized, they would number several tens of thousands. They all pretend to be Japanese. To be sure, those who actually come from Japan amount to no less than several thousand, but all the rest are Chinese subjects, scoundrels who attach themselves to the invaders."[22] Many such passages may be found, making it possible to assert that the proportion of Japanese among the brigands who pillaged the coastal regions of China in the 1550s was no greater than one in ten.

As easily found, however, are other accounts that indicate that the Japanese contribution to the exploits of the *wakō* was anything but insubstantial. The chief picaroons – the likes of Wang Chih, Hsü Hai, and Yeh Ming, alias Ma Yeh – may have been Chinese (although there is an argument that the characters Ma Yeh really represent a rebus for the Japanese name Asō), but knowledgeable Chinese sources also contain a veritable rogues' gallery of pirate captains with indisputably Japanese names and an extensive gazetteer of their nesting places in the Japanese archipelago. When *Jih-pen i-chien* (A mirror of Japan, c. 1564) states, for instance, that Sukegorō of Tanegashima, Kamon the Pilot of Satsuma, Hikogorō of Hyūga, and Hosoya of Izumi (the name smacks of a Sakai merchant) in 1556 at the behest of Hsü Hai organized a band of fifty thousand to sixty thousand pirates who set sail in one thousand vessels to pillage Kwangtung but suffered severe damage in a storm and hit South Chihli instead, we may assume that the numbers are exaggerated. But we have no reason to question the essential accuracy of the story of massive Japanese participation in this pirate fleet. Any reader of *Jih-pen i-chien* will conclude that its author, Cheng Shun-kung, was well informed – as well he might have been, for he had gone to Japan in that very year of 1556 as an official envoy charged with gathering intelligence on the *wakō* and enlisting the aid of the daimyo of Bungo, Ōtomo Sōrin, in their suppression. Cheng's "Mirror" reflects the observations of a half-year's stay in the country. Hence it is particularly interesting to see him first take a swipe at Chinese "exile drifters" who lurk in Japan and lure its inhabitants to cross the seas and plunder China but then draw the categorical conclusion: "From Kii on these barbarians' eastern seacoast to the south and west, through the San'yō and the San'in regions to Wakasa and the barbarians' west, there is no place where the people have not been

---

21 *Ming shih*, vol. 27, p. 8353; *Seishi no bu*, vol. 1, p. 295.   22 *Ch'ou-hai t'u-pien*, pt. 11, f. 1.

incited to join in the raids. They may call themselves merchants but are in actuality brigands."[23]

The "trade called bafan"

The term often used for these Japanese rovers in the contemporary lingua franca of the seas was *bahan*, or *bafan* in the Portuguese transcription. One encounters it written with a variety of Chinese characters, most often with the two that form the name of Hachiman (Ch: *pa-fan*), a deity of war whose cult was widespread in Japan. Presumably, the pirate vessels flew pennants bearing Hachiman's name, and the corsairs by extension came to be known by it. But this seems too facile an explanation and no longer enjoys the confidence of scholars. Of the several Chinese-character compounds that Cheng Shun-kung lists and glosses for the term, the most evocative is *p'o-fan*, "tattered sails," the bandits being called so because they are "nasty like sails that break." But whatever the term's derivation, its meaning is clear. Extensively practiced in such Japanese regions as Satsuma, "the trade called bafan . . . is to go make prizes and rob the maritime localities and settlements of China with many vessels armed for that purpose."[24]

According to *Ch'ou-hai t'u-pien*, Satsuma, Higo, and Nagato were the Japanese provinces that were the most prolific breeding grounds of pirates; next came Ōsumi, Chikuzen, Chikugo, Hakata (a city singled out for mention among provinces), Hyūga, Settsu, Harima, and the island of Tanegashima; natives of Buzen, Bungo, and Izumi also took part in the raids on occasion, notably so among them the traders who found themselves in Satsuma on business when the opportunity of joining an expedition to China presented itself. (Curiously enough, the only province of Kyushu that is *not* included on this roll of names is Hizen, the home of the Matsuura-tō and the base of Wang Chih. Perhaps "Higo" was a slip of the pen for its neighbor province, or possibly the identity of Hizen as a stronghold and refuge of the *wakō* was so well known that it was sometimes assumed as a given in such lists. To be sure, there is no lack of mentions of this province else-

---

23 Cheng Shun-kung, *Jih-pen i-chien* (Mikajiri Yutaka, ed., *Nihon ikkan*) (Kyoto, privately mimeographed, 1937; copy in the Library of the Faculty of Law, Kyoto University), pp. 132–8, 474. Also see the maps and descriptions of routes from the south of Kyushu to Kyoto, pp. 424–58.

24 On *p'o-fan*, see ibid., p. 108. On *bafan*, see Padre Luis Frois SJ, *Historia de Japam*, pt. 1, chap. 6, ed. Josef Wicki SJ (Lisbon: Biblioteca Nacional de Lisboa, 1976), vol. 1, p. 46; Matsuda Kiichi and Kawasaki Momota, trans., *Furoisu Nihonshi* (Tokyo: Chūō kōronsha, 1978), vol. 6, p. 72.

where. *Jih-pen i-chien*, for instance, names the Hizen ports Hirado and Arima as veritable sumps of pirates.)

After noting that it was the poor people of these places who provided the bulk of the pirate crews, *Ch'ou-hai t'u-pien* singles out the general lack of authority in Japan as the critical factor in the rise of piracy. Unlike in China, there was no central government in that country. Nobody listened to the orders of the "lord of Yamashiro," that is, the Ashikaga shogun in Kyoto. Of the three great military houses that had in the past maintained a measure of control over pirate areas even as they champed at one another, the Ōuchi of Yamaguchi had recently fallen; the Amako of Izumo were in a state of collapse; and only the Ōtomo of Bungo were left. Such authority as the Ōtomo had did not extend past the borders of six provinces in Kyushu, and naturally enough, the remainder of the island's nine provinces – Satsuma, Ōsumi, and Hyūga – ranked among the most notorious of the abiding places of the *wakō*. Then what were the prospects of seeking remedy in Japan? "To expect that country to keep the various barbarians in check is absolutely impossible."[25]

Indeed, in 1562, when *Ch'ou-hai t'u-pien* was compiled, no ready solution to the acute problem of authority was visible in Japan. In particular, Kyushu – the area of greatest concern to us – was in a state of turmoil. The Chinese "bible of *wakō* studies" was up to date in reporting on the six provinces of the lord of Bungo: Ōtomo Sōrin had by 1559 accumulated six military governorships (*shugoshiki*) in Kyushu and had even obtained the title of Kyushu *tandai*, the shogunal deputy in the island. But these distinctions granted by the Muromachi bakufu conveyed prestige, not power. At best, Sōrin exercised a tenuous hegemony over northern Kyushu, where he had many challengers and few trustworthy friends. The other three of Kyushu's military governorships – over those notorious provinces of Satsuma, Ōsumi, and Hyūga – had been, since the 1190s intermittently and since the 1390s constantly, in the hands of the Shimazu family.

This *shugo* family, however, had a history of violent internal quarrels. As a result, by the beginning of the sixteenth century, even its hold on Satsuma was shaky, and its ability to control affairs in the larger area of southern Kyushu was weak. In 1508, Shimazu Tadamasa committed suicide in despair or disgust at the seditiousness of his faithless relatives and overbearing liegemen. In the next eighteen years, four lords followed one another in quick succession, and the

25 *Ch'ou-hai t'u-pien*, pt. 2, f. 22rv.

house's main line was tested severely as it tried to maintain itself in the face of the revolts of other branches of the Shimazu, the fluctuating loyalties of vassals, and the perpetual attempts of petty local lords (*kokujin*) to assert themselves. The problem of authority was not fully resolved, even through the strenuous efforts of the famed "restorer" of the family's fortunes, Shimazu Takahisa (1514–71), who became *shugo* in 1526 and for the next forty years – until he passed on the office to his son Yoshihisa (1533–1611) – fought tenaciously to subject the recalcitrant barons to fealty. Throughout those years, southern Kyushu was a cockpit of contention.

It was not until Yoshihisa's day that the head of the Shimazu family managed to consolidate his dominion over southern Kyushu and establish himself as a Sengoku daimyo who would brook no opposition. In 1569, Yoshihisa subdued Hishikari Takaaki, a powerful baron of northern Satsuma; in 1570, the rebellious Irikiin and Tōgō families of Satsuma were reduced to submission; in 1574, Kimotsuki Kanesuke and Ijichi Shigeoki, magnates of Ōsumi whose families had been a law unto themselves for generations, surrendered to their Shimazu overlord; and by 1578, the Shimazu had destroyed the great house of Itō, lords of a major portion of Hyūga, and were ready to engage the Ōtomo in a contest for the ascendancy over all of Kyushu. Thus the Shimazu daimyo showed that he had the power to overawe the refractory. At the time of the great *wakō* raids on China in the 1550s, however, this development still lay in the future. The Shimazu had not yet managed to suppress the independence of various contending factions. The authority of the daimyo had not yet been imposed over all of the farming and fishing population. Disordered circumstances still prevailed in southern Kyushu.

Does not the history of this regional pell-mell help explain why Satsuma, Ōsumi, and Hyūga had such a reputation as rookeries of pirates? That reputation reached as far as Malacca, where the Jesuit Luis Frois, the future chronicler of the Roman Catholic mission in Japan, recorded on December 1, 1555, the news brought by Portuguese ships from China about the "very great conflicts and strife between China and Japan, and how a great armada had made ready at Cangoxima [Kagoshima, the central place of Satsuma] and had devastated many Chinese localities that were on the sea, as well as a very populous city, where the Japanese wrought great destruction."[26]

26 Irmão Luis Frois SJ to the Padres and Irmãos SJ in Goa, dated Malaqua, December 1, 1555, Josef Wicki SJ, ed., *Documenta Indica*, vol. 3, *Monumenta Missionum Societatis Iesu* 6, *Monumenta Historica Societatis Iesu* 74 (Rome: Monumenta Historica Societatis Iesu, 1954), p. 319.

Hangchow, which was attacked in June or July 1555, may be the large city meant here, but it is difficult to say, as that year's pirate band, organized by Hsü Hai with a following that reputedly consisted of Japanese from Izumi, Satsuma, Hizen, Higo, Settsu, and Tsushima, terrorized the entire populous area between Chiangyin on the Yangtze and Hangchow, striking inland as far as Soochow.[27] A stray group of sixty or seventy from this band penetrated as far as Nanking in the late summer, but could the news of this shocking event have traveled so fast that it reached the ears of Frois's informants before they sailed? In any event, unless we believe that those Portuguese informants – who were surely expert in the ways of the seafaring demimonde of the China Sea – were fooled by the Chinese goverment's propaganda and suborned into libeling the Japanese, we have no grounds to assume that the "great armada" of the pirates did not in fact have its origins or at least fit out in the Satsuma region.

Frois himself was at this time still a distant and unprejudiced observer. Later on, in *Historia de Japam*, he would reserve some of his most rancorous passages for Satsuma, the sworn enemy of his hero "King Francisco of Bungo," that is, Ōtomo Sōrin. When, for instance, he calls Satsuma such a miserable place that it had, of old, no claim to fame whatever but was despised by all and ignored by the central government, Frois is exaggerating. But it no longer sounds purely hyperbolical when he adds that the province was so poor that its people were driven to seek sustenance by plundering China, even at a terrible risk to their lives. In most years, the greater part of those who went there – Frois says – remained there. Others were lost on the sea in their small and fragile craft.[28]

Owing to the lack of contemporary Japanese sources, it is impossible to document an involvement of the Shimazu in the "trade called bafan," a trade that was without a doubt practiced widely in the three provinces under their nominal jurisdiction. Chinese sources, however, actually attribute membership in this daimyo family to two of the archest buccaneers. Ch'en Tung, who led the *bahan* fleet from Hizen, Chikuzen, Bungo, Izumi, Hakata, and Kii that attacked the Shanghai area in 1555, is described as "the younger brother of the lord of Satsuma, the chief of his secretariat." Naturally, "many of his followers were Satsuma men." And Hsü Hai's right-hand man, the ferocious

27 See *Ch'ou-hai t'u-pien*, pt. 8, ff. 27–28. Also see *Ming shih*, vol. 27, pp. 8352–3; *Seishi no bu*, vol. 1, pp. 294–5.
28 Frois, *Historia*, pt. 2 [B], chap. 40, ed. Wicki, vol. 4 (1983), pp. 292–3; Matsuda and Kawasaki, trans., *Furoisu Nihonshi*, vol. 8, pp. 168–9.

Shingorō, "whose venom infected the entire region of Wu, whose intent was to swallow up all of Chekiang, and who was on the lurk for Nanking," is called "the younger brother of the ruler of Ōsumi." This attribution of brotherhood with the mighty may rest on nothing more than the empty vaunting of the individuals in question or of their captors. In any event, their identities cannot be determined. Ch'en Tung may be the Chinese nom de guerre of a Japanese pirate, the garbled transcription of a Japanese name, or a rebus. Shingorō is as good a Japanese name as any, but the name by itself is in neither case a sure prognostic of nationality. The "lord of Satsuma" and "ruler of Ōsumi," Shimazu Takahisa, had two younger brothers, Tadamasa (d. 1561) and Naohisa, also called Matagorō. The latter, whose domain was in the Kawanabe district of Satsuma that juts into the east China Sea (the general area of what are now Bōnotsu-chō and the city of Makurazaki, Kagoshima Prefecture), is a shadowy figure reputed to have been the patron of pirates; the date of his death is unclear. Somewhat disappointingly, there is evidence that Naohisa was still alive in 1571, whereas the heads of Shingorō and Ch'en Tung are known to have been delivered to Peking in 1556, along with those of Hsü Hai and Ma Yeh.[29] Who the other Japanese captains and confederates of the *bahan* trade were – the picturesquely named Urumi ("Red-Brown") Tarō, Keiten ("The Sky's the Limit") Shinshirō, and Hakata Sukezaemon among them – likewise cannot be determined. Apparently, they did not seek notoriety in their native land.

"When they return to their islands from plundering," states *Ch'ou-hai t'u-pien*, "they say they have come back from trading. They will not speak of those who were captured or killed by our troops, keeping it a secret. Even the neighbors do not know, or [if they know], they think it honorable."[30] The reluctance of the perpetrators to publicize their part in plundering expeditions is understandable, although it is difficult to fathom how they could have kept it a secret in places such as Satsuma and Hirado. The "famed pirate and cruel killer of the sort that go to rob China" does make his appearance once or twice in Jesuit reports of deathbed conversions to Christianity.[31] In any event, al-

29 On Ch'en Tung, see *Ch'ou-hai t'u-pien*, pt. 8, f. 28v. On Shingorō, see ibid., pt. 9, ff. 22–23; and *Ming shih*, *chüan* 205: "Lieh-chuan 205, Hu Tsung-hsien," vol. 18, p. 5412; *Seishi no bu*, vol. 1, p. 205. On Shimazu Naohisa, see Ōta Akira, *Seishi kakei daijiten*, vol. 2 (Tokyo: Kadokawa shoten, 1963), p. 2874.
30 *Ch'ou-hai t'u-pien*, pt. 2, f. 35v.
31 For example, Frois, *Historia*, pt. 1, chap. 47 (Arima, 1563), and chap. 111 (Hirado, 1576), ed. Wicki, vol. 1, p. 330, and vol. 2 (1981), pp. 469–71; Matsuda and Kawasaki, trans., *Furoisu Nihonshi*, vol. 7, p. 17 and vol. 10 (1979), pp. 72–4.

though it must be reemphasized that contemporary Japanese sources on the *wakō* are next to nonexistent, it must also be stressed that their lack is not a convincing argument for the absence of Japanese from the *bahan* raids. Rather, it is beyond dispute that the pirate chiefs of the 1550s, whatever their nationality, had safe bases and powerful patrons in Japan and that they drew much of their fighting manpower from that island country. The best example is Wang Chih – also known as Captain Wu-feng (Gohō Senshu) and even styled Hui Wang, the King of Hui – who lived like a true sea king in Hirado, surrounded himself with luxury and a train of Japanese myrmidons, maintained cordial relations with not only the local petty eminence, Matsuura Takanobu (1529–99), but also with such great names as Ōtomo Sōrin and Ōuchi Yoshitaka, and sent bands of pirate-traders off to seek their and his fortunes in China.

The "trade called bafan" of the 1550s was the culmination of a long seafaring tradition in Japan. The political conditions of that confused time of Japanese history – at the climax of the Sengoku period (1467–1573), before unification – permitted the existence of armed groups that ventured overseas seeking gain. Although plunder was not their sole objective, what they could not get by peaceful trade they obtained by pillage.

What were the *wakō* after? According to Chinese sources, the Japanese above all sought raw silk (which fetched ten times its Chinese price in Japan), floss silk, cotton cloth ("because they do not have cotton wool"), pongee thread, brocade, red thread, quicksilver (ten times the Chinese price), needles, iron chains, iron pots, porcelain, old copper coins ("the Japanese do not mint their own but use old Chinese coins exclusively"), old paintings, old calligraphy, old books, pharmaceuticals, carpets, horse blankets, facial powder, bamboo ware, lacquer ware, and vinegar.[32] This, of course, looks like an ordinary shopping list, but it does not tell the whole story. It would appear that the sixteenth-century *wakō*, like their fourteenth-century predecessors, not only sought general merchandise but also engaged in slavery. Cheng Shun-kung reported the story of some two hundred or three hundred Chinese slaves kept by Japanese families in the vicinity of Takasu in Satsuma (actually, in Ōsumi; now part of the city of Kanoya, Kagoshima Prefecture). And the Jesuit Luis de Almeida wrote in 1562 of his efforts to safeguard the honor of a shipload of women he saw in the harbor of Tomari in the Kawanabe district of

---

32 *Ch'ou-hai t'u-pien*, pt. 2, ff. 32–33v.

Satsuma (now Bōnotsu-chō): They had been bought by some of his Portuguese compatriots from "the Japanese who seize them in war in China and then sell them." Almeida made sure that they were well protected on their voyage thence.[33]

By 1562, however, the peak of the *bahan* raids on China had passed. The greatest of the pirate bands were broken up in the late 1550s by the successful counteraction of the Ming authorities. In 1556, the governor of Chekiang, Hu Tsung-hsien, through a clever intrigue, first incited Hsü Hai to deliver Ch'en Tung and Ma Yeh into his hands, and then he destroyed Hsü Hai. This coup meant that three of the pirate chiefs having the closest connections with Japan had been eliminated at one blow. In 1557, Hu scored his greatest success when he lured Wang Chih, the godfather of organized *wakō* activity, back to China with the promise of a pardon for his past crimes and misdemeanors and a relaxation of the maritime prohibitions, with the effect of permitting trade with the Japanese – conditions that delighted not only Wang and his confederates but also his commerce-minded Japanese friend, Ōtomo Sōrin.[34] The promises of Hu Tsung-hsien turned out to be dross, and Wang Chih was beheaded at the end of 1559 or the beginning of 1560.

The capture and execution of the captain of all captains of the *bahan* trade presaged the end of the *wakō*. Buccaneers such as Hung Tse-chen, a former lieutenant of Wang Chih, continued to replenish their strength in Japan, and the *wakō* remained active for several more decades, but they had lost much of their sting. The focus of their activity shifted from the Yangtze Delta and Chekiang to the coasts of Fukien and Kwangtung, and given the increasing distance from Japan, the intensity of Japanese participation diminished. And then in 1567, the wind was taken out of the *bahan* sails when the Ming government finally – after two centuries – took its maritime prohibitions off the books. Mainland Chinese were permitted to travel overseas, and a prospering trade began with the Southeast Asian countries, removing some of the pressure that had initially led to the rise of the *wakō*. Because of the depredations associated with the Japanese, however,

---

33 *Jih-pen i-chien*, p. 136. Irmão Luis Dalmeida SJ to Irmãos SJ, dated Vocoxiura [Yokoseura in Hizen], October 25, 1562, *Cartas qve os Padres e Irmãos da Companhia de Iesus escreuerão dos Reynos de Iapão & China aos da mesma Companhia da India, & Europa, des do anno de 1549. atè o de 1580.* (Em Euora por Manoel de Lyra. Anno de M.D.XCVIII.), vol. 1, f. 106. Compare the slightly different version in Frois, *Historia*, pt. 1, chap. 33, ed. Wicki, vol. 1, p. 215; Matsuda and Kawasaki, trans., *Furoisu Nihonshi*, vol. 6, p. 270.

34 Hsü Hsüeh-chü (died c. 1617), *Chia-ching Tung-nan p'ing-wo t'ung-lu* (Nanking: Kuo-hsüeh t'u-shu-kuan, 1932 facsimile reprint). On Wang's capture, the debate on his fate, and his execution, see also *Ch'ou-hai t'u-pien*, pt. 5, ff. 31v–32 & 34v–35v, and pt. 9, ff. 24–9.

Japan officially remained off limits to the Chinese traders, and vice versa. But that continuing ban served the interests of the Portuguese, who established a highly profitable carrying trade between China and Japan. The raw silk that the Japanese sought so dearly thus came to Japan from China in Portuguese bottoms.

From pirate bands into navies

What happened to the Japanese pirates?[35] This question is intimately connected with the problem of the reestablishment of authority throughout the Japanese body politic during the second half of the sixteenth century. The pirates did not disappear; they were put under control. In the process of unification, the maritime armed bands (*kaizokushū*) lost their independent character and were transformed into navies (*suigun*) that served the major daimyo and then the national hegemon. In a few notable instances – the Kuki of the Kii peninsula and the Kurushima of the Inland Sea, not to mention the Matsuura of Hizen – their leaders themselves became daimyo whose families survived the Edo period as peers of the Japanese empire.

Pirates were recruited from a maritime populace that lived according to the principle enunciated by that expert on seafaring, Mephistopheles: "All that counts is a ready grip: / You catch a fish, you catch a ship."[36] In the Middle Ages, enterprising fishermen of this type were occasionally employed as guards of vessels transporting rents from landed estates (*shōen*) in outlying provinces to their proprietors in the Kyoto–Nara region, but they were not above attacking and plundering such shipments themselves. In some cases, their bosses established checkpoints at dominant spots on the waterways, where cargoes were controlled and fees had to be paid before a ship could proceed; in others, they simply exacted protection money from those who wanted to ensure an unmolested passage for themselves. Needless to say, they also took part in the *bahan* trade. Some of the locally prominent captains who headed groups of fishermen and on occasion used them for armed robbery came to exercise a dominant influence over similar seafaring entrepreneurs of a wider area. These newly risen maritime barons could easily sell their services as naval auxiliaries to one or the

---

35 A concise essay on this question is Utagawa Takehisa, "Chūsei kaizokushū no shūmatsu," *Nihon rekishi* 333 (February 1976): 22–39.
36 "Da fördert nur ein rascher Griff, / Man fängt den Fisch, man fängt ein Schiff." Goethe, *Faust*, II, 5:3 (11, 178–11,179).

other of the contending forces in a country that was rent by constant warfare.

Such a one was Murakami Takeyoshi (1533–1604), who ruled his fleets from an elaborate fortress located on the island of Noshima in Iyo Province (now Miyakubo-chō, Ehime Prefecture), at one of the narrowest but busiest straits of the Inland Sea. As the wars of unification entered a critical phase in the late 1570s with the beginning of the campaigns of Oda Nobunaga (1534–82) against the powerful Mōri family of western Honshu, both sides bid for Murakami's services with promises of rich enfeoffments and great prerogatives. As late as 1586, when the unification regime of Toyotomi Hideyoshi (1537?–98) had already made substantial inroads into the area all around Murakami's marine microcosm, the voice of this "greatest corsair of all Japan" evidently still sufficed either to raise or to assuage the terrors of a crossing of the Inland Sea. Indeed, we learn that the people of "the shores and seacoasts of other provinces each year pay him a tribute for fear of being destroyed" by him and his pirates, who "continually go out on raids."[37] Obviously, such a buccaneer's continued independence was incompatible with the aims of national unification, as was that of others like him. They were brought into line.

As Sengoku daimyo sought to extend their sway over regional domains, they tried to subordinate maritime armed bands to themselves by absorbing the chief corsairs into the body of their own vassals, if not to strengthen their military forces by adding a navy, then to secure the routes of commerce in and about their domains by eliminating piracy. When more and more daimyo became integrated into a grand structure of fealty as the process of unification advanced under Hideyoshi, it became possible for the hegemon to plan the elimination of all private arms-bearing nationwide. In 1588, Hideyoshi issued his famous "sword hunt" edict, in which "the farmers of the various provinces" were "strictly forbidden to keep swords, short swords, spears, firearms, and other types of military weapons." If they were permitted such "unnecessary implements," the document added, then they would be tempted to "evade their taxes" or even "plot uprisings" (*ikki*, perhaps the worst word in the vocabulary of the feudal ruler). Far less known, but as significant an illustration of the thoroughgoing effort of Hideyoshi's regime to reduce the capacity for violence or armed resistance on the part of any social group in Japan, is the other

---

37 Frois, *Historia*, pt. 2 [B], chap. 33, ed. Wicki, vol. 4, p. 248; Matsuda and Kawasaki, trans., *Furoisu Nihonshi*, vol. 5, p. 198.

edict that he issued on the very same day, a prohibition of piracy. If the former document decreed a sword hunt, then the latter ordered a dragnet through which must pass "the sea captains and fishermen of the provinces and the seashores, and all those who go in ships to the sea." They were to be subjected to an "immediate investigation" by the local representatives of their daimyo and made to "subscribe to written oaths that henceforth they shall not engage in the slightest piratical activity," for "pirate vessels are strictly prohibited on the seas of the various provinces." If, hereafter, the recipient of a fief were to prove so negligent that pirates should happen to be discovered in a place under his jurisdiction, then that fief "shall be confiscated in perpetuity."[38]

It has been argued that although Hideyoshi's sword hunt edict "may not have been class legislation in intent, it had the broadest social impact in practice, for it helped to underline the social distinction between samurai, whose profession it was to handle weapons, and farmers, whose job it was to till the soil and cultivate the mulberry."[39] *Mutatis mutandis*, much the same may be said about the decree concerning piracy; surely it is no accident that the two were issued together. The social distinction between samurai and farmers – *hei-nō bunri* – is often talked about. It may be time that the term for the separation between the warrior's and the fisherman's status – *hei-gyo bunri* – came into wider usage. In the Sengoku period, neither distinction was strict, but under Hideyoshi both became so. Unfortunately, the new definition of their status did not mean, for either farmers or fishermen, a total exemption from military service.

Just as peasants were mobilized as laborers (*jimbu*) and bearers (*bumaru*) in military camps and campaigns, so ordinary fishermen were drafted into service as sailors on naval vessels or transports. This fact and its consequences are dramatically illustrated in a document issued by Hideyoshi in 1593, which contains "strict orders" to round up "all the mariners from the age of fifteen up to the age of sixty that are left on the seashores of your domain," because the "sea captains

---

38 The two edicts, both dated Tanshō 16 (1588).7.8 and issued over Hideyoshi's vermilion seal, were meant to have a universal application; hence they have no particular addressee. For the prohibition of piracy, see Tōkyō daigaku shiryō hensanjo, ed., *Dai Nihon komonjo, iewake 11: Kobayakawa-ke monjo*, vol. 1 (Tokyo: Tōkyō daigaku shuppankai, 1979), no. 502, pp. 478–9. For the sword hunt edict, see ibid., no. 503, pp. 479–81.

39 John Whitney Hall, "Japan's Sixteenth-Century Revolution," in George Elison and Bardwell L. Smith, eds., *Warlords, Artists, & Commoners: Japan in the Sixteenth Century* (Honolulu: University of Hawaii Press, 1981), p. 15. On the applicability to fishermen, see Miki Seiichirō, *Teppō to sono jidai*, vol. 108 of *Kyōikusha rekishi shinsho "Nihonshi"* (Tokyo: Kyōikusha, 1981), pp. 175–7.

and mariners [*sendō kako*]" drafted the previous year had been so "sorely afflicted" that "the greater half of them died."[40] The service on which they had suffered such terrible losses was Hideyoshi's war of aggression in Korea.

WAR AND PEACE

The background of Japanese aggression in Korea

To the Koreans, Hideyoshi's invasion of their country meant the second coming of the *bahan* plague and the biggest *wakō* raid of all. In contrast, the Japanese participants who wrote accounts of the invasion – men of varied backgrounds, from the appropriately named Yoshino Jingozaemon, a samurai of Matsuura, to Shukuro Shungaku, a Zen monk in the retinue of the general Kikkawa Hiroie (1561– 1625) – invariably invoked the myth of a primordial conquest of Korea by Japan's empress Jingū as a historical precedent that justified their venture.[41]

Hideyoshi himself claimed a sanction that was even more grand: In broadcasting his plans to extend his dominion overseas, he asserted that the will to conquer had been bestowed on him by Heaven.[42] To the king of Korea, he wrote in 1590 that he was conceived when the wheel of the sun entered his mother's womb in a dream, a sure sign that the glory of his name should pervade the Four Seas, just as the sun illuminates the universe. Indeed, he had no purpose but to spread his fame throughout the Three Countries of Japan, China, and Korea. Now that he had pacified and prospered Japan and demonstrated his invincibility there, he would invade China to introduce Japanese customs and values to that country, and he wanted the Koreans to lead the way.[43]

Hideyoshi's ambassadors did their best to soften the rude force of his demand, by insinuating that the last phrase required the Korean

40 Hideyoshi to the home-province resident lieutenants (*rusui*) of Hashiba Kikkawa Jijū [Kikkawa Hiroie], dated [Bunroku 2.]2.5, in *Dai Nihon komonjo, iewake 9: Kikkawa-ke monjo*, vol. 1, no. 783, pp. 750–1.
41 *Yoshino Jingozaemon oboegaki*, in *Zoku gunsho ruijū*, XX-2 (Tokyo: Zoku gunsho ruijū kanseikai, 1923), 591:378; *Shukuro kō*, ibid, XIII-2 (1926), 356:1003.
42 *Kampaku* of Japan to Lesser Ryūkyū (i.e., the Philippine Islands), dated Tenshō 19 (1591).9.15, Murakami Naojirō, ed., *Ikoku ōfuku shokanshū, Zōtei ikoku nikki shō* (Tokyo: Sunnansha, 1929), p. 29.
43 *Kampaku* of Japan to King of Korea, dated Tenshō 18 (1590).11.–, *Zoku zenrin kokuhōki*, in *Zoku gunsho ruijū*, XXX-1 (1925), 881:404. Curiously enough, Wang Chih was another who was conceived when a "great star" entered his mother's womb in a dream; see *Ch'ou-hai t'u-pien*, pt. 9, f. 24.

government to do no more than clear the road to China for the Japanese (that is, grant them transit rights through Korea) or – milder yet – to smooth the path for a resumption of Japanese relations with China. But the Koreans would be neither fooled nor intimidated. They refused on principle to become party to an assault on the country that was their suzerain. To be sure, although they expressed themselves in terms of filial respect when they spoke of their duty to China, they also had a healthy fear of this parent; yet they trusted China to come to the aid of Korea, if need be.[44] Korea, in short, was comfortable with the international order of East Asia headed by China and sought security from it. Hideyoshi, however, wanted to overthrow that system. If Korea did not cooperate with him – and by the middle of 1591 it had clearly indicated that it would not – then it would have to suffer the consequences.

The notion of a continental invasion was not a thought that came to Hideyoshi suddenly. Indeed, in view of the prevalent image of Hideyoshi as a megalomaniac, which is based in large part on his foreign aggression, it is interesting to note that the idea was first broached not by him but by his predecessor. It was Oda Nobunaga who proclaimed in 1582 his intention to subdue China by force of arms once he had made himself "absolute master of all the sixty and six reigns of Japan."[45] In other words, a vision of the conquest of China was the common conceit of the two great unifiers, and both saw it as an extension of the conquests through which Japan was being subjected to their regime. For Nobunaga, the vision came to nothing when he was assassinated with less than half his Japanese objective in his grasp. For Hideyoshi, it grew less fanciful and more concrete as the process of Japan's unification advanced under his direction.

Significantly enough, the earliest-known documentary evidence of Hideyoshi's bellicose intentions toward the continent comes from 1585, that triumphal year when his armies were victorious in three different regions of Japan, when he won the appointment to the lofty

44 The arrival of Hideyoshi's letter in Korea, the efforts of his envoys, the priest Keitetsu Genso and Sō Yoshitoshi, the daimyo of Tsushima, to explain away the main issue, and the Korean court's reactions to these diplomatic proceedings are described in detail in Sŏnjo Sogyŏng Taewang sujŏng sillok, pt. 25, ff. 2–17v, entries for the third to sixth months of Sonjo 24 (1591): Chosŏn wangjo sillok, vol. 25 (1957), pp. 601–8. The response sent by the Korean court to Hideyoshi may be found in f. 14rv, p. 607. See also Chōsen Sōtokufu Chōsenshi henshūkai, ed., Chōsenshi, 4th series, vol. 9 (Keijō: Chōsen insatsu kabushiki kaisha, 1937), pp. 410–20.
45 Frois to General SJ, dated Cochinoççú (Kuchinotsu in Hizen), November 5, 1582, Cartas qve os Padres, vol. 2, f. 63v. Also in Frois, Historia, pt. 2, chap. 40, ed. Wicki, vol. 3 (1982), p. 336; Matsuda and Kawasaki, trans., Furoisu Nihonshi, vol. 5 (1978), p. 138.

aristocratic post of *kampaku* (imperial regent), and when the prospect of a country unified under his aegis first appeared as a real possibility. We find the mention in a letter in which the idea of a conquest of all Japan is coupled with that of China.[46] In 1586, as he planned the subjugation of the Shimazu and the pacification of Kyushu, Hideyoshi repeatedly referred to China and Korea as though to invade them were a course of action that would follow naturally from an occupation of southwestern Japan.[47]

By April 1587, when Hideyoshi departed Osaka on his Kyushu campaign, the scope of his ambitions had apparently increased along with their notoriety: There was talk of a "grand design" on his part to proceed onward and "slash his way" into Korea, China, and South Barbary (presumably somewhere in the region of the Indies or even farther, where pepper and the Portuguese came from).[48] That Hideyoshi, whose knowledge of world geography cannot have been great, indeed harbored a far-flung design that included even India would later become evident from his own words, but the immediate aftermath of the conquest of Kyushu was not yet the time to embark on a foreign venture. A great external exploit that would crown and safeguard his internal accomplishments was what Hideyoshi envisioned, but it had to be postponed while there were still important matters to be taken care of at home. The east and the north of Japan were as yet unconquered.

Accordingly, the machinery for the invasion of the mainland was not set in motion until 1591, when the provinces of Mutsu and Dewa, the

---

46 Hideyoshi to Hitotsuyanagi Ichinosuke (Sueyasu), dated [Tenshō 13.]9.3. See Iwasawa Yoshihiko, "Hideyoshi no Kara-iri ni kansuru monjo," in *Nihon rekishi* 163 (January 1962): 73–75. According to *Chōsen seibatsuki*, a history of the Korean invasion by the Neo-Confucian scholar Hori Kyōan (1585–1642), Hideyoshi on the occasion of his departure for the Chūgoku front against the Mōri in 1577 asked Nobunaga for the explicit permission to extend his conquests as far as Korea and China. Hideyoshi supposedly was concerned lest, without such orders, he be accused of *bahan* activity. Nobunaga laughed and then approved all of his campaign plans. This work, however, is not a primary source, and the anecdote cannot be accepted without question. See Nakamura, *Nissen kankeishi*, vol. 2 (1969), pp. 256–7.

47 See, for example, Hideyoshi's vermilion-seal letters to Mōri Uma no Kami (Terumoto), dated [Tenshō 14.] 4.10, and to Ankokuji (Ekei), Kuroda Kageyū (Yoshitaka), and Miyagi Uhyōe Nyūdō (Tomoyori), dated [Tenshō 14.] 8.5, in *Dai Nihon komonjo, iewake 8: Mōri-ke monjo*, vol. 3, nos. 949–50, pp. 227–31. Also see Frois's accounts of the Jesuit Vice-Provincial Gaspar Coelho's audience with Hideyoshi on May 4, 1586, when Hideyoshi asked the Jesuits to negotiate for him the charter of two well-equipped and well-officered Portuguese ships for his planned invasion of Korea and China: Frois to Alexandro Valignano SJ, dated Ximonoxèqui, October 17, 1586, *Cartas qve os Padres*, vol. 2, ff. 175v–7v; and Frois, *Historia*, pt. 2 (B), chap. 31, ed. Wicki, vol. 4, pp. 227–35; Matsuda and Kawasaki, trans., *Furoisu Nihonshi*, vol. 1 (1978, 4th printing), pp. 202–18.

48 Takeuchi Rizō, ed., *Tamon'in nikki*, vol. 4, in *Zōho zoku shiryō taisei* (Kyoto: Rinsen shoten, 1978), p. 68; entry for Tenshō 15.3.3.

northernmost reaches of Honshu, were finally subdued – all of Japan thereby becoming subject to Hideyoshi's authority – and the task of unification was completed. In the eighth month of that year, as his nephew and deputy Hashiba Hidetsugu (1568–95, soon to become the imperial regent of Japan) was reducing to fealty the last of the northern barons, Hideyoshi took two grave steps: First, he issued the famous edict that prohibited the change of status from samurai to townsman or farmer and forbade farmers to abandon their calling for a trade or for job work. Thereby Hideyoshi enacted the basic definition of a domestic social order that would last 280 years. Second, he set the date for the invasion of the mainland (to be the first day of the third month of the following year) and ordered the preparation of a headquarters and staging area at Nagoya in the Matsuura region of Hizen Province, at the point of Kyushu nearest to the mainland.[49]

It is clear that one of Hideyoshi's principal aims in invading the mainland was to demonstrate the unassailable power of Japan's national hegemon. But he wished to attain this goal not only externally, at the expense of the Koreans and Chinese; surely as important in his plans were the internal targets, the daimyo of Japan and the people of their domains. The object was to bend them to the unifier's will through the mobilization of their resources for the invasion, and they were put to tremendous exertions even before the first Japanese soldier crossed the strait of Tsushima to the continent. First, Hideyoshi's headquarters for the invasion, a huge two-ring fortress, had to be constructed from the ground up at Nagoya. This was accomplished in little more than six months by an enormous labor force rounded up by the lords of Kyushu. Having erected the elaborately ramparted and lavishly decorated castle, the peers of the Japanese realm were ordered to build their own residences in its vicinity, and a sizable castle town grew up around it. To this nonesuch in Kyushu, Hideyoshi traveled in style through twenty luxurious way stations prepared at his behest by daimyo along the route from Kyoto. These all were expensive and burdensome undertakings, and it was not Hideyoshi but the daimyo and their populations who shouldered the costs and the burdens.

According to the Jesuit chronicler Frois, the daimyo groaned at these impositions no less than at the thought that in taking ship for

---

49 Ōta Gyūichi, who knew Hidetsugu, wrote his name as Hidetsugi, but historians have not followed his example. The edict prohibiting the change of status, dated Tenshō 19.8.21, is found in many sources, such as *Mōri-ke monjo*, vol. 3, no. 935, pp. 216–17. An early statement regarding concrete preparations for the invasion of China is the letter from Ishida Moku Masazumi to Sagara Kunai no Daibu (Nagatsune), dated [Tenshō 19.] 8.23, in *Dai Nihon komonjo, iewake 5: Sagara-ke monjo*, vol. 2, no. 699, pp. 117–18.

Korea, they would be going to their deaths. There were rumors that a rebellion would surely spring up and put an early end to Hideyoshi's plans, but none among the daimyo wanted to bell the cat: They all were terror stricken and rendered incapable of conspiracy by the tyrant. Even as he intimidated and fleeced the Japanese lords, Hideyoshi sought to console them with expectations of rewards in Korea and China. For instance, he apparently promised three Chinese provinces to the "Christian daimyo" Dom Protasio Arima (Harunobu, the lord of Arima in Hizen, 1567–1612). It is likely that, as Frois states, the recipients of such assurances of future favor, profuse though they may have been with expressions of gratitude to Hideyoshi's face, in actuality wished nothing more than to hold on to their pieces of their native land and were scared stiff of their master's talk of a transfer to such distant if dilated dominions.[50] To be sure, there were also those like the lord of Saga in Hizen, Nabeshima Naoshige (1538–1618), who actively solicited reinvestment with a fief in China on the not-unreasonable grounds that his native province had close traditional ties with that country – "because a great many of the people of the Hizen seacoast have been over there on *bahan* business and are quite used and attached to China."[51]

Japanese historians have variously sought to explain the reasons for Hideyoshi's overseas venture. Their opinions range from that expressed by Tanaka Yoshinari, who wrote in 1905 that it was a type of manifest destiny – a "tidal force" – that drove the Japanese to expand overseas, to the more dyspeptic notion of Suzuki Ryōichi, who suggested in the early 1950s that the invasion of the mainland proceeded naturally from Hideyoshi's tyrannical character and that, in his urge to become an absolute ruler, he first used the daimyo to quash popular energies within Japan and then directed their aggressive impulses toward the neighboring country.[52] Suzuki's interpretation should at least be amended to allow for Hideyoshi's, that spectacular parvenu's, extra-

---

50 See Frois, *Historia*, pt. 3, chap. 51, ed. Wicki, vol. 5 (1984; note that the running headline of this volume, "Segunda parte," conflicts with its half-title, p. 1, "Terceira Parte da Historia de Japam"), pp. 382–6; Matsuda and Kawasaki, trans., *Furoisu Nihonshi*, vol. 2 (1977), pp. 160–6. Cf. *Tamon'in nikki*, vol. 4, pp. 337, 339–40, entries for Tenshō 20 (1592).2.28 and 3.15. A rebellion did occur in 1592, but it was abortive. The ringleader, Umekita Kunikane, a vassal of the Shimazu, was killed before he could accomplish anything. His wife was burned before the assembled grandees in a garden of Nagoya Castle, "pour encourager les autres." The episode caused a delay in the dispatch of Satsuma troops to Korea.

51 Katō Kiyomasa to Natsuka Masaie and Mashita Nagamori, Tenshō 20.6.24; quoted extensively by Nakamura, *Nissen kankei shi*, vol. 2, p. 262.

52 The major interpretations are synopsized by Kitajima Manji, *Chōsen nichinichiki, Kōrai nikki: Hideyoshi no Chōsen shinryaku to sono rekishiteki kokuhatsu* (*Nikki, kiroku ni yoru Nihon rekishi sōsho, kinsei* 4) (Tokyo: Soshiete, 1982), pp. 17–19.

ordinarily ardent desire for distinction, for this was "a social climber whose ambition knew no limits."[53]

In this context, it is interesting to speculate on the true significance of the dispositions that Hideyoshi was inspired to make, in the flush of his invasion's early success, regarding his future new order in Asia. In the notorious twenty-five-article vermilion-seal letter he sent on Tenshō 20 (1592).5.18 to the imperial regent Hidetsugu (the nephew and adopted son he had installed as *kampaku* in Kyoto not five months previously), Hideyoshi – if only on paper – moved the reigning Japanese emperor to the Chinese capital (allotting ten provinces in its vicinity to his support), assigned the rank of Emperor of Japan to either one of two imperial princes (one of them, Hachijō Toshihito, adopted by Hideyoshi as his own son), designated three of his other adopted sons as the candidates to rule over Korea, appointed Hidetsugi to the post of *kampaku* of China (promising him a hundred-province appanage near Peking), and put forward the names of two adopted sons as the possible successors to that dignity in Japan.[54] But where would that leave the paterfamilias, the man who thus disposed over reigns, regencies, and realms with the greatest of ease? He himself – we learn from a letter sent by his secretary on the same day to two of the ladies of Hideyoshi's entourage – would first go to Peking, but then he proposed to take up residence in Ningpo, "the anchorage of the Japanese"; later on, he expected to conquer India.[55]

What was the necessity for all these complicated moves and reassignments of positions? And what role did the conqueror of Korea, China, and India (not to speak of the lesser countries such as Ryūkyū, Taiwan, and the Philippines, all of which Hideyoshi also threatened with doom unless they submitted) consider worthy of himself after the final victory? Surely the maker of emperors and kings must have envisioned a dignity transcending all others. It is tempting to assume that the upstart Hideyoshi, foreseeing in the subjugation of Asia the triumphant climax of his career, planned the ultimate legitimation for him-

53 I have discussed the aristocratization of this lowborn hegemon in "Hideyoshi, the Bountiful Minister," in Elison and Smith, eds., *Warlords, Artists, & Commoners*, pp. 223–44; quotation from p. 233.
54 Hideyoshi to *Kampaku* (Hidetsugu), dated Tenshō 20.5.18, in Kitajima, *Chōsen nichinichiki*, pp. 67–70. It is difficult to tell what Hideyoshi meant by the term "province" (J: *kuni* or *koku*, Ch: *kuo*). If it refers to something of approximately the same size as the Japanese province, of which there were 68 in Hideyoshi's time, then the closest Chinese equivalent is the "district" (Ch: *hsien*, J: *ken*), of which there were 1,171 in the Ming period.
55 Yama(naka) Kichi(nai) (Nagatoshi) to Ohigashisama and Okyakujinsama (Dona Madalena), dated [Tenshō 20.]5.18, in Tokutomi Iichirō, *Toyotomi-shi jidai, chō-hen: Chōsen no eki*, pt. 1, vol. 7 of *Kinsei Nihon kokumin shi* (Tokyo: Min'yūsha, 1935), pp. 453–60.

self as a sort of universal monarch. What he actually had in mind, however, we shall never know, because his conquests did not get past the first obstacle, Korea.

Hideyoshi's plans were conceived in supreme confidence and the most abysmal want of knowledge of the conditions that the Japanese armies would confront on the mainland. Not so much megalomania as ignorance moved the entire enterprise. No systematic effort had been made to gather intelligence on the countries it was proposed to sweep into the maw (if there were Japanese books on Korea comparable to *Haedong chegukki* or on China analogous to *Ch'ou-hai t'u-pien*, they have not survived). Indeed, Hideyoshi's hazy knowledge of international relations for a good while made him suffer under the delusion that Korea was subject to Tsushima, hence causing him to insist that the king of Korea should come to Japan in order to pay obeisance.[56] Hideyoshi invaded Korea because it lay next to China, thinking that he could conquer China easily and that then all of the known world would fall into his lap. What he expected to do with it – beyond, undoubtedly, subjecting it to a round of cadastral surveys, sword hunts, and castle demolitions, the proven measures of Japanese unification – is unclear. Or is the true nature of his plans revealed in the unguarded language of the following wildly mixed metaphor? "To take by force this virgin of a country, Ming, will be [as easy] as for a mountain to crush an egg." India and South Barbary were next on the list.[57]

The invasion and the first Japanese offensive

According to the order of battle determined by Hideyoshi on Tenshō 20.3.13, the Japanese expeditionary army was composed of 158,800 men in nine divisions.[58] Two of these divisions, 21,500 men drawn from the provinces of Bizen, Mino, and Tango, were to be held in reserve on the islands of Iki and Tsushima; designated to make the

---

56 See Nakamura, *Nissen kankei shi*, vol. 2, pp. 248–9; and Kitajima, *Chōsen nichinichiki*, pp. 25–6, both citing *Kyūshū godōza no ki* (1587) by Ōmura Yūko.

57 Hideyoshi to Hashiba Aki no Saishō [Mōri Terumoto], dated Tenshō 20.6.3, *Mōri-ke monjo*, vol. 3, no. 903, p. 163. In another vermilion-seal letter addressed on the same day to Mōri Terumoto, Hideyoshi calls Ming "the country of long sleeves," the samurai's standard trope for effeminacy or genteel ineffectuality; see ibid., no. 904, p. 167.

58 See the chart set out by Kitajima, *Chōsen nichinichiki*, p. 36, on the basis of the order of battle detailed in Hideyoshi's memorandum to Hashiba Aki no Saishō, *Mōri-ke monjo*, vol. 3, no. 885, pp. 143–8, and synopsized with the addition of naval assignments, ibid., no. 886, pp. 149–50; both documents dated Tenshō 20.3.13. A total of 137,300 men may be calculated in another order of battle; ibid., no. 904, pp. 164–8, dated Tenshō 20.6.3.

assault on Korea were contingents from Kyushu, Shikoku, and the Chūgoku region. Almost all of the daimyo of western Japan were destined to make the crossing. Some 27,000 of Hideyoshi's own troops garrisoned his headquarters, Nagoya; more than 70,000 levies who had been marched to Kyushu by the eastern daimyo were disposed in encampments around the wider periphery of that castle. Another 100,000 men from the Kinai and Tōkai regions are said to have been concentrated around Kyoto. In other words, the mobilization for Hideyoshi's Korean venture encompassed the entire country of Japan, whether or not the troops were directly involved in operations on the continent. For obvious logistical reasons, however, most heavily affected by the mobilization were the populations of the Kyushu daimyo and the maritime lords – the former pirate chieftains – of the Inland Sea and the Kii peninsula. These had to furnish five men for each 100 *koku* (180 hectoliters) of rice that the particular domain was estimated under the *kokudaka* system to produce in rice yearly. Other domains were burdened relatively less.

It should be noted that the armies mobilized by Hideyoshi in this way were not composed entirely or even principally of members of a warlike caste, professional soldiers, and trained fighting men, that is, of samurai. A daimyo's quota was filled for the most part by ordinary farmers and fishermen impressed into service. For instance, in the contingent of 705 men led in the first wave of the invasion by Gotō Sumiharu (d. 1595), lord of the Gotō Islands in the Matsuura region, there were 27 mounted warriors, 40 dismounted men-at-arms, 120 foot soldiers (*ashigaru*), and 38 soldiers who served their officers as batmen (*kobito*). These 225, all that can be accommodated under the label "samurai," even if one stretches the term, were outnumbered by the 480 others identified as laborers (200) or master seamen and common sailors (280). Whether the last group, in particular, deserves to be called innocent islanders who were shanghaied into the invasion fleet is subject to doubt, given the past history of the Gotō Islands as a notorious lair of the *wakō;* moreover, it would be rash to generalize on the basis of this example alone. The muster rolls of other daimyo do, however, suggest that no more than half of those on the strength of a contingent drafted for service in Korea were fighting men; the rest did construction and transport duties. Even if the mariners were glad to carry on the piratical tradition of their *wakō* forbears, there is no reason to assume that the navvies and the bearers followed along enthusiastically in the train of the invasion armies. On the contrary, there is ample evidence of absconding and other forms of passive resistance by peasants who despaired of ever coming back to their native farmlands once they heeded the call to the war of aggression.[59]

The invasion began on Tenshō 20.4.12 (May 23, 1592) when the first division of the Japanese expeditionary force landed in Pusan. This division was composed of the contingents of Dom Agostinho Konishi (Yukinaga, daimyo of Uto in Higo, 1556?–1600), Dom Dario Sō (Yoshitoshi, daimyo of Tsushima, 1568–1615), Dom Sancho Ōmura (Yoshiaki, daimyo of Ōmura in Hizen, 1568–1616), Dom Protasio Arima, Matsuura Shigenobu (daimyo of Hirado in Hizen, 1549–1614), and Gotō Sumiharu. The prominent presence of "Christian daimyo" – not really odd, as they were concentrated in western Japan – gives at least this stage of the undertaking the air of a bizarre crusade. The Japanese again demanded free passage through Korea; the Koreans refused, choosing resistance over dishonor; and the hostilities commenced. Pusan fell the next day. (See Map 6.1.)

From Pusan, the Japanese forces advanced with startling speed northward up the peninsula. They were barely impeded by the totally unprepared Korean army. Many Korean commanders abandoned their posts, and others were overwhelmed by the Japanese, whose musketry inspired terror in the defenders. Eighteen days after the Japanese landing at Pusan, the king of Korea fled his capital, Seoul, for P'yŏngyang. A mere three weeks from the start of the invasion, on 5.3 (June 12), Seoul fell to the force led by Konishi and to the division made up of the units of Katō Kiyomasa (daimyo of Kumamoto, 1562–1611), Nabeshima Naoshige, and Sagara Nagatsune (daimyo of Hitoyoshi in Higo, 1574–1636). By 6.15 (July 23), Konishi's force had occupied P'yŏngyang, again causing the king of Korea to flee. It was destined, however, to get no farther than P'yŏngyang, remaining there until the beginning of 1593, when it was defeated and forced to withdraw by a Chinese army sent to the relief of Korea. In the meantime, the second division of Japanese troops, which had advanced jointly with Konishi's force from Seoul, split off from it at Ansŏng in Hwanghae Province and proceeded to the northeast. Its exploits there deserve our attention, as they illustrate nicely the policies and predicaments of the Japanese occupation army in Korea.

Having departed Ansŏng on 1592.6.10, the army of some twenty

---

59 See Miki Seiichirō, "Chōsen no eki ni okeru gun'yaku taikei ni tsuite" (1966), in Fujiki Hisashi and Kitajima Manji, eds., *Shokuhō seiken*, vol. 6 of *Ronshū Nihon rekishi* (Tokyo: Yūseidō, 1974), pp. 306–23; and cf. Fujiki Hisashi, *Oda–Toyotomi seiken*, vol. 15 of *Nihon no rekishi* (Tokyo: Shōgakkan, 1975), pp. 325–7, 341–9.

Map 6.1 Hideyoshi's invasions of Korea.

thousand led by Katō Kiyomasa and Nabeshima Naoshige traversed eastern Hwanghae and after a week's march entered Hamgyŏng Province, its objective. It took the Japanese little more than two months to subdue the populated portions of this huge and mountainous territory, the northeastern quarter of Korea, which stretched from south of the thirty-ninth parallel all the way to the forty-third, where it touches the Tumen River. In the process, Katō captured two Korean princes of the blood royal: Fleeing to the northernmost extremity of their country, the two had the ill luck or bad judgment to seek refuge in a penal colony, Hoeryŏng on the Tumen, where the political exiles lost no time in putting them and their retinue in chains and delivering them into the hands of the Japanese.[60]

Having scored this success, Katō permitted himself the luxury of an expedition across the Tumen into Manchuria, for no apparent purpose except to test the mettle of his troops against the Jürched tribesmen who roamed there. Nabeshima in the meantime kept himself busy in the rearward area of Hamgyŏng Province regimenting the populace, requisitioning supplies, and registering the land's capacity to be taxed. Still extant are the assessment rolls (*sashidashi*) of six districts, compiled for Nabeshima over the signatures of local Korean officials who vowed accuracy on pain of "having all our heads cut off." True to their master's orders that they treat their conquered areas "according to Japanese rules" (*Nihon okime no gotoku*), the generals of Hideyoshi's occupation forces in Korea taxed the peasants, confiscated their weapons, coerced them by taking hostages, and ruthlessly put down recalcitrants as though they were subjecting yet another Japanese province to his regime of unification through the methods of the Taikō *kenchi*.[61] Thus they took up in Hamgyŏng in 1592 where they had left off in Mutsu and Dewa in 1591.

On returning from his Manchurian expedition to his headquarters at Anbyŏn, Katō boasted that he had pacified the whole province, from north to south, in such a way that there was not the slightest opposition to the regimen laid down by him. Taxes and dues were being paid; in other provinces, where a slack hand was kept, disturbances might occur, but there need be no fear about Hamgyŏng, Katō

60 Shimokawa Heidayū, comp., *Kiyomasa Kōrai no jin oboegaki*, vol. 4 of *Zokuzoku gunsho ruijū* (Tokyo: Kokusho kankōkai, 1907), p. 299.
61 On the Japanese military administration and the tax rolls in Hamgyŏng, see Kitajima, *Chōsen nichinichiki*, pp. 97–107. Hideyoshi's orders of 1592.6.3 can be found in several collections of documents, for example, that addressed to Hashiba Kobayakawa Jijū (Kobayakawa Takakage), in *Dai Nihon komonjo, iewake 11: Kobayakawa-ke monjo*, vol. 1, no. 323, p. 292.

maintained.[62] But his bluster was misplaced. What Katō evidently did not know at the time of writing this report to Hideyoshi's headquarters at Nagoya was that a successful revolt had already broken out against the Korean collaborators whom he had left in charge of the province's northern reaches. A Japanese punitive force attacked the guerrillas but was defeated and bottled up in the fort of Kilchu for the winter. Indeed, as the people of southern Hamgyŏng also rose against the rule of Nabeshima, killing the rural administrators who served him and then taking to the hills, it became apparent that the Japanese controlled no more of the province than the string of forts that they garrisoned along the coastal highway. In the Japanese sources, these revolts are described as *Tōjin ikki. Tōjin* being a term with an opprobrious connotation, the phrase might be translated as "Chinamen's uprisings." Naturally enough, those who came to conquer in the name of Jingū Kōgō could not worry themselves about such tenuous details as calling the Korean people by their proper name, Koreans.

The early signs of a stalemate

It is noteworthy that the Japanese field staff in Seoul – Ishida Mitsunari (1560–1600) and others detailed by Hideyoshi to coordinate operations in Korea – should have sent Katō instructions to withdraw from Hamgyŏng even before Konishi's defeat at P'yŏngyang made the Japanese position in northern Korea untenable. Katō and his troops were more urgently needed in the southern part of the peninsula, and in particular in Kyŏngsang, the gateway province, where the Japanese hold was far from secure. There Korean guerrillas swarmed about the Japanese lines of communication. They threatened the main route of supply between Pusan and Seoul, and by year's end they had repelled all attempts by Hosokawa Tadaoki (daimyo of Miyazu in Tango, 1563–1646) to dislodge them from their stronghold at Chinju. Kyŏngsang Province, to be sure, had been a hotbed of resistance against the Japanese from the beginning of the invasion, but it was by no means unique.

Popular uprisings and the mobilization of irregular troops, typically led by members of the local gentry, took place sooner or later in every province of Korea that the aggressors entered. Irregular troops contained the penetration of the army of Kobayakawa Takakage (daimyo of Najima in Chikuzen, 1533–97) into Chŏlla Province in the seventh

62 Katō Kiyomasa to Ki(noshita) Hansuke, dated [Tenshō 20.] 9.20; Kitajima, *Chōsen nichi-nichiki*, pp. 117–19.

month of 1592 and cleared the province of invaders two months later. Guerrillas and militia harried the divisions led by Mōri Yoshinari (daimyo of Kokura, d. 1611) and Shimazu Yoshihiro (daimyo of Kurino in Ōsumi, 1535–1619) as they crisscrossed Kangwŏn Province. By the end of the eighth month, these Japanese forces were confined to garrisoning the towns that screened the approaches to Seoul along Kangwŏn's western border – Wŏnju, Ch'unch'ŏn, Kŭmhwa, and Ch'ŏrwŏn – and had abandoned the effort to dominate the rest of the province. In Hwanghae Province, Dom Damião Kuroda (Nagamasa, daimyo of Nakatsu in Buzen, 1568–1623) began his occupation with bravado, calling on the absconding peasants to return to farming or be killed, and compiling the inevitable taxation rolls. After he failed to take the strategic town of Yŏnan from guerrilla forces, however, Kuroda was by the beginning of the ninth month compelled to concentrate his troops in the southeastern corner of the province in order to protect the highway between Seoul and P'yŏngyang. For the Japanese, the days of easy victories were over. Everywhere, Hideyoshi's armies bogged down.

By the beginning of the new year Bunroku 2 (or, by the Chinese calendar which also applied to Korea, Wan-li 21), the Japanese had yet to suffer a major defeat on land, but they had been put on the defensive, almost without realizing it, by a pesky and persistent Korean resistance. Korean regular troops, unused to war, were no match for the Japanese soldiers, who had been made expert in their craft in the battles of unification. Korean guerrillas were beaten time and again when they could be cornered into a fight. And yet the Japanese failed to obtain a free hand in Korea. The areas they thought they had conquered refused to stay pacified; they held no more than corridors through a hostile countryside. Along those corridors, the Japanese did not dare to venture in bands of less than three hundred; north of Seoul, at least five hundred were needed for safety.[63]

Adding to their difficulties on land were the reverses the Japanese suffered at sea. Unlike the army, the Korean navy proved itself superior to the Japanese in the quality of its armament and leadership. The Japanese with their mixture of light raiding craft inherited from the *bahan* trade and the lubberly men-of-war called *atake-bune* could not match the more solid and also more maneuverable Korean vessels. In particular, the celebrated "turtle ships" (*kŏbuk sŏn*) gave them trouble.

63 Frois, *Historia*, pt. 3, chap. 75, ed. Wicki, vol. 5, p. 571; Matsuda and Kawasaki, trans., *Furoisu Nihonshi*, vol. 2, p. 261.

These were not ironclads, as is commonly asserted, but stoutly built wooden ships that had convex decks spiked with sharp pieces of metal to discourage boarding; they were armed with upward of fourteen cannon. There were never more than a few of them (ultimately perhaps as many as five), but they constituted the core of a formidable striking force that repeatedly surprised and beat the Japanese. Under the inspired tactical leadership of Naval Commander Yi Sun-sin, the Korean fleet fought a series of ten victorious engagements along the southern coast between Sach'ŏn and Pusan in the summer and early fall of 1592. These Korean victories forced the Japanese to reduce the scope of their naval operations to a passive defense of the sea-lane between Kyushu, Tsushima, and Pusan. The Japanese fleet was kept out of the Yellow Sea and thus was unable to establish communications with the land forces that had advanced north as far as P'yŏngyang, let alone supply them.

Supplies to the forward armies of the invaders therefore had to be carried on the backs of men or horses, along insecure roads, two-thirds of the way up the Korean peninsula. This logistical necessity severely taxed the organizational ability of the Japanese warlords and increased their manpower needs: They either had to impress more of the elusive Koreans into work gangs or transport more of the equally reluctant Japanese laborers across the sea. At first, the Japanese were confident that they could live off the land, especially as huge amounts of rice and other cereals stored in Korean government granaries had fallen into their hands. According to the chief state councilor of Korea, Yu Sŏng-nyong, they captured over 100,000 Korean sŏk (more than 767,000 U.S. bushels, or 270,000 hectoliters) of tax grains in P'yŏngyang alone.[64] But this cornucopia eventually had to run empty. Putting the peasants back to work in the fields and then requisitioning the product of their work from them became, accordingly, urgent tasks for the Japanese occupation forces. Whatever success the quartermasters had at these tasks evidently did not suffice to keep all their troops provisioned until the end of the campaign. The Jesuit Frois states that of the 150,000 Japanese soldiers and transport laborers who crossed over to Korea in the first invasion, one-third died – few of them through enemy action, and most from exhaustion, hunger, cold, and disease. The Korean losses in dead and in prisoners, he says, were incalculably greater.[65]

64 Yu Sŏng-nyong (Sŏae), Chingbirok, pt. 1, f. 35v, facsimile of the 1633 ed., in Sŏae munjip pu Chingbirok (Seoul: Sŏnggyungwan taehakkyo taedong munhwa yŏnguwŏn, 1958), p. 509.
65 Frois, Historia, pt. 3, chap. 79, ed. Wicki, vol. 5, p. 599; Matsuda and Kawasaki, trans., Furoisu Nihonshi, vol. 2, p. 304.

The intervention of Ming China

The Koreans, however, could not hope to expel the invaders from their land by themselves, and it was not the various logistical and organizational difficulties suffered by the Japanese that doomed the first invasion to failure. Rather, its fate was sealed by an external factor, the intervention of Korea's protector power, Ming China.

The first Chinese troops crossed the Yalu into Korea on the day P'yŏngyang was occupied by the Japanese, 1592.6.15. Amounting to no more than three thousand men, they were led into a debacle by an overconfident commander who had them attack the far superior Japanese garrison of P'yŏngyang a month later. The Chinese withdrew, but even in defeat they inflicted a rude shock on the Japanese generals, the more perspicacious among whom realized that it was only a matter of time before this new enemy would reappear in strength. At the other end of the theater of war, off the southeastern tip of the peninsula, the Japanese naval forces were in the meantime being battered by the Korean fleet of Yi Sun-sin and were finally ordered by Hideyoshi to avoid engagements at sea. Hence it was clear that the initiative was slipping from the Japanese.

Yu Sŏng-nyong observed correctly that the Korean naval victory spoiled the entire strategy of the invaders by "cutting off one of the arms" with which Japan tried to envelop Korea, isolating Konishi Yukinaga's army at P'yŏngyang and securing Chinese waters from the fear of a Japanese attack, so that "the Celestial Army could come by land to the assistance" of Korea.[66] The Chinese, however, could not commit major forces to Korea until they had dealt with a Mongol rebellion in Ning-hsia, on the distant northwestern frontier of the Ming Empire. They therefore initiated pourparlers with Konishi Yukinaga, who agreed to a fifty-day truce. The Ming emissary, Shen Wei-ching, may have intimated to Konishi that his government would

66 *Chingbirok*, pt. 1, f. 43, in *Sŏae munjip*, p. 513. The reference is to the victory of Admiral Yi Sun-sin at Hansan Island, 1592.7.7 (7.8 in the Korean and Chinese calendar), which was followed two days later by another off Angolp'o. See Yi Sun-sin's own report on these engagements, dated Wan-li 20 (1592).7.15: Chōsenshi henshūkai, ed., *Nanjung ilgich'o, Imjin changch'o / Ranchū nikkisō, Jinshin jōsō*, in *Chōsen shiryō sōkan*, vol. 6, (1935), pp. 337–48; Ha Tae-hung, trans., and Lee, Chong-young, ed., *Imjin Changch'o: Admiral Yi Sun-sin's Memorials to Court* (Seoul: Yonsei University Press, 1981), no. 9, pp. 56–68. Cf. *Wakisaka ki*, in *Zoku gunsho ruijū*, vol. 20, demivol. 2, *kan* 593(a), pp. 440–2. Hideyoshi's orders to cease naval operations until further notice, addressed to Tōdō Sado no Kami (Takatora), are dated [Tenshō 20.]7.16, the day of the Chinese defeat at P'yŏngyang; document in Kitajima, *Chōsen nichinichiki*, pp. 184–5.

not be averse to a partition of Korea at the Taedong River.[67] In any event, the Japanese considered the talks not only opportune but also promising. The Chinese, however, actually meant to use the truce period for no other purpose but to marshal their forces.

When Shen Wei-ching again came to P'yŏngyang for negotiations at the end of the truce, he would promise nothing more than that the Chinese government would consider resuming diplomatic and trade relations with Japan (and, as the precondition, investing a "King of Japan") if the Japanese first withdrew from Korea altogether. To be sure, Shen could afford a tough negotiating attitude, because he knew that a Chinese army of forty thousand men under the command of Li Ju-sung was about to march into Korea. Despite all the signs that pointed to a massive Chinese intervention, however, the Japanese were as surprised and as overwhelmed when it occurred as General Douglas MacArthur's United Nations forces would be in a similar situation three and a half centuries later. Unaware of the enemy army's approach until the Chinese were practically on top of them, the Japanese were routed from P'yŏngyang on Bunroku 2.1.7 (February 8, 1593) and retreated southward in great disorder. Nine days later, Dom Agostinho Konishi's frostbitten soldiers stumbled into Seoul, and a week after that, they put that city to fire and the sword, "killing to a man all the Chinamen [Tōjin] that there were in the capital and burning all the houses outside the [Japanese] fortifications."[68]

As this carnage was taking place in the streets outside their quarters, the members of Hideyoshi's field staff gathered to compose a gloomy report to their master on the unavoidable reasons for the withdrawal of his forward divisions as far back as Seoul, the critical need to secure the routes of communication south to Pusan, and the precarious supply situation of his troops. In short, they saw the imperative demand for going over to the defensive in Korea. As the Chinese closed in on the Korean capital, however, its Japanese occupiers showed that their forces were far from spent, by mounting a sharp counterattack. Sallying forth in eight detachments that totaled more than forty thousand men, they succeeded in trapping the vanguard of Li Ju-sung's army in a long and narrow valley at Pyŏkchegwan, some fifteen kilometers

---

67 Kitajima, Chōsen nichinichiki, p. 204.
68 Tajiri Akitane, Kōrai nikki, entry for Bunroku 2 (1593).1.23, in Kitajima, Chōsen nichinichiki, p. 384. Sŏnjo Sogyŏng Taewang sillok, 27:5, entry for Sŏnjo 26 (1593).1, states that Konishi and other Japanese, enraged by their defeat at P'yŏngyang and suspecting the Korean population of aiding the Chinese army, massacred the male citizens of Seoul but not the women, so that men who disguised themselves in female clothes escaped the slaughter. See Chosŏn wangjo sillok, vol. 25, p. 637.

north of Seoul, and slaughtered the Chinese cavalry as it floundered in the mud of this impasse. Li Ju-sung fled with the rest of his troops to P'yŏngyang. Left exposed by his headlong retreat was the fort of Haengju, at a strong hilltop position on the Han River fifteen kilometers downstream from Seoul, which was held by a Korean garrison. Intent on eliminating this thorn from their side, the Japanese tried to storm Haengju with an assault force of thirty thousand, but they were resoundingly defeated and fell back on Seoul.

Diplomacy, deceit, and disillusion

The victory of the Japanese at Pyŏkchegwan coupled with their defeat at Haengju showed that a stalemate had developed. The Japanese were no longer strong enough to pursue a sustained offensive against either the Chinese or the newly confident Koreans, but they were still too powerful to be displaced from Seoul if they chose to cling to it. Indeed, at the beginning of the third month of 1593, with the division of Katō and Nabeshima back from Hamgyŏng, there were no less than 53,000 of them in the city.

Two things were done to encourage the Japanese to leave. First, a Chinese commando penetrated Seoul and burned the storehouses at Yongsan, destroying most of what was left of the Japanese troops' depleted stocks of food. Next, Shen Wei-ching made another appearance to conduct negotiations. Threatened by Shen with an attack by an army of 400,000 Chinese and aware of their own weak position, Konishi and Katō agreed to an armistice under which the Japanese troops would be withdrawn to the Pusan area while the Ming forces were called back to China; a Ming embassy would be sent to Japan to discuss peace terms. Notably ignored in this agreement were the wishes of the Koreans, who vowed to fight on. Ten days after the talks, however – on 1593.4.18 – the Japanese evacuated Seoul, marching off to be redeployed in the southeastern corner of the peninsula and the islands off Pusan. Along with them went Shen Wei-ching and two special agents of the supreme commander of the Chinese forces in Korea, masquerading as regular diplomats. On 5.15, this group of Chinese negotiators arrived in Nagoya, where Hideyoshi received them as Ming imperial envoys. Among the several displays he organized to impress them was a tea ceremony in his golden tearoom, that ne plus ultra of ostentation.

As the Ming agents were about to depart late the next month, Hideyoshi set down his terms for peace in a document addressed to

Konishi Yukinaga and his other principal representatives in the negotiations, who were ordered to "explain the contents in detail to the imperial envoys of Great Ming." Seven conditions were put forward: a daughter of the Chinese sovereign to become the consort of the emperor of Japan; the tally trade between Japan and China to resume; high officials of the two countries to exchange pledges of amity; four provinces and the capital city to be returned to the king of Korea (that is, the four southern provinces of Korea to be annexed to Japan); high-ranking Korean hostages to be sent to Japan; the two captive Korean princes to be set free; and the Korean government to swear never again to oppose Japan. Given the existing situation in Korea, Hideyoshi was being overly optimistic if he really expected to get all that he demanded.

That Hideyoshi felt absolutely justified in making his demands, however, is clear from the language of a companion piece that he likewise addressed to Konishi and his other delegates but meant for the edification of the Ming agents. The tone of this undiplomatic note is established in its first sentence, "Japan is the Land of the Gods." Those gods have given Hideyoshi a special mandate. After rehearsing the story of his solar conception and reiterating that the power to unify Japan was a virtue bestowed on him by Heaven, Hideyoshi gets down to cases. It is true that Japanese pirates in the past had bothered China, but one of Hideyoshi's most radiant accomplishments in the "rectification of the eight heavenly directions" was to quell the *wakō* and secure the seas. For this favor, however, he never got any thanks from Ming. Assuming the reason to be that Ming despised Japan as an insignificant country, he decided to send an army to prove otherwise. Korea promised to cooperate but failed to keep that promise. When Hideyoshi accordingly set out to "correct" the Koreans, they had the temerity to defend themselves. As a result, many thousands of them had to be killed, and their capital was turned to ashes. China tried to save its client but failed. And so the present mutual predicament – the Chinese are informed in the peroration – is entirely Korea's fault.[69]

Would the man who used this sort of rhetoric ever be satisfied with investiture as "King of Japan," that is, as a vassal of the Ming Empire? How could a child of the sun ever accept tributary subordination? But

69 Both the list of peace conditions and the explanatory document are addressed to Konishi Settsu no Kami Yukinaga, Ōtani Gyōbu no Shō Yoshitsugu, Mashita Uemon no Jō Nagamori, and Ishida Jibu no Shō Mitsunari, and dated Bunroku 2.6.28 (the day the Chinese agents left Nagoya). See *Zoku zenrin kokuhōki*, pp. 404–6. The four Korean provinces that Hideyoshi wanted to annex were Kyŏngsang, Chŏlla, Ch'ungch'ŏng, and Kyŏnggi (less the Seoul area).

that ritual of subservience was China's traditional sine qua non for the conduct of foreign relations. Whether or not Hideyoshi knew it, it was the indispensable condition he would have to meet or surmount before he could press forward his and Japan's claims in Asia.

Hideyoshi's diplomatists (most notably Dom Agostinho Konishi), who appreciated the actualities far better than he did, were put in a quandary by their master's presumptuousness. They were expected to obtain a settlement that would aggrandize him; yet they knew that no accommodation with China could be gained on his terms. When Dom João Naitō (Naitō Hida no Kami Tadatoshi, d. 1626), the emissary that Konishi sent to the Ming court to explain away the Korean invasion, was held up in Liaotung Province because the Chinese authorities there considered his credentials incomplete without a message of submission from Japan, it became evident that this dilemma could be solved only by desperate means.

The matter was not referred back to Japan; rather, Konishi dealt with it in his Korean fort at Ungch'ŏn. Apparently persuaded by Shen Wei-ching that a forged letter was better than no letter at all, Konishi connived at the manufacture of a document in which "the former *kampaku* of Japan, [Your Majesty's] subject Taira no Hideyoshi" in the most abject terms declared himself to be in awe of the "power of heavenly protection" that flowed from the throne of China to keep the four corners of the world at peace, and proclaimed all of Japan to be the children of the emperor of Ming. Korea interfered with Hideyoshi's earlier desire to demonstrate his submissiveness to China, and hence he invaded Korea; a peaceful solution was achieved at P'yŏng-yang through the efforts of Konishi and Shen Wei-ching but was ruined by Korean bellicosity; nevertheless, the Japanese showed a "forbearing sincerity" toward the Koreans and returned them their land. Now – the forged document continued – Hideyoshi wished to bare his heart before the Chinese sovereign: "I prostrate myself and I beg Your Majesty to let that light of the sun and moon shine forth with which He irradiates the world, to extend that nourishing capacity of heaven and earth with which He overspreads and sustains all things that there are . . . and to bestow on me the title of an imperially invested vassal king."[70]

70 The text of the forged document, dated Wan-li 21 (1593).12.–, is cited and glossed with the appropriately skeptical comments in *Sŏnjo Sogyŏng Taewang sillok*, pt. 48, f. 14v, entry for Sŏnjo 27 (1594).2.[11], and again with minor variations, dated Wan-li 23(*sic;* error for 21).12.21 (February 10, 1594), ibid., pt. 51, f. 28rv, entry for Sŏnjo 27.5.[24]; *Chosŏn wangjo sillok*, vol. 22, pp. 221 and 276.

Conspicuously absent from this document is Hideyoshi's usual bombast about *his* glory illuminating the universe. Little wonder that at the Korean court, doubts were expressed regarding its authenticity as soon as the text became known in Seoul. But the letter evidently satisfied the Chinese government when Naitō finally bore it to Peking early in 1595. After Naitō had affirmed that Japan would withdraw all its forces from Korea, would seek no relationship (not even trade) with China beyond the investiture of its ruler, and would establish friendly relations with Korea as a fellow vassal state of Ming, the court of Peking decided to grant what was presented to it as Hideyoshi's plea and to bestow on him the title "King of Japan." Orders were given for a golden seal bearing this title to be cast and for royal raiments to be made, and ambassadors were appointed to conduct the ceremony of investiture in Japan.[71]

Toward the end of 1595, the Chinese ambassadors, conducted by Naitō, arrived in Japanese-occupied Pusan. Months before, Hideyoshi had, in expectation of their coming, sent Konishi in Korea a reiteration of his seven conditions for peace. It is possible that at this final stage of the journey to Japan, the chief Ming envoy, Li Tsung-ch'eng, was finally apprised of the inordinate and inflexible nature of Hideyoshi's actual terms or was persuaded by the rumors that he risked his life or his freedom once the true purpose of his mission became apparent to Hideyoshi. In any event, he abandoned his charge in Pusan, further delaying the progress of the embassy to its destination. Yet another ill omen was the great earthquake that destroyed the main buildings of Hideyoshi's palatial castle at Fushimi in the late summer of 1596, demolishing the enormous audience hall that had been especially designed for the reception of foreign embassies.

On Bunroku 5.9.1 (October 22, 1596), however, all difficulties appeared for the moment to be surmounted when Hideyoshi received the new envoys of the Ming Empire, Yang Fang-heng (gazetted as ambassador *vice* Ambassador Li, who had absconded) and Shen Wei-ching (the chief Chinese accomplice in the affair of the forged letter, now promoted to deputy ambassador) in audience at Osaka Castle. Hideyoshi showed nothing but pleasure at the delivery of his kingly robes

71 Naitō's reception in Peking and the Ming government's decision to invest Hideyoshi with the title "King of Japan" are reported in *Ming Shen-tsung shih-lu*, pt. 280, f. 2v to pt. 283, f. 3 *passim*, entries from Wan-li 22.12.[11] (January 20, 1595) to Wan-li 23.2.[3]: *Ming shih-lu*, vol. 108, pp. 5172–209. Relevant portions are extracted in *Min jitsuroku no bu*, vol. 3, pp. 705–10. Note that in the Ming sources, Naitō is called by the abbreviation of the name he adopted for the purposes of his mission as a delegate of Konishi Yukinaga: Konishi Hi(da no Kami), or Hsiao-hsi Fei in the Chinese pronunciation of the three characters.

and seal. The sole discord in the well-orchestrated spectacle was struck when he refused to kneel as a sign of respect before the imperial edict of investiture, but that dissonance was quickly resolved when a resourceful attendant improvised the excuse that a boil in the knee joint prevented his master from genuflecting.

At a banquet the next day, Hideyoshi appeared with crown and scepter in his Chinese costume before his paladins, some forty of them also freshly promoted to Chinese official ranks and richly caparisoned in Chinese ceremonial garb. At the end of the festive entertainments, he had his expert in diplomatic correspondence, the Zen priest Saishō Shōtai (1548–1605), read the message from the Chinese emperor. From that reading, Hideyoshi realized that this imperial rescript contained not one word about his seven demands and was nothing more than an instrument for binding him to vassalage. He burst into a rage, abused Konishi, threatened the Ming ambassadors with death, and then dismissed them abruptly. Having thus rung down the curtain on the tragicomedy of the false surrender document, the dupe of the show, Hideyoshi, was left susceptible to the argument of Katō Kiyomasa and others who maintained that to resume the war was the only way to expunge the humiliation. The Korean people would have to pay the price for a stratagem that had failed.[72]

The second campaign of aggression

In the meantime, the Japanese troops in Korea had settled down to garrison life in their string of forts that stretched from Ungch'ŏn in the west to Sŏsaeng in the northeast. Some 78,600 of the invasion force were left after the withdrawal from Seoul. They fought no significant military actions after the sixth month of 1593, when they took the great Korean fortress of Chinju by storm, thereby demonstrating once more that they could not so easily be forced off the peninsula. Instead, the common draftees cultivated the fields and rice paddies around their positions. The generals, too, engaged in activities little different from those they might have pursued in peacetime in their own country. They hobnobbed with one another and with the merchant burghers (machishū) of Sakai and other war profiteers attracted to their camps. They held tea ceremonies in tea houses of the sukiya type built by carpenters summoned from Japan, exercised their

---

72 A compendious summary of the sources regarding the failed ceremony of investiture may be found in Chōsenshi, 4th series, vol. 10, pp. 628–31; a photographic reproduction of the edict designating Hideyoshi as the King of Japan is appended as Figure 9.

literary skills at sessions of linked verse (*renga* and *wakan*) convoked in the properly Japanese ambience of chambers specially constructed in the *shoin* style of architecture, played the peculiarly Japanese game of kickball (*kemari*) on authentically laid out courts, and caroused in the Japanese manner at saké parties given diversity by amateur displays of dancing (*rambu*). In short, they made themselves right at home in Korea. If they were bored by lack of action, hunts relieved their ennui even as they served to supply one of their master's fancied needs: The tiger population of Korea had to suffer because Hideyoshi believed tiger meat to be a balm that would restore his tottering health.[73]

The pent-up energy of these garrison troops, augmented by new levies sent from Japan to form an army of 141,500, was released on Korea in Hideyoshi's second campaign of aggression, which began on Keichō 2.7.15 (August 27, 1597) with an event rare in this war, a Japanese naval victory. As a result of this battle, which was fought off Kŏje Island, the inept Korean commander, Wŏn Kyun (an intriguer who had succeeded in displacing Yi Sun-sin from his post half a year previously), lost his life; the Korean navy lost its base on Hansan Island and its domination of the southern coast, being obliged to withdraw far to the west; and the conditions were created for the Japanese to advance in force into Chŏlla Province, something they had not been able to do in the first campaign. Indeed, the occupation of Chŏlla and Ch'ungch'ŏng provinces, through the rapid deployment of a massive force from its bases in Kyŏngsang Province, was the operational plan of Hideyoshi's armies in their return venture to Korea. If they reached their objectives, the Japanese would dominate the southern half of the peninsula; if they held their gains, they would in effect obtain the partition of Korea, which was Hideyoshi's – vastly reduced – war aim of 1597. To be sure, boasts about a future conquest of China do not fail to appear in the marching orders he issued to the daimyo in advance of the second campaign, but they sound halfhearted.[74]

---

73 See, for instance, the letter addressed by Asano Danjō no Shōhitsu Nagayoshi and Kinoshita Daizen no Daibu Yoshitaka to Hashiba Kikkawa Jijū (Kikkawa Hiroie) on [Bunroku 3.]12.25 (February 5, 1595), in which Kikkawa is ordered to send Hideyoshi the "head, meat, and entrails" of a tiger, "well salted" and "without leaving anything out" but the skin, which "is not needed here"; *Kikkawa-ke monjo*, vol. 1, no. 769, pp. 737–8. Also see the vermilion-seal letters in which Hideyoshi thanks Kikkawa for tigers sent from Korea; ibid., nos. 132–3, pp. 98–100, dated [Bunroku 3.]12.20 and [Bunroku 4.]4.22.

74 The initial Japanese order of battle and Hideyoshi's basic strategy in the second campaign are outlined in two documents issued over his vermilion seal, dated Keichō 2 (1597).2.21, and sent to Hashiba Satsuma Jijū (Shimazu Yoshihiro); *Dai Nihon komonjo, iewake 16: Shimazu-ke monjo*, vol. 1, nos. 402–3, pp. 392–6 and 396–402.

Anticipating the Japanese resumption of the war, the Chinese court in the second month of 1597 decided to send a new expeditionary force to the support of its vassal state, Korea. By the middle of the sixth month, the advance guard of this army reached Namwŏn, a town in Chŏlla close to the Kyŏngsang border, fortified the place, and prepared to stand a siege there. Two months later, however, Namwŏn fell to a strong Japanese force under Ukita Hideie (daimyo of Okayama, 1573–1655), putting all of Chŏlla Province at the mercy of the invaders. At the same time another large Japanese army, under the overall command of Mōri Hidemoto (the future daimyo of Yamaguchi, 1579–1650), poured forth in three streams from Kyŏngsang and burst into Ch'ungch'ŏng Province to challenge the main body of the Ming expeditionary force, which was based in Seoul. A division of this army, led by Katō Kiyomasa, even penetrated Kyŏnggi Province, reaching Chiksan, less than seventy kilometers away from Seoul. This time, however, the Japanese got no farther. They were blocked on the border of Ch'ungch'ŏng and Kyŏnggi by the Chinese army. Their fleet, too, was blocked from coming to the support of the land forces. It had rounded the southwestern corner of the peninsula and was heading for the Yellow Sea through the Myŏngnyang Strait when it was intercepted and defeated by the Korean navy under its reinstated commander Yi Sun-sin.

The naval battle of Myŏngnyang, which took place on Keichō 2.9.14-16 (October 24–26, 1597), marked the turn of the tide in Hideyoshi's second Korean campaign. The Japanese lost the initiative, were again forced on the defensive, and withdrew to fortified places along the coast closest to Japan. This time, their fortress belt stretched farther than it had after the first campaign, forming an arc that extended more than two hundred kilometers from Sunch'ŏn in the west through Sach'ŏn and Pusan to Ulsan in the east. Soon enough, the Japanese generals in Korea were given ample reason to conclude that their forces were in fact overextended. Katō Kiyomasa's fortress at Ulsan, still under construction, was invested in January 1598 by a great Chinese–Korean army and could be relieved only with great difficulty. The siege of Ulsan was a near thing, and the experience impelled the Japanese commanders to request permission to reduce their perimeter by abandoning some of the more exposed forts.[75] This

75 Copy of a letter addressed by Ukita Hideie and twelve other captains to Hideyoshi's right-hand men Ishida Jibu no Shō (Mitsunari), Natsuka Ōkura no Daibu (Masaie), Mashita Uemon no Jō, and (Maeda) Tokuzen'in (Gen'i) on [Keichō 3.]1.26; *Shimazu-ke monjo*, vol. 3, no. 1206, pp. 59–63.

request fell on deaf ears, as Hideyoshi was determined to cleave to all of his bases in Korea, come what may.

Hideyoshi's death and the Japanese withdrawal

The moving spirit of the war did not, however, have long to live. In the late summer of 1598, as new Chinese and Korean armies assembled to prepare another offensive against his troops, Hideyoshi lay dying in his palatial castle at Fushimi. When he died on Keichō 3.8.18 (September 18, 1598), the management of affairs fell into the hands of his inner circle of councilors and commissioners, who knew that they must end the war quickly or themselves assume the responsibility for the continued squandering of Japanese manpower and resources in a foreign campaign that held little promise of success. Moreover, the members of that governing camarilla, who by no means formed a united group themselves, surely realized that they lacked the coercive power with which Hideyoshi had compelled daimyo of diverse interests to join together in the invasion of the mainland. They therefore had little choice but to seek as urgently as possible to disengage the Japanese troops from the enemy, extract them from the peninsula, and bring them safely home.

At first, they tried to keep the news of Hideyoshi's death from becoming public knowledge. A letter signed by Ishida Mitsunari and the rest of Hideyoshi's "Five Commissioners" (go bugyō) exactly a week after their master's demise tells Nabeshima Naoshige reassuringly that "the Taikō is at length recovering from his illness," while informing him that two special emissaries are being sent to inspect the situation on the Korean front. A companion piece orders Nabeshima to go to Pusan and receive further instructions from those emissaries in person. Another piece of official correspondence, addressed on the same day to Shimazu Yoshihiro by one of the "Five Commissioners," Mashita Nagamori (1545–1615), likewise maintains that "Our Lord has in the past few days at length been recovering from his illness," while asserting that "some time ago he issued instructions for peace." The details will be explained by the two inspectors being sent to Korea, and the daimyo are ordered to consult with them on how to bring about a settlement of the war. Copies of the memoranda issued to the inspectors reveal the terms on which the "Five Commissioners" were prepared to negotiate a withdrawal from Korea. In exchange for the surrender of the Japanese forts there, they were willing to accept that a Korean prince be sent as hostage to Japan or to content themselves with the delivery of an unspecified amount of rice, tiger skins, leopard skins, and honey from the Koreans.[76] How Japanese expectations had shrunk since the beginning of the war and since the heady days of Hideyoshi's seven demands!

But the Japanese were not to retire from Korea unopposed and unscathed. Before the special emissaries of the gobugyō and the orders they bore had had a chance to reach the peninsula, the Chinese and Korean armies struck hard at the key positions of the Japanese fortress belt. Ulsan was attacked first but once again was held by Katō Kiyomasa. Nine days later, on Keichō 3.10.1 (October 30, 1598), it was the turn of Sach'ŏn, which was assaulted by a Chinese and Korean force so large that the commanders of the successful Japanese defense, Shimazu Yoshihiro and his son Tadatsune (the future daimyo of Kagoshima, Shimazu Iehisa, 1578–1638), were officially credited with taking 38,717 heads in this one battle.[77] Although this figure is exaggerated, it is true that the mass of the attacking army was decimated after being lured into an exposed position under the walls of the well-designed Japanese fort, where it was raked by a terrific fusillade. Indeed, the effect of the victory of the Shimazu at Sach'ŏn can hardly be overestimated, as it was the Shimazu contingent, left intact after this fight, that later covered the withdrawal of the western wing of the Japanese army from Korea.

A day after the battle of Sach'ŏn, Konishi Yukinaga's fortress at Sunch'ŏn was attacked by yet another huge land force. When this attack by land was repelled, a combined Chinese and Korean fleet tried and failed to take Sunch'ŏn by sea. These were, however, only limited defensive successes for the Japanese: Having warded off the

76 Tokuzen['in] Gen'i, Asa[no] Dan[jō no Shōhitsu] Nagamasa, Ishi[da] Ji[bu no Shō] Mitsunari, Mashi[ta] U[emon no Jō] Nagamori, and Na(ga)[tsuka] Ō[kura no Daibu] Masaie to Nabeshima Kaga no Kami (Naoshige), dated [Keichō 3.]8.25; Nabeshima-ke monjo, nos. 131–2, in Saga kenshi hensan iinkai, ed., Saga-ken shiryō shūsei: komonjo-hen, vol. 3 (Saga: Saga kenritsu toshokan, 1958), pp. 402–3. Mashi[ta] U[emon no Jō] to Shimazu Hyōgo no Kami (Yoshihiro), same date, Shimazu-ke monjo, vol. 2, no. 986, p. 222; copies of the memoranda addressed by the "Five Commissioners" to the two special emissaries, Tokunaga Shikibu-kyō Hōin (Toshimasa) and Miyagi Chōji[rō] (Toyomori), same date, ibid., nos. 984–5, pp. 274–6; copy of the oath sworn by the two inspectors regarding their mission on Keichō 3.8.22, ibid., no. 982, pp. 271–2. Note that the announcement of Tokunaga's and Miyagi's mission to Korea, dated [Keichō 3.]8.25, was sent to Shimazu Yoshihiro and his son Tadatsune over Hideyoshi's vermilion seal, even though the hegemon had been dead a week; Shimazu-ke monjo, vol. 1, nos. 423 and 435, pp. 415, 425.
77 "Five Commissioners" to Hashiba Satsuma no Shōshō (Shimazu Tadatsune), dated Keichō 4 (1599).1.9; Shimazu-ke monjo, vol. 2, no. 1070, pp. 362–3. Cf. the memorandum written in similar language and addressed on the same day to Shimazu Tadatsune by the "Five Councilors" (gotairō) of the Toyotomi house, (Tokugawa) Ieyasu, (Maeda) Toshiie, (Ukita) Hideie, (Uesugi) Kagekatsu, and (Mōri) Terumoto; ibid., vol. 1, no. 440, pp. 429–30. Note that both documents are copies, not originals, and therefore suspect.

initial assaults, the contingents of Konishi and the other captains of the Sunch'ŏn garrison were blockaded in their fort by the Chinese squadron under Ch'en Lin and the Korean warships commanded by Yi Sun-sin. In the event, Konishi was able to evacuate Sunch'ŏn only because the Shimazu sent a naval force to his rescue. The Japanese relief force was mauled severely by the Chinese and Korean fleet, but the victorious admiral, Yi Sun-sin, was killed at the height of this encounter, which is called the battle of Noryang, and Konishi's division of the Japanese army made good its escape from Sunch'ŏn.

The naval engagement of Noryang, which took place on the night of Keichō 3.11.18–19 (December 16–17, 1598), was the last battle of the war. One week later, on Christmas Eve 1598, the weary troops of Dom Agostinho Konishi and the other rearguard elements of the army that Hideyoshi had sent to conquer the Asian mainland six and a half years earlier reembarked at Pusan and set sail for their home islands. The long Korean adventure was over.

The legacy of the Korean invasion

The Korean war was a complete failure for the Japanese, who won most of their battles but gained none of their objectives; having suffered grievous losses, they withdrew ignominiously from the peninsula. In the long run, the war was to prove a disaster for the victorious Ming Empire, which could ill afford the vast expenditures required by its intervention in Korea. The drain on its public treasury and its military manpower seriously weakened a Chinese regime that was already burdened with an enormity of external and internal problems and made it sink deeper into the dynastic decline that was to overcome it half a century later. Korea, the other ostensible victor, was left a land in ashes and anguish. Not only had it been ravaged by its Japanese invaders; it also had been humiliated and maltreated by its Chinese allies, whose concept of universal sovereignty permitted them to negotiate with the common enemy single-handedly and without concern for the wishes of the Koreans and whose sense of a mission of justice did not prevent them from raping and pillaging the very people they were supposedly protecting against aggression.

The war was fought with terrible cruelty, and its history is marked with atrocities that are amply attested in the contemporary records of the Japanese themselves. The manifestos published by the invading generals to announce the second coming of the Japanese in 1597 order all farmers to return to their homes and agricultural work or to be sought out and killed. They further declare that all officials will be killed as a matter of course, along with their wives and children, and that their houses will be burned, and they promise rewards for those who inform on officials in hiding.[78] The style is that of the *Bekanntmachung* that became altogether familiar in occupied Europe between 1939 and 1945, and the way the occupiers went about their task was also distressingly similar. In both cases, they suffered under the delusion that they could keep a resistance movement from forming by terrorizing the populace into collaboration.

In the manhunts conducted by the Japanese in the pursuit of this policy in Korea, many thousands of Koreans were killed or mutilated. No distinction was made among combatants and noncombatants, men, women, and children. The headhunters did not have to produce the head itself to obtain credit for a victim (in view of the numbers involved, that would have caused a logistical problem). Nor did they take scalps; instead, they collected noses. The noses taken by a unit were gathered together, preserved with salt, packed in casks, and sent on to the inspectors general of the field armies in Korea for forwarding to Hideyoshi's headquarters in Japan. A running account was kept, as the noses formed a sort of capital: Their number represented the quantification of that intangible quality, martial valor, and could be used as the basis for calculating future rewards for the captains of the search expeditions and their troops.

Some idea of the sanguinary excesses of the Japanese invaders in Korea may be obtained from the receipts preserved in the archives of two daimyo families, which record that Kikkawa Hiroie's contingent submitted no fewer than 18,350 noses to Hideyoshi's field staff in a period of little more than a month (between 9.1 and 10.9) in the year 1597 and that Nabeshima Katsushige's band was credited with at least 5,444 noses between 8.21 and 10.1 of the same year.[79] A mound made of the grisly trophies of the Korean invasion – known under the misnomer Mimizuka, "mound of ears" – may still be seen in Kyoto near Hideyoshi's foundation, the temple of Hōkōji, where it was erected in 1597. Like his contemporary Ivan the Terrible, who had masses said for the repose of the souls of his victims, Hideyoshi had Buddhist

---

78 See, for instance, the manifesto issued in the name of "Nihon Bizen no Chūnagon Hideie" (that is, Ukita Hideie) and dated Keichō 2.9.–, *Shimazu-ke monjo*, vol. 2, no. 970, pp. 253–4, and those signed by Shimazu Hyōgo no Kami Yoshihiro and twelve other captains, which were issued to various locales in the same month, ibid., nos. 971–3, pp. 254–60.
79 See *Kikkawa-ke monjo*, vol. 1, nos. 138–9 and 716–22, pp. 105–6 and 662–7; and *Nabeshima-ke monjo*, nos. 115–18 and 121, pp. 386–8 and 391–2. There are slight discrepancies in the chart summarizing these receipts that is set out by Kitajima, *Chōsen nichinichiki*, p. 305.

services performed over the miserable evidence of his continental expedition's true nature. The chief officiator at the ceremony, Saishō Jōtai, did not fail to mention the profound feelings of mercy and compassion that had moved his patron Hideyoshi to offer this spiritual bouquet to the dead.

A more genuine testimonial to the persistence of the spirit of commiseration amidst the horrors of war comes to us from a far less known Japanese Buddhist priest, Keinen, the resident of a provincial temple of the True Pure Land sect (Jōdo Shinshū). Keinen, who was the incumbent of the An'yōji in Usuki in Bungo – the recent domain of the dispossessed Ōtomo family – accompanied the town's new master Ōta Kazuyoshi (d. 1600) on the second Korean campaign, in the capacity of his physician. He wrote down his impressions of the campaign in the poetic diary Chōsen nichinichiki (Korean days), in which the record of the events he witnessed is interspersed with religious meditations, nostalgic reflections, and more than three hundred simple but affecting epigrams written in the form of tanka (thirty-one-syllable Japanese poems) on whatever most concerned Keinen on a particular day.[80] There is in this diary none of the bombast that is common in other Japanese accounts of the Korean invasion. Instead, it is an honest, vivid, and distraught portrayal of what went on. That the author was no hero, and indeed was somewhat of a naïf, does not diminish the force of his images of death, destruction, and depravity, or the strength of his expressions of faith in the Buddha's saving grace. That grace seemed to Keinen to be the only hope for men who did not stop to reflect on what they were doing. Everywhere about him, Keinen saw covetousness, anger, and the ignorance of right and wrong: From samurai to camp follower, all were infected with these Three Poisons, which formed the substance of this war.

People being led away in chains and tight bamboo collars through burning fields and hillsides that resounded with the wild voices of a soldiery intoxicated with their own arson; parents being killed before the eyes of their wailing children, who will be led away into captivity; the slaughter of the innocents after the capture of Namwŏn, where no

80 Keinen, Chōsen nichinichiki, ed. Naitō Shumpo, in Chōsen gakuhō 35 (May 1965): 55–154, accompanied by Naitō's explanatory article, "Sō Keinen no Chōsen nichinichiki ni tsuite," pp. 155–67. The text covers the seven months from Keinen's embarkation for Korea on Keichō 2.6.24 to his return to Usuki on Keichō 3.2.2. Quotations from pp. 102 and 104, entries for Keichō 2.11.15 and 19.

   For a more extended look at Keinen and his remarkable diary, see George Elison, "The Priest Keinen and His Account of the Campaign in Korea, 1597–1598: An Introduction," in Motoyama Yukihiko Kyōju taikan kinen rombunshū henshū iinkai, ed., Nihon kyōikushi ronsō: Motoyama Yukihiko Kyōju taikan kinen rombunshū (Kyoto: Shibunkaku, 1988), pp. 25–41.

prisoners were taken; the dreadful punishments meted out for the slightest remissness to Korean and Japanese laborers alike in the rush to complete the fortifications at Ulsan – these being the scenes from which he could not avert his eyes, it is no wonder that Keinen concluded, "Hell cannot be in some other place apart from this."

Keinen's most haunting image is that of the slaver:

Among the many kinds of merchants who have come over from Japan are traders in human beings, who follow in the train of the troops and buy up men and women, young and old alike. Having tied these people together with ropes about the neck, they drive them along before them; those who can no longer walk are made to run with prods or blows of the stick from behind. The sight of the fiends and man-devouring demons who torment sinners in hell must be like this, I thought.

How many people were taken thus into bondage? No accurate count is possible, but it appears that no fewer than fifty thousand or even sixty thousand Koreans were forcibly brought to Japan as a result of Hideyoshi's war of aggression.[81] Most were simple farmers forced to serve as laborers, but there were also numerous artisans and even some scholars.

If one can speak of a positive effect of the war, then surely it was the cultural contribution made to Japan by these captives. In particular, Korean potters taken willy-nilly to Japan, who brought superior techniques with them, caused a revolution in that country's ceramic production. Some of the most famous types of Japanese ceramics – for example, Arita ware and Satsuma ware – owe their origins to groups of Korean artisans who were resettled in the domains of their captors. A similarly great transformation in Japanese intellectual history has also been traced to Korean sources, for it has been asserted that the vogue for Neo-Confucianism, a school of thought that would remain prominent throughout the Edo period (1600–1868), arose in Japan as a result of the Korean war, whether on account of the putative influence that the captive scholar-official Kang Hang exerted on Fujiwara Seika (1561–1619), the soi-disant discoverer of the true Confucian tradition for Japan, or because Korean books from looted libraries provided the new pattern and much new matter for a redefinition of Confucianism. This assertion, however, is questionable and indeed has been rebutted convincingly in recent Western scholarship.[82]

81 Naitō Shumpo, "Jinshin, Teiyū no eki ni okeru hiro Chōsenjin no sakkan mondai ni tsuite: Chōsen shiryō ni yoru," pt. 3, Chōsen gakuhō (January 1965): 132.
82 See Willem Jan Boot, The Adoption and Adaptation of Neo-Confucianism in Japan: The Role of Fujiwara Seika and Hayashi Razan (Proefschrift, Rijksuniversiteit te Leiden, Netherlands,

The restoration of peaceful relations with Korea

In view of the war's dreadful ravages on Korea and of the heritage of bitterness engendered by Hideyoshi's aggression, it is remarkable how quickly normal relations between Japan and Korea were restored. Naturally enough, the need to make peace appeared most urgent to the Sō of Tsushima, whose island's economy depended on access to the peninsula. The Sō realized that the repatriation of the captives would be the principal issue of any peace talks between the two countries. Hence they pretended from 1599 onwards to play the part of an honest broker in the repatriation. They sought thereby to ingratiate themselves with the Koreans, while at the same time proving themselves to the Japanese national regime in their traditional role as experts in Korean relations. From 1600, that regime was in the hands of Tokugawa Ieyasu (1543–1616, r. 1603–5 as shogun) and of his successors in the Tokugawa shogunate. This fact at first facilitated the diplomatic tasks of the Sō, as the Tokugawa (whose armed contingents had not been required to cross over to Korea) could be dissociated from the outrages perpetrated by the armies of Toyotomi Hideyoshi and as their advent to power could be represented as an epochal turn in Japanese history. Eventually, however, the consolidation of the Edo bakufu caused difficulties for the mediators from Tsushima, whose wings were trimmed when the central government, intent on establishing its own preeminence, concluded that it could not permit a small, peripheral feudatory to remain in effective control of the conduct of relations with a foreign country.

By 1603, the Sō had returned some 800 prisoners to Korea; the next year, their efforts were rewarded when the Korean government sent the priest Yujŏng as an envoy to Tsushima with the welcome news that residents of the island would again be permitted to come to Pusan for trade. In the spring of 1605, Sō Yoshitoshi conducted Yujŏng and his retinue to Fushimi, where the Koreans were received in audience by Ieyasu and his son Hidetada (1579–1632, r. 1605–23), shortly to be proclaimed the second Tokugawa shogun. This meeting is noteworthy as the first direct contact between representatives of Korea and the highest personages of the new Tokugawa regime, even if Yujŏng was brought to Fushimi at Ieyasu's behest and without being accredited as an ambassador to him by the Korean government. There followed the

1982), chaps. 1–2, pp. 15–98, esp. pp. 83–5. Boot takes issue with the opinions Abe Yoshio expressed in his "definitive" work *Nihon Shushigaku to Chōsen*, 2nd ed. (Tokyo: Tōkyō daigaku shuppankai, 1971).

repatriation of a large number of Korean captives. More than 4,390 were sent back in the fourth and fifth months of 1605, bringing the total to 5,720 returnees.[83]

These gestures were meant to elicit the appointment of a fully constituted Korean embassy to Ieyasu, who exercised a dominant influence over Japan's foreign affairs even after retiring from the shogunate in 1605. The court of Seoul, however, refused to send one until it had received an official communication – a "document of state" (*kuksŏ*, J: *kokusho*) – from the Japanese ruler. But because the dispatch of such a message would show that the initial effort to resume relations after the war was Japanese and not Korean and could accordingly be interpreted as an admission of defeat on the part of the Japanese, it was apparent to the Sō and their diplomatic councilors that none would be forthcoming from Tokugawa Ieyasu. Hence they decided in 1606 to write the letter themselves in the name of the "King of Japan, Minamoto no Ieyasu." Although the Korean court knew this letter to be a forgery, it nonetheless determined to send a "return embassy" (*hoedapsa*, J: *kaitōshi*).

In order to keep their first fraud from being exposed, the nimble diplomatists in the Tsushima chancery next had to deliver to their overlords a document that was ostensibly the message of peace and friendship expected by the Tokugawa from the king of Korea and was moreover, free of the nuances of a response to a previous communication. They edited the text of the document that the Korean mission (purged by this hocus-pocus of the stain of a mere "return" embassy) actually bore with it and then, in a risky sleight of hand as the envoys were on their way to their audience in Edo Castle, they substituted their counterfeit for the original.[84] The Tsushima chancery's exertions proved fruitful, as the Korean ambassadors, who were, during the summer of 1607, received not only by Shogun Tokugawa Hidetada in Edo but also by the "retired" Ieyasu in Sumpu, concluded their business smoothly, and returned to Korea with 1,240 more former prisoners. The means used to bring about this embassy's success were more ingenious than honest; that success, however, was the indispensable precondition if normal relations were again to be established.

Two years later, when Korea and Tsushima concluded a formal agreement, Japanese–Korean relations were restored on the same ba-

83 Naitō "Jinshin, Teiyū no eki," pt. 2, *Chōsen gakuhō* 33 (October 1964):49.
84 The text of the Korean king's message, the emendations made by the diplomatists of Tsushima, and a brief discussion of this forgery may be found in Tashiro Kazui, *Kakikaerareta kokusho: Tokugawa, Chōsen gaikō no butaiura* (Tokyo: Chūō kōronsha, 1983), pp. 31–9.

sis that had prevailed before Hideyoshi's invasion, indeed, since the so-called Kakitsu treaty of 1443. To be sure, the terms of the 1609 agreement were the most severe yet: The Sō were permitted to send no more than twenty ships to Korea annually, and various other privileges previously enjoyed by the Japanese were likewise reduced. Pusan was to be the sole port of entry open to the Japanese; moreover, the Japanese were restricted to a trading factory on the outskirts of that city and were no longer allowed to travel to the capital of Korea, Seoul, as they had been permitted in the past. In their walled compound outside Pusan – called Waegwan (J: Wakan), "Japan House" – the Japanese traders were confined in just the way their Dutch colleagues in Japan would be sequestered on the artificial island of Dejima in Nagasaki harbor after 1641. And yet, notwithstanding all the restrictions imposed by the Korean government (which the Sō by various devices tried to circumvent), a flourishing trade was maintained between Japan and Korea by way of Tsushima throughout the Edo period.

In diplomatic relations, Tsushima continued to play a highly inventive role unhindered by higher authority for almost three decades. Although embassies were actually sent by Korea at the Japanese shogunal government's request, which was transmitted through the agency of Tsushima, for reasons of prestige it was thought necessary by the Japanese to disguise the fact that the initiative was theirs and not Korean. The Tokugawa wanted the gesture of recognition from the Korean government but did not wish to show deference to the neighbor country. The Koreans, for their part, were not unwilling to accommodate the bakufu, but they insisted on adherence to what they considered the proper forms of converse between nations. The differences between the expectations of the two parties were papered over by the original devices of the chancery of Tsushima, which handled the exchange of documents and the reception of the embassies in Japan.

An excellent example of the daring with which Tsushima's diplomatists went about their business is their management of the second official Korean embassy to the Edo bakufu, that of 1617. It took at least four separate missions from the Sō to Korea before that country's government agreed to appoint this embassy, which was ostensibly sent to congratulate the Tokugawa on their victory in the Osaka campaigns of 1614–15. (Because that victory involved the destruction of the Toyotomi family and Hideyoshi's heritage, it was depicted to the Koreans as an act of retribution exacted on their behalf by the Tokugawa.) The insistent emissary of the Sō, Tachibana Toshimasa, finally succeeded in swaying the Koreans when he presented them with a forged document purportedly sent by Shogun Hidetada. When the Korean "return embassy" bore with it merely a response to that forged communication instead of the felicitations commissioned by the Tokugawa, the congratulatory message expected at the shogunal court had to be fabricated in Tsushima. When the bakufu's diplomatic experts avoided using the title "King of Japan" (*Nihon kokuō*) in the reply that this embassy was to take back to Seoul and identified Shogun Hidetada only by the country he ruled, the "State of Japan" (*Nihonkoku*), the counterfeiters of Tsushima falsified this document, too, by adding the character for the missing syllable.[85] Although dissimulation is not unknown in the conduct of foreign affairs, this was a diplomacy based on outright forgery.

What caused the diplomatists of Tsushima so much toil? The Korean court expected the title "King" to be used in official correspondence with Japan, accepting it as the proper appellation of the ruler of a country within the East Asian international order dominated by China. The Edo bakufu (unlike its Muromachi predecessor) shunned the use of that title for the same reason, rejecting it as redolent of the language of enfeoffment used by Chinese emperors and an admission of subordinate status in the Sinocentric world system. Instead of communicating with the kings of Korea as with their peers – that is, as fellow vassals of China – the Tokugawa wanted to place themselves a level above them. Indeed, the Japanese rulers sought a supreme designation within an order of their own. Tsushima, the mediator, was caught in the middle of the conflicting interpretations of sovereignty.

On the occasion of the third official Korean embassy, which was sent in 1624 to congratulate Shogun Tokugawa Iemitsu (1604–51, r. 1623–51) on his accession, the diplomatists of Tsushima once again had to counterfeit a shogunal message to make it conform with Korean expectations: They adjusted the title "Sovereign of Japan" (*Nihon kokushu*), which was selected this time by the bakufu's secretariat, to the familiar "King of Japan" (*Nihon kokuō*). This was a serious manipulation, even if it required nothing more than the reduction of one of the characters in the compound *kokushu* by a single pen stroke. Could the bakufu have been completely unaware of such remarkable creativeness on the part of its island subjects? That is not very likely. It is more probable that for a time, the shogunate chose to turn a blind eye to the unorthodox activities of the editors of state papers in the service of

---

85 Tanaka Takeo, "Sakoku seiritsuki Nitchō kankei no seikaku," *Chōsen gakuhō* 34 (January 1965):36–7.

Tsushima, for they did, after all, smooth the relationship with Korea. At length, however, the manipulation of documents threatened to get out of hand and the bakufu had to crack down. In 1635, it took the opportunity of an internal power struggle on Tsushima to purge the forgers' group and install guardians against further diplomatic malpractice in the domain of the Sō.

The bakufu intervened when the history of forgeries became the central issue in a suit that pitted the daimyo of Tsushima, Sō Yoshinari (1604–57), against his vassal and accuser, Yanagawa Shigeoki (1603–84), one of the most influential samurai of the Tsushima domain, who also had excellent connections at the court of the Tokugawa in Edo. Shigeoki, who aimed at nothing less than Yoshinari's disenfeoffment and the displacement of the Sō from Tsushima, thought he could buttress his assertion that the daimyo was incompetent by denouncing the Sō family for decades of falsification of documents of state, forgery of shogunal seals, and gross malfeasance in the conduct of relations with Korea. Because Shigeoki had played a role almost surpassing that of the daimyo in Korean affairs – as had his father Toshinaga (d. 1613) and grandfather Shigenobu (d. 1605) before him – it could be assumed that he did, indeed, have intimate knowledge of such matters. But he fell into his own trap.

Yoshinari produced a number of witnesses who incriminated the Yanagawa in the planning, fostering, and actual execution of the forgeries, and Shigeoki was unable to discredit them. His Edo connections did not help him. On Kan'ei 12 (1635).3.11, after an investigation that dragged on for almost two years, he was summoned before Shogun Iemitsu, found guilty, and condemned to exile in a northern province. Some underlings of both the principals in the suit were sentenced to death. Sō Yoshinari, however, was vindicated and permitted to retain his position as daimyo of Tsushima.[86] No doubt the reason for exonerating him and also for sparing Yanagawa Shigeoki's life was that the bakufu wished to avoid a scandal that would disturb the Koreans. The last thing the bakufu wanted was draw attention to the fraud that had for years been perpetrated in its name. Instead, it sought above all to preserve the appearance that propriety and normalcy ruled at least the Japanese side of Japanese–Korean relations.

The conduct of those relations on behalf of the bakufu was, however, much more circumscribed after this so-called Yanagawa incident. What had been until then a regionally managed concern was put under

---

86 Tashiro, *Kakikaerareta kokusho*, pp. 133–60.

the supervision of the national government's emissaries. To be sure, the Sō were left in place, and they remained the key intermediaries between Japan and Korea until the end of the Edo period. But they were no longer in full charge.

In the seventh month of 1635 – a year of many institutional innovations – the bakufu started the practice of sending priests from the Five Great Zen Monasteries of Kyoto (Kyoto *gosan,* a traditional center of Chinese learning and source of expertise on correspondence in Chinese, the language of diplomacy in East Asia) to Tsushima, where they would keep a sharp eye on the management of official contacts with Korea. Because their residence was the cloister called Iteian and because they served on the basis of one to three years' rotation, this arrangement, which lasted until the fall of the shogunate, is called the Iteian rotational supervisory system (Iteian *rinbansei*). In the same year, a question that had long disturbed the diplomatists of both countries was resolved when the bakufu succeeded in establishing "Sovereign Lord of Japan" (*Nihonkoku taikun*) as the form of address to be used in official communications from Korea.[87] *Taikun* is the style that the Tokugawa shoguns bore thenceforth (with a brief interruption early in the eighteenth century) in their capacity as sovereigns of a nation engaged in intercourse with other nations. The English word "tycoon" derives from it.

The Japan-centered "international order" of the Tokugawa regime

That regularity had at length been achieved in the bakufu's foreign relations was demonstrated in 1636, when the Korean court for the first time appointed not a "return embassy" but a "diplomatic mission" (*t'ongsinsa;* J: *tsūshinshi*) to Japan. This large Korean embassy, which traveled to Edo for an audience with Shogun Iemitsu and then to Nikkō to pay its respects at the shrine of the deified Ieyasu, was followed in 1643 by one sent to offer congratulations on the birth of Iemitsu's heir Ietsuna (1641–80; r. 1651–80) and then between 1655 and 1811 by seven others dispatched to celebrate accessions to the shogunate. For the entire Edo period, that makes a total of twelve official embassies from Korea, the only foreign country with which the Tokugawa regime maintained diplomatic relations (*tsūshin,* as opposed to commerce, *tsūshō*) until the nineteenth century.

87 See Hayashi Akira, comp., *Tsūkō ichiran,* vol. 1 (Tokyo: Kokusho kankōkai, 1912), 28:336–7 and 30:365; and Kondō Morishige, comp., *Gaiban tsūshō,* no. 1, p. 11, in Kondō Keizō, ed., *Kaitei shiseki shūran,* vol. 21 (Tokyo: Kondō kappansho, 1901).

Commercial relations with the outside world were also extremely limited. Under the prohibition of foreign voyages (*kaigai tokō kinshi rei;* sometimes called *kaikin* in reference to the Ming Chinese model, *hai-chin*) issued by the bakufu in 1635, Japanese were forbidden on pain of death to travel abroad. Apart from the sanctioned commerce carried on by Tsushima through the Waegwan in Pusan, this measure left Japanese foreign trade in the hands of a few rigorously controlled groups of foreign traders resident in Japan. After the exclusion of the Portuguese in 1639, the Dutch were the only Westerners permitted to enter the country. Alongside them, there existed in Nagasaki a Chinese trading community that was, however, not officially countenanced by the Chinese imperial government. Relations with China were not reestablished during the Edo period, although there is some evidence of interest on Ieyasu's part in restoring them. Evidently, the Tokugawa shoguns were unwilling to demean themselves in the way the Ashikaga had, by submitting themselves to China's standards and entering into vassalage in order to enjoy the benefits of a tributary relationship with the "Central Country."

Between 1634 and 1806, the kingdom of Ryūkyū also sent fifteen embassies to the Tokugawa shoguns, but this could scarcely be called a foreign country insofar as Japan was concerned. Ryūkyū was not an independent or even an autonomous state: It had been conquered in 1609 by the Shimazu and was no more than a dependency of the daimyo of Kagoshima, whom the bakufu enfeoffed with Ryūkyū just as it did with Satsuma and Ōsumi. This colony, which was intensively exploited by the Shimazu, was permitted to call itself a "kingdom," that is, to maintain a tributary relationship with China, merely as a device that would give it continued trading access to that country. To be sure, in 1636 the bakufu ordered the Shimazu to cease referring to their puppet on the islands as a "king" and to call him "provincial governor" (*kokushi*) in future communications.

The colorful processions of the exotically garbed envoys from Korea and Ryūkyū may have impressed the populace along their route of progress to Edo with the notion that the bakufu enjoyed great authority among foreign nations. In actuality, however, they only masked the fact that after the 1630s Japan had a government that barely pursued foreign relations at all. The sham played with Ryūkyū's enforced participation and the facsimile of a formal relationship in which Korea acquiesced sufficed to create for the bakufu its own international order, in which Japan ranked first, even if it had to be *prima in vacuo.*

CHAPTER 7

CHRISTIANITY AND THE DAIMYO

The Tokugawa shogunate's self-serving conceit of a Japan-centered "international order," described in the conclusion of Chapter 6, could handily comprehend Ryūkyū, Korea, and even the mercantile Dutch, because these foreign entities either acquiesced to being fit or had no power to resist being forced into the Japanese derivative of the traditional East Asian model of international relations. Another group of foreigners posed a more difficult problem: The model of universal truth introduced by Roman Catholic Europeans who came to Japan with a missionary purpose could not be so easily accommodated by a regime intent on refashioning Japanese society in a mold of its own. Hence the Catholics' mission to Japan was ultimately condemned as subversive to the social order of the Tokugawa, and they were expelled as an alien element from the Japanese body politic.

At first, however, the Catholic Europeans were welcomed. At the time of their arrival, Japan was a splintered realm composed of the autonomous domains of many warring daimyo. For reasons that will be discussed in this chapter, some of those daimyo protected the foreigners, sought out their commerce, and even embraced the religion that the Europeans brought with them. The fragmented state of a nation that truly merited the label *sengoku*, a "country at war," made it possible for the Christian missionaries to disseminate their faith on a domanial and even regional basis.

Because those missionaries' activity in Japan lasted for roughly a hundred years, from the 1540s through the 1630s, Western historians have developed the practice of calling this Japan's "Christian Century." To be sure, the last half of that "Christian" period saw the paradoxical conditions that had once permitted the religion an entry into Japan eliminated and almost all traces of Christianity erased. As Japan passed from a state of extreme political dissolution and social upheaval to a new era of unity and peace, it also turned inward and away from the relative cosmopolitanism of the Christian Century's first half. From *sengoku*, Japan was transformed into *sakoku*, a "closed country."

For the daimyo, the establishment of a new order meant a reduction to fealty under the Tokugawa shogunate. For the Christian missionaries and their converts, it meant a bitter persecution and the nearly total eradication of their religion in Japan. For the country at large, it was the beginning of more than two centuries of national seclusion.

THE ARRIVAL OF THE EUROPEANS

The first contact between Japan and Europe, as far as can be determined, occurred in 1543, when two or three Portuguese traders arrived on board a Chinese junk in Tanegashima, the oblong island that forms a pendant to the southernmost tip of Kyushu at the entrance to Kagoshima Bay.[1] Scarcely a household word before that date, the island's name was destined to become famous throughout Japan on account of a Western product brought on this voyage, the harquebus. Tanegashima became synonymous with firearms when this weapon – introduced by those first Portuguese, imitated, improved, and produced in numbers by Japanese armorers, and employed in battle by daimyo fighting over a dismembered body politic – began to transform the methods of warfare in the "country at war."

The Portuguese traders' contribution of a new, modern instrument of mayhem to Japan's well-stocked but still medieval and, by European standards, obsolescent arsenal was one of those remarkable accidents of history that have a revolutionary effect. In the hands of the two or three warlords who had both the tactical acumen and the economic wherewithal to employ firearms massively, guns that evolved from the Tanegashima prototype would, later in the sixteenth century, become the indispensable tools of Japan's military reunification.

But the undoubted historical significance of their initial import notwithstanding, the traders were not the most important European actors in this first, dramatic encounter between Japan and the West. Their interest in Japan was exclusively material, and their activities there were, by and large, confined to a few spots on the country's periphery. For better or for worse, they had neither the inclination nor the capacity to play the parts of Europe's cultural emissaries to Japan

---

1 The date of the Portuguese traders' arrival in Tanegashima is given as Tembun [12].8.25 (September 23, 1543), and Wang Chih, alias Wu-feng, is identified as their interpreter, in the brief essay *Teppōki* (1607) by Nampo Bunji, a Zen priest and diplomatist in the employ of the Shimazu daimyo of Kagoshima. The text is most conveniently found in Okamoto Yoshitomo, *Jūroku seiki Nichiō kōtsūshi no kenkyū* (Tokyo: Kōbunsō, 1936), pp. 187–9.

or the disseminators of knowledge about Japanese civilization in Europe. Rather, those roles were to be filled by men with a definite cultural purpose and a special spiritual calling, the Christian missionaries who followed the merchants to Japan. The first of that dedicated and ultimately tragic group were three Jesuits led by the future saint, Francis Xavier, who were brought to Kagoshima in 1549 as passengers on another Chinese junk.

Both the merchants and the missionaries were carried to Japan in the backwash of the *wakō* tide. Indeed, in view of what has been observed in Chapter 6 regarding the character of the *bahan* trade and the role played by the Portuguese in its principal base of the 1540s, Shuang-hsü-kang or Liampoo, it was perhaps unavoidable that the first Europeans to visit Japan should have come in the company of Chinese illicit traders. For all that, it is rather startling to recognize in the "Confucian scholar" called Wu-feng, the fellow traveler who acted as an interpreter for the first Portuguese in Tanegashima, none other but the most notorious of all the *wakō* captains, Wang Chih, sailing under a nom de plume. Another noted interpreter who voyaged under "tattered sails" was Yajirō, the Kagoshima samurai who displayed natural qualities of such apparent excellence that Xavier was led to believe in the likely prospect of a rich harvest awaiting Christian missionaries in Japan: "For if all the Japanese are as eager to learn as [Yajirō], then it seems to me that, in all the lands that have been discovered, they are the people that is the thirstiest for knowledge." Yajirō was a *wakō*, if not when Xavier first met him in December 1547 in the Portuguese colony of Malacca as a fugitive from justice in his homeland, then certainly a few years later at the end of his days: He died on a pirate raid to China.[2] Needless to say, Xavier was conveyed from Malacca to Japan on the ship of yet another *wakō*, "a pagan Chinese pirate" named Aván.[3]

---

[2] On Yajirō's intellectual curiosity and the conclusions Xavier drew from it regarding the Japanese, see Xavier to Ignatius Loyola and other Jesuits, dated Cochín, January 20, 1548, in Georg Schurhammer SJ and Josef Wicki SJ, eds., *Epistolae S. Francisci Xaverii aliaque eius scripta*, vol. 1, *Monumenta Historica Societatis Iesu*, vol. 67 (Rome: Monumenta Historica Soc. Iesu, 1944), no. 59, pp. 391–2. On Yajirō's end, see Padre Luis Frois SJ, *Historia de Japam*, pt. 1, chap. 6, ed. Josef Wicki SJ, vol. 1 (Lisbon: Biblioteca Nacional de Lisboa, 1976), p. 46; Matsuda Kiichi and Kawasaki Momota, trans., *Furoisu Nihonshi*, vol. 6 (Tokyo: Chūō kōronsha, 1978), p. 72.

[3] Frois, *Historia*, pt. 1, chap. 1, Wicki, vol. 1, p. 22; Matsuda and Kawasaki, trans., *Furoisu Nihonshi*, vol. 6, p. 29. On Aván, also see Xavier to Dom Pedro da Silva, dated Cangoxima, November 5, 1549, *Epistolae*, vol. 2, *Monumenta*, vol. 68 (1945), no. 94, p. 230; and Xavier to various Jesuits in Goa, dated Malacca, June [20] and 22, 1549, ibid., no. 85, p. 124. Cf. Josef Wicki SJ, "Das neuentdeckte Xaveriusleben des P. Francisco Pérez S.I. (1579)," *Archivum Historicum Societatis Iesu* 34.67 (January–June 1965): 63–4.

As could be expected from these associations, the list of place names mentioned in the reports of the earliest Portuguese mariners who visited Japan overlaps considerably with the Japanese toponymy found in *Ch'ou-hai t'u-pien* and other Chinese sources on the home grounds of the *wakō*. From those reports, it is clear that the Portuguese traders were informed about routes beyond Kyushu, both through the Inland Sea and around the southeastern coast of Shikoku. But they never sailed to Sakai or any of the other harbors of the Kinai region in Honshu. Instead, they confined themselves to Kyushu ports. From 1550 to 1562, they mainly used Hirado, the ancient lair of the Matsuura-tō, although on occasion they called at Kagoshima and Yamagawa in Satsuma and such places as Hiji and Funai in Bungo. After 1564, they abandoned Hirado for other ports in Hizen. The most notable of those was Nagasaki, which became the recognized terminus of their trade with Japan from 1571 onward. Apart from the navigational and commercial, these changes had political and, indeed, also religious reasons.

The missionaries no less than the merchants sought a safe harbor, a place free of storms where they could anchor their enterprise in the hope that it would prosper under official protection. That type of security was not easy to find in Kyushu or, indeed, anywhere in Japan at the middle of the sixteenth century. The atrophy of Japan's central governing organism, the Ashikaga shogunate, had by that time reached an advanced stage. The malady of the central system of authority affected the political health of the entire country. The provinces were swept by disorder: Regional hegemonies emerged, only to disappear under what seemed to be the constant condition of war. Where, then, would their quest lead the foreigners through Sengoku's tempest?

THE CONDITION OF KYUSHU

When the first Portuguese and Jesuits arrived in Japan, Kyushu in particular was an arena of contention among many great or lesser warlords. No decision had yet been reached in that struggle, and the island would not be pacified until the great unifier Toyotomi Hideyoshi (1537?–98) invaded and conquered it in 1587. Hence missionaries and merchants alike repeatedly had to change their bases of operation in their search for a place of refuge and patronage. Eventually, they learned to utilize the political confusion that was endemic in Sengoku Japan to their own advantage.

Southern Kyushu was in turmoil because of the long-lasting internal

troubles of the Shimazu family, whose head had since the late fourteenth century held the title of *shugo* (military governor) of the three
provinces of Satsuma, Ōsumi, and Hyūga. These provinces, however,
remained full of independent-minded barons who continued to assert
themselves militarily against their supposed overlord, the daimyo
Shimazu Takahisa (1514–71), who was plagued by persistent party
taking and rebellion among his nominal vassals.

Takahisa made only slow progress in his effort to establish territorial
control over southern Kyushu, even if his early recognition of the
power of firearms aided that effort. At the siege of Iwatsurugi Castle in
1554, for instance, his general Shimazu Tadamasa (d. 1561) used the
novel tactic of "maneuvering five ships close in to the shore and shoot-
ing with firearms" upon the fort's defenders, two or three of whom
were killed by the new weapon.[4] After a few weeks, the castle fell, but
this success against a rebellious baron was no more than one step
forward for Takahisa in the bitter and protracted conflict between the
emergent Sengoku daimyo family of the Shimazu and the petty lords
(*kokujin*) of an entire region. Not until the 1570s, under the leadership
of Takahisa's son and successor Shimazu Yoshihisa (1533–1611), did
the Shimazu succeed in consolidating their authority over the area's
restive barons.

Northern Kyushu, too, was in an unsettled state at the time of the
first Europeans' arrival. For much of Japan's middle ages, ever since
the establishment of the Kamakura regime at the end of the twelfth
century, this area, which encompassed six of Kyushu's nine provinces,
was the sphere of influence of two great *shugo* families, the Shōni of
Chikuzen and the Ōtomo of Bungo. In the late fifteenth century,
however, these two traditional powers came under relentless pressure
from a relative newcomer, the Ōuchi family of Yamaguchi in Suō
Province across the Shimonoseki Strait in Honshu. That pressure
caused the collapse of the medieval power structure in northern
Kyushu.

The Shōni family was reduced to a nullity by 1536, when Ōuchi
Yoshitaka (1507–51) managed to destroy Shōni Sukemoto after enticing his principal vassal and most active general, Ryūzōji Iekane (d.
1546), to join the Ōuchi side. The Ōuchi, however, did not enjoy the
fruits of this victory for any length of time. Rather, it was their rivals,
the Ōtomo, to whom the elimination of the Shōni brought more last-

---

4 *Iwatsurugi kassen nikki*, quoted in *Kagoshima-ken*, vol. 46 of *Kadokawa Nihon chimei daijiten*
(Tokyo: Kadokawa shoten, 1983), p. 124. Iwatsurugi Castle was located near what is now
Shigetomi Beach in Aira-chō, just north of the Kagoshima city limits.

ing benefits. In the long run, however, the disappearance of the Shōni from the scene where they had played such a prominent role for centuries was significant mainly as the factor that permitted their former vassals, the Ryūzōji, to build a powerful new Sengoku daimyo domain. The Ryūzōji are of special interest to us because they were to play a baneful role in the history of the early Christian mission of Japan.

For the time being, Ōuchi Yoshitaka controlled most of Chikuzen and Buzen as well as parts of Hizen and Chikugo. Even after defeating the Shōni, however, Yoshitaka still had to confront the problem of the Ōtomo, who would never acquiesce in the Ōuchi family's ascendancy over northern Kyushu. Traditional enemies since the 1430s, the two great daimyo houses eyed each other warily. The tension along the borders of the Ōuchi and Ōtomo domains in Chikuzen, Buzen, and Chikugo never relaxed as the opportunistic petty barons of these provinces, ever on the lookout for the main chance, threw in their allegiances first with the one side and then with the other. There were recurrent local skirmishes.

In 1533, this habitually overstrained political situation had been aggravated when Ōtomo Yoshiaki (1502–50) succeeded in having his three-year-old son Shiobōshi-maru (later known as Yoshishige, as Sōrin, and as Francisco; 1530–87) designated *shugo* of Buzen by the Ashikaga shogunate. In the next year, Ōuchi Yoshitaka responded to this apparent challenge to his dominion over Buzen by sending an invasion force into Bungo. This invasion was stopped by the Ōtomo, and a tenuous peace was reestablished in 1535 through the intercession of Shogun Ashikaga Yoshiharu (1511–50, r. 1522–47) on condition that the Ōuchi return certain disputed territories in Chikuzen to Ōtomo Yoshiaki. But this agreement could not keep the two rivals satisfied for very long, and by 1543 Yoshiaki was complaining that the Ōuchi had failed to restore to the Ōtomo their rights in the port city of Hakata. For the time being, however, the truce freed both parties to turn their attention in potentially more profitable directions.

Ōuchi Yoshitaka used the respite to finish off Shōni Sukemoto, as just described. Ōtomo Yoshiaki moved against his own younger brother, Kikuchi Yoshitake (formerly known as Ōtomo Shigeharu, d. 1554), who had assumed this new name after being installed by Yoshiaki as the fictive heir of another tradition-rich, but extinct, *shugo* family, the Kikuchi of Higo. Far from being a complaisant puppet of the Ōtomo, Kikuchi Yoshitake placed his bets on the Ōuchi to prevail in northern Kyushu and took up arms against Yoshiaki. But Yoshitake was no match for his elder brother, who brushed him aside in order to grab his territory. By 1543, Ōtomo Yoshiaki's hold on Higo was solid enough to make his appointment as *shugo* over that province an appropriate recognition of his actual status.

Bungo and Higo were the foundations of the developing regional hegemony of the Ōtomo. This growing realm was disturbed severely in 1550 by a palace revolution in which Ōtomo Yoshiaki was killed after threatening to disinherit his eldest son Yoshishige. In the wake of this notorious affair, Yoshishige succeeded as the head of the Ōtomo family. He began his career as the lord over two provinces. In the stormy course of his life, he was to see the realm of the Ōtomo expand to a sum total of seven provinces and then shrink again until barely a small part of Bungo was left.

DEUS OR DAINICHI?

The daimyo Shimazu Takahisa, Ōuchi Yoshitaka, and Ōtomo Yoshishige, who were the most important political personages of western Japan, were also the Christian missionary Francis Xavier's most important collocutors in the country. To be sure, "collocutors" may not be the word, as the Basque priest's ability to learn foreign languages was poor, and he had to converse with his Japanese hosts through interpreters whose ability to convey his meaning was likewise highly limited. In any event, it is clear that Xavier was led badly astray by his first guide to Japan, Yajirō. This native informant may indeed have "learned in eight months to read, and write, and speak Portuguese" and even have been "very well indoctrinated in the faith of Jesus Christ Our Lord," as Xavier maintained.[5] For all that, he thoroughly misinformed his mentor. Yajirō's outline of the essentials of Japanese religion was the sometime *wakō*'s biggest disservice to the future saint.

According to Yajirō, the Japanese religious preached that "there is only one God, creator of all things." As if this sheer misstatement were not bad enough, the Christian neophyte proceeded to amplify it with fine-spun theological analogues. There was one order of priests, he said, who adored "the one and only God, whom they call *de ny chy* in their language. . . . Sometimes they depict this *de ny chy* with only one body and three heads, and then they call him *cogy.*" Yajirō added that

---

5 Xavier to Loyola, dated Cochín, January 12, 1549, *Epistolae*, vol. 2, no. 70, p. 10; Xavier to King of Portugal (João III), dated Malacca [June 20], 1549, ibid., no. 84, p. 117.

"he did not know the significance of these three heads; what he did know, however, was that all was one, *de ny chy* and *co ny gy*, just as among us are God and the Trinity."[6]

It is apparent that Yajirō had some casual acquaintance with the Shingon sect of Buddhism: What he meant by *de ny chy* is unquestionably that sect's central Buddha, Mahāvairocana, called Dainichi in Japanese. A more expert informant on Shingon Buddhism might have described Dainichi as the ultimate reality that is identical with the total functioning of the cosmos and also identical with the enlightened mind. The untutored Yajirō equated this totalist force with the personal Creator and Lord of All, the God of Christianity.

What this novice meant by *cogy* or *co ny gy* is obscure. In the extraordinarily rich iconography of Shingon, many figures are represented with multiple heads, but Dainichi as such is not one of them. In the well-known Shingon schema called *gochi nyorai*, "Tathāgatas of the Five Wisdoms," five forms of wisdom comprehended by Dainichi and personified by the Five Tathāgatas of the Diamond Realm are represented with Dainichi himself at the center and four other Buddhas either flanking him or surrounding him at the four cardinal points. Perhaps the term *cogy* reflects a distorted vision of that mandala; even so, the underlying Buddhist concept of course bears no resemblance to the Trinity of the Nicene Creed. But regardless of the background of Yajirō's garbled reference, the results of his altogether facile explanation are clear: Xavier began his mission in Japan by preaching Dainichi.

To be sure, it is likely that Xavier's unwitting decision to translate key Christian concepts by means of a terminology charged with Buddhist meanings actually eased his entry into Japan, as it created – if only temporarily and deceptively – a common ground of discourse with the "heathen" whom Xavier had come to convert. Moreover, the very fact that this religious teacher came from "Tenjiku," that is, India, the classical homeland of Buddhism, gave him charisma and gained him acceptance.

In Satsuma, for instance, Xavier was received amicably by the daimyo Shimazu Takahisa and also conversed on friendly terms with the eminent prelate Ninshitsu (d. 1556), the superior of Kagoshima's most important Buddhist temple, the Zen monastery Fukushōji. The

6 "Emformação da Ilha de Japão dada por mestre framçysquo que soube de pesoas muy autemtiquas pryncypalmente de huũ Japão q̃ se tornou crystão nesta cydade de Goa homẽ de gramde ẽgenho e abelydade," Biblioteca Municipal de Elvas, Mss. 5/381, ff. [6ov–62]; transcription by A. Thomaz Pires, "O Japão no seculo XVI," pt. 1, *O Instituto* 53 (1906): 760–1.

teacher who had come from India drew the curiosity of crowds of people as he sat on the steps to Fukushōji's entrance and read aloud from a summary of Christian doctrine that had been put into Japanese with Yajirō's assistance and painstakingly written out in roman letters by Xavier. According to Xavier's great successor in the apostolate of Asia, Visitator Alexandro Valignano SJ, the translation was such a bungled piece of work that it aroused "jeers and laughter; for neither was the truth of what the Padre was saying expressed well, nor was it written in such a way that it could be read before their men of letters without laughter."[7] For all that, in Kagoshima and in the castle of Ichiku, another key place of Shimazu Takahisa's domains, Xavier and his helpmates were able to convert more than one hundred people, who were drawn to the foreign priest by the force of his personality if not the power of his message. What the specific character of these converts' new religion was, however, cannot be said with certainty.

Once the missionaries learned enough Japanese to engage in intellectual debates, their easy familiarity with Buddhist monks would perforce have to come to an end. Learning enough of the language to understand their partners in debate, however, was evidently a weary two years' task for Xavier and the two Spanish Jesuits who accompanied him, Padre Cosme de Torres and Irmão Juan Fernandez. Not until the summer of 1551, and far away from Satsuma, did Xavier finally abandon the hopelessly compromised terminology with which Yajirō had encumbered him.

The occasion for that was Xavier's second visit to Yamaguchi. There Shingon priests applauded his insistence on the primacy of Dainichi as the self-generated "principle of all things," but their responses to his questions on the Trinity and on the Incarnation and Passion of Christ failed to satisfy him, and finally Xavier was enlightened. Having realized the gravity of his mistake, he sent Fernandez to preach in the streets that Dainichi and his religion were "an invention of the devil, as also were all the other sects of Japan."[8] Not surprisingly, this provocation aroused the fury of Yamaguchi's Buddhist clergy.

The Buddhists' protests merely underlined the fact that for the Jesuits, to establish Christian orthodoxy was, after all, their all-important mission. After this incident, the missionaries would disdain

7 Alexandro Valignano SJ, *Historia del principio y progresso de la Compañia de Jesús en las Indias Orientales (1542–64)*, ed. Josef Wicki SJ, *Bibliotheca Instituti Historici S.I.*, vol. 2 (Rome: Institutum Historicum S.I., 1944), p. 164.
8 Frois, *Historia*, pt. 1, chap. 5, Wicki, vol. 1, pp. 40–1; Matsuda and Kawasaki, trans., *Furoisu Nihonshi*, vol. 6, pp. 61–3.

anything that smacked of syncretism and would preach the uncompro-
mising law of Deus. As a result, the Japanese language was enriched
with a great number of neologisms, catechetical terms derived from
Latin or Portuguese.

THE SEARCH FOR SECURE PATRONS

If it was to survive and to grow in the face of opposition from the
native religious establishment, the fledgling Christian mission of Japan
had to find shelter under the protection of the powerful. Under the
conditions of Sengoku, however, that protection – if it could be obtained at all – rarely endured and was almost never disinterested. According to Valignano, the reason that the daimyo Shimazu Takahisa
and his principal deputies in Kagoshima accorded Xavier and his
party a good reception was because they "knew the credit and the
authority that the Padres had among the Portuguese and greatly desired that, through the [Padres'] mediation, [the Portuguese] would
come to that harbor with their ships." Hence they "detained the Padres there with many tricks and promises." A year into Xavier's stay
in their town, the lords of Kagoshima found out that their best efforts
notwithstanding, the Portuguese had chosen to anchor elsewhere. Consequently, the Shimazu prohibited any further conversions to Christianity and forced the missionaries to leave Satsuma.[9]

Naturally, Xavier then went to the harbor where the Portuguese
ship lay, Hirado. He thereby established the close association between
the bases of the Jesuit mission and the ports of call of the Portuguese
trading vessels in Japan that would continue until the country was
closed to commerce with Catholic lands in 1639.

In Hirado (where, it will be remembered, the Chinese sea king
Wang Chih had his Japanese abode), Xavier and his companions received a warm welcome from the local *tono* (lord), Matsuura Takanobu
(1529–99). The presence of the Portuguese traders and nothing else
accounted for Takanobu's show of favor to the missionaries – a temporary good grace, to be sure – and Xavier in any case had his eye on a
reception at the courts of princes far greater than this *wakō* chieftain.
He wanted legitimation not from petty barons but from national authorities, whom he planned to seek out in "Meaco" (Miyako, that is,
Kyoto), viewed by him as the capital of all Japan. He was to find out
that those authorities were ephemeral and not easily approached.

9 Valignano, *Historia del principio y progresso*, pp. 165, 167–8.

Even before traveling to Japan, Xavier had been given some idea of the peculiar division of sovereign powers that prevailed there. An imaginative report drawn up for him in India on the basis of information provided by Yajirō describes the Japanese polity as follows:

The principal king, who is called *Vo* in their language . . . apparently is among them such as the pope is among us. He has jurisdiction over laymen as well as over the clergy, of whom there are many in that country. But although he has full authority over everything – [Yajirō] says – he never orders the exercise of justice against anyone but leaves all that worry to another, who is among them as the emperor is among us and who is called *goxo*. The latter has the power and empire over all of Japan but nonetheless owes obedience to the aforesaid *Vo*. When *goxo* goes to visit *Vo*, [Yajirō] says, he does so kneeling on the ground; and – he says – if *goxo* commits a malfeasance, then *Vo* can take away his kingdom and cut off his head. And he says that those who are below strictly obey them who are above, as the exercise of justice there is so strict. . . .[10]

Actually, the regnant *"Vo"* (*ō*) at the time in question, Emperor Go-Nara (1497–1557, r. 1526–57), was so powerless that his enthronement had to be postponed for ten years, until 1536, because funds for the ceremony were lacking. To portray him as a mikado who could, if it suited him, make the punishment fit the crime throughout the country over which he had "full authority" does not quite capture Go-Nara's true historical image. And the ruling *"goxo"* (*gosho*) or shogun, Ashikaga Yoshifuji (1536–65, r. 1547–65; known as Yoshiteru from 1554), is barely recognizable under the description of a potentate who had "the power and empire over all of Japan." In fact, he was no more than a feeble pawn in the hands of his nominal deputies and rear vassals. Chased from his capital city of Kyoto in July 1549, Shogun Yoshifuji had to spend eight of the next nine and a half years as a refugee wandering from one provincial locality to another. He was permitted to return to Kyoto in 1559, but that turned out to be a dubious consolation to the shogun, who was murdered there in 1565 in his own residence.

It is evident that far from being a realm where "those who [were] below strictly obey[ed] them who [were] above," Japan at the time of Xavier's visit was a land that had fallen to the nadir of *gekokujō*, a seemingly anarchical condition in which those below endeavored, with considerable success, to overthrow the ones who were above them. Indeed, even as Xavier was on his way from Hirado via Yamaguchi to

10 "Emformação da Ilha de Japão dada por mestre framçysquo," Elvas Mss. 5/381, f. [53rv]; *O Instituto* 53: 758–9.

Kyoto in late December 1550, the upstart daimyo Miyoshi Nagayoshi (1522–64, also known as Miyoshi Chōkei) was assaulting Nagao Castle, Shogun Yoshifuji's last foothold on the northeastern outskirts of the capital. It was clearly not a propitious time to visit the seat of what remained of Japan's traditional establishment. Little wonder that Xavier's journey to Kyoto ended in failure.

Xavier set out for the Kansai with two principal goals in mind. The first was to visit and even to convert the "king of Japan," from whom he hoped to obtain permission to spread Christianity throughout the country. Not content with the vision of making the Son of Heaven into a Christian, Xavier also cherished the hope that he could make manifest the truth of the Christian religion at what were reputed to be Japan's leading institutions of higher learning. Accordingly, his second major objective was to gain entry to the "University of Meaco" (which had "five principal colleges," as he called the Five Great Zen Monasteries of Kyoto, know to us as the Gozan) and to the other "principal university" of the Kyoto area, located on "Fieson" (Hieizan, the site of Enryakuji, the great monastery of the Tendai sect and citadel of traditional Japanese Buddhism).[11]

After a month's harrowing journey from Yamaguchi by way of Sakai, the hazards and discomforts of the trip eased somewhat by the letter of introduction given him along the way by an "honored person" who had taken pity on the priest from "Tenjiku," Xavier arrived in the capital about the middle of January 1551. Apparently, he first tried to seek out the gosho, Shogun Yoshifuji, but failed to track down that refugee from Kyoto. He then tried to obtain an audience with the "Vo, the universal king of all Japan," but was turned away, in large part because he bore no legitimation and no presents. Thus frustrated in all his endeavors, Xavier after a mere eleven days shook the dust of Kyoto off his feet.[12]

XAVIER AND ŌUCHI YOSHITAKA

In the course of his travels, Xavier had, however, learned two important lessons. The first was that Japan's national authorities were not nearly as powerful as some of its regional rulers. The second was that

---

11 On the plan to convert the Japanese sovereign, "whereupon would follow much temporal profit for the king of Portugal," see Xavier to Padre Antonio Gomes SJ, dated Cangoxima, November 5, 1549, *Epistolae*, vol. 2, no. 93, p. 223. On Japanese "universities," see Xavier to the Jesuits of Goa, same place and date, ibid., no. 90, pp. 207–9.

12 On Xavier's journey to Kyoto, see Frois, *Historia*, pt. 1, chap. 4, Wicki, vol. 1, pp. 34–8; Matsuda and Kawasaki, trans., *Furoisu Nihonshi*, vol. 3 (1978), pp. 15–26.

courage and charisma did not suffice to gain and retain an entrée in the courts of princes: The petitioner who approached the gates of exalted personages barefooted and empty-handed would be turned away; apart from one's convictions, one had to bear with him gifts and credentials.

Having identified the "king of Yamaguchi," that is, Ōuchi Yoshi-taka, as the most powerful prince in Japan, Xavier determined to call on him again to seek his favor for the Christian mission. On his first visit to Yamaguchi, in November and December 1550, Xavier had succeeded in little more than annoying Yoshitaka, who had summoned the priest into his presence after being told that "this was a man from Tenjiku." It is difficult to say what caused the most offense on this occasion – Xavier's shabby appearance; the acknowledgedly barba-rous Japanese of his famous "summary of Christian doctrine," which he had his Jesuit companion Fernandez read before Yoshitaka and his suite (a performance Yoshitaka apparently endured for over an hour before abruptly breaking off the audience); or the intemperate lan-guage of the "summary's" condemnation of the sin of sodomy, at which "the king appeared to be severely conscience stricken and showed in his face that he was angered by this doctrine."[13] Although Fernandez feared the worst, the daimyo did not harm the missionar-ies; more to the point, however, he did not encourage them. This time, they made few converts in Yamaguchi.

On his second visit, which lasted four and a half months from the end of April 1551, Xavier appeared before Yoshitaka in the capacity of an envoy of the highest authorities of Portuguese India, equipped with letters from the governor and the bishop of Goa, bearing exotic pres-ents, and dressed in a splendid costume; that is, he comported with the official station of an ambassador. Yoshitaka was impressed. He responded by publicly posting his permission for the missionaries to preach and for the people to embrace the new religion in his domains. This was no small favor, because those domains at the time spread over all or parts of ten provinces, stretching from Bingo in the east to Hizen in the west.

As a result of the daimyo's evident approval of the missionaries' enterprise, the vacant monastery he had assigned them as their dwell-ing place attracted crowds of the inquisitive, who heard and debated the Jesuits' expositions of their doctrine. Notwithstanding Xavier's

13 Frois, *Historia*, pt. 1, chap. 3, Wicki, vol. 1, pp. 31–2; Matsuda and Kawasaki, trans., *Furoisu Nihonshi*, vol. 6, pp. 54–5.

previously discussed gaffe regarding Dainichi and despite the furious counterattacks of the Buddhist clergy, within two months some five hundred of the curious were converted. Many of the converts were from noble families, "*fidalgos*."[14] This success in Yamaguchi laid the foundation of the policy of reliance on the daimyo that the Jesuits subsequently pursued in their Japanese mission.

That Yoshitaka should have accorded privileges to Xavier was scarcely the product of a whim. Indeed, it might even be maintained that he was predisposed to extend a welcome to this spiritual teacher, even if – or, rather, particularly because – he came from abroad. The Ōuchi family, which itself pretended to a royal Korean ancestry, had a long history of diplomatic and economic relations with Korea and China and a tradition of cultural borrowing from overseas. Moreover, it was their aristocratic aspirations, which involved the patronage of the arts and of religion, that had made the Ōuchi famous in Japan, no less than their military prowess had. Yoshitaka, in particular, was a highly cultivated if eclectic man, one whose interests extended from the military and courtly accomplishments expected of a member of his class to more unusual intellectual pursuits. Gathered about him in Yamaguchi were a good number of the most accomplished litterateurs and religioners of the day. Under their guidance, he not only dabbled in poetry, linked verse, and courtly song but also inquired into philosophy.

Yoshitaka is especially known for his studies of Confucianism. He was trained in the traditional Confucian exegetics of the Kyoto academy, represented in Yamaguchi by such noted scholars as Kiyohara Yorikata (1520 – 90, also known as Kiyohara Ekata) and Ozuki Koreharu (d. 1551), but he was also familiar with Neo-Confucianism, still a relatively new intellectual vogue in Japan. He even charged an embassy to Korea with the mission of obtaining a complete edition of the Five Classics annotated by the great Neo-Confucian philosopher, Chu Hsi. He is known to have spent prodigious sums on Confucian texts, but his enthusiasm for this branch of learning was perhaps expressed best in the lecture series on the Four Books and Five Classics that he instituted in 1546 for his close retainers and palace attendants, giving some of the lessons himself. Buddhism, too, attracted Yoshitaka's interest and support, as did Shinto. His wide range of learning makes Yoshitaka appear an open-minded man, one blessed

14 Xavier to the Jesuits of Europe, dated Couchim, January 29, 1552, *Epistolae*, vol. 2, no. 96, pp. 262–6.

with a genuine intellectual curiosity.[15] That he should have given a hearing to the Christian message therefore appears in character, and that the messenger should have been as great a representative of his culture as Xavier seems entirely fitting.

But the association between the cosmopolitan daimyo Ōuchi Yoshitaka and the foreign missionaries, which seemed to open up such promising prospects to the Jesuits, was not destined to last. Indeed, it came to an end with a bewildering suddenness. Sometime toward the middle of September 1551, Xavier left for Bungo upon the receipt of news that a Portuguese ship had arrived there. A mere two weeks later, on September 30, Yoshitaka committed suicide, caught up in the vortex of a rebellion of his principal vassals led by Sue Takafusa (1521–55, known as Sue Harukata from 1552). To be sure, Padre Cosme de Torres, whom Xavier had left behind in Yamaguchi, escaped harm. Moreover, the regime installed by the rebels continued to treat the Christian missionaries with favor. But the rebellion had shaken the realm of the Ōuchi in its very foundations, and the new regime would fall in less than six years.

Takafusa, who had planned his revolt with the connivance of the Ōuchi family's traditional enemy, Ōtomo Yoshishige of Bungo, invited that daimyo's younger brother Ōtomo Haruhide (d. 1557) to assume the headship of the Ōuchi house (hence Haruhide was known as Ōuchi Yoshinaga from 1553). But this device could not paper over the multiple rifts ingrained in a vast domain where the daimyo's authority had never been properly established. The outlying provinces crumbled away. The realm that Sue Harukata and Ōuchi Yoshinaga themselves had gained by usurpation could not, at length, be defended against the determined attacks of their nominal vassal, the aggressive Sengoku daimyo Mōri Motonari (1497–1571) of Aki Province. When Motonari destroyed Yoshinaga in the spring of 1557, the properties deeded by Yoshinaga to the Jesuits were confiscated and turned over to a Buddhist priest. And that was the end of the mission of Yamaguchi for three decades. It was revived for a few months in 1586 and 1587, resurrected again from 1599 to 1602, and then it was suppressed once more until the modern era.

The protection of the powerful may have been indispensable to the Christian mission in sixteenth-century Japan, and reliance on the daimyo was no doubt an unavoidable policy. The Ōuchi episode

---

15 On Ōuchi Yoshitaka's cultural accomplishments, see Fukuo Takeichirō, *Ōuchi Yoshitaka*, vol. 172 of *Jimbutsu sōsho* (Tokyo: Yoshikawa kōbunkan, 1959), pp. 93–115.

shows, however, what perils inhered in that policy: If the power of the daimyo themselves was never secure, how could they guarantee security to others?

ŌTOMO SŌRIN YOSHISHIGE

The Jesuits had better luck with their next great patron, Ōtomo Yoshishige (known as Sōrin from 1562), who remained consistently sympathetic to them through all the ups and downs of fortune he experienced from his first meeting with Xavier in 1551 to his death in 1587. Yoshishige, too, may be considered a daimyo who was predisposed to accord the foreigners a good welcome. Like his rival Ōuchi Yoshitaka, Sōrin earned a reputation for wide-ranging cultural interests. The great Jesuit missionary and Japanologue João Rodrigues Tçuzzu (1561–1633), a man of many parts who knew Sōrin personally, attests to him a great desire for knowledge, especially in matters of religion, even at the early age of twenty-one, when he first heard Xavier preach Christianity.[16] Rodrigues also notes that Ōtomo was always well disposed toward the Portuguese, treated them with extreme politeness and generosity, and showed publicly the high regard he felt for them. Such displays of affection for the aliens may be regarded as evidence of this ambitious warlord's political vision and diplomatic skills. But his international-mindedness in fact had an internal objective. Sōrin sought to secure his position and expand his influence within Japan by establishing firm ties with an overseas power whose commerce would strengthen him economically and militarily.

A Portuguese ship had visited Bungo as early as 1544 or 1545, in the days of Sōrin's father Yoshiaki, and Portuguese merchants had established what amounted to a trading post in Funai, where the daimyo habitually resided; the trader Diogo Vaz de Aragão stayed there for almost five years, from around 1546 to 1551.[17] For the new daimyo Ōtomo Yoshishige, the arrival of the trading ship of Duarte da Gama and the resultant visit of the missionary Francis Xavier in the autumn of 1551 were a happy conjunction, one that offered him the chance to confirm the association between his house and the Portuguese. When da Gama set sail for India – with Xavier on board –

16 João Rodrigues Tçuzzu SJ, *Historia da Igreja do Japão*, pt. 2, chap. 3, in Doi Tadao et al., trans., *Nihon kyōkai shi*, vol. 2, vol. 10 of *Dai kōkai jidai sōsho* (Tokyo: Iwanami shoten, 1970), pp. 496–8.
17 Ōtomo Sōrin's own reminiscences, cited by Frois, *Historia*, pt. 2, chap. 3, Wicki, vol. 3 (1982), p. 24; Matsuda and Kawasaki, trans., *Furoisu Nihonshi*, vol. 7 (1978), p. 146.

Sōrin made sure to send along an ambassador to the Portuguese governor in Goa, as well as a letter and presents addressed to the king of Portugal himself. The relationship that was established in this way proved to be fruitful both for the daimyo of Bungo and for the Christian mission sponsored by Portugal. It is true that Portuguese ships only called at Bungo four or five times in the decade from 1551 and after that their visits there stopped altogether. On the evidence of no less an authority than Visitator Alexandro Valignano, however, it is known that Sōrin continued, through the mediation of the Jesuit mission superior of Japan, to gain "many advantages and great profit from the ship of the Portuguese," wherever it anchored.[18] It should also be noted that Ōtomo repeatedly wrote to the Portuguese base in Macao for munitions. Unctuous assurances of Sōrin's "hospitality, honours and favour" toward "the things of God" and "the Christians who are in my kingdom" accompany these appeals for arms.[19]

Ōtomo Yoshishige stopped short, however, of falling prostrate before the Jesuits in order to assure himself of profitable contacts with the Portuguese. That would be the expedient chosen by lesser names among the Kyushu daimyo; as for Sōrin, he did not accept baptism until 1578, after twenty-seven long years of flirtation with the missionaries. But in the meantime he did protect their Japanese enterprise. Under his patronage, the Jesuits founded an infant refuge in Funai, one of Bungo's two major towns, in 1555. A hospital run by Irmão Luis de Almeida, who was a skilled physician, was established in the same town in 1557. Indeed, by 1556, when Cosme de Torres moved there from war-torn Yamaguchi and was joined by two other priests and two postulants (irmãos), Funai had become the headquarters of the Christian mission in Japan. Sōrin installed the Jesuits in "some houses made of cedar wood, which were among the best in the country" and even promised them a benefice of five hundred ducats a year,

---

18 Valignano to General SJ, dated Goa, November 23, 1595, cited by Josef Franz Schütte SJ, *Valignanos Missionsgrundsätze für Japan*, vol. 1, pt. 1: *Das Problem (1573–1580)* (Rome: Edizioni di Storia e Letteratura, 1951), p. 328.
19 English translations of two letters from Ōtomo Sōrin to Bishop Belchior Carneiro SJ, dated 9.15 (October 17), 1567, and September 13, 1568, are included in C. R. Boxer, *The Great Ship from Amacon: Annals of Macao and the Old Japan Trade, 1555–1640* (Lisbon: Centro de Estudos Historicos Ultramarinos, 1959), pp. 317–19; for the Portuguese versions, see *Cartas qve os Padres e Irmãos da Companhia de Iesus escreuerão de Iapão & China aos da mesma Companhia da India, & Europa, des do anno de 1549. atè o de 1580.* (Em Euora por Manoel de Lyra. Anno de M.D.XCVIII.), vol. 1., ff. 249v–250. In the first letter, Sōrin asks for "ten piculs of good saltpetre each year," so that "the tyrant of Yamánguchi," namely, Mōri Motonari, may be dispossessed. In the second, he laments the loss in a shipwreck of a cannon being sent to him and urgently requests another.

"although these are not paid over faithfully by the person in charge."[20] Naturally, his advocacy of the Christian cause had the greatest resonance in northern Kyushu, an area that he came to dominate in the course of the ferocious war he fought against Mōri Motonari throughout most of the 1560s. But Sōrin's word on behalf of the Jesuits was heard as far as Kyoto, where he had useful connections at the shogunal court (an establishment that had managed to resettle in its capital in 1559). Sōrin was highly regarded in the councils of the Muromachi bakufu, as is apparent from the honors and titles that the shogunate lavished upon him.

THE BEGINNINGS OF THE CHRISTIAN MISSION IN THE KANSAI AREA

Ōtomo Sōrin's Jesuit protégés benefited from his prestige. The letter of introduction Sōrin is known to have written to an influential person in Kyoto – tentatively identified as Ise Sadataka (d. 1562), the chief (shitsuji) of the bakufu's Administrative Office (Mandokoro) – was most likely the key that opened the shogunate's doors to Padre Gaspar Vilela when the Jesuits in 1559 again conceived the plan to establish a mission in "the metropolis of all Japan and the fountainhead of all their laws." Vilela was received in audience by Shogun Ashikaga Yoshiteru, to whom he was represented as a "priest from Nanban [South Barbary], that is, the regions of India," and one moreover whose ecclesiastical rank was on a level with that of the principal religious dignitaries of Japan. Consequently, the bakufu on an unspecified date in 1560 favored "Bāteren, the priest from the Kirishitan Country," with the issue of a public off-limits notice (kinzei) that protected the missionary from having troops quartered and inappropriate imposts levied on him and prohibited intrusions, discourtesies, and other maltreatment.[21] This shogunal notice amounted to a permission to preach the Christian religion unharmed. With its posting, the Christian mission finally achieved the approbation of a national authority that Xavier had fruitlessly sought to obtain in 1551.

---

20 Padre de Torres SJ to Loyola (Bungo, November 7, 1557), cited in Josef Franz Schütte SJ, *Introductio ad historiam Societatis Jesu in Japonia, 1549–1650* (Rome: Institutum Historicum Soc. Iesu, 1968), p. 551.
21 See Frois, *Historia*, pt. 1, chap. 25, Wicki, vol. 1, pp. 159–63; Matsuda and Kawasaki, trans., *Furoisu Nihonshi*, vol. 3, pp. 76–83, with Matsuda Kiichi's comments on Ise Sadataka, p. 83, nn. 9–11, and the original text of the shogunal *kinzei* in n. 8, pp. 82–3. Cf. Vilela's own retrospective account in a letter to Irmãos SJ in India, dated Sacáy, August 17, 1561, *Cartas*, vol. 1, f. 91.

To be sure, that in itself did not guarantee the Jesuits security in the Kyoto area, let alone the entire country. In the Kinki region – the "Home Provinces" – no less than elsewhere, they had to cultivate the goodwill of the daimyo. This meant dealing with the likes of Miyoshi Nagayoshi and Matsunaga Hisahide (1510–77, also known as Sōtai), those veritable exemplars of gekokujō.

Miyoshi Nagayoshi (Chōkei), the warrior from Awa Province in Shikoku who first led an army to Kyoto in 1539, over the next two decades managed to pursue successfully a truly spectacular obstacle course through history. The stages of his progress, marked with treacheries as much as with acts of valor, led by way of the destruction of Nagayoshi's supposed betters, the Hosokawa and Hatakeyama families, to the establishment of his dominant influence in Awa, Sanuki, and Awaji as well as over the "Five Home Provinces" (Gokinai), namely, Yamashiro, Yamato, Kawachi, Settsu, and Izumi. Matsunaga Hisahide, a person of uncertain provenance, had entered Miyoshi's service by 1541. First, he turned himself into Nagayoshi's indispensable right hand. Eventually, he usurped his master's power. Matsunaga remained the nominal subordinate of Miyoshi and supported his campaigns.[22] But by 1560, when the Jesuit missionary Vilela first came into contact with these two model careerists of Sengoku, Hisahide had become prepotent in the Kinai region.

Vilela met Nagayoshi early in 1560 and obtained from him a patent of privileges similar to the public notice issued by the shogun in the same year.[23] Indeed, Hisahide also appears to have given the same sort of guarantees to the missionary. But Hisahide was, as the Jesuit reports describe him, a fervent adherent of the Hokke sect (also known as the Nichiren sect), a particularly intransigent branch of Buddhism. Hence he was inclined to be sympathetic to the pleas of the Buddhist priesthood of Kyoto when they insisted that the preacher of the foreign religion and his helpers, who had succeeded in making a handful of converts in the city, were subverting hallowed native traditions. Between 1560 and 1562, Buddhist priests and laymen repeatedly petitioned Hisahide to have the padre expelled not only from the city of

---

22 On the relationship between Miyoshi and Matsunaga, see V. Dixon Morris, "The City of Sakai and Urban Autonomy," in George Elison and Bardwell L. Smith, eds., *Warlords, Artists, & Commoners: Japan in the Sixteenth Century* (Honolulu: University of Hawaii Press, 1981), pp. 45–51.
23 See the letter from "Lourenço Iapão" (i.e., the quondam Irmão Lourenço) to the Jesuits of Bungo, dated Miaco, June 2, 1560, *Cartas*, vol. 1, f. 71. Cf. Frois, *Historia*, pt. 1, chap. 34, Wicki, vol. 1, p. 228; Matsuda and Kawasaki, trans., *Furoisu Nihonshi*, vol. 3, p. 129; note that the events described unquestionably took place in 1560, even if Frois's organization (and Wicki's gloss) appear to indicate 1562.

Kyoto itself but also from all the Home Provinces. Their sentiments were endorsed by certain of Matsunaga's samurai retainers, such as Takayama Zusho (d. 1596), the castellan of Sawa in Yamato, who advised his master to determine whether the new doctrine preached by Vilela and his Japanese translator Lourenço indeed countered the Japanese religions, and to "have their heads cut off" if it proved so.[24] Matsunaga decided on an official investigation.

The inquisition, which took place in Nara in the early summer of 1563, had startling results. Charged by Hisahide with establishing what he assumed – the presence of religious pravity – were two of the day's most highly reputed scholars, the astronomer Yūki Yamashiro no Kami Tadamasa and none other than Ōuchi Yoshitaka's former Confucian tutor, Kiyohara Ekata. On the basis of the evidence they heard, both judges accepted the truth of Christianity and requested to be baptized. The delator of the missionaries, Takayama Zusho, also embraced their new religion.

Of the three conversions, Takayama Zusho's was the most important. When this samurai led his entire family to baptism in 1564, he not only committed himself to the service of Japan's early church, but he also introduced into its ranks a young recruit who would become one of its greatest representatives. This recruit was Zusho's – or, to call him by his Christian name, Dom Dario Takayama's – son Ukon (Dom Justo, 1552?–1615). Takayama Ukon would develop into the Jesuits' prize pupil even as he pursued the bloody career of a Sengoku and Momoyama warlord. A striking exception among the Christian daimyo of Japan, he persevered in his faith under persecution. At the beginning of the Tokugawa era, he was exiled from his country for his religious convictions and died on foreign soil, in Manila.

The Kyoto mission's unexpected success was compounded when Yūki Tadamasa's son Yūki Saemon no Jō (Dom Antão), an officer in Miyoshi Nagayoshi's service, not only followed his father into the new religion but was so inspired by the new convert's proverbial zeal that he determined to make proselytes of his fellow samurai in Nagayoshi's castle town of Iimoriyama (now the city of Shijō Nawate, Osaka Prefecture). Toward the end of spring in 1564, Lourenço (a biwa hōshi, or blind jongleur, converted by Xavier) visited Iimoriyama, and the passionate sermons of this experienced public preacher swayed no fewer than seventy-three of Nagayoshi's bushi to become Christians. In-

---

24 See the panegyric on Takayama written by Frois and dated Vsuqui [Usuki], August 20, 1576, Cartas, vol. I, f. 364.

cluded among them were some of Nagayoshi's principal vassals, such as Sanga Hōki no Kami Yoriteru (Dom Sancho), the castellan of the fort at Sanga (now the city of Daitō, Osaka Prefecture), an important strong point in Iimoriyama's outworks.[25]

The baptisms of this elite group were a major breakthrough, as they put the mission of the Kyoto area on a solid footing. Men such as the Yūki, Takayama, and Sanga were to prove true stalwarts of Christianity in the difficult years ahead. They are especially worthy of note because, unlike some of the barons of Kyushu, these samurai were untouched by the motive of temporal profit when they converted. Instead, they appear to have been genuinely moved by the ethos of the Christian religion.

THE SYMBIOSIS OF DAIMYO, MISSIONARIES, AND MERCHANTS

Kyushu, however, remained the main base of Christianity in Japan, and the promise of temporal profit was the enticement consciously used by the Jesuits in their effort to fortify and expand that base. Geography made Kyushu the natural terminus of the trade between China and Japan. The intrusion of the Portuguese into that trade, which they came to monopolize after the main *wakō* bands were dissolved in the late 1550s, presented the missionaries with a golden opportunity that they recognized and exploited.

The assumption shared by all parties was that the Portuguese ships and their cargoes of Chinese silk would bring great profits to whatever Japanese lord managed to attract them permanently to his harbors. The traders, naturally enough, wanted a friendly environment for their commerce; the missionaries were willing and able to act as middlemen in bringing about an amiable arrangement between the Portuguese and the Japanese; the brokerage, apart from various forms of support given the Jesuits by the merchants, would involve the conversion of their common partner, the domanial lord (and, indeed, of his subjects), to Christianity. This equation, first developed in the 1560s, led to a fateful product, the cession of a piece of Japanese territory – the port city of Nagasaki and some of its environs – to the Society of Jesus in 1580.

The potential mutual profit of a trilateral partnership embracing

25 See Frois, *Historia*, pt. 1, chaps. 37–9, Wicki, vol. 1, pp. 245–69; Matsuda and Kawasaki, trans., *Furoisu Nihonshi*, vol. 3, pp. 159–200.

merchants, missionaries, and daimyo had, of course, been apparent even in Xavier's day. It has already been shown that the likes of Shimazu Takahisa and Ōtomo Yoshishige welcomed Xavier not so much out of sympathy with the Christian cause as from susceptibility to the Portuguese ships' allure: They had quickly and correctly identified the padres as likely brokers of influence with their coreligionists, the traders. At the time, however, Takahisa was too big a fish to be landed with the resources available to the missionaries, as indeed was the other great name, Yoshishige. (We should note that the number of Jesuits in Japan did not exceed nine at any time in the 1550s. Not until 1564 did it reach ten.[26]) Nor was Xavier's other Kyushu host, Matsuura Takanobu of Hirado, a good prospect. Tractable enough at first, he soon enough proved to be not only no friend of the Jesuits or their religion but also an extremely awkward customer for the Portuguese traders who came to his anchorages. Not for a decade after Xavier's departure would a genuinely promising target for solicitation be identified among the lords of Kyushu and a proper environment be found for the tripartite symbiosis.

In the meantime, the mission of Kyushu showed little growth. In a year's work beginning in late 1557, Padre Gaspar Vilela is said to have baptized thirteen hundred people on the islands of Ikitsukijima and Takushima and in the other holdings of Matsuura Takanobu's vassal, Dom Antonio Koteda Yasutsune (d. 1580), in the vicinity of Hirado. Even if one includes this considerable mass of new converts, it is unlikely that the number of Christians in Kyushu reached four thousand in that entire decade. To count the converts in Koteda's fiefdom as solid gains may, however, be delusive. The Christian mission there was interrupted after that one year, late in 1558, when Takanobu, objecting to the book burning and destruction of Buddhist images that were part of Vilela's method of evangelization, expelled the padre from the Matsuura territory.[27] No missionary was permitted to reside there for another five years, and it is doubtful that the majority of the neophytes could have sustained their faith during those years.

As he reviewed the faded prospects of the 1550s, Cosme de Torres must indeed have been "very sorry to see how time passed without there coming about any new conversion" of substance, one that would

---

26 See Josef Franz Schütte SJ, ed., *Textus catalogorum Japoniae, 1553–1654, Monumenta Historica Japoniae* I, *Monumenta Missionum Societatis Iesu* 34, *Monumenta Historica Societatis Iesu*, vol. 111 (1975), nos. 1–10, pp. 3–70.
27 Frois, *Historia*, pt. 1, chap. 18, Wicki, vol. 1, pp. 114–16, 121; Matsuda and Kawasaki, trans., *Furoisu Nihonshi*, vol. 6, pp. 188–91, 198.

bring in its train a large-scale catechetical project to which "he could devote the rest of his life." Having been disappointed yet again by Matsuura of Hirado, he sent Irmão Luis de Almeida to explore whether someone else among the barons of western Kyushu might not be persuaded to turn Christian, "by stirring their hopes that the Great Ship (*nao de carreira*) would come to their harbors, were they to have suitable ones." At Almeida's behest, a Portuguese ship's pilot in 1561 conducted secret soundings of Yokoseura (now a part of Saikai-chō, Nagasaki Prefecture), a harbor located at the northern tip of the west Sonogi peninsula and belonging to the territory of Ōmura Sumitada (1533–87). When Yokoseura was found to be a suitable port for the *nao*, Sumitada was approached with the suggestion that if he agreed to turn Christian and "permit the law of God to be preached in his land, great spiritual and temporal profits would follow for him therefrom." Sumitada was apparently more than willing to strike a bargain, for he promised "that he would give the harbor of Yocoxiura itself to the Church, so that a large Christian community might arise there, in whose houses the Portuguese traders and their merchandise could be sheltered securely; and that if the Portuguese would come to the aforesaid harbor, he would exempt them and free them of duties for a period of ten years."[28]

In 1562, the bargain was made perfect when the Jesuits not only arranged for the Great Ship of Pêro Barreto Rolim to come to Yokoseura but also caused another *nao* and a Portuguese junk from Macao to be brought round from Hirado, where they had already berthed, to Sumitada's harbor. Three more Portuguese ships visited Yokoseura in 1563. In late May or early June of that year, Ōmura Sumitada was baptized, taking the Christian name Bartolomeu. Reference works universally call him Japan's first Christian daimyo. Whether the status of a daimyo can be properly attributed to him in 1563 is, however, highly doubtful. Significantly enough, Visitator Alexandro Valignano – a man who knew how to make sharp distinctions – as much as two decades later described Dom Bartolomeu as a *kunishū*, using a term borrowed from the feudal vocabulary of Bungo and meaning the same as *kokujin*, that is, no more than a petty lord or baron.[29] What was it, then, that

28 Frois, *Historia*, pt. 1, chap. 40, Wicki, vol. 1, pp. 270–1; Matsuda and Kawasaki, trans., *Furoisu Nihonshi*, vol. 6, pp. 293–5. Also see Almeida's own report to Irmãos SJ, dated Vocoxiura (Yokoseura), October 25, 1562, *Cartas*, vol. 1, f. 109; and cf. Valignano, *Historia del principio y progresso*, pp. 445–6.

29 Valignano, *Sumario de las cosas de Japon (1583), Adiciones del Sumario de Japon (1592)*, ed. José Luis Alvarez-Taladriz, vol. 1, *Monumenta Nipponica Monographs*, no. 9 (Tokyo: Sophia University, 1954), p. 272; Matsuda Kiichi, Sakuma Tadashi, and Chikamatsu Hiroo, trans.,

enabled Sumitada to rise above his equals among the *kokujin* of Hizen? What laid the groundwork for the Ōmura family's emergence into daimyo status? In the final analysis, it was nothing other than Sumitada's adoption of Christianity.

Before he could claim a favorable outcome, however, Sumitada had to traverse a long, rocky, and perilous path. Apart from the maritime location of his domain in the Sonogi district of Hizen, his resources were few. From the very beginning, his lordship was insecure. By birth a member of the Arima family of Hizen's Takaku region – he was the second son of Arima Haruzumi (1483–1566) – Sumitada succeeded to the Ōmura house by means of adoption. His adoptive father, Ōmura Sumiaki (d. 1551), disinherited his own natural son Matahachirō (b. 1534) in the interest of forming, through Sumitada, an expedient alliance with the Arima. Matahachirō was in turn adopted into the Gotō family, a Hizen military house that had its seat in Takeo, on the borders of Ryūzōji Takanobu's sphere of influence. Better known under the name of Gotō Takaakira, Matahachirō owes his niche in history to his inexorable, but entirely understandable, hostility to the man for whose sake he had lost his heritage. He was the begetter, active accessory, or intended beneficiary of recurrent plots to do away with Sumitada.

The most notorious of those conspiracies is one that fed on the discontent aroused among some of Sumitada's closest liegemen by his conversion to Christianity and came to a climax in a coup de main they tried on his residence in Yokoseura in the late evening of August 15, 1563. The newly baptized Dom Bartolomeu barely escaped this attempt on his life, by fleeing precipitately to the wilderness of Taradake on the Sonogi district's eastern border. For weeks or months, it appeared that he could not recover his lordship. In the train of this violent disturbance that shook Yokoseura, a quarrel erupted between some of the Bungo merchants whom the presence of the foreign ships had attracted there and their Portuguese trading partners. Two or three of the latter were killed, while others fled with their goods to the safety of the vessels lying at anchor.

For a few days, the missionaries Cosme de Torres and Luis Frois found themselves in captivity, held hostage by the Bungo merchants until the Portuguese traders came back ashore to deliver the silks for

Nihon junsatsuki, vol. 229 of *Tōyō bunko* (Tokyo: Heibonsha, 1981), p. 127. Note that Ōmura is ranked only "*among* the principal lords of the realm of Hizen" and that there is a distinct contrast between his status and the higher one of a *yakata* held by his natural brother Arima Yoshisada, who is alternatively described as *rey de Arima*.

which they had already been paid more than sixty thousand cruzados' worth of silver. For three months thereafter, amity appeared to reign again between the Japanese and the Portuguese. Under the stage setting of good business relations, however, hostility continued to smolder until it burst forth in a spectacular finale to this melodrama

In late November, as the Portuguese ships were about to leave for Macao, the antiforeign party set fire to the Christian church and Jesuit house of Yokoseura and burned down the town that the missionaries had invested with the name "Port of Our Lady of Succor."[30] What may be called Japan's first treaty port had flourished for little more than a year. The triple alliance between the lord of the domain, the missionaries, and the merchants had, to all appearances, broken down.

But the deep links of that symbiosis had not, in fact, been dissolved. It was only the external conditions under which its formula had been tested that were inadequate. The essential validity of the equation continued to be recognized by all three concerned parties. Ōmura Sumitada, for one, certainly remained convinced that privileged access to the Portuguese ships and their cargoes was vital to his interests. And he wanted those cargoes – especially the Western firearms brought by the *nao* – kept out of the hands of his enemies, such as the Matsuura of Hirado.

In 1564, disregarding the Jesuits' advice to stay away from Hirado, the Portuguese traders insisted on going there, but they suffered for their pertinacity, losing a substantial part of their goods in a fire allegedly started with the knowledge (if not on the orders) of Matsuura Takanobu. In 1565, however, the Jesuits did manage to persuade Captain-Major Dom João Pereira to steer his Great Ship and its companion galliot to Fukuda in Ōmura Sumitada's domain. True to their *wakō* tradition, the Matsuura of Hirado now conspired with some Sakai merchants to seize the Portuguese ships and goods, mobilized a fleet of some eighty vessels, and attacked the *nao* at its anchorage. The galliot's artillery drove off the assault, inflicting severe casualties on the attackers and demonstrating the superiority of Western weapons. In 1566, when Sumitada was supplied with munitions by the *nao* of Dom Simão de Mendonça anchored at Fukuda, that superiority was proved once again. The weapons from the Great Ship enabled Sumi-

30 "Porto de nossa Senhora da ajuda," as Luis de Almeida calls it in the date of his letter to Irmãos SJ in India, November 17, 1563, *Cartas*, vol. 1, ff. 129–30. Frois describes the affair in his usual dramatic style in *Historia*, pt. 1, chap. 48, Wicki, vol. 1, pp. 333–41; Matsuda and Kawasaki, trans., *Furoisu Nihonshi*, vol. 9 (1979), pp. 95–111.

tada to recover a strategic fort in eastern Sonogi from the forces of his opponents headed by Gotō Takaakira of Takeo, saving Dom Barto-lomeu from a situation in which "there remained for him almost no human hope."[31] With the arms of the "Christian daimyo" blessed in this way, the tripartite relationship was obviously flourishing once again.

THE JESUIT COLONY OF NAGASAKI

Situated on a small bay that is exposed to the Sumō Sea, Fukuda was by 1570 found to be less than an ideal anchorage for the Portuguese ships. Hence the traders from 1571 onward shifted their activities to a more suitable site that lay across the Inasa Hills to the east. The Jesuits had been active at that site since 1568; it was called Nagasaki.

Nagasaki was at the time no more than a group of small and desolate hamlets clustered around the unprepossessing fort of Ōmura Sumi-tada's vassal Nagasaki Jinzaemon Sumikage. It had, however, the ines-timable advantage of being located on a magnificent natural harbor. Within a few years, a settlement of Christians expelled from such places as Hirado and Yamaguchi grew up on this spot, and by 1573, that settlement was surrounded with rudimentary fortifications.[32] Over the next few decades, Nagasaki developed into a prosperous port and a thoroughly Christian city. It would remain both the Christian missionaries' and the Portuguese merchants' main base of operations in Japan until the former were banned in 1614 and the latter expelled in 1639. (To be sure, in the intervening two and a half decades the missionaries continued their work in the city and its surroundings underground.) Even after that, and throughout the Tokugawa era's period of seclusion (1639–1854), Nagasaki continued to be Japan's window to the West, as the Dutch were permitted to maintain a trad-ing factory there from 1641.

The early history of the Christian city of Nagasaki and the continu-ing evolution of the symbiosis of daimyo, missionaries, and merchants were conditioned by the changing tides of war. In the late 1560s, northern Kyushu was the scene of a colossal conflict, as the armies of Ōtomo Sōrin clashed repeatedly with the forces of Mōri Motonari,

31 Frois, *Historia*, pt. 1, chap. 73, Wicki, vol. 2 (1981), p. 153; Matsuda and Kawasaki, trans., *Furoisu Nihonshi*, vol. 9, p. 277. Fukuda, now a part of the city of Nagasaki, is located on the western outskirts of the urban area.
32 Frois, *Historia*, pt. 1, chaps. 98 and 100, Wicki, vol. 2, pp. 377, 391; Matsuda and Kawasaki, trans., *Furoisu Nihonshi*, vol. 9, pp. 360, 387.

who had not only taken over the territories of the fallen power, the Ōuchi family, in western Honshu but had also inherited that family's tradition of interference in Kyushu affairs. In the autumn of 1569, the Mōri forces had to be withdrawn from that island when their home base in Honshu was threatened by the resurgence of scions of their conquered enemies, the houses of Ōuchi and Amako. Motonari's allies in Kyushu capitulated to Sōrin, who took control of Buzen and Chikuzen provinces, and all of northern Kyushu appeared to be in the grasp of the Ōtomo. But Sōrin had failed to checkmate a wily and durable enemy, Ryūzōji Takanobu. The invasion force he sent in 1570 to rout Ryūzōji out of his fortress of Saga in northeastern Hizen was repelled by Takanobu's captain Nabeshima Naoshige (1538–1618). Not only was Sōrin's advance into Hizen stopped by the failure of this expedition, but Takanobu also was freed by his victory to direct his attention to areas that lay to the west of his territory. Subduing or intimidating the likes of Gotō Takaakira, Matsuura Takanobu, and Arima Harunobu (1567?–1612), Ryūzōji in the course of the 1570s came to dominate Hizen.

Takanobu's ascendancy over Hizen greatly complicated the situation of Ōmura Sumitada, who had been hard pressed just to maintain himself even before the rise of this powerful new adversary. Between 1572 and 1574, Sumitada was beleaguered and nearly destroyed by a confederation of external and internal enemies led by his brother-in-law, the baron Saigō Sumitaka of Isahaya. His plight was made desperate when the Great Ship of 1573 was lost at sea, robbing Dom Bartolomeu of sorely needed sustenance and convincing his opponents that he had been "deprived of the strength to resist them."[33] Sumitada was saved from this deadly threat, however, when no fewer than four Portuguese ships came to his assistance in 1574. Under the stimulus of this latest close escape and seeking to ascertain himself of further relief and reinforcement, he decided to stake all on the Portuguese card. But that necessitated, in turn, a forceful demonstration of his bona fides to his Western allies.

The chronicler Luis Frois notes that Sumitada appreciated perfectly that "only the Christians, for all their small number, had stayed loyal to him in the hour of his greatest need." Hence Ōmura was entirely susceptible to the arguments of Padre Gaspar Coelho, the combative superior of the Jesuits' mission in western Kyushu, who importuned

33 Frois, *Historia*, pt. 1, chap. 98, Wicki, vol. 2, p. 380; Matsuda and Kawasaki, trans., *Furoisu Nihonshi*, vol. 9, pp. 365–6.

CHRISTIANITY AND THE DAIMYO

Dom Bartolomeu to repay the "great obligations" he had incurred to God for "freeing him of his enemies." The best way for Sumitada to do so, Coelho insisted, was by undertaking to "extinguish totally the worship and veneration of the idols in his lands" and to ensure, by the "universal conversion of his vassals," that "not a single pagan remained" there.[34]

According to another Jesuit who was fully familiar with the Ōmura mission, Padre Afonso de Lucena, Dom Bartolomeu achieved this goal admirably, after having "ordered and required all to become Christian, and those who did not want to do so should leave the land. And so those whom God did not call to Holy Baptism quitted Ōmura and exiled themselves to other lands with pagan lords."[35] Although neither Frois nor Lucena says so, these were the familiar, contemporary Iberian methods for ensuring political unity and ideological purity by means of Catholic uniformity. So that Christianity could flourish, traditional religious beliefs had to be extirpated among the populace, and the symbols of the native faith destroyed. Accordingly, beginning in November 1574, Buddhist temples and Shinto shrines were burned or demolished throughout the Ōmura domain. In this way, some sixty thousand of Dom Bartolomeu's subjects were indeed made Christian.

This was the realization of Cosme de Torres's dream and Gaspar Coelho's plan, the first "universal conversion" of a feudal domain in Japan. To be sure, according to the Jesuit missionaries themselves, it took years before this mass of converts, who had been forcibly brought to baptism, could be made fit to receive the other sacraments. For all that, Ōmura did become a stalwart Christian territory. It remained the very heartland of the Jesuits' Japanese mission until 1606, when Dom Bartolomeu's son and successor Ōmura Yoshiaki (Dom Sancho, 1568–1616), piqued at what he construed as the Jesuits' intrigues against his interests in Nagasaki, expelled them from his domain and himself abandoned the Christian religion for Buddhism. For years after that, however – although "almost all of the most noble among his retainers" had followed Dom Sancho into apostasy[36] – large portions of the populace of the Ōmura domain continued to practice Christianity.

---

34 Frois, *Historia*, pt. 1, chap. 104, Wicki, vol. 2, p. 424; Matsuda and Kawasaki, trans., *Furoisu Nihonshi*, vol. 10 (1979), pp. 9–10.

35 Padre Afonso de Lucena SJ, *Erinnerungen aus der Christenheit von Ōmura: De algumas cousas que ainda se alembra o Pᵉ Afonso de Lucena que pertencem à Christandade de Ōmura* [1578–1614], ed. and trans. Josef Franz Schütte SJ, *Bibliotheca Instituti Historici S.I.*, vol. 34 (Rome: Institutum Historicum S.I., 1972), pp. 96–7.

36 Padre Mattheus de Couros SJ to General SJ, *annua* dated Nagasaki, February 22, 1617, cited in Lucena, *Erinnerungen*, p. 268, n. 124.

The reduction of the populace of his domain to one common religious denomination did not, however, solve Ōmura Sumitada's external problems. Ryūzōji Takanobu, in particular, kept up the pressure on Ōmura, whose territory he invaded in 1577 and 1578. By 1580, it had become apparent that Sumitada could not continue indefinitely to resist Ryūzōji's overwhelming force and that he must, at length, submit to Takanobu as his liege. Neither Sumitada nor the missionaries, however, could countenance the "pagan" Ryūzōji's taking possession of Nagasaki (that is, establishing himself in control of the base of the Portuguese trade that sustained both Dom Bartolomeu and his Jesuit mentors) as he subjected Ōmura to fealty. The solution formulated jointly by Sumitada and the highest Jesuit authority on the scene, Visitator Alexandro Valignano – it is difficult to say who took the initiative – was the cession of Nagasaki to the Society of Jesus. If Sumitada could not retain possession of Nagasaki, then neither would Takanobu obtain it.

In real terms, the resulting "Donation of Bartolomeu" meant that Ōmura surrendered territorial sovereignty over the invaluable harbor and its environs to the Jesuits, instead of losing it willy-nilly to Ryūzōji. In doing so, he not only made certain that Portuguese ships would continue to call regularly at Nagasaki, a port that his donation had in a literal sense made a bastion of Christianity, but he also safeguarded for himself a substantial flow of income from the trade of those ships: Part of the deal was that the Jesuits were to be given the ships' anchorage fees (seven hundred to two thousand cruzados annually), but Sumitada would continue to collect the tariff duties on the goods that passed through the harbor. These tariffs amounted to several thousand cruzados each year. The Ōmura officials who collected those dues were pledged by the terms of the donation not to "intrude into any matter touching upon the jurisdiction or upon the government" of the place.[37]

The conveyance of cession that surrendered Nagasaki and the strategic neighboring locality of Mogi to the Society of Jesus "for always" was signed by Ōmura Sumitada and his son Yoshiaki on Tenshō 8.4.27 (June 9, 1580). On an unspecified date in 1580, Sumitada and his suite of relatives and retainers – the chief men of the Ōmura region – traveled to Saga, where they bound themselves in vassalage to Ryūzōji

37 More detail on the "Donation of Bartolomeu," including a translation of the Spanish text of Ōmura's conveyance of cession, may be found in George Elison, *Deus Destroyed: The Image of Christianity in Early Modern Japan* (Cambridge, Mass.: Harvard University Press, 1973), pp. 94–101; see pp. 98–9 on the fortification of the "Church domain."

Takanobu. The Jesuits were left with full administrative and judicial sovereignty in Nagasaki and Mogi "with all the terrains and arable lands that appertain thereto." It cannot be overemphasized that in accepting the donation, they assumed *capital* jurisdiction over their new domain. In the conveyance, Dom Bartolomeu states explicitly that the "Padres of the Society may put as captain over the said place whomsoever they please, and remove him from his charge; and to whomever they select I give the faculty, that he may kill and exercise all the justice necessary for the good government of the land and for the chastisement of those that should break the laws thereof."

How did the Jesuits propose to defend these responsibilities? No doubt they knew that Portuguese guns cast a long shadow, and they counted on the ambitious daimyo of Kyushu to be wary of those guns. But Nagasaki, contrary to what is sometimes asserted, never became a Portuguese colony. Instead, it was for a few years a Jesuit colony. Ultimately, the security of the missionaries' presence there depended on the degree to which whatever Japanese lord held the ascendancy over that region believed that advantages would accrue to him or the merchants patronized by him from the priests' mediation with the Portuguese. At the start of their tenure, however, the Jesuits were determined to hold on to their Japanese enclave by force of arms if need be. That much is evident from the orders Valignano gave on June 24, 1580, to fortify it militarily "in a manner to withstand any attack."

Hence "not only Nagasaki, the harbor of the *nao*, but also Mogi, which covers the Christian areas of [western Kyushu], Ōmura and Arima" were to be "protected with forts and equipped with munitions, weapons, and artillery." It may be true that such an elaborate system of defenses never came into existence, but even the *Apologia*, a polemical tract that Valignano wrote in 1598, eighteen years after he issued these orders, admits the construction of earthworks and their armament with five or six pieces of light artillery. (In actuality, a solid circumferential wall and bulwarks had been erected by 1581.) In short, the Jesuits made military plans and did not fail to act on them. They behaved *de facto* as what they indeed were *de jure:* a sovereign power (even if a small power) on Kyushu soil. This was the seedbed of their subsequent difficulties.

The Jesuits' jurisdiction over Nagasaki was a product of the peculiar state of political fragmentation that characterized Sengoku Japan. They had a chance of retaining their dominion as long as that state prevailed. But Sengoku was about to come to an end. The 1580s were the last decade of the century of universal conflict that had rent Japan to pieces. Even as rout continued in Kyushu, regeneration was well under way in central Japan, where the first of the great unifiers, Oda Nobunaga (1534–82), was putting the dismembered body politic back together by force. One of the principal items among his agenda was the elimination of the independent religious establishments that had developed into secular powers in the chaos of late medieval Japan. Indeed, the subjection of religious institutions to central hegemonic control was a major part of the general agenda of reunification.

The greatest triumph of that policy of subjugation had already been sealed two and a half weeks before Ōmura Sumitada deeded Nagasaki to the Jesuits: On May 22, 1580, Kennyo Kōsa (1543–92), the pontiff of the "religious monarchy" of the Honganji, the major branch of the Buddhist True Pure Land sect (Jōdo Shinshū), capitulated to Oda Nobunaga after a sanguinary ten years' war and went into exile. A few months later, on September 10, the great temple fortress of that sect, the Ishiyama Honganji in Osaka, was burned, and the most prominent Japanese symbol of the combined exercise of religious and secular authority thereby was destroyed.

Even if Nobunaga's power never did extend to Kyushu, that of his two great successors would. Hence it would be wise to recall that none of the "Three Heroes" of Japan's reunification – Nobunaga, Toyotomi Hideyoshi, and Tokugawa Ieyasu (1543–1616) – had any tolerance for the type of institution that the "Church domain" of Nagasaki was. Indeed, they all spent significant parts of their careers in fighting such institutions.

Against that historical background, it appears entirely logical that Hideyoshi, in the course of subjugating Kyushu to his central regime in 1587, should have objected to the Jesuits' pretensions to authority, their compacts with daimyo, and their forced conversions. These objections constituted the stuff of his indictment of the "Padres of the Society" and formed the rationale for the edicts he issued banning the missionaries. For them, the clear message of Hideyoshi's conquest of Kyushu was this: Sengoku had come to an end, and with it, the Jesuits' freedom of action had ended.

CHRISTIAN ADVANCES IN KYUSHU

Neither the extent to which Japan would be transformed by the Three Heroes in the coming decades nor the dire consequences that vast transformation would have on Japanese Christianity could be predicted by the Jesuits as they took possession of Nagasaki in 1580. They knew that their Japanese mission faced many difficulties, but on the whole they had reason to believe that it promised success. To be sure, they had experienced problems in settling on a mission method that would be rigorously orthodox and at the same time accommodative to Japanese customs, but those problems, caused in large part by the intransigence of their Japan Superior, Padre Francisco Cabral – a castebound Portuguese *fidalgo* of the most dour sort – were about to be resolved by the suave and politic Visitator Valignano, who dismissed Cabral from his charge in 1581. The mission's economic difficulties persisted, but they were eased substantially by the agreement Valignano had negotiated in 1578 with the city of Macao, which gave the Jesuits a fixed share in the cargoes of Chinese silk shipped annually by the Portuguese from Macao to Japan.

This direct involvement in commerce was, strictly speaking, inappropriate for members of a religious order, but the dearth of other reliable sources of income made it a necessity for the Jesuits, even if it involved severe risks. In 1582, for instance, eight thousand cruzados of the capital they had invested in silk – and, even more to the point, four thousand in expected profit – sank along with the large junk belonging to Bartolomeu Vaz Landeiro which was lost off the southwestern coast of Taiwan.[38] For all its risks and its unseemliness, however, this commercial venture appeared to be the only practical means of sustaining the Japanese mission's expansion and financing the ambitious institutional improvements planned by Valignano.

The mission was indeed expanding. As of the end of the year 1581, there were sixty-four members of the Society of Jesus in Japan, including twenty Japanese *irmãos* (at least eleven of these Japanese were actively engaged in preaching Christian doctrine, and six were novices undergoing probation). In addition, seven European Jesuits assigned to the Japan mission were in Macao, waiting to board ship for their final destination. Administratively, these missionaries constituted a vice-province of the Society (Padre Gaspar Coelho was the vice-provincial, with his seat in Nagasaki), which was divided into three main mission areas: Bungo, Shimo (that is, western Kyushu, including the Arima and the Ōmura regions, Hirado, and the Amakusa Islands), and Miyako (that is, Kyoto, the five "Home Provinces" of the Kinai, and the neighboring region; Padre Organtino Gnecchi-Soldo, the superior of this area, resided in Oda Nobunaga's

38 Ibid., pp. 101–6; and Boxer, *The Great Ship from Amacon*, p. 44. Valignano's own assessment of the problem of financing the Japanese mission may be found in *Sumario de las cosas de Japon*, vol. 1, chap. 29, pp. 331–9; Matsuda et al., trans., *Nihon junsatsuki*, pp. 148–53.

castle town of Azuchi). About 150,000 Christians were under their spiritual care.[39]

A considerable boost was given the number of their converts when Amakusa Shigehisa (baptized Miguel in 1571, d. 1582), a baron in the orbit of the Shimazu of Satsuma who had his main residence at Kawachi no Ura on one of the Amakusa Islands, was persuaded in 1577 to undertake the wholesale Christianization of his subjects. In the typical manner of such enterprises, the "bonzes" (bōzu, Buddhist priests) of Shigehisa's domain were confronted with the choice of either turning Christian or leaving Amakusa. Buddhist temples were destroyed, and churches arose in their place. In quick order, all of Dom Miguel's subjects, "ten or twelve thousand souls," submitted to baptism.[40]

An even greater advance came with the conversion of Arima Harunobu, the lord of the Takaku region of Hizen. Harunobu's father Yoshisada (Dom André, 1521–76), baptized in April 1576, had in little more than half a year brought about the conversion of more than twelve thousand of his subjects. After Dom André's death that same December, however, there followed a persecution in Arima. His successor Harunobu and his principal vassals "expelled the Padres, hewed down the crosses, burned the church, and forced the Christians of their region to apostatize."[41] But Harunobu, like his uncle Ōmura Sumitada, was the target not only of internal rebellions but also of external aggression on the part of the powerful Ryūzōji Takanobu; hence he, too, was susceptible to the lure of military assistance. The Jesuits appreciated and utilized that susceptibility. Indeed, when Valignano steered the Great Ship of 1579, a nao belonging to Leonel de Brito, to the port of Kuchinotsu in the Arima domain, he did so with the direct intention of inducing Arima Harunobu to favor Christianity.

The Jesuit chronicler Luis Frois tells us that early in 1580, as Arima's last forts were either in flames or under siege, Padre Alexandro Valignano, eager to keep Harunobu from "despairing entirely," ordered that "succor be given the fortresses that were under fire." Making sure to "provision them with victuals and some silver, as much as he could," Valignano also supplied them with "lead and

39 On the number of Jesuits in Japan, see Textus catalogorum Japoniae, no. 20, pp. 120–7. On the number of Christians, see the chart set out by Schütte in Introductio ad historiam Societatis Jesu in Japonia, pp. 429–30.
40 Frois, Historia, pt. 1, chap. 81, Wicki, vol. 2, p. 231; Matsuda and Kawasaki, trans., Furoisu Nihonshi, vol. 9, p. 321.
41 Valignano to General SJ, Kuchinotsu, December 10, 1579, cited in Schütte, Valignanos Missionsgrundsätze, vol. 1, pt. 1, p. 401.

saltpeter, of which he had laid in a good stock from the *nao* for this purpose (*para este effeito*)." Close to six hundred cruzados – a great sum, in view of the parlous state of the Jesuits' finances – were expended in these matters.

But there were dividends. According to Frois, the intelligence that Harunobu could suddenly avail himself of excellent munitions and provisions – thanks to the "aid that the Padre had given and would continue to give him" – impressed Ryūzōji Takanobu so much that he totally lost the confidence of being able to take the fortress of Arima and withdrew. Shortly before Easter, April 3, 1580, Arima Harunobu in turn let Valignano baptize him, taking the Christian name Protasio. The balance sheet for the three months spent by Valignano in Arima was as follows:

All the temples of their *camis* and *fotoques* [gods and Buddhas] were broken up and destroyed – more than forty of them, large and small, among them some of the most beautiful and renowned in all Japan; and all the bonzes either turned Christian or left [Dom Protasio's] lands. And apart from those who newly came to Holy Baptism, there rose again in these lands of Arima more than seven thousand souls, those that had either fallen in the persecutions of the previous years or had been living without Padres, without churches, and without doctrine. . . . The bonzes were married, the idols were broken up, and the number of converts grows day by day.

As Frois notes additionally, from this destruction of Shinto shrines and Buddhist temples "there were salvaged some remnants for the profit of the church," because Dom Protasio, "in accordance with a request" from Valignano, donated "the most important temples and their sites" for Jesuit projects.[42]

The buildings of one such temple were converted into the Jesuits' first formal educational institution in Japan, the boys' preparatory school known as the Arima *seminario*, which Valignano called into existence some time before the end of June 1580. By October, the school had enrolled twenty-two pupils, children of noble houses from all over Kyushu; most of them were eventually to enter the Society of Jesus.[43] Among the populace, too, the work of Christianization proceeded apace, and by the beginning of 1582, some twenty thousand Christians could be counted in the Arima domain.

With the contiguous territories of Ōmura, Arima, and Amakusa

42 Frois, *Historia*, pt. 2, chap. 20, Wicki, vol. 3, pp. 145, 149; Matsuda and Kawasaki, trans., *Furoisu Nihonshi*, vol. 10, pp. 160, 165–6.
43 José Alvarez-Taladriz provides a list of the pupils enrolled in the Arima *Seminario* between 1580 and 1583 in *Sumario de las cosas de Japon*, vol. 1, chap. 4, n. 75, pp. 85–8.

converted, a Christian bloc seemed to be coming into existence in the "Shimo" mission area. Although Arima Harunobu's motives for conversion appear questionable, in his long subsequent career as a daimyo he proved a staunch supporter of Christianity. Under his patronage, Takaku developed into a solidly Christian region, one where the practice of the Christian faith continued, resisting extinction to the uttermost, even after being driven underground by the general persecution pursued in earnest by the Tokugawa regime after 1614. No wonder that in 1637 and 1638, Arima and Amakusa became the scene of the so-called Shimabara Rebellion, a peasant uprising heavily colored with the tones of a millenarian Christianity.

THE VICISSITUDES OF BUNGO

Meanwhile, how did the cause of the missionaries fare in Bungo, their other major area of activity in Kyushu? For all of Ōtomo Sōrin's constant show of favor to the Jesuits, they were not held in high regard in his domain. As many as two thousand of the populace may have been baptized as early as the 1550s, but for a long time the upper levels of society remained barren ground for the seed of Christianity. In almost a quarter-century from Xavier's visit to Bungo's provincial capital, Funai, the Jesuits managed to convert no more than one member of its nobility, a man they had cured of a disease. Apparently, their works of charity among the distressed and downtrodden, such as the leper ward of their hospital in Funai, had if anything put them in disrepute among the upper crust – "a great impediment," Padre Francisco Cabral noted dyspeptically, "to the growth of Christianity."[44]

The missionaries' prospects changed markedly for the better only after Sōrin's second son, the fourteen-year-old Chikaie, was baptized at Christmastime 1575 at the behest of his father, taking the name Sebastião. A number of young samurai followed Chikaie's example, and the Christian religion began to gain esteem in Bungo. But greater things were yet to come. In 1578, Sōrin himself was converted.

Curiously enough, a marital problem and an extramarital affair formed the direct background of Sōrin's decision to become Christian. The wife he had taken in 1550, with whom he had three sons and five daughters, was a passionate adherent of Shinto and Buddhism and no friend of Christianity, as perhaps befitted a daughter of the grand

---

44 Padre Francisco Cabral SJ to General SJ, Kuchinotsu, September 9, 1576, cited in Schütte, *Valignanos Missionsgrundsätze*, vol. 1, pt. 1, pp. 288–9.

priest (*daigūji*) of the Nada Hachiman Shrine, one of the two most important Shinto sanctuaries in Bungo. Naturally, she was loathed by the Jesuits, who painted her in the most garish colors in their writings. Depicting her as a malicious and relentless opponent of all their pious designs, they made sure that they perpetuated her image as that of a righteous ruler's perverse consort: The only name by which she is known in history is the highly descriptive nickname they used every time they referred to her in their propaganda, "Jezebel."

According to Frois, by the beginning of 1578 this virago had driven her husband ill with her violent temper. Hence Sōrin sought consolation from a noblewoman who served "Queen Jezebel" as her chief lady-in-waiting. We are assured that it was not this court lady's comeliness – "which she did not have, for she was already a woman of forty" – that attracted the ailing "king of Bungo" but, rather, her spiritual qualities, the dedication with which she nursed him on his sickbed, and her excellent sense of how to manage a household; moreover, she was already related to him by marriage, as her daughter was the wife of Sōrin's son Sebastião. In any event, Sōrin abandoned the termagant "Jezebel," left his residential castle in Usuki for a seaside villa in a nearby spot called Gomiura, and one night ordered the lady "to be taken secretly from the palace [to Gomiura], where he kept her as his wife."

Removed from "Jezebel's" poisonous influence, the two could freely hear Christian instruction. First the lady was converted, receiving the name Julia in baptism. (At the same time her daughter was baptized, taking the name Cointa.) Then Sōrin quit the practice of Zen meditation, was tutored on the prerequisites and the obligations of a Christian marriage, accepted the truth of Christianity, and was baptized on August 28, 1578, with the name Francisco. The two could now properly be admitted to the sacrament of matrimony; "Jezebel" was no impediment, as she was an unregenerate pagan.

Frois, who was at the time in question the superior of the mission area of Bungo, tells this astonishing story demurely.[45] He has every intention of justifying Sōrin. Even this tendentious chronicler refers, however, to the great scandal that was aroused by Sōrin's actions among "Jezebel's" relatives and party takers; and some of these, such as her brother Tawara Chikakata, the head of the Tawara family (one of the three principal cadet branches of the house of Ōtomo), ranked

---

45 Frois, *Historia*, pt. 2, chaps. 2 and 3, Wicki, vol. 3, pp. 12–28; Matsuda and Kawasaki, trans., *Furoisu Nihonshi*, vol. 7, 128–55; quotations from p. 13 and p. 129, respectively.

among the highest grandees of the Bungo realm. This sort of affair was the stuff of legend. Looking at it and other real or imagined scandals from their own perspective, the Japanese chroniclers of the Edo period saw grounds to depict Ōtomo Sōrin as a selfwilled tyrant and a degraded, crapulent lecher.

The Jesuits, however, heroized their "good King Francisco of Bungo" as the ideal ruler. To them, his conversion was a triumph, one that was celebrated throughout their establishments in Portuguese Asia with high masses, edifying sermons, and solemn processions. In Cochin, for instance, it was the subject of a festive dramatic representation that aroused feelings of "gratification, exultation, and devotion." It was there that Matteo Ricci, a young missionary on his way to the memorable palaces of China, wrote that he and his friends all were filled with the hope that with Sōrin's baptism, "not only all his kingdoms, which number five or six, will be converted, but all of Japan."[46] As far as these optimists were concerned, this was a reasonable expectation. For all they knew, "King Francisco" was still at the zenith of his power, prepotent in Kyushu, one of the mightiest rulers in Japan. They were unaware that their triumph was but the prelude to a disaster.

At the beginning of the year 1578 (the time of Sōrin's break with "Jezebel"), a grave new strategic threat developed on the southeastern flank of the Ōtomo realm. This threat was the rise of the house of Shimazu, which had been plagued for a century by tumults among its own collaterals, nominal vassals, and the refractory *kokujin* of Satsuma and Ōsumi. By the middle of the 1570s, the Shimazu had managed to subject the barons of those two provinces to fealty. Under the leadership of the consolidator of the authority of his house, Yoshihisa (1533–1611, r. 1566–87 as daimyo), they then embarked on an ambitious program of expansion that was to transform the entire political complexion of Kyushu.

The first external target of the Shimazu was their old enemy, the Itō family of Hyūga, which had gained preeminence in that province during their time of troubles. By January 1578, the armies of Shimazu Yoshihisa and his brother Yoshihiro (1535–1619) had conclusively defeated the levies of the Itō, forcing the young head of that house, Yoshikata (1567–98), to flee Hyūga and seek the assistance of his maternal relatives, the Ōtomo. Sōrin had retired as daimyo in 1576,

---

46 Padre Manoel Teixeira SJ to General SJ, dated Cochym, January 30, 1580, *Documenta Indica* XI (1577–80), ed. Josef Wicki SJ, in *Monumenta Historica Societatis Iesu*, vol. 103 (1970), no. 110, p. 802; Padre Matteo Ricci SJ to Padre Martino de Fornari SJ, dated Coccino, January 30, 1580, ibid., no. 118, p. 847.

passing on the rulership of his great domain to his eldest son, Yoshimune (1558–1605). But the Ōtomo were more than willing to help the Itō. Rising to the challenge of the Shimazu, they decided on a massive intervention. A new daimyo eager to prove himself, Yoshimune in the late spring of 1578 sent into Hyūga an army variously estimated as forty thousand or sixty thousand strong.

To intervene in this way was not a wise decision. For one thing, committing such a large force to the south laid bare the Ōtomo realm's western frontiers, which could never be considered safe from Ryūzōji Takanobu's grasping reach. For another, it also exposed the north, if not to the risk of being invaded again by the Mōri (who had their hands full at the time trying to fight off Oda Nobunaga), then to the danger of destructive forays by lesser names among the independent barons and disaffected vassals of that area, such as Akizuki Tanezane (1545–96) of Chikuzen and Tsukushi Hirokado (1556–1623) of Chikugo.

At the start, however, the Ōtomo campaign in Hyūga went well. Between the Bungo border and the Mimikawa, a river that flows into the Hyūga Sea about one-third of the way down the long coastline of the invaded province, the only adherent of the Shimazu to put up serious opposition to the Ōtomo was Tsuchimochi Chikanari, the lord of Matsuo Castle in what is now the city of Nobeoka. On May 16, 1578, Matsuo Castle fell; Chikanari, who was captured alive, was forced to disembowel himself. To make certain that everyone understood that the Tsuchimochi territory had new masters, Sōrin and Yoshimune "ordered that the monasteries and temples of the *camis* and *fotoques* located there should be burned and laid waste; and so it was being done" when Sōrin himself – a Christian, it will be recalled, only since August (Yoshimune would not submit to baptism until 1587) – decided in October of that year to move to that territory and build there a model Christian community.[47]

Accompanied by his wife Julia, by the Japan Superior of the Jesuits Padre Francisco Cabral, and by three hundred Christian samurai, Sōrin settled his new residence at Mushika (now part of the city of Nobeoka). His plan was to found here a city that would be "ruled with new laws and institutions, different from those of Japan." This city would be the center of a province transformed into Utopia: "So that the natives of Fiunga [Hyūga] could form a more perfect union" with

---

47 Frois, *Historia*, pt. 2, chap. 2, Wicki, vol. 3, pp. 18–19, 38–40; Matsuda and Kawasaki, trans., *Furoisu Nihonshi*, vol. 7, pp. 135–6, 168, 170.

Sōrin and his people, "they would all have to become Christians and live with each other in brotherly love and concord." This may appear to be a more radically formulated policy than that of the other "Christian daimyo," but the methods used to attain the goal of Christian unity were to be the same.

To ensure that the new conquest of the Ōtomo would indeed be "ruled and governed according to the laws and customs of Europe," the "good King Francisco," encouraged by the missionaries, sought to make a clean sweep of the places of worship and the sacred images of Japanese religion in Hyūga. In Bungo, too, Sōrin ordered Shinto shrines and Buddhist temples to be destroyed. But Hyūga seems to have been a special case. The Christian neophyte Sōrin and his Jesuit mentors felt the need to be especially zealous and demonstrative in their work of demolition there, "because of the extraordinary veneration enjoyed by the *camis* and the cult of the *fotoques* in that land."

Throughout the territory occupied by the Ōtomo, those Buddhist priests who had not fled to other parts but had chosen to stay (although left "without their old benefices and reputation") had good reason to go about "downcast and disconsolate, their temples and their dwellings demolished, and their idols pulled down." But Sōrin's "holy enterprise" (*santo exercicio*) was brought to an abrupt end by an event that was unforeseen by the missionaries as totally as it was unexpected by the Ōtomo. Instead of conquering all Hyūga as they planned, the Ōtomo suffered a crushing defeat at the hands of the Shimazu. Before the year 1578 was out, Sōrin and his entourage of Jesuits had to flee Mushika, as whatever was left of the Ōtomo armies streamed back to Bungo in disorder.

The plural must be used in speaking of the "Ōtomo armies," as it is clear that one is discussing uncoordinated troop units led onward by constantly bickering rival captains, rather than an integrated body of men under the firm command of a single general in chief. It is remarkable that neither the daimyo Yoshimune – who lingered on in Notsu, no more than twelve kilometers (about 7.5 miles) from his home base of Usuki, instead of proceeding to the front – nor the "good King Francisco," who busied himself about his never-never *civitas Dei* in Mushika, was with those troops as they closed with the enemy. Instead, the man who presided over their march to the shambles was "Jezebel's" brother Tawara Chikakata, whom Western and Japanese sources with rare unanimity call an incompetent at the art of war and a coward. And yet, not having encountered much opposition along the way, the Ōtomo forces were full of confidence (and off their guard) as they debouched into the open ground of the river Omarugawa, the dividing line between northern and southern Hyūga.

There their progress was blocked by the fortress called Takajō (located in what is now Kijō-chō, Miyazaki Prefecture). An assault on the castle failed, due largely to the lack of unity and order among the captains of the attackers; they then agreed to settle down to a siege. Unfortunately for them and their soldiers, they neglected to take the elementary precaution of securing their flanks and rear. The while, unscouted and unrecognized by Bungo's captains, two strong formations of Shimazu troops, led by the daimyo Yoshihisa's brothers Yoshihiro and Iehisa (d. 1587), advanced to the relief of Takajō.

On December 10, 1578 (Tenshō 6.11.12), Yoshihiro's and Iehisa's pincers closed about the hapless forces of the Ōtomo. Twenty thousand of Sōrin's and Yoshimune's men are usually said to have perished in the ensuing slaughter. That figure may be exaggerated, as the number of the common soldiers (zōhyō) who lost their lives could only be estimated. It is known, however, that as many as three thousand men-at-arms (that is, heavy-armed and mounted samurai, hitakabuto) were either slain on this battleground or drowned in the eddies of the torrential Mimikawa River as they sought to escape. Among those who suffered death were a dozen top-ranking captains, but their general Tawara Chikakata, who was reported killed, had in fact managed to run away; he would reappear in Bungo more than a month after his defeat. The fearsome magnitude of the rout that overcame the "seven-province host of the Ōtomo" and the great and terrible extent of its killing ground may be surmised by considering that although the encounter began at Takajō on the Omarugawa, the running action continued as far as the Mimikawa, which flows some twenty-five kilometers (15.5 miles) to the north. Hence this great combat is known in history as the battle of Mimikawa.

The missionaries sought to find a meaning for the disaster that had befallen their patron "King Francisco" and his cause in the "lofty and mysterious judgments" of God. Luis Frois, for one, evidently thought that he had an insight into those judgments. As far as he was concerned, the chief cause of that disaster was God's desire to "punish the people of Bungo" for their sins, which "had accumulated to an extent that God could no longer choose to ignore."[48] Using a diametrically opposite line

48 Ibid., chap. 10, pp. 70–1 and p. 220, respectively. This chapter is a fine illustration of the dramatic bravura of the Counter-Reformation historian Frois. The passionate tirade on the faults of Bungo's captains is followed up by a truly magnificent, venomous indictment of Tawara Chikakata.

of reasoning, the "pagan" survivors of Mimikawa reached a similar-sounding conclusion regarding the main cause of their downfall. They, too, blamed the Christian God. Unlike the Jesuits, however, they heaped obloquy on his adherents. Prominent among those who blamed the Jesuits for all of Bungo's woes was the revenant Tawara Chikakata, but he was joined by many other peers of the dominions of the Ōtomo. The concerns and sentiments of those traditionalists are expressed most eloquently in the remonstrance that Sōrin's great vassal Tachibana Dōsetsu (1513?–85) addressed to a group of elders of the Ōtomo realm on Tenshō 8.2.16 (March 1, 1580).[49]

As the keeper of Tachibana Castle in Chikuzen (located in what is now Shingū-machi, immediately to the northeast of present-day Fukuoka), Dōsetsu was the guardian of that realm's northwestern reaches: His fortress was the cornerstone of the entire Ōtomo position in the perimeter that extended from Higo through Chikuzen into Buzen. Accordingly, Dōsetsu had to bear the full brunt of the consequences of the defeat in Hyūga, as the news of Mimikawa brought on a wave of defections from the ranks of Ōtomo vassals in that wide area. The perimeter crumbled.

There was no doubt that Sōrin's infatuation with Christianity at the expense of the traditional religious beliefs, practices, and institutions of the warrior class had exacerbated the retainers' disaffection from the Ōtomo. Hence Dōsetsu sounds particularly alarmed when he laments what he cannot comprehend, namely, the abandonment of customs that had prevailed among Ōtomo samurai from time immemorial: "to pray for the gods' and the Buddhas' protection, to stand on what is right and proper, and then to take up bow and arrow." Instead, according to Dōsetsu, what had been going on in Bungo was something unheard-of in previous generations: "young and old, men and women made willy-nilly into [adherents of] something that's supposed to be an Indian sect or whatever [Tenjiku-shū to yaran]; temples and shrines destroyed; [images of] the Buddhas and the gods either cast into the river or turned into firewood." To one who believed in the article of faith, "Japan is the Land of the Gods," as firmly as did Tachibana Dōsetsu, it was apparent that the impious excesses that had been latterly committed in the Ōtomo domain in the name of the

---

49 The remonstrance, addressed to Shiga Ise Nyūdō Dōki, Ichimada Hyōbu Nyūdō Sōkei, and eleven others, can be found in Takita Manabu, ed., Ōtomo shiryō, vol. 2 (Ōita: Kin'yōdō shoten, 1938), no. 89, pp. 56–66. For a synopsis of Tachibana Dōsetsu's career in the service of the Ōtomo, see Toyama Mikio, Ōtomo Sōrin, vol. 172 of Jimbutsu sōsho (Tokyo: Yoshikawa kōbunkan, 1975), pp. 60–3.

foreign faith – of Christianity – invited punishment from the Buddhas and the gods.

For all that, Tachibana Dōsetsu remained loyal to the Ōtomo. That was not the case, however, with the majority of the provincial gentry of Chikuzen, Chikugo, and Higo, to whom the news of the Mimikawa debacle was a clear signal to cast off their allegiance – an imposed, unwelcome, and always tenuous loyalty – to the Ōtomo. Some sought a new alliance with the Shimazu; others looked to Ryūzōji Takanobu for protection. Serious disturbances afflicted the very core of the domain: In Bungo itself, there was dissatisfaction with Yoshimune's leadership, discord within the ruling house, and discontent among close vassals of the Ōtomo.

Yet the crisis passed. The Ōtomo survived Mimikawa's immediate aftermath, because the victors did not press home their advantage. In 1580, the Shimazu made peace with the Ōtomo, ostensibly as a result of the intercession of the most powerful and the most prestigious authorities of Kyoto, the hegemon Oda Nobunaga joined by the former imperial regent (*kampaku*) and future grand chancellor of state (*daijō daijin*), Konoe Sakihisa (1536–1612).[50] In actuality – and quite paradoxically – it was Ryūzōji Takanobu's expansionist ambitions that, for the time being, removed the threat of destruction from the lords of Bungo. Takanobu rushed to fill the power vacuum created in Higo by the weakening of Ōtomo influence. By the middle of 1581, Ryūzōji had established a strong forward position in that province, thereby threatening Satsuma, the home of the Shimazu. Faced by the need to protect their northwestern flank, the Shimazu diverted their attention from Bungo. Inexorably, the Ryūzōji and the Shimazu headed for a showdown, one that would end with Ryūzōji Takanobu's defeat and death in 1584.

The respite granted the Ōtomo by this shifting of the fronts in Kyushu brought on a kind of Indian summer for the Jesuits in Bungo. But they failed to perceive that the Shimazu had vouchsafed "King Francisco" and his realm not a reprieve but only a temporary stay of execution. Valignano, who stayed in Bungo from September 1580 to March 1581 and then again in October 1581, found "happiness and consolation" in what he had accomplished there on his first visit;

50 Nobunaga to Konoe (Sakihisa), dated [Tenshō 8].8.12, in Okuno Takahiro, *Oda Nobunaga monjo no kenkyū*, 2nd ed., vol. 2 (Tokyo: Yoshikawa kōbunkan, 1973), no. 885, pp. 519–20; Nobunaga to Shimazu Shuri no Diabu (Yoshihisa), same date, and Konoe Sakihisa to Shimazu Hyōgo no Kami (Yoshihiro), dated [Tenshō 8].9.19, ibid., no. 886, pp. 520–2. Konoe Sakihisa, who had been *kampaku* from 1554 to 1569, was to be appointed *daijō daijin* in 1582.

hence he was cured, he stated, of his previous pessimism regarding the future of the Christian mission in Japan.

As late as December 1581, when the *visitator* and the padres of the Shimo area met in Nagasaki for a lengthy consultation on the questions that most affected their Japanese enterprise, they thought that all in all, Bungo was "the most secure kingdom" they knew in Japan. "Strong, belonging to one king only, and situated in the midst of other kingdoms belonging to the same king," the Ōtomo realm contrasted favorably with the Shimo and Miyako regions, "which are turned topsy-turvy every day and are kept perturbed by wars."[51] Hence the major formative institutions of the Society of Jesus in Japan were located in Bungo. A novitiate was formally opened in Usuki at Christmas 1580, with twelve candidate members of the Jesuit order (six of them Portuguese and six Japanese) starting on a period of probation that was prescribed to last at least one full year and, if possible, two. A Jesuit "college of studies," which was located in Funai, also began operations in the latter part of the year 1580. But these institutions were not destined to enjoy a long life: Both had to be closed in December 1586. Late that month, apprentice Jesuits and their professed masters, budding Latinists and aspiring Japanologists, all were forced to flee the domain of the Ōtomo and seek other and mightier patrons' protection from the Shimazu armies that flooded over Bungo and visited the last corners of that province with destruction.

THE END OF RYŪZŌJI TAKANOBU

It is another irony of history that this disaster suffered by "King Francisco" and his house should have had as its direct antecedent a famous victory celebrated by another "Christian daimyo" and great friend of the Jesuits, Dom Protasio Arima. Desperate to ward off Ryūzōji Takanobu, who continued to foment rebellion among his vassals and to whittle away his territory, Arima in 1582 turned for assistance to the Shimazu. It was high time, because by then the house of Arima – so prominent in Hizen once – had little left in its possession beyond a paltry coastal strip of the Shimabara peninsula. Seizing the opportunity to outflank Ryūzōji, the Shimazu agreed to help. In December 1582, they sent an expeditionary force across the Yatsushiro Sea and Shimabara Bay to Arima.

51 Japan Consultation, Question 8: "Whether it is good to establish some houses in Japan where Ours would live conjointly in the manner of a college," Point III (2), in Valignano, *Sumario de las cosas de Japon*, vol. 1, p. 107.

The allies made little progress, as transport difficulties, if nothing else, made a massive transfer of Satsuma troops from other fronts impossible. By the middle of April 1584, not many more than five thousand had arrived, but they were picked men serving under the command of a fine general, Shimazu Iehisa. Even so, the troops at the disposal of Iehisa and Dom Protasio only numbered about 6,300 when they laid siege to Shimabara, one of the important fortresses that had been played into Ryūzōji's hands by Arima's treacherous vassals.

Observing the numerical weakness of his enemy, Takanobu quickly moved to the relief of Shimabara with the whole glittering array of his main force, which is said, depending on the source, to have numbered between 25,000 and 50,000 men. On Tenshō 12.3.24 (May 4, 1584, by the Gregorian calendar), this huge force was routed at Okidanawate, a spot on the seashore between Shimabara and Mie (now part of the city of Shimabara), by the far smaller allied army of Arima and the Shimazu. An important role in the allies' dramatic success was played by a naval vessel belonging to an Arima nobleman and armed with two pieces of Western artillery, which bombarded the Ryūzōji troops clustered on the beach. "In the absence of a [trained] gunner, a Caffir loaded, a Japanese soldier aimed, and a Malabari fired the pieces." These three were no doubt all natives of Hizen; strange though it may seem, according to Frois, they praised the Lord as they passed the ammunition.[52]

Providentially, the marching orders issued by Ryūzōji reached Ōmura Sumitada, his constrained vassal, too late. On their way to Shimabara, Sumitada and his hastily gathered contingent were still some "6 or 7 leagues [36–42 kilometers] from the field of battle" when they "encountered much soldiery who were fleeing as fast as their horses' hooves would carry, away from the disaster that had befallen Tacanobu and his entire army."[53] Dom Bartolomeu wisely turned back to Ōmura Castle and escaped being caught up in the general rout. Thus the "Christian daimyo" of both the contending sides survived the battle of Okidanawate. But the "diabolical" Ryūzōji had been killed; the Christianity of western Kyushu was saved from his clutches.

And yet the Jesuits' troubles were far from over. No less infernal an

52 There is an extensive treatment of this campaign in Frois, *Historia*, pt. 2 [B], chaps. 6–9, Wicki, vol. 4 (1983), pp. 42–70; Matsuda and Kawasaki, trans., *Furoisu Nihonshi*, vol. 10, pp. 287–337; quotation from p. 59 and p. 316 (incomplete translation), respectively. Note that contemporary and near-contemporary Jesuit sources give the date of the battle of Okidanawate as April 24, 1584, that is, according to the Julian calendar, as the news of the reform that put the Gregorian calendar into effect in Catholic lands of Europe in October 1582 had not yet reached Japan at the time when the combat took place.
53 Lucena, *Erinnerungen*, pp. 254–5.

adversary, the Shimazu family, became the masters of western Kyushu as a result of Takanobu's demise and the subsequent collapse of the Ryūzōji realm. To be sure, the resounding victory of the Shimazu at Okidanawate did not immediately elevate them to unquestioned supremacy over that part of the island. They still had rivals in Kyushu. To start with, there were the Ōtomo, who either failed to recognize or sought to mask the weakness that had overcome them since the black day of Mimikawa in 1578; in any event, they thought they had the reputation of a major power to uphold. Naturally, they welcomed the chance to pick up the pieces left behind by the fall of one implacable enemy, Ryūzōji Takanobu, and at the same time to counteract, if not forestall, the rise of another, the Shimazu.

In the fall of 1584, Ōtomo Yoshimune accordingly sent troops into Chikugo. His intention was to intimidate and bring to heel Takanobu's son and successor, Ryūzōji Masaie (1556–1607), while at the same time checkmating Akizuki Tanezane, that old enemy of the Ōtomo. Yoshimune's envoys even proposed that the Shimazu join him in an offensive alliance directed against those two.[54] But their forcible-feeble policy availed the Ōtomo nothing. Their Chikugo army first encamped at Bandōji (now part of the city of Chikugo, Fukuoka Prefecture), then moved camp to Kōrasan (now Kurume), and after that hardly stirred from its lines. Its few offensive operations ended in failure, and in November 1585, even before the Shimazu could intervene in force against the Ōtomo, the Chikugo army finally withdrew from the field. One of its two generals, the famous Ōtomo loyalist Tachibana Dōsetsu, was dead. The other, Takahashi Jōun (1550–86), returned to his fortress at Iwaya in Chikuzen (now part of Dazaifu-machi, Fukuoka Prefecture) and braced himself to meet the onslaught that was sure to come. For it must be admitted that the futile maneuvers of this forlorn army, along with some feeble gestures made by Yoshimune toward the recovery of Higo, did have one concrete result. They provided the Shimazu with a casus belli against the Ōtomo.

At this juncture – in the late autumn and early winter of 1585 – it became vitally important for the Shimazu to consolidate their position in Kyushu and, if possible, to seize control of the entire island before an external force could intrude there to cross their plans and block their

54 According to what Ryūzōji's ambassadors reported to the Shimazu, the Ōtomo were at the same time proposing an anti-Shimazu alliance to Masaie. See Tōkyō daigaku shiryō hensanjo, ed., *Uwai Kakuken nikki*, vol. 2, *Dai Nihon kokiroku*, no. 5 (Tokyo: Iwanami shoten, 1954), pp. 125–6, entry for Tenshō 12.10.15 (November 17, 1584). Also see the entries for 9.21 and 9.25 of the same year, ibid., p. 113 and pp. 114–15, respectively.

triumphal progress. That such an intervention from the outside was more than likely became apparent to them with the arrival of an imperious message, dated the second day of the tenth month (November 23, 1585), from Toyotomi Hideyoshi. Speaking for the sovereign in the capacity of his imperial regent (*kampaku*) – a lofty appointment he had obtained through intimidation three and a half months previously[55] – Hideyoshi grandiloquently told Shimazu Yoshihisa that the whole realm, "as far as the outer limits of Ōshū," had now submitted to the imperial will and was at peace. This was balderdash, but it contained a serious threat. Kyushu alone, Hideyoshi asserted, was still plagued by war; this was a reprehensible state of affairs, and Yoshihisa must put a stop to it or suffer punishment.

The Shimazu, conscious of their status as a "house of unblemished lineage since the days of Yoritomo," were outraged at the bluster of this "parvenu" (*yurai naki jin*). Considering Hideyoshi obviously unfit for his new office and unworthy to be addressed with the deference ordinarily due a *kampaku*, they refused to dignify his ultimatum with the courtesy of a direct reply. Instead, Yoshihisa chose the expedient of writing back to an intermediary, the "literary daimyo" Hosokawa Fujitaka (1534–1610). Protesting the Shimazu party's solemn commitment and scrupulous adherence to the armistice agreement arranged by Oda Nobunaga and Konoe Sakihisa in 1580, and putting the blame on the Ōtomo for violating the peace of Kyushu with their recent incursions into Hyūga and Higo, Yoshihisa insisted that any countermeasures by the Shimazu were steps taken in justifiable self-defense. In other words, the Shimazu would not abandon their aggressive designs in order to placate Hideyoshi. Instead, they planned an intensification of the conflict in Kyushu.

The contents of this fateful correspondence were revealed to the principal captains of the Shimazu at a council of war held in Kagoshima in February and March 1586. The diary of Uwai Kakuken (or Uwai Satokane; 1545–89), the castellan of Miyazaki in Hyūga who was one of Yoshihisa's senior councilors, affords us an interesting glimpse into the proceedings.[56] The die was cast, or rather the lots (*mikuji*) were drawn,

55 See my "Hideyoshi, the Bountiful Minister," in Elison and Smith, eds., *Warlords, Artists, & Commoners*, pp. 229–32.
56 The text of Hideyoshi's message to Shimazu Yoshihisa may be found in *Uwai Kakuken nikki*, vol. 3 (1957), p. 89, entry for Tenshō 14.1.23 (March 13, 1586). Kakuken notes that Hosokawa Fujitaka and Hideyoshi's confidant, the interior decorator Sen no Rikyū (1522–91), had sent adjunct letters (*soejō*) supplementing that message. Yoshihisa addressed his reply to Hosokawa; the text, dated [Tenshō 14].1.11, is found ibid., pp. 89–90. The lots regarding the invasion of Bungo were drawn on 1.22; ibid., p. 88.

at this council. Their oracle made it evident that the gods wanted Bungo to be invaded from two directions. Shimazu Yoshihiro was to lead a force that would strike through Higo. Commanding another army in an advance through Hyūga would be the daimyo Yoshihisa in person.

THE ECCLESIASTICAL POLITICS OF VICE-PROVINCIAL COELHO

Their opponents did not stand idly by as the Shimazu prepared for war. In May 1586, Ōtomo Sōrin himself traveled to Osaka to seek Hideyoshi's pledge of military support. Although he got no such assurance directly from Hideyoshi, who was at his most garrulous as he conducted his awestricken guest on a tour through the sumptuous bedchambers, tearooms, and treasure houses of his nonesuch of the moment, Osaka Castle, Ōtomo could nevertheless go home with his fears assuaged, as the *kampaku*'s half-brother and right hand, Hashiba Hidenaga (1541?– 91), promised to take care of everything to Sōrin's complete satisfaction.[57] Among the others who were engaged in lobbying activities in Osaka that spring was the vice-provincial of the Jesuits, Padre Gaspar Coelho. His mission, too, was adverse to the interests of the Shimazu, whose oppressive dominance over the Christian areas of Kyushu he sought to resist at all costs. Indeed, he had undertaken the journey from Nagasaki to the Kansai in defiance of their express prohibition.

His trip was absolutely necessary, Coelho tried to tell the Shimazu, because he had an obligation to express his thanks to Hideyoshi for permitting the Jesuits to maintain an establishment in Osaka. Even while granting the mission superior of Japan the necessity of making such a courtesy visit, one wonders about its timing. The Jesuits had been enjoying the hegemon's protection in his great new castle town since 1583. What, then, was Coelho's hurry? No fools, the Shimazu suspected that the vice-provincial "went to Miaco for no other purpose than to arrange with Quambacu [the *kampaku* Hideyoshi] that he should favor Bungo and assist it against Sacçuma, which is the kingdom of the most inveterate and hard-bitten enemies that the Law of God has in Japan."[58]

---

57 Sōrin reported on his visit to Osaka in detail in a letter addressed to three of the elders of Bungo realm, Furusō Tango Nyūdō (Ikkan), Kasai Suō Nyūdō Sōsen, and Saitō Kii Nyūdō Dōreki, and dated Tenshō 14.4.6 (May 24, 1586, the day after the audience); a convenient synopsis may be found in Toyama, *Ōtomo Sōrin*, pp. 265–9.
58 Frois, *Historia*, pt. 2 [B], chap. 29, Wicki, vol. 4, p. 216; Matsuda and Kawasaki, trans., *Furoisu Nihonshi*, vol. 9, pp. 25–6. Also see *Uwai Kakuken nikki*, vol. 3, p. 47, entry for Tenshō 13.10.10 (December 1, 1585).

To be sure, it is clear that questions of even wider scope and greater import than the affairs of Kyushu occupied the visionary mind of the vice-provincial; his flights of fancy took him to the most rarefied regions of higher politics. Recall from Chapter 6 that Hideyoshi had at least since 1585 planned an invasion of Korea and China.

In the course of the audience that the *kampaku* granted him at Osaka Castle on May 4, 1586, Coelho proved only too eager to discuss that plan. Indeed, if we are to believe Organtino Gnecchi-Soldo, a fellow Jesuit who was present at this baneful interview, Coelho even volunteered to use his influence in getting two Portuguese Great Ships put at Hideyoshi's disposal when the time came for the assault on the Asian mainland. But an invasion of the continent could obviously not be mounted unless a base were secured for it in Kyushu, and Hideyoshi would first have to conquer the island for that reason if for no other. Coelho saw himself playing a not-insignificant part in this grand design.

How justified the Shimazu were in suspecting him of hostile intentions is apparent from the testimony of Padre Organtino, who affirms that Frois, addressing Hideyoshi as the interpreter on Coelho's behalf, began his speech by requesting the *kampaku*'s military intervention in Kyushu and promising in turn the vice-provincial's aid in putting all of that island's Christian lords on Hideyoshi's side. In actuality, Coelho lacked the power to deliver on such a promise: Try as he might to create a bloc of Christian daimyo, he never succeeded. That, however, is not really the point at issue. The paramount factor in the subsequent turn of events, one perceived clearly by Organtino, if only in retrospect, was that Hideyoshi had nothing but the greatest disdain for priests who meddled in military matters.[59] Hence Coelho's ambitious performance in Osaka, rash at best, was at worst – and proved to be in fact – suicidal.

For the time being, however, Hideyoshi hid his contempt. Apparently he found the prospect of cooperation outlined by Coelho attractive and useful. Assuming momentarily the mantle of a patron of the Christian mission, the *kampaku* made sure that the vice-provincial would be sent on his way in a contented state, by issuing him a charter that guaranteed the padres the right to reside and to preach their

59 A more detailed discussion of this audience can be found in my *Deus Destroyed*, pp. 112–14. Note that Frois and Organtino wrote conflicting versions of what was said in the course of the interview. Frois's report, which is dated October 4, 1586, was designed for publication throughout Europe. Organtino's confidential letter to the general of the Society of Jesus, written on October 10, 1589, is accordingly the more trustworthy even if less immediate source.

gospel unimpeded "in all the lands of Japan," freed them from the duty of quartering soldiers, and granted them exemption from other imposts.[60] The *kampaku's* decree, which is dated Tenshō 14.5.4 (June 20, 1586), gave Coelho an entrée even with those daimyo who had previously shown no disposition to favor Christianity or its apostles. Armed with this document, Coelho left Sakai on July 23 and proceeded westward by measured stages through the Inland Sea.

First Coelho crossed over to the island of Shikoku to call on Kobayakawa Takakage (1533–97), the lord of Iyo Province (now Ehime Prefecture), and was received by him with extreme courtesy. This may seem surprising, because Takakage was one of the main pillars of the great house of Mōri, a family with a history of hostility to the Christian religion. But the vast power complex of the Mōri, which covered the six westernmost provinces of Honshu as well as Iyo on Shikoku, had by 1586 been fully subordinated to Hideyoshi's national regime. It is evident that in welcoming the vice-provincial as lavishly as he did, Takakage was in fact deferring to the promulgator of the *kampaku's* pro-Christian decree rather than to its bearer and beneficiary. (The end result of that decree, so far as the Mōri were concerned, was the temporary reestablishment of the Jesuit residence in Yamaguchi after three decades of closure. It was promptly closed again when Hideyoshi turned anti-Christian in July 1587.) Along with his nephew Mōri Terumoto and his brother Kikkawa Motoharu (1530–86), Takakage was destined to play a key role in the vanguard of the invasion of Kyushu that Hideyoshi would shortly set in motion. Knowing Coelho's record, it is difficult to imagine him managing to stay away from that topic in his conversations with Takakage.

In early August, the vice-provincial proceeded from Iyo to Bungo, but he found little encouragement to tarry there. Gloom impended over the Ōtomo realm as the threat that had so long been in the offing grew ever more palpable: Having rejected yet another plan for the partition of Kyushu, the Shimazu on August 15 took the offensive.[61] After a month of early successes, their advance bogged down. But the

---

60 The charter's Portuguese translation, in which the standard chancery form of the exemption or "off-limits" decree (*kinzei*) is easily recognizable, can be found in Frois, *Historia*, pt. 2 [B], chap. 32, Wicki, vol. 4, p. 238. The original Japanese text does not survive.

61 The partition plan floated by Hideyoshi would have given Chikuzen to Hideyoshi himself, turned over Hizen to Mōri Terumoto, and assigned Chikugo, half of Higo, and half of Buzen to the Ōtomo, whereas the rest of Kyushu was to go to the Shimazu; see *Uwai Kakuken nikki*, vol. 3, p. 127, entry for Tenshō 14.5.22 (June 9, 1586). The Shimazu, required by Hideyoshi to reply to this plan by the seventh month or face his military intervention, decided at a council of war held on Tenshō 14.6.7 to spurn the proposal and two days later ordered a mobilization; ibid., pp. 133–4.

very awareness that Satsuma was on the march kept the Jesuit sympathizers of the Ōtomo in an undiminished state of anxiety.

This awareness evoked so vivid a specter of ruin before the eyes of Coelho's companion Frois that he thought he saw the enemy's grasp already extending over eight of the nine provinces of Kyushu – only "the wretched kingdom of Bungo" was left to stand by itself, and it was so denuded of resources and stripped of protection that "one could not help feeling sorry for its destitution." The causes of Bungo's derelict condition were obvious to this observer: The realm "lacked a head that would govern it, and its lords each went his own way without there being any sense of union among them." It was bad enough that Ōtomo Yoshimune "made light of the advice given him by his father, el-rey Francisco." Even worse, he shut his ears to Coelho's expostulations. The daimyo of Bungo refused to have Hideyoshi's decree regarding the free spread of Christianity officially proclaimed and enforced in his domains – not that the Society of Jesus "had any intention of forcing anyone," Frois reassures us. "Like another Pharaoh," Yoshimune failed to heed all admonitions and instead "repudiated the light," becoming ever more "obstinate and clouded with darkness in his heart." Cleaving to his dissolute ways, he "gave free rein to his appetites."[62]

The missionary's harsh words notwithstanding, Yoshimune's lack of enthusiasm for the Jesuits was not necessarily an instance of perversity. The daimyo of Bungo may simply have been afraid that any further encouragement of the Christian religion would exacerbate the deep cleavages that divided his realm and imperiled his rulership. If so, then there was reason in his recalcitrance.

Conversions to Christianity had increased dramatically in Bungo, even as the storm gathered over the domain of the Ōtomo: There were 2,000 adult baptisms in 1584, no fewer than 12,000 in 1585 (almost half that number in Funai and its vicinity alone), and 6,150 in the first nine months of 1586.[63] To note that is by no means to suggest that these Christians posed a threat to the Ōtomo because they were somehow disloyal or even seditious. But because many important vassals of the Ōtomo continued to cherish traditional religion, it is plain that the issue of the toleration – let alone the advancement – of the Christian

62 Frois, Historia, pt. 2 [B], chaps. 34 and 36, Wicki, vol. 4, pp. 254, 270–1; Matsuda and Kawasaki, trans., Furoisu Nihonshi, vol. 11 (1979), p. 40, and vol. 8 (1978), pp. 159–61.
63 See Schütte, Introductio ad historiam Societatis Jesu in Japonia, pp. 411–12; and Frois, Historia, pt. 2 [B], chaps. 27 and 28, Wicki, vol. 4, pp. 202–4, 215; Matsuda and Kawasaki, trans., Furoisu Nihonshi, vol. 8, pp. 136–8, 156.

cause by the daimyo family was highly divisive at the best of times and downright explosive during a time of crisis. In any event, Yoshimune resisted the Jesuits' entreaties, and Vice-Provincial Coelho departed for Shimonoseki on September 16, 1586, with his mission to Bungo an apparent failure.

Or is it possible that Coelho was undertaking these travels from Kyushu to Honshu and Shikoku and back on something other than a purely religious mission? If part of his task, self-appointed or not, was the coordination of military plans – decidedly not out of character for this adventurist – then he may even have left Bungo with a sense not of frustration but of expectation. When he landed in Shimonoseki some five days later, he found himself in the middle of a military camp, the staging area of an army drawn from the extensive domains of the Mōri and forming an advance echelon of the invasion of Kyushu ordered by Hideyoshi.

Early in October, Coelho went on to Yamaguchi to meet Dom Simeão Kuroda (Yoshitaka, also known as Kodera Kambyōe, 1546–1604), the inspector general charged by Hideyoshi with overseeing the operations of the Mōri forces. The two traveled back together to Shimonoseki, where they were shortly joined by another chief member of Hideyoshi's field staff who was a fervent Christian, Dom Agostinho Konishi (Yukinaga, 1556?–1600). Here the vice-provincial had the opportunity not only to consult again with Kobayakawa Takakage but also to make the acquaintance of Mōri Terumoto when that powerful daimyo arrived to take personal charge of his troops as they prepared to launch their assault across the Strait of Shimonoseki. By the middle of November, the Mōri army had occupied a strong beachhead in Kyushu, capturing the Shimazu side's fort at Kokura. For his part, Coelho left for Kyushu in the middle of December. In an odd throw-back to the association between *wakō* and missionaries that dated back to Xavier's day, the vice-provincial was convoyed to Nagasaki by an escort of seven armed vessels from the fleet of Kurushima Michifusa (1561–97), the "supreme captain of all the pirates of the sea," who had been baptized in Shimonoseki a few days previously.[64]

64 Frois, *Historia*, pt. 2 [B], chap. 38, Wicki, vol. 4, pp. 282–3; Matsuda and Kawasaki, trans., *Furoisu Nihonshi*, vol. 9, pp. 56–8. As noted by Frois, "Curuximadono" or Kurushima (more properly, Murakami) Michifusa ranked alongside Murakami Takeyoshi, the head of the Noshima branch of the Murakami family, at the top of the pirate hierarchy of the Inland Sea. Michifusa, whose fort dominated the narrows at Kurushima (now part of the city of Imabari, Ehime Prefecture), due to its swift tidal currents one of the most difficult passages in that sea, was one of the maritime barons whose fleets, mobilized in the service of Hideyoshi, played an indispensable part in the invasion of Korea. He died at the battle of Myŏngnyang, one of the key naval engagements of the second Korean campaign.

From Nagasaki, his own domain, Coelho went on to Arima, where he did his best to persuade the daimyo Arima Harunobu to abandon his temporal loyalties and join his fellow Christians, Konishi and Kuroda, in the war against the Shimazu. Dom Protasio, however, refused to turn his back on his erstwhile saviors, the lords of Satsuma, in order to take up the cause of the Jesuits. The vice-provincial thereupon ordered not only all missionaries but even the pupils of the *seminario* to leave Arima.[65]

One would attribute this extraordinary action to a random fit of temper, were there no similar examples of how Coelho conducted policy. In the early 1580s, for instance, at a time when Arima was being brutalized by Ryūzōji Takanobu, Coelho sought to inspire Dom Bartolomeu Ōmura – a sworn vassal of Takanobu – to rise against his lord, enter into a compact with Dom Protasio "so that Christianity would flourish," and "make war as best he could" against Ryūzōji. Ōmura raised scruples about this proposal. Among the concerns he mentioned was the safety of his son Sancho, a hostage under Takanobu's control, but to Coelho this was a small matter, one to be dismissed out of hand in view of any Christian's higher duty to his church. Hence Dom Bartolomeu's demur and the halfheartedness of his subsequent show of compliance with Coelho's fanciful anti-Ryūzōji scheme earned him the permanent ill will of the vice-provincial.

The ambitious Coelho failed to recognize that the lords he sought to influence had concrete interests other than Christianity and that his project for a Christian axis in Hizen, not to speak of his even more ambitious plan for a Catholic league in Japan, was therefore ungrounded in reality. What a chimera this particular vision of a holy alliance was may be judged from the fact that Dom Protasio Arima and Dom Bartolomeu Ōmura in 1586 actually fought a war with each other over a parcel of territory in the western Sonogi peninsula. This was a small war, but it was bloody nonetheless. Unfortunately, it is not the sole example of a military conflict in which Christians shed Christian blood in Japan.

In the event, Coelho applied to Ōmura Sumitada the very same sanctions that he had used against Arima Harunobu. According to the veteran Jesuit missionary Afonso de Lucena's reminiscences, "Our Japan Superior, for certain reasons and considerations that appeared to him to be just, ordered and required that all the Padres who were in

---

65 Padre João de Crasto SJ to Padre Alexandro Valignano SJ, dated Hirado, March 19, 1587, cited in Schütte, *Introductio ad historiam Societatis Jesu in Japonia*, pp. 698–9, n. 54.

Ōmura should remove *ad tempus* to Nagasaki, and [he did] this as a punishment he meted out to the *Tono* [Bartolomeu] for not doing certain things that [Bartolomeu] believed he could not do with respect to his honor and his temporal interests." Nor did Coelho's hostility to Sumitada end with this measure of coercion. When Dom Bartolomeu lay on his deathbed in the spring of 1587, Coelho twice refused urgent requests that he come to visit, to console, and to be reconciled with his prominent spiritual charge, the first of the "Christian daimyo."[66]

What sort of ecclesiastical politics was this? The distinguished Jesuit historian Josef Franz Schütte calls it "political willfulness" on the part of the Japan Superior.[67] Coelho's arrogance, however, was about to meet its match, and the vice-province he headed would presently suffer the grave consequences of his imprudent actions.

THE COLLAPSE OF THE ŌTOMO REALM

As if to mock the orderly processes of causation, the downfall of Coelho's and his fellow Jesuits' enterprise was compassed not by Satsuma, the enemy they feared, loathed, and tried to damage, but rather by the *kampaku* Hideyoshi, the self-decreed friend whose protection they cherished, whose interests they sought to further, and whose sweeping plans for conquest the vice-provincial had enthusiastically embraced. First, however, Hideyoshi brought about the humiliation of the Shimazu, by no means an easy endeavor. The campaign to break the power of the Shimazu, establish Hideyoshi's dominance over Kyushu, and (perhaps most important of all) show the mastery of the national hegemon over the daimyo of central and western Japan was a military operation of a scale and complexity unprecedented in Japanese history.

The *kampaku* is said to have ordered the mobilization of 200,000 men, drawn from no fewer than thirty-seven provinces, for his invasion of Kyushu.[68] At least half that total was to be assembled in the

---

66 See Lucena, *Erinnerungen*, pp. 108–15 on Coelho's anti-Ryūzōji scheme; pp. 114–25 on the war between Ōmura and Arima; pp. 134–9 on Dom Bartolomeu's final illness (he died on May 25, 1587); and pp. 138–41 on the withdrawal of missionaries from Ōmura.
67 See Schütte, "Einleitung" to Lucena, *Erinnerungen*, p. 29, and n. 54 to pt. 2 of Lucena's text, pp. 134–5.
68 Oze Hoan, *Taikōki*, ed. Kuwata Tadachika (Tokyo: Shin jimbutsu ōraisha, 1971), p. 230. Hoan's chronicle, which has a preface dated Kan'ei 2 (1625), is an anecdotal work not characterized by an attachment to accuracy. His statement regarding the mobilization of Hideyoshi's Kyushu army is apt to be an exaggeration. Historians, however, have by and large followed Hoan. The normally careful Fujiki Hisashi, for instance, even raises Hoan's number of troops to "more than 250,000" drawn from "nearly forty provinces"; see Fujiki Hisashi, *Oda–Toyotomi seiken*, vol. 15 of *Nihon no rekishi* (Tokyo: Shōgakkan, 1975), p. 202.

Kansai area as Hideyoshi's main striking force. This large army would then have to be provisioned, marched in echelons for some five hundred kilometers (310 miles) to the western extremity of Honshu, ferried across the Strait of Shimonoseki, and finally deployed to fight in a vast territory over which a resourceful enemy held preponderant control. The *kampaku* knew that he had to allow plenty of time for preparation; hence, setting the departure date of the several elements of his main force well ahead into the spring, he determined that he would lead his personal guard from Osaka on Tenshō 15.3.1 (April 8, 1587). He hoped that the Shimazu could be held in check until then by the Ōtomo and the advance contingents, made up of levies of his subject daimyo, that he had sent to their assistance.

In the meantime the Shimazu laid their own plans to conquer Bungo and entrench themselves in control of Kyushu. Shimazu Yoshihiro was to advance through Higo while his brother Iehisa struck at Bungo from Hyūga; their offensive was scheduled to begin on Tenshō 14.10.21 (December 1, 1586). Long before that date – in fact, at least since the autumn of the previous year – vassals and even members of the house of Ōtomo were covertly taking up contacts with the Shimazu, as though vying with one another to clamber aboard the juggernaut they saw rumbling their way.

When the Shimazu struck, Bungo's entire southern front caved in, as a rolling wave of defections from the vassal band of the Ōtomo smoothed the way onward for the invaders. As advised by his spies and collaborators, Shimazu Iehisa advanced with only a small force of his own, no more than three thousand men from Hyūga and five hundred from Satsuma. His ranks, however, were swelled by the troops of his fifth column in Bungo. This collapse of the vassalage structure of the Ōtomo in the face of an enemy attack showed once again how far behind the times their domain actually was. The Ōtomo had failed utterly to establish the direct control over their liegemen that was one of the identifying characteristics of the new breed of early modern daimyo. Theirs was still essentially a medieval realm built on the principle of coalition – a foundation, as it proved, of sand. The Shimazu knocked down their ramshackle dominion without much difficulty; then Hideyoshi restored it for a brief half-dozen years; but it would not survive the stewardship of Ōtomo Yoshimune.

Bungo did not fall without a fight. Saiki Koresada, the keeper of Togamure-jō (located on the boundary of what now are the city of Saiki and the township of Yayoi, Ōita Prefecture), sallied from his castle and mauled a force sent by Shimazu Iehisa to conquer eastern

Bungo, thereby stopping the enemy's advance into that territory. From a cluster of points of resistance he organized around his stronghold of Oka-jō (in what is now the city of Taketa), the Christian samurai Dom Paulo Shiga (Shiga Tarō Chikatsugu, Bungo's most intrepid captain throughout this conflict) and his adherents harassed the Shimazu and their collaborators with guerrilla warfare. The retired daimyo Ōtomo Sōrin, "King Francisco" himself, rallied the defenders of Niujima-jō, the seaside fortress that guarded Usuki, to defy the Shimazu army that occupied the castle town below its walls. Helped greatly by two 97-millimeter cannon supplied by the Portuguese in the past days of Bungo's glory (and named with the Delphian prognostic Kunikuzushi, "Domain Destroyers"), the outnumbered garrison of Niujima kept the attackers at bay, and the Shimazu never did take the castle of Usuki.

But these were practically all the creditable attainments of the Ōtomo arms in this war. The ruling daimyo, Ōtomo Yoshimune, certainly did not cut a heroic figure in the general debacle that overcame his domain. He took his stand against a Shimazu army in the field only once, and that one time was a disaster. In January 1587, Yoshimune ventured a sortie to the relief of Tsuruga-jō (located in what is now Ōaza Kami Hetsugi, Ōita City), the last obstacle that barred Shimazu Iehisa's route to Funai, Bungo's provincial capital. Hapless as always, Yoshimune permitted his troops as well as those of his allies, the Shikoku daimyo Chōsogabe Motochika (1540–99) and Sengoku Hidehisa (1551–1614) – auxiliaries sent by Hideyoshi – to be lured into a trap at the crossing of the river Hetsugigawa (now called Ōnogawa), where they suffered a crushing defeat. After this battle, Yoshimune left Funai to its fate and fled to Ryūō-jō (located in what is now Ajinmachi, Ōita Prefecture) in Buzen, abandoning Bungo to the enemy. His precipitate flight from the Ōtomo heartland prefigures, in a curious way, his disastrous performance six years later in Hideyoshi's invasion of Korea, when Yoshimune abandoned his post at Pongsan (Hwanghae Province) in the face of an enemy advance, thereby exposing the left flank of the entire Japanese army and forcing his comrades into a hasty and disorderly retreat. Hideyoshi disenfeoffed Yoshimune for that dereliction of duty, and so the Ōtomo family's long rule over Bungo came to an end in 1593.

In 1587, however, Hideyoshi was determined, for the time being, to revive, prop up, and sustain that rule as an element of his reorganization of the affairs of Kyushu. Hence he did not lay the blame for the fiasco of Hetsugigawa on Ōtomo Yoshimune. Instead, he put the responsibility for the "scandalous performance" on his own delegate in the field, Sengoku Hidehisa, whom he dispossessed from his Takamatsu domain as an admonishment to others. The reverses suffered by his side in Kyushu did not make Hideyoshi any less confident. He boasted that it was "a sure thing" that, no sooner in Kyushu, he would "chop off Shimazu's head."[69] Insofar as his promise to overwhelm Kyushu was concerned, Hideyoshi was as good as his word, even if he relented from his resolve to do grievous bodily harm to Shimazu Yoshihisa. In the end, the fact that they had overrun Bungo availed the Shimazu nothing. They were not permitted to rest, digesting their gains. Instead, they had to draw back before the massive force of the *kampaku*'s intervention.

Even before Hideyoshi could make his appearance in person on the stage they had come to dominate so spectacularly, the Shimazu concluded that prudence and self-preservation demanded that they vacate northern Kyushu and seek security in their home grounds to the south. Hence they left Bungo voluntarily. On April 22, 1587 (Tenshō 15.3.15), Hideyoshi reached Aki Province and camped in Yokkaichi (now part of the city of Higashi Hiroshima), about halfway from Osaka to Kyushu, and Shimazu Yoshihiro evacuated Funai. Two days later, harried by Dom Paulo Shiga and Saiki Koresada, the troops of Yoshihiro and his brother Iehisa crossed into Hyūga; other Shimazu detachments withdrew into Higo. The avenues used by the Shimazu five months previously to attack Bungo became the paths of their retreat.

HIDEYOSHI'S INVASION OF KYUSHU

Hideyoshi's invasion armies followed those same paths in their advance on Satsuma. On May 2 (3.25), Hideyoshi arrived in Shimonoseki, his last way station on Honshu, where he assigned the route through Chikuzen, Chikugo, and Higo to himself and put his half-brother Hashiba Hidenaga, the daimyo of Kōriyama in Yamato, in command of an army that would strike at the heartland of the Shimazu through Bungo and Hyūga, the eastern provinces of Kyushu.

For Hideyoshi, the march down the western side of the island was nothing less than a triumphal progress. He crossed over to Kokura on May 5 (3.28), and less than a month later, on June 3 (4.27), he had

69 Hideyoshi to Mōri Uma no Kami (Terumoto), vermilion-seal letter dated [Tenshō 14.]12.24 (February 1, 1587), in Tōkyō daigaku shiryō hensanjo, ed., *Dai Nihon komonjo, iewake 8: Mōri-ke monjo*, vol. 3 (Tokyo: Tōkyō daigaku shuppankai, 1979), no. 951, pp. 231–3.

reached Izumi in Satsuma, about three hundred kilometers (186 miles) away. He encountered no serious opposition along the way, where opportunists of the stamp of Akizuki Tanezane, Tsukushi Hirokado, Ryūzōji Masaie, the old *wakō* Matsuura Takanobu – and, in the end, also Dom Protasio Arima – flocked to the victor's banners.

Hidenaga had a more difficult time of it. As had been the case in the Ōtomo campaign of 1578, the powerful fortress Takajō in Hyūga stood in the way of the invaders from the north. As before, the castellan Yamada Shinsuke Arinobu defended his stronghold under siege; also as before, the Shimazu chieftains Yoshihisa, Yoshihiro, and Iehisa led an army to his relief. But unlike 1578, it was not the invaders who were surrounded and destroyed under the walls of Takajō. Rather, the relief army of the Shimazu was cornered and defeated on May 24, 1587 (Tenshō 15.4.17), by Hidenaga's superior numbers and the devastating force of his massed musketry. This battle decided the campaign. Four days later, the Shimazu initiated capitulation proceedings by sending hostages to Hidenaga. On June 13 (5.8), Shimazu Yoshihisa himself – his head shaven as a sign that he had abandoned worldly attachments – appeared before Hideyoshi to ask for his pardon.

A consummate master of statecraft, Hideyoshi showed magnanimity to the Shimazu. He had the power to dispossess them. Instead, he chose to reduce their holdings but leave them their status. Confirming Shimazu Yoshihisa in his lordship over Satsuma and assigning Ōsumi to Shimazu Yoshihiro, Hideyoshi left them as rulers over the provinces where their family had held authority since the end of the twelfth century. Pushed back to their borders of 1577, the Shimazu nevertheless still figured as the masters of southern Kyushu.

The great *shugo* family of northern Kyushu, the house of Ōtomo – for whose sake, ostensibly, Hideyoshi had intervened in the island's affairs – likewise had to content itself with a diminished estate: Losing whatever traditional claim he had on other provinces, Ōtomo Yoshimune was confirmed as the daimyo of Bungo alone. This was still a considerable domain (one valued, according to the new *kokudaka* system, at 378,000 *koku*), but it was a far cry from the "seven-province realm" Ōtomo Sōrin had once accumulated. Had Sōrin still been their head, Hideyoshi might well have been more generous to the Ōtomo. But his sweeping rearrangement of the domanial borders of Kyushu, undertaken in July 1587, no longer had to take account of Sōrin. "King Francisco of Bungo" had died on June 29 (5.24), apparently after having declined Hideyoshi's offer of Hyūga as an appanage.

For all his display of generosity toward a defeated enemy and of consideration toward a pitiable ally – who happened to be the two surviving pillars of the traditional structure of authority in Kyushu – the fact is that Hideyoshi imposed a completely new order on that island. Ryūzōji Masaie was left four districts in Hizen; also in Hizen, the Arima, the Ōmura, and the Matsuura all were confirmed in their possessions; the Sagara family retained their domain around Hitoyoshi in Higo. But the political map of the rest of Kyushu took on an entirely new appearance as a result of the *kampaku*'s actions.

Hideyoshi's old crony Terazawa Hiromasa (d. 1596) was given a 37,000-*koku* fief at Karatsu in Hizen. Except for the Sagara domain, the province of Higo was entrusted to Sassa Narimasa (d. 1588), another old comrade and sometime rival, whom Hideyoshi had fought, defeated, and pardoned in 1585. Narimasa was transferred to Kyushu from a fief in Etchū (now Toyama Prefecture). In a similar way, Kobayakawa Takakage was made to exchange his holdings in Shikoku for a new 307,000-*koku* domain centered in Najima (now Fukuoka) and covering Chikuzen as well as parts of Hizen and Chikugo. Takakage's younger brother and adopted son Hidekane (known as both Kobayakawa and Mōri Hidekane, 1566–1601) was installed in a 75,000-*koku* fief at Kurume in Chikugo. Baptized in the late spring of 1587, Hidekane (thereafter called Dom Simão) reinforced his status as a Christian daimyo by marrying Ōtomo Sōrin's daughter Maxentia later that year. Hideyoshi's confidant Dom Simeão Kuroda Yoshitaka, a baron from Harima, was made the lord of a 120,000-*koku* domain at Nakatsu in Buzen, whereas Kokura in the same province (a fief valued at 60,000 *koku*) was assigned to Mōri Yoshinari (d. 1611), Hideyoshi's retainer from Owari. All of these daimyo were newcomers with no roots in Kyushu.

Some of Kyushu's old, familiar names, however, were uprooted from their ancestral grounds and transplanted elsewhere. Thus Tachibana Muneshige had to leave Chikuzen for a new fief at Yanagawa in Chikugo; Akizuki Tanezane's son Tanenaga (1567–1614) and Takahashi Mototane (d. 1614) both were moved from the northwestern part of Kyushu to its southeast, the former to Takarabe (now Takanabe-chō, Miyazaki Prefecture) and the latter to Agata (now the city of Nobeoka) in Hyūga.

What, however, was the significance of all this scene shifting and rearrangement of the dramatis personae of Kyushu directed by Hideyoshi? He was putting on stage the finale of the long drama of Kyushu as a place with an independent identity in Japanese history. (He did not know that an epilogue remained to be played. The *kokujin* rebellion that swept the mainland of Higo and the Amakusa Islands from 1588 to 1590 would represent a last flare-up of the lost independence.) This dramatic production, moreover, gave a glimpse into the future of Japan's political organization. Anticipating the coinage of a phrase that became a truism in the Edo period, Hideyoshi treated the daimyo as potted plants, objects to be moved about at will. By the dispositions he made in Kyushu, the largest territory he had yet conquered, this grand *arriviste* showed that he had truly arrived: No longer could the Shimazu or any other military aristocrats, no matter how ancient their lineage, afford to treat Hideyoshi as a mere upstart.

Even if Hideyoshi's was a new regime, it had been legitimated by his elevation to the loftiest rungs of the old imperial hierarchy, the offices of *kampaku* and *daijō daijin* (grand chancellor of state). But it was deeds and not just titles that confirmed his authority. Although he still had eastern and northern Japan to subjugate, Hideyoshi demonstrated conclusively in these southern and western regions that he was in fact as well as in name the national hegemon. The daimyo he planted in Kyushu, rulers of autonomous regions in theory, were no more than his vicars in actuality.

HIDEYOSHI'S ANTI-CHRISTIAN EDICTS

One more would-be daimyo, the vicar general of the Society of Jesus in Japan, remained to be dealt with. In keeping with his dignity as the holder of administrative and judicial sovereignty over the port city of Nagasaki, Padre Gaspar Coelho traveled to Hakozaki to meet Hideyoshi in style and on his own naval vessel. Reputed to be the swiftest sail in Japanese waters, Coelho's *fusta armada* was apparently a ship of some two hundred to three hundred tons, built by a Portuguese shipwright in Nagasaki in the fashion of a light galley. Jesuit sources acknowledge that this *fusta* was armed with artillery, and Japanese chronicles allege that it had been used in military action against the Jesuits' unfriendly neighbors on the Nagasaki peninsula, the *wakō* band of Fukahori Sumikata.[70] The vice-provincial had several things to discuss with Hideyoshi on this visit, but no doubt what Coelho wanted most of all was a confirmation of the *kampaku*'s partiality for the missionaries and, if possible, an expansion of the privileges Hideyoshi had granted them by his decree of June 20, 1586.

---

70 See Alvarez-Taladriz, "Introduccion" to Valignano, *Sumario de las cosas de Japon*, vol. 1, p. 146; cf. Matsuda and Kawasaki, trans., *Furoisu Nihonshi*, vol. 1, p. 283, n. 18.

In the intervening year, Hideyoshi had kept up his show of favor toward the padres, and they had reciprocated by devoting "continuous masses and prayers" to the intention of "his good success and prosperous outcome in these wars."[71] Of all the Jesuits, however, surely it was Coelho himself who had the most reason to expect friendly regard if not gratitude from Hideyoshi: They both knew that the vice-provincial had exerted himself not only spiritually but also in a more direct way, politically, in the *kampaku*'s behalf. The meeting between the two, which took place aboard the notorious *fusta* on July 19, 1587 (Tenshō 15.6.14), was marked by outpourings of affability on Hideyoshi's part. Hence it came as a bolt from the blue when Hideyoshi, less than a week later, on July 24, 1587 (Tenshō 15.6.19), issued his edict condemning Christianity as a "pernicious doctrine" and giving the missionaries twenty days to get out of Japan.[72]

Hideyoshi's edict of 6.19 begins with the words, "Japan is the Land of the Gods," a nativist dictum that would be invoked again and again in subsequent anti-Christian pronouncements. Hideyoshi then asserts that the Christians' destruction of shrines of the native traditions "is something unheard of in previous ages." He stresses that "to corrupt and stir up the lower classes" by inciting them to commit these sacrileges, as the missionaries and the barons converted by them have done, "is outrageous." Naturally, those who are ultimately responsible for all those outrages – the Jesuit padres – must leave Japan and do so "within twenty days." The Portuguese merchants are specifically exempted from this antimissionary directive, as "the purpose of the Black Ships is trade, and that is a different matter."

Christianity and its servants had been the objects of suspicion, denigration, and occasional persecution in various parts of Japan from the day of Xavier's arrival in the country, but this was the first comprehensive anti-Christian decree issued by an effective national authority. What moved the *kampaku* to take this measure?

A "notice" dated Tenshō 15.6.18, the day before the edict of expulsion was issued, clearly explains Hideyoshi's motives. Particularly noteworthy is this document's prohibition of forced conversions. "That enfeoffed recipients of provinces, districts, and estates should force the peasants of Buddhist temples (*jian no hyakushō*), as well as

71 Frois, *Historia*, pt. 2 [B], chap. 53, Wicki, vol. 4, pp. 390–6; Matsuda and Kawasaki, trans., vol. 1 (1977), pp. 303–15.
72 See my *Deus Destroyed*, pp. 115–16, for a complete translation of Hideyoshi's edict dated Tenshō 15.6.19 (July 24, 1587); also see pp. 117–18, where an English version of the "notice" dated Tenshō 15.6.18 (July 23, 1587) is given.

others of their tenantry, against their will into the ranks of the sectarians of the Bateren [padres] is unreasonable beyond words and is outrageous," declares Hideyoshi, who then proceeds to outline in detail why he finds the "Bateren" so objectionable.

His most damaging aspersion is the elaborate comparison he makes between Christians and adherents of the Buddhist True Pure Land Sect (Jōdo Shinshū, also called the Ikkō, or "Single-Minded" sect). That sect's most prominent and belligerent branch, headed by the *hossu* (pontiff) of the Honganji, had in the sixteenth century developed into a religious monarchy that ruled whole provinces and competed with secular daimyo. The cohesiveness of this sectarian organization, drawn ever tighter by the "single-minded" nature of its members' commitment to the cause of their faith, made it the most formidable opponent of Hideyoshi's predecessor in the regime of national unification, Oda Nobunaga. That implacable hegemon did manage to defeat the Honganji's devotees and their pontiff, but not until they had fought him to the bitter end in a ten-years' war (1570–80) filled with sanguinary excesses.

Hence Hideyoshi could count on total agreement among his audience of military lords (many of whom had directly experienced that bitter conflict) when he asserted that the Ikkō sect had been patently "harmful to the realm" before it was put under control. In the context of Sengoku history, it was surely a damning judgment to state, as Hideyoshi does in his "notice," that the sectarians of the "Bateren" were "even more given to conjurations" than had been the case with the adherents of the Honganji, whose very byword was *ikki* (sworn league), a curse to the feudal ruler. This, if nothing else, made the Christians anathema.

With an eye on such Christian zealots as the daimyo of Akashi, Dom Justo Takayama Ukon, the *kampaku* reiterates: "That daimyo in possession of provinces and districts or of estates should force their retainers into the ranks of the sectarians of the Bateren is even more undesirable by far" than the activities of the Honganji's adherents; hence "these individuals of no discretion shall be subject to chastisement." Hideyoshi's "notice" of 6.18 then concludes by denouncing "the sale of Japanese to China, South Barbary, and Korea" by slavers who are implicitly identified as foreigners, and by banning the "trade and slaughter of cattle and horses for use as food."

The Jesuits reacted to Hideyoshi's determination with shock and indignant denials. In the propagandistic reports they sent to Europe, they maintained that the bill of indictment issued against them was nothing other than the unprovoked product of a tyrannical rage. Except for the allegation of the missionaries' complicity in the slave trade, however, all of the *kampaku*'s charges had a base in fact.

The name of Vice-Provincial Coelho was not mentioned explicitly in either of the two lists of particulars, but Hideyoshi's appreciation of the activities of this religious superior who pretended to secular authority, posed as the lawful ruler of Nagasaki, and paraded his military affectations on board his own naval vessel no doubt contributed much to his declared intent to expel the "Bateren" from Japan. Certainly, it did not take preternatural suspicion for Hideyoshi to identify Coelho as a competitor for the allegiances of his Christian vassals. Although Coelho's various plans to form a league of Christian daimyo had so far been unsuccessful, Hideyoshi was surely not unaware of the zeal with which he had pursued them (indeed, Coelho continued to entertain this figment of an armed holy alliance even after the edict of expulsion, going so far as to stockpile arms and ammunition for possible use against the anti-Christian tyrant). In short, the *kampaku*'s fear of the Christians' potential for "conjurations" was not groundless.

Hideyoshi had witnessed on the spot the inroads that Christianity had made into the nobility and the populace of Kyushu, and this made him all the more concerned about the number and the religious fervor of the Jesuits' converts in his own close entourage. These included such prominent figures as Dom Leão Gamō Ujisato (1556–95), Dom Agostinho Konishi, and Dom Simeão Kuroda, not to speak of Dom Justo Takayama. The last-named daimyo, thoroughly "Jesuited" from his youth, had made himself notorious by the forced Christianization of his domains in the Kansai area, first at Takatsuki and then, after 1585, at Akashi. In both those places, he had relentlessly pursued the eradication of native religious symbols and practices. Such excesses, Hideyoshi determined, must stop.

To make the other Christian lords toe the line, Hideyoshi dispossessed Takayama Ukon, reducing him to the existence of a *rōnin* forced to seek the protection (or, rather, submit to the supervision) of daimyo who retained Hideyoshi's trust. The others showed that they were daimyo first and Christians second. For the most part, they bent before the will of their master and abjured their faith, if only on the surface. To be sure, some of these chastened Christians, such as Konishi Yukinaga, continued to aid the missionaries discreetly. Kuroda Yoshitaka, too, remained loyal to the Christian religion to the end of his life. Such stalwarts, however, were few. The likes of Ōtomo

Yoshimune – hopefully but inappropriately named Dom Constantinho at his baptism on April 27, just three months earlier – reverted to type and resumed the persecution of Christianity.

Another matter of great concern to the national unifier as he prepared to leave Kyushu was the foreign Jesuits' status as the holders of domanial sovereignty over Nagasaki, a piece of Japanese soil made all the more important by its role as the terminus of the Portuguese trading vessels. In the aftermath of the edict of expulsion, Hideyoshi accordingly confiscated Nagasaki and appointed his own intendant (*daikan*) to administer the port city. The Jesuits' influence over that Catholic community was not erased, but it ceased being their colony. Nagasaki became instead the national hegemon's immediate domain.

The historical significance of the dispositions made by Hideyoshi in July 1587 was that the question whether to encourage, tolerate, or reject the Christian religion ceased being a matter that each daimyo could decide for himself. Hideyoshi made Christianity a national problem.

For the time being, however, the *kampaku* chose not to enforce his anti-Christian policy. To be sure, some churches were destroyed, and the missionaries were forced to reduce the scope of their public activities, but none of them had to leave Japan permanently as a result of the edict of 1587. So long as they remained discreet, Hideyoshi allowed them to exist without undue molestation, most likely because he continued to view the Catholic priests as valuable intermediaries in his contacts with the Portuguese traders. His forbearance caused some of the Jesuits to be optimistic regarding the chances of Japan's ultimate Christianization, especially because Hideyoshi seemed so enthusiastic about Western novelties. In fact, he himself led the period's fad for dressing *à la Portugaise*, a fashion complete with rosaries, reliquaries, and crosses worn as accessories around the neck. Hideyoshi did not, however, repeal his edict. The decree that stamped Christianity a subversive religion remained the law of the land. Hostility was but thinly hidden beneath the mask of tolerance.

What unleashed it and made it come into the open was a fortuitous event, the wreck of the Manila Galleon *San Felipe* off the coast of Shikoku in October 1596. Three years previously, in 1593, the Spanish colonial authorities in the Philippines had charged a group of Franciscan monks with an embassy to Hideyoshi; having concluded their diplomatic business, these friars remained in Kyoto as missionaries. Not only did their arrival mean the end of the Jesuit mission monopoly in Japan, the Franciscans conducted themselves with all the populist evangelical ardor characteristic of the early history of their order. According to the Jesuits, the fervency with which the friars proclaimed their faith amounted to recklessness. In any event, it is clear that it disturbed the tenuous *modus vivendi* that had developed between the Christian missionaries and Hideyoshi's regime.

The fact that the Jesuit mission was sponsored by the crown of Portugal whereas the Franciscans came to Japan under the patronage of Spain (two countries tied together since 1580 in a personal union under Philip II of Castile, a dynastic arrangement resisted by many Portuguese) aggravated the mutual antagonism between the two religious orders. Intent on fortifying its own position, each intrigued against the other, thus feeding the suspicions of the Japanese ruler.

Matters came to a head when the *San Felipe* was wrecked and Hideyoshi ordered the confiscation of the Spanish galleon's cargo. The ship's pilot sought to forestall that action by trying to impress Hideyoshi's agents with tales of his royal master's power, the might of the Spanish empire, and the thoroughgoing nature of the Spanish design for world conquest. An indispensable part of that design (so he alleged) was a fifth column of Spanish friars, sent ahead of military forces to Christianize the people of a country so that the land could then be easily taken over. At that, Hideyoshi "leapt to the conclusion that the friars of St. Francis, who had been in Meaco near unto three years, should also be taken for spies," and decided to do away with them and their Christians.[73]

That, at least, is the Jesuit side of the story, taken from the testimony of Dom Pedro Martins SJ, the bishop of Japan. The Franciscans, for their part, maintained that the Spanish pilot was blameless and that it was, in fact, the Jesuits who had slandered them before the Japanese authorities. A morass of recriminations between the missionaries has submerged the truth regarding who was responsible, but the fatal outcome of the *San Felipe* incident is clear. Hideyoshi was once more provoked to a draconian action. He ordered the execution of twenty-six Christians, including six Franciscan missionaries, three Jesuits, and seventeen Japanese laymen. And he renewed his general proscription of Christianity: "*I will that there be no more preaching of this law hereafter.*"[74] On February 5, 1597 (Keichō 1.12.19), there followed the martyrdom of the Twenty-Six Saints of Japan, who were crucified in Nagasaki. This was the first bloody persecution of the

73 Testimony of Bishop Pedro Martins SJ, cited ibid., p. 138.
74 Hideyoshi's orders, dated Keichō 1.11.10 (December 29, 1596), in Frois, "The report of the glorious death of xxvj persons," cited in my "The Cross and the Sword: Patterns of Momoyama History," in Elison and Smith, eds., *Warlords, Artists, & Commoners*, p. 79.

Christian religion in Japan and a grim first foreboding of the two and a half centuries of persecutions that were yet to come.

THE CHRISTIAN DAIMYO AND THE EARLY TOKUGAWA REGIME

There were no further martyrdoms of Christians in Japan under Hideyoshi: In the year and a half he had left to live, he was preoccupied with inflicting carnage on a far greater scale in Korea. Under his successor as national hegemon, Tokugawa Ieyasu, the Christian mission was to enjoy a decade of calm weather and clear sailing. But the missionaries were sailing in the eye of a storm.

Ieyasu at first took a conciliatory stance toward them, partially at least in consideration of the efforts of Christian daimyo who played important roles in the alliance that brought the Tokugawa to power in the great military conflict of 1600. To be sure, one of the principals of the anti-Tokugawa coalition that lost the battle of Sekigahara and, with it, the contest for Japan was also a Christian daimyo, Dom Agostinho Konishi Yukinaga. For every Konishi on the side of Ieyasu's adversaries, however, there was a Kuroda among the partisans of the Tokugawa.

That his coreligionists should have been instrumental in his defeat might be called poetic justice for Konishi, who had slaughtered large numbers of his fellow Christians only a decade earlier, in 1589 and 1590, in putting down a *kokujin* rebellion in the fief that Hideyoshi had assigned him in Higo Province. At least three of the "five Amakusa barons" (*goninshū*) who organized this *ikki* were Christians. But Konishi's brutal action as well as the uprising of the barons who wished to defend their regional autonomy should be considered as nothing more than further proof of the essential nature of the Christian daimyo: They pursued their own interests first and those of their religion second. It was an illusion to think that Christianity could be used to bind them in fraternal union, let alone a political alliance.

Thus Dom Protasio Arima Harunobu first promised to support Konishi in 1600 but then switched sides in time to help in the reduction of Dom Agostinho's fortress of Uto in Higo, and the Arima family thereby gained the confirmation of its daimyo status after the Tokugawa victory. Dom Simeão Kuroda Yoshitaka also took a stand against Konishi and was responsible for pacifying northern Kyushu in Ieyasu's behalf. Among those he defeated there was the ever-hapless Ōtomo Yoshimune, who had sought a last chance to recover Bungo but had bet on the wrong party in the national conflict. (Supposedly, Kuroda also managed to reconcile Ōtomo with Christianity, a task that surely took considerable powers of persuasion.) It is known that Yoshitaka's diplomatic skill was of great help to the missionaries, for whom he interceded with Ieyasu after the campaign's conclusion. No doubt as important in influencing Ieyasu to take a positive attitude toward the Christians was, however, the role played at the battle of Sekigahara by Yoshitaka's son, Dom Damião Kuroda (Nagamasa, 1568–1623).

His old and intimate political enmity against Ishida Mitsunari (1560–1600), the moving spirit of the anti-Tokugawa league, made Kuroda an early and fervent adherent of Ieyasu's cause, to which he made a critical contribution: It was Dom Damião who engineered the defection of the opposing general Kobayakawa Hideaki (1582–1602) and his army to Ieyasu at a crucial moment in the battle, thereby sealing the defeat of Ishida, Konishi, and their allies. For this service Kuroda was rewarded with a great domain at Fukuoka, a fief assessed at 523,100 *koku*, where he actively encouraged the Jesuit mission at the beginning of his tenure. But his affection for the missionaries would last only as long as his master, Ieyasu, permitted. Unlike in Sengoku, in Tokugawa Japan the daimyo danced to the shogunate's tune.

Interestingly, but not surprisingly, the inception of the Tokugawa regime's anti-Christian measures was intimately connected with the settlement of a problem of corruption in the Tokugawa house government. The man who set off this scandal was none other than Dom Protasio Arima.

Arima, who sought the addition of certain properties in Hizen to his fief, thought he could obtain this goal by the payment of large sums of money to Okamoto Daihachi, an aide of Ieyasu's senior councilor (*rōjū*) Honda Masazumi (1565–1637). Okamoto took the bribe but could do no better than forge the required documents. In 1612, this confidence game was inevitably exposed and Okamoto was executed, but not before he had had the chance to denounce Arima Harunobu for plotting the murder of the shogunate's commissioner (*bugyō*) in Nagasaki, Hasegawa Sahyōe.

For at least two reasons, this matter was far more serious than the melodrama that it may appear to be: That a vassal's investiture with land, a matter at the very pith and core of the feudal relationship, could be reduced to a business proposition between a subject daimyo and a relatively low-ranking member of their councils shocked the heads of the Tokugawa regime, the retired shogun Ieyasu (r. 1603–5) and his successor Hidetada (1579–1632, r. 1605–23). And the allegation that the magistrate charged with the government of one of the shogunate's most important direct holdings, the port city of Nagasaki, had become the object of an assassination plot raised broader questions regarding the loyalty of the western daimyo.[75] It did not help matters that both the principals in this nasty business, Protasio Arima and Paulo Okamoto, were Christians.

For his part in the Okamoto Daihachi incident, Dom Protasio Arima was first exiled from his province and then sentenced to death. But the incident had far broader consequences than the punishment of this one daimyo. The Tokugawa turned against Christianity with a vengeance, prohibiting the religion in shogunal domains. Needless to say, this measure was imitated by their subjects, the domanial rulers. One of the first who sought to ingratiate themselves with the Tokugawa that way was Harunobu's son, Dom Miguel Arima (Naozumi, 1586–1641), who apostatized, was installed by the shogunate as daimyo in Arima, and immediately began a massive effort to force his Catholic subjects into abandoning their faith. Not successful enough in that effort to please his masters, he was in 1614 transferred to another fief, Nobeoka in Hyūga. He left behind him a restive Christian populace and the seedbed of the Shimabara Rebellion, a large-scale disturbance that broke out in 1637 and confirmed the Edo bakufu in its cherished conviction that Christianity was a subversive faith.

The basic rationale for that judgment was laid out on February 1, 1614 (Keichō 18.12.23), for the rest of the Tokugawa era in a document that had the force of an ancestral law, because it was written at the behest of the founding father, Ieyasu. This "Statement on the Expulsion of the Bateren," which was drafted by the Zen monk Konchiin Sūden (1563–1633), first rehearses the standard traditionalist dictum, "Japan is the Land of the Gods," and then declares that the Christians seek to make Japan into "their own possession." Their religion teaches them to "contravene governmental regulations, traduce Shinto, calumniate the True Law, destroy righteousness, corrupt goodness" – in short, to subvert the native Japanese, the Buddhist, and the Confucian foundations of the social order. What else was this if not *jahō*, the ultimate "pernicious doctrine?"[76]

75 See Shimizu Hirokazu, *Kirishitan kinseishi*, vol. 109 of *Kyōikusha rekishi shinsho: Nihonshi* (Tokyo: Kyōikusha, 1981), pp. 98–101.
76 The original text can be found conveniently in Ōkubo Toshiaki, Kodama Kōta, Yanai Kenji, and Inoue Mitsusada, eds., *Shiryō ni yoru Nihon no ayumi (kinsei)* (Tokyo: Yoshikawa kōbunkan, 1963), pp. 124–5.

What undermined society, however, had to be uprooted. Hence, from this year 1614 onward, there followed a general persecution in Japan.

THE ANTI-CHRISTIAN SYSTEM OF THE TOKUGAWA

True to the "statement's" title and intent, the first and foremost measure of the general persecution was to order the expulsion of the missionaries from Japan. Many of them defied the bakufu's decree and stayed in the country in order to try keeping Japanese Christianity alive. Others, even more courageous, sought to slip into Japan from abroad, an adventure made all the more difficult by the prior need to find a sea captain prepared to take the risk involved in flouting the regime's explicit law. In some parts of Japan, the priests at first found ample protection from the populace. This was most notably the case in and around Nagasaki. In the seventeenth century's first decades, the port city had a population of some 25,000, almost all of them Christian. The neighboring areas of Hizen, too, were thoroughly Christian; indeed, many of the people of this region had been nourished in the Christian faith for three generations. Here the faith retained its vigor the longest, and here the persecution did its worst.

No less than forty-seven missionaries, including twenty-seven Jesuits, refused to leave in 1614, evaded the shogunate's agents, and continued their activities underground. Including those who were smuggled into Japan in trading ships, the number of Jesuits in that country had by the year 1621 actually increased to thirty-six.[77] Evidently, their zeal for the cure of souls did not diminish under persecution: Between 1614 and 1626, the Jesuits alone claimed seventeen thousand adult baptisms in Japan, and the total number of Japanese converted to Christianity under the grim conditions of those years must have been even higher, because members of other religious orders were also active in this mission.

Aware of the porous nature of his network of surveillance, Shogun Hidetada in 1616 ordered the daimyo to intensify their efforts to eradicate Christianity among the people of their domains. The persecution became more brutal. A sporadic bloodletting among the suspect populace followed, leading up to the so-called Great Martyrdom of Nagasaki in 1622, when fifty-five Christians were executed. But it

---

77 On the number of Jesuits in Japan between 1615 and 1644, see the charts set out by Schütte in *Introductio ad historiam Societatis Jesu in Japonia*, pp. 348–66. On the number of adults baptized by them under persecution, see ibid., pp. 415–18, 422–3.

was not until the reign of the third shogun, Tokugawa Iemitsu (1604–51, r. 1623–51), that the bakufu's anti-Christian system was perfected.

There were two faces to that system. Toward the inside, the bakufu asserted its supremacy by making the scrutiny of all possible traces of Christianity an instrument of social control throughout the country. The face directed toward the outside expressed the conviction that the "Christian peril" could be controlled and even eliminated if Japan were totally isolated from the sources of that contagion. Within Japan, all Catholic priests and their believers were to be hunted down, made to renounce their faith, or executed. Their sympathizers and sometime providers, the Portuguese traders were to be banned from the country.

In 1639, the Portuguese were expelled, and all contacts with Catholic lands were cut. In the next year, sixty-one members of an embassy sent by the Portuguese of Macao to seek a remission of that harsh ruling were beheaded: The world was to know that the shogunate meant what it said in its decrees. Thereafter, the Dutch were the only Europeans permitted an existence in Tokugawa Japan. Merchants imbued with a purely Protestant ethic, Christians who were enemies of the Catholics, they accommodated themselves to the shogunate's whims for the sake of profit and were content with their isolated niche in *sakoku*, a country under isolation.

How intimately the two sides of the system instituted by Iemitsu were associated may be seen from the so-called closed-country directives (*sakokurei*) issued over the names of his senior councilors and addressed to the bakufu's commissioners in Nagasaki. Five of these administrative directives were issued between 1633 and 1639, the year that ended the Christian Century. They deal in an increasingly rigorous fashion with three topics that the shogunate clearly thought to be interconnected: restrictions on Japanese travel abroad (after 1635, such travel was punishable by death), the reduction of the European presence in Japan, and the merciless persecution of Christianity.[78]

The very first of these directives proved fatal to the Jesuit missionaries in Japan. The document included a paragraph that offered financial incentives to inform on the whereabouts of Christian priests or their helpers, and this "infernal design" in short order led to the arrest of ten Jesuit padres and one *irmão* in Nagasaki. Another member of the Society of Jesus was arrested that year in Edo, and his capture reduced the number of Jesuits in Japan to six. By 1644, they all had been

78 See Asao Naohiro, *Sakoku*, vol. 17 of *Nihon no rekishi* (Tokyo: Shōgakkan, 1975), pp. 223–30.

rounded up, tortured, and killed or forced to apostatize.[79] There were no missionaries left, but the shogunate did not relax its watchfulness. Indeed, it urged redoubled vigilance on its subject daimyo.

A central Office of the Inquisition (Shūmon aratame yaku), established in Edo in 1640 and destined to remain in the bakufu's table of organization until 1792, coordinated the effort to purge Japan of Christians. In January 1665 (Kambun 4.11.25), the daimyo were told to emulate the shogunate and appoint inquisitors in their domains. From Yonezawa in the north through Okayama in the west of Honshu and down to Kagoshima in southernmost Kyushu, han governments instituted offices called "religious commissioner" (shūmon bugyō) and the like. To be sure, there was no real reason for this elaborate network's existence.

The fact is that there were practically no Christians left in Japan by the 1660s. Some three thousand Japanese Christians had died for their religion, including some six hundred captured in the Ōmura domain as late as 1657 and 1658, the last large group to be discovered. The mass of Japanese Christians had been driven into apostasy. All but a few, remote pockets of adherence to the "pernicious faith" had been eliminated, and it is doubtful that those few remaining groups of believers could properly be called Christian: Deprived of priests, cut off from the sources of their faith, their memories of its doctrines fading even as the Tokugawa era progressed, the "crypto-Christians" (kakure Kirishitan) of these isolated groups imperceptibly drifted from Catholicism into a syncretic folk creed tinctured with Buddhism and Shinto, the native Japanese religion.

And yet the machinery of surveillance did not rest. Indeed, at least one of the processes that the inquisition set in motion developed a dynamism that made it something more than a meaningless routine, a fruitless search for Christians where none was to be found. That process was the compilation of "religious inquiry census registers" (shūmon aratame ninbetsu chō), which were part of a more comprehensive scheme of social control. As no one was exempted from these surveys, which classified individuals according to the religious organization in which they claimed membership, they permitted the regime to keep tabs on all its subjects, whether or not there had ever been a Christian branch on their family tree.

79 The shock dealt to the Society of Jesus in Japan by the first sakoku directive and its immediate effects is described vividly in Visitator André Palmeiro SJ to General SJ, dated Macao, March 20, 1634, in Schütte, Introductio ad historiam Societatis Jesu in Japonia, pp. 256–8. Schütte painstakingly examines the process of the Society's extinction in Japan between 1639 and 1654, ibid., pp. 266–81.

The Buddhist ecclesiastical establishment was made responsible for verifying that a person was not a Christian through what became known as the "temple guarantee system" (*terauke seido*). By the 1630s, people were being required to produce a certificate of affiliation with a Buddhist temple as a proof of religious orthodoxy, social acceptability, and loyalty to the regime. In the Obama domain of Wakasa Province, for example, the daimyo Sakai Tadakatsu (1587–1662), a senior councilor of the shogunate, decreed peremptorily: "Everyone must have a [Buddhist] temple to go to for proof that he or she is not a Christian. Temple priests will therefore be required to issue guarantees." In 1639, newcomers who wanted to buy or rent houses in the city of Osaka were required to produce a temple's attestation before the contract could be signed. By the 1670s, such guarantees were required of anyone wishing to enter any type of service.[80]

When this system matured at the beginning of the eighteenth century, all members of the population were enrolled at birth in the Buddhist temple with which their family was affiliated and were listed as parishioners in the temple's *shūmon aratame ninbetsu chō*. The temple was responsible for keeping these registers up-to-date and for forwarding them periodically through the local officials to the domanial lord. So rigorously enforced was the *terauke* requirement that in many portions of Japan these documents provide modern demographers with extensive and reliable population data. Surely this is an effect that the inquisitors neither intended nor foresaw.

What does the sum total of the shogunate's policies amount to? The Edo bakufu seized control of the country's relations with the outside world even as it directed a nationwide network of vigilance aimed at what it regarded as the enemy within – the adherents of Christianity, the alien religion. In these two closely related realms of national policy, the shogunate was supreme. With the exception of the Sō of Tsushima, whose mediate role in relations with Korea was described in Chapter 6, the daimyo were kept out of foreign affairs. In the internal sphere, they followed the shogunate's lead and acted as its faithful agents in tracking down all those infected with the "pernicious faith."

Thus the daimyo, whose patronage had been so avidly sought by the missionaries of the sixteenth century and whose protection – once upon a time – had made Christianity flourish over wide regions of Japan, became in the seventeenth century the efficient instruments of

80 The "temple guarantee system" is discussed compendiously by Ōkuwa Hitoshi, *Jidan no shisō*, vol. 177 of *Kyōikusha rekishi shinsho: Nihonshi* (Tokyo: Kyōikusha, 1979), pp. 97–127. On Sakai Sadakatsu's decree, see ibid., p. 102.

a nationwide inquisition. They worked hard to eliminate from their domains and from their country what had been, in the case of daimyo families such as the Arima, Ōmura, and Kuroda, quite literally the faith of their fathers.

Just as some of their Sengoku ancestors had exerted themselves in forcing their populations to become Christian, mercilessly purging the priests, the symbols, and the practice of the "native" religions, Shinto and Buddhism, from the territories they ruled, so did the domanial lords of the Edo period seek to eradicate all traces of the "foreign" religion from the *han* entrusted to them by the shogunate. They forced the people subject to them to denounce Christianity, trample its symbols, and submit themselves to the officially sponsored Buddhist ecclesiastical structure.

What we see here is an extraordinarily vivid illustration of the extent to which the daimyo institution itself was transformed in the course of the Christian Century of Japan, the ninety years or so that passed from the arrival of Xavier and the first Jesuits to the promulgation of the final *sakoku* directives. With the advent of Oda Nobunaga, Toyotomi Hideyoshi, and Tokugawa Ieyasu, the regional hegemonies and petty baronies of Japan were integrated into a national body politic, and the daimyo, rulers over parts of that body, were subordinated to its head, the national hegemon. The Christian mission, which had established itself in a disjointed realm and had managed to survive the topsy-turvydom of Sengoku daimyo politics, lost its opportunity to thrive with the establishment of a strong central regime. The daimyo who once had sought profit by favoring the foreigners were henceforth bound by different rules of self-interest, needing to safeguard themselves in a world of constraints imposed on them by the Tokugawa shogunate.

CHAPTER 8

THOUGHT AND RELIGION: 1550–1700

Between the fourteenth and sixteenth centuries, Japanese society underwent fundamental changes that led to the dissolution of the traditional state structure and the appearance of new forms of state and social organization. This chapter focuses on the period from the middle of the sixteenth century to the end of the seventeenth century. It begins with the final stages of the era of social upheaval and ends a century after the formation of a unified political regime. During these 150 years a new state structure became firmly established, and the stable social environment that evolved led to a relatively steady improvement in the lives of the people. The factors that brought about this social change and the precise nature of its impact on the structure of society and the lives of the people are issues about which the opinions of researchers continue to differ. In this chapter, I would like to touch first on one social phenomenon that is central to the development of religion and thought in this period but has not received from researchers the attention it deserves. I refer to the establishment of the *ie* (house or lineage) as the basic unit of social organization among both the *bushi* (warrior class) and the rest of the population.

What I refer to here as the "house" is centered on the family. But the house was not identical with a consanguineous family unit; it incorporated as members unrelated persons such as employees (*hōkōnin*), and it was possible for an adopted heir who had no blood relationship to the other members to succeed to its headship. Rather than a natural kinship grouping, the *ie* may be described more accurately as an artificial functional entity that engaged in a familial enterprise or was entitled to a familial source of income.

The research of sociologists and anthropologists has made clear that beginning in the seventeenth century, "houses" of this kind constituted the basic units of Japanese society, and indeed the house has come to be recognized as a characteristic feature of Japanese society. It is believed that among the court aristocracy and the upper stratum of bushi, the house pattern took shape between the eighth to tenth centuries, but it probably did not become characteristic of the ordinary population until the fifteenth century, a period of widespread social upheaval that had a far-reaching impact on thought and religion.

The social structure that became established after the upheavals of the late medieval period was based on a system of functionally differentiated status categories: the bushi, peasant, artisan, and merchant classes. Within each category the house was the unit that performed the function associated with that status. In other words, the principle of a society organized around family units, each pursuing a hereditary "house occupation" (kagyō), emerged from the disintegration of the social structure of earlier times.

That the house became a characteristic phenomenon of the commoner stratum of society, a category that also encompassed the lower levels of the bushi class, was closely linked to an improvement in the standard of living of the ordinary populace. Researchers have found that from the fourteenth century the agricultural population began to establish solid ties to a particular piece of land, while merchants, artisans, and those engaged in various arts shifted from an itinerant to a more settled life-style. This development, as well as the closely related rise of cities during the sixteenth and seventeenth centuries, may be regarded as consequences of the spread of the house structure throughout society.

To be sure, not everyone could establish a "house" of his own. As late as the seventeenth century many people in the poorer strata of society were unable to form a house, and not all of those who were born into a house were able to preserve a place for themselves as regular members of it. The number of members that a house could accommodate was limited by the family enterprise and its total income. But even for those excluded from one house there remained the possibility of affiliating with another as an employee, servant, or adopted heir. And if one secured the economic wherewithal, one might eventually form a new house. The existence of various ways of pursuing a living within the framework of the house structure is evidence of the economic development that characterized the age.

Bushi enjoyed far fewer opportunities for economic advancement than did peasants and townsmen. The stipends and fiefs that constituted the bushi's sources of familial income were rigidly fixed according to hereditary criteria that allowed little room for expansion of the house or its division into separate branches. To rōnin (unattached samurai) or those second and third sons who faced exclusion from the house structure of bushi society, the world may indeed have appeared closed. However, if they did not cling to their bushi status, they could be adopted into the house of a peasant or townsman. Likewise, by taking up scholarship, religion, or one of the arts, they could establish a new house of their own. Society no longer assumed, as had often been the case in earlier ages, that birth into a particular lineage or social status was a prerequisite for making a living through cultural activities. The professional pursuit of such activities thus came to be regarded as a legitimate occupation, comparable to any other family enterprise. Consequently, regardless of one's birth, if one had scholarly or artistic talent, one could advance in one's field and thereby establish a house of one's own. This was true not only for bushi but also for those of townsman or peasant origin. The transformation of cultural activities into enterprises engaged in by the individual houses influenced in various ways the thought and religious outlook of this period. We shall leave fuller discussion of this influence for later, noting here only that the range of social activities expanded within the framework of the house structure.

As a result of the spread of the house structure throughout society, the majority of people were able to enjoy a modicum of security and even to look forward to a future improvement in their lives. Not surprisingly, then, much of the thought and religious writings of this period were characterized by a "this-worldly" outlook that basically affirmed reality and was primarily concerned with the question of how one should live within the existing society. This outlook found expression in an emphasis on ethics on the one hand and in the pursuit of hedonistic pleasures on the other. With the rise of a this-worldly outlook, the hold of the other world on the minds of the populace weakened, resulting in a relative decline in religiosity, as may be seen in the literature and art of the period.

We should not conclude, however, that religion itself had lost its vitality. To the contrary, it was in this period that Buddhism and Shinto first penetrated the populace as a whole and came to have a significant influence on the everyday lives of the people. What we regard as the traditional religion of Japan, which has survived even into the postmodern era, took shape at this time. Inevitably this religion took on a this-worldly coloration that constitutes its most distinctive feature. We should remember that a similar religious consciousness functioned as the spiritual backdrop to the seemingly secular thought and cultural activities of the age.

Although the dominant trend of the day was toward a this-worldly outlook, not everyone, needless to say, adopted such a perspective. What is of importance to us here is the link between this dominant trend and the individual's consciousness of himself or herself. If we assume that the rise of the house as a general social phenomenon sustained the trend toward a this-worldly outlook, then in what ways did the individual, reflecting these changes in religion and thought, actually perceive himself or herself in this relationship to the house?

The social conditions that enabled even the ordinary person to pursue a stable life within the framework of the house also brought about a general improvement in the lives of the house's members. The house system fostered in its members a growing awareness of themselves as individuals: not as free and independent entities but, rather, as discrete members of a particular house. As a result, the individual's perception of himself or herself was shaped by the dual role of the house as a unit of social organization.

On the one hand, the house was expected to carry out a particular function, to act as a gesellschaft. At the same time, it also had the characteristics of a familylike organic social unit, or gemeinschaft. As a gesellschaft, the house necessarily had to define its internal human relations in such a way as to fulfill the purpose (the conduct of the family enterprise) for which it was formed. Hence, each individual was assigned a role relative to the purpose of the group as a whole, whose successful performance became the guiding aim of his or her life. Roles within the group were diverse, and in many cases the relationship among members of the group was that of leader and follower. To that extent, the house's internal human relations were discriminatory and stratified. Discrimination and stratification also characterized the relationship between one house and another. The house as a unit carrying out its hereditary occupation was incorporated into the larger entity of the village and town or, in the case of samurai, the retainer band. But within that larger unit, the house was still responsible for performing its designated function. Even within the overall organization of the state, the house had a specified place within the structure of statuses, similarly based on function.

The clearly defined nature of the house fostered in the individual an awareness of his or her role as a member, and a consciousness of the responsibility in fulfilling his or her assigned role. However, that responsibility was rooted less in an objective perception of the individual function than in a sense of obligation to other members of the household, a moral obligation of devoted service typical of the relationship between parent and child or lord and retainer. Consequently, it was expressed not as an awareness of a clearly defined and demarcated accountability but, rather, as a feeling of unlimited responsibility.

The function of the house as a gemeinschaft was also conducive to the development of this sense of unlimited responsibility. Insofar as unrelated individuals were readily incorporated as full-fledged members of the house, the house as a gemeinschaft rested on the principle of equality, or commonality, among its members, as opposed to that of an innate hierarchy. As the representative of the house to the outside world, the house head exercised a functional authority over the other house members. But within the house, he did not enjoy any special privileges that set him above the others.

The premise of commonality rested on the understanding that each member of the house stood on equal ground and was responsible for some aspect of the underlying function of the house. This made it possible for each member of the house to regard the pursuit of his or her particular function as a self-generated responsibility rather than as something imposed from outside. The same premise was true of the external relations of the house. Although each house held a position within the village or town or state defined by its designated function within the hereditary status order, there was at the same time a sense of a commonality that linked houses, giving rise to a feeling of equality between members of different houses and thereby fostering the solidarity of the group.

Historians are intrigued by the questions of whether this sense of commonality was based on something more than the mutual bonds formed among those belonging to a particular organization and whether it could transcend the limits of an organizational framework and develop into a universal perception of the innate equality of human beings. This leads to the question of the extent to which this society could tolerate or guarantee freedom of the individual outside the bounds of the organization.

Scholars who study the history of Japanese social consciousness and thought have usually argued that this sense of commonality could not be extended beyond the particular group. Consequently, most have held that a universal notion of respect for the individual as such did not exist in traditional Japanese society. Such interpretations, however, may have resulted from facile comparisons with the individualism and universalistic systems of thought found in Europe and America. Although it can be argued that the sense of commonality that bound individuals in Japan was based on their mutual affiliation with a particular group, the scale of that group could be expanded from the house to the village, town, or retainer band and beyond that to the entire nation.

Given the gemeinschaft-like nature of the house, in which no fundamental distinction was made between those who were linked consanguineously to the house and those who were not, the sense of commonality in fact could transcend the state or ethnic group. Similarly, viewed from one angle, the consciousness of social responsibility as something that, rooted in direct affective ties, could not be sharply demarcated carried certain dangers. It might result in overly heavy demands on the individual and thus lead to the impairment of his or her sense of selfhood. However, considered from another angle, the very fact that the scope of responsibility was not rigidly defined meant that it was left up to the individual to decide how to accomplish his or her task. Thus it was also possible for the feeling of limitless responsibility to foster a sense of autonomous judgment. Whether or not that potential was realized within the actual historical context of early modern Japan is another question. Our aim is to try to answer this question, by examining Tokugawa society and thought.

RELIGION

The social upheaval during the fourteenth through the sixteenth centuries had a profound effect on Japanese religion, for it was during this period that what may be called a national religion was established in Japan. The religious beliefs and institutions regarded as characteristically Japanese reached maturity during this period and have continued to exist, with relatively little modification, until recent times. If one were to seek the origin of these religious beliefs, one undoubtedly could trace them back to antiquity. But it was only during the period under consideration that religion came to penetrate the lives of the general populace, not just as a primitive faith, but also as a system of beliefs that had undergone considerable intellectual refinement while sustained by the teachings and rituals of Buddhism and Shinto. The same period saw the establishment of a common religious institution throughout the country. And it is the spread of a common pattern of religious practice both geographically and socially that can be cited as evidence of the establishment of a national religion. We shall next look more closely at the specific features of this religion.

The structure of religious life

We have seen that a common pattern of religious practice spread throughout society in the fifteenth and sixteenth centuries, encompassing diverse lineages of faith. One of its identifying external features was the establishment of one shrine and one temple in each village. This made possible the simultaneous adherence of community members to Buddhism and to the worship of the native deities (*kami*). These disparate elements were brought together into a single entity by a common thread: the general desire of the populace to link themselves to something eternal while yet pursuing their everyday lives.

For the individual, religion served two basic functions. One was concerned almost exclusively with satisfying the needs of daily life, the other with the individual's fate after death. *Kami* worship, or Shinto, was largely oriented toward the former, Buddhism the latter. Once the two were identified with separate functions, a person could concurrently adhere to both. Although syncretism was practiced from antiquity, the practice of distinguishing between the customs and forms of worship that could be performed at Shinto shrines and at Buddhist temples, as well as the compartmentalization of these two religions into separate religious spheres, was essentially a post-sixteenth-century phenomenon.

To be sure, within the world of religion the inclination toward amalgamating Buddhism and Shinto continued to be strong, and it is not always easy to draw a line clearly separating the two. Although syncretistic practices were associated primarily with Shinto, the main form of religious activity at shrines remained *kami* worship.

Kami worship was believed to help achieve benefits in this world. At least two types of *kami* worship can be identified – one centering on the community and the other on the individual. For example, the shrine dedicated to the village's tutelary deity (*ujigami* or *chinju*) served as the center of village social life and was the focus of prayers for good harvests and a secure and peaceful existence. The shrine's significance in the lives of the villagers was largely limited to these functions, and the original religious nature of the object of worship was of no particular consequence. The deity worshiped may have been associated originally with syncretistic practices, such as Hachiman, but a deity's provenance had little bearing on the form in which it was worshiped.

The communal worship of *kami* could be called customary worship. People also engaged as individuals in a form of *kami* worship with a strong magical component, in the hope of obtaining good fortune or longevity for either themselves or their family. In this individual form of *kami* worship, prayers were normally directed at some specific deity whose spiritual authority was grounded in syncretistic beliefs. Gradually *kami* worship based on an amalgamation of Shinto and Buddhism (including Shugendō) came to be limited to the latter type of worship.

The new schools of Buddhism that arose in the Kamakura period were opposed in principle to the fusion of Buddhism and Shinto. The trend away from syncretism, in turn, influenced the older schools of Buddhism that had traditionally condoned such practices. The growing popularity of the Kamakura schools from the fourteenth century led to the further rejection of syncretism.

The new schools, unlike the traditional schools that were oriented primarily toward the concerns of the aristocracy, taught a new form of Buddhism that was concerned with the salvation of all people. This development in turn fostered the formation of a dual-structured, rather than syncretistic, religious outlook based on simultaneous faith in the *kami* as the protectors of one's day-to-day life and faith in the buddhas as entities who guided the individual to salvation in the other world.

As the new Buddhist schools spread among the populace, they began to accommodate themselves to the prevailing conditions of society, a process that inevitably led to changes in their orientation. More specifically, there was a significant shift in their interpretation of what salvation of the individual entailed. That is, salvation came to be understood principally as the salvation of the spirits of the dead. Therefore, greater emphasis was placed on guiding these spirits to the realm of the buddhas, and less attention was paid to the question of how the individual should seek salvation during his or her own lifetime. As a result, people came to regard the holding of funerals and masses for the dead as the main religious function of temples and priests.

"Funerary Buddhism" is the name often given to the type of religion that developed around these practices, and most of those who have written on the history of Buddhism in Japan have regarded it as marking a degeneration of Buddhism's original purpose. From the standpoint of Buddhist doctrine, such a conclusion is perhaps inevitable. A broader perspective, however, is necessary to understand the actual historical role of Buddhism as a social force. The founders of Kamakura Buddhism aimed to present Buddhist teachings in a form that would be accessible to the "ignorant masses," and therefore they were forced to make accommodations that would enable them to disseminate Buddhism as widely as possible.

The dissemination of Buddhism

The most prominent evidence of the establishment of Buddhism among the populace on a national scale in this period is the fact that a majority of the Buddhist temples surviving into the modern era were founded during this time. For example, studies based on records of the late seventeenth century have shown that a preponderant number of the temples of the Jōdo sect, one of the largest in Japanese Buddhism, were founded or reestablished between the late sixteenth and mid-seventeenth century. In the late seventeenth century, there were 6,008 Jōdo temples throughout the nation. A founding date can be ascertained for 4,435 of these temples; approximately 65 percent of them were established in the seventy-one years between 1573 and 1643. Because another 15 percent were founded between 1501 and 1572 and 10 percent were established between 1646 and 1696, all together about 90 percent of these Jōdo temples were established over the course of the sixteenth and seventeenth centuries. Moreover, the total number and the geographical distribution of these temples changed very little in the following centuries. A survey in 1941 recorded 6,974 Jōdo temples with a geographical distribution similar to that of the 6,008 temples that existed in the late seventeenth century. This evidence suggests that the main outlines of the Jōdo temple network as we know it today were established in the sixteenth and seventeenth centuries.[1] The results of other case studies suggest that a similar pattern of temple construction applies to other schools of Buddhism.[2]

The temples established during these two centuries fall into two major categories in terms of provenance. One type of temple can be traced back to the Buddhist sanctuaries (jibutsudō) set up by a local proprietary lord or influential warrior peasant within the grounds of his residence for the performance of funerary services for the repose of the spirits of his relatives and ancestors. The other type grew out of

---

1 Takeda Chōshū, *Minzoku bukkyō to sosen shinkō* (Tokyo: Tōkyō daigaku shuppankai, 1971), pp. 1171–91.
2 See Suzuki Taizan, *Zenshū no chihō hatten* (Tokyo: Unebi shobō, 1942), pp. 378–457; and Tamamuro Taijō, "Chūsei kōki bukkyō no kenkyū – toku ni sengokuki o chūshin toshite," *Meiji daigaku jimbun kagaku kenkyūjo kiyō* I (1962): 20–7.

the communal sanctuary (sōdō) established as a place of worship for the members of the local community. A local sanctuary was often transformed into a temple with a particular sectarian affiliation when a professional priest assumed responsibility for its affairs. The sanctuary was usually incorporated as a branch temple (matsuji) of the main temple of the school to which the priest belonged. This development also entailed a change in the priest's life-style. Before this time, most priests led an itinerant existence, traveling throughout the provinces to proselytize and carry on other religious activities, but with the proliferation of local temples, priests were able to take up permanent residence in a particular locality.[3]

The separation of warriors from the countryside carried out on a national scale during the last decades of the sixteenth century also had an impact on local sanctuaries, because it transformed most of rural society into agricultural communities made up solely of peasants. As a result, the local temple, even if formerly a personal sanctuary of the local proprietary lord, came to function as an institution serving the religious needs of all village members. At the same time, a large number of temples came to be established in urban areas where the bushi and commercial classes gathered after being driven from the land. Some existing temples were moved from the countryside to the city to serve the religious needs of the burgeoning urban population. But in most instances, the urban temples were new, a phenomenon that helps account for the expansion in the total number of temples across the nation during this period.

In both the village and the city, the religious function performed by these temples was different from that of the shrines. Whereas the shrines served as the center of communal life, the temples usually were linked to individual houses, and their main function was to serve as a venue for funerary services and masses for the dead performed on behalf of these houses. Hence, the establishment of houses among all social classes, as we just discussed, can be seen as another factor contributing to the dissemination of Buddhism.

The temple with which a particular house was affiliated was called a hereditary temple (bodaiji).[4] The families belonging to such a temple

---

3 Takeda Chōshū, "Kinsei shakai to bukkyō," in Iwanami kōza Nihon rekishi, vol. 9 (Tokyo: Iwanami shoten, 1975), pp. 265–8.
4 The term bodai (Sanskrit: bodhi) originally indicated the state of enlightenment. The latter state came to be equated with that of nirvana, and nirvana, in turn, came to mean death. Consequently, the recitation of prayers for the successful passage of the souls of the dead into the realm of the Buddha was referred to as "offering prayers for enlightenment" (bodai o tomurau). The bodaiji was the place where such prayers were offered.

were its parishioners (*danka*).[5] Houses at all levels of society, from the ruling classes down to the ordinary populace, formed ties to hereditary temples. The imperial family's *bodaiji* was Sennyūji, a Shingon temple in Kyoto, and that of the Tokugawa shogunal line was the Zōjōji, a Jōdo temple in Edo. These temples contained, respectively, the graves of members of the imperial family and the Tokugawa shogunal line.[6] Similarly, members of bushi and commoner families had tombs in the graveyard attached to their family's *bodaiji*. It is particularly noteworthy that even ordinary members of the populace came to have a temple and graveyard that they could regard as functioning on behalf of their family.

This development had an important influence on the system of grave construction within the Japanese village. Typically, two "graves" were established, one at the actual burial site (*umebaka*) and the other at a place set aside for the performance of rituals on behalf of the spirits of the deceased (*mairibaka*).[7] Centered on the Kinki area, this practice extended westward to the Chūgoku–Shikoku region, and eastward to the Kantō and has continued into recent times.

In 1854, S. W. Williams, the chronicler of Commodore Matthew Perry's expeditions to Japan, noted the existence of this custom in Yokohama, which at that time was still a small fishing village.[8] Japanese ethnographers and specialists in religion began to research the subject from around 1929. Today it is widely believed that the custom began in the fifteenth and sixteenth centuries, partly because dates on the stone steles erected at the site of the *mairibaka* date from that time. We should note also that the appearance of this custom coincides with the establishment of the village as a cohesive community.[9] It came to be regarded as obligatory to be buried in the graveyard shared communally by the villagers. At the same time, the autonomy of the

5 The term *danka* (*danna* house) derives from the term *danna* (an abbreviation of the Sanskrit *dana-pati*), meaning alms-offering believers. The *bodaiji* was also referred to as the *dannadera* (*danna* temple).
6 "Family" is used here in the narrow rather than the extended sense. For instance, in the case of the Tokugawa, Zōjōji was the *bodaiji* of only the immediate shogunal line, not of the Tokugawa family as a whole. The other branches of the Tokugawa family each had their own *bodaiji*. For example, the Owari branch of the Tokugawa had as its *bodaiji*, the Kenchūji, in Nagoya.
7 Although much research has been published on the dual-grave system, the most significant works have been collected in Mogami Takayoshi, ed., *Haka no shūzoku*, vol. 4 of *Sōsō bosei kenkyū shūsei* (Tokyo: Meicho shuppan, 1979).
8 Samuel Wells Williams, "A Journal of the Perry Expedition to Japan (1853–1854)," *Transactions of the Asiatic Society of Japan* 37 (1910): 116 (entry for February 25, 1854). The Japanese translation may be found in Hora Tomio, trans., *Perii Nihon ensei zuikōki* (Tokyo: Yūshōdō shoten, 1970), p. 191.
9 Satō Yoneshi, "Ryōbosei no mondaiten," and Mogami Takayoshi, "Sōsō," in Mogami, ed., *Haka no shūzoku*, p. 99 and pp. 144–6, respectively.

house as a constituent unit of the community grew stronger. People thus felt an increased need to maintain a sense of connection with the deceased members of the house, by conducting rituals for the repose of their spirits at a place specifically designated for that purpose. Such Buddhist funerary rites were performed to convey the spirits of the deceased to Amida's Pure Land or some other Buddhist paradise and thereby to transform the spirits into something pure. Because the actual burial site, which was associated with a state of pollution, was not regarded as a suitable venue for the performance of such rites, separate ritual graves were eventually established.

The changes in the common people's religious life that were occurring at this time can be understood only as a complex interaction with other developments. These we have noted as the evolution in ancestor worship, the spread of Buddhism among the populace, and the growth in the number of temples. Before this time, the ordinary people did not have clearly demarcated graves but simply disposed of their dead by abandoning corpses in uncultivated uplands or along riverbeds.[10] The legacy of this practice was apparent in the umebaka. Indeed, in some regions, the umebaka was referred to as the "dumping grave" (sutebaka). Corpses were generally placed in shallow pits, and after only a short interval the same ground was often dug up and used to bury another corpse. Thus, the site of the umebaka functioned less as a grave and more as a dumping ground for corpses. By contrast, the mairibaka, which first appeared in the late medieval period, usually was located within the sacred grounds of the village temple. Thus, whereas the umebaka preserved the traditional customs regarding disposal of the dead, the mairibaka marked the emergence of a new conception of the burial process and enabled even members of the ordinary agricultural population to possess graves.

Various attempts have been made to explain why the dual-grave system was most commonly practiced in the Kinki region and less frequently in outlying regions. Its emergence may have paralleled the appearance of the early modern village communities that developed first in the economically advanced Kinki region.[11] Judging by the dates engraved on village grave stones, it appears that individual houses did not begin to erect steles or stone markers for their

---

10 In ancient Japan the practice of disposing of the dead by exposing the body or burying it summarily was widespread, even among the aristocracy. See Tanaka Hisao, Sosen saishi no kenkyū (Tokyo: Kōbundō, 1959).
11 Satō Yoneshi, "Ryōbosei no mondaiten," and Takeda Chōshū, "Ryōbosei sonraku ni okeru mairibaka no nenrin (II)," Bukkyō daigaku kenkyū kiyō 52 (March 1968):152.

385

mairibaka until quite late. Before the eighteenth century, only prominent families in the village seem to have erected individual grave
stones; the majority of villagers made do with wooden memorial slips
at the village *bodaiji*, or with a communal stele or stone marker. This
indicates that both the *umebaka* and *mairibaka* were originally communal in nature, and it supports the hypothesis that the dual-grave system emerged in conjunction with the maturation of the communal
structure of the village.

Such a hypothesis also helps explain why the dual-grave system was
less likely to take root in peripheral areas. There the social stratification was more rigid, which tended to hinder the development of a
sense of community. Nonetheless, even in remote villages, similar
relationships developed at about the same time between the hereditary
family temples and its parishioners. Hence, the ordinary population in
remote regions also came to possess graves, even if they did not adopt
the dual-grave system.

It is important to note also that graveyards appeared at the same
time even among segments of the population that preferred a single
grave and so practiced cremation, namely, the townspeople and adherents of the Shin sect of Buddhism. Shin believers were among the first
to introduce the custom of cremating the dead and establishing a single
grave for both burial and ritual.

These changes in the role of the temple and that of burial customs
suggest that faith in Buddhism had come to play an important part in
the everyday life of most of the population. Accordingly, from the
1650s, the governing authorities began to use these developments for
various political purposes. For example, authorities seeking to enforce
the bakufu's prohibition of Christianity established a temple registry
system based on the relationship between the *bodaiji* and its parishioners. Bakufu officials sought to regulate the affairs of religious institutions by recognizing the authority of a main temple over its many
branches. Although the civil authorities were merely co-opting existing
relationships (between parishioner and *bodaiji*, and main and branch
temple) to achieve their own goals and not creating social institutions
anew, such manipulation brought about various changes in these religious institutions, many of which were ultimately detrimental.

For temples and priests to have taken on as their main function the
performance of funerary rites and ceremonies for the spirits of the
dead may have been a distortion of Buddhism's original spiritual intentions. However, by reassuring people about their own fate after death,
such practices fostered a sense of well-being that comes from knowing

that one has already been blessed with salvation, a development that was not without religious benefit.

It is significant as well that the practice of referring to the deceased as *hotoke* seems to have become common about this time.[12] The use of the term *hotoke*, which means buddha, indicates that people believed that the deceased would enter the realm of the Buddha as a result of the religious ministrations performed by the priest on the parishioner's behalf. The belief also developed that the spirits of the deceased returned to his or her family home every year during the Bon festival held in the summer and at the spring and autumn equinoxes, to receive the religious solace offered by his or her descendants and by priests engaged for this purpose. The regular performance of these seasonal religious ceremonies came to be a distinguishing characteristic of Japanese Buddhism.

From the perspective of Buddhist doctrine, it was contradictory to expect that spirits freed from the bonds of human existence would periodically return to this world.[13] Yet it was not perceived so because Buddhist beliefs had fused with the beliefs of traditional ancestor worship.[14] As a result, the deceased was regarded not simply as a *hotoke* but also as one of the ancestors who protected the house and preserved intimate ties with its living members. Likewise, the conviction that even after death one could continue to act as a member of the house offered further reassurance to the living about their own fate after death. This constellation of beliefs was reinforced by the spread of the custom of maintaining a Buddhist altar (*butsudan*) in each house, dating from about the seventeenth century.[15] The *butusdan* contained such objects as a Buddhist image and mortuary tablets of deceased family members, and it acted as the repository of the spirits of the ancestors (who had become *hotoke*).

Thus, Japanese Buddhism fostered a this-worldly orientation in two ways: It did not demand that ordinary believers pursue a particular religious regimen, which would set them apart from this world, and it sought to preserve ties with this world after death. The outlook characteristic of Tokugawa Buddhism linked the everyday life and human

12 Aruga Kizaemon, "Hotoke to iu kotoba ni tsuite," in Takeda Chōshū, ed., *Senzo kuyō*, vol. 3 of *Sōsō bosei kenkyū shūsei* (Tokyo: Meicho shuppan, 1979).
13 Hirayama Toshijirō, "Kamidana to butsudan," in Takeda, ed., *Senzo kuyō*, pp. 229–31.
14 Much research has been done on the fusion of Buddhism and the veneration of ancestors. Representative works are Yanagita Kunio, *Senzo no hanashi*, vol. 10 of *Teihon Yanagita Kunio shū* (Tokyo: Chikuma shobō, 1963); Takeda Chōshū, *Sosen sūhai*, vol. 8 of *Saara sōsho* (Kyoto: Heirakuji shoten, 1957); and also Takeda, ed., *Senzo kuyō*.
15 Hirayama, "Kamidana to butsudan," and Takeda Chōshū, "Jibutsudō no hatten to shū-shuku," in Takeda, ed., *Senzo kuyō*.

relations that centered on the house with the sacred. Although the evaluation of the spiritual quality of such a religion is not our task, we should note that what often is described simply as a secular outlook in fact rested on religious sentiments of this sort.

New forms of kami worship

Although Buddhism, which was by origin a foreign religion, did not take root among the ordinary population before the fourteenth century, *kami* worship was an indigenous religious practice that was widely disseminated much earlier. From ancient times, the formation of a social group was accompanied by the belief in the existence of a deity that would protect the group, and the members of the group assumed it to be their natural duty to conduct regular ceremonies honoring that deity. However, the form of such ceremonies and the popular understanding of the characteristics of the deities they honored changed over time. Let us examine these changes that resulted from the transformation of society characteristic of the fifteenth and sixteenth centuries.

The most important change was the emergence of the local tutelary deity (*ujigami*) as the center of the religious life of small regional communities like the agricultural village.[16] The word *ujigami* means the *kami* that protects a particular *uji* (a family or social group originally based on consanguinity). Although the *uji* often included people who were not blood relations, the tie among members of the *uji* was nevertheless usually conceived of as a blood tie. The custom of referring to the tutelary deity of such *uji* as *ujigami* existed from ancient times, and the practice continued into the medieval age. We see evidence of it, for example, in the Minamoto worship of Hachiman as its *ujigami*. However, the local *ujigami* that appeared in the fifteenth and sixteenth centuries were quite different. They had no connection with a particular lineage but instead were regarded as the protective deities of groups formed on a purely regional basis.

Early evidence of the use of the term *ujigami* in this new sense may be found in an entry for the year 1447, from the diary of the Zen priest Zuikei Shūhō. He wrote: "It is the general custom of people to refer to the deity who presides over the place in which they were born as their

16 The *ujigami* was also known as *ubusuna no kami* (natal deity) and as the *chinju* (protector); these names would seem somewhat more appropriate to the character of the *ujigami* as a local tutelary deity. However *ujigami* is the oldest and most generally used of these terms; the other two seem to have appeared later.

ujigami." Having been born in Sakai in Izumi Province, Zuikei noted that his own *ujigami* was the deity of Sumiyoshi. In this case his natal home lay within a *shōen* that already had become urbanized. Moreover, the shrine of the deity of Sumiyoshi that he identified as his *ujigami* was not located in Sakai itself but in the neighboring province of Settsu.[17] But though the *ujigami* of which Zuikei spoke was thus slightly different from the later village *ujigami*, his usage indicates that it had become the general practice to refer to the protective deity of a social unit with ties to a particular locality as a *ujigami*. In essence the *ujigami* to which he referred was the same as the *ujigami* of rural communities that existed from the seventeenth century on.

No fully convincing answer has been offered to the question of why a term that originally indicated the deity of a consanguineous group came to be used for a regional deity. Based on current information, my tentative hypothesis is that such a usage developed because the residents of a particular regional community regarded the *kami* in question as their common ancestral deity.[18]

The *ujigami* of antiquity – that is, the tutelary deity of a particular *uji* – was not necessarily the ancestral deity of that *uji*. This is clear from the fact that the Fujiwara *uji* of the Nara period took the *kami* of the Kashima and Katori shrines (located respectively in the provinces of Hitachi and Shimōsa) as their *ujigami*, whereas the Minamoto *uji* adopted Hachiman. None of these *kami* was regarded as the ancestor of the *uji* in question. At the same time, each *uji* had its own "parent deity" (*oyagami*) which it took to be its ancestor. Over time, the *ujigami* was also seen as an ancestral deity. With the dissolution of the *uji* and the emergence of the house as the fundamental unit of society, the belief that the souls of the dead ancestors of the house would act as a kind of deity to protect their descendants became widely held.

According to folklorists, one of the distinctive features of ancestor veneration in Japan is that in Buddhist services, the dead are first worshiped as *hotoke*, or spirits, but eventually (typically thirty-three

---

17 The deity of Sumiyoshi was the object of special veneration by those involved in sea commerce and fishing. It was presumably for this reason that it was worshiped as the protective deity of a port like Sakai. Sakai (literally, "border") was located on the border of the provinces of Settsu and Izumi; it combined within it what had originally been two separate *shōen*, Kita no shō (Settsu) and Minami no shō (Izumi).

18 Yanagita Kunio expresses a similar view in *Shintō to minzokugaku*, vol. 10 of *Teihon Yanagita Kunio shū*, originally published in 1943, and in *Ujigami to ujiko* (vol. 11), pp. 405–7, originally published in 1947. However, he holds that each house previously had its own *ujigami* and that these became combined into a common village *ujigami*. In fact, however, it appears that the concept of the village *ujigami* as the common ancestral deity of the villages existed before the practice of each house having its own *ujigami* became clearly established.

or, in some cases, fifty years after death), the soul of the deceased is believed to lose its individual characteristics. At that point, it becomes fused with the spirits of the ancestors in general and, as the ancestral deity of the house, enters the realm of the *kami*.[19] Although such beliefs are commonly referred to as "traditional folk religion," it is likely that this particular form of ancestral veneration, combining elements of both Buddhist and *kami* worship, spread widely throughout society only in the last several centuries.

We can assume that from antiquity people shared the vague notion that the spirits of the ancestors would protect their descendants. However, in an age when people simply abandoned the corpses of the dead instead of making a grave for them, the soul of a deceased individual was presumably not singled out for particular attention. But with the spread of Buddhism, which took the salvation of the individual as its mission, the idea took root that Buddhist services should be performed, for a certain length of time, for the dead as individuals. That period generally corresponded to the time during which family members retained a personal memory of the deceased. In other words, for that span of time the deceased "existed" simultaneously as an individual who needed the religious ministrations of his descendants and as one of the ancestors of the house. Eventually, however, the souls of the deceased became totally subsumed into the latter category.

Finally the question remained as to where the ancestors who had been transformed into *kami* should be enshrined. There were two plausible choices: the "god shelf" (*kamidana*) maintained by each household or the *ujigami* worshiped by the local community. Of these, the *ujigami* probably existed earlier. The relationship between the *ujigami* and the *kamidana* seems to have been similar to that between the temple and the *butsudan* in Buddhist practice. Just as the emergence of the temple as a communal site for funerary services and enshrinement of the dead appears to have preceded the establishment of *butsudan* in individual houses, it is likely that the members of the community gave priority to the *ujigami* that they worshiped as a community. They referred to this *kami* that served as the focus of the solidarity of their community as their *ujigami*, precisely because they regarded the *kami* as their common ancestral deity.

The people (actually the houses) who worshiped the *ujigami* were known as *ujiko*. Because the word *ko* (child) forms a natural pair with the word *oya* (parent), reference to the worshipers of a particular

19 See Yanagita, *Senzo no hanashi*.

ujigami as *ujiko* lends further support to the hypothesis that people saw the *ujigami* also as an *oyagami* (ancestral deity).[20] Treating the *ujigami* as an ancestral deity thus assumed the existence of an exclusive bond between the *ujigami* and the *ujiko*. The *ujigami* was believed to protect only its *ujiko;* likewise it was worshiped only by its *ujiko.* In the same way, the *ujigami* of ancient society had been worshiped only by those who belonged to the particular *uji* associated with that *ujigami.*

The worship of local *ujigami* began around the same time as did the formation of the village community. Initially, it is likely that the *ujigami* were enshrined not in permanent edifices but in *yashiro,* an ancient word that originally referred to a place where a temporary altar was erected to conduct services honoring a *kami.*[21] Agricultural villages traditionally held ceremonies to summon the presence of the *kami* only on particular occasions, such as before planting in the spring and after harvesting in the fall. During the rest of the year, the *kami* was believed to reside not in the village itself but at the top of a nearby mountain.

It is difficult to determine just when villages began to build a permanent shrine in each village or group of villages and to regard the *kami* as residing there permanently. The change may have occurred as the content of communal life grew more complex and as susceptibility to disasters such as drought, floods, and epidemic diseases fostered a need among the people to offer prayers to the *kami* on more than the traditional fixed occasions. The increased tendency by the individual house or village member to pray for the *kami*'s personal assistance could also have spurred the change.

In any case, permanent shrines were probably not constructed before the emergence of the house as a constituent element of the community was quite advanced, and thus we can safely date their establishment to sometime around the sixteenth century. The local *ujigami,* however, may have appeared somewhat earlier in economically advanced areas like the Kinki region. There large communities known as *sōshō,* which encompassed an entire *shōen* or an area of comparable size, had already emerged by the thirteenth century. The deity of the

20 The word *ko* originally meant one belonging to an occupational group, and the term *oya* meant the leader of that group; see Yanagita Kunio, *Ie kandan,* vol. 15 of *Teihon Yanagita Kunio shū.* However, because from antiquity on, the family or familial organizations such as the *uji* or *ie* functioned as the work group, it became common to refer as well to a blood parent or ancestor as *oya* and a child or descendant as *ko.*

21 The *ya* of *yashiro* means a building or altar, and *shiro* means the place where such a structure was erected. Originally the combination of these two linguistic elements seems to have referred to a space reserved for the construction of a temporary altar. Yanagita, *Shintō to minzokugaku,* and Hirayama, "Kamidana to butsudan."

RELIGION

shrine that formed the religious center of the *sōshō* was also referred to as its *ujigami*, and permanent shrines were built quite early. Another important feature of *sōshō ujigami* worship was the existence of the *miyaza*, an organization made up of bushi and petty proprietors acting as representatives of the community, which took responsibility for conducting and managing the religious ceremonies of the shrine.[22]

Whereas the formation of villages was the end result of communal efforts for economic survival, the *sōshō* (which may have consisted of groups of villages) was a political institution. Consequently, although the *sōshō* disappeared with the final disintegration of the *shōen* system in the sixteenth century, the village survived as the fundamental unit of social organization. These political developments were mirrored in the religious realm as the *ujigami* of the *shō* evolved into the *ujigami* of the village and the *miyaza* of the *shō* became the *miyaza* of the village.[23] The *ujigami* of a *sōshō* became the *ujigami* of a particular village or the common *ujigami* of a particular group of villages, and the ceremonies centering on that *ujigami* were handled by a *miyaza* made up of influential peasants from that village.

The same pattern of evolution in *ujigami* worship occurred among the urban commoner population. In place of a communal structure encompassing the entire city, various subdivisions of the city (referred to as *chō* or *machi*) became the locus of social activities, and several of these *chō* jointly managed the rites for a common *ujigami*.

In many ways the evolution of the *ujigami* resembled the evolution of the Buddhist temple. The difference is that the presence of a professional priest was a necessary prerequisite for the establishment of a temple. In the case of the shrine, however, the *miyaza* or a comparable local organization of the parishioners played the central role in the religious activities focused on the shrine. Even when a shrine functionary such as the *kannushi* had become responsible for the conduct of shrine rituals, in many cases the villagers had originally rotated the post among themselves. Shrines with a notable pedigree, like the *ujigami* of the *sōshō*, tended to have professional shrine functionaries. In ordinary villages the normal practice was to appoint a professional shrine priest only if the ritual to be performed grew too complex.

With the appearance of shrine priests in various parts of Japan, the need arose for some entity to oversee their activities. In response, the

22 Higo Kazuo, *Miyaza no kenkyū* (Tokyo: Kōbundō, 1941); Hagihara Tatsuo, *Chūsei saishi soshiki no kenkyū* (Tokyo: Yoshikawa kōbunkan, 1962).
23 Imai Rintarō and Yagi Akihiro, *Hōken shakai no nōson kōzō* (Tokyo: Yūhikaku, 1955); Andō Seiichi, *Kinsei miyaza no shiteki kenkyū* (Tokyo: Yoshikawa kōbunkan, 1960).

Yoshida family, whose original base was the Yoshida Shrine in Kyoto, supplied a doctrine of *kami* worship (known as either Yoshida Shinto or Yuiitsu Shinto) and came to exert great influence over the administration of shrines throughout the country.[24] Yoshida Shinto was founded by Yoshida Kanetomo (1453−1511), who established himself and his descendants as authorities who determined the proper way to perform shrine rituals and granted ranks and certificates to shrine functionaries. The Yoshida family also granted ranks and titles to shrines. Between the sixteenth and seventeenth centuries, the Yoshida family succeeded in bringing under their supervision the majority of the country's shrine functionaries.

Originally, the people's *ujigami* had no distinguishing characteristics, but from the eighteenth century onward it became common for local *ujigami* shrines to be identified as a branch of some major shrine, such as those devoted to Hachiman, Inari, or Tenjin (Sugawara no Michizane). In most cases, the affiliation of the local *ujigami* with a major central deity had relatively little impact on the actual content of *ujigami* worship. The spread of Ise worship among the populace, however, did have a major influence on local religious life.

The missionary activities of priests (*oshi*) associated with the Ise shrines were at first directed primarily at important local figures and bushi. However, from the end of the sixteenth century, the *oshi* began to enroll members of the ordinary populace as "parishioners" (*danna*), and as a consequence the number of both *oshi* and parishioners increased greatly. The number of Outer Shrine *oshi*, which had been about 150 at the end of the sixteenth century, grew to about 550 by the beginning of the eighteenth century. In addition there were about 140 Inner Shrine *oshi*. According to a document from the year 1777, the Outer Shrine *oshi* alone counted 4,961,370 households as parishioners, a figure nearly equal to the country's entire population.[25]

In contrast with communal worship of the *ujigami* as the tutelary deity of the community, Ise worship rested on the faith of the individual or his or her house. This was clearly a new development in popular *kami* worship. Worship of the Hachiman, Inari, or Tenjin deities, which became fused with the local *ujigami*, also entailed the selective worship of a particular deity for its distinctive spiritual authority.

24 Hagihara Tatsuo, "Yoshida shintō no hatten to saishi soshiki," in his *Chūsei saishi soshiki no kenkyū*, pp. 611−718; Emi Seifu, "Yuiitsu shintō ron," in Emi Seifu, *Shintō setsuen* (Tokyo: Meiji shoin, 1942).
25 Miyamoto Tsuneichi, *Ise sangū (Gendai kyōyō bunko)* (Tokyo: Shakai shisōsha, 1971); Shinjō Tsunezō, *Shinkō shaji sankei no shakai keizaishi-teki kenkyū* (Tokyo: Hanawa shobō, 1982).

Notably it was from the sixteenth century onward that faith in a particular Hachiman, Inari, or Tenjin shrine, apart from one's *ujigami*, spread among the general populace. The parallel existence of two types of *kami* worship, one at the level of the community and the other at the level of the house or the individual, became a new feature of the religious life of this period, and Ise worship was the most representative example of the latter type of *kami* worship.

From the eighteenth century it became common for households to set up *kamidana* (god shelves) and to place in them talismans from their local *ujigami* and from the Ise Shrine. The *kami* worship conducted at the level of the individual house thus retained a magical component, as did individual worship of *kami*. However, *kami* worship sustained by the individual's growing sense of self-awareness also came to acquire a rational, ethical orientation among some worshipers. This development may be seen in the appearance of religious teachings that stressed rectifying oneself in order to conform to the *kami*'s desire.

A key example of such teachings is the "Oracle of the Three Shrines" (Sanja takusen), which is believed to have been formulated some time in the fifteenth century.[26] The "Oracle of the Three Shrines" consisted of a piece of paper on which the names of the Ise, Hachiman, and Kasuga shrines were written. Below that was recorded the claim that the deity of each of these shrines taught the virtues of complete sincerity (*shōjiki*), purity (*shōjō*), and benevolence (*jihi*). From the sixteenth century onward this oracle was widely circulated, and it was common for ordinary people to mount a copy of it on a scroll that was placed in the alcove of their houses. This form of *kami* worship could be a denial of the efficacy of magical prayers and rituals. The popularity of the saying "If one's heart conforms to the way of complete sincerity (*makoto*), even if one offers no prayers, the *kami* will provide protection" may have reflected a trend away from magic.[27]

An example of yet another new form of *kami* worship that took shape in this period was the practice of enshrining human beings as *kami*. A key date in the development of this practice was the enshrinement in 1599 of Toyotomi Hideyoshi, who had died the previous year, as Toyokuni daimyōjin, at a shrine built in his honor in Kyoto. Before this time, historical figures had become the object of worship at cer-

---

26 Watanabe Kunio, "Sanja takusen no shinkō," in Watanabe Kunio, *Shintō shisō to sono kenkyūsha tachi* (Tokyo: Wataki, 1957).

27 In his *Yōtsuki*, written in 1650, Watarai Nobuyoshi argued that despite the prevalence of this formulation, it still was necessary to offer prayers to the *kami*.

tain specific shrines. Emperor Ōjin was identified with the deity Hachiman, an existing object of worship, and Sugawara no Michizane was deified as Tenjin, because he had died in a state of anger over a wrong done him. It was believed that enshrining his spirit would keep it from acting malevolently. But it was unprecedented for someone who had died under normal circumstances to be enshrined in his own right, and all the more unusual for the enshrinement to take place shortly after his death.[28]

Hideyoshi is said to have left instructions for his enshrinement. But why should he have had such an idea? And why was this new arrangement readily accepted by the court and other contemporary political and religious authorities? The traditional explanation that Hideyoshi's deification was due on the one hand to a grandiose sense of his own importance and on the other to a general adulation of him as a heroic figure is unsatisfactory. Perhaps the motive should be sought in the new kind of religious outlook just described.

In the new religious outlook, the kami and hotoke were not necessarily regarded as inhabiting a realm far removed from this world. If the dead became hotoke and the ancestors kami, it was also plausible to assume that the kami and hotoke were human, or at least a transformation of what once had been human. Further, although in name and form the hotoke and kami may have been different, the idea became widely established that fundamentally they were the same.

Both the view advocated by Buddhist Shinto (Ryōbu Shintō) that the kami were local manifestations of buddhas (honji suijaku) and the opposite assertion of Yoshida Shinto that the kami were fundamental and the buddhas secondary manifestations served the notion that the kami and the hotoke were essentially the same. This idea was further reinforced by the fact that Buddhist priests often assumed responsibility for performing shrine rituals. That a human being of extraordinary ability and accomplishments should have become a kami rather than a hotoke after his death was not perceived as particularly strange.

The teachings and ritual developed under the aegis of Yoshida Shinto unquestionably contributed to the acceptance of a recently deceased person as a kami. At the same time, from Hideyoshi's personal perspective, there were various reasons that he should have wanted to become a kami rather than a hotoke. As the founder of a new house rather than a successor to one with a long pedigree, it was

28 Miyaji Naokazu, "Hō taikō to Toyokuni daimyōjin," in his Jingi to kokushi (Tokyo: Kokon shoin, 1926); Katō Genchi, Hompō seishi no kenkyū (Tokyo: Chūbunkan, 1934); Miyata Noboru, Ikigami shinkō: hito o kami ni matsuru shūzoku (Tokyo: Hanawa shobō, 1970).

necessary for him to create an *ujigami* protector of his house, in the same way that Hachiman, for instance, protected the Genji and the Ashikaga houses. Moreover, as one who died fearing for the political future of the Toyotomi house, it was quite natural that Hideyoshi should wish to become a *kami*, capable of directly influencing this world, rather than a *hotoke*, whose power over this world would be limited. These various factors contributed to the creation of a new type of shrine, dedicated to the Toyotomi house. Apart from such factors particular to Hideyoshi, the general religious consciousness of the day was already prepared to accept the practice of enshrining a human being as a *kami*.

The enshrinement of Tokugawa Ieyasu, who succeeded Hideyoshi as the nation's dominant political figure, was a further manifestation of this religious trend. Ieyasu was deified as Tōshō Daigongen the year after his death in 1616, and the Tōshōgū Shrine at Nikkō was built to enshrine him. Moreover, from the seventeenth century on, not only political figures but also people of lesser stature came to be regarded as *kami*. Daimyo, Shinto teachers, and people who had accomplished some deeds of particular social merit frequently were enshrined as *kami* after their death or even during their lifetime. Connections might also be drawn between the growth of this religious consciousness that assumed a close linkage between this world and the world to come, and certain social phenomena of the seventeenth century. For example,there was the practice of self-immolation on the death of one's lord (a practice known as *junshi*), which achieved a certain currency among bushi in the first part of the century, and the wave of double suicides (*shinjū*), which swept commoner society in the latter half of the century. Both phenomena rested on the assumption that one could achieve after death what was unattainable in this world and hence may have been nourished by the same religious consciousness that sustained the practice of enshrining humans as *kami*.

THOUGHT

Ever since humans first became conscious of their own existence, they have posed the question of how they should live. When efforts to answer this question focused on the state of the human spirit or of a soul, which was presumed to survive the death of the individual, it was primarily a religious question. By contrast, when the issue of how the individual should behave within actual society was emphasized, it became mainly a matter of morality or ethics. The question of morality was inextricably bound up with the nature of the society or state within which the individual acted. Consequently, the discussion of morality extended naturally to the question of the kind of government needed to ensure social and political order. Discussions of morality also had a significant religious dimension, particularly when addressing the question of humanity's basic nature. And in the premodern world, speculation about the social or political order usually entailed the premise of some link between that order and a transcendental authority. Thus, the discussion of politics cannot be separated completely from religion. Nevertheless, in what follows I shall focus on thought in the sense of more or less systematic ideas about the problems of morality and politics, as distinguished from more purely religious conceptions.

In Japan, from the sixteenth century on, thought in this sense developed independently of religion. From antiquity, Confucianism, transmitted to Japan from China, had served as the source of ideas about morality and politics. However, up to the fifteenth century, Confucianism had remained a branch of scholarship of interest almost exclusively confined to Buddhist clergy and intellectuals of the upper, aristocratic, stratum of society; it had virtually no impact on society as a whole. Rather, the general population turned to religious teachings, in particular those of Buddhism, for intellectual guidance. Then, during the fifteenth century, a fundamental reorientation took place in the nation's religious life that reassured people concerning their fate after death and shifted their interest toward questions of politics and morality. The stabilization of people's livelihood and the possibility for future improvement that accompanied the spread of the house structure throughout society also encouraged such a shift in emphasis.

The development of thought in a form independent from religion sometimes is explained as the result of the separation of religion and thought, or even as the result of a trend toward the rejection of religion. More accurately, however, the new interest in the question of how to live in actual society should be seen as a consequence of the permeation of religion into the lives of the general populace. Confucianism, which played a central part in this intellectual activity, had a certain religious dimension, and several prominent Buddhist and Shinto clerics entered the debate over politics and morality from their own specialized, religious point of view. What distinguished the activities of these figures from those of both earlier and later periods is that they, like the Confucian thinkers of this era, characteristically took up as individuals rather than as the leaders of a religious movement the question of how to live in society. They may have attracted followers who were influenced by their ideas, but those followers did not form a religious sect. It as only in the nineteenth century that we would see the formation of such sects and the emergence of new religious movements.

One of the most noteworthy characteristics of the development of thought in the sixteenth and seventeenth centuries was that it was generally addressed to the concerns of society as a whole rather than to those of a particular social status or occupation. It was therefore able to achieve wide penetration into society. This phenomenon parallels the spread, noted earlier, of a common pattern of religious life throughout society, regardless of distinctions in social status.

In China, Confucianism was studied almost exclusively by officials and those who prepared for official examinations. In antiquity it was the aristocracy and, from the tenth century on, the scholar-gentry class who carried on the Confucian tradition of learning. Undoubtedly in part because of the difficulty of mastering the written language, Confucianism appears not to have been absorbed by the population at large. The situation was essentially similar in Korea, where Confucianism was established as the official school of learning in the fourteenth century. It remained a preserve of the upper stratum of society, the *yangban* class.

By contrast, in Japan from the seventeenth century on, not only did Confucianism serve as the medium for educating the rulers, the shogun and daimyo, but also its moral teachings spread widely among the populace. The publication of large numbers of didactic works (*kyōkunsho*), written in simple Japanese, and the establishment throughout the country of private Confucian academies (*shijuku*), brought a large percentage of the population into direct contact with Confucian teachings and ethics. Whereas in China and Korea Confucianism provided the subject matter for the examinations used to select officials, no comparable system of selection existed in Japan. Hence the study of Confucianism could not be expected to open doors to important political positions. Instead, scholars came to see their mission as the ethical training of not simply the rulers but society as a whole, including the ordinary bushi and commoner population.

A similar situation may be seen in the case of Zen Buddhism. In China, Zen was principally the religion of the educated elite, and temples relied on the financial support of the government and prominent aristocratic families for their maintenance. In Japan, Zen followed the Chinese example and established a network of official temples patronized by the government. But on the other hand, Zen priests

from the fourteenth century on proselytized widely among the populace and, through the support of local bushi and commoner adherents,
succeeded in establishing many small temples throughout the country.
This latter phenomenon, which resembled the developments in other
branches of Kamakura Buddhism, such as the Jōdo sect, led eventually to the popularization of Zen to a degree that did not occur in
China.[29]

This development also had important repercussions in the area of
thought. The tradition of Zen as the religion of the literati in China led
Japanese Zen priests to acquire a general familiarity with Chinese
culture, especially through the study of Confucian learning. By means
of their missionary activities, then, these priests spread an awareness
of Confucianism among the people. Moreover, by the early seventeenth century, many significant Confucian thinkers emerged from
among the ranks of Zen priests in Japan.

The spread of Chu Hsi Neo-Confucianism

Sung Neo-Confucianism, exemplified most fully in the writings of
Chu Hsi, was introduced into Japan in the twelfth century. Incorporated into the education of the aristocracy and Zen monks, it exerted a
visible influence on the historical writings of the Nambokuchō period
(1333-92), such as the *Jinnō shōtōki* by Kitabatake Chikafusa and the
historical chronicle *Taiheiki*.[30] Its practical character as a system of
thought that stressed the precise moral evaluation of political acts and
human behavior further encouraged its diffusion to all reaches of society, a trend that accelerated in the middle of the sixteenth century.

As a result, Confucian learning spread from the traditional cultural
center of Kyoto into the provinces. The Ashikaga *gakkō*, a notable
institution of Confucian learning based in eastern Japan and founded
in 1439 by Uesugi Norizane, reached the peak of its eminence under
its seventh head, the monk Kyūka, around 1550.[31] The number of

29 On the differences in the social situation of the Zen sect in China and Japan, see Tamamura
Takeji, "Nihon no shisō shūkyō to Chūgoku: Zen," in Bitō Masahide, ed., *Nihon bunka to
Chūgoku* (Tokyo: Taishūkan, 1968). The same work later was republished in Tamamura
Takeji, *Nihon zenshūshi ronshū* (Tokyo: Shibunkaku, 1976), vol. 1.
30 On medieval Confucianism, particularly Chu Hsi Neo-Confucianism, see Ashikaga Enjutsu,
Kamakura Muromachi jidai no jukyō (Tokyo: Nihon koten zenshū kankōkai, 1932); Ōe
Fumiki, *Hompō jugakushi ronkō* (Tokyo: Zenkoku shobō, 1943); and Wajima Yoshio, *Chūsei
no jugaku* (Tokyo: Yoshikawa kōbunkan, 1965).
31 Ashikaga Enjutsu, *Kamakura Muromachi jidai no jukyō*, pp. 586-664. Norizane is traditionally held to have "restored" rather than "founded" the school. But records concerning the
school before 1439 belong more to the realm of legend than history.

students who gathered at the school during this period is said to have numbered three thousand. From about 1560 the school was supported by the Go-Hōjō, the Sengoku daimyo who at that time controlled most of the Kantō region. This circumstance further enhanced the school's stature. Most of the students were Zen priests, but their studies centered on Confucianism, if not pure Chu Hsi thought. Particular emphasis was given to the study of the *Book of Changes*, a text of central importance to the practice of divination, and thus of interest to the daimyo, who were constantly confronted with the uncertainties of warfare. However, the interests of daimyo like the Go-Hōjō were not limited to divination but also encompassed Confucian teachings about morality and government.

For example, the *Hōjō godaiki*, which records the history of the Go-Hōjō house, describes the successive heads of the family and the major Go-Hōjō vassals as having emphasized the importance of Confucian moral values. A similar interest may be observed in the case of another major eastern daimyo, the Takeda of Kai. Apart from the fifty-seven-article legal code compiled under the direction of the famous general Takeda Shingen, there also exists a set of ninety-nine admonitions compiled in 1558 by Shingen's younger brother Nobushige, which cites references from Confucian texts such as the *Analects*.

Other Sengoku daimyo exhibited an interest in Confucianism as well. Known particularly for their influence on the intellectual world were the schools of Confucianism that developed under the sponsorship of the daimyo of Tosa and Satsuma. The Tosa school (the so-called Southern school) of Confucianism got its start under the Zen priest Nanson Baiken, who came to Tosa around 1548 or 1549. The Satsuma ("Satsunan") school claimed the fifteenth-century Zen priest Keian Genju (1429–1508) as its founder but began to flourish only under a later Zen priest, Nampo Bunshi (1556–1620). These priests all studied Confucianism at the Gozan temples in Kyoto, which stressed Chu Hsi's interpretations of Confucianism.

In both Tosa and Satsuma, Confucianism received the patronage of the daimyo and exerted an influence on the retainers of the house. In Satsuma, Shimazu Tadayoshi (1492–1568), the father of the domain lord Shimazu Takahisa, showed a deep interest in learning and composed the "Iroha uta," a set of forty-seven poems (*waka*) that conveyed Confucian moral principles in an easily comprehensible manner. The first poem states: "Merely to hear or study the way of antiquity is insufficient; merit derives from one's own practice of the way." Other poems propagated Confucian ethics together with faith in Buddhism and the qualities necessary for military success. The "Iroha uta" continued to play an important part in domain life until the end of the Edo period. Recited on various ceremonial occasions and used as a text at the *han* school and in *terakoya* (temple schools), it served as a central source of ethical teachings for all residents of the Satsuma domain.[32]

The formation of a new political and social order under the aegis of the Sengoku daimyo helped foster the spread of Confucianism. The warfare of the Sengoku period destroyed the court-based social order, and in its place arose a new political structure centered on the daimyo domain and resting on the new rural communal social structure, consisting of the house and the village. People living in this time of flux were conscious of having to take the initiative in deciding the course of their lives: The majority of the Sengoku daimyo and their major vassals had risen from a low social status. To be sure, there were those like the Shimazu who came from a notable lineage dating back to the Kamakura period, but even such daimyo as Shimazu Tadayoshi and Takahisa succeeded in consolidating their position only after a fierce struggle with rivals within their family. They differed little from the Sengoku daimyo in having to depend ultimately on their own ability. Most bushi were free to choose the lord they wished to serve, and the function they would perform depended to a considerable measure on their ability. For the upper stratum of peasants and townspeople as well, their occupation was not something imposed on them from the outside but, rather, depended on their own initiative. Living in such an age of both uncertainty and opportunity, people naturally felt the need for spiritual or intellectual guidance to how they should lead their daily lives. This perceived need was the major reason that Confucianism, which was concerned precisely with such issues, won wide acceptance among the people of the time, from the daimyo on down.

The teachings that circulated at this time were not necessarily pure Chu Hsi Neo-Confucianism. To read the classics, people tended to use the Han and T'ang commentaries as well as those of Chu Hsi. This eclecticism reflected the trends prevalent in Kyoto, the center of Japanese scholarship. Two groups dominated Kyoto scholarly activities: those who continued the tradition of the scholars of the court, and the Zen priests belonging to the Gozan temples. Whereas the former adhered rigidly to the traditions of scholarship preserved since antiquity, the latter were quite free in their approach. Because many Gozan priests had direct contact with China, they were influenced by trends

32 Ashikaga Enjutsu, *Kamakura Muromachi jidai no jukyō*, pp. 753-64.

in the continental scholarly world and thus tended to emphasize the latest interpretations of Chu Hsi, though they did not exclude other views. As might be expected, they did not draw a sharp distinction between Confucianism and Buddhism.

The trend toward eclecticism was also seen in the life-styles of the rulers. For instance, both Confucian and Buddhist paintings embellished the walls of Azuchi Castle, built in 1576 by Oda Nobunaga. Whereas the paintings for the topmost seventh floor depicted Confucius and the Confucian sages of antiquity, those for the sixth floor portrayed Sakyamuni and his disciples.[33] Toyotomi Hideyoshi and Tokugawa Ieyasu, who carried on the process of national unification inaugurated by Nobunaga, employed court scholars as well as Gozan priests and priests from the Ashikaga gakkō in their personal entourages. Ieyasu actively collected and printed Buddhist and historical books, but the only Confucian texts printed under his patronage were the *K'ung tzu chia yü* (*Kōshi kego:* Records of Confucius) and the *Book of Changes*, neither of which had a particular connection with Chu Hsi thought.

However, as Confucianism spread throughout society as a system of thought suitable for guiding the daimyo, bushi, and commoners in their daily lives, the Chu Hsi component in the existing eclectic mix of Confucian teachings was increasingly emphasized. Several factors appear to have been responsible for this development. First was the need to simplify Confucianism in order for it to function as a broadly applicable guide to responsible social life. For professional scholars it was possible to use the older commentaries together with those of Chu Hsi, but ordinary people could not be expected to sort out the different interpretations. Second, the Neo-Confucian teachings that had taken shape in China from the eleventh century in response to the concerns of the emergent gentry class possessed a rationalistic and universalistic component, as may be seen in the Neo-Confucian emphasis on the relatively accessible Four Books in place of the more archaic and difficult-to-understand Five Classics. Despite important differences in China's and Japan's social conditions, these rationalistic and universalistic aspects suited in many ways the new, communally oriented social structure characteristic of Japan in this period. Whereas Chu Hsi Neo-Confucianism was regarded as the official state ideology in contemporary China and Korea, the state seemed to have played a lesser role in the spread of Chu Hsi's thought in Japan.

33 Ōta Gyūichi, *Nobunaga kō ki* (Tokyo: Kadokawa shoten, 1963).

Scholarly opinion is divided on the question of whether Chu Hsi's thought was suited to the actual circumstances of early modern Japanese society.[34] Some hold that there was a close correspondence between the two, indeed, that the rulers of early modern Japan successfully promoted Chu Hsi's thought as an ideology to uphold the hereditary status order on which the society of this period was founded. Others point to the differences between Japanese society in this period and the Chinese social and political environment out of which neo-Confucianism emerged. For instance, the examination system, fundamental to Chinese society, was not adopted in Japan. These differences, they contend, limited the understanding and acceptance of Chu Hsi's thought in Japan.

These two polar views exist because both camps have focused primarily on institutional elements such as the social status system, and have not paid proper attention to the people's mental outlook. Clearly, there were substantial psychological reasons for those who lived in this period to be drawn to Confucian moral thought, particularly Chu Hsi's thought. On the other hand, the foreign origin of Chu Hsi Neo-Confucianism made its total absorption impossible. Eventually this led to the emergence of Japanized forms of Chu Hsi Neo-Confucianism and, on the other hand, to the appearance of new schools of thought that challenged the premises of the Chu Hsi school.

The key figure in both the diffusion of Chu Hsi's thought and the establishment of its independence from Buddhism was Fujiwara Seika (1561–1619), who came to be regarded as the founder of early modern Japanese Confucianism. Seika, descended from the Reizei branch of the Fujiwara family, became a monk and studied at the Kyoto Gozan temple of Shōkokuji. However, he later rejected Buddhism and became active in society as a Confucian scholar. He lectured on Confucian texts to Tokugawa Ieyasu and various other daimyo and, with the assistance of Kang Hang, a Korean scholar taken captive during Hideyoshi's invastions of Korea and brought to Japan in 1597, edited and punctuated for Japanese readers the classics as interpreted by Chu Hsi.[35] Later generations venerated Seika for his lofty vision of scholar-

---

34 The assumption that the premises of Chu Hsi thought were well suited to the circumstances of Tokugawa society was common among scholars from the mid-Tokugawa period on. It was given a theoretical grounding by Maruyama Masao in his *Nihon seiji shisōshi kenkyū* (Tokyo: Tōkyō daigaku shuppankai, 1952). The contrasting argument is developed in Bitō Masahide, *Nihon hōken shisōshi kenkyū: bakuhan taisei no genri to shushigaku teki shii* (Tokyo: Aoki shoten, 1961); and Watanabe Hiroshi, *Kinsei Nihon shakai to sōgaku* (Tokyo: Tōkyō daigaku shuppankai, 1985).
35 A biography of Fujiwara Seika may be found in Ōta Seikyū, *Fujiwara Seika* (Tokyo: Yoshikawa kōbunkan, 1985). His works have been published in Ōta Seikyū, ed., *Fujiwara*

ship and his devotion to learning that led him in his last years to lead the life of a recluse.

Many of those who studied with Seika embarked on scholarly careers, opening academies in Kyoto and becoming teachers or gaining employment as scholars with one of the daimyo. The most famous of his disciples was Hayashi Razan (1583–1657).[36] The son of a *rōnin*, Razan entered Buddhist training at the Gozan temple of Kenninji but left the temple in favor of life as a Confucian scholar. When, in 1604, Razan became a disciple of Seika, he presented him with a list of books he already had read. The list, which contains more than 440 Chinese works, offers evidence of the high level of scholarship pursued at the Gozan temples of the day. The previous year Razan, together with some friends, had begun a series of public lectures in Kyoto. Razan lectured on the *Analects* while another scholar, Matsunaga Teitoku, lectured on works of Japanese literature, such as *Tsurezuregusa*. These activities constituted a direct challenge to the premise that scholarship was the special province of a few aristocratic families and Zen priests, and signaled an effort to disseminate learning widely throughout society, a symbol of the new intellectual atmosphere of the age. It is said that one aristocratic scholar appealed to Ieyasu to prohibit such activities as contrary to the traditions of the court, but he was brushed aside. From 1607 Razan entered the service of Ieyasu. In the following fifty years he served four shoguns, and for generations, his descendants continued to serve as scholars to the bakufu.

Although known for his erudition, Razan was not an original thinker. Nonetheless, he contributed to the spread of knowledge about Confucian moral thought through writings such as the *Shunkanshō*, an exposition of the tenets of Neo-Confucianism written in simple Japanese and published in 1629. A similar work attributed to Seika, the *Kana seiri*, was published in 1650. Earlier, in 1635, Asayama Irin'an (1589–1664), another scholar active in Kyoto, although not a disciple of Seika, published the *Kiyomizu monogatari*, which presented Confucian ideas in the style of a popular form of literature, the *kana zōshi:* It is said to have sold two thousand to three thousand copies.[37] Thus, the

---

Seika shū, 2 vols. (Tokyo: Kokumin seishin bunka kenkyūjo, 1938–9); and Kanaya Osamu and Ishida Ichirō, eds., *Fujiwara Seika, Hayashi Razan* vol. 28 of *Nihon shisō taikei* (Tokyo: Iwanami shoten, 1975). Regarding the influence of Korean Confucianism on Seika and other early Tokugawa Confucians, see Abe Yoshio, *Nihon shushigaku to Chōsen* (Tokyo: Tōkyō daigaku shuppankai, 1965).

36 A biography of Razan may be found in Hori Isao, *Hayashi Razan* (Tokyo: Yoshikawa kōbunkan, 1964).

37 This figure is given in a similar work, *Gion monogatari*, published a little later.

development of the publishing trade also helped foster the dissemination of the ideas of Chu Hsi Neo-Confucianism.[38]

Views of politics and history

The concept of Heaven and the Way of Heaven (*tendō*, also pronounced *tentō*) had circulated even before the spread of Confucianism. First introduced to a wide audience through historical works and military tales, these concepts became part of the everyday vocabulary of the ordinary people as well as scholars and intellectuals.[39] In China there was widespread religious faith in Heaven as a transcendental entity that governed human destiny, and this faith had become an important element of Confucianism. The Japanese, by contrast, never developed a religious faith in the idea of Heaven. Nevertheless, the concept of Heaven and the Way of Heaven gained acceptance as an explanation for the vicissitudes of human existence.

From the thirteenth century on, the extreme shifts in political and individual fortunes caused a general anxiety among the populace. The first intellectual tradition to respond to their concern was Buddhism. For example, the *Heike monogatari* uses a Buddhist notion of fate in depicting the tragic destiny of both the Taira regime and the various individuals who figure in the tale. It propounds the view that however unfathomable the fate that one experiences in this world, by accepting that fate and putting one's trust in the Buddha, one can transcend this existence and obtain spiritual salvation. The spread of the Confucian concepts of Heaven and the Heavenly Way paralleled the emergence of this new concept of fate.

In Chinese Confucianism, the principles of Heaven regulated the entire universe, including the seasonal cycles. Adherence to the principles of Heaven made it possible to establish and preserve order in human society. The Heavenly Way provided moral guidelines for the individual, and the proper approach to governance. These principles were also linked to the notion of just retribution. If the individual behaved properly, eventually he or his descendants would be blessed with good fortune; conversely, improper behavior would bring misfor-

---

38 Until around 1630 the emergent publishing trade used movable wooden type; thereafter it was more common to carve a separate block for each page.

39 For the concepts of *ten* and *tendō* and the historical thought of this period that drew from those concepts, see Ozawa Eiichi, *Kinsei shigaku shisōshi kenkyū* (Tokyo: Yoshikawa kōbunkan, 1974); and Ishige Tadashi, "Sengoku Azuchi Momoyama jidai no shisō," in Ishida Ichirō, ed., *Taikei Nihonshi sōsho*, vol. 2 of *Shisōshi* (Tokyo: Yamakawa shuppansha, 1976).

tune. The notion of heavenly retribution served to legitimize the premise of dynastic change. Heaven, it was held, would grant its mandate (Ch: *t'ien-ming*, J: *temmei*) to rule the people to one whose virtue showed him to be worthy of Heaven's trust. If his descendants continued to devote themselves to ensuring the welfare of the people, they would continue to enjoy the mandate received by the founder. But if they failed to uphold their responsibilities as rulers, then Heaven would withdraw its mandate. The fact that the process of retribution was believed to take place over an extended period of time made it possible to attribute both the fate of a particular individual and the historical course of society to the operation of a basically rational principle.

Though the Japanese may not have accepted all the ramifications of the Confucian concept of Heaven, historical works and military tales written in the Edo period frequently explained the course of history by referring to such notions. And because the concept of Heaven and its way spoke to a number of concerns particular to the late medieval period, it was widely diffused. For those living through an era of tumultuous change, the notion of a Heavenly Way provided a rationale for ignoring the constraints of an outmoded social order. A challenge to that order or to one's lord could be justified in the name of *tendō* which thus provided an ideology for the phenomenon of *gekokujō* (the overthrow of the superior by the inferior).[40] The concept of Heaven and its way presumed, however, not the absence of order but, rather, the realization of an ideal social order. Thus it could be used not only to attack the old social and political structures but also to legitimize the creation of a new order in their place. The rationalistic view of history and human fate associated with the concept of Heaven gained support in this period in considerable measure because the people perceived the possibility of creating a new order and found in *tendō* an ideology appropriate to that endeavor.

The term *tendō* appears in various literary sources such as accounts of battles and biographies dating from the second half of the sixteenth century to the start of the seventeenth. The phrase "*tendō* is fearsome" appears frequently in *Nobunaga kō ki* (or *Shinchōki*) (Life of Lord Nobunaga) by Ōta Gyūichi (b. 1527), expressing the idea that human fate is frightening because it is unpredictable. Ōta Gyūichi regards Nobunaga's political success as extraordinary but legitimate and from that perspective, seeks to explain the historical process of his rise.

40 See Ishige, "Sengoku Azuchi Momoyama jidai no shisō," pp. 3–8.

Whereas most people fail to achieve their potential because of some sudden encounter with misfortune, Nobunaga, blessed with good fortune, repeatedly escaped unscathed. Moreover, although Gyūichi portrays the life of the individual as controlled by the fearsome power of fate, he also interprets *tendō* as a force that moved society as a whole toward the establishment of a new order centered on Nobunaga.

Nobunaga's successor, Toyotomi Hideyoshi, also employed the term *tendō* in his declaration of war against the Go-Hōjō. Their resistance to his efforts to unify the nation opened them up to the charge that they were going against "the principles of *tendō*." Hideyoshi simultaneously asserted that the new political structure he sought to create accorded with those principles.[41] Both Nobunaga and Hideyoshi were fond of referring to the entirety of Japan – the object of their policy of unification – as *tenka* (the realm, literally, "all under heaven"). Implicit in their use of this term is the premise that the unified state, the *tenka*, was the political structure that accorded with the will of Heaven. In Chinese thought, the will of Heaven was regarded as a projection of the popular will. Thus, the term *tenka*, as employed by Nobunaga and Hideyoshi, implied that the unification of the state under their authority was a reflection of the popular will.

From the seventeenth century on, the concept of *tendō* acquired an increasingly Confucian coloration. For example, in the *Kana seiri*, the term *tendō* was used to explain Chu Hsi's idea of principle (*tenri*) and human nature. A firmer grounding in Confucian theory enhanced the utility of these concepts as norms to guide the conduct of government. The phrase "The realm is not the realm of one person; it is that of the multitude" (*tenka wa hitori no tenka ni arazu, tenka no tenka nari*) frequently appeared in popular histories and didactic writings, and it served to remind the rulers of society that they should govern with the welfare of the people rather than their own interests in mind.[42]

The infusion of Confucian concepts imbued the political thought of this period with a new universality. A representative example of the political thought of the seventeenth century, the *Honsaroku* – said to be the work of the influential bakufu vassal Honda Masanobu – uses the conceptual framework of works like the *Kana seiri* but is noted for its discussion of various concrete political issues.

41 See the vermilion-seal edict issued by Hideyoshi in 1689 (Tenshō 17/11/24). Hideyoshi had copies of this edict sent to a large number of the major daimyo as well as to the Go-Hōjō, in effect promulgating it nationwide.
42 Regarding the wide diffusion of this phrase, see Tsuji Zennosuke, *Nihon bunkashi* (Tokyo: Shunjūsha, 1949), vol. 6, pp. 1–3.

The *Honsaroku* begins by declaring that the ruler of the realm is called the "son of Heaven" (*tenshi*) because he had been singled out by *tendō* as the man capable of ruling the realm and thus had been appointed "master of Japan" (*Nihon no aruji*). The *Honsaroku* does not specify whether this "son of Heaven" must be the emperor or the shogun; it simply sets forth in general terms the qualities that a ruler of the realm must possess. However, because the *Honsaroku* was intended to serve as a guide to governance, the term *tenshi* by implication referred to the shogun.

A similar premise may be found in the instructions that Ikeda Mitsumasa, daimyo of Okayama, handed down to his vassals in 1656. Mitsumasa declared that the shogun had been entrusted by Heaven with governing the people of Japan, that the daimyo had been entrusted by the shogun with governing the people of their respective domains, and that the retainers of the daimyo, from the elders on down, were responsible for assisting the daimyo with that task.[43] Both Mitsumasa and the author of the *Honsaroku* regarded a universal authority – heaven or *tendō* – as directly responsible for entrusting the ruler with the reins of government. Both ignored the traditional political role of the emperor as the source of the authority to govern.

The complex relationship between the court and bakufu and the legitimization of the actual political order cannot be explained simply in terms of abstract premises, and the *Honsaroku* remained vague on the issue of the locus of sovereignty. Nevertheless, when writers of this period dealt with this subject, they did not feel compelled to appeal to distinctively "Japanese" political traditions, in contrast with later political theorists of the eighteenth and nineteenth centuries. History as a motive force that adhered to the universalistic principles of *tendō* was often used to explain the shift in the locus of effective authority from the court to the bakufu. The *Honsaroku* simply declares that Emperor Go-Shirakawa (r. 1155–8; exercised authority as retired emperor 1158–92) lost the realm because he did not adhere to the "principles of Heaven," and it limits further discussion of governance of the realm in subsequent periods to the actions of the military (*buke*) rulers. Other political writers of the period generally recognized that a transfer of authority from the court to the military had occurred either with Go-Shirakawa (that is, at the time of the establishment of the Kamakura bakufu) or during the Nambokuchō period (namely, with the establish-

43 Hampō kenkyūkai, ed., *Okayama han*, vol. 1 (*Hampōshū*, no. 1) (Tokyo: Sōbunsha, 1959); Taniguchi Sumio, *Okayama hanseishi no kenkyū* (Tokyo: Hanawa shobō, 1964).

ment of the Muromachi bakufu). In their view, while the military regimes that came and went contributed to social turmoil, their rule eventually led to the establishment of a stable political order and a peaceful society.

The idea of restoring order by replacing the sovereign had much in common with the traditional Chinese notion of the "just revolution" (Ch: *ko-ming*, J: *kakumei* [literally "change of mandate"]). Although they did not necessarily employ the term revolution (*kakumei*) or explicitly declare that actual dynastic changes had taken place, Japanese writers depicted a historical process implicitly regulated by "changes of mandate" sanctioned by *tendō*. The Tokugawa bakufu was presented as the outcome of this historical process, which endowed it with an effective legitimacy transcending the more formalistic legitimacy it received through recognition by the court.

Among the major historical works of the early Edo period manifesting this view are *Honchō tsugan*, compiled under the auspices of the bakufu, and the *Dai Nihon shi*, compiled by the Mito domain. Both presented a comprehensive view of the history of Japan from ancient times. That both were official undertakings signaled a new awareness by the rulers of that time of the value of history as a mechanism for substantiating the contemporary political order. Previous military governments had not shown a comparable interest in the compilation of histories.

The *Honchō tsugan* was begun by Hayashi Razan. After his death, the bakufu ordered his son, Gahō, to continue the work of compilation. Working with a team of disciples, Gahō completed the some 300-volume enterprise in 1670. Written in Chinese and in the traditional Chinese chronological annals (*hennen*) style, the *Honchō tsugan* covered the period from Jimmu (the legendary first emperor who, according to the traditional account, established his reign in 660 B.C.) to the end of the reign of Go Yōzei (1611). In choosing the *hennen* style, Razan and Gahō followed the example of the six national histories, beginning with the *Nihon shoki*, that had been compiled in the Nara and early Heian periods.

As the name *Honchō tsugan* (Comprehensive mirror of Japan) indicates, Razan and Gahō also sought to emulate the *Tzu-chih t'ung-chien* (J: *Shiji tsugan*, or Comprehensive mirror for aid in government), the great comprehensive history of China compiled by the Northern Sung scholar and statesman Ssu-ma Kuang. However, unlike the latter work, the *Honchō tsugan* did not incorporate those sections in which the author expressed his own evaluation of the recorded events. In addition, the restrictions of the *hennen* style, which aimed at an objective presentation of the facts, made the *Honchō tsugan* a somewhat bland work rather than one conveying a distinct historical viewpoint.

By contrast, the *Dai Nihon shi*, compiled under the auspices of the Mito domain, employed the *kiden* style, consisting of annals, biographies, and treatises. Developed by Ssu-ma Ch'ien in the Han period, it was used in the Chinese dynastic histories.[44] The *Dai Nihon shi* was begun in 1657 at the direction of Tokugawa Mitsukuni (1628–1700), the second lord of the Mito domain. The work, in 397 volumes, was completed only in 1906. A large number of scholars participated in the collection and collation of data for the project. As a result, the project has had an important influence on the development of the study of history in Japan. At the same time, the historical perspective projected by the *Dai Nihon shi* had a direct influence on society. Moreover, the historical perspective that governed the compilation changed significantly between the first stage of writing in the seventeenth century and the second stage which began at the end of the eighteenth century. The perspective employed initially adhered closely to the Chu Hsi Neo-Confucian historical views held personally by Mitsukuni.

The *Dai Nihon shi* eventually incorporated four sections: the main annals, biographies, treatises, and chronological charts. However, the first stage of compilation dealt only with the annals and biographies. In the *kiden* style, as it developed in China, the annals were devoted to events centering on the emperor. Thus those whose lives were discussed in the annals were established *ipso facto* as legitimate rulers. The biographies, by contrast, took up the lives of those active during the reigns of the rulers discussed in the annals. The biographies were grouped by categories, and the inclusion of a historical figure in a particular category served to pass judgment on him. In addition, from the time of Ssu-ma Ch'ien, the compilers of this genre of history followed the practice of appending explicitly evaluative passages (*ronsan*) to both the main annals and the biographies. One of the premises of the Chu Hsi historical outlook was that these evaluations should clarify as meticulously as possible the moral issues illustrated by the life of the subject being evaluated.

Reflecting on his historiographical endeavors in his last years,

---

44 Regarding the compilation of the *Dai Nihon shi* and its intellectual background, see *Mito shishi, chūkan*, nos. 1,2,3 (Mito: Mito shiyakusho, 1968, 1969, 1976); Bitō Masahide, "Rekishi shisō," in Bitō Masahide, ed., *Nihon bunka to Chūgoku* (Tokyo: Taishūkan, 1968); and Bitō Masahide, "Mitogaku no tokushitsu," in *Mitogaku*, vol. 53 of *Nihon shisō taikei* (Tokyo: Iwanami shoten, 1977).

Mitsukuni wrote that he had sought to clarify which emperors were legitimate and whether the behavior of the emperors' subjects had accorded with the principles of morality.[45] In setting forth his own views on the first issue, Mitsukuni stressed three points. The first was the shift of Empress Jingū, the consort of Emperor Chūai – who was said to have exercised regnant authority after the death of her spouse – from the main annals to the biographies, to emphasize the impropriety of her exercising sovereign powers.

The second moral issue that Mitsukuni emphasized was the relationship between the later Emperor Temmu and his nephew, Ōtomo, at the time of the Jinshin rebellion in 672. In Mitsukuni's account, Ōtomo had succeeded his father (Temmu's brother) as emperor and was thus the legitimate ruler at the time of the rebellion. He thus included Ōtomo in the main annals, thereby indicating that the military contest between Ōtomo and Temmu in 672, which ended in victory for the latter, was in fact a rebellion by Temmu against the legitimate monarch. Mitsukuni's treatment of both Jingū and Ōtomo ran counter to accepted historical opinion, which adhered to the view of the *Nihon shoki,* the first of the official six national histories.

Mitsukuni's third innovation concerned the fourteenth-century division of the imperial line into the Southern and Northern courts. Diverging from the conventional view, the *Dai Nihon shi* treated the Southern Court as the legitimate line, and according to original plans the history was supposed to end with the absorption of the Southern line in 1392. Although this plan was subsequently modified, its basic contours shaped the content of the *Dai Nihon shi.*

What were the implications of terminating the *Dai Nihon shi* at the point when the Southern Court came to an end? In accordance with Confucian historical thought, it indicated that at that point there had been a "change in the mandate" and, consequently, the replacement of one dynasty by another. The *Dai Nihon shi,* then, was the history of a single dynasty that began with Emperor Jimmu and came to an end with the extinction of the Southern Court. Because the Northern Court did not possess sovereign authority, it could not be considered the legitimate successor to its southern counterpart. Neither could the Ashikaga, the military house in power at the time of the Southern Court's demise, because its power had not been acquired in a morally appropriate fashion.

Although the *Dai Nihon shi* does not explicitly designate a legitimate

45 *Bairi sensei hi.* After his death, Mitsukuni's account of his life and historiographical endeavors was inscribed on a stele erected in homage to him.

successor, it implicitly endorses the Tokugawa as heirs to the mandate, in the evaluative passages appended to the main annals and biographies, particularly in its depiction of the Nitta family, the putative ancestors of the Tokugawa. The Nitta, who had loyally served the Southern Court, the legitimate dynasty by Mitsukuni's account, had met with misfortune at that point. However, in accordance with the principle of Heaven's just retribution, their moral propriety was appropriately and eventually compensated when their descendants, the Tokugawa, assumed authority over the realm. Thus the emphasis on the legitimacy of the Southern line served indirectly to provide a historical grounding for the legitimacy of the Tokugawa.

A *tour de force* analysis of Japanese history according to Confucian historiographical principles is the *Tokushi yoron* by Arai Hakuseki (1657–1725).[46] This work was based on notes of lectures that Hakuseki gave before the sixth shogun, Tokugawa Ienobu, in 1712. Though dating from the eighteenth century, the work exemplifies the seventeenth-century historical outlook just discussed. *Tokushi yoron* traces the start of the decline of the ancient court to the succession of the eight-year-old Emperor Seiwa in 858 and the subsequent establishment of the Fujiwara regency.

Hakuseki divides the period between those events and the end of the Southern Court into nine eras, which he treats as a process of the steady disintegration of the imperial dynasty. He separates the rise of the military into five eras spanning the time of the establishment of the Kamakura bakufu to the founding of the Edo bakufu. After the demise of the Southern Court, Hakuseki writes, the people were not even aware of the emperor's existence. The emperor of the Northern Court was no more than an "empty vessel" set up by the Ashikaga to further the shogun's interests, and not a legitimate ruler. By contrast, Ashikaga Yoshimitsu, the third Ashikaga shogun, acted in effect as the king of Japan, and with the appearance of Tokugawa Ieyasu, who possessed the virtues of a true Confucian king, the military state was fully established.

According to Hakuseki, the Southern Court represented the legitimate line, but it failed to survive because of Go-Daigo's "lack of virtue." Instead, the warriors fell heir to the heavenly mandate forfeited by the Southern Court because in the Muromachi period their

---

46 Regarding Hakuseki's historical thought, see Bitō Masahide, "Arai Hakuseki no rekishi shisō," in Bitō Masahide et al., eds., *Arai Hakuseki*, vol. 35 of *Nihon shisō taikei* (Tokyo: Iwanami shoten, 1975). In English, see *Lessons from History: Arai Hakuseki's Tokushi Yoron* (St. Lucia: University of Queensland Press, 1982). Translation & commentary by Joyce Ackroyd.

leaders were relatively more virtuous than the emperor was, and they eventually produced a truly virtuous ruler in the Edo period. Whether or not Hakuseki's account of these developments corresponds to the historical record, it completely fits the Chinese concept of dynastic change through a "just revolution." Hakuseki does not explicitly take up the ties between the Tokugawa and the Nitta, but he does frequently refer to the concept of "Heaven's just retribution" to explain the rise and fall of various other regimes and political figures.

Both the *Dai Nihon shi* and *Tokushi yoron* contain well-developed arguments, though marred perhaps by excessive abstraction. People generally were responsive to the notion that the flow of history followed the principles of *tendō* or the logic of the concept of just retribution, but the association of those notions with the idea of dynastic change (through the transfer of Heaven's mandate) did not, in fact, fit well either the actual events in Japanese history or the general perceptions of history among the people. Historiographical developments in the eighteenth century would better mirror historical circumstances. They also would reflect a shift away from the universalistic political thought of the seventeenth century exemplified by the notion of Heaven and *tendō* toward an emphasis on the political traditions particular to Japan.

New directions in ethical thought

The growth of the individual's self-awareness that spurred the seventeenth-century diffusion of Chu Hsi's thought sustained as well the activities of various other original intellectuals who concerned themselves with matters of morality and ethics, that is, with the question of how the individual should live in society and of what spiritual qualities were needed to lead a proper life. Like the Chu Hsi thinkers, when considering governance and other sociopolitical issues, they tended to give priority to the moral qualities of the ruler rather than to questions of structure and function. This emphasis, together with their universalistic outlook, may be considered a general characteristic of the thought of this period. Their expression of a consciousness grounded in the particularities of Japanese society but based on universalistic ethical premises exhibits a historical significance comparable to the emergence of Kamakura Buddhism.

A number of Zen priests were among the first major intellectual figures to put forth original views in the area of ethics. Compared with the Confucian scholars, who were inclined to become caught up in a pedantic quest for academic knowledge, the Zen priests, having personally submitted themselves to a rigorous discipline in pursuit of spiritual enlightenment, tended to be more conscious of the need for an intellectual outlook geared to the actualities of human life. To be sure, the tradition of Zen discipline had not continued uninterrupted from the medieval age. In the latter half of the medieval period (the fourteenth to the sixteenth centuries), the social power and influence of Zen had increased greatly, but its religious appeal had declined.

In the big central monasteries like the Gozan temples, Zen priests became specialists in Confucianism and Chinese literature, and in the local temples, priests initiated disciples into the "correct" responses to the questions intended to ascertain whether they had attained enlightenment. As a consequence, Zen acquired an increasingly esoteric orientation.[47] But from the seventeenth century a movement arose within Zen to reject such tendencies and to restore the original religious spirit of Zen. One of the representative figures in this movement was Takuan Sōhō (1573–1645), a monk from the Kyoto temple of Daitokuji.

In 1628 Takuan played a central part in the so-called purple vestment (shie) incident in which the temples of Daitokuji and Myōshinji mounted a resistance to the bakufu's efforts to regulate their activities and restrict their links to the court.[48] The incident was touched off by the bakufu's revoking all grants of the privilege to wear purple vestments awarded by the court to priests of these two temples, between 1615 (the year the bakufu issued comprehensive regulations to major temples) and 1627. It also entailed the temples' rejection of bakufu directives specifying, among other things, the standards of spiritual accomplishment that a monk in training should achieve. For instance, the regulations handed down to Myōshinji and Daitokuji declared that a monk could not be regarded as having completed his training unless he had answered seventeen hundred kōan (Zen conundrums). This formalistic approach to Zen spiritual discipline assumed a continuation of the esoteric tradition of "secret transmission" that had developed in the preceding centuries.[49] However, to Takuan, such formalistic regulation was meaningless. The resolution of one kōan alone, if it

47 Tamamura Takeji, "Nihon chūsei zenrin ni okeru Rinzai Sōtō ryōshū no idō: rinka no mondai ni tsuite," Shigaku zasshi 59 (July–August 1950); later this article was included in the author's Nihon zenshūshi ronshū (Tokyo: Shibunkaku, 1979), vol. 2, no. 1.
48 The "purple vestment" incident is discussed in detail in Tsuji Zennosuke, Nihon bukkyōshi (kinsei 2) (Tokyo: Iwanami shoten, 1953).
49 This interpretation of the "purple vestment" incident was developed by Tamamura Takeji, "Takuan sōhō: shii jiken ni taisuru ichi kenkai," in his Nihon zenshūshi ronshū, vol. 1 (Tokyo: Shibunkaku, 1976).

reflected true spiritual insight, should be sufficient testimony to a monk's religious achievements.

Takuan fiercely criticized the bakufu's interference in the temples' religious affairs. His overt rejection of the bakufu's regulations was in turn condemned by the bakufu as disrespectful, and he and several other monks were sentenced to exile. But although the leaders of the bakufu felt compelled to uphold their authority to issue such regulations, they did not necessarily object to Takuan's religious position. That the dispute was as much a matter of face as a fundamental disagreement may be deduced from the fact that Takuan's forced exile was retracted three years later and that thereafter the third shogun, Iemitsu, showed him great favor, summoning him regularly to Edo for consultation.

The Zen reform movement attempted to institute more rigorous training for the priesthood, but it also attempted to make Zen accessible to the general populace, teaching the lay believer the true spirit of Zen. Takuan's efforts to make Zen an effective guide to life for the individual may be seen in such works as *Riki sabetsu ron* (On the distinction between *ri* and *ki*), in which he set forth the similarities shared by Buddhism and Neo-Confucianism, and *Fudōchi shimmyōroku* (Miraculous records of the immovable spirit), in which he declared that the ultimate essence of swordsmanship was the same as the spirit of Zen. These works advocate "nothingness" or "no-mind," that is, a state of mind unimpeded by outside constraints, as the essential foundation for all human activities.

Suzuki Shōsan (1579–1655) was another monk who sought to make the essence of Buddhist teachings accessible to ordinary people.[50] Shōsan originally served and fought for the Tokugawa as a bushi. Later, at the age of forty-two he became a Zen monk. He wrote several works for the edification of the general public, such as *Bammin tokuyō* (Teachings for the multitude), which argued that the occupations pursued by those living in society were universally endowed with religious significance.

According to Shōsan, one's ideal as a human being should be to live in a spiritually free, autonomous fashion. To achieve that ideal, unremitting and determined commitment to a spiritual regimen was essential. For a bushi, that spiritual regimen was none other than the correct pursuit of his daily duties as a bushi. Moreover, by pursuing those

---

50 Nakamura Hajime, *Kinsei Nihon ni okeru hihanteki seishin no ichi kōsatsu* (Tokyo: Sanseidō, 1949).

duties he would in some manner contribute to the functioning of society, thereby conforming to the intention of the Buddha, who had sought to be of use to the people of the world. In other words, the performance of one's allotted function or vocation was a spiritual means of attaining one's true nature, that is, becoming a Buddha; at the same time it constituted a realization of the will of the Buddha. Shōsan held the same to be true for peasants and tradesmen.

The attempt to present Buddhist truth not as something attainable only in the distant future or after death but as something to be used in the context of one's daily life was common at this time. In the Pure Land tradition, for example, there was a widespread saying: "The Pure Land exists within one's heart; in this form one is Amida."[51] Shosan regarded Zen and the *nembutsu* (invocation of the name of Amida), as nearly the same.

Another figure who tried to elucidate the lofty state of enlightenment in a simple manner for the people was Bankei Eitaku (1622–93).[52] Bankei expressed the spiritual state attained through rigorous Zen training as one of "nonbirth" (*fushō*). "Nonbirth" referred to the mind in its original, unadulterated condition, and Bankei held that because all beings were endowed with "the Buddha-nature of nonbirth," the individual needed only to become aware of that innate endowment. The straightforward manner in which he presented his teachings and his personal integrity won Bankei some fifty thousand followers, ranging from daimyo to ordinary people.

The efforts of Shōsan and Bankei to carry the teachings of Zen to the general population were inspired by religious motivations and had a significant social impact. Nevertheless, considered from the perspective of traditional Zen doctrine, their approach might lead to the misconception that a rigorous religious discipline was not needed to achieve enlightenment. The figure who took on the task of resolving this problem was Hakuin Ekaku (1685–1768).[53] Revitalizing the traditional Zen discipline based on *zazen* (meditation) and the use of *kōan*, Hakuin established the approach that has characterized Rinzai Zen from the latter part of the early modern period to modern times.

Religious figures belonging to the Shinto tradition also made intel-

51 Ōkuwa Hitoshi, "Bukkyō shisōron: shokyō itchi ron no keisei," in Hongō Takamori and Fukaya Katsumi, eds., *Kinsei shisōron*, vol. 9 of *Kōza Nihon kinseishi* (Tokyo: Yūhikaku, 1941).
52 *Bankei zenji goroku* (Tokyo: Iwanami shoten, 1941); Suzuki Daisetsu, *Zen shisōshi kenkyū*, vol. 1 (Iwanami shoten, 1942); Suzuki Daisetsu and Furuta Shōkin, eds., *Bankei zen no kenkyū* (Tokyo: Sankibō busshorin, 1942).
53 Tsuji Zennosuke, *Nihon bukkyōshi (kinsei 3)*.

lectual contributions in this period. The most noteworthy of these was Watarai Nobuyoshi (1615–90), a priest attached to the Outer Shrine (*gekū*) of the Ise Shrine, who endeavored to reform Ise Shinto as it was established in the medieval period. In works like *Yōfukki*, Nobuyoshi argued in a clear, rationalistic fashion that devoted performance of one's allotted social function conformed to the teachings of the *kami* and that on this point the moral philosophy of Shinto and Confucianism were the same. Nobuyoshi's attempt to free Shinto from a ritualistic, magical orientation paralleled the efforts of reformers like Takuan. It also fit in with the ethical dimension seen in the popular *kami* worship of this period and encouraged its further growth.

In addition to Nobuyoshi, other contemporary figures who contributed to the development of Shinto include Yoshikawa Koretaru (1616–94), who came out of the Yoshida Shinto tradition, and Yamazaki Ansai (1618–82), also active as a Neo-Confucian scholar, who founded the Suiga school of Shinto. All three thinkers, however, adhered to a Confucian interpretation of Shinto; it was only in the next century that scholars of "national learning" (*kokugaku*) broke out of this Confucian framework and presented Shinto as a religion indigenous to Japan. In this connection we may note that the foundations for the emergence of *kokugaku* also were established in this period through the accumulation of scholarly studies of the Japanese classics. Particularly Keichū (1640–1701) broke new scholarly ground through his adoption of a philological approach to the study of the classics.

In this period, Buddhist and Shinto thought shared the view that the individual's committed pursuit of his or her allotted social function would ensure his or her autonomy and thus would serve as a means of spiritual salvation. To a certain extent this notion coincided with the premises of Chu Hsi's thought, which helps explain its successful diffusion and the acceptance among Zen and Shinto thinkers of the essential unity of their teachings with those of Chu Hsi's thought.

According to the premises of Chu Hsi's thought, the fundamental principles of reason and morality (Ch: *li*, J:*ri*) were identical with humanity's original nature (Ch: *hsing*, J: *sei*). Consequently, the pursuit of *ri* was at the same time a means of developing the potential of one's inner nature to guide one in behaving correctly. Through sustained effort, one would eventually succeed in making the principles of morality one's own and be able to act appropriately simply by following the promptings of one's mind.

Moreover, because all beings were endowed with the original nature, they possessed the potential of achieving this ideal state of human existence. To fulfill that potential, it was essential to carry out faithfully one's moral duty as a member of society. The diversity of social roles meant that these duties differed from individual to individual, as did the principles underlying them. But did this mean that through the performance of one's duty, one could grasp only the principle specific to it? To the contrary, because these diverse specific principles derived from the general principles of human morality present in each individual's innate nature, they were fundamentally different manifestations of one principle. The distinctive feature of Chu Hsi's moral view lies in this positing of a universal entity common to diverse circumstances and in the premise that pursuit of the latter is the proper means of achieving the former.

An example of one who correctly understood this essential feature of Chu Hsi's thought and sought to put it into practice was Nakae Tōju (1608–48).[54] At the age of twenty-seven, Tōju abandoned his bushi status and returned to his native village to devote himself to scholarship. In *Okina mondō*, which he wrote at the age of thirty-three, he explained in a simple fashion the essential points of Chu Hsi Neo-Confucianism as they applied to actual life.

Beginning with a discussion of the familiar virtue of filial piety, Tōju went on to show that whether one was lord, retainer, or commoner, to pursue one's vocation in an appropriate manner was to practice the tenets of Confucianism. Moreover, because all were endowed by nature with "illustrious virtue" (*meitoku*), if the individual took into account the "time, place, and his or her status" and acts on this innate virtue, he or she could respond spontaneously in a correct manner to any situation. Through the criteria of "time, place, and status," Tōju sought to establish a basis for the individual to carry out his or her allotted social function while preserving his or her own spiritual autonomy.

The postulation of the simultaneous pursuit of these ends as the ideal way of life corresponded closely to the premises of Chu Hsi's thought. At the same time Tōju sought through the principle of "time, place, and status" to reduce some of the alien dimensions of Confucianism as a product of Chinese social experience, thereby making the essential elements of Chu Hsi's thought more applicable to the circumstances of Japanese society. For example, Tōju held that the principle of conforming to "time, place, and status" made it unnecessary for contemporary Japanese to adhere rigidly to the formal rules of behavior stipulated by the Chinese Confucian tradition.

54 Regarding Tōju, see Bitō, *Nihon hōken shisōshi kenkyū*, pp. 136–216.

To be sure, there was a contradiction between Tōju's assertion that one should not feel unduly constrained by formalistic rules of behavior and the Chu Hsi school's position that rectification of the self through the study of "principle" (kyūri) depended on scrupulous observance of the moral criteria specific to a particular circumstance. Inevitably those criteria were the product of social custom and tradition. Seeking a means of resolving this dilemma, in his last years Tōju turned increasingly to the Wang Yang-ming school of Neo-Confucianism. As a consequence, he frequently has been called the founder of the Wang Yang-ming school in Japan. But this tag is somewhat of a misnomer. Tōju's grasp of Wang Yang-ming's ideas remained incomplete; moreover his work that circulated most widely and had the greatest impact on society was Okina mondō, which belongs to the period of intellectual searching before his turn to the thought of Wang Yang-ming.

The most influential of those who inherited Tōju's intellectual tradition was Kumazawa Banzan (1619–91) who served for a time as adviser to the daimyo of Okayama.[55] Adopting Tōju's advocacy of acting in accordance with "time, place, and status," Banzan applied that principle to the actual conduct of government. He criticized the growing trend toward autocracy in the politics of the day and tried to expand the possibilities for individuals to act autonomously. Such views, however, made Banzan the object of suspicion, and bakufu officials ordered him to be kept under strict supervision, an order that remained in effect until the end of his life.

The respective fates of Tōju and Banzan suggest that there were major obstacles to incorporating the full dynamics of Chu Hsi's thought into Japanese society. Both men understood the essential Chu Hsi ideal of perfecting one's inborn potential to act as an autonomous being. However, Tōju failed to find an effective means to realize that ideal, and Banzan's efforts to act in accordance with these principles led to his political isolation. For this reason, although Tōju and Banzan were acclaimed by later generations, they had no immediate intellectual successors.

Other contemporary figures were more successful in gaining a large following. Particularly notable in this regard was Yamazaki Ansai (1618–82), a fervent believer in the Chu Hsi tradition who emphasized putting the tenets of that tradition into practice.[56] Ansai started out as a Zen monk but turned to Neo-Confucianism under the influence of

55 For Banzan, see Bitō, Nihon hōken shisōshi kenkyū, pp. 217–76.
56 For Ansai, see Bitō, Nihon hōken shisōshi kenkyū, pp. 40–99. In English, Herman Ooms, Tokugawa Ideology: Early Constructs, 1570–1680 (Princeton: Princeton University Press, 1985.)

the Tosa Southern school of Confucian scholars. In 1655 he established a private school in Kyoto that attracted a large number of disciples. Besides instructing students, Ansai published works by Chu Hsi and wrote commentaries on them. He also traveled regularly to Edo where he lectured before a number of daimyo.

To Ansai, practicing the tenets of the Chu Hsi tradition meant that one should endeavor, to the best of one's abilities, to carry out faithfully the moral obligations specific to the social circumstances in which one was placed. This required an attitude of "reverence" (Ch: *ching*, J: *kei* or *tsutsushimi*), a mental state characterized by stability of mind and circumspect behavior. The emphasis that Ansai put on the cultivation of an attitude of "reverence," as opposed to the "plumbing of principle," is one of the distinctive features of his approach. In Chu Hsi's thought, reverence was originally held to be a precondition for the plumbing of principle. Ansai, however, interpreted reverence as summing up the essence of the Chu Hsi tradition. He did not explicitly deny the importance of principle, but he believed the plumbing of principle to be something not readily attainable by the average person and so relegated it to a place of secondary importance.

As a consequence, the ideal that Ansai delineated differed substantially from that of Tōju. Tōju envisioned an individual enabled by the process of self-cultivation to choose on the basis of his or her own innate reason the proper course of action. By contrast, Ansai regarded the ultimate goal as preservation of the correct social order, which consisted of the totality of specific moral standards, and he called on each individual to contribute to this goal by striving unremittingly to uphold the particular moral standard appropriate to his or her situation. This task was described by the term *meibun*, or action in accordance with "names," in other words, action appropriate to the relative social status of all parties concerned. The stricture to uphold *meibun* was stressed particularly in the context of the relationship between lord and vassal, leading to the exaltation of an attitude by the retainer of devotion and unquestioning loyalty to the lord. However, Ansai did not see the person of the lord as the sole object of such commitment. Rather, he emphasized the extension of devoted service to the social organization that the lord represented and to the function that the individual was expected to perform within that organization. This expansion of the object of service constitutes one of the distinctive features of the moral outlook associated with Ansai.

The mysticism inherent in this outlook may have stimulated Ansai's deep interest in Shinto. The conviction that one could find the basis for the proper moral stance in the myths of ancient Japan led Ansai to engage in an elaborate reinterpretation of the language of the myths and eventually to formulate a new school of Shinto, the Suiga school. That development resulted, in turn, in the split of Ansai's disciples into two opposing factions, Shinto and Confucian, and the expulsion from his coterie of disciples of the two leading representatives of the Confucian camp, Asami Keisai (1652–1711) and Satō Naokata (1650–1719). Ironically, however, most of Ansai's school (said at one time to number as many as six thousand followers) coalesced around the Confucian faction rejected by Ansai. Naokata, Keisai, and a third scholar, Miyake Shōsai (1662–1741), came to be known as the three exemplars of the Ansai school (*kimon sanketsu*), and their teaching exerted a substantial influence on society. Ansai's interpretation of Chu Hsi's thought, calling for devoted performance of one's particular social function, obviously responded effectively to the actual circumstances and needs of Japanese society in this period.

If the meaning of existence is identified with one's contribution to society through the performance of one's particular function, the "plumbing of principle" advocated by Chu Hsi not only ceases to be necessary, but its emphasis on the development of the rational faculties may even come to be regarded as wrongly encouraging the individual to separate himself or herself from society at large. Ansai sought to overcome this dilemma by stressing will instead of reason. Eventually, however, scholars appeared who rejected the premises of Chu Hsi's thought as such and sought to establish a new intellectual system in its place. Foremost among them were Yamaga Sokō (1622–85) and Itō Jinsai (1627–1705) who, together with the early-eighteenth-century scholar Ogyū Sorai, are known as the formulators of the Ancient Learning school (*kogakuha*).

The term "Ancient Learning" refers to the effort to approach directly the Confucian classics of antiquity, without relying on the commentaries and interpretations of later scholars such as Chu Hsi. On this point, all three of these scholars were in agreement. However, in regard to questions of actual methodology and the theoretical implications they drew from their studies, each followed his own path. Their successors likewise formed distinct groups. Thus, despite the common denomination of these scholars as adherents of Ancient Learning, they did not constitute a single, consistent school of thought.

The Tokugawa Ancient Learning scholars are often likened to the Empirical Learning school which arose in Ch'ing China, and indeed the philological studies of Jinsai and Sorai achieved results comparable in many ways to those of the Empirical Learning scholars. Where the Ch'ing and Tokugawa scholars differed, however, was that the former, while rejecting the commentaries of Chu Hsi, tried to clarify the original meaning of the classics by using earlier commentaries written in the Han period. By contrast, the Tokugawa Ancient Learning scholars rejected reliance on all commentaries, including those of the Han period. To interpret accurately works written more than two thousand years earlier, even Chinese scholars found it necessary to use the oldest commentaries available. It inevitably was difficult for Japanese scholars, working with a foreign tradition and setting aside all commentaries, to reach the same level of scholarly achievement. But if the Ancient Learning scholars may be faulted on the point of scholarly precision, considered from the perspective of the history of Japanese thought they achieved much. They succeeded both in developing a systematic interpretation of Confucianism that accorded with the actualities of Japanese life and, to a considerable degree, in providing plausible textual support for that interpretation.

Both Sokō and Jinsai began as followers of Chu Hsi, but around 1662–3 each shifted to an Ancient Learning position. The two lived in different circumstances and were not in contact with each other. Of bushi origins, Sokō was active primarily in Edo, while Jinsai grew to maturity in a townsman's family in Kyoto – Thus it was coincidental that each shifted to a new intellectual stance at approximately the same time. Yet this very coincidence points to the intellectual trends of the time.

Sokō acquired a notable reputation in his youth, not so much as a Confucian, but as a specialist in military affairs (*heigakusha*).[57] Confucianism, in essence, served as the theoretical foundation for his approach to military affairs. According to Sokō, the Confucian sages put particular emphasis on "knowledge" (J: *chi*, Ch: *chih*). The object of this knowledge was the concrete standards of correct behavior specific to the individual human relationships, such as those between lord and vassal and father and son. In their totality those relationships formed the structure of society and the state. Consequently, the standards of behavior specific to each such relationship derived from the public purpose of maintaining the social order. Because the human relationships that formed the larger social order were different, the criteria of behavior proper to each must also be different; that is, one could not "know" them by extrapolating from one general principle. It was

---

57 For Sokō's biography, see Hori Isao, *Yamaga Sokō* (Tokyo: Yoshikawa kōbunkan, 1959); and for his thought, see Bitō Masahide, "Yamaga Sokō no shisō teki tenkai," *Shisō* 560–1 (1971).

necessary, therefore, to build up a concrete knowledge of particular relationships and the standard of behavior specific to each.

"Knowledge" in the context of Chu Hsi thought was directed internally toward the heart or mind. It referred to the effort to perceive directly through a spiritual awakening the original nature of the mind, that is, the general principles of morality. By contrast, for Sokō what was to be "known" were things that could be perceived objectively, such as the social order and human relationships as they should exist within the framework of that order. By correctly understanding such things the individual would realize more precisely the social function allotted him or her and also would obtain a concrete knowledge of how to carry out that function.

Seeing the dissemination of such knowledge to be his mission as a scholar, Sokō wrote many books. These included not only works setting forth the fundamental principles of his intellectual approach, such as *Seikyō yōroku* (The essential teachings of the sages), but also historical works such as *Chūchō jijitsu* (The records of the central nation), which dealt with the ancient history of Japan, and *Buke jiki* (Account of the military houses), which dealt with the period of military rule from the thirteenth to the sixteenth centuries. The last covered various topics like methods of warfare, weapons, and the construction of castles. In essence it was a kind of encyclopedia – a *heigaku* textbook – intended to give the bushi, whose function was to fight, systematic knowledge of the matters necessary for the performance of that function. In Sokō's eyes, those who like himself belonged to the bushi class had to acquire this kind of historical and practical information in order to fulfill appropriately their social role.

Sokō looked to the surrounding social order, rather than the individual's inner being, to provide the criteria for action. In this regard, Sokō's intellectual outlook resembled that of Ansai. However, Ansai's emphasis on the need for an attitude of devoted service to the social order in effect postulated a kind of religious transfiguration in which the individual became one with the social order. On this point Ansai drew from the Chu Hsi premise that the individual's original nature (*sei*) and the principles of morality (*ri*) were one and the same and that the individual should seek to unify subjective and objective knowledge through the realization of this identity. Sokō, by contrast, sharply divided the object of intellectual perception from the individual engaged in the act of perception. As a consequence, although Sokō's concept of knowledge offered a rational foundation for the standards of behavior demanded of the individual, it lacked the appeal to the emotions necessary to stimulate the drive to fulfill those standards. It presumably was for this reason that compared with his military and political writings, Sokō's interpretation of Confucianism itself had little social impact.

Itō Jinsai also held that the meaning of life was to be found in the performance of the role allotted to one in the context of specific human relationships such as those between lord and subject and father and son. He saw those relationships as constituting the actuality of human life and Confucianism as what taught the correct way of living in accordance with that actuality. He further assumed that as human relationships as a whole formed the social order, the manner of life of an individual should properly be considered within the framework of society as a whole (literally, the "realm," *tenka*). Up to this point Jinsai and Sokō held essentially the same ideas. But then Sokō focused on how to grasp objectively and concretely one's position in the total structure of society and one's corresponding responsibilities (*shoku-bun*). Jinsai, by comparison, concerned himself primarily with the problem of the inner moral sense which he believed should guide the individual in his or her relations with others.[58]

On the surface Jinsai would seem to resemble the Chu Hsi school in his emphasis on a moral sense rooted in the heart of the individual. Yet Jinsai was highly critical of the Chu Hsi outlook. According to Chu Hsi, the foundation of morality lay in the "original nature," something akin to an intellectual capacity for moral judgment that constituted one aspect of the human heart. If it were allowed to function unimpeded by the passions or selfish desires, this capacity for moral judgment would enable the individual not only to act appropriately in his or her own life but also to exert positive influence on others, thereby helping bring society into conformity with its proper form. Although the Chu Hsi moral view thus started with the individual, indeed with the intellectual dimensions of the individual's mind or heart, Jinsai argued that morality transcended the level of the individual. By this he meant that morality existed within society as the overall structure in which were subsumed the multiplicity of human relationships. In that this overall structure reflected social purposes and desires common to all people, it broadly accorded with the individual's natural sentiments. However, Jinsai held, the moral judgments reached by the individual through intellectual reasoning were not always congruent

---

58 Bitō Masahide, "Itō Jinsai ni okeru gakumon to jissen," *Shisō* 524 (1968); and "Itō Jinsai no shisō ni okeru jō no igi," *Tōhō gakkai sōritsu yonjūshūnen kinen tōhōgaku ronshū* (1987); Koyasu Nobukuni, *Itō Jinsai – jinrinteki sekai no shisō* (Tokyo: Tōkyō daigaku shuppankai, 1982).

with what was appropriate to society as a whole. Thus to follow un-swervingly one's own judgment, regardless of the general movement of society, might well be morally improper in the larger sense.

Jinsai did not mistrust the human mind as such; to the contrary, faith in the propriety of people's natural sentiments is a major charac-teristic of his intellectual outlook. But he did fear that overdependence on the intellect might lead one to regard others coldly and to distance oneself from society, and so he opposed the Chu Hsi moral view as susceptible to such tendencies. In place of the intellect, Jinsai saw feelings, particularly the capacity to love and sympathize with others, as the essence of the human mind. Moveover, because human relations and the social order were founded on these feelings of love and em-pathy basic to the human heart, morality, in his view, should not be regarded as something lofty and difficult to achieve. Instead, it was rooted in the context of ordinary social life, and to conduct one's life properly in accordance with one's natural feelings of love for others was to practice morality.

Among the Confucian classics Jinsai gave particular emphasis to the *Analects* and *Mencius*, which he interpreted in light of his concept of morality. In addition to commentaries in which he set forth this inter-pretation, he also wrote works such as *Dōjimon* (Dialogue with a child), which systematically elaborated his own ideas. His approach to scholarship, which was continued by his son Itō Tōgai (1670–1736), attracted many followers to the private academy that he founded on Horikawa Street in Kyoto and had a major influence on the late-seventeenth and early-eighteenth-century intellectual world. The disci-ples of Jinsai and Tōgai formed what is known as the Horikawa or "Ancient Meaning" (*kōgi*) school of scholarship.

The Confucian thought exemplified by the *Analects* and *Mencius* was essentially an intellectual abstraction and systematization of the hu-man relations characteristic of the family-oriented community of an-cient China. Jinsai likewise tried to articulate a moral consciousness geared to the mentality of those living in the new communal social structure of sixteenth- and seventeenth-century Japan. In that the social base of early Tokugawa Japan and ancient China were different, Jinsai's interpretation of works like the *Analects* did not always con-form entirely to the meaning of the original text. But by the same token, his interpretations fit closely the mental reality of his own society. As such, they represent one culmination of the intellectual endeavors of the Confucian scholars of the seventeenth century.

CHAPTER 9

POLITICS IN THE EIGHTEENTH CENTURY

By the middle of the seventeenth century, the government of Japan in many important respects had assumed the shape it was thereafter to maintain for the next two hundred years.[1] The emperor, nominal head of state, was kept in Kyoto, isolated and virtually powerless. In Edo, the administrative center of the country, was the bakufu, a government staffed by a large group of samurai officials. Already they were at work producing a voluminous and dense body of statutes, precedents, and procedural instructions to cope with the increasingly complex society over which they presided. The sixty-eight provinces were divided among 250 feudal lords, or daimyo, all to some extent autonomous but all having sworn – with a greater or lesser degree of sincerity – undying loyalty to the Tokugawa shogun. None of them had found the first fifty years of the new regime particularly easy. Some had been plucked abruptly from the Tokugawa vassal band to assume independent responsibilities for the first time; others, once Tokugawa equals and even rivals, had suffered in various ways, their domains now surrounded by Tokugawa watchdogs or shifted from favorable locations to areas more distant or less prosperous. Even so, they were the lucky ones – luckier by far than those 175 of their peers who lost all or part of their domains during the first half of the seventeenth century.

Once the first fifty years had passed, however, there were undeniable signs that having attained a certain measure of security, the Tokugawa revolution in government was coming to a halt. After 1650, it used its powers against the daimyo much less, the rate of both attainders and fief transfers falling decisively. To no small extent this was due to the recognition of the principle of deathbed adoption; failure to produce an heir had once been one of the major causes of daimyo

---

1 Tsuji Tatsuya, " 'Geba shōgun' seiji no seikaku," *Yokohama shiritsu daigaku ronsō* (Humanities) 2–3 (August 1979):30–31.

attainder, but after 1651 it no longer applied. Slowly, almost imperceptibly, the social structure of the samurai class, after decades of constant flux, began to settle down, starting, appropriately enough, at the top. Daimyo families, unless they committed the grossest of indiscretions, were now safe; as institutions, they could continue even if the bloodline itself failed. The same held true for families all the way down the samurai hierarchy. What you were born to, you could rely on keeping, regardless of talent or suitability.[2]

The imposition of the shogun's authority over the other power centers, however, did not bring a halt to political transformations during the Tokugawa period. The politics of the eighteenth century were lively and significant in their own right. In large part, this was due to the appearance of new social and economic problems that forced creative responses from the governmental structure.[3] One of the most pressing problems was fiscal, for by the turn of the eighteenth century the growing shogunate had begun to discover that its need for revenue outstripped its capacity to tax the peasantry on its own lands. With quickening tempo, the control that government exercised over the farming communities that sustained them began to weaken, and tax revenues began to decline. New policies were called for, and successive regimes struggled with the problem of how to extract more taxes from a population that, in turn, was increasingly reluctant to part with its surpluses.[4]

Political life in the eighteenth century was also affected by the increases in agricultural productivity. New crops and new farming methods generated continuously larger rural surpluses, and these provided the fuel for unprecedented commercial development during the second half of the seventeenth century. Quickly trade and commerce grew beyond the government's ability to control it. In towns and villages alike, new opportunities and new risks brought about by commercial development began to reshape patterns of social organization. From the shogunate's perspective, this threatened to pull the farmer from his land and to erode the loyalty of the samurai class, whose incomes lagged behind those of their merchant neighbors. This commercial assault on the basis of the social status system would draw the attention of almost every eighteenth-century reformer.

2 Asao Naohiro, "Shōgun seiji no kenryoku kōzō," in *Iwanami kōza Nihon rekishi*, vol. 10 (Tokyo: Iwanami shoten, 1975), pp. 39–40.
3 Tsuji, " 'Geba shōgun'," p. 42; and Matsumoto Shirō, "Kambun–Genroku-ki ni okeru daimyo-gashi no tokushitsu," in *Mitsui bunkō ronsō*, no. 1 (1967):81–94.
4 Tsuji, " 'Geba shōgun'," pp. 40–3; and Satō Takayuki, "Kinsei zenki no nengu shūshu to nōson kin'yū," in *Tokugawa rinsei-shi kenkyūjo kenkyū kiyō* (1979):391–414.

None of the new fiscal or commercial challenges, however, were amenable to easy solution. As problems mounted during the eighteenth century – or sometimes as proposed solutions created newer and equally vexing predicaments – various reform factions fought for control over the shogunate and sought to promote their own reform programs. At times, this pitted the shogun against entrenched bureaucratic interests; at other times reform groups within the bureaucracy ruthlessly moved against their opponents. These struggles so colored the politics of the eighteenth century that the story of reformers and reformism provides a convenient framework for understanding the direction of political change during the middle years of the Tokugawa shogunate.

TOKUGAWA TSUNAYOSHI

The first great reformer was Tokugawa Tsunayoshi (1646–1709). The fifth of the Tokugawa rulers, Tsunayoshi nearly never became shogun at all. True, he was the son of Tokugawa Iemitsu, the third shogun, but he was the fourth son, with therefore only the slightest prospect of obtaining the succession. When in 1651, at the age of six, he became a daimyo with a fief of 150,000 *koku,* he seemed destined to follow the classic career of a younger son – comfortable and not particularly demanding. His removal, ten years later, to a larger fief rated at 250,000 *koku* at Tatebayashi, in the province of Kōzuke, was much in the same tradition. But then in 1680, his elder brother, the fourth shogun, Tokugawa Ietsuna, died without issue, and Tsunayoshi was returned to the main Tokugawa line as his successor. From 1680 until his death in 1709, Tsunayoshi did all he could to bring the central government into line with commercial and social development.

His years as shogun began with an extraordinary demonstration of autocratic power. Sakai Tadakiyo, who as grand councilor since 1666 had been undeniably the most powerful and prominent member of Ietsuna's government, was abruptly dismissed, much to the surprise of everyone. This was a flagrant break with convention. In the past, officials of such eminence were expected to remain in their posts until they died. Typically, they were not permitted to resign, even if desperately ill, as convention decreed that both status and office were granted for life. What made all this even more remarkable was Sakai Tadakiyo's own family background, for he came from a line known for its firm support for the Tokugawa house. Naturally enough, because no official explanation was ever offered, Edo was filled with rumors, one of the most widely accepted (although never substantiated) claiming that the grand councilor had disapproved of the new shogun and had unsuccessfully tried to have him replaced with an imperial prince.[5]

It is more likely, however, that Tsunayoshi, by eliminating the experienced and influential elder statesman, had sought to transfer Sakai's powers to himself. With the grand councilor gone, the entire bureaucratic apparatus would become more responsive to the shogun's demands. A subsidiary aim might have been to inject some urgency into an administration grown stagnant; by removing the bureaucracy's highest official with such dispatch, Tsunayoshi had placed all other officials on notice. Certainly, if such were his motives, Tsunayoshi was to see them accomplished to a very large extent.

Tokugawa Iemitsu, Tsunayoshi's father, had always been conscious of his lack of formal education and took some pains to see that his own sons did not suffer in the same way. Tsunayoshi therefore had been exposed from childhood to formal educational training, together with the Confucianism with which it was virtually synonymous. As a youth he had taken to this learning with great enthusiasm, and now as shogun, he at last had the opportunity to put his Confucian principles into practice. He particularly urged bakufu officials to pay close attention to their studies and obliged them to attend lectures on the Confucian classics, some of which he delivered personally. To some extent this may be seen simply as the whim of an autocrat basking in the adulation of those around him, but there is no question about his intention. Tsunayoshi desperately wanted to create a loyal, learned, and effective bureaucracy, one in which the spirit of Confucianism might be given tangible form.[6]

The same impulse lay behind Tsunayoshi's attitude toward the common people. For their benefit he had a series of public notice boards erected throughout the country in 1682 to publicize the key Confucian virtues of loyalty, filial piety, thrift, and diligence. His famous laws aimed at the protection of the animal kingdom, with dogs a special favorite – the so-called Shōrui awaremi no rei, or Instructions concerning compassion for all living creatures – are yet another example. Ultimately, by enjoining people not to abandon sick cows or horses, by prohibiting the sale of creatures such as birds and tortoises for food, by jailing those who injured animals, and by threatening with death or

5 Tsuji Tatsuya, Kyōhō kaikaku no kenkyū (Tokyo: Sōbunsha, 1963), pp. 43–46.
6 Tsuji, Kyōhō, p. 36; and Tsuji Tatsuya, "Bakusei no shindankai," in Iwanami kōza Nihon rekishi, vol. 11 (Tokyo: Iwanami shoten, 1963), pp. 12–13.

exile anyone who killed a dog, Tsunayoshi may have oppressed the people, but this was never his intention. Rather, he was trying to foster a true benevolence among them, one that would embrace the whole of creation, even its meanest members. He was in fact trying to create the perfect Confucian society, peopled by none but the benevolent and docile.[7]

It was Tsunayoshi's Confucianism, too, that led him to institute a rigorous policy of rewarding or punishing bakufu officials for their efficiency, or lack of it. This resulted, on the one hand, in a number of promotions, as many administrators were raised far beyond their normal expectations, in tribute to their honesty or diligence. On the other hand, an enormous number of officials in both the shogunate and the daimyo domains were punished for their alleged mistakes.

Much of this unprecedented behavior has been attributed to Tsunayoshi's own personal idiosyncracies. The poet Toda Mosui, a contemporary, wrote in his *Gotōdaiki:*

When so many were penalized for the most trifling errors, people's uncertainty grew; no one knew who would be punished next, nor what his punishment would be. During the rule of the fourth shogun, men had tried to win official appointment for the honor of their ancestors and their descendants; now, should they be given an official post, they pray to gods and buddhas that they might safely be allowed to resign.

Indeed, some did see their estates confiscated when they dared to step down.

Certainly there was an element of caprice in Tsunayoshi's policy reflecting both the authority of the shogun and his instability. Nevertheless, it cannot be explained away simply in terms of the shogun's own individual peculiarities. There was an important political issue underlying this new severity as an examination of Tsunayoshi's treatment of the daimyo so clearly demonstrates.

In the sixth month of 1681, Tsunayoshi sat in judgment on a difficult and long-unsettled dispute that had taken place in Echigo, in the Takada domain. Characteristically, his judgment was severe. Not only did he punish the leaders of both sides of the dispute, but he also confiscated the entire domain, on the grounds that Matsudaira Mitsunaga, the daimyo, had been at fault. In its way this was a momentous decision, for the Echigo Matsudaira family, of which Mitsunaga was the head, was an eminent branch of the three major cadet houses at

7 Tsuji Tatsuya, "Seidan no shakai-teki haikei," in Yoshikawa Kōjirō and Maruyama Masao, eds., *Ogyū Sorai,* vol. 36 of *Nihon shisō taikei* (Tokyo: Iwanami shoten, 1973), pp. 778–82.

Kii, Mito, and Owari. Tsunayoshi's decision to destroy it, therefore, startled contemporaries as much as his dismissal of Sakai Tadakiyo had six months earlier. This decision foreshadowed a new severity in the fifth shogun's attitude toward the daimyo class.

Under Tsunayoshi a total of forty-six daimyo were stripped of all or part of their domains, surrendering a total of 1.6 million *koku* in the process. During the previous regime only half that number of daimyo had felt the shogun's displeasure. Further, an analysis of those forty-six daimyo reveals several interesting insights. First, seventeen of them were outside lords (*tozama daimyō*), men whose rise had been independent of, and often predated, that of the Tokugawa house itself. But nearly twice as many – twenty nine, in fact – were *fudai*, the daimyo who up to now had been most cherished by Tokugawa shoguns. Furthermore, in seventeen examples the cause for punishment was reasonably clear-cut: for insanity, physical violence against another, and failure to produce an heir. In all such cases, punishment was mandatory. Nine of these seventeen men were *tozama* and eight were *fudai*. Of the twenty-nine remaining cases, the more problematical decisions, only eight were *tozama*, and a totally disproportionate twenty-one were *fudai*, a clear indication that Tsunayoshi's displeasure was leveled far more at the traditional supporters of the Tokugawa than at those who had always kept their distance. Indeed, beginning with his dismissal of Sakai Tadakiyo, one of the most eminent of *fudai* daimyo, proceeding through his destruction of the Echigo branch of the Matsudaira family and culminating in an onslaught on the *fudai* as a group, Tsunayoshi seemed to be attacking the very underpinnings of Tokugawa authority.

Not all of this was deliberate. Like all lords and indeed like the bakufu itself, the *fudai* daimyo had not been spared the consequences of social change. To a greater or lesser degree, all had been troubled by political difficulties within their own domains. Often the result was a factional dispute like that which had occurred at Takada – open, acrimonious, and not infrequently bloody. Such arguments, known as *oiesōdō*, offered Tsunayoshi an ideal pretext for action, as all could be manifestly attributed to maladministration at the highest levels of domain government. Further, not only were the *fudai* daimyo as vulnerable on such issues as the *tozama*, but they also ran an additional risk. They were far more likely to win office within the bakufu than anybody else and so were far more likely to provoke the unpredictable shogun with an administrative blunder of some sort.

This does not mean that Tsunayoshi was able to shrug off completely the traditional *fudai* influence. The authority conferred by lineage and status remained, and occasionally served to restrain the shogun. All in all, however, within the administration, the strength of the *fudai* class was diminished, and its hold over the shogun weakened perceptibly.[8] Tsunayoshi, as a result, enhanced his own authority to a considerable degree. Such at least is the impression conveyed by Date Tsunamura, daimyo of Sendai. "When I had an audience with the fourth shogun Ietsuna," he is reported to have said, "I could always look him in the face; now, in the august presence [of Tsunayoshi] I automatically bow my head." Whether or not Tsunamura actually said this – and the source, the *Sannō gaiki*, is not the most reliable – the currency of this, and many other such stories, suggests the fifth shogun's heightened powers.

Tsunayoshi's attempt to reform the bakufu administration, however, did not run smoothly. It was not easy to replace a bureaucracy determined on the basis of family status with one recruited more widely, and by attempting to do so, Tsunayoshi forfeited the confidence of many of those whose support would have been helpful. He was quickly obliged, therefore, to turn to his own friends and cronies for support. In 1681, within a year of his succession, he restructured the administration of the shogunal household, creating the new position of *sobayōnin* (lord chamberlain), with rank equivalent to that of senior councilor, and installing his old friend and adviser Makino Narisada in it. Narisada was the first to achieve what was seen by many as unwarranted influence through his personal association with the shogun. *Fudai* daimyo like Matsudaira Terusada and Matsudaira Tadachika followed, as did *tozama* like Nambu Naomasa and Kanamori Yoritoki, and finally, Yanagisawa Yoshiyasu, who, like Makino Narisada, had served Tsunayoshi even before his accession. The same shogunal patronage also took Kitami Shigemasa from the position of *hatamoto* (bannerman), with a stipend of one thousand *koku*, to that of *sobayōnin*, with twenty thousand. In his case, however, this was followed by an equally abrupt fall from favor, and dismissal.

Nevertheless, such reversals apart, it was clear that many newcomers, even those of low rank, were being elevated to positions of considerable power in both the shogun's own household and the external administrative hierarchy. Inevitably, many of those not so favored would seek their assistance and would offer bribes to ensure their success.

8 Tsuji, *Kyōhō*, pp. 46–55; and Tsuji, "Bakusei," pp. 9–12, 14–15.

The rise of Makino Narisada within the shogun's own household was paralleled by the growing eminence of Hotta Masatoshi within the bakufu. As a senior councilor, Hotta had certainly been eminent enough under the previous shogun, but in 1681 Tsunayoshi appointed him to the position of grand councilor left vacant by Sakai Tadakiyo, granting him at the same time a fief increase that took him from a 40,000-*koku* domain to one of 130,000 *koku*. Hotta seemed to be replacing Sakai, literally as well as figuratively, for he was also given his predecessor's official residence near the main Ōte gate of Edo Castle. Such a transfer may seem normal enough now, but the Sakai family had been prominent in the Tokugawa service since the sixteenth century, even before the battle of Sekigahara; the Hotta, by contrast, were newcomers. The first of the Hotta family to serve the Tokugawa house had been Masatoshi's father, Hotta Masamori, who joined Tokugawa Iemitsu as a personal attendant in 1620. Nor was that all. Masatoshi, as his father's third son, was even further removed from the status rank demanded by the highest office in the shogun's administration. He too, therefore, like Makino Narisada, must be seen as one brought to power by Tsunayoshi's personal patronage, and by that alone.[9]

By filling in such an arbitrary way the top positions in the shogunate and in his own personal household, Tsunayoshi sought to provide himself with a staff composed of those he trusted and to make the government more responsive to his wishes. There were some difficulties, however, particularly in regard to Hotta Masatoshi. The latter's relations with the shogun, for example, were far from ideal – perhaps because of his reluctance to commit himself completely to Tsunayoshi's policies. Hotta's relations with his own subordinates, who found him somewhat dictatorial, were even worse. Indeed his relations with one of them, the junior councilor Inaba Masayasu, must be considered calamitous, as Inaba was to assassinate him in the summer of 1684.

After Hotta's death, Tsunayoshi promoted no more capable politicians to the bakufu administration. Those who became senior councilors were, to borrow Arai Hakuseki's description of them, "daimyō's sons" – in other words, those with nothing but their birth to recommend them, men incapable of comprehending the state of national finances, much less of offering adequate political leadership.

In consequence, the deliberations of the Senior Council, the highest organ of government, and that responsible for handling bakufu affairs

9 Tsuji, *Kyōhō*, pp. 57–8; and Tsuji, "Bakusei," pp. 15–16.

became more and more involved with empty ritual. Effective political leadership passed instead to the shogun's own cronies, the lords chamberlain who alone were privy to his wishes. Among these lords chamberlain, Yanagisawa Yoshiyasu was especially noteworthy. In 1698 he was allowed precedence over the senior councilors, and in 1704 he was enfeoffed at Kōfu Castle, previously held only by members of the Tokugawa family. Just how effective this new style of shogunal autocracy was can be seen by the readiness with which even the more eccentric of Tsunayoshi's laws were put into effect. They may have been inspired by the shogun's own fantasies, but complaisant followers like Yanagisawa were prepared to enforce them without question.

Not all of Tsunayoshi's new policies were strange. Some, like his attempt to reform the administration of the bakufu's own domain (tenryō), were eminently sensible. Immediately upon becoming shogun in 1680, Tsunayoshi gave Hotta Masatoshi, then still a senior councilor, sole authority over the management of the Tokugawa domain, nominating a council of six others – the two Kyoto magistrates and four finance officials – to help with the task. This was a significant departure from tradition. First, it mixed officials of different rank, in this case senior councilors and magistrates. Second, whereas senior councilors normally rotated responsibility for routine administration among themselves, a month at a time, now an individual was given total control over one particular policy area. Clearly, the management of the Tokugawa domain was sufficiently important in the estimation of the new shogun to warrant some dramatic changes.

The establishment of a unit of inspectors in the Finance Office in 1682 was another move in the same direction. Experienced finance officials were assigned the task of scrutinizing the performance of their colleagues. They were given a rank one grade below that of magistrate but were no longer responsible to the superintendents of finance. Rather, they reported to the senior councilors, which meant that their former superiors also came under their scrutiny. Not only that, there were also changes in the way that superintendents of finance themselves were appointed. Previously, such posts had never gone to anyone within the Finance Office itself; they went instead to middle- or upper-level *hatamoto* who had reached a career level appropriate to such a promotion. Consequently, appointees were not necessarily skilled in either financial matters or public administration. Their subordinates, whether in Edo or the provinces, also tended to inherit their positions from their fathers, with no expectation of either transfer or further advancement. Tsunayoshi changed all this. Acting in the belief that so important an arm of government needed capable administrators, he began promoting subordinates particularly experienced or skilled in matters of finance or local administration, as well as those showing more general promise. Before long this policy was to bear fruit with the elevation of a small number of men from the post of the comptroller of finance to superintendent of finance.

It was also to bear fruit of a less palatable kind as these new officials turned their attention to the activities of the rural intendants (*daikan*), the men primarily responsible for local administration. As early as 1680, intendants had received a set of instructions alerting them to their obligations and reminding them that the people over whom they presided were the very foundation of the state. The following year, the bakufu began to investigate the activities of individual intendants, and within the next eight years some twenty-six intendants were dismissed from office. When one realizes that there were, at the most, only forty-five intendants in office at any one time, then the massive scale of the purge becomes apparent. By 1704, when the wave of dismissals came to an end, a total of thirty-five men had been ousted from their posts, and some of them had even been sentenced to death.

There are other interesting aspects of this policy. At least eighteen of the thirty-five men dismissed came from families accustomed to providing intendants ever since the Tokugawa period began – families that, in all likelihood, had been prominent in their localities long before that. The records enable the positive identification of only eighteen families of this type, but there may well have been more involved. Those who escaped outright dismissal, too, did not necessarily go unscathed, as some of them – again from the same sort of background – were transferred from their traditional areas to places where they had no private authority. Obviously, Tsunayoshi was trying to break the private links between specific local officials and the areas they administered and was prepared to use whatever pretext necessary. In most cases, too, the alleged reason for dismissal was that the officials concerned had failed to remit local taxes to the bakufu intact; in other words, they were guilty of embezzlement. No fewer than twenty-five of the thirty-five dismissals were on these grounds. Under Ietsuna, Tsunayoshi's predecessor, it had been a matter of common knowledge that intendants were dishonest, but it took Tsunayoshi to confront the issue directly.[10]

10 Tsuji, *Kyōhō*, pp. 62–75; and Tsuji, "Bakusei,", pp. 19–21; and Tsuji, " 'Geba shōgun'," pp. 37–43, 63–4.

The evidence of embezzlement was clear enough; the reasons for it, however, perhaps not so clear. Later, many attributed the cause to the bakufu's failure to supply its local administrators with adequate salaries, as well as to pressures on the intendants to lend money for the relief of local distress.[11] But there were other factors at work as well. The problem lay with the bakufu's entire system of tax collection and with the position of intendant itself. In the beginning, the government had found it useful to appoint established local leaders as its rural administrators – not just intendants but also lower officials such as village headmen (*nanushi* and *shōya*). Such men, already respected and closely acquainted with local people and conditions, were invaluable in introducing Tokugawa authority into the rural districts.

By the late seventeenth century, however, the situation had changed. The local magnates found their old economic status had begun to erode, while those about them, even the small farmers, were growing increasingly independent. Commercial development was already turning the class structure of the traditional farming village on its head, thereby weakening both local gentry and village authorities to such an extent that they could no longer function adequately as tax officials. Tsunayoshi's policy toward the intendants, therefore, attempted not just to control their peculations but also to remove the conditions that either tempted or obliged them to steal. Creating a new kind of intendant was a first step toward a new kind of local administration.[12]

Politically, Tsunayoshi's attempt to strengthen the shogunal prerogative had a profound impact on the bakufu's faltering administrative machinery. From the very highest official down to the humblest intendant, the bakufu's bureaucrats were forced to be responsive to the shogun's own personal wishes. The daimyo domains, too, were being obliged to accommodate themselves to recent social developments. In terms of centralized control and administrative rationality, what the fifth shogun was trying to do was commendable. Yet Tsunayoshi's reputation – among his contemporaries and even today – has been far from good. Even the *Tokugawa jikki*, the official chronicles compiled for posterity on the order of the Tokugawa shoguns themselves, was ready to concede the misgovernment of his regime, offering only the excuse of mental instability in his defense. "Extraordinary rulers are

11 Tsuji, *Kyōhō*, pp. 74, 152–3; and Sone Hiromi, "Zaichi daikan shihai to shoki jinushi kosaku kankei no tenkai," in Kitajima Masamoto, ed., *Bakuhansei kokka seiritsu katei no kenkyū* (Tokyo: Yoshikawa kōbunkan, 1978), pp. 380–405.
12 Tsuji, *Kyōhō*, pp. 68–70;. Tsuji, "Bakusei," pp. 21–3; Asao Naohiro, *Kinsei hōken shakai no kisō kōzō* (Tokyo: Ochanomizu shobō, 1967), pp. 340–53; and Fujimoto Yukio, "Kawachi no kuni ichi shōya-ke no ken'i to sono tokushitsu," *Nihon rekishi* 353 (October 1977): 57–70.

prone to such excesses," it noted; ". . . more conventional rulers are never so extreme."[13]

The truth of the matter is that eccentricities (and there were many of them) apart, even the most rational of Tsunayoshi's new initiatives failed. They raised new possibilities and suggested new solutions, but they did not themselves solve any of the problems Japan had begun to encounter as the seventeenth century shaded into the eighteenth. By trying to create a new government, one more trustworthy and efficient than the old, Tsunayoshi succeeded only in installing his cronies in positions of authority, leaving those no less talented (if not so fortunate) disoriented, forced into either passivity or flattery to protect themselves and their careers. Even within the Treasury itself, to which no criterion other than efficiency applied, the shogun's policy failed, bestowing total control on a man like Ogiwara Shigehide, who achieved little beyond corruption and confusion.

Tsunayoshi's recoinage policy, too, failed to solve anything. In 1698, faced with massive financial difficulties (attributable to some extent to the unrestrained spending of the shogun and his colleagues), the shogunate decided to increase the amount of coinage in circulation. This in itself was not particularly new; previously, during Ietsuna's time, the government had also decided to buy itself out of trouble by minting large quantities of gold and silver coins. It was hardly a long-term solution, however, as Tsunayoshi discovered when confronting the same difficulties with depleted reserves. What he did, therefore, was something quite innovative: He elected to increase the quantity of coins by the simple expedient of calling them in and reminting them, adulterating them with baser metals in the process. The end product was a greater quantity of coins with the same face value but with an inferior metal content. Having done it once effectively, Tsunayoshi's government thereafter proceeded to repeat the process several times.

Not all the effects of this initiative were uniformly bad. By devaluing the currency, Tsunayoshi had increased bakufu revenue. Not only that, but the daimyo were also better off, as the size – or at least the value – of their debts had been reduced. Recent scholarship has also come to accept that Tsunayoshi's policy worked in favor of the moneylenders, too, simply because it got loans moving again. Further, as devaluation automatically raised prices, it helped those, whether farmers or merchants, with anything to sell.[14] Ultimately, however, the

---

13 Tsuji, *Kyōhō*, p. 39.
14 Nakai Nobuhiko, "Hōreki–Temmei-ki no rekishiteki ichi," *Rekishigaku kenkyū* 299 (April 1965):16; and Matsumoto, ed., *Bakuhansei*, pp. 87–94.

result of this first experiment with devaluation was confusion, accompanied by a dramatic leap in prices. It was also, incidentally, to offer Ogiwara Shigehide, the superintendent of finance, an opportunity for peculation on a massive scale.

THE SHŌTOKU ERA

The death of Tokugawa Tsunayoshi early in 1709 and the accession of his nephew (and adopted son) Ienobu were greeted with general enthusiasm, both inside the bakufu and elsewhere. The new shogun, as if in response to popular expectations, began by quickly repealing the laws for the protection of birds and animals, which had been the most oppressive of his predecessor's policies, and by releasing 8,831 prisoners under a general amnesty. This did not indicate that Ienobu was any less fervent a Confucian than the fifth shogun had been but, rather, that he chose to display his fervor somewhat differently. Tsunayoshi had been determined that his people would be made virtuous or that they should suffer the consequences. By contrast, Ienobu – influenced perhaps by the scholar Arai Hakuseki, who was his tutor – preferred his officials to act virtuously, thereby setting an example to those over whom they presided and to encourage rather than to force them to act more responsibly.

This attitude surfaced quite early in the new shogun's regime, in 1711, when farmers rioted in the province of Echigo on the Japan Sea coast. Opinion within the Supreme Court of Justice (hyōjōsho) was divided on the issue. Although some members urged punitive action, Arai Hakuseki, observing that "officials must listen like parents to the complaints of the people," argued in favor of sympathetic investigation, a view that the shogun accepted. Further, when plans for reversing the currency debasements of the previous decade were discussed, Hakuseki advocated a humane approach. Instead of thinking only of the shogunate's profits, he said, the government should try to win the people's trust rather than to trick them. Here too, once recoinage began, Hakuseki's position seems to have been endorsed.

Clearly, Ienobu made use of Arai Hakuseki's ideas, although perhaps not to the extent the Confucian scholar would have wished. Hakuseki wanted the shogun to be a model of Confucian rationalism, a ruler comparable to Yao and Shun, the sage kings of Chinese antiquity, and in his lectures to Ienobu he spared no effort to show him what his duty was. Yet at the same time Hakuseki worked no less diligently for the enhancement of shogunal prestige and for a system of ceremonies by which order and stability might be preserved forever. As one might have anticipated, he failed in these two key objectives, but he nevertheless succeeded in much else.

The new government was by no means totally committed to the policies of its predecessors; had it been, there would have been no general amnesty and no currency revaluation, and Tsunayoshi's laws for the protection of animals would have been maintained. On the other hand, there were substantial areas of agreement. For instance, the general pattern of government represented by Yanagisawa Yoshiyasu, Tsunayoshi's right-hand man who retired on his master's death, remained in effect. The senior councilors were not restored to political power – at least not during Ienobu's time in office – and the shogun himself, assisted by Arai Hakuseki and Manabe Akifusa, dominated his government just as surely as had Tsunayoshi before him.

Indeed, superficial differences apart, the political functions of Hakuseki and Manabe were much in the Yanagisawa mold. Like him, they both had joined Ienobu's retinue when the future shogun was still only daimyo of Kōfu and had won his trust and friendship long before his accession. Both had come from modest origins – Manabe beginning life as an apprentice noh dancer – and rose to influence together with their master. Thereafter, even though Manabe achieved the rank of daimyo, with a domain of fifty thousand *koku* at Takasaki and a status comparable to that of a senior councilor, the Confucian scholar Hakuseki was content to remain a mere *yoriai*, that is, a *hatamoto* with a modest stipend but no formal appointment. As personal friends of the shogun, both were as much his men as Yanagisawa had been Tsunayoshi's. "I humbly proffered my personal opinions," Arai noted with customary modesty, "not all of which were ignored."[15]

This system of administration was strong enough to survive Ienobu's death in 1712, although not without some modification. Ietsugu, the new shogun, was only four years old and unable to offer his father's two associates anything like the same degree of support. Without a strong shogun to enforce their views, therefore, both Hakuseki and Manabe found their effectiveness diminished, and the government, in consequence, often brought to a standstill. Nevertheless, these two personal advisers to the shogun, even if that shogun were a mere infant, still had a formidable degree of authority. Accordingly, the rule of the seventh shogun, like those of the fifth and sixth, can be considered one in which the shogun's personal staff was dominant.

15 Tsuji, *Kyōhō*, pp. 81–86; and Tsuji, "Bakusei," pp. 27–9.

For that matter, the major issues of the period were also precisely as they had been in Tsunayoshi's time, that is, the reconstruction of the bakufu's financial base and the reform of the bakufu's administrative machinery. Finances were still very much under the control of Ogiwara Shigehide, Tsunayoshi's superintendent of finance, so much so, indeed, that even those senior councilors assigned special responsibility for financial matters retained only nominal authority. Ogiwara, just as before, continued to raise money through recoinage, reducing the content of precious metal each time. Arai Hakuseki, to whom Ogiwara and his policies were anathema, urged Ienobu to get rid of him on three separate occasions, and on the last of these, just a month before the sixth shogun's death, he finally succeeded.[16]

Earlier, in 1712, on the Confucian scholar's recommendation, the post of the comptroller of finance was revived. This office, originally established by Tsunayoshi in the hope that it would prove useful in reforming government finances, had been allowed to wither, to suit Ogiwara's convenience. Resuscitating it, therefore, was a step toward Ogiwara's removal. It was also a step in the direction of financial reform, for Arai's main purpose in this measure was to bring talented and sympathetic finance officials back into direct contact with the problems of the common people. A secondary aim was to make sure that nobody would ever again be able to amass the kind of power Ogiwara had.

More immediately, reviving the office gave Hakuseki new sources of influence over policy. Hagiwara Yoshimasa, one of Hakuseki's favorite pupils and a man on whom the scholar could rely, was the first of the two officials appointed to the position of comptroller. Through him, Hakuseki gained the detailed knowledge of the shogunate's finances needed for the program of fiscal reforms he introduced in 1714. Through him, too, and one of Hagiwara's friends, a certain Tani Chōemon, thought to have been a Sakai merchant, Arai Hakuseki was able to set about reforming the currency, a project that had been Ienobu's dying wish.

Hakuseki's position on the question of currency was quite straightforward, as doctrinaire solutions tend to be. In his view, the fundamental cause of the current economic ills was the bakufu's unwise commitment to a policy that reduced the value of money while at the same time increasing its volume. The only way out of the morass, he be-

---

16 Kate W. Nakai and Nakai Yoshiyuki, "Arai Hakuseki jihitsu Ogiwara Shigehide dangai-sho soko," *Shigaku zasshi* 89 (October 1980):38–49.

lieved, lay in revaluation, by which Japan's currency might be restored to its pristine, pre-Ogiwara purity.[17]

Of course, currency reform alone would not solve the government's financial difficulties, and Arai Hakuseki had other weapons in his armory. He was well aware that enormous quantities of gold, silver, and copper had been leaving Japan ever since the beginning of European trade in the sixteenth century. In a pamphlet entitled *Honchō hōka tsūyō jiryaku* (A brief treatise on the circulation of money), he advocated imposing restrictions on the amount of precious metals shipped abroad, and in 1715 he issued instructions that the number of Dutch and Chinese vessels entering Nagasaki was to be limited, as was the amount of metal they could take away with them. At the same time, in an effort to reduce imports, he urged his fellow countrymen to produce for themselves those things that, like silk and medicinal herbs, would otherwise have to be imported. On the whole, Hakuseki was opposed to foreign trade and hoped to wean the Japanese from their dependence on it.

Hakuseki was no less active in the field of law reform, attempting through the intervention of Ienobu and Manabe Akifusa to make the processes of the Supreme Court of Justice both more prompt and more equitable. In his autobiography, *Oritaku shiba no ki,* he describes the confusion then prevailing in the resolution of disputes by the shogunate's legal agencies. Long delays were common, with examples of people kept waiting for as long as fifteen years before their cases were heard – long enough, in some instances, for the details of the original offense to have been forgotten. Those plaintiffs who came to Edo from distant corners of Japan and were forced to live there for long periods of time were financially disadvantaged. Other cases were impeded by trivia or obstructed by partiality or bribery. Arai Hakuseki did what he could to speed up the process, as he notes in his autobiography, but some of the abuses were far too well entrenched to be reformed at second hand.[18]

With the death of Shogun Ienobu and the accession of the four-year-old Ietsugu, both Arai Hakuseki and Manabe Akifusa found their positions that much more difficult. The senior councilors could oppose as they pleased, on the flimsiest of grounds, whatever policies Hakuseki might bring forward. In the legal field, for example, it seems to have become standard practice among the various magistrates

---

17 Itō Tasaburō, "Edo bakufu Shōtoku no kahei kaichū," *Shakai keizaishigaku* 18 (1953):1–25; and Tsuji, *Kyōhō,* pp. 187–94.

18 Tsuji Tatsuya, *Ōoka Echizen no kami* (Tokyo: Chūō kōronsha, 1964), pp. 104–20.

not to keep Manabe apprised of current affairs. Hagiwara Yoshimasa, Hakuseki's right-hand man in the area of currency reform, was moved out of his position as comptroller of finance in 1716 and transferred to the sinecure of keeper of the second enclosure (*ni no maru rusui*) of Edo Castle, there deprived of both power and responsibility.

In fact, as matters stood, senior officials could now bring the machinery of government to a grinding halt, a situation in which only bribery could restore it to fitful life. The shogunate was deadlocked, with the new men Arai Hakuseki and Manabe Akifusa on the one side, and the traditional officials, led by senior councilors, on the other. Ultimately, it was settled in the only way such deadlocks could be resolved, by death. The seventh shogun, Tokugawa Ietsugu, only seven years old, died early in 1716. With the accession of a new shogun from outside the main Tokugawa family line, both Arai Hakuseki and Manabe Akifusa, experience and abilities notwithstanding, were driven from public life.[19]

TOKUGAWA YOSHIMUNE

The new shogun, Tokugawa Yoshimune, came to the shogunate with his reputation as a reformer already well established. As daimyo of the Kii domain he had proved an outstanding economic manager, particularly through his irrigation projects along the Kino River. His concern for education and military arts was also well known.[20] Much was, therefore, expected of him as shogun, and Yoshimune acquitted himself with great distinction during the thirty years of his rule, from his accession in 1716 to his retirement in 1745. In particular, he set in motion the Kyōhō Reforms, a series of profoundly important initiatives that took their name from the Kyōhō era (1716–36) when they were introduced.

To contemporaries, it seemed obvious that Yoshimune's accession changed the entire tone of government; historians ever since have confirmed this view, and not without reason. There was, to begin with, the undeniable fact that the new shogun was very different from his predecessors. Both Tsunayoshi and Ienobu had been cultivated men, absorbed in Confucianism and fond of noh (to the extent of performing on stage themselves); Yoshimune, by contrast, although no dunce, had no great interest in poetry or philosophy. Instead, he

19 Tsuji, *Kyōhō*, pp. 91–7.
20 Tsuji Tatsuya, *Tokugawa Yoshimune-kō den* (Nikkō: Nikkō Tōshōgū, 1962), pp. 2–12.

was devoted to the martial arts, hunting, and falconry – during which, so it was said, he had been known to rip the heads from newly caught birds to drink their blood. This certainly could not have endeared him to Tsunayoshi and probably not to Ienobu either. Yoshimune was no less impulsive in seizing control of government. He quickly removed Manabe Akifusa and Arai Hakuseki, together with others of the previous regime, from their positions of influence. He was no less quick to rid bakufu life of much of the ceremony that the punctilious Arai Hakuseki (who set great store in rites) had introduced. It is not surprising, therefore, that to contemporaries, and to generations of later historians as well, the eighth shogun should have seemed opposed to both the persons and the policies of the previous ruler and therefore was inclined to do something quite new.

These expectations were exaggerated. True, Yoshimune differed from his predecessors in personality and habits, and such differences naturally came to be reflected in the morale and efficiency of the administration he headed. Yet it is questionable how far differences on the individual level could affect the general direction of government policy. In this particular case, although Yoshimune did abandon some of Arai Hakuseki's projects, those projects themselves were of no major significance, and their demise did not indicate a critical shift in policy direction. Moreover, the removal of Arai Hakuseki and Manabe Akifusa from their former positions of influence was predictable. Given the hostility between these men and the senior councilors, which had brought government to a standstill, some such action was necessary to get it moving again. It was far simpler to dismiss the "new men" and reaffirm the traditional authority of the *fudai*, those daimyo from whose ranks senior councilors were customarily chosen. Yoshimune, of course, had brought some of his own advisers with him from Kii, but he tactfully refrained from institutionalizing their positions and made it his business to see that they did not acquire too much power.[21]

This was the way in which Yoshimune dissipated the anxieties of senior bakufu officials who, ever since the rule of the fifth shogun, had seen their authority, and their entitlement to all the tangible signs of shogunal regard, pass to newcomers. In fact, however, Yoshimune was no more ready to allow his councilors to dictate to him than the earlier shogun had been. On the contrary, he continued to enhance his own position. Often, for instance, he would bypass

21 Tsuji, *Kyōhō*, pp. 98–107.

senior officials to confer directly with their own subordinates in order to make himself familiar with both the broad outlines and the minutiae of government affairs. Further, he formed his own intelligence agency, the *oniwaban*, a group of some twenty handpicked men charged with providing him with information concerning daimyo and shogunal officials.[22] In 1721 he decreed that three times each month a suggestion box should be set in front of the Supreme Court of Justice to give him access to even more information, thereby confirming and institutionalizing his personal approachability. This suggestion box served two purposes: First, it injected new ideas into the system, and second, it offered an avenue through which dishonesty and incompetence might be exposed.[23]

The eighth shogun also proved himself especially interested in, and adept at, the selection of administrative personnel. Indeed, his adroit use of capable men was one of the chief characteristics of the reforms. In 1720, for example, much to everyone's amazement, he retrieved Hagiwara Yoshimasa from the obscurity of his position as keeper of the second enclosure and reinstated him as comptroller of finance, the post that Arai Hakuseki had originally bestowed on him. Presumably Yoshimune had felt that his government could ill afford to waste a man of such talent.

At the same time, however, Yoshimune was always careful to pay due respect to the claims of status and family lineage, seeming to honor the prestigious even as as he nudged them further and further away from real political power. For example, he maintained the traditional distinction between *bankata* (those who manned the shogunate's standing army) and *yakukata* (those who staffed its civil service), by making sure that the former were made to seem more highly esteemed. But this was no more than a formality, for in practice the civil component emerged in the Kyōhō period as much the more influential of the two. The military, by contrast, declined in everything save prestige, as its members, although continuing to be granted sonorous titles of one sort or another, were nevertheless distanced from power.

In civil administration, Yoshimune encouraged the appointment of officials on the basis of talent alone and increasingly relied on such men to spearhead the government's reform program. This process was accelerated in 1723 with the introduction of the *tashidaka* system, which also facilitated the promotion of capable officials. Under this

22 Fukai Masaumi, "Edo bakufu oniwaban to bakusei," *Tokugawa rinsei-shi kenkyūjo kenkyu kiyō* (1979):351–7.
23 Tsuji, *Kyōhō*, pp. 119–26.

new system, any officials promoted above their hereditary status expectations were to have their stipend augmented – not permanently, as had previously always been the consequence of any promotion, but only for their period of office. The administration could therefore make use the skills of various people, regardless of their station, and reward them handsomely, but always with the knowledge that the arrangement was temporary and conditional. This proved an important step in the process by which the bakufu became a bureaucracy, and its officials salaried bureaucrats. Given that large numbers of officials saw their stipends increase dramatically – often doubled or redoubled – for their term of office, and the implications such an arrangement had for the traditional stipend system, it could hardly have been otherwise.

One of the most important personnel problems Yoshimune had to confront related to the *rōjū*, the members of the Senior Council. At the time of his accession, they had been five in number – Tsuchiya Masanao, Inoue Masamine, Abe Masataka, Kuze Shigeyuki, and Toda Tadazane. Arai Hakuseki, who had been obliged to deal with these men as adversaries, had considered them all unutterably stupid, but not so the new shogun. After all, these men represented the *fudai* (those families traditionally associated with the Tokugawa house), and perhaps of even more immediate consequence, they had brought Yoshimune over from the Kii branch of the Tokugawa house into the main line. Not unexpectedly, Yoshimune treated them with consideration. Yet, external tokens of respect notwithstanding, Yoshimune steadily brought them all under his control, and then, as they died or retired one by one, he failed to replace them, unobtrusively allowing the system of government they represented to disappear with them. By the time Inoue Masamine died in the middle of 1722, only one, Toda Tadazane, was left of the original five, and he, being old and passive, hardly counted. Effectively, therefore, the shogun no longer needed to defer to anybody. It is true that Mizuno Tadayuki had been promoted from Kyoto deputy to senior councilor in 1717, but he was definitely the shogun's own man. After Inoue's death in 1722, therefore, Yoshimune was free to remake the system of government. In this reform, as in many others, he was assisted by Mizuno, and by another new senior councilor, Matsudaira Norimura, promoted from keeper of Osaka Castle in 1723.[24]

24 Tsuji, *Kyōhō*, pp. 108–11, 128–9, 131–3.

KYŌHŌ REFORMS: THE FIRST STAGE

It is sometimes claimed that the Kyōhō Reforms began only in 1722, the year in which the shogunate set about rearranging its finances, and that the first six years of Yoshimune's regime were merely a time of preparation.[25] This view is somewhat distorted. There is, in fact, reason to believe that the years from 1716 to 1722 produced some important and distinctive reform policies in a variety of areas. The national economy and the shogunate's own finances were generating far too much concern to allow any government to overlook them for six years. Yoshimune, therefore, began his administration with a strict frugality campaign. This in itself was not unusual: Exhortations to frugality were as characteristic of the "normal" governments of Tokugawa Japan as they were of those self-consciously committed to reform. But this was a campaign with a difference. So thoroughly did Yoshimune pare government expenditures that even Confucian scholars, themselves normally the most vociferous advocates of frugality, were led to complain when ceremonial life was adversely affected. "There is a difference between economy and parsimony," complained Muro Kyūsō, "and this is parsimony."

On the other hand, critics found another of Yoshimune's early economic reforms far more palatable. This was his recoinage policy, introduced in 1718 with a series of instructions governing the use of gold and silver coins. These called for a total currency revaluation, exactly the same measure advocated previously by Arai Hakuseki, save for one important difference. The Confucian scholar had aimed at a gradual standardization of the currency in a process taking twenty years or so, but Yoshimune intended to work much more rapidly. He called for complete revaluation and standardization within the space of four years, and he succeeded. The conditions were not at all propitious, as Japan's gold and silver mines had virtually ceased production. Revaluation, therefore, could be achieved only by melting down currency already in use, skimming off the dross, and then casting new coins from the unalloyed residue. It sounds simple enough, but it contained one obvious difficulty: For any given number of coins recalled, the government would inevitably return a smaller amount – better in quality, certainly, but deficient in quantity. The volume of coin in circulation would be reduced, as Arai Hakuseki had realized when urging a

25 Ōishi Shinzaburō, *Kyōhō kaikaku no keizai seisaku* (Tokyo: Ochanomizu shobō, 1961), pp. 161–4.

cautious approach. Yoshimune, however, far more politically secure, plunged straight in and succeeded.[26]

Another of Yoshimune's early reforms, predating even his currency revaluation, concerned regulations relating to Edo money changers. He began by restricting their numbers, continued by requiring them to register with the authorities, and finally, from 1718 onward, forced them into cooperating with the currency revaluation. Yoshimune extended this policy of merchant control in 1721 by requiring the formation of guilds for ninety-six different categories of merchants and artisans who were designated as being involved in the production or sale of extravagant and luxurious goods. Yoshimune hoped that once they were formed, he could compel these guilds to observe official prohibitions against the manufacture and sale of luxury items and novelties. These actions represented a totally new kind of initiative in the area of shogunate–business relations.[27]

Before long, these early economic reforms had led to others in related fields. By restricting its own spending, for example, the shogunate had brought on something of an economic recession, the first effects of which were felt by the moneylenders. They in turn felt obliged to seek legal redress against defaulting debtors. So immediate was the increase in lawsuits that it effectively crippled those bodies officially concerned with resolving money disputes – the Supreme Court of Justice, and the office of the city magistrates. To relieve this pressure, the shogunate declared in 1719 that disputes over money-lending were private affairs and were to be settled without recourse to the official judicial system. This was the famous Kingin aitai sumashi rei, or Instruction for the private settlement of money disputes,[28] a measure that, though in one sense resulting directly from the policy of financial retrenchment, was also a first step toward reform of the legal system.

As we have already seen, the Edo law courts had long been inadequate. Arai Hakuseki had done what he could, but Yoshimune was determined to make further improvements. The appointment of Ōoka Tadasuke to the position of Edo city magistrate in 1717 was one of his first steps in this direction, and it was followed by a succession of practical measures, particularly in 1721, when Yoshi-

---

26 Tsuji, *Kyōhō*, pp. 205–14; and Itō Tasaburō, "Kinsei kahei-shi no ichi mondai," *Rekishi chiri* 85 (1954):15–36.
27 Tsuji, *Kyōhō*, pp. 246–59.
28 Tsuji, *Kyōhō*, pp. 215–17; Ōishi, *Kyōhō*, pp. 102–19; and Sone Hiromi, "Kyōhō-ki no soshō saiban-ken to uttae," in Matsumoto Shirō and Yamada Tadao, eds., *Genroku, Kyōhō-ki no seiji to shakai* vol. 4 of *Kōza Nihon kinsei-shi* (Tokyo: Yūhikaku, 1980), pp. 267–72.

mune held a special session in Edo Castle so that he might see how his magistrates operated.

The main object of this legal reform was to speed up the legal process. To this end there was an attempt to simplify the presentation and hearing of petitions, but it is also noteworthy that efforts were made to have disputes settled informally at a lower level, by the mediation of such figures as ward headmen, before they could become a formal lawsuits – exactly the principle applied to disputes concerning money.[29] Further, at the beginning of 1720 the shogun ordered those involved in the Supreme Court of Justice – the superintendents of temples and shrines, the Edo city magistrates, and the superintendents of finance – to collect and make public those regulations concerning the prompt reporting of grievances and the proper form for contracts, in the hope that this might reduce the volume of lawsuits.[30]

This was by no means all, for at the same time officials were to designate which punishments were appropriate to which crimes, the first time in Tokugawa history that an attempt was made to establish and publicize a set of judicial procedures. Clearly, this was an attempt to create an impartial legal system. Precedents and legal instructions themselves were codified in 1724 under the title Kyōhōdo hōritsu ruiyose (A collection of laws of the Kyōhō period), although it is not clear to what extent they were actually used. Also, in the interests of an impartial legal system, restrictions were imposed in 1722 on the use of torture, the object being to save people from being vigorously persuaded into confessing to crimes they had not committed. The suggestion box also played a part here, as it provided a safe way of complaining about dishonest or biased judgments.[31]

A third strand in Yoshimune's legal reforms concerned the amelioration of punishment. In 1721 it was decreed that families of those common people found guilty of serious crimes were to be spared the automatic charge of complicity that otherwise would have followed. This was no more than sensible in a society in which single men were moving from the country to towns and cities, leaving friends and family behind. Limits were also placed on terms of banishment, and instructions were given that such sentences be commuted to fines; this too seemed more appropriate now that unification under the Tokugawa government had robbed banishment of much of its significance.

---

29 Sone, *Kyōhō*, pp. 275–9.   30 Tsuji, *Ōoka*, pp. 125–7.
31 Tsuji, *Ōoka*, pp. 145–50, 133–5; Tsuji, *Kyōhō*, pp. 119–26; Sone, "Kyōhō," pp. 279–90.

Both cases, therefore, exhibit a degree of rational adjustment to changing circumstances.

Mention should also be made of other reforms: a statute of limitations on criminal offenses, for example, and improvements in prison conditions, including efforts to keep the prisons clean, the prisoners healthy, and the jailers honest. Yoshimune's education policy also has its place in a catalog of legal reforms, simply because one of its aims was to teach the common people respect for the law. All in all, these legal reforms in the first years of Yoshimune's rule were among the most outstanding intiatives of the period, and their impact on Tokugawa society, then and later, was profound. Certainly they left their mark on the common people, among whom stories involving the law and above all Yoshimune's chief legal adviser, Ōoka Tadasuke, were still circulating long after the Tokugawa government itself had disappeared.[32]

Another important initiative of the early Kyōhō period concerned the intendants, the shogunate's local administrators. In 1719 a total of twenty-one men, some of them currently intendants, others either former officeholders or their sons, had their stipends confiscated or were required in some other way to reimburse the government for money they, or their fathers had embezzled. Not since the years of Tsunayoshi, the fifth shogun, had intendants been treated so brusquely. In this case, as with Tsunayoshi's purge, most of those threatened also came from families traditionally associated with the office of intendant. The fifth and the eighth shogun, between them, virtually destroyed the old hereditary intendant class, setting something new in its place. The old intendant had been a tax farmer, a wealthy local identity with family ties in his area stretching back into the medieval period, but his replacement now became a tax-collecting bureaucrat.[33]

The first six years of Yoshimune's rule, the years between 1716 and 1722, therefore saw what was in some respects a continuation of policies laid down by earlier officials and advisers – Arai Hakuseki, and even to some extent by Tokugawa Tsunayoshi. All these policies were backed by the shogun's personal authority, and all brought to some sort of conclusion. Currency was revalued and standardized; inflation was brought under control; government expenditures were reduced; and adjustments were made to the legal system and to local government. Yet the Tokugawa government was by no means free of its difficulties. Once the issues of currency chaos and inflation had been settled, other problems, no less menacing, began to emerge from their shadow.

32 Tsuji, Ōoka, pp. 138–50.   33 Tsuji, Kyōhō, pp. 146–51; and Ōishi, Kyōhō, pp. 86–91.

KYŌHŌ REFORMS: THE SECOND STAGE

The most critical of these new problems concerned the shogunate's own finances, which had failed to keep pace with national productivity. By the early eighteenth century, Japan's agricultural production was roughly 60 percent more than it had been a century earlier; by contrast, however, the central government's own financial position was declining year by year. In a nation bustling with all kinds of agricultural and commerical activity, the central government was simply unable to secure enough for its own needs. From 1722 onward, having stabilized the currency and free now from the threat of opposition from the Senior Council, Tokugawa Yoshimune turned to the task of financial reconstruction. His first step was an organizational one. He reestablished the position of senior councilor with special responsibility for financial affairs, set it in charge of long-term planning, and gave it to his friend and protégé Mizuno Tadayuki.

Still, the government's economic plight was desperate, and something had to be done immediately to relieve the situation. In 1722 the shogunate notified the daimyo of its difficulties and ordered them all to supply rice to its storehouses at the rate of one hundred *koku* for each ten thousand *koku* of domain assessment. In return, the alternate residence system (*sankin kōtai*), under which daimyo were required to reside in Edo at specified times, was to be modified, requiring them to spend only six months, rather than twelve, in Edo every alternate year. The special imposition, together with the *sankin kōtai* concession, continued until 1730.

Naturally, the shogunate did not neglect more conventional methods of raising funds. Land reclamation, always a sure way to gain more income, was also to play its part. In the middle of 1722, Ōoka Tadasuke, one of the Edo city magistrates, was assigned responsibility for agricultural policy, with special reference to land reclamation, irrigation, and flood control in the Kantō area. The following month a notice was posted at Nihonbashi, in the very center of the city, calling for proposals for land reclamation anywhere in Japan, whether on the shogun's territory or in daimyo domains. A year later, Izawa Tamenaga, a flood control expert from the shogun's old domain, was brought into central government employment and set to work at land reclamation.[34]

At this time too, the shogunate revised its methods of assessing

34 Tsuji, *Kyōhō*, pp. 175–80; Tsuji, *Ōoka*, pp. 175–8; and Ōishi, *Kyōhō*, pp. 170–201.

taxes on lands under its direct jurisdiction, in an effort to bring the fruits of increasing agricultural productivity into its own ambit. The result was an overall tax increase, by no means uniform across the breadth of its holdings but, rather, varying from village to village. From 1724 onward, a new taxation rate was hammered out in discussion among the intendants, finance officials, and farmers. Those villages agreeing to the new rate were offered, in return, assessment by a new system. Previously, each year's harvest had been estimated by groups of traveling officials, who had to be courted and entertained – and not infrequently bribed – by those villages they passed through. Now, as an incentive to securing agreement to a higher tax rate, the shogunate offered farming villages a permanently fixed assessment set at a notional figure, thereby offering an escape from the nuisance of an annual inspector and the sometimes-arbitrary exactions that accompanied the older system. With this carrot-and-stick approach, the government hoped first to raise, and then to stabilize, its land-tax income.[35]

There were other changes as well. Formerly, people on bakufu land in western Japan had been allowed to declare one-third of their holdings as upland (and therefore unsuitable for growing rice), a technicality that allowed them to pay one-third of their taxes in cash rather than in rice, but now the custom was revised. In 1722 the bakufu decreed that in principle all land taxes should be paid in rice, and it instructed intendants to set rates as high as possible – higher even than the local cost of rice – when farmers requested permission to pay in cash. This in fact was another way of increasing taxes, as the farmers of western Japan were known to prefer growing such lucrative cash crops as tobacco, cotton, and rapeseed.[36]

Through such means the shogunate managed to increase its tax income considerably in 1727 and 1728. Between 1716 and 1723, its average annual income from the land tax had been 1.37 million *koku*; between 1724 and 1730 it rose to 1.52 million *koku*, an increase of nearly 11 percent.[37] In 1727, particularly, the land-tax income of 1.62 million *koku* represented an increase of 320,000 *koku* over 1723, when only 1.3 million *koku* had been collected.[38]

35 Mori Sugio, "Kinsei chosahō no tenkan," in *Osaka furitsu daigaku kiyō* (Jimbun, shakai kagaku 12) (1964), pp. 169–94; Tsuji, *Kyōhō*, pp. 162–72.

36 Ōishi, *Kyōhō*, pp. 122–60.

37 These figures are taken from *Otorika tsuji kakitsuke*, which provides a reliable annual breakdown of bakufu finances over the period 1716 to 1841. See Tsuji Tatsuya and Matsumoto Shirō, "*Otorika tsuji kakitsuke* oyobi *Onengū-mai, onengūkin hoka shomuki osame watashi kakitsuke* ni tsuite," *Yokohama shiritsu daigaku ronsō* (Jimbun kagaku keiretsu 15) (March 1964), pp. 181–216.

38 Tsuji, *Kyōhō*, pp. 173–5.

Nevertheless, although the shogunate's land-tax income may have been growing steadily, it was not long before opposition to the new economic policies began to appear in the towns and villages of Japan. In the villages, in particular, the opposition mounted until it was strong enough to impede the policies themselves. The government, as we have seen, was trying to guarantee high annual tax revenue through a fixed assessment that admitted no variation except in the case of famine. The farmers, for their part, were complaining that they were left without food and without seed rice for the following year's crop, and they soon began to bombard local officials with petitions. Ultimately, the government was forced to relax its policy. In 1727 it was decided that in the event of a 50 percent crop loss, the farmers could revert temporarily to the old system of annual inspection. In 1730 this was further relaxed, with the cutoff point lowered to 30 percent. The new system of assessment, therefore, was becoming meaningless, and land-tax revenues plummeted again, to an annual average of 1.3 million *koku* during the period from 1731 to 1736, a level similar to that recorded at the beginning of Yoshimune's years as shogun.[39]

Another problem emerged when the price of rice fell. For various reasons – currency confusion, inflation, crop damage of sundry kinds (including that caused by an eruption of Mt. Fuji in 1707) – the price of rice had risen in the last years of the seventeenth century and remained high well into the Kyōhō period. Especially meager harvests in 1720–2 had sent the price of one *koku* of rice up to around 70 to 80 *momme* of silver (a *momme* being 3.75 grams), the highest yet recorded in the eighteenth century. Thereafter, however, a succession of normal harvests drove the price down by 50 percent in 1723 and by 75 percent in 1730–1. The impact on the samurai class, which lived by exchanging its rice stipends for cash, was to reduce its available income dramatically. Consequently, during the opening decades of the eighteenth century, the shogunate tried several remedies: buying up rice itself, storing tax rice rather than selling it, stimulating the rice market by allowing speculation (previously prohibited), and imposing new controls over the activities of the Osaka rice market, which set the price for national rice trading. All were to no avail.[40]

Then in 1732, the situation suddenly changed. In the summer of that year, swarms of locusts appeared in the Inland Sea area, ruining much of the rice crop of western Japan. In the resulting famine, rice in Edo and Osaka cost five to seven times as much as it had during the

39 Tsuji, *Kyōhō*, pp. 280–3.   40 Tsuji, *Tokugawa*, pp. 143–50.

glut of the previous years, and a *koku* of rice could now fetch as much as 150 *momme*, the normal price being 40 to 50 *momme*. City dwellers, at the mercy of these price fluctuations, grew restless – just how restless became apparent at the beginning of 1733 when a crowd of seventeen hundred Edo residents, inflamed by rumors of hoarding, attacked and destroyed the residence of Takama Dembei, one of the government's specially licensed rice dealers, in Japan's first instance of *uchikowashi* (property smashing), in an urban area.[41] The pressure on the cities was soon to be relieved, as rice prices began to slump once more, but this left the shogunate with the original problem untouched. What could be done to stop falling rice prices? The government was not to find an answer; an attempt to halt the slide by enforcing a minimum price was evaded by dealers with ridiculous ease.

Falling rice prices did not necessarily indicate a glut. On the contrary, many parts of Japan were complaining of crop failures. The root of the problem lay in the overaccumulation of rice in Osaka, and this in turn can be traced back to the economic depression brought about by the shogunate's economic policies. By restricting expenditures and then reducing the amount of currency in circulation, the government had unintentionally created a depression, thereby reducing the buying power of the business community at precisely the time when daimyo were increasing their rice shipments to Osaka to earn money. Despite the shogunate's best efforts, therefore, unbought rice began to fill up the storehouses at Dojima. Prices fell accordingly. It was not the first time that daimyo interests had diverged from those of the shogunate, nor was it to be the last.[42]

The difficulty over rice prices also drew the attention of government authorities to the question of commodity prices in general, particularly in Edo and other large cities. It was generally assumed that a fall in the price of rice would bring about commensurate reductions in the cost of other commodities. In fact, the opposite was more often the case, with some items becoming more expensive rather than less. To counter this, the shogunate in 1724 ordered a general lowering of prices and imposed heavy fines on lamp-oil dealers suspected of willfully raising prices. Further, it demanded the registration of all wholesalers dealing in such commodities as lamp oil, soy sauce, and *miso* (bean paste) whose prices had risen most noticeably. These dealers were formed into associations through which the government could assert some

---

41 Hara Heizō and Tōyama Shigeki, "Edo jidai kōki ikki oboegaki," *Rekishigaku kenkyū* 127 (May 1947): 24–6; and Tsuji, *Tokugawa*, pp. 150–6.
42 Tsuji, *Tokugawa*, pp. 157–68; and Tsuji, *Kyōhō*, pp. 216–18, 283–7.

degree of price control. By 1726 the government had succeeded in registering many individual dealers, but it had not been nearly so successful in forcing them into formal associations, perhaps because commercial life was now far too complex to allow such a simple solution. Without any real understanding of market mechanisms, Yoshimune and his advisers were inevitably frustrated in their efforts at price control, just as were their successors throughout the rest of the Tokugawa period.[43]

They could, however, help break the economic depression, at least to the extent of rectifying the shortage of currency. In 1736, the shogunate reversed its position and decided to increase the amount of money in circulation by devaluing its gold and silver coins. The number of gold coins in circulation was increased by 65 percent and silver by 50 percent. At the same time, to balance this, a massive amount – six billion, in fact – of copper coins was to be minted. Between 1736 and 1746, more than half the copper cash ever issued in the Tokugawa period was produced. This new currency provided a basis of stability such that no more gold coins were minted for another eight decades, until 1819, and no silver coins until 1820.[44]

Still, the problem of financial reform remained. Earlier attempts to settle this, it will be recalled, had been brought to a halt by other difficulties: the rice price, the famine, and peasant resistance among them. In 1737, Yoshimune took yet another organizational initiative by giving senior councilor Matsudaira Norimura the finance portfolio (previously left vacant by the retirement of Mizuno Tadayuki in 1730) and promoting Kan'o Haruhide to the post of superintendent of finance. Between them, these two men set about spurring the intendants into action in an effort to restore government tax revenues which, as we have seen, had begun to decline after reaching a peak in 1730.

In particular, these men began to look closely at shogunal lands in western Japan, where revenues were far lower than the high productivity of the region warranted. Kan'o made a tour of the region in 1744 and recommended that stern measures be applied to any farmers who refused to pay higher taxes, even if this meant executing them by the thousand. It was even rumored at the time than Kan'o had been heard to mutter the old maxim "Peasants and oil seeds are much alike; the harder you squeeze them, the more they will give." In the hands of

---

43 Tsuji, *Kyōhō*, pp. 259–62.
44 Tsuji, *Kyōhō*, pp. 226–38; Itō Tasaburō, "Edo bakufu gembun no kahei kaichū," *Shirin* 38 (May 1955): 24–45.

men like this, the shogunate's finances took a sudden upward turn. Tax revenues in 1737 showed a jump of 340,000 *koku* over those of the previous year, and for the next nine years up until 1745 the annual average was 1.6 million *koku*, or some 80,000 more than the average for the years 1724 to 1730, when Yoshimune first turned his attention toward the land tax. Indeed, in 1744, the government's revenue from the land tax climbed to 1.8 million *koku*, the highest recorded during the entire Tokugawa period.[45]

The years surrounding 1740 also marked a high point in the government's efforts at legal renovation, comparable in its own way to the reforms of 1719–21. This time the major activity took place in 1742, with the appearance of that collection of laws known as the Kujikata osadamegaki. Just when its compilation was begun is uncertain, but the Supreme Court of Justice in 1738 drew up a preliminary draft that served as a model for the revised and augmented version that appeared in two volumes in 1742. This code was never made public, but its significance as the central government's first comprehensive legal code is nevertheless enormous. The first volume was a collection of instructions on legal procedure; the second, the so-called Osadamegaki hyakkajō, was a collection of legal precedents consisting of 103 articles divided into more than five hundred paragraphs.

On the whole, the legal code's juridical connections with earlier Tokugawa law were minimal, for only a quarter of the cases predated the Kyōhō period. In many respects, therefore, it represented a change in emphasis. One example of this concerns the penalties for peasants involved in acts of defiance against the authorities. Before the Kyōhō period it was recognized that peasants with a legitimate grievance against their local lord could desert their villages en masse, always provided, of course, that they had paid their taxes before leaving. Such behavior was now forbidden, under threat of severe punishment. On the other hand, the free sale of land by peasants, prohibited since 1643, was now given official sanction. Both departures from precedent were prompted, not unnaturally, by the government's immediate needs – first to keep peasant resistance in check and then to increase tax revenues, even at the expense of social polarization in the countryside.[46]

45 Tsuji, *Kyōhō*, pp. 287–9; and Mori Sugio, "Kano Wakasa no zōchō o megutte," *Rekishi kenkyū* 9 (1965): 32–56.
46 Tsuji, *Tokugawa*, pp. 230–42; Koide Yoshio, "*Osadamegaki hyakkajō* hensan jijō ni tsuite," *Shichō* 4 (November 1934): 112–37; Kukita Kazuko, *Edo bakufu hō no kenkyū* (Tokyo: Gannandō shoten, 1980), pp. 7–11, 31–119.

The significance of the Kujikata osadamegaki was enhanced by the appearance of two other legal collections. The first of these was the Ofuregaki Kampō shūsei, compiled by the shogunate in 1743, which consisted of 3,550 official decrees issued from 1615 onward, and the Sen'yō ruishū, completed separately by the office of the Edo city magistrates.

Culturally, too, the Kyōhō period marks a new epoch. On the one hand, we have already seen that Yoshimune and those under him displayed no great interest in traditional scholarship and education. Yet Confucianism was still an important element in official thinking, and education, particularly that of the common people, remained a matter of concern. In 1717, the series of Confucian lectures held at the Seidō at Yushima, the academy patronized by the shogunate, was opened to the public for the first time. Then, in 1721, the shogunate issued a textbook specifically for the use of the commoners. This was the *Rikuyu engi taii*, a translation, with commentary, of a set of precepts issued in China nearly a century earlier. Yoshimune had had it rendered into Japanese in the hope that it might be used as a text in the *terakoya*, the thousands of little schools throughout Japan where commoners learned to read and write. It was also during this period that the bakufu encouraged the opening of private academies, again with the intention of fostering the education of the common people, although the ultimate goal was more the creation of a docile and tractable public than a concern with pure intellectual achievement.[47]

The shogunate was also especially interested in learning that had practical applications. Scholars like Muro Kyūsō and Ogyū Sorai were often approached for advice on current affairs or else were asked to search ancient Chinese and Japanese histories for legal and historical precedents.[48] Approaches were also made to the Dutch in the hopes of discovering what conditions were like in Europe or of acquiring new technical skills. Yoshimune himself contributed enormously to the development of Western learning in Japan simply because of his own keen personal interest in science and technology. He put entire generations of future scholars in his debt by allowing Chinese translations of Western books into Japan after 1720.[49]

By emphasizing the more immediately useful branches of learning,

---

47 Tsuji, *Tokugawa*, pp. 254–60; and Tsuji Tatsuya, "Kyōhō kaikaku to jugaku," in Saigusa Hiroto kinen ronshū iinkai, ed., *Saigusa Hiroto kinen ronshū: Sekai ni okeru Nihon no bunka* (Tokyo: Daiichi hōki shuppan, 1965), pp. 46–51.
48 Tsuji, *Tokugawa*, pp. 261–70, 229–30; and Tsuji, "Kyōhō kaikaku to jugaku," pp. 40–46.
49 Tsuji, *Tokugawa*, pp. 271–8; Itō Tasaburō, "Kinsho no kenkyū," *Rekishi chiri* 58 (October–November 1936): 313–46, 421–70.

Yoshimune's administration undeniably helped change the direction of Japanese thought, deflecting it away from speculative philosophy and toward the areas of natural science, classical study, and textual analysis, a shift that helped clear the way for the intellectual revolution of the eighteenth century. It is doubtful, however, whether the shogun or any of his advisers had ever really foreseen such a consequence. Their aim was far more restricted, for in this, as in everything else they did, they tried only to stabilize the form of government that they had inherited and that was, they knew, beginning to totter.

THE HŌREKI PERIOD

Tokugawa Yoshimune retired in the autumn of 1745, installing as ninth shogun his eldest son Ieshige. There seems to have been no political reason for this change. In all probability Yoshimune, now past his sixtieth year, simply felt it appropriate to give way to his thirty-five-year-old heir apparent. Some misgivings must have accompanied the transfer, however, for the new shogun was an invalid, the consequence perhaps of too many years of intemperance.

Even though Ieshige was one of the least capable of all the shoguns, however, the government ran smoothly enough, at least on the surface, throughout the 1750s. Of course, the land-tax revenues never again reached the level of 1744, but between 1746 and 1764 collections averaged 1.65 million *koku* yearly, a level slightly ahead of the 1737-to-1745 period, producing the highest sustained averages for the entire Edo period. Land-tax revenues during the years 1746 to 1764 were remarkably stable, with very little fluctuation. Under these conditions the government treasury, which in 1742 held a reserve of 1 million gold pieces, swelled to 2.5 million by 1753, and to 3 million by 1770, the largest reserve ever produced during the Tokugawa period.[50]

Underneath this apparent tranquillity, however, there were reasons for suspecting that the Tokugawa bakufu, by the 1750s, had already reached the limits of its power and that crises of various sorts were beginning to emerge. One of them, in fact, may have been a succession crisis, for no sooner had Yoshimune retired than his old ally, Senior Councilor Matsudaira Norimura, was removed from office and deprived of ten thousand *koku* of his domain. The *Tokugawa jikki* cov-

50 Tsuji Tatsuya, "Bakusei-shi kara mita Kyōhō yori Tanuma e no katei ni tsuite," *Rekishigaku kenkyū* 264 (April–May 1962): 63–66; and Tsuji Tatsuya, "Hōreki–Temmei-ki no seiji jōsei," in Kitajima Masamoto, ed., *Seijishi*, vol. 11 of *Taikei Nihon-shi sōsho*, pt. 2 (Tokyo: Yamakawa shuppan-sha, 1965), pp. 247–8.

ered over the incident by observing that "nobody knew the reason, which was kept secret." The *Zoku sannō gaiki,* on the other hand, claimed that Matsudaira Norimura, believing Ieshige to be too frail to make a good shogun, pressed the case of Yoshimune's second son, Tayasu Munetake, thereby incurring Yoshimune's hostility. This latter is not an especially reliable source, but it is clear that some tension existed between Ieshige and his younger brother, for just two years after Matsudaira's dismissal, Munetake was ordered to spend three years under house arrest, so a succession dispute of some kind is by no means an implausible hypothesis.[51]

After Matsudaira's departure, government in the Tokugawa administrative structure devolved on a number of people, all of them judged by historians to have been mild and conscientious. One of these was Ōoka Tadamitsu, a man whose spectacular rise from obscurity matched that of Arai Hakuseki and Manabe Akifusa. For some scholars, Ōoka was the prototype of Tanuma Okitsugu, who later dominated the shogunate from a similar position, but the fact is that Ōoka was deficient in both ability and authority. It was almost as if all involved in shogunal politics had agreed that power should not be monopolized by any single individual.[52]

One of the most obvious characteristics of Ieshige's administration was the relatively severe treatment of the daimyo. The earlier Kyōhō Reforms had concentrated on the shogunal level, and few daimyo had been called to account for maladministration within their domains. If we exclude those cases in which daimyo domains were confiscated or reduced because of the daimyo's inability to produce an heir, only two daimyo were punished by Yoshimune for breaches of discipline. As it happens, both of those concerned had gone mad and murdered people. Other flagrant breaches were punished by simple sentences of house arrest rather than by confiscation. Such, at least, was the punishment meted out to Tokugawa Muneharu of Owari, who publicly criticized the shogunate's frugality drive, preferring to beggar his own domain through an alternative policy of free spending, and to the notoriously dissolute Sakakibara Masamine of Himeji, whose purchases of Yoshiwara courtesans had raised many eyebrows.

Ieshige's government, on the other hand, initiated a succession of confiscations, beginning with Senior Councilor Matsudaira Nori-

51 Mikami Sanji, *Edo jidai shi,* vol. 2 (Tokyo: Fuzambō, 1944), pp. 286–90; Tsuji, "Hōreki–Temmei," pp. 239–41; and Tsuji, *Tokugawa,* pp. 301–2.
52 Mikami, *Edo,* pp. 290–6; Tsuji, "Bakusei-shi," pp. 63–4; Matsuo Masaji, "Hōreki-ki seikyoku no dōkō ni tsuite," *Rekishi chiri* 91 (April 1968): 21–36.

mura's loss of ten thousand *koku* in 1745. This was followed by the punishments of Uemura Tsunetomo of Katsuura in 1751, Andō Nobutada of Kanō in 1755, Kanamori Yorikane of Gujō in 1758, and Honda Tadanaka of Sagara in the same year. All, with the exception of Norisato, were punished for supposed misrule, whether in their domains or in their personal households. The 1758 punishments of Kanamori and Honda came in the wake of peasant uprisings, for example. Clearly, despite the deficiencies of the shogun himself, his administration could sense a looming crisis and displayed its concern by giving renewed attention to the conduct of local government throughout Japan.

It was this same concern that also gave rise to a far stricter attitude toward the shogunate's own finances and the administration of the Tokugawa house domain, bringing with it a spate of penalties against local officials. In the twelve years between 1748 and 1759, for example, a total of thirty-two finance and local officials were either dismissed or deprived of their stipends. Previous purges undertaken by Tsunayoshi and Yoshimune had emphasized punishments for embezzling and misappropriation of taxes by members of the traditional official class in rural areas. As a result, these families had been largely removed from office by 1720 and replaced by bureaucrats held more directly accountable to top administrators in Edo. As a result, the shogunate's income from the land tax had increased.

In the purges of the 1750s, however, the victims came almost entirely from among those bureaucrats introduced into local government by Yoshimune; not a few of them had built up considerable reputations for their efforts in the Kyōhō Reforms. Just why they were now being punished is far from clear – records offer little in the way of explanation beyond laconic statements like "corruption" or the even more cryptic "with reason." Whatever the case, the heroes of the Kyōhō period had become the villains of the Hōreki period (1751–64), a development from which it is possible to deduce that the nature of the shogunate's problems was changing.

Not all administrators involved in local government were purged, however. Several families, the Okada and Ibi among them, were commended in 1767 for their management of the areas entrusted to them, which meant that they had produced greater tax revenues without alienating the common people. This latter fact was particularly significant, for the high tax yields of the Kyōhō period, won at the cost of peasant disaffection, had, by the Hōreki period, come to be seen as counterproductive. Instructions to local officials in 1745, 1748, and

1756 all had cautioned against excessive taxation, so for the Hōreki period the model official was one who could keep the peasants happy and at the same time provide stable tax revenues.[53]

Underlying this new, more conciliatory attitude toward local administration lay the fear of mounting popular unrest. This had been growing steadily since the latter stages of the Kyōhō Reforms. In the thirty-five years between 1681 and 1715, there had been 426 incidents of peasant protest; the succeeding thirty-five-year period, from 1716 to 1750, produced 724, or almost twice as many.[54] Their scale was growing, too. A revolt in Iwakitaira in 1738 eventually involved an estimated 84,000 farmers, and later that year a similar protest near the silver mines at Ikuno was put down only through the intervention of troops from thirteen different daimyo domains. Not since the great Shimabara Rebellion of a century before had Japan seen such an emergency.[55]

In one sense the incidence and scale of peasant protest can be seen as simply an extension of earlier patterns. The nature of the protests themselves, however, was quite different. Previously, such incidents had been directed against oppressive rulers and increased taxes and had only a limited measure of success. Now, in some instances, plans to increase taxation were brought to a standstill, and in others – as in the case of Kanamori Yorikane – peasant protest was enough to force the removal of the daimyo himself, together with a number of high officials who had been bribed to keep quiet about the affair.[56] Several domains were also to see faction disputes among their samurai linked with, and echoed by, peasant revolts, one of the most notable examples taking place at Kurume in 1754.[57]

Clearly, the authority of Japan's ruling class was coming under challenge more and more during the 1750s. Ultimately, not even the shogun was exempt from criticism. In 1759, for example, a Shinto scholar named Takenouchi Shikibu was banished from Kyoto for having expressed his belief that Japan was displaying all the classic signs of a realm in disarray. This was also the year in which Yamagata Daini, in his *Ryūshi shinron*, called attention to the shortcomings of Tokugawa rule. Both Takenouchi and Yamagata were idealists, but in their mis-

53 Tsuji, "Bakusei-shi," pp. 64–6.
54 Aoki Kōji, *Hyakushō ikki sōgō nempyō* (Tokyo: San-ichi shobō, 1971), pp. 29–31.
55 Tsuji, *Tokugawa*, p. 196.
56 Hayashi Motoi, "Hōreki, Temmei-ki no shakai jōsei," in *Iwanami kōza Nihon rekishi*, vol. 12 (Tokyo: Iwanami shoten, 1963), pp. 106–13; and Yamada Tadao, "Hōreki, Meiwa-ki no hyakushō ikki," in *Nihon keizai-shi taikei*, vol. 4 (*kinsei* 2) (Tokyo: Tōkyō daigaku shuppankai, 1965), pp. 134–49.
57 Itō Tasaburō, *Nihon kinsei-shi*, vol. 11 (Tokyo: Yūhikaku, 1952), pp. 222–9.

givings about the stability of Japanese government and society, they expressed the criticisms of a great many of their fellow countrymen. The same mood was also reflected in the work of the Tōhoku philosopher Andō Shōeki, who was currently writing his own critique of the Tokugawa class system.[58]

THE TANUMA PERIOD

In the summer of 1760, Ieshige resigned, leaving the office to his son Ieharu. His actions were likely prompted by his despondency over the death the previous month of Ōoka Tadamitsu, reputedly the only high official capable of understanding the shogun's stammerings and interpreting them to the outside world. Intimation of his own mortality may also have played a part, as Ieshige was to die the following year.

Ieharu took no greater part in government than his father had. He ruled for twenty-six years, from his accession in 1760 to his death in 1786 but, during this time government policy was guided chiefly by Ieharu's personal adviser, Tanuma Okitsugu, whose immense influence earned these years the title of "the Tanuma period." It is often claimed that Tanuma deliberately excluded the shogun from government, or at the very least manipulated him into doing what Tanuma himself wished, but this is far too simple.[59] The processes at work were much more impersonal and were related not so much to individual strengths and weaknesses as to the fact that the task of government was now far too complex for any one man to control.

Tanuma Okitsugu is so commonly associated with corruption, at least in the popular mind, that even today any political scandal is likely to evoke highly colored journalistic comparisons with the eighteenth-century politician. Certainly, the stories of Tanuma's cupidity and venality are greatly exaggerated, often wildly so, but undoubtedly Tanuma and those around him accepted bribes more or less openly.

Similarly, there were others no less willing to offer bribes to Tanuma and his circle. Even the sanctimonious Matsudaira Sadanobu later confessed to having occasionally given money to Tanuma in order to obtain more influence. It should be remembered, however, that this kind of corruption was part of the fabric of Tokugawa political life. Nobody was immune to it, nor was the practice condemned as it is today. Senior Councilor Matsudaira Takemoto, held by posterity to

---

58 Tsuji Zennosuke, *Tanuma jidai* (Tokyo: Nihon gakujutsu fukyū-kai, 1915), pp. 260–3; and Hayashi, "Hōreki," pp. 128–31.
59 Tsuji, *Tanuma*, pp. 21–7.

have been a model of decorum, was no less guilty than Tanuma in this respect. Date Shigemura of Sendai, writing to his retainers in 1765, noted that if he wanted a higher court rank he would have to buy off both Matsudaira and Tanuma.[60]

The issue of corruption aside, Tanuma Okitsugu faced some very severe problems. To begin with, the living standards of all bakufu vassals, regardless of rank, continued to decline. In particular, those who did not hold official positions in the bureaucracy, and were accordingly totally dependent on their inherited stipends, were subject to sharp financial distress. Living in Edo, surrounded by temptations to spend money they did not have, only made their deteriorating standards of living more difficult to tolerate. So much had already become apparent during the Kyōhō period; the passage of time simply made matters worse.[61] This exacted its toll in both human and institutional terms. These retainers constituted the bakufu's standing army, and their progressive impoverishment meant the inevitable erosion of the government's military capabilities.

Government finances also began to collapse during the 1760s. True, between 1746 and 1764 the annual revenue from the land tax averaged 1.65 million *koku*, the highest sustained level during the Tokugawa period, but thereafter, from 1765 to 1779, that figure slumped to 1.52 million *koku*. Then from 1780 to 1786 – even excluding the two famine years of 1783 and 1786 (1.21 million and 1.08 million *koku*, respectively) – the annual average fell an additional 12 percent, to 1.45 million *koku*. Government reserves dropped accordingly, from 3 million gold pieces in 1770 to 2.2 million in 1788. The great Temmei famine, which lasted from 1782 to 1787, and the disastrous Edo fire of 1772 also contributed to this financial downturn, as both caused loss of income and both required massive government relief measures.[62]

The economic measures implemented by the bakufu to combat this problem were far from popular among conservatives, who saw in them palpable proof of corruption within the administration. More recently, however, some historians have come to judge these policies in a more positive light.[63] They interpret the various new measures – among them the development of mines; the establishment of government monopolies in ginseng, camphor, copper, iron, and brass; the creation of associations of merchants specifically authorized to handle such commodities as seed-oil and sulfur; and the levying of licensing fees

60 Ibid., pp. 11–21, 60–6, 234.   61 Ibid., pp. 67–92, 339–40.
62 Tsuji, "Hōreki," pp. 252–3; Tsuji, *Tanuma*, pp. 116–34.
63 Tsuji, "Hōreki," pp. 186–219, 337–8.

(*myōgakin*) – as attempts to broaden the government's economic base and allow it to take advantage of commercial development.[64]

Yet, the impact of these new initiatives on the bakufu's finances is still questionable. The lack of detailed records does not permit any certainty, but there is reason to doubt that they had much effect at all. Certainly the licensing fees demanded of merchants were not burdensome. According to guidelines announced in 1770, members of the licensed oil-seed guild of Osaka were obliged to pay an initial sum of twenty gold pieces and, thereafter, an annual fee of three gold pieces – a ludicrously small sum in view of the volume of oil-seed trade at the time. Other guilds appear to have paid at much the same rate, so it is more appropriate to conceive of the licensing fees simply as registration dues rather than as an attempt to tap commercial wealth.[65]

The more convincing explanation of Tanuma's attempt to force merchants into monopolistic associations concerns his desire to control prices. Previously, during the Kyōhō Reforms, the shogunate had become concerned about fluctuations in the price of rice as well as the increase in other commodity prices and had first tried its hand at commercial controls. At that time, the main object of official attention was the various Edo wholesalers (*ton'ya*) as the authorities tried to regulate the price of goods sent from Osaka. In subsequent years the shogunate shifted its attention from Edo to Osaka and tried to police directly the Osaka wholesalers who shipped goods to Edo. With seed-oil used in lamps, for example, the government strengthened the monopoly of the Edo wholesalers in 1741, by refusing to allow any other merchants to import directly from Osaka. From 1753 onward it also began to bolster the Osaka wholesalers, insisting in 1770 that all involved in oil pressing in the Osaka area form an association and come under the supervision of the Osaka oil market. This reinforced the privileged position of the Osaka oil wholesalers and also depressed the price of oil, as it maximized the quantity handled in Osaka, an area under constant bakufu supervision.[66]

One feature of the Tanuma period was the emergence of speculators, men from outside the normal commercial establishment who came to have an inordinate degree of influence on Tanuma and his associates. Through their political activities, these men – known as *yamashi* by their contemporaries – were responsible for several new

64 Itō, *Nihon*, pp. 160–8.
65 Miyamoto Mataji, *Kabunakama no kenkyū* (Tokyo: Yūhikaku, 1938), pp. 132–45.
66 Tsuda Hideo, *Hōken keizai seisaku no tenkai to shijō kōzō* (Tokyo: Ochanomizu shobō, 1961), pp. 26–62.

initiatives. Some of these were successful; many failed. It was at the urging of these men, for example, that government offices were set up to oversee the activities of the rice market, to regulate the flow of goods from Osaka to Edo, and to lend out money at low rates of interest. Elsewhere, these speculators were responsible for a plan to set up ten inspection posts in the Kantō area to check the quality of silk and silk goods produced there, with the costs of inspection to be borne by the purchaser. This proved to be one of the failures, as the scheme resulted in considerable opposition from local peasants, who ultimately expressed their anger by destroying the houses of the scheme's originators and by marching into Takasaki, the castle town of Senior Councilor Matsudaira Terutaka. The bakufu had no option but to dismantle the whole enterprise.[67]

Another new element in Tanuma's economic policies involved moneylending. During the Kyōhō Reforms the government had tried to stabilize the price of rice by permitting the use of promissory notes in speculative ventures into the rice market, but this had only encouraged various daimyo domains – all of them under financial pressures – to issue promissory notes without the money to guarantee them. In 1761, therefore, the government forbade daimyo to issue any promissory notes unless they were able to redeem them, and in 1767 it further ordered Osaka merchants not to accept such notes. Then, in 1782, the shogunate appointed the cloth merchant Gotō Nuinosuke as inspector of rice promissory notes in Osaka and assigned to him the task of restoring confidence in the paper currency.

The practice of moneylending between merchants and peasants had also grown, as farmers increasingly required help in meeting their farming expenses or their taxes. In 1767 the shogunate intervened and established an agency in Osaka to oversee any loans in which houses had been pledged as security. Already in 1760, the government had set up an office to deal with small loans in copper cash and followed this in 1770 with a similar office dealing with silver cash. Finally in 1786, the bakufu issued a law under which, for the next five years, money was to be collected from all peasants, townspeople, and religious foundations in Japan, at a predetermined rate, and such money, augmented by the bakufu's own funds, was to be lent out to the daimyo. Tanuma was removed from office, however, before this could be put into effect.[68]

67 Matsumoto Shirō, "Shōhin ryūtsū no hatten to ryūtsū kikō no saihensei," in *Nihon keizaishi taikei*, vol. 4 (*kinsei* 2) (Tokyo: Tōkyō daigaku shuppankai, 1965), pp. 92–3, 96–9, 127–30; and Tsuji, *Tanuma*, pp. 204–7.
68 Matsumoto, "Shōhin," pp. 96–9; and Tsuji, *Tanuma*, pp. 207–12.

There were also noteworthy developments under Tanuma in the area of coinage. One of these concerned silver coins, always a vexed issue, as no specific weights had ever been established for them. This was a matter of considerable inconvenience, for it meant that coins had to be weighed for every transaction involving silver. Tanuma tried to put an end to that in 1765 by issuing a coin that conformed to the precious metal content established by Yoshimune in 1736 and weighed precisely five *momme* (a little over half an ounce). It was a praiseworthy initiative but, as with so many of Tanuma's ideas, did not translate into reality quite as anticipated. First, the coin was regarded with very great suspicion, perhaps because the coin and the concept behind it were unfamiliar. Two years later, when the bakufu declared that twelve of these silver coins were to be worth one gold piece, rumors attributed the change to a plot by moneychangers who wished to profit from the fluctuations in the exchange rate.

In 1722 another new silver coin was minted, the *nanryō nishuban*, which was given the official but arbitrary value of one-eighth of a gold piece. This coin was therefore an oddity, a silver coin whose value was defined only in terms of gold. In all probability the shogunate was hoping to use this coin to break down the inconvenient dual-currency system under which western Japan carried out its affairs in silver, and eastern Japan in gold. Unfortunately, because Tanuma was associated with it, this initial attempt failed, being interpreted as yet another example of the senior councilor's shiftiness.[69] Yet, this attempt to convert the whole country to a gold standard was a rational approach to the problem, and indeed, later politicians were to try it again successfully in the nineteenth century.

Tanuma also introduced great changes in foreign trade. Ever since the beginning of Japan's isolation in the early seventeenth century, the general tendency in matters of foreign trade had been toward greater restriction, aimed at preventing the outflow of Japan's gold, silver, and copper reserves. Tanuma, however, adopted a vigorous export policy in an attempt to reverse these trade imbalances. By the late eighteenth century, there was a growing demand for what were referred to as *tawaramono*, that is, the various marine products like shark fins, sea slugs, and seaweed so prized in Chinese cooking. Tanuma proceeded to urge increased production and export of these items to help reverse Japan's trade imbalance. This initiative, at least, would seem to have been successful, as it was claimed that Tanuma's new silver pieces were actually minted from silver brought into Japan through the sale of exports.[70]

The development of Hokkaido was another issue to which Tanuma devoted much thought. Always aware of their vulnerability to foreigners from the south, the Japanese at the end of the eighteenth century were beginning to look northward as well, and not without reason. The Russians had crossed Siberia, colonized portions of Kamchatka, and had even started to press southward toward the Kurile Islands. Russian ships were being sighted along Japanese coasts with increasing frequency. In 1777, indeed, a group of Russians approached the authorities of the Matsumae domain in Hokkaido with a request for trade. This was officially rejected, but there seems to have been some surreptitious trade, for some Russian goods were later to be found in the Osaka markets.

News of these developments came to Tanuma's attention in a curiously roundabout fashion. Some of his friends had passed on to him a work entitled *Aka Ezo fūsetsukō*, written by Kudō Heisuke, a medical practitioner from Sendai. Kudō's argument in favor of commercial exchange with Russia was so convincing that the senior councilor dispatched a team to Hokkaido in 1785 to investigate the possibilities of opening trade relations. As events transpired, the resulting report was notably unenthusiastic, putting an immediate end to any prospect of Japan's trading with its northern neighbor. On the other hand, the investigating team did urge the development of Hokkaido, contending that land reclamation there could bring the shogunate an additional 5.83 million *koku* annually in tax revenues, an amount that would have more than doubled its income. Given the state of agricultural technology at the time, this may well have been too optimistic an assessment, but in any case, like other plans, this too would collapse along with Tanuma's own political career.[71]

While Tanuma's government was experimenting with these new policies, a series of crises overtook Japan. The farming community, on whose revenues all political power rested, was beginning to fall apart under the combined pressure of mounting agrarian unrest and successive natural disasters. Protest in rural areas, already formidable by the end of the Kyōhō period, had risen, by the 1780s, to an average of more than fifty incidents a year.[72] Their scale was growing too, as was the level of violence. More importantly, the nature of protest had also

70 Tsuji, *Tanuma*, pp. 312–29; and Numata Jirō, "Nisshin bōeki ni okeru ichi mondai," *Rekishi chiri* 68 (November–December 1936): 421–34, 543–8.
71 Tsuji, *Tanuma*, pp. 295–312.   72 Aoki, *Hyakushō ikki*, p. 31.

changed. In the 1750s, protest had usually been in the form of demands from village communities that their feudal overlord – whether the bakufu or daimyo – reduce taxes or provide them with extra rice for food or seed. By the 1770s and 1780s, however, poor farmers were beginning to unite in attacks on the more prosperous members of the village community itself, particularly the village headmen (nanushi), landlords, and wealthy rural merchants. In some cases, these uprisings were echoed in Japan's towns and cities. To combat this alarming trend, the shogunate in 1769 instructed all daimyo that such outbreaks of violence were to be stamped out, irrespective of the merits of their grievances. In 1770, signs were posted throughout Japan offering rewards to those ready to inform on agitators. Despite this increased government attention, however, agrarian unrest continued to grow.[73]

The situation was not helped by an extraordinary succession of natural disasters: storms, droughts, volcanic eruptions, crop failures, famines, and epidemics throughout the countryside and fires in the cities. All of these made the life of the common people that much more precarious. They also focused resentment on the government, for in a Confucian society natural disasters were taken as Heaven's way of reproving earthly misrule. No one knows how many people died in the great Temmei famine, which began in 1782 and continued until 1787, but its severity can perhaps be gauged by the fact that the shogunate's land-tax revenues fell by more than half during its duration.

Certainly there is no doubt that one of its casualties was Tanuma Okitsugu himself, the man held directly accountable for all his country's maladies.[74] The first blow came with the assassination of his son in the spring of 1784. At the end of the following year Matsudaira Sadanobu, the man destined to supplant Tanuma as leader of the government, bribed his way into the shogunate's highest advisory body, the Tamarinoma, and began to work toward the senior councilor's overthrow. This was not long in coming. In the autumn of 1786, Tokugawa Ieharu, the tenth shogun, fell gravely ill and died. Even before his death, Tanuma's projects had been stopped, and now, left without a protector, Tanuma was turned out of office. Subsequently he lost twenty thousand koku of his domain and was placed under house arrest. Then early in the summer of 1788, he too died, in his seventieth year, leaving to his grandson Okiaki a domain that had shrunk to a mere ten thousand koku.[75]

73 Hayashi, "Hōreki," pp. 113–17; and Yamada, "Hōreki," pp. 149–74.
74 Tsuji, Tanuma, pp. 116–34.   75 Tsuji, Tanuma, pp. 32–59, 220–42.

THE KANSEI REFORMS

With the accession of the thirteen-year-old Ienari as shogun, Matsu-daira Sadanobu's rise to political prominence was assured. As daimyo of Shirakawa, Sadanobu had already won the support of the new shogun's natural (as distinct from his adoptive) father, Hitotsubashi Harusada. A prominent leader of one of the three Tokugawa cadet branches descended from Yoshimune, Harusada was able to enlist the support of the prestigious Owari, Kii, and Mito branches for Sada-nobu as well. All were ready to encourage the young politician in his plan to mount a program of reforms, for not only was Sadanobu a grandson of Yoshimune, the Kyōhō reformer, but he had also proved himself a capable administrator in his own domain at Shirakawa, where he had managed to keep the impact of the Temmei famine to an absolute minimum.

Nevertheless, the initial steps in the campaign to install Sadanobu in the inner circles of the shogunate proved unexpectedly difficult. Tanuma Okitsugu may have been dismissed, but his associates still remained, in both the bureaucracy and the shogun's household, and particularly in the ōoku, the women's quarters. The political tussle between Sadanobu's faction and the Tanuma diehards continued into the new year, until popular unrest brought it to a stop. In 1786, two years earlier, there had been 57 peasant protests, and in just the previ-ous year, 1787, violent riots had rocked Edo, Osaka, and other major cities. Finally, in 1788 there were 117 separate revolts.

They were exactly what Tanuma's opponents needed to drive the last of his adherents from the shogunal household and clear the way for Matsudaira Sadanobu to be elevated to the post of senior councilor and shortly thereafter to chief senior councilor (rōjū shūseki). At his urging, the newly installed shogun quickly called together the senior administrators and ordered them to perform their duties in accordance with the spirit of Yoshimune, the reforming shogun of fifty years before. Following this command, Sadanobu told the bureaucrats in considerable detail exactly what was expected of them. This consti-tuted the opening maneuver in what came to be known as the Kansei Reforms.

There were still some obstacles, however. The new shogun, Ienari, was just fifteen and unable to offer much assistance. Moreover, only two members of Sadanobu's own faction had thus far been brought into the administration – Honda Tadakazu as junior councilor, and Kanō Hisanori as assistant chamberlain (sobayaku goyō toritsugi).

Against this, Tanuma's old supporters were still strongly entrenched in important posts. Matsudaira Yasuyoshi still served as senior councilor and Mizuno Tadatomo as the titular senior councillor (*rōjū kaku*). Faced with this much opposition, Sadanobu petitioned the heads of the Kii, Owari, and Mito branches of the Tokugawa house for some additional sign of official approval to help him implement his reform program. This petition had some success, although not as much as he would have wished. He had in mind promotion to grand councilor but had to settle for the ancient position of shogunal adviser (*hōsa*), a post unfilled for more than 150 years. Once this step had been taken, early in 1788, both his major opponents, Mizuno and Matsudaira, resigned from the Senior Council, to be replaced with Sadanobu's own friends – Matsudaira Nobuakira as senior councilor, Honda Tadakazu as chamberlain, and Toda Ujinori as superintendent of temples and shrines. These changes gave Matsudaira Sadanobu the commanding position he needed inside the bakufu and the shogun's own household. With this base and the support of the three cadet daimyo, as well as Ienari's father Hitotsubashi Harusada, Sadanobu could now begin his own reforms.[76]

Of all the manifold problems confronting him, the legacy of social chaos left by the events of the last years of the Tanuma period was the most disturbing. To cope with this, Sadanobu believed it necessary to rebuild the entire social system, to restore morale, and to revive the economy, and all as quickly as possible. In particular, the problem of the bakufu's own samurai retainers, now largely demoralized, called for urgent attention. To restore morale, the government exhorted the samurai to improve their general behavior and encouraged them to devote themselves to scholarship and to training in the martial arts. The administration also promised to identify men with the necessary skills and qualities to take charge of such a program, and so orders went out to promote even subordinate, low-ranking samurai who might be considered for such responsibilities.

Then, in mid-1790, the government issued the Igaku no kin (Prohibition of heterodoxy). The administration believed that the orthodox Chu Hsi philosophy espoused by Tokugawa officials for nearly a century and a half had been undercut by new philosophies. To the authorities, members of the Ancient Learning school and the proponents of

76 Kikuchi Kenjirō, "Matsudaira Sadanobu nyūkaku jijō," *Shigaku zasshi* 26 (January 1915): 1–22; Inobe Shigeo, *Bakumatsu shi no kenkyū* (Tokyo: Yūzankaku, 1927), pp. 1–17; Takeuchi Makoto, "Kansei kaikaku," in *Iwanami kōza Nihon rekishi*, vol. 12 (*Kinsei* 4) (Tokyo: Iwanami shoten, 1976), pp. 5–14; Tsuji, *Tanuma*, pp. 151–7, 237–8.

eclecticism seemed to be turning people away from the practical application of Confucian ethics and, instead, promoting undesirable habits of mind, antiquarianism and pedantry among them.

Accordingly, Matsudaira Sadanobu took steps to protect Chu Hsi Confucianism, as it was defined by the Hayashi school, long the shogunate's custodian of doctrinal purity. Hayashi Nobutaka, head of the school, was instructed to see that the official orthodoxy was maintained and that all other branches of philosophy were avoided as heretical. Because the underlying intent was to reform all Japanese, not just the samurai, through proper Confucian morality, the Igaku no kin was accompanied by other similar measures. Stricter censorship was announced, with an absolute ban on pornography, a step that led to the prosecution of some well-known figures, including the writer Santō Kyōden. On a more positive note, the shogunate also ordered a national search for cases of exemplary behavior and later published appropriate examples under the title *Kōgiroku* (Records of righteousness and filial piety).

There was also another side to the Igaku no kin, and this concerned the training of capable officials. To demonstrate its commitment to promoting scholarship and the martial arts, the shogunate also turned its attention to training students at its own academy, where future bureaucrats were instructed. To this end, it established in 1792 a five-tier system of annual examinations for shogunal vassals and their sons. These examinations were open to any samurai who wished to sit for them, but the government directed senior administrators to invite capable subordinates to apply, whether or not they wished to. In practice, however, this system did not prove as praiseworthy as expected: Anyone could score well with hasty and mindless cramming, and the odds were still stacked against candidates of humble status, no matter how able. Still, the impulse itself was a good one, and it was revived later by the Meiji government with the introduction of competitive public service examinations.

The Igaku no kin was significant in another way as well. By encouraging scholarship in such a decisive manner, the bakufu, perhaps coincidentally, was staking its claim to ultimate authority over Japan's academic and technological development. This impulse can be seen clearly in its approach to the matter of medical training. Before 1791, the government gave no more than unenthusiastic support to the Igakukan, one of the country's many medical schools. In that year, however, the administration reversed course and took over the Igakukan, which then became the official medical school. Igakukan students received exemptions from formal examinations, whereas all other doctors in bakufu employ were obliged to be examined there before they could be registered. Similarly, the government also took the first steps toward controlling the study of Western science and technology. In 1797, for example, the preparation of a new calendar became a pretext for bringing the country's best astronomers into employment in its own observatory. If many aspects of the Kansei Reforms were reactionary attempts to resolve the crisis of the late eighteenth century by restoring the older, feudal-based order, here, at least, they anticipated several late-nineteenth-century developments, for the Meiji academic establishment was ultimately created along lines suggested by Matsudaira Sadanobu's experimental efforts.[77]

Samurai demoralization was not the only problem confronting the shogunate. Farming communities, too, were in desperate need of stabilization. In many areas, agriculture had been so damaged by natural disasters that there was little any government could do to restore productivity. In the Kantō and Tōhoku regions, for example, the events of the previous decade had driven many peasants to abscond, leaving their farms to revert to wilderness. This was hardly a problem that the shogunate could ignore, so from the late 1780s onward the authorities began to devise strategies to cope with the phenomenon of "deserted villages." One plan was to encourage more well-to-do farmers to begin their own land reclamation projects, using the labor of less fortunate fellow villagers. Another was to identify "honest vagabonds" (*mushukumono*), that is, men who had left their villages and were no longer registered at any temple, and to grant them parcels of land in areas that needed more cultivators.

The government also severely restricted the drift of seasonal workers from the country to the city. Toward the end of 1790 the shogunate announced that men who had come to Edo from the country would be provided with money for travel, food, and agricultural implements, provided they agreed to go home again. If for any reason they could not do so, or no longer had relatives or farms there, then the authorities would offer to settle them somewhere else.

Abortion and infanticide, common in some parts of Japan during the famine of the 1780s, were seen as another cause of declining rural population. To cope with this, the government ordered local adminis-

77 Tahara Tsuguo, "Kansei kaikaku no ichi kōsatsu," *Rekishigaku kenkyū* 178 (December 1954): 9–21; Kumakura Isao, "Kasei bunka no zentei," in Hayashiya Tatsusaburō, ed., *Kasei bunka no kenkyū* (Tokyo: Iwanami shoten, 1976), pp. 47–59; and Takeuchi, "Kansei kaikaku," pp. 15–17.

trators to instruct village officials and the mutual responsibility groups (*goningumi*) to watch over the health of pregnant women. Such women were to be given every assistance, even sums of money to use to rear their children when necessary, but local officials were also instructed to rigorously investigate the death of any of these children. All in all, these efforts to rebuild rural Japan cost the shogunate a good deal. In 1800, for example, almost 150,000 gold pieces, some 10 percent of its total expenditures for that year, were devoted to this cause.[78]

In the end, however, agriculture could not be revived without the help of competent local administrators. Consequently, the bakufu again removed several local officials believed to be incompetent and replaced them with new appointments. Some of the dismissals were quite spectacular: Both Chigusa Senjūrō, district magistrate (*gundai*) of Mino, and Ōkusa Masatada of Hida were banished in 1789. The following year Ina Tadataka of the Kantō had his stipend confiscated and was placed under permanent house arrest, and in 1793 Ibi Miki-nosuke, another prominent district magistrate, was dismissed from office. All four men were of extremely high status, far higher than usual for this level of local administrator, and all had been responsible for very large areas of shogunal land. Their fates, therefore, warrant special attention.

Take, for example, the case of Ina Tadataka, the Kantō district magistrate, whose family had held that position for over two hundred years, ever since Tokugawa Ieyasu had moved into the region at the end of the sixteenth century. The family was very well liked and also trusted by the people in the region, as Tadataka had discovered in 1781 and again in 1787, when he had used his popularity to quiet a series of violent local disturbances. Back in 1764 his grandfather Tadaoki, too, had used his personal standing in the community to disperse mobs of angry peasants. Why then, should the shogunate place such a man under permanent house arrest? The official reason was that Tadataka had failed to control a dispute among his own subordinates and that his report of the matter to higher levels of the bureaucracy had been less than frank. It is more likely, however, that the real reason concerned his poor handling of government loan funds. Yields on high-

78 Takeuchi, "Kansei kaikaku," pp. 22–23; Kishimoto Junkichi, *Kishimoto Budayū kun jiseki* (Tokyo, 1919), pp. 26–30; Nagayama Usaburō, *Hayakawa daikan* (1929), pp. 190–201; Kanazawa Harutomo, *Teranishi daikan jiseki shū* (Tsunetoyo, Fukushima: Tsunetoyo kyō-doshi kankōkai, 1930); and Murakami Tadashi, *Daikan* (Tokyo, Jimbutsu ōrai sha, 1963), pp. 144–5, 151–2, 154–65, 181–6, 195.

interest loans had become extremely important to administration finances. Early in the Tanuma period the government had decided to offset falling land-tax revenues by turning moneylender and had dragooned its local administrators into helping. They were compelled personally to borrow funds from the shogunate, as well as from wealthy farmers in their areas, and then to lend out the monies to local farmers at high rates of interest. Under normal conditions this scheme might have worked, but the turmoil in the Kantō during the 1780s, the area for which Ina Tadataka was responsible, made it impossible. People simply could not repay their debts, and consequently, neither could Tadataka. In 1789, when he requested a twenty-year extension of his debt of fifteen thousand gold pieces, the shogunate refused. At the same time, his local reputation also suffered because of his role as moneylender, and he came to be seen as an ally of the rich against the poor. When a dispute erupted among his retainers, therefore, the shogunate simply took advantage of the opportunity to replace him.

Ibi Mikinosuke was a man of similar eminence. In 1767 the bakufu announced that the office of west county magistrate would be granted to the Ibi family in perpetuity in honor of its exemplary record in local administration over the previous three generations. Some two decades later, however, Ibi Mikinosuke was denied the traditional privilege of an audience with the shogun. Two years later the shogunate dismissed Mikinosuke from office on the grounds that his predecessor had raised large sums of money from wealthy farmers on the pretext of lending it out to the needy and had then proceeded to use it for his own benefit. That same success in moneylending that had brought the family official recognition in the first place had also led to their downfall.

Disgrace also awaited the Ōkusa family of Hida, who had been piling up debts for generations, ever since the time of Ōkusa Masatada's grandfather, Masanaga. They too were charged with misappropriating public money. Such corruption, linked as it was with moneylending, had little to do with the Kansei Reforms but, rather, was the legacy of an earlier period.[79]

Having unmasked and punished one lot of local administrators, Sadanobu's administration then set about replacing them with new ones. Nine intendants were appointed in 1788 and another ten the following year. Several of these men went on to become famous offi-

79 Takeuchi Makoto, "Kantō gundai Ina Tadataka no shikkyaku to sono rekishi-teki igi," *Tokugawa rinsei-shi kenkyūjo kenkyū kiyō* (1966), pp. 173–203; and Tsuji Tatsuya, "Edo Bakufu Policy in the Late Eighteenth Century," *Yokohama shiritsu daigaku ronsō* 19 (1967): 34–49.

cials. Okada Hakaru (better known by his pen name of Kansen) was a well-known Confucian scholar who, together with Shibano Ritsuzan, had been active in the shogunate's academy. His appointment was a gamble on Sadanobu's part, but it was a successful one. Some changes were made further down the hierarchy as well. Instead of using local peasants or commoners as clerks, a practice that had led to much corruption in the past, the government now decided that its local officials should appoint their subordinates from among the shogunate's own vassals.[80]

Despite all this activity, however, the bakufu never overcame corruption at the local level, especially the problems associated with moneylending. Sadanobu's administration never considered a straightforward program of distributing grants of money for purposes like land reclamation or the care of orphaned children. Instead, it entrusted large sums of money – as much as twenty thousand gold pieces in some cases – to local officials with instructions that the funds be lent out to wealthy peasants and merchants, and the interest used to create a fund from which the poor could then be assisted. This was precisely what Ina Tadataka and others had done, except that the Kansei Reforms had reasserted government authority, rather than leaving it in the hands of people who, like the Ina, Ibi, and Ōkusa, were compromised by their connections with the wealthy families of their areas.

Toward the end of 1788, the bakufu tried to establish a closer association between the Finance Ministry and seven prominent Edo merchants. The significance of this may not be immediately apparent, but the government was effectively offering tacit recognition to a new commercial force. Formerly, two distinct merchant groups had dominated Edo's commercial life. One consisted of semiofficial merchants who ran the gold and silver guilds and managed the cloth trade. The other comprised entrepreneurs from elsewhere – places like Kyoto, Osaka, Ōmi, and Ise – whose nationwide interests dictated that they maintain branches in Edo. During the eighteenth century, and particularly after the Kyōhō Reforms, a third group had emerged. These were local Edo entrepreneurs who had found new routes to wealth and influence. By enticing representatives of this group into its service, the bakufu hoped to tap their resources and to use them to supervise the activities of the city's rice and money markets. Already, earlier in that

---

80 Kumakura, "Kasei bunka," pp. 59–67; and Takeuchi, "Kansei kaikaku," pp. 17–18; Murakami, *Daikan*, pp. 140–74, 179–204.

same year of 1788, the government had asked them to contribute funds for repairing the Imperial Palace in Kyoto.

The second objective was to enlist the efforts of these merchant elites in fund-raising schemes. The administration lent the men money at low interest and had them put that money to work in various spheres. At the same time the men could also commit their own capital, in full expectation of guaranteed government support on debt collections. It was not long before the government needed their services. In the autumn of 1789 the regime ordered the cancellation of all debts incurred by the samurai. This, it was hoped, would remove one of the government's most pressing concerns, but it was also recognized that unless something further was done, this measure might well have unfortunate repercussions, namely, that the rice brokers and moneylenders, whose loans had been abruptly and unilaterally wiped out, would simply refuse to lend money to samurai again. The government, therefore, asked their new merchant allies, whose numbers had increased from seven to ten, to open a bureau at Saruyachō where distressed rice brokers and moneylenders could borrow money at advantageous rates.

Then in 1791, the bakufu instructed each of the residential wards in Edo to economize on administrative costs and to keep 70 percent of what they saved in a ready reserve. These funds, augmented by money from the bakufu, were to be administered by another bureau for poor relief or for low-interest loans. Naturally, the administration's new allies would manage this as well and thus have control over the city's moneylending system. By using them, rather than representatives of Osaka or Kyoto, it was coincidentally helping raise Edo's own financial status.[81]

Foreign affairs had already begun to emerge as a political issue during the Tanuma period, when there were indications that the policy of seclusion might be modified.[82] The development of Hokkaido was being planned in precisely this context. Matsudaira Sadanobu, on the other hand, believed that traditional policies should not be tampered with, and he also argued that an undeveloped Hokkaido provided the best-possible buffer against foreign encroachment. Looking inward,

81　Takeuchi Makoto, "Kansei kaikaku to 'Kanjōsho goyōtashi' no seiritsu," pts. 1 and 2, *Nihon rekishi* 128 (February 1959): 23–32; and vol. 129 (March 1959): 44–56; and Takeuchi Makoto, "Bakufu keizai no hembō to kin'yū seisaku no tenkai," *Nihon keizaishi taikei*, vol. 4 (Tokyo: Tōkyō daigaku shuppankai, 1965), vol. 4, pp. 197–207.
82　Tsuji, *Tanuma*, pp. 295–7; and Numata Jirō, "Tanuma jidai to Isaac Titsingh," *Nihon rekishi* 380 (January 1980): 101–6.

he committed himself enthusiastically to the task of rebuilding and extending Japan's coastal defenses.

His efforts were stimulated by the arrival of Adam Laksman at Nemuro in 1792. A lieutenant in the Russian army, Laksman came with orders from Catherine the Great to repatriate Japanese castaways, but he also requested the opening of diplomatic and commercial relations between Russia and Japan. The bakufu avoided giving an immediate reply. But eventually it nominated Nagasaki as the port where all contact should take place, and then it gave Laksman an entry permit that proved to be invalid until the middle of the following year. The intention was to gain time so that the shogunate could organize its defense with, as a fallback position, the possibility of permitting trade until they were ready. As events transpired, however. Laksman soon returned to Russia, and Japan saw no more of its northern neighbors until 1804.

Meanwhile, the bakufu was not idle. It ordered all daimyo with coastal domains to improve their defenses, and it drew up its own plans for the fortification of Edo Bay. Further, it dispatched officials to inspect the coasts of the Kantō, Izu, and Suruga regions. Matsudaira Sadanobu himself made a tour of the Izu and Sagami coasts. He also gave some thought to creating new daimyo domains along the shores of Edo Bay to replace the multitude of small domains, and he made plans for the fortification of Hokkaido. But he was to resign before any of these possibilities reached fruition, leaving the pressing problem of defense to bedevil his successors in the nineteenth century.[83]

One of the new issues to cast its shadow over politics during the Kansei period concerned relations with the imperial court. The trouble came in 1789 when Emperor Kōkaku requested that his natural father be accorded the title *dajō tennō*, or retired emperor. Were this to be granted, the father could take precedence over imperial ministers on ceremonial occasions. Otherwise, as a mere imperial prince, he would be obliged to yield precedence, as decreed by Tokugawa Ieyasu in his 1615 instructions to the imperial court. The emperor's request was therefore refused, on the grounds that it lacked precedent. After several more overtures, matters came to a head in 1792 when Emperor Kōkaku declared his intention to promote his father, whether or not the shogunate approved. Quickly, the shogun summoned two senior

83 Suematsu Yasukazu, *Kinsei ni okeru Hoppō mondai no shinten* (Tokyo: Shigundō, 1928), pp. 204–44: Shibusawa Eiichi, *Rakuō kō den* (Tokyo: Iwanami shoten, 1939), pp. 273–317; and Tabohashi Kiyoshi, (*Zōtei*) *Kindai Nihon gaikoku kankei shi* (Tokyo: Tōkō shoin, 1943), pp. 148–57.

court officials to Edo and the following year punished them for their role in the incident.

Unfortunately for Kōkaku and his father, they had chosen the least opportune time to approach the shogunate with such a request. By coincidence, Matsudaira Sadanobu was already committed to resisting a similar initiative from the shogun Ienari, who had expressed the wish that his own father, Hitotsubashi Harusada, might be given the title of retired shogun (completely unwarranted, for he was no such thing). Although Sadanobu owed a great deal to the head of the Hitotsubashi branch, including his own promotion to senior councilor and subsequently to shogunal guardian, his debt was not so heavy that he would countenance quite such a promotion. Were it to eventuate, Hitotsubashi might very well become so strong as to threaten the political supremacy of the shogun's own cabinet of advisers. Were the government to accede to the emperor's request, the same privilege could hardly be refused to the shogun.[84] The punishment of the Kyoto envoys in 1790 laid both issues to rest, but it left an open sore between Kyoto and Edo.

There is no doubt that by this time Matsudaira Sadanobu had become generally unpopular. When he announced his intention to resign in 1791, a move designed, perhaps, to gauge the depth of his support, his followers prevailed on him to remain in office. The following year, he tested his standing a second time. After learning that several ladies-in-waiting had become involved with Buddhist priests, Sadanobu instigated a purge of the shogunal women's quarters. Then, feeling vulnerable, he formally requested permission to surrender some of his duties. In particular he asked to be relieved of his financial responsibilities within the bakufu, his supervision of the shogun's household, and his position as shogunal guardian. Once again he was reassured. The shogun relieved him only of his duties as supervisor of the shogunal household, confirming Sadanobu in everything else and showering him with gifts. In 1793, however, Sadanobu decided to test Ienari's confidence in him for the third, and to his surprise, the last time. Asking to be relieved of his duties as shogunal guardian, he found his request granted – and was stripped of his office of senior councilor into the bargain.[85]

In the short term, Sadanobu's departure made little difference to the general thrust of government policy. His office passed to his friend

---

84 Tsuji Zennosuke, *Nihon bunkashi* (Tokyo: Shunjūsha, 1950), vol. pp. 138–327. The Kyoto affair is referred to as the *songō* (title) incident.

85 Shibusawa, *Rakuō kō den*, pp. 318–33.

and colleague Matsudaira Nobuakira, to whom Sadanobu continued to offer advice, despite his retirement. Nevertheless, the reform impulse eventually ebbed away, leaving ominous jetsam in its wake.

The Russian threat may have retreated for the moment, but Japan was hardly prepared to respond to future emergencies. In Kyoto, the long dormant imperial court had unaccountably begun to stir, and the reverberations, already felt in Edo, would soon be evident everywhere. Above all, the bakufu, having spent more than a hundred years trying to cope with changing circumstances, had failed, leaving problems of rural distress, shrinking finances, and samurai demoralization not only intact but far more daunting and intractable than they had ever been. It was no basis on which to face the crises of the coming century.

CHAPTER 10

THE VILLAGE AND AGRICULTURE DURING THE EDO PERIOD

Near the end of the Tokugawa period, officials from the shogunate's Finance Office undertook a survey of villages in Musashi and Sagami provinces.[1] During the course of their investigations, the bakufu officials consulted documents preserved by prominent village families that traced their lineages back in time to samurai society of the sixteenth century. Some of the documents from the villages of Sagami had been issued by the Hōjō house of Odawara, and many of the Musashi documents carried the seal of the Uesugi daimyo. Among them were directives requiring the recipient to provide horses for military service, whereas others bestowed fiefs in reward for distinguished service in battle, an indication that some of the villagers' ancestors had served, nearly three centuries earlier, as warriors under the Sengoku daimyo. Other evidence corroborates this notion. In many cadastral survey registers from the early seventeenth century, it is not uncommon to find two persons listed as cultivators (*sakunin*). Usually the name of a samurai or priest appears first, below which is entered the name of the man who was presumably the actual cultivator, separated by the term *bun*. From this it is clear that many former samurai who had lived in the villages while serving the Sengoku daimyo as warriors remained on the land in the seventeenth century, thus establishing the lineages revealed in the survey at the end of the Edo period. Why these persons chose to remain on the land, abandoning samurai status for a life on the soil, remains an intriguing question that can be answered only by examining how the relationships among land tenure, taxation, agricultural technology, and the social composition of villages subtly yet irrevocably shifted over the course of time that separated the late Edo from the late Sengoku period.

Social stratification within the *shōen* estates of the medieval period

---

[1] For a comprehensive explanation of these surveys, see Furushima Toshio, *Nihon nōgyōshi* (Tokyo: Iwanami shoten, 1956), pp. 177–9.

was very complex. Local landholders, known as *myōshu*, were the principal cultivators, and they paid an annual land rent to the estate's proprietors, most often temples or aristocratic families in Kyoto. These local landholders possessed legally protected entitlements to their lands, including the right to buy, sell, and bequeath their holdings. Landownership was transferable not only between fellow landholders but also to officials of the shogunate such as the military estate stewards (*jitō*), some of whom might reside within the boundaries of any given estate and ultimately become the vassals of that estate's proprietors. At this time in the Tōkai region, small-scale private landholders, who also constituted a portion of the lower stratum of the warrior class, were referred to as *kumon*, or native estate officers. Like the *myōshu* these men could buy and sell land, expand agricultural production, and open markets.

Many of the landholders of the medieval period had to fight when called upon by the daimyo with whom they had entered an alliance. To this end, members of this landowning warrior class were expected to supply their own provisions and military equipment and to lead their own retainers into battle. Moreover, this upper stratum of warrior-villagers also managed groups of "vassal peasants" (*hikan-byakushō*), who in peacetime worked land leased from the samurai but who in time of war accompanied their samurai masters into battle. More numerous were the villagers called *jige-byakushō*, men who engaged solely in agriculture under the direction of the *myōshu* and *kumon* but who were not required to fulfill any military service obligation. These numerous social differences indicate that the sharp division between the warrior and peasantry that distinguished the class structure of Tokugawa society had not yet come into existence even in the late Sengoku era.

Although the proprietary control wielded by the temples, shrines, and nobility over their *shōen* in the Kinai region gradually diminished, their vestigial authority over the land lingered on until Toyotomi Hideyoshi, as part of his drive to achieve national hegemony, began a comprehensive survey of Japanese agricultural land, the famous Taikō cadastral survey, which permanently altered the nature of rural land tenure in the final decades of the sixteenth century. Consequently, the offices of military estate steward (*jitō*) and estate officer (*shōkan*) also remained until Hideyoshi's time. Some of these officials had been able to accumulate considerable holdings within the villages that comprised the *shōen* and had built up sizable military followings. Some had even managed to acquire court rank by virtue of their political connections with court-based proprietors, allowing them to become directly involved in the political machinations of the Kyoto court.

The cultivators-cum-samurai and the villagers who farmed but did not fight constituted different social classes in villages, living together and performing complementary functions. A community of such small-scale landowners usually constituted a *sō*, an autonomous body entrusted with resolving any problems that arose within its boundaries.[2] The right to convene assemblies to resolve *sō* matters was generally limited to samurai. Within the community, members with samurai status were called *otona-byakushō*, or senior farmers, and they had many special privileges. All festival activities of the village shrine dedicated to the local tutelary deity, for instance, were conducted by this group. The rise of the samurai marked an important stage in the transition from the increasingly ineffectual *shōen* system to the social institutions of Tokugawa society.

As Toyotomi Hideyoshi established his hegemony over the country, he and his fellow daimyo enacted policies that obliterated the old social composition of rural society.[3] Of all his policies, Hideyoshi's nationwide survey of all land under cultivation did more than anything else to redefine the composition of the peasant class and to establish the amount of land tax that the cultivators were capable of delivering to the overlord. Political motivations accompanied the social and economic aspects of the survey, for this was also Hideyoshi's means for safeguarding the authority he had acquired through conquest, as it enabled him to measure more accurately the worth of the fiefs he granted to his band of retainers.

The first land survey was carried out in Yamashiro Province in 1582, a month after Hideyoshi had hunted down Akechi Mitsuhide and extracted revenge for his having killed Oda Nobunaga. As the survey teams moved out across Japan, they discovered that not all villages were equally receptive to the inspection. In Kyushu, for instance, Hideyoshi was obliged to proceed more cautiously, because of the strength of the hostile local samurai. When one of Hideyoshi's commanders did begin a survey there, the indigenous samurai rose up in an ill-fated rebellion that was quashed by daimyo forces mobilized

---

2 The historical significance of *sō* is discussed in Keiji Nagahara, with Kozo Yamamura, "Village Communities and Daimyo Power," in John Whitney Hall and Takeshi Toyoda, eds., *Japan in the Muromachi Age* (Berkeley and Los Angeles: University of California Press, 1977), pp. 107–23.

3 Hideyoshi's career and policies are covered in Mary Elizabeth Berry, *Hideyoshi* (Cambridge, Mass.: Harvard University Press, 1982); and George Elison, "Hideyoshi, the Bountiful Minister," in George Elison and Bardwell L. Smith, eds. *Warlords, Artists, & Commoners: Japan in the Sixteenth Century* (Honolulu: University of Hawaii Press, 1981), pp. 223–44.

from throughout Kyushu. But soon after this, Hideyoshi was finally able to open up the entire island of Kyushu to survey teams. In 1590, after the Kantō and the Tōhoku regions were subjugated, Hideyoshi ordered a survey for the entire Tōhoku region. To encourage compliance, he promised to destroy the castles of any warrior who resisted and to slaughter all peasants who complained.

Survey teams measured the area of land cultivated by individual farmers, estimated the average productivity of the region, and on this basis calculated the potential yield of each plot of land. This calculation was referred to as the *kokudaka*, an assessment of the land's productive capacity in terms of *koku* (approximately five bushels) of rice. The name of the cultivator was entered into the cadastral register next to this figure. Before Hideyoshi's survey, landownership was usually verified through a process known as *sashidashi*, or a call for the submission of pertinent documents. The landowner would present documents describing his holdings, both fiefs and hereditary lands, together with documentary evidence to support his claims. Under Hideyoshi's procedures, however, verification of landownership by initiative from below was no longer considered adequate. Instead, the impetus now came from above. Typically, a proprietor dispatched his own officials to the countryside to measure all of the agricultural and residential land in a certain region, using the *chō* (approximately one hectare) as their standard. The "cultivator" listed in each entry of the register was then held responsible for paying the annual land rent, whether or not he actually tilled the land.

Regional differences were common, however. For instance, Yamashiro, the province surrounding the capital city of Kyoto, never came under the control of a strong, independent daimyo. Rather, it long remained an area of competition among small warrior families seeking influence in the Muromachi bakufu. The *myōshu* who served as estate officials or military estate stewards were rewarded with benefice land (*kyūbun*) for their service, and they were also allowed to buy up *myōshu* rights to additional landholdings. These privileges enabled many of the *myōshu* to accumulate extensive holdings, and a growing number became samurai. As a result, the gap widened between those with samurai status and those who remained mere peasants. Some of the landed samurai left their villages to become vassals of the nobility, but most chose to remain in their villages. When Hideyoshi's survey teams came to the lands in Yamashiro that belonged to the nobility and the religious organizations, the samurai and functionaries of the religious establishment who still resided in the villages were classified as "cultivators" (*sakunin*), even though they served simply as collectors of rent from the actual families who tilled the land. This meant that the actual cultivators, in this instance, were not accorded any status in the registers.

Consequently, historical debate has focused on questions of when and under what conditions the separation of status in rural society eventually took place.[4] In regions where the aims of Hideyoshi's survey were fully realized, the actual cultivator was usually recognized in the survey registers as the *sakunin;* in such areas most of the former warrior families, having relinquished their lands, did not appear on the register. Registration became more complex when Hideyoshi reassigned daimyo to different domains, however. In such circumstances, some of the rural vassals accompanied their lords to the new domains, but most remained behind in their villages. At this point they lost their official status as samurai and were carried on the village registers as *sakunin*, which meant that now the actual cultivator of the land might be listed below them in the register, separated by the character *bun*. This practice was known as *bunzuke kisai*, or joint registration, and was most common to Shinano and the provinces of the Kantō.

One objective that Hideyoshi hoped to achieve through the use of surveys was to establish a system of agriculture based on the small, independent farmer (*shono*). Discrete social units consisting of members of the immediate family were to become the principal source of the annual land revenues, and the act of cultivation was now deemed as the most important criterion for determining who possessed the land and who paid the annual rent. This basic intent can be further discerned from pertinent pronouncements issued during the late sixteenth century. A decree promulgated by Hideyoshi in 1594, for instance, forbade any peasant family from living with a collaterally related family if both families had independent incomes, and it further ordered such families to construct separate residences.[5] Similarly, Asano Nagamasa's decree of 1587 prohibited the upper stratum of

4 Among the major interpretive works are Araki Moriaki, *Taikō kenchi to kokudakasei* (Tokyo: Nihon hōsō shuppan kyōkai, 1959, 1982); Wakita Osamu, *Shokuhō seiken no bunseki*, 2 vols. (Tokyo: Tōkyō daigaku shuppankai, 1975–7); Osamu Wakita, "The Emergence of the State in Sixteenth Century Japan: From Oda to Tokugawa," *Journal of Japanese Studies* 8 (Summer 1982): 343–67; Kanzaki Akitoshi, *Kenchi* (Tokyo: Kyōikusha, 1983); and Miyakawa Mitsuru, *Taikō kenchi ron*, 3 vols. (Tokyo: Ochanomizu shobō, 1957–63).

5 Editor's note: Unless otherwise specified, the factual material for this article is contained in the very rich corpus of scholarship that Professor Furushima has published in Japanese. Those wishing further details should see his *Nihon nōgyōshi* and his *Kinsei keizaishi no kiso katei – nengu shūdatsu to kyōdōtai* (Tokyo: Iwanami shoten, 1978); *Tochi ni kizamareta rekishi* (Tokyo: Iwanami shoten, 1969); and *Sangyōshi* (Tokyo: Yamakawa shuppansha, 1966). These have been reprinted in *Furushima Toshio chosakushū*, 10 vols. (Tokyo: Tōkyō daikaku shuppankai, 1974).

peasantry from employing tenant farmers to work their lands, and it
stipulated that the actual cultivator of the land had to forward the
annual land rent directly to the proprietor in order to fulfill his obligations as a cultivator, thus preventing the village upper class and officialdom from employing peasants without remuneration.

The nature of Hideyoshi's prohibition against peasant ownership of
weapons was revealed in another of his well-known policies, the
"sword hunt," announced in a decree dated 1587/7. The previous year
a rebellion in the province of Higo, led by local samurai and supported
by elements of the cultivator-warrior stratum of rural society, had been
suppressed only with great difficulty. In the wake of this incident,
Hideyoshi punished many samurai, and in the following year he prohibited peasants from bearing weapons of any kind. Impounded were
long swords as well as short swords, bows, spears, and firearms.

The total disarmament of the peasantry throughout the country
moved in pace with the pacification of the daimyo. Previously,
Nobunaga had depended on village warriors to fill out the ranks of his
spear columns and infantry corps, and when the flintlock became the
major weapon of warfare, they constituted the bulk of his musket
corps and were officially designated as samurai. On the other hand, as
Hideyoshi conducted land surveys and sword hunts, the former samurai who elected to remain in the village were no longer permitted to
bear arms. They now had their lands confirmed by being listed in the
survey registers as cultivators. Thus, these measures helped support
the newly erected barrier between the farmer and warrior, and the two
most important social groups of society were henceforth differentiated
not only economically but also by social status, as symbolized by the
bearing of swords. Of course, in rural areas farmers were permitted to
keep guns for hunting and to fire blanks in order to prevent wildlife
from destroying crops. They were, however, expected to register these
guns with regional officials. The size of the ammunition they used was
regulated, and the number of guns held by a village was checked
annually.

Hideyoshi also sought to implement what can be called his small,
independent farmer policy by prohibiting cultivators from migrating
from their home villages or changing occupations. Consequently, although the samurai would accompany a daimyo who was transferred
to a new domain, the peasants remained in place in their home villages. Daimyo sought to maintain or, if possible, to increase the number of households subject to payment of the annual land tax (*nengu*).
This aim was repeatedly stressed in the ordinances banning the flight

of cultivators, especially those who held official posts. When the number of farm families within a village decreased because of unavoidable
mishaps, such as the death of a household head, the samurai officials
demanded that village officials seek assistance from the farmer's
widow and his surviving children to make certain that either their
family or another would continue to cultivate the holding and pay
taxes.

Still other policies, enacted later during the Tokugawa period, also
promoted stability for the small-scale independent farmer. One matter
of special concern was the effort to maintain the viability of agricultural households. A decree in 1649 dealt with a father's bequest to his
children, and his wish to register each of his children who were engaged in agriculture. Not only did this decree acknowledge the
farmer's right to divide the property, but it also recognized each of the
inheritors as independent farmers. In the Kinai region in the seventeenth century, many personal servants (genin) began to acquire their
own homes, and most gained official recognition as independent cultivators and full members of the village as well.

Two important decrees that significantly influenced affairs in the
countryside were the prohibition against the permanent alienation of
farmlands (dempata eitai baibai no kinshi) and the decree limiting the
division of land (bunchi seigen rei).[6] Such prohibitions codified many
measures announced earlier by individual daimyo before the appearance of Hideyoshi. According to the house laws issued by the Imagawa
family of Tōtōmi in 1553, for instance, the sale (or mortgage) of
private lands for a fixed time period after prior notification of the
authorities was permitted, but the decree still prohibited the permanent alienation of land.[7] A placard from Kaga domain dated 1615
prohibited the sale of agricultural land, and a 1631 decree stipulated
that when rice fields were sold, the purchaser was required to collect
the annual land-tax payments from the original cultivator, serve as
proxy for the seller, and promise not to sell the land later.[8] The prohibition against the permanent alienation of land was not incorporated into
bakufu law until 1643. Up to that time, village deeds clearly recorded
instances of the permanent sale of agricultural land. Thereafter, instances of mortgaging and foreclosure continued to occur, and al

---

6 Furushima, Nihon nōgyōshi, chap. 7. See also Furushima Toshio chosakushū, vol. 3, pp. 49–59
7 Katsumata Shizuo, "Imagawa Kana mokuroku," in Chūsei seiji shakai shisō, vol. 21 of Nihon
   shisō taikei (Tokyo: Iwanami shoten, 1972).
8 Nakamura Kichiji, Kinsei shoki nōseishi kenkyū (Tokyo: Iwanami shoten, 1938), p. 364.

though the prohibition was often repeated, the transfer of land became quite widespread by the beginning of the eighteenth century.[9]

Decrees that limited the subdivision of land also restricted the redistribution of land to children other than the eldest son in those cases in which the family head held less than a defined minimum amount of land. This minimum requirement varied from domain to domain and not infrequently changed over time, but a figure of ten *koku* was common. The first appearance of this sort of inheritance restriction came in the year 1673, when most people considered approximately one hectare of land as the minimum needed to support an ordinary small family for a year, and hence to ensure perpetual consanguineous possession.[10]

The cadastral surveys generally dealt only with cultivated land and residential plots. Individual possession and utilization of forestland and communal brushland, as well as the use of the lakes, seas, and coastlands, did not come under the jurisdiction of any clearly stated measure similar to the survey. In the sixteenth century, the rapid growth of waterborne commerce led to an increased demand for shipbuilding materials which, along with the growing demand for building materials for castles, warrior residences, and the houses and stores of the merchants, stipulated the demand for lumber. Consequently, many villages began communally to cut timber to sell commercially. Forestland also served as a crucial source of fuel necessary for the farmer's subsistence. Grass from pastures and forests provided fodder for both the samurai's riding horses and the farmers' own workhorses and oxen.

Even more importantly, woodlots became the single most important source of green fertilizer. Under the *shōen* system, the use of mountain woodlands, the collection of grasses for fertilizer, and fishing in the lakes and seas usually were regulated according to long-established customs that obviated the need for official guidelines. Local custom also prevailed with respect to the use of village communal forests and brushlands. Such lands might be owned by an estate proprietor or his officials who were empowered to grant access to the stewards, the *myōshu*, and the peasants who depended on such lands. Even after the Taikō survey clearly established the peasantry as a landed class, such long-standing local practices would not change until well into the Edo period.

9 *Furushima Toshio chosakushū*, vol. 3, pp. 57–8.   10 Ibid., pp. 59–61.

THE SOCIAL COMPOSITION OF THE EARLY MODERN VILLAGE

Although the basic intent of the Taikō cadastral survey was to record the names of the heads of small peasant families that cultivated the land in order to bring social stability to the countryside and to make these families responsible for paying annual land taxes, this goal was not completely realized everywhere. Had it been, it would have resulted in a situation in which all peasants owned and worked parcels of land of approximately the same size. However, entries in registers dating from the late sixteenth and early seventeenth centuries reveal a considerable disparity in the assessed value of the lands held by individual farmers, even among inhabitants of the same village. A few large families might cultivate lands whose productive capacities amounted to as much as two hundred or three hundred *koku* of rice. On the other hand, some individual peasant families held less than five *koku,* and the putative yields of others did not amount to even one *koku.* This inequity arose because many village samurai in the regions of Kinai and the mountainous reaches of Kantō and Tōsan (the old provinces of Hida, Shinano, and Kai) were permitted to retain rights of possession and cultivation over their hereditary lands. These samurai-turned-peasants might hold lands assessed at upwards of three hundred *koku,* and they were able to manage such large possessions only by incorporating branch families into their own households and by employing hereditary servants, known as *hikan, nago,* or *kadoya.* These house servants were owned by the heads of households and could be sold or traded.

In contrast, a more common pattern could be seen among the farmers who worked lands estimated at ten to twenty *koku* and who cultivated these lands by relying on the labor of their immediate family and relatives. Those farm families who worked only tiny plots were forced to lease land from wealthier farmers and to pay rent in kind or in labor service. In some very remote villages, there were even some farmers who still used the primitive slash-and-burn and field rotation techniques, and these lands were usually not subject to the annual land tax.

Inequality in the distribution of individual family holdings was also reflected in social relationships within the villages. Those farmers who possessed large landholdings were able to monopolize the prized, honorary functions in ceremonies that evoked the village's protective deities. In villages near Kyoto such families in fact were considered to have the status of samurai. In Honden village in Kawachi, for example, only the upper-class villagers participated in the local religious ceremonies, and they claimed to be descended from the founders of the village.[11] Such farmers were referred to as "the rooted" (*neoi*) or as "the pioneers" (*kusawake*).

Quite common in the Kinki region and certain other areas in western Japan was the monopoly of religious and ceremonial duties by a *miyaza*, or shrine council, composed of the heads of landholding village families.[12] Moreover, in the early Togugawa period, village ceremonies were typically conducted by a select "privileged council," or *kabuza*. Still other customs that served to differentiate the older families who constituted the village's upper class from the rest of the villagers survived throughout Japan well into the Tokugawa period. Even in the early nineteenth century, elite villagers in Mino Province were still referred to as "elder" or "head" farmers (*otona-* or *kashira-byakushō*). In Kanō domain, official government edicts gave legal sanction to the traditional housing and clothing privileges that were reserved for this class. The smaller, more ordinary farmers were called "lower" or "adjunct" farmers (*jige-* or *waki-byakushō*), and they were supposed to live in more humble dwellings.[13] In some villages, the older and lower-class farmers even patronized separate shrines.

The gap between the upper-class farmers and the rest of the farming population was both a product of traditional social custom and a consequence of economic privileges and laws favorable to the elite rural families. For instance, in the Sengoku period it was common for only head farmers to have the right to own forestlands. Moreover, riparian works were often carried out by either a *sō* or a coalition of *myōshu*, and this often meant that the village's upper class was able to retain authority over the distribution of reservoir water. Such privileges and the concomitant economic advantages continued to be enjoyed by select groups well into the Edo period, and the accompanying social differences that had arisen among the inhabitants of pre-Tokugawa villages were often preserved for a considerable length of time.

Although the nationwide land surveys of the late sixteenth and early seventeenth centuries established a rough kind of horizontal equity among the cultivators, by requiring everyone listed in the survey registers to work the land and to pay the annual land taxes, in fact, condi-

11 See chap. 5 of Furushima Toshio and Nagahara Keiji, eds., *Shōhin seisan to kisei jinushisei* (Tokyo: Tōkyō daigaku shuppankai, 1954).
12 See the entry "miyaza" in Terao Hirotaka, comp., *Nihon keizaishi jiten*, vol 2 (Tokyo: Nihon hyōronsha, 1940).
13 See doc. 119 ("Motorogun Miederamura teishō") in *Gifu kenshi shiryō*, vol. 4.

tions in the early Tokugawa period allowed a privileged subclass to continue to dominate village politics. In some part this can be attributed to the concern of many daimyo governments with protecting small-scale farmers from falling victim to the insolvency that could be brought on by the combined onus of tax payments and the frequently heavy expenses associated with conducting official village duties. It should also be remembered that early Tokugawa village officials were often descended from a privileged class of local elites who had held official posts assigned by the earlier civilian proprietors or military lords. Thus they could claim that a prestigious lineage entitled them to positions of authority, especially as village headmen.

Beginning about the mid-seventeenth century, however, the practice of limiting formal membership in village organizations as well as positions of leadership to select members of the village's upper class gradually began to change, especially in response to transformations in the village economy and domain politics. Sometimes the initiative came from below. In many places where the "privileged councils," or *kabuza*, had dominated village affairs, for instance, protests by lower-class villagers, who not infrequently took their demands to daimyo or shogunal courts, brought about the establishment of "village councils," or *muraza*, which permitted all village families to be represented in such ceremonies. Another example, this time concerning access to forestlands, comes from Horado village in the mountainous region of northern Mino. In 1655 the long-standing claim by wealthy village landholders to the exclusive use of nearby forestlands was challenged by lower-class farmers who had been denied entry into the forest to collect materials for use as fertilizers. The dispute was eventually settled in favor of the lower-status farmers, and most of the forestland was opened for communal use.[14]

Another factor leading to change was the increasing tendency to apportion taxes and other dues in proportion to a family's holdings relative to the entire village *kokudaka*. This process can be traced in some detail for the villages of Tōdō domain, located in the ancient provinces of Iga and Ise.[15] In principle the annual land rent was based on the putative yields recorded in the cadastral survey, and it was paid by the cultivators as a percentage of these assessments. During the

14 Furushima, *Kinsei keizaishi no kiso katei*, pp. 189–92.
15 See the 1750 document "Sōkokushi," edited by Tōdō Kōbun, for specific ordinances. Particularly relevant are the details for 1692. This document was published in 1941 by the Kyōiku kai of Ueda-machi in Mie Prefecture.

early Tokugawa period, however, the Tōdō village officials, not the common cultivators, came to be held responsible for ensuring that their village as a unit delivered the specified amount of its total tax assessment to the appropriate domain official. Indeed, village leaders were sometimes even held hostage when defaults occurred.

At first, documents imposing the annual land tax tended merely to list a figure that represented the total *kokudaka* for all old and new paddies and dry fields within the village and then demanded a certain percentage of tax based on that total, thus treating the village as a single tax entity. Consequently, within any given village, taxes often were not apportioned according to an individual farmer's assessment as specified in the original cadastral survey records. Eventually the annual tax assessment documents began to include clauses providing that village meetings, in which all village households were represented, would decide how to apportion the village's tax burden. The earliest instances in Tōdō domain of villagewide participation in the apportionment process date back to 1610, but the practice did not appear in the tax documents of Tōdō domain until approximately 1650. Furthermore, the apportionments agreed upon within the Tōdō villages had to be written down and witnessed by everyone, and even other minor taxes, originally paid exclusively by upper-class households, were now divided into equal amounts and paid by all village households.

To continue with the Tōdō example, in 1649 the domain government conducted a survey of the rural households within its boundaries. A document summarizing the results of the survey noted that the number of village households had increased markedly, but it remarked on a decline in the number of so-called official farmers (*yakugi no hyakushō*), a term used in Tōdō to refer to households that had existed in the late Sengoku period and that were traditionally held responsible for paying an annual household levy known as the *yanami yaku*, a cash substitute for an older corvée levy. Based on this finding, domain officials recommended that the number of households subject to this levy be decreased in poor villages and increased in wealthier villages. This policy enabled the domain to restore the number of households obligated to pay this levy to a figure roughly equivalent to what it had been in previous years. Consequently, the term "official farmers" had now come to indicate one's degree of wealth, and not one's pedigree. Status within the village was now bestowed according to the farmer's actual holdings and his ability to pay the village assessment. Those who were able to pay the entire family allotment were considered "full" members. Less wealthy peasants who only paid seven or eight tenths of the tax were called "seventy percenters" or "eighty percenters."

Policies designed to alter the number and composition of officially recognized village members reflect a shift in the pattern of landholding that was taking place as a result of the sale of farmland. There was an increasing tendency among villagers to apportion all taxes, not just the land tax, in accordance with the *kokudaka* assessment for each family. For example, a 1690 decree in Tōdō ordered that village maintenance fees (*muranyūyō*) were to be borne by the entire village. Village officials were also prohibited from taking other farmers along on trips to the domain capital, nor were they to employ other farmers to cultivate their own lands. The decree also stipulated that servants and members of extended families, who had previously been denied standing as separate householders, now could become independent farmers if they received partitioned lands and established separate, detached domiciles. Two years later, in 1692, another decree stipulated that "from this date village maintenance fees are to be paid as a proportion of an individual family's *kokudaka* and are not to be divided among village households in a manner that fails to reflect differences in wealth." This decree also stated that "official farmers" had to pay the village maintenance fee as a proportion of their *kokudaka*. Significantly, the document justified this policy by noting that if equal fees were paid by all village households, the poorer farmers would be put at a disadvantage.

In short, the social structure commonly found in most villages in the latter half of the Tokugawa period emerged after tax assessments began to be levied in proportion to the size of an individual farmer's holdings and started to take account of disparities in wealth. New nomenclature also appeared that reflected these changes in village social stratification. For example, from the beginning of the eighteenth century, all cultivators with independent holdings were referred to as *hyakushō* or *hombyakushō*, and the poorer families who did not possess their own holdings, and hence did not have a *kokudaka* assignment, were known as *mizunomi* (literally, "those who drink water").

As the possession of holdings included in a village's official *kokudaka* became the sole criterion for determining *hyakushō* status, official administrative posts, such as village headmen, elder, group household head, and farmers' representative (*hyakushōdai*), gradually replaced the mixed bag of village-level positions that had been recognized in the early Tokugawa years.[16] Moreover, the method of selecting village officials became more open. In the early years of the Tokugawa period, village officials were usually appointed by the domain government, and almost all were drawn from the same traditional upper-class families, often referred to as the *otona-byakushō*, or elder farmers, who had dominated so many other aspects of village life. But as landholding patterns and taxation methods changed, new people felt that they had achieved a more equitable standing in the village, and so they began to press for administrative changes that would give them a larger voice in village political affairs.

In 1841, for example, a coalition of village officials and *otona-byakushō* of a village in Mino Province submitted a document to the local lord that set out guidelines for resolving a dispute that had erupted over nominating a man to serve as village headman.[17] These guidelines established new rules to govern the election of future village officials by providing that two members from a group of six former elders (*toshiyori*) would serve alternately as headman for three years while the other four continued to serve as elders. This measure essentially created a six-member council to govern the village. Routine village functions were to be carried out by the six elders in consultation. All "elder farmers" were allowed to participate in discussions of special matters such as the apportionment of the annual land tax, the official domain inspection of the rice crop, and the provision of lodging for visiting officials. Among the thirteen signatories of the document, social distinctions remained. Only one wrote *hyakushō* under his name. The remaining twelve listed themselves as *otona-byakushō*, one of whom was a farmer's representative, and six of whom were elders.

The sharp social barriers between farmers who had the status necessary to become village officials and the lower-class farmers began to crumble even more after the 1720s when disturbances and even violent demonstrations flared up concerning the election of ordinary peasants as village officials, usually in regions where viable markets had developed for agricultural goods.[18] For instance, in 1642 the shogunate

---

16 For a discussion of village offices in English, see Harumi Befu, "Duty, Reward, Sanction and Power: The Four Cornered Office of the Tokugawa Village Headman," in Bernard S. Silberman and Harry D. Harootunian, eds., *Modern Japanese Leadership* (Tucson: University of Arizona Press, 1966), pp. 25–50; and Harumi Befu, "Village Autonomy and Articulation with the State," in John Whitney Hall and Marius B. Jansen, eds., *Studies in the Institutional History of Early Modern Japan* (Princeton, N.J.: Princeton University Press, 1968), pp. 301–14.

17 *Gifu kenshi shiryō*, vol. 4, doc. 133, pp. 594–6.

18 A detailed discussion of this process in Kurashiki can be found in Thomas C. Smith, *The Agrarian Origins of Modern Japan* (Stanford, Calif.: Stanford University Press, 1959), pp. 180–200.

stationed an administrative representative (*daikan*) at Kurashiki in Bitchū, and the town prospered as a port from which the shogunate's rice tax was shipped. From this time, thirteen men, known as the *koroku* (ancient lineages), held positions of authority as village officials and landlords.

Beginning in 1700, new fields were developed near the sea, and cotton cultivation became increasingly widespread around Kurashiki. At the same time, wealthy men who engaged in the cotton trade began to appear. They became known as the *shinroku* (new lineages), and beginning in the late eighteenth century they opened a contest, at times edging on violence, with the old lineages for positions of authority in the village. By the 1818–30 period the so-called new lineages had emerged as the community's political elite. Under conditions such as these, elections in which ballots were formally cast for candidates began to be held in many areas throughout Japan. Peasant grievances over the unfair distribution of the land-tax burden and the unequal imposition of the village maintenance fees were the primary catalysts for these disturbances. Important also was dissatisfaction over the monopoly by an elite few of honorary positions in village festivals. More ordinary farmers now questioned the governing abilities of the once-wealthy farmers whose fortunes had declined but who nonetheless continued to hold sway over village politics.

LAND-TAX REVENUE AND GOVERNMENT FINANCES

Wealth came from many sources in the Tokugawa period. The mines and forests produced important primary resources, and Chapter 11 in this volume explains the dynamic growth in commerce during the seventeenth and eighteenth centuries. Yet for all the vitality and excitement associated with the expansion of cities and trade, it must be remembered that the rice taxes collected from rural villages constituted the basic wealth of the country throughout the entire early modern epoch. An appreciation of the important role of the peasantry in the economy can be gained from examining the income of the largest and most important of the military families, the Tokugawa house, for the last century of the regime.

The extensive Tokugawa domain was officially assessed at between 3.5 million to 4 million *koku*. By comparison, the domain of the next largest lord, the Maeda house of Kaga, was officially appraised at just over 1 million *koku*, although the annual rice crop was usually nearly a third more than that. The Tokugawa family enjoyed many other economic advantages beyond its landholdings. First, the Tokugawa house had the benefit of the services of an enormous bureaucracy that it entrusted with the task of administering its lands scattered throughout Japan. This bureaucracy was distinguished by its extensive organization, its systematic auditing of accounts, and other features that were later adopted by the Meiji civil service. Moreover, the Tokugawa house acquired control over the output of all mines throughout Japan, including the rich gold mines of Sado and the extensive silver mines of Ikuno and Ōmori. In addition the Tokugawa house managed the large tracts of forests situated in the Hida and Kiso mountains. And finally, the Tokugawa family was able to levy taxes on commerce and industry in Edo, Osaka, Kyoto, and other cities under its direct administration and to collect revenues from the Nagasaki trade.

Because only secondary sources survive, we do not have accurate figures on the shogunate's revenues for the entire Edo period. However, it is possible to make calculations derived from documents that are extant for certain years. In 1844, for instance, a year for which good documentation exists, gross bakufu revenues amounted to 4,011,766 ryō of gold, of which 1,827,879 ryō was categorized as "regular income" and 2,183,887 ryō as "extraordinary revenues."[19] The single most important source of revenue was the land tax, which amounted to the equivalent of some 1,660,000 ryō in 1844. The shogunate also netted about 583,000 ryō from loan repayments; 839,000 ryō as profits garnered from a recoinage that lowered the precious metal content of the coins it issued; and 23,629 ryō from forced loans and gifts extracted from wealthy merchants and peasants. Lesser but still significant amounts of income were derived from mining revenues (62,000 ryō) and transport fees (71,000 ryō).

Clearly, the land tax was the major source of revenues. Such tax payments made up 41 percent of the bakufu's total revenues in 1844, almost twice the 21 percent of total earnings represented by the second largest source of income: recoinage profits. Daimyo who could not avail themselves of the special sources of income restricted to the Tokugawa house were even more dependent on the land tax. In Kaga domain, to take but one example, the land tax during the early decades of the nineteenth century accounted for well over 80 percent of all domain revenues, or nearly 560,000 koku of rice annually. Although Kaga's landed income was exceptionally large in absolute terms, most

19 Furushima, *Kinsei keizaishi no kiso katei.*

domains derived approximately the same percentage of their total revenues from the rice tax.[20]

It is easy to imagine the burden that fulfilling the annual tax obligations presented to the average household farm. Many specific taxes
were typically lumped together to make up the average family's annual
tax obligation. The most important of these was the "basic tax"
(*honnengu*), calculated as a proportion of the official, estimated yields
on surveyed lands. Added to this were the various miscellaneous taxes
(*komononari*) that were imposed on fixed assets: the boats that plied
the rivers and seas, the soaking bins used for making paper, the large
pots used for boiling seawater to make salt, and even the possession
and use of forestland. These taxes were usually small sums paid as user
or licensing fees rather than as a percentage of output or profit. In the
early Edo period, there was also a labor corvée imposed on each registered farm household, and this was later converted into a cash payment calculated as a percentage of *kokudaka* holdings. Another levy –
one that won little favor with local farmers – was imposed from the
mid-Tokugawa period and required the villages located along the major highways maintained by the shogunate, the Tōkaidō, Nakasendō,
Nikkō Kaidō, and Kōshū Kaidō, as well as those dotting the highways
constructed by individual daimyo, to provide packhorses for official
communications and transport.

The payment of these taxes resulted in severe hardships for most of
the peasantry, and official policies often seemed to be designed to leave
the peasants with only the minimal income necessary for their continued existence. The draconian spirit of the shogunate's officials is revealed in a few well-known sayings that have come down to us.[21]
Honda Masanobu (1538–1616), a daimyo closely allied with Tokugawa
Ieyasu, urged his officials to estimate a peasant's annual output and his
consumption needs and then to calculate the basic tax so that it would
soak up every surplus grain of rice. "The proper way to govern is to
ensure that peasants don't accumulate wealth yet don't starve either."
Ieyasu advised his rural intendants to govern the peasant by "making
certain they can neither live nor die." Kan'o Haruhide, the finance
magistrate in 1749 when the shogunate increased its tax levies, com-

20 For a general discussion of domain finances, see Aono Shunsui, *Daimyō to ryōmin* (Tokyo:
Kyōikusha, 1983); pp. 70–91; and Kitajima Masamoto, *Bakuhansei kokka kaitai katei no
kenkyū* (Tokyo: Yoshikawa kōbunkan, 1978), esp. pp. 1–28.
21 This quotation and others similar to those that follow can be found in many texts. See
Furushima, *Nihon nōgyōshi*, pp. 173–6, as well as vol. 22 (*Shiryō-hen, Nihon, kinsei-hen*) of
the *Sekai rekishi jiten* (Tokyo: Heibonsha, 1955).

pared the peasants to sesame seeds: "The harder you squeeze them, the more you can extract from them."

The harshness of the tax burden is also revealed in the expenditure records of village officials from several domains. During a normal harvest year, most peasant families could usually manage to make ends meet with the income left to them after paying the land tax. Successive poor harvests, however, could make it impossible for some households in hard-hit areas to survive. Rice production was frequently ruined by insect plagues, especially in the southwestern regions, by extended spells of cold weather during the summer growing season in the northeast, and by rain and wind damage during the autumn typhoon season across the entire country. Unseasonally cold weather brought special dread to farm villages throughout the Tokugawa period. During cool summers, outbreaks of rice blast could wipe out the year's entire rice harvest over large regions. Cold temperatures usually damaged other grain crops as well, leaving peasant families without any food at all to subsist on. During the Temmei famine, which lasted from 1782 to 1785, and the great Tempō famines that occurred in the 1830s, tens of thousands of peasants throughout Japan died from starvation and disease.

Adding to the crushing weight placed on the peasantry were the revised tax collection procedures authorized by the shogunate during the early eighteenth century in order to counter its own gradual decline in revenue collection. Many of these revisions were first ordered by the eighth shogun, Yoshimune, as part of his famous Kyōhō Reforms. Surviving documents permit a glimpse at the effect these new procedures had on tax rates and gross tax collections on shogunal lands over the subsequent century.

These changes can be divided into four distinct phases, the first covering the twenty years of the Kyōhō period itself, from 1716 to 1736. Among the reforms instituted during this period was the so-called *jōmen*, or fixed-rate system, first introduced to selected villages in 1724. Under this system, a village's tax rate would be set for a fixed period, usually three, five, or ten years. If more than 30 percent of the anticipated harvest was then destroyed by natural causes during one of the fixed periods, the tax rate would be temporarily lowered. Under the new procedures the taxation rate was reviewed after each period, and the government probably expected regular upward revisions. This reform had an immediate impact on the shogunate's income. Total annual revenues, which had previously hovered around 1.4 million *koku*, leapt immediately to 1.5 million *koku*. In 1727, the shogunate collected 1.62 million *koku*, and this caused rice prices to plunge. Five years later, in 1732, however, crop failures occurred in Kyushu and the Chūgoku region, and subsequent annual revenues returned to the 1.4 million-*koku* level.

During the second stage of reform, from 1737 to 1764, tax collections rose to new peak levels. Early in this phase, the shogunate initiated the use of the "actual inspection" method (*arige kemi*) in which the levy for each field was calculated as a fixed percentage of the putative yield, as determined by a visual inspection of the crop. This new practice permitted the shogunate's officials to monitor more closely the crop conditions, and it resulted in enhanced revenue collections. The well-known scholar and government adviser Honda Toshiaki (1744–1821), however, believed the actual inspection system to be a pernicious practice, and he attributed the frequent outbreaks of famine in the Kantō and Tōhoku regions to its widespread adoption. Be that as it may, in 1744, the revenues derived by the shogunate from land taxes reached a record high of 1.8 million *koku*. Five years later, in 1749, the system was officially extended over the entire country, and for the next sixteen years the shogunate's annual land-tax revenues ranged between 1.65 million and 1.7 million *koku*, with the exception of one year when they temporarily fell to 1.55 million *koku*.[22]

Such high levels of tax collection could not be maintained for long without inviting protest from the peasantry, who were wont to interpret any perceived hike in tax collections as unjust and unfair. Peasant attitudes had changed since 1710, the eve of the Kyōhō Reforms. Before the Kyōhō era, there were rarely more than ten incidents of violent protests by peasants in any given year. But fifteen violent protests erupted in the year following the record tax collections of 1744, and in 1749, thirty-one violent outbursts took place, with more than ten incidents recorded for each of nine of the thirteen years of the Hōreki era (1751–63).[23]

The third stage of tax reform witnessed even more agrarian unrest. In 1766, tax collections had receded to the 1.55 million-*koku* level, where they remained until 1780, only to decline rapidly again after the disastrous harvests of 1783 and 1786. These nationwide crop failures were caused by summer cold spells, which were due chiefly to the large

22 Furushima, *Kinsei keizaishi no kiso katei*, pp. 335–41.
23 Ibid., p. 271. A convenient introduction to recent interpretations concerning popular protest is Aoki Michio et al., eds., *Ikki*, 5 vols. (Tokyo: Tōkyō daigaku shuppankai, 1981–2). The most comprehensive listing of popular dissent is Aoki Kōji, *Hyakushō ikki no nenji-teki kenkyū* (Tokyo: Shinseisha, 1966).

amounts of volcanic ash thrown into the atmosphere by an eruption of Mt. Asama. The poor harvests brought on a significant number of peasant demonstrations, and the shogunate announced that penalties would be imposed on leaders of such protests and that government forces would be empowered to fire on rebellious peasants. Despite the threat of government suppression, continuing outrage against tax increases made it difficult for the shogunate to consider any further hikes.

The fourth stage spanned the period from 1787 to 1819, corresponding to the years that Matsudaira Sadanobu (1758–1829) served as senior councilor and to the first half of Shogun Ienari's administration. Although the shogunate's expenditures for the construction of temples, shrines, and coastal fortifications suddenly increased, the shogunate was able to keep its budget under control by compelling the daimyo to contribute significant portions of the expenses for these projects. Consequently, the shogunate was able to manage with less revenue, often with just 1.55 million *koku* a year, and tax rates fell accordingly. Indeed, the principal dissimilarity between the second and fourth stages was in the different rates of taxation. During the last sixteen years of the second stage (1748–64), the taxation rate hovered between 37 and 39 percent of the tax base, with the exception of one year. By contrast, during the fourth stage there were only three years in which the taxation rate approached 35 percent, and for three years the rate fell below 32 percent.

Despite the extreme hardship brought on by periodic famines and unpredictable yet sharp tax increases from time to time, living conditions for much of the peasantry improved during the course of the Edo period, thanks in part to advances in agricultural technology. A key factor in this process was that the rural upper classes accumulated large agricultural surpluses which they then used to develop and introduce the new technologies. These surpluses were a consequence of certain features of the tax collection system at the time it was first implemented. During the Taikō survey, all villages within a specified region were classified into three categories according to their total yields, and all farmland within a village was further graded as superior, average, poor, or even "especially poor" quality land. In mountainous regions, land was classified as either "mountain paddy" or "mountain field" land. In the Kinai region, the rank of "especially superior" was given to land of extremely high quality, and in other regions, similar distinctions were made among different grades of land to reflect expected variances in yields. Despite this multiplicity of grades, however, the documentary record for specific regions reveals that the gradations in the tax scale applied to lands of very different quality were actually quite small.

In the early Tokugawa period, moreover, land taxes were typically assessed as a percentage of the total village *kokudaka*, and this tended to translate into a low percentage tax rate for high-yield lands, and a relatively high tax rate for low-yield lands, if for no other reason than that the farmers who owned the better lands often had more influence in the village assemblies that apportioned the tax levy. Thus, the burden of meeting the annual tax payments fell inequitably on the small-scale farmers. Those who found themselves unable to pay their dues were forced to sell part or all of their land, falling into the status of indentured servant. While the small farmer eked out his living, the agrarian upper class, paying a lesser proportion of their yield as taxes, accumulated surpluses that provided the funds to develop and introduce new technology.

Changes in peasant life during the Edo period were also related to fluctuations in the amount of annual land-tax revenues collected over time. Thus the decline in the shogunate's tax revenues that began in the 1760s, as we noted, as well as the drop in percentage rates in the early nineteenth century, permitted some members of the agrarian class to gather funds to invest in technology. Moreover, it is clear that the amount of rice extracted through land taxes also began to level off in many individual daimyo domains during the eighteenth century.[24] This was the case in such widely separated domains as Satsuma, Kaga, and Aizu–Wakamatsu. As with shogunal lands, this left a surplus in the hands of the peasants, who could then plow them back into technological improvements or buy the new kinds of foods, clothing, and housing that did so much to change the quality of life in rural villages, as described in Chapter 13 in this volume.

IRRIGATION AND LAND RECLAMATION

Many of the rural upper classes who accumulated surpluses increasingly invested them in irrigation and land reclamation projects. They were joined in this effort by the daimyo, who anticipated that such projects would broaden their tax base by expanding rice production.[25]

24 Land taxes are discussed in Aono, *Daimyō to ryōmin*. In English, Thomas C. Smith examined the stabilization of rates, especially in Kaga domain, in his "The Land Tax in the Tokugawa Period," in Hall and Jansen, eds., *Studies*, pp. 283–99.
25 A thorough discussion of irrigation and land reclamation projects can be found in Kozo Yamamura, "Returns on Unification: Economic Growth in Japan, 1550–1560," in John Whitney Hall, Keiji Nagahara, and Kozo Yamamura, eds., *Japan Before Tokugawa: Political*

Indeed, in the late Sengoku and early Edo periods, the daimyo often took the initiative in sponsoring such projects, as they had the political authority needed to mobilize large labor forces and the capital necessary to finance these efforts.

One of the most noteworthy flood control and irrigation projects of the late sixteenth century was undertaken by the daimyo Takeda Shingen (1521–73) in the area between the Kamanashi and Fuefuki rivers to the south of Kōfu city, an area already blessed with one of Japan's highest per acre yields for wet-field rice. The Midai River, which fed into the Kamanashi, was redirected north to join the Kamanashi at a point where there are cliffs on the opposite shore. Over time, Shingen then constructed dikes that would direct water toward the Kamanashi in such a manner that whenever the rivers flooded, the spillover would flow gently onto the farmland behind the dikes. During the Edo period, these dikes were gradually moved closer to the river, and by the 1750s riparian technology had improved to a level that enabled the completion of a continuous dike encircling the entire southern section of Kōfu. During this period, the tributaries of the original Kamanashi River were then converted into irrigation canals.

Even more sophisticated projects later became possible as the Japanese improved the riparian technology available to them. For example, engineers learned how to construct sluices near the rapids that usually formed at the point where mountain rivers spilled out onto the plains, thus converting natural waterways into irrigation canals, so that a constant flow of water could be maintained through both dry and rainy seasons. Moreover, by the seventeenth century, domain construction offices were able to plan more complexly designed systems of reservoirs. In Sanuki Province on Shikoku, for example, construction teams blocked off ravines to provide reservoir storage during the autumn and winter, drawn from the upper reaches of rivers in that area.[26] These new reservoirs were linked to older, existing reservoirs in order to form an interlocking irrigation system that would ensure a steady supply of water throughout the growing season.

The new castle towns often benefited from these riparian projects. In Kanazawa, for instance, engineers designed a system of inter-

Consolidation and Economic Growth, 1500–1650 (Princeton, N.J.: Princeton University Press, 1981), pp. 327–72. Also see William W. Kelly, "Water Control in Tokugawa Japan: Irrigation Organization in a Japanese River Basin, 1600–1870," in Cornell University East Asian Papers, no. 31 (Ithaca, N.Y.: Cornell University Press, 1982).
26 Furushima, Nihon nōgyōshi, pp. 231–2.

linking canals several dozens of miles in length that drew water from two rivers and delivered it to key points within the city. They even invented a unique siphon pump to move the water uphill at one point.[27] Initially, the city of Edo relied on Inogashira Pond, located some twenty kilometers to the west of the city, for its water supply. But from 1650, the city began to channel water in from the upper reaches of the Tama River, after an extensive canal system was laid out on the plateau west of Edo.[28]

Providing for a more constant supply of water was only one of many methods used to increase agricultural production during the Edo period. Land was also reclaimed from the bays and shallow tidal marshes facing the Pacific Ocean and the seas off western Kyushu, as well as from Seto Inland Sea. Most of this land was very fertile, as it was composed of rich silt deposited by rivers. Engineers constructed breakwaters, and the trapped saline water was pumped or allowed to flow out through the gates at low tide. The scale of reclamation projects grew considerably as technology improved. Often by the 1700s more than one hundred hectares of land were being reclaimed at a time.

At first, only the daimyo had the resources to carry out large-scale reclamation schemes, but during the seventeenth century, wealthy merchants and peasants also began to finance coastal projects. The funding provided by Yoshida Kambei (1611–86) for the reclamation of a portion of Edo Bay was one of the earliest examples of the merchants' participation in large-scale land development.[29] There, fields were reclaimed from the delta region of the Ōoka River, situated just behind what would later become the port of Yokohama. Drainage work for the project was initiated in 1656, although construction had to be halted the next year owing to tidal damage. Work was resumed in 1659, and the project was completed only after Edo merchants responded to a call for additional investment funds from Yoshida, whose name then became linked with the project. Another example comes from Osaka, where in 1685 merchants began to invest in the reclamation of the marshland located near the delta of the Yodo River.[30] Merchant-inspired land development projects continued for several decades in this region. The reclamation of an old riverbed of the

---

27 The siphon system is described in Nishi Setsuko, "Tatsumi yōsui repōto," *Rekishi techō* 2 (May 1974): 31–4.

28 Doboku gakkai, ed., *Meiji izen Nihon dobokushi*, vol. 7 (Tokyo: Iwanami shoten, 1936), pp. 1436–42.

29 Yokohama shiyakusho, ed., *Yokohama-shi shi*, vol. 3 (Yokohama: Yokohama shiyakusho, 1958), pp. 670–8.

30 Matsuyoshi Sadao, *Shinden no kenkyū* (Tokyo: Yūhikaku, 1936).

Yamato River, begun in 1707, as well as the drainage of additional marshes helped make the Osaka area the nation's most productive agricultural region, starting in the 1700s.

Many projects during the Edo period were made possible by the joint effort and investments of both political overlords and wealthy farmers and merchants. Governing officials, of course, saw such projects as a means of expanding the tax base, whereas farmers and merchants viewed them as a means of enhancing their own income. One famous example of such a joint effort occured in Echigo in the 1720s when the shogunate authorized Edo merchants to provide the financial backing that permitted local farmers to convert coastal swamps into paddy fields.

In some cases, however, land reclamation became a new source of friction that threatened village harmony or led to disagreements between farmers and government authorities. Kumazawa Banzan (1619–91), a seventeenth-century Confucian scholar, noted that the large amount of reclaimed paddy in Bizen Province would deprive the older fields of water and fertilizer.[31] To take another example, the increase in the amount of arable land forced some daimyo in Sanuki to measure the water level of the reservoirs during the spring and then to set limits on the acreage that the farmers could plant in rice during that year.[32]

Farmers everywhere were keen to secure sufficient supplies of water for the spring planting season and the months of rapid plant growth during the summer. This not infrequently set off a sharp competition among farmers from the same, or even different, villages whose irrigation systems shared the same water source. Consequently, care had to be taken to allocate water equitably over the entire irrigation system. Gates, locks, and other facilities were constructed to guarantee a fair distribution of water, and watering was often done on a daily or even hourly rotational basis. Decisions regarding the dispensation of water essentially defined the length of the rice-planting season and determined where the seedlings, later transplanted to rice paddies, were first set and the amount of land that could be planted with a winter grain crop. Because individual households were unable to secure water supplies on their own, they were forced into cooperating with other members of their or neighboring villages in order to carry out their

---

31 See Kumazawa's "Shugi gaisho," in Takimoto Seiichi, ed., *Nihon keizai sōsho*, vol. 33 (Tokyo: Nihon keizai sōsho kanōkai, 1917), p. 222. Chapter 3 in vol. 3 of my *Furushima Toshio chosakushū* has many examples in which people complain to the shogunate concerning the opening of new fields.
32 Furushima, *Nihon nōgyōshi*, pp. 234–5.

agricultural tasks. When quarrels erupted, officials often had to be called in to mediate a settlement.

The same was especially true in areas where double cropping was practiced. Typically, the second crop was barley, wheat, or rapeseed. In order to plant such grains, a farmer had to drain and till the fields after the fall harvest. Because the fields were kept dry during the winter, they required proportionately more water when reflooded in the spring, a time of peak demand. This contributed to water shortages and sparked additional disagreements among neighbors. To dissipate such frictions, officials in Tōdō domain in 1649 moved to discourage double cropping, ordering its peasants to reduce the size of the winter grain crop to two-thirds of normal yields. The same decree also stipulated that the land-tax rate would remain unchanged even when there were crop failures, and the officials warned that farmers who diverted their labor to tilling their newly reclaimed fields, to the detriment of their registered paddy fields, would not be granted tax relief.

AGRICULTURAL USE OF FORESTLAND

The availability of good land and an adequate supply of water were not, in themselves, sufficient to guarantee stable agricultural outputs during the early modern period. Farmers also had to maintain the fertility of their paddy fields by gathering shrubs, shoots, and grasses from marginal lands for use as green manure or for mixing with horse and cow manure. Nearby woodlands provided many of life's other necessities – wood for sheds, outbuildings, irrigation canals, and firewood; roof thatch; and such supplementary foods as greens, fruits, and mushrooms. Tree buds, grass shoots, and roots also served as emergency foods that helped the peasants survive, however miserably, through the worst stretches of famine. Because the woodlands played an indispensable role in the agricultural process and the daily lives of the agrarian population, the peasantry was intensely concerned about their supervision and use.

During the Sengoku period, the valuable woodlands and marginal wastelands usually belonged to the estate proprietor, and individual peasants could gain entry only on the basis of negotiations worked out between the proprietor and the village community, which over time tended to coalesce into an accepted definition of custom and precedent governing access to the bounty of the forests. In the Edo period, two forces worked to change these local traditions. The first came from the top down as daimyo moved to assert their authority over their realm.

From the late sixteenth century, daimyo needed building materials in order to construct their castle towns. Even later, demand remained high as the country's cities were ravaged periodically by fires. Consequently the daimyo regulated the felling of trees that could be used for construction materials. At first, they tended to declare the dense forests in remote mountains that contained the largest trees as being off limits to the farmers, though the lords still permitted villagers access to the smaller woodlands that surrounded the agricultural plots. Later, many daimyo barred the peasants from cutting zelkova, cedar, cypress, fir, hemlock, and other prime timber on these smaller woodlands. In time, the shogunate and most daimyo designated all timber stands as "the lord's forest" and strictly prohibited any unauthorized cutting of trees.[33]

The second force for change came from inside the village community itself. In the medieval period, the local conventions worked out with proprietors had typically provided only for a village's elite, landholding families to have access to the forests, whereas the commoner farmers usually could enter the forest only by virtue of their established relationships with the elites. In time, however, the commoner farmers became inclined to consider such privileges as rights, and they came to view nearby forestland as communal property from which they could gather firewood and materials for building and for aging into fertilizer. In many places by the mid-seventeenth century, villagers were demanding that the forests be opened to the whole community. Government officials were usually invited to mediate such disputes, and the typical solution was to reserve a small portion of the forestland for the person claiming ownership and to open most of the remaining land for communal use.

Although the documentation for this evolution of rights to forestland is sketchy, it appears that as elite control broke down, the use of communal forests came to be regulated by the village covenant, which guaranteed equal access to the forests.[34] Infractions of the village covenant could be punished by the withdrawal of such rights, and the eyes of the village youth association (*wakamonogumi*) enforced compliance. The covenant determined the opening day and length of the periods during which entry into the forests would be allowed. The first day of each gathering season was usually referred to as the day of "opening the gates to the mountains." After inspecting the growth of

33 Forestry policy is the subject of Conrad Totman, *The Origins of Japan's Modern Forests: The Case of Akita* (Honolulu: University of Hawaii Press, 1985).
34 Furushima, *Kinsei keizaishi no kiso katei*, pp. 186–94.

rice seedlings and meadow grasses, the village officials would designate a day during which grass used for mulch could be cut, usually two
or three days before the seedlings were transplanted to the paddies.
There were separate opening days and periods for collecting fodder
that would be used for farm animals, for gathering the hay spread on
barn floors during the winter, and for cutting firewood and roof
thatch.

Daimyo and village alike enforced other restrictions so as to protect
the forests' resources. Most daimyo permitted peasants to use only
sickles and scythes when in the woodlands so that they would not
damage large, valuable trees. Frequently, village covenants included a
provision prohibiting the sale of harvested grasses, especially to peasants from other villages. Similarly, a farmer's consumption of forest
products was limited to the amount of grass required to fertilize his
paddy fields and the amount of hay that had to be mixed with the
manure in his compost pits. Equal access did not mean equal division
of forest and meadow products among all households. Instead, the
yield from the meadows and forests was typically divided among farmers according to the size of a farmer's landholdings and the number of
people in his family.

This system underwent additional changes during the latter half of
the Tokugawa period. A farmer's yearly take from the woodlands came
to be perceived as a right held by every farming household, and these
allotments began to be bartered and sold. Some households were assigned plots in woodlands, initially for limited periods of time. Such
assignments gradually became permanent, and individual households
began to ignore village or communal claims to the forests and woodlands. Some farmers planted thickets in order to sell the yield as
firewood, and others produced and marketed charcoal. Forestland was
cleared and converted into paddy land, and meadowland was forested
so that farmers could sell trees for use as lumber. This privatization
and commercialization of communal lands became especially prevalent
after 1800.

TECHNOLOGY AND COMMERCIAL AGRICULTURE

The previous sections have examined how several aspects of agricultural life changed over the seventeenth and eighteenth centuries. It is
now possible to take a more comprehensive view of the evolving agricultural community and to elaborate on the relationship between the
transformations in village life and the changes in the mode of agricul-

tural production. During the Edo period, agriculture passed through three technological stages of varying degrees of complexity: the slash-and-burn technique, the self-contained village economy, and the commercialized cash crop economy – and the shift from one stage to another lay at the bottom of three different life-styles.[35]

Slash-and-burn farming

The most rudimentary type of farming relied on slash-and-burn techniques. The so-called agricultural servants such as *hikan* and *nago,* as well as other subordinate peasant families who provided labor services for the large farming households, often used this method on their marginal holdings in poor, upland areas. But in secluded mountains and on isolated islands, whole villages employed this primitive technology. The isolated regions of the Chichibu district in Musashi, the Shibayama district of Hyūga, and Tsushima Island are prominent examples. In these areas, farmers would typically raze sections of forestland. Trees, shrubs, and grasses within delineated areas were cut and burned on the site, and farmers could then grow crops in the ashes for two to five years. The farmers did not bother to apply fertilizers to preserve the soil's fertility, as the ashes usually provided sufficient nutrients to produce crops for several years. After yields fell to inefficient levels, the farmers would abandon the land. However, the land could be used again after a lapse of several years, once it had become overgrown with small trees and shrubs.

Another aspect of slash-and-burn farming was that fields did not need to be plowed. Plots were kept small enough to be leveled with rakes and bamboo brooms after removing any branches that had not been reduced to ashes in the fire. Hence, the only tools needed for cultivation were a sickle for cutting grass, hand axes for felling trees, and the rakes and bamboo brooms used to level the ashes. These plots were usually planted with such crops as buckwheat, soybeans, and foxtail millet, and farmers on Tsushima also grew wheat and barley. Productivity, however, was quite low; yields amounted to only three or four times the amount of seed sown, whereas ordinary rice paddies usually yielded between thirty to fifty times the amount of seed sown.

Because fields created with slash-and-burn techniques were often situated in hilly or mountainous areas, crops were vulnerable to dam-

35 Ibid., pp. 238–72, for additional details.

age from wildfowl, boar, and deer. When harvest time approached, the villagers put up temporary huts near the fields from which they kept watch in order to ward off predators. On Tsushima, for instance, farmers constructed wooden palisades to keep out wild boar. Hence, once fields had been burned over on this island, they had to be left idle until enough wood for making palisades could be cut from nearby trees. Good land thus had to be held out of production for fifteen years, poor land for up to twenty-five years.

Self-sufficient farming

The phrase "self-sufficient farming," used here in contrast with "commercialized farming," should not be taken to mean that individual farmers, or even entire villages, relied completely on the goods and crops they produced themselves. Rather, villagers who engaged in these self-sufficient practices had a traditional peasant mentality. That is, they did not engage in commercial agriculture in order to accumulate wealth that could then be used to create new and different modes of living. Rather, their aim was more modest and was bound by the concerns of their ancient village customs. Thus, they grew commercial crops and engaged in trade only to the extent necessary to acquire commodities that would permit them to sustain life at a traditional level. To this end, they tended to shun the market whenever possible and to produce items for sale only within the context of an assured production for subsistence. Typically, the proceeds from such sales would then be used to buy goods that could not be produced on the homestead.[36]

Examples of this kind of production are abundant for the early Tokugawa period. With the exception of those living near the sea, for instance, most farmers were forced to rely on outsiders for salt, because of the lack of rock salt deposits in Japan. Moreover, iron and other metals used for farm tools and household goods usually had to be acquired from a limited number of mining regions. After 1680, cotton replaced cruder fibers as the most common material for clothing, and peasants began to buy secondhand cotton clothes, ginned cotton, and cotton cloth from external sources. At first, the farmers simply bartered their crops for the goods they needed from outside, but then they started to pay for them more frequently with cash. People in the

---

36 Most readers will be aware of the similarity between this sort of peasant mentality in Japan and the general ideas about peasant attitudes toward commerce expressed by Eric Wolf in his *Peasant Wars of the Twentieth Century* (New York: Harper & Row, 1964), pp. xiv–v.

Tsuzuki district (*gun*) in Musashi, for example, acquired their salt in the early Tokugawa period from villages in the neighboring Kuraki district. The exchange was by barter, with the salt producers in Kuraki receiving firewood, which they used as a fuel to make the salt. Later, the Tsuzuki villagers began to sell their firewood to inns in Edo and along the Tōkaidō highway, where they got a better price, and they used that cash to buy salt.[37]

Villagers in many regions were able to remain self-sufficient during the early modern period because of their access to water and forestland. An abundant water supply was necessary for wet-rice cultivation, which provided the bulk of the land tax, and free use of forests provided the basis for self-sufficiency in everyday essentials. We have already noted that the ready availability of materials for constructing flood control and riparian works made cash expenditures unnecessary in most daily transactions. But even more important to agricultural self-sufficiency were the fertilizers gathered from the forests and the wild fodder collected from marginal lands. Farmers were thus able to continue self-sufficient farming on the same farmland despite intensive cultivation because they could maintain the fertility of the soil with these self-gathered fertilizers.

The three most important fertilizers were "gathered mulch" (*karishiki*), livestock manure, and human waste. Tall grasses, shoots that grew from the stumps of felled broad-leaved trees, and the leaves of shrubs were used for mulch and were laid directly on the paddies. Livestock manure was mixed with leftover fodder, dried autumn grasses, forage, and rice straw. Horses and cattle were used to till the fields and to transport goods, but their most important role was as a source of manure. This is revealed in the design of stables of this period. Stable floors were dug out to accommodate the addition of straw and grass, and the roofs were raised in order to allow the manure – hay mixture to pile up into large heaps. The stable manure was shoveled out monthly and piled in the yard. When it reached a sufficient age and height, the manure would be transferred to the fields. Farmers' almanacs recommended that hay and grasses be fed to animals from all four sides of the stable to ensure a proper blend of the manure and uneaten fodder.[38] Farmers who fertilized paddy fields with cut grasses used this fodder–manure mixture for dry fields. In villages without livestock, pits were dug in the yard and filled with cut

37 *Yokohama-shishi*, vol. 4, pp. 504–5. See also vol. 11, pp. 971–4.
38 Furushima, *Nihon nōgyōshi*, chap. 6, esp. pp. 250–3.

grass, straw, chaff, wastewater from the kitchen, and human waste. This mixture was allowed to decompose and then was then applied to the fields in place of the animal manure and fodder mixture.

Fertilization with night soil has often been viewed as a hallmark of Japanese agriculture. Naturally, the bodily waste from an average household was not sufficient to maintain the fertility of its farmlands. But farmers from villages located near cities and post towns were able to collect human waste from these communities in exchange for a few vegetables and some glutinous rice cakes during the New Year's season. Night soil was used to fertilize land planted with rice, grain, or, quite often, vegetables. A thriving night soil trade developed in cities like Edo and Osaka, as well as regional castle towns such as Kanazawa, and "ladler guilds" were formed in these cities to cater to outlying villages.[39]

Improved tools and their expanded availability were also responsible for helping Tokugawa villagers achieve self-sufficiency. Advances in agricultural efficiency came slowly in those isolated areas where most holdings were too small to utilize the new technology efficiently. Consequently, the farmer who held less than one hectare of farmland continued to rely on the hoe, which he used as an all-purpose tool for tilling, leveling the ground, preparing the soil, and even for cutting grass. In most regions, however, change came more quickly and was a product not only of the farmer's desire to grow more but also of his lord's will that he do so.

Studies of several domains reveal that blacksmiths residing in castle towns were frequently ordered by the daimyo to produce iron-bladed hoes for farmers who were unable to make them on their own. Initially, the blades were paid for in rice when the land tax was collected. By the 1680s, blacksmiths had begun to move permanently to villages so that they could expand their business of repairing and selling farm tools and blades. In some instances, the villages paid a small part of the village maintenance fee to the blacksmith for his services, and most repairs were probably paid for in kind. By the 1730s such smiths had invented several kinds of highly specialized hoes. The split-bladed "Bitchū hoe" was designed for improved tilling, and a hoe especially for cutting grass was also being manufactured. Wealthy farmers who employed servants and kept livestock would, of course, have used horse- or ox-drawn plows, but the ordinary peasants had to make do with a *nagatoko*. This was a plow with a long wooden base and a cast-

39 Kobayashi Shigeru, *Nihon shinyō mondai genryūkō* (Tokyo: Akashi shoten, 1984).

iron blade that had to be pushed by hand, and it could not cut even as deeply as a hoe could.[40]

The second most important farm tool was the sickle. It was usually used for weeding and cutting grass, as well as for chopping down shrubs, trimming branches, and even hacking down trunks of small trees. Sickles were even pressed into service as weapons by the disarmed peasantry. With the sickle and hoe, the peasants could carry out all of their farm duties. Moreover, they needed to buy only the blades for these tools, as the handles and all other farm implements could be made by using material gathered from the communal forestlands.[41]

Self-sufficient agriculture was also defined and limited by the variety of crops cultivated and by the tiny amount of land available to grow these different crops. Self-sufficient farmers paid their land taxes in kind and usually planted all of their arable paddies with rice. If they double-cropped their fields, they would most often grow wheat and barley (usually more of the former than the latter) as winter crops to feed their households. Wheat was usually ground into flour and eaten as noodles or dumplings. For home consumption, dry fields were planted with soybeans, millet, buckwheat, large white radishes, sweet potatoes (in western Japan), and taro, especially along the Pacific seacoast from Ise eastward into Suruga. Bits and pieces of spare land around residences were also turned into gardens and planted with a variety of vegetables.

An agricultural manual from a secluded mountain village in Shimotsuke with a preface dated 1808 describes a typical harvest.[42] The writer was a village headman (*nanushi*) who held nearly seven hectares of land, about half of which was cultivated by his household in 1814. However, the average peasant who appears in this manual farmed only 0.2 hectares of paddy and an equal amount of dry field. In one case mentioned in the document, a peasant who worked a tiny plot of land planted the paddy entirely with rice and cultivated other grains on the dry fields, typically millet, soybeans, cotton, adzuki beans, buckwheat, tobacco, and cowpeas. The borders of these fields and any remaining land were used for vegetables such as eggplant, autumn radishes, and taro. This peasant's fields gave only minimal yields.

40 Furushima, *Nihon nōgyōshi*, pp. 244–8.
41 Dai Nihon nōkai, ed., *Nihon no kama, kuwa, suki* (Tokyo: Nōsei chōsa iinkai, 1979). For a brief discussion in English of agrarian technology, see Kee Il Choi, "Technological Diffusion in Agriculture Under the Bakuhan System," *Journal of Asian Studies* 30 (August 1971): 749–59.
42 Furushima, *Nihon nōgyōshi*, pp. 344–6.

Cotton production for this secluded mountain village was perhaps no more than three to five *kan* per *tan* (1 *kan* = 8.267 lb.), which meant that in the average year this man grew only enough to meet the clothing needs of his own family. The tobacco yield was also not large enough to market. However, by 1808 even a small household such as this sold some of its produce, most often the surplus rice that remained after paying the land tax. This household ate almost none of its rice crop, instead relying chiefly on the grains from its dry fields. But this farmer owned a horse, and by using night soil, grass mulch, and the animal's manure, he was able to maintain the fertility of his fields without having to buy commercial fertilizers.

Commercialized agriculture

In some parts of Japan during the seventeenth century, and in most parts of the country after that, subsistence farming gave way to more commercialized forms of agriculture, and the traditional peasant mentality was increasingly displaced by more modern attitudes toward farm production. The key to this transformation was increased interaction with the marketplace. If the older peasant kept the market at arm's length, the new farmer embraced it more fully, opening his land and labor to competition and exploring alternatives to the factors of production so as to maximize returns. In this process the new cultivator came to favor those products with a potential of commercial profit over the more traditional, less risky crops cultivated for family subsistence. The changeover to cash crops was first seen among the upper-class farmers in the Osaka region around the middle of the seventeenth century. By 1770 commercial crops were grown by all peasant classes in the Kinai region. Within the next half-century, they were also being widely adopted in the Kantō region.

The first great cash crop of Tokugawa Japan was cotton. Even as early as the Muromachi period, cotton was imported, first as cloth and later as thread, which was woven into "Ise cotton cloth" and other designed cloths, and then sold to the nobility and clergy. During the Sengoku period, cotton was used to pay the fees charged at checkpoints along major transportation routes. Later, as farmers began to cultivate cotton for commercial purposes, cotton fields acquired sufficient importance to be listed separately in the land survey registers of Mikawa, Tōtōmi, and Shinano provinces, as well as those from the Kantō region. By the beginning of the nineteenth century, the area stretching west from Kyoto along the Inland Sea and east as far as Mikawa had become a major cotton-growing region.[43]

The agrarian upper class was most responsible for introducing cotton as a cash crop, for their lands generated the surpluses that permitted them to risk introducing such an innovation. From a village in the Ōtori district of Izumi in 1605 comes an example of a farm household that possessed lands assessed at ninety-five *koku* and given over entirely to growing rice as well as a small amount of other cereals. By contrast, seventy years later, in a neighboring village within the same Ōtori district, farmers grew rice and cotton on alternate years.

One household in this village that rotated between rice and cotton cultivation had its total landholdings assessed at 69 *koku* during the 1594 survey. By 1647, the family's holdings (including scattered possessions in neighboring villages) had swollen to 165 *koku*, 8 *to*, and by 1666 had increased to 190 *koku*. From harvest records, we discover that this family planted dry fields near the foot of the mountains with cotton, but they rotated cotton and indigo on the other dry fields and alternately grew cotton and rice in the paddy fields. The family leased the paddy fields to tenant farmers during the years when they were planted with rice. Because this region was subject to water shortages, portions of the paddy land were left unirrigated and used for cultivating cotton during drought years. This family could afford to purchase sardine-meal fertilizer by selling the surplus from their cotton crop. In 1665 the family fertilized between seven *tan* to one *chō* of its lands with sardine meal, and the cotton yield from these lands far surpassed the clothing needs of the family's four members and twelve servants.[44] Although there are no extant records that document the transition from a rice-based to multicrop agriculture, the introduction of cotton can safely be attributed to farmers from the agrarian upper class.

Clearly, we have evidence here of the influence of demand on supply. The emergence during the seventeenth century of massive urban populations, especially in Edo, Osaka, Kyoto, and Kanazawa, increased the demand for cotton and other commercial crops. Yanagita Kunio in his "Before Cotton Wear" (*Momen izen no koto*) concludes from the description of clothing colors and textures found in *haikai* poems that cotton clothing had become quite widely used by urban

43 The most detailed study in English examining the spread of cotton as a commercial crop is William B. Hauser, *Economic Institutional Change in Tokugawa Japan: Osaka and the Kinai Cotton Trade* (Cambridge, England: Cambridge University Press, 1974).
44 Furushima, *Nihon nōgyōshi*, chap. 6, esp. pp. 217–19.

residents before the Genroku era (1688–1704).[45] Indeed, sumptuary regulations promulgated in many domains in the 1650s and 1660s called for merchants and peasants to use cotton rather than silk.[46] Other kinds of documentary evidence from the early 1700s show that 40 to 50 percent of the land in some villages surrounding Osaka were given over to the cultivation of cotton.

In this region, farmers from all economic strata grew cotton. A detailed study of a village in the Kawachi district found that in 1705 nearly 41 percent of this village's paddy fields were planted with cotton; by 1747 this figure had climbed to 50 percent. By then the villagers had even blocked off the irrigation ditches leading to the paddies, in order to concentrate the village's water resources on the fields planted with rice. Sections for growing cotton were rotated annually. This meant that each farmer had to grow on his land the crop selected by the village for that portion of fields during that year.[47]

Other changes accompanied the increasingly widespread cultivation of cotton by large- and medium-scale farmers in the Osaka area. During the 1700s, for instance, live-in servants began to build their own homes, and many were able to establish themselves as full-fledged independent farming households on the basis of their increased output. In addition to household reorganization, several technological innovations also played an important role in increasing production. These were designed to improve yields for all crops, and the most remarkable were related to methods of fertilization, farm tools, and agricultural management.

Commercial fertilizers appeared during the seventeenth century. As early as 1673 sardine meal had been adopted by the wealthier members of the agrarian class to fertilize cotton fields. Initially, merchants sold dried sardines to urban dwellers for consumption as an ordinary foodstuff. Chapter 11 in this volume explains in some detail how dried sardines came to be used as a fertilizer and how merchant guilds that specialized in this product were formed in response to this new and growing demand. Sardine guilds cooperated in helping increase the size of sardine hauls, because the farms consumed sardines in much greater volume than did the urban consumers, and extremely large seines, which had to be hauled in by several fishermen, were intro-

45 Yanagita Kunio, *Momen izen no koto*, in *Teihon Yanagita Kunio shū*, vol. 14 (Tokyo: Chikuma shobō, 1962).
46 Furushima, *Nihon nōgyōshi*, pp. 209–10.
47 Furushima, *Nihon nōgyōshi*, pp. 347–50; and Hayama Teisaku, *Kinsei nōgyō hatten no seisanryoku bunseki* (Tokyo: Ochanomizu shobō, 1969).

duced. These nets required large sandy beaches and were used only during sardine runs. Sardine fishing required large amounts of capital, both to purchase the nets and to mobilize a large force of fishermen. Osaka's sardine merchants provided the necessary capital and opened up many new fishing grounds. At first, sardines were caught off the coasts of Bungo, Hyūga, and Iyo, and later off the coasts of Kujūkuri-gahama beach in modern-day Chiba Prefecture, from whence they were shipped to Osaka. During the nineteenth century, herring and whale by-products were shipped from ports in Hokkaido to Osaka.

In time, bricks or cakes of pressed rapeseed, sesame seed, and cottonseed were used as fertilizers. Merchants tested the fertilizing potential of numerous organic materials and began to market a variety of new products as well. The result of the opening of new fishing grounds and the ensuing leaps in the quantities and varieties of catches not only boosted the quantity of fertilizers produced but also led to the adoption of fertilizers for all crops, resulting in the greater productivity of food crops as well as cash crops. For example, some documents show that farmers who once had averaged one *koku*, six *to* of rice per *tan* on high-quality fields were, by the beginning of the nineteenth century, able to harvest between two *koku*, five *to*, and two *koku*, eight *to*.[48]

Throughout Japan new fertilizers naturally led to new methods of fertilization. At first, grass–manure mixtures had been applied once a year to fields before sowing or transplanting seedlings. When first introduced, dried whole sardines were also laid on the fields just once a year. But later, sardines were ground in mortars and applied several times a year in quantities that corresponded to the crops' rate of growth. These methods were later applied to traditionally self-supplied fertilizers. Urine, for instance, was separated from night soil and ladled around crops late in the growing season as a supplemental fertilizer.

Farmers in the Osaka region who grew commercial crops such as cotton and rapeseed led the move to new fertilizers as a way of improving yields. These same cultivators also sought to improve farm tool technology, although here their interest was directed as much at reducing labor costs as at increasing yields. For instance, on an average farm with a yield of nineteen *koku*, threshing done by hand required approximately 111 days of labor, more time than any other farm task took after fertilizers were improved. To reduce this cost, some farmers

48 Furushima Toshio, *Kinsei Nihon nōgyō no tenkai* (Tokyo: Tōkyō daigaku shuppankai, 1963), p. 345.

first employed a new tool known colloquially as the "threshing chopsticks," two, thirty-centimeter-long bamboo sticks used to scissor ears
and kernels of grain. By the 1680s, the "threshing chopsticks" had
been replaced in the Osaka area by the one-thousand-tooth thresher,
whose split bamboo teeth were fastened in rows to a wooden block.
This one-thousand-tooth thresher was reputed to be ten times more
efficient than the threshing chopsticks. These farm implements helped
decrease labor requirements during the autumn harvest and threshing
season and reduced the total labor input for cotton and rapeseed cultivation. In 1720, iron teeth had replaced the bamboo in the one-
thousand-tooth thresher, and this version was subsequently introduced to all regions of Japan.

These many improvements in agricultural technology, when applied
systematically by farm households, led to intensive cultivation. The
literature of the Edo period, especially that written by Confucian scholars, often gives the impression that farmland in general was tilled only
once in several years and that seeds were sown in a haphazard fashion.
Casual cultivation methods were, however, limited to the fields opened
up by slash-and-burn techniques. Otherwise, seeds were sown on upland dry fields in rows or clusters. Although rice seedlings were not
transplanted to paddies in precise rows, they were planted in bunches
adjusted so that a certain number covered a fixed area. Moreover, the
more effective management of nursery beds and rice seed meant that
fewer seeds had to be sown per *tan* of paddy, and upland fields were
managed with more care as cash crops were introduced.

As rice came to be grown as a commercial crop, wealthy, elite farmers, especially village headmen, often kept farm journals in which they
recorded the types of crops, amounts of fertilizer, strains of rice, and
annual yield for each plot of village farmland.[49] Strains were selected
after comparing the yields recorded in such documents. In this manner, farmers were able to discover rice plants with especially productive ears, and eventually even to breed new varieties systematically. At
the same time, farmers tried to reduce the amount of seed sown. In the
Kantō region, where seeds were thickly sown, one *tan* of rice paddy
usually was sown with somewhere from one *to*, two *shō*, to one *to*, five
shō of unhulled rice. By 1720, farmers were only sowing three *sho* of
rice per *tan*. This improvement resulted from the adoption of new
sowing methods. Previously, unhulled rice was sown after being

49 A general discussion of this kind of manual can be found in Jennifer Robertson, "Japanese
   Farm Manuals: A Literature of Discovery," *Peasant Studies* 11 (Spring 1984).

soaked in water until sprouts began to appear. But by soaking the unhulled rice for only one day, draining the seeds, and sowing them immediately, farmers were able to save seeds. Additional savings were achieved by selecting seeds through testing for resistance to wind and water damage.

Innovative methods of intensive agricultural management were also devised by farmers who grew fruits and vegetables for sale to the urban market. In the Kyoto region, for instance, melons known as *makuwa uri* were highly prized. By 1680 several villages had become well-known for producing handsome melon specimens, the best of which were produced near Tōji (temple) and sold with an affixed seal testifying to their origin.[50] Farmers prepared and fertilized the plots for these melons during the preceding winter. When the plants first appeared in the spring, the farmers carefully observed each plant, keeping the most promising and thinning out the others. They even counted the leaves and cut the tops of branching vines to permit the main stem to grow larger and stronger. The top of the main vine was also pruned, and the next generation of vines was then allowed to bear fruit. Though time-consuming, such intensive horticultural techniques were already widely employed before the eighteenth century in regions where agriculture had been influenced by the growth of markets.

COOPERATIVE ASPECTS OF VILLAGE SOCIETY

Despite the great changes that surged through the villages during the Edo period, many cooperative aspects of village life provided elements of continuity that linked together the new and the old. The inhabitants of the early modern village may have possessed differing levels of political responsibility and observed distinctions based on lineage, but they also worked together, functioning as a coordinated unit to engage in agriculture. Village unity was fostered by a system of social relationships that encouraged cooperation and promoted a sense of community. Moreover, all village inhabitants were obliged to work together for mutual advantage in a variety of agricultural and social activities, of which irrigation provides a good example.

The construction and maintenance of an irrigation system was a complex undertaking. In addition to the initial investment of labor for

50 Furushima Toshio, *Nihon nōgyō gijutsushi*, vol. 6 of *Furushima Toshio chosakushū*, pp. 426–7, 543–8.

the construction of the irrigation canals that enabled the expansion of rice cultivation, constant maintenance was necessary to keep the irrigation system in operation. Locks, sluice gates, and other flood control devices that were erected to hold back rivers during the typhoon season required periodic maintenance and frequent repair. These facilities were made of wood, bamboo, stone, and sand, that is, from materials gathered by mutual consent and effort from the village's communal lands. Furthermore, irrigation ditches had to be dredged and repaired before the planting season, and the weeds that sprouted along ditches during the summer required constant attention. Villages that shared water supplies with neighboring villages or that were allowed to irrigate their fields only during certain times of the day shared the responsibility for opening and closing the water locks at the water sources, yet another task that required the full cooperation of all villagers.

In regions where double cropping was possible, rice seedling nurseries were begun before the winter grain was harvested. The young rice plants had to be irrigated as soon as they were put into the nursery plot, but diverting water to the seedbeds often lowered the level of the groundwater in adjacent fields that were planted in a winter grain crop. Consequently, where to locate a seedling nursery was a delicate question, requiring the consent of the entire village. As a general rule, farmers had to cooperate in order to be ensured of adequate water supplies. Moreover, they were forced to work their lands according to identical schedules, because adjoining fields in the same irrigation system were watered at the same time.

Cooperation was also the order of the day in villages that specialization in commercial crops. Cotton farming required dry fields, which were often constructed from paddy fields by cutting off the flow of irrigation water. Hence, cotton could be grown only with the cooperation of farmers whose lands shared the same irrigation ditch, as all land downstream within an irrigation system would be simultaneously converted into dry fields when the irrigation water was blocked off, unless the cultivators were willing to expend the time and funds to redirect the irrigation canals.

The rethatching of roofs was typically a community matter as well. Although it was possible for the average farmer to save enough straw from successive wheat harvests to cover his roof, the accumulated straw would not be of uniform age or dryness. Hence, special roof thatch was grown for covering roofs, and villagers set aside specific fields to grow enough thatch to reroof one or two villages homes every year, although the large houses of wealthy villagers usually required a double portion of thatch. All healthy male members of the village would help harvest the reeds and thatch the house selected for that year, and all families contributed to providing the bamboo supports and straw ropes needed for tying down the thatch. Because thatching the eaves of roofs required special skills, one person from every village (or sometimes every other village) was usually trained for this task, and the more elementary chores would be performed by ordinary villagers under his guidance.

Close cooperation among village members and the need for joint effort and consensus also had another side, making it difficult for innovations in life-styles, farm tools, and crops to penetrate village life. Traditions of cooperation tended to survive longest in those villages that were most self-sufficient and isolated from the outside world. On the other hand, the relative importance of village cooperation tended to diminish in areas where the market economy had made inroads and market-bound crops were widely cultivated.

CONCLUSION

When the farmers in Musashi and Sagami dug out their old family records to show the officials of the shogunate's Finance Office near the end of the Tokugawa period, what they found must have excited them. Verification of one's lineage, especially a tie to samurai origins nearly three centuries earlier, would have provided psychological satisfaction by placing one in the great flow of tradition and the village's history. Even more pleasing, one could now boast with confidence about one's elite heritage and claim a special niche in village lore.

But if one reads between the lines of those musty documents, what is even more startling is the change that time had wrought. The shift from subsistence to commercial farming; the appearance of new implements, seeds, and farming techniques; the expanded use of irrigation and fertilizers; the development of new means of village administration; and the steady improvement of diet, clothing, and housing – all of these had so far removed the farmer of the mid-nineteenth century from his samurai ancestors that he must have wondered whether his predecessors had ever existed at all.

The late Edo period farmers also stood, perhaps unknowingly, at the brink of another revolutionary transformation that would propel their own successors into the modern age. The shift from "peasant" to "farmer" that had occurred over the course of two centuries had not been simply a psychological reorientation. Rather, as depicted in the other chapters in this volume, it had also involved a major shift in the institutional context within which the Japanese farmer lived. That institutional context was powerfully conditioned by the massive commercial developments in central Japan, developments that are beyond the purview of this chapter and that are treated in Chapter 11 of this volume and in volume 5 of *The Cambridge History of Japan*.

As a result of these changes, the expansion of national and international markets in the 1850s and 1860s would shake the foundations of Japan's institutional structure, inviting a group of leaders from western Japan to overthrow the shogunate and launch Japan on the course of modernization. Few farmers participated in the revolutionary struggles – perhaps because commercialization had proceeded so far as to dissolve the traditional cohesiveness of the peasant community – but all would be profoundly affected by its outcome.

CHAPTER 11

COMMERCIAL CHANGE AND URBAN GROWTH IN EARLY MODERN JAPAN

AN ERA OF URBAN GROWTH

During the first century and a half of the early modern period, between 1550 and 1700, Japan became one of the most urbanized societies in the world. At the beginning of this era, the ancient imperial capital of Kyoto was the only city with more than 100,000 residents, and a mere handful of other settlements held as many as 10,000 persons. But by the year 1700, four new Japanese communities had exceeded the 100,000 mark, and approximately 5 to 7 percent of all Japanese lived in such large cities. This compared with a figure of 2 percent in Europe, where only fourteen cities had reached the 100,000 level, and only the Netherlands and England–Wales could boast of urban concentrations greater than Japan's. Edo had become the world's largest city by the end of the seventeenth century, and the populations of Osaka and Kyoto approached those of London and Paris, the two largest cities in the West.

The meteoric urban growth that occurred in Japan at the beginning of the early modern period had profound and diverse consequences for Japanese history. First, the cities acted as large magnets, creating energy fields that set in motion large-scale population movements and propelled hundreds of thousands of persons into the cities to fill burgeoning job opportunities. The growing urban centers served as enormous consumption centers as well, and across Japan farmers changed their cropping patterns to meet new demands for vegetables, fruits, and plant materials for clothes. Consequently, regional specialization increasingly became a feature of early modern commerce, and new transportation networks and post towns sprang up everywhere to cater to mobile traders. In time, a fresh, spirited set of urban entertainments came into being as well, thus enriching the texture of Japanese cultural history. Finally, the unprecedented concentrations of people – vigorous, creative, and at times unruly – compelled the authorities to devise new kinds of political and administrative institutions.

The Sengoku period background

The quest to understand how and why this urban growth took place, and to appreciate as well the historical significance of the cities, takes us back in time to the middle of the sixteenth century – to the Sengoku period and the genesis of Japan's extraordinary epoch of urban development.[1] There were three principal types of urban settlement at that time. The most common, and the seed of what ultimately would become the dominant urban force in the early modern period in Japan, was the castle town, or *jōkamachi*, literally a community that grew up around a castle. During the first half of the sixteenth century, the bushi tended to live in agricultural villages, where they managed their fiefs and the affairs of the villagers. Gradually, during the decades of continual warfare that marked this era, these bushi emerged as an elite, arms-bearing class. As this happened, their leaders began to move out of the villages and to establish fortified residences at more easily defended locations. As revealed in names such as Negoya (literally, the huts at the base of the mountain) and Yamashita (at the foot of the mountain), these strongholds were usually situated where plains meet mountains, and they provided assembly points where, in times of crisis, the lord could gather his military band of retainers, relatives, and vassal samurai.[2]

These military centers quickly came to be the home for civilians as well. As combat spread into even remote parts of the country during the later decades of the sixteenth century, the castellans (now more familiarly known as daimyo), found it advantageous to gather into their castle headquarters larger and larger numbers of artisans who could manufacture weapons such as swords, lances, and even firearms; merchants who could transport these goods; and finally, groups of laborers to work on construction projects. It was also useful for the daimyo to establish within the precincts of the new castle towns officially authorized marketplaces where commodity transactions could

---

1 For a convenient overview of the issues that have occupied the attention of historians concerning Sengoku period cities, see Nakabe Yoshiko, "Sengoku jidai daimyō kyojū toshi ni kansuru shomondai," in Chihōshi kenkyū kyōgikai, ed., *Toshi no chihōshi* (Tokyo: Yūsankaku, 1980), pp. 56–79. In English, see Haruko Wakita, with Susan B. Hanley, "Dimensions of Development: Cities in Fifteenth-Century Japan," in John Whitney Hall, Keiji Nagahara, and Kozo Yamamura, eds., *Japan Before Tokugawa: Political Consolidation and Economic Growth, 1500–1650* (Princeton, N.J.: Princeton University Press, 1981), pp. 295–326.
2 Nishikawa Kōji, *Nihon toshishi no kenkyū* (Tokyo: Nihon hōsō shuppan kyōkai, 1972), pp. 167–202.

take place peacefully, and this too encouraged permanent residence in the towns.[3]

As the daimyo's policies gave rise to larger and more prosperous communities, the towns also became centers of local religious and cultural activities. Moreover, as life in the imperial capital of Kyoto became less secure after the Ōnin War (1467–77), men of artistic and literary accomplishment, such as the landscape artist and garden designer Sesshū, left the capital and took refuge in the provinces. And like Sesshu, who was employed by the Ōuchi daimyo of western Japan, such persons often were taken into service by the daimyo, thus ultimately bringing a measure of cultural refinement to the lives of the bushi and cementing the tie between artist and military figures that would endure into the early modern period.

Some notion of the vitality of these communities can be found in the epistles of the Jesuit missionaries, who openly admired the castle towns of the Sengoku period.[4] When visiting Gifu in 1575, for instance, Luis Frois wrote: "At this point I wish I were a skilled architect or had the gift of describing places well, because I sincerely assure you that of all the palaces and houses I have seen in Portugal, India, and Japan, there has been nothing to compare with this as regards luxury, wealth, and cleanliness." And after visiting Azuchi in 1584, Lourenço Mexia remarked that Japanese houses were as neat and clean as sacristies and that at Nobunaga's palace "the gardens and corridors were such that one could not spit in them." Such praise, however, should not obscure the fact that these castle towns were still relatively small; even in the 1580s most had populations of only a few thousand persons. Still, more than a hundred such settlements dotted the countryside of Japan, and these would provide one of the seedbeds for the rapid urbanization of the seventeenth century, growth that would propel Japan into the leading ranks of the urbanized countries.

Although these rustic castle towns represented the principal urban creation of the late Sengoku period, they were not without competitors. The warfare of that age was fought at two different levels. The first and most visible was the struggle among daimyo to expand their domains by military means; the other was the contest for supremacy within domains between individual daimyo and armed elements of the peasantry. In some instances, groups of such peasants were members

3 Nakabe Yoshiko, *Jōkamachi* (Kyoto: Yanagihara shoten, 1978), pp. 9–64.
4 Michael Cooper, ed., *They Came to Japan: An Anthology of European Reports on Japan, 1543–1640* (Berkeley and Los Angeles: University of California Press, 1965), pp. 131, 145.

of secularly powerful Buddhist sects, such as the Ikkō, or True Pure
Land sect (*Jōdo Shinshū*), which permitted the peasants, together with
merchants and artisans who were also sect members, to take up residence in and around a sect temple. These settlements then became
known as "temple towns" (*jinaimachi*), and their residents often
claimed autonomy from daimyo control.[5]

These temple towns were distinct from the so-called *monzenmachi*
(literally, towns in front of the gates), which were concentrations of
inns and souvenir shops clustered together around the entrances to
those famous shrines and temples that attracted large numbers of
worshipers and pilgrims.[6] The essential difference between the two
urban types is that the temple towns formed under the auspices of
major temples had a distinctive religious character and asserted their
independence from the daimyo's authority. That is, these communities as corporate groups exercised judicial and police powers, apportioned and at times even levied their own tax dues, and undertook self-
defense projects such as the construction of moats. The possession of
these special immunities permitted the temple towns to carry out certain functions outside the direct purview of daimyo authority, and it is
this latitude for independent action that has prompted historians to see
them as autonomous, self-governing communities.[7]

Historians have identified seventeen temple towns, all founded in the
middle decades of the sixteenth century.[8] These settlements, however,
tended to have very short life spans. As daimyo put together greater and
greater concentrations of military and political might during the latter
half of the sixteenth century, they attacked the major religious sects and
cut away the independent power basis of the temple towns. In some
cases, the daimyo actually converted the temple towns into their own
castle headquarters. For instance, Osaka was known at that time as
Ishiyama and was built up as an armed community of Honganji believers. In 1580, Oda Nobunaga destroyed this fortified town after a decade
of fighting, and subsequently Toyotomi Hideyoshi erected his own

5 The term is also read as *jinaichō*. A good introduction to this type of settlement can be found in
   Wakita Osamu, "Jinaimachi no kōzō to tenkai," *Shirin* 41 (January 1958): 1–24.
6 Harada Tomohiko, "Kinsei no monzenmachi," in Toyoda Takeshi, Harada Tomohiko, and
   Yamori Kazuhiko, eds., *Kōza: Nihon no hōken toshi*, 3 vols. (Tokyo: Bun'ichi sōgō shuppan,
   1981–2), vol. 3, pp. 201–23.
7 In certain *jinaimachi* the temple priests retained ultimate political authority and managed the
   affairs of the community. See Osamu Wakita, with James L. McClain, "The Commercial and
   Urban Policies of Oda Nobunaga and Toyotomi Hideyoshi," in Hall, Nagahara, and Yamamura, eds., *Japan Before Tokugawa*, pp. 231–7.
8 For a careful discussion of the origins of temple towns and their historical significance, see
   Wakita Osamu, "Jinaimachi no rekishi-teki tokushitsu," in Toyoda, Harada, and Yamori,
   eds., *Kōza: Nihon no hōken toshi*, vol. 1, pp. 143–64.

castle headquarters on its ashes. Similarly, the castle town of Kanazawa, which by 1700 would become the fourth largest city in Japan under the rule of the Maeda family of daimyo, was built on the site of an earlier temple town named Kanazawa Gobō, which had existed under the protection of the Ikkō sect. In other instances, conquering daimyo left the towns in place as local merchant settlements. But in these cases as well, the military lords stripped the communities of their self-governing responsibilities and fully incorporated them into the tightening web of daimyo authority. The town of Imai, associated with Yanenji temple in Nara Prefecture, is a typical example of a temple town that lost its immunities and became purely a commercial settlement populated by small-scale merchants.

If the temple towns represented impediments to daimyo power, there was another type of sixteenth-century community that served an essential purpose for the daimyo. These were centers of trade and transshipment, or what might be called entrepôt towns. Some of these were inland post towns, but most were ports, such as Sakai on Osaka Bay, Kuwana on Ise Bay, and Hakata on the bay of the same name in Kyushu. In some instances, these settlements exercised self-governing powers similar to those claimed by the temple towns. In Sakai, for example, influential merchants managed urban administration and maintained armed forces.[9] But whether fortified or not, these merchant communities received different treatment from the daimyo than did the temple towns. Their strategic locations made them useful to daimyo, almost all of whom had to engage in some trade in order to acquire goods that were produced beyond their own borders. Indeed, most daimyo believed these entrepôt towns to be so central to their own ultimate economic success that they adhered to a tacit agreement to maintain a policy of nonaggression toward the settlements.

Interestingly enough, certain features of urban life and the cityscape in sixteenth-century Japanese cities reminded the first Westerner visitors of European urban settlements. One missionary noted the similarity between Japanese temple towns and Venice, which was also governed through administrative offices staffed by merchants. When visiting Nara, Gaspar Vilela wrote, "I spent some days there and saw three outstanding things of note. One of them is a great

9 For a detailed study of Sakai, see Izumi Chōichi, *Sakai: chūsei jiyū toshi* (Tokyo: Kyōikusha, 1981). In English, see V. Dixon Morris, "Sakai: From Shōen to Port City," in John W. Hall and Takeshi Toyoda, eds., *Japan in the Muromachi Age* (Berkeley and Los Angeles: University of California Press, 1977), pp. 145–58; and V. Dixon Morris, "The City of Sakai and Urban Autonomy," in George Elison and Bardwell L. Smith, eds., *Warlords, Artists, & Commoners: Japan in the Sixteenth Century* (Honolulu: University of Hawaii Press, 1981), pp. 23–54.

metal idol as big as the tower of the gate of Evora."[10] However impressed those European visitors might have been, no medieval city would survive unscathed the wars of reunification at the end of the sixteenth century, and the powerfully centralized state that resulted from that unification would call into being new cities, larger and more grand than anything those first European visitors saw.

National unification and early modern castle towns

It has become a historical truism to say that Oda Nobunaga initiated the political and economic programs that resulted in the early modern state; that Toyotomi Hideyoshi amplified them; and that Tokugawa Ieyasu supplied the final institutional refinements. As familiar as that paradigm might be, however, it is still relevant to a discussion of those social policies that had the most significant impact on urban growth – the separation of the peasants from the warriors (*heinō-bunri*) and of the peasants from the merchants (*nōshō-bunri*).

Oda Nobunaga's first step in imposing a new social order came after a bitter and bloody campaign against the forces of the Honganji sect gathered at their stronghold at Ishiyama. It took Nobunaga the full decade of the 1570s, and the sacrifice of tens of thousands of lives, before he could defeat the Honganji army, a mix of peasants, local samurai, and even merchants and artisans from the local temple town. As a consequence of this victory, Nobunaga acquired the strength and reputation to begin a policy of disarming peasants on some portions of his holdings. He also initiated steps to separate the warriors from agricultural management by conducting a cadastral survey (*kenchi*) in his home provinces of Yamato and Harima.

What lay behind Nobunaga's actions was the fear of an aroused peasantry and of an alliance between his retainers and villagers.[11] As long as the vassal warriors resided in the countryside and oversaw village affairs, they held the potential to threaten the lord. Indeed, in the middle decades of the sixteenth century, so many retainers turned their village holdings into independent power bases from which they defied daimyo orders, or even rose in revolt against their masters, that these years became popularly known as the era of *gekokujō*, of the inferiors overthrowing their superiors. The ultimate motive of Nobunaga, and of the daimyo who followed his example, was to drive a

---

10 Cooper, eds., *They Came to Japan*, pp. 282.
11 On the importance of peasant actions, see Keiji Nagahara, with Kozo Yamamura, "Village Communities and Daimyo Power," in Hall and Toyoda, eds., *Japan in the Muromachi Age*, pp. 107–23.

wedge between the retainers and vassals in order to bring each under more direct control.

Hideyoshi extended these policies of status separation.[12] As detailed in Chapters 2 and 4 of this volume, from the mid-1580s Hideyoshi began to expand the survey of rice-producing lands first started by Nobunaga, a policy that eventually produced a new village and administrative system, as well as a much more closely regulated peasantry. In 1588 he ordered a nationwide "sword hunt" to confiscate arms from villagers and to etch more clearly the status lines between peasant and warrior. Three years later, in 1591, Hideyoshi instructed the daimyo to conduct a village-by-village census (*hitobarai*) of their domains, a recording of the population and the numbers of households in rural areas that was designed to prevent the peasants from absconding and to bind them more tightly to the land. In that same year Hideyoshi also issued his famous edict that prohibited changes of status from samurai to merchant or from farmer to merchant. Although none of these policies could ever be fully enforced, they did provide a clear conceptual and legal differentiation of warrior, peasant, and merchant.

Tokugawa Ieyasu and his successors brought these policies to their completion. During the seventeenth century, the Tokugawa line of shoguns completely disarmed the peasantry and summoned the bushi class into the areas around its castles, moves that were repeated in nearly every daimyo domain. To be sure, in places where agriculture developed more slowly – generally in Shikoku, Kyushu, and in the north of Honshu – some lower-ranking bushi continued to live in villages. But with these exceptions, the imposition of status distinctions and the severing of the samurai from the management of agricultural affairs gave the shogun and daimyo the opening they needed to compel the warriors to move out of the villages and to take up residence around the lord's castle. At the same time, the overlords held out more positive incentives, by granting their vassal warriors residential sites and guaranteeing them annual stipends.

One consequence of these social policies was the large-scale growth of castle towns.[13] If the populations of the rudimentary castle towns of the Sengoku era tended to number in the low thousands, now cities of

---

12 Cities and the policies of the first two unifiers are discussed in Takamaki Minoru, "Shokuhō seiken to toshi," in Toyoda, Harada, and Yamori, eds., *Kōza: Nihon no hōken toshi*, vol. 3, pp. 189–211.

13 A discussion of the historiographical issues can be found in Matsumoto Shirō, "Kinsei toshiron," in Fukaya Katsumi and Matsumoto Shirō, eds., *Bakuhansei shakai no kōzō* (Tokyo: Yūhikaku, 1980), pp. 109–21.

thirty, forty, and even a hundred thousand persons became commonplace. The core population for these cities were those samurai who had
been forcefully uprooted from the countryside by the social policies of
the unifiers. Between the 1580s and the 1650s, for example, some
50,000 samurai, including their families and attendants, moved into
the shadow of the Maeda daimyo's castle at Kanazawa. By the end of
the seventeenth century, more than half that number had taken up
residence at Sendai, the headquarters of the Date family of daimyo,
while nearly 25,000 samurai and their dependents lived at Tottori and
18,000 at Okayama. In all, the bushi class comprised approximately 5
to 8 percent of Japan's total population. As they settled into the areas
around some 250 or so daimyo castles that dotted the Japanese countryside, they became the stable nucleus around which the urban population formed.[14]

A second migration, this one among rural villagers who hoped to
become the merchants, artisans, and laborers of the new cities, accompanied the movement of the samurai into the communities around the
castles. The construction of the castle and samurai residences entailed
a tremendous outlay of capital expenditures, and thousands of rural
men poured into the city to take up jobs in the booming construction
trades. As the samurai set up urban households, they hired servants –
even a humble warrior family would usually employ an attendant, a
valet, and a couple of women servants – thus creating additional employment opportunities for rural immigrants.

Urban bushi households also generated enormous consumption demands. Restricted by daimyo fiat to military and bureaucratic careers,
the samurai relied on the commoners to provide them with both military equipment and a variety of everyday goods and services, a situation
that naturally attracted would-be merchants and artisans to the city. A
fraction of them came because they were invited to sell specialty goods
such as swords and armor to the daimyo and his warrior followers, but
most of the prospective merchants arrived on their own, hoping to take
advantage of the new commercial opportunities by setting up shops to
sell more ordinary goods: umbrellas, footwear, wooden buckets, and
pots and pans. It was this civilian migration that pushed the population
of Tottori to 35,000 persons, Okayama to 40,000, Sendai to 50,000, and
Kanazawa to nearly 120,000 persons by the year 1700.

14 The three classic works on premodern Japanese cities are Ono Hitoshi, *Kinsei jōkamachi no
kenkyū* (Tokyo: Shibundō, 1928); Toyoda Takeshi, *Nihon no hōken toshi* (Tokyo: Iwanami
shoten, 1952); and Harada Tomohiko, *Nihon hōken toshi kenkyū* (Tokyo: Tōkyō daigaku
shuppankai, 1973).

Although the castles and surrounding environs were originally planned as defensive enclaves, the mass migration of merchants and artisans into the new communities quickly gave them well-defined economic functions, as nodes of both consumption and production, so that their commercial significance far exceeded the capacities of the Sengoku period towns. The economic needs of the daimyo lords during the seventeenth century also contributed to the burgeoning importance of these castle town communities. Probably no daimyo domain was ever totally self-sufficient in goods or currency. Some had to import crockery or clothing materials such as cotton or silk; others had to acquire foodstuffs such as tea, salt, or fish from outside sources. Moreover, whenever the Tokugawa shogunate made demands on the daimyo for contributions to construction projects, some lords had to go outside the local economy for cash or building materials. Consequently, no daimyo could escape the need to participate, at least to some extent, in the broader, national network of economic exchange that was taking shape around these cities.

The policies of the shogunate toward currency and the minting of coins also encouraged an expansion in the volume of commercial transactions and contributed to the emergence of castle towns as nodes of economic exchange. Most major daimyo minted their own coins in the early decades of the seventeenth century. The shogunate, however, began to produce gold and silver coins in 1601 and copper coins five years later, and it soon claimed a monopoly on the right to issue currency that circulated throughout the entire nation. This meant that coins minted by the daimyo could be spent legitimately only inside the domain of origin and that the lords were compelled to spend the shogunate's currency to pay for imported goods, as well as to meet the extraordinary construction levies imposed by the shogunate and the expenses associated with the alternate residence system (*sankin-kōtai*) that was institutionalized during the decade of the 1630s. To acquire these coins meant that each daimyo had to sell a portion of his tax rice in the national, shogunate-controlled markets of Edo and Osaka, thus contributing to their growth and importance.

In addition, most daimyo also marketed some exportable local specialty products that could be collected from the peasantry in place of rice. These specialty goods were determined by the topographical conditions within each domain but many, at least in the early seventeenth century, consisted of raw materials such as lumber or hemp harvested from mountainous regions, copper and iron dug from the earth, and dried fish and salt hauled from the sea. During the opening decades of the seventeenth century, castle towns soon became the focal points not only of commercial activity but also of the collection and transshipment of these items.

The geographic location of the new castle towns within the daimyo domains reflected their twin importance as military and economic centers.[15] Toward the end of the sixteenth century, as the daimyo began to consolidate their grasp over increasingly large territorial units, they moved out of the narrow confines of the mountains and built new, more massive moat-and-tower fortresses on the wide plains that constituted the strategic and economic heart of their holdings. Here, the daimyo could assemble and hold in readiness their growing warrior bands, protected by walls and moats constructed at sufficient distance from the castle nerve center to safeguard it from musket and cannon, the new implements of siege and destruction. But the new locations conferred economic advantages as well, for these citadels towered over the villages of the domains and permitted the daimyo easier access to the agricultural surpluses that they could tax and use for trade and to support their regimes. Most of the new castle towns were also situated directly on or close to major transportation routes, an important consideration for the merchants and artisans whom the daimyo lords hoped to attract to their communities.

Because most bulk commodities were transported by ship, the daimyo took into consideration the proximity of bays and harbors when choosing locations for their castle towns. If a castle could not be located directly on the coast, a daimyo would often construct port facilities as close to the castle town as possible and then dig a connecting canal so that barges and small boats could transport goods into the castle town. The castle town of Kanazawa, for instance, was located several kilometers inland from the Sea of Japan, and so the Maeda daimyo encouraged the development of Miyanokoshi as a port and in the early seventeenth century went to considerable expense to dredge out two rivers connecting the port to Kanazawa so that the castle town merchants could profit from easier access to oceangoing transportation. Between the 1580s and 1630s, several dozen new port towns

15 The bulk of research in Japan concerning the relationship between economic growth and the geographic distribution of castle towns has been conducted not by historians but, rather, by specialists known as historical geographers, who have tended to use one variety or another of central place theory. Two of the more influential works in this genre are Yamori Kazuhiko, *Toshizu no rekishi: Nihon hen* (Tokyo: Kōdansha, 1974); and Matsumoto Toyotoshi, *Jōkamachi no rekishi chirigaku-teki kenkyū* (Tokyo: Yoshikawa kōbunkan, 1967). In English the fullest discussion of economic linkages among Tokugawa period cities can be found in Gilbert Rozman, *Urban Networks in Ch'ing China and Tokugawa Japan* (Princeton, N.J.: Princeton University Press, 1974).

sprang up along the harbors of Japan, one example of the secondary urban construction stimulated by the growth of the early modern castle towns.

One disadvantage of the new locations was that the castles and their adjoining communities were usually located at some distance from the materials necessary to construct them. The mammoth stones used for the walls of Edo Castle, for example, had to be quarried in the higher mountains along the rugged western coast of the Izu peninsula. They then had to be lowered by ropes down the steep, treacherous mountainsides and loaded onto the nearly three thousand barges that had been assembled to ship the stone blocks to Edo.[16] In Kanazawa, the stones were carved out of Mt. Tomuro, nearly eighty miles to the east of the city. Labor gangs rolled them overland on logs to a staging area near the castle where they were cut to shape by stone masons before being lifted and fitted into place. Such undertakings were hazardous. Countless numbers of men died while lowering the stones down the Izu mountains, and in Kanazawa portions of the walls collapsed twice during construction, killing dozens and injuring hundreds of laborers.[17]

Indeed, the epic nature attributed to these endeavors became part of the country's folklore as the peasant families who were compelled to supply the labor for these construction project left their feelings in a tradition of sorrowful folk songs and legends about those who toiled, and sometimes died, to erect the castles. For others, however, the sacrifices of the laborers were quickly overshadowed by the magnificence of the new castles, which were praised both as works of beauty as well as strength. In Kanazawa, one samurai wrote with pride that the long sweep of the walls gave the castle a sense of permanence, while the white stucco watchtowers gracefully, yet dramatically, set off the massive turrets and gates. Awed, he boasted that Kanazawa Castle was equal to the Toyotomi fortress in Osaka.[18]

To a large degree, the military and economic requirements of the age influenced the internal spatial arrangement of the castle towns.[19] Cer-

16 For a wonderfully illustrated history of the building of Edo, see Naitō Akira, *Edo no machi*, 2 vols. (Tokyo: Sōshisha, 1982).
17 James L. McClain, *Kanazawa: A Seventeenth-Century Japanese Castle Town* (New Haven, Conn.: Yale University Press, 1982), p. 33.
18 McClain, *Kanazawa*, p. 33. The construction of Osaka Castle is discussed in William B. Hauser, "Osaka Castle and Tokugawa Authority in Western Japan," in Jeffrey P. Mass and William B. Hauser, eds., *The Bakufu in Japanese History* (Stanford, Calif.: Stanford University Press, 1985).
19 The most detailed mapping of the castle towns has been completed by historical geographers. Especially influential has been Yamori's *Toshizu no rekishi*. Yamori divided castle town layouts into five general types, a classification that has been generally accepted as a working model by most researchers.

tainly, the physical layout of the communities embodied the status assumptions imposed by the lord on his domain. In the most common pattern, the residence of the daimyo lord and his family, as well as the most important administrative offices, were located in an area known as the *naikaku,* or central keep, an enclosure securely protected by stone walls and a network of moats, canals, and rivers. Around this inner redoubt lay the residences assigned to the band of vassal retainers, generally in two zones. The more important and unquestionably loyal samurai received rather large residences with perhaps as many as a dozen or more rooms and graced with landscape gardens. These were generally clustered together near the castle walls, protected by the ramparts and close to the administrative offices where these high-ranking retainers spent their working hours. Quarters for lower-ranking retainers were located in a second belt, usually far removed from the castle and often unprotected except perhaps for a single outer moat or sometimes a simple earthen barricade. The accommodations here accorded with the more humble status of these warriors, who, divided by occupational rank (riflers, foot soldiers, and the like), were crowded together with their families into tiny apartments inside long, narrow, barracks-style tenement houses known as *nagaya.*

Most of the merchants and artisans lived between the two groups of warriors. This residential area for the urban commoners was divided into wards (*machi*). Most commonly, these were oblong quarters, strung out along the roads which were planned to cross at right angles, with the houses facing each other across a street constituting a single ward. To some extent, the composition of these wards reflected the status and economic gradations that subdivided the merchant and artisan classes. Within any castle town, some wards were made up almost entirely of a small group of elite merchants who supplied certain crucial military or prized luxury goods to the daimyo, items such as munitions or arms, rice in bulk shipments, silks and other quality clothing materials, or cakes and saké. The daimyo would grant charters to these men, vouching that he would buy their products and thus coining the generic term, *goyō shōnin,* purveyors to the lord, that defined this distinctive group. In addition to the charters, the lord often bestowed on these merchants tax exemptions and residential housing plots within the better wards, generally known as the *hommachi,* that were close to the castle and among the first laid out, locations that had the additional advantage of being near the wealthier samurai customers.

Also given preferential treatment were the forwarding agents, the men who procured packhorses, arranged coolie labor, and otherwise managed the details of the daimyo's export trade.[20] Typically they received residential plots in the center of the commercial section, an area that then became known as Temmamachi, literally the post horse ward. Similarly, each daimyo required the services of certain kinds of artisans – swordsmiths, armorers, carpenters, stone cutters, plasterers, and tatami makers – and to entice them to his domain he would offer guarantees of employment, tax exemptions, and housing that was conveniently situated close to the castle.[21] Often those with the same occupation were clustered together in a specific ward, and even today ancient names such as carpenters' ward, swordsmiths' ward, and so forth can be found in the modern cities that evolved from former castle towns.[22]

Beyond the quarters dominated by the commoner elites were the more numerous wards populated by the merchants who dealt in ordinary goods such as vegetables, tea, oil, charcoal, and paper, and by artisans such as umbrella makers, coopers, dyers, and barbers.[23] Although separated from the elite areas, these wards usually still enjoyed a favorable location within the belt between the two main zones of samurai residences. Beyond the outer ring of lower-ranking samurai, on the outskirts of the town, were the slumlike areas of the urban poor, outcast groups, and day laborers who toiled in the lowest-paid and least-skilled construction jobs.[24]

The rapid growth of the castle towns during the late sixteenth century and early seventeenth centuries forced the Japanese daimyo to devise new systems of urban administration. Such a task defied easy solution, however, and it was not until the middle of the seventeenth century that most daimyo could set in place the administrative structures that served as the basis of urban government for the balance of the Tokugawa period. Unfortunately, the specific steps that the daimyo took to build these urban political structures cannot be easily traced, for natural disasters have destroyed much of the documentary base in most cities, and so the events in the first half of the seventeenth

20 Tsuchida Ryōichi, "Kinsei jōkamachi no temmayaku," in Chihōshi kenkyū kyōgikai, ed., Nihon no toshi to machi (Tokyo: Yūzankaku, 1982), pp. 146–75.
21 The residential clustering of persons according to occupation is the topic of Fujimoto Toshiharu, "Toshi no dōgyōsha-machi to sangyō," in Toyoda, Harada, and Yamori, eds., Kōza: Nihon no hōken toshi, vol. 2, pp. 35–7.
22 For a recent study of artisan groups, see Yokota Fuyuhiko, "Shokunin to shokunin dantai," in Rekishigaku kenkyūkai, ed., Kōza Nihon rekishi, vol. 5 (Tokyo: Tōkyō daigaku shuppankai, 1985), pp. 189–226.
23 Fukai Jinzō, "Kinsei toshi no hattatsu," in Matsumoto Shirō and Yamada Tadao, eds., Genroku, Kyōhō-ki no seiji to shakai (Tokyo: Yūhikaku, 1980), pp. 148–59.
24 For a discussion of outcast groups, see Harada Tomohiko, "Kinsei toshi no hisabetsu buraku," in Toyoda, Harada, and Yamori, eds., Kōza: Nihon no hōken toshi, vol. 2, pp. 389–412.

century often must be conjectured from the later records of the eighteenth and early nineteenth centuries.

One exception to this rule is the castle town of Kanazawa, where a variety of early-seventeenth-century documents have been preserved. Although there was perhaps no such creature as a perfectly typical castle town, the general evolution of Kanazawa paralleled that of other such cities. Consequently, the details observed there can provide a useful example of how urban government commonly developed. Moreover, because urban governance has received little attention from historians to date, a close examination of Kanazawa can help illuminate how the castle towns served as important units of local government and how the daimyo's efforts to govern the cities fit into the pattern of domain and village governance, as explained in Chapters 4, 5, and 10 of this volume.[25]

The administrative arm of the city government in Kanazawa, as in other castle towns, could be functionally divided into two principal components: one designed to rule the merchants and artisans and the other to govern the samurai. The samurai's administrative apparatus was the direct heir of the battlefield chain of command established in the late sixteenth century as the Maeda daimyo fought their way to power in the hills and plains of the Hokuriku region. During their rise to power, the Maeda had put into place a military organization in which authority passed from daimyo to individual retainers through a hierarchy of command that permitted the daimyo to mobilize and deploy military personnel easily during the years of constant warfare. As the Maeda summoned the samurai into the castle town between 1580 and 1620, they began to add civil administrative functions to this system of command. The highest level of the Maeda band of retainers, known collectively as the Eight Houses (*hakka*), served as the lord's leading military tacticians and commanders during times of warfare, but after the move into Kanazawa they were named as chief advisers and made responsible for formulating the political and administrative policies for the entire domain. Consequently, after the 1620s every important political decision that affected life in Kanazawa was made by either the daimyo or this body of chief advisers. In addition, these men were responsible for overseeing the activities of the next lower status group, the commanders (*hitomochi*).[26]

---

25 The most complete general coverage of castle town governments can be found in Nakabe, *Jōkamachi*, pp. 239–300; Tanaka Yoshio, *Jōkamachi Kanazawa* (Tokyo: Nihon shoin, 1966); and McClain, *Kanazawa*, pp. 85–101.

26 This pattern was similar to that observed in other domains; see, for example, John Whitney Hall, "The Ikeda House and Its Retainers in Bizen," in John W. Hall and Marius B. Jansen, eds., *Studies in the Institutional History of Early Modern Japan* (Princeton, N.J.: Princeton

The commanders were relatively high-ranking samurai (they had stipends ranging between one thousand and fourteen thousand *koku*), who had led troops on the field of battle. After being withdrawn to the city, they were assigned to significant posts in the civilian government. Four of the most influential domain offices, for example, were the offices of comptroller, rural magistrates, city magistrates, and magistrates for shrine and temple affairs, and all were staffed by men from this status group. Strictly speaking, these posts were not usually endowed with specific policymaking powers. However, the incumbents had frequent contact with the daimyo and the chief advisers, who often solicited their opinions, and this gave the commanders an informal mechanism for influencing policy decisions. Thus, for example, when the daimyo and the chief advisers were deadlocked over whether or not to license a kabuki and prostitution district in Kanazawa in the 1820s, the decision turned on the recommendations submitted by the city magistrates.

In addition to their posts within the formal administrative structure, the commanders were also held accountable for the civil conduct of the samurai under their jurisdiction. Any one commander might oversee as many as 150 warriors, who were then divided into several units, each captained by a unit leader (*kumigashira*). The commander was responsible for ensuring that all members of these units, as well as their families and attendants, obeyed the laws and edicts issued by the daimyo. If a rear vassal committed a crime involving violence, for instance, he had to be turned over to the appropriate domain police officials for punishment. In other cases, however, the unit leaders would meet with the parties involved in a dispute and attempt to arrange a mutually agreeable settlement. If that proved impossible, the commander would enter the case and could even mete out punishments, subject to the approval of his own superiors.

A much more elaborate administrative apparatus specifically designed to handle the affairs of the merchant and artisan status groups was created during the opening decades of the seventeenth century. In its final form, the city government became highly bureaucratic. Perhaps the most crucial officials were the city magistrates (*machi bugyō*). The first appointments to this office were made irregularly from the 1590s and permanently from 1641. These officials were entrusted with

University Press, 1968), pp. 79–88; and Madoka Kanai, "Fukui, Domain of a Tokugawa Collateral Daimyo: Its Traditions and Transition," in Ardath W. Burks, ed., *The Modernizers* (Boulder, Colo.: Westview Press, 1985), pp. 33–68.

implementing policies established by the daimyo and the chief advisers, and to this end, they supervised the City Office (Machi kaisho) that by the end of the seventeenth century had come to include more than three hundred employees.

A great number of merchants and artisans also served as lesser officials in urban administration. The post of city elder (*machidoshiyori*) was the most important of these. This term appears in documents as early as 1594, but appointments were not made on a regular basis until the late 1640s and early 1650s, when the number of elders was fixed at twenty.[27] The daimyo appointed as city elders merchants who had made their marks in business, men who possessed administrative skills and enjoyed a high reputation, as defined in terms of commercial success. Not unexpectedly, many came from the ranks of the chartered merchants, the merchant elite who enjoyed commercial privileges and an especially close relationship with the lord and high retainers.

The elders performed a variety of duties. They received written requests and complaints from the townspeople, attached their own opinions, and then submitted the paperwork to the samurai officials at the City Office. They also checked tax receipts and submitted statements that the proper amount had been collected. The elders accompanied the police officials who investigated the crimes of merchants and artisans and then attended hearings. Finally, they helped supervise the activities of other commoners who worked at the City Office. In a more general way, they were expected to promote good behavior and filial piety among the townspeople, to mediate civil disagreements between commoners, and to encourage diligence by merchants and artisans.

Several dozen other offices that functioned under the jurisdiction of the city elders in Kanazawa also became institutionalized during the middle decades of the seventeenth century. It became common practice, for example, to appoint inspectors (*yokome kimoiri*) and ward representatives (*machi kimoiri*) to assist the city elders. The inspectors helped with tax collection and investigated charges of questionable administration by city officials. Each representative served several wards (in the 1690s there were approximately forty representatives and slightly more than one hundred commoner wards), and they were specifically instructed to help compile census reports, examine commoner com-

---

27 The number was reduced to ten in 1669. *Machidoshiyori rekimei narabi ni tsutomekatachō*, ms. copy, Kanazawa City Library.

plaints about allegedly exorbitant and unfair prices, hold conciliation talks in commercial disputes, and investigate suspicious deaths. For this, the representatives were paid a salary of a little less than five *koku* of rice each, about one-half of what the city elders received.

The groups of ten households (*jūningumi*) constituted the final link in the administrative chain. The groups had a long history in Kanazawa, and the term can be found in early-seventeenth-century documents. Apparently not all urban commoners formed themselves into such groups, however, until domain proclamations issued in the 1640s instructed them to do so. These groups of ten households (in reality, the number of households in any one group often exceeded that number) were the functional equivalent of the household groups established in the rural villages in most domains.

In one sense, the groups preserved the interests of the merchant and artisan neighborhoods, since they functioned as units of mutual aid and self-help. In Kanazawa, for instance, members were supposed to assist neighbors who fell on hard times financially, and from the mid-seventeenth century each group maintained firefighting equipment such as ladders, rakes, and rain barrels. Looked at from another perspective, the groups reflected an effort by the daimyo to extend his authority and laws over the commoner populace, as the group members were held jointly responsible for obeying the law and, in theory, could be collectively punished for the actions of any single member. Beyond this, the groups also carried out a variety of administrative functions. They assembled periodically to hear a reading of legal codes, enforced the provisions of wills and decided the disposition of property when a member died without leaving such a document, and verified that any member who moved to a new ward left no debts behind. Moreover, they conducted conciliation talks whenever quarrels, commercial disagreements, or land disputes among group members interrupted neighborhood tranquility. If no satisfactory solution could be found, then the ward representative, and ultimately the city elder if necessary, would be called in for further rounds of negotiation. Only if the mediation at all these levels failed did the dispute move up the ladder for settlement by samurai officialdom.

In pace with the amplification of the urban administrative apparatus during the first half of the seventeenth century, Kaga's officials acted to establish a written, legal basis for their political authority by issuing codifications of laws and ordinances. These were promulgated according to status group, with different codes for the samurai and for the urban commoners. During the early years of the castle town's growth, the Maeda daimyo issued three separate codes regulating the samurai life: in 1601, 1605, and 1612 (with a set of supplements in 1613). Here, daimyo law was very limited in scope and intent. For instance, the 1605 code, issued under the personal seal of Maeda Toshinaga (1562–1614), prohibited the following:

1. Walking on the streets at night.
2. Loitering on the streets.
3. Singing on the streets.
4. Playing the flute (*shakuhachi*).
5. Holding sumo matches on the street.
6. Dancing in the streets.
7. Masking one's face with a scarf.

Clearly, the government's chief concern was to preserve law and order and to establish procedures for the adjudication of disputes. The other samurai codes played on the same themes: They forbade cliques, declared that retainers should not harbor thieves or suspected criminals among their rear vassals, specified that all parties involved in violent quarrels were to be judged equally guilty, irrespective of who was at fault, and prohibited gambling, with specific rewards for anyone who supplied information about violators.

The laws directed at the merchants and artisans were much more numerous, and major codifications were issued in 1642 and 1660. A concern with peace on the city streets could also be detected in these documents. The 1642 code, for instance, carried prohibitions against gambling, gossiping, and keeping dogs as pets; whereas the 1660 edition repeated earlier injunctions against prostitution, wearing swords, and urinating from the second floor of houses.

But these merchant codes could intrude more into the lives of the urban commoners than did the samurai codes. Particularly noticeable was the expansion of government involvement in the economic life of the townspeople. The 1660 code stipulated that maximum interest rates be fixed at 1.7 percent per month and prohibited any joint samurai–merchant business ventures. Yet another article announced that a representative from the City Office would visit any person who fell behind in his debt repayments or credit obligations, an especially important clause for the merchants and artisans of Kanazawa, as it promised government assistance in collecting all debts. Another feature of merchant codes was a concern with public services. The 1660 code contained clauses concerning garbage disposal, the firefighting responsibilities of the household groups, and the duties of the ward patrols (*teishūban*), whose chief responsibility, which rotated among the residents of each ward, was to patrol nightly the ward's streets, watching for fire and criminal activity.

In addition to the major legal codifications, the domain government issued a mass of ordinances during the middle of seventeenth century that attempted both to regulate behavior and to further refine status distinctions. An important ordinance in 1661, for example, attempted to synchronize clothing with status. Regulations that took effect on New Year's Day of that year established the types of clothing fabrics permitted to peasants, townspeople, and each major subdivision of the samurai status group. Accordingly, high-level retainers such as members of the Eight Houses and the commanders could wear thirteen kinds of high-quality silk; retainers from the middle ranks were permitted four kinds of lesser silk; and those such as the more minor archers and riflers were restricted to pongee, cotton, and the rougher fibers of flax, hemp, and vines, known collectively under the rubric of *nuno*. The regulations provided that townspeople could wear plain silk (*kinu*) and pongee, whereas the peasants were held to pongee and the rougher fibers.

The domain complemented these clothing regulations with other status decrees. Some laws set limits on the amounts and kinds of foods that could be served on holidays and ceremonial days, with the samurai permitted more opulent indulgences than merchants were. According to other laws, townspeople were not supposed to have carved wooden beams or doors made from cedar in their homes, because these were perquisites of the samurai class. Nor could townspeople, unless they were seriously ill or over sixty years of age, ride in palanquins, whose use was normally restricted to high-ranking samurai and certain city officials.

The establishment of patterns of urban governance in early modern Japan paralleled the transformations in the exercise of political authority in rural areas and on the domain level, as explained in Chapters 5 and 9 of this volume. The daimyo of the late sixteenth century had been personal autocrats who led armies, enfeoffed retainers, issued decrees, and set policy. By the second half of the seventeenth century, most of their successors had withdrawn from the direct, day-to-day management of the affairs of government and, instead, had become more nominal rulers whose chief function was to serve as the legitimizing agent of the administrative structure.

The retreat of the daimyo as personal leaders, however, did not portend a decline in state powers, for the new bureaucracies of the seventeenth century had more ability to tax, legislate, and punish than did the daimyo of the previous age. Yet, in a profound historical twist, the exercise of this power was also newly tempered; first, by the government's need to harmonize its policies with the aspirations and wishes of the merchants and artisans in the cities and, second, by the obligation of government to subordinate its impulses to the requirements imposed by the new bureaucratic practices, legal codes, and standardized procedures that grew up during Japan's transition from the medieval to the early modern polity. The history of cities such as Kanazawa demonstrate how castle towns brought together the concentrations of wealth and power that made possible this shift away from personal forms of authority toward a new style of bureaucratic statism.

CITIES AND COMMERCE IN THE SEVENTEENTH CENTURY

Castle towns and the agricultural revolution

The commercial economy grew significantly during the period of Japan's political unification, from the middle sixteenth down to the end of the seventeenth century. The point of departure for this expansion was a revolution in agricultural production. Although the statistical data are not without shortcomings, some scholars have estimated that the amount of cultivated paddy more than doubled in the century from 1550 to 1650 alone.[28] Productivity and yields also increased as better fertilizers, improved farm tools, and new strains of seeds made their appearance. Important as well were reclamation and large-scale irrigation projects, many underwritten by daimyo who hoped to expand the taxable revenue base of their domains. Another factor was the role played by the individual peasant household. As rural residents acquired more secure rights to their holdings, a process discussed in Chapters 3 and 10 in this volume, the farmers came to believe that significant portions of any increase in yield would accrue to them, and thus they were more willing to make the investments necessary to boost productivity and to bring formerly marginal fields into cultivation.[29] Indeed, signs of a growing rural prosperity – new and larger houses, improved diet, better clothing – were evident in most areas of Japan by the middle of the seventeenth century.

These improvements in the nation's productive capacity touched off

28 Kozo Yamamura, "Returns on Unification: Economic Growth in Japan, 1550–1650," in Hall, Nagahara, and Yamamura, eds., *Japan Before Tokugawa*, p. 334.
29 Ibid., pp. 339–57.

a dynamic spurt in population growth. Although accurate statistics were not kept at that time, some demographers and historians place the growth rate in the range of 0.78 to 1.34 percent annually between 1550 and 1700. Others posit an accelerating rate during the seventeenth century, rising from 0.5 percent in the early decades of the century to nearly 1.4 percent between 1650 and 1670.[30] Despite these differences of opinion, most scholars agree that the greatest population increases took place in the last half of the seventeenth century and that, in aggregate, the country's total population grew from roughly 12 million persons to approximately 26 million to 30 million at the time of the shogun's census in 1721.

The rapid increase in both productive capacity and population also brought about changes in household composition. The number of individual farm households increased at a faster rate than did overall production growth, and this statistic indicates a rearrangement of household configuration away from a complex, extended family toward smaller nuclear families, many of which were created as branches and given land by the stem family. The disappearance of the extended farm family meant that the small independent cultivator (*jisakushonō*) who farmed his holding with the labor of his own family became the most common type of peasant household. As the process of subdivision continued, however, there eventually came into being a growing number of families who possessed land that was barely sufficient for their needs. Indeed, by the 1670s the shogunate had become so concerned about the destabilizing aspects of the further subdivision of farmland that it issued a "law restricting the division of farmland" (*bunchi seigen-rei*).[31]

The evolution of the farm family also brought about conditions that favored urban migration. As families shed surplus members during the first half of the seventeenth century, there were always some who did not have enough land to establish branch families. These disfranchised men and women often moved into the growing castle towns, where they could hope to find work as day laborers or unskilled artisans, although the poorest of the women were sometimes forced into prostitution. Similarly, those new branches who had received only marginal amounts of land were in a position of continuous economic

30 Hayami Akira, *Kinsei nōson no rekishi jinkōgaku-teki kenkyū* (Tokyo: Tōyō keizai shimpōsha, 1973), p. 23; and Shakai kōgaku kenkyūjo, ed., *Nihon rettō ni okeru jinkō bumpu no chōki jikeiretsu bunseki* (Tokyo: Shakai kōgaku kenkyūjo, 1974), pp. 42–57.
31 The fullest discussion of the relationship between the commercialization of agriculture and household composition remains Thomas C. Smith, *The Agrarian Origins of Modern Japan* (Stanford, Calif.: Stanford University Press, 1959).

jeopardy, and in years of even slight drought or cold weather they might have to abandon their homes to search for work, or even to beg, in the castle towns.

There is no way of knowing the exact magnitude of migration in the seventeenth century, but given the rapid growth of the castle towns, surely several hundreds of thousands of persons were on the move in the middle decades of the century. In Kanazawa alone, to take one example, between 1660 to 1663, arriving would-be merchants and artisans leased well over 300,000 square meters of farmland on the fringes of the city.[32] Regardless of the exact scale of migration, however, local officials were clearly worried, and many castle towns enacted special ordinances in the middle of the seventeenth century that discouraged further movement into their cities and that attempted to bring beggars under closer supervision.[33]

The ongoing migration from village to city also prompted the shogunate to introduce the system of family census registers (*koseki*) as one way of gaining some measure of control over this migrant population. Before this, the shogunate had compelled each temple to conduct a religious investigation (*shūshi aratame*) as a means of suppressing Christianity. It had also ordered a census and household count in each village for the purpose of making corvée levies, and at the same time, it instructed peasants to report the number of cattle and horses they were raising. In 1670, however, these two records were combined in the religious and census investigation (*shūmon aratame*). This new reporting system began the practice of requiring all the households of each domain, without exception, to register the names of their members with ward or village officials and to identify their temple of affiliation. Once a person was registered, if he wanted to migrate, he had to prove that he had obtained the permission of his temple and his ward or village.

In addition to provoking the imposition of stricter political controls, the large influx of population into the cities in the middle decades of the seventeenth century affected the physical layout of the castle towns. First, the castle towns started to expand into areas beyond the geographic limits that the daimyo founders had envisioned. The migrants, mostly poor, tended to live where rents were lowest, on the rural fringes of the castle towns. Increasingly, the boundaries between urban wards and agricultural villages became blurred as men and

---

32 Tanaka Yoshio, "Kinsei jōkamachi hatten no ichi kōsatsu – 'Aitaiukechi' kara mita jōkamachi, Kanazawa no baai," *Hokuriku shigaku* 8 (1959): 19–37.
33 For a specific example, see McClain, *Kanazawa*, pp. 124–32.

women who worked as laborers, craftsmen, or bushi household servants rented lodgings in settlements that were under the administrative jurisdiction of the rural magistrates (*kōri bugyō*). Moreover, theaters and houses of prostitution often sprouted up in these fringe areas. This growth caused, in turn, a whole new set of problems, as farmers complained about the newcomers trampling over fields, breaking down dikes, or otherwise disrupting the rhythm of agricultural life. Many urban governments responded by transferring these areas to the jurisdiction of the city magistrates, thus making the merchant–farmer wards part of the cityscape.

The physical expansion of the cities played havoc with older notions of urban planning. Originally, for instance, most daimyo had preferred, for defensive purposes, to situate their foot soldiers and the large Buddhist temples in a concentric circle around the outer limits of the city. Now many had to abandon that design or else undertake considerable expense and trouble to relocate the warrior residences and religious institutions. Predictably, this kind of urban reorganization most frequently occurred in cities that had the misfortune of suffering a major fire. Such conflagrations provided a convenient pretext for the daimyo to relocate people who otherwise would have been reluctant to move to strange neighborhoods, away from old friends and familiar shops and places of worship. Following such fires, many daimyo also widened the streets and established open areas as firebreaks at strategic points.

Concurrently, the principle that persons of the same occupation ought to live together in the same wards suffered serious erosion, and except for some special occupations such as that of gunsmith or swordsmith, artisans as well as merchants began to reside in scattered locations throughout the expanding cities. One reason contributing to this process was that some established merchants and artisans voluntarily moved into the newly created fringe wards, in search of new customers or lower shop rents. A second reason was that the forced relocation of some bushi turned the fringe areas into real residential hodgepodges, adding samurai to the merchant, artisan, and day laborer populations. In Kanazawa, for instance, seven of the households in one ward on the outskirts of the city belonged to artisans, twenty-eight to merchants, six to day laborers, and thirteen to samurai.[34]

The complexion of the inner city changed as well. As some of the

34 For this and other examples, see Tanaka, *Jōkamachi Kanazawa*, pp. 103–106; and Tanaka Yoshio, *Kaga han ni okeru toshi no kenkyū* (Tokyo: Bun'ichi sōgō shuppan, 1978), pp. 140–5.

newcomers prospered, they moved into the older, more prestigious sections of the city, usually choosing sites that suited their fancy and commercial needs, rather than adhering to the artificial occupation divisions of an earlier age. Finally, many were tempted by the empty land within the new firebreaks. Not uncommonly, poorer merchants and artisans squatted on this land, much to the chagrin of those domain authorities who were still wedded to the notion of a planned city. But the perseverance of the homesteaders to stay was usually greater than the resolve of the city authorities to evict them.

The expansion of cities in the middle and later decades of the seventeenth century was only one factor working to change the character and function of cities. By the end of the century, the commoners of the castle towns had also achieved new levels of economic prosperity and brought into being a distinctive urban-based culture. The interaction of the population migration with the commercial and cultural developoment inside the city created a new kind of castle town, as we shall see, one that was very different from the expectations of the daimyo during the period of urban creation at the beginning of the century.

Commercial development and castle town merchants

Paralleling the agricultural revolution was a spectacular expansion in the volume of commercial exchange that began during the middle decades of the sixteenth century and continued until the end of the seventeenth century. Historians have identified several causes that contributed to this process, including the policies implemented by the daimyo during the late Sengoku period in order to strengthen the economic basis of their rule, such as the abolition of toll gate barriers and the promotion of periodic markets that would be open to all traders.[35]

Daimyo of the seventeenth century continued these policies and also vigorously promoted the expansion of permanent markets within the new castle towns, such as when the Maeda daimyo set aside two plots of land in the commercial heart of Kanazawa to be used by fish and vegetable dealers.[36] Other significant stimulants included the standard-

---

35 The classic work on this topic is Sasaki Gin'ya, *Chūsei shōhin ryūtsū no kenkyū* (Tokyo: Hōsei daigaku shuppankyoku, 1972). In English, see Gin'ya Sasaki, with William B. Hauser, "Sengoku Daimyo Rule and Commerce," in Hall, Nagahara, and Yamamura, eds., *Japan Before Tokugawa*, pp. 125–48; and Kozo Yamamura, "Returns on Unification," on pp. 327–72 of the same volume.

36 Kanazawa-shi Ōmichō ichiba-shi hensan iinkai, ed., *Kanazawa-shi Ōmichō ichiba-shi* (Kanazawa: Hokkoku shuppansha, 1979), pp. 10–25.

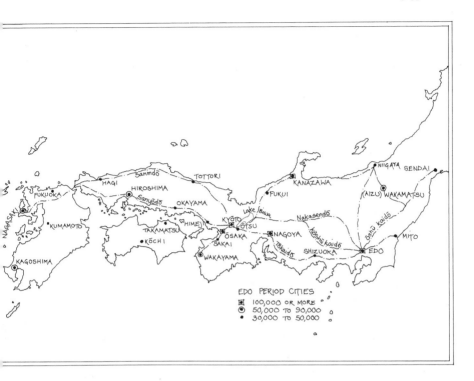

Map 11.1 Major cities and transportation routes, eighteenth century.

ization of weights and measures and the minting of coins by the Toku- ✓
gawa shogunate that were accepted nationwide as units of exchange.
Important, too, was the growth of transportation facilities.[37] Beyond
constructing port facilities and dredging rivers and canals to link castle
towns to ports, the Tokugawa shogunate and individual daimyo also
laid out large sums of money to develop overland transportation facilities. The keystone of these projects was the linking of Edo with distant
localities by the construction of several major roadways, including the
great Tōkaidō highway between Edo and Kyoto, whose more than
fifty post towns provided the supplies, horses, and resting places that
made possible transportation between the emperor's and the shogun's
home cities. Within the domains, too, the daimyo built roads and
bridges to ease the transport of foodstuffs and raw materials from the
rural villages into the castle towns.[38] (See Map 11.1)

37 Maruyama Yasunari, "Toshi to rikujō kōtsū," in Toyoda, Harada, and Yamori, eds., *Kōza:
Nihon no hōken toshi*, vol. 2, pp. 119–44.
38 For a very useful study of the post towns, see Haga Noboru, *Shukuba-machi* (Kyoto:
Yanagihara shoten, 1977).

Another factor was the institutionalization of the system of alternate residence. Although the custom of personal attendance on one's superior and the submission of hostages as an expression of loyalty had become fairly common during the sixteenth century, these practices were made a permanent obligation for the daimyo only after 1633. From that date, daimyo were compelled to alternate their residences between Edo and their home domains, to build elaborate mansions in Edo, and to leave appropriate retinues, including their wives and children, permanently in the shogun's city. This system was designed to permit the shogunate to maintain a close surveillance over the daimyo, but it also had the consequence of stimulating the nation's volume of commercial exchange as the daimyo processions moved back and forth along the new highways that crossed Japan.[39]

The growing wave of commercial transactions had several important consequences. Agricultural patterns changed enormously, for now farmers were able to concentrate more profitably their energies on growing commercial crops, such as cotton, tea, hemp, mulberry, indigo, vegetables, and tobacco, for sale to the urban markets.[40] Regional specialization also became a feature of economic life, as great numbers of villagers around Osaka, for instance, started to switch over to cotton cultivation while farmers in northern Japan began to raise horses and cattle for sale as draft animals.[41] Individual rural households began to develop by-employments or simple rural industries, so that even within a single domain certain villages became known for their production of goods such as paper, charcoal, ink, pottery, lacquer ware, or spun cloth.

Concurrent with the commercial growth of Tokugawa Japan was the daimyo's increasing need for cash revenues, which could come only through participation in interregional trade. One part of the story is simply that the daimyo needed money to buy the growing number of specialized goods that were produced outside their own domains. But the system of alternate residence also put a strain on the daimyo's finances. The experience of the Maedo daimyo of Kaga was fairly typical. By the end of the seventeenth century, their journeys to Edo

39 The most complete treatment of the alternate residence system in English is Toshio George Tsukahira, *Feudal Control in Tokugawa Japan: The Sankin Kōtai System*, Harvard East Asian Monographs, no. 20 (Cambridge, Mass.: Harvard University Press, 1966).
40 This shift in cropping patterns is discussed in Watanabe Zenjirō, *Toshi to nōson no aida* (Tokyo: Ronsōsha, 1983), esp. pp. 121–49, 241–76.
41 For examples of this sort of regional specialization in the Kinai, Morioka, and Okayama, see Susan B. Hanley and Kozo Yamamura, *Economic and Demographic Change in Preindustrial Japan, 1600–1868* (Princeton, N.J.: Princeton University Press, 1977), pp. 91–198.

and the expenses associated with maintaining the nearly three thousand persons from Kaga who lived year-round in the Edo mansion often consumed at least one-third and sometimes as much as one-half of all annual domain expenditures.[42]

The occasional extraordinary levies made by the shogunate were also burdensome. The Tokugawa rulers demanded economic assistance when they rebuilt Osaka Castle after the siege of 1614–15, constructed a castle residence for the retired Ieyasu at Sumpu, and repaired Edo Castle after fires in 1636, 1657, and 1658. The shogunate also made fairly regular exactions for the construction of roads, bridges, and waterways. The cash requirements dictated by the shogun's levies, when added to burdens associated with the system of alternate residence, contributed greatly to the domains' growing indebtedness. By the end of the seventeenth century, nearly all domains were spending in some years more than they could collect in agricultural levies, and many daimyo had turned to borrowing funds from wealthy merchants in Edo and Osaka. To return to the Kaga example, annual domain expenses amounted to nearly 15 percent more than its revenues in the 1690s, and within another two generations the total of its outstanding loans to wealthy merchants probably amounted to more than twice the sum of all annual domain revenues.[43]

Commercial growth and the expanding needs of most domains for new sources of revenues prompted many daimyo to revise their policies toward the merchants in their castle towns. In particular, many daimyo began to cast aside their ties with the older class of privileged merchants, the *goyō* purveyors to the lord, and, instead, began to nurture relationships with other groups of businessmen who could best meet the changing requirements for increasing the flow of goods into castle towns and promoting interdomain trade.

In most castle towns, the daimyo and their governments now forged ties with *ton'ya*, or groups of wholesalers and forwarding agents, to whom the lords granted monopoly rights over specific commodities and commercial crops. Some of these associations participated in interregional trade. In Kaga domain, for instance, an association of tea wholesalers had been formed by the 1650s and had been granted sole rights to import tea from other domains. The wholesalers' own profits came from a commission, which was authorized by the domain and added to the basic price before the wholesalers sold the tea to peddlers

42 For the figures for Kaga and several other domains, see Tsukahira, *Feudal Control*, pp. 81–102.
43 Kuranami Seiji, *Kaga: Hyakumangoku* (Tokyo: Hachiyo shuppan, 1974), pp. 101–28.

who then retailed it throughout the domain.[44] Other wholesale groups specialized in moving goods from the closer rural hinterlands to castle town customers. Thus by the 1680s several different wholesale groups were authorized to buy charcoal, paper, ink, cloth, cooking oil, and firewood from villagers throughout Kaga domain, who produced these items at slack times in the agriculture season, and to sell them, after adding a commission, to retailers in the castle town of Kanazawa.[45]

In other cases, wholesalers were responsible for directing the complex flow of raw materials that were used to produce local specialities for sale outside the domain. An example of how many layers of wholesalers might be involved in such a process comes from the castle town of Hikone, headquarters of the famous Ii family of *fudai* daimyo. There, the most marketable local product was clothing made from jute (*asa*), which was prized for its coolness and breathability in the warmer, more humid regions of Japan. Farmers in mountainous areas around Hikone collected the jute and sold it to designated groups of wholesalers, who in turn resold it to artisans, who then spun it into thread. A different group of wholesalers known as *asaya*, or jute dealers, then purchased this thread, added an authorized markup, and sold it to craftsmen who wove it into cloth. Finally, yet another authorized group of wholesalers purchased the cloth and marketed it outside the domain.

In other circumstances, a domain might pursue policies that favored particular artisan groups. In the castle town of Wakamatsu in Aizu domain (the present-day city of Aizu–Wakamatsu), about 10 percent of all the artisans in the city produced lacquer ware, a local product that won fame nationwide and was in great demand in central markets such as Edo and Osaka. The domain designated the trees and bushes from which lacquer base was extracted as *yakuboku*, or "tax trees," and the domain ordered the peasants to collect the liquid extracted from the trees and to pay it as a tax. The government later sold the extract to castle town artisans and then purchased the output, mostly wooden soup bowls, for sale outside the domain. Although no figures for the seventeenth century are available, by the middle of the eighteenth century, exports of such lacquer ware accounted for 84 percent of all domain exports. Indeed, the fact that the domain imported beech and magnolia trees, which provided sap that could be turned into the lacquer base, indicates that demand for Aizu lacquer ware far outstripped the amount of raw material available in the domain.

44 Heki Ken, eds., *Kaga han shiryō*, 18 vols. (Tokyo: Ishiguro bunkichi, 1928–58), vol. 4 (Kambun 3 [1663]/3/6), pp. 10–12.
45 McClain, *Kanazawa*, pp. 131–4.

Government policy in almost every castle town gave preferential treatment to rice dealers. The reason for this had to do with the tax and stipendiary systems. When the diamyo across Japan pulled the samurai into the castle towns and abolished their prerogative to extract dues from the peasants directly, the lords began to compensate their retainers by providing stipends, denominated in units of rice. By the middle of the seventeenth century, it had become standard practice in most parts of Japan to pay samurai with certificates, good for the amount of their stipends and collectible from the daimyo's granary. Very soon, rice dealers who bought the certificates from the samurai, and even from the daimyo himself, and then sold the rice on the open market became a prominent part of the merchant class in nearly every castle town.

Because it was in the daimyo's interest to have rice sell at as high a price as possible, most daimyo governments enacted laws that, in effect, gave special protection to the rice dealers. For example, almost every daimyo strictly prohibited the importation of rice from outside his home domain, except during times of famine. Moreover, most daimyo formally recognized groups of rice dealers, who could then form a protective association, or *kabunakama*, with monopoly rights to purchase rice certificates from the samurai.

Finally, many daimyo enacted policies that favored saké brewing as a way of encouraging rice consumption. One way that they did this was to specify the amounts of rice to be set aside for saké production. Beyond this, many daimyo also protected the brewers by authorizing the formation of protective associations, prohibiting the importation of saké from outside the domain, and granting special payment terms to brewers for the rice they used in their business.[46] By the end of the seventeenth century, saké brewers in the castle towns had become as important as their rural counterparts and were among the more prosperous elements of the urban merchant class.

Local towns

Closely related to the increasing volume of commercial exchange was the appearance of what were called local towns, or *zaigōmachi*. As

---

46 Numerous restrictive regulations concerning saké brewing can be found in compilations of laws in the Tokugawa period, and so it has been argued that saké brewing was generally carried out under very severe production restrictions. However, these regulations were typically issued on a temporary basis during the periods of poor harvest or crop failures. In normal times, saké brewers were valued as large-scale consumers of rice.

farmers engaged more and more in by-employments, merchants began to move into rural areas in order to help the farmers assemble raw materials, process those into finished products, and then transport the goods into the urban retail markets. In time, the percentage of the rural population engaged in trade grew, and many of the villages lost their agricultural identity. The evolution of villages into local towns is often considered to be a nineteenth-century phenomenon, but the process certainly began earlier. For instance, in Kaga domain alone, by the close of the seventeenth century the government had recognized the commercial growth of fifteen villages by redesignating them as towns (*machi*) and placing them under the jurisdiction of their own town magistrates.[47]

The village of Jōhana, located not far from Kanazawa in Kaga domain, can serve as a useful example of the trend toward small-scale rural urbanization.[48] Jōhana sits on a large alluvial delta at the point where the famous Mt. Gokayama faces Tonami Plain. Farmers who lived in the foothills around the mountains grew cocoons that were used to manufacture silk thread. These farmers, however, had only a few plots of rice paddy, and after they paid their taxes and fed their families, few had enough capital to cover the cost of producing the cocoons. Consequently, certain urban-based rice merchants and financiers came to Jōhana and began to lend rice and money to farmers so that they could raise cocoons, with the understanding that these merchant financiers would be permitted to buy the crop. The merchants then turned over the cocoons to artisans in Jōhana who would spin them into thread, which in turn was sold to another group for weaving into silk cloth. Finally, wholesalers, also based in Jōhana, would sell the silk cloth outside the domain, especially to merchants in Kyoto. This kind of commercial opportunity transformed Jōhana from an agricultural village at mid-century into a community in which the majority of households in 1693 were engaged in some aspect of the silk business. Indeed, about 30 percent of Jōhana's residents had migrated there between 1683 and 1693 in order to take advantage of these commercial opportunities.

Raw cotton was another commercial crop whose increased popular-

---

47 *Kaga han shiryō*, vol. 5 (Genroku 13 [1700]), p. 515. For more on Japan in general, see Thomas C. Smith, "Pre-modern Economic Growth: Japan and the West," *Past and Present* 43 (1973): 127–60.

48 Jōhana is the topic of several articles in Mizushima Shigeru, *Kaga han, Toyama han no shakai keizaishi no kenkyū* (Tokyo: Bunken shuppan, 1982), pp. 41–64.

ity had significant repercussions on urbanization and the emergence of local towns.[49] Cotton was first grown extensively as a cash crop in the Yamato region (present-day Nara Prefecture), and the provinces of Settsu, Kawachi, and Izumi quickly became centers of cotton cultivation. Later, production moved further into western Japan. The rapid expansion of cotton production at the end of the seventeenth century touched off a clothing revolution, for farmers and lower-class urban dwellers quickly began to replace their rough hemp and jute clothing with cotton products.

At first cotton was grown on dry fields in the Yamato region, but farmers soon changed to wet-field production. In many villages, more than 50 percent of the wet-field area was given over to cotton production. At the beginning of the eighteenth century, the shogunate sponsored a construction project on the Yodo River, which flowed into the sea at Osaka, and completed a channel that emptied into the ocean at Sakai. At that time, old residences, ponds, and swamps along the river were converted into wet fields, most of which were used to grow cotton. Indeed, there were even some villages where all the land was turned over to cotton cultivation.

Farmers typically held back a portion of the cotton crop that they harvested and processed it themselves by stripping the seeds and spinning the cotton into thread for weaving into cloth on home looms. Normally, they did this as a form of by-employment in the slack season and sold the output to cotton cloth dealers. The farmers sold any remaining portion of the crop in its unprocessed state to wholesale agents, who turned it over to local artisans who ginned the cotton, some using an instrument called a *wataguri*, a tool imported from China through the port of Nagasaki. Next, other local artisans spun the cotton into thread and wove it into cloth for sale by retailers. Any remaining portion was bought up by traveling wholesalers who peddled it in various individual domains across Japan.

In the Yamato region, the collection of raw cotton from farmers and the processing into thread and cotton cloth took place chiefly in the castle town of Kōriyama.[50] But in the Osaka area, where cotton growing developed on a wide scale, several local towns sprang up to house

49 For a study of the causes leading to the growth of local towns in one region, see Omura Hajime, "Echigo no zaigō-machi," in Toyoda, Harada, and Yamori, eds., *Kōza: Nihon no hōken toshi*, vol. 3, pp. 354–91.
50 Kobayashi Shigeru, "Kinai no zaigō-machi," in Toyoda, Harada, and Yamori, eds., *Kōza: Nihon no hōken toshi*, vol. 3, pp. 392–422.

the merchants and artisans engaged in the trade.[51] Examples include Hiranogō, Kashiwabara, Furuichi, Tondabayashi, Daigazuka, Izumisano, and Kaizuka, many of which once had been temple towns.

The largest of these old temple towns that emerged as a commercial center was Hiranogō, which, according to a 1704 census, had 2,543 households and 9,272 persons. Among these households, 1,331 were listed as agriculturalists, and thus Hiranogō might be labeled an "agricultural town" (nōson-toshi), that is, one in which approximately half the population engaged in agriculture and half in commerce. Among the 1,212 households engaged in commerce in Hiranogō, 254 were involved in some aspect of the cotton business, from the wholesaling through the winnowing stages. In addition, 60 households purchased cottonseeds and manufactured oil. If the dyers of cotton cloth, dealers in used cotton clothing, fertilizer manufacturers, and shipping agents are also included, then 44 percent of all the merchants in the city managed businesses that were related in some way to the cotton trade. Day laborers accounted for 313 households, and many were undoubtedly employed in some aspect of the cotton business. Thus it is clear that Hiranogō was supported by the cotton production of surrounding agricultural areas and that the cotton trade within the city was characterized by a highly developed functional specialization.

There were some ten other, similar "agriculture towns" in the region, including Kaizuka, which also had previously been a temple town. Kaizuka was the home port for eleven oceangoing ships and forty-one coastal boats used to export cotton and cloth and to import rice from Shikoku and Hokuriku and fish fertilizer from Edo and Uraga. This indicated that the production of cotton was not dominated solely by capital financiers from Osaka but, rather, flourished in the various "agricultural towns" and in large part involved small-scale, independent traders and producers. Moreover, the Kaizuka example shows how the development of the cotton business brought about a new marketing structure that stimulated the commercial rice business in Shikoku and Hokuriku as well as the fish business in the Kantō region.

The commercialization of agriculture and the emergence of new patterns of marketing during the seventeenth century also created fresh opportunities for new groups of men to compete with the older,

51 For a full discussion of the spread of the cotton trade into local towns, especially those such as Hiranogō and Kaizuka in the Osaka region, see Nakai Nobuhiko, *Tenkan-ki bakuhansei no kenkyū* (Tokyo: Hanawa shobō, 1971), pp. 237–321. In English, see William B. Hauser, *Economic Institutional Change in Tokugawa Japan: Osaka and the Kinai Cotton Trade* (Cambridge, England: Cambridge University Press, 1974), pp. 143–60.

established shipping agents who were based in castle towns and who monopolized the transportation of goods under charters authorized by their daimyo. That is, during the first half of the century, goods were typically transported along a limited number of prescribed roadways by officially designated transportation agents or shippers, who handled cargo at prescribed places called *toiyaba* within the cities. In exchange for this monopoly right, the shippers had to handle freight for the daimyo and his retainers either free of charge or at reduced rates. However, some commodities, especially those that had to be carted into a castle town from its hinterland villages, were transported outside of the official system. In these cases, farmers simply packed goods that they had made themselves onto horses or other draft animals, which they otherwise used for agricultural purposes, and took these products into the cities.

During the seventeenth century, some of these farmers started to transport goods to more distant places, shipping agricultural products and rural handicrafts, and even finished goods from the castle towns, to central markets outside of their own domains. For many merchants the new services offered by the farmers turned part-time shippers were cheaper and more convenient than the official system, which by law required that loads be placed on fresh horses at the *toiyaba* of each post town, which were located about ten kilometers apart along the major roadways. Consequently, many customers began to use the services of these farmer-agents. As they accumulated capital, some of these new shippers also became wholesalers, buying up goods in rural areas and selling them to urban merchants. In this way there emerged a new group of former agriculturalists who moved into the cities during the final decades of the seventeenth century and who came to specialize in the purchase, handling, storage, and sales of various commodities.

Because the public transportation system had been set up by the shogunate and the individual daimyo domains, the older, officially recognized forwarding agents and wholesalers in the post towns now protested to the shogunate and requested that prohibitions be directed against the newly emerging shippers and wholesalers in both cities and rural areas. Often, however, daimyo supported the newer shippers. The reason was that the daimyo were hoping that the greater volume of commerce generated by the new shippers would help enhance the prosperity of their domains, especially the castle towns.[52]

---

52 For a study of the transportation system and of some of the contentions that could arise, see Constantine N. Vaporis, "Post Station and Assisting Village," *Monumenta Nipponica* 41 (Winter 1986): 377–414.

It was also during the latter half of the seventeenth century that ocean transport developed rapidly, especially between Edo and Osaka. The enormous consumption demands generated by the residents of Edo, the de facto political capital of the country, were satisfied in large part by supplies from advanced economic areas in western Japan. Consequently, great importance was attached to the development of an ocean link with Osaka, which had emerged as a collection and distribution center. The Inland Sea, used for shipping from the earliest times, formed the principal route between Osaka and Kyushu, Shikoku, and western Honshu. Usually goods sent to Edo from the Pacific coast region of northern Japan were shipped by oceangoing transport to Naha Bay (near Mito in present-day Ibaraki Prefecture) where they were off-loaded and forwarded to Edo via land, river, and lake routes. A second ocean link involved shipping the goods to Chōshi Bay (present-day Chiba Prefecture) and then sending them up the Tone River on barges to Edo. Ships avoided going around Bōsō peninsula and directly into Edo Bay because of the danger of shipwreck off the southern tip of the peninsula. Goods from the Japan Sea side of Tōhoku and from Hokuriku were first shipped to Tsuruga (Fukui Prefecture) or Obama on Wakasa Bay. They were off-loaded at these ports and sent overland to the northern shore of Lake Biwa where they were put on boats and transshipped to Ōtsu before being forwarded overland to Kyoto and Osaka.

Shipping was still divided into these circuits at the middle of the seventeenth century, although all had the disadvantage of requiring that the goods be hauled overland for a portion of the journey. That state of affairs was remedied and the Japan Sea coast transformed into one complete circuit when the shogunate instructed the entrepreneur Kawamura Zuiken to develop the sea routes known as the eastern sea circuit (*higashi mawari*) and the western sea circuit (*nishi mawari*). Kawamura accomplished this by charting coastal waters, erecting beacons and lighthouses at dangerous points where the shipping lanes came close to rocks, and providing disaster relief facilities. With the backing of the shogunate, he was also able to convince many daimyo to abolish port taxes and to issue regulations that permitted freedom of cargo handling so that ships from every domain could enter all ports. Ultimately, the eastern sea circuit connected the most distant parts of Tōhoku directly with Edo, and the western sea circuit went from the Japan Sea coast side of Tōhoku through Hokuriku, then around the Straits of Shimonoseki and into the Inland Sea, before continuing directly to Osaka. The Edo–Osaka route connected the two circuits.[53]

The establishment of the two coastal shipping circuits in 1671 and 1672 was a direct response to the growth of Edo's population. In other words, Edo's demands for foodstuffs, which had increased markedly just before this period, far outstripped supplies from the city's nearby hinterland, which were unusually scarce because of several poor harvests, and this threatened social unrest in the city. Consequently, the shogunate was anxious to find a way to ship tax rice from its holdings in the Tōhoku area quickly and safely to Edo.

The consolidation of the shipping circuits, however, also encouraged private traders and stimulated the development of a nationwide commercial economy by fostering the manufacture of goods for export outside the area of production. One example of this is commercial fertilizers which became necessary for the cultivation of raw cotton as the acreage dedicated to that crop expanded explosively in the Nara and Osaka areas. The most common kind of fertilizer was made from dried sardines, and at first fish taken from the Inland Sea were used for this purpose. In response to the rapid increase in demand for this kind of commercial fertilizer, new businesses were established on Bōsō peninsula, especially at Kujūkuri beach. At first, the fishing grounds around Bōsō were worked by fishermen who came up from Wakayama during the fishing season and toiled for a daily wage on boats owned and managed by men who lived in the Kujūkuri area. They dried the sardines on the sands of the beach and then sent them to ports in Uraga. Fertilizer merchants from Kansai opened branch stores in the port towns around Uraga Bay to buy up fertilizer for shipment to cotton-growing areas in western Japan.[54]

Until this time, the broad sands of Kujūkuri beach had been used to produce modest amounts of salt, which the local farmers made by boiling off salt water in large cauldrons. Now, however, the farmers learned from the men of Wakayama new methods of netting fish. In time, some of the villagers even abandoned their agricultural homes in

---

53 For a thorough study in English, see E. Sydney Crawcour, "Kawamura Zuiken: A Seventeenth Century Entrepreneur," *Transactions of the Asiatic Society of Japan* 9, 3rd series (1966): 1–23. A detailed analysis of the impact of the new routes on local commerce is contained in Takase Tamotsu, *Kaga han kaiunshi no kenkyū* (Tokyo: Yūhikaku, 1979).

54 For an account of how the development of shipping routes influenced commercial production on the opposite side of Japan, see Makino Ryūshin, *Kitamaebune no jidai* (Tokyo: Kyōikusha, 1979). In English, see Robert G. Flershem, "Some Aspects of Japan Sea Trade in the Tokugawa Period," *Journal of Asian Studies* 23 (May 1964): 405–16.

order to establish fishing villages on the seashore. An improved, larger net that could be stretched between two boats came into general use, and this made the Kujūkuri area Japan's richest sardine-fishing grounds. The farmers-turned-fishermen capitalized on this by opening up a wholesale office on the banks of the Fuka River in Edo, and even the fertilizer dealers from the Kansai region had to purchase supplies through this office. Gradually, the Edo wholesale office also took over the collection of cargoes, which had previously been handled by merchants in Uraga.

In this way, the fishing villages located along the Bōsō coastline increased their catches of fish that were processed into fertilizer for use in cotton cultivation in the Kansai region, and the residents of Kujūkuri beach, who had given up making salt to concentrate on producing fish fertilizer, began instead to purchase salt that was produced in villages along the Inland Sea, an area where salt production grew rapidly at the end of the seventeenth century. The abandonment of salt production at Kujūkuri beach was not an isolated event. The demands of the great urban markets at Edo and Osaka stimulated the production of salt in the villages along the Inland Sea, and this salt, cheaper because of large-scale production techniques, came to be sold commercially along the western circuit and almost completely displaced local, small-scale salt manufacturers, such as those at Kujūkuri. The only exception to this trend were those special cases in which daimyo supported salt production through the grant of special privileges.

In short, the expansion of urban markets was closely linked to the emergence of local towns, such as Jōhana, where businessmen could produce competitively priced goods, and to the more intensified regional specialization in the production of commercial items such as fertilizers and salt. In turn, the new production locales and marketing networks triggered further transformations in the three major metropolises of Edo, Kyoto, and Osaka, as we shall see next.

The three metropolises

Kyoto. Nestled at the top of the urban hierarchy in early modern Japan were the three large metropolises of Edo, Osaka, and Kyoto. Of these, Kyoto was the most ancient and the most highly regarded as a cultural center. Kyoto's artistic and literary achievements had sparkled most brightly during the classical golden age of the early eleventh century, when court mimes, pageants, and processions were held regularly at palatial residences around the city, when artists unrolled their stories on narrative scrolls (*emakimono*), and when court ladies such as Mura-saki Shikibu and Sei Shōnagon penned novels and literary diaries of unsurpassed elegance and style.

During a large portion of the medieval period, Kyoto functioned as the nation's undisputed administrative center.[55] From its founding in 794 Kyoto had been home to the emperor and his court, but from 1338 until 1573 Kyoto became as well the headquarters for the shogunate. From the thirteenth century, the city also served as Japan's primary religious center when the new, popularly oriented Jōdo and Nichiren sects, as well as the more rigorous Rinzai branch of the Zen sect, established their chief temples in Kyoto or else in the city's immediate environs. Concurrently, as the priesthood and warrior class joined the nobility in the city as a consuming elite, Kyoto became a center of trade, manufacturing, and exchange. Artisans who produced handi-crafts of exceptional quality for the courtiers had long been a perma-nent feature of Kyoto life, but now they worked alongside merchants, known as *toiya* or *ton'ya*, who served the military elite by forwarding to the city tax revenues and other goods from the warriors' home prov-inces. Within Kyoto, the Ashikaga shogunate also encouraged the development of guilds (*za*) to control the production and distribution of certain crucial commercial products such as lamp oil and salted fish.[56]

Kyoto reached another crossroads in 1573 when Oda Nobunaga forced the last Ashikaga shogun to flee and then burned and pillaged Kamigyō, the aristocratic northern half of the city. Hideyoshi began to refashion the city into a military strongpoint by girdling the city with an earthen rampart and compelling religious establishments to congre-gate in Teramachi and Tera-no-uchi, areas set aside for that specific purpose. Tokugawa Ieyasu then capped this process by placing Nijō Castle and a military garrison in the midst of the city.[57]

The rich history of the city during the early modern period is re-flected in an occupation register compiled in 1685.[58] According to this

55 The leading scholar on premodern Kyoto is Hayashiya Tatsusaburō. See especially his *Ma-chishū: Kyōto ni okeru "shimin" keisei shi* (Tokyo: Chūō Kōronsha, 1964). In English, see Tatsusaburō Hayashiya, with George Elison, "Kyoto in the Muromachi Age," in Hall and Toyoda, eds., *Japan in the Muromachi Age*, pp. 15–36.
56 These issues are covered in Takeshi Toyoda and Sugiyama Hiroshi, with V. Dixon Morris, "The Growth of Commerce and Trades," in Hall and Toyoda, eds., *Japan in the Muromachi Age*, pp. 129–44.
57 Ashikaga Kenryō, "Kyōto jōkamachi no keisei," in Toyoda, Harada, and Yamori, eds., *Kōza: Nihon no hōken toshi*, vol. 3, pp. 68–97.
58 Nakai Nobuhiko, "Kinsei toshi no hatten," in *Iwanami kōza Nihon no rekishi*, vol. 11 (*kinsei* 3) (Tokyo: Iwanami shoten, 1963), pp. 37–100. The population composition of the city is also discussed in Moriya Takeshi, *Kyō no chōnin* (Tokyo: Kyōikusha, 1980), pp. 55–70.

document, Kyoto was home to 51 doctors, categorized as physicians, surgeons, pediatricians, obstetricians, ophthalmologists, and dentists. In addition, two other registers list 41 "men of letters" (*bungakusha*), including poets and specialists of Chinese classics; 16 "experts" (*kanteinin*) on painting and calligraphy; and 125 "masters" (*shishō*) of the tea ceremony, flower arrangement, the noh theater, and the board games *go* and *shōgi*.

Skilled artisans also made Kyoto the nation's center of traditional fine arts and handicrafts. The population registers of 1685 also list famous shops by specialty, and among these we can find dealers with national reputations for their musical instruments, writing brushes, and implements for the tea ceremony. A separate register contains the names of craftsmen who produced such high-quality artistic goods as crowns, folding fans, porcelain, *tabi* footwear, special clothing for use in the tea ceremony, fixtures for Buddhist household altars, and high-quality paper used by the emperor, courtiers, and the warrior elite.

Beyond this, the weaving of silk goods and textile dyeing added a distinctive touch to craft production in Kyoto. The number of weavers in the seventeenth century is not known for certain, but some documents state that a fire in 1730 destroyed nearly three thousand looms, out of a total of more than seven thousand in the city.[59] If this is so, then it would seem likely that more than ten thousand persons were engaged in textile production at that time, if the dyers are included. During the late medieval period, weaving spread to Kaga and then other parts of the country, but in general regional production concentrated on more ordinary, plain silk, whereas the techniques for expert dyeing and for making complicated patterns and crests remained an exclusive monopoly of the Kyoto craftsmen.

The great economic transformation of the seventeenth century changed the nature of the silk trade in Kyoto. The growth in wealth nationwide generated new demands for Kyoto silk, and over the century the ancient imperial capital became as well known for its commercial production as it had been for its aristocratic traditions. Some of the new demand came from daimyo and upper-level samurai, who had become the country's new social nobility. Keenly aware of the need to develop symbols of their new status, they began to consider the expensive, high-quality silk of Kyoto as indispensable for use in their own clothing. They also gave presents of this silk to the shogun and his

59 Hayashiya Tatsusaburō and Katō Hidetoshi, *Chōnin kara shimin e* (Tokyo: Kōdansha, 1979), pp. 65–83.

officials. Many daimyo even sent retainers to Kyoto to purchase silk so that they could make certain that they were acquiring genuine, Kyoto-produced textiles.

Other specific policies implemented by the Edo shogunate also had an impact on the high-quality silk-weaving trade that was concentrated in the Nishijin section of Kyoto. The restriction of foreign trade to Nagasaki, a city under direct shogunal administration; the beginning of the tally trade in silk thread with China; and the granting to designated merchants of exclusive rights to deal in imported raw silk thread (referred to as *shiraito*) all affected business conditions in Kyoto. The raw silk thread imported through Nagasaki was shipped to Kyoto, along with high-quality silk cloth and other textiles produced in China. These goods passed from the tally-trade merchants, who were the importers, to the thread-shipping agents (*nakagai*), who were concentrated in Nishijin, and then to the weavers. The 1685 occupation register lists seventy-six tally-trade merchants, thirty-eight shipping agents for imported silk thread, and thirteen wholesalers who handled imported goods other than raw silk thread.

This same register also lists forty-six silk wholesalers who dealt in unfinished silk cloth that was produced outside Kyoto. Silk cloth usually was not shipped directly from local production areas to large consumption centers such as Edo and Osaka. Rather, because the Kyoto craftsmen had exclusive knowledge of certain dyeing and processing techniques, silk cloth from other regions was sent to Kyoto where it was glossed, dyed, embroidered, and rolled into finished bolts. The Kyoto-based wholesalers not only handled unglossed silk cloth, but they also acted as purchasing agents and wholesalers for raw silk thread that was produced in various regions in Japan. These same purchasing agent–wholesaler houses also helped establish silkworm cultivation in various regions at the end of the seventeenth century, and Nishijin weavers quickly began to use this locally produced raw silk thread instead of imported thread. As a consequence, Nagasaki's importance as an entry point for foreign trade rapidly declined.

The 1689 occupation register lists fifty-four money changers in the city of Kyoto.[60] These coinage specialists not only assayed and exchanged coins minted in various domains, but they also provided several forms of rudimentary banking services, by advancing loans and issuing letters of credit. The cash holdings of wealthy persons such as importers of raw silk thread were concentrated in Kyoto by the

---

60 Nakai, "Kinsei toshi no hatten," pp. 37–100.

middle of the seventeenth century. The daimyo, who had no means of obtaining cash other than from the sale of tax rice and who needed large amounts of cash for obligations to the shogunate, often borrowed money from wealthy merchants, using future tax proceeds as collateral. Moreover, merchants found it necessary to exchange among themselves coins minted in various parts of Japan in order to purchase semiprocessed goods and raw materials such as silk thread and cloth and also to complete the sales of processed goods to outlets in Edo and Osaka. These kinds of monetary conditions gave rise to the business of money exchanging, the buying and selling of cash, and the issuing of letters of credit – all of which served to transform Kyoto into one of Japan's leading financial, as well as production, centers.

Osaka. Like Kyoto, Osaka could trace its history back into antiquity. A settlement had come into existence in prehistoric times, and this later served as a point of embarkation for embassies to Korea. The community then became the temporary site of an imperial capital before more permanent ones were established, first at Nara and then at Heian early in the eighth century. Several centuries later, in 1496, the monk Rennyō (1415–99) chose this site on Osaka Bay as the location for his Ishiyama Honganji temple complex. Over the next century, the population expanded rapidly, at first because of a sudden influx of migrants when the main Ishiyama temple in Kyoto was overrun by rivals in 1532, and then thanks to more modest but steady growth as merchants and artisans arrived to serve the needs of the temple personnel and their followers.[61]

In 1580 Oda Nobunaga, during his quest to unify Japan, overwhelmed this fortress after several unsuccessful attacks. Two years later Nobunaga's successor, Toyotomi Hideyoshi, took over what remained of the fortress and erected a large, formidable castle on the site. The city expanded under Toyotomi control, as several daimyo built residences near the castle to signify their loyalty to Japan's new military hegemon. Still more merchants and artisans arrived to cater to the daimyo's needs, and the city also expanded physically as the government filled in portions of the adjoining bay. By the battle of Osaka Castle in 1614–15, when Tokugawa Ieyasu obliterated the Toyotomi house and subsequently placed the city under the administrative super-

61 For a classic survey of Osaka's history, see Miyamoto Mataji, *Ōsaka* (Tokyo: Shibundō, 1957). More current is Wakita Osamu, *Kinsei Ōsaka no machi to hito* (Kyoto: Jimbun shoin, 1986). In English, see William B. Hauser, "Osaka: A Commercial City in Tokugawa Japan," *Urbanism Past and Present* 5 (Winter 1977–8).

vision of the shogunate, Osaka rivaled, and perhaps even surpassed, Kyoto in population.[62]

In the decades after the battle of Osaka Castle, the city was reconstructed, and by the middle of the seventeenth century Osaka had become one of the two greatest commercial and manufacturing centers in the country.[63] At the heart of this dramatic growth was Osaka's emergence as the central rice market for western Japan. Hideyoshi had shipped some of his tax rice from Shikoku to Osaka before his death in 1598, but the city's transformation into the nation's most important rice market followed the establishment of the Tokugawa hegemony and the imposition of the shogunate's authority over the city. As Osaka continued to grow in the early decades of the seventeenth century, daimyo from western Honshu, Kyushu, and Shikoku began to ship tax rice into the city. Concurrently, daimyo along the coast of the Japan Sea sent rice to Tsuruga or Obama, where it was transshipped overland and across Lake Biwa. In all, some estimates for the first quarter of the seventeenth century place the quantity of rice shipped into Osaka in the range of one million koku annually, and a century later, by the 1720s, this figure had increased more than fourfold.[64]

But Osaka did not prosper simply because of rice sales. According to 1714 statistics, the following categories of goods were shipped into Osaka: farm products, 40.9 percent of total imports; forest products, 24.4 percent; marine products, 14.1 percent; and mining products, 8.9 percent. The fertilizer made from sardines was 7.8 percent. The kinds of goods shipped out from Osaka in the same year were as diverse: farm products and processed agricultural goods, 72.8 percent; mining products, 12.6 percent; and processed forestry products, 12.6 percent.[65]

These statistics reveal a number of interesting points. Aside from rice, for example, forestry products constituted the chief imports. Most of the lumber was consumed in construction projects within the city, and the remainder were manufactured into household utensils and furniture, and then exported to other urban markets. After forest prod-

62 Osamu Wakita, with James L. McClain, "The Commercial and Urban Policies of Oda Nobunaga and Toyotomi Hideyoshi," in Hall, Nagahara, and Yamamura, eds., *Japan Before Tokugawa*, pp. 243–4.

63 The layout of the city is discussed in Yanai Akira, "Kinsei Ōsaka keikan fukugen e no kokoromi," in Toyoda, Harada, and Yamori, eds., *Kōza: Nihon no hōken toshi*, vol. 3, pp. 122–42.

64 Hauser, *Economic Institutional Change*, p. 13.

65 Nakai, "Kinsei toshi no hatten," p. 46. Occupation statistics are also a concern of Yasuoka Shigeaki, "Edo chūki no Ōsaka ni okeru torihiri soshiki," *Dōshisha shōgaku* 16 (November 1964): 290–307; and 16 (February 1965): 589–625.

ucts, the next largest import into Osaka was oil (15.8 percent), which was processed for use in lamps and cosmetics. Surplus oil not consumed in the city was exported. Similarly, mining products and imported raw materials were processed into iron or copper goods, or into refined copper, and also shipped out to other consumption centers.

Other statistics corroborate Osaka's emergence as a manufacturing and commercial center during the seventeenth and eighteenth centuries. Records dating from the 1710s, for instance, indicate that some two thousand ship's carpenters resided in the city, a clear indication that shipbuilding had become a major industry in Osaka. These statistics also record that fifty rapeseed oil producers and twenty-seven cottonseed oil producers lived in the city, and they turned out approximately seventy thousand kiloliters of oil annually. This should be regarded as a very large amount as no producers used waterwheels at that time but, rather, relied on the labor of humans and animals. Special wholesalers who shipped processed oil to Kyoto and Edo had made their appearance as early as the decade of the 1610s, and within a century a total of 360 wholesale houses handled raw, unprocessed seeds. Nine others shipped processed oil to Edo and Kyoto, and 250 agents shipped it to cities and villages in Hokuriku, Tōhoku, and western Japan. An additional 25 wholesalers dealt in oil cakes (shimakasu), a by-product of the oil-manufacturing process that was used for fertilizer.[66]

Perhaps the largest production facility in Osaka at this time was a copper-refining plant.[67] Virtually all mined copper in the entire country, about 3,257 tons annually, was brought to Osaka. There it was refined and nearly all, about 3,000 tons yearly, was reshipped to Nagasaki for export overseas. There were seventeen refiners in Osaka, and a total of approximately ten thousand men worked in the smelting plants. At that time, the Sumitomo family operated copper mines in Kyushu and was the largest refiner in Osaka. They later became, along with the Mitsui family, one of Japan's largest zaibatsu.

Osaka profited greatly from the nation's expanded agricultural production during the second half of the seventeenth century, as well as from the new opportunities afforded by the establishment of the Western Sea Circuit. Osaka quickly surpassed Kyoto in economic importance as it drew on products from many sections of Japan. Kyushu, Shikoku, and regions in northern Honshu supplied raw materials from

66 Exports are discussed in Nakai, "Kinsei toshi no hatten," p. 80.
67 Nakai, "Kinsei toshi no hatten"; and Yasuoka, "Edo chūki no Ōsaka ni okeru torihiki soshiki."

the primary sector, such as rice, soy beans, lumber, minerals, and fish, as well as a limited number of finished goods from the secondary sector such as paper, wax, and tatami-mat facing. The Kinki region emerged as the leading source of certain commercial agricultural goods such as cotton and rapeseed, processed goods made from these farm products, and such manufactured items as saké, soy sauce, and cotton cloth which were made from raw materials supplied from as far away as Kyushu and Shikoku. The coastal areas of the Inland Sea region, on the other hand, developed primary industries such as commercial agriculture and fishing.

All of these different goods were shipped to Osaka, where they were either consumed or reexported to other consumption centers such as Edo, Kyoto, and the cities and villages of the Kinki and Horuriku regions. Processed goods brought into Osaka were redistributed in that form, and the raw materials were manufactured into various products by artisans in the city. As Osaka became a hub of manufacturing and distribution, its population grew, and the city became the leading commercial center in western Japan, pushing Kyoto into the economic background.

As Osaka developed its commercial potential, new types of financial and credit institutions were established. These played an especially important role in promoting the flow of goods and raw materials into Osaka from surrounding rural areas. Essentially, there were two kinds of wholesalers: "provincial wholesalers" (*kunidoiya*) and "specialized wholesalers" (*semmondoiya*). As can be seen from such names as "the Satsuma wholesalers" and "the Awaji wholesalers," the provincial wholesalers derived their names from the old provincial units of the ancient imperial system established as part of the Taika Reforms in the seventh century, and they handled a complete line of commercial products and raw materials from that particular area. These provincial wholesalers were especially common in those regions that were linked to Osaka by shipping routes, and they sometimes included descendants of the wealthy merchants who helped make the Yodo River more suitable for shipping in the early Tokugawa period, as well as influential merchants who from the beginning had been engaged in ocean transport, cargo-handling, and warehousing services.

In the latter half of the seventeenth century there was a tendency for specialized wholesalers to split off from the provincial wholesalers.[68]

68 Nakabe Yoshiko, "Kinsei toshi Ōsaka no kakuritsu," in Toyoda, Harada, and Yamori, eds., *Kōza: Nihon no hōken toshi*, vol. 3, pp. 106–15.

For example, the Bingo tatami mat-cover wholesalers separated from the Bingo provincial wholesalers, and the Bizen pottery wholesalers amicably divorced themselves from a larger set of Bizen provincial wholesalers. In all, the number of provincial wholesalers tended to decline, and the specialized wholesalers started handling key commercial goods such as cotton and oil. Then, during the final decades of the seventeenth century, the number of specialized wholesalers increased sharply and subspecializations began to appear. For example, fish wholesalers broke away from the provincial groups, exerted their dominance over the market, and then subdivided into more narrowly specialized groups that dealt exclusively in fresh fish, dried and salted fish, dried bonito (*katsuobushi*), and river fish. In pace with these developments, the kinds and numbers of brokers and shipping agents multiplied, and nearly ten thousand were recorded in an Osaka census report from the 1710s.

New instruments of finance and credit were necessary in order to support this increased volume of trade. Among the first to invent these were the financiers associated with the marketing of daimyo rice. These financiers were known as *kakeya,* and they replaced the daimyo's own retainers as managers of the daimyo's warehouses (*kuramoto*). Serving on a contract basis, these *kakeya* disbursed warehouse rice, held cash on deposit, and supplied additional capital to the daimyo by making loans to them. So great was the lords' need for capital, however, that a daimyo often would approach a set of merchants in the same line of business, who would then pool their funds to make a joint loan and thus to share the risk of default. There were also financiers who solicited money from a number of merchants involved in different lines of business in order to acquire sufficient funds to make loans to daimyo.

The latter half of the seventeenth century also witnessed the growth of transactions among rice merchants who handled the sales of large volumes of daimyo tax rice after it reached the Osaka warehouses. In the 1710s, there were already some thirteen hundred rice brokers (*komenakagai*) in the city. These brokers bought and sold tax rice shipped through the daimyo warehouses at the new rice market established in a section of the city known as Dōjima. Soon they also started to deal in futures by buying and selling rice certificates as negotiable instruments that entitled the bearer to withdraw a specified amount of rice from the warehouses. By the 1710s some seventy money changers attached themselves to the rice market and offered guarantees for transactions made in the market.

As the Dōjima market flourished, the price of rice sold there tended to become the standard rice price for the entire nation, and this lent a certain stability to the finances of the daimyo who pledged their future tax levies as collateral for loans. Previously, the daimyo had frequently defaulted on the loans advanced by merchants, who understandably then became wary of making such loans. The establishment of the market at Dōjima, however, gave renewed confidence to Osaka merchants concerning the collectibility of daimyo loans. As a consequence, many money changers began to specialize in daimyo loans. One obvious example is the Kōnoike family, which became one of the wealthiest merchant houses of the Tokugawa period.[69]

In addition to the money changers associated with the rice market and those who specialized in daimyo loans, there were also many moneylenders who performed more generalized commercial services in Osaka. Like the money changers in Kyoto, these men issued letters of credit, bought and sold coins, changed coins, and advanced loans to wholesalers. As Osaka became the nation's largest commercial city, economic activity outpaced that of Kyoto and stimulated the development of a credit system whose most outstanding feature was the circulation of promissory notes, or *tegata*, which were secured by real estate or by current accounts.[70]

The moneylenders of Osaka devised other credit instruments as well. Merchants in Edo and Osaka, for instance, had often exchanged letters of credit, but the continuance of too many unbalanced accounts hindered the expansion of business activities. The solution to this problem came when the shogunate and daimyo accepted a new means of transmitting to Edo the proceeds from the sale of their tax rice through Osaka warehouses. Until the final decade of the seventeenth century, the shogunate and daimyo had sent cash overland to Edo. But from 1694 the warehouse managers began to take the receipts from the sale of tax rice to Osaka money exchangers, who would then purchase what was termed a "collectible credit draft" (*gyakugawase*) from a merchant who had an accounts receivable due from an Edo merchant. The Osaka money exchanger would then send this collectible credit draft to his own branch shop in Edo (or to a merchant in the same line of business), who would then collect the amount due from the Edo

69 Sakudō Yōtarō, "Kinsei Ōsaka ryōgae shō keiei no keisei katei – jūnin ryōgae no sōsetsu to Kōnoike ryōgaeten," *Bankingu* 175 (October 1962): 32–54.
70 For an informed discussion of new credit devices, see Sakudō Yōtarō, "Tokugawa chūki ni okeru shin'yō seido no tenkai – toku ni kin'yū to zaisei no kanren o chūshin to shite," *Rekishigaku kenkyū* 264 (April–May 1962): 66–70.

merchant. This money would then be turned over to the shogunate or to the Edo mansion of the daimyo within a fixed time limit, generally set at sixty days after the issuance of the draft in the case of the shogunate.

The Osaka money changers profited greatly from the commissions charged for such services. But even more significant was the impact that the use of these drafts had on the national economy. Because the person who held a collectible credit draft could in effect use it as collateral for sixty days, this system permitted a dramatic expansion in the volume of available commercial credit. As the system evolved in the early eighteenth century, promissory notes and credit drafts in circulation frequently amounted to several times the amount of actual currency in circulation, and this stimulated the growth of manufacturing and production throughout the entire country. The new credit system also drew more business to Osaka, making it a hub of finance as well as manufacturing and distribution. This contributed to the further centralization of economic activity in this city rather than Kyoto, so that by 1700 Osaka and Edo had emerged as Japan's leading commercial cities.

Edo. Of early modern Japan's three great cities, Edo was the youngest, and it grew the fastest.[71] The settlement was a small agricultural village until 1457, when Ōta Dōkan (1432–86), a retainer of the Uesugi family, built a small fortress on the site.[72] In 1590 Tokugawa Ieyasu, newly settled in the Kantō region, took over the castle, and after Ieyasu was appointed shogun in 1603, the surrounding community began to develop rapidly, both as the castle town headquarters of the Tokugawa family and also as the effective political and administrative capital of the country.[73]

Edo's population exploded in the seventeenth century. The nucleus for this growth was provided by the direct retainers of the shogun, the army of bannermen (*hatamoto*) and housemen (*gokenin*) who, together with their families and attached service personnel, were compelled to take up residence near the castle, just as the vassals of the daimyo were moved into the castle towns of their lords across all of Japan.[74] Once

71 A summary of the early growth of the city can be found in Haga Noboru, *Ō Edo no seiritsu* (Tokyo: Yoshikawa kōbunkan, 1980), pp. 1–64.
72 A fascinating introduction to the early history of the settlement can be found in Naitō Akira, *Edo to Edojō* (Tokyo: Kashima kinkyūjo shuppankai, 1966), pp. 14–40.
73 A fluent overview of the history of Edo can be found in Nishiyama Matsunosuke and Haga Noboru, eds., *Edo no sambyakunen*, 3 vols. (Tokyo: Kōdansha, 1975).
74 Nomura Kentarō, *Edo* (Tokyo: Shibundō, 1966), pp. 49–70.

the system of alternate residence was institutionalized in the 1630s, the daimyo, some members of their immediate families, and their extensive entourages established residences within the city, adding perhaps another third of a million persons to the city's growing population.[75] Merchants, artisans, and construction workers flowed into the city in response to the burgeoning occupational opportunities, and by the time this phase of rapid growth had exhausted itself in the 1720s, Edo's commoner population of merchants and artisans surely stood above the half-million mark, and the city's total population easily surpassed one million persons.

Some of these merchants and artisans accumulated considerable wealth and fame. The principal merchant wards of the city were referred to as *hommachi,* and many of these streets were lined with the shops of clothing and lumber merchants, who have come to represent the popular stereotype of the great Edo merchants.[76] In part, the popular image grew out of the special favors that the shogunate bestowed on some of these families. For instance, the headman (*tōryō*) of the chartered artisans (*goyō shokunin*) who were entrusted with minting coins on behalf of the shogunate, together with the headman of the chartered merchants (*goyō shōnin*) who specialized in silk goods, lived on large estates that were given to them by the shogunate. These were situated near the entrance to the castle, a location of very high status (today the Bank of Japan is located on the grounds of the former residence of the headman of the minters). In other cases, the stereotype derives from the lavish way in which these merchant princes displayed their wealth. In particular, the extravagant lifestyles of the lumber merchants, who took on construction projects during the great building booms of the second half of the seventeenth century and who made enormous fortunes, became central characters in folktales that still remain well known today. These men allegedly often reserved several large rooms in the pleasure quarters, summoned prostitutes beyond number, and threw gold coins around with reckless abandon.

Despite some similarities in growth patterns between Edo and the

75 Edo's population structure is discussed in Gilbert Rozman, "Edo's Importance in the Changing Tokugawa Society," *Journal of Japanese Studies* 1 (Autumn 1974): 93–4.
76 Some of the most imaginative research on the layout of Edo has been undertaken by Naitō Akira. See, for instance, his *Edo no machi* (cited in note 16); *Edo no toshi no kenchiku* (Tokyo: Mainichi shimbunsha, 1972); and "Edo no machi kōzō," in Nishiyama Matsunosuke and Yoshiwara Ken'ichirō, eds., *Edo jidai zushi,* vol. 4 (Tokyo: Chikuma shobō, 1975). A useful account of the spatial relationships between old Edo and modern Tokyo can be found in Jinnai Hidenobu, "Tōkyō no machi o yomu," *Bunka kaigi* (November 1985): 20–33.

other major metropolises, the city in eastern Japan retained a distinctive identity. Not only did more warriors live in Edo, but the city's merchant and artisan cultures also provided a contrast with those of Osaka and Kyoto. An Edo occupation register published in 1694 lists a total of 161 employment classifications and includes the names of important merchants and artisans. Among these are 68 doctors and 280 persons are identified as scholars, poets, painters, and noh actors, thus giving the impression that Edo was emerging as a city of culture and learning. But set against this is the fact that almost all the artisans were employed in the rougher construction trades or in the production of weapons. Moreover, there were in Edo no distinctive industries that were innovative technically or aesthetically, such as the copper refiners and shipbuilders of Osaka or the weavers and dyers of Kyoto.

In many ways the most visible merchants in Edo were those who dealt in fresh foods such as vegetables and fish. Edo's residents dined on a great variety of regional specialties shipped in from the city's hinterland: *daikon* radishes from Nerima, burdock from Iwafu (in modern-day Saitama), native Japanese melons from Kawagoe and Fuchū, and watermelons from Hachiōji.[77] Vegetables grown in villages within a forty-kilometer radius of Edo were sold daily by retailers at six markets in the city. Fish from nearby Tokyo, Sagami, and Suruga bays, as well as the coastal areas of Chiba and Ibaraki, were sent by ship from the fishing villages to riverside fish markets, and they were then sold at four markets in Edo. Because the volume of fresh foods consumed by all urban residents, including both warriors and commoners, was enormous, both the forwarding agents and retailers who handled goods needed in daily life, such as oil and wood and charcoal, together with the rice merchants, occupied an important niche in Edo's commercial activity.

Craft production developed slowly in the Edo region, and for a long time the city had to depend on the more economically advanced Kansai region, and on Osaka in particular, for supplies of those consumer goods that required sophisticated processing.[78] Other cities of the Kantō and Tōhoku regions faced similar circumstances, and wholesalers in Edo in the early seventeenth century functioned chiefly to

77 An early and still influential study concerning the spread of commercialized agriculture is Furushima Toshio, *Edo jidai no shōnin ryūtsū to kōtsū* (Tokyo: Ochanomizu shobō, 1951).
78 For a discussion in English of the relationship between Edo and its hinterland and Edo's dependence on Osaka, see William B. Hauser, *Economic Institutional Change*, pp. 14, 30; and Rozman, "Edo's Importance," pp. 105–6. For a classic study of Edo's commercial development, see Hayashi Reiko, *Edo ton'ya nakama no kenkyū* (Tokyo: Ochanomizu shobō, 1967).

distribute goods to outlets in these regions on behalf of shippers head-quartered in the Kansai region. However, by the end of the seventeenth century, wealthy merchants from Ise, Ōmi, and Kyoto who had extensive experience and reserves of capital expanded their operations into the Kantō area and Edo's extended hinterland. At that time they no longer functioned as simple forwarding agents on behalf of others, but, rather, they themselves directly purchased goods in Kansai and Osaka for sale in Edo. In this fashion, real economic power slipped from the hands of the old forwarding agents who handled sea shipping and warehousing services and passed into the hands of these more aggressive merchants.

Not unexpectedly, the more intense competition from these outside merchants set off a reaction among the merchants in Edo, first visible in their efforts to organize trade associations to meet the new challenges. In 1694, to take the most notable example of this, wholesalers in Edo who dealt in eighteen different kinds of goods shipped by sea from Kansai formed what was referred to as the *tokumidon'ya*, or ten groups of wholesale guilds.[79] As was the case with the formation of protective associations in the castle towns, the Edo wholesalers, through this agency, hoped to be able to better protect markets and restrict the operation of outsiders.

The Edo wholesalers also discovered ways to use their organization to provide more regular business practices and some degree of protection against the unexpected. Thus, they forbade group members from engaging in shipping practices that might give one house an unfair competitive advantage. To promote stability for the entire group, they also started to indemnify members whose goods were lost or damaged in transit. It was not uncommon at this time for the crews of hired ships to fake a shipwreck and then secretly sell the cargoes. Also, it was standard practice for a ship's captain to jettison deck cargoes in order to improve his ship's stability and seaworthiness whenever storms stirred up rough seas. Among the more valuable of these cargoes were casks of refined saké brewed in the Nada sections of Osaka. Because Nada saké enjoyed an especially proud reputation in Edo, wholesalers there quickly sold whatever stock they had, and the loss of a cargo of Nada saké represented an immediate and substantial financial loss. Indeed, the system of joint indemnification initiated by the Edo wholesalers was originally designed to cover losses of saké car-

79 For a recent study of the development of merchant associations, see Kagawa Takayuki, "Toshi shōten no hatten," in Rekishigaku kenkyūkai, ed., *Kōza Nihon rekishi*, vol. 6 (Tokyo: Tōkyō daigaku shuppankai, 1985), pp. 195–228.

goes, although indemnities were soon extended to cover the loss of any cargo that was tossed overboard or went down with a ship.

As the curtain fell on the seventeenth century, it was obvious that Japan's commercial economy had become urban centered. On the regional level, the castle town of each domain had become a nodal point of trade, drawing in raw materials, agricultural surpluses, and processed goods from the village and towns in its hinterland. Much of this was consumed by the residents of the castle towns, but an increasing fraction – either in its original state or after further processing – entered the new transportation conduits that served as the arteries of the emerging national economy. The great centers of Edo, Osaka, and Kyoto were the poles that defined the national economy's magnetic field. Their enormous populations needed to be fed, and this generated the currents that set in motion the transfers of materials, finished products, and the development as well of financial instruments that had come to define Japan's early modern economy.

CITIES AND COMMERCE IN THE EARLY EIGHTEENTH CENTURY

The expanding commercial activity of the seventeenth century produced new and unprecedented levels of well-being and prosperity in Japan, especially for those segments of society that were most directly involved in economic production. Yet at the same time, the economic changes that surged through Tokugawa society also caused dislocations, created fresh problems for government, and stirred up waves of concern among the nation's political leaders. Ultimately, in the 1710s and 1720s the shogunate would address these challenges through a set of policies known as the Kyōhō Reforms. Chapter 9 in this volume details the political significance of this political program, but as we shall see, the reforms also held important implications concerning the economic life and well-being of Japan's urban residents.

The impact of the Kyōhō Reforms on the urban economy can best be understood by recalling some of the events and concerns that led up to them. Among these were the apprehensions of the nation's political leaders, who feared at the end of the seventeenth century that continued and unrestrained economic growth might have adverse consequences for the system of rule by status that they had worked so hard to implement earlier. Merchants were supposed to occupy the lowest rung of the Neo-Confucian hierarchy, but in some cases their business success had given them wealth and a reputation inconsistent with their theoretical position in society. As one city magistrate in Kanazawa noted in his office diary:

Merchants deal in goods. They buy and sell things which people need in their daily lives – food, shelter, and clothing. Merchants transport goods from one area to another. . . . They accumulate money. They lend out money and make a profit. Merchants who have a plan of operations and a good sense for profits do a large volume of business and make a great deal of money. When they have a favorable destiny, they can become rich in a single generation. Among the newly rich are some whose descendants are lazy and lack a profit sense, and they squander all of the accumulated wealth. In these troubled times, samurai households are suffering vicissitudes and changes of fortune. Persons who excel in business have become society's heroes. . . . A samurai can inherit [his father's] fief, but he cannot inherit his father's standing as a great man.[80]

The uneasiness of the political elite sprang from other, practical fiscal considerations as well. Despite the growth in the commercial economy, tax rice still remained the foundation of wealth for the shogun and daimyo. Too much commercial development, officials feared, might prompt farmers to take land out of rice production, thus jeopardizing their tax collection. Moreover, as ever more wealth flowed into the countryside to pay for commercial crops or the products of rural handicraft industries, the political leadership became increasingly concerned that farmers might become lazy and spendthrift, and thus less diligent in their efforts to produce rice and less able to pay taxes.

Finally, the shoguns Ietsuna (1651–80) and Tsunayoshi (1680–1709) pursued currency debasements in order to offset their well-known extravagant expenditures and to finance the resultant budget deficits. Specifically, for a fifteen-year period beginning in 1668, the shogunate minted large volumes of copper coins and then authorized the issuance of great amounts of gold and silver coins as well. This expansion of the money supply was designed to cover the increasing budgetary shortfalls of the period and to counterbalance the loss of coins that flowed out of Nagasaki to finance the export trade with Chinese, Dutch, and Korean merchants.

The shogunate's other chief concern at this time was to compensate for dislocations caused by the expansion of the commercial economy and its penetration into peasant villages. This is evident from the fact that the increase in minting activity emphasized those kinds of silver coins that were used in the Kansai regions and points farther west, where economic development and the commercialization of agricul-

80 Quoted in McClain, *Kanazawa*, p. 121.

ture had been most rapid.[81] Whatever the specific causes, however, the increase in the minting of silver coins took place at a time when the production of silver at Japan's mines was declining rapidly. As a result, the shogunate was forced to reduce the proportion of silver used in the coins to less than one-third of the coins' par value. In all, these various debasements sparked an inflationary fire, and, in the minds of policy-makers during the opening decade of the eighteenth century, fear of inflation combined with the apprehensions concerning the nature of economic growth to bring on a sense that an economic crisis was sweeping the country and undermining political authority.

The Kyōhō Reforms, merchant associations, and urban violence

The Kyōhō Reform program bundled together several specific policies that were aimed at dampening inflationary pressures, including calls for austerity in government; the issuance of detailed sumptuary regulations designed to encourage frugality in private life; the promulgation of moral injunctions exhorting the samurai to revive their martial spirit; a tightening up of rice-tax collections through the implementation of a fixed, annual payment system; a return to hard currency; and the wide-scale licensing of merchant protective associations (*kabuna-kama*) in the cities under the shogunate's jurisdiction. This set of policies, especially the authorization of merchant associations, would redefine the relationship between the urban and rural sectors of the economy, and the deflationary trends set in motion by the reforms would also have an impact on urban living standards, contributing, as we shall see, to the appearance of the first examples of organized violence by commoners in the urban centers of early modern Japan.

Merchant protective associations endowed with monopoly rights were not entirely new, of course.[82] We noted earlier how many individual daimyo during the seventeenth century had come to rely on certain wholesalers and transportation agents for the conduct of interregional trade and had consequently accorded exclusive prerogatives to these merchants houses. Similarly, those craftsmen who could produce certain goods – lacquer ware in Aizu–Wakamatsu, jute cloth in Hikone, and paper, ink, and charcoal in Kanazawa, to note but a few already familiar examples – not infrequently received special privileges as

---

81 Classic studies on currency problems include Kobata Atsushi, *Nihon no kahei* (Tokyo: Shibundō, 1958); and Sakudō Yōtarō, *Kinsei Nihon kaheishi* (Tokyo: Kōbundō, 1958).
82 An early and still frequently cited study of such associations is Miyamoto Mataji, *Nihon kinsei ton'yasei no kenkyū* (Tokyo: Tōkō shoin, 1951).

well. In all cases, the government and merchants could hope to derive certain obvious benefits. The merchants received monopoly rights and were able to reduce intragroup competition, while the government could offer protection to business enterprises that were important to the city's overall economy and well-being.

The authors of the Kyōhō Reforms also saw in these examples of protective associations, however, a way in which government might gain greater leverage over economic activity and the structure of prices. So excited were they by these possibilities that between 1721 and 1726 the reformers organized nearly all merchants in Edo into protective trade associations, a pattern followed by many daimyo in their own domains. Out of this burst of licensing came the form of protective association that is most familiar to historians. That is, the government authorized specific monopolies in exchange for the payment of annual licensing fees (myōgakin) and annual taxes (unjōkin), monies that could help the shogunate and the domains address their financial difficulties. In addition to a guaranteed monopoly, each merchant group acquired the rights to define its exact business activities, fix the number of licenses to be issued, decide who would be eligible to buy or inherit a license, determine their own internal regulations, and confiscate the licenses of those who violated the bylaws. They also jointly decided prices to be charged and apportioned the percentage of the licensing fees and annual taxes to be paid by each member. Moreover, the government typically required each association to include in its bylaws a promise to observe the laws of the shogunate or daimyo domain and to submit periodic reports to the appropriate officials concerning prices, fees, and recent business activities.

The shogunate, and the daimyo in their castle towns, had certain specific intentions in mind when they licensed protective associations, and they found ways to impose their policy considerations on association merchants. First, they used the submission of the periodic reports as opportunities to jawbone merchants into holding the line on prices. In addition, political leaders hoped to prohibit the production and sale of certain expensive luxury goods, such as some types of clothing, and of all kinds of new products, in order to be able to restrain consumption and, by extension, inflation. Moreover, government officials sought to regulate the volume of goods being shipped, in order to prevent unscrupulous merchants from buying up and hoarding commodities, and they acquired yet another means of influencing prices when they began to insist on making public their approval (or disapproval) of the handling fees and commissions that middlemen proposed charging. Finally, the shogunate and most daimyo wanted to prevent urban wholesalers from making purchases in producing areas and local towns, so as to isolate the producers, especially farmers, from what were seen as the debilitating effects of trade and commerce. One means they used to accomplish this was to enforce the descriptions of business activities included in association bylaws, although many daimyo governments also chose to issue new ordinances on the subject as well.

The impact of the Kyōhō Reforms on Japan's residents cut many ways. Some prospered. It is clear, for instance, that the leading houses within the merchant associations were sometimes able to amass considerable wealth in regional castle towns, such as Kanazawa, and that they came to constitute a new elite that could compete for the social and political prerogatives accorded the older, established merchant families.[83] In the major metropolises of Edo and Osaka as well, it was not difficult in the early eighteenth century to discover evidence of better housing and food in the wealthier merchant wards and, despite the disappearance of some of the vigor of Genroku culture, to find a proliferation of entertainment establishments that catered to the more well-to-do merchants, such as the leaders of the protective associations. Indeed, by mid-century some merchant houses had grown so rich that they were well known throughout the country, houses such as the Echigoya (the Mitsui family of the modern era) and the Shirokiya (founders of today's chain of Tōkyū department stores).

Yet, whatever prosperity the Kyōhō Reforms brought to merchant elites, on another social level the new policies caused distress that found its outlet in acts of collective violence. These were most common in the countryside, where the reforms squeezed the peasantry under a more severe tax system. Indeed, before the Kyōhō period, there had seldom been more than one or two examples a year of organized, violent rural protest, but by 1750 such incidents averaged more than six a year. The Kyōhō Reforms led to economic hardship for some segments of urban society as well. In urban centers, the policies of reducing consumption, controlling prices, and, from the 1710s, issuing gold and silver coins at previous standards of purity while prohibiting the circulation of older, debased coins all combined to produce a sharp, if short, depression toward the end of the 1720s.

In the midst of these economic difficulties, a widespread infestation of locusts in 1732 caused severe damage to the rice crop in western

---

83 Tanaka, *Kaga han ni okeru toshi no kenkyū*, pp. 129–98.

Japan, especially on the island of Kyushu. In order to stave off a famine in that region, the shogunate quickly purchased large amounts of rice in Osaka and Edo for shipment to western Japan. As a consequence, prices rose dramatically in these major cities. In Edo, some two thousand poor persons, believing that the price increases were due to a sinister plot by the rice merchants, rioted and broke into the shops of the largest chartered rice merchants (*kome goyō shōnin*). This disturbance occurred in 1733 and constituted the first riot by urban commoners in the city of Edo, the shogun's castle town.[84]

In that same year, riots also broke out in Nagasaki on Kyushu, and in Hida–Takayama (present-day Gifu Prefecture) where the city's residents smashed rice shops.[85] As was the case in the countryside, such urban food riots became increasingly common over the last century of Tokugawa rule. With increased numbers came, ultimately, new demands as well. Whereas the 1733 rioters had engaged in a typical struggle for control over the food supply and had simply demanded that government function as it ought to in accordance with Neo-Confucian concepts of benevolence and order, by the beginning of the nineteenth century the rioters were denouncing the entire political and social order. Even this was only a prelude to the call for a radical reordering of the polity that would resound throughout Japan at the middle of that century.

The Kyōhō Reforms, urban financiers, and marketing networks

As stressful as were the economic dislocations and human suffering associated with the deflationary period of the 1720s and 1730s, it is also important to note that in the long run of economic development, the Kyōhō Reforms accelerated already existing trends concerning Japan's protoindustrialization and the development of an integrated national marketing network.[86] This can be seen in the subsequent history of the merchant houses and associations: By the middle of the eighteenth century, for instance, there were more than five thousand wholesalers in over four hundred different kinds of businesses in Osaka alone, and

---

84 For a discussion of this event within the broader context of Edo period urban violence, see Sasaki Junnosuke, *Hyakushō ikki to uchikowashi* (Tokyo: Sanseidō, 1974), pp. 47–61, and Takeuchi Makoto, *Edo to Ōsaka* (Tokyo: Shōgakkan, 1989), pp. 112–38.
85 The most comprehensive listing of popular dissent can be found in Aoki Kōji, ed., *Hyakushō ikki no nenji-teki kenkyū* (Tokyo: Shinseisha, 1966). A convenient introduction to popular protest is Aoki Michio et al., eds., *Ikki*, 5 vols. (Tokyo: Tōkyō daigaku shuppankai, 1981–2).
86 Two influential studies concerning the development of national markets and regional commerce are Toyoda Takeshi and Kodama Kōta, eds., *Ryūtsūshi*, vol. 1 (Tokyo: Yamakawa shuppansha, 1969); and Hayashi, *Edo ton'ya nakama no kenkyū*.

despite what the Kyōhō Reforms had said about urban–rural separation, the Echigoya and the other urban retailers maintained large purchasing establishments that sometimes contracted for the textile output of an entire region.

The extensive commercial activity generated by the wholesalers injected fresh bursts of energy into the arteries of interregional trade, stimulating new growth and creating a need for larger sums of capital.[87] As the wholesalers fanned out across Japan, it became standard practice for them to make partial payments in advance of receiving orders and to lend capital for production purposes as well as for purchasing raw materials. In time, some merchants made as much or more from the interest earned on these loans as they did from the commissions they received for their shipping and marketing services.

The elaboration of the marketing activities of these wholesalers held other implications for capital formation. That is, although some merchants had functioned solely as wholesalers in the seventeenth century, more typically, men in local areas who themselves engaged in production also arranged to ship their goods and those of their neighbors and fellow villagers to customers of their own choosing. The appearance of the new wholesaler associations, however, meant that the local producer-cum-shipper was relegated to functioning as an agent who filled orders from the urban-based wholesalers, by using the wholesalers' capital to buy and transport goods. Now the incomes of the rural merchants no longer derived from profits they made on sales but, rather, came from commissions on the volume of goods they handled. In effect, the local men now functioned as buyers' representatives. In this capacity, they would host members of the wholesaler's shop who were dispatched to the producing areas, help them select and purchase goods, and arrange for shipping. For these services, the local merchants received their expenses and a commission. These local merchants were typically referred as *kaiyado*, or purchasing houses, and in many cases they had an exclusive contract with a particular wholesale association. Moreover, as local shippers came to function as the purchasing agents for urban-based wholesalers, they were increasingly isolated from the local commercial distribution system. In turn, this often meant that still new kinds of financing arrangements were necessary. In time, the producers themselves began to borrow money from the urban-based wholesalers, which they repaid in the form of manufactured goods.

87 Matsumoto Shirō, "Genroku, Kyōhō-ki no seiji to keizai," in Matsumoto and Yamada, eds., *Genroku, Kyōhō-ki no seiji to shakai*, pp. 1–35.

This process of commercially inspired changes came full circle when the new methods of finance and distribution began to influence the business practices of the great financiers. For example, large wholesale houses now had to create complex accounting systems, and some even developed a form of double-entry bookkeeping that permitted them to compare credits against debits and to register both capital accounts and profit accounts. Moreover, in accordance with an expansion in the scale of operations, shops began to separate business finances from household finances.

Increasingly as well, in a practice known as "dividing the shop curtain," some wholesale houses began to provide training for their most skilled employees and to help them establish their own branch shops.[88] Men were often first employed by a shop at the age of twelve or thirteen and were given training in mathematics at the shop while carrying out their job obligations. Future shop managers were chosen from this group. Even though an employee might not ultimately become a manager, if he worked diligently for a fixed number of years, he might be given a lump sum of money, the hereditary family shop name, and other assistance in order to help him start his own shop. The day-to-day management of the main shop was often entrusted to managers who were employed for life, were granted use of the hereditary family name, and were treated much like a family member. This style of operation became widespread after the 1820s, and a century later Japanese modern industrialists were able to refer back to this system and to use it to rationalize the new schemes of permanent employment and promotion by seniority that they were attempting to fashion.

The Kyōhō Reforms, fires, and local government

Although the economic consequences of the Kyōhō Reforms were complex and subtle, it should be remembered that the guiding motive behind them was simple and direct: The shogunate was seeking to regulate the economy more closely. The same desire for greater control can be seen in the shogunate's attempt to reorganize the Edo city government during the decade of the 1720s. As was the case with the economic side of reform, the administrative changes constituted a response to a century of growth and to many unexpected problems that had arisen during the era of unparalleled urbanization.

88 One standard account of this process can be found in Miyamoto Mataji, "Kinsei no shōka hōkōnin to shōten soshiki," in his *Kinsei shōgyō keiei no kenkyū* (Kyoto: Ōyashima shuppan, 1948), pp. 111–47.

One of these unanticipated problems was fires, often poetically referred to as "the flowers of Edo." Pestilence would be more like it, especially for the city's commoners. The merchants and artisan wards of Edo were densely populated, houses were constructed of wood and paper; and firefighting equipment was rudimentary. The hand-operated pump first came into use in Osaka only during the latter half of the eighteenth century; but even in the nineteenth century, this pump was used in just a few places and the most common means of stopping fires was simply to demolish wide rows of homes in order to create firebreaks.

Under these conditions, any fire could quickly become a major disaster, and the documentary record reveals that the central wards of Edo were destroyed by fire on the average of once every six years in the 178-year period between the middle of the seventeenth century and the 1830s.[89] In particular, exceptionally large numbers of fires occurred in the decades of the 1650s, 1710s, 1770s, and 1830s, and all of them contributed to the social unrest of those decades.[90]

Among these four periods, the largest number of fires broke out during the decade of the 1710s. Then in the 1720s, the shogunate changed its urban policy by forming a firefighting association and offering rewards to those who could identify arsonists. The transformation in urban policy also involved a reorganization of the city.[91] In order to prevent the spread of fires, the shogunate increased the number of public squares (*hiroba*) and issued an ordinance instructing people to use adobe or mud plaster in home construction and to tile their roofs, which previously had been made of wood or thatch. Although this decree was not uniformly observed in every ward, especially those whose residents had sunk into serious economic straits, the government did try to enforce it more strictly in certain designated wards, mainly those that had been rebuilt following a fire. In time, the practice of using the new building materials spread, and by the nineteenth century, streets with rows of houses constructed of adobe or plaster and roofed with tiles gradually started to appear in cities in all parts of Japan.

The government also began to organize firefighting brigades in almost all sections of Edo. Officials actually used red ink to divide a map

89 A useful introductory study to fires and fire fighting is Minami Kazuo, "Shōbō," in Toyoda, Harada, and Yamori, eds., *Kōza: Nihon no hōken toshi*, vol. 2, pp. 457–71.
90 Harada Tomohiko, *Kinsei toshi sōjōshi* (Kyoto: Shibunkaku shuppan, 1982), pp. 92–123.
91 Yoshioka Yuriko, "Kyōhō-ki Edo machikata ni okeru sogan undō no jittai," in Chihōshi kenkyūkai kyōgikai, ed., *Toshi no chihōshi*, pp. 108–58.

of the city into forty-seven firefighting precincts. Each administrative subdivision within a precinct had to supply a brigade of thirty men, and all of the brigades would be mustered whenever a fire broke out anywhere within the precinct. The individual brigades were captained by the ward elders, and the new post of precinct fire chief was rotated among them, each serving for a period of one month. All of the city's firefighting precincts were placed under the authority of six newly appointed fire superintendents (nine in winter), who reported to the city magistrates. Since the forty-seven precincts that served as the basis of the new system were named after the forty-seven characters of the syllabary, this was known as the *i-ro-ha* system.

Firefighting officials often enlisted special artisans known as "scaffolding men" (*tobi*), who normally worked in high places on construction projects, to help demolish houses in order to create firebreaks. In time, these scaffolding men were placed on fixed retainers, with the aim of ensuring a supply of reliable reinforcements for the firemen in each ward. However, scaffolding men were also infamous as *abare-mono*, or rowdy, undisciplined members of the day laborer class of that era, and fights among the scaffolding men broke out at each fire, sometimes actually adding to the problems of the average urban dweller.

This attempt to fold the responsibility for firefighting into the general administrative duties assigned to the City Office should be seen as part of a broader attempt to restructure urban government and to redefine the tax responsibilities of the merchant class in Edo at the beginning of the eighteenth century.[92] The main thrust of this administrative reorganization was to restrict the number of ward elders while expanding the scope of their jurisdiction and strengthening their powers. As a consequence, their duties came to resemble closely those noted earlier for the ward representatives in the castle town of Kanazawa.

At the same time, the entire city of Edo was divided into seventeen "townships," each consisting of several of the original wards. An organization of ward elders (*machikuchō kumiai*) was established, and a ward elder head (*kumiaichō*) was appointed from among the ward elders for a one-year term for the purpose of maintaining a proper liaison with higher units of government. Specifically, there were 254 designated wards in the city and a total of 263 ward elders, with some

92 Yoshiwara Ken'ichirō, *Edo no machi yakunin* (Tokyo: Yoshikawa kōbunkan, 1980), pp. 92–128.

wards having joint appointments. In addition, some peripheral areas were not included among these designated wards. These were not eligible to have their own elder and so were placed under the supervision of an elder from a neighboring ward.

Below the elders, the urban residents in each ward were organized into neighborhood associations, or groups of households, just as in the castle towns and rural villages. Originally, the official, recognized members of a ward were those who could claim proprietary rights of possession to land within the ward. The individual members of the neighborhood associations would alternately serve one month each as household group head and assist the ward elders in the performance of their duties. For instance, all reports, petitions, and lawsuits had to bear the seal of the household group head and the ward elder before they could be submitted to higher officials.

In general, the wards' fiscal obligations to the shogunate, as well as other expenses such as the salaries of the ward elders, originally were apportioned among those who possessed land and who were thus formal members of the ward, in accordance with the physical size of each individual's landholdings. Many merchants, however, claimed that the value of any particular plot of land depended on location as well as size. To do away with the alleged irregularities, then, the reformers of the early eighteenth century created three new categories of land value, assigned each merchant plot to one of these categories, and made uniform levies based on territorial size on all plots in each category.

For the wards where the artisans lived, the shogunate imposed corvée obligations that were different from the property taxes levied in the merchant wards. For example, the members of the carpenters' ward owed a fixed number of days of service when they had to work on shogunal construction projects. However, after the artisans moved out of their original wards and began to live in scattered locations around the city, the service obligations that had been levied on artisan wards as a whole were redistributed and levied on the individual members of an occupational group, regardless of their place of residence. Thus, another reason that the shogunate, as part of the Kyōhō Reforms, decided to authorize and encourage the formation of protective associations of artisans throughout the city was to make it easier to identify those individuals subject to service levies.

These kinds of changes that the shogunate effected in the urban administrative machinery of Edo in the 1720s were also replicated to a large degree in Kyoto and Osaka, which the shogunate governed directly and which generally had been subject to the same social and economic transformations that had swept through Edo.[93] Then from the 1750s the daimyo throughout Japan instituted similar reforms in their castle towns, and although other, lesser reforms were introduced afterwards in response to the changing circumstances of the nineteenth century, the framework constructed in the early seventeenth century tended to endure until the collapse of the Tokugawa shogunate in the 1860s.

CITIES AND COMMERCE IN THE LATE EIGHTEENTH CENTURY

The regional spread of commercial production

As discussed in detail in Chapter 9 in this volume, the Kyōhō Reforms did not provide permanent solutions to the ongoing problems of economic growth that were satisfactory to the shogunate. In particular, the shogunate was not able to halt further commercialization of agriculture, and that, together with the explosive growth of processing industries in local areas, eventually led the shogunate, and many individual daimyo as well, to yet another round of economic reforms in the 1770s and 1780s.

Signs that the Japanese economy was moving into a new stage of development during the middle decades of the eighteenth century were first visible in the textile industry. Cotton cultivation, which had been concentrated at first in the Kinki region, spread throughout almost the entire nation during the middle and late eighteenth century, except for the Tōhoku area, where climatic conditions made such farming nearly impossible. As cotton cultivation spread out from the Osaka region, it soon became a particularly important crop on the Ise peninsula and in areas along the coast of the Inland Sea. As the farmers in these locales started to cultivate cotton, farm families also began to engage in spinning and weaving as forms of by-employment. Later, the bleaching of cotton and the processing of bleached cloth became concentrated along the southern and eastern shores of Lake Biwa, before spreading into the Ise area in the latter half of the eighteenth century.

In the 1760s the silk textile industry became established in the Kiryū region (modern-day Gumma Prefecture) when local weavers

93 See, for instance, Nakabe Yoshiko, "Kinsei toshi Ōsaka no kakuritsu," in Toyoda, Harada, and Yamori, eds., Kōza: Nihon no hōken toshi, vol. 3, pp. 98–121.

mastered some of the dyeing techniques for silk that previously had been an exclusive possession of craftsmen in the Nishijin section of Kyoto. As Kiryū silk became known for its fine quality and as sales increased, other farmers and merchants in the area started to engage in silkworm cultivation, silk thread manufacture, and the production of a variety of silk textiles. About the same time, farmers in the mountainous areas of the southern Kantō region started to produce raw silk thread and cotton cloth for use by the great mass of urban commoners. As this happened, towns like Hachiōji and Ōme became important collection and transshipment points. A similar story could be told for Hokuriku, when the area around the city of Toyama became a thriving center for the production of silk and cotton textiles.[94] This localization of production and the development of new networks of exchange during the last half of the eighteenth century meant that Kyoto's importance as the center of the silk trade diminished greatly.

There were similar changes in the production of lamp oil, another important product. Originally, a variety of fish and vegetables were refined into oil in Kobe and Nishinomiya, where waterpower was abundant. Later, refining spread into a great number of local areas that grew rapeseed, which producers, until that time, had exported in its raw state although they also processed small amounts for individual use. Not surprisingly, the emergence of competitive marketing systems for cotton, silk, and rapeseed generated some sharp tensions between the established merchants of Osaka and the local upstarts. Some sense of this can be felt in the organization of a new protective association of lamp-oil traders in Osaka in 1759, whose members then pressured the shogunate to decree that all oil seeds, including rape and cotton seed, be sent to Osaka for processing.[95]

It is also important to note that the regional growth of processing industries often stimulated the production of raw materials in local areas. For example, in the early seventeenth century, people in Edo relied on imports of soy sauce from areas in the Kinki region such as Yuasa (present-day Wakayama Prefecture) and Tatsuno (Hyōgo Prefecture). Then, by mid-century, the sardine fishermen discussed earlier took with them from Yuasa to Chōshi the manufacturing techniques employed by the soy sauce brewers of western Japan. From there, the brewing process became generally known among producers in such localities as Sawara and Noda (Chiba Prefecture) and Tsuchiura

94 See Mizushima Shigeru, "Etchū orimono no hattatsu," *Toyama shidan* 34 (1966): 35–51.
95 For further details, see Nakai, *Tenkan-ki bakuhansei no kenkyū*, pp. 118–23.

(Ibaraki Prefecture), and merchants in those areas started to brew soy sauce to suit the tastes of the residents of Edo, fond of a saltier, more intensely flavored seasoning than was marketed in Osaka. Soon, soy sauce manufactured in the urban centers of the Kansai region was driven from the markets of Edo. Thus in a variety of products ranging from soy sauce and cooking oil to silk and cotton cloth, rural producers were challenging the previously predominant position of the older, more established shops of Kyoto and Osaka, many of whom had enjoyed some form of favored government protection.

Commercial growth and new economic policies

Tanuma Okitsugu. The 1760s and 1770s witnessed the initiation of new economic policies by the leaders of the shogunate and individual domains. Often historians have focused less on this set of events than on the subsequent Kansei Reforms; yet the policies of the 1760s and 1770s had a significant impact on the structure of economic activity in Japan, and they deserve our close attention. To some extent, the new policies constituted a response to the problems brought on by the regional spread of commercial activity and the growth of local marketing systems. As we shall see, the aggressive behavior of rural-based merchants and the decline of the central role of Osaka merchants caused dislocations and difficulties that would force their attention on government officials when the established but threatened merchants appealed for protection.

The new policies also addressed some older, and frustratingly persistent, fiscal problems that had plagued the shogunate and daimyo governments. The central concern here was to find some way to eliminate what had by now become chronic budgetary shortfalls and to reduce reliance on loans from merchant houses. Moreover, government officials hoped to acquire some control over prices, in order to overcome the inflation that had reappeared after the economic recession of the late Kyōhō period and that was seen as being responsible for both driving up government expenditures and causing serious financial problems for the samurai status group.[96]

The contemporaries who struggled with these problems and the historians who have reviewed their policy decisions have not had an easy time understanding the causal relationships between persistent budgetary

96 An early and still useful study of domain indebtedness is Sekiyama Naotarō, *Nihon kahei kin'yūshi kenkyū* (Tokyo: Shinkeizaishi, 1943).

shortfalls and the resurgence of inflation. Research has shown that currency debasements and other policies concerning coinage were clearly a factor. On more than sixty occasions, for instance, the shogunate issued new varieties of gold or silver coins, typically in order to debase the currency and thus augment official revenues.[97] These debasements, some historians contend, acted to drive up commodity prices. Others, however, have suggested that despite the infusion of new coinage into the economy, the shogunate never did mint enough coins to meet demand, so that the gap between supply and demand for currency became the chief source of inflationary pressures.[98]

Yet other historians place the blame for inflation on the unwise policies of domain governments. The lords of many domains, for instance, began to issue paper notes (*hansatsu*) during the eighteenth century. But frequently these were inconvertible, and even when convertibility to coins was promised, domain officials tended to pay little or no attention to the relative quantities of paper currency issued or to the amount of metallic money that they were supposedly holding on reserve to back the issuance.[99] That was precisely what happened in Kanazawa in 1775 when the domain first printed an excessive amount of paper currency and concurrently banned the use of silver coins. The popular action was immediate: People shunned the notes; the currency rapidly depreciated in value; and prices rose sharply.[100]

As frustrating as it has been for historians to obtain a full understanding of the relationship between currency policies and inflation, they have had even more difficulty with other related questions, which constitute an agenda for future research. We still, for instance, do not know the exact extent to which the shogunate and daimyo bureaucracies taxed the growing merchant wealth; nor do we fully understand why they did not put into place more systematic methods for moving that wealth into official coffers, especially after the Kyōhō Reforms had secured the unquestioned right of governments to levy annual dues and licensing fees on protective associations. Moreover, we have not yet fully analyzed the relationship between the spread of commercial production and rising commodity prices. On the one hand, we might well expect

97 John Whitney Hall, *Tanuma Okitsugu: Forerunner of Modern Japan* (Cambridge, Mass.: Harvard University Press, 1955), p. 69.
98 Shimbō Hiroshi, "Kinsei kōki ni okeru bukka, kin sōba, kawase uchigin sōba, 1787–1867," in Umemura Mataji et al., eds., *Nihon keizei no hatten* (Tokyo: Nihon keizai shimbunsha, 1976), pp. 261–79; and Sakudō, "Tokugawa chūki ni okeru shin'yō seido no tenkai," pp. 66–70.
99 Sekiyama, *Nihon kahei*, presents several case studies; and a detailed analysis of Okayama can be found in Kokushō Iwao, *Hōken shakai no tōsei to tōsō* (Tokyo: Kaizōsha, 1928), pp. 53–102.
100 Tsuchiya Takao, *Hōken shakai hōkai katai no kenkyū – Edo jidai ni okeru shokō no zaisei*, pt. 2 (Kyoto: Kōbundō, 1927), pp. 239–309.

that the diffusion of commercial enterprises and technology would enhance competition, cut production costs, and reduce the prices of commercial goods; yet, officials in domains across Japan constantly complained of higher prices as people within their jurisdictions became more actively involved in the commercialized sector of the economy.[101] Further, we need to know more about the linkage between prices and the formation of official merchant groups.[102] Useful, too, would be more amply documented analyses of the impact on prices of other daimyo policies, such as the frequent bans on the import into any one domain of goods that competed with local products. Finally, it is necessary to uncover more precise and detailed information about the relationship between rice prices and commodity prices in general. It has become somewhat of a truism that the eighteenth century witnessed a rise in commodity prices in general, but a decline in rice prices.[103] Indeed, one can find documentation that would support this conclusion.[104] Yet, most studies assume this inverse correlation between the two price indices without offering a convincing explanation of why the growth of the commercial economy should depress the rice price and thus reduce the relative value of tax revenues and samurai incomes.[105]

Although shogunal and daimyo officials frequently had an even less precise understanding than do modern-day historians about how their economy worked, many in the 1760s realized that a new fiscal crisis was at hand, and so they put together a set of fresh economic policies to address the problems confronting them. On the national level, Tanuma Okitsugu (1719–88) became the chief architect of the sho-

101 Dohi Noritaka, "Kinsei bukka-shi no ichi kōsatsu," in Nishiyama Matsunosuke sensei koki kinenkai, ed., Edo no minshū to shakai (Tokyo: Yoshikawa kōbunkan, 1985), pp. 415–37.
102 The Edo city magistrates, for instance, in 1723 thought that creating licensed groups of wholesalers would give them a way to reduce prices. "Prices have risen," they claimed, "because of competition between traders, shippers, and producers. If producers were authorized to sell only to ton'ya, monopoly profits could be controlled." Quoted in Hauser, Economic Institutional Change, p. 36. Yet, other officials would later condemn protective associations on the grounds that their monopolistic practices acted to increase prices. See James L. McClain, "Failed Expectations: Kaga Domain on the Eve of the Meiji Restoration," Journal of Japanese Studies 14 (Summer 1988).
103 See, for instance, Hauser, Economic Institutional Change, pp. 34–5; and Kitajima Masamoto, Edo jidai (Tokyo: Iwanami shoten, 1958), pp. 125–40.
104 See, for example, Ono Takeo, Edo bukka jiten (Tokyo: Tembōsha, 1982). For information on a local area, see Takase Tamotsu, "Kaga han no beika hyō," in Toyoda Takeshi, ed., Nihonkai chiikishi kenkyū, vol. 1 (Tokyo: Bunken shuppan, 1980), pp. 319–60.
105 See, for instance, Sasaki Junnosuke, Daimyō to hyakushō, vol. 15 of Nihon no rekishi (Tokyo: Chūō kōronsha, 1966), p. 160; and Kitajima Masamoto, Nihonshi gaisetsu, vol. 2 (Tokyo: Iwanami shoten, 1968), pp. 201–8. As might be expected, given the nature of the data available, scholars do not even agree that all members of the samurai class suffered a relative loss of income. See, for instance, Kozo Yamamura, A Study of Samurai Income and Entrepreneurship (Cambridge, Mass.: Harvard University Press, 1974), pp. 26–69.

gunate's economic initiatives. In the 1760s and 1770s he reversed the old, Kyōhō-inspired policies of restraint and, instead, began to encourage the growth of the economy's commercial sector, in the hopes that this would increase supplies, bring down prices, and create new sources of revenues.[106]

Perhaps the most conspicuous aspect of Tanuma's program was to add to the existing number of protective associations and to broaden the official patronage of the great merchant families, in the hope that this would stimulate production. Thus the 1760s witnessed the appearance of many new retail groups in Edo and Osaka with exclusive privileges in the retail marketing of iron, brass, lime, and other staple commodities. Concurrently, selected wholesale houses were granted newly authorized monopsony rights over such products as oil, cottonseed, and sulfur. Similarly, the shogunate authorized associations to organize all shipping on the Tone and Kinu rivers as well as along the Kasumigaura coastal region, so as to reduce transportation fees.

Individual merchant houses also prospered from the acquisition of new privileges. The Sumitomo family, for instance, had been involved in the pharmaceutical and iron-goods business in Kyoto from the early years of the Tokugawa period. Later, it started to trade in copper, opened a refinery in Osaka, and, as we saw, rose to a position of economic and social prominence. Thus, when Tanuma decided to establish a copper monopoly in 1783, the Sumitomo were given exclusive rights to the copper trade in the Kansai region and later were permitted to develop the rich Besshi mines.[107]

The desire to promote development and growth was evident in other initiatives as well. Tanuma, for instance, provided funds to bring new lands under cultivation, and after the eruption of Mt. Asano in 1783 had raised the bed of the Tone River, the shogunate arranged for flood prevention and other riparian works to be undertaken. In a more grandiose and controversial move, Tanuma encouraged foreign trade through Nagasaki to China. Particularly attractive as export items were the so-called *tawaramono*, or bales of dried sea products such as tangle (*kombu*), sea slugs (*iriko*), and abalone. Then he turned his

---

106 For a full study in English of this policymaker, see Hall, *Tanuma Okitsugu*.

107 The expanded licensing of protective associations in the 1760s and 1770s is often interpreted as an attempt by the shogunate to sell special privileges in order to increase its revenues, as each association had to pay an annual licensing fee to the shogunate. Licensing had this advantage, of course, but because the annual fees were rather small and contributed little to the shogunate's financial well-being, historians in recent years have come to see licensing only as part of a broader set of economic objectives designed to stimulate production and promote lower commodity prices. For a discussion of the importance of these revenues for the shogunate, see Hauser, *Economic Institutional Change*, pp. 41–46.

attention to developing fishing around Hokkaido, an island also reputed to be rich in gold and other minerals, and he converted the existing baled-goods business into a shogunal monopoly. In 1786 Tanuma ordered all merchants who had formerly engaged in the trade to become government agents, and he then established a Baled Goods Office (*tawaramono yakusho*) at Nagasaki to supply capital to fishermen, set prices, and establish strict domestic consumption limits for exportable marine products. So successful were these efforts that some members of the shogunate even contemplated extending such activities into Sakhalin and the southern part of the Bering Sea, a move that would have reversed Japan's traditional seclusion policy.

Finally, Tanuma tried to reform the currency. Notable here was the introduction of a new silver coin known as the *nanryō nishu*, minted at 98 percent pure silver. In an innovative move, the shogunate tried to fix the coin's exchange rate by stamping onto its face the legend "Eight *nanryō* will exchange for one gold *ryō*," and officials further announced that the shogunate would accept only the *nanryō* for the obligations owed to it. In a related policy development, Tanuma tried to overcome the shogunate's chronic scarcity of copper for minting purposes, not only by relying on important merchant families such as the Sumitomo, but also by actually taking over the direct operation of some mines. In Akita, for instance, the shogunate confiscated from the local Satake daimyo the lands surrounding the family's famous Ami mine so that the shogunate could take over its production. Finally, the shogunate augmented the supply of coins by opening a mint for *zeni* at Nagasaki in 1768 and also by issuing a new four-*mon* copper piece known as the *shimon sen* in that same year.

Historians have not generally credited much success to these currency reforms, chiefly because the new policies aroused so much opposition that Tanuma was rather quickly driven from office, when stories of unprecedented shogunal extravagance and corruption also came to light. Some of the strongest opposition to specific Tanuma policies came from merchants.[108] Many of them, for instance, refused to have anything to do with the new *nanryō nishu* silver coin, and so it was used only for the intrinsic value of the silver it contained, not the artificial rate stamped on its face.[109] Moreover, the government seems to have

---

108 Kitajima Masamoto, *Kinsei no minshū to toshi* (Tokyo: Meicho shuppan, 1984), pp. 292–313.
109 The popular rejection of the *nanryō nishu* was first reported by Getaya Jimbei in a 1787 memorial. Shortly thereafter, popular attitudes changed when people realized that the coin had a high degree of purity, and it continued to circulate until 1824. See Hall, *Tanuma Okitsugu*, pp. 71–3.

been somewhat too enthusiastic in minting *zeni* and copper coins, and it issued more than markets would accept. *Zeni,* for example, circulated at approximately 2,800 to one gold *ryō* in the late 1730s but fell to 5,780 to one *ryō* in 1773. The consequence was an immediate and disastrous rise in commodity prices that produced loud complaints from people all across Japan.

Even more troublesome for Tanuma was the manner in which the licensing of new protective associations created tensions between those merchants and the older, established families, leading the shogunate to exhaust considerable credibility in trying to resolve such conflicts. One example of this concerns oil dealers in and around Osaka. Before Tanuma's tenure as grand chamberlain, merchants in Osaka had monopolized the oil business. In order to encourage expanded production, Tanuma divided the area between Osaka and modern-day Kōbe into five geographic districts and granted special rights to purchase all raw materials in these districts to five newly created associations of oil dealers. When the established Osaka merchants complained, Tanuma shifted gears and gave them the right to buy specified amounts of raw materials for processing into oil in all five of the districts, although the Osaka merchants were instructed to pay a fee to each of the new rural associations for this privilege. This solution satisfied no one, and both sides bombarded the local daimyo and the shogunate's officials with objections, petitions, and protests. The bitterness ran deep, and ultimately a frustrated shogunate tried to demonstrate its authority by announcing a shocking final solution: It confiscated from the local daimyo most of the territory where the oil was being produced, placed towns such Nishinomiya under the direct jurisdiction of the Osaka city magistrates, and gave its own rural attendants (*daikan*) stationed in Osaka administrative authority in the rural areas.[110]

If merchants protested some policies, the daimyo were even more apprehensive about other ways in which Tanuma flexed the shogunate's muscles. The confiscation of land in the Kansai brought no joy to the daimyo there, of course, and those in the north were equally frightened by Tanuma's confiscation of territory surrounding the copper mines in Akita, although there a strong protest by the Satake family ultimately succeeded in getting the family lands returned.

Even more daimyo felt threatened by Tanuma's new policies concerning the way in which they financed their own debts. Throughout the

---

110 Nakai, *Tenkan-ki bakuhansei,* pp. 118–23.

Tanuma years, the shogunate held to the belief that its fiscal problems, as well as those of the daimyo, were caused essentially by a combination of falling rice prices and rising commodity prices. Tanuma and his associates further argued that one of the primary reasons for the decline in rice prices came from false market surpluses created when daimyo – who sold rice certificates in Osaka in order to finance their own domain governments – began to issue certificates for more rice than their domains could actually produce.

Consequently, the shogunate began to require each daimyo to report officially the total amount of rice certificates issued as well as the actual amount of tax rice that he shipped into the city. The shogunate also permitted the merchants at the rice market in Dōjima to buy and sell only those certificates that bore the seal of the rice certificate inspector, an official newly appointed by the shogunate. The shogunate added still more restrictions on the diamyo's financing when it began to impose extraordinary levies on moneylenders and then to lend these funds back to the moneylenders with instructions to make these monies available to daimyo. As complicated as these fiscal arrangements seem on the surface, the new system meant that loans to the daimyo in theory were now originating with the shogunate, and as a condition for receiving such loans, the shogunate could require that daimyo pledge as collateral a portion of the domain tax rice equal in value to the loan. Thus, whenever a particular daimyo defaulted on the repayment of a loan, the rights to that portion of the domain's tax rice could be transferred in theory to the shogunate until the loan was fully repaid. In hopes of making this a more general method for all daimyo financing, the shogunate even went so far as to announce that it was considering extracting forced loans from peasants and urban dwellers throughout the country. Had such a scheme materialized, it would have marked the first time in the shogunate's history that it had bypassed the daimyo and directly taxed the residents of individual domains.

Many daimyo were severely handicapped by the new financing system, and all were shaken by the shogunate's threat to usurp their taxing prerogatives. Soon the dissatisfactions of these daimyo boiled to the surface, and when Tanuma's protector, the shogun Ieharu, died in 1786, Tanuma's enemies conspired to force his resignation and to appoint Matsudaira Sadanobu (1758–1829) as senior adviser to the shogun. Together with his own supporters, Sadanobu then launched the so-called Kansei Reforms of the late 1780s and early 1790s, whose self-declared purpose was to "return to Yoshimune" by recreating the alleged golden age of Sadanobu's grandfather and the author of the Kyōhō Reforms.

As we have learned from Chapter 9 in this volume, the core of the Kansei Reforms consisted of the abolition of many of the protective associations, a reissuing of sumptuary regulations, retrenchment programs, decrees ordering reductions in commodity prices, and exhortations against corruption, prostitution, and bribery. The Kansei Reforms came to an abrupt halt when Sadanobu himself was removed from office in 1793, and they were not particularly successful. The reforms treated symptoms, not causes. They did not adequately address such fundamental problems as the growing gap between commercial reality, on the one hand, and the frequent misconceptions of the daimyo and shogun about how the economy worked, on the other. Nor did the reforms eliminate the destructive aspects of the rivalry between urban merchants and the producers and wholesalers based in local towns and commercial villages. With economic policy in near chaos, commercial and urban problems would continue to mount in the early decades of the nineteenth century, forming part of the process that ultimately led to the Meiji Restoration.

Daimyo commercial policies. As many daimyo confronted increasingly severe problems with deficit financing during the latter half of the eighteenth century, they began to encourage commercial development within their domains and attempted to develop new mechanisms for tapping that wealth.[111] The centerpieces of these efforts were usually the creation of domain monopolies over certain products that could profitably be produced locally and sold in the great urban metropolises. Some domains had established such monopolies as early as the seventeenth century, but the techniques employed at that time were not nearly as sophisticated as those deployed in the late eighteenth century, when domain governments introduced new products and encouraged production by importing technology and supplying raw materials and capital to producers. Another important difference was that whereas the domains established the earlier monopolies in order to increase official revenues by collecting annually taxes and licensing fees, in the late eighteenth century many domains hoped to accomplish the same ends by capturing a portion of the profits of the trade,

---

111 For a recent discussion of the spread of commerce into local areas, see Yamaguchi Tetsu, "Bakuhansei ichiba no saihen to shōhin seikatsu," in Rekishigaku kenkyūkai, Nihonshi kenkyūkai, eds., *Kōza Nihon rekishi*, vol. 6 (Tokyo: Tōkyō daigaku shuppankai, 1985), pp. 229–65.

typically by marketing themselves the final product or by taking a percentage of the price of the goods as they moved from producer to wholesaler or from wholesaler to retailers outside the domain.

Kumamoto provides a good example of a domain that actively moved into new commercial endeavors. In the latter half of the eighteenth century, domain officials established a local silkwork culture industry by importing techniques originally developed at Nishijin in Kyoto. Those same officials promoted wax tree cultivation by advancing to farmers in producing areas interest-free loans for fertilizer, tools, and household expenses.[112] Similarly, officials in Yonezawa domain imported silkworms and technical advisers from the nearby Date and Fukushima domains, distributed pamphlets with advice on mulberry cultivation throughout the domain, and advanced loans to producers. In Kaga, the government coupled similar incentives with tax exemptions in order to promote the lacquer and gold leaf industries.[113]

In most instances, the domain governments also attempted to control distribution and thereby to reserve the bulk of the profits for themselves. That is, the monopolies' actual day-to-day operations were entrusted to wholesale merchants within the local castle town, who were placed under the jurisdiction of newly created offices that typically bore names such as the Office of Domain Products (Kokusankata) or Office for Domain Prosperity (Kokuekikata). These offices usually carried out a full range of services, such as researching production problems, introducing technology, advancing capital and loans, and setting up distribution systems for the sale of the final products. Thus, the Kaga Office of Domain Products, established in 1813, oversaw the production – and took a percentage on the sale of – a variety of products, including textiles, lacquer, gold leaf, pottery, gold and silver inlay, ink, and paper.[114] In Mito, the domain established an office to handle the sale of locally produced *konnyaku* (devil's tongue) and then applied the profits to discharge loans contracted earlier between the domain and merchants in Edo and Osaka.

The system of domain monopolies had a mixed record. Some suc-

112 Several examples of specific domain monopolies can be found in Fujino Tamotsu, *Daimyō: sono ryōkoku keiei* (Tokyo: Jimbutsu ōraisha, 1964), pp. 229–37.
113 For additional details, see Shimode Sekiyo, *Kaga Kanazawa no kimpaku* (Kanazawa: Hokkoku shuppansha, 1972); Mori Yoshinori, "Kanazawa no haku," *Gakuhō* 26 (1982): 79–85; Miyamoto Masahisa, *Ishikawa ken* (Tokyo: Shōheisha, 1982), pp. 43–5; and Wajima shishi hensan semmon iinkai, ed., *Wajima shishi*, vol. 1 (Wajima: Wajima shiyakusho, 1976), pp. 286–314.
114 See Tabata Tsutomu, "Bunsei, Tempō-ki no Kaga han sanbutsukata seisaku no igi ni tsuite," in Tanaka Yoshio, ed., *Nihonkai chiikishi no kenkyū*, vol. 4 (Tokyo: Bunken shuppan, 1982), pp. 67–9.

ceeded and provided revenues that the daimyo could use to decrease their indebtedness. But many more failed, leaving domain finances in worse shape than ever.[115] In other instances, the monopolies drew the ire of established merchants and commercial farmers, who saw them as new threats to their own enterprises, and there were several incidents when peasants and merchants banded together to protest violently the new monopolies, thus adding to the challenges to daimyo authority that began to mount as the eighteenth century gave way to the nineteenth. The monopolies also presented new problems to the shogunate, for the monopolies once again challenged the role of Osaka and Edo merchants and disrupted the established marketing systems that centered on these urban centers. In all, their intention ran counter to the policies of Matsudaira Sadanobu, and their legacy was a new set of problems with which the shogunate ultimately would have to contend.

CONCLUSIONS

Viewed from the long run of Japanese history, the emergence of a more urbanized society and the growth of a commercialized economy during the Tokugawa period contained significant implications for Japan's development after 1868. Others have explained in some detail, for instance, how such Tokugawa period innovations as insurance systems and improved facilities for banking and credit contributed to Japan's relatively rapid economic transformation in the second half of the nineteenth century.[116] As we have seen, the merchants of Osaka and Edo created a system of marine insurance, and the moneylenders in those two urban centers put in place a sophisticated set of practices concerning deposits, advances, bill discounting, exchange transactions, and financing programs for rural industry that anticipated many of the functions of a modern banking system.

Equally important were the economic developments that took place outside the major cities. The protoindustrialization that occurred in the local towns and commercialized villages of the Tokugawa period stimulated the growth of light industry in such diverse endeavors as

---

115 Yoshinaga Akira, "Sembai seido to shōhin ryūtsū," in *Rekishigaku kenkyū* 229 (March 1959): 48–54.
116 See, for instance, E. Sydney Crawcour, "The Tokugawa Period and Japan's Preparation for Modern Economic Growth," *Journal of Japanese Studies* 1 (Autumn 1974): 113–25, as well as his "The Tokugawa Heritage," in William W. Lockwood, ed., *The State and Economic Enterprise in Japan* (Princeton, N.J.: Princeton University Press, 1965), pp. 17–44. A particularly influential article concerning banking is Kozo Yamamura's "The Role of the Samurai in the Development of Modern Banking in Japan," *Journal of Economic History* 27 (June 1967): 198–220.

the production of textiles, pottery, saké brewing, lacquer ware, tatami matting, roofing tiles, and farm equipment. Historians have found it difficult to quantify precisely the exact level to which such production had risen by the 1860s, but most agree that from this base, these industries grew quite rapidly during the final decades of the nineteenth century. Again, the precise rates of growth in the modern period are disputed by historians, and in any case they seem to have varied regionally, but it is clear that after 1868 the broader diffusion of traditional technology, the importation of new materials and technology from the West, the availability of new markets, and an increase in personal incomes in Japan all combined to stimulate considerable growth in the rural-based industries. Over time, this confluence of factors created greater sources of capital accumulation, increased the level of output of the economy, and provided useful experience with early forms of mechanized manufacturing that made possible the growth of modern, heavy industry in Japan at the turn into the twentieth century.[117]

However salutary the long-term consequences of commercialization and urbanization, in the shorter run they generated dislocations, contention, and competition, all of which contributed to the growing domestic crisis that formed a prelude to the Meiji Restoration. One example of this was the change in the internal composition of urban populations seen in Japanese cities during the opening decades of the nineteenth century. An especially prominent trend was a growing gap between the wealthier and the poorer members of the population, as well as an apparent increase in the absolute number of very poor.

Although the documentation is not complete, it seems likely that the percentage of urban residents who rented lodgings in major cities such as Edo and Osaka increased rapidly, often by as much as one-third.[118] These renters worked as peddlers, day laborers, or artisans who, to use the shogunate's own contemporary parlance, "eke out their living one day at a time."

It is difficult to explain why the proportion of urban poor should have been growing at a time when the total urban population had

---

117 The classic study that initiated research concerning the role of traditional industries in Japan's transition to modern economic growth is Furushima Toshio, *Sangyōshi*, vol. 3 of *Taikei Nihonshi sōsho* (Tokyo: Yamakura shuppansha, 1966). One of the more optimistic estimates of the growth of traditional industries in the Meiji period, and still widely cited, is Yamada Yuzō, *Nihon kokumin shotoku suikei shiryō* (Tokyo: Tōyō keizai shimpōsha, 1957); and lower growth rates for western Japan are documented in Nishikawa Shunsaku, *Nihon keizai no seichōshi* (Tokyo: Tōyō keizai, 1985).
118 An insightful study about the urban poor is Minami Kazuo's *Edo no shakai kōzō* (Tokyo: Hanawa shobō, 1977).

leveled off and when there is compelling evidence, as demonstrated in Chapter 13 of this volume, that standards of living were improving for many segments of urban society. Some demographers argue that the marriage age in cities was relatively high, compared with that of the agricultural villages, and that consequently in-migration from rural areas was necessary in order to maintain urban populations at a steady level. Such migrations did in fact take place in many regions, and most likely it was the poorer elements of peasantry who moved into the cities in the late eighteenth century. Most were formerly independent farmers who had lost their lands when the commercial economy reached agricultural villages.

Moreover, poor harvests hit Japan several times in the late eighteenth century, resulting in widespread starvation. At that time, the poor in several cities, including Edo and Osaka, took part in food riots, inspiring the shogunate to fashion new social welfare schemes for urban centers. The system implemented in Edo came to serve as a model for many other cities. There, each person who owned land contributed annually to his ward an amount of money that was determined by the value of his land. The collected monies constituted a reserve fund that ward representatives used to buy and store rice for emergencies, to make grants to elderly persons who lived alone, and to finance low-interest loans for the construction and maintenance of homes and shops. These funds were referred to as the City Office reserve fund (*machi kaisho tsumikin*) and still existed at the time of the Meiji Restoration, when Edo passed to the control of the new Meiji oligarchy, and the office that controlled the funds became the focal point of the new movement to establish a City Assembly (*shikai*) in Tokyo after 1868.[119]

The economic and social problems of the early nineteenth century, especially the rapid increase in budget deficits on both the shogunal and domain levels, contributed to the well-known, relative decline of the economic lot of many samurai retainers in the decades immediately before the Meiji Restoration.[120] Equally obvious, both to the samurai who lived through the times and to modern historians, was the fact

119 For more on the life of the urban poor at this time, see Matsumoto Shirō, "Kinsei kōki no toshi to minshū," in *Iwanami kōza Nihon no rekishi*, vol. 12 (*kinsei* 4) (Tokyo: Iwanami shoten, 1976), pp. 89–146.
120 Discussions of domain deficits and the impact on the samurai can be found in Aono Shunsui, *Daimyō to ryōmin* (Tokyo: Kyōikusha, 1983); Kitajima Masamoto, "Tempō-ki no rekishiteki ichi," in Kitajima Masamoto, ed., *Bakuhansei kokka kaitai no kenkyū* (Tokyo: Yoshikawa kōbunkan, 1978), pp. 1–22; and Hanley and Yamamura, *Economic and Demographic Change*, pp. 131–60.

that the shogunate and the country's daimyo had been generally unable to implement policies that would provide long-term solutions to the economic problems experienced by the samurai. Tokugawa Ieyasu and his fellow daimyo had built a society based on the concept of rule by status, but two centuries of urbanization and commercial growth had created a new world in which such a political ideal no longer corresponded to economic and social reality. Agriculture had become commercialized and oriented toward the urban markets, and even domain governments had become involved in the production and sale of commercial products. While inflation ate away at the samurai's incomes, some merchants, and even peasants, grew wealthy and enjoyed life-styles that drew the envy of even the highest-ranking elements of the samurai status group. Yet during times of drought and famine, the rural poor would crush into the castle towns, and the sounds of the food riots and of shops being smashed could be heard even within samurai mansions. Increasingly, society seemed out of kilter.

Confusion and anger led many to question the legitimacy of the shogunate and daimyo governments, and the samurai seemed to grow less loyal. This was manifested in subtle ways: some warriors took handsomely dowered wives from the merchant class; others sold their birthrights and drifted off into mercantile occupations; and a few simply gave up in despair and committed suicide. From the 1830s, other samurai, no longer willing to bear the hardships forced on their class, began to pay more attention to domain affairs. For some, this meant listening more closely to critics of government policy, whereas others tried to gain bureaucratic positions that would enable them to redirect domain policy. Thus, when the nation's crisis worsened in the 1850s and 1860s, a great many samurai were prepared to enter the political arena, eager to defend Japan from without and to reform its political structure from within.

During the early nineteenth century, the bonds that had shaped the nation's status groups into a coherent whole began to fray along other seams as well. In the seventeenth century, society was symbiotically organized, held together by mutual obligations and the trust that each of society's status groups would perform the duties assigned to it. The daimyo relied on merchants and artisans to supply goods and services, and the lords reciprocated by providing an environment within the castle towns and domains that responded to the merchants' needs and desires. Samurai and merchants were also organically linked. The samurai handled military responsibilities and staffed the most important, decision-making offices in the domain government. The merchants catered to the samurai's daily needs for commercial goods and also fleshed out the lower, enforcement ranks of urban administration.

During the late eighteenth and early nineteenth centuries, however, the pressures of commercial growth and the problems associated with urbanization eroded the old organic bonds of interdependence. Derision replaced trust. Daimyo no longer voiced confidence in merchants but, rather, condemned them. The bitterness in the new attitudes is clearly revealed in the speeches and behavior of the lord's officials in Kaga domain. In 1835 the leading adviser to the Maeda daimyo called the city magistrates to his office. "Among the households of urban commoners," he complained, "are many, both high and low, rich and poor, who are audacious and who do not preserve their status." The more humble merchants, he lamented, purchased splendid clothing when attending ceremonial functions, or even worse, he cried out, borrowed large sums with which to rent such clothing. Criticisms rolled from his tongue. Some merchants "coveted the houses of those of higher status," whereas others served "expensive banquets at weddings, beyond their status and financial means. . . . Yearly the excesses have become greater as people strive to impress their neighbors." Sadly, he concluded, "There are many who no longer observe the status regulations, who spend too much money, who have a poor sense of social responsibility." In response to this outburst, the city magistrates reissued sumptuary regulations and instructed lower officials to make certain that they were read aloud to all of Kanazawa's residents.[121]

It was a short step from scorn for the merchants' social behavior to condemnation of their business ethics. In 1842 several of the lord's advisers in Kaga jointly set forth their complaints about higher commodity prices:

In recent years, there has been adequate production of rapeseed. However, merchants have spread rumors that shortages exist, and they charge higher prices. Merchants have claimed shortages of paper, firewood, and charcoal and then raised their prices. All merchants and artisans have been forgetting the dictates of status and moral behavior. The attitude that one can neglect to work hard and yet still make a large profit has become widespread. . . . Originally, in the past, people worked at their jobs with passion and sincerity, and they made a reasonable profit. Now, however, people concoct elaborate

121 *Kaga han shiryō*, vol. 14 (Tempō 6 [1835]/intercalary 7), pp. 597–602.

schemes that allow them to neglect the proper conduct of their profession but still make enormous profits.[122]

The new abusive rhetoric displaced the more expected discourse of respect and deference and thus put into place paving stones that others would tread when they moved toward a new formulation of the political norm at mid-century. Even in the face of such frustration and complicated economic change, the shogunate and daimyo stubbornly continued to cling to the tenets of class separation, agrarianism, and rule by status, and their dogmatism was increasingly interpreted as an arrogant attempt to preserve artificially their dominant position in politics and society. The failure of the Tempō Reforms in the 1830s and 1840s opened the door for even more doubts and questioning, and the edifice of shogunal and daimyo authority collapsed quickly when a foreign policy crisis became intertwined with domestic upheavals during the 1850s and 1860s. It was only in the process of building a new system to respond to the changing modern environment after 1868 that the Meiji leadership finally adopted policies that reached an accommodation with the forces set in motion by the waves of urban and commercial growth that Japan experienced during the seventeenth and eighteenth centuries.

122 *Kanshi zuihitsu* (The public service records of Okumura Hidezane), ms copy, Kanazawa City Library, Tempō 13 (1842)/5/29.

CHAPTER 12

HISTORY AND NATURE IN EIGHTEENTH-CENTURY TOKUGAWA THOUGHT

INTRODUCTION

Of all the years that spanned the Tokugawa period (1600–1868), the middle years, Tokugawa *chūki*, here called the "eighteenth-century," are distinguished by the creative achievements realized along a broad front. Important innovations were introduced in theater, literature, and printmaking in the arts and, more pertinent to this chapter, into reflections on history, nature, and political economy. Coming in the era directly before the Industrial Revolution in modern times, this century offers key insights into the philosophical foundations of modern Japanese civilization that are grounded in the history prior to Japan's intense engagements with the Western world. It comes as no surprise that intellectuals have continued to turn to that history as a resource for critical inspiration.[1]

An obvious point must be made before continuing. As historical time was not recorded according to the Christian calendar, "eighteenth-century Japan" is no more than a rough Western "translation" of a period of time following the well-known era of Genroku (1688–1704), essentially commencing with the Kyōhō (1716–36), and ending with the Ka-sei, an elision of Bunka and Bunsei, 1804–18 and 1818–30, respectively.

The opening years present a sobering aftermath of the ebullient commercial revolution identified with the Genroku. Often cited as a specific event to demarcate that moment of uneasiness is the famous

---

1 In the area of political thought, the outstanding figure is Maruyama Masao, known for his theory of creative political fabrication and fiction that he traced to the historical philosophy of Ogyū Sorai: *Nihon seiji shisōshi kenkyū* (Tokyo: Tōkyō daigaku shuppankai, 1952). This was translated by Mikiso Hane, *Studies in the Intellectual History of Tokugawa Japan* (Princeton, N.J.: Princeton University Press, 1974). The terms for the discussion of postwar politics were set decisively by Maruyama's reflective writings on Tokugawa thought. Also of interest are Bitō Masahide, *Nihon hōken shisōshi kenkyū* (Tokyo: Aoki shoten, 1961); Yoshikawa Kōjirō, *Jinsai–Sorai–Norinaga* (Tokyo: Tōhō gakkai, 1983); Minamoto Ryōen, *Tokugawa shisō shōshi* (Tokyo: Chūō kōronsha, 1973); Matsumoto Sannosuke, *Kinsei Nihon no shisōzō* (Tokyo: Kembun shuppan, 1984); and a special issue on Tokugawa thought in *Shisō* 4 (1988).

vendetta incident of the "forty-seven samurai" in 1702. This celebrated act of loyal revenge, admired by many, was also legally treason-
ous, and after much agonizing debate, the Tokugawa bakufu ordered
the execution of these "loyal" retainers through ritual suicide. Political
thinking concentrated on the meaning of the new commerce that had
come to dominate the economy of the nation and, more pointedly, on
whether or not this new history could be brought under control by
loyal men committed to the system and its laws. Shortly after the end
of the century and signifying the beginning of yet another tempestu-
ous era, is the rageful rebellion of 1837, led by the philosophical
radical and former official of the regime, Ōshio Heihachirō (1794–
1837). With Ōshio's rebellion, overt militant action against the regime
itself as an expression of true loyalty and not of personal revenge was
injected with unprecedented forcefulness into the waning years of the
Tokugawa bakufu, a period known as Bakumatsu.

Between these eventful markers, the legitimacy of the Tokugawa
order was rarely doubted nor was it frontally challenged. There was
much faith in reason and the possibility of objective knowledge, as
exemplified by Ogyū Sorai in the beginning, and Honda Toshiaki,
Kaiho Seiryō, and Yamagata Bantō at the end. It would be erroneous,
however, to conclude that the Tokugawa regime governed during this
century in "peace and tranquility under heaven," or *tenka taihei*, the
moral epithet with which the bakufu embellished its rule.

Hardly tranquil, the eighteenth century presents a troubled landscape dotted with periodic famines and rebellions in the countryside,
rice riots and bankruptcies among merchant houses in the towns and
cities, and deepening indebtedness among the regional barons, the
daimyo, and their samurai retinues. Indeed, historians generally agree
that the bakuhan system, with the bakufu at the center in Edo and two
hundred or so semiautonomous domains in the regions, had entered a
period of severe unrest, *dōyōki*, which was reflected in the carefully
planned reforms from within the system to rectify that unrest. Known
as the "Three Great Reforms" – *sandai kaikaku* – of Kyōhō, Kansei
(1787–93), and Tempō (1830–44), historians often rely on these reforms to provide chronological coherence to the political history of the
eighteenth century.[2]

Although all of these reforms failed to offer lasting solutions, despite the intelligent purpose behind them, they reveal a consistent aim
worthy of notation, namely, to resolve the discordance between what

2 See *Iwanami kōza Nihon rekishi*, vols. 11–13 (Tokyo: Iwanami Shoten, 1964).

had been envisioned by the founders of the Tokugawa order – peace and tranquility in seclusion and agricultural self-sufficiency – with the unintended consequences of that settlement, centering mainly on the commercial revolution and the turbulent economic forces unleashed by it. A money and market economy of unexpected magnitude had been generated by the movement of aristocratic retinues to and from Edo. Anchored in Osaka, the merchant city of large and small banking and trading houses, this new economy witnessed the spillage of resources from the countryside into the cities, in the form of rice stipends that were converted into cash and that fueled the expanding commercial economy.

It was in this troubled middle period, when the sudden demise of the regime was not thought to be imminent but its competence was frequently held in doubt, that the meaning of history, nature, and political economy was pondered, constituting a major intellectual experience in Japanese history and indeed East Asia more generally. Commonsensical questions came increasingly to be asked toward the end of Genroku as a sober mood replaced the optimism of the generation before: Why was there so much inefficiency and misery in the secluded kingdom? Why had the initial vision of peace and tranquility gone awry? Was the apparent errant flow of history due to passionate and vulgar forces underlying commerce and hedonistic play? Was it due to the overall structure of the political order itself? Or was it due at some deeper level to faulty epistemology adopted by the regime that could not serve as a reliable guide to action?

There was virtually universal agreement that the problem was not the general design of the political structure itself, although this consensus would undergo steady erosion over the century. There were always warnings about the decline of human virtue and the rise of reckless passion as the source of political failings. But the more fundamental concern was directed at the question of epistemology, the manner in which knowledge was to be approached, ordered, and translated into action. Attracting the attention of the leading thinkers of the time, this question informed a good deal of the contentious and polemical debates that went into the compilation of prodigious scholarly works for which this era is noted.[3]

3 A comprehensive summary of such works is Inoue Tetsujirō, *Nihon Yōmeigakuha no tetsugaku* (Tokyo: Fuzambō, 1900); and two sequels, *Nihon kogakuha no tetsugaku* (1902) and *Nihon Shushigakuha no tetsugaku* (1905). Valuable collections are Seki Giichirō, ed., *Nihon jurin sōsho*, 14 vols. (Tokyo: Tōyō tosho kankōkai, 1927–38); Inoue Tetsujirō, ed., *Nihon rinri ihen*, 10 vols. (Tokyo: 1901–3); and Takimoto Seiichi, ed., *Nihon keizai taiten*, 60 vols. (Tokyo: Meiji bunken, 1966–). For this essay, I have relied primarily on volumes in Ienaga Saburō and

The central issue was the reliability of the philosophy utilized by the Tokugawa regime to justify its claim to moral and secular knowledge. This was the philosophy systematized by the Sung scholar Chu Hsi (1130–1200) and known in Western historiography as Neo-Confucianism. Although it would be unwarranted to claim Neo-Confucianism to be a comprehensive ideological "orthodoxy" for the *bakuhan* system, owing to the bakufu leaders' syncretic approach to ideas and rituals, Neo-Confucianism contained an epistemology that Buddhism and Shinto did not, as to how objective knowledge could be acquired and on the basis of which the flow of history could be managed in a predictable manner.

Thus, even though the Tokugawa rulers did not sever their ties with either Buddhism or Shinto, the former provided the rituals related to death, and Shinto those that sanctified sacred territory under a protective deity – an image the shogunal figures projected for themselves – they also saw in Neo-Confucianism a set of broad philosophical propositions on which servitors in positions of administrative responsibility could agree to govern according to predictable rules and not by arbitrary and whimsical acts. In time, these propositions became the primary "foil" behind which criticism was leveled against the politics of the day, with the intended aim of explaining the apparent lack of control over the course of events.[4]

As a cosmological system authorized by a transcendent moral absolute, the "Great Ultimate" or *taikyoku*, Neo-Confucianism articulated a sharp division between the Tokugawa era of peace and tranquility and the immediately preceding Sengoku period of constant warfare. A timeless and absolute norm drawn from outside historical time and transcending the chaotic warfare of the recent past was called on to establish the *bakuhan* structure of noncentralizing governance as being "principled."

Above all, it was theorized that this cosmology could be verified through the diligent and disciplined observation of things close at hand. The cognitive procedure would lead the human mind to uncover norms that informed categories of phenomena, each category anticipating higher and more universal levels that culminated in the "great ultimate" or "univeral reason" – *ri*. This perfect virtue, in turn,

Shimizu Shigeru et al., eds., *Nihon shisō taikei*, 67 vols. (Tokyo: Iwanami shoten, 1970–82); and Itō Sei et al., eds., *Nihon no meicho*, 50 vols. (Tokyo: Chūō kōronsha, 1972–82). Multivolume collected works of most of the major thinkers have also been published in modern form.
4 Divergent interpretive views are presented in Maruyama, *Studies;* Bitō, *Nihon hōken shisōshi;* and Herman Ooms, *Tokugawa Ideology – Early Constructs, 1570–1680* (Princeton, N.J.: Princeton University Press, 1985).

logically encompassed those abiding moral values such as goodness, benevolence, wisdom, and loyalty, in short, the very ethic of trust on which the Tokugawa government relied to regulate itself internally at the ground level of ordinary administration. Within such a cosmological scheme, the *bakuhan* system gained an intrinsic moral essence that went beyond military hegemony secured on the field of battle. Thus the Tokugawa regime presented itself as capable of humane and just rule in accordance with the norms of peace and tranquility.

The procedure of acquiring knowledge through observation, however, yielded disturbing evidence that was at odds with the ostensive goals of "ordering" and "saving" the people – *keisei saimin* – that governments universally should realize. No heady theorizing was required to realize that many trends of the day were not in accord with prevailing moral beliefs, such as merchants dominating the economy, samurai living in debt, peasants rebelling and townspeople flocking to vulgar theater. Agreeing on a persuasive alternative approach to knowledge, however, was quite another matter that required addressing broad theories of epistemology. If observing things close at hand was unreliable, as they did not yield general meaning, where then should the inquiring mind seek stable knowledge with which to better steer the course of history? In short, what was the proper object of cognition from which stable norms might be extracted? Two broad responses to this problem dominated much of the intellectual history of the eighteenth century.

One powerful resolution identified history, as expressed in language and text, to be the reliable object of knowledge, in contrast with speculative cosmology. Within this historicist frame of reference, there were those who insisted that the field of history be defined in terms of origin and the first articulation of principles. To grasp the present, the seeker must detach himself or herself from indigenous history and the convenient references to recent history and clarify a creative movement, this most often being ancient China where civilization presumably began. However, others denied the validity of such a search for beginnings in a "foreign" culture, arguing instead for the sufficiency of norms as shaped within indigenous history either as a result of a lengthy evolutionary political history, as in the inexorable rise of the *bakuhan* system, or in a moment of divine creation when the sacred community of the Japanese people first came into existence.

The alternative position to these theses of history proposed that all human knowledge, including documentation of the past, were relative, vis-à-vis universal nature. Although history was obviously a valuable source of inspiration to show how people sought to gain deeper empirical and emotional insights into nature, thereby strengthening the bonds of trust among themselves in society, it was to nature that the human mind must ultimately orient its quest for knowledge. What was normative here was not a fixed and refined moment in human time, but nature as infinite and thus ontological. The human mind could never fully comprehend nature, and therefore knowledge would remain relative even as it expanded. Human morality, then, was not so much a replication of nature as it was a series of human understandings based on the reverential and objective study of nature as an inexhaustible resource of knowledge. Modern Japanese scientific thought may be traced to this view of nature.

Though these two major themes of history and nature hardly deplete the range and richness of eighteenth-century Tokugawa thought, they provide an introductory perspective into some of the conceptual events of that important era.

HISTORY

It was Ogyū Sorai (1666–1728) who best articulated the basic proposition that reliable knowledge was to be located in history, in documented human experience itself and not outside human time in a transcendent absolute. It was captured in his famous dictum: "The ultimate form of scholarly knowledge is history."[5] Undoubtedly the most provocative and influential of the historicist thinkers, Sorai argued that although nature was certainly universal and infinite, the human mind was finite. Nature could not serve as a stable source of social norms precisely because it was beyond the grasp of human intelligence, and the procedure of directly observing nature to deduce moral norms was therefore flawed and arbitrary. Historical text, on the other hand, could be authenticated through the systematic philological "study of ancient language," or *kobunjigaku*. The intellectual choice that scholars faced regarding the proper object of study, therefore, was not between nature and history but between a textual field in one period of time as compared with another. While affirming that the source of knowledge was external to the human self and thus needed to be observed, Sorai insisted that the object was not, in the first instance, nature or the immediate social universe but a distant epoch,

---

5 *Gakumon wa rekishi ni kiwamari sōrō koto ni sōrō.* From Sorai's *Tōmonsho,* in Inoue, ed., *Nihon rinri ihen* vol. 6, pp. 146–203, esp. p. 153. A modern rendering is by Bitō Masahide, ed., *Nihon no meichō,* vol. 16 (Tokyo: Chūō kōronsha, 1974), pp. 297–358.

detached from the present and the recent past, when social norms were first created. Only after these norms and the intent behind their creation were clarified could the scholar then objectively "observe" things in the present. Without this knowledge, the act of observation was simply relative and subjective. Studying the ancients was not mere antiquarianism for Sorai. Rather, it was aimed at locating refined moral norms locked in ancient language that might guide the political order and control of the rapidly changing present.

Sorai's thinking was prefigured by Itō Jinsai (1627–1705), a renowned philosopher of merchant background who taught during the latter part of the seventeenth century.[6] Observing things close at hand did not yield to Jinsai a moral perspective on universal reason. He moreover rejected the claim that natural and social hierarchies were morally fixed by a cosmological absolute. This minimized the virtue of ordinary human beings and belittled their capacity to order and control, in a moral manner, the world around them. Jinsai had thus concluded that the scholar must first sever his analytical view of things from existing reality – the hierarchical order received from the immediate past – and seek out the initial creative formulation of the universal moral worth of all human beings, regardless of their social and political status.

Bypassing the history of Japan that had yielded the present as well as that of imperial China that had relied on deceptive metaphysics, Jinsai proceeded to study ancient language and texts. Significantly, he identified as fundamental to all subsequent humankind the writings of Mencius. Here was the first clear expression of the universalistic idea that all human beings possessed a potential for goodness and that goodness was not a static virtue or an unchanging absolute available only to the knowledgeable few or the influential. Kings, Mencius had emphasized, could be powerful and also wicked. Viewing virtue as an active potential residing in all human beings, regardless of status, Jinsai separated virtue from an abstract absolute and emphasized the "horizontal" dimension of it as a universal human possession, a ceaseless tendency toward action found everywhere in society. Although hierarchy was necessary for social existence, Jinsai emphasized that virtue persisted at every level.

6 Jinsai's key essays *Gomō jigi* and *Dōjimon* are in Yoshikawa Kōjirō and Shimizu Shigeru, eds., *Itō Jinsai – Itō Tōgai*, vol. 33 of *Nihon shisō taikei* (Tokyo: Iwanami shoten, 1971), pp. 11–113; and Ienaga Saburō and Shimizu Shigeru et al., eds., *Kinsei shisōka bunshū* vol. 97 of *Nihon koten bungaku taikei* (Tokyo: Iwanami shoten, 1966), pp. 49–200. See also Yoshikawa, *Jinsai, Sorai, Norinaga;* and Koyasu Nobukuni, *Itō Jinsai – jinrinteki sekai no shisō* (Tokyo: Tōkyō daigaku shuppankai, 1982).

The ultimate value of Mencius, then, was the existential emphasis given to human virtue as never static, and not an absolute to be recovered through diligent meditation or study. Virtue was constantly being acted out by ordinary individuals as a continuous part of human history, in small and unspectacular ways that never led to final resolutions, as in total enlightenment. It was best to speak of the "way," Jinsai thus concluded, not as an ultimate and unchanging reason but as small pathways that human beings journeyed over in daily life, with compassion, fairness, humility, and truthfulness. This included for Jinsai a healthy appreciation of the inevitable human passions, *jō*, of fear, sadness, joy, and anger as essential to human life. The active tendency toward goodness was thus to be found in the actual world of work, play, learning, and commerce without regard to distinctions previously imposed by metaphysical and political hierarchies. Through Jinsai, Mencius took on a fresh moral and intellectual cogency among commoners often not adequately appreciated by historians of thought. Through Mencius, ancient text had framed action in the present at whatever level in society that could be moral in a universally human sense.

Ogyū Sorai found much in Jinsai's thinking to admire, especially as he too had independently reached similar conclusions regarding the unreliability of Neo-Confucian metaphysics, the centrality of historical genius as the proper source of moral knowledge, and the importance of leaving the present and identifying with that genetic moment. Sorai, moreover, did not dispute Jinsai's propensity to see virtue in human action at all levels of society. He disagreed profoundly, however, on where the ultimate genesis of moral knowledge should be located and on what this knowledge should clarify in the first and most fundamental instance. Whereas Jinsai directed his historicism to expand the spaces for universal moral action among commoners, stressing the horizontality of human potential, Sorai insisted that this perspective did not address the question of why there was hierarchy and governance at all, and what these meant to history and to the ongoing present as a moral field.

Sorai's admiration for Jinsai, therefore, was qualified on firm conceptual grounds, as he reiterated in his key writings on the way and on names – *Bendō* and *Benmei*.[7] He expressed particular dissatisfaction

7 The *Bendō* and *Benmei* are in Yoshikawa Kōjirō and Maruyama Masao, eds., *Ogyū Sorai*, vol. 36 of *Nihon shisō taikei* (Tokyo: Iwanami shoten, 1973). See also Bitō Masahide, ed., *Ogyū Sorai*, vol. 16 of *Nihon no meicho* (Tokyo: Chūō kōronsha, 1974). See also Tahara Tsuguo, *Tokugawa shisōshi kenkyū* (Tokyo: Miraisha, 1967); Imanaka Kanshi, *Soraigaku no kisoteki kenkyū* (Tokyo: Yoshikawa kōbunkan, 1966); Hiraishi Naoaki, *Ogyū Sorai nempukō* (Tokyo: Heibonsha, 1984); J. R. McEwan, *The Political Writings of Ogyū Sorai* (Cambridge, England:

with Jinsai's conception of moral potential which he thought hardly differed from the Neo-Confucian view that all human beings possessed an innate goodness. For Sorai, Jinsai had succumbed to a simple theory of human virtue and had not explained why structures and hence history had come into existence in the first place. The ideas of Mencius, Sorai argued, were inadequate and inappropriate to the study of this problem, as they were articulated as part of a passionate polemic against the proponents of legalism and Taoism. Thus, although Jinsai had addressed the question of commoners managing and controlling their immediate lives in ways that were moral in a universalistic sense, Sorai focused on the broader issue of governance as a structured presence and further sought to resolve this problem by theorizing about historical and social genesis.

Sorai reasoned that human history was not "natural," but was "created," fashioned with artificial means. Unlike nature, which was infinite, having neither beginning nor end and thus being in this sense timeless, human history had a determinable beginning, an epoch when societies were forged and thus separated from nature. In a state of nature human beings did not possess history, but in society they did. Once the intent behind that creation could be uncovered, however, history, like natural time, could persist indefinitely into the future. Yet that vision of endless and dynamic continuity that all regimes, including the Tokugawa bakufu, must first grasp in order to rule wisely could be clarified only through the systematic philological analysis of the textual evidences of ancient history. It was on the basis of this knowledge of the "beginning" that political societies would survive and flourish or decline and fall, as could easily be demonstrated in the fate of Chinese dynasties and regimes in Japan's history before the rise of the Tokugawa.

Though he conceded that many of the texts existed in fragmentary form only, requiring historians to explore without prejudice a wide variety of evidence, including formal texts on law and ritual as well as the songs that conveyed the true feelings of princes and commoners, Sorai went on to formulate a grand and provocative perspective. In the ancient world well before Mencius and even Confucius, great, heroic kings, or *sen'ō*, grasped the original mandate of Heaven to bring peace and well-being among humankind. They replaced strife and struggle in nature with rites, laws, administrative procedures, moral norms,

Cambridge University Press, 1962); and Olof G. Lidin, *Ogyū Sorai's Distinguishing the Way* (Tokyo: Sophia University Press, 1970).

poetry, songs, and so forth that would nourish all human virtues in society, including those of the weak and lowly.

The great virtue of benevolence – *jin* – Sorai thus concluded must be identified only with these ancient kings who created society and with it human history, and it should not be confused as a general and innate human possession. Later kings, princes, lords, scholars, and commoners may be endowed with specific virtues, but these were not the same as the great virtue of historical creation. Confucius himself must be seen in this light as a compiler and transmitter of received wisdom, not as the creator of social norms. And similarly, because the norm of benevolence is external to humankind, it is neither transcendent and timeless nor to be found in the natural order, as theorized by Neo-Confucian cosmologists. "The way," as Sorai put it explicitly, "was created by the ancient kings. It is not natural. . . . The way of the ancient kings most assuredly is not to be found in nature."[8]

Much of human history presented itself as a record of decline and failure, Sorai argued, precisely because the creative norm of the ancient kings had not been used by kings and ministers, who accepted instead the deceptive metaphysical idea that the essence of Heaven and human goodness were identical. Human beings were coerced into believing that they could transform their flawed virtue into true timeless virtue. This idea was totally contrary to the reality of multiple virtues among humans and the indisputable fact that limited human intelligence could not possibly "know" the essence of Heaven, or what its moral intent (*ten'i*) might be in distributing virtues.

The great sages of antiquity, therefore, scrupulously avoided claiming to know Heaven as a universal norm and, instead, expressed reverence for Heaven and its infinite mystery. Even when Confucius spoke of "knowing Heaven's mandate" (*tenmei o shiru*), he certainly did not mean by this that he had gained an authoritative understanding of Heaven but simply that, as he gained wisdom with the advancement of age, he had finally become aware of his heavenly endowed personal virtue and thus now knew his imperative in life to be a scholar and not a political minister. Nowhere, Sorai claimed, did Confucius speak of his personal virtue as being in accord with the moral essence of Heaven. Indeed, much of human history reveals a fundamental misunderstanding of this meaning of virtue and universal and transcendent

8 Sorai's views on nature as institutional creation are scattered throughout his writings. A clear statement is sec. 5 of *Bendō*.

norm, by claiming the former to have a normative significance as meaning innate benevolence located in the human self.

The meaning of virtue, Sorai insisted, must be distinguished in two basic ways. There was first the great virtue specific to the ancient kings, who created history by separating society from nature with the intent of bringing peace and well-being among humankind. This virtue to be called Benevolence is located only at the beginning of history and is not a possession of subsequent kings and scholars. There is another virtue, the "little virtue" (shōtoku) that is granted by Heaven to each individual. It is the "imperative" (mei) within each self that the individual alone can realize. How little virtues are distributed among individuals in society is entirely unpredictable, as this is determined by a transnatural force to be referred to as Heaven. Virtue in this human sense should not be thought of as normative, in that it is entirely plural and relative from one person to the next. Indeed, virtue among humankind may be thought of as infinite, as there is no way to predict what sorts of virtues will appear as history unfolds. Expressing deep skepticism regarding the view that human virtues were common and shared, Sorai contended that each individual must conform to the virtue that is given by Heaven and, relying on benevolence, strive to realize fully that personal virtue.

Sorai practiced this theory of virtue as a teacher. Denying that he could mold others to become scholars, Sorai insisted that each student must realize his own virtue from within himself as a personal quest or imperative. Only when this effort had reached a moment of excruciating frustration could he, as a teacher, be useful by offering suggestions and encouragement. Despite his reputation as a dogmatic scholar, Sorai in fact assumed a laissez-faire attitude toward his students in accordance with his belief that a teacher, like a ruler, should not attempt to reshape the virtues of others.[9]

Sorai's theory of virtue contained an elitist implication that did not elude his many critics: If virtue is relative and specific to the individual, it followed that only few would be endowed with the "political" virtue to govern or the "scholarly" virtue to study ancient history. The bulk of society would be outside these crucial spheres of human activity and would simply rely on others who did possess these virtues. Although Sorai criticized the aristocracy for posing as a class endowed at birth with political virtue, his theory also created intellectual limits

9 Sorai's ideas about human virtue are presented in his *Gakusoku*, in Yoshikawa and Maruyama, eds., *Ogyū Sorai*, pp. 187–98; and also in his *Bendō*, as in sec. 14.

that especially educators of commoners found unacceptable. Lenient in the sense that it allowed for a wide variety of virtues to flourish, this theory was constraining to intellectual versatility and creative expansion beyond more than one field, meaning, practically, that it limited individuals to a functional occupation.[10]

At the same time, however, Sorai's concept of little virtues was intertwined with a broader theory of moral purpose in government. Although human virtues could not serve as a political norm, they were nonetheless the object of moral rule. The ancient kings created laws and political structures to nourish the myriad virtues that Heaven had bestowed on human beings. This was the substance of benevolence as the great virtue of the kings, and it therefore was also termed the way of human nourishment (*yashinai no michi*). Recognizing Heaven to be the sole source of human virtues and hence beyond human control, the kings forged political instruments to nourish all of these virtues with equanimity and without exception.

To the kings, all virtues were precious and worthy of fulfillment, no virtue being too trivial to be wasted. It was the vision of the kings that no virtue that appeared in the unfolding of future history would ever exceed the boundaries of the norm of nourishment. Virtues not yet known would find nourishment in their way. It allowed men to seek deep enjoyment in the arts. The way of the ancient kings, therefore, was vast and expansive, not inflexible, rigid, and legalistic. Indeed, as Sorai emphasized, if the broad way is in place, all the little virtues may move to and fro without interference. And in this free-flowing intermixing of human virtues that Sorai idealized, the king or prince would represent that comprehensive and broad norm of benevolence symbolizing thereby the individual virtues of each; he would scrupulously refuse to tamper with those virtues to make them conform to a single moral standard. In short, for Sorai, the prince did not stand for a moral norm to which men should aspire to approximate. Nor for that matter did he stand as a personal symbol of power and wealth. "The prince," as Sorai observed, "is always a social prince."[11]

To Sorai, then, all governments must be evaluated according to the norm of benevolence, not according to principle in nature, essence in Heaven, or universal virtue in human beings. Quite simply, any exist-

---

10 Scholars of commoner background argued against Sorai all through the eighteenth century. See my *Visions of Virtue in Tokugawa Japan – The Kaitokudō Merchant Academy of Osaka* (Chicago: University of Chicago Press, 1987).

11 *Sore kun naru mono wa gun nari.* See Ogyū Sorai's *Bemmei*, Yoshikawa and Maruyama, eds., *Ogyū Sorai*, pp. 37–185, esp. pp. 48, 54.

ing system of rule must nourish human virtues and refrain from coerc
ing them into something other than what Heaven had endowed. It wa:
this historical norm of benevolence fashioned by the ancient kings that
Sorai believed, must be brought to bear in the observation of the pres
ent. Goverments that maintain moralistic distinctions in status must b(
seen as coercive and as having failed to meet the demands of tha
original norm. And at this level of historical actuality, it was no longe1
the language or rhetoric of men who ruled that mattered, but th(
structured practice of nourishment that did. Of immense importance
Sorai's conception of politics held that no system of laws and procedur(
of governance should be taken prima facie as fixed in perpetuity, a:
being sacrosanct in terms of cosmological ideals, but instead must b(
constantly evaluated in accordance with the external norm of benevolence, the proposition enunciated by the ancient kings at the beginning
of history on which all human societies must be made to rest.

The true purpose of observation as an epistemological procedure
therefore, was not to find principle in nature to anchor moral norms,
but to analyze the state of political economy in light of the constant
intent underlying historical creation. As observation based on this aim
took precedence over other considerations, such as maintaining the
integrity of the aristocracy, it followed that specific political prescriptions must be directly oriented to the relative discrepancy perceived
between historical norm and the ongoing present. Sorai's theory of
history and virtue, in short, called on critical scholars to focus on this
discrepancy and not on stable continuity, which was to be Sorai's
lasting legacy in the discourse on political economy.

Viewing the historical present in terms of his theoretical perspective, Sorai drew the pessimistic conclusion that the Tokugawa peace
would not last far into the future unless major structural reforms were
carried out. Although in the past, systems were known to have corrected themselves in times of crisis, trends in the present suggested to
Sorai a bleak and irreversible process under way that would lead before long to popular insurrections that would prove fatal to the regime.
Men in positions of authority, he complained, lacked the proper virtue
to govern, leading inevitably to "men of talent and wisdom emerging
from below to overthrow the order." Before the faith of the people in
the government faltered even further, Sorai concluded, talent from
below must be nourished and elevated to positions of political responsibility to serve the needs of peace and well-being among the populace.[12]

12 Ogyū Sorai, *Seidan*, in Yoshikawa and Maruyama, eds., *Ogyū Sorai*, pp. 259–445, esp. p. 366.

Sorai's critical perception was entirely consistent with his overall thesis that human virtues were distributed by Heaven at random, and not in relation to socially determined status, and that therefore the monopoly of power by the aristocracy was inappropriate to the exercise of benevolence. This discrepancy between fixed status and the historical mission of social well-being, moreover, could be traced to a systemic failure to adapt from conditions of general warfare to one of peace, from the movement of marching armies to fluid commerce, from logistical encampments to hotels and pleasure quarters – in short, the entire transition from Sengoku to Genroku. Although it may be said in retrospect that Sorai's anticipation of swift decline was unfounded, as the regime maintained itself for another century and a half, his long-term vision of its fate was unerring.

In his analysis of the current state of the political economy, Sorai found widespread poverty among the general populace, not the nourishment of human virtues.[13] The discrepancy with the basic norm of benevolence was indeed of crisis proportion, as the aristocracy had failed to identify with the way of the ancient kings and had used cosmology instead to fix its own virtue in place as a privileged ruling group. The actual norms defining this class, however, were entirely inappropriate to historical actuality. The aristocracy was organized on principles fashioned under conditions of generalized warfare, which did not apply to normal conditions of peace that the regime was committed to maintain. Even though military techniques were useful in preserving the status of the aristocracy, they could not serve the needs of society over the long duration. Talent judged according to the norms of military standards was inadequate for providing peace and well-being. The rules that had separated the military aristocracy from the soil, compelling it to live in castle towns and to travel back and forth from Edo to reconfirm loyalty to the shogunal center, all were outmoded, relevant only to a country in a state of endemic military siege but not one living in peace yet experiencing extreme poverty.

Under these circumstances, Sorai concluded, "there is no real alternative except to reconstruct the laws." He meant by this specifically returning the aristocracy to the soil, not to reunite sword and land literally, but to avoid the erroneous assumption that sword and talent were coincidental, a fiction sustained by authoritative law. By returning the samurai to the land, Sorai argued, they would once again mix with the general population as commoners as they had been before

13 Ibid.

their rise as men of military ability. After the ruling class was reconstituted in this manner, new and appropriate talent (*jinzai*) would be sought to govern the land in ways appropriate to the original vision of the ancient kings. True to his theory that no single class intrinsically possessed the virtue of governing others, as political authority did not influence how virtues were distributed in society, Sorai prescribed far-reaching reforms vis-à-vis the present. Through his outline of practical prescriptions, moreover, he insisted that the norm of benevolence be used consistently so that reforms would not be whimsical and purposeless or gauged merely to self-centered needs of status preservation.

Thus, whereas Jinsai had oriented his historicism to clarify personal moral action without regard to the status structure, Sorai turned his framework to challenge the fiction of aristocratic virtue, articulating forcefully the idea that political talent was to be found distributed throughout society, a provocative concept that would grow in importance all through the rest of the eighteenth century and, indeed, on into modern times.[14]

Sorai's critical pragmatism steered some of his students away from the prolonged study of ancient texts that the philological approach demanded and oriented their scholarly attention to the immediate world of political economy. The most prominent among these was Dazai Shundai (1680–1747), whose principal work on political economy, *Keizairoku*,[15] would be among the most widely read treatises on this subject throughout the remainder of the Tokugawa period. Unlike others among Sorai's students, most notably Hattori Nankaku (1683–1759) who maintained a lifelong focus on the study of ancient poetics and philology, a commitment that Sorai tolerated in accordance with his appreciation of divergent virtues, Shundai found this to be antiquarian and dilettantish and felt nothing but impatience toward it. To Shundai, scholarly priority must always go to the careful assessment of the changing conditions of the present. The ancient kings, as he had learned from Sorai, did not establish a fixed set of laws that would be appropriate to all historical circumstances. On the contrary, these kings had taught that history would change and that conditions would differ from one epoch to the next. Although the original vision of benevolence would remain unchanged as the underlying way, the means by which this vision would be realized must adapt to the actualities of historical change itself. Without objective adaptation, Shundai

14 Ibid., pp. 273, 420–1.
15 The *Keizairoku* and the addendum, *Keizairoku shūi*, are in Rai Tsutomu, ed., *Sorai gakuha*, vol. 37 of *Nihon shisō taikei* (Tokyo: Iwanami shoten, 1972), pp. 7–57.

reasoned, the original norm of benevolence would simply be an abstraction differing little from the metaphysical concepts that Sorai had found to be unsound.

Referring to the world of the ancient kings metaphorically rather than as supportive of sacrosanct structures and fixed procedures, Shundai took his thinking to an extreme position consistent with the pessimistic appraisal of the present he shared with Sorai. Given the severity of the economic crisis, Shundai reasoned, only the drastic and comprehensive redesigning of the existing semiautonomous *bakuhan* system could produce the desired result of peace and well-being. Having argued his theory to this radical conclusion, however, Shundai retreated from it as being tactically infeasible in the present and prescribed instead reform within the existing order. His prescription nonetheless called for a departure from received moral ideas that extolled the primacy of rice agriculture as the fundamental basis for virtue and decried the political engagement in market and trade. Shundai's thinking in this regard may be seen as a major epistemological breakthrough, marking a key beginning in the conceptualization of politics in economic terms.

Shundai proposed a systematic creation of wealth through trade, utilizing the principle of exporting plentiful goods from one domain and importing scarce ones from another. History, as it currently presented itself, Shundai reasoned, was driven helter-skelter by an economic crisis that could be resolved only in economic terms. The sudden emergence of money and a market economy was new, to be found in neither ancient China nor Japan. In the present, aside from a few minor matters, "everything is money," and "the best way to earn money is through trade."[16]

No longer seeing trade and market economies as functionally specific to the merchant class, but as politically necessary, Shundai advised that there was no alternative but to increase the income of cash through trade and thereby carry out the true ethical aims of governance. Trade was simply another means, in this regard, to a moral end, just as were law, rites, language, and other legacies handed down from the distant past. In Shundai's eyes, no legal artifact could be thought of as being sacrosanct. Institutions must continuously adapt to the requirements of promoting peace and well-being in society. Consistent with this view, Shundai urged that the aristocracy not be allowed to maintain their houses through the "unnatural" act of adop-

16 Ibid., pp. 45–47.

tion in order to maintain the fiction of house immortality. The artifi
cial maintenance of a large aristocracy, he maintained, was inconsis
tent with the pressing need to generate wealth. Should these measure:
not be adopted, he predicted the quick demise of the *bakuhan* systen
in which scholars like himself would have no choice but to "do noth
ing" (*mu-i*) which Shundai claimed idiosyncratically, to be the tru<
meaning of Taoism, to become a recluse in nature and let the politica
order collapse of its own accord, as it should.[17]

Shundai's conceptual breakthrough regarding trade was one of sev
eral similar tendencies that developed within the framework of Toku
gawa historicism. His reference to ancient texts to provide a critica
perspective on the present can be detected in other historicist think
ers, as witnessed in Jinsai's incorporation of commoners througl
Mencius and Sorai's denial of aristocratic virtue. Historicism as a
mode of thought, in other words, provided a variety of related ye
distinct uses. It was in this respect a creative conceptual framework
that illuminated certain major intellectual trends other than those o
governance and trade. An intriguing variant, for example, proposed a
radical skepticism regarding all history, and another affirmed history
politically as well as culturally.

Skepticism as to whether any historical text contained normative
ideas relevant to the present was articulated best by the precocious
scholar Tominaga Nakamoto (1715–46).[18] Trained at the Osaka mer
chant academy, the Kaitokudō, Nakamoto shared with Jinsai and
Sorai certain general presuppositions: Metaphysics and cosmology as
well as the subjective interpretation of nature were unreliable, and
history was indeed the proper object of study from which to gair
insight into the present. However, Nakamoto went well beyond the
limits of what his predecessors would have allowed. Unlike them
Nakamoto challenged the view that language and text could ever serve
as objective data from which to make universal statements, and he
argued instead that texts were always manifestations of particular cul
tural contexts. History was thus relative and fundamentally unreliable
as a resource for ethical guidance in the present.

Because all texts, be they ancient or recent, were in the final analysis

17 I have commented on Shundai's idiosyncratic reading of Taoism in "Political Economism in
   the Thought of Dazei Shundai (1680–1740)," *Journal of Asian Studies* 31 (1972): 821–39
18 Tominaga Nakamoto's writings are in Mizuta Norihisa and Arisaka Takamichi, eds.
   Tominaga Nakamoto–Yamagata Bantō vol. 43 of *Nihon shisō taikei* (Tokyo: Iwanami shoten
   1973), pp. 11–138; and in Ienaga Saburō et al., eds., *Kinsei shisōka bunshū*, vol. 97 of *Nihon
   koten bungaku taikei* (Tokyo: Iwanami shoten, 1966). I have written about Nakamoto in
   relation to merchant ideology in *Visions of Virtue*, pp. 99–121.

distorted, the important issue for Nakamoto was to clarify what made texts, and hence all of history, unstable. History, Nakamoto reasoned, underwent constant change. Language and the meaning of words also changed. Each historical present was continuously interpreting its past and changing its mind about basic philosophical ideas. Underlying this instability, moreover, was human ambition, which led scholars to manipulate language and impute new meanings to articulate mythmaking claims as to what was orthodox, as opposed to heterodox.

All through history, each new generation of philosophers sought in this manner to outdo their predecessors and to seek hegemony over their competitors as to what constituted "true" history. The pure origins, as in the original vow of Buddhism or, for that matter, the normative purpose in the first creation of history, were therefore impossible to reconstruct. The overlay of claims and counterclaims was simply too intricate to unravel. If there was a dimension to history that was stable, Nakamoto noted, it was the rhetorical patterns by which scholars distorted received knowledge. He identified these patterns as exaggeration, generalizing from the concrete, reducing the meaning of the concrete from a priori abstractions, and using polarity and contradictions in deceiving ways. Religious history was particularly guilty of relying on rhetorical dishonesty. It could be found easily in the mysticism of Buddhism, the scholasticism of Confucianism, and the superstition of Shinto.[19]

Received moral wisdom should therefore be viewed with extreme skepticism, and the present, in turn, must be appreciated in its own terms, without regard to history. Referring to this approach to the present as "the way of truthfulness" (*makoto no michi*), Nakamoto called for ethical filial relationships and trust among human beings, for their own authenticity in the world of the living and not because of textual authorizations from the past.

Nakamoto added another provocative idea to his theory of history. Just as historical texts were irrelevant to the present, Nakamoto further reasoned that the intellectual and cultural history of one country could not be transferred to another. Historical lines were parallel and distinct rather than sympathetic and comparable. The history of Buddhism, for example, became increasingly distorted as it was grafted onto the history of China and Japan. Religious ideas, customs, and cultural styles, he concluded, could not be transferred from one his-

19 Nakamoto's views in his "Jottings of an Old Man" (*Okina no fumi*) are in Ienaga et al., eds., *Kinsei shisōka bunshū*, pp. 519–36.

torical sequence to another. Japan especially had suffered by incorporating Chinese scholasticism and Indian mysticism, disfiguring the indigenous cultural ideal of "unadorned honesty" (*naoki no kokoro*).

Although Nakamoto was harshly critical of Shinto as a body of simple and superstitious ideas, he had also posited the concept of distinctive historical cultures that could not be transferred to other societies. It was this conception of history that attracted the attention of scholars of national studies such as Motoori Norinaga (1730–1801) and Hirata Atsutane (1776–1843). These were scholars who turned historicist reasoning to affirm an authentic indigenous history untouched by the moral and scholastic ideas imported from abroad. Whereas Jinsai and Sorai had left the present and set their scholarly attention on ancient origins, Nakamoto saw this procedure as flawed and called for a return to the present in and for itself. Yet in reorienting historicist thinking in this direction, he also confirmed the particularity of historical sequences and hence the distinctiveness of cultural experience.[20]

Nakamoto's return to indigenous culture as separate and distinctive was in keeping with a general tendency in Tokugawa historical thought. Even Sorai, who had dramatized the beginning of history in ancient China, was not entirely untouched by this intellectual current. His conceptual scheme affirmed the Tokugawa system of noncentralized rule (*hōken*) as conforming more closely to the ancient model than to the more recent centralized imperial regimes in China. He believed the latter to be unduly harsh and legalistic, with the examination system especially stifling to intellectual life.

Sorai's forerunner in the development of ancient studies, Yamaga Sokō (1622–85), was even more explicit in his affirmation of indigenous political history.[21] After identifying ancient norms in Confucius's *Analects*, Sokō tried to show how, during the course of some five hundred years, equivalent values had been created within Japan itself by the aristocracy. These values as a coherent whole he termed the "way of the warrior" (*bushidō*). Filial piety, loyalty, truthfulness, trust, and so forth that are central to the *Analects* were also fashioned independently in Japanese history. It was thus incumbent on the aristocracy to continue to identify with the values of its class rather than on metaphysics and cosmology, in order to rule effectively and morally.

20 Nakamoto's critique on Buddhism, *Shutsujō gogo*, is in Mizuta and Arisaka, eds., *Tominaga–Yamagata*, pp. 11–105.
21 Sokō's writings are in Tahara Tsuguo and Morimoto Jun'ichirō, eds., *Yamaga Sokō*, vol. 32 of *Nihon shisō taikei* (Tokyo: Iwanami shoten, 1970).

Sokō's leap outside the present into the world of the ancients was thus followed by a return to a point in indigenous history from which ideals were extracted, in order to explain and critique current history. Sorai did not rely on this evolutionary scheme of narration, choosing to bring the norm of creative historical genesis directly to the present, although the option was clearly there, as is evident in Shundai's own recounting of the rise of noncentralized governance in Japan.

It was Sorai's political rival Arai Hakuseki (1657–1725) who most effectively used the evolutionary reconstruction of the rise of noncentralized governance as a comprehensive representation of Japan's political history. A scholar-bureaucrat of considerable reputation in the inner councils of the bakufu between 1709 and 1716, Hakuseki turned Sokō's emphasis on values embodied by the aristocracy into a political history involving relationships of power. Significantly, Hakuseki separated that history from the normative underpinnings of ancient texts and provided an interpretation that was grounded primarily in developments within the Japanese nation. In his influential history of 1712 (*Tokushi yoron*), Hakuseki presented the unfolding of national history in which the present was made to seem like an inevitable outflow of the past. The emphasis, moreover, was not on the creation of value over time but on the steady emergence of a political class. Although Hakuseki's history covers the entire span from the mythical beginnings, his emphasis was clearly on the six hundred years that had culminated in the founding of the Tokugawa regime.[22]

Hakuseki identified two crucial trends that had intersected in the earlier portion of this history and had permanently and irreversibly altered the character of Japanese history. One was the steady decline of imperial authority all through the tenth and eleventh centuries under the Fujiwara regency and especially with the establishment of the Kamakura bakufu in the late twelfth century. The other was the ascendancy of the aristocracy of the sword and, with it, a comprehensive tradition of noncentralized rule. What had been cast as centuries of warfare, to be distinguished from the new era of peace and tranquility, was now rendered by Hakuseki as explicable in terms of coherent linkages between the peaks and valleys covering a vast epoch. A political tradition was shaped in these centuries, irrevocably

22. On Hakuseki, see Matsumura Akira, Bitō Masahide, and Katō Shūichi, eds., *Arai Hakuseki* vol. 35 of *Nihon shisō taikei* (Tokyo: Iwanami shoten, 1975); and translations by Joyce Ackroyd of *Tokushi yoron*, *Lessons from History* (New York: University of Queensland Press, 1982); and of Hakuseki's autobiography, *Oritaku shiba no ki*, *Told Round a Brushwood Fire* (Princeton, N.J.: Princeton University Press, 1979). See also Kate Wildman Nakai, *Shogunal Politics: Arai Hakuseki and the Premises of Tokugawa Rule* (Cambridge: Harvard University Press, 1988.)

setting into place an institutional mode of governance that made perfect sense in the light of the previous flow of history. It followed that the rise of the aristocracy was a central feature of this history, thus confirming the special status of the Tokugawa samurai class in relation to that history.

In legitimating the present in this manner, Hakuseki did not resort to ancient textual sources to authenticate his account. In his view, history did not evolve out of individuals making moral choices and thereby altering the course of events. The imperial decline was not due to faltering moral conviction, nor was the rise of the aristocracy of the sword a reflection of moral superiority. History, in short, was not chosen, as one does in conventional life, weighing the advantages of doing things in one way as against another. The decisive overall trend in one direction and not the other, however, was unmistakable. And this transformational flow, though not willed by the whims of heroic choices nonetheless swept all along with it, inexorably, irresistibly, and cumulatively into a recognizable and coherent political tradition of *hōken* manifested in the political forms of the present.

Although this evolutionary reconstruction of history clearly contained a critique of centralized imperial rule, it also, more fundamentally, confirmed the adaptive capacities of the Tokugawa *bakuhan* system in the present. Produced by a long political history, the system of noncentralized rule could not be drastically altered, even if men chose to do so. Existing structures, therefore, must be used in creative and enlightened ways to bring order and peace to the general populace. Moving the aristocracy back to the soil, as Sorai had prescribed, was obviously not acceptable to Hakuseki. To him, the rise of the aristocracy of the sword was inevitable, the product of a pervasive historical evolution that could not be undone and to which no one in Japan from the emperor and court nobles down to the general populace could be exempted.

The dissociation of internal political history from external legitimation found further expression in the intellectual movement known as "national studies" (*kokugaku*). Here too the conception that historical sequences are separate and distinctive, regulated by patterns that owe nothing to exogenous influences, was strongly underscored. The return, however, was not to political history but to comprehensive cultural autonomy, found at the nation's birth. The devotees of national studies focused their intellectual attention on the indigenous cultural spirit that unified the entire people. Their concern was not to represent the most salient aspect of political tradition, as they were not interested in political structures such as the *hōken* form of governance, and similarly with the rise of the aristocracy.

National studies, instead, was a "populistic" search for a common spiritual and emotive culture that preceded the formation of political structures, aristocracies, and, most pointedly, the imposition of foreign historical values, language, and modes of thinking. It thus clearly occupied a distinctive place in the development of eighteenth-century historical consciousness. Its relationship with the broader discourse on history, however, is at the same time unmistakable: in Sorai's quest for ancient historical genesis, Tominaga's thesis on the inapplicability of foreign ideas for indigenous culture, and Hakuseki's representation of national political history in its own terms.

Of particular importance is the emphasis of national studies on the aesthetics that unified the indigenous culture. What needed to be shown in terms of ancient origin, distinctive internal patterns, and comprehensive meaning to history was the irreducible cultural level at which members of a community knew without reflection and analysis the beauty and hence the truthful meaning in beings and things. A powerful stimulus to this aesthetic perspective of national history was provided by the late-seventeenth-century Buddhist scholar-priest Keichū (1640–1701).[23] A devotee of the Shingon sect, Keichū also studied at Itō Jinsai's school and used the method of ancient studies to approach the life and writings of the patron saint and founder of Shingon, Kūkai (or Kōbō Daishi) (774–835) and to seek the spiritual resources of this great and celebrated saint.

Kūkai had insisted in his teachings that true religious experience could be attained in Japan, on the native land itself, without having to travel to the holy sources of scripture on the Asian continent, establishing from this point of view the famous pilgrimage sites around the island of Shikoku. Keichū focused on Kūkai's spirituality within Japan and identified Japanese poetics in Kūkai's writings as crucial to understanding the saint's religious faith. It was here that Keichū believed Kūkai had expressed in unadorned manner his innermost faith in the religiosity of the universe inclusive of all things. Keichū proceeded from that aesthetic perception of Kūkai to the poetics of the ancient *Man'yōshū* and the *Kojiki*.

Keichū's scholarship remained a touchstone for all subsequent advocates of national studies. Although specifically Buddhistic elements

23 See Hisamatsu Sen'ichi, *Keichū* (Tokyo: Yoshikawa kōbunkan, 1963); and Taira Shigemichi and Abe Akio, eds., *Kinsei Shintō ron zenki kokugaku*, vol. 39 of *Nihon shisō taikei* (Tokyo: Iwanami shoten, 1972).

were to be shorn from his works, the emphasis on faith in a true communal origin of the nation would be retained as an elaboration of the way of truthfulness. Subsequent scholars relying on a similar philological scheme sought to clarify the unique foundations of Japanese cultural history rather than to seek the faith of Buddhism, to make clear the origins of Japan as a sacred community and thereby expose the superficiality of cultural glosses drawn from foreign sources such as Buddhism and Confucianism. Scholars such as Kada no Azumamaro (1669–1736), Kamo no Mabuchi (1697–1769), and especially Motoori Norinaga (1730–1801) were decisive in shaping this idealistic view of national history that celebrated its uniqueness, its sacred land and community, and the aesthetics of the people's language and feelings.

The common strategy employed by these men in their writings was to establish binary contrasts between Japanese and foreign, most pointedly Chinese, cultures. For example, China's monosyllabic language with its thirty-odd thousand characters is compared with Japan's syllabic one of fifty phonetic letters; artificial scholasticism and rhetoricism with the natural unity of speech and language; the separations among the human spirit, nature, and society and the undifferentiated world of humankind, things, and creatures; the belief in the universe as being reason and hence subject to rational distinctions with an allowance for life, and the universe as being beyond reason and full of divine mystery – life not being rational but mystical; the emphasis on scholastic reason leading to the construction of elitist and artificial cultural and political constructions that were inaccessible to the populace at large, with a sacred community in which language and feelings were conjoined in poetics of the heart, devoid of artificiality yet reverential to the mystery of life and nature; artificial social constructs that rise and fall, with a sacred community that is immortal from ancient origins into the indefinite future as it precedes structures; and an imperial monarch being all-powerful yet distant from the people, with an archaic king that is part of the sacred community, mediating between nature and human life through the rite of eternal renewal and hence one and inseparable from the feelings of the people.[24]

These binary constructs clearly outline the principal aims of national studies. Foreign cultural ideas and beliefs must be discarded as artificial and replaced with an identification with communal genesis, a pure moment in an ancient world when the natural and sacred commu-

---

24 Saegusa Yasutaka, *Kamo no Mabuchi* (Tokyo: Yoshikawa kōbunkan, 1959); and for Makuchi's *Kokuikō*, Endo Ryūkichi et al., eds., *Nihon kokusui zensho* (Tokyo: Nihon kokusui zensho kankokai, 1916), vol. 3, pp. 1–35.

nity first came into existence, that moment when "national" history may be said to have begun. From such identification, the meaning of culture and politics in the present must be recomprehended. Although Sorai had used this scheme to identify a utopian origin as located in the records of the ancient kings and although Nakamoto had argued that such a transference across time and space was extremely misleading, the scholars in national studies absorbed both Sorai's concept of pure, normative beginning and Nakamoto's concept of the distinctiveness of cultural histories, to fashion a potent conception of Japanese culture and the basis on which to evaluate its meaning. By uncovering the original meaning of Japanese culture, these men contended, all of the artificialities of subsequent history could be erased. The way of truthfulness (*makoto no michi*) thus would not be fragmentary and momentary but anchored to the ideal of sacred community when word, feelings, and human trust all were conjoined. When such a reidentification with origin occurred, it would then be possible to reconstitute and reorder the meaning of the present as well.

A good many of these themes were expressed by Motoori Norinaga, the pivotal thinker in this entire intellectual development. It is perhaps safe to say that without Norinaga's scholarship, works such as the *Tale of Genji* and the mythic *Kojiki*, which had been referred in the past in sporadic and fragmentary ways, would not have survived into the modern era as sacred cultural classics. That they have survived as such is in no small measure a creation of the national studies movement of the late eighteenth century. To Norinaga, too, the beginning moment was the emergence of the Japanese people as a sacred community. In that beginning, he wrote, humankind, the gods, and nature were in a state of peace and harmony. The world of infinite mystery and natural community were one. Words and things were joined in divine fashion (*kannagara*). Sophistry and deception were absent, and truthfulness reigned. The sacred king oversaw this wondrous community and mediated between the needs of human life and nature, a role he confirmed in the rite of eternal renewal (*Daijōsai*).[25]

25 Endo et al., eds., *Nihon kokusui zensho*, vol. 13; and Yoshikawa Kōjirō, Satake Akihiro, and Hino Tatsuo, eds., *Motoori Norinaga* vol. 40 of *Nihon shisō taikei* (Tokyo: Iwanami shoten, 1978). See also Koyasu Nobukuni, *Norinaga to Atsutane no sekai* (Tokyo: Chūō kōronsha, 1977); Watanabe Hiroshi, " 'Michi' to 'Miyabi' – Norinaga gaku to 'kagaku' ha kokugaku no seiji shisōshiteki kenkyū," *Kokka gakkai zasshi* 87 (1974): 477–561, 647–721; and 88 (1975): 238–68, 295–366; and Shigeru Matsumoto, *Motoori Norinaga 1730–1801* (Cambridge, Mass.: Harvard University Press, 1970); and H. D. Harootunian, *Things Seen and Unseen: Discourse and Ideology in Tokugawa Nativism* (Chicago: University of Chicago Press, 1988).

History, however, went awry. The Chinese idea of the Way was introduced, deceiving the people with the belief that reason controlled human time rather than faith in the divine ways of ancient times and convincing people to stray from the immediate and practical ethics of human truthfulness. As the result of the introduction of these foreign ideas, history actually declined from its communitarian origins to one of treachery and deception. The sacred king and the community retreated from the mainstream of popular life. Artificial ways came to dominate. It was clear from all of this that Norinaga had come through his historicist thinking to conclude rather dimly about the cultural realities around him. And although he avoided making political prescriptions as to what specifically to do about the present, Norinaga envisioned, nonetheless, a renewal of the pure and sacred native land, which would be wrought not by human reason and planning but by chaotic divine cleansing. The idea here that history is not intrinsically evolutionary and decided by inexorable forces, as argued by Arai Hakuseki, but, rather, determined by divine intervention or what might be termed "accident" beyond the control of human and bureaucratic reason was a potent one, for in time, it could serve as a theory of action to identify the individual will with the idea of divine instrumentation.

The previous examples from ancient and national studies illustrate the divergent directions in which historical thinking could travel. That the impact of Sorai's was enormous in all this is readily evident. Indeed, in his assessment of Confucian thinkers, the late Tokugawa scholar Hirose Tansō (1782–1856)[26] observed that the Confucian tradition in Japan underwent sudden and irreversible change after Sorai and that no scholar could revert to Neo-Confucian metaphysics without first stating his clear reservations. Thus although many chose not to align themselves with ancient studies, they adopted an intellectual stance of philosophical syncretism (setchūgaku), which, Tansō noted, became the mainstream of intellectual thought from then on. Syncretism, in Tansō's view, resulted directly from the impact of Sorai and the countervailing arguments leveled against him. Yet this attack on Sorai in order to protect the metaphysics of Neo-Confucianism had the net effect of also ensuring the continuation of Sorai's conception of history and political economy, as his theoretical position could not be entirely discredited and displaced. Most granted Sorai a distinguished place in

---

26 Tansō's view in *Jurin hyō* (1836) is in Seki Giichirō, ed., *Kinsei Juka shiryō*, vol. 1 (Tokyo: Hanchō shobō, 1942), pp. 1–22.

the discourse on political economy, while admitting at the same time the importance of the idea of natural reason in Neo-Confucianism.

The syncretic resistance to historicism indeed suggests the dynamic role played by the idea of universal reason. Anchored by a theory of natural ontology, this philosophical position rested on a rationalistic view in which human affairs and hence history were seen as relative to nature. No particular epoch, such as an ancient origin, could assume an absolutely privileged status vis-à-vis nature, as one era was no more or less insightful than another. When based on natural ontology, syncretism regarding history did not mean indecisiveness, as this development is sometimes characterized to be.

NATURE

Parallel to the expanding discourse on history, a distinct tradition within the related conceptual universe of Tokugawa Confucianism had also gained favor among articulate segments of the various classes. Based on the Neo-Confucian theory of the universality of natural principle (*ri*), this intellectual tradition underwent important metamorphoses from a cosmology that fixed in place the status quo into a body of scientific thinking and, reminiscent of Itō Jinsai's use of Mencius, a philosophy that validated new moral spaces among commoners. In this new science, nature was conceptualized as the ultimate field of knowledge that should engage scholarly attention, differing fundamentally in this regard from the historicist position that had placed primary focus on historical experience and hence on language rather than on nature, which, as Sorai had observed, was beyond human comprehension. Moreover, although advocates of natural principle agreed with historicists that the purpose of scholarship was to nourish, or "save," the general populace, they stressed the importance of a sound knowledge of nature as taking precedence over the reliance on political hierarchy. Again, the difference with Sorai in this regard is particularly striking.

As articulated in the thinking of Kaibara Ekken (1630–1714) in his development of agronomy for the peasantry, Nishikawa Joken (1648–1724) and Goi Ranju (1697–1762) in their instruction to merchants, and Miura Baien (1723–89) in his theory of economic value based on broad social utility, we find in common the view that the people are to be saved by teaching them about the importance of objectively grasping natural principle and dealing with the world around them in a practical, accurate, nonarbitrary, and hence moral fashion. To these men, history was less significant as a philological field to be studied as it was a continuing present to be ordered and acted out, through the empirical reliance on natural reason. There was also the mutually consistent understanding that the study of nature as the universal text would yield nourishment to commoners in general. Knowledge was not thought to be the special privilege of the aristocracy. Thus, though the exponents of natural ontology did not produce counterstructural radicalism, they generated a good deal of eccentricity and defiance toward conventions regarding social structure.

A good deal of eighteenth-century thought on nature can be traced to Kaibara Ekken.[27] An extremely prolific writer on such varied subjects as ethics for commoners, childbearing, education for women, and even the natural history of plants and minerals in Japan, his *Yamato honzō* is a monumental work that, through the eighteenth century, remained a testimony of his intellectual convictions. Ekken dedicated his last efforts to a sweeping critique of Neo-Confucian metaphysics and cosmology. Entitled *Taigi roku* (A record of grave doubts; ca. 1713), the treatise argued for the disengagement of the empirical study of nature from its moralistic and political uses. Though Ekken believed in the necessity of politics, he stressed that nature could not provide metaphysical sanctions for it. He viewed cosmology as simply a convenient device to confirm status and authority. It did not, in his eyes, direct men to address the basic moral question of social order, namely, providing nourishment for the people, which he believed an objective reference to nature did. Nature, he contended further, did not embody a timeless moral norm, as posited in Neo-Confucian metaphysics. It was characterized more fundamentally by ceaseless life activity, whose underlying principle ought not be intuited or meditated on in quietistic fashion, presupposing nature to be in essence static and unchanging. How nature changed and reconstituted itself and underwent change again, therefore, involved systematic observation that would result in moral action.

Ekken related the study of nature and moral action in the following manner: Human beings possessed within themselves at birth a universal "principle of life" (*seiri*). All were, in this sense, "children" of nature, the "great parent" (*dai fubo*). Human morals, however, were not inherent in nature, as theorized in Neo-Confucianism. By sharing

27 Araki Kengo and Inoue Tadashi, eds., *Kaibara Ekken – Muro Kyūsō*, vol. 34 of *Nihon shisō taikei* (Tokyo: Iwanami shoten, 1970). I have focused on Ekken in "Intellectual Change in Early Eighteenth Century Tokugawa Confucianism," *Journal of Asian Studies* 34 (1975): 931–44.

a common understanding of being governed by one natural principle, human beings related to others in humane and trustworthy ways that in fact made moral society possible. The principle of life that one received from nature, therefore, ought to be thought of as a "blessing" (*on* or *megumi*) or, indeed, the "great blessing" that transcended conventional ones that came from rulers or parents. Nature was the ultimate and absolute source of human blessings, and it was the reverence toward this ontological truth that, in turn, informed the human "spirit of truthfulness" (*makoto no kokoro*).[28]

Ekken further insisted that compassion based on reverence for nature must extend beyond social relations to encompass all natural things. The idea that humankind stood in a dominant relationship vis-à-vis nature, or even as being separate from it, as Sorai had argued, was repugnant to Ekken. Because nature was the primary object of study, in the final analysis, history, language, and other forms of organizing knowledge were significant only in relation to it.

Historical texts must thus be seen as relative insights into the complexities of nature. They reveal that human knowledge of nature had expanded from the ancient period down to the present and that the most reliable insights were not those stemming from passive and meditative engagements with nature as an unchanging norm, but the active observation of nature as a dynamic reality. And because human knowledge had expanded in history, the accumulation of knowledge should not be viewed as embodiments of truths, but only as relative insights into a natural universe that would never be fully known. In the quest for knowledge, therefore, the human mind must always proceed from a position of skepticism, doubting things and facts that had been documented and, in the end, doubting once again what had been organized and ordered as reliable knowledge. Ekken found flawed and unacceptable the belief that the human mind could realize ultimate truth through the spiritual identification between moral self and transcendent absolute.

A major feature of Neo-Confucianism was a dualism in which all phenomena were categorized as being either beyond shape (*keijijō*) or with shape (*keijika*), as in the world of observable physical objects. The former preceded physical experience and hence the nonvisible principle or reason that defined one category of things as opposed to another. Being beyond the constraints of time and physical changes, it was constant, universal, ultimate, and good in serving as an unchang-

28 See Araki and Inoue, eds., *Nihon shisō taikei*, vol. 34, pp. 9–64.

ing moral norm. The principle defining particular things was thus identified with this ultimate norm and was also rendered good and moral in being constant and transcendent of form. It was this moral philosophy that Ekken found to be conceptually misleading, as it was speculative and similar to Buddhist and Taoist thinking about human immortality.

Expressing much impatience with the religious impulse embedded in Neo-Confucianism, Ekken redefined this philosophy in terms of a strict monism. Visible and invisible would be understood with reference to a unified principle of matter. Principle or reason was thus not a timeless essence of matter but matter itself, one and identical with it. Reason, in his view, was the reason of matter and not separable into two categories. By focusing on the physical world as theoretically central and not relative to another metaphysically conceived reality, Ekken had effectively denied the claims made in Neo-Confucian cosmological reasoning of an abstract moral norm more universal than and hence transcendent of physical nature. Nature itself was the ontological basis on which all human considerations of knowledge, including history and ethics, must be made to rest.[29]

Owing to Ekken's skeptical view of Neo-Confucian metaphysics, scholars of ancient studies took immediate notice of the treatise on grave doubts. Sorai himself was shown a copy of the manuscript shortly after Ekken's death and was much impressed with it. So too was Dazai Shundai, who noted his surprise that a scholar so closely identified with Neo-Confucianism should enunciate his objections to that philosophical system with such devastating succinctness. Although Shundai argued that Ekken had not spelled out the logical conclusion to his thesis, namely, the total unreliability of Neo-Confucianism as a framework to organize knowledge, he admitted that Ekken had in fact vitiated it to an irreparable degree by rejecting its philosophical dualism.[30]

Despite the interconnectedness in Ekken's thinking with that of Sorai's school in their shared skepticism regarding Neo-Confucian metaphysics, a profound intellectual distinction separated Ekken's from the historicists. The latter firmly anchored their conception of knowledge on human and hence historical experience, whereas Ekken insisted on the proposition that nature ought to remain the ultimate object of knowledge. In this respect, the Neo-Confucian method of

29 Ibid., pp. 17–20.
30 Shundai's piece, "Sonken Sensei no Taigi roku o yomu" is in *ibid.*, pp. 59–62.

observing things remained vital to Ekken. His doubt about dualism did not lead him to view history as being a superior source of knowledge over nature. Indeed, despite an eclectic interest in a wide variety of intellectual fields, he remained consistent in the orientation to first principle in nature.

Throughout his life, Ekken insisted that nature should not be received passively as a given, but that it should be viewed as an infinite source of knowledge that the human mind would continuously explore but never exhaust. The human mind in every present age, therefore, takes part in an ongoing process of uncovering insights into nature as an inexhaustible source of knowledge. In this continuing process, knowledge once believed to be unshakably true will constantly be altered through the exercise of doubt.

A key teacher of the philosophy exemplified by Ekken was Goi Ranju (1697–1762) who taught merchants in Osaka.[31] Ranju turned the theory of natural ontology into a pedagogical principle on which to instruct commoners. Lectures, and informal comments taken down by his students, clearly reveal a consistent theoretical stance in regard to the relationship between historical texts and nature. The observation of things, Ranju taught, led to the indisputable conclusion that nature and the entire universe of phenomena, humankind included, were organized internally by an ordering principle.

This theory of knowledge held that the fundamental "thing" to be examined was not language, as Sorai, Jinsai, Nakamoto, and other historicists had argued but, rather, the natural order itself. Ranju, like Ekken, did not discount the importance of language fields and history in general; but language was relative to nature, a tool with which human beings sought in ever-expanding ways to grasp more persuasively and effectively the meanings that were apparent in nature. Language texts were thus to be appreciated in accordance with the insights they provided into universal nature. The ancient classics were classics for this reason. And so too were the writings of Chu Hsi and other Neo-Confucianists, especially in their discussion of observation and principle. These texts were not to be seen as absolute, as no human text could ever contain a complete statement of the reason embedded in the universe. That historical texts were thus flawed was not only inevitable but utterly human. To reject Neo-Confucianism and, through philological reduction, to isolate only one or a certain cluster of historical texts, as

31 Ranju has not been anthologized as have been the other thinkers in this chapter, although he played a pivotal role at the merchant academy of Osaka, the Kaitokudō. I have written about him in *Visions of Virtue*, pp. 121–48.

Sorai and Jinsai had done, was to Ranju and his students, the brothers Nakai Chikuzan (1730–1804) and Riken (1732–1817), prejudicial and unsound scholarship, a viewpoint they outlined in polemical arguments directed against Sorai.[32]

To Ranju and his students, Sorai's scholarship was even more seriously flawed than the excesses of Neo-Confucian metaphysics. Assuming that historical origin could be demonstrated with philological tools, Sorai went on to minimize the importance of some of the other great classics such as the *Doctrine of the Mean* and *Mencius*, labeling these as merely polemical. To his critics, however, Sorai's evidence did not warrant these interpretations, or his grandiose claim that he had uncovered the intention of the ancient kings in creating history thereby clarifying the meaning of human virtue for all subsequent history. Ranju denounced this dogmatic reading of Sorai's historicism.

To Ranju, historical texts in general were to be read, evaluated, and appreciated in terms of the relative insights offered into the infinite wonders of nature. And from this perspective it was unreasonably restrictive to isolate only the most ancient texts as normative and to assess all subsequent ones as polemical glosses. Recent texts such as those of Chu Hsi were also valuable, Ranju believed, as were literary expressions that contained honest human perceptions of nature as a universal phenomenon. Ranju could thus without apology encourage commoners to study Japanese literature as important philosophical texts. Although Sorai had also emphasized literature as important evidence for the cultural spirit of the ancients, to Ranju, literature represented the continuing imperative among humankind to gain relative insights into the universality of nature.

The human mind, like historical texts, was and always would be relative to infinite nature. This principle of relativity, furthermore, was universal and encompassed all human beings, regardless of class and status. To Ranju this meant the human capacity to observe and know, in relative ways, certain general truths. Never absolute, such knowledge was relative from one individual to the next, and it was never predetermined by one's birth. As all humans shared the potential to know, to gather and organize external knowledge, and to act on that knowledge, this meant more than knowing about things close at hand, or one's little virtue, but, rather, comprehending broad moral concepts that related to matters large and small.

32 Ranju's *Hi-Butsu hen* of 1766 remains unpublished in modern print. The main thesis of Nakai Chikuzan's *Hi-Chō* is in Nakamura Yukihiko and Okada Takehiko, eds., *Kinsei kōki juka shū*, vol. 47 of *Nihon shisō taikei* (Tokyo: Iwanami shoten, 1972), pp. 43–62.

Here again the disparity with Sorai was striking: Whereas Sorai had insisted that most human beings could not fathom the meaning of external norms and thus should not seek to do so but should rely on them (*yorashimubeshi*), Ranju countered vehemently that ordinary human beings indeed could "know" such norms, just as they were inherently capable of grasping the order of things in nature. Human knowledge of nature would always be incomplete and relative. The quest for a better comprehension of nature, however, would remain the continuing epistemological imperative for all humankind, and not the special occupation of the talented few. Thus although the knowledge that human beings acquired from within, vis-à-vis external nature, would remain incomplete, the relationship between inner and outer, for Ranju, could not logically be in a state of disjuncture, as Sorai had theorized.

The insistence we see here on the moral unity between inner virtue and outer knowledge was especially important to commoner education. The inner virtues of commoners were taught within this framework as not being inferior to those of other classes, including the aristocracy. It also allowed teachers to claim that all commoners possessed the capacity to know a wide variety of external things, such as general moral norms and the truthfulness or righteousness of the objective calculation of the workings of the agricultural cycle or the marketplace. The strong stance taken against Sorai's historicism, therefore, carried far-reaching implications. At stake was the prerogative of commoners, in general, to acquire knowledge and thus to study classical texts, even though they might be merchants and not scholars.

The articulate defense of the potential of commoners to acquire general knowledge underscores an important pattern in the metamorphosis of Tokugawa Neo-Confucian thought. A philosophical system favored at first, because it fixed in place law, social order, and political hierarchy, had come to take on a much broader significance, namely, the universality of virtue in terms of a human capacity to study and know moral knowledge.

This idea received powerful moral reinforcement from Ishida Baigan (1685–1744) who taught among the humble townsfolk in Kyoto.[33] Known as *shingaku* (teachings of the human spirit), his teachings spread through various cities and regions of the country as an educational movement among commoners, and the young in particular. In

33 Shibata Minoru, *Baigan to sono monryū* (Kyoto: Minerva shobō, 1977); and Robert Bellah, *Tokugawa Religon: The Values of Pre-Industrial Japan* (New York: Free Press, 1985).

Baigan's works, too, the strong resistance to Sorai's historicism is readily evident. Against Sorai, who had particularized human virtue, denying the universal moral potential of human beings to transform themselves in terms of a common norm of goodness, Baigan argued exactly the opposite. Humans possessed a mutually shared virtue that allowed all to gain an inner knowledge of moral truths. Individuals, therefore, should not rely on an externally fixed norm created at the dawn of history but instead should actively seek that knowledge of virtue in the present and transform themselves from within the spiritual self.

Moreover, external activity, whatever the particular field of action, was potentially a true moral extension of one's inner virtue. Baigan thus combined with his idealistic ethic a practical message that affirmed as potentially moral both commerce and the menial activities that accompanied trade and agriculture. The exchange of goods of reliable quality, he taught, involved an expression of trust among men that contributed to the ethical and material well-being of society. By emphasizing the moral coherency between inner and outer realms in this manner. Baigan found receptive audiences especially among the lower strata of the cities' new commercial segments.[34]

Baigan's moral teachings, it should also be stressed, differed from Ranju's in significant ways. In Baigan's teachings, an idealistic theory of the human spirit served as the basis of his syncretism. To Baigan, the aspects of all of the major religions – Buddhism, Confucianism, and Shinto – that affirmed the inner human spirit, or the heart, were equally valid, and moral men should accept them. To claim one religion to be superior to another was prejudicial and contrary to the inner spirit. Ranju found this view to be unacceptable. Because the basis of selection must be based on natural reason, religions that did not accept that premise must be rejected as unreliable. Buddhism, for example, advanced a philosophy that nature could not serve as a stable ontological reference because it was in a constant state of impermanence and flux. Shinto, moreover, based its ideas on superstition.

Due to the different philosophical premise on which their syncretic ideas rested, the thrust of Baigan's and Ranju's teachings was distinct, even as they both affirmed the new commerce. The accuracy or righteousness of knowledge was less critical to Baigan than was the inner spirit of truthfulness that informed external action. Ranju, on the other

---

34 See Ishikawa Ken, *Nihon shomin kyōikushi* (Tokyo: Tōkō shoin, 1925); and his *Ishida Baigan to 'Tohi mondo'* (Tokyo: Iwanami shoten, 1968).

hand, stressed universal nature as the source of human accuracy, emphasizing therefore the crucial internal potential to observe natural phenomena rather than to introspect on the inner spirit. Ranju, in short, tended to be decidedly secular and rational, situating himself squarely in the naturalistic tradition of Neo-Confucianism and targeting within this framework the universality of virtue and the inevitability of natural passion (jō). Although he did not endorse the reckless pursuit of worldly pleasures, Ranju denied the view held by some of his moralistic contemporaries that human life was to be guided by the idealistic heart alone. The exclusive emphasis on the primacy of the human spirit, he argued, was the source of much deception, as it denied the great virtue of nature, life, which included human passions.

Reminiscent of Itō Jinsai, Ranju insisted that human goodness was to be realized in the daily world of active and passionate interactions and not in meditative concerns about the truth of one's inner spirit. His entire moral philosophy was informed by this naturalistic realism. People assigned names to certain kinds of action that were deemed supportive of human society, he taught, but what people termed "good" or "evil," or "pure" or "corrupt," were customary agreements and hence relative, and not a manifestation of a universal moral absolute that is consistent with the human spirit. For example, in nature a wolf is not deemed to be wicked for its instincts; men kill fish and fowl but are not named wolves. The limits that the sages proposed in order to clarify the excessive pursuit of human wants were thus relative and not fixed extensions of natural principle. As practical and necessary measures for social well-being, they should not be taken as idealistic denials of the natural passions of people that are part of universal life.

The inquisitive and flexible approach to knowledge found in Ranju's rationalism was articulated by other philosophers of commoner background as well. Ranju emphasized the justifiable prerogative of ordinary men to study texts from all periods of history, but others stressed the importance of history as a continuing life process to be acted out in the present in relation to natural reason. This practical orientation to the study of nature was evident in Kaibara Ekken's colleague in the shaping of agronomical studies, Miyazaki Yasusada (1623–97).[35] Best known for his compilation of the enormously influential Nōgyō zensho (Compendia of agricultural knowledge, ca. 1697), Yasusada wrote in

---

35 Takimoto, Nihon keizai taiten, vol. 3; Furushima Toshio and Aki Kōichi, eds., Kinsei kagaku shisō – jo, vol. 62 of Nihon shisō taikei (Tokyo: Iwanami shoten, 1972), pp. 67–168; and Thomas C. Smith, The Agrarian Origins of Modern Japan (New York: Atheneum, 1966), pp. 88–95.

the easily accessible language of the day about the fundamentals of scientific farming, the accurate assessment of seasonal, weather, climatic, and soil conditions to maximize agricultural production. Handbooks based on Yasusada's work proliferated throughout villages in the country, greatly enhancing the science of agriculture among the Tokugawa peasantry in one of the most momentous developments in the intellectual history of commoners. To Yasusada, the proper object of knowledge was not so much history – although he did not deny the importance of the subject for scholars – but natural history, the actual conditions bequeathed by natural legacy that determined how people must act in accordance with it to save society. Commoners must not wait for benevolent barons from above to nourish them or meditate about their spirit but must alleviate suffering based on the firm epistemological control of natural reason.

This theme was popularized still further by Nishikawa Joken (1648–1724). A merchant astronomer in Nagasaki, Joken penned two enormously successful didactic tracts aimed specifically at commoners, one entitled *Chōnin bukuro* (A bagful of knowledge for merchants, 1719) and the other *Hyakushō bukuro* (A bagful for peasants, 1721).[36] As implied in the metaphor of the bag, these works were a miscellany of ethical and practical ideas that ranged from nature, politics, history, language, custom, infanticide, and even to diet, in regard to the baneful effects of consuming red meats and wines in the manner of Westerners. In short, bits and pieces of knowledge drawn from a wide variety of sources, some scholarly, others not, were assembled in a convenient and readable format and with certain consistent themes emphasized through repetition. More than moral didacticism pure and simple, these themes add up to the affirmation of the epistemology based on natural ontology that accorded closely with the thinking of Ekken, Antei, and Ranju.

Emphasizing that all human beings existed within a broad and universal natural order, not apart from or superior to it, Joken drew from this premise the conclusion that all people, regardless of status or genealogy, were therefore relative to that absolute. Because at some ultimate level all human beings shared a common natural essence, the moralistic claims assigned to social hierarchy regarding superior and inferior were unacceptable. That natural essence, however, was the relative capacity possessed by all to acquire universalistic knowledge

---

36 These two works are, respectively, in Nakamura Yukihiko, ed. *Kinsei chōnin shisō*, vol. 59 of *Nihon shisō taikei* (Tokyo: Iwanami shoten, 1975), pp. 85–174; and Takimoto Seiichi, ed., *Nihon keizai taiten*, vol. 4 (Tokyo: Meiji bunken, 1967), pp. 493–534.

of external phenomena. As an example Joken cited the commonsense knowledge that all humans possessed in regard to the predictable and nonarbitrary character of natural time and their ability to make accurate judgments and to act in accordance with this knowledge. Because commoners could acquire knowledge of natural principle, they also could know moral norms and control moral action. Commoners, in short, should not distance themselves from these general human problems merely because they were not learned scholars of language and history.

Joken went on to argue that the exercise of natural reason by peasants and merchants was social and public in character and not passionate or inferior. Commerce, for example, was vital to distributing agricultural and handicraft products through a system of exchange. Hardly the expression of human greed, commerce served the well-being of the entire country. Money, in his view, belonged to everyone in the nation. By conceptualizing commerce as an extension of natural reason (*tenri*) and as public in its ramifications, Joken provided sturdy endorsement to the actions of traders. Exchange through trade was presented as reflecting a universal norm, expressing a non-arbitrary reason or principle. It followed from this line of thinking that "wealth" itself was also part of natural reason. Like nature, wealth was always in a state of dynamic movement and flow. It was in this regard not a static possession of an individual, but relative to different segments of society. It was not an item that an individual ruler or merchant could fix absolutely in place. All this was also to say that poverty, like wealth, was not fixed by natural reason. It, too, was in a constant process of dynamic flow. And as poverty was not absolute, it behooved peasants and merchants alike to grasp the natural principle of commerce to better manage the constant flow between wealth and poverty.[37]

Joken's "bagful of knowledge" clearly set out to create a realm of political economy for commoners, articulated with reference to the theory of natural ontology. He did not believe that nature contained a principle regarding the superior and inferior among human beings. These distinctions resulted from custom only. Indeed, as nature had no selfish or private purpose and so blessed all without prejudice, no object or creature in nature should be seen as inherently inferior or wicked. Just as a wicked parent was likely to raise a child in his or her image, so too it must be said that a lowly peasant could be raised by a samurai to become a samurai. In this manner, Joken emphasized hu-

---

37 Nishikawa, *Chōnin bukuro*, p. 105.

man potential, regardless of social status, denying emphatically that status was a hierarchical ideal reflecting natural reason. And by exhorting commoners to control their own ongoing present in accordance with natural principle, reasoned calculation, the nonarbitrary flow of commerce, and the regularity of Heaven's time, Joken claimed for merchants and peasants their universal capability to acquire knowledge without reference to considerations of power and hierarchy, as a privilege they possessed as much as the aristocracy did.[38]

To Joken as to Ranju, natural philosophy was utilized to create a moral basis for commoners that bypassed the formal definitions of status set by the legal order. Ideological certitude was thus offered to commoners in their everyday lives. As with historicist thinking, in other words, the idea of natural principle could be used in various ways, revealing a migratory dynamic that crossed the boundaries of status and regions.

In the case of Andō Shōeki (1707–55) the identification with nature was applied to affirm the validity of indigenous community in a distant corner of northern Japan. Here nature was used to argue the need to retreat from received history and formally constituted structures. Although Shōeki exhibited traces of nativist thinking akin to the students of national studies, the idea of true history found in Kamo Mabuchi and Norinaga is not evident in Shōeki. There is, rather, the affirmation of natural community vis-à-vis artificially constructed legal society. Referring to this latter as selfish "fabrications" (*koshiraegoto*) designed to protect and enhance the authority of the privileged few, Shōeki posited the true way of human life as being based ultimately on nature or the natural way of doing things. In the final analysis, the human community must be close to nature, whose members are one under Heaven in relation to nature so that status distinctions between male and female and high and low do not exist and all are simply human. In his words, "In the way of nature, there is no superior and inferior . . . no division between one and another."[39]

Analogous to Nakamoto's use of ancient studies to denounce the major religious tradition, Shōeki, relying on natural existence, attacked Confucianism and Buddhism for reinforcing artificial social distinctions. In Confucianism, abstract moral concepts were used to

38 Ibid., p. 134; also my *Visions of Virtue*, pp. 47–57.
39 Shōeki's *Shizen shin'ei dō* is in Ienaga, et al., eds., *Kinsei shisōka bunshū*, pp. 567–682. See also Bitō Masahide, "Andō Shōeki to Motoori Norinaga," *Bungaku* 36 (1968): pp. 882–92; and E. H. Norman, "Andō Shōeki and the Anatomy of Japanese Feudalism," *Transactions of the Asiatic Society of Japan* 2, 3rd series, 1949.

distinguish between high and low; Buddhism identified natural passions as the source of pain, evil, and suffering. Even in the imperial tradition in Japan, the position of the emperor was altered from its true role of preserving the life principle in nature to a cloistered figure in exile. The specific occupational functions – farming, fishing, craftsmanship, and so forth – that served as fundamental distinctions among men were disregarded by Shōeki, as they did not contradict the commonality of humanity. However, abstract categories drawn from metaphysics or history were responsible for reinforcing the hierarchical control of human life. The ancient sages, Shōeki contended, built hierarchies to maintain order but created evil systems instead, imposing poverty among the populace. Better, he noted ironically, to do neither good nor evil and simply to withdraw to the natural community based on trust and respect for other natural selves.

The idea that history was to be controlled in the present in relation to nature and not to ancient models or moral philosophy was also present in the thinking of pioneering scientists such as Sugita Gempaku (1733–1817) of Dutch studies (*rangaku*), as well as the epistemologist Miura Baien (1723–89). These were men who avoided the utopian and "Taoistic" orientation of Shōeki and addressed themselves more squarely to questions of applying scientific knowledge of nature and formulating a theoretical basis on which to seek such knowledge. Sugita Gempaku shared with Ranju the perspective of relativity of insight into knowledge, which allowed a view of modern science as relatively, though never absolutely, superior. For Gempaku, the appropriate text to be studied was not to be found in Asian history but in Western and primarily Dutch works on anatomy. The language to be examined, therefore, was not the ancient Chinese characters but the Dutch alphabet, grammar, and vocabulary. The purpose of scholarship remained the same: saving the people from suffering and misery in the most objective and effective manner possible. The general method was also related: The approach was to be systematic and empirical. But the field of knowledge had been dramatically displaced by philology, anatomy, and medicine. And the specific procedure had likewise been altered from reading and dissecting language texts to practicing vivisection.[40]

40 Gempaku's *Rangaku kotohajime* is in Haga Tōru, ed., *Sugita Gempaku, Hiraga Gennai, Shiba Kōkan*, vol. 22 of *Nihon no meicho* (Tokyo: Chūō kōronsha, 1971), pp. 87–136. A translation of it is by Ryōzō Matsumoto and Eiichi Kiyooka, *Dawn of Western Science in Japan* (Tokyo: Hokuseido Press, 1969). See also Akagi Akio, *Rangaku no jidal* (Tokyo: Chūō kōronsha, 1980).

Gempaku, however, had been influenced by the sensitivity to language taught in the intellectual tradition of Ogyū Sorai, which was manifested most pointedly in his early awareness that the Dutch language must first be mastered before the most advanced texts on anatomy and science could be grasped. The result of this approach was the translation from Dutch of a work on human anatomy of pivotal importance in the development of medical sciences in Japan – *Kaitai shinsho*. Although only a handful of scholars were then interested in Dutch medicine, virtually every practitioner of the art of healing only a generation later had read and accepted the knowledge contained in Gempaku's first work on human anatomy. Indeed, the study of Dutch medicine would expand enormously beyond Gempaku's pioneering days and reach its culmination in the first half of the 1800s, as witnessed in the school of Ogata Kōan (1810–63), the Tekijuku, to which some six hundred young scholars from virtually every domain in the country would go to study the Dutch language and medicine in the 1840s and 1850s. Among them were leaders of the modern intellectual movement for reform and "enlightenment" such as Hashimoto Sanai (1834–59) and Fukuzawa Yukichi (1835–1901).[41]

Although Dutch studies represented natural ontology as an applied science, emphasizing practical experience and diagnosis, it was not a framework for theoretical reasoning. Dutch was a language to translate, not to theorize with. This attitude remained within the existing language field and, more specifically, the Confucian discourse on nature. Undoubtedly the most original thinker in this regard was Miura Baien. Although fascinated with Dutch science, Baien felt that certain fundamental questions about nature had not been answered by it, and so he turned his intellectual energies to address the problem of epistemology, by creating new meanings out of the system of communication he had before him, a language of objective science that was not a translation from another language. Convinced that his project as a student of nature was to address the fundamental norm or reason underlying nature, Baien, with single-minded dedication, took up this task and expanded Tokugawa thinking on natural ontology to its extreme conceptual limits.

Following in the footsteps of Kaibara Ekken, Baien based his overall epistemology on the familiar idea that nature was the ultimate object of knowledge, and although it would never be totally fathomed, as its mysteries were infinite, people should strive continuously to

41 See Ogata Tomio, *Ogata kōan den* (Tokyo: Iwanami shoten, 1963).

uncover what there was to know about nature, revising received knowledge on the subject and expanding the horizon of human understanding. Going beyond Ekken in shaping an objective perspective on nature, Baien challenged not only the reliability of particular history but also language itself. History for him was primarily the accumulation of social habits that added up to what people called custom. He saw in this repetition and accretion of human habits the shaping of mental prejudices toward nature. Though he did not characterize history as passionate and ambitious distortions over time, as Tominaga Nakamoto had hypothesized, and he moreover attributed a practical necessity to moral precepts for social existence, Baien still did not assign a fundamental place to history and language, and hence to historical and literary texts in general, as guides to objective knowledge.

Despite his breadth of learning in classical literature, Baien emphasized the fundamental importance of the origins of knowledge as it related to nature. As his skepticism dictated that this genesis was not located in history, he was moved to seek a new vocabulary, a new language, to convey his thinking on nature. His insistence that knowledge about nature or political economy be based on ultimate or fundamental premises is best illustrated in his philosophical treatise on basic propositions (*Gengo*).[42]

Human beings, Baien observed, lived within the overall confines of the natural order, not apart from or in opposition to it, and nature therefore should be the primary focus of study. Although knowledge of the universe had increased manifold, especially through the contributions of Western astronomy, the understanding of the underlying principle of nature (*tenchi no jōri*) remained well beyond the grasp of human reason. Western scholars were not, in Baien's view, any closer to resolving this issue than he and his colleagues were. The major obstacle to understanding natural principle was conventional reasoning itself, which relied on the senses which were invariably conditioned by social habits – traits acquired through the repetition of assumed truths. History and religion were especially influential in this regard. They deceived human perception, leading people to believe in their superiority over other natural forms such as insects and fishes that were classified as handicapped and belonging to a lower order. The principle that governs the shaping and unfolding of life, however, did not have definable organic parts. There was, moreover, the ten-

42 Baien's works are in Yamada Keiji, ed., *Miura Baien*, vol. 20 of *Nihon no meichō* (Tokyo: Chūō kōronsha, 1982). See also Saigusa Hiroto, *Miura Baien no tetsugaku* (Tokyo: Dai-ichi shobō, 1941).

dency to infer humanlike elements in nature, reminiscent of cartoon books for children. Animals such as badgers and foxes were thus made into goblins intertwined mysteriously with human life, and plants such as the wisteria and pines were made to convey or reflect human feelings of sadness or loneliness. Projections of human emotions of this kind onto the natural landscape should not be used as an approach to firm knowledge.

Baien questioned the procedure of observing things that was prescribed in Neo-Confucian philosophy. The human eye, he argued, cannot observe certain things in nature, and the theory that predictable repetition in nature only constituted a basis of generalization as to the universality of categories but failed to raise the important question "why" of any given phenomenon. On the other hand, observation often draws the mind to anomalies, to the strange happenings in nature, as in a blooming flower on a dying tree. Yet here again, the curiosity aroused does not lead one to question why flowers bloom at all, in young flourishing trees as well as old ones. This question is not asked because such happenings are assumed by the human senses to be normal, the way that nature ought to be, thus requiring no further explanation. Similarly, to be intrigued by thunder and lightning should yield the query as to why the skies are quiet and clear on most other days. The fundamental approach to knowledge, Baien reasoned, must involve the self-conscious detachment from the forces of habit handed down from history and the commonsense empiricism that relied on the immediate senses and, instead, introduce constantly an attitude of doubt, so that nothing would be accepted as unequivocally and self-evidently true.

Baien's view of knowledge led him to doubt the utility of received names and language itself and to seek out a new set of terms and a provisional method. His approach relied on a theory of oppositional or binary configurations in all phenomena. As the truth of any given datum is always more than meets the eye, there must always be a hidden oppositional dimension that the mind should ponder. The sun, in one example, appeared to move westward while moving constantly in fact to the east. The outward and observable thus must always be seen as a sign of another dynamic set of opposite features. In a similar vein, he hypothesized that all phenomena were part of a dialectical process of counteraction and synthesis in an infinite sequence. This infinite process could be reduced to the mathematical principle that one is always two and two continuously unfolds as one. The process also could be conceptualized in the oppositional categories of form and nonform, of internal constructions gridded along horizontal and vertical or longitudinal and latitudinal lines, and of movement that was rotative and linear.[43]

Baien hypothesized that these general concepts were universal to all things, despite apparent discrepancies in physical appearances. As they suggest phenomena in nature to be without origin or end, without direction, and not limited by location, they should not be confused with human demarcations of time and place or conventional ethics. Nor were they guidelines to metaphysical moral concepts about goodness and hierarchy.

Baien's assessment of political economy closely paralleled his approach to knowledge in terms of first principles, as was clear from his ideas about money and the origins of value in *Kagen*.[44] Offered as prescriptions to the lord of Ueda domain on how to rescue the faltering economy, Baien's treatise, despite passing references to stylized ideas about political ethics, did not base its appeal on ancient custom or the classics. He offered instead the provocative thesis that the ultimate source of economic value was social utility (*riyō kōsei*). The tiny lantern that gives light to thousands of homes, in his phrasing, surpassed in value the precious stones or the markers surrounding a mighty castle. Unfortunately, the principle of social utility had been abandoned in favor of the concept of scarce, and hence relatively useless, items as being of value. The virtuous ruler, however, should not prize scarce jewels but should adopt the basic norm of utility. According to this norm, the most useful metal among the people is iron and then copper and lead; rarely is it silver and gold.

All economic transactions in society should be gauged in terms of social utility. The prevailing view that the value of money was determined by the content of scarce metal – gold, silver, copper, in that order – should be abandoned. The use of cash minted with scarce metal gained importance in the Tokugawa era owing to the large amount of goods transported over long distances, which required less bulky monetary equivalences. This function, however, should not be confused with the fundamental value of money, which is the general *social* utility of exchanging goods. If this principle were firmly subscribed to, then paper could be substituted for gold. The more fundamental corrective, however, was to realign the production and consumption of goods so as to reduce the need for exchanging large amounts of goods over long distances and to return the exchange and

43 Saigusa, *Miura Baien no tetsugaku*, pp. 9–31.   44 Ibid., pp. 37–82.

consumption of goods close to the source of production. This meant returning value to the producers of goods, to labor itself. In such an economy, iron, the most widely available metal, would serve as money, and the wise lord could then claim to have promoted the nourishment of human life and to have brought politics into accord with natural reason (jōri).

Convinced that the conventional view of money would not be altered, thus perpetuating poverty in the countryside, Baien called on nearby peasants to organize themselves into self-help communes of "unlimited trust" (mujin kō) to nourish life from below and not to wait for political benevolence from above. In his particular village in Kyushu, Baien drafted a written contract or compact that each member signed to confirm that trust. Though this withdrawal into the natural village strikes sympathetic chords with Andō Shōeki, Baien's conceptual framework was far less romantic and aggressively analytical in its application of a consistent and, from his point of view, basic principle of knowledge.[45]

Baien explored in radical ways (for which he is justly remembered) eighteenth-century Tokugawa theorizing about nature. His skepticism vis-à-vis received custom as being emotive and deceptive and his related search for a new abstract language and method detached from time and space reveal a conceptual readiness to study Western natural and physical science. By stretching the outward boundaries of Tokugawa Neo-Confucian thinking on nature, Baien and his disciples Waki Guzan (1764–1814) and Hoashi Banri (1778–1852) generated the intellectual momentum that led to the incorporation of Western science into modern Japan.[46]

HISTORY AND NATURE IN THE LATE EIGHTEENTH
CENTURY

Eighteenth-century Tokugawa thought as expressed by such thinkers as Ogyū Sorai, Dazai Shundai, and Kamo no Mabuchi, on the one hand, and Kaibara Ekken, Andō Shōeki, and Miura Baien, on the other, suggests a complex and uneasy intellectual history. Indeed, the conceptual unfolding of this history suggests a growing sense of moral crisis, especially in the recognition from diverse points of views of the discrepancy between conventional moral language and the actualities

45 See Shinozaki Tokuzō, Jihi mujin no sōshisha Miura Baien (Tokyo: Chūō shakai jigyō kyōkai shakai jigyō kenkyūjo, 1936).
46 Saigusa Hiroto, ed., Nihon kagaku koten zensho, vol. 1 (Tokyo: Asahi Shimbunsha, 1978).

of political economy. As Tokugawa history moved into the late eighteenth century, however, the categories of history and nature would continue to serve as resources from which thinkers would draw to help resolve the perceived dissonance between received history and what properly should be and to clarify thereby the future course of events. The proliferation of critical insights along a broad front reflects this general intellectual concern. Some of the perspectives were harshly critical of the existing regime, others were moderate; some offered grand epistemological frameworks, others were more specific and prescriptive. Many of the thinkers were viewed as eccentrics by their contemporaries. Almost all were syncretists, not meaning here men without intellectual convictions but individuals who, out of a dissatisfaction with the world around them, reformulated received conceptual language in ways that were experimental, adventurous, and sometimes desperate. What seems common to all of them was the awareness that beneath the surface of administrative order was a world of uncertainty, nervousness, and fretful impatience that perhaps the Tokugawa order should not continue as it had during the previous one hundred years. Although the forms of thought were manifold and complex, the following examples will suffice to illustrate the general theme.

One of the most potent of these was the school of thought identified with the domain of Mito. A blood-related collateral house of the ruling Tokugawa family itself, Mito was nonetheless denied administrative responsibility in the bakufu government in Edo. Its collateral status was dignified, in part, by being assigned the privilege of compiling "The Great History of Japan" (*Dai Nihon shi*). What began in the early 1700s as a project to outline the splendid culmination of history with the founding of the virtuous Tokugawa order gradually turned into a glorification of the imperial court, an understandable shift, as much of ancient history was written from that perspective. During the late eighteenth century, however, this shift in emphasis came to be combined with the spiritual idealism of national studies. It was indeed through the Mito scholars that the full political implications of national studies were spelled out.

National studies lacked a coherent theory of political structure, as its primary intellectual concern was clarifying the genesis of national history as a sacred community preceding bureaucratic formation. The intellectual energies of thinkers such as Motoori Norinaga were addressed to refining the elemental cultural ideal informing Japanese culture and not to describing the rise of feudal government. Yet, when

synthesized within a scheme of thought such as that of the Mito school
that was concerned with the problem of governance, national studies
did serve as a vital thesis on which reformist prescriptions could be
made to rest, such as in the writings of Mito scholars Fujita Tōko
(1806–55) and especially Aizawa Seishisai (1782–1863) and his influential treatise of 1825, *Shinron* (A new thesis).[47]

Mito scholars melded the previous ideas about structures, including
those identified with Ogyū Sorai, with the ideal of sacred community
emphasized in national studies. A provocative synthesis, it contained a
radical splitting of structures from the moral values of genesis, which
allowed for an ideology oriented to reform from within the existing
order, without in any way violating the moral foundations of historical
culture. This culture the Mito scholars termed the "national historical
essence" (*kokutai*). As expressed by Seishisai, the moral values of
trust, loyalty, filial piety, peace, and well-being among the people – in
short, those values that society agreed to be essential for orderly life –
all were part of that national essence that was transferred as a mandate
from Heaven to the divine line of archaic kings through the sun goddess Amaterasu. Moral values were thus inherent to the Japanese
sacred community and were not imported from the Asian continent at
a later time. Echoing Yamaga Sokō, this line of thinking had the net
effect of saying that the moral values of sacred community and those of
the Confucian tradition were not contradictory but essential to Japan
as absolutes from the beginning of national history. They were not
special only to Chinese civilization, as equivalences were easily found
in indigenous historical experience.

The particular importance of this form of syncretic thinking was to
underscore the general proposition that moral values were part and
parcel with the sacred community when national history first began
and thus preceded the subsequent formation of structures. They had a
continuous history as part of the national essence, without regard to
the rise and decline of particular institutional arrangements. The persistent faith among the populace in the unbroken imperial line stemming from the sun goddess (sanctified in the rite of eternal renewal, or
Daijōsai, in which the emperor mediated between sacred community
and nature to symbolize social immortality) provided convincing evi-

47 J. Victor Koschmann, *The Mito Ideology – Discourse, Reform, and Insurrection in Late Tokugawa Japan 1790–1864* (Berkeley and Los Angeles: University of California Press, 1987); and
Harry D. Harootunian, *Toward Restoration* (Berkeley and Los Angeles: University of California Press, 1970), pp. 47–128. See also Bob Tadashi Wakabayashi, *Anti-foreignism and Western
Learning in Early Modern Japan: The New Theses of 1825* (Cambridge, Mass.: Harvard University Press, 1986) for a full translation.

dence to the people of Mito of this essential history. In short, the values of sacred community were sacrosanct; structures were not. The latter could be altered without causing injury to the former.

This reformist proposition was conceptually at odds with the proposition subscribed to by the Tokugawa bakufu, in which moral norms and structures were argued to be mutually inseparable, the former always reinforcing and sanctioning the latter. It was hardly surprising that the bakufu did not view the Mito scholars with favor and in fact imprisoned some of them and sent their domain lord, Tokugawa Nariaki (1800–60), into house exile. Although the actual prescriptions advanced by the Mito school need not be detailed here, a few of the general proposals are worth noting. Although hardly revolutionary, they were at the same time quite provocative. Echoing the thinking of Sorai, the Mito scholars called for the return of the aristocracy to the land so that it could provide effective leadership over the countryside and engage in productive activity. The peasantry, Seishisai and others insisted, should not be feared and kept separate from the rest of society. Rather, it should be taught new skills and mobilized for the greater good of the domain. Above all, the Mito scholars recommended increased administrative autonomy for regional domains such as Mito so that they could institute reforms that would provide peace and well-being to the populace at the village level, which was an approach that ran contrary to the bakufu's policy of separating the sword from village society.

Despite the moderate character of the proposals, it should be emphasized that the Mito thesis regarding structure and sacred community carried with it rebellious action consequences. In late Tokugawa times, young radicals from Mito armed with the ideas of Tōko, Seishisai, and others would engage in direct terrorist action against bakufu leaders and also throw the domain of Mito into civil war (1864–5) in what is sometimes known as the "uprising of the party of mountain goblins" (*tengu tō no ran*).[48]

The articulation by the Mito scholars of the aesthetic historicism of national studies as a political concept of national essence, contributed mightily to shaping a critical discourse on institutional reform in the late eighteenth century that, in the following generation, would be used to topple the Tokugawa order itself. That the Mito thinkers did not have in mind such a drastic consequence is clear enough. Tōko and Seishisai firmly believed that the *bakuhan* structure provided suffi-

---

48 J. Victor Koschmann, "Action As a Text: Ideology in the Tengu Insurrection," in Tetsuo Najita and J. Victor Koschmann, eds., *Conflict in Modern Japanese History – The Neglected Tradition* (Princeton, N.J.: Princeton University Press, 1982), pp. 81–106.

cient flexibility to remedy the economy. The issue was how to integrate that system so that it would resolve the crisis at hand. Yet the dilemma was equally evident. Although the system of noncentralized government was to be preserved, policies must be directed to solve the ills of the whole. To reduce the discordance between name and reality, terms often used by the Mito scholars, the efficiency of structure must be made to accord with the earlier norm of national essence.

The reformist prescriptions of Mito, based on this fusion of instrumentalist and historicist thinking, encouraged sympathetic expression from other politically articulate parts of society. In some instances, the comprehensive representation of *hōken* narrated by Arai Hakuseki was used as a critical perspective. Although initially used to confirm the existing aristocracy, the same outline could be used with other purposes in mind that called, for example, for institutional alteration of the sort that Hakuseki would not have prescribed. A good case in point is Nakai Chikuzan (1730–1804) student of Goi Ranju and a teacher among merchant leaders in Osaka.

Despite the reliance on Hakuseki's overall historical scheme, the resulting orientation of Chikuzan's thinking was not to offer ideological affirmation of the aristocracy.[49] In explaining the Tokugawa order as the glorious achievement of recent rather than ancient history, Chikuzan was implying that the existing order could accommodate the virtue of all human beings in society, particularly commoners. Despite his confirmation of the existing order in terms of the history that produced it, therefore, Chikuzan's prescriptions were decidedly reformist in certain crucial ways. His assessment of the Tokugawa world suggests a realization of a once-glorious regime in a state of crisis that, in fact, overlapped with the thinking of the men of Mito.

Chikuzan's critical perspective is best stated in his prescriptive opus *Sōbō kigen*, which ranks along with the writings of Sorai's *Seidan* and Dazai Shundai's *Keizairoku* as one of the three most widely read works on political economy. Chikuzan brought to the attention of the bakufu all subjects that teachers of virtue should have under intellectual control. The subjects were broad and all-inclusive. But among them, Chikuzan called for major structural alterations such as the curtailment and ultimate abandonment of the hostage system of alternative attendance in Edo by regional daimyo and their retinues. The costs to these daimyo, he reasoned, were unbearable and the impact on the economy too extensive to be controlled through political means.

49 Najita, *Visions of Virtue*, pp. 149–86.

Chikuzan also recommended the termination of guaranteed stipends for the aristocracy, urging the institution of a merit system by which to compensate the aristocracy, which meant, in effect, the abolition of that class.

Above all, Chikuzan proposed a unified educational system that would instruct all classes, with the talented at various levels being promoted to higher levels of accreditation until, regardless of social background, those who had achieved the highest status would be recognized as scholars and be awarded certificates and appropriate salaries. One center of the educational system, he believed, should be in Edo, especially for the training of administrative skills. The other, he advised, should be in the Kyoto–Osaka area, and its specialization should be in cultural studies, that is, history, morals, and the letters in general. This vision of a national educational system, it might be noted, was endorsed by other scholars such as Hoashi Banri, a disciple of Miura Baien who also studied with Chikuzan and who developed Chikuzan's ideas on education, advocating a similar construction but adding to the curriculum in the university of arts and letters a program of translation and research in Western science.[50]

The critical though sanguine vision that Nakai Chikuzan and Hoashi Banri projected through educational reform was not shared by others in that closely related intellectual world. Chikuzan's brother Riken (1732–1817) offered an alternative view, although it was quite obviously drawn from a common conceptual grounding, as both were students of Ranju. Riken did not agree with his brother that the downward course of Tokugawa history could be halted. He agreed on the universality of human virtue and took part in the polemic against Ogyū Sorai. Riken also agreed that history should be explained in terms of an evolutionary framework more in keeping with Hakuseki's perception rather than advocates of ancient studies. Yet his relationship to both perspectives was ambivalent. Toward Sorai (and Itō Jinsai), Riken adopted the method of philological analysis used in ancient studies to reencounter the classics (*nanakei hōgen*) and to confirm human virtue as the epistemological capacity of all human beings to judge what was accurate or just in the external world. He remained true to Ranju in this regard and shared this moral point of view with his brother Chikuzan.

Riken's interpretation of history, however, was decidedly different. Whereas Chikuzan believed in reform, Riken did not think this to be

50 See Nakamura and Okada, eds., *Kinsei kōki juka shū*, pp. 163–219.

possible. Riken used the evolutionary framework to disagree with what the previous generation, including Chikuzan, had said, namely, that the history of the previous five hundred years had resulted in the virtuous Tokugawa regime. In Riken's eyes, that same evolutionary history revealed a consistent pattern of deceit, the unwarranted usurpation of legitimate kingly authority, and steady decline. Having read the Mito school's "Great History," Riken could not reconcile this account with the broad representation of the present as the inevitable outcome of the past. The decline of justice over that long history was not inevitable but attributable to passionate warlords seeking power against the imperial center that sought peace and tranquility for the populace. Although Riken retained intact the evolutionary perspective, he had sharply altered the interpretive intent into an indictment of received history. The Tokugawa shogunate could now be framed as the culmination of a vast conspiracy and incessant betrayal. Riken's pessimism led him to withdraw from political society and to lead a life as a scholarly recluse.[51]

Riken was not alone in reinterpreting history in this harsh manner. A near contemporary, Yamagata Daini (1725–67) had taken this alternative scheme and shaped a theory of rebellion against the bakufu itself.[52] History revealed, for Daini, treachery by ambitious men, whose manifestation in the present was the privileged aristocracy. As a class that depended on the sword, it retained the norms of emergent military rule to govern society in inappropriately brutal ways. Governance in times of peace should rest on cultural means, which required that the aristocracy be dismantled and returned to the soil and new talent from below recognized.

The key issue that Daini addressed was that of action. If the injustices received from history were perpetuated through systemic procedures and power and were enforced as legitimate law, how should moral men of knowledge proceed? Dazai Shundai had raised this question too and had advised that the sage had no choice but to do nothing and let the system falter and collapse on its own. Daini did not believe that the existing order would allow such an ignominious fate and that injustices backed up by the force of law would persist. Rather than do nothing, therefore, the sage must meet power with power. Curiously, Shundai himself had discussed this alternative in connection with the

51 I have written about Riken in *Visions of Virtue*, pp. 186–221.
52 See Ichii Saburō, *Meiji ishin no tetsugaku* (Tokyo: Kōdansha, 1967), pp. 33–53; and my "Restorationism in the Political Thought of Yamagata Daini (1725–67)," *Journal of Asian Studies* 31 (1971): 17–29.

vendetta case of the forty-seven *rōnin* (masterless samurai). Rather than attack a single wicked lord, Shundai had argued, these wronged *rōnin* should have either turned their domain into a military bastion from which to launch rebellion or directly attacked the bakufu center in which formal laws were produced and enforced. Daini opted for this latter, in the cause of justice and well-being for the populace. Daini proposed, therefore, that a popular army be raised in the countryside, that it capture a regional domain, and that it lead a rebellion against the bakufu center.

Scholars supportive of the bakufu argued strenuously against Daini's use of history to show illegitimate rule, siding instead with the perspective that Hakuseki had presented. History should be studied to show how and why the present was an inevitable outflow of the past and that absolute moral judgments were therefore abstract and improper. Daini remained adamant that a government based on military norms that punished people on the ground that it possessed the legal authority to do so was in fact committing illegitimate and criminal acts and ought to be attacked relentlessly from within. Executed by the bakufu in 1767 for teaching this principle of treason, Daini believed that the future would vindicate him.

The historical interpretation argued by Yamagata Daini and Nakai Riken was turned into a persuasive history by Rai San'yō (1780–1832) and aimed at the politically articulate strata of the times. A frequent visitor in Osaka, San'yō derived the main thesis of his masterpiece from Riken. Called innocuously "A General History of Japan" (*Nihon gaishi*), this elegantly crafted opus would become the single most influential interpretive history of late Tokugawa. An immediate sensation, it was read by all reformers and activists of that era. And as with Daini and Riken, the received present and the history underlying it were cast in terms of betrayal, broken trust, and chicanery. True history was shown to have belonged to the defeated cause identified with the fallen imperial forces. The rise of the aristocracy of the sword was not inevitable, undergirded by some irrepressible force or energy as Hakuseki had narrated, but a process of passionate and illegitimate usurpation of power.[53]

The theme of rebellion and withdrawal evidenced in Daini's and Nakai Riken's works requires some interpretation. This theme was far more widespread than historians tend to report. We are reminded of

---

53 Rai San'yō's *Nihon gaishi* is in Rai Tsutomu, ed., *Rai San'yō*, vol. 28 of *Nihon no meicho* (Tokyo: Chūō kōronsha, 1972). See also Nakamura Shinichirō, *Rai San'yō to sono jidai* (Tokyo: Chūō kōronsha, 1971).

such well-known intellectual eccentrics of the time as Shiba Kōkan (1738–1818), Watanabe Kazan (1793–1841), and Takano Chōei (1804–50), and more broadly of the three or four out of every ten aristocrats who went to Edo and chose to cut their ties with their domain.

Many of these aristocrats entered the "classless" status of being Confucian scholars (*jusha*) which was often synonymous with being a physician, in short, a mixed group of itinerant teachers and healers eking out a life outside the formal status system and seeking intellectual adventure out of a sense of dissatisfaction with the present. They romanticized their freedom as entering the world of eccentric play and dreams, which meant leaving the universe of bureaucratic rule. The intellectual significance of play and dreams, however, should not be misunderstood. These are mediating metaphors that suggest minds searching for detachment and hence truer objectivity. The intention was to gain closer and stricter epistemological control of the observation of things, without the intercession of received history or, in the language of Miura Baien, custom and accumulated habit.

In this respect, the eccentrics were very much part of the eighteenth-century discourse on history and nature even as they sought ways to escape the constraints of their age. The quest for sure epistemological control of knowledge, whether the object was in the past or in nature, remained central to the intellectuality of the late eighteenth century. And the faith remained that this knowledge would contribute in some direct manner to a surer understanding of history in process and thus of what the future might hold. This optimism remained essential to many of the eccentrics.

The functional relationship between play and objectivity might be illustrated by the example of Kaiho Seiryō (1755–1817).[54] A high-ranking domainal samurai of ministerial rank, Seiryō declassed himself from the aristocracy and sought intellectual refuge in Osaka and west-central Japan among merchants and enterprising peasants. Describing his separation from Edo, the city of aristocracy and the universe of fixed statuses, as entering the world of play, Seiryō journeyed among the commoners in search of a new principle that might explain more objectively the meaning of history as it appeared before him. He rejected ancient models of genesis and drew on Shundai's perception

54 Tsukatani Akihiro and Kuranami Seiji, eds., *Honda Toshiaki – Kaiho Seiryō*, vol. 44 of *Nihon shisō taikei* (Tokyo: Iwanami shoten, 1970). See Hiraishi Naoaki, "Kaiho Seiryō no shisōzō," *Shisō* 11 (1980): 47–65; and my "Method and Analysis in the Conceptual Portrayal of Tokugawa Intellectual History," in Tetsuo Najita and Irwin Scheiner, eds., *Japanese Thought in the Tokugawa Period – Methods and Metaphors* (Chicago: University of Chicago Press, 1978), pp. 3–83.

of the crucial significance of trade or, more fundamentally, the principle of economic exchange, agreeing with him that land alone could no longer sustain society. Seiryō therefore entered the world of play to uncover the reasons for the merchants' effectiveness in controlling the process of commerce.

As he journeyed in Osaka and the countryside lecturing on Taoism – the philosophy of play – Seiryō formed a perspective on the historical present that said that the future belonged to the merchants and, more specifically, to the economic epistemology they controlled. The so-called way of the merchants contained a principle of mathematical precision that served as a controllable norm. The very idea of an exact interest rate was calculated so as to be fair and beneficial to the exchanging parties. The emotional reading that trade was a passionate act motivated by greed, Seiryō therefore contended, was irrational and indeed arbitrary, determined by the customary views of Confucian ethics. The calculation of profit, he emphasized, was in fact the exercise of universal mathematical reason (*sansu*). From this observation that commoners in fact dealt with their world in terms of universal norms of knowledge, Seiryō decided that the future belonged to the merchants, as men in government did not govern in terms of that principle. The principle of exactitude, of precise measurability (*menokozanyo*), a term widely used among merchants, must indeed be the dynamic in the present. It was a principle, moreover, that accorded with nature in the sense that peasants calculate accurately what is to be derived from nature in accordance with what is given to it. That principle of exchange applied to society was trade as measured in mathematical terms.

The iconoclasm issuing from this excursion into the world of play is quite clear. It did not mean for Seiryō doing nothing, as Shundai suggested ironically. It meant, rather, uncovering, through severance from the existing structure of authority in the world of play, epistemological certitude with which the present, as received from the past, might be objectively assessed. The system of social classes that was justified in ethical historical terms, Seiryō now argued to be erroneous. Classes were functional and internally defined as terms of the universal principle of exchange so that, in the end, classes were not moral but economic in character. Although the aristocracy may have more bureaucratic responsibilities, Seiryō argued, merchants and peasant entrepreneurs knew this principle far better than do those in positions of power.

Seiryō thus challenged the existing conceptions of virtue. Virtue was not pinned to a universal moral norm, but to a principle of calculation.

A virtuous individual was one who had a better knowledge of that principle of exactitude. Because the extent to which a class knew this determined its relative superiority, it followed that the aristocracy should not be at the top of the status structure in society. What history had determined to be superior was not to be found in chartered domain land or in guaranteed status supported by fixed stipends; not in historical scholarship in Confucian ethics or in possessing the sword. The present and the future would be determined by that principle of exactitude as it was applied to the exchange of things of value through trade.

Holding firmly to this economic view of the future, Seiryō readdressed the problem of politics and governability, the concerns of the class he had abandoned. Politics, he observed, must adapt to the principle that shaped history at the ground level of economic actuality. First, the aristocracy must surrender its privileged position that it holds as a birthright. Next, the polity must be reconstituted so that the high and low are united in a community that agrees on knowledge and are dedicated to the peace and well-being of the whole. The future must be seen less in terms of house or domain but in terms of an entire national society that interacts according to the universal principle of exactitude.

The interplay between principle and play provides us with a key perspective into late-eighteenth-century syncretism. Critics such as Riken and Seiryō reveal self-conscious struggles to gain a new objectivity vis-à-vis a Tokugawa world ostensibly under control yet in apparent disarray. Within the boundaries of rationality and romantic retreat, related conceptual fragments were assembled to project creative visions very much within the conceptual universe outlined so far: Honda Toshiaki (1744–1821) conceptualized a new political center armed with technology; Ninomiya Sontoku (1787–1856) taught peasants to order their lives in accordance with the principle of exactitude; Yamagata Bantō (1748–1821) formulated a comprehensive statement of the rationality of principle against dreams; and Ōshio Heihachirō (1793–1837), at the end, objected to reason and also to play in favor of a theory of active revolt. These extraordinary figures took eighteenth-century thought to the outer limits of its discursive range.

Among the eccentrics, Honda Toshiaki formulated perhaps the most provocative theory of political economy.[55] Although Shundai prescribed reform within the domain to create wealth, as did the scholars of Mito, Toshiaki challenged all of the existing political and social arenas as

---

55 Tsukatani and Kuranami, eds., *Honda – Kaiho*, pp. 9–212. See also Nakazawa Morito and Mori Kazuo, *Nihon no kaimei shisō* (Tokyo: Kinokuniya, 1970), pp. 134–84.

anachronistic. He rejected the status system, the domain, the house, and the overall conception of noncentralized governance (*hōken*) on which the regime rested. Indeed, the bakufu's policy of territorial seclusion, of limiting political space in order to exercise virtue, Toshiaki believed to be, in the long run, self-defeating. To create wealth and save the nation, political spaces must be thoroughly redefined, a fact that in turn would require the acquisition of new knowledge and the selection of talent based on this knowledge. In short, the ideas of reform conceived within the domain and of principle as systematic calculation were now, in the hands of Toshiaki, rearticulated in terms of a restructured and centralized nation state and state interest.

The crisis in Japan, Toshiaki reasoned, was not attributable to moral decline but to the contradiction between fixed land area and hence the limited production of goods, relative to the natural growth of the population. The problems afflicting the nation could not be resolved until that elemental relationship between land and population was first grasped. The very concept of territorial seclusion was untenable. As this contradiction was not peculiar to Japan and all nations faced it in relative degrees, the problem was best seen as being not merely domestic but also international in character. The provocative appearance of Western ships in Asian waters in the 1790s Toshiaki interpreted as extensions of that very contradiction in European nations. The abandonment of the static idea of splendid isolation, moreover, entailed the added consequence that the nation must pursue its interest as a competitive trading nation on the high seas. Whereas Shundai had earlier urged that domains involve themselves in active interdomainal trade, exchanging surplus for scarce goods, Toshiaki now extended this idea to the international level.

The creation of wealth through international trade, however, must include the adoption of new knowledge appropriate to a dynamic, as opposed to a static, conception of space. Here Toshiaki pointed to the vast scientific and technological knowledge of Western trading nations, compared with that of Japan which still relied on moral aphorisms drawn from Confucianism, Buddhism, and Shinto, all of which Toshiaki denounced as pedantic, superstitious, or ludicrous.

In his *Keisei hisaku* (Secret proposals on political economy, 1798), Toshiaki explained what he meant by the kind of new technological knowledge and the specific uses for it that he had in mind.[56] First, he

---

56 Tsukatani and Kuranami, eds., *Honda – Kaiho*, pp. 12–43. See also Donald Keene, *The Japanese Discovery of Europe, 1720–1830* (Palo Alto, Calif.: Stanford University Press, 1969), pp. 59–122, 175–226, for translations of Honda.

urged the incorporation of the technology of manufacturing explosives, not only for the obvious military uses but also to create new ports, waterways, and rice fields – in general to pursue projects that could not be achieved through human energy. His second proposal was the institution of mining engineering to extract strategic and precious metals to reinforce the nation's wealth and power. As metals were the "backbone" of the nation, they should be held in concentrated amounts by the central government and not squandered as an item for export. Third, he urged the construction of a national merchant marine so that trade could be carried out through centrally owned and managed ships. And fourth, he advocated the application of technology to explore and survey neighboring islands for defensive purposes. Expansive naval powers from the West fueled by the contradiction of growing population and limited land would invariably impinge on Japan, Toshiaki reasoned, and so it behooved Japan to meet that challenge on the high seas well beyond the existing parameters of the national coastline.

Toshiaki's conception of the nation state is clearly that of a mercantilist. The production and accumulation of wealth were the responsibility of the central government, whether this wealth was acquired through trade or mining. Given this clear endorsement of centralization over noncentralized governance, Toshiaki unequivocally criticized the history from the eleventh century onward that had produced the existing *bakuhan* system, sharing a historical perspective consistent in this regard with that of Yamagata Daini, Nakai Riken, and Rai San'yō. It followed from this too that Toshiaki would be impatient with the aristocracy, which he saw as ineffectual and parasitic, totally out of step with the momentum of the times. Toshiaki legitimated his radical mercantilism with the ethical idea that all government owed their existence to the agreement (*yakusoku*) to provide peace and well-being for the general populace. Drawing on Sorai and Shundai, Toshiaki defined the imperative of the prince, by which he meant the central government, as being, above all else, the alleviation of the people's suffering.

As part of this agreement, governments were obliged to seek talent throughout society and not the aristocracy alone. Reminiscent of Nakai Chikuzan's thinking, Toshiaki advocated the establishment of a centralized educational system headed by a "great school" (*dai gakkō*) that would train the most talented in the nation without regard to class and to oversee the study and application of new scientific knowledge. To facilitate the incorporation of new knowledge, moreover, the custom of relying on Chinese characters would be abandoned, as memorizing the tens of thousands of them was intellectually distracting and anachronistic. Just as Europe made creative achievements in science by ending its relationship with Roman civilization, so too Japan must now end its cultural ties with China and, by relying on the Japanese syllabary, set out to study the sciences of mathematics and physics.

Toshiaki's vision should not be seen as an isolated one. In other parts of society, too, as in the villages, the issue of organization and knowledge had become pressing issues. At stake were peasants saving themselves without relying on the exercise of benevolence from above. Perhaps the most revered and influential sage to emerge from this development was Ninomiya Sontoku, a self-educated peasant who created a vision of peasants controlling their destiny through systematic knowledge. Whereas Toshiaki's vision called for a reorganized political center "saving" people, Sontoku addressed his to peasants saving the nation. These were parallel yet related visions emerging out of the late-eighteenth-century intellectual history of political economy.

Sontoku drew from a variety of sources to form a coherent body of ideas oriented to peasant action in the expanding universe of commercial agriculture.[57] Consistent with the tradition of agronomy begun by Kaibara Ekken and Miyazaki Yasusada, Sontoku emphasized the importance of action vis-à-vis nature as the universal absolute. One did not study history to act in nature, although history may provide suggestive insights into the attitude that one might adopt. History more basically was resolving the immediate problems of poverty in relation to nature as a given.

All human beings, Sontoku believed, were endowed by nature or Heaven with a virtue (*toku*) that was unrelated to the status distinctions made in society. As this virtue was a universal blessing (*on*), it was the responsibility of all human beings to act it out in works of thanksgiving. And because the gift was neither haphazard nor arbitrary, people must likewise respond in a manner that was systematic and principled, regardless of the particular function. For farmers, Sontoku elaborated, the engagement with nature must be objective and based on firm knowledge, never on guesswork. It involved knowing precisely what nature could or could not yield. Forms of knowledge that did not contribute to this exercise of virtue ought to be

57 Naramoto Tatsuya and Nakai Nobuhiko, eds., *Ninomiya Sontoku – Ōhara Yūgaku*, vol. 52 of *Nihon shisō taikei* (Tokyo: Iwanami shoten, 1973), pp. 10–234; and Yokokawa Shirō, ed., *Ninomiya Sontoku shū*, vol. 5 of *Kinsei shakai keizai gakusetsu taikei* (Tokyo: Seibundō shinkōsha, 1935). See also Bellah, *Tokugawa Religion*, pp. 127–30.

discarded – for example, moral homilies, fairytales, gossip, and super-stition. The exercise of virtue, in other words, required the objective observation of principle and the use of this knowledge to annihilate poverty first in one village and ultimately throughout the nation. The alleviation of poverty and suffering among the populace was not to come as benevolence from above but as the exercise of virtue from below.

In viewing the exercise of virtue in human or social space, Sontoku distinguished between natural principle, or the way of Heaven (*tendō*), and society, or the way of humankind (*jindō*). Reminiscent of Ogyū Sorai, he argued that the utilization of nature was not natural and that the artifacts that they produced were no longer of nature. Men fashioned the wheel with natural elements, but the wheel was no longer natural. The wheel was used to draw the energy of the flowing stream, but the energy produced from it was not of nature, this being a result of men's use of natural principle. Similarly, men relied on this principle to induce the apricot to bear fruit annually rather than in alternate years, by applying fertilizer to enhance the richness of the soil. These acts were part of the way of humankind and not *of* nature itself.

Like Sorai, Sontoku did not see humanity in opposition to or in a superior relationship over nature, but in an infinite relationship of nourishment. But unlike Sorai, Sontoku viewed nature as the ultimate object of knowledge and felt a deep reverence for it as the universal reality within which people everywhere shaped their social existence. This reverence he translated into acts of thanksgiving to that universal source of life itself; he did not lecture about relying on the benevolence of the ancient kings.

What is important is that Sontoku emphasized the virtuous use of nature to realize social ends that could be distinguished from the natural order. The realization of peace and well-being meant the creation of wealth through increased agricultural production and commerce, not to enrich the state, but to realize the ends that politics had failed to achieve, the alleviation of famine and poverty in the countryside. Accordingly, Sontoku organized the peasantry around him in "mutual trust cooperatives" (*hōtoku shin'yū*) to manage the local political economy.

To be distinguished from the villages per se, these cooperatives were in fact economic resources from which members could draw support in emergencies. All participants were thus required to contribute a certain amount of money as their right to membership. The commercial principle operating here is extremely important. Over the long term, these cooperatives came to function as commercial banks for commoners. Sontoku personally shunned the use of the mutual trust fund for personal ventures, and he insisted that all members agree to the principle of virtuous action in relation to nature. Yet he also encouraged the use of that fund for communal advantage, as in enhancing the exchange of agricultural and manufactured goods to increase the capital fund of the cooperative and in charging interest in these transactions. It is clear that he saw the commercial uses of the cooperative as enhancing the agricultural community's economic viability and hence its survival. In Sontoku's cooperative, all of the members were given a voice in establishing its governing rules, and loans to individual members were determined by the entire group. Here we see that virtue was not restricted to working with nature for social ends. It also was an economic community based on mutual trust to manage capital generated among the membership in the countryside. Knowledge of natural principle and of trade mesh in the ideal of thanksgiving that would guide commoners to save the people.

The idea of saving the people from below also found expression among merchant intellectuals such as Kusama Naokata (1753–1831) and especially Yamagata Bantō.[58] A financier of Osaka, Bantō, more than any other late-eighteenth-century thinker, refashioned the received discourse on history and nature into a comprehensive statement of knowledge. His tour de force, *Yume no shiro,* (In place of dreams, ca. 1805) is a thorough summation of eighteenth-century epistemology. A student of Nakai Chikuzan and Riken, Bantō totally rejected dreams of all forms imagined or artificially fabricated. Between principle and play, Bantō unequivocally grabbed the former and not the latter. He was in this sense closer in temperament to Chikuzan and his single-minded institutional vision of a new educational system for the future. But in his fascination with Western science, he was closer intellectually to Riken.

As the branch manager (*bantō*) of the Osaka banking house of Masuya, Yamagata Bantō had gained considerable visibility and prestige managing the finances of the Sendai domain. He served unbeknownst to himself as one of the primary examples on which Kaiho

58 See Suenaka Tetsuo, *Yamagata Bantō no kenkyū,* 2 vols. (Osaka: Seibundō, 1971 and 1978); Mizuta and Arisaka, eds., *Tominaga Nakamoto – Yamagata Bantō* (Tokyo: Iwanami shoten, 1973); and Matsumoto Sannosuke, ed., *Kindai no hoga* vol. 1 of Gendai shisō taikei (Tokyo: Chikuma shobō, 1966). See also Albert Craig, "Science and Confucianism in Tokugawa Japan," in Marius B. Jansen, ed., *Changing Japanese Attitudes Toward Modernization* (Princeton, N.J.: Princeton University Press, 1965), pp. 133–60. I discuss Yamagata Bantō and Kusama Naokata in *Visions of Virtue*, pp. 222–84.

Seiryō based his theories about the principle of mathematical exactitude that merchants seemed to him to have mastered. Seiryō, on the other hand, was unaware that the branch manager of Masuya whose ideas he extolled was himself a scholar of considerable intellectual power who had begun to pen his famous compendium on knowledge, which echoed his own ideas about how to order history and save the general populace.

Yamagata Bantō's epistemology was based on the theory of natural ontology, which was in keeping with the teachings of Ranju, as handed down to him through the Nakai brothers. He used this premise, however, to synthesize all other forms of knowledge known to him, while maintaining without compromise his intellectual commitment to the rationality of all things, and the potential that he identified with virtue. His book thus begins with a comprehensive statement on the universe and the universality of principle, claiming all human knowledge to be preastronomy or postastronomy; moving from that to geography, the variety of physical spaces occupied by people, creatures, and things; prehistory, the era of oral tradition and the reliance on the divine; history, the documentation of human events with formal language; the formation of a political order within that history; the current status of political economy; and finally, as an overall conclusion, the affirmation of the rationality of all phenomena and the unreliability of a priori moral abstractions and superstitions, including tales of strange spirits, goblins and gods, faith in religious claims about heaven and hell, and speculations about the divine origins of national society, all of which could be summed up under the metaphor of dreams.

Bantō's proposition that all objective knowledge must proceed from the premise of a science of the universe, or astronomy, informed his entire treatise. Having studied science with Riken and Asada Goryū (1734–99), Bantō began by affirming the Copernican theory of the universe. Just as the earth was not the center of the universe, so too on that earth, no geographical location was logically the center or the source of the entire globe. By thus proceeding from the universality of science, Bantō could then, through comparative geography, address himself to the particularity of Japanese history, denying its having divine privilege, as claimed by Motoori Norinaga and his colleagues in national studies, especially regarding the character of the Japanese people and their culture. Universal principle, Bantō argued, did not exist to favor one country or region over another. The universe, in short, was ontologically before physical land, society, history, religion, hierarchy, language, culture, and so forth. It was only out of this recognition of the relativity of human experience and knowledge vis-à-vis universal nature, Bantō believed, that human reason could gain objectivity, for this allowed the mind to see history and custom as relative.

Using natural ontology as his premise, Bantō thus could turn to relative history and bring that history down to the imperfect present and his relative view of the state of the national economy. Bantō presents an unequivocal affirmation of the knowledge that merchants possessed as crucial to the goal of saving people. If Shundai at the beginning of the century had posited a political view of the economy and trade in particular, Bantō at the close presented, in this carefully constructed piece against dreams, a case for an economic view of politics, claiming knowledge of the former as a precondition for proper governance, regardless of the relative merit of the political structure that might be received from history.

The two central sections of the treatise are thus termed "economics." And here, while referring to agricultural production as the base of society, because it supplies food for the populace, Bantō concentrated on the relationship among money, price, and trade that had thrown the economy into disarray and caused famines and uprisings among the people. Political leaders had failed to grasp certain basic principles of political economy from which to regulate the economy. By minting money with uneven metallic content, for example, they had brought on inflation and price instability.

The politicality in Bantō's thinking is striking. Merchants must see their work not merely as the extensions of their virtue but as fundamental to the well-being of the nation. Politics, he contended, could no longer rely on military norms, or on cultural ones either. The ongoing historical crisis called for emergency action as being the normal course to take. This constant need for emergency action also called for merchants to alter their view of the political world and see their knowledge of wealth as essential to promoting the national well-being. Here then was yet another vision formulated in the late eighteenth century, parallel and distinct from Toshiaki's and Sontoku's, and articulated from the perspective of the merchant leaders. It is a vision that clearly anticipates the status given to wealth as a key ideological component to the modern polity.

What is impressive about Bantō's claim for merchant knowledge is that it is placed in the broadest possible conceptual framework. He used the Copernican theory, in particular, to state from the outset that the center of the universe was elsewhere and not in the immediately inhabited globe or in received history. This construction, which Ranju had used as a basis of syncretism, to choose relatively insightful texts, Bantō now used to decentralize the globe and other presumably fixed objects, such as national history and its language, and the status structure received from history that placed the aristocracy at the top and merchants at the bottom. Bantō's rejection of this in the sections on economics is angry and insistent and reveals his use of natural ontology, in a radical manner consistent with the thinking of Seiryō, Toshiaki, and Sontoku.

EPILOGUE

The eighteenth century left in its wake a profound ambivalence regarding the integrity of the aristocracy as the custodians of political history. From Sorai and Shundai on down through the Nakai brothers, Seiryō, Toshiaki, and Daini, there is a consistent theme of skepticism regarding the validity of the aristocracy that was contained in general discussions about history and nature. Sorai had expanded the discourse by arguing that because virtue was distributed randomly by Heaven, the social institution of aristocracy was at odds with this general theory. His prescription that the samurai be returned to the soil was a pragmatic consequence of his view that the aristocracy was at once conceptually unstable – as it was not an extension of nature – and, more importantly, economically disruptive. This view was echoed in the thinking of the Mito scholars, who were not devotees of Sorai studies, and it was also in the ideas of the Nakai brothers who, as teachers among merchants, were staunchly opposed to the elitist and restrictive implications of Sorai's conception of political virtue. Whether addressed from the historicist perspective of Sorai or of Motoori Norinaga in his national studies or in the scientific perspective of Ekken, Joken, Ranju, Baien, and Bantō, the idea that the aristocracy had a special claim on virtue steadily lost credibility during the eighteenth century. The study of national history no longer provided a secure projection for the ruling aristocracy.

Throughout the eighteenth century, then, the reliance on *hōken* as a comprehensive representation of virtuous noncentralized rule in Japanese history became increasingly problematical. For thinkers such as Yamagata Daini and Nakai Riken, the rejection of it was firm, but for Yamagata Bantō there was an ambivalence based on a deep-seated reservation about the viability of centralized bureaucratic rule. Viewed earlier as a glorious achievement in indigenous history, *hōken* by the end of the century had come to convey the opprobrious implication of betrayal, in which ambitious and passionate men seized power totally contrary to the values of loyalty and benevolence. The positive evolutionary flow of history over some six hundred years was now shown to be one of steady decline to the ineffectual political present. The thinking of men in the countryside resonated with this perception. Andō Shōeki, Miura Baien, and Ninomiya Sontoku shaped epistemologies and communal strategies that called on the peasantry to seize their own history by acquiring firm knowledge without anticipating the benevolent mediations of domain lords.

Somewhat analogous to the fate of feudalism as a broad characterization of Western history, *hōken* underwent a similar transformation. Entirely positive and celebrative at the beginning of the century, *hōken*, like feudalism, acquired the negative implication of aristocratic privilege gained at the expense of both the emperor and the people as a whole. (We shall only mention in passing that the term *hōken* would be used to translate feudal in modern Japanese, thereby infusing into feudalism much of the late-eighteenth-century understanding of *hōken* as a stage in history belonging to a failed past and embodied in the Tokugawa aristocracy of the sword, outwardly proud and autocratic yet ineffectual in its leadership.)

Yamagata Bantō's synthesis of eighteenth-century thought also provides suggestive insight. Though situating his ideas clearly in the tradition of natural ontology as articulated by Ranju, his summation is innovative. Instead of emphasizing the choice of different texts based on their relative perspective on universal nature, Bantō imposes categories of knowledge arranged from the most universal to the particular: astronomy, geography, prehistory, history, and political economy. Although the various fields are relative to the universe as the ultimate reference, the entire force of reasoning is to bring the problem of knowledge down from the universal to the theoretically decentralized yet immediate world of cognition, which was the concrete reality of political economy in the Tokugawa present and his own perception of it as a merchant intellectual. There is here an ideological force in the entire conceptual procedure that is informed throughout by an austere dedication to principle and the self-conscious denial of play, faith, and dreams as mediations to objectivity. It was indeed this relentlessness that marks Bantō's treatise against dreams as a radical consummation of eighteenth-century thought.

If Bantō took eighteenth-century epistemology to such an extreme, the other side of that closure, during the Tempō era that ends the eighteenth century, was the idealism of his younger contemporary, Ōshio Heihachirō.[59] In an equally radical fashion, he rejected the supremacy of rational principle. In contrast with Bantō's polemic against dreams and irrational thinking of all kinds, Ōshio attacked reason as the source of deception. A low-ranking bakufu official in Osaka who studied at the same merchant academy that Bantō had, Ōshio shaped an idealistic philosophy of action that denounced the epistemology of rational observation as having failed to address the problem of action against perceived injustice. The very claim to objectivity, Ōshio lectured, was the source of distinctions on which human prejudices rested, so that the entire discourse on history and nature was useless as a moral resource for action in the present. While agreeing with his friend Rai San'yō that received history revealed a pattern of disloyalty and betrayal, he did not find in the writing of history the resolution to the problem of action against that history.

Convinced, then, that the corruptions of received history could not be rectified through observing nature or studying that history itself, Ōshio turned his philosophy into a moral theory of active resistance and revolt. He called this radicalism the way of truthfulness. Earlier, Tominaga Nakamoto had used this ethical concept of truthfulness to indicate, from his historicist stance, action that was reasonable, meaning accurate and fair, without reference to classical language and text. And Ishida Baigan used this to teach commoners about their inner spiritual worth, regardless of their function or status in life. Ōshio transformed it to mean action against received history. Whereas Nakamoto advised men to ignore the past as unreliable, and Baigan, to select from the various great religious traditions, Ōshio called on them to attack the past as a corrupt present.

Ōshio's theory of action, therefore, called for the anarchic leveling of the present as morally unacceptable and recommended directly saving the people. Unlike Andō Shōeki, who urged a withdrawal to the natural community at the periphery of the nation, Ōshio revolted against the public order in his shocking uprising in Osaka in 1837. Expecting the beleaguered peasants in the area to respond in a populist revolt, Ōshio in fact met defeat in a tragic and violent end, one to which Rai San'yō had anticipated his philosophy would take him. Yet with Ōshio the possibility of revolt was forcefully introduced in the

59 Miyagi Kimiko, *Ōshio Heihachirō* (Tokyo: Asahi shimbunsha, 1977); Miyagi Kimiko, ed., *Ōshio Chūsai*, vol. 27 of *Nihon no meicho* (Tokyo: Chūō kōronsha, 1978); and my "Ōshio Heihachirō (1793–1837)" in Albert Craig and Donald Shively, eds., *Personality in Japanese History* (Berkeley and Los Angeles: University of California Press, 1970), pp. 155–79.

political discourse of the day. If the eighteenth century may be said to have begun in 1702 with the forty-seven *rōnin* carrying out the vendetta against a single wicked bureaucrat in the name of loyalty, in 1837 Ōshio struck against the reason of that century that Bantō epitomized and called for a *public* revenge against the political order on behalf of the suffering populace. This theme was repeated even after the eighteenth century in the tumultuous end of Tokugawa rule, known as the Bakumatsu.

The interfacing of Ōshio's radical commitment to idealism and action with Bantō's singular faith in reason marks the end of the eighteenth century. Bantō remained within the outer limits of the eighteenth century because he held to the optimism of that period. Even as his sense of crisis and historical decline deepened, Bantō did not surrender the view that through the effective control of knowledge, history could also be brought under intelligent management. This conviction was shared by thinkers before him such as the historicists Sorai and Shundai and by Baien, Sontoku, and others who based their ideas on nature. Toward the end of the century, this conviction often was mediated by emotive metaphors such as dream, play, and death.

Although despairing of their present, eighteenth-century thinkers created autonomous spaces to better control knowledge and to live their lives as eccentrics. Kaiho Seiryō, it will be recalled, abandoned the aristocracy to seek a principle of knowledge among commoners, and he called this arena the world of play. And although death to Ōshio meant the ultimate sacrifice of the moral sage, to Miura Baien and Yamagata Bantō it was a phenomenon in nature about which people had imperfect knowledge and should not use, therefore, as an emotive metaphor. Death was part of a universe that the human mind would continuously gain more knowledge about but never exhaust. People in the present, these thinkers were convinced, knew more about nature than the ancient sages did, and future minds would correct the misconceptions of the present. In short, nothing in the universe, including death, was to be treated as being beyond the universe of reason. It was the eighteenth-century faith in reason that Baien and Bantō embodied that would now flow into a new era of idealistic political activism and the concurrent quest for a new political order.

CHAPTER 13

TOKUGAWA SOCIETY: MATERIAL CULTURE, STANDARD OF LIVING, AND LIFE-STYLES

Our material possessions, however mundane or trivial, are extremely important to determining the quality of our lives. Indeed, the houses we live in, the possessions that provide our creature comforts, and what we eat and drink – which combine to create what can be called our material culture – are of more immediate concern and interest in our day-to-day existence than is our higher culture, namely, our religion, ideology, and arts. Also, our material possessions and our perceptions of them are essential elements to the formation of our values, goals, philosophy, and much of what we consider to be culture. A study of the material aspects of life is also more capable of illuminating the lives of the majority of most populations, the common people who form the backbone of the economy but about whom little is written in most historical documents.

The level or quality of our material culture can also serve as a principal measure of what we refer to as our standard of living, an abstract concept determined by the quantities of goods and services we consume and the amount of leisure we enjoy. The level of material culture, codetermined by income (flow) and wealth (stock), can also be used as an indicator or proxy for the standard of living in societies for which reliable statistics on income and wealth are not available.

Both material culture and standard of living are, in turn, major components of what we term *life-style*, the way of life or the patterns of how people live. Not only does material culture influence life-style, but conversely, life-styles help determine which mix of material goods people choose to obtain and how they divide current disposable income between consumption and savings. The nature of the material culture also affects well-being as defined by quality of life. For example, different kinds of foodstuffs or housing may cost approximately the same – and hence will be regarded as similar in measuring the standard of living – but they can result in very different levels of health and therefore stamina and energy (hence productivity) and life expectancy. These three aspects of life – material culture, standard of living, and life-style – all are affected by the availability of resources, the levels of technology and interregional trade, the social and political systems that determine the pattern of income distribution and the level of government imposts, and a host of other factors.

Until the 1970s, few professional Japanese historians regarded material culture and life-styles as subjects of serious inquiry. Of the three topics, only the premodern standard of living was of academic concern, because it was an integral part of the debate between Marxist and non-Marxist economic historians. That is, scholars using a Marxist framework of analysis emphasized a low standard of living for commoners in the Tokugawa period, focusing on what they saw as exploitation of the cultivators and others at the bottom of society. Their questions centered on distribution, or who gets how much.

In the last two decades, however, the small but growing group of Japanese economic historians trained in neoclassical economic theory have found increasing evidence to support the view that total output was growing ever larger (though not at a fast rate compared with twentieth-century growth rates) and that the shares of all grew as the economy grew. In the 1980s, Marxists and non-Marxists alike found evidence that during the Tokugawa period the standard of living did rise. Finally, the material culture and life-styles of the common folk have become acceptable as objects of academic inquiry, just as they have in the West, and now research on all three topics is being pursued in Japan.

Although numerous sources, such as government records, diaries, novels, household budgets, and laws, reveal how people lived in Tokugawa times, these tend to be partial, random, and specific to regions, so that it is difficult to obtain a comprehensive picture of the life-styles and levels of living of larger groups and classes. Nor are there sufficient data from which to compile statistics, except for limited times and locales. The records, though far better than those for earlier centuries in Japan, are not so good with regard to life-styles as are those for eighteenth- and nineteenth-century Europe or the United States. Nevertheless, there is sufficient evidence from the seventeenth century on to enable us to discover how people must have lived.

Because of the nature of the sources, arguments over interpretation are to be expected. For instance, rice is considered to have been the staple food, but many histories report that rice was a luxury for most people and was consumed only infrequently, for ceremonies and during festivals. Then how many Japanese actually ate rice as the staple of their diet? Also, historians have usually considered that life for most people improved with industrialization in the late nineteenth century, which has caused them to underestimate the standard of living in the preceding centuries. However, recent studies on the course of industrialization in Japan suggest that the standard of living and quality of life may instead have fallen for many Japanese during the early years of industrialization.[1] Arguments about the standard of living and quality of life are as heated for early modern Japan as they are for Western Europe in the century following industrialization.[2]

Not only does a study of the material culture fill out our picture of Japan from the sixteenth to the nineteenth centuries, but it also changes some of the accepted outlines. Because the formal sociopolitical structure did not change for over two centuries, we tend to assume that life, too, was unchanging. However, a study of the material culture and living standards provides evidence that Japan was always changing, albeit more slowly than in the twentieth century. Although many "traditional" life-styles had their origins in the Sengoku and early Tokugawa periods, and even earlier, many of the key elements of the material culture were developed, refined, and diffused as late as the second half of the Tokugawa period. Examples of these elements are wooden houses with raised floors covered with rush matting (tatami); meals of white rice with soup, pickles, and possibly a simple side dish; and bedding consisting of quilts filled with cotton batting and spread directly on the flooring.

The civil wars of the sixteenth century and the concurrent social and economic developments were catalysts in the transformation of the material culture and life-styles of the common folk. Artisans and merchants were increasingly drawn into the towns and cities, as were the samurai. Farmers and fishermen, left in the rural areas, were organized into formal governmental entities called *mura* (villages) which were also the major social and economic units. This development led to the creation of the three main social classes – the villager, the urban commoner, and the samurai – from which developed the three major life-styles and patterns of consumption of the Tokugawa period. The civil wars affected the material culture as well: Daimyo

---

1 For an analysis of change and continuity from the late Tokugawa through the Meiji periods, see Marius B. Jansen and Gilbert Rozman, eds., *Japan in Transition: From Tokugawa to Meiji* (Princeton, N.J.: Princeton University Press, 1986), especially the chapters by Hayami Akira, Nishikawa Shunsaku, Saito Osamu, Kozo Yamamura, and Susan B. Hanley.
2 For two examples, see Susan B. Hanley, "A High Standard of Living in Nineteenth-Century Japan: Fact or Fantasy?" *Journal of Economic History* 43 (March 1983): pp. 183–92; and Yasuba Yasukichi, "Standard of Living in Japan Before Industrialization: From What Level Did Japan Begin? A Comment," *Journal of Economic History* 46 (March 1986): 217–24.

imported cotton for military use – sails, uniforms, and fuses – and it was produced domestically and spread throughout the population in the following centuries. During the late sixteenth century, the sweet potato was introduced into western Japan, and by the early eighteenth century it provided a bulwark against famine in years of poor rice crops.

With the Tokugawa peace, the new institutional arrangements encouraged economic development, which in turn spurred on social changes.[3] Freed from the need to be ever-prepared for war, domains could allocate more effort and resources to economic development. Large engineering projects to reclaim land for cultivation and provide flood control and irrigation were sponsored by both daimyo and the bakufu during the seventeenth century. The amount of arable land is estimated to have doubled during the Tokugawa period, and much of the increase occurred during the seventeenth century. New agricultural techniques also enhanced productivity. Paralleling the increases in output and productivity in agriculture was the accelerated commercialization of the economy. By the early eighteenth century, the major goods traded included rice, cotton, rapeseed oil, saké, silk, fertilizer (dried fish cakes), draft animals, salted and dried marine products, and scores of regional specialties. The rapid urbanization in the seventeenth century stimulated the demand for products of all kinds in the towns and cities.

The first peak of this economic growth was reached by the late seventeenth century, in the Genroku era (1688–1703), noted not only for economic prosperity but even more for the cultural flowering of the first mass culture centered in the metropolises of Kyoto and Osaka. The new commoner prosperity and cultural boom were not confined to the metropolises but spread to the castle towns throughout Japan, and then to the towns that grew up in the countryside and even to the villages. The *sankin kōtai* system, which had many samurai traveling to Edo and living there for part of the time, the growing trade, regional specialization, and increasing participation by villagers in the national economy all contributed to the economic growth. Villagers not only traded over wide areas, often national in scope, but themselves traveled to find work and to make religious pilgrimages. The growing contact among Japanese gradually brought about cultural unification.

With the lasting peace and the economic development of the early

3 For an analysis and description of both the economic and the accompanying social changes, see Susan B. Hanley and Kozo Yamamura, *Economic and Demographic Change in Preindustrial Japan, 1600–1868* (Princeton, N.J.: Princeton University Press, 1977).

Tokugawa years, the population grew, though no one is certain by how much. The national population survey of 1721, the first of its kind in Japan, gave a figure of just over 26 million for the commoner population. Estimates for the population in 1600 range from just over 10 million to 18 million, but whichever figure is accurate – and the latter is probably closer – the population growth rate was considerable during the seventeenth century.[4] Part of this growth may be accounted for by the absence of warfare, but at least part was due to the trend for landowners to shift from managing the labor themselves to parceling out their land to tenants, who were then free to marry.[5]

During the Tokugawa period, patterns of income distribution in city and countryside alike changed as a result of economic growth, led by continued growth in the agricultural sector and the accelerated growth of commerce. Both farmers and merchants benefited by the inability of the samurai elite to tax commercial activities effectively or to capture the productivity gains in agriculture. By the early nineteenth century at the latest, the social groupings no longer indicated income, as the samurai elite would have liked. Also, the transmission of ideas and goods flowed across class as well as regional boundaries, and by the end of the Tokugawa period, commoners were imitating the life-styles of the samurai and had adopted many of their values. By the late eighteenth century, some well-to-do farmers lived in houses resembling samurai residences, and the lowest-ranking samurai in most respects lived the life-style of an ordinary townsman. There were poor among the samurai as well as among the commoners, and a small number of merchants rivaled or even exceeded many high-ranked daimyo in personal disposable income. Thus there were differences in standard of living and life-styles by social class, by income stratum within each class, and by region and locale as well as by city and village.

Material culture, as defined by Japanese scholars, is composed of three basic elements: *i-shoku-ju*, or clothing, food, and housing. In this chapter, we shall examine these three major components and then analyze how the material culture differed by class and income, what daily life was like, and how the material culture affected the physical well-being of the Japanese. Finally, we shall look at the implications of

4 The population figures can be found in Sekiyama Naotarō, *Kinsei Nihon no jinkō kōzō* (Tokyo: Yoshikawa kōbunkan, 1958), pp. 137–9. A discussion of these figures and the various estimates can be found in Hanley and Yamamura, *Economic and Demographic Change*, chap. 3.
5 For a discussion of these changes and the effect of the market on agriculture, see Thomas C. Smith, *The Agrarian Origins of Modern Japan* (Stanford, Calif.: Stanford University Press, 1959).

the changes in the material culture and life-styles and attempt to assess the changes in the living standard over the Tokugawa period.

HOUSING: SAMURAI, TOWN, AND FARM

Housing is the least difficult of the three aspects of material culture to study, not only because many houses have been preserved, at least those belonging to the well-to-do, but also because we still have floor plans and paintings for numerous buildings that no longer exist. It is also easier to examine architecture because buildings and floor plans can be dealt with as a whole, a unit, in contrast with an isolated article of clothing or a household utensil. Furthermore, in many ways, housing influenced the life-style of a family, to a great extent determining how members carried out their daily work, related to one another, and learned their place in the world. Housing is probably the best indicator of family wealth, as it is the major investment for most households.

All Tokugawa housing shared certain basic characteristics, owing to the scarcity or availability of resources on the Japanese islands. The scarcity of usable space was certainly a major determinant in housing, life-style, social behavior, and communication. By the early eighteenth century, there were nearly thirty million people in an area the size of Montana, and only 15 percent of Japan is flat enough to be arable. The population was crowded into the few plains and along the coasts. Farm housing was in clusters – hamlets or villages – either along a road or a river or nestled up in the foothills where it would be difficult to create a paddy. However, the large metropolises of Edo, Osaka, and Kyoto were less densely populated per square mile than the European capitals were, because the Japanese did not build up; few buildings were more than one and a half or two stories high.

Premodern Japanese buildings were built of tensile materials such as wood, bamboo, and thatch. Most of the land was forested mountains, and so these materials were plentiful, but their use also meant that houses had to be rebuilt more frequently than did those of brick or stone. However, tensile materials were an advantage in a country plagued by earthquakes. Safety seems to have been a major consideration in the development of Japanese architecture; hence the limitations on height, the lack of cellars, and the use of foundation stones on which support posts merely rested, permitting lateral movement without the destruction of the building. The primary drawback to this type of architecture is that it was subject to fires, particularly in the densely-packed cities. Fires were the "flowers of Edo": The worst, in

1657, destroyed over half the city and part of the castle. The main mansion of the Oda domain of Tamba burned down sixteen times, and most domains had to rebuild their mansions several times during the Tokugawa period.[6]

Over the course of Japan's history, the main floor level of the house was gradually elevated. A prehistoric house was basically a thatched roof over a circular hole in the ground a couple of feet deep. Only the elite lived in houses with raised flooring. But by the sixteenth and seventeenth centuries, raised flooring was the standard for the well-to-do and the samurai, whereas the common folk and poor had houses with earthen floors. As people could afford it, they put in flooring of various kinds, but only in the section of the house that was used for sitting, eating, and sleeping. The gradual change represents both a rise in the living standard and a healthier environment, as people moved up off the damp ground.

By the Tokugawa period, virtually every house that was not a mere hovel was divided into two parts: a "living" area and a "service" (or work) area. The service area was used for preparing meals, as a workplace, and for storage. Privies and stables were part of the service area, and often all were under the same roof. The floor of the service area in every house (the *doma*), no matter how wealthy the occupants, was invariably packed earth, though it was an integral part of the house. The floors of living rooms were made of boards, split bamboo, or tatami, or a combination of these in houses that had raised flooring. In those houses in which flooring was beyond the family means, the living section of the dwelling was separated from the work area by a sill, and the ground was covered with husks, hulls, and straw which were then covered with straw mats for sitting and sleeping.

Posts hold up a traditional Japanese house, so that walls are not structurally necessary. Depending on the architectural style, posts are located throughout the house where necessary to hold up the building. These structural elements are not hidden, even in the most luxurious of houses, but become part of the design and decoration of the rooms. Because supporting walls are not necessary, Japanese have freedom of use of space not only within the building but also with regard to the outside walls. Large doors can be built into the service area for ease in bringing work materials and supplies inside. Whole walls can be

6 Toshio George Tsukahira, *Feudal Control in Tokugawa Japan: The Sankin Kōtai System*, Harvard East Asian Monographs, no. 20 (Cambridge, Mass.: Harvard University Press, 1966), p. 93. Tsukahira provides good examples of daimyo expenses and hence life-styles.

opened up to let in the sun and air the house. However, in the mid-to-late Tokugawa period this usually was possible only in the houses of the well-to-do who could afford sliding doors of translucent paper, and flooring.

The most striking element in traditional housing is the development of tatami flooring. This may be one feature of Japanese culture that is truly unique. In the Heian period, the floors in aristocratic buildings were wooden, and mats were used for sitting and sleeping, as they were in China. But the Japanese progressed to putting rush mats in wooden frames for use in various parts of the room and, finally, to covering an entire floor with matting. From the Muromachi period on, tatami were made of a base of straw covered by woven rush in rectangles of approximately three by six feet. The size was gradually standardized by region, with the mats made to fit between the set intervals of the support posts. Finally, they became the modules for designing a room, and the dimensions of Japanese-style rooms are still based on a set number of tatami, usually three, four and a half, six, eight, ten, or twelve. Tatami performed a number of functions: (1) They provided a firm yet comfortable floor covering for both sitting and sleeping that obviated the need for most furniture; (2) they made it possible to use a room for multiple functions when necessary, with minimum adjustments; and (3) they provided a uniform measure for constructing buildings of all types. Although tatami date from medieval times, their extensive use as standard flooring among the elite, their gradual adoption by commoners, and the role they played in the standardization of the basic components of housing all took place during the Tokugawa period. Scarce resources may have played a part in the development of this type of flooring: Mature forests were becoming scarce during the Tokugawa period, but rush could easily be grown throughout much of Japan.

Despite common housing characteristics and similarities in housing at both ends of the income scale, whatever the class, people in different occupations had different housing needs. Samurai required reception areas, whereas families in commerce had to have a store front for selling foods, storage space, and a delivery entrance for wares and materials. Farmers needed space for farm work and draft animals. There also was a wide variation by region in housing styles, but these occupational requirements resulted in similar floor plans for each class throughout Japan.

Samurai housing was the ideal for housing during the Tokugawa and even the Meiji period. It was the most innovative and the best adapted to new life-styles as incomes rose for all classes. The basic elements of the style date from the late Muromachi period when Japanese began to build *shoin* into their house plans. *Shoin* refers to the writing table that was built into one wall of the room. Later it became a general designation for the style of a house that had this feature.[7] This built-in desk, combined with the *tokonoma* (an alcove for decorative display) and the *chigaidana* (stepped decorative shelves) are usually considered basic to the *shoin* type of architecture. By the Tokugawa period, other essential elements added to this style of architecture were a formal entrance known as a *genkan,* raised floors covered with tatami, *fusuma* (built-in sliding room dividers covered with thick paper on both sides), *shōji* (sliding panels with wooden frames covered by translucent paper and used between a room and the outside corridor), and often square pillars instead of round for the supporting posts. Very few of the formal buildings in the *shoin* style survive. What many consider to be the epitome of *shoin* style can be seen in the Katsura Detached Palace, which was built in the seventeenth century just outside Kyoto.

Samurai housing is also known for incorporating gardens as an integral part of the architecture, rather than merely adding them on as decoration. Rooms for guests were situated so that views of the garden became the backdrop for the room when the *shōji* and outside protective wooden sliding doors were removed. There was usually an *engawa,* or veranda, several feet in width, between the room and the outside of the house. *Shōji* divided the room from this corridor, and wooden shutters, called rain doors (*amado*) usually enclosed the *engawa.* On fine days, both sets of sliding doors could be opened to let the sun and cool breezes into the house, which had the effect of bringing the outdoors into the house. Westerners had to resort to house plants to achieve this effect, and then less successfully.

Because the Japanese climate is humid nearly year-round, good ventilation is essential to both comfort and health, as dark, damp houses promote lung infections. Japan has a month-long rainy season beginning in mid-June, followed by a very hot summer with high

---

7 For information on the *shoin* style of architecture, see Itō Teiji with Paul Novgorod, "The Development of Shoin-Style Architecture," in John Whitney Hall and Toyoda, eds., *Japan in the Muromachi Age* (Berkeley and Los Angeles: University of California Press, 1977), pp. 227–39; Fumio Hashimoto, *Architecture in the Shoin Style* (Tokyo: Kōdansha and Shibundō, 1981); and Kiyoshi Hirai, *Feudal Architecture of Japan* (New York: Weatherhill/Heibonsha, 1973). A variation of the *shoin* style is the *sukiya,* which developed in buildings in which the tea ceremony was performed. The *sukiya* style is simpler and less formal and allows for more variation in the placing of the elements that make up the *shoin* style. Most residences in the Tokugawa period were in fact in this *sukiya* variation.

humidity, a typhoon season in the early autumn, and a winter that ranges from usually snowless in the west to areas in the north and east where snow accumulates up to the first story of houses for months at a time.

Throughout medieval Japan, housing fulfilled the primary function of providing shelter from the elements, but samurai housing during the early modern period shifted to a design that emphasized summer comfort rather than merely shelter from rain, snow, and cold. This development began in central and western Japan where protection from the winter elements was not a major consideration. During the Tokugawa period, samurai built their houses above the damp and dusty ground, open to the winter sun but protected from the high summer sun, making them more comfortable in the summer months and less damp in the rainy times of the year. What they sacrificed was warmth in winter, but how much colder the Japanese were than the Europeans in stone or brick houses is debatable.

Although most samurai houses were simple, independent structures, the mansions of high officials were built as a series of rooms or small buildings connected together in and around various courtyards, which enabled many rooms to have garden views. They were usually asymmetrical, so that from the Western standpoint the floor plans of daimyo mansions look almost as if the rooms and buildings were tacked on at random when additional space was required. This all was carefully planned, however, for both functions and aesthetics, with a good deal of traditional wisdom – and not a little superstition – about where the toilets, kitchen, gate, and well should be located.[8] When building large houses, it was easier to construct a number of smaller buildings connected to one another so that one large roof did not have to be engineered. The style of a number of buildings or rooms strung together was also a legacy of the palace-style architecture of the Heian period, in which each room had a separate roof and covered corridors led from one room to the next. By Tokugawa times the rooms were connected so that the houses were all part of one floor plan inside, and this trend toward more compact buildings accelerated as urban populations soared and space was at a premium.

The *shoin* style was used as the model for the formal audience halls

8 The Japanese have followed the Chinese art of geomancy in designing buildings, from at least the seventh century until today. The positioning of the front gate, the toilet, the kitchen, and the like all are considered, and this sometimes results in what seem to be unlikely positioning of rooms. See Bruno Taut, *Houses and People of Japan* (London: John Gifford, 1937), pp. 26–8, for an explanation of how geomancy is applied in the twentieth century. Taut's reaction to Japanese architecture is revealing both of the Japanese and the Westerner and is highly recommended.

of the shogun and daimyo, where the emphasis was on size and splendor to denote status, and for residences and teahouses, where there was a more relaxed and gracious atmosphere. By the late Tokugawa period, the homes of the upper-strata samurai were built in this style, and even the tiny two-room apartments of the lowest echelons of samurai had one room in which guests were received that had some of the elements of the *shoin* style. Commoners were forbidden to build houses in the samurai style, but by the late Tokugawa period, *tokonoma* and other *shoin* features could be found in the houses of well-to-do farmers and village headmen who had to have formal guest rooms for the reception of samurai officials. It is the samurai style that became the preferred style of housing in the Meiji period, the forerunner of modern Japanese architecture. Status symbols were certainly a factor in this preference, but so were the drier, lighter, more healthy environment and the increased comfort that became available as the standard of living rose.

In contrast with the samurai residences, which were typically detached houses situated on their own grounds, the houses of merchants, artisans, and other commoners in a town or urban setting were usually row houses. Lots were priced by the amount of frontage, as it was crucial for a merchant to have access to the street, hence the long narrow shape of the lots. Business was carried out in the part of the building facing the street, the living quarters were usually in the midsection, and a small courtyard and any storehouses were located in the rear of the lot. In western Japan in particular, city houses were usually one room in width and two to three rooms in depth, with a dirt-floored passage called the *tōriniwa* running along one side from front to back. The *tōriniwa* not only served as a corridor, but had the same function as the *doma* in farmhouses. Along one side were the cooking facilities and often a well and, a short distance from these, the privy.

The commoner sections of cities were usually laid out in large blocks, whose outer edge faced the main streets. Lots fronting these main streets were more expensive than back lots reached by narrow alleyways. In the center of these blocks were built the *nagaya* (long houses) or tenements that housed the daily laborers and the poor. Most *nagaya* were in effect one-story apartment houses, with the families sharing a well or other access to water and the privies. Typically, families lived in one room, often only nine feet by nine feet. The entrance was an earth-packed area three feet by nine, which also served as the kitchen, the work area, and the place to store any tools and equipment. These *nagaya* were the forerunners of today's small apartments, in which people carry on all daily activities from eating to sleeping in one small room with virtually no furniture.

The majority of houses in the Tokugawa period, however, were farmhouses, which were sufficiently different from samurai and urban housing that architects categorize them separately.[9] The main difference between samurai and farm housing is that the floor plan of the farmhouse was designed to fit into the framework of the building, whereas the floor plan of the samurai house could be drawn to taste and the structure designed to fit these plans. The most common farmhouses throughout the period were essentially rectangular boxes with roofs of thatch or wooden shingles. These wooden dwellings had few openings except for a large door and some slatted windows to let in a bit of light and air. Presumably they were divided into *doma* and living space, but in the early part of the period, few would have had raised floors. As people could afford them, they built larger houses, and those with sufficiently large houses added floors of wood or bamboo slats and later, when they could, tatami. Dwellings with no flooring could be found in poor rural areas even after World War II, but the trend for the past several hundred years has been to build houses with flooring in the living areas.

Because of the lack of extant examples, little is known about how the farm housing – that is, housing for 80 percent or more of the Japanese – changed from medieval Japan into the Tokugawa period. It is known that up until the seventeenth century, foundation posts were usually set directly into the ground, which eventually caused them to rot. In short, houses were not built to be long lasting, even if they withstood warfare, fires, typhoons, and other disasters. There were wider regional variations during the seventeenth century and earlier, but evidence from archaeological digs and historical records suggests that in many parts of Japan the various activities of a major landholder took place in separate buildings. Even in smaller households, there were two buildings: one for family life and a second for cooking and related activities. Examples exist for such widely separated areas as the present Fukuoka Prefecture in Kyushu and in Ibaraki Prefecture in the northern Kantō plain. Sunken pit dwellings, characteristic of late

---

9 Farmhouses from the early modern period through about the end of the nineteenth century are termed *minka* (literally, "commoners' houses"). *Minka* refers to no one particular style but usually applied only to the larger farmhouses. For a discussion in English of this style of housing, see Teiji Itoh, *Traditional Domestic Architecture of Japan* (New York: Weatherhill/ Heibonsha, 1972).

prehistoric times, could also still be found in the very early seventeenth century.

By the seventeenth century, foundation stones were starting to be used in new buildings, so that the posts did not directly touch the ground. Thicker and higher-quality materials were used; braces were fitted between the posts; and walls were covered with mud plaster or boards. Increasingly, doors were made of wood rather than split and woven bamboo, and they were built to slide open in frames, rather than as a part of the wall that would open upward. Wooden floors gradually became more common than earthen ones. These developments reflected the new techniques in carpentry and also a rise in the standard of living that enabled commoners to build houses of higher quality.

In the eighteenth and nineteenth centuries, commoner housing underwent further change, reflecting developments in samurai housing made possible by new carpentry techniques. For those who could afford it, houses were transformed from dark boxes to the open style that we think of as characteristic of Japanese domestic architecture. The *engawa*, translucent *shōji*, and wooden rain doors sliding on tracks opened up the entire side of a house. The *engawa* progressed from a projection on the outside of the house to an integral part of the house as the rain doors were moved to enclose the *engawa*. Wood floors became standard, and many houses had tatami in at least one room. As people could afford to, they erected ceilings over all of the living rooms except, of course, the area over the hearth (*irori*). The well-to-do also began installing *tokonama* and other features of the *shoin* style.

By the late Tokugawa period, the average house size was larger than that in the seventeenth century. However, the trend was probably not one of steady, gradual increase. An analysis of house sizes in the village of Kosugaya in Owari Province in central Japan for the seventeenth and eighteenth centuries reveals a decrease during the eighteenth century.[10] The average house size increased between 1646 and 1684 from 27.65 square yards to 32.78 square yards but then fell to 29.23 in 1734. During the same period, the number of houses in the village increased from fifty-six to sixty and then seventy, but because the population was growing, the average amount of floor space per person fell by more than 25 percent between 1684 and 1734. Kosugaya is a very small and isolated sample, but it indicates that house size varied

10 Hayami Akira, "Kinsei Chita chihō no jūkyo to kazoku keitai," *Shakai keizai shigakkai daigojūni-kai taikai hōkoku-shū*, 1983, pp. 7–9.

greatly in accordance with economic position and that the average house was very small by modern standards. A house of 27.65 square yards, the 1646 average, measured approximately 12 by 21 feet. Other evidence that seventeenth-century houses were small comes from restrictions on building sizes. For example, in 1656, in a newly reclaimed area in Musashi Province, just outside Edo, the magistrate in charge of the area issued specifications for the kind of housing that newcomers could build. The size of house permitted depended on the size of the family. A couple could build a house only 12 feet by 21, whereas a family with four to five members was allowed a house 15 by 27 feet.[11]

However, from the eighteenth to the nineteenth century, both the size of dwellings and the average amount of space per person rose. Houses not only contained more rooms and living space, but the number of members per family also decreased. In Okayama, for example, the average household size decreased from seven in the early eighteenth century to five by the turn of the nineteenth century. The most important factor was that families had fewer children. Although the government tried to regulate house sizes, given the changes in family size over time because of changes in the members' life cycles, it would have been impossible to regulate house size by the number of family members for more than the year in which the house was built.

The Japanese were also very clever in circumventing regulations: Usually the distance between the main posts holding the roof was limited by statute, but farmers could build larger houses by adding space under the eaves. Because most roofs were high, whole rooms could be added in this way, while keeping the size of the house within the letter of the law. City regulations often included a provision that commoner housing be no more than one and one-half stories high. Townsmen circumvented this clause, however, by building houses that were precisely one and one-half stories at the front, but with a rising roof that slanted up from the street front which made it possible to construct full-sized rooms in the middle and rear of the house, even on an upper floor. The authorities must certainly have been aware of this mass flouting of regulations, but clearly the need, the desire, and the means to build larger-than-legal structures, with the growing commerce and rising incomes, led the officials to ignore anything but the most flagrant violations.

11 Kimura Motoi, "Nōmin seikatsu no shosō," *Seikatsu shi*, vol. 2 (Tokyo: Yamakawa shuppansha, 1965), pp. 207–8. This is not only the best summary article on the farmer's lifestyle in the Tokugawa period, but it is replete with contemporary examples.

THE HOUSE AND LIFE-STYLES

Just as the size and style of housing changed during the Tokugawa period, so did the use of the house. Some of the changes were due to advances in technology, growing incomes, and the availability of resources for building better-constructed housing, but many resulted from a change in life-styles and then in the function of houses. Residence indicated both occupation and status in premodern Japan. Thus status as well as function was a concern of all classes when designing or renovating houses.

At the top of the social hierarchy, daimyo were required to maintain formal residences in Edo to be used during their stay at the capital, and the specifications for these mansions depended on the status and size of the respective domains. High officials, as well as daimyo, had to have rooms suitable for meetings, for receiving important guests, and for entertaining anyone of high rank. Thus, a major consideration in the houses built for officials was these formal guest rooms, and so the floor plans of samurai housing indicate that what might seem to be an inordinate amount of space was devoted to ostentatious rooms that may have been infrequently used.

In a society so ruled by status, the treatment of guests was both governed by etiquette and often prescribed in regulations.[12] This meant that certain features became a necessary part of samurai residences. The one that is stressed most by Japanese scholars is the *genkan*, or formal entrance, where guests were received and which led to the formal guest or reception rooms of the buildings. The number, size, and decoration of the reception rooms depended on the wealth and status of the homeowner. To the untutored eye, most of the rooms in a samurai residence are indistinguishable from one another, covered as they are with tatami and all leading one into another through sliding room dividers (*fusuma*). However, viewing empty rooms in a Japanese house is as misleading as looking at an unoccupied Western house. Each room had a separate function, and how the rooms were used by persons of which status was clearly delineated. Originally, those persons with the highest status were seated on the tatami, but when the entire floor was covered with this matting, distinctions had to be made, either by raising the floor several inches in the section of the room in which the person of superior status would sit, or by designat-

12 Hirai, *Feudal Architecture*, p. 151.

ing a special part of the room for guests or the master. Usually guests or those of high status were seated in front of the focal point of the room, the *tokonoma* or other decoration, facing the others and with their backs to the art objects displayed.

A samurai house can be divided into three basic uses of space: formal, family, and service. Typically, the largest percentage of space in the building was devoted to the formal area which had larger rooms than did the rest of the house and a separate formal entryway and entry hall, which were not used by family, tradesmen, or callers of low status. The family rooms were usually in an inner section, and the master's private room had the same decorative elements – *tokonoma*, fixed writing table, and the like – as the formal reception rooms. The third area can aptly be termed the "service area" because this was where the work of the house was carried out. A large *doma* would adjoin a wooden-floored kitchen, storage areas, and maids' rooms. In former times the formal, family, and service areas were housed in separate buildings, but by the Tokugawa period they all were part of the same structure.

Even in the tiny apartments of the lowest-echelon samurai, the same division of space can be seen, although clearly the living space was so small that most areas had to serve dual functions. But there was always a work space (*doma*) and usually a wooden-floored area, as well as a main room designed to receive guests and a second, smaller, tatami room for sleeping and storage. This type of housing became the predominant pattern for all classes in Japan in the nineteenth century and was the model for Japanese dwellings until the last few decades, with clear divisions among service areas, family living quarters, and separate reception areas for guests.

Farmhouses looked very different from samurai residences from the outside, but even in the seventeenth century, the houses built by well-to-do farmers had floor plans indicating uses similar to those of the samurai. Gradually other features of samurai housing were adopted as well. The biggest and most frequently used entrance was through the *doma*. Though headmen often put in formal entries for their reception rooms, many farmhouses that had formal guest rooms had access to them only through the *doma* and family rooms. Styles of farmhouses were so varied that it is impossible to depict a representative model. Those who could afford three- or four-room houses – and the number increased during the Tokugawa period – typically had one or two rooms used by the family, usually with a wooden or bamboo floor with an open hearth in one of them, an inner room used for sleeping and storage, and a room for guests. These rooms were, of course, in addition to the *doma*.

Scholars of Japanese architecture and aesthetics have made much of the point that there is not as clear a demarcation between inside and outside in traditional Japanese housing as there is in Western houses. One reason is that sliding doors often fill an entire wall, and when the doors are open, the garden seems to become part of the room. An even more important reason is the tradition of building *engawa* onto rooms. These long, narrow wooden passageways are built either as walkways between the main rooms and the outside of the house or as shelflike projections onto the outside of the house at floor level. In either case, when the storm doors and inner sliding doors are opened up, the *engawa* become extensions of the rooms inside. On sunny days, occupants can move to the *engawa* to chat or work. On the other hand, persons in the garden can rest a few moments by sitting on the edge of the *engawa*. Informal calls can even be made without entering the house, for a visitor can sit on the edge of the *engawa* and chat with a family member sitting inside. In modern times the *engawa* can accommodate chairs and a small table.

Despite this seeming tradition of blurring the distinction between inside and outside, Japanese in fact make as clear distinctions as Westerners do. One is that any part of a Japanese house that can be closed off from the outside, including the *doma*, is part of the house, even though footgear is worn in this area. But outer footgear is removed when entering any section of the house covered by flooring or mats. A social equal or superior, for example, would enter a house through the formal entrance if there was one. But a neighbor, friend, or social inferior faced a two-stage process when entering a house. First he would make his presence known at the entry to the *doma*, and if the visit was to take some time or involve the serving of food, he would next be invited to come up to the living quarters (two or three feet above ground level), whereupon he would remove his footgear. In informal situations, a guest could sit casually on the edge of the raised floor of the living quarters with his feet on the *doma*, or he could stand in the *doma*.

A major reason that the *engawa* becomes an extension of the house is because so little furniture is used in traditional housing. Decoration is largely built into the structure itself, and thus support posts are chosen for aesthetic as well as practical reasons. The shelves and space to hold ornaments are built into the room itself in the form of the *tokonoma* and *chigaidana*. Walls are not hung with heavy paintings, nor are large pieces of furniture like dining tables and sofas used, as in the West. The Japanese elite ate from individual tray tables while sitting on cushions on the floor, and thus virtually the only furniture necessary were chests for storing clothing, bedding, and other household goods. The poor, as in any country, had few possessions and often ate sitting around the fire on which their pot of food cooked.

Because they used tatami, the Japanese needed neither chairs nor beds. The well-to-do slept on either tatami or the rush matting that was its forerunner, covering themselves with their outer garments for warmth. The rich used silk for their quilts; the rest of the population used anything available. Paper bedding was common; heavy paper made of mulberry bark, hemp, or other fibers was used as a quilt cover stuffed with straw. But many people simply slept in or under their clothing. There is even the record of a samurai who did not have bedding made for several years but instead slept under his garments.

The Japanese began to use quilts stuffed with cotton batting only during the Tokugawa period, but it is difficult to trace the history of *futon*, as these were called, because the Japanese wrote little about the commonplace and private aspects of their lives. We do know that these quilts gradually evolved from clothing. Ieyasu was said to have used an early version, and there is increasing mention of cotton quilted bedding from the 1620s on. The term *futon* originally referred only to the quilt spread on the floor for sleeping. In eastern Japan, the top quilt clearly evolved from the kimono, and even nineteenth- and twentieth-century examples can be found that are roughly the shape of a kimono with a neck and sleeves. The neck was covered with a cloth collar that could be removed for washing, as this was the only part of the covering that would come into contact with the sleeper's face.

It is probable that most people slept with little or no bedding during the Tokugawa period. Although it would have been cold, it is conceivable for people in western Japan to have used little or no bedding. In colder regions in the north, people slept near the fire. When and where it was really cold, they used bedding made from whatever materials were at hand. A traveler to Akita in 1789 noted that people dried seaweed and wove it into quilts. Hemp was also used, and even straw. An 1835 document from the Toyama–Niigata area reports that people in Akiyama just slept in their clothing, even through most of the winter, but when it was really cold, they slept in straw bags, one couple to a bag.[13]

13 Ogawa Kōyō, *Shinjo to shingu no rekishi* (Tokyo: Yūzankaku, 1973), p. 171.

The poorest people slept in a corner of their one-room earthen-floored cottage, but those who had the space, sectioned off a portion of floor, dividing it from the work space by a wooden sill. They filled the sleeping space with hulls or straw and spread straw mats on top for sleeping and sitting. People who could afford floors used the inner-most corner – the farthest from the entrance to the *doma* – as the sleeping room (*nando*). This room had walls on three sides and was entered through a door from the living room, and hence it was dimly lit at best. Usually there was a sill at this door to keep the straw and hulls spread out on the floor from spilling into the next room. During the Tokugawa period, as tatami were gradually installed in sleeping areas, this door lost its function and was often eliminated from new houses.

For the well-to-do in the Tokugawa period, samurai and commoner alike, ostentation seems to have been more important than comfort in designing housing. The Japanese make much of the point that their houses are built for summer rather than winter and how open they are to gardens. But in fact, the Japanese shut up their houses at night with sliding wooden doors, even during the heat of the summer, and some of the inner rooms in the largest and most extravagant buildings were dark and gloomy inside because light could not penetrate them. In contrast with the light and airy housing that came into fashion among those with money, the huts of the poor and even the ordinary farm-houses of early Tokugawa had no windows save a few barred spaces for light and air, and thus the dwellings would have been cold and smoky in winter and hot and stuffy in summer. The sleeping room was often six by nine feet or even smaller, and as it was enclosed it would have been a dark, dank place. Although the addition of bedding added warmth, it was also likely to attract bugs, and when cotton was used, the bedding would have become damp as well. The small, unventi-lated construction of these sleeping rooms attests to the use of body warmth for heating purposes.

Most farmhouses did not have ceilings, and though this allowed the smoke to escape through a hole in the roof made for ventilation, it also meant that the heat, too, went into the rafters. The only means of heating houses, samurai and commoner alike, were the open hearths, and for those who could afford them, *hibachi* (charcoal braziers). By the latter half of the Tokugawa period, fuel was hard to come by, and so in central and western Japan many people in the cities and the poorer in the countryside went without heat altogether. The lack of sufficient fuel may be one reason for the development of raised flooring in Japanese houses. The introduction of floors of raised bamboo slats meant that people no longer had to sit or sleep near the cold, damp ground. Moreover, such flooring would be cool in the summer.

One of the factors in the development of the Japanese bath must certainly have been the need to warm the body in winter.[14] Their primary purpose was, of course, to cleanse the body. The original bath was a type of steam bath that used little water but produced a sweat that was intended to open the pores and rid the body of dirt. After leaving the steam bath, bathers would pour water over their bodies to rinse off the dirt. Baths for the well-to-do, and the first public baths in the early Tokugawa period, were steam rooms that could be enjoyed by a number of people simultaneously. The less elaborate, individual bath that commoners could afford was the forerunner of the modern Japanese bathtub, but until the early part of the twentieth century, these too were more commonly steam baths, rather than tubs of hot water. The bather would enter through a small door in the side of the bath, shut the door, and cover the bath with a woven straw lid. In the Tokugawa period, the Japanese distinguished between *furo*, the present term for baththub, which referred to the steam bath, and *oyu*, which means hot water and referred to actually getting into a tub full of hot water.[15]

It is difficult to determine how prevalent bathing was in the seventeenth and eighteenth centuries. The public bath in Japan is considered to date from the construction of Edo in the late sixteenth century. Public baths in urban areas during the Tokugawa period enjoyed the same sort of reputation that Roman baths did; they combined hygienic functions with socializing. Various styles of bathtub are extant from diverse regions in Japan, and many can be found in the surviving farmhouses, but precisely when these were built and what percentage of the population used them are completely unknown. European visitors to Japan from the sixteenth century on were so impressed by the cleanliness of the Japanese that the standards must surely have been higher in Japan than in the West, but certainly the standards of cleanliness in both parts of the world were lower than they are today.

In the farmhouse the bath was in a corner of the *doma*. Also located

---

14 Although the Chinese and Koreans developed methods of heating houses, mainly heating the floors from below, the Japanese did not. Despite all the elements of material culture the Japanese adopted from the continent, they did not borrow the concept of central heating. Instead, they developed a system of bathing that thoroughly heated the entire body.

15 Shiraki Kosaburō, *Sumai no rekishi* (Osaka: Sōgensha, 1978), pp. 54–5.

in the *doma* were the well, if inside the house, the hearth, and later the stove (*kamado*). The cooking, cleaning up, and quick meals or snacks all took place in the *doma*, as did various types of farm work, especially in inclement weather. At least in southern Japan, activities related to food preparation were undertaken in a separate building, but the typical Tokugawa pattern was for all household activities to take place in the same structure. Over time, some of these activities moved to the family room next to the *doma*, which usually had an open hearth and wooden flooring. This family room became the location for relaxed family meals and food preparation, and it later held the sink. There was thus a gradual shift toward using a raised, wooden-floored room for household tasks, which culminated in the modern houses in which the earthen-floored area is nothing more than a few square feet of space immediately inside the back door.

FOOD, NUTRITION, AND OTHER DIETARY FACTORS

For some two thousand years, rice has been the preferred staple of the Japanese diet, but how much of it was consumed by whom in any given period is undergoing intense debate. Rice was first introduced into the Japanese islands in prehistoric times. By the Tokugawa period it was the staple of the elites and well-to-do and also was consumed to some extent by most commoners. It was also the unit by which daimyo domains were valued, samurai stipends were calculated, and taxes were assessed. Because rice occupied such a dominant place in the Japanese economy and diet, it may seem puzzling that there is so much debate on who consumed how much rice during the Tokugawa period.

First, it is clear that rice was only one of many grains consumed during the Tokugawa period and earlier. The government recognized that rice was a luxury food, and in a famous ordinance the bakufu in 1649 exhorted peasants not to give rice to their families at harvest time. Instead they were to eat vegetables, millet, and other coarse grains. They were also not to buy saké, a wine made from rice.[16] Even after the economic prosperity of the late seventeenth century, not everyone was eating rice. Frequently quoted is the report from the Kyōhō period (1716–36) stating that farmers living in the flatlands where rice was grown regularly ate rice in the form of gruel (*zōsui*), but

---

16 *Keian no furegaki*, described in Watanabe Minoru, *Nihon shoku seikatsu shi* (Tokyo: Yoshikawa kōbunkan, 1964), p. 244.

those in the mountainous regions who had to purchase it could afford to eat it only on the first three days of the New Year.[17]

Unfortunately, nearly all scholars who touch on the subject of diet in the Tokugawa period cite little more than these two sources, and most are doing so in order to support the position that commoners lived badly in premodern Japan. Other scholars, who must rely on late-nineteenth-century figures if they are to use any data at all, probably overestimate the amount of rice consumed. In all probability, during the Tokugawa period the consumption of rice steadily increased, but most of the population ate many other staple foods as well.

The argument for the widespread consumption of rice comes from both the beginning and the end of the period.[18] If rice had not been the staple by an overwhelming proportion in the early seventeenth century, it would not have made sense to have an economy in which rice was the basis for calculating salaries, taxes, and land values. More than two and a half centuries later, in 1874, rice comprised 63 percent of the value of all farm products. One of the few estimates we have on output and food consumption for any part of the Tokugawa period is for Chōshū in western Honshu for 1840.[19] An estimate based on output and population places the average daily consumption of rice in 1840 at 53 percent of the grains consumed.

It would be unusual to find any premodern society that depended on one grain crop for its staple; not only would it make poor use of human and natural resources, but it also would be dangerous, for a crop failure would cause widespread starvation. The Japanese, like most peoples, relied on a number of staple foods. The preferred grains were rice, barley, and wheat, but a number of others were consumed as well. The oldest cultivated grains in Japan were two kinds of millet (*awa* and *kibi*) and deccan grass (*hie*). By the Tokugawa period the Japanese also ate buckwheat (*soba*) and sorghum (Indian millet, called *morokoshi*). From prehistoric times, nuts, roots, and various tubers have been part of the Japanese diet. But rice, introduced into Japan some two thousand years ago, is the preferred staple, and other grains have been considered merely substitutions, supplementary foods, or foods to be eaten in times of famine.

17 Tanaka Kyūgū in *Minkan seiyo*, cited in Kitō Hiroshi, "Edo jidai no beishoku," *Rekishi kōron* 89 (April 1983): 43. Tanaka, first a local and then a bakufu administrator, published *Minkan seiyō* in 1721. An astute observer and an expert on conditions in the Kantō region, he is widely cited because of his insight and detail.
18 The best article on this subject is Kitō, "Edo jidai no beishoku," pp. 43–9.
19 Shunsaku Nishikawa, "Grain Consumption: The Case of Chōshū," in Jansen and Rozman, eds., *Japan in Transition*. See Table 16.4, p. 435.

The most important new food crop was the potato which arrived in both Asia and Europe from South America in the sixteenth century. The sweet potato is thought to have been introduced to Japan in 1605, and the white potato at about the same time. The reaction of the Japanese was the same as the Europeans: to grow potatoes for the pretty flowers and then to use the tubers for horse fodder. But by the second quarter of the seventeenth century, people in western Japan had begun to eat them. White potatoes became valued as a versatile food but were also used in the production of saké, *miso* (bean paste), and soy sauce. However, it is the sweet potato that is credited with reducing the death rate from famine in Japan. In 1732, locusts caused a major crop failure in Kyushu, but the death rate was low in both Satsuma and Nagasaki because people were not relying entirely on grain; now they had sweet potatoes to fall back on. Sweet potatoes could be grown upland, in contrast with rice, and they produced more calories per acre than did almost any other crop. Sweet potatoes may well have been an important factor in maintaining a dense population in Japan in the eighteenth and nineteenth centuries and also in explaining why the population of western Japan grew faster than did that of the rest of the country.[20]

The Japanese also relied on a wide variety of beans, greens, and other vegetables, in addition to wild plants, mushrooms, bamboo, and the like. Included in what would have to be a very long list of Tokugawa foods were white radishes, green onions, soybeans, melons, turnips, ginger, eggplant, cucumbers, and many more that do not translate into English. Wild plants eaten included a variety of ferns, burdock roots, and, in times of famine, bark and tubers that would not be considered food in normal times. Fruits included persimmons, peaches, plums, Japanese pears, and various kinds of citrus fruits.

For protein, the Japanese relied primarily on plant protein plus protein from the sea. Meat from four-legged animals was proscribed by Buddhism, but those who could afford to hunt ate wild birds, and the outcast classes are known to have eaten animal flesh. *Tōfu* (bean curd) is a good source of protein but was a luxury for many. Unless they lived near a source of seafood, commoners would rarely if ever have had fresh fish in their daily diet; dried or salted fish was more usual. The sea provided the Japanese with protein and also greens, as

20 Watanabe, *Nihon shoku seikatsu shi*, pp. 246–9; and Adachi Iwao, *Nihon shokumotsu bunka no kigen* (Tokyo: Jiyū kokuminsha, 1981), pp. 257–9.

seaweed was dried and used widely in a variety of ways, from adding it to soup, brewing it as tea, and even using it as medicine.

Although it is possible to add to the list of foods known to have been eaten in Japan in any period, calculating who ate how much of what and in what combination is impossible. Estimates based on the amount of rice paddy and population – which are in themselves only very rough estimates – indicate that Japan was not producing sufficient rice to feed everyone but that probably most people in cities were eating rice and that most farmers were eating rice mixed with other grains.[21] In every social class from samurai down to commoners, the amount of rice in the diet depended on income. The amount of arable land, including irrigated paddy, was substantially increased in the seventeenth century, and the flourishing rice market combined with the greater number of farmers paying their rice tax in cash instead of in kind from the 1660s and 1670s into the eighteenth century all tell of a surplus in rice for cultivators and the establishment of a rice diet.

Just as farmers ate more rice over time, so did they eat better-milled and more highly polished rice. In the seventeenth century, people ate rice that was partially polished; it appeared whitish, but part of the bran remained. Late in the century, a process was developed that would completely remove the hull but leave the bran. White, or polished, rice was considered the highest quality, and this tended to be eaten in cities. But those who could afford white rice tended to develop a vitamin B deficiency, and thus beriberi became known as the "Edo affliction." People who became ill while working as servants in Edo found that when they went back to the country, they improved, but it was not until the early twentieth century that the cause of this disease was discovered.

In the countryside, the diet consisted of mixed grains and vegetables. Rice was often the "glue" that held together the coarse grains, and it was added to create the desired consistency. Often various seasonal greens were added to make a kind of vegetable–grain stew. This type of dish might be eaten only once a day; at other meals there would be gruel, according to a description of the diet in Kawasaki along the Tōkaidō.[22] In Musashino, on the outskirts of Edo, the diet from the mid-Tokugawa period on was said to consist mostly of coarse grains, usually a mixture of three parts millet (awa) and seven parts barley.

21 See Kitō, "Edo jidai no beishoku"; and Nishikawa, "Grain Consumption."
22 Tanaka Kyūgū, cited by Kimura, "Nōmin seikatsu no shosō," p. 201.

What people ate and how they prepared it depended to a large extent on the utensils and technology available.[23] This not only varied by region but also changed over the course of the Tokugawa period, and these changes transformed the Japanese diet. Traditionally the Japanese had two basic methods of cooking: One used the *irori*, an open hearth with a pot set over it on a hook suspended from the ceiling; and the other used the *kamado*, an enclosed stove with pots set into the top. The *kamado* used less fuel, but by the same token it could not be used for warming the family. In families depending on the *irori* for cooking, one-pot dishes were popular because the various ingredients could be added at the appropriate times and just left to cook in the pot, as could gruels. Families who could afford a *kamado*, which usually had more than one place for a pot, could use it to cook more complicated meals, including the rice or grain as a separate dish from the soup and vegetables.

By the Tokugawa period, the *kamado* was widely used in towns and cities where it was difficult and expensive to obtain fuel, whereas the *irori* predominated in the cold regions of the north. In mansions and monasteries, a *kamado* was used in the *doma* for cooking, and a *hibachi* provided what little heat there was for at least warming the hands. Farmhouses of the well-to-do often had a *kamado* in the *doma* and one or more *irori* in the living rooms. The smoke from the *irori* could also be used to dry and preserve foods – and it also preserved the roof – but it damaged the eyes of the people gathered around the fire for light and heat.

A related development was an iron ring on which to rest a pot in the *irori* so that it did not rest directly on the fire. The use of this ring meant that earthenware pots, instead of precious iron, could be used for cooking and that less heat was necessary. Charcoal, which used fewer resources than burning wood directly did and which could be more readily transported, was sufficient for this new method of cooking. By the late Tokugawa period, the methods that used less fuel and iron were increasingly popular, particularly in urban areas.

The present method of steaming polished rice is a relatively new technique. The method gradually developed from the mid-Tokugawa period but was perfected and became widespread only a century ago. Originally two methods were used. One was the same as the present method, in which exactly the right amount of water is used from the

23 For good descriptions of cooking utensils and methods, see Ekuan Kenji, *Daidokoro dōgu no rekishi* (Tokyo: Shibata shoten, 1976).

start and the rice is steamed until the liquid is completely absorbed. The second was to start with more water than was needed. The excess was removed during the cooking process, and then the rice was left to steam. The first method is the more difficult because the temperature must be gauged precisely; the rice must be cooked at a high temperature at first; and after the midpoint, the heat must be lowered but the top not opened until the cooking is completed and the rice has sat for some time. The rice can easily be burned and ruined, and thus considerable cooking skill was needed to prepare rice using this method, in contrast with boiling it in a pot on the *irori*. Clearly only the elite and well-to-do had the resources, time, and skill to prepare rice using this method, but the growth of its popularity over time clearly attests to a rise in the standard of living.

The development of Japanese cuisine accompanied these changes in rice preparation methods from the mid-Tokugawa period on. As cities grew, the first restaurants began to appear. By the late Tokugawa period numerous cookbooks had been written and circulated, and the chefs for the rich were even experimenting with exotic new spices, such as cinnamon, that were introduced to Japan in the early nineteenth century. Clearly, many Japanese had reached a level of culture and income at which they could afford a varied diet and wished to experiment with food.

The main seasoning for most Japanese was *miso*, a paste based on soybeans. Although this was commercially produced during the Tokugawa period, most families made their own, usually once a year, in February or March. This seasoning was used daily in soup and could be used to flavor vegetables or fish. Soy sauce was also available but was seldom used. It was hard to make, and the quality varied considerably. Thus it was only an upper-class seasoning. It was not until the last century that the quality of soy sauce was perfected to the point that it could be used without cooking. As in every other premodern society, salt was both a seasoning and a preservative. Mountain villagers seldom saw fish that had not been dried and salted, and any green vegetables eaten in the long winter months were in the form of pickles.

To summarize, the center of the Edo period diet was staple grains. The word for cooked rice is the same word for meal in Japanese: *gohan*. Everything else was considered a side dish (*okazu*). Most families ate *miso* soup and pickles at meals at which the main dish was not a gruel or grain-based stew. At ceremonial occasions, bean curd and salted fish were served, and when the technique was known, steamed white rice with red beans cooked in it was a special treat.

From the evidence available, it is possible to argue either that the Japanese had a very poor and boring diet in the Tokugawa period or that the diet was rich and varied. Even samurai families were often restricted to a daily diet of coarse grains or rice and other grains with a side dish of fish or something special for the master but only soup, pickles, and possibly boiled vegetables for the rest of the family and the servants. Accounts can be found of mountain villages in which virtually no rice was eaten because none was grown and the villagers were too poor to buy it. Oral histories tend toward this picture of daily life in the late nineteenth century, but diets reconstructed from memory are notoriously unreliable.

On the other hand, there are numerous accounts of meals at inns, feasts on special occasions, and the delicacies given to the elite and wealthy that lead to the conclusion that the diet for at least some was at the gourmet level. For instance, in Yonezawa in the mid-Tokugawa period, a group of men who formed the governing body of a village held a meeting after the fall harvest at which they ate the following foods: salted salmon, tuna, bean curd, dried bonito, squid, herring roe, and dried herring – all purchased in a nearby town – eggs, dried *nameko* (a kind of mushroom), sea bream, fried bean curd, *ayu* (sweetfish), horseradish, and the list goes on.[24] Clearly many of the items were not part of the daily diet, and certainly not in this combination, but they all were available, and farmers had the income to purchase them for special occasions. Sugar was a luxury item and purchased only in small quantities, but it is significant that even people in the northern, poorer sections of the country could buy it and did by the mid- to late Tokugawa.

Saké, rice wine, was the most popular drink and was produced all over the country. The best was Nada saké, made in Settsu (just west of the modern Kobe), and this was shipped to Edo from Osaka in such quantity that special ships were developed for this purpose. Farmers produced in their own homes a "home brew," an unrefined version of saké. Saké was in such demand that when regulations ordered a reduction in saké production in times of famine, many disobeyed. This is a clear indication that by the Tokugawa period not everyone suffered in times of crop failure.

At least two attempts have been made to ascertain the nutritional level during this period. This is an overwhelming task, given the lack of information to determine even what the typical diet was. The most

24 Kimura, "Nōmin seikatsu no shosō," p. 204.

successful efforts so far are based on data from the mid-nineteenth century. This evidence, though scattered, seems to indicate that nutrition probably improved over time, and so the quantitative studies would represent the highest levels that nutrition probably reached during the Tokugawa period. The most ambitious studies are for the Hida area of Gifu and for the domain of Chōshū in western Honshu.

The data for Hida are for 1874 and include the amounts of 168 foodstuffs produced and the amount of food imported and exported from the area.[25] By dividing the total amount of food retained in the region by the total population and by 365 days, one can obtain a rough estimate of the nutrition available to the "average" person in 1874. The results of the study of Hida indicate a heavy dependency on rice and millet, which led to a deficiency of certain essential vitamins and minerals, notably vitamins A and C, calcium, and iron. The diet was somewhat lacking in protein and very high in salt content. This evaluation is borne out by the leading causes of death as analyzed from the records of a local temple. Among the major causes were childbirth complications (in which calcium deficiencies can play a part), cerebral hemorrhage (connected to a high salt intake), and epidemics (whose incidence is worsened by a low level of nutrition). The Hida estimates are for a mountainous area, and the authors of the study admit that some items known to have been consumed were not included in the survey, such as sweets, eggs, seaweed, some kinds of mushrooms, and certainly wild greens that individuals could gather from the mountainside. These would never be included in the figures on output, but they may have contributed to raising somewhat the vitamin content of the diet. From the data available for Hida, the average daily caloric intake has been estimated at roughly 1,850 calories.

The Hida estimate can be considered at the same nutritional level as Chōshū's diet, which in the 1840s contained an average per-capita intake of 1,664 calories from staple foods, including rice, barley, wheat, millet, buckwheat, soybeans, red beans, and sweet potatoes.[26] This does not include fish, seaweed, vegetables, fruit, or sweets. Even though fish and vegetables were a minor part of the diet, they would almost certainly have added a couple hundred calories per day and been significant in balancing the diet. By the 1890s, the Japanese in

25 The implications of this study with regard to the diet for the people in this area can be found in Fujino Yoshiko, "Meiji shoki ni okeru sanson no shokuji to eiyō: 'Hida go-fūdoki' no bunseki o tsūjite," *Kokuritsu Minzokugaku Hakubutsukan kenkyū hōkoku* 7 (September 1982): 632–54.
26 Nishikawa, "Grain Consumption," pp. 435–6.

this region obtained on the average 1,902 calories from the staples, just above the Hida estimate for a decade earlier. What is significant about both the estimates is that the number of calories would probably have been sufficient for the body stature of the time, given that the army recruits in the last two decades of the nineteenth century had an average height of 156.5 centimeters, or 5 feet 1.5 inches.[27] Also, the very young and the elderly would have consumed less, leaving more calories for the adult males.

Many members of the samurai class and well-off commoners in the prospering flatlands of Japan almost certainly had a better diet than the average diet in either Hida or Chōshū. One lower official in the bakufu, who was something of a gourmand, kept a travel diary in 1856 that listed the menus of the inns he stayed in while making an official tour to the north of Edo.[28] Based on these menus, the diet of travelers would have been adequate, with the possible exception of vitamin A. But because sweet potatoes, pumpkin, and squash, plus numerous greens, were eaten in the home, many would have had a well-balanced diet.

It would be difficult to argue, of course, on the basis of fragments of evidence that the Japanese as a people were well nourished or that they were better nourished than the Europeans were during the seventeenth and eighteenth centuries. However, the rapid growth of the Japanese population during the seventeenth century and the relatively few famines and deadly epidemics reported during these centuries corroborate the conclusion that the Japanese must have been fairly well fed. By 1700, Japan not only contained three of the world's largest cities but was over 10 percent urbanized by conservative estimate. It was also one of the most densely populated countries in terms of the man–land ratio. Yet two major crop failures of multiple-year duration (in the 1730s and 1780s) plus other poor harvest years did not decrease the population of this already-crowded country. The Japanese had sufficient surplus in normal or good years so that food could be stored. A single year of poor harvest thus could be weathered without the loss of life recorded for earlier centuries.

The new foods introduced during the late medieval period, rises in agricultural productivity during the Tokugawa period, improvements

27 The heights of military recruits from the Meiji period on can be found in the *Nihon teikoku tōkei nenkan* of the Naikaku tōkei kyoku. These are cited in Carl Mosk, "Fecundity, Infanticide, and Food Consumption in Japan," *Explorations in Economic History* 15 (July 1978): 279.
28 Hayami Akira, "Bakumatsu-ki 'Kemi nikki' ni miru tabiyado no shokuji," *Rekishi kōron* 73 (December 1981): 80–87.

in transportation, and a more varied diet for much of the population during the seventeenth and eighteenth centuries not only meant a lower incidence of disease and less fear of starvation but also an increase in longevity for many Japanese.

CLOTHING

Clothing in any society is a reflection of the standard of living and the quality of life, as well as the structure of society. The Tokugawa period saw a distinct rise in the quality of life, owing to the introduction of a new fiber for cloth. In addition, changes in clothing styles resulted from both the occupational class structure and the new distinctions in wealth. The most striking development was the introduction of cotton in the late Sengoku period, which transformed clothing and bedding for commoners and samurai alike over the next two hundred years.

The introduction of cotton was so unspectacular that it has almost been ignored by historians. It was first imported from the continent, mostly Korea, by the Sengoku daimyo, who were interested in it for three reasons: for sails, for fuses for the newly introduced firearms, and for uniforms. Canvas was more durable than straw for sails and more resistant to weather; cotton fuses were more reliable than those made of cypress bark or bamboo; and cotton uniforms were more durable than paper, warmer than hemp, and wore and looked better in battle. The Japanese had known of the superiority of cotton to other fabrics from the fifteenth century, but it took about a century and the military needs of the civil wars leading to unification before the Japanese managed to grow it for themselves.

In the seventeenth century, when the Japanese learned how to grow their own cotton, it came to be the preferred material for clothing for commoners. Because it was superior to hemp, it gradually replaced the coarser fiber for all who could afford it. Its popularity is indicated by the fact that in Osaka in 1736 the value of all cotton products far exceeded the value of rice traded in this major transshipment center.[29] It may well have had the same kind of impact on the Japanese population that it had in the West, in terms of making life more comfortable and more hygienic – possibly even helping lower mortality, thereby being a factor in the rapid population growth of the seventeenth century.

Silk remained the preferred material for the rich as it had been for over a millennium. Though fashions varied widely over time, women's

29 Kimura, "Nōmin seikatsu no shosō," p. 200.

formal dress from the eighth century on and men's formal wear from about the twelfth were versions of the kimono. The basic garment was made of straight pieces of cloth, rectangular in shape and with rectangular sleeves. To hold the garment on, the left front panel was closed over the right one and some kind of belt or sash was wrapped around the waist. In earlier periods, court dress and even the everyday dress of the aristocrats was often extremely impractical, with the length of the garment several feet longer than the person wearing it, so that walking was next to impossible. By the Tokugawa period, even formal dress was simplified so that the longest garments were floor length or shorter. Social distinctions were made by style, type of material, and impractical fashions such as very long sleeves that would preclude any kind of manual work for wealthy young women. Little jewelry was worn other than hair ornaments; instead brocade, richly dyed materials, and gold and silver embroidery were used by the wealthy.

By the seventeenth century, the basic garment for formal and casual wear of all classes was the *kosode*, which fits the description of what Westerners envision when the word *kimono* is used. The *kosode* was so widely adopted that by the eighteenth century, people were calling it kimono, which literally means clothing. Originally an undergarment, the *kosode* became the article of clothing worn immediately under outerwear, such as rain gear or the formal outer garments worn for public ceremonies. Until the seventeenth century, a sash tied above the hips held the clothing together – no buttons, ties, or hooks were used. But in the Tokugawa period, women started using a wide, stiff band, called an *obi*, that encircled them from under the breasts to the top of the hips, giving them a rather tubular look. As cotton became widely used, both men and women added cotton underwear and men usually wore a loincloth. A Japanese of any period could tell the status, wealth, and age of any other Japanese merely by looking at his or her clothing, but the basic pattern of the *kosode* changed little over time.[30]

All kimono for adults are made even today from one long, rectangular length of cloth that is cut into eight pieces. The pattern and length of the bolt of cloth is the same for every adult. Because the pieces are cut in straight lines, there is no waste. Adjustments for variations in size are made by tucking up the kimono under the sash. Kimono are sewn together with basting stitches. Thus the thread can be removed and the garment taken apart when it is washed.

30 For illustrations and fuller explanations of what people wore, see the entry "clothing" in the *Kōdansha Encyclopedia of Japan* (Tokyo: Kōdansha, 1983), pp. 329–33.

This type of clothing was extremely economical in a premodern society in which clothing was expensive. No material was wasted in the cutting and sewing, and the standard kimono size meant that fabric could be produced in standard lengths. Clothing could be passed from one person to another without alteration, as the garments were one-size-fits-all. And when a garment was taken apart for laundering, it could be refurbished by bleaching and redyeing if necessary. Children's clothing was made in the same way, with huge tucks taken at the shoulders and the waistline which could be let out as the child grew. Finally, when a garment was too old to be worn any longer, it would be taken apart one last time and the material cut up for diapers, rags, and other household items. Clearly, Japanese clothing was designed for making maximum use of scarce resources. Even for the rich who wore elaborately woven and dyed materials, the standardization meant minimum waste.

Footgear was also standardized. The poor wore sandals of straw called *waraji* which could be woven very quickly and cheaply. *Waraji* were also the basic footgear for travelers. Wooden clogs (*geta*) of varying heights were useful in the mud and rain but were difficult to wear when walking long distances. For dress the Japanese wore *zori*, a kind of thonged sandal. The only form of stocking worn was a short sock (*tabi*) with a mittenlike separation for the big toe so that it could fit into both sandals and *geta*. All footgear could be easily slipped on and off, as they had to be removed before entering any building with floors.

None of the clothing described was very useful for working in the fields or at heavy manual labor in the towns. One of the most detailed descriptions of village life dates from 1857 but portrays the conditions prevailing from the mid-Tokugawa period on.[31] In a village in Tosa in southern Shikoku, the daily working garb for both men and women was a type of pants said to have been derived from the Portuguese outfits of the sixteenth century, over which was worn a short type of jacket. Over this might be worn a protective bib and an apron, and some workers wore fingerless gloves. In summer the outfit was much abbreviated; often only a brief undergarment and an apron were worn, plus a sun visor or hat to protect the head and face from the sun. The *hachimaki* – a towel tied around the forehead to catch sweat – was popular as well. The official who wrote about the Tosa village was much impressed by the diligence of the people, but not with their

31 Kimura, "Nōmin seikatsu no shosho," p. 199.

sense of cleanliness or etiquette. He also commented that most slept in their working clothes directly on the floor.

The Japanese did not have the sense of shame regarding their bodies that Westerners were taught. Because clothing was expensive, many people worked nearly naked during the summer, and women doing manual labor often stripped to the waist, particularly middle-aged and older women. Those with social pretensions would not have appeared in anything less than full dress, and neither would farmers on a formal occasion, but being caught naked was not something to worry the ordinary person. Houses had little privacy, and people were brought up to ignore anyone not in proper dress.

Although the well-to-do Japanese did not wear jewelry in the form of bracelets, brooches, or earrings, women often wore elaborate hairstyles and hair ornaments. In fact, these were so elaborate that hairdressers were called in once or twice a week to create the styles. In order not to displace the hair, women began to sleep on neck rests that supported only the base of the head and so kept the hairdo from mussing. This meant that women had to sleep on their backs and train themselves not to roll over in their sleep. Men, too, wore fairly elaborate though more practical styles, the most conspicuous being that of the *chommage* which was originally a samurai style. The head was shaved on the top, but the rest of the hair was allowed to grow long and was pulled into a topknot that was either folded forward onto the top of the shaven head or tied so that it stuck out from the back of the head like a stiff ponytail. The hairstyles clearly varied by class and status, so that one could tell at a glance the person's age, social status, and wealth and, for women, marital status as well.

Many women also wore elaborate makeup. The customs that offended the taste of Westerners were women's shaving their eyebrows and blackening their teeth with a mixture made of iron shavings and an adhesive. Women also wore face powder and rouge, according to social status. The *geisha* and prostitutes were distinguished from other women not only by their dress but also by their makeup, both of which were in the extreme of fashion. Farm women, on the other hand, had neither the time nor the money for makeup or elaborate hairstyles.

Although one would expect to find that dress varied by class and income in a highly stratified society, what is remarkable for Tokugawa Japan is how similar the basic cut of the clothing was for each class. Samurai clothing, even for the most formal occasions, was a much simplified version of that worn in earlier periods, and much more practical. At the same time, commoners gradually became better off and started wearing simplified versions of the same basic style. The daily wear of men of both the samurai and merchant classes was remarkably similar in basic style. And though one could determine the status of women from their clothing, again the basic pattern was similar for all. Thus, during this period when many historians emphasize class distinctions, dress in fact was gradually being standardized and class differences minimized.[32]

IMPLICATIONS OF CHANGES IN THE MATERIAL CULTURE AND LIFE-STYLES

Because the institutional structure remained much the same from the early seventeenth until the mid-nineteenth century, the Tokugawa period is usually viewed as a time when the Japanese life-style underwent little if any change. But recent studies of the material culture, particularly in relation to economic, demographic, and social conditions, reveal much about change in the standard of living and the quality of life, as well as in the relationships among the social classes and in their lifestyles.

Two of the most important influences on all aspects of life in the Tokugawa period were Japan's large population combined with a relative scarcity of resources. The Japanese therefore made a virtue of necessity and created a material culture that focused on the simple – on one or a few rather than on the many. The result was an almost total elimination of waste. The unifiers and especially the early shoguns patronized luxurious art and architectural styles, but even in the early seventeenth century they continued to follow an earlier tradition of simplicity. Katsura Detached Palace near Kyoto is a prime example of this merging of traditions.

One can find simplicity and economy in the material culture of all classes. Houses, by Western standards, were almost without furniture. The decorative focus of the main room was an alcove in which were usually displayed only two objects: a ceramic vase and a hanging scroll. The rich owned many objects of art, but these were stored and brought out to be appreciated only one at a time. Japanese flower

---

32 *Mon*, the crests adopted by families as emblems, differed from the European coats of arms, in that although they originated as warrior insignia, they also functioned as design and their use was never monopolized by the ruling elites. All daimyo and samurai had family crests, but crests also served as commercial trademarks, even those designs associated with the ruling families.

arrangements were elaborate, but they were created from what are actually only a few flowers plus leaves, branches, and materials that would be thrown out in the West.

The scarcity of resources affected housing, the diet, and daily life, as well as aesthetic traditions. Houses and their furnishings were made from what was available, not just wood, but often bamboo, rush, and, for the poor, even straw and husks. Even clay for pottery was often unobtainable, given Japan's volcanic soils. Metals were used only when there was no substitute; one can even find wooden knives from the Tokugawa period. The well-to-do Japanese built their houses for summer and chose to ignore when possible the winter cold. When they did use heat, it was efficiently to heat bodies rather than entire rooms.

The Japanese ate almost every kind of plant and seafood. Many of the foods appreciated for their delicate flavor and eaten in small quantities are not considered edible in Europe and in fact have little or no nutritional value. The sea was especially important as a source of foodstuffs. Not only was it readily accessible from many parts of Japan, but by the sixteenth century, Japan could no longer afford the land it took to raise livestock for food – pasture land and grain fields could be better used to provide food for people rather than feed for animals. One could argue that the Japanese were following Buddhist proscriptions against the eating of meat, but why did the Chinese not follow such strictures? As their population grew denser, the Japanese began to rely almost exclusively on grains, whenever possible rice, along with sweet potatoes for their calories.

One can see that almost every element of the Japanese life-style resulted from an attempt to live well using the least amount of resources. Despite the Japanese emphasis on economy of resources, or perhaps because of the Japanese aversion to waste, the average standard of living rose during the Tokugawa period. That the Japanese had an economic surplus during these centuries is suggested by the fact that the country as a whole was able to support an urban population of between 10 and 20 percent of the total population.

Urban demand stimulated rural production. No one disputes that the economy was growing at a good pace during the seventeenth century, but some controversy still exists among Japanese historians as to whether the economy continued to grow in the eighteenth and nineteenth centuries and who the beneficiaries were. Marxist scholars still write of burdensome taxes, harvest failures, lack of savings, and exploitation of the peasants by other classes, all of which led to famines, to peasants who were forced off their land when they could not pay rent or taxes, and to lives of poverty and hardship in the villages. But even historians in this school offer evidence to the contrary, even for the poorest regions of the northeast. They acknowledge an increase in the consumption of sugar (which had to be imported from western Japan) and fresh fish, an increase in the consumption of white rice and saké, and much improved clothing. Even in Morioka, in the extreme north, the deaths reported to the bakufu in the famine of the 1780s were largely fictitious; certainly such vast numbers are not to be found in the domain's own books.[33]

Economic historians trained in modern economic theory are publishing a growing number of quantitative studies that demonstrate that the economy continued to grow in the eighteenth century, even if not at the rate of the seventeenth, and that the standard of living by the early to mid-nineteenth century was at Meiji levels in many respects.[34] Those doing the quantitative studies have yet to obtain results that support the Marxist case. This is not to say that no one died from lack of food or as a result of malnutrition but, rather, that during this period the Japanese were not only able to support their large population – well over 25 million by the eighteenth century – but also to improve the life of the average Japanese as well.

Dramatic evidence of the improvement in the rural standard of living can be inferred from regulations governing goods permitted to be sold in the rural districts of the daimyo domain of Okayama.[35] In order to prevent the cultivators from wasting on small luxuries any cash they might have, the domain first tried to place a total ban on rural peddlers, but this was so openly violated that by 1666 peddlers were allowed to sell eleven items considered necessities: fishing nets, dried fish, salt, dried seaweed, tea, rapeseed oil, kindling, wooden water dippers, oars, basket tops, and farm tools. As demand grew, the rules had to be relaxed accordingly, and by 1705, thirty-one items were permitted to be sold, including pottery, cotton, pans, rice pots, straw mats, paper, fans, and rulers. The number of peddlers more than doubled between 1652 and 1707, and by the 1720s the domain discov-

33 For elaboration on Morioka, see chap. 6 of Hanley and Yamamura, *Economic and Demographic Change*, pp. 126–60.
34 These economic historians have organized a group for the study of quantitative economic history. Key members include Hayami Akira and Nishikawa Shunsaku of Keiō University, Umemura Mataji and Saitō Osamu of Hitotsubashi University, and Yasuba Yasukichi and Miyamoto Matao of Osaka University.
35 Discussions of the regulations, their violations, and what was sold and how in the villages are found in Andō Seiichi, *Kinsei zaikata shōgyō no kenkyū* (Tokyo: Yoshikawa kōbunkan, 1958), pp. 125–8; and in Okayama shiyakusho, *Okayama shishi, sangyō keizai hen* (Okayama: Okayama shiyakusho, 1966), pp. 164–5.

ered that many merchants were selling in farm villages without bothering to obtain a license.

By the eighteenth century, the castle town no longer controlled all commerce in Okayama. Rural towns had sprung up and many peddlers were based in them, and by late in the century many villages had their own stores, making goods available on a daily basis. To cite one example, by 1813, a much-cited shop in the village of Oi sold, among other things, ink, paper, writing brushes, pots, needles, pipes, tobacco and pouches, teapots, various containers and dishes, vinegar, soy sauce, bean paste, salt, noodles, kelp, saké, cakes, tea and teacups, rice crackers, grain, oil, candles, hair oil, hair cords and hairpins, cotton, towels, socks, various kinds of footgear, funeral necessities, and "other everyday necessities." Other shops in the same village sold various kinds of food and farm necessities, such as tools and fertilizers.[36] All of these goods were common items in traditional Japanese material culture, and they had long been available in towns and cities. What is significant is that during the Tokugawa period, rural villagers were gradually able to buy goods that had been previously available only in urban centers or to purchase items that had formerly been made in the household, such as bean paste and soy sauce.

By the nineteenth century, goods sold in Okayama included products made all over Japan, and the domain itself was producing an impressive number of goods that it sold within the domain as well as exported to other parts of Japan. This area was particularly well known for its cotton products and rush for tatami covers. It produced saké, pottery, tobacco, paper, tea, sugar and sweets, medicine, dyes, furniture, and household goods made of iron. By this time, some people even in the farming villages were able to afford linen, medicines, and furniture, specialty goods imported from distant parts of Japan.[37]

Although Okayama is a domain in the more advanced area of western Japan, even the domains considered the most "backward" showed clear evidence of a rising standard of living. In Morioka in the northeast, people in the mountainous regions and poorer villages were eating fresh fish by the late eighteenth century, and candies made with sugar imported from the west were sold widely. Clothing improved, to the point that the domain began to issue decrees admonishing the

36 Andō, *Kinsei zaikata shōgyō*, p. 95.
37 Okayama-ken, *Okayama-ken no rekishi* (Okayama: Okayama-ken, 1962), pp. 392–5; and Andō, *Kinsei zaikata shōgyō*, pp. 95, 125.

peasants and prohibiting "luxuries."[38] The most luxurious consumer goods were, of course, available in the large cities, and the stories and histories of the pleasure quarters provide ample evidence of what could be purchased.[39]

The rising standard of living both brought the Japanese more goods and some luxuries and also improved the quality of their life. The changes in housing that made life more comfortable often made the people healthier as well. Cotton was as much a boon to the Japanese as it was to the Europeans. But the quality of life was also affected by the Japanese social customs and personal patterns of behavior, particularly by the Japanese response to scarce resources. Despite the high value that Japanese place on the group, many items in daily life were given to one individual for private use, in contrast with shared utensils used in the West. For example, chopsticks, rice bowls, and teacups were portioned out to the family members, and no one used anyone else's. Thus it did not much matter that these were not washed carefully between meals, if at all. In merchant houses with numerous employees resident, each person took his or her own meal on a separate tray table, and often the dishes and chopsticks were wiped off after each meal and stored in a drawer at the bottom of the tray until the next meal. Lower on the economic scale, family meals were more casual, with individuals picking bits of food out of the communal pot or pickle dishes. Also, it was not customary to drink water; a kettle was kept on the fire with cheap tea in it, and family members dipped into it when thirsty. These customs almost certainly helped limit the spread of disease.

Resource scarcity had an unexpected effect on sanitation. Even in the early Tokugawa period, fertilizer was in inadequate supply. With little animal manure available, the Japanese resorted to human waste, and in the farming areas surrounding the largest cities, night soil was transformed from a waste to a "good," one that was bought and sold. For example, in the seventeenth century, vegetables brought by boat to Osaka were exchanged for night soil. But by the early eighteenth century, the demand for this type of fertilizer had risen so much that farmers had to pay for night soil in cash, and groups of villages fought over collection rights.[40] Under these circumstances, city dwellers were unlikely to dispose of human wastes by throwing them out on the

38 Mori Kahei, *Nihon hekichi no shiteki kenkyū*, vol. 1 (Tokyo: Hōsei daigaku shuppankyoku, 1969), pp. 519, 524, 536–40, 572.
39 See Chapter 14 in this volume.
40 Wakita Osamu and Kobayashi Shigeru, *Ōsaka no seisan to kōtsū* (Osaka: Mainichi hōsō, 1973), p. 127.

street, as many Europeans did, nor were there the problems with cesspools that many American cities faced. Although bath and dish-water ran through uncovered drainage ditches in the middle of or alongside the road, this did not produce either the stench or the un-healthy conditions that prevailed in London and other cities because of their open sewers. Thus, because wastes were useful in Tokugawa cities, they were collected, rather than allowed to seep into the water table and contaminate wells and underground pipes. By the late nineteenth century, the quality of the water in Edo was higher than that in London was in the same period.[41]

The net result of Japanese customs with regard to sanitation was a much lower incidence of epidemic diseases than in Europe and other parts of the world.[42] Cholera was absent until the mid-nineteenth century and then was readily contained, and typhoid seems not to have been a problem. Both of these diseases are spread through polluted water. Even dysentery, which almost certainly affected the death rate of the very young in Japan, was not the killer of children that it was in the West in the nineteenth century. The closing off of Japan from anything but the most limited contact with other countries certainly helped keep cholera and bubonic plague from the Japanese population. Japan's rapidly running and short rivers did much to prevent water pollution. Equally important were waste disposal, boiling of the drinking water, and other sanitation measures routinely practiced by all Japanese.

The data do not exist to enable a direct comparison between the Japanese standard of living and quality of life with those of European or other countries, but information on the population can be used for comparison. Many of the estimates of mortality and life expectancy are for small samples, but the studies made by various scholars have such consistent results that they can be considered to apply to a much larger area, in fact much of central and western Japan.[43] The crude death rates in village samples dating from the late eighteenth century to the end of the Tokugawa period indicate that most crude death rate averages were in the twenties per thousand, even in years of hardship. Death rates were more frequently below twenty than above thirty. The

41 R. W. Atkinson, "The Water Supply of Tokio," *Transactions of the Asiatic Society of Japan* 6 (October 27, 1877–January 26, 1878), from the reprinted version of 1888, pp. 87–105.

42 For an excellent study of diseases and their causes and incidence in the Tokugawa period, see Ann Bowman Janetta, *Epidemics and Mortality in Early Modern Japan* (Princeton, N.J.: Princeton University Press, 1986).

43 For a summary and analysis of many of these studies, see chap. 11 of Hanley and Yamamura, *Economic and Demographic Change*, pp. 292–319.

sole exception for these samples is for the period of the Tempō famine in the 1830s, when the death rate for a village in the northeast rose to thirty-seven per thousand and that for the city of Takayama was nearly forty-five. Estimated life expectancies for the same samples are higher than many Japanese scholars find believable, but the challengers have not been able to furnish contradictory evidence. Estimated life expectancies of over forty years meant that two-year-olds in the late Tokugawa period had a life expectancy similar to those in Western Europe in the mid-nineteenth century, and one not much different from that in Japan in the early twentieth century.

Japan's birthrates from the eighteenth century on were in the same range as the death rates. The effect of the low birthrates combined with low death rates was to create a very slow rate of population growth for the latter half of the Tokugawa period. Neither famines nor epidemics had the devastating effect on the population that they did in earlier times or other countries. The question, then, is why the Japanese had low birthrates during centuries of gradual but clear upward growth of the economy, a rise in income, and an improved standard of living. The answer is that Japanese were limiting family size through a variety of measures, and they were doing so to maintain and improve their standard of living, rather than as a means of coping with dire circumstances, as the older generation of Japanese scholars (that is, the ones writing in the 1930s to the 1960s) has contended. All scholars agree that the Japanese resorted to abortion and infanticide as a means of limiting the number of children within marriage, but studies in historical demography at the village level reveal that these methods were practiced equally in good times and bad, in villages with growing economies, and in those with limited resources for growth.[44]

Farmers sought to optimize the size of their families. In rural village samples, the average number of children in the completed family from the end of the eighteenth century and well into the nineteenth was only three and a half children. This would have ensured a male heir for most but would have prevented numerous children who would have been a burden on the family and village when grown. Families used a number of means to regulate family size, of which birth control was only one. Some methods were in the form of generalized social customs enforced through social and economic pressure. Women married

44 See especially the studies by Hayami Akira and Susan B. Hanley, cited in Hanley and Yamamura, *Economic and Demographic Change;* Thomas C. Smith, *Nakahara* (Stanford, Calif.: Stanford University Press, 1977); and Susan B. Hanley and Arthur P. Wolf, eds., *Family and Population in East Asian History* (Stanford, Calif.: Stanford University Press, 1985).

in their early to mid-twenties, which delayed childbearing and reduced the number of childbearing years. It was also the custom for only one son in each household to marry. And in periods of economic hardship, marriages were postponed until better years.

Within marriage, one of the methods used to limit children seems to have been sex-selective infanticide, although there is limited statistical evidence for this practice.[45] However, descriptions of abortion, abortionists, and the effects of this practice are abundant, and this form of birth control is known to have been widely practiced throughout Japan. Abortion was an undesirable practice but not a "sin." Infanticide was even condoned by the euphemism that it was a means of "returning" an infant at birth before it had become an individual and a part of society. That is, it was thought of as a form of postpartum birth control. Though these were considered undesirable practices by contemporaries, they were possibly less cruel than the premodern European custom of doing away with unwanted children through carelessness, or gin and laudanum, or abandoning them at church doors.

The social pressure to compel the Japanese to limit family size in a growing economy can be understood only by examining Japan's social values. Although the Japanese are noted for being group oriented, and certainly the Tokugawa village formed a tightly knit group, within each social unit or level the competition was intense. The measures taken to lower to the minimum the number of nonproductive members in the household lead us to conclude that Japanese were seeking to create a population favorable to economic production.

At the heart of Japanese society, rural or urban, commoner or samurai, was the house or family unit, called the *ie*. The *ie* was conceived of as a corporate body, and its members were expected to sacrifice personal desires for the benefit of the group as a whole. The goals of the current members of the *ie*, whether they had been born in the family or were married or adopted into it, were to maintain the current level of prosperity and, if at all possible, to increase its future wealth and status.

Wealth and family status were important at all levels of Japanese society. Few samurai, from the middle of the Tokugawa period on, could expect to improve the family status, and even with intense competition by all, they had to struggle merely to maintain their present position. In the village, there was strong incentive to maintain the *kakaku*, the status of the house. There were no explicit rules governing

---

45 See the studies cited in the preceding footnote for evidence.

how status was determined, but there was implicit consent as to how it was assigned. The status the family had in past generations held some weight, but the primary determinant was economic position within the village. Status determined who became village headman, who assumed the other posts of village government, and even who sat where at village meetings.[46]

To maintain status, it was not enough merely to maintain the same standard of living as in the past; families had to maintain their relative position vis-à-vis other families in the village. When ranks began to change within a village, often conflict would break out as people jockeyed for power. In the tightly knit Tokugawa village, the struggle to maintain position was felt continually – at weddings, funerals, and at times of crisis, such as in a year of poor harvest or when a family in the village needed aid. As more goods came into the village and were purchased by a few, the rest of the people would feel a need to own the same items.

From Tokugawa times comes the propensity for formal gift giving on every conceivable occasion, but especially to superiors and those to whom one owes something. There was an equal emphasis on giving a gift in return for one received, a focus on entertaining in order to maintain business and status relationships, and a penchant for conspicuous consumption. People might eat boiled grains with greens day after day but then splurge at a level unthought of in the West when entertaining guests who had to be impressed, or even at an annual village meeting attended by one representative from each household. Daily life might be very simple and austere so that at appropriate times the family could spend large sums to maintain its status and not dishonor the *ie*.

Actual household budgets dating from the Tokugawa times are hard to find, but a number of case studies have been pursued by modern historians. For example, one farmer in the 1840s spent 29 percent of his cash income on social obligations. A carpenter in Kyoto in the 1820s who was spending two-thirds of his income on food and fuel spent 7.5 percent of his income on social obligations. An upper-income samurai in the service of the bakufu who was spending just over half of his income paying off loans, debts, and interest spent nearly double the carpenter's annual income in 1779 on social expenses connected with the birth of a daughter.[47] Thus, the Japanese econo-

---

46 Kodama Kōta, *Kinsei nōmin seikatsu shi* (Tokyo: Yoshikawa kōbunkan, 1957), p. 277.
47 For a fuller description and analysis of these examples, see Hanley, "A High Standard of Living in Nineteenth-Century Japan."

mized on creature comforts for themselves but spent large proportions of their incomes on status goods, gifts to maintain and enhance their social network, and payments or donations to maintain and advance their social status within the community.

A study of the material culture of Tokugawa Japan provides overwhelming evidence that people of all classes sought to improve their social position. Everything from style in dress and housing, appropriate forms of recreation, and even who was officially permitted to drink tea was set down in law. However, a look at the changes in these regulations over time indicates that a lot of people were not strictly conforming to the class codes. Class distinctions were violated, both overtly and covertly, but the violations were so widespread that it was impossible for authorities to enforce compliance. The first violations were subtle; no one wanted to flout the law openly. For example, townsmen might wear fine silks, but only as linings to cotton outer garb.

Because the size, design, and decoration of residences denoted status, it was important to prevent persons of low status from adopting the status symbols of their betters. Commoners were forbidden to use styles that belonged to the samurai, and regulations spelled out what was prohibited. In Osaka, as late as 1843, a set of regulations forbade commoners from making doors of cryptomeria, installing fixed reading tables (the *shoin* or, more properly, the *tsuke-shoin*), using silver and gold foil on their *fusuma*, and putting lacquer on posts in the house.[48] However, it was impossible for the authorities to police what people installed in their private residences, and more and more of the well-to-do violated such sumptuary regulations.

Just as residences denoted status among the samurai, so they did among the farmers. The most important family in the village was supposed to have the grandest house, with the largest roof and the longest, thickest, and most beautiful posts and rafters. In some villages, status was shown by the number of decorations on the ridge post of the house. In the Niigata area, the *chumon-zukuri*, an L-shaped plan containing living quarters, work area-cum-kitchen, and stable, seems originally to have been a style used by the samurai. Despite seventeenth-century regulations banning the use of this plan for lower-level samurai and commoners, in time the *chumon-zukuri* became the favored house style for the upper levels of the farming communities. However, this style does not seem to have been used by those of low socioeconomic status in

48 Shiraki, *Sumai no rekishi*, p. 135.

the villages, but by designated farmers who owned their own land.[49] Examples of sumptuary laws and status symbols from all parts of Japan testify to the imitation of samurai status symbols by commoners and also to the observance of status differences within local communities.

What was occurring during the Tokugawa period was a mingling of status symbols to reflect income and wealth as well as social group. Those not born into the samurai class could not hope to govern, but if they became rich, they could afford many of the luxuries of life that were supposed to be limited to the samurai. Even by the early eighteenth century a Confucian adviser to the shogunate was opposed to the "increase in consumers [that] has come about because there are no regulative institutions." Country people who migrated into Edo quickly adopted a style of life not considered suitable for commoners: drinking saké, purchasing clothes instead of making them, and installing *shōji*, ceilings, and mosquito nets in their houses.[50]

The authorities not only knew of the violations of the sumptuary laws and unwritten behavior codes, they themselves helped bring about the loss of clear class distinctions. by the late Tokugawa period, many domains were in financial difficulties and therefore allowed commoners to purchase the privilege of wearing swords and using a surname. The major reason for the blurring of class lines, however, was the growing discrepancies in the income of samurai and commoners, more so in the various daimyo domains than in the lands controlled by the bakufu. Even in Edo, the commoners' incomes were steadily rising while the samurai in the service of the bakufu found themselves with more or less constant incomes and facing a rising tide of goods and services that the townspeople could afford but they could not. Real wages were rising throughout Japan, so that samurai families gradually had to let most of their servants go, and many of the lower-ranked samurai had to take in piecework to supplement their stipends. For example, in the domain of Odawara, samurai produced lanterns, dyed paper, fishhooks, toothpicks, and umbrellas, and seven hundred samurai in Mito notified their domain that they were engaged in part-time work.[51]

If we look only at how Japanese society was supposed to operate, we will find a rigid class society in place throughout the Tokugawa period.

---

49 Itoh, *Traditional Domestic Architecture*, pp. 118–20.
50 Ogyū Sorai, translated into English by J. R. McEwan, *The Political Writings of Ogyū Sorai* (Cambridge, England: Cambridge University Press, 1962), p. 44.
51 For an analysis of this topic, see Kozo Yamamura, *A Study of Samurai Income and Entrepreneurship* (Cambridge, Mass.: Harvard University Press, 1974).

But Japan lost its class distinctions far more quickly and far more thoroughly than England did, and much of the reason has to be a blurring of class lines before the Meiji Restoration. Commoners were aping samurai in material culture and in cultural ways as well. Textbooks for children provided a common Confucian philosophy and ethic for samurai and commoners alike, and a "samuraization" of society was at work. But the influence was not just in one direction: The samurai were fascinated by the townspeople's culture and were avid theatergoers and readers of popular fiction, even though they were not supposed to lower themselves to this level.

A major cause for the blurring of class lines was economic. From the eighteenth century on, if not earlier, social class determined occupation, but it did not determine income. Although the average income of samurai was higher than that of commoners, vast numbers of both townspeople and villagers had higher incomes than did the lowest ranks of the samurai. In fact, in some domains, samurai and commoners worked side by side in the same jobs. In Okayama, for example, a listing of persons working in the castle for the daimyo for the 1840s reveals that both samurai and commoners were filling the same positions at the lower supervisory levels.[52] Above all, it is important to emphasize the point made in Chapter 3 that the samurai were not a landed gentry whose presence in the village might have reinforced the social differences on a personal level. Nor did they constitute a class of urban absentee proprietors. This separation of the samurai from the rural population meant that there was virtually no daily contact that would reinforce class differences. Instead, members of the farming communities competed among themselves for wealth and position – tenants aspiring to become landowners, and landowners village leaders. People were well aware that they might move up the social and economic ladder within their own class or occupation, but they also knew that being born a samurai was no guarantee of high income.

Although the standard of living gradually increased over the Tokugawa centuries, the changes took place within the framework of the traditional economy and in the context of the indigenous Tokugawa culture, with little foreign influence. Thus the increases achieved are apparent if this period is studied in isolation, but when contrasted with the West, which was undergoing industrialization, Japan seems to have been very backward by the mid-nineteenth century. Westerners who visited Japan in the sixteenth and seventeenth centuries were

52 Ibid., pp. 126–7.

much impressed by the Japanese government, society, cleanliness, housing, and technology. But by the nineteenth century, the Industrial Revolution had so transformed the West that visitors saw little in Japan to impress them, despite improvements that had in fact taken place over several centuries.

The views of these nineteenth-century Westerners, along with the Japanese who themselves felt Japan to be backward in comparison with the Western powers, have continued to color our view of traditional Japanese life. Although the Japanese may have been relatively poor by Victorian standards, the record indicates that they may have been just as healthy; Japanese life expectancy in the nineteenth century was similar to that in the advanced Western industrial nations. And although the Japanese are resource poor by any standard, they have developed a material culture and an aesthetic tradition that are admired throughout the world today.

CHAPTER 14

POPULAR CULTURE

INTRODUCTION

Among the developments of the early Edo period that distinguish it most clearly from preceding eras is the emergence of a distinctive popular culture among the urban commoners. From Nara times the imperial court had been the fountainhead of poetry, literature, the arts, and scholarship. After the court's decline in resources and strength in the twelfth century, members of the military elite increasingly came to serve as patrons for cultural and intellectual developments in their mansions and in Buddhist monasteries. In the Edo period, while the shogun and daimyo continued their patronage of the higher culture and learning, the most original and lively developments took place among the populace of the cities. For the first time, commoners, the nonelite, became culturally important.

Major economic and social changes followed political unification and the establishment of a stable political order under the Tokugawa in the years after 1600. The rapid development of trade and commerce was accompanied by the dramatic growth of the three major cities – Kyoto, Osaka, and Edo. Much of this growth came from the function of these cities as national markets for goods from all areas. Because the increase in population was largely among those engaged in commercial activities – merchants, craftspeople, shopkeepers, rice brokers, builders, and laborers – and because it was they who benefited most from the economic expansion, the social composition of cities and also the distribution of wealth took on entirely new patterns. The rise in income of many *chōnin*, as the urban commoners were called, brought an increasing demand for goods and services, as they had leisure to engage in a more active social and cultural life and to seek entertainments. The requirements of business led to a rise in literacy that, in turn, encouraged the writing and publication of a variety of books for the edification and entertainment of city residents. The interest in popular entertainment and culture in the major cities developed rapidly, especially in the second half of the seventeenth century, culminating in a brilliant flowering of popular culture known as the golden age of Genroku. Although Genroku is the era name for the years 1688 to 1704, the name is used more broadly to designate the cultural period that encompasses the half-century centered on the rule from 1680 to 1709 of the fifth shogun, Tsunayoshi.

These years spanned the careers of a remarkable number of creative writers, performers, and artists who are among the most celebrated names in the history of Japanese culture. The novels and short stories of Ihara Saikaku (1642–93) provide the most incisive accounts of the merchants' business methods and the life of the prostitutes' quarters. Chikamatsu Monzaemon (1653–1725) wrote for both the kabuki and puppet theaters and was the first playwright to give plays a dramatic structure, especially in the domestic tragedies he composed. A third literary figure of great creativity and influence was Matsuo Bashō (1644–94) who reshaped the aesthetics of haiku composition.

Kabuki became a full-fledged dramatic form during these years, thanks in part to the appearance of its first great actors, Sakata Tōjūrō (1647–1709) and Ichikawa Danjūrō I (1660–1704), and the development of the art of playing female roles by Mizuki Tatsunosuke (1673–1745) and Yoshizawa Ayame (1673–1729). Performers of puppet plays rivaled kabuki in popularity because of the artistry of the reciters of *jōruri* texts, most notably Takemoto Gidayū (1651–1714), whose name came to designate the new style of *gidayū* recitation. During the same years the *ukiyoe* (pictures of the floating world) style of painting and woodblock illustration emerged from the brushes of Hishikawa Moronobu (d. 1694), Torii Kiyonobu (1664–1729), and many others. The pleasure quarter of the city, with its prostitutes of celebrated beauty and cultural accomplishments, was the social stage for much of the new urban culture. The quarter was the main subject of ukiyoe prints and Saikaku's stories.

This new popular culture, which had wide appeal to urban commoners, is the focus of this chapter. In addition, however, there were artistic achievements in the Genroku that responded to the interests of a more exclusive number of wealthy commoners. These were the counterpart to the high style produced by officially patronized artists for the upper bushi (samurai), imperial court, and Buddhist clergy – a style epitomized by the paintings of the Kanō and Tosa schools, the metal craft of the Gotō, the colored porcelain of Nabeshima, and lacquer in the Kōami and Igarashi traditions. Ogata Kōrin (1658–1716) developed a rich, decorative style of painting and lacquer work

and also designed textiles for affluent commoners. His brother Kenzan (1663–1743) and another Kyoto ceramist, Nonomura Ninsei (fl.
1660s), made works of great originality. Miyazaki Yūzensai pioneered
the *yūzen* style of intricate dyeing which provided commoners with a
substitute for the brocade and embroidered garments that were forbidden to them. The woodcut artist Moronobu and Hanabusa Itchō
(1652–1724) painted screens and handscrolls for urban clients. Most
of these men came from families of craftspeople, but when they created new styles they had a keen consciousness of their identity as
master artists; Ninsei and Kenzan, for example, freed themselves
from the tradition of earlier craftsmen by signing their work. Moronobu was the first artist to put his name on woodcuts (*Buke hyakunin
isshu*, 1672), and Chikamatsu was the first popular playwright to claim
authorship.

Underlying the conspicuous successes of this popular culture was a
new audience, a large number of urban commoners who were not only
literate but increasingly discriminating. They were informed by popular books, simply written and published for their consumption. Their
demand for entertainment was met not only by brothels and theaters
but more commonly by many other diversions that leisure and city life
offered. For the first time, commoners discovered the pleasure of
reading, and many went beyond popular books to classical and medieval literature or Chinese texts. The study and enjoyment of cultural
pastimes was open to them: tea and flower arrangement, composition
of poetry, recitation of noh plays, playing of musical instruments, and
singing of *kouta*.

Popular culture developed first in the three great cities. It is usually
referred to as *chōnin* culture – suggesting that it was made by urban
commoners for urban commoners – to distinguish it from court culture and bushi culture. This is a simplification, as of course the new
culture drew on traditions existing in the upper classes, and moreover,
some of its creators, such as Bashō and Chikamatsu, were of samurai
background. Furthermore, there was great interest in this culture
among other classes as well.

From the early Edo period, the government recognized the order of
the four classes as samurai (*shi*), farmer (*nō*), craftsman (*kō*), and
merchant (*shō*). Although Confucianists often spoke of this class order,
it was never given a legal basis, and its artificiality and imprecision
must be kept in mind. Indeed, the system served primarily to separate
the rulers from the ruled. In principle, the bushi were paid stipends,
and the other classes had tax obligations. The class system distin-

guished the proper samurai of substance – with his rights to bear a surname, wear two swords, occupy a larger residence, and receive deference – from the rest of the population. But for administrative purposes, even foot soldiers and the servants of proper samurai were considered as belonging to the bushi class. Including wives and children, the bushi made up about 6 or 7 percent of the national population, which stood at approximately thirty million by the end of the seventeenth century.

Farmers ranked second, in recognition of their labors that provided the sustenance of the country. This ranking derived from the physiocratic principle that land was the source of the country's wealth. Farmers were followed by craftsmen (or artisans), many of whose products in pre-Edo times were weapons, military equipment, and buildings required by the bushi. In practice, no attempt was made to distinguish craftsmen from merchants: Both were treated as a single group and referred to as *chōnin*, "people of the blocks," the term usually being translated as townsmen or townspeople. They made up 5 to 6 percent of the population.[1]

The four-class designation, when first applied by warlords, did have some rough correspondence to the relative usefulness of the groups to the bushi. The honor accorded farmers was an empty one, as they were treated far more harshly than the other classes were. Because income from the bakufu's agricultural lands (*tenryō*) was the government's financial basis, careful attention was given to the systematic collection of taxes and to restricting the movements of farmers. The bakufu's 1649 regulations for farmers exhorted them to work hard in the fields from sunrise to sunset and to spend their evenings making straw rope and sacks. They were told to eat coarse grains rather than the rice they produced, not to buy tea or saké, and to divorce wives who were overly fond of tea and excursions to temples.[2] In the early Edo period, peddlers were prohibited from entering villages in some districts, in an attempt to protect farmers from being tempted by nonessential articles. In some regions, village stores were actually forbidden to sell books, so as to prevent farmers from wasting their time reading.[3]

By comparison, the treatment of the city commoners was milder

---

1 The estimate by Harada Tomohiko includes commoners resident in cities, castle towns, and ports, but artisans, tradesmen, innkeepers, and so on in rural areas are counted as farmers. See his entry "Chōnin" in *Nihon fūzokushi jiten* (Tokyo: Kōbundō, 1979), p. 416.
2 Hōseishi gakkai, ed., *Tokugawa kinreikō* (Tokyo: Sōbunsha, 1959–61), vol. 5, pp. 159–64.
3 Kodama Kōta, *Kinsei nōmin seikatsu shi* (Tokyo: Yoshikawa kōbunkan, 1951), p. 9; Donald H. Shively, "Sumptuary Regulation and Status in Early Tokugawa Japan," *Harvard Journal of Asiatic Studies* 25 (1964–5): 153–5.

and more diplomatic. The third shogun, Iemitsu, remitted the land taxes of Osaka, Sakai, and Nara in 1634 (those of Edo and Kyoto had been canceled earlier), a gesture of psychological importance to encourage the residents to cooperate with the bakufu. The Tokugawa kept the major cities and ports under direct control because of their commercial importance. They were interested mainly in the essential services that the *chōnin* supplied: shipping and marketing rice and other produce from the shogunal and daimyo domains, and making and distributing goods of all kinds. Furthermore, because the provinces around Edo lagged behind the Kyoto–Osaka region in both agriculture and manufacturing, the government was constantly concerned that the needs of Edo's enormous population be met and that shortages not occur. The bakufu, therefore, placed few restraints on trade and was concerned with providing security of person and private property for the commercial populations of its cities. Because Kyoto and Osaka served increasingly as national markets, the wealth of the country flowed into the hands of urban businessmen. However, the bakufu was unable to tax this wealth effectively, deterred not only by the physiocratic notions of economics but also by a lack of understanding of the new commercial processes.

The Tokugawa honored – or perhaps we should say took advantage of – the traditions of self-rule that had developed in commercial towns under the chaotic conditions of the sixteenth century, by assigning to the merchant families of Kyoto and Osaka considerable responsibility for self-administration. Under the direction of two *hatamoto* (bannermen) sent as city magistrates (*machi bugyō*) to each of these cities, the bakufu appointed the heads of old merchant families as city elders to arrange and oversee the necessary administrative work. Although this self-administration placed a considerable burden of time and money on the urban commoners (effectively negating before long the advantage of remitting land taxes), it minimized the intrusion of bushi into the daily lives of the people and fostered an atmosphere of considerable freedom for the *chōnin*, especially in Kyoto, Osaka, and other primarily commercial cities.

Chōnin were not subject to as much regimentation as were the shogun's samurai vassals, nor were they in constant jeopardy of the demotion or expropriation suffered by many daimyo during the seventeenth century. Samurai were required to be ready to perform military or administrative services, and their personal conduct was governed by an ethical system. The *chōnin*, however, were free to follow their self-interests in making money and spending it. They had the freedom of the city – with its shops and sights and pleasure quarters – where money talked. Their lack of political and social status was not, therefore, without its compensations.

The meaning of class is diminished also by the vast differences in level within each class. Bushi included not only the shogun and the daimyo but also the humble servants of samurai. Farmers ranged from rich landowners and village headmen to tenants and agricultural servants. *Chōnin* included privileged purveyors to the rulers and merchants of fabulous wealth but also large numbers of poor laborers.

The meaning of class was undercut most of all by the gradual erosion of the financial position of much of the samurai class in the middle of the seventeenth century, while at the same time the income of urban commoners was rising. The real income of samurai declined, for they were living on fixed stipends paid in rice, the price of which fluctuated and, in general, did not keep pace with the prices of other commodities. Samurai were required to live in cities and towns, where everything had to be purchased. The variety of goods available increased constantly, and more and more articles came to be regarded as necessities. It was the government's belief that to maintain the proper relationship between the bushi and the other classes, there should be hierarchal distinctions, not only in their functions, but also in the quality of their dress, food, and housing, in behavior and speech, and in intellectual and cultural activities. (For example, noh drama, which had been adopted by the courts of the Ashikaga and Hideyoshi, was the appropriate "music" of the bushi and hence was not to be public entertainment for commoners.) It became more and more difficult for ordinary samurai to keep up appearances. To preserve at least the outward distinctions among classes, *chōnin* were chided in sumptuary laws not to dress in expensive silks (ordinary silk was allowed), to decorate their rooms with gold and silver leaf, or to furnish them with objects of gold lacquer.[4] It is apparent that the authorities had already conceded a level of luxury that was remarkably at variance with the living style prescribed for farmers.

Intermarriage between samurai and commoners was considered inappropriate, but bushi were permitted, not uncommonly, to take commoner wives, doubtless for reasons of financial advantage. A kind of cultural leveling occurred, especially in the case of bushi who were permanent residents of large cities and lived in daily contact with *chōnin*. Many family members were attracted to the popular novels,

---

4 Shively, "Sumptuary Regulation and Status," pp. 123–31.

plays, music, and fashions considered more appropriate to *chōnin*, whereas commoners aspired to the education, ethical values, and cultural pastimes of their betters. The elite among the commoners – privileged merchants, government contractors, city elders – adopted a style of life similar to that of the bushi. The most affluent enjoyed more luxuries than the minor daimyo did.

Social class meant less in Kyoto than elsewhere, for there the population was more diversified, and *machishū* residences had long been scattered throughout even the upper city (*kamigyō*), the preserve of the aristocracy. A few merchant houses, prominent long before the rise of the Tokugawa, associated in social circles or salons with court nobles, high clergy, cultivated bushi, and poets and artists. Some amassed important collections of tea bowls and utensils, paintings, and rare Chinese books. The skill of some merchants in cultural accomplishments such as *waka* and *renga*, poetry and tea, painting, and noh, also speaks to the social position of these individuals.

During the Hideyoshi and early Tokugawa years, some samurai became purveyors or commercial agents for their daimyo in Kyoto and other cities. Others became merchants to seek a better fortune, and as they came from bushi stock, they were more congenial contractors for government and daimyo business. The presence of former samurai among the merchant houses served to enhance the status of the upperclass merchants.

Kyoto had a richer diversity of residents than did the other cities. The proportion of bushi was far smaller than in Edo or other castle towns. Among the samurai were the bakufu representative (the *shoshidai*) and his staff, the Nijō Castle guard, the two city magistrates and their samurai staffs, the eighteen Kamigata *daikan* who administered the *tenryō*, and so forth. Also in the city were samurai hired as guards and retainers by court nobles and by some Buddhist temples. Most daimyo continued to post retainers in Kyoto as agents, especially to procure clothing and other fine articles from the city's artisans and to borrow money from wealthy merchants. At least eighty-five daimyo maintained official residences (*yashiki*) there in the 1680s, even though they themselves could not ordinarily enter the city.[5] Countless *rōnin* drifted to Kyoto, samurai who had lost employment because their daimyo lords were attainted by the bakufu; this confiscation of daimyo domains continued unabated until at least 1651 and, to a lesser degree, until the end of Tsunayoshi's rule.

5 *Kyōto no rekishi* (Tokyo: Gakugei shorin, 1968–76), vol. 5, p. 19.

Among those not included in the four classes were both the nobles and the monks and nuns of Kyoto. The upper city accommodated the imperial family and members of the court nobility – 150 families which provided officials for the imperial government – and their attendants.[6] There was, in addition, a large religious establishment associated with fifteen hundred temples and shrines in the capital and its immediate environs. Kyoto's population further included many physicians, scholars, teachers, artists and noh performers, and masters of other arts, some of whom did not fit exactly into class categories. They were among the best educated residents of the city. Those descended from noble or religious or samurai families regarded themselves as distinct from the commercial class. From this kind of background came many of the writers of seventeenth-century popular books – romances, edifying texts, and travel stories and guides.

The development of popular culture, during its early stages, took place largely within the urban environment of Kyoto. Although this capital had long been the country's only real city, it was not repaired or restored to prosperity until the Hideyoshi years. It had been largely destroyed during the Ōnin War of 1467–77 and did not recover fully during the following century, as one warlord after another failed to establish a durable regime. If Kyoto had ever had as many as 200,000 people, it had certainly fallen far below that number. The main urban area in these years, the economic heart of the country, was the Kyoto–Sakai–Nara triangle. Osaka was not a city until Hideyoshi began to rebuild the Ishiyama Honganji market town in 1583. Edo was a very small castle town when it became the Tokugawa headquarters in 1590. In this situation there was no hint of the enormous surge of urbanization that was about to begin. In just over a century, by 1700, Kyoto, Osaka, and Edo each had a *chōnin* population of 350,000.[7] Edo had, in addition, a bushi population at least as numerous as the *chōnin*. In another two decades it probably embraced 1 million people and had become larger than any Western European city. During these years, some regional cities reached considerable size: Kanazawa, Nagoya, Kagoshima, Hiroshima, Sendai, Nagasaki, and Sakai all were in the range of 50,000 to 100,000.[8]

The three large cities (*santō*, or three capitals) each were of a rather

---

6 Ibid., p. 509.
7 Nakabe Yoshiko, *Kinsei toshi no seiritsu to kōzō* (Tokyo: Shinseisha, 1967), p. 637; Wakita Osamu, *Genroku no shakai* (Tokyo: Haniwa shobō, 1980), pp. 154–68.
8 Wakita, *Genroku no shakai*, pp. 155–9; Takeo Yazaki, *Social Change and the City in Japan* (Tokyo: Japan Publications, 1968), pp. 103–37, 237–78, 255–6.

different type, and they played different roles. Kyoto, which had already been the imperial capital for eight hundred years, was the home of the court aristocracy, the repository of the classical arts, and the source of most high-quality articles. It had changed from a Chinese-style *ritsuryō* capital, to shogunal headquarters under the Ashikaga, to castle town under Hideyoshi. It was also the religious center of the nation as the headquarters of most Buddhist sects, the principal commercial market until late in the seventeenth century, and it continued even longer as the fountainhead of culture.

Osaka under the Tokugawa was almost exclusively a commercial city. There were even fewer bushi than in Kyoto, and these were concentrated in the east near the castle. There were, of course, no court nobles and far fewer members of religious and cultural professions. Some of its populace had been drawn from Kyoto, but much more from other nearby commercial towns such as Sakai, Nara, and Fushimi. Functioning as the principal market to which most daimyo shipped their rice, Osaka also became the chief market for trading special products from all parts of the country. Before 1700, Osaka displaced Kyoto as the leading national market.[9] With its energetic, prosperous *chōnin* population, this city began to make major contributions to popular literature and drama by the last decades of the century.

If Osaka came to function as a purely commercial city, Edo became the political center. It was the Tokugawa's castle town, the bushi administrative headquarters where samurai always outnumbered *chōnin*. Edo's growth to great size came with the formalization of the *sankin kōtai* after 1635, which required the daimyo, then almost three hundred in number, to spend half their time in Edo and maintain large residential compounds there. The land occupied by the shogun and his vassals and by the daimyo establishments covered between 60 and 70 percent of the city area. Because temples and shrines occupied half of the remainder, the *chōnin* had only 15 to 20 percent of the city land area for their residences and businesses.[10] They were crowded into districts that were segregated from the far more spacious and greener areas assigned to the bushi for their residences. The numerical and geographical superiority of the bushi, not to mention their monopoly

9 William B. Hauser, *Economic Institutional Change in Tokugawa Japan: Osaka and the Kinai Cotton Trade* (Cambridge, England: Cambridge University Press, 1974), pp. 11–32, 38–40; Wakita, *Genroku no shakai*, pp. 179–86; Wakita Osamu, *Kinsei Ōsaka no machi to hito* (Kyoto: Jimbun shoin, 1986), pp. 112–3; Kodama Kōta, *Genroku jidai*, vol. 16 of *Nihon no rekishi* (Tokyo: *Chūō kōronsha*, 1966), pp. 260–76.
10 Kōda Shigetomo, *Edo to Ōsaka* (Tokyo: Fuzambō, 1942), p. 17.

on political power, gave a coloration to city life in Edo that differed markedly from the freer atmosphere of Kyoto and Osaka. It took time for Edo to outgrow its raw, frontier personality. Because it was a new city, teachers and masters of the arts had to be drawn from Kyoto. The development of popular culture also lagged until the last decades of the seventeenth century. But as the city matured, stimulated by the traffic of commoners as well as bushi from all parts of the country, it gradually replaced Kyoto in the middle of the Edo period as the creative center of popular culture.

EDUCATION

The increase in literacy during the seventeenth century among both samurai and urban commoners was an important factor in the functioning of the administration and the expansion of commerce. It brought a profound change in the level of knowledge and cultural life of both classes. As evidence of the spread of literacy, writers have pointed to the accumulation of village archives, administrative and legal documents of all kinds, and commercial records. More impressive, however, are the founding and rapid growth of a large publishing industry, offering not only serious books but also, from the middle of the century, popular books on a wide range of topics. The brisk sales of Saikaku's books of stories from 1682 on, for example, informs us that the number of sophisticated readers among the commoners had already grown impressively.

During the century of warfare preceding the establishment of the Tokugawa bakufu, there was little time or necessity, even among the daimyo, for extensive formal education. Most members of the military elite were literate, but it was the exceptional daimyo who received much tutoring in the Japanese literary or historical works or in the Chinese classics. For the most part, military men relied on Zen monks to draft important documents and records and also to provide political advice based on their knowledge of Japanese and Chinese history and Chinese works on statecraft.

Tokugawa Ieyasu was aware that the peace he had finally attained in a lifetime of military campaigns would not be lasting unless the daimyo and their vassals, brutalized by generations of warfare, could be tamed. He thus took steps to civilize them, by promoting education among their ranks through supporting libraries and subsidizing the publication of books on law and administration and military statecraft.

His design to encourage the education of the upper samurai was made clear in the article placed first in the Buke shohatto (Laws for the military houses) issued to the daimyo in 1615 for their own guidance and the direction of their retainers. This article expressed the principle that the samurai should be prepared equally well in the literary arts (*bun*) and in the military arts (*bu*). *Bun* means not only "writing" or "literature" but, in its fullest sense, means "civilization" and includes the moral teachings that are handed down in texts. If *bu* is the art of war, *bun* is the art of peace. In later revisions of the Buke shohatto, as in 1635, 1663, 1683, and 1710, the principle of *bumbu* was always given primacy.[11]

There was a powerful incentive for the daimyo to acquire the knowledge to govern wisely. On many occasions during the first century of Tokugawa rule, daimyo were transferred to lesser domains or lost their domains entirely as punishment for maladministration, such as taxing farmers unfairly, failing to avert succession quarrels, or causing disharmony within their own houses. The Tokugawa made it clear that the world had changed: Daimyo and *hatamoto* who could not learn to administer benevolently or practice moderation in their expenditures and in the conduct of their personal lives were in jeopardy.

In a nation at peace, ordinary samurai had little opportunity to advance their careers through military prowess. The advantage of an education for gaining appointment to supervisory or administrative work was a strong incentive for study. Both the bakufu and daimyo encouraged education, but rather than establish schools, they were at first more inclined to attract and subsidize scholars under whom their retainers could study. Acquiring an education was a personal matter, undertaken as an act of self-cultivation.[12]

Most bushi children were educated at home by tutors or were taught in small groups by a Buddhist monk or a samurai man or woman. By the end of the seventeenth century, almost all samurai probably had some ability to read and write. Saikaku, writing about 1690, stated: "There is nothing in the world as shameful as being unable to write." He followed this with an anecdote about a samurai with a stipend of

---

11 The laws appear in *Gotōke reijō:* Ishii Ryōsuke, ed. *Kinsei hōsei shiryō sōsho* (Tokyo: Sōbunsha, 1959), vol. 2, pp. 1–11. The Buke shohatto of 1615 is translated in Ryusaku Tsunoda, William Theodore de Bary, and Donald Keene, comps., *Sources of the Japanese Tradition* (New York: Columbia University Press, 1958), pp. 335–38.
12 Tsuda Hideo, "Kyōiku no fukyū to shingaku," in *Iwanami kōza Nihon rekishi*, vol. 12 (*kinsei* 4) (Tokyo: Iwanami shoten, 1976), pp. 149–51. By 1715 only 20 official domain schools (*hankō*) had been established, but there were 215 by the end of the Edo period. Ishikawa Matsutarō, *Hankō to terakoya* (Tokyo: Kyōikusha, 1978), pp. 18–29.

two hundred *koku* who, remarkably, did not know characters: "a retainer who does not fit the times."[13] Bushi who sought more than a basic education continued their studies with a tutor in the domain or sought permission to study under a scholar in Edo or Kyoto.

Readers and copybooks made up of edifying quotations from the Chinese classics and histories were the basic texts used in learning to read. Chinese moral and humanistic ideas were absorbed in the process. These books served well to strengthen the ethics of loyalty to lord, devotion to parents and family, and other Confucian social principles that had long been the premises of conduct among samurai. It was in the interest of shogun and daimyo alike to propagate this value system as a formal code of personal conduct to maintain discipline in an age when feudal relationships were no longer cemented by personal loyalties formed on the battlefield.

The education of a samurai boy was to include the military arts and training to read and write both Chinese and Japanese and to extend as well to other accomplishments expected of a gentleman. A model program of study is set forth in a 1670 work called *Shison kagami* (A mirror for sons and grandsons):

Those born to a bushi family should have lessons in sequence as follows: first, from ages seven or eight, practice in writing the first characters; from eleven, twelve, or thirteen, reading the words of the Four [Confucian] Books, and also learning tea ceremony, deportment, recitation of noh, and playing the noh hand drum; from fourteen to seventeen, defensive fencing [*iai*], swordsmanship, handling the spear, horseriding, archery, musketry, and next falconry and board games [*go*, chess, and backgammon]; and from eighteen or nineteen, military administration, tactics, the composition of Chinese and Japanese poetry, and medicine.[14]

This ideal regime, perhaps designed for sons of upper-class bushi families, included instruction in etiquette and deportment according to the rules handed down by the Ogasawara family since the fifteenth century; these rules prescribed the proper formal postures, ways of greeting, manners at mealtime, and graceful movements in archery, swordsmanship, and other martial arts.

The authorities may at first have seen little purpose in the education of the common people, but they did not discourage it, at least in the cities. It was, of course, necessary to have headmen of villages and city

---

13 *Saikaku nagori no tomo*, in *Teihon Saikaku zenshū* (Tokyo: Chūō kōronsha, 1951), vol. 9, p. 370; cited by Ronald Dore, *Education in Tokugawa Japan* (Berkeley and Los Angeles: University of California Press, 1965), p. 22.
14 Quoted by Munemasa Isoo, *Kinsei Kyōto shuppan bunka no kenkyū* (Kyoto: Dōhōsha, 1982), p. 22.

quarters (*chō*) who could record and transmit the regulations and orders passed down to them and maintain accurate tax and property records. Some writers expressed the view that farmers should not read or engage in any activities that would take time from farm work, but generally the warnings were only against too much learning that might distract from essential tasks. Nishikawa Joken (1648–1724), a bakufu scholar of astronomy, wrote in his *Hyakushō bukuro* (A bag of advice for farmers, 1721): "Even farmers should follow the trend of the times and, as appropriate to their status, learn to write. They should listen to the explanations of learned people so as to rectify their minds."[15]

Although no steps were taken in the seventeenth century to encourage literacy among urban commoners, officials were mindful that reading was useful for encouraging respect for the laws and inculcating ethics. It became common in the middle of the century to post a few basic laws on notice boards mounted on posts (*kōsatsu*) at major crossroads and at the ends of bridges. The practice also arose of prefacing both the annual registers of the village or quarter population (*shūshi nimbetsu chō*) and the oaths of the five-family groups (*gonin gumi*) with at least the text of the basic three-article law forbidding gambling, unlicensed prostitution, and Christianity. The noted Confucian scholar Itō Jinsai (1627–1705), himself the son of a lumber merchant, observed: "It will not do for *chōnin* and farmers not to have learning."[16] Literacy was taken for granted in a book for merchants: "It goes without saying that those of low status should also learn writing and arithmetic and should also learn to read a little."[17]

The impetus to acquire an education came from the urban commoners themselves who wished to prepare their children to engage in business and participate in the social intercourse related to success in a trade. In addition to professional advantages, there was the desire to acquire something of the culture and values of their betters – the bushi and privileged merchants – in the hope of moving upward within *chōnin* society. But the danger of too much education, if it led to an enthusiasm for scholarship or a passion for the dilettantish pursuit of polite accomplishments, was feared by parents in merchant families. Books of advice to merchants and the *ukiyo zōshi* of Saikaku and Ejima Kiseki (1666–1735) provide many cautionary tales of mer-

15 Takimoto Seiichi, ed., *Nihon keizai sōsho* (Tokyo: Nihon keizai sōsho kankōkai, 1914), vol. 5, p. 182.
16 Quoted by Konta Yōzō, *Edo no hon'ya san* (Tokyo: Nihon hōsō shuppan kyōkai, 1977), p. 51.
17 Quoted from *Akindo heijō ki* (1738), in Ishikawa Ken, "Terakoya" entry in *Sekai daihyakka jiten* (Tokyo: Heibonsha, 1966), vol. 15, p. 626.

chants' sons who neglected the family business because of elegant avocations and, in the end, brought financial ruin.

The educating of commoners in the Edo period calls to mind the image of the *terakoya*, the small, one-room schools in the cities and villages. By the end of the Edo period there were more than ten thousand of these institutions. Almost nothing is known about such schools in the seventeenth century, however, and the name *terakoya* has not been found in literature until 1716. Yet there are several book illustrations and paintings that depict schools of this type in the decades before 1700.[18] The teacher was most frequently a commoner, but sometimes a samurai, *rōnin*, monk, doctor, or Shinto priest, who wished to supplement his income by teaching a dozen or more students in his home or in rooms provided by the community. Often commoner and samurai children were taught together. Much of the study time was taken up with learning to write characters and character phrases with a brush, copying over and over the fair copy provided by the teacher. There was also reading aloud and memorization of the maxims in the copybook and, for commoners, instruction in the use of the abacus.[19]

Even at the end of the Edo period, several of the most frequently used school texts were surprisingly ill suited to the needs of either samurai or *chōnin*. The classic was the *Teikin ōrai*, a text that had been used since the early Ashikaga period. It was made up of pairs of letters and answers (*ōrai*), ingeniously working in the vocabulary of various subjects. Unfortunately, some of the words were obsolete and even incomprehensible by the seventeenth century. Nonetheless, this text was printed at least 170 times in the Edo period. Two other works frequently used were the *Jitsugo kyō* and the *Dōji-kyō*, dating from the Heian period and written in Chinese. Their content was largely Confucian in tone – urging the virtues of fidelity, reverence for teacher, and so forth – but with a generous admixture of popular Buddhist thought: the ephemerality of the present life, the horrors of the hells, the possible rewards of paradise, and even the prospects for happiness and wealth in this world.

One of the most frequently used texts was the *Shōbai ōrai* (Merchants' *ōrai*), written in 1693. Abandoning the letter format, it is merely a list of business vocabulary, names of commodities, and techni-

18 Three examples are Sumiyoshi Gukei's handscroll, "Tohi zukan," detail reproduced in Konta, *Edo no hon'ya san*, p. 11; illustration from *Nan chōhōki* (1693) reproduced in Dore, *Education in Tokugawa Japan*, facing p. 267; and Saikaku's *Munesan'yō* (1692), in Noma Kōshin, ed., *Saikaku shu*, pt. 2, vol. 48 of *Nihon koten bungaku taikei* (Tokyo: Iwanami shoten, 1957), p. 299.
19 Dore, *Education in Tokugawa Japan*, pp. 258–9.

cal terms of commerce. Similar ōrai (the term came to mean simply a primer) appeared for farmers, craftsmen, warehousers, carpenters, seamen, booksellers, clothiers, and so on. Yet other ōrai took a geographical theme, describing, for example, a journey along the Tōkaidō from Edo to Kyoto, listing the names of places along the highway, the local products, scenic places, and legends or historical incidents associated with them.[20] In all, some seven thousand books compiled during Edo times have been classified as ōrai in its broad sense.[21]

Many other books appeared in print that, like some of the ōrai, were probably not intended as schoolroom texts but, rather, for use in the home to aid in preparing the young for adult life. Such books had the word chōhōki (record of accumulated treasures) in their title, as in "Gathered things one needs to know for living in the world."[22] Some listed useful words accompanied by an illustration – household utensils, furnishings, items of clothing, proper dress and objects for ceremonial occasions, and the like. Among some twenty chōhōki published in the last decade of the seventeenth century, when they were most in vogue, was the Nan chōhōki (1693), designed to teach boys, especially of the bushi class, what they should know: the qualities of men of noble and daimyo rank, the skills of calligraphy, poetry in Chinese, waka, renga, haikai, tea ceremony, flower arrangement, board games, and model letters to be written when offering condolences and congratulations and when presenting gifts.[23] The author wrote a companion volume for women, the Onna chōhōki (1692). There was also chōhōki designed to instruct the bridal couple. Others provided specialized information on human relations, weapons and equipment of bushi, medicine, geomancy, spell casting, correct language usage, letter writing, Chinese poetry, character learning, and other topics. As these works became more detailed, the word mampō (myriad treasures) was prefixed to the title (Mampō chōhōki, Mampō zensho, and so on), and they served as encyclopedic household reference works.

Another variety of educational book was the illustrated lexicon, such as the Kimmō zui (Illustrations and definitions to train the untutored) of 1666 in fourteen slim fascicles or stitched volumes. Arranged in the topical categories of Chinese and Japanese encyclopedias, it provided for each of its twelve hundred words the readings, a syn-

20 Ibid., pp. 278–83.
21 Ishikawa, "Terakoya," p. 318. Seventeen volumes of ōrai texts appear in Ishikawa Ken, Nihon kyōkasho taikei: ōrai-hen (Tokyo: Kōdansha, 1968–77).
22 Konta, Edo no hon'ya san, p. 38.
23 These works by Namura Jōhaku, once a bushi physician, appear in Kinsei bungaku shiryō ruijū: sankō bunken hen, vols. 17–18 (Tokyo: Benseisha, 1981).

onym or line of definition and, in most instances, a drawing.[24] During the last two decades of the seventeenth century, *kimmō zui* were published also to teach the vocabulary and rudiments of special subjects: military equipment, noh drama, the occupations, and flower arranging; there was even one on sex (*Kōshoku kimmō zui*, 1686) with ample illustrations of practitioners and equipment.

A more substantial dictionary was the *Setsuyō shū*, originally compiled about 1444. It was frequently revised and expanded, and some eight hundred editions were printed between the late sixteenth century and the early Meiji period. A 1680 edition, *Setsuyō taizen*, had thirty thousand words. By 1704 at the latest, publishers added a great deal of prefatory material concerning the geography and history of Japan: maps of the three cities, lists of famous places, a who's who, and a chronology of Japanese history. Next came practical information for daily life: sample letters and legal documents, instruction in etiquette, a calendar of annual events, correct methods of dressing and folding clothes, the proper ways to present food, rules of mourning, and so forth. These elements of a household encyclopedia grew successively until they occupied almost as many pages in a book of nine hundred pages as did the dictionary itself.[25]

Learning to read and write at a *terakoya* or at home was only part of a child's education for life. It was assumed that boys would follow in the family trade. The son of a merchant or craftsman began to learn the trade from about the age of ten by becoming an apprentice (*detchi*), either at home or, more commonly, in another household. If he were apprenticed out, the term was usually ten years. He would live as a member of his master's household with the other apprentices and servants and would receive only his meals and, twice a year, a seasonal change of clothing. His own family was expected to provide pocket money and any other necessities. In the first years the boy would work as a servant, sweeping and cleaning, helping in the kitchen, and running errands, but his education in reading and writing would be continued. This was a hard life for a young boy, but its hardness was training for life: "You should think of the hard time you have as an apprentice as sowing the seeds for getting on later in life – for growing the flowers of success."[26]

24 By Nakamura Tekisai (1629–1702), reproduced in *Kinsei bungaku shiryō ruijū: sankō bunken hen*, vol. 4 (1976).
25 Toshio Yokoyama, "Setsuyōshū and Japanese Civilization," in J-P. Lehmann and Sue Henny, eds., *Themes and Theories in Modern Japanese History* (London: Athlone, 1986).
26 Quoted from *Chōka shikimoku bungen tama no ishizue* by Dore, *Education in Tokugawa Japan*, p. 267.

At about the age of fifteen the apprentice would have his *gembuku* ceremony and advance to semiadult status; his hairstyle would be changed and he would be given a proper name in place of his childhood name. He would be taught the proper words and polite expressions to use and how to handle merchandise and tell good coins from poor. Gradually he would be sent on more responsible errands and would accompany senior clerks on purchasing and bill-collecting trips about the city. At about eighteen such a young man became a clerk (*tedai*). At a ceremony recognizing his adulthood, he received a set of adult clothes, a pipe, and a tobacco pouch. He now became fully involved in the business, dealing with clients and suppliers. Within a few years he faced opportunities to make important decisions, to gain experience, and to test his business judgment. He was expected to stay on for about five years after his term of indenture had ended, as an expression of gratitude for the training he had received. An especially promising clerk might be promoted to *bantō* (manager) and given the responsibility of supervising all the clerks and overseeing the day-to-day operation of the business. A further advancement was sometimes possible: He might be given his own shop as head of a branch family (*bunke*). Should the master lack a male heir, a marriage might be arranged between a daughter of the house and a *bantō* or *tedai* who would be adopted as heir to the business and house.

The system of apprenticing had the advantage for less prosperous families of providing to second sons the opportunity to learn a trade and gain achievement. They would also acquire something of the culture of better families. For richer merchants (and rural landowners also), apprenticeship was a way to make a man of a son who might be spoiled at home. He would be exposed to the realities of life – hard work and discipline, getting along with strangers, the value of money – as well as the experience of learning a business in operation.

There were also opportunities for a daughter to be apprenticed in the household of a wealthy merchant, court noble, daimyo, or upper samurai as a servant or a companion for children. There she could acquire something of the feminine culture of the upper classes and improve her chances of marriage into a bushi or upper *chōnin* house.[27]

Most manuals of advice on raising daughters gave attention to moral guidance, and there were many books devoted solely to this subject.

27 The description of the apprentice system is based on Dore, *Education in Tokugawa Japan*, pp. 266–9; Sakata Yoshio, *Chōnin* (Tokyo: Kōbundō, 1939), pp. 61–6; and Charles David Sheldon, *The Rise of the Merchant Class in Tokugawa Japan, 1600–1868*, Monographs of the Association for Asian Studies, no. 5 (Locust Valley, N.Y.: J. J. Augustin, 1958) pp. 52–3.

Among the best known were *Honchō onna kagami* (1661), a collection of biographies of exemplary women of China and Japan, and *Onna daigaku* (Greater learning for women, 1715). A work called *Onna shisho* (The four books for women, 1656) was an adaptation of four minor Chinese classics. The author, Tsujihara Gempo, in explaining the purpose of his work, wrote that one should not let children read licentious and amorous stories like the *Ise* and *Genji monogatari;* instead they should be taught accounts of the chaste and virtuous women of China.[28]

Whether or not daughters were taught to read and write, all learned the basic skills of making clothes and sewing bedding, cooking and cleaning, taking care of children, and properly greeting and serving guests. The illustrations as well as the text of manuals such as the *Joyō kimmō zui* (1700) and the *Onna chōhōki* (mentioned earlier) taught them the correct names for different articles of clothing, furniture, household utensils, how to wear garments and apply cosmetics, and how to wrap a present and attach the correct knots and presentation message. The latter book went further, giving instruction in developing the proper mental attitude toward life, taking care of one's health, and being attentive to mind and body during pregnancy. Depending on the family's status and ambitions, there were accomplishments that could be learned as preparation for marriage or going into service in a good household, such as flower arranging, tea, painting, calligraphy, composition of *waka* and *haikai* poems, singing and dancing, or playing a musical instrument. Some skills might be learned from accomplished relatives or friends, others from professional teachers.

Some of these arts, and others such as noh singing (*utai*), were often studied by men as well, not only for personal pleasure, but also to acquire performing skills (*gei*) desirable at parties, on such occasions as entertaining prospective clients, attending meetings of guild and fraternal groups, and in social intercourse with restaurant waitresses or prostitutes.

The preceding discussion of education and training in the arts has been concerned with only the elementary stage of instruction for both samurai and commoners. For those proceeding to a more advanced level of proficiency, there were teachers offering private instruction, and in Kyoto, in particular, there were master practitioners. The first good list appears in a guide to Kyoto, the *Kyō habutae* (1685), which

---

28 "Onna shisho" entry in Nihon koten bungaku daijiten henshū iinkai, ed., *Nihon koten bungaku daijiten*, 6 vols. (Tokyo: Iwanami shoten, 1983–5), vol. 1, p. 536c.

lists the names of 241 masters in 47 specialties in the city. Twenty-eight scholars are listed: 6 Confucians, 6 lecturers on Confucian books, 4 lecturers on medical books, 1 in Chinese phonology, 2 in Chinese poetry, 1 in the calendar, 2 in Shinto, 1 in court practices, 2 in mathematics, and 3 in calligraphy. The masters of poetry numbered 5 classical, 3 *renga*, and 12 *haikai*. A list of Kyoto masters compiled by the Tokugawa city administration not later than 1717 mentions 440, of whom 288 were in the arts: 4 *go*, 4 chess, 11 flower arrangement (*rikka*), 3 tea, 5 kickball (*kemari*), 17 painting, 1 cuisine, 4 massage, 116 music (probably mostly blind *biwa* players), 11 noh recitation, 35 noh acting, 15 noh flute, 19 noh small hand drum, 20 noh large hand drum, 7 noh stick drum, and 16 *kyōgen* actors.[29] Some of the masters (especially scholars, physicians, teamen, and noh actors and musicians) received residential land and stipends from court nobles or daimyo. The upper-class *chōnin* were also prominent among the patrons and students of these practitioners. The names of the masters indicate that the greater number were from commoner background. This is confirmed by Nishikawa Joken, writing in 1692, who said that *chōnin* became masters of the arts because prosperity provided them with leisure time: "Since the last hundred years has been an age when the realm is at peace, many of the Confucian scholars, physicians, masters of poetry, and those accomplished in tea and other elegant arts have come from among the *chōnin*."[30]

The teachers who had the most far-reaching influence were the new generation of Confucian scholars who gave instruction in the explication of classical Chinese texts and lectured on their inner meaning. In the past, this knowledge had been the special province of court nobles and Zen monks, but now it became accessible to samurai and commoners as well. The first and most important of the private academies were established by men who studied under Fujiwara Seika (1561–1619), the founder of Edo period Confucianism. Hayashi Razan (Dōshun) (1583–1657) opened a private school in Edo in 1630. (Razan had entered the employ of Ieyasu in 1607 as a scholar and researcher, and the Hayashi house continued as one of bakufu scholars until the end of the Tokugawa period.) Matsunaga Sekigo (1592–1657) and Kan Tokuan (1581–1628) began to teach in Kyoto in the 1620s. Many of

29 *Kyōto no rekishi*, vol. 5, pp. 509–10. *Kyō habutae*, in (*Shinshū*) *Kyōto sōsho* (Kyoto: Rinsen shoten, 1976), vol. 2, pp. 200–4. The official source is *Kyōto oyakusho-muki taigai oboegaki*, a collection of official memoranda and reports, revised to 1717, edited by Iwao Seiichi (Osaka: Seibundō, 1973), vol. 2, pp. 121–44.
30 *Chōnin bukuro* (1692), in *Nihon keizai sōsho*, vol. 5, p. 65; Takeshi Moriya, "*Yūgei* and *Chōnin* Society in the Edo Period," *Acta Asiatica*, no. 33 (1977): 44.

their followers were employed by daimyo as Confucian scholars; others opened their own schools in Kyoto, Edo, and other cities. Among the most distinguished of Sekigo's "five thousand followers" were Kinoshita Jun'an (1621–98), the most influential teacher of his generation, and the commoner Itō Jinsai who, with his son Tōgai (1670–1736), attracted large numbers of students. Yamazaki Ansai (1618–82), who opened a school in Kyoto in 1655, is said to have had six thousand followers.[31] Yamaga Sokō (1622–85) in Edo also taught many students.

The impressive progress among bushi in study of the Chinese classics and in cultural accomplishments from early in the seventeenth century was given by far its greatest official encouragement during the time of Tsunayoshi. He was the most scholarly of the Tokugawa shoguns. He attempted to spread knowledge of the Chinese texts by requiring daimyo and officials to join him in attending lectures of textual exegesis. In fact, he himself delivered hundreds of lectures to captive audiences. These were antic performances, but his intentions were serious. Tsunayoshi even built a large Confucian shrine at Yushima, close to Edo Castle, in 1690, and converted the Hayashi school into the official bakufu school.[32]

Although fewer commoners than samurai pursued advanced studies, their numbers and achievements were significant. The Itōs' academy in Kyoto is said to have had over three thousand students. In Osaka, a group of benefactors founded the Kaitokudō in 1724 as a school of Chinese studies for commoners. It soon received government recognition and continued to prosper until the beginning of the Meiji period.

BOOKS AND PUBLISHING

The spread of knowledge and culture could not have taken place at such a pace without a flourishing publication trade. Before 1590 there was almost no printing except in Buddhist monasteries. Except for some editions of the Confucian classics and collections of Chinese poetry, they printed only Buddhist works, all in very small editions.

31 *Kyoto no rekishi*, vol. 5, pp. 419–37; Robert Rubinger, *Private Academies of Tokugawa Japan* (Princeton, N.J.: Princeton University Press, 1982), pp. 42–56. The remarkable intellectual achievements of these and other Confucian scholars during the seventeenth century are discussed in Chapter 8 in this volume.
32 Donald H. Shively, "Tokugawa Tsunayoshi: The Genroku Shogun," in Albert M. Craig and Donald H. Shively, eds., *Personality in Japanese History* (Berkeley and Los Angeles: University of California Press, 1970), pp. 85–126, esp. pp. 114–17.

Not a single work of the large corpus of Japanese literature had been put in print. But within a century, well over ten thousand books were in print, sold or rented by more than seven hundred bookstores. The availability of books on all subjects, including illustrated and easy-to-read books written mostly in *kana*, was a stimulus to learning to read.

Hideyoshi's military campaign in Korea in 1592 helped bring about the end of the monastic monopoly on printing. The Japanese generals, and the Zen monks who served as their secretaries and interpreters, found collections of beautifully printed, large-format books in the homes of the Korean gentry. Korean libraries were seized as prized booty, and fonts of copper movable type and even presses were brought back to Japan.

Printing private editions in movable type became a pastime at the imperial court and among daimyo. Doctors, scholars, and other educated men in their entourages, fascinated by the novel technology, also began to print the Chinese classics and books on military tactics, statecraft, and medicine. The most dramatic development was the printing of the classics of Japanese literature which had perilously survived for many centuries in manuscript. The first to be printed in movable type from about 1601 were works most desired by the bushi: collections of noh texts and military epics such as the *Taiheiki* and *Heike monogatari*. At last the notion was overcome that Japanese prose, with its flowing *kana* syllabary, could be copied only by brush. The cursive style was laboriously replicated in the most inefficient medium of movable type. In rapid succession the great works of Heian and Kamakura prose came into print, and they appeared in edition after edition – as many as eighteen of some works – as no preferred text had yet been established.

During the first two decades, publication was a cultural activity of the privileged, not unlike the manuscript copying of scribes, for only a few impressions were made for distribution as gifts. Buddhist monasteries were also active in printing in their workshops but soon engaged publishers who began to appear in the city blocks of Kyoto to carry out the work. These shops also printed Chinese texts required by Confucian scholars and their pupils. As publishing became increasingly a commercial enterprise, the more economical method of printing from woodblocks, used in Japan for at least six hundred years, soon replaced movable type. Of the five hundred works known to have been printed between 1593 and 1625, 80 percent were printed by movable type, but movable type accounted for less than 20 percent of the printing occurring during the next quarter-century, and for virtually none after 1650.[33]

Until 1650 the three most numerous categories of books aimed at the serious reader: Chinese classics and commentaries and works on Chinese history, governance, and poetry; Buddhist works, mostly in Chinese; and classical Japanese literature. The number of these editions is remarkable. A fourth category of increasing importance embraced books of instruction, the earliest of which addressed samurai: the seven books of military science, texts of feudal law, the *Azuma kagami* (important for its lessons on Minamoto governance), samurai etiquette according to the Ogasawara school, and aids to the composition of poems in Chinese. Other instructive works were of practical interest to *chōnin* as well: dictionaries, lexicons, *ōrai mono* and other elementary textbooks, books of moral instruction and deportment for women, and illustrated household reference books. In 1670, the same year that *Shison kagami* (A mirror for sons and grandsons) prescribed the ideal regime of instruction for a young samurai, a booksellers' list (*shojaku mokuroku*) noted publications that could serve as texts for cultural studies as well: 27 collections of noh plays, 31 of dance pieces (*mainohon*), 4 on the noh hand drum, 12 on board games, 7 on tea, and 77 on calligraphy and stone rubbings. Among the many works on Chinese poetry, *waka*, and *renga*, there were 133 titles on *haikai* poetry.[34] Many of these books would appeal to *chōnin* families as well.

The next two decades saw the addition of practical books on many other subjects such as the playing of musical instruments, flower arranging, garden design, teahouse architecture, clothing design, the care of birds, cooking, mathemathics, descriptions of scenic and historical places, and travel accounts and guidebooks.

A fifth category of books included popular publications, written mostly in simple language for easy reading, which appeared in large

33 Kawase Kazuma, "Kokatsuji-ban kankō nempyō," in his (*Zōho*) *Kokatsuji-ban no kenkyū* (Tokyo: Antiquarian Booksellers Association of Japan, 1967), vol. 2, appendix. In addition, the following books were consulted on early Edo printing: Konta, *Edo no hon'ya san*, pp. ii, 21–26; Suwa Haruo, *Shuppan koto hajime: Edo no hon* (Tokyo: Mainichi shimbunsha, 1978), pp. 24–39, 49–55, 61–73; Kawase Kazuma, (*Nyūmon kōwa*) *Nihon shuppan bunka shi* (Tokyo: Nihon editā sukūru shuppambu, 1983), pp. 99–155, 178–79, 199–200; Okano Takeo, *Nihon shuppan bunka shi* (Tokyo: Shumpodō, 1959), pp. 3–15; and David Chibbett, *The History of Japanese Printing and Book Illustration* (Tokyo: Kōdansha, 1977), pp. 67–85. The Jesuit Mission Press in Hirado printed over thirty works in roman script using European techniques, beginning in 1591, but there is no evidence of influence on Japanese publishing (Chibbett, *The History of Japanese Printing*, pp. 61–67).

34 Munemasa, *Kinsei Kyōto shuppan*, pp. 23–24. The 1670 list appears in Shidō Bunko, ed., (*Edo jidai*) *Shorin shuppan shoseki mokuroku shūsei* (Tokyo: Inoue shobō, 1962–4), vol. 1, pp. 53–109.

numbers from the middle of the century. Using far more *kana* than Chinese characters, they are known as *kana zōshi*, and they were made up in several slim volumes or fascicles of twenty to thirty leaves each. They were intended to be entertaining reading – romances, miscellanies of unusual tales, stories of the supernatural, humorous anecdotes – but too often the story form was really a device to make the didactic message palatable.[35]

A few *kana zōshi* had begun to appear in the first decades of the Edo period. These were mostly old-fashioned romances, probably written by court nobles or physicians and storytellers attached to military houses. Composed for amusement, some came out in movable-type editions for circulation among friends. They were soon reprinted commercially, but the readers at first may have been mainly from the upper classes. These books included contemporary touches – settings at famous temples of Kyoto, descriptions of the city's sights, and the mention of living persons – and differed from their medieval models in being specific as to time and place. *Urami no suke*, written just after 1612, is a disguised account of a scandal of 1606, an illicit liaison between a *hatamoto* and a lady of the imperial court.[36] The stories came to reflect changes in society as the young gallant was transformed from courtier to samurai, and the beautiful lady of the court was replaced by a prostitute. When the role of the lover was given to a *chōnin*, in *Zeraku monogatari* of about 1658, the *kana zōshi* had become part of the popular culture.[37]

Another type of *kana zōshi* that began to appear just before 1640 had the purpose of presenting in popular form ethical ideas for a new age. Some propagated Confucian morals; others offered Buddhist teachings; and still others argued for a unity of the doctrines. The authors were not of the privileged circle who anonymously wrote the romances but, rather, were men of samurai background who, in most cases, had become Confucian teachers or monks or remained *rōnin*. They wrote for commercial publication, attempting to make their message more

---

35 On *kana zōshi*, see Richard Lane, "The Beginnings of the Modern Japanese Novel: Kana-zōshi, 1600–1682," *Harvard Journal of Asiatic Studies* 20 (1957): 644–701; Donald Keene, *World Within Walls* (New York: Holt, Rinehart and Winston, 1976), pp. 149–66. For texts and discussion, see Maeda Kingorō, in Maeda Kingorō and Morita Takeshi, eds., *Kana zōshi shū*, vol. 90 of *Nihon koten bungaku taikei* (Tokyo: Iwanami shoten, 1965), pp. 3–12; Noma Kōshin, in Ichiko Teiji and Noma Kōshin, eds., *Otogi zōshi. Kana zōshi*, vol. 26 of *Kanshō Nihon koten bungaku* (Tokyo: Kadokawa shoten, 1976), pp. 133–42; Kishi Tokuzō, in Jimbō Kazuya et al., eds., *Kana zōshi shū, ukiyo zōshi shū*, vol. 37 of *Nihon koten bungaku zenshū* (Tokyo: Shōgakkan, 1971), pp. 7–19.

36 Noma, *Otogi zōshi*, pp. 221–7; Maeda, *Kana zōshi shū*, pp. 14–15; Keene, *World Within Walls*, pp. 150–1.

37 Lane, "The Beginnings of the Modern Japanese Novel," pp. 661–4.

attractive by presenting it in literary form: short stories, conversations, or exchanges of letters. The message typically emerged in a dialogue between a knowledgeable person (the author) and his hapless companion. These books had the patronizing air of a man of education introducing the traditions and morality of educated society to a newly literate strata of bushi and commoners.

The *Kiyomizu monogatari* (1638) by Asayama Irin'an (1589–1664), later to become a prominent Confucian teacher, was one of the most widely known of these books. It is said to have sold two or three thousand copies, considered a large number at that time.[38] The *Iguchi monogatari* of 1662 has a double-page illustration, a scene of ten people seated in a parlor looking at *kana zōshi* of this didactic genre, the titles of which are clearly legible: *Kashōki* (1642), *Kanninki* (1659), *Inga monogatari* (1661), and the *Iguchi monogatari* itself. Among the readers we can identify are a monk, samurai, *rōnin*, court lady, and catamite, all but the last of whom are people of a status expected to read traditional literature rather than popular works. But this illustration is more likely promotion by the author than a reliable record of readership.[39]

The most prolific writer of *kana zōshi* was Asai Ryōi (1612?–91). At about the time of his birth, his father was expelled from his position as head of a Jōdo Shinshū temple near Osaka, and the child seems to have grown up under trying circumstances. He did manage to acquire a good education, however, and while supporting himself as a physician and by writing popular books, he harbored the ambition of becoming head of a Shinshū temple, a goal that he achieved in his late years. The twenty or more *kana zōshi* he wrote ranged from books of moral guidance to collections of comic stories, adaptations of Chinese stories of the supernatural (*Otogi bōko*, 1666), and three well-known guidebooks: *Tōkaidō meishoki*, *Edo meishoki*, and *Kyō suzume*.[40] Because these works were written for publication and in part, at least, to make a living, he has been called Japan's first professional writer.[41] In his later years he became head of a Shinshū temple in Kyoto and wrote voluminous commentaries on Buddhist texts as well as popular explanations of Shinshū doctrine.

Ryōi's best-known work, *Ukiyo monogatari* (A tale of the floating

38 According to the *Gion monogatari* (c. 1644), a critique of *Kiyomizu monogatari*. See Tenri toshokan shisho kenkyūbu, ed., *Kana zōshi hen*, vol. 1 of *Kinsei bungaku mikambon sōsho* (Nara: Yōtokusha, 1947), p. 51.
39 Nagatomo Chiyoji, *Kinsei kashihon'ya no kenkyū* (Tokyo: Tōkyōdō, 1982), p. 22. The illustrations appear in a facsimile edition of the text, *Kana zōshi hen*, vol. 33 of *Kinsei bungaku shiryō ruijū* (Tokyo: Benseisha, 1977), pp. 312–13.
40 Noma, *Otogi zōshi*, pp. 271–3.   41 Keene, *World Within Walls*, p. 156.

world), appeared about 1665. The book traces the experiences of a man by the name of Hyōtarō (*hyō* means gourd) as he is carried through life as by a current. His adventures are prefaced by an explanation of the change in meaning of the word *ukiyo*, which in medieval stories had meant the transient world of suffering and misery. In the new meaning of "floating world," the character *uki*, meaning "sad," is replaced by one meaning "floating" or "drifting." The floating world is the up-to-date, fashionable, carefree life of pleasure lived by the new urban sophisticates:

> Living only for the moment, turning our full attention to the pleasures of the moon, the snow, the cherry blossoms and the maples, singing songs, drinking wine, and diverting ourselves just in floating, floating, caring not a whit for the poverty staring us in the face, refusing to be disheartened, like a gourd floating along with the river current: This is what we call *ukiyo*.[42]

Hyōtarō's father, who abandoned the samurai profession out of desire to make a fortune as a merchant, and his son, who carelessly squandered the wealth he inherited, exemplify the new age. The young rake dresses extravagantly in the latest style and devotes himself completely to the pleasures of the Shimabara prostitutes' quarter in Kyoto. His family and friends try to save him from his excesses, lecturing him on the fate of financial ruin and recourse to crime that awaits him. The author, in this first expression of the hedonistic abandon of the floating world and the odyssey of the rake, appears to anticipate by two decades the first of the *ukiyo zōshi*, Saikaku's *The Man Who Spent His Life in Love*. But from this suggestive beginning Ryōi turns to a heavy-handed detailing of the selfishness and greed in society that extends from daimyo to merchant. His moralizing overwhelms the plausibility of his main character.[43]

Whatever the limitations of *kana zōshi* as literature, these books were a vital stage in the transition from medieval to early modern society. Books for the first time were written for publication. The books were popular, and they sold immediately to waiting readers. Although only 54 are known to have been printed by 1655, 178 appeared in the next eighteen years.[44] They differed from the received literature, which described an aristocratic society of a different age or

---

42 Adapted from Lane, "The Beginnings of the Modern Japanese Novel," pp. 671–2.
43 Keene, *World Within Walls*, pp. 156–60; Lane, "The Beginnings of the Modern Japanese Novel," pp. 671–5; Maeda, *Kana zōshi shū*, pp. 18–19, text pp. 241–354; Taniwaki Masachika, in Jimbō et al., eds., *Kana zōshi shu*, pp. 28–33.
44 Akai Tatsurō, "Genroku ki no toshi seikatsu to minshū bunka," *Iwanami kōza Nihon rekishi*, vol. 10 (*kinsei* 2) (Tokyo: Iwanami shoten, 1975), p. 334.

stories underlain by Buddhist concerns for the next world and the intercession of deities in human affairs. Writing for a contemporary audience changed the focus to the this-worldly, to the conveying of information that was of interest to those living in contemporary society. With the additional step to Saikaku's stories and Chikamatsu's plays, literature began to acquire the realism of everyday life.

By 1659 the publication and sale of books had so expanded that Kyoto dealers began to publish, for the benefit of booksellers, lists of works currently available. Starting with 1,600 titles in twenty-two subject categories, the classifications expanded to seventy-two as more and more different kinds of books were published. The fourteenth of these lists, published in Edo in 1696 (*Zōeki shojaku shomoku daizen*), ran to 674 pages and listed author, number of volumes, publisher, and price for its 7,800 titles.[45] Yet this was far from a complete list of current books, because not all publishers were included and because most scripts of the puppet and kabuki theater, *haikai* poetry, picture books (*ukiyo ehon*), *kusa zōshi*, and a number of other types of light books were excluded. Books published privately also were not included: publications of the bakufu, daimyo, temples, and other nontrade books.

Publishing houses, like other craftsmen's workshops, were family concerns. Members of the family and a few apprentices directed the entire process: They had a calligrapher write out the manuscript in an elegant hand, commissioned illustrations, had an engraver cut the woodblocks, and then printed the pages and sewed the bindings. The same shop handled retail as well as wholesale marketing. From the 1660s, most books included colophons bearing the date of the woodblocks, the name and address of the publisher, and, in later decades, the names of participating publishers or distributors in other cities. By about 1720 there were 200 publishers in Kyoto who were members of the publishers' association, 47 in Edo, and 24 in Osaka. For the entire Edo period, 3,753 publishers have been identified.[46] Some concerns continued in business for as long as two hundred years, but keen competition drove others out after a short time. The publishers in each of the three cities organized themselves into trade associations (*nakama* or *ton'ya*) in an attempt to protect exclusive claims to books they

45 Konta, *Edo no hon'ya san*, p. 12; Munemasa, *Kinsei Kyōto*, p. 32; Suwa, *Shuppan koto hajime*, pp. 116–18, 189–94. Fifteen of the twenty-three lists are reproduced and indexed in (*Edo jidai*) *Shorin shuppan shoseki mokuroku shūsei*, 4 vols.
46 Konta, *Edo no hon'ya san*, pp. 75–7; Suwa, *Shuppan koto hajime*, pp. 51–2. Sakamoto Muneko added 2,613 publishers to Inoue Kazuo's list of 1,140, compiled in 1916, in reprinting his book as (*Zōtei*) *Keichō irai shoko shūran* (Osaka: Takao shoten, 1972).

had already published and to deter newcomers from entering the trade. Although these associations, like most other trade groups, were illegal at this time, they gained recognition between 1716 and 1723 as the authorities realized their usefulness in policing the trade and enforcing censorship.[47]

Most bookstores, whether or not they published books, were known to favor certain types of publication: imported Chinese editions, Buddhist books, literature, poetry, noh texts, old books, light popular *zōshi* or picture books, maps, and so forth.[48] Many also rented out books, extending greatly the number of readers who could enjoy books at a quarter or a third of the retail price. Peddlers went about the streets and into the countryside with book frames on their backs piled high with books for sale or rent.[49]

Who were the commoners who bought books, and what kind did they buy? Little evidence has been found for the city residents of this period, but there are data of great interest concerning three families in villages in the prosperous hinterland of Kawachi Province, about fifteen kilometers east of Osaka. We have the surviving library of the merchant Sugiyama of Tondabayashi, with books dating from the 1660s on; a book inventory of the fertilizer dealer Sanda of Kashihara, compiled about 1730, listing the 803 volumes acquired in the previous two generations; and the diary of Mori Chōzaemon, headman of Kusaka village, recording books he bought, rented from, or sold to four energetic book peddlers from Osaka who visited him every month or two from 1727 to 1729. *The Great Learning* and several other Confucian classics were found in these households, as well as Buddhist texts, early Japanese prose and poetry, noh texts, and many educational and practical books: advice for merchants, textbooks for school or home instruction, guides for women, and household reference works such as the *chōhōki*. Because two of Saikaku's collections of stories about merchants also were found, we know that these rural families read of the pleasures and travails of Kyoto and Osaka businessmen. Sugiyama was an enthusiastic performer of noh plays. Sanda Jōkyū is mentioned by Saikaku as a *haikai* poet; in 1679 he compiled and published in a fine edition an illustrated guide to notable places of Kawachi Province (*Kawachi kagami meishoki*) and in the appendix listed the names and addresses of 260 associates who contributed poems to the book. Mori,

47 Konta, *Edo no hon'ya san*, pp. 75–7, 80.
48 Nagatomo, *Kinsei kashihon'ya no kenkyū*, pp. 4–11.
49 Ibid., pp. 6, 19–22, 26–33, 61–2; illustrations of book peddlers, pp. 25–31, 247–8; Suwa, *Shuppan koto hajime*, pp. 213–20.

the village headman, recorded that he stayed at home all one day to read a book he had rented, *Naniwa gunki*, probably an account of the Tokugawa's attack on Osaka Castle. Among Mori's purchases was the *Wakan sansai zue*, a Sino-Japanese encyclopedia in eighty-one volumes, compiled by an Osaka physician in 1712.[50]

KYOTO THE SOURCE

Kyoto continued as the center of learning and culture during the seventeenth century. It was also the model of what a city should be, as for many centuries the imperial capital had remained the only real city in the country. In early Tokugawa times, Kyoto came to be thought of as a place to be enjoyed, rich in attractions and entertainments, not for the elite alone, but for residents and visitors of all classes.

Kyoto enjoyed a virtual monopoly on places and sights with cherished historical or literary associations. These were celebrated in large painted screens of the cityscape – with its palaces, Buddhist temples, and Shinto shrines – that were made for daimyo to carry off to their castles in locales far from the capital. Also depicted in the screens were places of scenic beauty around the city, popular for excursions and picnics and dance performance under flowering cherry trees or autumn maples. The screens provided a continuous narrative of the pleasures of the capital that the viewer could tour vicariously. The panoramic design and the conventions used in the pairs of screens called *rakuchū rakugai zu* (pictures of the capital and its environs) were already fully evolved in the Machida pair of the 1520s, the earliest of these works to survive. A magnificent pair by Kanō Eitoku was sent by Nobunaga as a gift to Uesugi Kenshin in 1573; the names of 223 of the buildings and scenic places that appear on the screens are identified by inscriptions.[51]

So great was the appeal of the capital that some sixteenth-century daimyo reproduced in their provincial castle towns certain distinctive features of Kyoto: streets laid out in a grid, shrines with the name Gion, or temple buildings duplicating Kyoto models, such as Kiyomizu-dera.

50 Konta, *Edo no hon'ya san*, pp. 41–48; Nagatomo, *Kinsei kashihon'ya no kenkyū*, pp. 21, 78–101; Noma Kōshin, "Ukiyo zōshi no dokusha sō," *Bungaku* 26 (1958): 66–7.

51 The screens are illustrated and discussed in Ishida Hisatoyo, Naitō Akira, and Moriya Katsuhisa, comps., *Rakuchū rakugai zu taikan*, 3 vols. (Tokyo: Shōgakukan, 1987), vols. 1, 2; *Fūzoku ga: Rakuchū rakugai*, vol. 11 of *Nihon byōbu-e shūsei* (Tokyo: Kōdansha, 1977–80); Kyōto kokuritsu hakubutsukan, comp., *Rakuchū rakugai zu* (Tokyo: Kadokawa shoten, 1966).

Some named the hills outside their castle towns Higashiyama or Hiei and Atago; some likened their rivers to the Kamo and Oi. Yamaguchi, Hida Takayama, and Tosa Nakamura are among the Sengoku cities now referred to as "Little Kyoto" (Shō-Kyōto) because such traces can still be found.[52]

Kyoto had undergone extensive changes in the last years of the sixteenth century. For example, Hideyoshi ordered more than a hundred temples removed to temple "zones" along Teramachi, Teranouchi, and Shimo Teramachi. He rebuilt the imperial palace, razed blocks in the commoner district to create a new palace compound for the retired emperor, and constructed the Daibutsu-den of Hōkōji to house a colossal statue of the Buddha. He also built an earthen wall around the city, the *odoi,* the only city wall to be completed in Kyoto's history, which defined the boundary between city and country. The growth of the city and its prosperity began again during Hideyoshi's years and continued unabated under the Tokugawa. Ieyasu had Nijō Castle constructed and required many daimyo to establish residences nearby. Visitors came in increasing numbers for commerce, pilgrimage, and tourism once the coming of peace made travel safe.

Detailed information about this larger and more complex city became available for the first time when maps and guidebooks were published for the convenience of both residents and visitors. But even earlier, *kana zōshi* had begun to enumerate the pleasures of life in the capital.

Inu makura (c. 1606) was one of the earliest books by a contemporary author to be printed. In imitation of Sei Shōnagon's catalogs in her *Pillow Book,* to which the title refers, the author makes ninety-odd lists. Starting with contrasting categories of likes and dislikes, he notes under "Things one likes to do": "(possessing) stylish articles fashionable today," "constructing a teahouse," and "outings and seeing sights." Under "Things one likes to see," he lists "skillful noh," "articles for a teahouse," and "famous sights, famous sights" (*meisho, meisho*). On the other hand, under "Things one hates to do," he includes "going with one's master on outings and to see sights." "Things that make one rejoice" includes "finding a great bargain in an [antique] shop."[53] Such boons of life in the capital are those depicted in the screen paintings: sightseeing, watching performances of noh, and shopping.

52 *Kyōto no rekishi,* vol. 3, pp. 663–73.
53 *Kyōto no rekishi,* vol. 5, p. 289; Moriya Takeshi, *Kyō no chōnin* (Tokyo: Kyōikusha, 1980), pp. 19–20. The text appears in Maeda and Morita, eds., *Kana zōshi shū,* p. 35.

Famous sights in the capital are also mentioned in early *kana* romances, even when they have no relevance to the story. In *Urami no Suke* there is a long passage describing the lacquer design on the sound box of an "up-to-date samisen" which depicts some thirty-seven sights of the capital and Osaka, each one lovingly listed.[54] In a comic travel account (*Chikusai monogatari,* printed in the early 1620s), the quack doctor Chikusai, before setting off for the provinces, first makes a tour of ten or more of Kyoto's most famous places, composing poems at each. Near Kitano Shrine he comes upon a series of scenes largely unique to the capital: Chikusai glimpses an elegant court lady in her carriage (which reminds Chikusai of the *Tale of Genji*), and then he sees a *renga*-composing party, young samurai playing kickball, prostitutes playing the samisen and fiddle, actors performing noh plays, men gambling at backgammon, an incense-judging party, sumo wrestling, and a bevy of ladies-in-waiting from the palace having a drinking party. These scenes too are like the subjects of the *rakuchū rakugai* screens. Chikusai also witnesses a self-indulgent abbot attempting to seduce the ladies from the court, and his description of the abbot's costume becomes a catalog of shops: "His sash is from Mukade-ya on Nijō, famous through the realm," his cap from Karamono-ya Jinkichi on Sanjō, his rosary from Ebi-ya at Shijō and Teramachi, and his fan from the capital's Tawara-ya. The last named is the house of the painter Sōtatsu.[55]

The first of the proper guidebooks to Kyoto was the *Kyō warabe* (The Kyoto youth), written in 1658 by a physician, Nakagawa Kiun. The account starts with the palace and proceeds to shrines, temples, famous sights, and historical remains, in all 88 places in the capital and its environs. This guide describes the places to which Kyoto people flocked – the temples and shrines they visited in the appropriate season, the new pleasure quarters at Shimabara, the riverbank at Shijō and its kabuki theaters, and the Kamo Shrine where horses were raced. Each place is illustrated with a drawing and capped with a poem.[56] Another much larger work written the same year (*Rakuyō meisho shū*) lists 307 famous places to see in and about the capital. Following the example of Kyoto, a guidebook to Edo, Asai Ryōi's *Edo meisho ki,* was published in Kyoto in 1662. A guide to Osaka followed

54 Moriya, *Kyō no chōnin,* pp. 20–21; text in Maeda and Morita, eds., *Kana zōshi shū,* pp. 55, 481–3.
55 Moriya, *Kyō no chōnin,* p. 21; *Kyōto no rekishi,* vol. 4, pp. 647–8, vol. 5, pp. 290–1; Maeda and Morita, eds. *Kana zōshi shū,* pp. 89–159, esp. pp. 94–101. There is a partial translation by Edward Putzar, "Chikusai monogatari," *Monumenta Nipponica* 16 (1960–1): 161–95.
56 (*Shinshū*) *Kyōto sōsho,* vol. 1, pp. 1–88.

in 1675. Most of the guidebooks appearing in the next decade or two, like those just mentioned, are sprinkled with poems, anecdotes, and historical asides, with attempts at literary flourishes. Others, more substantial and scholarly, appeared shortly: The *Yōshū fushi* (1686), for example, was written in Chinese and modeled on Chinese gazetteers that provide information on topography, local products, and customs of the area. Another contemporary guide records 1,138 temples and 105 shrines in the city and its environs.[57]

One genre of guidebook, the *machi kagami* (mirror of the quarters), concerned itself with explanations of the city streets and the kinds of shops and artisans that could be found on each of them. The preface to *Kyō suzume* (Kyoto chatterbox, 1665) announces that the work will canvas the entire city from Ichijō to Kujō, from Suzaku to Higashi Kyōgoku. The account covers the history and enterprises of each street and the trades assembled there; it includes illustrations of streets and shop fronts, indicating where one can buy dry goods, paper, fans, toys, lumber, tombstones, and so forth. A sequel, *Kyō suzume atooi* (1678), provides an even more detailed guide to the establishments of craftsmen and merchants. The trades are first listed in alphabetical (*i-ro-ha*) order, followed by addresses. A second list classifies enterprises into ninety trades, and a supplement lists the trades in yet a third fashion, by address, *chō* by *chō*.[58] A pocket version of a shopping guide, *Kyō hitori annai tebiki shū* (The self-directed guide to Kyoto, 1694), lists the clothiers of Kyoto under the name of the daimyo who patronized them.[59] Although these guides to shops were certainly valuable to buyers and wholesalers who came to the city, they also served the window shoppers who browsed not merely to buy essentials but also to seek amusement.

That Kyoto's shops deserved their fame is corroborated by the German physician Engelbert Kaempfer, who visited the city (which he refers to as Miaco [capital]) in 1691. To quote from the 1727 English translation of his account:

Miaco is the great magazine of all Japanese manufactures and commodities, and the chief mercantile town in the Empire. There is scarce a house in this large capital, where there is not something made or sold. Here they refine copper, coin money, print books, weave the richest stuffs with gold and silver

57 Kojima Tokuemon's *Kyō habutae*, in (*Shinshū*) *Kyōto sōsho*, vol. 2, pp. 93–154. The government compilation gives 1,430 temples and 138 shrines in 1715 (*Kyōto oyakusho-muke taigai oboegaki*). *Kyōto no rekishi*, vol. 5, p. 509.

58 *Kyōto no rekishi*, vol. 5, pp. 291–2; Moriya, *Kyō no chōnin*, pp. 23–5; (*Shinshū*) *Kyōto sōsho*, vol. 1, pp. 173–270, 271–386.

59 (*Shinshū*) *Kyōto sōsho*, vol. 3, pp. 1–50.

flowers. The best and scarcest dies, the most artful carvings, all sorts of musical Instruments, pictures, japan'd cabinets, all sorts of things wrought in gold and other metals, particularly in steel, as the best temper'd blades, and other arms are made here in the utmost perfection, as are also the richest dresses, and after the best fashion, all sorts of toys, puppets, moving their heads of themselves, and numberless other things, too many to be mention'd. In short, there is nothing that can be thought of, but what may be found at Miaco. . . . There are but few houses in all the chief streets, where there is not something to be sold, and for my part, I could not help admiring, whence they can have customers enough for such an immense quantity of goods.[60]

The pleasure of finding a bargain in a stall or even coming upon a treasure (already mentioned in the *Inu makura*), is described in the diary of the priest Hōrin of Rokuonji. Strolling one day in 1638 at Kitano, not far from his temple, he came upon an antique dealer from whom he bought an Iga vase, an old Seto tea caddy, and a Korean jar. He then stopped at the home of a physician friend, and they called in a dealer who lived in that quarter to appraise his wares as well. Hōrin went on to make purchases from this dealer and from yet another whose shop he visited in the Juraku district. He concluded in his diary: "I passed judgment on the pieces. Did I not find great bargains?"[61]

The addition of many new streets and the continuing changes in street names created a demand for maps and street guides. Publishers began to print sheet maps of Kyoto from woodblocks from about 1624. The earliest surviving of these maps are confined to the grid of the city proper, but they bear the name of every street and *chō*.[62] Around 1641, maps began to show the Buddhist temples and Shinto shrines around the periphery of the grid. They are shown pictorially, as they were added for the benefit of tourists and pilgrims. By 1654, publication commenced of large, attractive maps with three colors applied by hand. These included more and more information useful to both tradesmen and visitors. In addition to the names of streets, now listed in a table keyed to the streets, there were also tables identifying the residences of 119 court nobles and the incomes of each. The residences of bakufu officials, their names and incomes,

60 Engelbert Kaempfer, *The History of Japan, Together with a Description of the Kingdom of Siam 1690–92* (Glasgow: James MacLehose, 1906), vol. 2, pp. 3, 21–2.
61 *Kyōto no rekishi*, vol. 5, p. 278; Moriya, *Kyō no chōnin*, pp. 26–7.
62 "Heian-jō machinami zu" (116.7 × 55.6 cm), before 1641, described and illustrated in Yamori Kazuhiko, *Toshizu no rekishi: Nihon hen* (Tokyo: Kōdansha, 1974), pp. 129–30 (fig. 37), p. 147; also in Nakamura Hiroshi, ed., *Nihon kochizu taisei* (Tokyo: Kōdansha, 1974), p. 166 (fig. 80). A similar map, probably earlier, appears in Kyōto-shi, comp., *Kyōto-shi shi: Chizu hen* (Kyoto: Kyōto shiyakusho, 1947), p. 47 (fig. 14).

and the location of daimyo mansions appeared as well. Temples, shrines, and palaces came to be boldly marked and color coded. The word *rakugai* added to the title informs us that famous temples and historical sites in the environs of the capital have been crowded into the margins.[63]

A new generation of large, five-colored maps began in 1686. In these maps, Hideyoshi's Great Buddha was clearly the prime tourist attraction: The dimensions of all of its parts and other trivia were also listed in map tables.[64] Tourists could find, too, in the northeast corner of some of the maps, a description and history of Enryakuji on Mt. Hiei. Additional lists and tables accounted for the major Buddhist sects, and the number of their branch temples and landholdings, the names of the entrances to the city, the distances to other towns and cities in the vicinity, the length and width of major bridges, and so forth. In fact, maps of Kyoto became a type of guidebook. In the eagerness to include factual information, the effectiveness of the map was somewhat compromised: The tables obscure, for example, streets and roads on the west side of the southern suburb of Fushimi. When drawing roads outside the grid, any notion of scale was abandoned in favor of including the outlying sights of Mt. Hiei, Uji, and Yodo within the corners of the map. Indeed, the attention to illustration and artistry was so keen that publishers employed recognized artists to embellish their maps and, so, to tempt buyers. Like the multivolume guidebooks, the large, attractive maps had lasting appeal as precious souvenirs of the capital and entertainment for the vicarious traveler. Several Kyoto publishers reissued their maps every few years, recarving sections of the woodblocks to update information. Evidently there were map collectors, for one shop advertised a supply of old maps for antiquarians.[65]

As some of the tables on maps suggest, interest in Kyoto's notable people was as intense as interest in Kyoto's notable places. Thus it is not surprising that a guidebook called *Kyō habutae* (Warp and woof of Kyoto, 1685) devotes its last two fascicles to a who's who of the city's important residents. Under the name of each imperial prince and court noble we find his rank, crest, annual income, address, age, and the names of his main retainers. Following a similar catalog of daimyo, this guide lists the bakufu officials stationed in Kyoto. In addition, to

---

63 "Shimpan Heian-jō tōzai namboku machinami rakugai no zu" (134.9 × 87.0 cm), published by Muan (1654), in Yamori, *Toshi zu no rekishi*, pp. 141–5. A 1662 revision is reproduced in *Kyōto-shi shi: Chizu hen*, pp. 52–3 (fig. 18).
64 "Shinsen zōho Kyō ōezu" (165.2 × 124.8 cm), 1686, in Yamori, *Toshi zu no rekishi*, p. 144 (fig. 47), p.146. Reproduced in *Kyōto-shi shi: Chizu hen*, pp. 54–55 (fig. 19).
65 Yamori, *Toshi zu no rekishi*, p. 148.

the catalog of 241 master-teachers described earlier, there is also a list of leading artisans and dealers.[66]

Information concerning the names and addresses of bushi resident in Edo was of particular importance to the tradesmen of that city, and as early as 1647 and 1651, registers of *buke* (warrior) houses, called *bukan* ("mirror of the *buke*"), were privately compiled and printed by book dealers. The daimyo *bukan* list name, domain, assessed yield in *koku*, court rank, name of heir, dates of arrival and departure for *sankin kōtai*, crest, design of pikes and standards used in processions, locations of the daimyo's several residences in Edo, and other information. In later times annual revisions were published. There were also *bukan* of bakufu officials and of *hatamoto* (bannermen).

A characteristic of Japanese culture that has found expression in literature and painting since Heian times is an awareness of changing seasons and a desire to engage in activities appropriate to the phase of the calendar. Hence guidebooks included information on which places were best visited, and when. Screen paintings had earlier represented Kyoto places in their best seasons: Higashiyama and its cherry trees in spring, the Kamo River bank with its cool breezes in the evenings of summer, Arashiyama to the west with its maples in the fall, Inari on the south for the fire festival in winter. In the same way that poems since the *Kokinshū* (the first imperial anthology of 905) had associated celebrated sights around the capital with a season, Edo paintings and popular songs made seasonal references to Kyoto places.

Published handbooks, such as the *Annaisha* (1662), which were exclusively guides to the calendar for the Kyoto resident, recorded events through the year (*nenjū gyōji*) that were observed in the capital. Among the more detailed was the *Hinami kiji* (1685) which listed events day by day under seven categories: observances in the imperial household, celebrations at Shinto shrines, official ceremonies, practices of the common people, memorial anniversaries, the showing of hidden treasures by temples and shrines, and Buddhist services. Of the 3,100 events recorded in this work, over half are still observed in Kyoto today. If the guides described earlier dealt with city space, these charted city time – the rhythm of urban life.[67] It is evident from popular stories as well as guides to the calendar that visiting temples and shrines on days of festivals or other special events was a favorite form of entertainment. Temples drew crowds by announcing the days on

66 (*Shinshū*) *Kyōto sōsho*, vol. 2, pp. 155–238; *Kyōto no rekishi*, vol. 5, pp. 508–10.
67 Akai, "Genroku ki no toshi seikatsu to minshū bunka," pp. 335–6; Moriya, *Kyō no chōnin*, pp. 30–1; *Kyōto no rekishi*, vol. 5, pp. 293–6.

which their most sacred treasures would be shown. Called *kaichō*, or opening the curtain, it involved unveiling a secret statue or painting of the principal deity or founder of the temple or some other treasure. For temples lacking scenic locations or impressive buildings and grounds, the *kaichō* was a rare opportunity to attract visitors. As the practice became popular in the seventeenth century, temples from all over Japan sent their treasures to Kyoto where large numbers of people would see them and make offerings. In later times, when Edo had become the crossroads of the country, that city became the center for *de-kaichō*.

Another entrepreneurial activity favored by temples was the designation of touring routes through the city that would lead the pilgrim to the fifteen places where Hachiman was worshiped, or to the twenty-nine places were Benzaiten was worshiped, or to the thirty-three Kannon, the thirty-six Jizō on Teramachi, the forty-eight Honganji, and so on and so on. Five such tours are described in *Kyō habutae* (1685). Among the eighteen tours in *Miyako suzume annaisha* (1708), one passed eighteen temples that were associated with Gansan Daishi (the Tendai monk, Ryōgen 911–85).[68] The route, described as covering three *ri* (twelve kilometers), proceeded south along Higashiyama, passed the Gion entertainment quarter, crossed west through the Shijō and Sanjō commercial districts, and north to Sembon Imadegawa, and ended near the Kitano Shrine and its amusement quarter. If the showing of secret icons and the prescribing of tour routes by the temples – abetted no doubt by shopkeepers among their parishioners – was inspired not solely by the religious mission of the Buddhist institutions but also by their financial needs, the appeal to laymen might also have been more than pilgrimage: Such excursions were group social outings that combined pious acts with sightseeing and visiting shops and might conclude with a picnic or a visit to a teahouse of whatever variety.

Shinto festivals played a larger role in the life of the community than such Buddhist pilgrimages. In particular, the Gion *matsuri* (festival) of the main business district, which continued for more than two weeks of celebrations during the summer, was one of the most enjoyable occasions of the year. Its parade of colorful floats, famous throughout the country, drew crowds of visitors to the city.

The glory of Kyoto in the seventeenth century is most ideally depicted in paintings, beginning with the Funaki *rakuchū rakugai zu*

68 Moriya, *Kyō no chōnin*, pp. 31–4; *Kyōto no rekishi*, vol. 5, pp. 297–8.

screens of the 1620s and followed by handscrolls by Sumiyoshi Gukei (1631–1705) and other artists in the last decades of the century. The Funaki screens show the city of the new guidebooks.[69] Between the Toyotomi's Daibutsuden on the right (southeast) and the Tokugawa's Nijō Castle on the extreme left (northwest), we see dramatic performances in progress at two noh, two kabuki, and two puppet theaters. The Misuji-machi prostitute quarter appears prominently, and the Gion festival procession passes through the streets. The entrance curtains (*noren*) and merchandise of dozens of stores and craftsmen's shops are shown in detail. The scroll and screen paintings seem to bring together all of the delights and beauties of the bustling city that set it a world apart from the countryside. On a single surface painted in clear colors, the city opens before us – palace and castle, temples and shrines, hills and gardens in foliage and flower of the four seasons, theaters and houses of pleasure, and festivals in progress. All the buildings are represented in perfect repair; the streets are clean; the shops tidy; the people beautifully dressed in bright colors. They pass through the streets as in a costume parade. There is no end to the interesting things to see and do. Kyoto appears to be a paradise.

The most sensational attractions of the three great cities were the entertainment districts – the brothel quarter and the theaters. Kyoto guidebooks gave them as much attention as they did the imperial palace and Kiyomizu temple. There were also specialized manuals published as early as the 1650s as guides to these districts. The bakufu, while deploring as necessary evils the brothels and theaters, the "two wheels of the vehicle of pleasure," nevertheless recognized their importance in making the cities under its control lively places that would attract and accommodate commerce. It adopted a policy of concentrating the prostitutes and actors in separate quarters where each group could be better supervised and contact between these semioutcasts and the rest of society controlled. These enclaves were frequently referred to as the two "bad places" (*akusho*).

The traveler on a first visit to the great city would not want to return home without at least venturing into the streets of these specially licensed quarters, in the hopes of having a glimpse of one of their stars. The names of the great beauties of the pleasure quarter were known throughout the city, and the leading actors were lionized. Prostitute and actor were the main subject of *ukiyo* prints and picture books, and

---

69 The Funaki screen is illustrated in *Rakuchū rakugai zu taikan*, vol. 3; and in the other works mentioned in footnote 51.

details of their lives were publicized outrageously. To the end of the Edo period, the life of the brothel quarter, especially, was an absorbing subject in the *ukiyo zōshi* and later literary genres such as *sharebon* and *gōkan*. It was a rare kabuki or puppet play that did not locate a scene in a brothel. The two pleasure quarters were the source of up-to-date fashions, music, song, and other elements of popular culture that spread throughout urban society. Both quarters became centers of social life, not simply for personal places of recreation, but also for wining, dining, and entertaining customers.[70]

THE SOCIETY OF PROSTITUTES

In 1589 Hideyoshi had the brothels in the city of Kyoto brought together in one licensed quarter known as Nijō Yanagi-machi, in the eastern part of the strip of land that still remained deserted between the upper and lower city.[71] In 1602, when the Tokugawa built Nijō Castle, they moved the brothels away to a quarter known as Rokujō Misuji-machi and in 1640 transferred them for the last time to an even more remote location, the fields in the extreme southwest corner of the city wall, beyond the great compounds of Buddhist temples. This quarter, which came to be called the Shimabara, measured 200 by 240 meters and was surrounded by an earthen wall and a moat 3 meters wide. The single entrance, a guarded gate on the east side, made it possible to keep under surveillance those entering the quarter – fugitives who might seek refuge there and *rōnin* and other troublemakers. It also prevented prostitutes from leaving to ply their trade outside the quarter.[72]

A similar policy was followed in Edo. In 1617 the various brothels were brought together to form the Yoshiwara quarter on reclaimed land a short distance east of Nihombashi. But the business district developed around the quarter, and Edo Castle itself was not far away. When the Meireki fire of 1657 destroyed this part of the city, the bakufu seized the opportunity to move the houses to a location given the name Shin Yoshiwara, outside the city in the open fields beyond

---

70 Donald H. Shively, "The Social Environment of Tokugawa Kabuki," in James R. Brandon, William P. Malm, and Donald H. Shively, eds., *Studies in Kabuki: Its Acting, Music, and Historical Context* (Honolulu: University of Hawaii Press, 1978), pp. 1–61, esp. pp. 50–4.

71 Hideyoshi established a licensed quarter in Osaka in 1585 at the time when he was constructing Osaka Castle. This is believed to be the first instance of a segregated, licensed quarter. Ono Takeo, *Yoshiwara, Shimabara* (Tokyo: Kyōikusha, 1978), p. 32. However, there was licensing of prostitutes from at least the late twelfth century.

72 *Kyōto no rekishi*, vol. 4, pp. 590–2, vol. 5, pp. 167–72.

Asakusa Temple, a distance of six kilometers from the center of Edo. A walled enclave like the Shimabara was constructed, with the bakufu contributing generously to help finance the relocation.[73] In Osaka, too, the authorities began in 1631 to bring brothels together to form the Shimmachi quarter on swampy land on the western edge of the city.

The licensing of these quarters followed a common pattern. Hideyoshi issued the Kyoto license to two former samurai who organized and administered the quarter. Decades later, the Tokugawa contracted with individuals of samurai background when the Edo and Osaka quarters were established. They received extensive authority to administer the quarters and keep order. Because the clientele in the early decades of the Edo period was predominantly bushi of all ranks, it was essential to take a firm hand to prevent outbreaks of violence among the pleasure seekers. The cavorting of samurai, foot soldiers, monks, and *chōnin* in the streets and houses of the Misuji-machi quarter is clearly recorded in the Funaki screens.[74]

Although the quarter offered women of a wide range of rank and price to all comers, it was the presence of a few celebrated beauties of wit and cultural accomplishments who created the mystique of the courtesan. A small number of the highest rank were known as *tayū*, a title (originally meaning "great minister") used by noh actors, but also assumed by the kabuki actors and actresses who performed the leading roles on the Shijō stages. Some were proficient in dancing, singing, or playing musical instruments, of course, and also in classical poetry, *haikai*, tea, and other arts. They dressed in magnificent robes and were sought by daimyo, upper bushi, and court nobles who summoned them to their residences and, in a few instances, even bought them from their proprietors. *Tayū* were, in fact, known as daimyo *dōgu*, or daimyo's articles, as though they were tea bowls or other treasured objects collected by the great lords.[75] Some participated in the social life of the elite, according to an early record of the Yoshiwara, which says: "During the Keichō and Genna eras [1596–1624], men of the most distinguished families invited intimates, telling them that a certain *tayū*, engaged for several days, would make tea at a certain person's house."[76] There also were reports that *tayū* were

73 Ishii Ryōsuke, *Yoshiwara* (Tokyo: Chūō kōronsha, 1967), pp. 4–12, 21–7; Gunji Masakatsu, *Kabuki to Yoshiwara* (Tokyo: Awaji shobō, 1956), pp. 96–102.

74 *Rakuchū rakugai zu taikan*, vol. 3, pp. 56–9, 64–67; *Kyōto no rekishi*, vol. 4, p. 590.

75 *Kyōto no rekishi*, vol. 5, pp. 268–72; Ishii, *Yoshiwara*, pp. 13–18, 94–5, 119; Gunji, *Kabuki to Yoshiwara*, pp. 140–1.

76 Sakata, *Chōnin*, p. 20, quoting (*Ihon*) *Dōbō goen* (1720), *Enseki jisshu*, III, vols. 27–29 of *Kokusho kankokai sōsho*, series 1, 1908, p. 3.

sent to appointments in such fine palanquins that they were mistaken for ladies of the highest court nobility.[77]

The bakufu endeavored to correct the unseemly behavior of daimyo by warnings in the Buke shohatto (Laws for the military houses) against extravagance and excesses in drinking and sex.[78] Daimyo could be punished by reduction or loss of their domains. The successive moves of the prostitute quarters in Kyoto and Edo and closer supervision also worked to discourage conspicuous patronage of prostitutes by the upper bushi. They were replaced as clients of tayū by merchants of great wealth who appeared in the 1660s. Ukiyo zōshi provide many legendary stories of the vast sums spent by these merchants on entertainment in the quarters.

Commoners inherited the quarters in Kyoto and Osaka, in part because of the decreasing numbers of bushi in these cities. The situation was different in Edo, where bushi outnumbered commoners. Tens of thousands of daimyo retainers were there on sankin kōtai every year, and estimates suggest that bushi (presumably middle and lower bushi) made up 70 percent of the customers of the Yoshiwara. Those of some stature felt constrained to be discreet about their visits. It was their practice, and that of some chōnin as well, to rent large woven hats near the entrance to the quarter to conceal their faces. Above all, bushi were careful to avoid quarrels or behavior that might bring them to the attention of the authorities.

The highest rank of houses in the quarter were much employed as places of business entertainment. At these fine establishments merchants who were purveyors or contractors to the bakufu and daimyo could entertain fiscal officials with drink and choice cuisine, followed by performances of music and dance and, if desired, sexual pleasures. A building appropriate to the entertainment of men of rank and discrimination still survives in the Shimabara. Constructed soon after 1640, the Sumiya has large, well-designed parlors – the Fan Room, Damask Room, Cypress-fence Room, and so forth, with fusuma painted by leading masters, tokonoma alcove and shelves of expensive woods, and elaborately designed shōji lattices.[79] No less care was taken in the design and construction of this building than in the Katsura Villa of Prince Hachijō, four kilometers to the east, which dates from the same years. In recognition of its architectural and cultural importance, the Sumiya has been designated an Important Cultural Property by the Agency for Cultural Affairs.

77 Kyōto no rekishi, vol. 5, p. 172.   78 Article 2 of the law of 1615, Gotōke reijō, p. 1.
79 Kyōto no rekishi, vol. 5, pp. 207–9.

One of the first descriptions of the Kyoto courtesans appears in the *kana zōshi* entitled *Tsuyudono monogatari* (c. 1625). When Tsuyu arrives in Kyoto, his innkeeper shows him a scroll containing descriptions of thirty-two of the leading women of the Misuji-machi quarter. This passage may be the earliest example of this genre, critiques comparing the talents and personalities of beauties of the quarter.[80]

The first guide to the pleasure quarter and its inmates, known as *yūjo hyōbanki*, is the illustrated *Azuma monogatari* of 1642 concerning the old Yoshiwara quarter. It describes the higher ranking among the 75 women of *tayū* rank, 31 *kōshi*, and 881 *hashijorō*.[81] Guidebooks produced during the next years, such as the *Tōgenshū* (1655) on the Shimabara quarter, went into even greater detail in describing the houses and women. Because of the wide range of prices charged for women of different rank, not to mention differences among them in artistic accomplishments and in traits of personality and beauty, information about them could be of practical as well as vicarious interest. Sketch maps showing the location of each house in the quarter, and a price by the woman's name, were often included. Over two hundred books of information on the quarters had been published by 1700.

The *Keisei iro shamisen* (1701) lists the names of the prostitutes of the major official licensed quarters in eleven cities, reporting their rank, fee, and house. For the three cities, the totals by rank are shown in Table 14.1.[82]

Guidebooks and critiques gave attention mostly to prostitutes of the two or three highest ranks and to the best houses. It was the quarter at its most elegant and glamorous that became the material of literature and kabuki and puppet plays. This picture bore little relationship to the sordid work of prostitution to which the great majority of the inmates were subjected. But the idealized image in popular culture presents the *tayū* as a cultivated lady living in luxury.

In addition to beauty and cultural achievements, a *tayū* was said to have qualities of character – spirit (*iki*) and pride (*hari*) – that she demonstrated in her independence, refusing suitors she did not like. Some early *tayū* were held up as models of womanhood in books for

80 Jimbō et al., eds., *Kana zōshi shū*, pp. 95–104. Colored paintings from a handscroll depicting Tsuyu's adventures are reproduced in *Kinsei fūzoku zukan* (Tokyo: Mainichi shimbunsha, 1973–4), vol. 2, pp. 21–36.
81 Gunji, *Kabuki to Yoshiwara*, p. 99; *Azuma monogatari*, in Asakura Haruhiko, ed., *Kana zōshi shūsei*, vol. 1 (Tokyo: Tōkyōdō, 1980), p. 361.
82 The *ukiyo zōshi* by Ejima Kiseki (1666–1735) is included in Hakubunkan henshū kyoku, ed., *Chimpon zenshū*, pt. 1, vol. 31 of *Teikoku bunko* (Tokyo: Hakubunkan, 1927), pp. 174–80, 211–24, 248–65; Gunji, *Kabuki to Yoshiwara*, p. 135; Howard Hibbett, *The Floating World in Japanese Fiction* (New York: Oxford University Press, 1959), pp. 52–3.

TABLE 14.1
Number and rank of prostitutes in Kyoto, Osaka,
and Edo, c. 1700

Shimabara (Kyoto)	Shimmachi (Osaka)	Yoshiwara (Edo)
Tayū, 13	*Tayū*, 37	*Tayū*, 5
Tenjin, 57	*Tenjin*, 91	*Kōshi*, 99
Kakoi, 54	*Kakoi*, 53	*Sancha*, 493
Hashi jorō, 184	*Hashi jorō*, 424	*Umecha*, 280
	Gobun jorō, over 150	*Gosun tsubone*, 426
		Sanzun tsubone, 44
		Other *tsubone*, over 400
Total: 308	Total: over 760	Total: over 1,750

the education of girls because of their constancy, dignity, and generosity toward the less fortunate. The *tayū*'s proprietor had her educated and trained in deportment to qualify her as a suitable companion for men of rank and wealth. The most thorough treatise on the quarter, Fujimoto Kizan's *Shikidō ōkagami* (The great mirror of sex, 1678) holds up a standard of ladylike behavior for the *tayū*, admonishing that she should never laugh out loud or open her mouth without covering it with her sleeve. Like a great lady she should refrain from mentioning the names of foods. She was also to be able to compose poetry. The author adds:

It is unfortunate for *anyone* not to be able to write, but for a courtesan it is a disaster. . . . As long as a courtesan writes well, it does not matter if she is incompetent at the samisen, but even for a samisen virtuoso it would be unfortunate if people said she wrote a bad hand or that her grammar was shaky.[83]

A *tayū* was given an elegant name that evoked figures from classical literature, like Yūgiri of the *Tale of Genji*, or places of scenic beauty, such as Yoshino and Takao. To enhance her image, she was addressed by her maids in the language of formal deference accorded a daimyo's consort by her ladies-in-waiting. She was treated as a celebrity in the small world of the quarter. The *tayū* was cultivated as an increasingly exclusive product that few could afford. The title was reserved for only a few women in Kyoto and Osaka, and although there had been

83 Quoted by Donald Keene, "Fujimoto Kizan and the Great Mirror of Love," in his *Landscapes and Portraits: Appreciations of Japanese Culture* (Tokyo: Kodansha, 1971), p. 246, also p. 245. Only fascicle 5 out of sixteen (or eighteen) of Kizan's large manuscript was published in the Edo period. The complete work was printed by Noma Kōshin, (*Kampon*) *Shikidō ōkagami* (Kyoto: Yūzan bunko, 1961).

seventy-five in Edo in 1642, the title was no longer used there by the 1750s. *Tayū* and courtesans of the second rank (*tenjin* or *kōshi*) did not meet their clients at their proprietors' establishments, as did the lower orders of prostitute, but were sent a written invitation by the proprietor of an *ageya* such as the Sumiya. The *tayū*'s transit to the *ageya* was a deliberate parade on which she was accompanied by two young *kamuro*, an attendant, a matron, and, in later times, a parasol bearer. The cost of carrying on a relationship as a regular client is discussed by Saikaku: It required the wealth of a millionaire.[84] It also required preparation on the part of the client to know the proper procedures and how to conduct himself (*showake*) in the quarter. Guidebooks and novels provided examples of how to act with sophistication and how to exhibit *savoir-faire* (*sui* and *tsū*) and, above all, how to avoid being taken for a boor (*yabō*). The rules of etiquette and the rituals that applied to the *tayū* and patron gave a remarkable refinement to the business of prostitution. Indeed, the artistic emphasis on the pleasures of social and cultural intercourse made the sex act almost incidental. Remarkably, a "sex ceremony" (*shikidō*) was created.

The quarter was a small island free of class restrictions, where a hierarchy of services corresponded to what the customer was willing to pay. Here, as Saikaku wrote, lineage of birth was replaced by the pedigree of money. The affluent commoner could find refuge from the humiliation of his position in the samurai world by commanding luxurious surroundings and the greatest esteem that flattery and enthusiastic attentions could convey. The inflation of the *tayū* was designed to increase the gratification of the merchant who succeeded in commanding her. The ordinary businessman or craftsman, seeking services and pleasure within his means, could gain similar, but more moderate, attentions from women of lower rank.

For the *chōnin* the quarter became a refuge from restrictions, not only of the class system, but also of family and community. Marriage was not governed by expectations of romantic attachment or sexual compatibility but was arranged by parents and go-betweens concerned with finding optimal arrangements likely to ensure the family's continuity and strengthening the family trade. No particular stigma was attached to a man's visiting the quarter as long as such dalliance did not jeopardize the security of family and business. That is, the *chōnin* was not to form a strong emotional attachment in the quarter or spend

---

84 Ivan Morris, trans., *The Life of an Amorous Woman and Other Writings by Ihara Saikaku* (New York: New Directions, 1963), pp. 287–8.

too much money there. The freedom of individual action, restricted by family responsibilities, was qualified, too, by subordination to corporate groups – the residential quarter (*chō*) and the trade association (*nakama* or *ton'ya*). Moreover, the increasing influence of Confucian ethics, which emphasized family obligations, loyalty, and harmony, added to the underlying controls of Buddhism with its teaching of forbearance, suppression of desire, and deferment of rewards until the next world. The quarter therefore offered a brief respite from this outside world of complex responsibilities and ethical constraints.

However pleasurable the atmosphere of the quarter or solicitous the attentions of its women, it was not possible to shut out entirely the harshness of the world. The customer's partner was essentially a slave, condemned to prostitution because her parents, unable to pay their land taxes or burdened by other debts, had been forced to sell her, to indenture her for ten years or more. The underlying sadness of the quarter surfaces in the popularity of plaintive songs of homesickness and fickle lovers. This mood predominates in scenes of the quarter in drama.[85]

According to regulations, there was to be no prostitution outside the licensed quarters, but this was never the situation. Because of the inconvenience of traveling the distance to the Yoshiwara, brothels continued to spring up in different parts of Edo. Particularly popular were the bathhouse girls (*yuna*) who scrubbed customers' backs, washed their hair, and provided sexual attentions. Hundreds were rounded up and moved to the Yoshiwara in 1665, installed in buildings that looked like bathhouses to carry on the familiar tradition. Yet brothels flourished elsewhere as well – in Shinagawa, Shinjuku, Itabashi, Senju, and dozens of other locations (*oka basho*). After periods of tacit tolerance, they were closed during the great reforms of Kansei and Tempō and their inmates sent to the Yoshiwara. Samurai wives, caught in adultery, were also sent there to serve without pay as *yakko*. In Kyoto, brothels continued to reopen in parts of the city where they had formerly existed: Gion, Nijō, Shichijō, and Kitano. When the popular writer Bakin visited Kyoto in 1802, he found the Gion quarter superior to the overly formal Shimabara. In both Kyoto and Osaka, where the attitude of the authorities was more lenient than in Edo, a number of the informal quarters acquired semiofficial status.

The yearly issuance of laws banning private prostitution throughout the Edo period suggests that little progress was made in stemming this

85 *Kyōto no rekishi*, vol. 5, pp. 481–2.

practice. The literature also notes, routinely, the presence of accommo-
dating maids at inns, post stations, restaurants, tea shops, and bathhouses. Indeed, the large variety and gradations among sexual practitioners may best be indicated by the almost five hundred words used
to designate prostitutes.

THE THEATER WORLD

The second type of district for entertainment and pleasure seeking –
the quarter of kabuki and puppet theaters and the teahouses that
surrounded them – also flourished in the Genroku period. Kabuki is
conventionally dated in origin to 1603, when a woman called Okuni
appeared with her troupe on a stage outside Kitano Shrine to perform
dances and skits. She had appeared there before, claiming to solicit
funds for Izumo Shrine. For some decades earlier, in fact, troupes of
female dancers had been coming to Kyoto from the provinces to perform exuberant dances called *furyū odori* or to put on *kyōgen* and noh in
a not very proper style. What distinguished Okuni's act in 1603 was
her miming and dancing the role of a dandy visiting a brothel. Her skit
caused a sensation. The word *kabuki* had originally meant "inclined"
or "tipped," suggesting deviant, wild behavior, and it was used first
for *kabuki mono*, gangs of young men dressed in outrageous clothes,
carrying overly long swords, who swaggered about the streets of
Kyoto causing trouble.

Okuni went on to perform at Edo Castle in 1607, and other troupes
of women were quick to imitate Okuni's skits. Brothel owners at
Misuji-machi and Fushimi set up stages on the east bank of the Kamo
River near Shijō in order to show their women. Painted screens record
these performances of women's kabuki (*onna* kabuki) and prostitutes'
kabuki (*yūjo* kabuki). The most talented performers, the *tayū*, are
shown seated in the middle of the stage on stools covered with tiger
skins, playing the samisen, while dancers circle them, swinging their
hips and throwing their arms about with great abandon.[86] In the
prostitute-accosting skits, the role of the rake was often played by a

86 *Kyōto no rekishi*, vol. 4, pp. 697–714; vol. 5, pp. 250–8. On early kabuki, see Donald H.
Shively, "Bakufu *versus* Kabuki," *Harvard Journal of Asiatic Studies* 18 (1955): 326–56,
reprinted in John Whitney Hall and Marius B. Jansen, eds., *Studies in the Institutional History
of Early Modern Japan* (Princeton, N.J.: Princeton University Press, 1968), pp. 231–61;
Keene, *World Within Walls*, pp. 230–43; Benito Ortolani, *Das Kabukitheater: Kulturgeschichte
der Anfänge*, *Monumenta Nipponica* Monographs no. 19 (Tokyo: Sophia University Press,
1964); Gunji Masakatsu, "Kabuki no rekishi to honshitsu," in Gunji Masakatsu, *Kabuki
ronsō* (Kyoto: Shibunkaku shuppan, 1979), pp. 12–26; Hattori Yukio, *Kabuki seiritsu no
kenkyū* (Tokyo: Kazama shobō, 1968), pp. 168–82, 214–34.

woman sporting a man's name, and the prostitute's part was played by a man, providing the opportunity for a great deal of confused and indecent pantomime. The shogun's scholar, the Confucian Hayashi Razan, reports:

The men wear women's clothing; the women wear men's clothing, cut their hair, and wear a man's topknot, have swords at their sides, and carry purses. They sing base songs and dance vulgar dances; their lewd voices are clamorous, like the buzzing of flies and the crying of cicadas. The men and women sing and dance together. This is the kabuki of today.[87]

An earlier diary entry of 1608 notes: "I saw women's kabuki at Shijō. Several thousands of people flocked there. It was something that astounded the eyes."[88]

We even have an Englishman's testimony about the female kabuki players. Richard Cocks, head of the English trading post at Hirado from 1615 to 1622, referred in his diary to the local variety of performer as "*caboques* or Japan players (or whores)." He mentions being entertained by a Japanese merchant who "provided *caboques*, or women plears, who danced and songe; and when we returned home, he sent eavery one one of them."[89]

In the first decades, the star performers of the Kyoto and Edo stages were the first *tayū* prostitutes described in the preceding section of this chapter. Kabuki troupes of women performed from time to time between 1612 to 1615 at the imperial court, and Yoshiwara women performed kabuki at Nihombashi and Nakabashi.[90] Troupes also toured the provinces and were even engaged by the daimyo of Kumamoto and Sendai.

The first kabuki "theaters" to be licensed in 1617 in Kyoto resembled noh stages surrounded by a simple fence. Most were in the Shijō riverside amusement district which sprang up across the Kamo River on undeveloped land just outside the formal boundaries of the city as defined by Hideyoshi's wall. This area, close to the business district, along the extension of Shijō that led to Gion Shrine, became a lively quarter and a favorite theme of paintings on screens and handscrolls. In addition to kabuki, puppet and noh stages, they show arenas for sumo wrestlers, and a large variety of sideshows. There are performances of

87 *Razan sensei bunshū*, quoted in *Dai Nihon shiryō*, series 12 (Tokyo: Tōkyō teikoku daigaku, 1901), vol. 1, pp. 260–1.
88 *Kyōto no rekishi*, vol. 4, p. 708.
89 Edward M. Thompson, ed., *Diary of Richard Cocks* (London: Hakluyt Society, 1933), vol. 1, pp. 156, 177, 180, 193, 211, vol. 2, p. 27.
90 *Kyōto no rekishi*, vol. 5, pp. 250–1.

dance and music, storytellers, reciters of military epics, fortunetellers, magicians, jugglers, acrobats, tightrope walkers, and freaks – the female giant and the armless woman archer. Exhibitions of exotic animals such as tigers, bears, porcupines, eagles, and peacocks appear in the paintings, as do performing monkeys and dancing dogs. Barkers in outlandish costumes – Portuguese hats and pantaloons – call to the passing throngs; samurai, *rōnin*, and town gallants parade about. Among the stalls offering food and drink saunter women from the nearby unlicensed houses of Gion and the riverbank to the south. Men and women in colorful summer kimono dance in a circle on the riverbed, and swimmers splash in the stream.[91]

Excitement over the kabuki women sometimes ignited brawls and duels among hot-blooded bushi, and daimyo's retainers were killed. To avoid such volatile incidents, the government banned women from the stage permanently in 1629. The Misuji-machi prostitutes were confined to their quarter and in 1640 were moved to the Shimabara on the opposite side of the city from the theaters.[92] Prostitutes and actors were separated in other cities as well. The removal of Edo's Yoshiwara in 1657 left kabuki, limited to four playhouses, in the business district at Sakai-chō and Kobiki-chō. In Osaka the authorities designated a separate theater district at Dōtombori.

Even before the women were banned, at least as early as 1612, there emerged troupes made up entirely of boys performing *wakashu* kabuki (youths' kabuki). Following the tradition of young noh actors of the Ashikaga period, they too were available as sexual partners. Homosexuality, long associated with monasteries, became prevalent among the upper bushi during the military campaigns of the fourteenth and fifteenth centuries. In the early Edo period, some shogun and daimyo and Buddhist clergy continued to show a preference for their beautiful pages, and even *chōnin* emulated their betters who had bestowed on pederasty a certain prestige. There is an extensive literature in the Edo period, in addition to guides to actors, which debates the relative romantic and sexual merits of "the two ways of love."

The playlets performed in youths' kabuki were designed to display the beauty and allure of the young actors: The skits featured homosexual love (*shudō goto*) and the accosting of prostitutes. Assignations of

91 For late-seventeenth-century paintings of the amusement quarter by the Kamo River, see the two handscrolls, "Shijō-gawara zukan," in *Kinsei fūzoku zukan*, vol. 2, pp. 73–122; *Shijō-gawara*, vol. 5, and *Kabuki*, vol. 10, of *Kinsei fūzoku zufu* (Tokyo: Shōgakukan, 1982–4); Ichitaro Kondo, *Japanese Genre Painting: The Lively Art of Renaissance Japan*, trans. R. A. Miller (Tokyo: Tuttle, 1961), plates 4, 66–71, pp. 22, 24.
92 *Kyōto no rekishi*, vol. 5, pp. 167–72, 271–73.

bushi with actors and quarrels over them repeated the experience with the *tayū*. Although even the shogun Iemitsu patronized kabuki, summoning troupes to Edo castle to divert him during the last months of his fatal illness, directly after his death the bakufu banned all kabuki in 1652.

Following repeated entreaties by theater operators, an agreement was reached that permitted kabuki performances to be staged again. Thereafter, laws required female impersonators to dress their hair in the masculine fashion, shaving the forelock. At first prohibited from covering the bald area, which diminished their appeal, they were later permitted to cover it with a small patch of purple silk. By late in the century, they wore wigs on stage. The effect of government repression, which banned women from the stage and placed restrictions on boys, was to force kabuki to turn from burlesque skits toward more substantial plays and to replace (to some extent) the parade of youths with mature male actors – men who, of necessity, developed technique and skill in dramatic acting. The beneficial results of the reforms of 1652 were felt only gradually. Drawing material from noh plays, military epics, and puppet texts, longer dramas with more plot began to appear. In 1664 the prevalent "Shimabara plays" about accosting prostitutes were banned, and "continuous plays" (*tsuzuki kyōgen*) of four short acts strung together were introduced.[93]

In spite of the reforms, the first guides to actors (*yarō hyōbanki*) found their model in books on prostitutes. The earliest extant guide, the *Yarō mushi* (1660), is an illustrated work that describes forty-one young actors. Like other early books in this genre, it gives more attention to their erotic appeal than to their talent for the stage. Written by men of education who were aficionados, such works bore literary pretensions and, like the books on prostitutes, were embellished with witty poems in Chinese and Japanese appropriate to each individual under discussion. Toward the end of the century, books on actors (then called *yakusha hyōbanki*) gave more attention to dramatic ability and critiqued performances in plays. They usually rated the *kaomise* performance offered in the eleventh month and the program of the seventh month, and some included introductory material on the theaters, their locations, and managerial personnel. The system of rating performers was modeled on the prostitute booklets. The earliest guide to rate actors, dating from 1687, employed only three grades, but by 1702 six were in use – from "medium" (*chū*) up to "superior-

93 Shively, "Bakufu *versus* kabuki," pp. 338–44.

superior-excellent" (jōjōkichi). The Yakusha nichō jamisen of that year listed 302 actors in the three cities, placing 26 in the highest category and 135 in the lowest. Variations on this scheme were used for some years, but in time the schedule of ratings was devalued by overuse of the higher grades.[94]

Kabuki gained greatly in popularity in the last two decades of the seventeenth century with the appearance of actors of great ability, it seems, who pioneered roles that shaped kabuki. The style of the great lover (wagoto, or tender business) was developed in Kyoto and Osaka by Sakata Tōjūrō. He was called the "original master of love scenes" and "the first in the line of engagers of prostitutes." In Edo, Ichikawa Danjūrō developed the aragoto (rough business) style to enact the great feats of strength of rash heroes. His bravado suited the impetuous temperament of the Edo plebs in the pit.

The most crucial development of the kabuki theater centered on defining techniques that men could use to play women's roles, the onnagata parts. Almost all of the onnagata had, of course, been kabuki youths, but as they grew older, they needed to develop a more subtle and abstract way to play women. They singled out the essential elements of a woman's gestures and speech and gave to these a special emphasis, in much the same way that puppets exaggerate human gestures so as to appear alive. A distinctive cracked vocal style was also cultivated. The stylized manner of playing women became so well established as an integral characteristic of kabuki, particularly in the interplay between the onnagata and the male lead (tachiyaku), that attempts in modern times by women to take the female roles have not been accepted by the audience. The beauty of onnagata acting lies in its formalized grace. Women, placed in these roles, appear too natural, too realistic. Furthermore, because the male roles are played in a strong, somewhat exaggerated manner, women often lack the physical stature to project an equal stage presence. And again, women do not exude the peculiar eroticism with its homosexual overtones that is inherent in kabuki. Actresses thus become suitable for kabuki roles only if they play their parts not by miming women but by imitating onnagata.

On the stage, the onnagata portrayed the fidelity, modesty, and forbearance of the ideal woman. As models of etiquette in their bows, their elegant gestures, and deferential attitudes, the onnagata were

94 Iizuka Tomoichirō, Kabuki gairon (Tokyo: Hakubunkan, 1928), p. 238; Shively, "The Social Environment of Tokugawa Kabuki," pp. 49–50.

emulated by women of the audience. It was common for *onnagata* to lead feminine lives off the stage as well, that is, to live their art. They continued to practice the motor habits of women in hand gestures, walking, and sitting and to use women's language and intonation. Some wore only women's clothes and dressed their hair in feminine coiffures. Some, indeed, are said to have entered the women's side of public bathhouses, and "no one thought this strange."[95] The famous actor Yoshizawa Ayame said that an *onnagata* should continue to experience the feelings of an *onnagata* even in the dressing room, eating only the kind of food appropriate to women, and modestly turning away from the leading man while eating.[96]

The popularity of players of male roles was enhanced by accounts of their lives off the stage. Scandal was good publicity. Critical booklets cultivated their notoriety as lovers. It was said of the Osaka actor Arashi San'emon (1635–90): "There is not a prostitute with whom he is not intimate." The details of actors' lives, the astonishingly high salaries that the most popular reputedly received, and their extravagance were matters of endless anecdotes. The craze for actors reached extremes among fans in Edo. A delicious scandal occurred in 1714 when a love affair was uncovered between the handsome Ikushima Shingorō (1671–1743), who played love scenes "realistically and provocatively," and Ejima (1681–1741), a ranking lady official in the service of the shogun's mother. The authorities reacted with another attempt to reform kabuki; among other steps they demolished the Yamamura-za theater and limited the number of licensed kabuki playhouses in Edo to three for the remainder of the Edo period.[97]

From its beginnings, leading players dominated kabuki. Material was selected and speeches blocked out to give an actor the best opportunity to display his talents. Even when playwrights replaced actors as writers, toward the end of the seventeenth century, the actors themselves filled in the chief speeches and action. Hence complete scripts of a play were not made, and the sketchy scenarios, which date from about 1685, have little literary merit. Talented writers, notably Chikamatsu, therefore turned to writing more for the puppet theater than for kabuki. As kabuki developed into a more serious dramatic form, it drew increasingly on puppet plays for its material, for both plot structure and literary language.

95 Ihara Toshirō, "Kabuki no fūzoku," in *Nihon fūzokushi kōza*, Vol. 11 (Tokyo: Yūzankaku, 1929), p.17; Shively, "The Social Environment of Tokugawa Kabuki," pp. 34–42.
96 In *Ayame gusa*, translated by Charles J. Dunn and Bunzo Torigoe, *The Actors' Analects* (Tokyo: University of Tokyo Press, 1969), pp. 61–2.
97 Shively, "The Social Environment of Tokugawa Kabuki," pp. 29–45.

Puppet texts in their origin were more like literary narratives than plays. They developed out of fifteenth- and sixteenth-century narratives known as *jōruri* which were recited to the accompaniment of a lute called the *biwa*. In the late sixteenth century the samisen replaced the *biwa*, and soon after, puppets were added to accompany the recitation. These performances became popular with all classes, and troupes were frequently summoned to the imperial court and the residences of daimyo. The texts, which could be read as storybooks, were published from the 1630s on, and more than four hundred printed between 1625 and 1686 are extant.[98]

Takemoto Gidayū created a bold new style of recitation. Chikamatsu, who enjoys a reputation as Japan's greatest playwright, wrote particularly for Gidayū and for his successor, Masadayū (1691–1744). He composed in a rich, literary style for the rhythmical narrative portions of the text and gave to his plays more plot structure. From Chikamatsu's time on, an especially beneficial exchange of influences developed between the puppet and kabuki theaters. Most of the classical pieces of the kabuki repertoire today are adaptations of mid-eighteenth-century puppet plays. Puppet performances were made more theatrical by increasing the portion of recitation delivered in dialogue, rather than in third-person narrative form. Also, the puppets came to command more attention as they became more lifelike, increasing to two-thirds human size. The principal puppets had movable parts – eyes, eyebrows, mouths, and fingers – and three men manipulated them.

Most puppet plays were *jidaimono*, or period pieces. They concerned heroes of earlier ages, and facts and legends about them were drawn from military epics, noh texts, and popular stories. Occasionally the playwright located a scene in an Edo-style brothel or commoner's home, anachronistically placed in the twelfth century. From these beginnings, Chikamatsu developed the *sewamono* – a domestic piece or, better, a gossip piece – of three acts which was added to the more serious five-act period piece to fill out the all-day program. *Sewamono* concerned commoners – shopkeepers, farmers, prostitutes – and were often based on a recent incident – a murder, theft, swindle, or arson case. The subject matter was similar to Saikaku's stories, in several instances the same event, but was treated with more emotion and sympathy for the plight of the simple protagonists.

The most representative of the *sewamono* concern a hopeless love that leads to a double suicide (*shinjū*). In most of these plays, the girl is a

98 Charles J. Dunn, *The Early Japanese Puppet Drama* (London: Luzac, 1966), pp. 42, 70–2.

prostitute and her lover a *chōnin* who lacks the money to buy her freedom. As neglect of his family business responsibilities threatens disaster, the imprudent young couple embraces in desperation the belief that by killing themselves they will be reborn together in Amida Buddha's Western Paradise. Yet, they are torn by a sense of duty (*giri*) that conflicts with their personal feelings (*ninjō*). The effectiveness of these plays depends on the author's skill in spinning around the thwarted young couple a web of circumstances that makes death the only escape, at least in the minds of the audience. Beginning with *Sonezaki shinjū* in 1703, thirteen of Chikamatsu's twenty-four domestic pieces were *shinjū* plays. The romantic, poetic treatment of these suicides was suggestive to rash young men and women who anticipated that their deaths would be publicized, if not immortalized. The bakufu thus proscribed both the suicides and plays and stories about them in 1723.[99]

The staple of both the puppet and kabuki theaters continued to be the period piece, but it was increasingly enriched by *sewamono*-like scenes. With the better development of plot structure by Chikamatsu in the last of his nearly one hundred period plays, the story lines became more and more complicated, the unexpected twists and turns in the plots more astonishing. *Jidaimono* usually dealt with historical events familiar to the audience. Most concerned samurai exploits of long ago: the heroic struggles of the Taira and Minamoto clans in the twelfth century, the revenge of the Soga brothers, and the fourteenth-century battles and intrigues recorded in the *Taiheiki*. The occasional play treated remote figures of the imperial court or great religious leaders. Sources for the plays included not only early histories and military epics but later, and highly fictionalized, literature of the Muromachi period as well: noh plays, *kōwakamai*, *otogi zōshi*, and old *jōruri*. Needless to say, such materials added only legend and fanciful embellishment to the original histories. The dramatic products contained as much folklore as fact.

Most performances in both the puppet and kabuki theaters were not revivals of earlier hits but adaptations of those plays that traded on their popularity while adding new complications to their plots. Rival theaters often staged plays on the same familiar theme in the same month, competing ingeniously in exploiting scenes that had won acclaim, adding new love affairs or revelations that, for example, familiar characters were actually long-lost relatives.

99 Donald H. Shively, *The Love Suicide at Amijima*, Harvard–Yenching Institute Monograph Series, no. 15 (Cambridge, Mass.: Harvard University Press, 1953), pp. 12–29; Keene, *World Within Walls*, pp. 253–63.

Kabuki and *jōruri* plays were written primarily for the entertainment of *chōnin*, although samurai and members of their families went as inconspicuously as they could to see performances. Catering to commoners of less cultivated taste, popular plays lacked the restraint of the samurai's noh dramas and piled one emotional event on another, to agonizing effect. The separation of families, the sacrifice of an only child, the identification of the severed head of a son or parent, the *seppuku* (*harakiri*) of a hero found to have been unnecessary only moments after the fatal dagger was thrust into the belly – all such scenes were played in a cathartic style. For commoners, the theater was a place of escape where they could fantasize about the superhuman feats of brave men and the noble sacrifices of virtuous women, the palaces of shogun and emperor, the quarrels and love affairs in the families of great lords, and high living in the finest houses of assignation.

The topics that most excited the curiosity of people in the seventeenth century were the dramatic events of the wars of unification: the intrigues and battles of Nobunaga and Hideyoshi and, above all, the steps by which Tokugawa Ieyasu broke solemn oaths and stole the nation. The Tokugawa were so sensitive on the issue that they forbade any plays or stories that discussed bushi houses in the sixteenth century. Of course, no events of Edo times involving bushi could be mentioned. Thus playwrights and storytellers could feed the commoners' fascination only by making up stories about succession quarrels in daimyo houses (*oiesōdō*) and vendettas (*katakiuchi*) that bore no recognizable parallels to the actual outbreaks of violence in the seventeenth century. In time, however, resourceful authors developed ways of treating sensitive events, even the affairs of the unification years, by elaborately camouflaging the stories. They moved events to earlier centuries and folded into the familiar cycles of the period piece twelfth-century heroes who represented Ieyasu and other great generals. Historical anachronisms and jumbled chronology were already characteristic, in any case, of the stock period piece.[100]

The first forbidden topic to be treated successfully in this way was the revenge of the forty-seven *rōnin*. The affair began in 1701 when Asano, daimyo of Akō, drew his sword in the shogun's court against Kira, an official of the bakufu. Evidently provoked by Kira, Asano slashed at him but inflicted only a slight wound. To draw a sword at court was a capital offense, and Asano was sentenced immediately to

---

100 Donald H. Shively, "Tokugawa Plays on Forbidden Topics," in James R. Brandon, ed., *Chushingura: Studies in Kabuki and the Puppet Theater* (Honolulu: University of Hawaii Press, 1982), pp. 29–33.

perform *seppuku*. Thereupon his retainers plotted revenge against Kira. Waiting twenty-two months to the day for the opportune moment, forty-seven of the *rōnin* made a night raid on Kira's mansion in Edo. They killed or wounded a number of his retainers and, after a desperate search of the premises, at last found Kira hiding in the charcoal storage room. They cut off his head and carried it through the streets of Edo to their lord's tomb.

The problem of how to deal with the Akō men posed a dilemma for the Tokugawa government. The *rōnin* exemplified traditional feudal virtues, but they had violated the government's regulations for the preservation of law and order by secretly forming a league and carrying out a revenge without authorization. Almost two months after the attack, following extensive debate within the bakufu councils, the shogun sentenced the *rōnin* to *seppuku*.

After generations of peace throughout the country, the bold raid on the mansion of one of the shogun's officials within the city of Edo was an electrifying event. In these Genroku years of prosperity and pleasure seeking, when feudal values were said to have gone soft, the courage and dedication of the *rōnin* – their resolve to sacrifice their lives to uphold honor and atone for what they regarded as the unjust sentencing of their lord – won the admiration of samurai and commoner alike. It seemed to some that the old virtues of loyalty and sacrifice, which survived only in idealized form in textbooks and stories, had unexpectedly reemerged.

Although the government issued a special order warning writers not to touch this story, in the following years playwrights and storytellers gingerly hinted at parts of it. But it was not until 1748 that all of the major ingredients were finally included in a masterful eleven-act puppet play, *Kanadehon Chūshingura* (A copybook of the treasury of loyal retainers). This became the most famous play in the history of both the kabuki and the puppet theater and has since inspired countless modern plays, films, and television dramas. It is significant that the commoners' most beloved play should be a story of samurai loyalty.[101]

The purpose of playwrights in venturing into forbidden territory was not to criticize the regime but, rather, to excite the spectators by their daring. Nor was their purpose to instruct their listeners but, rather, to entertain them. In fact, however, the theater was a classroom. It taught through performances and also through the many

101 Ibid., pp. 23–4, 33–44. The play has been translated by Donald Keene, *Chūshingura: the Treasury of Loyal Retainers* (New York: Columbia University Press, 1971).

different publications of *jōruri* texts, synopses of kabuki plays, and many genres of storybooks that drew their material from the stage. The theater taught historical names and facts, however unreliably. More important, it taught the common people a consciousness of the past and the culture's inherited traditions.

The plays taught ethics more effectively than they taught history. Exemplifying the values taught to bushi was the stuff of the period plays, even if in vulgarized form. The heroes emerged as models of self-discipline, uprightness, honesty, and compassion. Plots revolved around conflicts that arose in maintaining loyalty to one's lord and obedience to one's father, or around the necessity to sacrifice one's wife, child, or friend in the service of the supreme loyalty. Never questioned was the inevitability of capitulation to the ethical code, which supported the political and social system. In the clash between (*giri*) and personal wishes (*ninjō*), *giri* always prevailed in the period piece. There could be no suicides for love among bushi. Evil was defeated and good triumphed, sometimes in a glorious death.

The theater was also a peculiar classroom of etiquette, the arts, fashion, and music. It fed the curiosity of the commoners with an approximation of the dress and deportment of their betters. And it provided, too, an example of the proper way for persons of every station and both genders to walk, sit, bow, and speak in different social situations. In portrayals of daimyo ladies and courtesans, viewers also learned something of poetry composition, calligraphy, and playing musical instruments. Not least important, the stage became a showroom for the display of what was new in fashion – clothing design and fabrics, weaving, dyeing, embroidery, hairstyles, combs, bodkins, makeup, and personal ornamentation. Some styles originated in the prostitute quarters and were introduced through plays to a wider public, even as moralists decried the adoption of these fashions by merchants' wives and daughters and, more seriously, by bushi women as well. Trading on their mounting popularity, actors gave their names as endorsements for cakes, cosmetics, sashes, and clothing material for sale in the city's shops.

Artistically, both the prostitute and theater quarters shared in the creation of music, popular songs, and styles of recitation. The standard instrument of both quarters was the samisen, introduced from the Ryūkyū Islands in about 1570. The samisen of the kabuki and the pleasure quarters was higher pitched than that of the puppet theater and had a plaintive, sensuous quality scandalous to Confucian scholars, who considered it the most harmful of "licentious music."

The two worlds were also linked by styles of dance. Female dancers from the prostitute quarter adopted stage movements, whereas kabuki performers promptly assimilated new material developed in the brothel.

The interconnection between the two worlds appears most fully in those acts of kabuki plays set in houses of assignation. There the glamorous, mysterious life of a fine establishment is revealed for an audience to savor what only a rich man could afford. The manner of speaking of the inhabitants of the quarter – the jargon of their trade, the unique honorific verb endings, the peculiar intonation – all attracted great interest. The cultural accomplishments of the *tayū*, focus of so many improbable claims, could be "proved" on the stage as she answered the challenge of a guest to perform virtuoso pieces on a zither or samisen and to compose poems in a skillful hand. The dramatization of a customer's first meeting with a courtesan, its protocol and witty banter, emerged as the ultimate refinement of the prostitute-accosting skits of primitive kabuki.[102]

The common people, while regarding actors and prostitutes as somewhat disreputable, found them endlessly intriguing; they admired their beauty and splendid clothes, their poise and *savoir-faire*. The fame of the leaders of both professions was spread by prints, picture books, and critical guides. Indeed, woodcuts developed in technique and sophistication in the effort to cope ever more imaginatively with subjects so voraciously consumed by the public. Hishikawa Moronobu who, more than any other artist, shaped the early development of *ukiyo* painting and prints, divided his work largely between the two quarters in Edo. Torii Kiyomoto pioneered the professional style of drawing actors, producing his first poster for the Ichimura-za in 1690. From the middle of the eighteenth century, prints displaying actors posed in their roles were regularly issued with the change of the Edo programs. The depiction of a single bold figure against a plain ground was also used in courtesan paintings and prints of the Kaigetsudō school from early in the eighteenth century. Although actors were usually identified by name in prints by 1700, it was not until the middle of the century that the courtesan of the single print was specified by name and house.[103]

The intimate connection between the two worlds in the public mind may be best illustrated by prints that pose actor with prostitute. The

102 Shively, "The Social Environment of Tokugawa Kabuki," pp. 42–5, 50–4.
103 Ibid., pp. 45–9.

consummate works on this theme were those erotic prints, delicately called "spring pictures" (*shunga*), which showed in breathtaking detail a popular actor and a prostitute in the act of love. Considered neither libelous or invasions of privacy, the prints simply depicted leaders of the two professions behaving as the public expected.

THE *CHŌNIN*

The observer who left the most revealing record of *chōnin* life in the Genroku period was Saikaku. An Osaka merchant by birth, a *haikai* poet most of his life, he turned in his last twelve years to writing short stories, the first of the *ukiyo zōshi*. In more than twenty books written between 1682 and 1693, Saikaku was eloquent on the topics that most attracted his fellow residents in Osaka: making love and making money. His best stories were on the affairs of rakes, the love lives of prostitutes, the adventures of forward young maidens of the town, and the making and breaking of fortunes. Saikaku also met the demand for critiques of actors, stories of homosexual affairs among young actors and samurai, accounts of travel in the provinces, and detective stories about judicial cases.

Saikaku's most memorable passages were quick sketches of the city people he knew best. In a few deft phrases he brought to life the hardworking merchant who made a fortune but spoiled his children, the merchant's son who was interested only in the pleasure quarters, the daughter who thought only of clothes and actors. Saikaku's lovers were profligate and dissipated, his shopkeepers tightfisted to the extreme. They were, alike, single-minded, in the pursuit of either profit or love. Still other characters were interested neither in business nor in lovemaking, instead pursuing with great dedication such inappropriate avocations as playing the samisen, studying Chinese classical texts, or learning the martial arts of the samurai, all to disastrous ends. Always in a hurry, Saikaku never had time to develop his characters fully. His are not moderate or balanced individuals. But from Saikaku's overdrawn characters emerges the picture of the Genroku *chōnin:* energetic, spirited, unconcerned by his position as commoner, and reveling in the enjoyment of the floating world or an ability to accumulate wealth.

Saikaku aimed to dazzle his readers with his style and wit. He wrote swiftly, carrying over to his prose his technique as an avant-garde poet of the Danrin school of *haikai*, who competed for speed records in composition. He was acclaimed the ultimate champion for his improbable record of composing 23,500 verses in a twenty-four-hour marathon. Excelling in unexpected twists and turns within his sentences, Saikaku substituted word associations or pivots on a pun for logical progression. He could not resist the ironic turnabout – things were not as they seemed – and he often changed direction before he could complete a serious thought. But this irreverent style effectively reflected the brash confidence of the new Osaka chōnin.[104]

Saikaku's first book, Kōshoku ichidai otoko (The man who spent his life in love, 1682), traces the progress of a rake, the son of a wealthy Kyoto merchant, from his precocious initiation through escapades with women of all classes in brothels throughout the country. By the age of sixty, tiring of what Japan has to offer after encounters with 3,742 women and 725 young men, the rake sails off with his companions in search of the fabled Island of Women. In shaping his work in fifty-four chapters, Saikaku had in mind the eleventh-century Tale of Genji, and he made occasional references to episodes in that classic. But in contrast to the leisurely, sentimental affairs of Prince Genji in mansions of the court nobility, the Genroku lover hurries along his commercial course. The entire book is a celebration of unrestrained sex, although it is not explicit in an erotic sense. The work was an immediate success, was republished repeatedly, and was followed by other books authored by Saikaku with kōshoku, meaning "to love love" or "to enjoy sex" as the first word of the title.[105]

Kōshoku ichidai onna (1686) is in form the confession of an old crone who reviews a life of lovemaking, first as a girl at court, then as concubine to a daimyo, later as a tayū, and eventually as an ever-descending prostitute who ends her days as a streetwalker.[106] Kōshoku gonin onna, of the same year, is a collection of five stories of the love affairs of commoner women. Contrary to the expectation that women are modest and deferential, these young maidens (three of them were only fifteen) and indiscreet wives were surprisingly bold and enterprising in consummating illicit affairs which led, in all but one instance, to

104 On Saikaku's works and his style, see Hibbett, The Floating World in Japanese Fiction, pp. 36–49, 65–96; Keene, World Within Walls, pp. 167–215; Morris, trans., The Life of an Amorous Woman, pp. 15–51. Saikaku's chief works appear in Noma Kōshin, ed., Saikaku shū, vols. 47–48 of Nihon koten bungaku taikei (Tokyo: Iwanami shoten, 1957–60); and a full collection in Noma Kōshin, ed., Teihon Saikaku zenshū, 15 vols. (Tokyo: Chūō kōronsha, 1949–70).
105 The work is discussed in Hibbett, The Floating World in Japanese Fiction, pp. 36–44; Keene, World Within Walls, pp. 167–74; G. W. Sargent, trans., The Japanese Family Storehouse (Cambridge, England: Cambridge University Press, 1959), pp. xli–xlii. There is a translation by Kengi Hamada, The Life of an Amorous Man (Tokyo: Tuttle, 1964).
106 Translated in part by Hibbett, The Floating World in Japanese Fiction, pp. 153–217; and Morris, trans., The Life of an Amorous Woman, pp. 119–208.

their ruin.[107] These latter two books, unlike Saikaku's first work on the rake, show the unhappy consequences of the thoughtless pursuit of love.

Saikaku's books about merchants, his *chōnin mono*, celebrate the pursuit of wealth and are based for the most part on the experience of actual tradesmen. *Nihon eitaigura* (The everlasting storehouse of Japan, 1688, with the subtitle The new bible for getting rich), contains thirty stories about ingenious or unpredictable ways in which businessmen made or lost money. The ideal that runs through the stories is establishing a fortune or perpetuating a prosperous family enterprise. These are the success stories of a rising middle class.[108] *Seken munesan'yō* (1692) tells how tradesmen contrive to pay outstanding accounts that fall due on New Year's Eve.[109] In his stories about business, Saikaku relishes describing how *chōnin* pursue money and the effect that wealth has on them. He assumes throughout that the accumulation of wealth is a proper goal: His *chōnin* are unconcerned that their course is antithetical to the values of bushi and are undeterred by Buddhist teachings that disapprove of seeking rewards in this world. With a characteristic touch of cynicism, Saikaku observes the materialism of his fellow *chōnin:* "People are not so fond of having plum, cherry, pine and maple around the house as gold and silver, rice and hard cash."[110] Saikaku's own background as a merchant is evident in his attention to what everything costs – from a pair of chopsticks to a night with a *tayū* – and he makes arithmetical calculations to demonstrate costs and profits, showing off his intimate knowledge of how business is conducted. He tosses off advice lightly, as in his prescription for the secret of wealth: the "millionaire pill" (*chōja-gan*) is compounded of early rising (five parts), application to the family trade (twenty parts), working after hours (eight parts), thrift (ten parts), and sound health (seven parts). Taken twice a day, the pill will make a person a millionaire if, during treatment, the user only abstains from sixteen specified practices, one of which is "familiarity with kabuki actors and with the brothel quarters."[111]

---

107 William Theodore de Bary, trans., *Five Women Who Loved Love* (Tokyo: Tuttle, 1956); and in part in Morris, trans., *The Life of an Amorous Woman*, pp. 53–118.
108 Sargent, trans., *The Japanese Family Storehouse*, pp. xlviii–xlix.
109 Ben Befu, trans., *Worldly Mental Calculations* (Berkeley and Los Angeles: University of California Press, 1976); and Masanori Takatsuka and David Stubbs, trans., *This Scheming World* (Tokyo: Tuttle, 1965).
110 Quoted by Hibbett, *The Floating World in Japanese Fiction*, pp. 36–7, from *Nihon eitaigura*, in Noma, ed., *Saikaku shū*, vol. 2, p. 36.
111 *Nihon eitaigura*, in Noma, ed., *Saikaku shū*, vol. 2, p. 87; Sargent, trans., *The Japanese Family Storehouse*, pp. 59–60.

In recording the ways in which *chōnin* enjoy money, Saikaku gives particular attention to the ostentation of the wealthy and its consequences:

Fashions have changed from those of the past and have become increasingly ostentatious. In everything people have a liking for finery above their station. Women's clothes in particular go to extremes. Because they forget their proper place, extravagant women should be in fear of divine punishment. Even the robes of the awesome high-ranking families used to be of nothing finer than Kyoto *habutae*. Black clothing with five crests cannot be called inappropriate to anyone from daimyo down to commoner. But in recent years, certain shrewd Kyoto people have started to lavish every manner of magnificence on men's and women's clothes and to put out design books in color. With modish fine-figured patterns, palace-style hundred-color prints, and bled dapple tie-dye, they go the limit in unusual designs to suit any taste. Such behavior by wives and the marriages of daughters have drained the household finances and impaired the family business of countless merchants. Prostitutes make a daily display of beautiful clothes toward earning a living. But beautiful wives of commoners, when they are not blossom viewing in spring or maple viewing in autumn or going to weddings, should forgo these many layers of conspicuous garments.

Saikaku then goes on to refer to the many sumptuary laws that, in an attempt by the authorities to make appearances correspond to social status, prescribed the fabrics appropriate to various gradations of class:

The recent clothing laws are for all the provinces and all the people. If we give this some thought we realize that we can be grateful for them. It is distressing to see a merchant wearing good silks. Pongee suits him better and looks better on him. But fine clothes are essential to a samurai's status, and therefore even a samurai who is without attendants should not dress like an ordinary person.[112]

The extravagance of the wives of some wealthy merchants is illustrated by an incident of 1680. When Ichikawa Rokubei of Edo visited Kyoto, his wife dazzled the residents of the capital with her costumes. Not to be outdone, the wife of the Kyoto merchant Naniwa-ya Juemon appeared in a satin kimono embroidered with the famous sights of the capital. Ishikawa's wife thereupon promenaded through the streets in black *habutae* with an embroidered pattern of nandina. Observers thought this a poor match for the kimono of the Kyoto woman until they noticed that the red berries of the nandina were coral. Although the Edo woman won that round in the interurban rivalry, her displays of finery came to the attention of the shogun himself. He confiscated all of Ichikawa's property and banished the merchant from Edo.[113]

Sumptuary laws were issued continually in the attempt to check

---

112 *Nihon eitaigura*, in Noma, ed., *Saikaku shū*, vol. 2, pp. 46–7.
113 Shively, "Sumptuary Regulation and Status in Early Tokugawa Japan," pp. 128–9.

extravagance and display by *chōnin*, both men and women, in clothing and articles of personal adornment. Prohibitions also appeared against three-story houses, the use of gold and silver leaf and gold-lacquer articles, and extravagance in weddings, funerals, memorial services, and dining and entertainment. These laws sought, of course, to curb the luxurious living of prosperous merchants which, because it was superior to the comforts enjoyed by samurai, might provoke jealousy and hence undermine morale and discipline. They remained, however, little more than outbursts of indignation by the ruling class against the presumptuousness of social inferiors. Because the laws were directed at the display of wealth – attacking as they did the symptoms rather than the economic causes of fundamental changes in society – they were of limited effectiveness. But the reminder to *chōnin* that they should live like inferiors, together with a few exemplary confiscations and the frequent repudiation by daimyo of their enormous debts to merchants, served to sap some of the exuberance of the more pretentious *chōnin*. Such developments encouraged some *chōnin* to reflect again on their proper role and behavior in Edo society, and to bear in mind Saikaku's warning of "divine punishment."[114]

This theme was taken up by others who wrote words of advice for chonin. Nishikawa Joken wrote a practical guide called *Chōnin bukuro* (A bag of advice for townsmen, 1692), in which he admonishes:

Chōnin are at the bottom of the four classes. . . . Being at the bottom, they should not exceed their superiors. They should not be envious that others have prestige and majesty. They should keep to simplicity and plainness and be content with their status. If they keep to their kind, like oxen enjoy being with other oxen, they will achieve lifelong enjoyment.

Joken adds the warning: "If lowly *chōnin* wear fine clothes and go on outings, they will be accosted by robbers who will strip them. As people of humble birth, if they imitate the behavior of their superiors, they will bring ruinous misfortune on themselves."[115]

Ishida Baigan (1685–1744), who formulated a body of social and ethical teachings for *chōnin*, known as *shingaku*, gave advice on which materials should be worn appropriately to reflect one's status. "Be grateful for these established forms," he said, "do not violate them, but observe them strictly. Know the lowliness of oneself. It is good to observe these distinctions."[116] For Baigan, the avoidance of extravagant

114 Ibid., pp. 126–35. 115 *Nihon keizai sōsho*, vol. 5, pp. 65, 67.
116 *Tohi mondo* (1739), Akabori Matajirō, ed., in *Shingaku sōsho* (Tokyo: Hakubunkan, 1904), vol. 3, p. 206. On Shingaku, see Robert N. Bellah, *Tokugawa Religion: The Values of Pre-Industrial Japan* (Glencoe, Ill.: Free Press, 1957), pp. 133–77.

clothing was not merely prudence; it had ethical value: "Lowly *chōnin* who are ostentatious are criminals who violate moral principles."[117] The heads of merchant houses also left words of advice and admonition to their descendants. Some formulated house laws (*kahō*) as guides to the management of business and personal conduct. During the seventeenth century, many merchant houses did not continue to prosper long after the death of the founder. They proverbially failed in the third generation, putatively because of extravagance or inattention. Notable among the families that continued to prosper through the Edo period is the Mitsui house (which was, in fact, among the few to make the transition into modern times). The Mitsui left the fullest record of their commercial history and also of family rules and advice.

The Mitsui house law of 1695 includes detailed rules for the operation of their shops. The instructions concerning hours of rising, dress, food, relations with customers, and restrictions on leaving the premises provide a picture of a disciplined, austere style of life. The parallel drawn between the duty of managers to defend the Kyoto shop as their "main castle" and the duty of the shogun's guard to defend Nijō and Osaka castles expresses a concern, which runs throughout the document, with the dangers to business lurking on every side and the necessity for constant vigilance in an extremely competitive commercial world.[118] Both this law and the 1722 testament of Mitsui Takahira (Sōchiku, 1653–1737) enumerate business procedures to be followed and the types of transactions to be avoided. The documents emphasize cooperation and harmony among the nine Mitsui branch shops, and they caution repeatedly against extravagance and forgetting one's place as a merchant.

Sōchiku's views on merchant imprudence also appear in a work called *Chōnin kōken roku* (Some observations on merchants) which he completed about 1727. This is an account of the downfall of some fifty merchant houses, almost all in Kyoto, and the lessons to be drawn from the disastrous consequences of lending to daimyo, speculating in currency and commodities, living luxuriously, collecting expensive antiques, mixing with court nobles or noh actors, becoming too engrossed in religion and giving buildings to temples, and, in any variety of ways, forgetting one's proper station. "Never waste your attention

---

117 *Seikaron* (1744), in Akabori, ed., *Shingaku sōsho*, vol. 1, pp. 142–3. Naramoto Tatsuya, *Chōnin no jitsuroku*, vol. 17 of *Nihon no rekishi* (Tokyo: Chūō kōronsha, 1966), pp. 396–404.
118 "Kanai shikihō chō" (1695), in "Kōhon Mitsui-ke jigyō shiryō, Dai-ichi gofuku ten no bu, Dai-ni hen seido" (microfilm). Ōishi Shinzaburō, *Genroku jidai* (Tokyo: Iwanami shoten, 1970), pp. 66–71.

on matters which have nothing to do with your work. . . . Remember that it is the family business that must not be neglected for a moment."[119] Sōchiku illustrates here the principles expressed earlier in the house laws and testament. But in addition to citing unsound business practices that lead to financial failure, he draws attention to those moral failings that contribute to the decline of families. Although there can be no doubt that neglect and extravagance were factors in some cases, we must surely expect that many business failures of the time ensued from unforeseen changes in a rapidly developing economy.[120] Nonetheless, moralizing and didactic advice were included among the practical instructions of even the most hardheaded of Edo-period businessmen.

Just as merchant house laws and patriarchal admonitions followed in the traditions of house codes (*kahō*) and family admonitions (*kakun*) that had been prevalent in bushi families from the thirteenth century on, some *chōnin* writers suggested that there was also a *chōnin* equivalent to the way of the samurai. To the extent that its elements have been articulated, they may be found in the writings of moralists such as Joken and Baigan and in the laws and precepts of houses like the Mitsui. Such writings sought to bring respectability to the work of *chōnin*, especially tradesmen, by asserting their essential role in society. *Chōnin* were to fulfill this role by behaving at all times appropriately to callings assigned them by Heaven. They were to follow Confucian teachings in social relationships: obedience to parents, harmony in family relationships and in the community, observance of the ruler's laws, loyalty to the master, thrift, hard work, honesty in business dealings, securing only a moderate profit from work, and so forth. To violate these principles was to commit a crime against the government, against society, and against Heaven. These teachings express the sober and responsible side of *chōnin* behavior, the dedication of the individual to the continuation and prosperity of his family trade. And they put into better perspective the hedonistic view of *chōnin* life found in Saikaku's *kōshoku* books.

The principles embodied in the way of the *chōnin* fostered social discipline and conformity. Although the Tokugawa authorities had done little, if anything, to encourage this code, it served their purposes admirably. In particular, the code supported official policy of relying

119 Translated by E. S. Crawcour, "Some Observations on Merchants: A Translation of Mitsui Takafusa's *Chōnin Kōken Roku, Transactions of the Asiatic Society of Japan* 8, series 3 (1961): 115.
120 Ibid., p. 25.

768   POPULAR CULTURE

on leading merchants to ensure the cooperation of city residents. Although the government did determine the policies of city government and issued urban regulations, authorities appointed established merchant families to see to the routine, day-to-day administrative work, drawing on traditions of self-rule that had evolved in commercial towns in the century preceding Tokugawa rule. Unlike their counterparts in Europe during medieval and early modern times, when the interests of merchant councils occasioned conflict with aristocratic rulers, Japanese merchants of the early period were engaged especially in supplying the needs of the ruling class, and their privileged position was dependent on patronage by the rulers.

The government appointed respected merchant families to serve under the *machi bugyō*, both as senior elders at the highest level (for example, the *sōdoshiyori* of Osaka) and as headmen (*toshiyori* or *nanushi*) of the hundreds of quarters (*chō*) into which the cities were partitioned. Within the quarter, a unit of several hundred residents, the individual householder was also assigned responsibility for family members, servants, employees, and tenants. At each level, therefore, from citywide administration down to household management, there were *chōnin* who were obliged to ensure conformity by each individual within their jurisdictions to official regulations and to foster quiet neighborhoods and harmonious relationships.

Should an individual commit an offense, his family members and associates and headman were variously liable for punishment, depending on the gravity of the infraction. Further, neighborhoods, and sometimes trades, were divided into five-family groups (*gonin gumi*) responsible for the actions of all individuals in the group. Similarly, members of a guild or trade association could be held liable for the actions of any member. The various lines of accountability formed networks of corporate responsibility from top to bottom of commoner society. This system put heavy pressure on the individual to conform to the interests of the group. Headman urged parties in dispute to accept settlement by mediation rather than to take suits to the magistrate's court. People learned to keep a close eye on their relatives, neighbors, and business associates in order to deter them from any action that would cause difficulties for the group.

Restrictive as the social and financial obligations that shaped the daily life of *chōnin* might have been, they were less severe than the constraints on the rural population. City life also differed from life in the country in the range of diversions and entertainments that developed during the seventeenth century. Nonetheless, as the opportunity for better earnings increased in the countryside, rural life did become less restricted. Better conditions in many areas, accompanied by the spread of knowledge through books as well as through travel, worked to diffuse more widely the elements of urban culture, from education to entertainments. Villagers read popular literature, and they performed kabuki or puppet theatricals in the village shrine compound. Some learned the genteel arts and accomplishments that the *chōnin* had derived from samurai culture, such as noh recitation and drum playing. Others learned the samisen music and the love songs of the brothel and theater. By the end of the Edo period, the urban popular culture became the popular culture of the country.

WORKS CITED

Abe Yoshio 阿部吉雄. *Nihon shushigaku to Chōsen* 日本朱子学と朝鮮. Tokyo: Tōkyō daigaku shuppankai 東京大学出版会, 1965, 2nd ed., 1971.

Ackroyd, Joyce, trans., *Lessons from History: The Tokushi Yoron by Arai Hakuseki*. St. Lucia: University of Queensland Press, 1982.

Ackroyd, Joyce, trans., *Told Round a Brushwood Fire: The Autobiography of Arai Hakuseki*. Princeton, N. J.: Princeton University Press, 1979.

Adachi Iwao 安達巌. *Nihon shokumotsu bunka no kigen* 日本食物文化の起源. Tokyo: Jiyū kokuminsha 自由国民社, 1981.

Aizu-Wakamatsu-shi shuppan iinkai 会津若松史出版委員会, ed. *Aizu-Wakamatsu-shi* 会津若松史. Aizu-Wakamatsu: Aizu-Wakamatsu-shi 会津若松市, 1967.

Akabori Matajirō 赤堀又次郎, ed. *Shingaku sōsho* 心学叢書. 6 vols. Tokyo: Hakubunkan 博文館, 1904-5.

Akagi Akio 赤木昭夫. *Rangaku no jidai* 蘭学の時代. Tokyo: Chūō kōronsha 中央公論社, 1980.

Akai Tatsurō 赤井達郎. "Genroku-ki no toshi seikatsu to minshū bunka" 元禄期の都市生活と民衆文化. In *Iwanami kōza Nihon rekishi* 岩波講座日本歴史. Vol. 10. Tokyo: Iwanami shoten 岩波書店, 1975.

Andō Hideo 安藤英男, ed. *Chiritsubo: Kawai Tsugunosuke nikki* 塵壺：河井継之助日記. Vol. 257 of *Tōyō bunko* 東洋文庫. Tokyo: Heibonsha 平凡社, 1974.

Andō Seiichi 安藤精一. *Kinsei miyaza no shiteki kenkyū* 近世宮座の史的研究. Tokyo: Yoshikawa kōbunkan 吉川弘文館, 1960.

Andō Seiichi 安藤精一. *Kinsei zaikata shōgyō no kenkyū* 近世在方商業の研究. Tokyo: Yoshikawa kōbunkan 吉川弘文館, 1958.

Anno Masayuki 安野真幸. " 'Kirishitan kinrei' no kenkyū"「キリシタン禁令」の研究. In Bitō Masahide sensei kanreki kinenkai 尾藤正英先生還暦記念会, ed. *Nihon kinseishi ronsō* 日本近世史論叢. Vol. 1. Tokyo: Yoshikawa kōbunkan 吉川弘文館, 1984.

Aoki Kōji 青木虹二, ed. *Hyakushō ikki no nenji-teki kenkyū* 百姓一揆の年次的研究. Tokyo: Shinseisha 新生社, 1966.

Aoki Kōji 青木虹二, *Hyakushō ikki sōgō nempyō* 百姓一揆総合年表. Tokyo: San-ichi shobō 三一書房, 1971.

Aoki Michio 青木美智雄 et al., eds. *Ikki* 一揆. 5 vols. Tokyo: Tōkyō daigaku shuppankai 東京大学出版会, 1981-2.

Aono Shunsui 青野春水. *Daimyō to ryōmin* 大名と領民. Tokyo: Kyōikusha 教育社, 1983.

Araki Kengo 荒木見悟 and Inoue Tadashi 井上忠, eds. *Kaibara Ekken - Muro Kyūsō* 貝原益軒·室鳩巣. Vol. 34 of *Nihon shisō taikei* 日本思想大系. Tokyo: Iwanami shoten 岩波書店, 1970.

Araki Moriaki 安良城盛昭. *Bakuhan taisei shakai no seiritsu to kōzō* 幕藩体制社会の成立と構造. Tokyo: Ochanomizu shobō 御茶の水書房, 1959.

Araki Moriaki 安良城盛昭. *Taikō kenchi to kokudakasei* 太閤検地と石高制. Tokyo: Nihon hōsō shuppan kyōkai 日本放送出版協会, 1969, 1982.

Arano Yasunori 荒野泰典. "Taikun gaikō taisei no kakuritsu" 大君外交体制の確立. In Katō Eiichi 加藤栄一 and Yamada Tadao 山田忠雄, eds. *Sakoku* 鎖国. Vol. 2 of *Kōza Nihon kinseishi* 講座日本近世史. Tokyo: Yūhikaku 有斐閣, 1981.

Aruga Kizaemon 有賀喜左衛門. "Hotoke to iu kotoba ni tsuite" ホトケという言葉について. In Takeda Chōshū 武田聴洲, ed. *Senzo kuyō* 先祖供養. Vol. 3 of *Sōsō bosei kenkyū shūsei* 葬送墓制研究集成. Tokyo: Meicho shuppan 名著出版, 1979.

Asakawa, Kan'ichi, trans. and ed. *The Documents of Iriki*. Tokyo: Japan Society for the Promotion of Science, 1955.

Asakawa, Kan'ichi. *Land and Society in Medieval Japan*. Tokyo: Japan Society for the Promotion of Science, 1965.

Asakura Haruhiko 朝倉治彦, ed. *Azuma monogatari* あづま物語. Vol. 1 of *Kana zōshi shūsei* 仮名草子集成. Tokyo: Tōkyōdō 東京堂, 1980.

Asao Naohiro 朝尾直弘. *Kinsei hōken shakai no kiso kōzō* 近世封建社会の基礎構造. Tokyo: Ochanomizu shobō 御茶の水書房, 1967.

Asao Naohiro 朝尾直弘. " 'Kinsei' no hajimari - Higashi Ajia no keizai hendō to sankasei." 「近世」のはじまり-東アジアの経済変動と三貨制. *Zusetsu Nihon bunkashi taikei, geppō* 図説日本文化史大系, 月報 8 (1966).

Asao Naohiro 朝尾直弘. *Sakoku* 鎖国. Tokyo: Shōgakkan 小学館, 1975.

Asao Naohiro 朝尾直弘. "Sakoku no seiritsu" 鎖国の成立. In Rekishigaku kenkyūkai 歴史学研究会 and Nihonshi kenkyūkai 日本史研究会, eds. *Bakuhansei shakai* 幕藩制社会. Vol. 4 of *Kōza Nihonshi* 講座日本史. Tokyo: Tōkyō daigaku shuppankai 東京大学出版会, 1970.

Asao Naohiro 朝尾直弘. "Shōgun kenryoku no sōshutsu" 将軍権力の創出. Pts. 1-3. *Rekishi hyōron* 歴史評論 241 (August 1970): 70-78; 266 (August 1972): 46-59; and 293 (September 1974): 20-36.

Asao Naohiro 朝尾直弘. "Shōgun seiji no kenryoku kōzō" 将軍政治の権力構造. In *Iwanami kōza Nihon rekishi* 岩波講座日本歴史. Vol. 10. Tokyo: Iwanami shoten 岩波書店, 1975.

Asao Naohiro 朝尾直弘. "Toyotomi seiken ron" 豊臣政権論. In *Iwanami kōza Nihon rekishi* 岩波講座日本歴史. Vol. 9. Tokyo: Iwanami shoten 岩波書店, 1963.

Asao, Naohiro, with Marius B. Jansen. "Shogun and Tennō." In John W. Hall, Keiji Nagahara, and Kozo Yamamura, eds. *Japan Before Tokugawa: Political*

Consolidation and Economic Growth, 1500–1650. Princeton, N. J.: Princeton University Press, 1981.

Ashikaga Enjutsu 足利衍述. *Kamakura Muromachi jidai no jukyō* 鎌倉室町時代之儒教. Tokyo: Nihon koten zenshū kankōkai 日本古典全集刊行会, 1932.

Ashikaga Kenryō 足利健亮. "Kyoto jōkamachi no keisei" 京都城下町の形成. In Toyoda Takeshi 豊田武, Harada Tomohiko 原田伴彦, and Yamori Kazuhiko 矢守一彦, eds. *Kōza: Nihon no hōken toshi* 講座：日本の封建都市. Vol. 3. Tokyo: Bun'ichi sōgō shuppan 文一総合出版, 1981.

Atkinson, R. W. "The Water Supply of Tokio." *Transactions of the Asiatic Society of Japan* 6 (October 27, 1877; January 26, 1878) (reprinted 1888): 87–105.

Bankei zenji goroku 盤珪禅師語録. Tokyo: Iwanami shoten 岩波書店, 1941.

Befu, Ben, trans. *Worldly Mental Calculations*. Berkeley and Los Angeles: University of California Press, 1976.

Befu, Harumi. "Duty, Reward, Sanction and Power: The Four Cornered Office of the Tokugawa Village Headman." In Bernard S. Silberman and Harry D. Harootunian, eds. *Modern Japanese Leadership*. Tucson: University of Arizona Press, 1966.

Befu, Harumi. "Village Autonomy and Articulation with the State." In John W. Hall and Marius B. Jansen, eds. *Studies in the Institutional History of Early Modern Japan*. Princeton, N. J.: Princeton University Press, 1968.

Bellah, Robert N. *Tokugawa Religion: The Values of Pre-Industrial Japan*. New York: Free Press, 1985; 1st ed., 1957.

Berry, Mary Elizabeth. *Hideyoshi*. Cambridge, Mass.: Harvard University Press, 1982.

Bitō Masahide 尾藤正英. "Andō Shōeki to Motoori Norinaga" 安藤昌益と本居宣長. *Bungaku* 文学 36 (August 1968): 882–94.

Bitō Masahide 尾藤正英. "Arai Hakuseki no rekishi shisō" 新井白石の歴史思想. In Bitō Masahide 尾藤正英 et al., eds. *Arai Hakuseki* 新井白石. Vol. 35 of *Nihon shisō taikei* 日本思想大系. Tokyo: Iwanami shoten 岩波書店, 1975.

Bitō Masahide 尾藤正英. "Itō Jinsai ni okeru gakumon to jissen" 伊藤仁斎における学問と実践. *Shisō* 思想 524 (February 1968): 66–79.

Bitō Masahide 尾藤正英. "Itō Jinsai no shisō ni okeru jō no igi" 伊藤仁斎の思想における常の意義. In *Tōhō Gakkai sōritsu yonjisshūnen kinen tōhōgaku ronshū* 東方学会創立四十周年記念東方学論集, 1987.

Bitō Masahide 尾藤正英. "Mitogaku no tokushitsu" 水戸学の特質. In Imai Usaburō 今井宇三郎, Seya Yoshihiko 瀬谷義彦, and Bitō Masahide 尾藤正英, eds. *Mitogaku* 水戸学. Vol. 53 of *Nihon shisō taikei* 日本思想大系. Tokyo: Iwanami shoten 岩波書店, 1977.

Bitō Masahide 尾藤正英. *Nihon hōken shisōshi kenkyū: bakuhan taisei no genri to shushigaku-teki shii* 日本封建思想史研究：幕藩体制の原理と朱子学的思惟. Tokyo: Aoki shoten 青木書店, 1961.

Bitō Masahide 尾藤正英. *Ogyū Sorai* 荻生徂徠. Vol. 16 of *Nihon no meicho* 日本の名著. Tokyo: Chūō kōronsha 中央公論社, 1974.

Bitō Masahide 尾藤正英. "Rekishi shisō" 歴史思想. In Bitō Masahide 尾藤正英, ed. *Nihon bunka to Chūgoku* 日本文化と中国. Tokyo: Taishūkan, 大修館, 1968.

Bitō Masahide 尾藤正英. "Society and Social Thought in the Tokugawa Period." *Japan Foundation Newsletter* 9 (June–September 1981): 4–6.

Bitō Masahide 尾藤正英. "Yamaga Sokō no shisō teki tenkai" 山鹿素行の思想的転回. *Shisō* 思想 560 (1971): 22–37; 561 (1971): 82–97.

Bolitho, Harold. "The Dog Shogun." In Wang Gungwu, ed. *Self and Biography*. Sydney: Sydney University Press, 1975.

Bolitho, Harold. "The Tempō Crisis." In Marius B. Jansen, ed. *The Nineteenth Century*. Vol. 5 of *The Cambridge History of Japan*. Cambridge, England: Cambridge University Press, 1989.

Bolitho, Harold. *Treasures Among Men: The Fudai Daimyo in Tokugawa Japan*. New Haven, Conn.: Yale University Press, 1974.

Boot, Willem Jan. *The Adoption and Adaptation of Neo-Confucianism in Japan: The Role of Fujiwara Seika and Hayashi Razan*. Proefschrift, Rijksuniversiteit te Leiden, Netherlands, 1982.

Boot, Willem Jan. "The Deification of Tokugawa Ieyasu." *Japan Foundation Newsletter*, Vol. xiv, No. 5, February 1987.

Borton, Hugh. "Peasant Uprisings in Japan of the Tokugawa Period." *Transactions of the Asiatic Society of Japan* 16, 2nd series (May 1938): 1–219.

Boxer, C. R. *The Christian Century in Japan, 1549–1650*. Berkeley and Los Angeles: University of California Press, 1951.

Boxer, C. R. *The Great Ship from Amacon: Annals of Macao and the Old Japan Trade, 1555–1640*. Lisbon: Centro de Estudos Historicos Ultramarinos, 1959.

Buraku mondai kenkyūjo 部落問題研究所, ed. *Burakushi no kenkyū: zenkindaihen* 部落史の研究：前近代篇. Kyoto: Buraku mondai kenkyūjo shuppanbu 部落問題研究所出版部, 1978.

Buzen sōsho 豊前叢書. 22 vols. Kita-Kyūshū: Buzen sōsho kankōkai 豊前叢書刊行会, 1962–7.

Ch'en Mou-heng 陳懋恆. *Ming-tai wo-k'ou k'ao-lueh* 明代倭寇考略. Peking: Jenmin Ch'u-pan-she 人民出版社, 1957.

Cheng Shun-kung. *Jih-pen i-chien*. In Mikajiri Yutaka, ed. *Nihon ikkan*. Kyoto: privately mimeographed, 1937.

✓ Chibbett, David. *The History of Japanese Printing and Book Illustration*. Tokyo: Kōdansha, 1977.

Chihōshi kenkyū kyōgikai 地方史研究協議会, *Chihōshi kenkyū hikkei* 地方史研究必携. Tokyo: Iwanami shoten 岩波書店, 1961.

Choi, Kee Il. "Technological Diffusion in Agriculture Under the Bakufu System." *Journal of Asian Studies* 30 (August 1971): 749–59.

Chōsenshi henshūkai 朝鮮史編修会, ed. *Chōsenshi* 朝鮮史, 4th series. Keijō: Chōsen insatsu kabushiki kaisha 朝鮮印刷株式会社, 1937.

Chōsenshi henshūkai 朝鮮史編修会, ed. *Chōsen shiryō sōkan* 朝鮮史料叢刊. 36 vols. Keijō: Chōsen sōtokufu 朝鮮総督庁, 1933– .

Chosŏn wangjo sillok 朝鮮王朝実録. 48 vols. Seoul: Kuksa p'yonch'an wiwonhoe 国史編纂委員会, 1955-63.

Cooper, Michael, ed. *They Came to Japan: An Anthology of European Reports on Japan, 1543-1640*. Berkeley and Los Angeles: University of California Press, 1965.

Craig, Albert. "Science and Confucianism in Tokugawa Japan." In Marius B. Jansen, ed. *Changing Japanese Attitudes Toward Modernization*. Princeton, N. J.: Princeton University Press, 1965.

Crawcour, E. Sydney. "Kawamura Zuiken: A Seventeenth Century Entrepreneur." *Transactions of the Asiatic Society of Japan* 9, 3d ser. (1966): 1-23.

Crawcour, E. Sydney. "Some Observations on Merchants: A Translation of Mitsui Takafusa's *Chōnin Kōken Roku*." *Transactions of the Asiatic Society of Japan* 8, 3d ser. (1961): 1-139.

Crawcour, E. Sydney. "The Tokugawa Heritage." In William W. Lockwood, ed. *The State and Economic Enterprise in Japan*. Princeton, N. J.: Princeton University Press, 1965.

Crawcour, E. Sydney. "The Tokugawa Period and Japan's Preparation for Modern Economic Growth." *Journal of Japanese Studies* 1 (Autumn 1974): 113-25.

Dai Nihon komonjo 大日本古文書. Tokyo: Tōkyō teikoku daigaku 東京帝國大學, 1901- .

Dai Nihon nōkai, 大日本農会, ed. *Nihon no kama, kuwa, suki* 日本の釜・鍬・犁. Tokyo: Nōsei chōsa iinkai 農政調査委員会, 1979.

Dai Nihon shiryō 大日本史料. Tokyo: Tōkyō teikoku daigaku 東京帝國大學, 1901- .

Davis, David L. "Ikki in Late Medieval Japan." In John W. Hall and Jeffrey P. Mass, eds. *Medieval Japan: Essays in Institutional History*. New Haven, Conn.: Yale University Press, 1974.

de Bary, William Theodore, trans. *Five Women Who Loved Love*. Tokyo and Rutland, Vt.: Tuttle, 1956.

Doboku gakkai 土木学会, ed. *Meiji izen Nihon dobokushi* 明治以前日本土木史. Tokyo: Iwanami shoten 岩波書店, 1936.

Dohi Noritaka 土肥鑑高. "Kinsei bukka-shi no ichi kōsatsu" 近世物価史の一考察. In Nishiyama Matsunosuke sensei koki kinenkai 西山松之助先生古希記念会, ed. *Edo no minshū to shakai* 江戸の民衆と社会. Tokyo: Yoshikawa kōbunkan 吉川弘文館, 1985.

Dore, R. P., *Education in Tokugawa Japan*. Berkeley and Los Angeles: University of California Press, 1965.

Dunn, Charles J. *The Early Japanese Puppet Drama*. London: Luzac, 1966.

Dunn, Charles J., and Bunzo Torigoe. *The Actors' Analects*. Tokyo: University of Tokyo Press, 1969.

Ekuan Kenji 栄久庵憲司. *Daidokoro dōgu no rekishi* 台所道具の歴史. Tokyo: Shibata shoten 柴田書店, 1976.

Elison, George. "The Cross and the Sword: Patterns of Momoyama History." In George Elison and Bardwell L. Smith, eds. *Warlords, Artists, & Commoners: Japan in the Sixteenth Century*. Honolulu: University of Hawaii Press, 1981.

Elison, George. *Deus Destroyed: The Image of Christianity in Early Modern Japan*. Cambridge, Mass.: Harvard University Press, 1973.

Elison, George. "Hideyoshi, the Bountiful Minister." In George Elison and Bardwell L. Smith, eds. *Warlords, Artists, & Commoners: Japan in the Sixteenth Century*. Honolulu: University of Hawaii Press, 1981.

Elison, George. "The Priest Keinen and His Account of the Campaign in Korea, 1597–1598: An introduction." In Motoyama Yukihiko Kyōju taikan kinen rombunshū henshū iinkai 本山幸彦教授退官記念論文集編集委員会, ed. *Nihon kyōikushi ronsō: Motoyama Yukihiko Kyōju taikan kinen rombunshū* 日本教育史論叢：本山幸彦教授退官記念論文集. Kyoto: Shibunkaku shuppan 思文閣出版, 1988.

Elison, George, and Bardwell L. Smith, eds. *Warlords, Artists, & Commoners: Japan in the Sixteenth Century*. Honolulu: University of Hawaii Press, 1981.

Emi Seifū 江見清風. "Yuiitsu Shintō ron" 唯一神道論. In Emi Seifū 江見清風, *Shintō setsuen* 神道説苑. Tokyo: Meiji shoin 明治書院, 1942.

Endo Ryūkichi 遠藤隆吉 et al., eds. *Nihon kokusui zensho* 日本國粹全書. Vol. 3. Tokyo: Nihon kokusui zensho kankōkai 日本国粋全書刊行會, 1916.

Flershem, Robert G. "Some Aspects of Japan Sea Trade in the Tokugawa Period." *Journal of Asian Studies* 23 (May 1964): 405–16.

Frois, Luis, SJ. *Furoisu Nihonshi* フロイス日本史. 12 vols. Trans. by Matsuda Kiichi 松田毅一 and Kawasaki Momota 川崎桃太. Tokyo: Chūō kōronsha 中央公論社, 1977–80.

Frois, Luis, SJ. *Historia de Japam*. Edited by Josef Wicki SJ. Lisbon: Biblioteca Nacional de Lisboa, 1976–82.

Fujii Sadafumi 藤井貞文 and Hayashi Rikurō 林陸朗, eds. *Han shi jiten* 藩史事典. Tokyo: Akita shoten 秋田書店, 1976.

Fujiki Hisashi 藤木久志. *Oda-Toyotomi seiken* 織田・豊臣政権. Vol. 15 of *Nihon no rekishi* 日本の歴史. Tokyo: Shōgakkan 小学館, 1975.

Fujiki Hisashi 藤木久志. *Toyotomi heiwa rei to sengoku shakai* 豊臣平和令と戦国社会. Tokyo: Tōkyō daigaku shuppankai 東京大学出版会, 1985.

Fujimoto Toshiharu 藤本利治. "Toshi no dōgyōsha-machi to sangyō" 都市の同業者町と産業. In Toyoda Takeshi 豊田武, Harada Tomohiko 原田伴彦, and Yamori Kazuhiko 矢守一彦, eds. *Kōza: Nihon no hōken toshi* 講座：日本の封建都市. Vol. 2. Tokyo: Bun'ichi sōgō shuppan 文一総合出版, 1983.

Fujimoto Yukio 藤本幸雄. "Kawachi no kuni ichi shōya-ke no ken'i to sono tokushitsu" 河内国一庄屋家の権威とその特質. *Nihon rekishi* 日本歴史 353 (October 1977): 57–75.

Fujino Tamotsu 藤野保. *Bakuhan taisei shi no kenkyū* 幕藩体制史の研究. Tokyo: Yoshikawa kōbunkan 吉川弘文館, 1961; rev. ed. 1975.

Fujino Tamotsu 藤野保. *Bakusei to hansei* 幕制と藩制. Tokyo: Yoshikawa kōbunkan 吉川弘文館, 1979.

Fujino Tamotsu 藤野保. *Daimyō: sono ryōgoku keiei* 大名：その領国経営. Tokyo: Jimbutsu ōraisha 人物往来社, 1964.

Fujino Tamotsu 藤野保. "Hansei kakuritsu-ki no shomondai – seihoku Kyūshū sho han (Hirado, Ōmura, Saga kaku han o chūshin to shite)" 藩政確立期の諸問題 – 西北九州諸藩 (平戸，大村，佐賀各藩を中心として). *Shakai keizai shigaku* 社会経済史学 24 (1958): 111–42.

Fujino Yoshiko 藤野淑子. "Meiji shoki ni okeru sanson no shokuji to eiyō: 'Hida go-fudoki' no bunseki o tsūjite" 明治初期における山村の食事と栄養 – 斐太後風土記の分析を通じて. *Kokuritsu minzokugaku hakubutsukan kenkyū hōkoku* 国立民族学博物館研究報告 7 (September 1982): 632–54.

Fujiwara Teika 藤原定家. *Meigetsuki* 明月記. Vol. 2. Tokyo: Kokusho kankōkai 国書刊行会, 1911.

Fukai Jinzō 深井甚三. "Kinsei toshi no hattatsu" 近世都市の発達. In Matsumoto Shirō 松本四郎 and Yamada Tadao 山田忠雄, eds. *Genroku, Kyōhō-ki no seiji to shakai* 元禄・享保期の政治と社会. Tokyo: Yūhikaku 有斐閣, 1980.

Fukai Masaumi 深井雅海. "Edo bakufu oniwaban to bakusei" 江戸幕府御庭番と幕政. *Tokugawa rinseishi kenkyūjo kenkyū kiyō* 徳川林政史研究所研究紀要 (1979): 351–86.

Fukui-ken 福井県, ed. *Fukui-ken shi* 福井県史. 5 vols. Tokyo: Sanshūsha 三秀舎, 1920–2.

Fukuo Takeichirō 福尾猛市郎. *Ōuchi Yoshitaka* 大内義隆. Vol. 16 of *Jimbutsu sōsho* 人物叢書. Tokyo: Yoshikawa kōbunkan 吉川弘文館, 1959.

Fukuyama-shi shi hensankai 福山市史編纂会, ed. *Fukuyama-shi shi* 福山市史. 3 vols. Fukuyama-shi, 1963–7.

Furushima Toshio 古島敏雄. *Edo jidai no shōhin ryūtsū to kōtsū* 江戸時代の商品流通と交通. Tokyo: Ochanomizu shobō 御茶の水書房, 1951.

Furushima Toshio 古島敏雄. *Furushima Toshio chosaku shū* 古島敏雄著作集. Vols. 3, 6. Tokyo: Tōkyō daigaku shuppankai 東京大学出版会, 1974.

Furushima Toshio 古島敏雄. *Kinsei keizaishi no kiso katei – nengu shūdatsu to kyōdōtai* 近世経済史の基礎過程 – 年貢収奪と共同体. Tokyo: Iwanami shoten 岩波書店, 1978.

Furushima Toshio 古島敏雄. *Kinsei Nihon nōgyo no tenkai* 近世日本農業の展開. Tokyo: Tōkyō daigaku shuppankai 東京大学出版会, 1963.

Furushima Toshio 古島敏雄. *Nihon nōgyōshi* 日本農業史. Tokyo: Iwanami shoten 岩波書店, 1956.

Furushima Toshio 古島敏雄. *Sangyōshi* 産業史. Pt. 3. Vol. 12 of *Taikei Nihonshi sōsho* 体系日本史叢書. Tokyo: Yamakawa shuppansha 山川出版社, 1966.

Furushima Toshio 古島敏雄. *Tochi ni kizamareta rekishi* 土地に刻まれた歴史. Tokyo: Iwanami shoten 岩波書店, 1969.

Furushima Toshio 古島敏雄 and Aki Kōichi 安芸皎一, eds. *Kinsei kagaku shisō, jō* 近世科学思想・上. Vol. 62 of *Nihon shisō taikei* 日本思想大系. Tokyo: Iwanami shoten 岩波書店, 1972.

Furushima Toshio 古島敏雄 and Nagahara Keiji 永原慶二. *Shōhin seisan to kisei jinushisei* 商品生産と寄生地主制. Tokyo: Tōkyō daigaku shuppankai 東京大学出版会, 1954.

Furuta Ryōichi hakase kanreki kinen-kai 古田良一博士還暦記念会, ed. *Tōhoku shi no shin kenkyū* 東北史の新研究. Sendai: Bunri tosho shuppansha 文理図書出版社, 1955.

Fūzoku ga: Rakuchū rakugai 風俗画 - 洛中洛外. Vol. 11 of *Nihon byōbu-e shūsei* 日本屏風絵集成. Tokyo: Kōdansha 講談社, 1978.

Gaspar da Cruz, OP. *Tractado em que se cōtam muito por estēso as cousas da China* (title page: 1569; colophon: Euora em casa de Andre de Burgos impressor, 1570). Translated and edited by C. R. Boxer, "Treatise in which the things of China are related at great length." In *South China in the Sixteenth Century*, 2d ser., vol. 106. London: Hakluyt Society, 1953.

Gifu-shi 岐阜市, ed. *Gifu kenshi: shiryō hen* 岐阜県史・史料編. Gifu: Gifu-shi 岐阜市, 1976-80.

Gotō Tanji 後藤丹治 and Okami Masao 岡見正雄, eds. *Taiheiki* 太平記, Pt. 3. Vol. 36 of *Nihon koten bungaku taikei* 日本古典文学大系. Tokyo: Iwanami shoten 岩波書店, 1962.

Gunji Masakatsu 郡司正勝. "Kabuki no rekishi to honshitsu" 歌舞伎の歴史と本質. In Gunji Masakatsu 郡司正勝, *Kabuki ronsō* かぶき論叢. Kyoto: Shibunkaku shuppan 思文閣出版, 1979.

Gunji Masakatsu 郡司正勝. *Kabuki to Yoshiwara* 歌舞伎と吉原. Tokyo: Awaji shobō 淡路書房, 1956.

Ha, Tae-hung, trans., and Lee, Chong-young, ed. *Imjin Changch'o: Admiral Yi Sun-sin's Memorials to Court*. Seoul: Yonsei University Press, 1981.

Haga Noboru 芳賀登. *Ō Edo no seiritsu* 大江戸の成立. Tokyo: Yoshikawa kōbunkan 吉川弘文館, 1980.

Haga Noboru 芳賀登. *Shukuba-machi* 宿場町. Kyoto: Yanagihara shoten 柳原書店, 1977.

Haga Tōru 芳賀徹, ed. *Sugita Gempaku, Hiraga Gennai, Shiba Kōkan* 杉田玄白・平賀源内・司馬江漢. Vol. 22 of *Nihon no meicho* 日本の名著. Tokyo: Chūō kōronsha 中央公論社, 1971.

Hagiwara Tatsuo 萩原竜夫. *Chūsei saishi soshiki no kenkyū* 中世祭祀組織の研究. Tokyo: Yoshikawa kōbunkan 吉川弘文館, 1962.

Hagiwara Tatsuo 萩原竜夫. "Yoshida Shintō no hatten to saishi soshiki" 吉田神道の発展と祭祀組織. In Hagiwara Tatsuo 萩原竜夫, *Chūsei saishi soshiki no kenkyū* 中世祭祀組織の研究. Tokyo: Yoshikawa kōbunkan 吉川弘文館, 1962.

Hakubunkan henshū kyoku 博文館編輯局, ed. *Chimpon zenshū* 珍本全集. Pt. 1. Vol. 31 of *Teikoku bunko* 帝国文庫. Tokyo: Hakubunkan 博文館, 1927.

Hall, John Whitney. "The Castle Town and Japan's Modern Urbanization." In John W. Hall and Marius B. Jansen, eds. *Studies in the Institutional History of Early Modern Japan*. Princeton, N. J.: Princeton University Press, 1968.

Hall, John Whitney. "The Confucian Teacher in Tokugawa Japan." In David S. Nivison and Arthur F. Wright, eds. *Confucianism in Action*. Stanford, Calif.: Stanford University Press, 1959.

Hall, John Whitney. "E. H. Norman on Tokugawa Japan." *Journal of Japanese Studies* 3 (Summer 1977): 365-74.

Hall, John Whitney. "Feudalism in Japan - A Reassessment." In John W. Hall and Marius B. Jansen, eds. *Studies in the Institutional History of Early Modern Japan*. Princeton, N. J.: Princeton University Press, 1968.

Hall, John Whitney. "Foundations of the Modern Japanese Daimyo." In John W. Hall and Marius B. Jansen, eds. *Studies in the Institutional History of Early Modern Japan*. Princeton, N. J.: Princeton University Press, 1968.

Hall, John Whitney. *Government and Local Power in Japan, 500 to 1700: A Study Based on Bizen Province*. Princeton, N. J.: Princeton University Press, 1966.

Hall, John Whitney. "The Ikeda House and Its Retainers in Bizen." In John W. Hall and Marius B. Jansen, eds. *Studies in the Institutional History of Early Modern Japan*. Princeton, N. J.: Princeton University Press, 1968.

Hall, John Whitney. *Japanese History: A Guide to Japanese Reference and Research Materials*. Ann Arbor: University of Michigan Press, 1954.

Hall, John Whitney. "Japan's Sixteenth-Century Revolution." In George Elison and Bardwell L. Smith, eds. *Warlords, Artists, & Commoners: Japan in the Sixteenth Century*. Honolulu: University of Hawaii Press, 1981.

Hall, John Whitney. "Kyoto As Historical Background." In John W. Hall and Jeffrey P. Mass, eds. *Medieval Japan: Essays in Institutional History*. New Haven, Conn.: Yale University Press, 1974.

Hall, John Whitney. "Materials for the Study of Local History in Japan: Pre-Meiji Daimyo Records." In John W. Hall and Marius B. Jansen, eds. *Studies in the Institutional History of Early Modern Japan*. Princeton, N. J.: Princeton University Press, 1968.

Hall, John Whitney. "The Nature of Traditional Society: Japan." In Robert E. Ward and Dankwort A. Rustow, eds. *Political Modernization in Japan and Turkey*. Princeton, N. J.: Princeton University Press, 1964.

Hall, John Whitney. "Rule by Status in Tokugawa Japan." *Journal of Japanese Studies* 1 (Autumn 1974): 39-49.

Hall, John Whitney. *Tanuma Okitsugu: Forerunner of Modern Japan*. Cambridge, Mass.: Harvard University Press, 1955.

Hall, John Whitney. "Terms and Concepts in Japanese Medieval History: An Inquiry into the Problems of Translation." *Journal of Japanese Studies* 9 (Winter 1983): 1-32.

Hall, John W., and Marius B. Jansen, eds. *Studies in the Institutional History of Early Modern Japan*. Princeton, N. J.: Princeton University Press, 1968.

Hall, John W., Keiji Nagahara, and Kozo Yamamura, eds. *Japan Before Tokugawa: Political Consolidation and Economic Growth, 1500-1650*. Princeton, N. J.: Princeton University Press, 1981.

Hampō kenkyūkai 藩法研究会, ed. *Hampōshū* 藩法集. 12 vols. Tokyo: Sōbunsha 創文社, 1959-75.

Hanley, Susan B. "A High Standard of Living in Nineteenth-Century Japan: Fact or Fantasy?" *Journal of Economic History* 43 (March 1983): 183-92.

Hanley, Susan B., and Arthur P. Wolf, eds. *Family and Population in East Asian History*. Stanford, Calif.: Stanford University Press, 1985.

Hanley, Susan B., and Kozo Yamamura, *Economic and Demographic Change in*

Preindustrial Japan, 1600–1868. Princeton, N. J.: Princeton University Press, 1977.

Hanseishi kenkyūkai 藩政史研究会, ed. *Hansei seiritsushi no sōgō kenkyū – Yonezawa han* 藩制成立史の総合研究 - 米沢藩. Tokyo: Yoshikawa kōbunkan 吉川弘文館, 1963.

Hara Heizō 原平蔵 and Tōyama Shigeki 遠山茂樹. "Edo jidai kōki ikki oboegaki" 江戸時代後期一揆覚書. *Rekishigaku kenkyū* 歴史学研究 127 (May 1947): 24–26.

Harada Tomohiko 原田伴彦. "Kinsei no monzenmachi" 近世の門前町. In Toyoda Takeshi 豊田武, Harada Tomohiko 原田伴彦, and Yamori Kazuhiko 矢守一彦, eds. *Kōza: Nihon no hōken toshi* 講座：日本の封建都市. Vol. 3. Tokyo: Bun'ichi sōgō shuppan 文一総合出版, 1981.

Harada Tomohiko 原田伴彦. "Kinsei toshi no hisabetsu buraku" 近世都市の被差別部落. In Toyoda Takeshi 豊田武, Harada Tomohiko 原田伴彦, and Yamori Kazuhiko 矢守一彦, eds. *Kōza: Nihon no hōken toshi* 講座：日本の封建都市. Vol. 2. Tokyo: Bun'ichi sōgō shuppan 文一総合出版, 1983.

Harada Tomohiko 原田伴彦. *Kinsei toshi sōjōshi* 近世都市騒擾史. Kyoto: Shibunkaku shuppan 思文閣出版, 1982.

Harada Tomohiko 原田伴彦. *Nihon no hōken toshi kenkyū* 日本の封建都市研究. Tokyo: Tōkyō daigaku shuppankai 東京大学出版会, 1973.

Harafuji Hiroshi 腹藤弘司. "Kaga han kahō no seikaku" 加賀藩家法の性格. *Kanazawa daigaku hō-bungakubu ronshū* 金沢大学法文学部論集 (*Hōkei hen* 法経編 5), 1958. Reprinted in Harafuji Hiroshi 腹藤弘司. *Bakufu to hampō* 幕府と藩法. Tokyo: Sōbunsha 創文社, 1980.

Harootunian, Harry D. *Things Seen and Unseen: Discourse and Ideology in Tokugawa Nativism*. Chicago: University of Chicago Press, 1988.

Harootunian, Harry D. *Toward Restoration*. Berkeley and Los Angeles: University of California Press, 1970.

Hashimoto, Fumio. *Architecture in the Shoin Style*. Tokyo: Kodansha and Shibundo, 1981.

Hattori Yukio 服部幸雄. *Kabuki seiritsu no kenkyū* 歌舞伎成立の研究. Tokyo: Kazama shobō 風間書房, 1968.

Hauser, William B. *Economic Institutional Change in Tokugawa Japan: Osaka and the Kinai Cotton Trade*. Cambridge, England: Cambridge University Press, 1974.

Hauser, William B. "Osaka: A Commercial City in Tokugawa Japan." *Urbanism Past and Present* 5 (Winter 1977–8): 23–36.

Hauser, William B. "Osaka Castle and Tokugawa Authority in Western Japan." In Jeffrey P. Mass and William B. Hauser, eds. *The Bakufu in Japanese History*. Stanford, Calif.: Stanford University Press, 1985.

Hayama Teisaku 葉山禎作. *Kinsei nōgyō hatten no seisanryoku bunseki* 近世農業発展の生産力分析. Tokyo: Ochanomizu shobō 御茶の水書房, 1969.

Hayami Akira 速水融. "Bakumatsu-ki 'Kemi nikki' ni miru tabiyado no shoku-ji" 幕末期「検見日記」にみる旅宿の食事. *Rekishi kōron* 歴史公論 73 (December 1981): 80–87.

Hayami Akira 速水融. "Kinsei Chita chihō no jukyō to kazoku keitai" 近世知多地方の儒教と家族形態. *Shakai keizai shigakkai dai-52-kai taikai hōkoku shū* 社会経済史学会第52回大会報告集 (1983): 7-9.

Hayami Akira 速水融. *Kinsei nōson no rekishi jinkōgaku-teki kenkyū* 近世農村の歴史人口学的研究. Tokyo: Tōyō keizai shimpōsha 東洋経済新報社, 1973.

Hayami Akira 速水融. "Tokugawa Nihon seiritsu no sekaishi – Philip II to Toyotomi Hideyoshi" 徳川日本成立の世界史 - フェリペ II 世と豊臣秀吉 *Mitagakkai zasshi* 三田学会雑誌 77 (February 1985): 50-61.

Hayashi Akira 林煒, comp. *Tsūkō ichiran* 通航一覧. 8 vols. Tokyo: Kokusho kankōkai 国書刊行会, 1912-13.

Hayashi Motoi 林基. "Hōreki, Temmei-ki no shakai jōsei" 宝暦·天明期の社会情勢. In *Iwanami kōza Nihon rekishi* 岩波講座日本歴史. Vol. 12. Tokyo: Iwanami shoten 岩波書店, 1963.

Hayashi Razan 林羅山. *Razan sensei bunshū* 羅山先生文集. Kyoto: Heian kōkogakkai 平安考古学会, 1981; also in *Dai Nihon shiryō* 大日本史料, 12th series. Tokyo: Tōkyō teikoku daigaku 東京帝國大學, 1901.

Hayashi Reiko 林玲子. *Edo ton'ya nakama no kenkyū* 江戸問屋仲間の研究. Tokyo: Ochanomizu shobō 御茶の水書房, 1967.

Hayashi Tōichi 林董一. *Owari han kōhōshi no kenkyū* 尾張藩公法史の研究. Tokyo: Nihon gakujutsu shinkōkai 日本学術振興会, 1962.

Hayashiya Tatsusaburō 林屋辰三郎. *Machishū: Kyōto ni okeru "shimin" keiseishi* 町衆:京都における「市民」形成史. Tokyo: Chūō kōronsha 中央公論社, 1964.

Hayashiya, Tatsusaburō, with George Elison. "Kyoto in the Muromachi Age." In John W. Hall and Takeshi Toyoda, eds. *Japan in the Muromachi Age*. Berkeley and Los Angeles: University of California Press, 1977.

Hayashiya Tatsusaburō 林屋辰三郎 and Katō Hidetoshi 加藤秀俊. *Chōnin kara shimin e* 町人から市民へ. Tokyo: Kōdansha 講談社, 1979.

Heki Ken 日置謙, ed. *Kaga han shiryō* 加賀藩史料. 18 vols. Tokyo: Ishiguro bunkichi 石黒文吉, 1928-58.

Hibbett, Howard. *The Floating World in Japanese Fiction*. New York: Oxford University Press, 1959.

Hidemura Senzō 秀村選三, Kuwabata Kō 桑波田興, and Fujii Jōji 藤井讓治. "Hansei no seiritsu" 藩政の成立. In *Iwanami kōza Nihon rekishi* 岩波講座日本歴史. Vol. 10. Tokyo: Iwanami shoten 岩波書店, 1975.

Higo Kazuo 肥後和男. *Miyaza no kenkyū* 宮座の研究 Tokyo: Kōbundō 弘文堂, 1941.

Hirai, Kiyoshi. *Feudal Architecture of Japan*. New York: Weatherhill/Heibonsha, 1973.

Hiraishi Naoaki 平石直昭. "Kaiho Seiryō no shisōzō" 海保青陵の思想像. *Shisō* 思想 11 (1980): 46-68.

Hiraishi Naoaki 平石直昭. *Ogyū Sorai nempukō* 荻生徂徠年譜考. Tokyo: Heibonsha 平凡社, 1984.

Hirao Michio 平尾道雄. *Tosa han* 土佐藩. Tokyo: Yoshikawa kōbunkan 吉川弘文館, 1965.

Hirayama Toshijirō 平山敏治郎. "Kamidana to butsudan" 神棚と仏壇. In Takeda Chōshū 竹田聴洲, ed. *Senzo kuyō* 先祖供養. Vol. 3 of *Sōsō bosei kenkyū shūsei* 葬送墓制研究集成. Tokyo: Meicho shuppan 名著出版, 1979.

Hisamatsu Sen'ichi 久松潜一. *Keichū* 契沖. Tokyo: Yoshikawa kōbunkan 吉川弘文館, 1963.

Hompukuji atogaki 本福寺跡書. In Kasahara Kazuo 笠原一男 and Inoue Toshio 井上鋭夫, eds. *Rennyo, Ikkō ikki* 蓮如・一向一揆. Vol. 17 of *Nihon shisō taikei* 日本思想大系. Tokyo: Iwanami shoten 岩波書店, 1972.

Honjō Eijirō 本庄栄治郎, ed. *Kinsei Nihon no san dai kaikaku* 近世日本の三大改革. Vol. 4 of *Keizai shiwa sōsho* 経済史話叢書. Tokyo: Ryūginsha 龍吟社, 1949.

Honjō Eijirō 本庄栄治郎, comp. *Nihon keizaishi jiten* 日本経済史辞典. 2 vols. Tokyo: Nihon hyōronsha 日本評論社, 1940.

Hora Tomio 洞富雄, trans. *Perii Nihon ensei zuikōki* ペリー日本遠征随行記. Tokyo: Yūshōdō shoten 雄松堂書店, 1970. (See also Williams, Samuel Wells.)

Hori Isao 堀勇雄. *Hayashi Razan* 林羅山. Tokyo: Yoshikawa kōbunkan 吉川弘文館, 1964.

Hori Isao 堀勇雄. *Yamaga Sokō* 山鹿素行. Tokyo: Yoshikawa kōbunkan 吉川弘文館, 1959.

Hōseishi gakkai 法制史学会, ed. *Tokugawa kinreikō* 徳川禁令考. 11 vols. Tokyo: Sōbunsha 創文社, 1959-61.

Hsü Hsüeh-chü 徐薛朱. *Chia-ching Tung-nan P'ing-wo t'ung-lu* 嘉慶東南平倭通錄. Nanking: Kuo-hsueh T'u-shu-kuan 郭薛圖書館, 1932 (facsimile reprint).

Ichii Saburō 市井三郎. *Meiji ishin no tetsugaku* 「明治維新」の哲学. Tokyo: Kōdansha 講談社, 1967.

Ichiko Teiji 市古貞次 and Noma Kōshin 野間光辰. *Otogi zōshi, kana zōshi* 御伽草子・仮名草子. Vol. 26 of *Kanshō Nihon koten bungaku* 鑑賞日本古典文学. Tokyo: Kadokawa shoten 角川書店, 1976.

Ienaga Saburō 家永三郎 et al., eds. *Nihon shisō taikei* 日本思想大系. 67 vols. Tokyo: Iwanami shoten, 1970-82.

Ienaga Saburō 家永三郎 and Shimizu Shigeru 清水茂 et al., eds. *Kinsei shisōka bunshū* 近世思想家文集. Vol. 97 of *Nihon koten bungaku taikei* 日本古典文学大系. Tokyo: Iwanami shoten 岩波書店, 1966.

Iezusu kai Nihon nempō, ge イエズス会日本年報, 下. Trans. by Murakami Naojirō 村上直次郎 and ed. by Yanagiya Takeo 柳谷武夫. Tokyo: Yūshōdō shoten 雄松堂書店, 1969.

Ihara Saikaku. *Five Women Who Loved Love*. Trans. by Wm. Theodore de Bary. Tokyo and Rutland, Vt.: Tuttle, 1956.

Ihara Saikaku. *The Life of an Amorous Man*. Trans. by Kengi Hamada. Tokyo: Tuttle, 1964.

Ihara Toshio 伊原青々園. "Kabuki no fūzoku" 歌舞伎の風俗. In *Nihon fūzokushi koza* 日本風俗史講座. Vol. 11. Tokyo: Yūzankaku 雄山閣, 1929.

Iizuka Tomoichirō 飯塚友一郎. *Kabuki gairon* 歌舞伎概論. Tokyo: Hakubunkan 博文館, 1929.

Ikeda Kōen 池田晃淵. *Tokugawa jidai shi* 徳川時代史. Tokyo: Waseda daigaku shuppan-bu 早稲田大学出版部, 1909.

Imai Rintarō 今井林太郎 and Yagi Akihiro 八木哲浩. *Hōken shakai no nōson kōzō* 封建社会の農村構造. Tokyo: Yūhikaku 有斐閣, 1955.

Imaizumi Shōzō 今泉省三. *Nagaoka no rekishi* 長岡の歴史. 6 vols. Sanjō: Nojima shuppan 野島出版, 1968-72.

Imanaka Kanshi 今中寛司. *Soraigaku no kisoteki kenkyū* 徂徠学の基礎的研究. Tokyo: Yoshikawa kōbunkan 吉川弘文館, 1966.

Inobe Shigeo 井野邊茂雄. *Bakumatsu shi no kenkyū* 幕末史の研究. Tokyo: Yūzankaku 雄山閣, 1927.

Inoue Kazuo 井上和雄. *(Zōtei) Keichō irai shoko shūran* (増訂) 慶長以来書賈集覧. Osaka: Takao shoten 高尾書店, 1970.

Inoue Tetsujirō 井上哲次郎. *Nihon kogakuha no tetsugaku* 日本古学派之哲学. Tokyo: Fuzambō 冨山房, 1902.

Inoue Tetsujirō 井上哲次郎. *Nihon rinri ihen* 日本倫理彙編. 10 vols. Tokyo: Fuzambō 冨山房, 1901-3.

Inoue Tetsujirō 井上哲次郎. *Nihon shushigakuha no tetsugaku* 日本朱子学派之哲学. Tokyo: Fuzambō 冨山房, 1905.

Inoue Tetsujirō 井上哲次郎. *Nihon yōmeigakuha no tetsugaku* 日本陽明学派之哲学. Tokyo: Fuzambō 冨山房, 1900.

Ishida Hisatoyo 石田尚豊, Naitō Akira 内藤昌, and Moriya Katsuhisa 森谷尅久, comps. *Rakuchū rakugai zu taikan* 洛中洛外図大観. 3 vols. Tokyo: Shōgakkan 小学館, 1987.

Ishige Tadashi 石毛忠. "Sengoku Azuchi Momoyama jidai no shisō" 戦国安土桃山時代の思想. In Ishida Ichirō 石田一良, ed. *Shisōshi* 思想史. Pt. 2. Vol. 23 of *Taikei Nihonshi sōsho* 体系日本史叢書. Tokyo: Yamakawa shuppansha 山川出版社, 1976.

Ishihara Michihiro 石原道博. *Wakō* 倭寇. Vol. 7 of *Nihon rekishi sōsho* 日本歴史叢書. Tokyo: Yoshikawa kōbunkan 吉川弘文館, 1964.

Ishihara Michihiro 石原道博. "Wakō no onjō ni tsuite" 倭寇の温情について. *Nihon rekishi* 日本歴史 166 (April 1962): 38-45.

Ishii Ryōsuke 石井良助, ed. *Kinsei hōsei shiryō sōsho* 近世法制史料叢書. Tokyo: Sōbunsha 創文社, 1959.

Ishii Ryōsuke 石井良助. *Yoshiwara* 吉原. Tokyo: Chūō kōronsha 中央公論社, 1967.

Ishikawa Ken 石川謙. *Ishida Baigan to 'Tohi mondō'* 石田梅岩と「都鄙問答」. Tokyo: Iwanami shoten 岩波書店, 1968.

Ishikawa Ken 石川謙, ed. *Nihon kyōkasho taikei: ōrai-hen* 日本教科書大系：往来編. Tokyo: Kōdansha 講談社, 1968-77.

Ishikawa Ken 石川謙. *Nihon shomin kyōiku shi* 日本庶民教育史. Tokyo: Tōkō shoin 刀江書院, 1925.

Ishikawa Matsutarō 石川松太郎. *Hankō to terakoya* 藩校と寺子屋. Tokyo: Kyōikusha 教育社, 1978.

Itō Sei 伊藤整 et al., eds. *Nihon no meicho* 日本の名著. 50 vols. Tokyo: Chūō kōronsha 中央公論社, 1972-82.

Itō Tasaburō 伊東多三郎. "Bakuhan taisei ron" 幕藩体制論. In *Shin Nihonshi kōza* 新日本史講座. Tokyo: Chūō kōronsha 中央公論社, 1947.

Itō Tasaburō 伊東多三郎. "Edo bakufu gembun no kahei kaichū" 江戸幕府元文 の貨幣改鋳. *Shirin* 史林 38 (May 1955): 24-45.

Itō Tasaburō 伊東多三郎. "Edo bakufu Shōtoku no kahei kaichū" 江戸幕府正徳 の貨幣改鋳. *Shakai keizaishigaku* 社会経済史学 18: 6 (1953): 1-25.

Itō Tasaburō 伊東多三郎. "Kinsei kahei-shi no ichi mondai" 近世貨幣史の一問 題. *Rekishi chiri* 歴史地理 85 (1954): 15-36.

Itō Tasaburō 伊東多三郎. *Nihon kinsei shi* 日本近世史. Vol. 11. Tokyo: Yūhikaku 有斐閣, 1952.

Itō, Teiji with Paul Novgorod. "The Development of Shoin-Style Architecture." In John W. Hall and Takeshi Toyoda, eds. *Japan in the Muromachi Age*. Berkeley and Los Angeles: University of California Press, 1977.

Itoh, Teiji. *Traditional Domestic Architecture of Japan*. New York: Weatherhill/ Heibonsha, 1972.

Iwami Hiroshi 岩見宏 and Taniguchi Kikuo 谷口規短雄. *Dentō Chūgoku no kansei* 伝統中国の完成. Vol. 4 of *Chūgoku no rekishi* 中国の歴史. Vol. 4 of *Shinsho Tōyōshi* 新書東洋史. Tokyo: Kōdansha 講談社, 1982.

Iwanami kōza Nihon rekishi 岩波講座日本歴史. 23 vols. Tokyo: Iwanami shoten 岩波書店, 1962-4; 26 vols., 1975-7.

Iwao Seiichi 岩生成一, ed. *Kyōto oyakusho-muki taigai oboegaki* 京都御役所向大 概覚書. Osaka: Seibundō 清文堂, 1973.

Iwasawa Yoshihiko 岩沢愿彦. "Hideyoshi no Kara-iri ni kansuru monjo" 秀吉 の唐入りに関する文書. *Nihon rekishi* 日本歴史 163 (January 1962): 73-5.

Izumi Chōichi 泉澄一. *Sakai: Chūsei jiyū toshi* 堺：中世自由都市. Tokyo: Kyōikusha 教育社, 1981.

Janetta, Ann Bowman. *Epidemics and Mortality in Tokugawa Japan: 1600-1868*. Princeton, N. J.: Princeton University Press, 1986.

Jansen, Marius B., ed. *Changing Japanese Attitudes Toward Modernization*. Princeton, N. J.: Princeton University Press, 1965.

Jansen, Marius B., and Gilbert Rozman, eds. *Japan in Transition: From Tokugawa to Meiji*. Princeton, N. J.: Princeton University Press, 1986.

Jimbō Kazuya 神保五彌 et al., eds. *Kana zōshi shū, ukiyo zōshi shū* 仮名草子集・ 浮世草子集. Vol. 37 of *Nihon koten bungaku zenshū* 日本古典文学全集. Tokyo: Shōgakkan 小学館, 1971.

Jinnai Hidenobu 陣内秀信. "Tōkyō no machi o yomu" 東京の町を読む. *Bunka kaigi* 文化会議 (November 1985): 20-33.

Kaempfer, Engelbert. *The History of Japan, Together with a Description of the Kingdom of Siam, 1690-92*. Glasgow: James MacLehose, 1906.

Kagawa Takayuki 賀川隆行. "Toshi shōten no hatten" 都市商店の発展. In Rekishigaku kenkyūkai 歴史学研究会, ed. *Kōza Nihon rekishi* 講座日本歴史. Vol. 6. Tokyo: Tōkyō daigaku shuppankai 東京大学出版会, 1985.

Kanai Madoka 金井圓, ed. *Dokai Kōshūki* 土芥寇讎記. Tokyo: Jimbutsu ōraisha 人物往来社, 1976.

Kanai, Madoka. "Fukui, Domain of a Tokugawa Collateral Daimyo: Its Tradition and Transition." In Ardath W. Burks, ed. *The Modernizers: Overseas Students, Foreign Employees, and Meiji Japan.* Boulder, Colo.: Westview Press, 1985.

Kanai Madoka 金井圓. *Hansei* 藩政. Tokyo: Shibundō 至文堂, 1962.

Kanaya Osamu 金谷治 and Ishii Ryōsuke 石井良助, ed. *Fujiwara Seika, Hayashi Razan* 藤原惺窩・林羅山. Vol. 28 of *Nihon shisō taikei* 日本思想大系. Tokyo: Iwanami shoten 岩波書店, 1975.

Kanazawa Harutomo 金沢春友. *Teranishi daikan jiseki shū* 寺西代官事績集. Tsunetoyo, Fukushima: Tsunetoyo kyōdoshi kankōkai 常豊郷土史刊行会, 1930.

Kanazawa-shi Ōmichō ichiba-shi hensan iinkai 金沢市近江町市場史編纂委員会, ed. *Kanazawa-shi Ōmichō ichiba-shi* 金沢市近江町市場史. Kanazawa: Hokkoku shuppansha 北国出版社, 1979.

Kanzaki Akitoshi 神崎彰利. *Kenchi* 検地. Tokyo: Kyōikusha 教育社, 1983.

Karatsu-shi shi hensan iinkai 唐津市史編纂委員会, ed. *Karatsu-shi* 唐津市. Kara-tsu, Fukuoka, 1962.

Kasahara Kazuo 笠原一男 and Inoue Toshio 井上鋭夫, eds. *Rennyo, Ikkō ikki* 蓮如・一向一揆. Vol. 17 of *Nihon shisō taikei* 日本思想大系. Tokyo: Iwanami shoten 岩波書店, 1972.

Katō Genchi 加藤玄智. *Hompō seishi no kenkyū* 本邦生祠の研究. Tokyo: Chūbunkan 中文館, 1934.

Katsumata Shizuo 勝俣鎮夫. "Imagawa kana mokuroku" 今川仮名目録. In Ishii Susumu 石井進 et al., eds. *Chūsei seiji shakai shisō jō* 中世政治社会思想・上. Vol. 21 of *Nihon shisō taikei* 日本思想大系. Tokyo: Iwanami shoten 岩波書店, 1972.

Katsumata Shizuo 勝俣鎮夫. "Rakuichiba to rakuichi-rei" 楽市場と楽市令. In "Chūsei no mado" dōjin 「中世の窓」同人, eds. *Ronshū chūsei no mado* 論集中世の窓. Tokyo: Yoshikawa kōbunkan 吉川弘文館, 1977.

Katsumata Shizuo 勝俣鎮夫. *Sengokuhō seiritsu shiron* 戦国法成立史論. Tokyo: Yoshikawa kōbunkan 吉川弘文館, 1979.

Katsumata, Shizuo, with Martin Collcutt, "The Development of Sengoku Law." In John W. Hall, Keiji Nagahara, and Kozo Yamamura, eds. *Japan Before Tokugawa: Political Consolidation and Economic Growth.* Princeton, N. J.: Princeton University Press, 1981.

Kawase Kazuma 川瀬一馬. "Kokatsuji-ban kankō nempyō" 古活字版刊行年表. In Kawase Kazuma 川瀬一馬, ed. *(Zōho) Kokatsuji-ban no kenkyū* (増補)古活字版之研究. Tokyo: Antiquarian Booksellers Association of Japan, 1967.

Kawase Kazuma 川瀬一馬. *(Nyūmon kōwa) Nihon shuppan bunka shi* 入門講話日本出版文化史. Tokyo: Nihon editā sukūru shuppanbu 日本エディタースクール出版部, 1983.

Keene, Donald. *Chūshingura: The Treasury of Loyal Retainers.* New York: Columbia University Press, 1971.

Keene, Donald. *The Japanese Discovery of Europe 1720–1830.* Palo Alto: Stanford University Press, 1969.

Keene, Donald. "Fujimoto Kizan and the Great Mirror of Love." In Donald Keene, *Landscapes and Portraits: Appreciations of Japanese Culture*. Tokyo: Kodansha, 1971.

Keene, Donald. *World Within Walls*. New York: Holt, Rinehart and Winston, 1976.

Kelly, William W. "Water Control in Tokugawa Japan: Irrigation Organization in a Japanese River Basin, 1600-1870." Cornell University East Asian Papers, no. 31. Ithaca, N. Y.: Cornell University Press, 1982.

Kikuchi Kenjirō 菊池謙二郎. "Matsudaira Sadanobu nyūkaku jijō" 松平定信入閣事情. *Shigaku zasshi* 史学雑誌 26 (January 1915): 1-22.

Kikuchi Sadao 菊地貞夫 et al., eds. *Kinsei fūzoku zukan* 近世風俗図巻. Tokyo: Mainichi shimbunsha 毎日新聞社, 1973-4.

Kimura Motoi 木村礎. "Nōmin seikatsu no shosō" 農民生活の諸相. In *Seikatsu shi* 生活史. Pt. 2. Vol. 16 of *Taikei Nihonshi sōsho* 体系日本史叢書. Tokyo: Yamakawa shuppansha 山川出版社, 1965.

Kimura Motoi 木村礎 and Sugimoto Toshio 杉本敏夫, eds. *Fudai hansei no tenkai to Meiji ishin* 譜代藩政の展開と明治維新. Tokyo: Bungadō ginkō kenkyūsha 文雅堂銀行研究社, 1963.

Kinsei bungaku shiryō ruijū 近世文學資料類従. *Kana zōshi hen* 仮名草子編. Tokyo: Benseisha 勉誠社, 1977.

Kinsei bungaku shiryō ruijū 近世文學資料類従. *Sankō bunken hen* 参考文献編. Tokyo: Benseisha 勉誠社, 1981.

Kinsei fūzoku zufu 近世風俗図譜. Tokyo: Shōgakkan 小学館, 1982-4.

Kishida Tsutomu 岸田勉. "Kyūshū no bunjinga" 九州の文人画. In Mikami Tsugio 三上次男, ed. *Kyūshū no kaiga to tōgei* 九州の絵画と陶芸. Tokyo: Heibonsha 平凡社, 1975.

Kishimoto Junkichi 岸本順吉. *Kishimoto Budayu kun jiseki* 岸本武太夫君事蹟. Tokyo, 1919.

Kitajima Manji 北島万次. *Chōsen nichinichiki, Kōrai nikki: Hideyoshi no Chōsen shinryaku to sono rekishiteki kokuhatsu* 朝鮮日々記・高麗日記：秀吉の朝鮮侵略とその歴史的告発 (*Nikki, kiroku ni yoru Nihon rekishi sōsho, kinsei* 4 日記・記録による日本歴史叢書 - 近世). Tokyo: Soshiete そしえて, 1982.

Kitajima Masamoto 北島正元. *Bakuhansei kokka kaitai katei no kenkyū* 幕藩制国家解体過程の研究. Tokyo: Yoshikawa kōbunkan 吉川弘文館, 1978.

Kitajima Masamoto 北島正元, ed *Bakuhansei kokka seiritsu katei no kenkyū* 幕藩制国家成立過程の研究. Tokyo: Yoshikawa kōbunkan 吉川弘文館, 1978.

Kitajima Masamoto 北島正元. *Edo bakufu* 江戸幕府. Vol. 16 of *Nihon no rekishi* 日本の歴史. Tokyo: Shōgakkan 小学館, 1975.

Kitajima Masamoto 北島正元. *Edo bakufu no kenryoku kōzō* 江戸幕府の権力構造. Tokyo: Iwanami shoten 岩波書店, 1964.

Kitajima Masamoto 北島正元. *Edo jidai* 江戸時代. Tokyo: Iwanami shoten 岩波書店, 1958.

Kitajima Masamoto 北島正元. *Kinsei no minshū to toshi* 近世の民衆と都市. Tokyo: Meicho shuppan 名著出版, 1984.

Kitajima Masamoto 北島正元. " 'Meikun' no higeki" 「名君」の悲劇. In Itō

Tasaburō 伊東多三郎, ed. *Kokumin seikatsu shi kenkyū* 国民生活史研究. Vol. 1 of *Seikatsu to seiji* 生活と政治. Tokyo: Yoshikawa kōbunkan 吉川弘文館, 1957.

Kitajima Masamoto 北島正元. *Nihonshi gaisetsu* 日本史概説. Vol. 2. Tokyo: Iwanami shoten 岩波書店, 1968.

Kitajima Masamoto 北島正元, ed. *Oie sōdō* 御家騒動. Tokyo: Jimbutsu ōraisha 人物往来社, 1965.

Kitō Hiroshi 鬼頭宏. "Edo jidai no beishoku" 江戸時代の米食. *Rekishi kōron* 歴史公論 89 (April 1983): 43-49.

Kobata Atsushi 小葉田淳. *Nihon no kahei* 日本の貨幣. Tokyo: Shibundō 至文堂, 1958.

Kobayashi Shigeru 小林茂. "Kinai no zaigō-machi" 畿内の在郷町. In Toyoda Takeshi 豊田武, Harada Tomohiko 原田伴彦, and Yamori Kazuhiko 矢守一彦, eds. *Kōza: Nihon no hōken toshi* 講座：日本の封建都市. Vol. 3. Tokyo: Bun' ichi sōgō shuppan 文一総合出版, 1981.

Kobayashi Shigeru 小林茂. *Nihon shinyō mondai genryū kō* 日本屎尿問題源流考. Tokyo: Akashi shoten 明石書店, 1984.

Kōda Shigetomo 幸田成友. *Edo to Ōsaka* 江戸と大阪. Tokyo: Fuzambō 冨山房, 1942.

Kodama Kōta 児玉幸多, ed. *Azuchi Momoyama jidai* 安土桃山時代. Vol. 8 of *Zusetsu Nihon bunkashi taikei* 図説日本文化史大系. Tokyo: Shōgakkan 小学館, 1956.

Kodama Kōta 児玉幸多. *Genroku jidai* 元禄時代. Vol. 16 of *Nihon no rekishi* 日本の歴史. Tokyo: Chūō kōronsha 中央公論社, 1967.

Kodama Kōta 児玉幸多. *Kinsei nōmin seikatsu shi* 近世農民生活史. Tokyo: Yoshikawa kōbunkan 吉川弘文館, 1951.

Kodama Kōta 児玉幸多 and Kitajima Masamoto 北島正元, eds. *(Dai ni ki) Monogatari han shi* 第2期物語藩史. Tokyo: Jimbutsu ōraisha 人物往来社, 1966.

Kodama Kōta 児玉幸多 and Kitajima Masamoto 北島正元, eds. *Monogatari han shi* 物語藩史. 8 vols. Tokyo: Jimbutsu ōraisha 人物往来社, 1964-5.

Kodansha Encyclopedia of Japan. 9 vols. Tokyo: Kodansha, 1983.

Koide Yoshio 小出義雄. "*Osadamegaki hyakkajō* hensan no jijō ni tsuite" 御定書百箇條編纂の事情に就いて. *Shichō* 史潮 4 (November 1934): 112-37.

Kokushi daijiten henshū iinkai 国史大辞典編集委員会, comp. *Kokushi daijiten* 国史大辞典. Tokyo: Yoshikawa kōbunkan 吉川弘文館, 1979- .

Kokushō Iwao 黒正巌. *Hōken shakai no tōsei to tōsō* 封建社会の統制と闘争. Tokyo: Kaizōsha 改造社, 1928.

Kokushō Iwao 黒正巌. *Hyakushō ikki no kenkyū* 百姓一揆の研究. Tokyo: Iwanami shoten 岩波書店, 1928.

Kondo, Ichitaro. *Japanese Genre Painting: The Lively Art of Renaissance Japan*. Translated by R. A. Miller. Tokyo and Rutland, Vt.: Tuttle, 1961.

Kondō Keizō 近藤圭造, ed. *(Kaitei) Shiseki shūran* 改定史籍集覧. Tokyo: Kondō kappansho 近藤活版所, 1900- ; reprinted by Rinsen shoten 臨川書店, 1967-9.

Kondō Moku 近藤杢 and Hiraoka Jun 平岡潤, eds. *Kuwana-shi shi* 桑名市史. 3 vols. Kuwana: Kuwana-shi kyōiku iinkai 桑名市教育委員会, 1959-65.

Kondō Morishige 近藤守重, comp. *Gaiban tsūsho* 外蕃通書. In Kondō Keizō 近藤圭造, ed. *(Kaitei) Shiseki shūran* 改定史籍集覧. Vol. 21. Tokyo: Kondō kappansho 近藤活版所, 1901.

Konta Yōzō 今田洋三. *Edo no hon'ya san* 江戸の本屋さん. Tokyo: Nihon hōsō shuppan kyōkai 日本放送出版協会, 1977.

Koschmann, J. Victor. "Action As a Text: Ideology in the Tengu Insurrection." In Tetsuo Najita and J. Victor Koschmann, eds. *Conflict in Modern Japanese History - The Neglected Traditon.* Princeton, N. J.: Princeton University Press, 1982.

Koschmann, J. Victor. *The Mito Ideology - Discourse, Reform, and Insurrection in Late Tokugawa Japan, 1790-1864.* Berkeley and Los Angeles: University of California Press, 1987.

Koyasu Nobukuni 子安宣邦. *Itō Jinsai - jinrinteki sekai no shisō* 伊藤仁斎・人倫的世界の思想. Tokyo: Tōkyō daigaku shuppankai 東京大学出版会, 1982.

Koyasu Nobukuni 子安宣邦. *Norinaga to Atsutane no sekai* 宣長と篤胤の世界. Tokyo: Chūō kōronsha 中央公論社, 1977.

Kugyō bunin 公卿補任. Vol. 55 of *Kokushi taikei* 国史大系. Tokyo: Yoshikawa kōbunkan 吉川弘文館, 1964.

Kukita Kazuko 茎田佳寿子. *Edo bakufu hō no kenkyū* 江戸幕府法の研究. Tokyo: Gannandō shoten 巖南堂書店, 1980.

Kumakura Isao 熊倉功夫. "Kasei bunka no zentei" 化政文化の前提. In Hayashiya Tatsusaburō 林屋辰三郎, ed. *Kasei bunka no kenkyū* 化政文化の研究. Tokyo: Iwanami shoten 岩波書店, 1976.

Kumazawa Banzan 熊沢蕃山. "Shūgi gaisho" 集義外書. In Takimoto Seiichi 瀧本誠一, ed. *Nihon keizai sōsho* 日本経済叢書. Vol. 33. Tokyo: Nihon keizai sōsho kankōkai 日本経済叢書刊行会, 1917.

Kuranami Seiji 蔵並省自. *Kaga: Hyakumangoku* 加賀：百万石. Tokyo: Yachiyo shuppan 八千代出版, 1974.

Kurita Mototsugu 栗田元次. *Edo jidai shi* 江戸時代史. Tokyo: Kokushi kōza kankōkai 国史講座刊行会, 1934.

Kurita Mototsugu 栗田元次. *Sōgō Nihonshi gaisetsu, ge* 総合日本史概説・下. Tokyo: Chūbunkan 中文館, 1943.

Kuroda Toshio 黒田俊雄. "Chūsei kokka to shinkoku shisō" 中世国家と神国思想. In Kuroda Toshio 黒田俊雄, *Nihon chūsei no kokka to shūkyō* 日本中世の国家と宗教. Tokyo: Iwanami shoten 岩波書店, 1975.

Kuroita Katsumi 黒板勝美, ed. *Tokugawa jikki* 徳川実記. Vols. 38-47 of *Shintei zōho Kokushi taikei* 新訂増補国史大系. Tokyo: Yoshikawa kōbunkan 吉川弘文館, 1964-6.

Kuroya Naofusa 黒屋直房. *Nakatsu-han shi* 中津藩史. Tokyo: Hekiun-so 碧雲荘, 1940.

Kuwata Tadachika 桑田忠親. *Tokugawa Ieyasu, sono tegami to ningen* 徳川家康 - その手紙と人間. Tokyo: Shin jimbutsu ōraisha 新人物往来社, 1971.

Kyōto daigaku bungakubu kokushi kenkyūshitsu 京都大学文学部国史研究室,

ed. *Hirado Matsuura ke shiryō* 平戸松浦家資料. Kyoto, 1951.

Kyōto kokuritsu hakubutsukan 京都国立博物館, comp. *Rakuchū rakugai zu* 洛中洛外図. Tokyo: Kadokawa shoten 角川書店, 1966.

Kyōto-shi 京都市, ed. *Kyōto no rekishi* 京都の歴史. Tokyo: Gakugei shorin 学芸書林, 1968-76.

Kyōto-shi 京都市, comp. *Kyōto-shi shi: Chizu hen* 京都市史：地図編. Kyoto: Kyōto shiyakusho 京都市役所, 1947.

Lane, Richard, "The Beginnings of the Modern Japanese Novel: Kana-zōshi 1600-1682." *Harvard Journal of Asiatic Studies* 20 (1957): 644-701.

Lidin, Olof G. *Ogyu Sorai's Distinguishing the Way*. Tokyo: Sophia University Press, 1970.

Lu, David John, comp. *Sources of Japanese History*. 2 vols. New York: McGraw-Hill, 1974.

Lucena, Alfonso de, SJ. *Erinnerungen aus der Christenheit von Ōmura: De algumas cousas que ainda se alembra o pᵉ Alfonso de Lucena que pertencem à Christandade de Ōmura (1578-1615)*. Edited and translated by Josef Franz Schütte SJ. *Bibliotheca Instituti Historici S.I.* Vol. 34. Rome: Institutum Historicum S.I., 1972.

McClain, James L. "Failed Expectations: Kaga Domain on the Eve of the Meiji Restoration," *Journal of Japanese Studies* 14 (Summer 1988): 403-47.

McClain, James L. *Kanazawa: A Seventeenth-Century Japanese Castle Town*. New Haven, Conn.: Yale University Press, 1982.

McEwan, J. R. *The Political Writings of Ogyū Sorai*. Cambridge, England: Cambridge University Press, 1962.

McMullin, Neil. *Buddhism and the State in Sixteenth Century Japan*. Princeton, N. J.: Princeton University Press, 1984.

Maeda Kingorō 前田金五郎 and Morita Takeshi 森田武, eds. *Kana zōshi shū* 仮名草子集. Vol. 90 of *Nihon koten bungaku taikei* 日本古典文学大系. Tokyo: Iwanami shoten 岩波書店, 1965.

Makino Ryūshin 牧野隆信. *Kitamaebune no jidai* 北前船の時代. Tokyo: Kyōikusha 教育社, 1979.

Maruyama Masao 丸山真男. *Nihon seiji shisōshi kenkyū* 日本政治思想史研究. Tokyo: Tōkyō daigaku shuppankai 東京大学出版会, 1952.

Maruyama Masao. *Studies in the Intellectual History of Tokugawa Japan*. Trans. by Mikiso Hane. Tokyo: University of Tokyo Press; and Princeton, N. J.: Princeton University Press, 1974.

Maruyama Yasunari 丸山雍成. "Toshi to rikujō kōtsū" 都市と陸上交通. In Toyoda Takeshi 豊田武, Harada Tomohiko 原田伴彦, and Yamori Kazuhiko 矢守一彦, eds. *Kōza: Nihon no hōken toshi* 講座：日本の封建都市. Vol. 2. Tokyo: Bun'ichi sōgō shuppan 文一総合出版, 1983.

Matsuda Kiichi 松田毅一 and Kawasaki Momota 川崎桃太, trans. *Furoisu Nihonshi* フロイス日本史. 12 vols. Tokyo: Chūō kōronsha 中央公論社, 1977-80.

Matsumoto, Ryōzō, and Eiichi Kiyooka. *Dawn of Western Science in Japan*. Tokyo: Hokuseidō Press, 1969.

Matsumoto Sannosuke 松本三之介, ed. *Kindai shisō no hōga* 近代思想の萌芽. Vol. 1 of *Gendai Nihon shisō taikei* 現代日本思想大系. Tokyo: Chikuma shobō 筑摩書房, 1966.

Matsumoto Sannosuke 松本三之介. *Kinsei Nihon no shisōzō* 近世日本の思想像. Tokyo: Kembun shuppan 研文出版, 1984.

Matsumoto, Shigeru. *Motoori Norinaga 1730–1801*. Cambridge, Mass.: Harvard University Press, 1970.

Matsumoto Shirō 松本四郎. "Genroku, Kyōhō-ki no seiji to keizai" 元禄享保期 の政治と経済. In Matsumoto Shirō 松本四郎 and Yamada Tadao 山田忠雄, eds. *Genroku, Kyōhō-ki no seiji to shakai* 元禄・享保期の政治と社会. Tokyo: Yūhikaku 有斐閣, 1980.

Matsumoto Shirō 松本四郎. "Kambun-Genroku-ki ni okeru daimyō-gashi no tokushitsu" 寛文・元禄期における大名貸しの特質. *Mitsui bunko ronsō* 三井文 庫論叢 1 (1967): 33–112.

Matsumoto Shirō 松本四郎. "Kinsei kōki no toshi to minshū" 近世後期の都市 と民衆. In *Iwanami kōza Nihon rekishi* 岩波講座日本歴史. Vol. 12. Tokyo: Iwanami shoten 岩波書店, 1976.

Matsumoto Shirō 松本四郎. "Kinsei toshiron" 近世都市論. In Fukaya Katsumi 深谷克巳 and Matsumoto Shirō 松本四郎, eds. *Bakuhansei shakai no kōzō* 幕 藩制社会の構造. Tokyo: Yūhikaku 有斐閣, 1980.

Matsumoto Shirō 松本四郎. "Shōhin ryūtsū no hatten to ryūtsū kikō no saihensei" 商品流通の発展と流通機構の再編成. In *Nihon keizaishi taikei* 日本 経済史大系. Vol. 4 (kinsei 近世 2). Tokyo: Tōkyō daigaku shuppankai 東京大 学出版会, 1965.

Matsumoto Toyotoshi 松本豊寿. *Jōkamachi no rekishi chirigaku-teki kenkyū* 城 下町の歴史地理学的研究. Tokyo: Yoshikawa kōbunkan 吉川弘文館, 1967.

Matsumura Akira 松村明, Bitō Masahide 尾藤正英, and Katō Shūichi 加藤周一, eds. *Arai Hakuseki* 新井白石. Vol. 35 of *Nihon shisō taikei* 日本思想大系. Tokyo: Iwanami shoten 岩波書店, 1975.

Matsuo Masaji 松尾政司. "Hōreki-ki seikyoku no dōkō ni tsuite" 宝暦期政局の 動向について. *Rekishi chiri* 歴史地理 91 (April 1968): 21–36.

Matsushita Shirō 松下志朗. *Bakuhansei shakai to kokudakasei* 幕藩制社会と石高 制. Tokyo: Hanawa shobō 塙書房, 1984.

Matsuyoshi Sadao 松好貞夫. *Kanemochi daimyō bimbō daimyō* 金持大名貧乏大 名. Tokyo: Jimbutsu ōraisha 人物往来社, 1964.

Matsuyoshi Sadao 松好貞夫. *Shinden no kenkyū* 新田の研究. Tokyo: Yūhikaku 有斐閣, 1936.

Mikami Sanji 三上参次. *Edo jidai shi* 江戸時代史. 2 vols. Tokyo: Fuzambō 冨山 房, 1944.

Miki Seiichirō 三鬼清一郎. "Chōsen no eki ni okeru gun'yaku taikei ni tsuite" 朝鮮の役における軍役大系について (1966). In Fujiki Hisashi 藤木久志 and Kitajima Manji 北島万次, eds. *Shokuhō seiken* 職豊政権. Vol. 6 of *Ronshū Nihon rekishi* 論集日本歴史. Tokyo: Yūseidō 有精堂, 1974.

Miki Seiichirō 三鬼清一郎. "Hitobarai-rei o megutte" 人掃令をめぐって. In Nagoya daigaku bungakubu kokushi kenkyūshitsu 名古屋大学文学部国史研究

室, ed. *Nagoya daigaku Nihonshi ronshū* 名古屋大学日本史論集. Vol. 2. Tokyo: Yoshikawa kōbunkan 吉川弘文館, 1975.

Miki Seiichirō 三鬼清一郎. "On'okite, on'okite tsuika o megutte" 御掟・御掟追加をめぐって. In Bitō Masahide sensei kanreki kinenkai 尾藤正英先生還暦記念会, ed. *Nihon kinsei shi ronsō* 日本近世史論叢. Vol. 1. Tokyo: Yoshikawa kōbunkan 吉川弘文館, 1984.

Miki Seiichirō 三鬼清一郎. "Taikō kenchi to Chōsen shuppei" 太閤検地と朝鮮出兵. In *Iwanami kōza Nihon rekishi* 岩波講座日本歴史. Vol. 9. Tokyo: Iwanami shoten 岩波書店, 1975.

Miki Seiichirō 三鬼清一郎. *Teppō to sono jidai* 鉄砲とその時代. Tokyo: Kyōikusha 教育社, 1981.

Minami Kazuo 南和男. *Edo no shakai kōzō* 江戸の社会構造. Tokyo: Hanawa shobō 塙書房, 1977.

Minami Kazuo 南和男. "Shōbō" 消防. In Toyoda Takeshi 豊田武, Harada Tomohiko 原田伴彦, and Yamori Kazuhiko 矢守一彦, eds. *Kōza: Nihon no hōken toshi* 講座：日本の封建都市. Vol. 2. Tokyo: Bun'ichi sōgō shuppan 文一総合出版, 1983.

Minamoto Ryōen 源了圓. *Tokugawa shisō shōshi* 徳川思想小史. Tokyo: Chūō kōronsha 中央公論社, 1973.

Minegishi Kentarō 峯岸賢太郎. "Seiritsu-ki han keizai no kōzō" 成立期藩経済の構造. In Furushima Toshio 古島敏雄, ed. *Nihon keizaishi taikei* 日本経済史大系. Vol. 3. Tokyo: Tōkyō daigaku shuppankai 東京大学出版会, 1965.

Ming shih, chüan 明史, 巻 322: "Lieh-chuan 列伝 210, wai-kuo 外国 3, Jih-pen 日本," Vol. 27. Peking: Chung-hua-shuchü 中華書局, 1974.

Ming shih-lu 明實録. Taipei: Chungyang yen-chiu-yuan li-shih yu-yen yen-chiuso 中央研究院歴史語言研究所, 1962.

Mito-shi shi hensan iinkai 水戸市史編纂委員会. *Mito-shi shi* 水戸市史 (chūkan 中巻 1-3). Mito: Mito shiyakusho 水戸市役所, 1968, 1969, 1976.

Miura Toshiaki 三浦俊明. "Hamamatsu-han ryōiki no keisei to shukueki joseikin" 浜松藩領域の形成と宿駅助成金. *Chihōshi kenkyū* 地方史研究 79 (1966): 1-29.

Miyagawa Mitsuru 宮川満. *Taikō kenchi ron* 太閤検地論. 3 vols. Tokyo: Ochanomizu shobō 御茶の水書房, 1957-63.

Miyagi Kimiko 宮城公子, ed. *Ōshio Chūsai* 大塩中斎. Vol. 27 of *Nihon no meicho* 日本の名著. Tokyo: Chūō kōronsha 中央公論社, 1978.

Miyagi Kimiko 宮城公子. *Ōshio Heihachirō* 大塩平八郎. Tokyo: Asahi shimbunsha 朝日新聞社, 1977.

Miyaji Naokazu 宮地直一. "Hō taikō to Hōkoku daimyōjin" 豊太閤と豊国大明神. In Miyaji Naokazu 宮地直一, *Jingi to kokushi* 神祇と国史. Tokyo: Kokon shoin 古今書院, 1926.

Miyamoto Masahisa 宮本又久. *Ishikawa-ken* 石川県. Tokyo: Shōheisha 昌平社, 1982.

Miyamoto Mataji 宮本又次. *Kabunakama no kenkyū* 株仲間の研究. Tokyo: Yūhikaku 有斐閣, 1938.

Miyamoto Mataji 宮本又次. "Kinsei no shōka hōkōnin to shōten soshiki" 近世

の商家奉公人と商店組織. In Miyamoto Mataji 宮本又次, *Kinsei shōgyō keiei no kenkyū* 近世商業経営の研究. Kyoto: Ōyashima shuppan 大八洲出版, 1948.

Miyamoto Mataji 宮本又次. *Nihon kinsei ton'yasei no kenkyū* 日本近世問屋制の研究. Tokyo: Tōkō shoin 刀江書院, 1951.

Miyamoto Mataji 宮本又次. *Ōsaka* 大阪. Tokyo: Shibundō 至文堂, 1957.

Miyamoto Tsuneichi 宮本常一. *Ise sangū* 伊勢参宮. Tokyo: Shakai shisōsha 社会思想社, 1971.

Miyata Noboru 宮田登. *Ikigami shinkō: hito o kami ni matsuru shūzoku* 生き神信仰：人を神に祀る習俗. Tokyo: Hanawa shobō 塙書房, 1970.

Miyazaki Michio 宮崎道生. *Aomori-ken no rekishi* 青森県の歴史. Tokyo: Yamakawa shuppansha 山川出版社, 1970.

Miyazaki Michio 宮崎道生, ed. *Teihon "Oritaku shiba no ki" shakugi*. 定本折たく柴の記釈義. Tokyo: Shibundō 至文堂, 1964.

Mizushima Shigeru 水島茂. "Etchū orimono no hattatsu" 越中織物の発達. *Toyama shidan* 富山史壇 34 (1966): 35–51.

Mizushima Shigeru 水島茂. *Kaga han, Toyama han no shakai keizaishi no kenkyū* 加賀藩・富山藩の社会経済史の研究. Tokyo: Bunken shuppan 文献出版, 1982.

Mizuta Norihisa 水田紀久 and Arisaka Takamichi 有坂隆道, eds. *Tominaga Nakamoto – Yamagata Bantō* 富永仲基・山片蟠桃. Vol. 43 of *Nihon shisō taikei* 日本思想大系. Tokyo: Iwanami shoten 岩波書店, 1973.

Mogami Takayoshi 最上孝敬, ed. *Haka no shūzoku* 墓の習俗. Vol. 4 of *Sōsō bosei kenkyū shūsei* 葬送墓制研究集成. Tokyo: Meicho shuppan 名著出版, 1979.

Mori Kahei 森嘉兵衛. *Nihon hekichi no shiteki kenkyū* 日本僻地の史的研究. Vol. 1. Tokyo: Hōsei daigaku shuppankyoku 法政大学出版局, 1969.

Mori Sugio 森杉夫. "Kano Wakasa no zōchō o megutte" 鹿野若狭の増長をめぐって. *Rekishi kenkyū* 歴史研究 9 (1965): 32–56.

Mori Sugio 森杉夫."Kinsei chōsohō no tenkan" 近世徴租法の転換. *Ōsaka furitsu daigaku kiyō* 大阪府立大学紀要 (*Jimbun shakai kagaku* 人文社会科学 12) (1964): 169–94.

Mori Yoshinori 森嘉紀. "Kanazawa no haku" 金沢の箔. *Gakuhō* 学報 26 (1982): 79–85.

Moriya Takeshi 守屋毅. *Kyō no chōnin* 京の町人. Tokyo: Kyōikusha 教育社, 1980.

Moriya, Takeshi. "*Yūgei* and *Chōnin* Society in the Edo Period." *Acta Asiatica* 33 (1977): 32–54.

Morris, Ivan, trans. *The Life of an Amorous Woman and Other Writings by Ihara Saikaku*. New York: New Directions, 1963.

Morris, V. Dixon. "The City of Sakai and Urban Autonomy." In George Elison and Bardwell L. Smith, eds. *Warlords, Artists, & Commoners: Japan in the Sixteenth Century*. Honolulu: University of Hawaii Press, 1981.

Morris, V. Dixon. "Sakai: From Shōen to Port City." In John W. Hall and Takeshi Toyoda, eds. *Japan in the Muromachi Age*. Berkeley and Los Angeles: University of California Press, 1977.

Mosk, Carl. "Fecundity, Infanticide, and Food Consumption in Japan." *Explorations in Economic History* 15 (July 1978): 269–89.

Munemasa Isoo 宗政五十緒. *Kinsei Kyōto shuppan bunka no kenkyū.* 近世京都出版文化の研究. Kyoto: Dōhōsha 同朋舍, 1982.

Murai Masuo 村井益男. *Edo-jō* 江戸城. Tokyo: Chūō kōronsha 中央公論社, 1964.

Murai Shōsuke 村井章介. "Chūsei Nihon no kokusai ishiki ni tsuite" 中世日本の国際意識について. In *Minshū no seikatsu, bunka to henkaku shutai* 民衆の生活・文化と変革主体 (*Rekishigaku kenkyūkai 1982 nendo taikai hōkoku* 歴史学研究会 1982 年度大会報告). Tokyo: Aoki shoten 青木書店, 1982.

Murakami Naojirō 村上直次郎, ed. *Ikoku ōfuku shokanshū, Zōtei ikoku nikki shō* 異国往復書翰集・増訂異国日記抄・Tokyo: Sunnansha 駿南社, 1929.

Murakami Tadashi 村上直. *Daikan: bakufu o sasaeta hitobito* 代官：幕府を支えた人々. Tokyo: Jimbutsu ōraisha 人物往来社, 1963.

Nagahara Keiji 永原慶二, ed. *Sengoku-ki no kenryoku to shakai* 戦国期の権力と社会. Tokyo: Tōkyō daigaku shuppankai 東京大学出版会, 1976.

Nagahara, Keiji, with Kozo Yamamura. "The Sengoku Daimyo and the Kandaka System." In John W. Hall, Keiji Nagahara, and Kozo Yamamura, eds. *Japan Before Tokugawa: Political Consolidation and Economic Growth, 1500–1650.* Princeton, N. J.: Princeton University Press, 1981.

Nagahara, Keiji, with Kozo Yamamura. "Village Communities and Daimyo Power." In John W. Hall and Takeshi Toyoda, eds. *Japan in the Muromachi Age.* Berkeley and Los Angeles: University of California Press, 1977.

Nagaoka shiyakusho 長岡市役所, ed. *Nagaoka-shi shi* 長岡市史. Nagaoka: Nagaoka shiyakusho 長岡市役所, 1931.

Nagatomo Chiyoji 長友千代治. *Kinsei kashihon'ya no kenkyū* 近世貸本屋の研究. Tokyo: Tōkyōdō 東京堂, 1982.

Nagayama Usaburō 永山卯三郎. *Hayakawa daikan* 早川代官. Okayama: Okayamaken kyōikukai 岡山県教育会, 1929.

Naikaku tōkeikyoku 内閣統計局, ed. *Nihon teikoku tōkei nenkan* 日本帝國統計年鑑. Tokyo, 1886–1936.

Naitō Akira 内藤昌. *Edo no machi* 江戸の町. 2 vols. Tokyo: Sōshisha 草思社, 1982.

Naitō Akira 内藤昌. "Edo no machi kōzō" 江戸の町構造. In Nishiyama Matsunosuke 西山松之助 and Yoshihara Ken'ichirō 吉原健一郎, eds. *Edo jidai zushi* 江戸時代図史. Vol. 4. Tokyo: Chikuma shobō 筑摩書房, 1975.

Naitō Akira 内藤昌. *Edo no toshi no kenchiku* 江戸の都市の建築. Tokyo: Mainichi shimbunsha 毎日新聞社, 1972.

Naitō Akira 内藤昌. *Edo to Edojō* 江戸と江戸城. Tokyo: Kashima kenkyūjo shuppankai 鹿島研究所出版会, 1966.

Naitō Shumpo 内藤雋輔, ed. *Chōsen nichinichiki* 朝鮮日々記 (by Keinen 慶念). *Chōsen gakuhō* 朝鮮学報 35 (May 1965): 55–154.

Naitō Shumpo 内藤雋輔. "*Chōsen nichinichiki* ni tsuite"「朝鮮日々記」について. *Chōsen gakuhō* 朝鮮学報 35 (May 1965): 155–67.

Naitō Shumpo 内藤雋輔. "Jinshin, Teiyū no eki ni okeru hiryo Chōsenjin no sakkan mondai ni tsuite: Chōsen shiryō ni yoru." Pts. 2-3. 壬辰・丁酉の役における被虜朝鮮人の刷還問題について(中, 下). *Chōsen gakuhō* 朝鮮学報 33 (October 1964): 48-103; 34 (January 1965): 74-140.

Najita, Tetsuo. "Intellectual Change in Early Eighteenth Century Tokugawa Confucianism." *Journal of Asian Studies* 34 (1975): 931-44.

Najita, Tetsuo. "Method and Analysis in the Conceptual Portrayal of Tokugawa Intellectual History." In Tetsuo Najita and Irwin Scheiner, eds. *Japanese Thought in the Tokugawa Period: Methods and Metaphors*. Chicago: University of Chicago Press, 1978.

Najita, Tetsuo. "Ōshio Heihachirō (1793-1837)." In Albert Craig and Donald H. Shively, eds., *Personality in Japanese History*. Berkeley and Los Angeles: University of California Press, 1970.

Najita, Tetsuo. "Political Economism in the Thought of Dazai Shundai (1680-1740)." *Journal of Asian Studies* 31 (1972): 821-39.

Najita, Tetsuo. "Restorationism in the Political Thought of Yamagata Daini (1725-67)." *Journal of Asian Studies* 31 (1971): 17-29.

Najita, Tetsuo. *Visions of Virtue in Tokugawa Japan - The Kaitokudō Merchant Academy of Osaka*. Chicago: University of Chicago Press, 1987.

Najita, Tetsuo, and Irwin Scheiner, eds. *Japanese Thought in the Tokugawa Period: Methods and Metaphors*. Chicago: University of Chicago Press, 1978.

Nakabe Yoshiko 中部よし子. *Jōkamachi* 城下町. Kyoto: Yanagihara shoten 柳原書店, 1978.

Nakabe Yoshiko 中部よし子. *Kinsei toshi no seiritsu to kōzō* 近世都市の成立と構造. Tokyo: Shinseisha 新生社, 1967.

Nakabe Yoshiko 中部よし子. "Kinsei toshi Ōsaka no kakuritsu" 近世都市大阪の確立. In Toyoda Takeshi 豊田武, Harada Tomohiko 原田伴彦, and Yamori Kazuhiko 矢守一彦, eds. *Kōza: Nihon no hōken toshi* 講座:日本の封建都市. Vol. 3. Tokyo: Bun'ichi sōgō shuppan 文一総合出版, 1981.

Nakabe Yoshiko 中部よし子. "Sengoku jidai daimyō kyojū toshi ni kansuru shomondai" 戦国時代大名居住都市に関する諸問題. In Chihōshi kenkyū kyōgikai 地方史研究協議会, ed. *Toshi no chihōshi* 都市の地方史. Tokyo: Yūzankaku 雄山閣, 1980.

Nakai, Kate Wildman, *Shogunal Politics: Arai Hakuseki and the Premises of Tokugawa Rule*. Cambridge: Harvard University Press, 1988.

Nakai, Kate W. ケイト・W・ナカイ, and Nakai Yoshiyuki 中井義幸. "Arai Hakuseki jihitsu 'Ogiwara Shigehide dangai-sho' sōkō" 新井白石自筆「荻原重秀弾劾書」草稿. *Shigaku zasshi* 史学雑誌 89 (October 1980): 38-49.

Nakai Nobuhiko 中井信彦. *Bakuhan shakai to shōhin ryūtsū* 幕藩社会と商品流通. Tokyo: Hanawa shobō 塙書房, 1961.

Nakai Nobuhiko 中井信彦. "Hōreki-Temmei-ki no rekishiteki ichi 宝暦-天明期の歴史的位置. *Rekishigaku kenkyū* 歴史学研究 299 (April 1965): 14-23, 50.

Nakai Nobuhiko 中井信彦. "Kinsei toshi no hatten" 近世都市の発展. In *Iwanami kōza Nihon rekishi* 岩波講座日本歴史. Vol. 11. Tokyo: Iwanami shoten, 1963.

Nakai Nobuhiko 中井信彦. *Tenkanki bakuhansei no kenkyū* 転換期幕藩制の研究. Tokyo: Hanawa shobō 塙書房, 1971.

Nakamura Hajime 中村元. *Kinsei Nihon ni okeru hihanteki seishin no ichi kōsatsu* 近世日本における批判的精神の一考察. Tokyo: Sanseidō 三省堂, 1949.

Nakamura Hidetaka 中村栄孝. *Nissen kankeishi no kenkyū* 日鮮関係史の研究. 3 vols. Tokyo: Yoshikawa kōbunkan 吉川弘文館, 1965-9.

Nakamura Hiroshi 中村拓, ed. *Nihon kochizu taisei* 日本古地図大成. Tokyo: Kōdansha 講談社, 1974.

Nakamura Kichiji 中村吉治. *Bakuhan taisei ron* 幕藩体制論. Tokyo: Yamakawa shuppansha 山川出版社, 1972.

Nakamura Kichiji 中村吉治. "Hōken jidai kōki sōsetsu" 封建時代後期総説. In *Shin Nihonshi kōza* 新日本史講座. Tokyo: Chūō kōronsha 中央公論社, 1947.

Nakamura Kichiji 中村吉治. *Kinsei shoki nōseishi kenkyū* 近世初期農政史研究. Tokyo: Iwanami shoten 岩波書店, 1938.

Nakamura Kichiji 中村吉治. *Nihon hōkensei saihenseishi* 日本封建制再編成史. Tokyo: Mikasa shobō 三笠書房, 1940.

Nakamura Naokatsu 中村直勝, ed. *Hikone-shi shi* 彦根市史. 3 vols. Hikone-shi: Hikone shiyakusho 彦根市役所, 1960-4.

Nakamura Shin'ichirō 中村真一郎. *Rai San'yō to sono jidai* 頼山陽とその時代. Tokyo: Chūō kōronsha 中央公論社, 1971.

Nakamura Yukihiko 中村幸彦, ed. *Kinsei chōnin shisō* 近世町人思想. Vol. 59 of *Nihon shisō taikei* 日本思想大系. Tokyo: Iwanami shoten 岩波書店, 1975.

Nakamura Yukihiko 中村幸彦 and Okada Takehiko 岡田武彦, eds. *Kinsei kōki jukashū* 近世後期儒家集. Vol. 47 of *Nihon shisō taikei* 日本思想大系. Tokyo: Iwanami shoten 岩波書店, 1972.

Nakazawa Morito 中沢護人 and Mori Kazuo 森数男. *Nihon no kaimei shisō* 日本の開明思想. Tokyo: Kinokuniya shoten 紀伊国屋書店, 1970.

Naramoto Tatsuya 奈良本辰也, *Chōnin no jitsuryoku* 町人の実力. Vol. 17 of *Nihon no rekishi* 日本の歴史. Tokyo: Chūō kōronsha 中央公論社, 1966.

Naramoto Tatsuya 奈良本辰也, ed. *Hagakure*葉隠. Vol. 17 of *Nihon no meicho* 日本の名著. Tokyo: Chūō kōronsha 中央公論社, 1969.

Naramoto Tatsuya 奈良本辰也, Hosokawa Morisada 細川護貞, and Murakami Genzō 村上元三, eds. *Edo daimyō hyakke* 江戸大名百家. Vol. 22 of *Taiyō bekkan* 太陽別巻. Tokyo: Heibonsha 平凡社, 1978.

Naramoto Tatsuya 奈良本辰也 and Nakai Nobuhiko 中井信彦, eds. *Ninomiya Sontoku, Ōhara Yūgaku* 二宮尊徳・大原幽学. Vol. 52 of *Nihon shisō taikei* 日本思想大系. Tokyo: Iwanami shoten 岩波書店, 1973.

Nihon fūzokushi gakkai 日本風俗史学会, ed. *Nihon fūzokushi jiten* 日本風俗史事典. Tokyo: Kōbundō 弘文堂, 1979.

Nihon koten bungaku daijiten henshū iinkai 日本古典文学大辞典編集委員会, ed. *Nihon koten bungaku daijiten* 日本古典文学大辞典. 6 vols. Tokyo: Iwanami shoten 岩波書店, 1983-5.

Nihon shiryō shūsei hensankai 日本史料集成編纂会, ed. *Chūgoku, Chōsen no shiseki ni okeru Nihon shiryō shūsei* 中国・朝鮮の史籍における日本史料集成: *Min jitsuroku no bu* 明實録之部; *Richō jitsuroku no bu* 李朝實録之部; *Seishi no bu* 正史之部. Tokyo: Kokusho kankōkai 国書刊行会, 1975.

Nishi Setsuko 西節子. "Tatsumi yōsui repōto" 辰巳用水レポート. *Rekishi techō* 歴史手帳 2 (May 1974): 31-4.

Nishikawa Kōji 西川幸治. *Nihon toshishi no kenkyū* 日本都市史の研究. Tokyo: Nihon hōsō shuppan kyōkai 日本放送出版協会, 1972.

Nishikawa, Shunsaku. "Grain Consumption: The Case of Chōshū." In Marius B. Jansen and Gilbert Rozman, eds. *Japan in Transition: From Tokugawa to Meiji*. Princeton, N. J.: Princeton University Press, 1986.

Nishikawa Shunsaku 西川俊作. *Nihon keizai no seichōshi* 日本経済の成長史. Tokyo: Tōyō keizai 東洋経済, 1985.

Nishiyama Matsunosuke 西山松之助 and Haga Noboru 芳賀登, eds. *Edo sambyakunen* 江戸三百年. 3 vols. Tokyo: Kōdansha 講談社, 1975-6.

Noma Kōshin 野間光辰, ed. (*Kampon*) *Shikidō ōkagami* 色道大鏡 (by Fujimoto Kizan 藤本箕山). Kyoto: Yūzan bunko 友山文庫, 1961.

Noma Kōshin 野間光辰, ed. *Saikaku shū* 西鶴集. Pt. 2. Vol. 48 of *Nihon koten bungaku taikei* 日本古典文学大系. Tokyo: Iwanami shoten 岩波書店, 1960.

Noma Kōshin 野間光辰, ed. *Teihon Saikaku zenshū* 定本西鶴全集. 15 vols. Tokyo: Chūō kōronsha 中央公論社, 1949-70.

Noma Kōshin 野間光辰, "Ukiyo zōshi no dokusha sō" 浮世草子の読者層. *Bungaku* 文学 26 (1958): 63-73.

Nomura Kanetarō 野村兼太郎. *Edo* 江戸. Tokyo: Shibundō 至文堂, 1966.

Nonaka Jun 野中準, comp. *Dai Nihon sozeishi* 大日本租税志. 3 vols. Tokyo: Chōyōkai 朝陽会, 1926-7.

Norman, E. H. "Andō Shōeki and the Anatomy of Japanese Feudalism." *Transactions of the Asiatic Society of Japan* 2, 3rd ser. (1949).

Norman, E. H. "Feudal Background of Japanese Politics." In John W. Dower, ed. *Origins of the Modern Japanese State: Selected Writings of E. H. Norman*. New York: Random House, 1975.

Norman, E. H. "Japan's Emergence As a Modern State." In John W. Dower, ed. *Origins of the Modern Japanese State: Selected Writings of E. H. Norman*. New York: Random House, 1975.

Norman, E. H. "Late Feudal Society." In John W. Dower, ed. *Origins of the Modern Japanese State: Selected Writings of E. H. Norman*. New York: Random House, 1975.

Nosco, Peter, ed. *Confucianism and Tokugawa Culture*. Princeton, N. J.: Princeton University Press, 1984.

Numata Jirō 沼田次郎. "Nisshin bōeki ni okeru ichi mondai" 日清貿易における一問題. *Rekishi chiri* 歴史地理 68 (November-December 1936): 421-34, 543-8.

Numata Jirō 沼田次郎. "Tanuma jidai to Isaac Titsingh" 田沼時代とイザーク・ティチング. *Nihon rekishi* 日本歴史 380 (January 1980): 101-6.

Ōe Fumiki 大江文城. *Hompō jugakushi ronkō* 本邦儒学史論考. Osaka: Zenkoku shobō 全国書房, 1943.

Ōgaki shiyakusho 大垣市役所, ed. *Ōgaki-shi shi* 大垣市史. 3 vols. Ōgaki, 1930.

Ogata Tomio 緒方富雄. *Ogata Kōan den* 緒方洪庵傳. Tokyo: Iwanami shoten 岩波書店, 1963.

Ogawa Kōyō 小川光暘. *Shinjo to shingu no rekishi* 寝所と寝具の歴史. Tokyo: Yūzankaku 雄山閣, 1973.

Ōishi Shinzaburo 大石慎三郎. *Genroku jidai* 元禄時代. Tokyo: Iwanami shoten 岩波書店, 1970.

Ōishi Shinzaburo 大石慎三郎. *Kyōhō kaikaku no keizai seisaku* 享保改革の経済政策. Tokyo: Ochanomizu shobō 御茶の水書房, 1961.

Okamoto Yoshitomo 岡本良知. *Jūroku seiki Nichi-Ō kōtsūshi no kenkyū* 十六世紀日欧交通史の研究. Tokyo: Kōbunsō 弘文荘, 1936.

Okano Takeo 岡野他家夫. *Nihon shuppan bunka shi* 日本出版文化史. Tokyo: Shumpodō 春歩堂, 1959.

Okayama shiyakusho 岡山市役所. *Okayama-shi shi, sangyō keizai hen* 岡山市史, 産業経済編. Okayama: Okayama shiyakusho 岡山市役所, 1966.

Okayama-ken 岡山県. *Okayama-ken no rekishi* 岡山県の歴史. Okayama: Okayama-ken 岡山県, 1962.

Ōkubo Toshiaki 大久保利謙, Kodama Kōta 児玉幸多, Yanai Kenji 箭内健次, and Inoue Mitsusada 井上光貞, eds. *Shiryō ni yoru Nihon no ayumi (Kinsei)* 史料による日本の歩み－近世. Tokyo: Yoshikawa kōbunkan 吉川弘文館, 1963.

Okuno Takahiro 奥野高広, ed. *Oda Nobunaga monjo no kenkyū* 織田信長文書の研究. 2 vols. Tokyo: Yoshikawa kōbunkan 吉川弘文館, 1969-70.

Okuno Takahiro 奥野高広. "Oda seiken no kihon rosen" 織田政権の基本路線. *Kokushigaku* 国史学 100 (November 1976): 29-58.

Ōkuwa Hitoshi 大桑斉. "Bukkyō shisōron: shokyō itchi ron no keisei" 仏教思想論：諸教一致論の形成. In Hongō Takamori 本郷隆盛 and Fukaya Katsumi 深谷克巳, eds. *Kinsei shisōron* 近世思想論. Vol. 9 of *Kōza Nihon kinseishi* 講座日本近世史. Tokyo: Yūhikaku 有斐閣, 1981.

Ōkuwa Hitoshi 大桑斉. *Jidan no shisō* 寺檀の思想. Vol. 177 of *Kyōikusha rekishi shinsho: Nihonshi* 教育社歴史新書：日本史. Tokyo: Kyōikusha 教育社, 1979.

Ōmori Eiko 大森映子. "Daimyō kayaku to bakuhan kankei" 大名課役と幕藩関係. In Rekishigaku kenkyūkai 歴史学研究会, ed. *Sekaishi ninshiki ni okeru minzoku to kokka* 世界史認識における民族と国家 (*1978 nendo Rekishigaku kenkyūkai taikai hōkoku* 1978年度歴史学研究会大会報告). Tokyo: Aoki shoten 青木書店, November 1978.

Omura Hajime 小村弌. "Echigo no zaigō-machi" 越後の在郷町. In Toyoda Takeshi 豊田武, Harada Tomohiko 原田伴彦, and Yamori Kazuhiko 矢守一彦, eds. *Kōza: Nihon no hōken toshi* 講座：日本の封建都市. Vol. 3. Tokyo: Bun'ichi sōgō shuppan 文一総合出版, 1981.

Ono Hitoshi 小野均. *Kinsei jōkamachi no kenkyū* 近世城下町の研究. Tokyo: Shibundō 至文堂, 1928.

Ono Kōji 小野晃嗣. "Kyōto no kinsei toshika" 京都の近世都市化. *Shakai keizai shigaku* 社会経済史学 10 (October 1940): 1-32.

Ono Takeo 小野武雄. *Edo bukka jiten* 江戸物価事典. Tokyo: Tembōsha 展望社, 1982.

Ono Takeo 小野武雄, comp. *Kinsei jikata keizai shiryō* 近世地方經濟史料. 10

vols. Tokyo: Kinsei jikata keizai shiryō kankōkai 近世地方經濟史料刊行会, 1931-2.

Ono Takeo 小野武雄. *Yoshiwara, Shimabara* 吉原・島原. Tokyo: Kyōikusha 教育社, 1978.

Ooms, Herman. *Tokugawa Ideology – Early Constructs, 1570-1680.* Princeton, N. J.: Princeton University Press, 1985.

Ortolani, Benito. *Das Kabukitheater: Kulturgeschichte der Anfänge. Monumenta Nipponica* Monographs, no. 19. Tokyo: Sophia University Press, 1964.

Ōta Akira 太田亮. *Seishi kakei daijiten* 姓氏家系大辞典. Vol. 2. Tokyo: Kadokawa shoten 角川書店, 1963.

Ōta Gyūichi 太田牛一. *Nobunaga kō ki* 信長公記. Tokyo: Kadokawa shoten 角川書店, 1969.

Ōta Heisaburō 太田兵三郎, ed. *Fujiwara Seika shū* 藤原惺窩集. 2 vols. Tokyo: Kokumin seishin bunka kenkyūjo 國民精神文化研究所, 1938-9.

Ōta Seikyū 太田青丘. *Fujiwara Seika* 藤原惺窩. Tokyo: Yoshikawa kōbunkan 吉川弘文館, 1985.

Ōtsuka shigakkai 大塚史学会, ed. *(Shimpan) Kyōdoshi jiten* (新版)郷土史辞典. Tokyo: Asakura shoten 朝倉書店, 1969.

Ōyamazaki-machi chōshi hensan iinkai 大山崎町町史編纂委員会, ed. *Ōyamazaki chōshi, shiryō hen* 大山崎町史史料編. Kyoto: Ōyamazaki-machi 大山崎町, 1981.

Ozawa Eiichi 小沢栄一. *Kinsei shigaku shisōshi kenkyū* 近世史学思想史研究. Tokyo: Yoshikawa kōbunkan 吉川弘文館, 1974.

Oze Hoan 小瀬甫庵. *Taikōki* 太閤記. Edited by Kuwata Tadachika 桑田忠親. Tokyo: Shin jimbutsu ōraisha 新人物往来社, 1971.

Pires, A. Thomaz. "O Japan no seculo" XVI. Pt. 1. *O Instituto* 53 (1906).

Putzar, Edward. "Chikusai monogatari." *Monumenta Nipponica* 16 (1960-1): 161-95.

Rai Tsutomu 頼惟勤, ed. *Rai Sanyō* 頼山陽. Tokyo: Chūō kōronsha 中央公論社, 1972.

Rai Tsutomu 頼惟勤, ed. *Sorai gakuha* 徂徠学派. Vol. 37 of *Nihon shisō taikei* 日本思想大系. Tokyo: Iwanami shoten 岩波書店, 1972.

Reischauer, Edwin O. *Japan: The Story of a Nation.* New York: Knopf, 1970; 3d ed., 1981.

Robertson, Jennifer. "Japanese Farm Manuals: A Literature of Discovery." *Peasant Studies* 11 (Spring 1984): 169-94.

Rodrigues Tçuzzu, João, SJ. *Historia da Igreja do Japao.* Pt. 2. In Doi Tadao 土井忠生 et al., trans. *Dai kōkai jidai sōsho* 大航海時代叢書. Pt. 2. Vol. 10 of *Nihon kyōkai shi* 日本教会史. Tokyo: Iwanami shoten 岩波書店, 1970.

Rozman, Gilbert. "Edo's Importance in the Changing Tokugawa Society." *Journal of Japanese Studies* 1 (Autumn 1974): 91-112.

Rozman, Gilbert. *Urban Networks in Ch'ing China and Tokugawa Japan.* Princeton, N. J.: Princeton University Press, 1974.

Rubinger, Robert. *Private Academies of Tokugawa Japan.* Princeton, N. J.: Princeton University Press, 1982.

Saegusa Yasutaka 三枝康高. *Kamo no Mabuchi* 加茂真淵. Tokyo: Yoshikawa kōbunkan 吉川弘文館, 1959.

Saga kenshi hensan iinkai 佐賀県史編纂委員会, ed. *Saga-ken shiryō shūsei: komonjo-hen* 佐賀県史料集成古文書編. Vol. 3. Saga: Saga kenritsu toshokan 佐賀県立図書館, 1958.

Saigusa Hiroto 三枝博音. *Miura Baien no tetsugaku* 三浦梅園の哲学. Tokyo: Dai-ichi shobō 第一書房, 1941.

Saigusa Hiroto 三枝博音, ed., *Nihon kagaku koten zensho* 日本科学古典全書. Vol. 1. Tokyo: Asahi shimbunsha 朝日新聞社, 1978.

Sakata Yoshio 坂田吉雄. *Chōnin* 町人. Tokyo: Kōbundō 弘文堂, 1939.

Sakudō Yōtarō 作道洋太郎. *Kinsei Nihon kaheishi* 近世日本貨幣史. Tokyo: Kōbundō 弘文堂, 1958.

Sakudō Yōtarō 作道洋太郎. "Kinsei Ōsaka ryōgae shō keiei no keisei katei – jūnin ryōgae no sōsetsu to Kōnoike ryōgaeten" 近世大阪両替商経営の形成過程 – 十人両替の創設と鴻池両替店. *Bankingu* バンキング 175 (October 1962): 32-54.

Sakudō Yōtarō 作道洋太郎. "Tokugawa chūki ni okeru shin'yō seido no tenkai – toku ni kin'yū to zaisei no kanren o chūshin to shite." 徳川中期における信用制度の展開 – とくに金融と財政の関連を中心として. *Rekishigaku kenkyū* 歴史学研究 264 (April-May 1962): 66-70.

Sansom, G, B. *Japan: A Short Cultural History*. New York: Appleton Century, 1943.

Sanyō shimbunsha 山陽新聞社, ed. *Nene to Kinoshita-ke monjo* ねねと木下家文書. Okayama: Sanyō shimbunsha 山陽新聞社, 1982.

Sargent, G. W., trans. *The Japanese Family Storehouse*. Cambridge, England: Cambridge University Press, 1959.

Sasaki Gin'ya 佐々木銀弥. *Chūsei shōhin ryūtsū no kenkyū* 中世商品流通の研究. Tokyo: Hōsei daigaku shuppankyoku 法政大学出版局, 1972.

Sasaki, Gin'ya, with Willam B. Hauser, "Sengoku Daimyo Rule and Commerce." In John W. Hall, Keiji Nagahara, and Kozo Yamamura, eds. *Japan Before Tokugawa: Political Consolidation and Economic Growth, 1500-1650*. Princeton, N. J.: Princeton University Press, 1981.

Sasaki Junnosuke 佐々木潤之介. "Bakuhansei kokka ron" 幕藩制国家論. In Hara Hidesaburō 原秀三郎 et al., comps. *Kinsei* 近世. Vol. 3 of *Taikei Nihon kokka shi* 大系日本国家史. Tokyo: Tōkyō daigaku shuppankai 東京大学出版会, 1975.

Sasaki Junnosuke 佐々木潤之介. *Daimyō to hyakushō* 大名と百姓. Vol. 15 of *Nihon no rekishi* 日本の歴史. Tokyo: Chūō kōronsha 中央公論社, 1966.

Sasaki Junnosuke 佐々木潤之介. "Gun'yaku ron no mondaiten" 軍役論の問題点. In Toyoda Takeshi 豊田武 et al., eds. *Bakuhan taisei* 幕藩体制. Pt. 1. Vol. 7 of *Ronshū Nihon rekishi* 論集日本歴史. Tokyo: Yūseidō shuppan 有精堂出版, 1973.

Sasaki Junnosuke 佐々木潤之介. *Hyakushō ikki to uchikowashi* 百姓一揆と打ちこわし. Tokyo: Sanseidō 三省堂, 1974.

Sasaki, Junnosuke, with Ronald P. Toby. "The Changing Rationale of Daimyo

Control in the Emergence of the Bakuhan State." In John W. Hall, Keiji Nagahara, and Kozo Yamamura, eds. *Japan Before Tokugawa: Political Consolidation and Economic Growth, 1500-1650*. Princeton, N. J.: Princeton University Press, 1981.

Satō Takayuki 佐藤孝之. "Kinsei zenki no nengu shūshu to nōson kin'yū" 近世前期の年貢収取と農村金融. *Tokugawa rinseishi kenkyūjo kenkyū kiyō* 徳川林政史研究所研究紀要 (1979): 387-436.

Satō Yoneshi 佐藤米司. "Ryōbosei no mondai ten" 両墓制の問題点. In Mogami Takayoshi 最上孝敬, ed. *Haka no shūzoku* 墓の習俗. Vol. 4 of *Sōsō bosei kenkyū shūsei* 葬送墓制研究集成. Tokyo: Meicho shuppan 名著出版, 1979.

Satow, Sir Ernest. *A Diplomat in Japan*. Oxford, England: Oxford University Press, 1968.

Scheiner, Irwin. "Benevolent Lords and Honorable Peasants: Rebellion and Peasant Consciousness in Tokugawa Japan." In Tetsuo Najita and Irwin Scheiner, eds. *Japanese Thought in the Tokugawa Period: Methods and Metaphors*. Chicago: University of Chicago Press, 1978.

Schurhammer, G., SJ, and J. Wicki, SJ, eds. *Epistolas S. Francisci Xaverii aliaque eius scripta*. Pt. 1. In *Monumenta Historica Societatis Iesu*. Vol. 67. Rome: Apud Monumenta Historica Societatis Iesu, 1944.

Schütte, Josef Franz, SJ. *Introductio ad historiam Societatis Jesu in Japonia 1549-1650*. Rome: Apud Institutum Historicum Societatis Iesu, 1968.

Schütte, Josef Franz, SJ, ed. *Textus catalogorum Japoniae, 1553-1654*. *Monumenta Historica Japoniae* 1, *Monumenta Missionum Societatis* 34, *Monumenta Historica Societatis Iesu*. Vol. 111 (1975), nos. 1-10.

Schütte, Josef Franz, SJ. *Valignanos Missionsgrundsätze für Japan*. Vol. 1. Pt. 1. *Das Problem (1573-1580)*. Rome: Edizioni di storia e Letteratura, 1951.

Sekai hyakka daijiten 世界百科大事典. Tokyo: Heibonsha 平凡社, 1981.

Sekai rekishi jiten 世界歴史事典. Vol. 22: *Shiryō-hen* 史料篇, *Nihon* 日本. Tokyo: Heibonsha 平凡社, 1955.

Seki Giichirō 関儀一郎, ed. *Kinsei juka shiryō* 近世儒家史料. Vol. 1. Tokyo: Ida shoten 井田書店, 1942.

Seki Giichirō 関儀一郎, ed. *Nihon jurin sōsho* 日本儒林叢書 14 vols. Tokyo: Tōyō tosho kankōkai 東洋図書刊行会, 1927-38.

Sekiyama Naotaro 関山直太郎. *Kinsei Nihon no jinkō kōzō* 近世日本の人口構造. Tokyo: Yoshikawa kōbunkan 吉川弘文館, 1958.

Sekiyama Naotaro 関山直太郎. *Nihon kahei kin'yūshi kenkyū* 日本貨幣金融史研究. Tokyo: Shinkeizaisha 新経済社, 1943.

Shakai kōgaku kenkyūjo 社会工学研究所, ed. *Nihon rettō ni okeru jinkō bumpu no chōki jikeiretsu bunseki* 日本列島における人口分布の長期時系列分析. Tokyo: Shakai kōgaku kenkyūjo 社会工学研究所, 1974.

Sheldon, Charles David. *The Rise of the Merchant Class in Tokugawa Japan, 1600-1868*. Monographs of the Association for Asian Studies, no. 5. Locust Valley, N. Y.: J. J. Augustin, 1958.

Shibata Akimasa 柴田顯正, ed. *Tokugawa Ieyasu to sono shūi* 徳川家康と其周圍.

3 vols. Okazaki-shi: Okazaki shiyakusho 岡崎市役所, 1926.

Shibata Minoru 柴田実. *Baigan to sono monryū* 梅岩とその門流. Kyoto: Mineruva shobō ミネルヴァ書房, 1977.

Shibusawa Eiichi 渋沢栄一. *Rakuō kō den* 樂翁公傳. Tokyo: Iwanami shoten 岩波書店, 1939.

Shidō bunko 斯道文庫, ed. *(Edo jidai) Shorin shuppan shoseki mokuroku shūsei* 江戸時代書林出版書籍目録集成. Tokyo: Inoue shobō 井上書房, 1962-4.

Shiga-ken 滋賀県, ed. *Shiga kenshi* 滋賀県史. 6 vols. Tokyo: Sanshūsha 三秀舎, 1927-8.

Shihōshō 司法省. *Tokugawa kinrei kō* 徳川禁令考. 6 vols. Tokyo: Yoshikawa kōbunkan 吉川弘文館, 1931-2.

Shimbō Hiroshi 新保博. "Kinsei kōki ni okeru bukka, kin sōba, kawase uchigin sōba, 1787-1867" 近世後期における物価・金相場・為替打銀相場, 1787-1867. In Umemura Mataji 梅村又次 et al., eds. *Nihon keizai no hatten* 日本経済の発展. Tokyo: Nihon keizai shimbunsha 日本経済新聞社, 1976.

Shimizu Hirokazu 清水紘一. Kirishitan kinseishi キリシタン禁制史. Vol. 109 of *Kyōikusha rekishi shinsho: Nihonshi* 教育社歴史新書：日本史. Tokyo: Kyōikusha 教育社, 1981.

Shimode Sekiyo 下出積与. *Kaga Kanazawa no kimpaku* 加賀・金沢の金箔. Kanazawa: Hokkoku shuppannsha 北国出版社, 1972.

Shinjō Tsunezō 新城常三. *(Shinkō) Shaji sankei no shakai keizaishi-teki kenkyū* 新稿社寺参詣の社会経済史的研究. Tokyo: Hanawa shobō 塙書房, 1982.

Shinotō Mitsuyuki 篠藤光行. "Hansei kaikaku no kenkyū – jōkamachi shōgyō no kiki o tsūjite mita Nakatsu han hōken kōzō no hōkai katei" 藩政改革の研究－城下町商業の危機を通じて見た中津藩封建構造の崩壊過程. *Keizaigaku kenkyū* 経済学研究 21: 2 (1955).

Shinozaki Tokuzō 篠崎篤三. *Jihi mujin no sōshisha Miura Baien* 慈悲無尽の創始者三浦梅園. Tokyo: Chūō shakai jigyō kyōkai shakai jigyō kenkyūjo 中央社会事業協会社会事業研究所, 1936.

Shinshū Kyōto sōsho kankōkai 新修京都叢書刊行会, ed. *(Shinshū) Kyōto sōsho* (新修)京都叢書. 22 vols. Kyoto: Rinsen shoten 臨川書店, 1967-76.

Shiraki Kosaburō 白木小三郎. *Sumai no rekishi* 住まいの歴史. Osaka: Sōgensha 創元社, 1978.

Shively, Donald H. "Bakufu *versus* Kabuki." *Harvard Journal of Asiatic Studies* 18 (1955): 326-56; reprinted in John W. Hall and Marius B. Jansen, eds. *Studies in the Institutional History of Early Modern Japan*. Princeton N. J.: Princeton University Press, 1968.

Shively, Donald H. *The Love Suicide of Amijima*. Harvard-Yenching Institute Monograph Series, no. 15. Cambridge, Mass.: Harvard University Press, 1953.

Shively, Donald H. "The Social Environment of Tokugawa Kabuki." In James R. Brandon, William P. Malm, and Donald H. Shively, eds. *Studies in Kabuki: Its Acting, Music, and Historical Context*. Honolulu: University of Hawaii Press, 1978.

Shively, Donald H. "Sumptuary Regulation and Status in Early Tokugawa

Japan." *Harvard Journal of Asiatic Studies* 25 (1964-5): 123-64.

Shively, Donald H. "Tokugawa Plays on Forbidden Topics." In James R. Brandon, ed. *Chushingura: Studies in Kabuki and the Puppet Theater.* Honolulu: University of Hawaii Press, 1982.

Shively, Donald H. "Tokugawa Tsunayoshi: The Genroku Shogun." In Albert M. Craig and Donald H. Shively, eds. *Personality in Japanese History.* Berkeley and Los Angeles: University of California Press, 1970.

Shōda Ken'ichirō 正田健一郎 and Hayami Akira 速水融. *Nihon keizaishi* 日本経済史. Vol. 4 of *Keizai gaku zenshū* 経済学全集. Tokyo: Sekai shoin 世界書院, 1965.

Smith, Bardwell L. "Japanese Society and Culture in the Momoyama Era: A Bibliographic Essay." In George Elison and Bardwell Smith, eds. *Warlords, Artists, & Commoners: Japan in the Sixteenth Century.* Honolulu: University of Hawaii Press, 1981.

Smith, Thomas C. *The Agrarian Origins of Modern Japan.* Stanford, Calif.: Stanford University Press, 1959.

Smith, Thomas C. "The Japanese Village in the Seventeenth Century." In John W. Hall and Marius B. Jansen, eds. *Studies in the Institutional History of Early Modern Japan.* Princeton, N. J.: Princeton University Press, 1968.

Smith, Thomas C. "The Land Tax in the Tokugawa Period." In John W. Hall and Marius B. Jansen, eds. *Studies in the Institutional History of Early Modern Japan.* Princeton, N. J.: Princeton University Press, 1968.

Smith, Thomas C. *Nakahara.* Stanford, Calif.: Stanford University Press, 1977.

Smith, Thomas C. "Pre-modern Economic Growth: Japan and the West." *Past and Present* 43 (1973): 127-60.

Sŏae munjip pu Chingbirok 西屋文集附懲毖録. Seoul: Sŏnggyungwan taehakkyŏ taedong munhwa yŏnguwŏn 成均館大學校大東文化研究院, 1958.

Sone Hiromi 曽根ひろみ. "Kyōhō-ki no soshō saibanken to uttae" 享保期の訴訟裁判権と訴. In Matsumoto Shirō 松本四郎 and Yamada Tadao 山田忠雄, eds. *Genroku, Kyōhō-ki no seiji to shakai* 元禄・享保期の政治と社会. Vol. 4 of *Kōza Nihon kinseishi* 講座日本近世史. Tokyo: Yūhikaku 有斐閣, 1980.

Sone Hiromi 曽根ひろみ. "Zaichi daikan shihai to shoki jinushi kosaku kankei no tenkai" 在地代官支配と初期地主小作関係の展開. In Kitajima Masamoto 北島正元, ed. *Bakuhansei kokka seiritsu katei no kenkyū* 幕藩制国家成立過程の研究. Tokyo: Yoshikawa kōbunkan 吉川弘文館, 1978.

Strayer, Joseph R. "The Tokugawa Period and Japanese Feudalism." In John W. Hall and Marius B. Jansen, eds. *Studies in the Institutional History of Early Modern Japan.* Princeton, N. J.: Princeton University Press, 1968.

Suematsu Yasukazu 末松保和. *Kinsei ni okeru hoppō mondai no shinten* 近世における北方問題の進展. Tokyo: Shibundō 至文堂, 1928.

Suenaka Tetsuo 末中哲夫. *Yamagata Bantō no kenkyū* 山片蟠桃の研究. 2 vols. Osaka: Seibundō 清文堂, 1971, 1976.

Sugiyama, Hiroshi, with V. Dixon Morris. "The Growth of Commerce and Trades." In John W. Hall and Takeshi Toyoda, eds. *Japan in the Muromachi*

Age. Berkeley and Los Angeles: University of California Press, 1977.

Susser, Bernard. "The Toyotomi Regime and the Daimyo." In Jeffrey P. Mass and William B. Hauser, eds. *The Bakufu in Japanese History*. Stanford, Calif.: Stanford University Press, 1985.

Suwa Haruo 諏訪春雄. *Shuppan koto hajime: Edo no hon* 出版事始：江戸の本. Tokyo: Mainichi shimbunsha 毎日新聞社, 1978.

Suzuki Daisetsu 鈴木大拙. *Zen shisōshi kenkyū* 禅思想史研究. Vol. 1. Tokyo: Iwanami shoten 岩波書店, 1942.

Suzuki Daisetsu 鈴木大拙 and Furuta Shōkin 古田紹欽, eds. *Bankei zen no kenkyū* 盤珪禅の研究. Tokyo: Sankibō busshorin 山喜房仏書林, 1942.

Suzuki Taizan 鈴木泰山. *Zenshū no chihō hatten* 禅宗の地方発展. Tokyo: Unebi shobō 畝傍書房, 1942.

Tabata Tsutomu 田畑勉. "Bunsei, Tempō-ki no Kaga han sanbutsukata seisaku no igi ni tsuite" 文政・天保期の加賀藩産物方政策の意義について. In Tanaka Yoshio 田中喜男, ed. *Nihonkai chiikishi kenkyū* 日本海地域史研究. Vol. 4. Tokyo: Bunken shuppan 文献出版, 1982.

Tabohashi Kiyoshi 田保橋潔. *(Zōtei) Kindai Nihon gaikoku kankei shi* 増訂近代日本外国関係史. Tokyo: Tōkō shoin 刀江書院, 1943.

Tahara Tsuguo 田原嗣郎. "Kansei kaikaku no ichi kōsatsu" 寛政改革の一考察. *Rekishigaku kenkyū* 歴史学研究 178 (December 1954): 9-21.

Tahara Tsuguo 田原嗣郎. *Tokugawa shisōshi kenkyū* 徳川思想史研究. Tokyo: Miraisha 未来社, 1967.

Tahara Tsuguo 田原嗣郎 and Morimoto Junichirō 守本順一郎, eds. *Yamaga Sokō* 山鹿素行. Vol. 32 of *Nihon shisō taikei* 日本思想大系. Tokyo: Iwanami shoten 岩波書店, 1970.

Taira Shigemichi 平重道 and Abe Akio 阿部秋生, eds. *Kinsei Shintō ron, Zenki kokugaku* 近世神道論・前期国学. Tokyo: Iwanami shoten 岩波書店, 1972.

Takagi Shōsaku 高木昭作. "Edo bakufu no seiritsu" 江戸幕府の成立. In *Iwanami kōza Nihon rekishi* 岩波講座日本歴史. Vol. 9. Tokyo: Iwanami shoten 岩波書店, 1975.

Takahashi Tomio 高橋富雄. *Miyagi-ken no rekishi* 宮城県の歴史. Tokyo: Yamakawa shuppansha 山川出版社, 1969.

Takamaki Minoru 高牧実. "Shokuhō seiken to toshi" 織豊政権と都市. In Toyoda Takeshi 豊田武, Harada Tomohiko 原田伴彦, and Yamori Kazuhiko 矢守一彦, eds. *Kōza: Nihon no hōken toshi* 講座：日本の封建都市. Vol. 1. Tokyo: Bun'ichi sōgō shuppan 文一総合出版, 1982.

Takase Tamotsu 高瀬保. *Kaga han kaiunshi no kenkyū* 加賀藩海運史の研究. Tokyo: Yūzankaku 雄山閣, 1979.

Takase Tamotsu 高瀬保. "Kaga han no beika hyō" 加賀藩の米価表. In Toyoda Takeshi 豊田武, ed. *Nihonkai chiikishi kenkyū* 日本海地域史研究. Vol. 1. Tokyo: Bunken shuppan 文献出版, 1980.

Takatsuka, Masanori, and David Stubbs, trans. *This Scheming World*. Tokyo: Tuttle, 1965.

Takatsuki-shi shi hensan iinkai 高槻市史編さん委員会, ed. *Takatsuki-shi shi* 高

槻市史. Takatsuki: Takatsuki-shi 高槻市, 1973.

Takeda Chōshū 竹田聽洲. "Jibutsudō no hatten to shūshuku" 持仏堂の発展と収縮. In Takeda Chōshū 竹田聽洲, ed. *Senzo kuyō* 先祖供養. Vol. 3 of *Sōsō bosei kenkyū shūsei* 葬送墓制研究集成. Tokyo: Meicho shuppan 名著出版, 1979.

Takeda Chōshū 竹田聽洲. "Kinsei shakai to bukkyō" 近世社会と仏教. In *Iwanami kōza Nihon rekishi* 岩波講座日本歴史. Vol. 9. Tokyo: Iwanami shoten 岩波書店, 1975.

Takeda Chōshū 竹田聽洲. *Minzoku bukkyō to sosen shinkō* 民族仏教と祖先信仰. Tokyo: Tōkyō daigaku shuppankai 東京大学出版会, 1971.

Takeda Chōshū 竹田聽洲. "Ryōbosei sonraku ni okeru mairibaka no nenrin (2)" 両墓制村落に於ける詣墓の年輪(二). *Bukkyō daigaku kenkyū kiyō* 佛教大學研究紀要 52 (March 1968): 17-170.

Takeda Chōshū 竹田聽洲. *Sosen sūhai* 祖先崇拝. Vol. 8 of *Saara sōsho* サーラ叢書. Kyoto: Heirakuji shoten 平楽寺書店, 1957.

Takeuchi Makoto 竹内誠. "Bakufu keizai no hembō to kin'yū seisaku no tenkai" 幕府経済の変貌と金融政策の展開. In *Nihon keizaishi taikei* 日本経済史大系. Vol. 4. Tokyo: Tōkyō daigaku shuppankai 東京大学出版会, 1965.

Takeuchi Makoto 竹内誠. *Edo to Ōsaka* 江戸と大阪. Tokyo: Shōgakkan 小学館, 1989.

Takeuchi Makoto 竹内誠. "Kansei kaikaku" 寛政改革. In *Iwanami kōza Nihon rekishi* 岩波講座日本歴史. Vol. 12. Tokyo: Iwanami shoten 岩波書店, 1976.

Takeuchi Makoto 竹内誠. "Kansei kaikaku to 'Kanjōsho goyōtashi' no seiritsu" 寛政改革と「勘定所御用達」の成立. Pts. 1, 2. *Nihon rekishi* 日本歴史 128 (February 1959): 23-32; 129 (March 1959): 49-56.

Takeuchi Makoto 竹内誠. "Kantō gundai Ina Tadataka no shikkyaku to sono rekishiteki igi" 関東郡代伊奈忠尊の失脚とその歴史的意義. *Tokugawa rinseishi kenkyūjo kenkyū kiyō* 徳川林政史研究所研究紀要 (1966): 173-203.

Takeuchi Rizō 竹内理三. *(Zōho) Zoku shiryō taisei* 増補続史料大成. Kyoto: Rinsen shoten 臨川書店, 1978.

Takimoto Seiichi 瀧本誠一, ed. *Nihon keizai sōsho* 日本経済叢書. Vol. 33. Tokyo: Nihon keizai sōsho kankōkai 日本経済叢書刊行会, 1917.

Takimoto Seiichi 瀧本誠一, ed. *Nihon keizai taiten* 日本経済大典. 60 vols. Tokyo: Meiji bunken 明治文献, 1966- ; 54 vols. Tokyo: Keimei shuppansha 啓明出版社, 1928-30.

Takita Manabu 田北學, ed. *Ōtomo shiryō* 大友史料. Ōita: Kin'yōdō shoten 金洋堂書店, 1938.

Tamamura Takeji 玉村竹二. "Nihon chūsei zenrin ni okeru Rinzai Sōtō ryōshū no idō: rinka no mondai ni tsuite" 日本中世禅林に於ける臨済・曹洞両宗の異同—「林下」の問題について. *Shigaku zasshi* 史学雑誌 59 (July 1950): 1-18; 59 (August 1950): 43-69.

Tamamura Takeji 玉村竹二. "Nihon no shisō shūkyō to Chūgoku: Zen" 日本の思想宗教と中国:禅. In Bitō Masahide 尾藤正英, ed. *Nihon bunka to Chūgoku*

日本文化と中国. Tokyo: Taishūkan, 大修館, 1968.

Tamamura Takeji 玉村竹二. *Nihon zenshūshi ronshū* 日本禅宗史論集. 3 vols. Kyoto: Shibunkaku 思文閣, 1976–81.

Tamamura Takeji 玉村竹二. "Takuan Sōhō: shie jiken ni taisuru ichi kenkai" 沢庵宗彭：紫衣事件に対する一見解. In Tamamura Takeji 玉村竹二, *Nihon Zenshūshi ronshū* 日本禅宗史論集. Vol. 1. Kyoto: Shibunkaku 思文閣, 1976.

Tamamuro Taijō 圭室諦成. "Chūsei kōki Bukkyō no kenkyū – toku ni sengoku-ki o chūshin toshite" 中世後期仏教の研究－特に戦国時代を中心として. *Meiji daigaku jimbun kagaku kenkyū kiyō* 明治大学人文科学研究所紀要 1 (1962).

Tamura Hiroyuki 田村洋幸. *Chūsei Nitchō bōeki no kenkyū* 中世日朝貿易の研究. Kyoto: Sanwa shobō 三和書房, 1967.

Tanaka Hisao 田中久夫. *Sosen saishi no kenkyū* 祖先祭祀の研究. Tokyo: Kōbundō 弘文堂, 1959.

Tanaka Takeo 田中健夫. *Chūsei taigai kankei shi* 中世対外関係史. Tokyo: Tōkyō daigaku shuppankai 東京大学出版会, 1975.

Tanaka Takeo 田中健夫. "Sakoku seiritsuki Nitchō kankei no seikaku" 鎖国成立期日朝関係の性格. *Chōsen gakuhō* 朝鮮学報 34 (January 1965): 29–62.

Tanaka Takeo 田中健夫. *Wakō: umi no rekishi* 倭寇：海の歴史. Tokyo: Kyōiku-sha 教育社, 1982.

Tanaka Yoshio 田中喜男. *Jōkamachi Kanazawa* 城下町金沢. Tokyo: Nihon shoin 日本書院, 1966.

Tanaka Yoshio 田中喜男. *Kaga han ni okeru toshi no kenkyū* 加賀藩における都市の研究. Tokyo: Bun'ichi sōgō shuppan 文一総合出版, 1978.

Tanaka Yoshio 田中喜男 "Kinsei jōkamachi hatten no ichi kōsatsu – 'Aitaiukechi' kara mita jōkamachi, Kanazawa no baai" 近世城下町発展の一考察－相対請地から見た城下町，金沢の場合. *Hokuriku shigaku* 北陸史学 8 (1959): 19–37.

Taniguchi Sumio 谷口澄夫. *Okayama hanseishi no kenkyū* 岡山藩政史の研究. Tokyo: Hanawa shobō 塙書房, 1964.

Tashiro Kazui 田代和生. *Kakikaerareta kokusho: Tokugawa, Chōsen gaikō no butaiura* 書き替えられた国書：徳川・朝鮮外交の舞台裏. Tokyo: Chūō kōron-sha 中央公論社, 1983.

Taut, Bruno. *Houses and People of Japan*. London: John Gifford, 1937.

Tenri toshokan shisho kenkyū-bu 天理図書館司書研究部, ed. *Kana zōshi hen* 仮名草子篇. Vol. 1 of *Kinsei bungaku mikambon sōsho* 近世文學未刊本叢書. Nara: Yōtokusha 養徳社, 1947.

Thompson, Edward M., ed. *Diary of Richard Cocks*. London: Hakluyt Society, 1933.

Toby, Ronald P. "Reopening the Question of *Sakoku*: Diplomacy in the Legitimation of the Tokugawa Bakufu." *Journal of Japanese Studies* 3 (Summer 1977): 323–63.

Toby, Ronald P. *State and Diplomacy in Early Modern Japan: Asia in the Development of the Tokugawa Bakufu*. Princeton, N. J.: Princeton University Press, 1984.

Tokutomi Iichirō 徳富猪一郎. *Toyotomi-shi jidai, tei hen: Chōsen no eki* 豊臣氏時代・丁篇:朝鮮役. Pt. 1. Vol. 7 of *Kinsei Nihon kokumin shi* 近世日本国民史. Tokyo: Min'yūsha 民友社. 1935.

Tōkyō daigaku shiryō hensanjo 東京大学史料編纂所, ed. *Tokushi biyō* 讀史備要. Tokyo: Naigai shoseki 1933; Kōdansha 講談社, 1966.

Tōkyō daigaku shiryō hensanjo 東京大学史料編纂所, ed. *Uwai Kakuken nikki* 上井覚兼日記. Tokyo: Iwanami shoten 岩波書店, 1954-57.

Totman, Conrad. *The Origins of Japan's Modern Forests: The Case of Akita.* Honolulu: University of Hawaii Press, 1985.

Totman, Conrad. *Politics in the Tokugawa Bakufu, 1600-1843.* Cambridge, Mass.: Harvard University Press, 1967.

Toyama Mikio 外山幹夫. *Chūsei no Kyūshu* 中世の九州. Tokyo: Kyōikusha 教育社, 1978.

Toyama Mikio 外山幹夫. *Ōtomo Sōrin* 大友宗麟. Vol. 172 of *Jimbutsu sōsho* 人物叢書. Tokyo: Yoshikawa kōbunkan 吉川弘文館, 1975.

Toyoda Takeshi 豊田武. *Nihon no hōken toshi* 日本の封建都市. Tokyo: Iwanami shoten 岩波書店, 1952.

Toyoda, Takeshi and Hiroshi Sugiyama, with V. Dixon Morris, "The Growth of Commerce and the Trades." In John W. Hall and Takeshi Toyoda, eds. *Japan in the Muromachi Age.* Berkeley and Los Angeles: University of California Press, 1977.

Toyoda Takeshi 豊田武 and Kodama Kōta 児玉幸多, eds. *Ryūtsūshi* 流通史. Vol. 1. Tokyo: Yamakawa shuppansha 山川出版社, 1969.

Tsuchida Ryōichi 土田良一. "Kinsei jōkamachi no temmayaku" 近世城下町の伝馬役. In Chihōshi kenkyū kyōgikai 地方史研究協議会, ed. *Nihon no toshi to machi* 日本の都市と町. Tokyo: Yūzankaku 雄山閣, 1982.

Tsuchiya Takao 土屋喬雄. *Hōken shakai hōkai katei no kenkyū - Edo jidai ni okeru shokō no zaisei* 封建社会崩壊過程の研究－江戸時代における諸侯の財政. Kyoto: Kōbundō 弘文堂, 1927.

Tsuda Hideo 津田秀夫. *Hōken keizai seisaku no tenkai to shijō kōzō* 封建経済政策の展開と市場構造. Tokyo: Ochanomizu shobō 御茶の水書房, 1961.

Tsuda Hideo 津田秀夫. "Kansei kaikaku" 寛政改革. In *Iwanami kōza Nihon rekishi* 岩波講座日本歴史. Vol. 12. Tokyo: Iwanami shoten 岩波書店, 1963.

Tsuda Hideo 津田秀夫. "Kyōiku no fukyū to shingaku" 教育の普及と心学. In *Iwanami kōza Nihon rekishi* 岩波講座日本歴史. Vol. 12. Tokyo: Iwanami shoten 岩波書店, 1976.

Tsuji Tatsuya 辻達也. "Bakusei no shindankai" 幕政の新段階. In *Iwanami kōza Nihon rekishi* 岩波講座日本歴史. Vol. 11. Tokyo: Iwanami shoten 岩波書店, 1963.

Tsuji Tatsuya 辻達也. "Bakusei-shi kara mita Kyōhō yori Tanuma e no katei ni tsuite" 幕政史からみた享保より田沼への過程について. *Rekishigaku kenkyū* 歴史学研究 264 (April-May 1962): 63-66.

Tsuji, Tatsuya. "Edo Bakufu Policy in the Late Eighteenth Century." *Yokohama shiritsu daigaku ronsō* 横浜市立大学論叢 19 (1967): 34-49.

Tsuji Tatsuya 辻達也. *Edo kaifu* 江戸開府. Vol. 4 of *Nihon no rekishi* 日本の歴史. Tokyo: Chūō kōronsha 中央公論社, 1966.

Tsuji Tatsuya 辻達也. " 'Geba shōgun' seiji no seikaku" 「下馬将軍」政治の性格. *Yokohama shiritsu daigaku ronsō* 横浜市立大学論叢 (Humanities) 3 (August 1979).

Tsuji Tatsuya 辻達也. "Hōreki-Temmei-ki no seiji jōsei" 宝暦・天明期の政治情勢. In Kitajima Masamoto 北島正元, ed. *Seijishi* 政治史. Vol. 11 of *Taikei Nihonshi sōsho* 体系日本史叢書. Tokyo: Yamakawa shuppansha 山川出版社, 1965.

Tsuji Tatsuya 辻達也. "Kinsho no kenkyū" 禁書の研究. *Rekishi chiri* 歴史地理 58 (October–November 1936): 313–46, 421–70.

Tsuji Tatsuya 辻達也. *Kyōhō kaikaku no kenkyū* 享保改革の研究. Tokyo: Sōbunsha 創文社, 1963.

Tsuji Tatsuya 辻達也. "Kyōhō kaikaku to jugaku" 享保改革と儒学. In Saigusa Hiroto kinen ronshū henshū iinkai 三枝博音記念論集編集委員会, ed. *Saigusa Hiroto kinen ronshū: Sekai ni okeru Nihon no bunka* 三枝博音記念論集：世界における日本の文化. Tokyo: Dai-ichi Hōki shuppan 第一法規出版, 1965.

Tsuji Tatsuya 辻達也. *Ōoka Echizen no kami* 大岡越前守. Tokyo: Chūō kōronsha 中央公論社, 1964.

Tsuji Tatsuya 辻達也. "Seidan no shakaiteki haikei" 政談の社会的背景. In Yoshikawa Kōjirō 吉川幸次郎 and Maruyama Masao 丸山真男, eds. *Ogyū Sorai* 荻生徂徠. Vol. 36 of *Nihon shisō taikei* 日本思想大系. Tokyo: Iwanami shoten 岩波書店, 1973.

Tsuji Tatsuya 辻達也. *Tokugawa Yoshimune* 徳川吉宗. Tokyo: Yoshikawa kōbunkan 吉川弘文館, 1958.

Tsuji Tatsuya 辻達也. *Tokugawa Yoshimune kō den* 徳川吉宗公傳. Nikko: Nikkō Tōshōgū 日光東照宮, 1962.

Tsuji Tatsuya 辻達也 and Matsumoto Shirō 松本四郎, "Otorika tsuji kakitsuke oyobi *Onengu-mai, onengukin hoka shomuki osame watashi kakitsuke* ni tsuite." 「御取箇辻書付」および「御年貢米・御年貢金外諸向納渡書付」について. *Yokohama shiritsu daigaku ronsō* 横浜市立大学論叢 (Jimbun kagaku keiretsu 人文科学系列 15) (March 1964): 181–216.

Tsuji Zennosuke 辻善之助. *Nihon bukkyōshi* 日本佛教史. 10 vols. Tokyo: Iwanami shoten 岩波書店, 1953.

Tsuji Zennosuke 辻善之助. *Nihon bunkashi* 日本文化史. 7 vols. Tokyo: Shunjūsha 春秋社, 1952–3.

Tsuji Zennosuke 辻善之助, ed. *Tamon'in nikki* 多聞院日記. 5 vols. Tokyo: Kadokawa shoten 角川書店, 1967.

Tsuji Zennosuke 辻善之助. *Tanuma jidai* 田沼時代. Tokyo: Nihon gakujutsu fukyū kai 日本学術普及会, 1915.

Tsukahira, Toshio George. *Feudal Control in Tokugawa Japan: The Sankin Kōtai System*. Harvard East Asian Monographs, no. 20. Cambridge, Mass.: Harvard University Press, 1966.

Tsukatani Akihiro 塚谷晃弘 and Kuranami Seiji 蔵並省自, eds. *Honda Toshiaki,*

Kaiho Seiryō 本多利明・海保青陵. Vol. 44 of *Nihon shisō taikei* 日本思想大系. Tokyo: Iwanami shoten 岩波書店, 1970.

Tsunoda, Ryusaku, William Theodore de Bary, and Donald Keene, comps. *Sources of the Japanese Tradition.* New York: Columbia University Press, 1958.

Tsuruoka shiyakusho 鶴岡市役所, ed. *Tsuruoka-shi shi* 鶴岡市史. Tsuruoka: Tsuruoka-shi 鶴岡市, 1962.

Utagawa Takehisa 宇田川武久. "Chūsei kaizokushū no shūmatsu" 中世海賊衆の終末. *Nihon rekishi* 日本歴史 333 (February 1976): 22–39.

Valignano, Alejandro, SJ. *Historia del principio y progresso de la Compañía de Jesús en las Indias Orientales (1542–1564).* Ed. by Josef Wicki, SJ. *Bibliotheca Instituti Historici S. I.* Vol. 2. Rome: Institum Historicum S. I., 1944.

Valignano, Alejandro, SJ. *Nihon junsatsuki* 日本巡察記. Translated by Matsuda Kiichi 松田毅一, Sakuma Tadashi 佐久間正, and Chikamatsu Hiroo 近松洋男. Tokyo: Heibonsha 平凡社, 1973.

Valignano, Alejandro, SJ. *Sumario de las cosas de Japón* (1583), *Adiciones del sumario de Japón* (1592). Vol. 1. Ed. by José-Luis Alvarez-Taladriz. *Monumenta Nipponica Monographs,* no. 9. Tokyo: Sophia University, 1954.

Vaporis, Constantine N. "Post Station and Assisting Villages." *Monumenta Nipponica* 41 (Winter 1986): 377–414.

Wajima shishi hensan semmon iinkai 輪島市史編纂専門委員会, ed. *Wajima shishi* 輪島市史. Vol. 1. Wajima: Wajima shiyakusho 輪島市役所, 1976.

Wajima Yoshio 和島芳男. *Chūsei no jugaku* 中世の儒学. Tokyo: Yoshikawa kōbunkan 吉川弘文館, 1965.

Wakabayashi, Bob Tadashi, *Anti-Foreignism and Western Learning in Early Modern Japan: The New Theses of 1825.* Cambridge, Mass.: Harvard University Press, 1986.

Wakita Haruko 脇田晴子. "Muromachi-ki no keizai hatten" 室町期の経済発展. In *Iwanami kōza Nihon rekishi* 岩波講座日本歴史. Vol. 7. Tokyo: Iwanami shoten 岩波書店, 1976.

Wakita, Haruko, with Susan B. Hanley, "Dimensions of Development: Cities in Fifteenth-Century Japan." In John W. Hall, Keiji Nagahara, and Kozo Yamamura, eds. *Japan Before Tokugawa: Political Consolidation and Economic Growth, 1500–1650.* Princeton, N. J.: Princeton University Press, 1981.

Wakita, Osamu. "The Emergence of the State in Sixteenth Century Japan: From Oda to Tokugawa." *Journal of Japanese Studies* 8 (Summer 1982): 343–67.

Wakita Osamu 脇田修. *Genroku no shakai* 元禄の社会. Tokyo: Hanawa shobō 塙書房, 1980.

Wakita Osamu 脇田修. "Jinaimachi no kōzō to tenkai" 寺内町の構造と展開. *Shirin* 史林 41 (January 1958): 1–24.

Wakita Osamu 脇田修. "Jinaimachi no rekishi-teki tokushitsu" 寺内町の歴史的特質. In Toyoda Takeshi 豊田武, Harada Tomohiko 原田伴彦, and Yamori

Kazuhiko 矢守一彦, eds. *Kōza: Nihon no hōken toshi* 講座：日本の封建都市. Vol. 1. Tokyo: Bun'ichi sōgō shuppan 文一総合出版, 1982.

Wakita Osamu 脇田修. *Kinsei hōken shakai no keizai kōzō* 近世封建社会の経済構造. Tokyo: Ochanomizu shobō 御茶の水書房, 1963.

Wakita Osamu 脇田修. *Kinsei hōkensei seiritsu shiron* 近世封建制成立史論. Tokyo: Tōkyō daigaku shuppankai 東京大学出版会, 1977.

Wakita Osamu 脇田修. *Kinsei Ōsaka no machi to hito* 近世大阪の町と人. Kyoto: Jimbun shoin 人文書院, 1986.

Wakita Osamu 脇田修. "Kinsei shoki no toshi keizai" 近世初期の都市経済. *Nihonshi kenkyū* 日本史研究 200 (April 11, 1976): 52-75.

Wakita Osamu 脇田修. "Kinsei toshi no kensetsu to gōshō" 近世都市の建設と豪商. In *Iwanami kōza Nihon rekishi* 岩波講座日本歴史. Vol. 9. Tokyo: Iwanami shoten, 1975.

Wakita Osamu 脇田修. "The *Kokudaka* System: A Device for Reunification." *Journal of Japanese Studies* 1 (Spring 1975): 297-320.

Wakita Osamu 脇田修. *Oda seiken no kiso kōzō* 織田政権の基礎構造. Tokyo: Tōkyō daigaku shuppankai 東京大学出版会, 1975.

Wakita Osamu 脇田修. *Shokuhō seiken no bunseki* 織豊政権の分析. 2 vols. Tokyo: Tōkyō daigaku shuppankai 東京大学出版会, 1975-7.

Wakita Osamu 脇田修 and Kobayashi Shigeru 小林茂. *Ōsaka no seisan to kōtsū* 大阪の生産と交通. Osaka: Mainichi hōsō 毎日放送, 1973.

Wakita, Osamu, with James L. McClain, "The Commercial and Urban Policies of Oda Nobunaga and Toyotomi Hideyoshi." In John W. Hall, Keiji Nagahara, and Kozo Yamamura, eds. *Japan Before Tokugawa: Political Consolidation and Economic Growth, 1500-1650*. Princeton, N. J.: Princeton University Press, 1981.

Watanabe Hiroshi 渡辺浩. *Kinsei Nihon shakai to Sōgaku* 近世日本社会と宋学. Tokyo: Tōkyō daigaku shuppankai 東京大学出版会, 1985.

Watanabe Hiroshi 渡辺浩. " 'Michi' to 'miyabi' - Norinaga gaku to 'kagaku' ha kokugaku no seiji shisōshiteki kenkyū"「道」と「雅び」-宣長学と「歌学」派国学の政治思想史的研究. *Kokka gakkai zasshi* 国家学会雑誌 87 (1974): 477-561, 647-721; and 88 (1975): 238-68, 295-366.

Watanabe Kunio 渡辺国雄. "Sanja takusen no shinkō" 三社託宣の信仰. In Watanabe Kunio 渡辺国雄, *Shintō shisō to sono kenkyūsha tachi* 神道思想とその研究者たち. Tokyo: Wataki 渡喜, 1957.

Watanabe Minoru 渡辺実. *Nihon shoku seikatsu shi* 日本食生活史. Tokyo: Yoshikawa kōbunkan 吉川弘文館, 1964.

Watanabe Zenjirō 渡辺善次郎. *Toshi to nōson no aida* 都市と農村の間. Tokyo: Ronsōsha 論創社, 1983.

Watson, William, ed. *The Great Japan Exhibition: Art of the Edo Period 1600-1868*. New York: Alpine Fine Arts Collection, 1981.

Wicki, Josef, SJ. "Das neu entdeckte Xavieriusleben des P. Francisco Perez S. I. (1597)." *Archivum Historicum Societatis Iesu* 34 (January-June 1965).

Wicki, Josef, SJ., ed. *Documenta Indica* III. In *Monumenta Missionum Societatis*

Iesu 6, *Monumenta Historica Societatis Iesu* 74. Rome: Apud Monumenta Historica Societatus Iesu, 1954.

Wicki, Josef, SJ. *Documenta Indica* XI (1577-1580). In *Monumenta Historica Societatis Iesu* 103. Rome: Apud Institutum Historicum Societatis Iesu, 1970.

Williams, Samuel Wells. "A Journal of the Perry Expedition to Japan (1853-1854)." *Transactions of the Asiatic Society of Japan* 37 (1910). (See also Hora Tomio.)

Wheelwright, Carolyn. "A Visualization of Eitoku's Lost Paintings at Azuchi Castle." In George Elison and Bardwell L. Smith, eds. *Warlords, Artists, & Commoners: Japan in the Sixteenth Century*. Honolulu: University of Hawaii Press, 1981.

Wolf, Eric. *Peasant Wars of the Twentieth Century*. New York: Harper & Row, 1964.

Yamada Keiji 山田慶児, ed. *Miura Baien* 三浦梅園. Vol. 20 of *Nihon no meicho* 日本の名著. Tokyo: Chūō kōronsha 中央公論社, 1982.

Yamada Tadao 山田忠雄. "Hōreki-Meiwa-ki no hyakushō ikki" 宝暦・明和期の百姓一揆. In Furushima Toshio 古島敏雄, ed. *Kinsei* 近世. Vol. 4 of *Nihon keizaishi taikei* 日本経済史大系. Tokyo: Tōkyō daigaku shuppankai 東京大学出版会, 1965.

Yamada Yūzō 山田雄三. *Nihon kokumin shotoku suikei shiryō* 日本国民所得推計資料. Tokyo: Tōyō keizai shimpōsha 東洋経済新報社, 1957.

Yamagata-ken 山形県, ed. *Yamagata-ken shi (Shiryō-hen)* 山形県史(資料編). Tokyo: Gannando 巌南堂, 1961.

Yamaguchi Keiji 山口啓二. *Bakuhansei seiritsushi no kenkyū* 幕藩制成立史の研究. Tokyo: Azekura shobō 校倉書房, 1974.

Yamaguchi Tetsu 山口徹. "Bakuhansei ichiba no saihen to shōhin seikatsu" 幕藩制市場の再編と商品生活. In Rekishigaku kenkyūkai 歴史学研究会 and Nihonshi kenkyūkai 日本史研究会, eds. *Kōza Nihon rekishi* 講座日本歴史. Vol. 6. Tokyo: Tōkyō daigaku shuppankai 東京大学出版会, 1985.

Yamamura, Kozo. "Returns on Unification: Economic Growth in Japan, 1550-1650." In John W. Hall, Keiji Nagahara, and Kozo Yamamura, eds. *Japan Before Tokugawa: Political Consolidation and Economic Growth, 1500-1650*. Princeton, N. J.: Princeton University Press, 1981.

Yamamura, Kozo. "The Role of the Samurai in the Development of Modern Banking in Japan," *Journal of Economic History* 27 (June 1967): 198-220.

Yamamura, Kozo. *A Study of Samurai Income and Entrepreneurship*. Cambridge, Mass.: Harvard University Press, 1974.

Yamori Kazuhiko 矢守一彦. *Toshizu no rekishi: Nihon hen* 都市図の歴史:日本編. Tokyo: Kōdansha 講談社, 1974.

Yanagita Kunio 柳田国男. *Ie kandan* 家閑談. In *Teihon Yanagita Kunio shū* 定本柳田国男集. Vol. 15. Tokyo: Chikuma shobō 筑摩書房, 1963.

Yanagita Kunio 柳田国男. *Momen izen no koto* 木綿以前の事. In *Teihon Yanagita Kunio shū* 定本柳田国男集. Vol. 14. Tokyo: Chikuma shobō 筑摩書房, 1962.

Yanagita Kunio 柳田国男. *Senzo no hanashi* 先祖の話. In *Teihon Yanagita Kunio shū* 定本柳田国男集. Vol. 10. Tokyo: Chikuma shobō 筑摩書房, 1962. [Fanny Hagin Mayer and Ishiwara Yasugo, trans. *About Our Ancestors – The Japanese Family System.* Tokyo: Japanese National Commission for UNESCO, 1970.]

Yanagita Kunio 柳田国男. *Shintō to minzokugaku* 神道と民俗学. In *Teihon Yanagita Kunio shū* 定本柳田国男集. Vol. 10. Tokyo: Chikuma shobō 筑摩書房, 1962.

Yanagita Kunio 柳田国男. *Ujigami to ujiko* 氏神と氏子. In *Teihon Yanagita Kunio shū* 定本柳田国男集. Vol. 11. Tokyo: Chikuma shobō 筑摩書房, 1963.

Yanai Akira 矢内昭. "Kinsei Ōsaka keikan fukugen e no kokoromi" 近世大阪景観復元への試. In Toyoda Takeshi 豊田武, Harada Tomohiko 原田伴彦, and Yamori Kazuhiko 矢守一彦, eds. *Kōza: Nihon no hōken toshi* 講座：日本の封建都市. Vol. 3. Tokyo: Bun'ichi sōgo shuppan 文一総合出版, 1981.

Yasuba, Yasukichi. "Standard of Living in Japan Before Industrialization: From What Level Did Japan Begin? A Comment." *Journal of Economic History* 46 (March 1986): 217-24.

Yasuoka Shigeaki 安岡重明. "Edo chūki no Ōsaka ni okeru torihiki soshiki" 江戸中期の大阪における取引組織. *Dōshisha shōgaku* 同志社商学 16 (November 1964): 290-307; and 16 (February 1965): 589-625.

Yazaki, Takeo. *Social Change and the City in Japan.* Tokyo: Japan Publications, 1968.

Yi Kyŏng-sok 李炯錫. *Imjin chŏllan sa* 壬辰戰亂史. Seoul: Ch'ungmuhoe, 1975.

Yobuko Jōtarō 呼子丈太朗. *Wakō shikō* 倭寇史考. Tokyo: Shin jimbutsu ōraisha 新人物往来社, 1971.

Yokohama shiyakusho 横浜市役所, ed. *Yokohama-shi shi* 横浜市史. Vol. 3. Yokohama shiyakusho 横浜市役所, 1958.

Yokokawa Shirō 横川四郎, ed. *Ninomiya Sontoku shū* 二宮尊徳集. Vol. 5 of *Kinsei shakai keizai gakusetsu taikei* 近世社会経済學説大系. Tokyo: Seibundō shinkōsha 誠文堂新光社, 1935.

Yokota Fuyuhiko 横田冬彦. "Shokunin to shokunin dantai" 職人と職人団体. In Rekishigaku kenkyūkai 歴史学研究会, ed. *Kōza Nihon rekishi* 講座日本歴史. Vol. 5. Tokyo: Tōkyō daigaku shuppankai 東京大学出版会, 1985.

Yokoyama, Toshio. "Setsuyōshū and Japanese Civilization." In J. P. Lehmann and Sue Henny, eds. *Themes and Theories in Japanese History.* London: Athlone, 1986.

Yoshida Tōgo 吉田東伍. *Tokugawa seikyō kō* 徳川政教考. 2 vols. Tokyo: Fuzambō 冨山房, 1894.

Yoshihara Ken'ichirō 吉原健一郎. *Edo no machi yakunin* 江戸の町役人. Tokyo: Yoshikawa kōbunkan 吉川弘文館, 1980.

Yoshikawa, Kōjirō. *Jinsai, Sorai, Norinaga.* Tokyo: Toho Gakkai, 1983.

Yoshikawa Kōjirō 吉川幸次郎 and Maruyama Masao 丸山真男, eds. *Ogyū Sorai* 荻生徂徠. Vol. 36 of *Nihon shisō taikei* 日本思想大系. Tokyo: Iwanami shoten 岩波書店, 1973.

Yoshikawa Kōjirō 吉川幸次郎, Satake Akihiro 佐竹昭広, and Hino Tatsuo 日野龍夫, eds. *Motoori Norinaga* 本居宣長. Vol. 40 of *Nihon shisō taikei* 日本思想大系. Tokyo: Iwanami shoten 岩波書店, 1978.

Yoshikawa Kōjirō 吉川幸次郎 and Shimizu Shigeru 清水茂, eds. *Itō Jinsai, Itō Tōgai* 伊藤仁斎・伊藤東涯. Vol. 33 of *Nihon shisō taikei* 日本思想大系. Tokyo: Iwanami shoten 岩波書店, 1971.

Yoshinaga Akira 吉永昭. "Sembai seido to shōhin ryūtsū" 専売制度と商品流通. *Rekishigaku kenkyū* 歴史学研究 229 (March 1959): 48–55.

Yoshioka Yuriko 吉岡由利子. "Kyōhō-ki Edo machikata ni okeru sogan undō no jittai" 享保期江戸町方における訴願運動の実態. In Chihōshi kenkyū kyōgikai 地方史研究協議会, ed. *Toshi no chihōshi* 都市の地方史. Tokyo: Yūzankaku 雄山閣, 1980.

Yoshizumi Mieko 善積美恵子. "Tetsudai bushin ichiran-hyō" 手伝普請一覧表. In *Gakushūin daigaku bungaku-bu kenkyū nempō* 学習院大学文学部研究年報 15 (1968): 87–119.

Zoku gunsho ruijū 続群書類従. Tokyo: Zoku gunsho ruijū kanseikai 続群書類従完成会, 1923; rev. 3d ed., 1984.

Zoku zoku gunsho ruijū 続々群書類従. Tokyo: Kokusho kankōkai 國書刊行会, 1906– .

GLOSSARY-INDEX